EXAMINATION
REGULATIONS
2013

UNIVERSITY OF OXFORD

EXAMINATION REGULATIONS

2013

[FOR THE ACADEMIC YEAR 2013–14]

OXFORD UNIVERSITY PRESS

OXFORD
UNIVERSITY PRESS

Great Clarendon Street, Oxford, OX2 6DP,
United Kingdom

Oxford University Press is a department of the University of Oxford.
It furthers the University's objective of excellence in research, scholarship,
and education by publishing worldwide. Oxford is a registered trade mark of
Oxford University Press in the UK and in certain other countries

© Oxford University Press 2013

The moral rights of the author have been asserted

First Edition published in 2013

Impression: 1

Published in the United States of America by Oxford University Press
198 Madison Avenue, New York, NY 10016, United States of America

British Library Cataloguing in Publication Data
Data available

ISBN 978-0-19-967897-6

Printed in Great Britain by
Clays Ltd., St. Ives plc.

PREFACE

This book contains the regulations of the University relating to the various degrees, diplomas and certificates conferred by the University together with regulations made by boards, and certain other relevant information.

There is a range of other documents of importance to those involved in examinations:

Essential Information for Students (Proctors' and Assessor's Memorandum) available online at: http://www.admin.ox.ac.uk/proctors/info/

Policy and Guidance for Examiners and others involved in University Examinations available online at: http://www.admin.ox.ac.uk/proctors/policyandguidanceforexaminers

Comprehensive information about undergraduate, postgraduate and Continuing Education programmes, including programme specifications with assessment information, is available through the Education Committee's website: http://www.admin.ox.ac.uk/edc/qa/prog info

The Examination Regulations are now available online at: http://www.admin.ox.ac.uk/examregs/. The functionality, particularly archiving, contents, printing and search facility, is expected to be considerably improved during the course of 2013. The online version, along with the print version, is maintained by the Education Policy Support Section, who may be contacted via examinationregulationsenquiries@admin.ox.ac.uk. It may help your search to know that the constituent files of the Examination Regulations online (as displayed in the 'contents' listing) are in the same order as they appear in the print version.

This print version of the Examination Regulations, commonly referred to as 'the Grey Book', is currently published annually at the beginning of Michaelmas Term. Print copies are provided to students and members of the collegiate University, however steps are being taken to substantially reduce the print run with a view to making the online version the principal source of information in the near future.

At present, the authoritative version of the Examination Regulations remains the most recent printed edition (as published in October of each year) plus the further changes published in the *University Gazette*. This version therefore takes precedence over Examination Regulations reproduced elsewhere e.g. in programme handbooks. The 2013 Grey Book contains gazetted changes at least up to the beginning of Trinity Term 2013. Further changes may have been approved since that date and will appear in the *Gazette* which is available online at: http://www.ox.ac.uk/gazette/.

DATES OF TERMS 2013–2014

2013
Michaelmas: Tuesday 1 October to Tuesday 17 December

2014
Hilary: Tuesday 7 January to Tuesday 25 March
Trinity: Wednesday 23 April to Sunday 6 July
Michaelmas: Wednesday 1 October to Wednesday 17 December

†DATES OF FULL TERM 2013–2014

2013
Michaelmas: Sunday 13 October to Saturday 7 December

2014
Hilary: Sunday 19 January to Saturday 15 March
Trinity: Sunday 27 April to Saturday 21 June
Michaelmas: Sunday 12 October to Saturday 6 December

DATES OF EXTENDED TERMS 2013–2014

For Part I candidates in Materials, Economics and Management
2014
Trinity: Friday 25 April to Saturday 28 June

For Part II candidates in Molecular and Cellular Biochemistry
2013
Michaelmas: Friday 20 September to Saturday 14 December

2014
Michaelmas: Friday 19 September to Saturday 13 December

For Part II candidates in Chemistry
2013
Michaelmas: Thursday 26 September to Tuesday 24 December

2014
Hilary: Tuesday 7 January to Wednesday 16 April
Trinity: Monday 28 April to Saturday 12 July
Michaelmas: Thursday 25 September to Tuesday 23 December

---

† Undergraduates will be required by their colleges to come into residence in the week preceding the beginning of Full Term.

For Part II candidates in Materials Science

2013
Michaelmas: Friday 13 September to Saturday 14 December

2014
Hilary: Friday 10 January to Saturday 12 April
Trinity: Friday 25 April to Saturday 5 July
Michaelmas: Friday 12 September to Saturday 13 December

For Master of Business Administration

2013
Michaelmas: Saturday 28 September to Friday 20 December

2014
Hilary: Monday 13 January to Friday 28 March
Trinity: Monday 21 April to Friday 4 July
Long Vacation: Monday 7 July to Sunday 31 August
                Monday 1 September to Saturday 13 September

DATES OF ENCAENIA

2014   Wednesday 25 June
2015   Wednesday 24 June*
2016   Wednesday 22 June*
2017   Wednesday 21 June*

For further information please see the notice published by Council in the University Gazette of 7 February 2013 at http://www.ox.ac.uk/gazette/2012–2013

* Provisional dates.

CONTENTS

x   *Contents*

PROVISIONAL DATES OF EXAMINATIONS

The provisional start dates of examinations and examination entry deadlines which were previously published in this volume are now produced as a separate document. This document is published in mid-September in the *University Gazette* and on the University website (www.ox.ac.uk), and is circulated directly to colleges and departments. The reason for this change is that the publication lead-time for this volume requires the inclusion of dates likely to change before the start of the academic year. The revised publication arrangements have led to greater reliability of published information on examination dates and entry deadlines, to the benefit of those who make use of it.

NOTE ON CONVENTIONS GOVERNING THE REVISED USE OF HEADINGS IN THIS EDITION

As a result of changes in the structure of University legislation, with effect from 1 October 2002, all former decrees concerning examinations were formally converted into regulations. In order to maintain continuity with earlier editions of this volume the following conventions have been observed as far as is practicable:

1. All former decrees governing the award of a degree, diploma, or certificate in general terms (as opposed to those decrees dealing with examinations in particular subjects leading to the award of such a qualification) are headed GENERAL REGULATIONS.

2. All former decrees relating to a particular subject course are headed SPECIAL REGULATIONS.

3. All elements of examination legislation which were regulations under the previous dispensation, and remain so under the new structure, are also to be found under the heading SPECIAL REGULATIONS.

4. In order to distinguish between the two types of Special Regulation described above, those which were formerly decrees are to be found, printed in larger type, under a sub-heading 'A', while those which were formerly regulations are printed in smaller type (as in previous editions) under a sub-heading 'B'.

REGULATIONS ON THE NUMBER AND LENGTH OF TERMS

Made by Council on 8 May 2002

1. The academic year shall be divided into three terms and three vacations.

2. (1) The first, or Michaelmas, Term shall begin on and include 1 October and end on and include 17 December.

    (2) The second, or Hilary, Term shall begin on and include 7 January and end on and include 25 March or the Saturday before Palm Sunday, whichever is the earlier.

    (3) The third, or Trinity, Term shall begin on and include 20 April or the Wednesday after Easter, whichever is the later, and end on and include 6 July.

3. (1) In each term there shall be prescribed by Council a period of eight weeks to be known as Full Term, beginning on a Sunday, within which lectures and other instruction prescribed by statute or regulation shall be given.

    (2) The dates on which each Full Term will begin and end in the next academic year but one shall be published by the Registrar in the *University Gazette* during Hilary Term.

REGULATIONS FOR MATRICULATION OF STUDENT MEMBERS

Made by Council on 8 May 2002

1. In these regulations, unless the context requires otherwise, 'college' means any college, society, or Permanent Private Hall or any other institution designated by Council by regulation as being permitted to present candidates for matriculation.

Academic qualifications

2. (1) In order to be matriculated as student members candidates must show evidence of an appropriate educational background and good standards of literacy and numeracy.[1]

(2) The University sets no formal 'Course Requirements' other than for the First Examination for the Degree of Bachelor of Medicine; candidates must, however, show that they are qualified to study the particular course they wish to take at Oxford.

(3) Acceptance by a college for presentation for matriculation will be deemed to be adequate evidence of an appropriate educational background, of good standards of literacy and numeracy, and of qualifications to study the course.

3. All candidates for matriculation shall supply to the Registrar such particulars as Council may from time to time determine, and may be required to produce to the Registrar (through the authorities of their colleges) evidence of their qualification to be matriculated.

4. Certificates in a language other than English must be accompanied by an English translation certified as correct by a duly authorised official of the country to which the candidate belongs.

Presentation for matriculation

5. Unless regulation 6 below applies, every head of a college or in their absence their deputies shall present to the Vice-Chancellor for

---

[1] GCSE passes at grade C and above in English Language, in a Mathematics or Science Subject, and in a language other than English and at least two A-level passes (or the equivalent in AS levels or a mixture of A and AS levels) would normally satisfy these requirements, as would an appropriate level of attainment in other qualifications such as Scottish Highers, the Irish Leaving Certificate, BTEC National Certificate, an Open University Foundation Course Credit, the European and International Baccalaureates, and degrees of other universities.

matriculation all members of their college who are prospective student members of the University within a fortnight from the date of their admission to the college.

6. A person who wishes to become a Senior Student under the provisions of the Regulations for Senior Student Status, or a graduate of another university who is applying for admission as a Probationer Research Student or as a student for any of the Degrees of Master of Fine Art, Master of Letters, Master of Philosophy, Master of Science, Master of Studies, Magister Juris, Master of Business Administration, Master of Public Policy, Bachelor of Philosophy, Bachelor of Civil Law, or Bachelor of Divinity must be presented to the Vice-Chancellor for matriculation by the head of his or her college or deputy within one month from the date of his or her admission to membership of his or her college.

7. A candidate who is matriculated during vacation shall be deemed to have been matriculated on the first day of the term following the vacation.

8. A person who becomes a student member by incorporation under regulations 1.7–1.18 of the Regulations for Degrees, Diplomas, and Certificates shall be deemed to have been matriculated on the first day of the term in which he or she was incorporated (or, in the case of a person incorporated during vacation, on the first day of the term following the vacation).

9. The procedure at the matriculation ceremony shall be in accordance with the arrangements laid down in the Regulations of Congregation for the Conduct of Ceremonies in Congregation.

Provisional matriculation

10. (1) Any person who is eligible to be matriculated may, if in the opinion of the head of his or her college there is good reason for that person not to be presented for matriculation under regulation 5 above, and on payment of the matriculation fee (if payable), be 'provisionally matriculated' (in absence) in accordance with arrangements made by Council and shall then be treated for all purposes as a member of the University until the end of the term in which he or she is provisionally matriculated.

(2) The duty under regulation 5 above of a head of a college to present any person for matriculation within a specified period from the date of his or her admission to the college shall be deemed to have been satisfied by that provisional matriculation, subject to the following conditions:

(*a*) any person who is matriculated not later than the term following the date of his or her provisional matriculation shall be deemed for all purposes to have been matriculated on the date of his or her provisional matriculation;

(*b*) if any person has not been matriculated in or before the term following his or her provisional matricula- 5 tion, his or her provisional matriculation shall, unless Council determines otherwise, be cancelled but the fee shall not be returned.

11. Notwithstanding the provisions of regulation 10 above, any person who has been provisionally matriculated and who is a stu- 10 dent for the degree of M.St in International Human Rights Law, or who, in accordance with arrangements approved by Council, spends the first two terms of his or her studies at any of the universities approved by Council under the ERASMUS postgrad- uate exchange scheme for Law and Economics may be matriculated 15 up to the end of the third term after the term in which he or she was provisionally matriculated, and the duty under regulation 5 above of a head of a college to present any person for matriculation within a specified period from the date of his or her admission to the college shall be deemed to have been satisfied by that provisional 20 matriculation, subject to the following conditions:

(1) any person who is matriculated not later than the third term after the term in which he or she was provisionally matriculated shall be deemed for all purposes to have been matriculated on the date of his or her provisional 25 matriculation;

(2) if any person has not been matriculated in or before the third term after the term in which he or she was provisionally matriculated, his or her provisional matriculation shall, un- less Council determines otherwise, be cancelled but the fee 30 shall not be returned.

12. The matriculation fee (if payable), the particulars which the candidate is required to supply under the provisions of regulation 3 above, and (if requested) evidence of his or her qualification to be matriculated shall be sent by the authorities of the candidate's 35 college to the Registrar with a request that the candidate be provi- sionally matriculated.

St Catherine's Society

13. All persons who were matriculated through St Catherine's Society shall be deemed to have been matriculated through 40 St Catherine's College, except that those who were matriculated in Michaelmas Term 1961 or later and who were not reading for the

Degree of Bachelor of Arts shall be deemed to have been matriculated through Linacre College.

Matriculation for Theological Courses of members of certain institutions in Oxford

14. In each academic year, subject to the approval of Council, Ripon College, Cuddesdon, shall be permitted, subject to the conditions laid down in regulations 15–17 below, to present for matriculation by the University:

(1) not more than twenty-two full-time-equivalent qualified candidates offering themselves for the qualifications listed in regulation 17 below other than the M.Th. in Applied Theology or the Diploma in Applied Theology; and

(2) not more than fourteen qualified candidates offering themselves for the M.Th. in Applied Theology or the Diploma in Applied Theology.

15. No person may be matriculated under the authority of these regulations unless the institution presenting that person for matriculation can certify that he or she is a minister of religion or a genuine candidate for the ministry.

16. Before presenting any candidate for matriculation under the authority of these regulations, the institution presenting him or her shall consult the Board of the Faculty of Theology or such nominee or nominees as the board may appoint to act for it.

17. Persons matriculated under the authority of regulations 14–16 above shall have in relation to the University the same privileges and obligations as if they had been matriculated through a college, except that they may not (unless they migrate to a college listed in Statute V) offer themselves for any degree, diploma, or certificate examinations of the University other than those for:

(1) the Honour School of Theology or any joint Honour School which includes Theology;

(2) the Diploma in Theology or a Certificate in Theology or the Degree of Bachelor of Theology;

(3) the Degree of Master of Studies or Master of Philosophy in Theology, or Master of Studies or Master of Philosophy in Philosophical Theology, or Master of Theology in Applied Theology, or the Diploma in Applied Theology;

(4) the Degree of Bachelor of Divinity or Doctor of Divinity.

REGULATIONS FOR RESIDENCE
IN THE UNIVERSITY

Made by Council on 8 May 2002

1. Where under any statute or regulation a student member is required, in order to be admitted to any examination or degree or obtain any other qualification of the University, to keep a number of terms or any other period of residence in the University these regulations shall apply for the purpose of:

(1) defining the place or places of residence; and

(2) calculating any period of residence necessary to satisfy that requirement.

2. Residence as defined by those regulations is called 'statutory residence'.

3. In these regulations, unless the context otherwise requires, 'college' means any college, society, or Permanent Private Hall or any other institution designated by Council by regulation as being permitted to present candidates for matriculation as student members of the University.

Place of residence

4. (1) Unless regulations 4(2), 6, or 7 below apply, student members who are reading for a degree awarded on passing the Second Public Examination must reside, for the period prescribed for that degree, within six miles from Carfax.

(2) A student member to whom paragraph (1) above applies may reside within twenty-five miles from Carfax if he or she:

(*a*) holds the status of Senior Student or has already satisfied the examiners in a Second Public Examination; or

(*b*) resides in the home of his or her parent or guardian.

5. Unless regulations 6 or 7 below apply, student members who are reading for any other degree of the University shall reside, for the period prescribed for that degree, within twenty-five miles from Carfax.

6. The Proctors may, upon the application in writing of the head or another officer of the applicant's college, authorise a student member to reside and keep terms in a house or flat situated more than the number of miles from Carfax prescribed in his or her case if

there are special circumstances which appear to the Proctors to justify such authorisation.

7. All student members who are engaged on part-time courses, or who are exceptionally permitted to undertake their research in a well-found laboratory outside Oxford under the provisions of the Regulations for the Degree of Doctor of Philosophy, shall be exempt from the residence limit.

8. If any student member (other than one engaged on a part-time course, or one exceptionally permitted to undertake his or her research in a well-found laboratory outside Oxford under the provisions of the Regulations for the Degree of Doctor of Philosophy) shall reside more than the number of miles from Carfax prescribed in his or her case without the permission of the Proctors, he or she shall not be permitted to count such residence towards any period or periods during which he or she is required to reside to obtain a degree or other qualification from the University.

9. (1) If any student member is dissatisfied with a decision by the Proctors under regulation 6 above or regulation 14 below, he or she, or his or her college, may within fourteen days of the date of the decision appeal in writing to the Chair of the Education Committee of Council.

(2) The appeal shall be adjudged expeditiously by the Chair or another member of that committee, other than one of the Proctors, nominated by the Chair.

Calculating periods of residence

10. Whenever the required time for any degree or other qualification is reckoned in terms, 'term' shall mean a term as prescribed in regulation 2 of the Regulations on the Number and Length of Terms.

11. A person on whom any degree has not yet been conferred shall not be reckoned as having completed a term of residence for his or her degree unless he or she has resided within the University for six weeks of each such term.

12. Whenever the required time for any degree or other qualification is reckoned in years, a year shall be deemed to be the equivalent of three terms. (For example, if three years are required, nine terms shall be understood, if four years, twelve terms, and so on.)

13. If a student member is presented for matriculation during the course of a term he or she shall be entitled to count the whole of that term as one term's residence if he or she has been residing at a place

of residence authorised under these regulations for the whole of that term.

14. A person who wishes to become a Senior Student under the provisions of the Regulations for Senior Student Status, or a graduate of another university who is applying for admission as a Probationer Research Student or as a student for any of the Degrees of Master of Fine Art, Master of Letters, Master of Philosophy, Master of Science, Master of Studies, Magister Juris, Master of Business Administration, Master of Public Policy, Bachelor of Philosophy, or Bachelor of Civil Law, may be given permission by the Proctors to count towards his or her statutory residence any period not exceeding one calendar month during which he or she has resided, before his or her matriculation, under conditions approved by his or her college, within the relevant distance from Carfax as specified in these regulations.

15. Any person who has been given dispensation from the requirements of regulation 11 (1) of the Regulations for Matriculation of Student Members only after he or she has come into residence shall be permitted to reckon as part of his or her statutory residence under these regulations any period, not exceeding one term, during which he or she has resided before his or her matriculation, under conditions approved by his or her college, within the appropriate distance from Carfax as specified in these regulations.

16. If a student member is suspended from access to the premises and facilities of the University, the period of suspension shall not count towards the fulfilment of that student's statutory residence requirements.

Dispensations

17. Council may by regulation provide for student members to be excused from any required period of statutory residence up to a specified limit.

REGULATIONS FOR SENIOR STUDENT STATUS

Made by Council on 8 May 2002

1. The following may be admitted to the status and privileges of a Senior Student, subject to the decision of the Education Committee of Council in any case of doubt or difficulty:

   (1) persons who have obtained a degree at another university after having pursued a course of study extending over three years of full-time study, or its equivalent on a part-time basis;

   (2) persons who, having been a student at a university in a European country, have successfully completed a course of study on a full-time, or equivalent part-time, basis deemed to be equivalent to that of an undergraduate degree qualification;

   (3) persons who have obtained a degree at another university and have also been selected to come to Oxford by some body recognized for the purposes of this regulation by the University;

   (4) persons who, though not eligible under paragraphs (1) or (2) or (3) above, have satisfied the Education Committee of Council that they are well-qualified to be admitted as Senior Students.

2. The status and privileges of Senior Students shall be as follows:

   (1) The term in which they are matriculated shall be reckoned, for the purposes of any provisions respecting the standing of members of the University, as the fourth term from their matriculation.

   (2) They shall not be required to pass the First Public Examination as a condition for the Degree of Bachelor of Arts or of Master of Biochemistry or Chemistry or Computer Science or Earth Sciences or Engineering or Mathematics or Mathematics and Computer Science or Computer Science and Philosophy or Mathematics and Philosophy or Mathematics and Physics (after transfer to that Honour School for their Part C examination from the Master of Mathematics in Mathematics, the Master of Physics in Physics, or the Master of Physics and Philosophy in Physics and Philosophy following their Part B examinations) or Physics or Physics and Philosophy, or the Preliminary Examination in Fine Art as a condition for the Degree of Bachelor of Fine Art, as the case may be.

(3) They shall be entitled to supplicate for the Degree of Bachelor of Arts, or of Bachelor of Fine Art, or of Master of Biochemistry or Chemistry or Computer Science or Computer Science and Philosophy or Earth Sciences or Engineering or Mathematics or Mathematics and Computer Science or Mathematics and Philosophy or Mathematics and Physics (after transfer to that Honour School for their Part C examination from the Master of Mathematics in Mathematics, the Master of Physics in Physics, or the Master of Physics and Philosophy in Physics and Philosophy following their Part B examinations) or Physics or Physics and Philosophy, as the case may be, if they have kept statutory residence, as defined in the relevant regulations, for six terms in the case of courses of study lasting three years, or nine terms in the case of courses of study lasting four years, and have obtained a place, or have been declared to have deserved Honours under the Regulations for the Conduct of Examinations, in the Results List of an Honour School of the Second Public Examination or the Final Examination in Fine Art, or they are entitled under the relevant regulations to supplicate for one of those degrees as if they had obtained Honours in such an examination.

3. Any persons who desire to become Senior Students under the provisions of these regulations shall send their applications, through an officer of a college, society, or Permanent Private Hall or another institution designated by Council by regulation as being permitted to present candidates for matriculation, to the Registrar and shall at the same time produce all necessary certificates and information in support of their applications.

REGULATIONS FOR READMISSION AND MIGRATION

Made by Council on 8 May 2002

1. In these regulations, unless the context requires otherwise, 'college' means any college, society, or Permanent Private Hall or any other institution designated by Council by regulation as being permitted to present candidates for matriculation.

2. If any person has been expelled by any college, that person shall not be readmitted to the college without the written permission of the Proctors if:

(1) his or her expulsion has taken place while he or she was still subject to any penalty imposed by the Proctors or the Disciplinary Court or the Appeal Court; or

(2) the Proctors have given specific notice in writing to the college that the consent of the Proctors will be required.

3. A student member of the University may migrate from any college to any other, and a graduate of the University who is a minister of religion or a candidate for the ministry may migrate to Ripon College, Cuddesdon, in order to read for the Honour School of Theology, for any joint Honour School which includes Theology, for the Diploma in Theology, for the Certificate in Theology, or for the Degree of Bachelor of Theology, if in each case he or she has first obtained:

(1) written permission for his or her migration from the college to which he or she belongs; and

(2) a certificate signed by the two Proctors that they have seen that permission and do not oppose his or her migration.

4. If the Proctors decline to give their consent under regulation 2 above, or to sign the certificate specified in regulation 3 (2) above, the person concerned may dispute the Proctors' decision in accordance with Statute XVII.

5. No person who has previously been admitted as a member by any college within the University shall be admitted as a member by any other without the production of the proper certificates.

6. In granting a certificate of migration, the Proctors, with the consent of the Vice-Chancellor, may append such conditions

as to residence during the next three terms as may appear to them desirable.

7. If any permission or testimonial required under the provisions of regulations 2 and 3 above is refused, the Vice-Chancellor may nevertheless, if he or she thinks fit, grant consent in writing for the migration.

8. If any student member of the University has been expelled by the authorities of any college, that person shall not be readmitted to membership of the University unless the Vice-Chancellor has heard the case and has given consent in writing for the readmission of that person; and it shall be the duty of the authorities of colleges to satisfy themselves that any person applying to them for admission has not previously been so expelled.

9. Any student member of the University migrating or having been readmitted to membership of the University except under the conditions laid down above shall forfeit all the privileges of the University from the date of his or her migration or readmission; except that the two Proctors, if they are satisfied that there was no reason why that person should not have been allowed to migrate or to be readmitted, may exempt him or her from the penalties imposed by this regulation, and any person so exempted shall pay to the University through the Registrar a further sum equivalent to one-half of the matriculation fee payable at the date of the exemption.

10. (1) Nothing in regulations 2–9 above shall be taken to apply to any person:

    (*a*) who becomes a member of another college by virtue of his or her election to any office or emolument;

    (*b*) who, being a graduate of the University, becomes a member of another college in order to pursue a further course of study (other than one which continues the academic programme for which he or she has already been admitted as a Probationer Research Student).

(2) It shall be the responsibility of the head or bursar of the college of which a person becomes a member under paragraph (1) (*a*) or (*b*) above to include the name of that person in the termly schedule of the names of the members of the college who are liable to pay composition fees to the University, unless that person's name is included in the schedule prepared by the head or bursar of any other college of which the person is already a member.

NOTES

I

REGULATIONS FOR THE CONDUCT OF UNIVERSITY EXAMINATIONS

*It is suggested that these regulations are read
in conjunction with the Policy and Guidance for Examiners
and others involved in University Examinations*[1]

Part 1
Introduction

1.1. (1) These regulations shall, unless otherwise stated in any statute or in these or any other regulations, apply to University Examinations (including the First as well as the Second Public Examination) for all degrees except those referred to in paragraph (3) below.

(2) They also apply to University Examinations for all certificates and diplomas awarded by the University, and to any Examination described as a qualifying examination.

(3) They do not apply to University Examinations for the degree of Doctor of Divinity, Medicine, Civil Law, Letters, Science, Music and Philosophy or Master of Letters, Master of Science by Research, and Master of Studies in Legal Research, or Bachelor of Divinity.

1.2. In these regulations unless the context otherwise requires:

(1) 'college' means any college, society, or Permanent Private Hall or any other institution designated by Council by regulation as being permitted to present candidates for matriculation;

(2) 'examiners' includes all persons approved to examine candidates for University Examinations to which these regulations apply;

(3) 'examination' includes the submission and assessment of a thesis, dissertation, essay, practical work, or other coursework and any other exercise which is not undertaken in formal examination conditions but counts towards or constitutes the work for a degree or other academic award;

---

[1] Available at: http://www.admin.ox.ac.uk/edc/qa/policies

    (4) 'University Examination' means a group or number of examinations which a candidate must pass to obtain a degree or other award or to qualify as a candidate for a degree or other award of the University;

    (5) 'supervisory body' means a Board of the Division or Faculty or other university body which has supervision over a University Examination;

    (6) 'Board of Examiners' means the body of examiners, including external examiners, who are appointed to conduct a University Examination but does not include assessors.

    (7) 'Senior Tutor' means the Senior Tutor or other proper officer of a candidate's college.

    (8) words and expressions in the singular include the plural and those in the plural include the singular.

1.3. For the purpose of these regulations unless regulation 1.4 below applies a person is a member of the college through which he or she pays fees or has compounded for the payment of fees to the University, and of no other college.

1.4. A person who is a tutor or fellow of a college shall for the purpose of these regulations be deemed to be a member of that college.

1.5. Where in these regulations examiners are distinguished as junior and senior, seniority shall, unless the context reguires otherwise, be determined in accordance with regulations made by Council.

1.6. References in these regulations to Full Term and any other University Term shall bear the meaning attributed to them by Council Regulations on the Number and Length of Terms.

1.7. Council may authorise a supervisory body to make special regulations for a University Examination modifying the effect of these regulations on that Examination to the extent permitted by Council.

Part 2
Number of Examiners

2.1. It is the duty of every supervisory body:

    (1) to ensure that there is a sufficient number of suitably qualified examiners to prepare and examine every part of the University Examination for which it is responsible;

    (2) to arrange for their nomination in accordance with Part 4 below.

2.2. Except in the cases mentioned in regulation 2.3 below, every candidate in an examination shall be examined by at least two examiners or by one examiner and one assessor.

2.3. Regulations 2.2 above shall not apply to:

(1) an examination which is part of a Preliminary Examination or Moderations (but not Honour Moderations) in the First Public Examination; or

(2) an examination which is exempted from the requirement set out in regulation 2.2 with the written permission of the chair of the Education Committee.

Doctor of Clinical Psychology

2.4. (1) The membership and terms of reference of the Board of Examiners for the Degree of Doctor of Clinical Psychology shall be determined by the Directorate of the Oxford Doctoral Course in Clinical Psychology.

(2) The Course Director shall deposit annually with the Proctors the procedures for nomination of examiners, and the terms of reference and conventions of the Board of Examiners.

(3) Nominations of examiners shall be subject to regulation 4.8 and 4.13 in Part 4 of these regulations.

Part 3
Qualifications of Examiners

3.1. Examiners, other than examiners appointed under regulation 2.4 above or external examiners appointed under Part 4 of these regulations, must be members of a Faculty or department of the University.

3.2. The Pro-Vice-Chancellor (Education) and Proctors may for good cause dispense with the requirements of regulation 3.1 above.

3.3. Except in the cases referred to in regulation 3.4 below, no more than two persons who are, or have been during the two preceding years, on the teaching staff of the same college shall be nominated to serve at the same time:

(1) as moderators in the same part of a First Public Examination; or

(2) as public examiners in the same Final Honour School.

3.4. Regulation 3.3 above does not apply to persons who are appointed to examine in separate subjects or in the separate parts of a University Examination which is divided into separate formal parts.

3.5. The Pro-Vice-Chancellor (Education) and Proctors may for good cause dispense with the requirements of regulation 3.3 above.

Part 4
Examiners: Nominations and Vacancies[1]

4.1. It is the duty of every supervisory body to establish and maintain standing orders for:

(1) the number of examiners for any University Examination for which that supervisory body is responsible;

(2) the examiners' period of office;

(3) the appointment of a chair of examiners;

(4) the composition and constitution (including the arrangements for appointment of the chair and rules as to quorum) of any nominating committee to whom responsibilities are delegated under regulations 4.4 or 4.5 below; and

(5) the period of service of the members of that committee and the filling of vacancies.

4.2. The standing orders made under regulation 4.1 above shall be submitted:

(1) to the Proctors and the Registrar[2] before the beginning of each academic year; and

(2) the Education Committee with the examiners' report at the conclusion of the Examination.

4.3. Examiners must be nominated to the Pro-Vice-Chancellor (Education) and Proctors by the supervisory body in accordance with those standing orders.

4.4. Unless there is provision to the contrary in any regulation, the responsibility for making nominations in respect of any University Examination which is under the joint supervision of more than one supervisory body shall be delegated to a nominating committee appointed jointly for this purpose by the supervisory bodies concerned.

4.5. A single supervisory body responsible for making nominations in respect of any other University Examination may delegate its responsibility to a nominating committee consisting of not fewer than three persons appointed by it for this purpose.

4.6. The Proctors and the Registrar shall be informed annually of the membership of each nominating committee.

---

[1] Reference should also be made to Policy and Guidance for Examiners and others involved in University Examinations available via: www.admin.ox.ac.uk/edc/qa/policies

[2] References to the Registrar in this section should normally be taken to refer to the Head of Examinations and Assessments at the Examination Schools, who acts on behalf of the Registrar.

4.7. (1) Every nomination shall be made by a majority of votes.

(2) When the votes are equal the chair of the relevant board or other body or nominating committee acting on its behalf shall have an additional, casting vote.

(3) Where a nomination is made by a casting vote and is forwarded to the Pro-Vice-Chancellor (Education) and Proctors for their approval, they shall be informed that it has been made by a casting vote.

Degree of Doctor of Clinical Psychology

4.8. (1) Nominations of examiners for the Degree of Doctor of Clinical Psychology shall be made by a committee comprising two persons elected by the Directorate of the Oxford Doctoral Course in Clinical Psychology and two persons elected by the Medical Sciences Board.

(2) Nominations made under this regulation must be made in writing by at least three of the members of the nominating committee and shall be subject to the approval of the Pro-Vice-Chancellor (Education) and Proctors.

Notice of vacancies

4.9. By the Friday of the last week of each Full Term the Registrar shall send to each supervisory body, or its nominating committee acting on its behalf (as the case may be), the vacancies in examinerships to be filled in the following term.

Notice of nominations

4.10. Each supervisory body, or its nominating committee acting on its behalf (as the case may be), shall, unless regulation 4.11 below applies, submit to the Registrar, by 5 p.m. on the first Tuesday of the Full Term in which any vacancy has to be filled in accordance with Part 5 of these regulations, nominations of new examiners, signed by not fewer than two of the members of the board or other body or committee in question.

4.11. Nominations of new examiners for the Degree of Bachelor of Philosophy and Master of Philosophy in subjects other than Classical Archaeology shall be submitted by 5 p.m. on Friday in the sixth week of the Full Term in which a vacancy has to be filled in accordance with Part 5 of these regulations.

4.12. If notice of a vacancy in an examinership is not received by the Monday before the Full Term in which it is to be filled in accordance with regulation 4.09 above, the Pro-Vice-Chancellor (Education) shall fix the date by which nominations in writing must be received in accordance with those regulations, and the date for any meeting of the board or other body or nominating committee which may be necessary to make a nomination.

Submission of nominations

4.13. The chair of the board or other body or of the nominating committee acting on its behalf shall be responsible for the submission of nominations under regulations 4.10–4.12 above duly signed by the persons specified.

External examiners

4.14. Regulations 4.15–4.19 below apply to the appointment of external examiners.

4.15. Each supervisory body or nominating committee acting on its behalf *must* nominate as an external examiner for each University Examination for the Second Public Examination for which it is responsible a person to act as an external arbiter of standards and *may* nominate a person as an external examiner to provide academic expertise not otherwise obtainable from within the University.

4.16. A person nominated under regulation 4.15 above may be approved and designated by the Pro-Vice-Chancellor (Education) and Proctors as an external examiner. An external examiner who fails to submit the annual report required by the University may continue in office only with the permission of the Pro-Vice-Chancellor (Education) and the Proctors.

4.17. A person holding a post in the University or any college or other Oxford institution associated with the University in the examination of candidates may not be approved or designated as an external examiner.

4.18. Unless they are appointed to examine separate subjects or in separate parts of a University Examination divided into formal parts, no two persons who are, or have been during the preceding two years, on the teaching staff of the same university or other institution shall normally be nominated to serve at the same time as external examiners in the same University Examination.

4.19. External examiners shall be entitled to a retaining fee up to but not exceeding an amount determined from time to time by the Planning and Resource Allocation Committee of Council.

Additional examiners

4.20. A supervisory body may at any time, if it is necessary or desirable to do so, nominate additional examiners to serve on a Board of Examiners for one University Examination only, and the provisions of any standing orders shall not apply to the time of their nomination.

Final Honour Schools divided into Parts

4.21. If any Final Honour School is divided into Parts there shall be a separate Board of Examiners for each Part.

Part 5
Examiners: Period of Office, Casual Vacancies, Resignation, and Removal

5.1. (1) Examiners (except additional examiners) shall take up their office on the first day of the Full Term following the approval of their nomination by the Pro-Vice-Chancellor (Education) and Proctors.

(2) Additional examiners shall take up their office immediately after that date.

5.2. (1) Subject to the provisions of this Part examiners shall serve for the period designated in its standing orders by the supervisory body responsible for the University Examination for which they are appointed.

(2) Each supervisory body shall notify the Proctors and the Registrar before the beginning of each academic year of the number of examiners and the period of their office.

5.3. Examiners who have not held office for the full period may be renominated either for a full period or for such period as together with the period of office thay have in fact completed will constitute a full period.

5.4. If it is necessary for the due regulation of the succession among examiners in any University Examination that an examiner or examiners shall retire before the end of the normal period of service, then the junior shall retire.

5.5. The Pro-Vice-Chancellor (Education) and Proctors may dispense from any of the requirements of regulations 5.1–5.4 above if they consider it reasonable to do so.

5.6. (1) An examiner may, on account of sickness or other urgent cause, obtain from the Pro-Vice-Chancellor (Education) and Proctors leave of absence for a period extending over not more than one University Examination, and a suitably qualified person shall be appointed to act as his or her substitute during that period.

(2) If leave of absence is granted before the first day of the Full Term in which or following which the University Examination in question is to begin, the substitute shall

be nominated by the supervisory body or (as the case may be) the nominating committee concerned.

(3) If leave of absence is granted on or after that day the substitute shall be appointed by the Pro-Vice-Chancellor (Education) and Proctors.

5.7. If an examiner appears to the Pro-Vice-Chancellor (Education) or the Proctors to be acting in the conduct of his or her office in a manner which is inconsistent with proper standards of academic rigour, integrity, impartiality, or fairness, or may otherwise bring discredit upon the examination process or the University, he or she shall (without prejudice to any other action which may be taken) be removed from office by the Pro-Vice-Chancellor (Education) or Proctors as the case may be.

5.8. (1) If an examiner dies or resigns or is removed from office under this Part a suitably qualified person shall be appointed to act as his or her substitute.

(2) Where death, resignation, or removal occurs before the first day of Full Term in which or following which the University Examination in question is to begin, the substitute shall be nominated in accordance with regulation 5.6 (2) above and shall serve for the residue of the period of office of the person whom he or she succeeds.

(3) Where death, resignation, or removal occurs after that date the substitute shall be appointed by the Pro-Vice-Chancellor (Education) and Proctors and shall serve for the next University Examination only.

5.9. Examiners appointed under regulations 5.6 and 5.7 above shall:

(1) take up their office forthwith; and

(2) receive such remuneration (if any) as is determined from time to time by the Pro-Vice-Chancellor (Education) and Proctors.

5.10. If a person who is appointed an examiner by virtue of his or her office is for any reason unable to act he or she shall nominate a deputy who shall be a member of a faculty to act in his or her place with the approval of the Pro-Vice-Chancellor (Education) and the Proctors.

Part 6
Chairs of Examiners

6.1. The supervisory body responsible for a University Examination shall appoint a chair of examiners as soon as practicable and in accordance with its standing orders and shall notify the Registrar of the appointment.

6.2. Except with the permission of the Pro-Vice-Chancellor (Education), an external examiner shall not be eligible to serve as chair.

6.3. The Registrar shall arrange a notice of the appointment of each chair of examiners to be published in the *University Gazette*.

6.4. Until a chair has been appointed the senior examiner who is a member of a Faculty shall fulfil the duties of the chair. Seniority shall be determined by reference to the rules for academic precedence and standing as made from time to time by Council.

6.5. As well as performing the specific duties laid down in these or any other regulations the chair shall be responsible generally for ensuring that the business of his or her Board of Examiners is properly conducted and that the requirements of these regulations are fulfilled by that Board.

6.6. It shall be the duty of each chair of examiners to ensure that account is taken of the *Policy and Guidance for Examiners and others involved in University Examinations* published periodically by the Proctors and the Education Committee so far as it is applicable to the University Examination for which his or her Board of Examiners is responsible.

6.7. (1) The chair shall convene at least one meeting of the examiners before each University Examination for which they are responsible and by this and other means ensure that all arrangements for its proper conduct have been made and understood.

(2) An external examiner shall not be required to attend such a meeting but shall be informed by the chair of its proceedings and decisions.

6.8. The chair of the Board of Examiners for each single Final Honour School shall designate the examiners required for any joint Final Honour School in which any of the examinations correspond with an examination in the single School.

Part 7

Assessors

7.1. A Board of Examiners may in accordance with the provisions of this Part appoint as assessors other persons who are not examiners in the same University Examination to act with them in setting and/ or marking any particular part of a University Examination.

7.2. (1) Unless paragraph (3) below applies an assessor must hold the same qualifications as an examiner as provided in regulation 3.1 above.

(2) The Pro-Vice-Chancellor (Education) and Proctors may for good cause dispense with the requirements of regulation 7.2 (1) above.

(3) A person who holds a post of lector in either the University or one of the colleges in the language concerned may be appointed to act as an assessor in an oral examination in any of the following Final Honour Schools:

Modern Languages

History and Modern Languages

Philosophy and Modern Languages

Classics and Modern Languages

English and Modern Languages

European and Middle Eastern Languages.

7.3. Where an examination forms part of more than one University Examination a person may be appointed to act as an assessor of that examination for all University Examinations of which it forms a part.

7.4. The chair of the Board of Examiners concerned must apply to the Pro-Vice-Chancellor (Education) and Proctors for their approval of the appointment of any assessor, and an appointment shall not be effective until that approval is given.

7.5. The Proctors shall inform the Registrar of the names of all persons appointed as assessors.

7.6. Persons acting as assessors shall make a report to the Board of Examiners on the parts of the University Examinations submitted to them, but shall have no right of voting on the place of any candidate in a Results List nor on the question of his or her having satisfied the examiners or having been adjudged worthy of distinction.

7.7. An assessor shall if invited by the Board of Examiners take part in any *viva voce* examination.

7.8. The remuneration of assessors shall be according to a scale drawn up by the Planning and Resource Allocation Committee of Council.

7.9. The provisions of regulations 5.6, 5.7, and 5.8 above which concern leave of absence, death, resignation, and removal in the case of examiners shall apply, with any necessary modifications, to assessors.

7.10. The Pro-Vice-Chancellor (Education) and Proctors shall have power to give and vary directions necessary for the carrying out of the provisions of this Part.

Part 8
Approval of Conventions and Submission of Papers to Examiners

Approval of conventions

8.1. The conventions to be used in the assessment of candidates in any University Examination shall be approved by the supervisory body responsible for the course and the Examination and be published to prospective candidates not less than one whole term before the Examination takes place or, where assessment takes place in the first term of a course, at the beginning of that term.

Submission of papers to examiners

8.2. The papers proposed for any written examination shall be submitted to all the examiners in the University Examination concerned according to a timetable determined by the chair of the examiners under this Part.

8.3. Each chair of examiners shall determine a timetable for the submission of papers under regulation 8.2 above which shall allow sufficient time for

(1) the due consideration and approval of the proposed papers by all the examiners;

(2) the production and proof-reading of the papers and their presentation in camera-ready copy; and

(3) the delivery of two camera-ready copies of each paper to the Examination Schools not later than five weeks before the first day of the University Examination in question.

8.4. In the Final Honour School of Oriental Studies it shall be sufficient if the paper in each main subject and, where appropriate, additional language, is submitted to the chair of the examiners and the examiners acting together in the conduct of the examination in that main subject and additional language.

Part 9
Times for Holding Examinations and Entry of Names of Candidates

Times for holding Examinations

9.1. The Registrar and the Education Committee shall, after consultation with the Pro-Vice-Chancellor (Education) and Proctors, fix the days on which each University Examination shall begin and shall give public notice of such days.

9.2. The chair of examiners in each University Examination shall, on the advice of the Registrar, state and give public notice of the date time and place of the beginning of each examination, and shall afterwards give such notice as he or she shall deem necessary of the further attendance required of candidates.

9.3. (1) The Registrar shall be given the names of all candidates for all University Examinations except those referred to in paragraph (2) of this regulation.

(2) For the Examination for the Postgraduate Certificate in Education names shall be given in the manner prescribed by the regulations governing that Examination.

9.4. The Registrar shall devise and issue to all candidates an entry form on which candidates shall

(1) state the University Examination for which they intend to enter;

(2) state the options they intend to offer, if the regulations of the University Examination for which they are entering permit the offering of options;

(3) secure the confirmation of their college through the signature of the Senior Tutor or his or her nominee that their entry is valid;

(4) declare their intention of abiding by all University Regulations governing the conduct of examinations; and

(5) provide such other declaration as may be required by the special regulations for the University Examination in question.

9.5. The Registrar shall fix the days for entering names after consultation with the Education Committee, and he or she shall give public notice of the place and hour at which he or she will receive names.

Late entries

9.6. Where a candidate whose name has not been entered for an examination by the date fixed by the Registrar under the provisions of regulation 9.5 above wishes his or her name to be entered after that date, the procedure shall be as follows:

(1) the candidate shall apply in writing through the Senior Tutor to the Registrar for his or her name to be so entered;

(2) the Registrar shall determine whether the candidate proposes to offer part of the examination which has not already been offered by some other candidate whose name has been entered under the provisions of regulation 9.5 above and whether any other change in the conduct of the examination, as already arranged, would be involved;

(3) if no change in the conduct of the examination as referred to in paragraph (2) would be involved, the Registrar shall, subject to the payment by the candidate of a late-entry fee, grant permission for the candidate to be admitted to the examination;

(4) if some such change would be involved, the Registrar shall ask the chair of examiners whether he or she is, nevertheless, willing to consent to the candidate being admitted to the examination, and if the chair consents the Registrar shall, subject to the payment by the candidate of a late-entry fee, grant permission for the candidate to be admitted to the examination;

(5) if the chair of examiners refuses to give the consent referred to in paragraph (4), the Registrar shall refer the matter to the Proctors for decision, and, if they give permission, this shall be subject to the payment by the candidate of a late-entry fee;

(6) the late-entry fee payable under paragraphs (3), (4) and (5) shall be such sum as the Education Committee shall from time to time determine, and different sums may be specified in respect of permission given under different paragraphs.

9.7. (1) Notwithstanding the provisions of regulation 9.6 above, the Divisional Board of Social Sciences may make provision for late entry, as appropriate, in the regulations for the Postgraduate Certificate in Education.

(2) Candidates permitted to enter late for these examinations shall pay such sum as the Education Committee shall from time to time determine.

Late alteration of options

9.8. Where the regulations for a University Examination permit the offering of options and a candidate wishes to alter his or her choice of options, the procedure shall be as follows:

(1) The candidate shall apply in writing through the Senior Tutor to the Registrar for the alteration to be made.

(2) The Registrar shall determine whether the candidate proposes to offer a part of the examination which has not already been offered by some other candidate whose name has been entered under the provisions of regulations 9.3–9.5 above and whether any other change in the conduct of the examination, as already arranged, would be involved.

(3) If no change in the conduct of the examination as referred to in paragraph (2) would be involved, the Registrar shall, subject to the payment by the candidate of a late-alteration fee, grant permission for the alteration to be made.

(4) If some such change would be involved, the Registrar shall ask the chair of examiners whether he or she is, nevertheless, willing to consent to the alteration, and, if the chair consents, the Registrar shall, subject to the payment by the candidate of a late alteration fee, grant permission for the alteration to be made.

(5) If the chair of examiners refuses to give the consent referred to in paragraph (4), the Registrar shall refer the matter to the Proctors for decision, and, if they give permission, this shall be subject to the payment by the candidate of a late-alteration fee.

(6) A candidate or his or her college may within fourteen days of the date of the Proctors' decision appeal in writing to the chair of the Education Committee (who may nominate another member of the committee, other than one of the Proctors, to adjudicate the appeal).

(7) The late-alteration fee payable under paragraphs (3), (4) and (5) above shall be such sum as the Education Committee shall from time to time determine, and different sums may be specified in respect of permission given under different paragraphs.

Waiver of fees

9.9. The Proctors may waive the payment of any fee payable under regulations 9.6 and 9.8 above if it appears to them to be reasonable to do so.

Processing of forms

9.10. The Registrar shall acknowledge to the candidates the receipt of all completed entry forms and shall return to the candidate for completion or correction any form which is incomplete or is not in accordance with any relevant regulation.

9.11. Candidates must notify the Registrar of any subsequent changes in the information given on their form.

9.12. If, through change of name, migration or otherwise the Registrar entertains any reasonable doubt about the identity of a candidate offering himself or herself for any University Examination, he or she may require such further evidence of identity as he or she may deem necessary.

Transmission of names of candidates and their options to the examiners

9.13. From the entry forms the Registrar shall assign a candidate number to each candidate and shall send the lists of numbers to the chair of the examiners in the University Examination for which the candidates have been entered.

Examination for the Degree of Doctor of Clinical Psychology validated by the University

9.14. Notwithstanding any provision of regulations in this Part to the contrary, the entry of names, late entries, late alterations of names and candidates, and transmission of names of candidates and lists of subjects to the examiners for the examination for the Degree of Doctor of Clinical Psychology shall be governed by regulations laid down from time to time by the Directorate of the Oxford Doctoral Course in Clinical Psychology and lodged annually with the Proctors.

Part 10
Candidates with Special Examination Needs

Application of Part 10

10.1. (1) This Part is concerned with candidates for University Examinations who have a physical or mental impairment which has a substantial and long-term adverse effect on their ability to carry out normal day-to-day activities.

(2) This Part shall apply to them if the impairment which they have significantly affects their ability to undertake any examination at or within the time allotted to it, or at the place where it is to be held, or in the manner in which it is normally undertaken by candidates.

(3) This Part in any case applies to every candidate who has a specific learning difficulty such as dyslexia, dyspraxia, dysgraphia, dyscalculia or attention deficit disorder.

(4) Candidates to whom this Part applies are called 'candidates with special examination needs' and those falling within paragraph (3) of this regulation are called 'candidates with specific learning difficulties'.

General Rules

10.2. A candidate in any University Examination with special examination needs may apply to the Proctors through the Senior Tutor of his or her college:

(1) for alternative examination arrangements relating to his or her condition; and

(2) for the condition to be taken into account by the examiners as a special factor that may affect his or her performance in examinations.

10.3. (1) An application under regulation 10.2 above shall be made as soon as possible after matriculation and in any event not later than the date of entry of the candidate's name for the first examination for which alternative arrangements are sought.

(2) The application must be supported by a statement from an educational psychologist or other suitably qualified medical practitioner (called in these regulations 'the consultant') approved by the Proctors.

(3) The consultant's statement must be based on an assessment of the candidate carried out by that person and on such further assessment of the candidate as the consultant considers necessary in order to form a judgement.

(4) The Proctors shall issue guidance periodically on the qualifications of consultants and the nature of the assessments that will be considered appropriate.

10.4. (1) Where an application is made in respect of a candidate who is confirmed under regulation 10.3 above to have special examination needs, the Proctors shall ensure that arrangements are made for the examination of that candidate which are appropriate for him or her and fair in all the circumstances.

(2) These arrangements may include but are not limited to the provision of a room for the examination of the candidate, permission under Part 13 of these regulations for the dictation of papers and the use of a word-processor or other materials and equipment, the provision of an amanuensis, and the granting of extra time for the examination.

(3) The Proctors shall have regard to any recommendation made by the consultant in deciding what arrangements they should make.

10.5. Candidates who are confirmed under regulation 10.3 above to have a specific learning difficulty shall, where appropriate, be given extra time by the Proctors. Additional examination adjustments may be permitted on the recommendation of the consultant.

10.6. In the case of a candidate with a specific learning difficulty the Proctors shall also ensure that the appropriate statements explaining the effects of a specific learning difficulty are supplied to the chair of the examiners of the relevant University Examination and the Registrar shall ensure that they are placed on the candidate's examination scripts and any other work submitted for assessment, in order to assist the examiners in adjudicating the merits of the candidate's work.

Visually-impaired candidates

10.7. (1) This additional regulation applies to candidates who are visually-impaired.   5

(2) Where any college has a visually-impaired candidate for any University Examination, the Senior Tutor shall, not less than three months before the date of the Examination, inform the Proctors who will make the necessary arrangements (including provision for papers   10 in Braille if appropriate) in consultation with the Chair of Examiners and the Registrar.

(3) When papers in Braille or another format are required, the chair concerned shall submit a copy of the necessary manuscripts to the Registrar at least eight weeks before   15 the date of the beginning of the University Examination.

Codes of practice

10.8. In exercising their powers under this Part the Proctors and chairs of examiners shall take full account of any relevant code of practice or other guidance adopted by the University in relation to   20 persons who have a disability.

Invigilation

10.9. The invigilation of candidates with special examination needs for whom an examination room is provided shall be carried out in accordance with regulation 15.5 below.   25

Continuity of arrangements

10.10. Alternative arrangements approved by the Proctors under this Part shall normally apply to all University Examinations taken by the candidate during his or her course of study.

10.11 (1) It shall be the responsibility of the candidate to apply for   30 any subsequent change to these arrangements which he or she may wish, and to inform the Proctors of any material change in his or her circumstances which might affect the suitability of those arrangements.

(2) In considering any request made under paragraph (1)   35 the Proctors shall obtain and take into account the views of the consultant.

Appeals under this Part

10.12. A candidate who is dissatisfied with any decision made by the Proctors under this Part, or his or her college, may appeal   40 against that decision in accordance with the provisions of regulation 18.1 below.

Costs

10.13. The costs of arrangements made under this Part shall not fall on the candidate.

Part 11
Acute Illness or other Urgent Causes Affecting Candidates

Application of Part 11

11.1. This Part is concerned with candidates whose performance in a University Examination may be significantly affected by acute illness or some other urgent cause, not falling within regulation 10.1 above, which comes to the notice of a candidate's college before, during or after an examination.

Non-appearance at an examination

11.2. (1) A candidate in any University Examination may, through his or her college, request the Proctors to accept a submission that the candidate will be or has been prevented by illness or other urgent cause from presenting himself or herself at the appointed time or place for any part of a University Examination.

(2) For the purposes of this regulation a candidate will be deemed to have presented himself or herself for a written paper if he or she was present in the place designated for that examination and had the opportunity to see the question paper there.

11.3. (1) A request under regulation 11.2 above must be submitted in writing by the Senior Tutor or other proper officer of the candidate's college, with sufficient evidence to support it.

(2) Where non-appearance is caused by illness a medical certificate from a qualified medical practitioner must be sent, and this certificate must specify, with dates, the reason why the illness will prevent or has prevented the candidate from attending the examination.

11.4. (1) If the Proctors accept a submission under regulation 11.2 above they shall send a copy of their decision promptly to the chair of examiners of the University Examination concerned and inform the candidate's college and the Registrar.

(2) If the Proctors decide not to accept the submission they shall give reasons for their decision.

11.5. If the Proctors accept a submission under 11.2 above they may authorise the examiners either:

(1) to examine the candidate at another place or time under such arrangements as they deem appropriate; or

(2) if other work that the candidate has already submitted in the Examination is of sufficient merit, to act as if he or she had completed the part of the University Examination which he or she was unable to attend.

11.6. Where it is decided under paragraph (1) of regulation 11.5 above that a candidate is to be examined at a place or time other than that appointed for the examination the invigilation of the candidate shall be carried out in accordance with regulation 15.5 below.

11.7. (1) Where it is decided under paragraph (2) of regulation 11.5 above that the examiners are to act as if the candidate had completed the part of the University Examination concerned, and the University Examination is one in which Honours may be awarded, the examiners may adopt one of the following courses:

(a) if they consider the candidate has submitted enough work to allow them to determine his or her proper class, they may award the candidate the class his or her performance merits;

(b) if they are unable to adopt course (a) but consider, on the basis of the work submitted, that but for the candidate's absence he or she would have obtained classified Honours, they may deem the candidate to have obtained Honours and publish his or her name accordingly at the foot of the Results List under the words 'declared to have deserved Honours';

(c) if they are unable to adopt course (a) or course (b) but are nevertheless satisfied with the work submitted, they may include the candidate's name on the Results List to show that the candidate has satisfied the examiners;

(d) if they are unable to adopt course (a), (b), or (c) they shall fail the candidate.

(2) Where the examiners have adopted course (b), (c), or (d) above it shall be open to the candidate to apply to Council for consideration of his or her standing for Honours at a future examination.

(3) Where it is decided under paragraph (2) of regulation 11.5 above that the examiners are to act as if the candidate had completed the parts of the University Examination concerned, and the University Examination is one in which Honours are not awarded, the examiners may adopt one of the following courses:

    (*a*) if they consider the candidate has submitted enough work to allow them to determine whether it is of a sufficient standard to enable the candidate to pass the Examination they may include his or her name in the Results List;

    (*b*) if they are unable to adopt course (*a*), they shall fail the candidate.

Factors affecting performance

11.8. If it comes to the notice of a candidate's college before, during or after an examination that the candidate's performance in any part of a University Examination is likely to be or has been affected by factors of which the examiners have no knowledge, that college shall through the Senior Tutor inform the Proctors of this factor.

11.9. (1) The Proctors shall pass this information on to the chair of the examiners unless in their judgement it is irrelevant to the performance of the candidate in the examination.

    (2) If the Proctors decide not to pass the information on they shall give reasons for their decision.

    (3) The Proctors will normally not pass such information to the chair of examiners if it is received after marks have been finalised by examiners.

11.10. (1) If the University Examination is one in which Honours may be awarded the examiners may adopt one of the following courses, taking account of the information passed to them:

    (*a*) if they consider the candidate has submitted enough work to allow them to determine his or her proper class, they shall award the candidate the class his or her performance merits;

    (*b*) if they are unable to adopt course (*a*) but consider, on the evidence of the work submitted, that but for the illness or other urgent cause affecting the candidate's performance, he or she would have obtained Honours, they may deem the candidate to have obtained Honours and publish his or her name accordingly at the foot of the Results List under the words 'declared to have deserved Honours';

(c) if they are unable to adopt course (a) or course (b) but are nevertheless satisfied with the work submitted, they may include the candidate's name on the Results List to show that the candidate has satisfied the examiners;

(d) if they are unable to adopt course (a), (b), or (c) they shall fail the candidate.

(2) Where the examiners have adopted course (b), (c), or (d) above it shall be open to the candidate to apply to Council for consideration of his or her standing for Honours at a future examination.

(3) If the University Examination is one in which Honours are not awarded the examiners may adopt one of the following courses, taking account of the information passed to them:

(a) if they consider that the candidate has submitted enough work to allow them to determine that it is of sufficient standard to enable the candidate to pass the Examination, they shall include his or her name in the Results List;

(b) if they are unable to adopt course (a) they shall fail the candidate.

Appeals under this Part

11.11 A candidate or his or her college who is dissatisfied with any decision made by the Proctors or by the examiners under this Part, may appeal against that decision in accordance with the provisions of regulations 18.1 or 18.2 below.

Part 12

Religious Festivals and Holidays Coinciding with Examinations

12.1. A candidate in any University Examination who is forbidden, for reasons of faith, from taking papers on religious festivals or other special days which may coincide with days on which examinations are set, may, through his or her Senior Tutor, apply to the Proctors for approval of alternative examination arrangements.

12.2. A candidate in any University Examination who is fasting, for reasons of faith, during religious festivals or other special days which may coincide with days on which examinations are set, may, through his or her Senior Tutor, apply to the Proctors for approval of alternative examination arrangements.

12.3. An application under 12.1 or 12.2 above shall be made as soon as possible after matriculation and in any event not later than the date of entry of the candidate's name for the first examination for which alternative arrangements are sought and shall specify the faith of the candidate concerned and the details of any days specially affected.

12.4. (1) If the Proctors approve the application they shall notify the Registrar who shall make reasonable efforts to ensure that an examination timetable is set such that alternative arrangements are not required.

(2) If the Proctors do not approve the application they shall give reasons for their decision.

(3) Where a request is made after the date specified in 12.3 the Proctors may still approve the application and shall follow the procedure set down in 12.4 (1) above.

12.5. If it is not practicable to adjust the timetable in the manner described in regulation 12.4 (1) above, the Registrar shall notify the Proctors and the candidate's Senior Tutor and identify another date or time when the candidate must take that part, which will, whenever possible, be no earlier than the date prescribed for the part in question.

12.6. Following such notification, the Senior Tutor shall make arrangements for the candidate to be examined at that alternative time and shall submit these arrangements to the Proctors for approval.

12.7. The Proctors shall notify the Chair of Examiners and the Registrar of alternative arrangements approved under this regulation.

12.8. When a candidate is to be examined on a date or at a time fixed by the Registrar under regulation 12.5 above, the invigilation of the candidate shall be carried out in accordance with regulation 15.5 below.

Costs

12.9. The costs of arrangements made under this Part shall not fall on the candidate.

Appeals under this Part

12.10. A candidate who is dissatisfied with a decision made by the Proctors under regulation 12.4 above, or his or her college, may appeal against that decision in accordance with the provisions of regulation 18.1 below.

Part 13
Dictation of Papers and the Use of Word-Processors, Calculators, Computers, and other Materials in Examinations

Dictation and the use of word-processors

13.1. Unless permitted by the Proctors under Parts 10 or 11 of these regulations or under any other regulation, the use of word-processing and the dictation of papers in any University Examination is prohibited.

13.2. (1) If the Proctors permit the use of a word-processor, whether for the candidate's own use or for use by an amanuensis during the dictation of papers, the Proctors shall specify in each case such detailed arrangements as they deem appropriate for the preparation and use of any equipment and computer software during the examination and for the conduct of the examination.

(2) The Proctors shall also specify the detailed arrangements to be made for the printing, handing in and recording of the candidate's script, and the number of copies to be made.

(3) The Proctors shall send the details of these arrangements promptly to the chair of the examiners of the relevant examination, with copies to the Senior Tutor, and to the Registrar.

(4) The arrangements for the collection of the examination paper by the invigilator and for the invigilation of the candidate shall take place in accordance with regulation 15.5 and 15.6 below.

13.3. The costs of arrangements made under regulation 13.2 above shall not fall on the candidate.

Use of calculators

13.4 Unless any regulation provides otherwise the following conditions shall apply in any University Examination in which candidates are permitted to use hand-held pocket calculators.

(1) The candidate shall ensure that the power supply of the calculator is adequately charged.

(2) No calculator for which a mains supply is essential will be allowed.

(3) Any calculator deemed by the Proctors or examiners to cause a disturbance will be prohibited.

(4) Output by the calculator shall be by visible display only.

(5) Candidates shall clear any user-entered data or programmes from the memories of their calculators immediately before starting each examination.

(6) No storage media external to the calculator are permitted.

(7) Input to the calculator during the examination shall be by its own keys or switches only.

(8) The examiners, invigilators, Proctors and the Registrar may inspect any calculator during the course of the examination.

Use of computers

13.5. Unless any regulation provides otherwise, in any University Examination which requires use of computers the following conditions apply:

(1) No material such as cassettes, discs, or any other device on which machine readable files can be stored may be taken into the examination room.

(2) No password or user name other than any specified on the examination paper shall be used.

(3) The examination paper shall contain a list of files, if any, which it is permitted to access. None of these files shall be deleted, written to, or tampered with in any way. No other file shall be accessed (except any files created by candidates during the course of the examination).

(4) Any files which candidates are permitted to access during the examination shall be previously submitted for approval to all examiners conducting that examination.

(5) If it is permitted to access remotely held files which are held in a file store containing other files, the permitted files shall be accessed by user names and passwords which are used solely for the purposes of the examination, and they shall not be revealed to the candidates until the start of the examination and shall be specified on the examination paper.

(6) In the event of any computer failure not involving the loss of any files in use in the examination and lasting less than one half hour, or not more than two separate failures, together lasting less than one half hour, the examination shall be extended by the amount of time lost.

(7) In the event of any computer failure not covered by (6), the examination in question shall cease forthwith. An entirely new paper shall be set at a time and place which shall have been previously announced in the timetable for the examination: but it shall be open to any candidate who shall have submitted work during or at the end of the sitting of the original paper to elect to be assessed upon that work and not to sit the new paper.

(8) If any examination is aborted on a second occasion the examiners shall determine the outcome of that examination by an alternative method after consultation with the Proctors.

Use of pencils

13.6. Except for the drawing of diagrams, no candidate may use pencil for the writing of an examination unless prior permission has been obtained from the Proctors.

Use of dictionaries

13.7. (1) Unless any regulation provides otherwise, the use of dictionaries of any kind shall not be permitted in any University Examination.

(2) This regulation shall not apply to candidates whose course of study commenced prior to Michaelmas Term 2009. Such a candidate whose native language is not English and who wishes to take into any examination a bilingual dictionary (covering English and the candidate's native language) must at the time of entering for the examination obtain permission from the Proctors through the Senior Tutor. Permission shall not be given where regulations or examiners' instructions have previously forbidden the use of dictionaries.

Part 14
Withdrawal from Examinations and Non-appearance

14.1. This Part provides for candidates who wish to withdraw from any University Examination after their names have been entered under Part 9 of these regulations or who do not appear at the time or place appointed for taking any examination for which they have been entered.

Withdrawal before the Examination begins

14.2. A candidate whose name has been entered for a University Examination may withdraw from that Examination at any time before the start or (as the case may be) date for submission of the first paper or other exercise in the Examination.

Withdrawal after the Examination has started

14.3. A candidate who wishes to withdraw from a University Examination at any time after the start of the first paper or date for submission of the first paper or other exercise must inform an invigilator and the Registrar at once and his or her college as soon as possible.

14.4. (1) A candidate may not withdraw from a University Examination at any time after the start or date for submission of the first paper or other exercise in the

Examination unless regulations 11.2–11.7 above apply to his or her case.

(2) If the candidate's college is satisfied with the reason given the Senior Tutor must as soon as possible notify the Registrar.

(3) On receipt of the notice given under paragraph (2) above the Registrar shall inform the chair of the relevant examiners.

Non-appearance at an examination

14.5. (1) Except in cases to which regulations 11.2–11.7 or 14.3 and 14.4 above apply a candidate who fails to appear for any part of a University Examination (including a viva voce examination other than as specified in (2) below) will be deemed to have failed the entire Examination or, in the case of a Second Public Examination taken over more than one year, the entire Part of the Examination.

(2) This regulation shall not apply where candidates (a) fail to appear for, or to submit work in respect of, optional papers supplementary to the compulsory elements of the examination; (b) fail to appear for a viva voce examination which has the sole purpose of confirming their final position in a Results List.

Part 15
Supervision and Invigilation of Examinations

Attendance at examinations by examiners

15.1. (1) Before the start of any examination at least one examiner shall be present to check the question paper and shall remain for the first 30 minutes of the examination (or for the duration of the paper if so required by the chair of the examiners) in case of query.

(2) An external examiner shall not be required to attend.

(3) The chair of the examiners may appoint an assessor to attend in the place of an examiner.

Invigilators

15.2. (1) The Registrar shall draw up for the approval of the Proctors a list of persons whom he or she deems suitable to invigilate examinations.

(2) No student member of the University shall be eligible to act as an invigilator unless he or she is a graduate

student in at least the third year of his or her registration for graduate study.

(3) Approved invigilators shall comply with any requirements made by Proctors, in consultation with the Registrar, with regard to their training, conduct, attendance or the discharge of their duties.

(4) The Proctors may remove from the list the name of any person who in their opinion should no longer act as an invigilator.

(5) The Registrar shall, in consultation with the chair of the examiners, arrange for individuals from the approved list to invigilate each examination.

(6) No person who is appointed to act as an amanuensis in any examination may also invigilate that examination.

Invigilation

15.3. Unless the Proctors otherwise determine, one invigilator shall be required for the first fifty candidates and one for each additional fifty candidates or fraction of that number.

Remuneration of invigilators

15.4. Persons other than examiners appointed to supervise or to invigilate under this Part shall be paid in accordance with the scale drawn up by the Education Committee.

Invigilation in cases to which Parts 10, 11 or 12 or regulation 13.2 apply

15.5. (1) When a candidate is to be examined on a date or at a time or place fixed by the Proctors, or as the case may be by a chair of examiners, under Parts 10, 11 or 12 or regulation 13.2 above, paragraphs (2)–(6) of this regulation and regulation 15.6 below shall apply.

(2) Whenever possible the examination shall take place in a room managed by the Registrar who shall be responsible for the appointment of an invigilator and other necessary arrangements.

(3) If the examination takes place in a room provided by the candidate's college, the Senior Tutor shall appoint as invigilator for that part of the examination a person whose name is on the list of invigilators or some other suitable person whose name shall be approved by the Proctors.

(4) If the examination is to take place at a time different from the time fixed for other candidates the Senior Tutor shall make arrangements to be approved by the

Proctors for the isolation and supervision of the candidate during the period which begins at the time when the part of the examination is due to be taken by him or her and ends at the time at which it is taken by other candidates (or the other way round) which will ensure   5
that the candidate is unable directly or indirectly to communicate in person, by telephone or by electronic or any other means with any other candidate, unless the Proctors otherwise permit.

(5) When these arrangements are approved by the Proctors   10
they shall communicate them to the chair of the examiners and the Registrar.

(6) The provisions of this regulation shall apply with any necessary modification to practical examinations.

15.6. (1) Where the Proctors have given permission for an examination to be held in a place or at a time other than that   15
appointed for the examination, the invigilator or another person approved by the Proctors shall attend the Examination Schools at least 15 minutes before the examination begins, to receive the examination paper and   20
any necessary writing materials from the Examination Schools, and should bring their University Card or other reliable evidence of their identity.

(2) The invigilator should sign the list kept by the Registrar of examination papers which are issued in this way.   25

(3) The candidate's work must be handed as soon as possible after the time appointed for the collection of papers to the Registrar, who shall make the appropriate entry in his or her register.

Part 16   30
Marking and Assessment

Adjudication on the merits of candidates

16.1. (1) Every examiner who takes part in adjudicating on the merits of a candidate shall give careful attention to the examination of such candidates.   35

(2) No examiner adjudicating on the merits of any candidate shall take account of any circumstances, not forming part of, or directly resulting from, the examination itself, except as provided in Parts 10 or 11 of these regulations.   40

(3) The work of any candidate to whom Part 10 or 11 of these regulations applies shall be assessed with due and careful regard to the circumstances of that candidate and any relevant code of practice or guidelines adopted by the University in relation to such candidates.

(4) In the case of a candidate against whom an order has been made by a University Court under section 11 (3) or section 21 (1)(*e*) of Statute XI or by the Appeal Court in similar terms (intentional or reckless breach of examination regulations), the examiners shall give effect to that order.

(5) Where the Proctors have a recommendation to the examiners in respect of a candidate under section 32 (3) of Statute XI (breach of examination regulations which is neither intentional nor reckless) the examiners shall give due weight to the recommendation in assessing the candidate's work.

Examination conventions

16.2. (1) In adjudicating on the merits of candidates the examiners shall follow and apply the conventions approved under regulation 8.1 above subject to the right of the Board of Examiners in exceptional circumstances to make minor adjustments to the conventions during any particular Examination.

(2) In cases of doubt or difficulty arising under (1), the examiners shall consult the Proctors.

(3) Nothing in this regulation shall affect the authority of the examiners in the making of academic judgements on the performance of each candidate.

Viva voce Examination

16.3. In any University Examination in which candidates are examined viva voce the examiners shall determine the order in which they are to be examined.

16.4. Only one candidate at a time shall be examined viva voce in any one University Examination, but in cases approved by the Pro-Vice-Chancellor (Education) and Proctors the examiners in any University Examination may be permitted to divide themselves into groups which may examine candidates simultaneously.

16.5. (1) Except in the circumstances referred to in paragraph (2) below no examiner, other than an examiner in the Preliminary Examination in Medicine or in the

Second Examination for the Degree of Bachelor of Medicine, or in the Honour School of Oriental Studies shall examine viva voce any candidate who belongs to any college in which he or she is tutor or in which he or she has been tutor during the previous two years or who has been instructed by him or her (otherwise than at a lecture or class open to all members of the University) within the previous two years.

(2) The Pro-Vice-Chancellor (Education) and Proctors may relieve any Board of Examiners of the restriction imposed by this regulation if it would cause difficulty in the conduct of the Examination in question.

Submission of theses or other exercises: exceeding word limits and departure from title or subject-matter

16.6. (1) Where a candidate for any University Examination in which a thesis (or other exercise) may be, or is required to be, submitted as part of that Examination presents a thesis (or other exercise) which exceeds the word limit prescribed by the relevant statute, or regulation, the examiners, if they agree to proceed with the examination of the work, may reduce the mark by up to one class (or its equivalent).[1]

(2) Where a candidate submits such a thesis (or other exercise), the title or subject matter of which differs from that which was approved by the supervisory body concerned, the examiners (if they agree to proceed with the examination of the work) may similarly reduce the mark by up to one class (or its equivalent).[1]

Illegible scripts

16.7. (1) If a chair of examiners considers that a script of a candidate in an examination is illegible (whether the whole script or any part thereof as identified by the chair), he or she shall inform the Senior Tutor of that candidate's college.

(2) Should the Senior Tutor dispute the illegibility of any such script (or part thereof as identified by the chair of examiners), the question shall be referred to the Proctors, whose ruling on the question shall be conclusive.

---

[1] 'Reduction by one class' means a reduction from a II(i) to a II(ii) in the case of a mark which would otherwise have led to classification as a II(i).

(3) Where it is accepted that a script (or part thereof) is illegible. The Senior Tutor shall either:

  (*a*) arrange with the Registrar for the script to be transcribed in accordance with the procedure agreed between the Proctors and the Registrar;

  or

  (*b*) arrange for the candidate to dictate his or her script (or each required part thereof) to a typist under the invigilation of a Master of Arts of the University or any other person who is deemed by the Proctors to be suitable, having first submitted in advance to the Proctors proposals for (i) the appointment of a typist and an invigilator for the transcription of the script and (ii) the timing and venue for the exercise.

(4) It shall be the responsibility of the Registrar or the Senior Tutor, as the case may be, to ensure that the transcription exercise is conducted in accordance with the arrangements approved by the Proctors.

(5) During the transcription exercise the candidate shall dictate his or her script (or each required part thereof) to the typist in the presence of the invigilator, with the exception (unless otherwise identified by the chair of examiners) of work which constitutes rough notes. The candidate shall ensure that the typescript is in every respect identical in form and content to the original script. The use of any recording device is not permitted. Only one fair copy shall be made of each dictated script (or required part thereof), for submission to the examiners.

(6) Academic dress and sub-fusc clothing need not be worn by any of the participants during the transcription exercise.

(7) The cost of the typing and invigilation shall not be a charge on the University.

(8) Following completion of the transcription exercise, it shall be the responsibility of the Registrar (for transcriptions under (3)(*a*) above) or the Senior Tutor (for transcriptions under (3)(*b*) above) to make available to the chair of examiners both the original script and the typescript.

(9) The examiners shall read the typescript page by page with the original script beside it and shall immediately report any discrepancy to the Proctors.

Late submission of work

16.8. (1) Where a candidate for any written examination in which a thesis (or other exercise) may be, or is required to be, submitted as part of that examination wishes on some reasonable grounds to be permitted 5 to present such thesis (or other exercise) later than the date prescribed by any statute, or regulation, the procedure shall be as follows:

(*a*) the candidate shall apply in writing through the Senior Tutor of his or her college to the Proctors 10 for such permission enclosing the grounds for the application;

(*b*) in cases where a significant extension of time is requested, or where the proposed new submission date is beyond the date by which the thesis (or other 15 exercise) may reasonably be assessed for consideration at the relevant meeting of the examiners, the Proctors shall consult the chair of examiners about any such application and shall then decide whether or not to grant permission. 20

(*c*) in cases where an extension of time is requested which results in the submission date being beyond the term of office of the current examiners, the application shall be considered by the Chair of the Education Committee or another member of the Committee, other than one 25 of the Proctors, nominated by the Chair.

(2) If permission is granted, the examiners shall accept and mark such a thesis (or other exercise) as if it had been submitted by the prescribed date.

(3) If a candidate fails to submit a thesis (or other written 30 exercise) on time without prior permission, but submits it on the prescribed date of submission, the examiners shall mark the submitted work and impose an academic penalty according to the established conventions agreed by the relevant supervisory body and the candidate 35 shall pay a late presentation fee. A candidate may apply to the Proctors in writing through the Senior Tutor of his or her college to request that the examiners take into account the circumstances of the late submission. Such an application should be made within five 40 working days of the prescribed date of submission. If the Proctors accept the application, they shall forward

it to the chair of examiners. If the Proctors decide not to accept the application, they shall inform the Senior Tutor in writing of the reasons why.

(4) If a candidate fails to submit a thesis (or other written exercise) on time without prior permission, but submits after the prescribed date of submission, the Proctors shall enquire into the circumstances. If they permit the candidate to remain in the Examination, then they shall instruct the examiners to accept and mark the work, and forward to the chair of examiners an account of the circumstances of the late submission. They may give leave to the examiners to impose an academic penalty according to the established conventions agreed by the relevant supervisory body. It shall be a condition of any permission granted under this regulation that the candidate shall pay a late presentation fee.

(5) Where provided for by regulation, submissions must be accompanied by a declaration of authorship and originality. The examiners are under no obligation to mark any submission not so accompanied. This declaration should be in a sealed envelope (which may be included inside the envelope used to hand in the written work). In the event that the Declaration of Authorship is submitted late, the Proctors may recommend that the examiners apply an academic penalty.

(6) A candidate who is dissatisfied with a decision made by the Proctors under this regulation may, or his or her college may, appeal against it in accordance with the procedure set out in regulation 18.1 below.

Voting on candidates

16.9. (1) If in voting upon the place to be assigned to a candidate in any Results List the examiners shall be equally divided, the chair of the examiners in that Examination shall (unless paragraph (2) below applies) have a second or casting vote.

(2) If the candidate in question shall be of the same college as the chair of the examiners or of any college in which he or she is tutor or in which he or she has been tutor during the previous two years, or shall have been privately taught by him or her during the past two years, then the casting vote shall be with the senior of the examiners who is not disqualified on that ground.

16.10. Candidates whose performance is not sufficient for the award of Honours but have satisfied the examiners at 'pass' standard shall be awarded a pass.

Part 17
Publication of Results

Honours Examinations

17.1. As soon as the examiners in an Honours Examination have examined and fully considered the work of all the candidates they shall:

(1) distribute candidates (identified only by their examination numbers) judged to have shown merit into three classes according to merit;

(2) except in the case of Honour Moderations (other than Classics) distribute the candidates in the second class into two divisions;

(3) forthwith provide the information determined under (1) and (2) above to the Registrar using the Registrar's Results List.

17.2. Where a University Examination in which Honours are awarded is divided into several Parts then (unless the regulations for the specific Examination otherwise provide) in respect of all Parts save the last:

(1) the examiners shall determine the candidates (identified only by their examination numbers) who have shown sufficient merit to obtain Honours in each Part; and

(2) forthwith provide the information determined under paragraph (1) above to the Registrar; and

(3) the respective chairs of the examiners shall deposit the candidates' exercises with the Registrar for the use of the examiners in any succeeding Examination.

17.3. If a candidate in any Honour Moderations has not been judged by the moderators to be worthy of Honours but has satisfied the moderators at 'pass' standard they shall give notice of that fact at the close of the Examination to the Registrar.

17.4. If a candidate in any Final Honour School or in the Final Examination for the Degree of Bachelor of Fine Art has not been judged by the examiners to be worthy of Honours but has satisfied them at 'pass' standard the examiners shall give notice of that fact at the close of the Examination to the Registrar.

17.5. (1) If a candidate in any Honour School of the First or Second Public Examination or in the Final

Examination for the Degree of Bachelor of Fine Art is disqualified by standing from obtaining Honours in that Examination, but has in the judgement of the examiners shown sufficient merit to entitle him or her to obtain Honours but for such disqualification, the examiners shall give notice of that fact on the Results List Submitted to the Registrar at the close of the Examination.

(2) A candidate to whom this regulation applies shall be entitled to supplicate for the Degree of Bachelor of Arts or of Fine Art (as the case may) in the same manner as if he or she had obtained Honours in the Examination.

17.6. If the regulations for any University Examination in which Honours are awarded also permit the award of a merit or a distinction in any part of that Examination the examiners shall give notice to the Registrar at the close of the examination of the names of all the candidates whose work in that part has been adjudged worthy of either accolade.

Preliminary or Qualifying Examinations for Master's Degrees, Diplomas and Certificates

17.7. The examiners in any Preliminary or Qualifying Examination or in any examination for a course of special study for the Degree of M.Phil. or Master of Science or in any examination for the degree of Master of Studies or for a diploma or certificate except the Diploma in Law or the Certificate in Management Studies shall:

(1) determine the candidates (identified only by their examination number) who have satisfied them;

(2) if the regulations governing the particular Examination permit, determine the candidates who have shown sufficient merit to obtain a distinction; and

(3) forthwith provide the information determined under paragraphs (1) and (2) above to the Registrar using the Registrar's Results Lists.

17.8. In an Examination where a candidate is not required to pass in all subjects at one and the same Examination the examiners shall provide a Results List with the agreed results to date.

Approved musical exercises for the Degree of Bachelor of Music

17.9. At the close of the Examination of the Musical Exercises for the Degree of Bachelor of Music submitted to them in any term, the examiners shall notify the Registrar of the candidates whose exercises have been approved by them.

Candidates who have failed

17.10. If a candidate in any University Examination has been judged by the examiners to have failed the examination the examiners shall give notice of that fact, at the close of the examination to the Registrar by inclusion on the Registrar's Results List.

Notification of results

17.11. All notifications submitted to the Registrar under this Part shall be made in a form of Results List as provided by the Registrar, unless he or she otherwise agrees.

17.12. All information submitted to the Registrar under this Part shall (unless any examiner shall have been excused by the Proctors) be certified by the signature of all the examiners who have acted together in the assessment of the candidates in the Examination.

17.13. On receipt of the information provided under regulations 17.11 and 17.12 above the Registrar shall arrange the publication of results to each candidate.

17.14. (1) After results have been released to candidates, examiners shall have no power to alter such Results Lists except under paragraph (2)–(4) below.

(2) Examiners may submit to the Deputy Registrar a change in an individual assessment mark or grade without further consent in instances where an examination overall outcome is not changed.

(3) Examiners may, with the written consent of the Pro-Vice-Chancellor (Education) and Proctors, amend an individual assessment mark or grade where such change will result in a change in the overall examination outcome.

(4) Examiners may, with the written consent of the Pro-Vice-Chancellor (Education) and Proctors, issue a further Results List or Lists to provide results of candidates omitted from the original list.

Custody of records

17.15. The Results Lists drawn up and duly signed shall be circulated and published by the Registrar according to the requirements of the Education Committee and subject to the provisions of the Data Protection Act and the signed copy shall remain in the custody of the Registrar, and any question thereafter arising, with respect to the result of any Examination, shall be determined by reference to such lists.

Forms of Certificates

17.16. (1) Degree certificates and other certificates for diplomas and other certificate courses shall be issued to successful candidates in forms prescribed by the Registrar.

(2) When a candidate has obtained a distinction in his or her Examination, or in any part of it for which a distinction may be awarded, the certificate or diploma, as the case may be, which is issued shall record that fact.

Part 18
Appeals from Decisions of the Proctors and Examiners

Appeals from decisions under Parts 10, 11, 12, and regulation 16.8

18.1. (1) A candidate who is dissatisfied with a decision made by the Proctors under Parts 10, 11, 12, or regulation 16.8 above, may, or his or her college may, appeal against it in accordance with the procedures set out in this regulation.

(2) An appeal must be made within 14 days of the date of the Proctors' decision.

(3) Any such appeal must be made in writing to the Chair of the Education Committee.

(4) The appeal shall be determined expeditiously by the Chair or another member of the Committee, other than one of the Proctors, nominated by the Chair.

Appeals from decisions of examiners

18.2. Appeals from decisions of examiners shall be made in accordance with the Procedures for Handling Complaints (including Academic Appeals) laid down and published by the Proctors under section 20 of Statute IX and any Council Regulations made under that section and not otherwise.

Part 19
Proctors' Disciplinary Regulations for Candidates in Examination

Made by the Proctors on 1 October 2003
Approved by Council on 30 October 2003

1. These regulations are made by the Proctors in the exercise of their powers under section 22 of Statute IX and are designated by Council as disciplinary regulations under section 6 (2) of Statute XI.

2. In these regulations: (1) 'examination' includes where the context so permits the submission and assessment of a thesis, dissertation, essay, Transfer of Status materials, Confirmation of Status materials, or other coursework which is not undertaken in formal examination conditions but is a requirement for, counts towards or   5
constitutes the work for a degree or other academic award; and (2) 'examination room' means any room designated by the University's Registrar or his or her deputy or approved by the Proctors as a place for one or more candidates to take an examination.

3. No candidate shall cheat or act dishonestly, or attempt to   10
do so, in any way, whether before, during or after an examination, so as to obtain or seek to obtain an unfair advantage in an examination.

4. No candidate shall present for an examination as his or her own work any part or the substance of any part of another   15
person's work.

5. In any written work (whether thesis, dissertation, essay, coursework, or written examinations) passages quoted or closely paraphrased from another person's work must be identified as quotations or paraphrases, and the source of the quoted or   20
paraphrased material must be clearly acknowledged.

6. Unless specifically permitted by the special Subject Regulations for the examination concerned, no candidate shall submit to the Examiners any work which he or she has previously submitted partially or in full for examination at this University   25
or elsewhere. Where earlier work by the candidate is citable, he or she shall reference it clearly.

7. No person shall dishonestly give help to a candidate before, during or after an examination so as to give, or attempt to give, that candidate an unfair advantage in an examination.   30

8. No candidate shall take, or attempt to take, into an examination any unauthorised material (including revision notes), item or device (including a mobile telephone or any device capable of receiving or communicating information) nor use or attempt to use such material, item or device.   35

9. No candidate shall copy from the script of another candidate or in any other way dishonestly receive help from another person in an examination.

10. Candidates may not communicate with any person other than an invigilator during an examination.   40

11. No candidate may leave or re-enter an examination room unless permitted by an invigilator.

12. No candidate shall enter an examination room more than thirty minutes after an examination has started except with the permission of the Proctors or an invigilator.

13. No candidate shall unless permitted by the Proctors or an invigilator leave an examination room:

(1) within thirty minutes of the beginning of an examination; or

(2) within thirty minutes of the time at which it is due to end.

14. No candidate may smoke in an examination room or in any building in which an examination is being held, or behave in any other way which distracts or is likely to distract other candidates.

15. Candidates may not use paper in an examination except that which is provided for them.

16. At the end of each examination candidates must hand back to an invigilator all the paper provided for writing their answers, including paper used for rough drafts and paper which has not been used. No paper shall be removed from the examination room other than the question-paper for the examination that has just been completed.

17. Unless regulation 18 below applies, all articles or equipment to be used in an examination must be carried into the examination room in a transparent bag.

18. Candidates must offer non-transparent bags for inspection and, unless special permission is given by an invigilator, must deposit them at the place designated for the deposit of bags and other personal belongings.

19. Candidates must present themselves for examinations in full academic dress.

20. Candidates must follow the directions of the invigilators and the Proctors during an examination, including a direction to leave the examination room and the building in which the examination is being held.

Part 20
Proctors' Administrative Regulations for Candidates in Examinations

Made by the Proctors on 1 October 2005

1. These regulations shall apply to all university examinations, including any examination described in any regulation as a qualifying examination.

2. In these regulations 'college' means any college, society, or Permanent Private Hall or any other institution designated by Council by regulation as being permitted to present candidates for matriculation.

3. It is the responsibility of each candidate to ensure that he or she hands in all the material he or she wishes to be considered by the examiners and to comply with regulations relating to the submission of written work such as dissertations, essays and project reports. Once a candidate has submitted a piece of work, he or she may not withdraw that piece of work and substitute a revised version in the same examination without the Proctors' consent.

4. During every written paper, each candidate shall display his or her University Card face up on the desk at which he or she is writing.

5. A candidate who is taken ill while sitting a written paper may (with an invigilator's permission) leave the room and return while the examination is in progress, to resume the paper on one occasion only (and no extra time shall be allowed). If the candidate is unable to complete the paper concerned because he or she has been taken ill a second time, he or she should inform an invigilator so that the incomplete script can be handed in. It is the candidate's responsibility to obtain a medical certificate, in accordance with the relevant provisions of the General Regulations for the Conduct of University Examinations, explaining how his or her performance in the paper concerned may have been affected by illness.

6. A candidate may not withdraw from an examination after the written part of the examination is complete. The point of completion shall be deemed to be the conclusion of the last paper for which the candidate has entered, or the time by which a dissertation or other written material is due to be submitted, whichever is the later.

7. Concerns about the conduct of an examination must not be raised directly with Examiners. A candidate on a taught course may communicate with Examiners about such matters only through the Senior Tutor or equivalent officer of his or her college. If such a candidate wishes to raise a query or make a complaint about the conduct of his or her examination, such query or complaint must be notified to the Senior Tutor or equivalent officer of his or her college not later than three months after the notification of the results of the examination concerned (when the matter will be dealt with in accordance with the Council Regulations governing the handling of complaints submitted to the Proctors). A candidate

for a research degree or higher doctorate may communicate a query or complaint about the conduct of his or her examination direct to the Proctors: this must be done not later than three months after the notification of the results of the examination concerned (in accordance with the procedures set out in the Council Regulations governing the handling of complaints submitted to the Proctors).

5

NOTES

2

GENERAL REGULATIONS FOR ADMISSION TO DEGREES AWARDED ON PASSING THE SECOND PUBLIC EXAMINATION

Made by Council on 8 May 2002

Part 1
General

1.1. These regulations apply to the following degrees of the University:

Bachelor of Arts	Master of Engineering
Bachelor of Fine Art	Master of Mathematics
Master of Biochemistry	Master of Mathematics and Computer Science
Master of Chemistry	Master of Mathematics and Philosophy
Master of Computer Science	Master of Mathematics and Physics
Master of Computer Science and Philosophy	Master of Physics
Master of Earth Sciences	Master of Physics and Philosophy

1.2. In these regulations where the context admits:

(1) the expression 'statutory residence' means residence at any place authorised by the Regulations for Residence in the University ('the Residence Regulations');

(2) references to divisions and faculty boards shall include a reference to the Committee for the Ruskin School of Art; and

(3) 'college' means any college, society, or Permanent Private Hall or any other institution designated by Council by regulation as being permitted to present candidates for matriculation.

1.3. Any member of the University may be admitted to a degree to which these regulations apply if he or she:

(1) has kept statutory residence for the period prescribed in these regulations for the degree in question; and

(2) has employed himself or herself in study and hearing lectures and has (unless exempt) passed the First and Second Public Examinations in accordance with the requirements laid down by regulation.

Part 2
Residence

2.1. A member reading for the Degree of Bachelor of Arts or of Fine Art must unless regulation 2.2 below applies keep nine terms of statutory residence.

2.2. A member who has taken Honour Moderations in Classics as the First Public Examination or who intends to apply for Honours in the Second Public Examination in Mathematics and Philosophy (Part II) or Physics and Philosophy (Part C) must keep twelve terms of statutory residence.

2.3. A member reading for any of the Master's degrees referred to in regulation 1.1 above must keep twelve terms of statutory residence.

2.4. The Proctors may, for any reason judged by them to be sufficient and on such conditions as they think fit, excuse a member reading for a degree to which these regulations apply from up to three terms of statutory residence.

2.5. (1) If any member is dissatisfied with a decision by the Proctors under regulation 2.4 above, he or she, or his or her college, may within fourteen days of the date of the decision appeal in writing to the Chair of the Education Committee of Council.

(2) The appeal shall be adjudged expeditiously by the Chair or another member of that committee, other than one of the Proctors, nominated by the Chair.

2.6. Applications for dispensation under regulation 2.4 above must be made through the applicant's college.

2.7. A member who is granted dispensation from statutory residence under regulation 2.4 above must nevertheless, unless expressly exempted, pay in respect of any term for which he or she is excused residence any university fee which would have been payable if he or she had actually resided.

2.8. Council may permit time spent outside Oxford, as part of an academic programme approved by it, to be counted towards residence for the purposes of these regulations.

Part 3
First Public Examination

3.1. The First Public Examination shall include Honour Moderations, Moderations, and Preliminary Examinations in the subjects respectively listed in Table 1, Table 2, and Table 3

3.2. The examinations shall be conducted by Moderators under the supervision of the divisional and faculty boards assigned to each subject respectively in Table 1, Table 2, and Table 3

TABLE 1: HONOUR MODERATIONS

Subject	*Board(s)*
Archaeology and Anthropology	Social Sciences Division
Classics	Faculty of Classics

TABLE 2: MODERATIONS

Subject	*Board(s)*
Law	Faculty of Law

TABLE 3: PRELIMINARY EXAMINATIONS *(For the explanation of the asterisks see regulation 3.10)*

Subject	*Board(s)*
Ancient and Modern History	Faculties of Classics and History
*Archaeology and Anthropology	Social Sciences Division
Biological Sciences	Mathematical, Physical and Life Sciences Division
Biomedical Sciences	Medical Sciences Division
Chemistry	Mathematical, Physical and Life Sciences Division
Classical Archaeology and Ancient History	Social Sciences Division and Faculty of Classics
*Classics	Faculty of Classics
Classics and English	Faculties of Classics and English Language and Literature

Computer Science	Mathematical, Physical and Life Sciences Division	
Computer Science and Philosophy	Mathematical, Physical and Life Sciences Division and Faculty of Philosophy	5
Earth Sciences	Mathematical, Physical and Life Sciences Division	
Economics and Management	Social Sciences Division	
Engineering Science	Mathematical, Physical and Life Sciences Division	10
English and Modern Languages	Faculties of English Language and Literature and Medieval and Modern Languages	
English Language and Literature	Faculty of English Language and Literature	15
European and Middle Eastern Languages	Faculties of Medieval and Modern Languages and Oriental Studies	
Fine Art	Committee for Ruskin School of Art	
Geography	Social Sciences Division	20
History	Faculty of History	
History and Economics	Faculty of History and Social Sciences Division	
History and English	Faculties of History and English Language and Literature	25
History and Modern Languages	Faculties of History and Medieval and Modern Languages	
History and Politics	Faculty of History and Social Sciences Division	
History of Art	Faculty of History	30
Human Sciences	Social Sciences Division	
Materials Science	Mathematical, Physical and Life Sciences Division	
Mathematics	Mathematical, Physical and Life Sciences Division	35
Mathematics and Computer Science	Mathematical, Physical and Life Sciences Division	
Mathematics and Philosophy	Mathematical, Physical and Life Sciences Division and Faculty of Philosophy	40

Mathematical and Theoretical Physics (after transfer to that Honour School for the Part C examination from the Honour Schools of Mathematics, Physics, or Physics and Philosophy)	Mathematical, Physical and Life Sciences Division
Modern Languages	Faculty of Medieval and Modern Languages
Molecular and Cellular Biochemistry	Medical Sciences Division
Music	Faculty of Music
Oriental Studies	Faculty of Oriental Studies
Philosophy and Modern Languages	Faculties of Philosophy and Medieval and Modern Languages
Philosophy, Politics, and Economics	Faculty of Philosophy and Social Sciences Division
Physics	Mathematical, Physical and Life Sciences Division
Physics and Philosophy	Mathematical, Physical and Life Sciences Division and Faculty of Philosophy
Psychology, Philosophy, and Linguistics	Medical Sciences Division and Faculties of Philosophy and Linguistics, Philology and Phonetics
Theology	Faculty of Theology

3.3. The boards shall from time to time make and publish Special Regulations respecting the examinations under their supervision and shall publish lists of subjects and (where appropriate) of books which may be offered for examination, maintaining as far as possible a distinction between the subjects and any books prescribed in the First and Second Public Examinations respectively.

3.4. Special Regulations made and lists drawn up by boards under regulation 3.3 above shall not have effect until:

(1) they have been approved by or on behalf of the Education Committee of Council;

(2) in the case of regulations made and lists drawn up by faculty boards or other bodies within the Humanities and Social

Sciences Divisions, they have also first been approved by the Humanities Board or the Social Sciences Board as appropriate;

(3) they have then been duly published, and if necessary approved by Congregation, in accordance with the procedure laid down in sections 13–18 of Statute VI.

Method of examining

3.5. Subject to regulation 3.6 below the examinations shall be conducted in writing.

3.6. A board may specify by Special Regulation that an examination shall be partly aural, oral, practical, or visual.

Admission to the First Public Examination

3.7. No person who is not a student member of the University may be admitted to the First Public Examination.

3.8. Candidates may be admitted to Honour Moderations at any time not earlier than the third term from matriculation, but no candidate who has exceeded the sixth term from matriculation inclusively, or the eighth term in the case of candidates for Honour Moderations in Classics, shall be capable of obtaining Honours.

3.9. Candidates may be admitted to each of the Moderations listed in Table 4, not earlier than the term from matriculation specified in each case.

TABLE 4: ADMISSION TO MODERATIONS

Moderations	*Earliest term from matriculation*
Law	2nd

3.10. (1) Candidates shall not be admitted to any of the Preliminary Examinations which has the same title as any Honour Moderations or Moderations, and which is one of those marked with an asterisk in Table 3, unless they have either failed the examination for the Honour Moderations or Moderations with the same title or, subject to the consent of the Proctors, have been prevented by illness or other urgent and reasonable cause from taking that examination.

(2) If any member of the University is dissatisfied with a decision by the Proctors under paragraph (1) above, he or she, or his or her college, may within fourteen days of the date of the decision appeal in writing to the Chair of the Education Committee of Council.

(3) The appeal shall be adjudged expeditiously by the Chair or another member of the committee, other than one of the Proctors, nominated by the Chair.

3.11. Candidates may be admitted to each of the Preliminary Examinations listed in Table 5, not earlier than the term from matriculation specified in each case.

TABLE 5: ADMISSION TO PRELIMINARY EXAMINATIONS

Preliminary Examination	*Earliest term from matriculation*
Ancient and Modern History	3rd
Biological Sciences	3rd
Biomedical Sciences	3rd
Chemistry	2nd
Classical Archaeology and Ancient History	3rd
Classics	2nd
Computer Science	3rd
Computer Science and Philosophy	3rd
Earth Sciences	2nd
English and Modern Languages:	
English	3rd
Modern Language	2nd
Fine Art	3rd
History	3rd
History and Economics	3rd
History and English	3rd
History and Modern Languages	3rd
History and Politics	3rd
Mathematics	3rd
Mathematics and Computer Science	3rd
Mathematics and Philosophy	3rd
Modern Languages	2nd
Molecular and Cellular Biochemistry	2nd
Music	3rd
Oriental Studies:	
Arabic, Chinese, Egyptology and Ancient Near Eastern Studies, Japanese, Turkish	3rd
Other languages	2nd

Philosophy and Modern Languages	2nd
Philosophy, Politics, and Economics	2nd
Physics	3rd
Physics and Philosophy	3rd
Psychology, Philosophy, and Linguistics	2nd
Theology	2nd

3.12. No person whose name has been placed in any Results List issued by Moderators shall be admitted again as a candidate in the same Honours Examination.

Passing the First Public Examination

3.13. A candidate shall be deemed to have passed the First Public Examination if he or she has satisfied the Moderators in any one of the parts of the examination as set out in Table 1, Table 2, and Table 3

3.14. Any person who has satisfied the Moderators in Part I of the First Examination for the Degree of Bachelor of Medicine shall be deemed to have passed the First Public Examination.

3.15. (1) A candidate who fails to satisfy the examiners in his or her initial examination for the First Public Examination shall be permitted to re-enter for the examination on one further occasion in accordance with the special regulations governing re-sits in the programme concerned.

(2) A further exceptional opportunity to re-sit the examination at the next opportunity shall require application to and approval on behalf of the Education Committee.

(3) A candidate who passes the First Public Examination whether at the first attempt or after re-sitting the examination shall be deemed to have reached the University's threshold standard for embarking on the Final Honour School.

Part 4
Second Public Examination

4.1. The Second Public Examination shall, except in the case of the Degree of Bachelor of Fine Art, consist of a Final Examination in the Honour Schools in each of the subjects listed in Table 6.

Table 6: honour schools

Subject	Board(s)	
Ancient and Modern History	Faculties of Classics and History	
Archaeology and Anthropology	Social Sciences Division	
Biological Sciences	Mathematical, Physical and Life Sciences Division	5
Cell and Systems Biology	Medical Sciences Division	
Chemistry	Mathematical, Physical and Life Sciences Division	
Classical Archaeology and Ancient History	Social Sciences Division and Faculty of Classics	10
Classics and English	Faculties of Classics and English Language and Literature	
Classics and Modern Languages	Faculties of Classics and Medieval and Modern Languages	15
Classics and Oriental Studies	Faculties of Classics and Oriental Studies	
Computer Science (three-year and four-year)	Mathematical, Physical and Life Sciences Division	20
Computer Science and Philosophy (three-year and four-year)	Mathematical, Physical and Life Sciences Division and Faculty of Philosophy	
Earth Sciences (four-year)	Mathematical, Physical and Life Sciences Division	25
Economics and Management	Social Sciences Division	
Engineering, Economics, and Management	Mathematical, Physical and Life Sciences and Social Sciences Divisions	
Engineering Science	Mathematical, Physical and Life Sciences Division	30
English Language and Literature	Faculty of English Language and Literature	
English and Modern Languages	Faculties of English Language and Literature and Medieval and Modern Languages	35
European and Middle Eastern Languages	Faculties of Medieval and Modern Languages and Oriental Studies	
Experimental Psychology	Medical Sciences Division	
Geography	Social Sciences Division	40
Geology (three-year)	Mathematical, Physical and Life Sciences Division	

History	Faculty of History	
History and Economics	Faculty of History and Social Sciences Division	
History and English	Faculties of History and English Language and Literature	5
History and Modern Languages	Faculties of History and Medieval and Modern Languages	
History and Politics	Faculty of History and Social Sciences Division	
History of Art	Faculty of Modern History	10
Human Sciences	Social Sciences Division	
Jurisprudence	Faculty of Law	
Literae Humaniores	Faculties of Classics and Philosophy	
Materials, Economics, and Management	Mathematical, Physical and Life Sciences and Social Sciences Divisions	15
Materials Science	Mathematical, Physical and Life Sciences Division	
Mathematics (three-year and four-year)	Mathematical, Physical and Life Sciences Division	20
Mathematics and Computer Science (three-year and four-year)	Mathematical, Physical and Life Sciences Division	
Mathematics and Philosophy	Mathematical, Physical and Life Sciences Division and Faculty of Philosophy	25
Mathematical and Theoretical Physics (after transfer to that Honour School for the Part C examination from the Honour Schools of Mathematics, Physics, or Physics and Philosophy)	Mathematical, Physical and Life Sciences Division	30
Mathematics and Statistics (three-year and four-year)	Mathematical, Physical and Life Sciences Division	
Medical Sciences	Medical Sciences Division	35
Modern Languages	Faculty of Medieval and Modern Languages	
Molecular and Cellular Biochemistry	Medical Sciences Division	
Music	Faculty of Music	40

Neuroscience	Medical Sciences Division
Oriental Studies	Faculty of Oriental Studies
Philosophy and Modern Languages	Faculties of Philosophy and Medieval and Modern Languages
Philosophy, Politics, and Economics	Faculty of Philosophy and Social Sciences Division
Philosophy and Theology	Faculties of Philosophy and Theology
Physics (three-year and four-year)	Mathematical, Physical and Life Sciences Division
Physics and Philosophy	Mathematical, Physical and Life Sciences Division and Faculty of Philosophy
[Until 1 October 2014: Physiological Sciences	Medical Sciences Division]
[Until 1 October 2015: Psychology and Philosophy	Medical Sciences Division and Faculty of Philosophy]
[From 1 October 2014: Psychology, Philosophy, and Linguistics	Medical Sciences Division and Faculties of Philosophy and Linguistics, Philology and Phonetics]
[Until 1 October 2014: Psychology, Philosophy, and Physiology	Medical Sciences Division and Faculty of Philosophy]
Theology	Faculty of Theology
Theology and Oriental Studies	Faculties of Theology and Oriental Studies

4.2. The examinations shall be conducted by the Public Examiners under the supervision of the divisional or faculty boards assigned to each school in Table 6.

4.3. The Second Public Examination for the Degree of Bachelor of Fine Art shall consist of a Final Honour School under the supervision of the Committee for the Ruskin School of Art.

4.4. The boards shall from time to time make and publish Special Regulations respecting the examinations under their supervision and shall publish lists of subjects and (where appropriate) of books which may be offered for examination.

4.5. Special Regulations made and lists drawn up by boards under regulation 4.5 above shall not have effect until:

(1) they have been approved by or on behalf of the Education Committee of Council;

(2) in the case of regulations made and lists drawn up by faculty boards or other bodies within the Humanities and Social Sciences Divisions, they have also first been approved by the Humanities Board or the Social Sciences Board as appropriate;

(3) they have then been duly published, and if necessary approved by Congregation, in accordance with the procedure laid down in sections 13–18 of Statute VI.

Method of examining

4.6. Every candidate in a Second Public Examination shall be examined in writing; and any candidate who seeks Honours may be examined viva voce where Special Regulations made by the divisional board, board of a faculty, or other body responsible for an examination (or jointly by the relevant bodies where an examination is a joint responsibility) expressly provide.

4.7. A board may specify by Special Regulation that an examination shall be partly aural, oral, practical, or visual.

Admission to the Second Public Examination

4.8. No person who is not a student member of the University may be admitted to the Second Public Examination.

4.9. No person may be admitted to the Second Public Examination unless he or she has passed or been exempted from the First Public Examination.

4.10. No person may be admitted as a candidate in any Final Honour School unless he or she:

(1) has satisfied the conditions, if any, which are required by regulations (including Special Regulations) relating to the School in which he or she is a candidate; and

(2) will by the end of the term in which the examination is taken have kept statutory residence for the number of terms which, under Part 2 or 5 of these regulations or the Regulations for Senior Student Status, is appropriate to his or her status and to the School in which he or she is a candidate.

Maximum time allowed for Honours

4.11. No person may be admitted as a candidate in any Final Honour School after the lapse of twelve terms from the term of matriculation inclusively, except in the following cases:

(1) A candidate who has obtained Honours in some other Final Honour School may be admitted not more than

six terms after the date on which he or she first obtained Honours in a Final Honour School.

(2) A candidate who has obtained Honours (or has satisfied the Moderators under the Regulations for the Conduct of Examinations) in Honour Moderations may be admitted as a candidate in Part II of the examination in Chemistry or in Molecular and Cellular Biochemistry or in Materials Science up to the end of the eighteenth term.

(3) A candidate in any of the following Final Honour School examinations may be admitted up to the end of the fifteenth term:

(*a*) any Final Honour School, if the candidate has obtained Honours (or has satisfied the Moderators under the Regulations for the Conduct of Examinations) in Honour Moderations in either the fifth or sixth term, or the eighth term in the case of Honour Moderations in Classics, from matriculation;

(*b*) the second part of any Final Honour School which is divided into two parts, except the Honour School of Biological Sciences, the Honour School of Geology, and the Honour School of Physics (three-year course);

(*c*) the third part of any Final Honour School which is divided into three parts;

(*d*) the Honour School of Classics and Modern Languages, English and Modern Languages, European and Middle Eastern Languages, Jurisprudence, Modern Languages, Modern History and Modern Languages, or Philosophy and Modern Languages, if the candidate is certified by his or her college to have spent an academic year of approved residence in an appropriate country or appropriate countries;

(*e*) the examination in Chinese or Japanese, or, if the candidate is certified to have spent an academic year abroad on a course approved by the Board of the Faculty of Oriental Studies, the examination in Arabic, or Hebrew, or Persian, or Turkish, in the Honour School of Oriental Studies.

(4) A person whose position is not covered in any of paragraphs 4.11 (1)–(3) may be admitted as a candidate in a Final Honour School for which there is at least one other candidate, subject to the approval of the Education Committee.

(5) A person who is admitted under (4) above within six terms of the term in which they were originally due to be examined for a part of a Final Honour School or the relevant Part, shall normally be examined in accordance with the regulations pertaining to the orginal examination.

(6) A person who is admitted under (4) above seven or more terms after the term in which they were originally due to be examined for a part of a Final Honour School or the relevant Part, shall normally be examined in accordance with the current regulations.

4.12. The candidate's college shall be required to certify on the entry form, by the time determined for entry, whether or not the candidate will have met the requirement for statutory residence by the end of the term in which the examination is held, and to notify the University of any change in the candidate's status in this respect between entry and the date of the examination.

4.13. No person whose name has been placed in any Results List by the Public Examiners (other than a candidate who has been declared to have deserved Honours under the Regulations for the Conduct of Examinations) shall be admitted again as a candidate in the same Final Honour School, but this regulation shall not affect the regulations concerning the Final Honour Schools of Modern Languages and Oriental Studies which enable candidates under certain conditions to offer themselves again in the same School.

4.14. (1) No person whose name has been placed in any Results List by the Public Examiners (with the exceptions in regulations 4.12 and 4.13 above) shall be admitted as a candidate in a second Final Honour School having papers in common with the first, except with the permission of the Proctors.

(2) If any member of the University is dissatisfied with a decision by the Proctors under paragraph (1) above, he or she, or his or her college, may within fourteen days of the date of the decision appeal in writing to the Chair of the Education Committee of Council.

(3) The appeal shall be adjudged expeditiously by the Chair or another member of the committee, other than one of the Proctors, nominated by the Chair.

Passing the Second Public Examination

4.15. Candidates shall be deemed to have passed the Second Public Examination if they either have obtained Honours, or satisfied the examiners, in any one of the Honour Schools listed in Table 5, and Table 6 or in the Final Examination in Fine Art.

Part 5
Foundation Courses at the Department for Continuing Education

5.1. Any member of the University who has successfully completed the course for a Foundation Certificate at the Department for Continuing Education (whether or not he or she was a member when he or she did so) may apply for admission to the Degree of Bachelor of Arts if he or she has:

(1) kept statutory residence in accordance with regulations 5.2 and 5.3 below; and

(2) passed the Second Public Examination.

5.2. A person who has successfully completed the course for the Foundation Certificate in English Language and Literature may be admitted as a candidate in the Final Honour School of English Language and Literature if by the end of the term in which the examination is held he or she has kept statutory residence for six terms.

5.3. A person who has successfully completed the course for any Foundation Certificate may not be admitted as a candidate in any Final Honour School more than nine terms inclusively from the term of matriculation.

Part 6
Degrees awarded on passing the Second Public Examination

6.1. The Degree of Bachelor of Arts shall be awarded to members of the University who have obtained Honours, or have satisfied the examiners but have not obtained Honours, in any Final Honour School other than the School of Fine Art or the Schools listed in Table 7 below, subject to these regulations and to the Special Regulations for the Second Public Examination concerned.

6.2. The Degree of Bachelor of Fine Art shall be awarded to members of the University who have obtained Honours, or who have satisfied the examiners, in the Final Honour School for that degree, subject to these regulations and to the Special Regulations for that School.

6.3. The Master's Degrees to which these regulations apply shall be awarded to members of the University who have obtained Honours in the Second Public Examination in the relevant Final Honour Schools, as set out in Table 7 below, subject also to the conditions laid down in the Special Regulations for each School.

TABLE 7: MASTER'S DEGREES

Degree	Final Honour School
Master of Biochemistry	Molecular and Cellular Biochemistry
Master of Chemistry	Chemistry
Master of Computer Science	Computer Science (four-year course)
Master of Computer Science and Philosophy	Computer Science and Philosophy (four-year course)
Master of Earth Sciences	Earth Sciences
Master of Engineering	Engineering Science
	Engineering, Economics, and Management
	Materials, Economics, and Management
	Materials Science
Master of Mathematics	Mathematics (four-year course)
	Mathematics and Statistics (four-year course)
Master of Mathematics and Computer Science	Mathematics and Computer Science (four-year course)
Master of Mathematics and Philosophy	Mathematics and Philosophy (four-year course)
Master of Mathematics and Physics	Mathematical and Theoretical Physics (after transfer to that Honour School for the Part C examination from the Honour Schools of Mathematics, Physics, or Physics and Philosophy)
Master of Physics	Physics (four-year course)
Master of Physics and Philosophy	Physics and Philosophy (four-year course)

SPECIAL REGULATIONS FOR SPECIFIC FIRST PUBLIC EXAMINATIONS

Special Regulations for the Honour Moderations in Archaeology and Anthropology

A

Honour Moderations in Archaeology and Anthropology shall be under the supervision of the Social Sciences Board and shall consist of such subjects as it shall by regulation prescribe.

B

1. Every candidate shall offer four papers of three hours each, as follows:

Paper (1) Introduction to world archaeology.
Paper (2) Introduction to anthropological theory.
Paper (3) Perspectives on human evolution.
Paper (4) The nature of archaeological enquiry.

2. All candidates will be required to undertake a course of practical work, including laboratory work.

All candidates will be assessed on their practical ability.

Class co-ordinators shall make available to the chair of the examiners records showing the extent to which each candidate has pursued an adequate course of practical work.

Special Regulations for the Honour Moderations in Classics

A

The subjects of the examination shall be as prescribed by regulation from time to time by the Board of the Faculty of Classics and the Board of the Faculty of Philosophy.

B

Candidates shall take one of the following courses: IA, IB, IC, IIA, IIB.

Any candidate whose native language is not English may bring a bilingual (native language to English) dictionary for use in any examination paper where candidates are required to translate Ancient Greek and/or Latin texts into English.

Course IA

The examination will consist of the following papers.

I. HOMER *ILIAD*

One paper (3 hours) of translation and questions. Compulsory passages for translation and commentary will be set from *Iliad* I-IX and XVI-XXIV. Candidates will be expected to have knowledge of the whole poem. They will also be required to scan a short passage.

II. Virgil, *Aeneid*

One paper (3 hours) of translation and questions. Compulsory passages for translation and commentary will be set from *Aeneid* I-VI and XII. Candidates will be expected to have knowledge of the whole poem. They will also be required to scan a short passage.   5

III, IV. Texts and Contexts

An essay paper and a translation paper (each 3 hours). Candidates are expected to have considered the general topics as well as the particular texts and archaeological material specified. In the essay paper they will be required to answer a compulsory picture question, and three essay questions. A syllabus of images from   10
which items will be selected for the picture question will be posted on WebLearn under "Texts and Contexts". In the translation paper candidates will be required to translate six passages, three Greek and three Latin, set from the texts listed under α for each topic.

1. *The Persian Wars and Cultural Identities*   15

   α Herodotus 7.1–53, 8.56–110
   β Aeschylus, *Persians*
     Herodotus 1.1–32, 131–40; 3.61–88, 150–160; 7.54–239; 8.1–55
     Bisitun Inscription of Darius 1–15, 51–76
   Archaeological material: Identities in Greek and Persian art   20

2. *Dionysus, Drama, and Athens*

   α Euripides, *Bacchae* 1–1167
     Aristophanes, *Frogs* 1–459, 830–1533
   β Remainder of *Bacchae*
     Remainder of *Frogs*   25
   Archaeological material: Theatres, theatre images, and Dionysian iconography

3. *Love and Luxury*

   α Cicero, *pro Caelio* 17–53 (... *dedisti.*)
     Catullus 1–16, 31–7, 42–5, 48–51, 53, 69–70, 75–6, 79, 83–6, 95, 99–101, 116
     Propertius 1.1–3, 6, 11, 14   30
   β Remainder of *pro Caelio*
     Catullus 64.31–266
     Remainder of Propertius 1
   Archaeological material: Love pictures and Vesuvian villas

4. *Class*   35

   α Petronius, *Cena Trimalchionis* 26.7–36, 47–78
     Juvenal 3, 5
   β Remainder of *Cena Trimalchionis*
     Juvenal 1, 4, 6, 7, 9
     Pliny, *Epistulae* 7.29, 8.6   40
     Tacitus, *Annals* 14.42–5
   Archaeological material: Houses, tombs, and the archaeology of public entertainment.

V. Philosophy Special Subject

All candidates must offer one Philosophy Special Subject, chosen from either Group A or Group B. Candidates may not combine a subject from Group B with   45
a Classical Special Subject (VI) from Group E. One three-hour paper will be set in each subject.

A.

1. *Early Greek Philosophy*

Candidates will be expected to have studied:
(*a*) Heraclitus, Parmenides, Empedocles, and Anaxagoras; and **any one** of the following:
(*b*) Early Ionian Philosophy;
(*c*) Zeno;
(*d*) Early Atomism.

A general knowledge of pre-Socratic philosophy will also be expected. The subject shall be studied in Diels, *Die Fragmente der Vorsokratiker*, sixth or any later edition, edited by Kranz (Berlin, 1951 and later).

The texts prescribed are:
(*a*) Heraclitus (Diels-Kranz 22), B 1, 2, 10, 12, 17, 18, 21, 26, 28–32, 40, 41, 45, 50–62, 64, 67, 78–80, 88, 90, 93, 94, 101, 101a, 102, 103, 107, 108, 111, 113–15, 117–19, 123–6, and the first part of A 22 (Aristotle *Eudemian Ethics* 1235^{a}25–7); Parmenides (Diels-Kranz 28), B 1–9, 19; Empedocles (Diels-Kranz 31), B 6, 8, 11–13, 17, 28–30, 35, 112, 115, 117, 134, 146; Anaxagoras (Diels-Kranz 59), B 1–17, 21, 21*a*;
(*b*) (i) early Ionian philosophy: Anaximander (Diels-Kranz 12) A 9 and B 1; Anaximenes (Diels-Kranz 13) B 2; Aristotle *Metaphysics* A 3.983^{a}24–984^{a}18, *Physics* III 4.203^{a}16–18 and 203^{b}3–15; Xenophanes (Diels-Kranz 21), B 1, 7, 10–12, 14–16, 18, 23–9, 32, 34–6, 38; Aristotle *Metaphysics* A 5.986^{b}10–27;
(ii) Zeno: Zeno (Diels-Kranz 29) B 1–4; Plato *Parmenides* 127a7–128e4; Aristotle *Physics* VI 2.233^{a}21–31 and 9.239^{b}5–240^{a}18;
(iii) early atomists: Leucippus (Diels-Kranz 67) B 2; Democritus (Diels-Kranz 68) B 4, 6–8, 9, 10, 11, 117, 118, 125, 156, 164, 167; Aristotle *De Generatione et Corruptione* I 8.324^{b}35-325^{a}36, *Metaphysics* A 4.985^{b}3–22.

Where Diels-Kranz B-texts are prescribed, the prescription includes only what Diels-Kranz print in spaced type.

A compulsory question will contain passages for translation and comment from (*a*). A second compulsory question will contain passages for comment (not for translation). At least one passage will be taken from (*a*), and at least one from each of (*b*)–(*d*). Essay questions will also be set which will include questions on (*a*) and on each of (*b*)–(*d*).

2. Plato, *Meno* and *Euthyphro*

The paper will include questions on the philosophical topics discussed in the dialogues. Candidates will be expected to have read *Meno* in Greek and *Euthyphro* in English. There will be a compulsory question containing passages for translation and comment from *Meno*; any passages for comment from *Euthyphro* will be accompanied by a translation (to be taken from *The Last Days of Socrates*, tr. Tredennick & Tarrant (Penguin, revised 1993)).

B.

1. *General Philosophy*

As specified for section I of Introduction to Philosophy in the Preliminary Examination for Philosophy, Politics and Economics.

2. *Moral Philosophy*

As specified for section II of Introduction to Philosophy in the Preliminary Examination for Philosophy, Politics and Economics.

3. *Introduction to Logic*

As specified for section III of Introduction to Philosophy for the Preliminary Examination for Philosophy, Politics and Economics.

VI. CLASSICAL SPECIAL SUBJECT

All candidates must offer one Classical Special Subject, chosen from one of the groups C-F. Candidates must not combine a subject from Group E with a Philosophy Special Subject (V) from Group B. One three-hour paper will be set in each subject.

C.

1. *Thucydides and the West*

The prescribed text is Thucydides VI. Compulsory passages for translation and comment will be set from this book. Candidates will also be expected to be familiar with Thucydides VII and Plutarch, *Nicias*.

2. *Aristophanes' Political Comedy*

The prescribed plays are *Knights, Wasps* and *Lysistrata*. Compulsory passages for translation and for comment will be set from *Wasps* and from *Lysistrata* 387–613 and 980–1220. Candidates will also be expected to be familiar with the 'Old Oligarch'.

D.

1. *Cicero and Catiline*

The prescribed texts are: Sallust, *Catiline*; Cicero, *In Catilinam* I-IV, *Pro Sulla*; Asconius, *In orationem in toga candida*. Compulsory passages for translation and comment will be set from these.

2. *Tacitus and Tiberius*

The prescribed text is Tacitus, *Annals* I and III. Compulsory passages for translation and comment will be set from these books. Candidates will also be expected to be familiar with *Annals* II and IV-VI.

E.

1. *Homeric Archaeology and Early Greece from 1550 BC to 700 BC*

Evidence on the composition and history of the poems provided by extant archaeological remains, with special emphasis on burial practices, architecture, metals, and the world outside the Aegean. An overall knowledge will be required of the archaeological evidence for the Late Bronze Age and Early Iron Age of the Aegean from 1550 BC to 700 BC. The examination will consist of one picture question and three essay questions.

2. *Greek Vases*

The study of the general history of Greek decorated pottery from c. 800 BC to c. 300 BC, including study of the Attic black-figure and red-figure styles and of South Italian Greek vase painting. Knowledge will be required of the techniques used in making Greek pottery and in drawing on vases, and also of the ancient names for vases and the shapes to which they refer. Candidates should in addition study the subjects of the paintings and their treatment by painters as compared with their treatment by writers and should be familiar with actual vases, for example those in the Ashmolean Museum. The examination will consist of one picture question and three essay questions.

3. *Greek Sculpture, c. 600–300 BC*

The major monuments of archaic and classical Greek sculpture—their context and purpose as well as their subjects, styles, and techniques. Candidates will be expected to have some knowledge of the external documentary evidence, such as literary and epigraphic texts, on which the framework of the subject depends, and to be acquainted with the major sculptures of the period represented in the Ashmolean Cast Gallery. The examination will consist of one picture question and three essay questions.

4. *Roman Architecture*

The subject comprises the study of Roman Architecture from the Republic to the Tetrarchy in Italy and in the provinces, with particular reference to form, materials, technology, and function, and the movement of both materials and ideas. The examination will consist of one picture question and three essay questions.

F.

1. *Historical Linguistics and Comparative Philology*

The subject includes an introduction to the methods and aims of historical and comparative linguistics, the reconstruction of the Indo-European protolanguage and its development into Latin and Greek. The questions set will require specific competence in one of the two classical languages but not necessarily in both. An opportunity will be given for (optional) commentary on Greek or Latin texts.

VII. UNPREPARED TRANSLATION FROM GREEK

One paper (3 hours).

VIII. UNPREPARED TRANSLATION FROM LATIN

One paper (3 hours).

IX. GREEK LANGUAGE

One paper (3 hours). The paper will be divided into two main sections.
Candidates are required to offer *either* (*a*) *or* (*b*):

(*a*) a selection of passages from D. A Russell, *An Anthology of Greek Prose* (OUP, 1991), on which questions on accidence, syntax and style will be set (for the prescribed passages see the Mods Handbook) AND a short passage for translation into Greek prose;

(*b*) a passage for translation into Greek prose.

X. LATIN LANGUAGE

One paper (3 hours). The paper will be divided into two main sections.
Candidates are required to offer *either* (*a*) *or* (*b*):

(*a*) a selection of passages from D. A Russell, *An Anthology of Latin Prose* (OUP, 1990), on which questions on accidence, syntax and style will be set (for the prescribed passages see the Mods Handbook) AND a short passage for translation into Latin prose;

(*b*) a passage for translation into Latin prose.

XI. (OPTIONAL PAPER) VERSE COMPOSITION *OR* ADDITIONAL TRANSLATION *OR* ADDITIONAL TRANSLATION AND METRE

This paper (3 hours) will consist of the following:

(*a*) passages for translation into Greek iambics and Latin elegiacs and hexameters, of which candidates will be required to translate one;

(*b*) passages for translation into English from each of the following ten books below, and a question on metre; candidates will be required to attempt *either* (i) three passages *or* (ii) two passages and the question on metre.

    1. Archilochus 3, 60, 79a, frr. 23* and 196A* West; Mimnermus 1, 2, 5, 13; Solon 3, 5, 23, 24; Sappho 1, 2, 16, 31, 81b, 94, 96, 130; Alcaeus 38a, 129, 130, 332, 333, 335, 338, 362; Ibycus 286, 287, 288; Anacreon 356, 358, 359,

---

* Indicates a poem not included in D.A. Campbell, *Greek Lyric Poetry*. These are in a leaflet, available on WebLearn. All the poems not asterisked are in the Campbell edition.

360, 376, 388, 395, 396, 398, 417; Xenophanes 1, 3; Theognis as in D.A.
Campbell, *Greek Lyric Poetry*; Simonides 542, fr. 22 West*; Scolia 884,
889, 890, 892, 893, 900, 901, 902, 903, 907; Bacchylides fr. 20B; Pindar frr.
123*, 124a*.b*, 127*, 128* Maehler

2. Sophocles, *Antigone*   5
3. Demosthenes 54 [*Against Conon*], 59 [*Against Neaera*]
4. Plato, *Symposium* 172a–178a5, 188e2–223d
5. Plutarch, *Antony* 1–9, 23–36, 53–87
6. Plautus, *Menaechmi*
7. Horace, *Epistles* I   1C
8. Livy 30
9. Ovid, *Metamorphoses* 7.661–8.884
10. Apuleius, *Cupid and Psyche* (*Metamorphoses* 4.28–6.24)

Candidates will be required to offer *either (a) or (b)*.

Course IB   1▪

The examination will consist of the following papers.

I. HOMER, *ILIAD*

One paper (3 hours) of translation and questions. Compulsory passages for translation and commentary will be set from *Iliad* I, IX, XXII, XXIV. Candidates will
be expected to have knowledge of the whole poem. They will also be required to scan   2▪
a short passage.

II. VIRGIL, *AENEID* [COURSE IA PAPER II]

III, IV. TEXTS AND CONTEXTS

An essay paper and a translation paper (each 3 hours). Candidates are expected to
have considered the general topics as well as the particular texts and archaeological   2▪
material specified. In the essay paper they will be required to answer a compulsory
picture question, and three essay questions. A syllabus of images from which items
will be selected for the picture question will be posted on WebLearn under "Texts and
Contexts". In the translation paper candidates will be required to translate six
passages, three Greek and three Latin, set from the texts listed under α for each topic.   3C

1. *The Persian Wars and Cultural Identities*

    α Herodotus 8.56–110
    β Aeschylus, *Persians*
      Herodotus 1.1–32, 131–40; 3.61–88, 150–160; 7.1–239; 8.1–55
      Bisitun Inscription of Darius 1–15, 51–76   3▪
      Archaeological material: Identities in Greek and Persian art

2. *Dionysus, Drama, and Athens*

    α Euripides, *Bacchae* 1–169, 370–518, 643–976
      Aristophanes, *Frogs* 1–459, 1004–98, 1378–1481
    β Remainder of *Bacchae*   4▪
      Remainder of *Frogs*
      Archaeological material: Theatres, theatre images, and Dionysian iconography

3. *Love and Luxury*

    α Cicero, *pro Caelio* 17–53 (...*dedisti.*)
      Catullus 1–16, 31–7, 42–5, 48–51, 53, 69–70, 75–6, 79, 83–6, 95, 99–101, 116   4▪
      Propertius 1.1–3, 6, 11, 14
    β Remainder of *pro Caelio*
      Catullus 64.31–266
      Remainder of Propertius 1
      Archaeological material: Love pictures and Vesuvian villas   5C

4. *Class*

  α Petronius, *Cena Trimalchionis* 26.7–36, 47–78
    Juvenal 3, 5
  β Remainder of *Cena Trimalchionis*
    Juvenal 1, 4, 6, 7, 9
    Pliny, *Epistulae* 7.29, 8.6
    Tacitus, *Annals* 14.42–5
Archaeological material: Houses, tombs, and the archaeology of public entertainment.

V PHILOSOPHY SPECIAL SUBJECT

All candidates must offer one Philosophy Special Subject chosen from either Group A or Group B. Candidates may not combine a subject from Group B with a Classical Special Subject (VI) from Group E. One three-hour paper will be set in each subject.

A.

1. *Early Greek Philosophy*

Candidates will be expected to have studied:

  (*a*) Heraclitus, Parmenides, Empedocles, and Anaxagoras; and any one of the following:
  (*b*) Early Ionian Philosophy;
  (*c*) Zeno;
  (*d*) Early Atomism.

A general knowledge of pre-Socratic philosophy will also be expected. The subject shall be studied in (i) Aristotle, *Metaphysics* A 1–8; (ii) G.S. Kirk, J.E. Raven, and M. Schofield, *The Presocratic Philosophers* (second edition, Cambridge, 1981); and (iii) a Faculty Supplement (available on WebLearn).
The prescribed texts under (ii) and (iii) are as follows:

  (*a*) Heraclitus Diels–Kranz B 1, 2, 10, 12, 17, 18, 21, 26, 28–32, 40, 41, 45, 50–62, 64, 67, 78–80, 88, 90, 93, 94, 101, 101a, 102, 103, 107, 108, 111, 113–15, 117–19, 123–6, and the first part of A 22 (Aristotle *Eudemian Ethics* 1235^{a}25–7); Parmenides Diels–Kranz B 1–9, 19; Empedocles Diels–Kranz B 6, 8, 11–13, 17, 28–30, 35, 112, 115, 117, 134, 146; Anaxagoras Diels–Kranz B 1–17, 21, 21a;
  (*b*) Early Ionian philosophy: Anaximander Diels–Kranz A 9 and B 1; Anaximenes Diels–Kranz B 2; Aristotle *Metaphysics* A 3.983^{a}24–984^{a}18, *Physics* III 4.203^{a}16–18 and 203^{b}3–15; Xenophanes Diels–Kranz B 1, 7, 10–12, 14–16, 18, 23–9, 32, 34–6, 38; Aristotle *Metaphysics* A 5.986^{b}10–27;
  (*c*) Zeno: Zeno Diels–Kranz B 1–4; Plato *Parmenides* 127a7-128e4; Aristotle *Physics* VI 2.233^{a}21–31 and 9.239^{b}5–240^{a}18;
  (*d*) Early Atomism: Leucippus Diels–Kranz B 2; Democritus Diels–Kranz B 4, 6–8, 9, 10, 11, 117, 118, 125, 156, 164, 167; Aristotle *De Generatione et Corruptione* I 8.324^{b}35–325^{a}36, *Metaphysics* A 4.985^{b}3–22.

There will be a compulsory question containing passages for translation and comment from Aristotle, *Metaphysics* A 1–8. A second compulsory question will contain passages for comment (not for translation). At least one passage will be taken from (*a*), and at least one from each of (*b*)–(*d*); all the passages for this question will be accompanied by a translation (to be taken from Kirk, Raven, and Schofield (eds), and/or the Faculty Supplement). Essay questions will also be set which will include questions on (*a*) and on each of (*b*)–(*d*).

2. Plato, *Euthyphro* and *Meno*

The paper will include questions on the philosophical topics discussed in the dialogues. Candidates will be expected to have read *Meno* 70a–86d2 in Greek and the rest of *Meno* and *Euthyphro* in English. There will be a compulsory question containing passages for translation and comment from *Meno*; any passages for comment from *Euthyphro* and the other parts of *Meno* will be accompanied by a translation (to be taken from *Euthyphro* in *The Last Days of Socrates*, tr. Tredennick & Tarrant (Penguin, revised 1993) and *Meno*, tr. Sharples (Aris & Phillips)).

3. Lucretius, *De Rerum Natura* IV

There will be a compulsory question containing passages for translation and comment from the prescribed book.

The paper will also include questions on the philosophical topics examined in that book, together with some questions of a more general character on Epicurean philosophy as expressed in *De Rerum Natura* as a whole.

B.

1. *General Philosophy* [Course IA, paper V B(1)]
2. *Moral Philosophy* [Course IA, paper V B(2)]
3. *Introduction to Logic* [Course IA, paper V B(3)]

VI. CLASSICAL SPECIAL SUBJECT

All candidates must offer one Classical Special Subject, chosen from one of the groups C-F. Candidates may not combine a subject from Group E with a Philosophy Special Subject (V) from Group B. One three-hour paper will be set in each subject.

C.

1. *Thucydides and the West*

The prescribed text is Thucydides VI. Compulsory passages for translation will be set only from chapters 1–61. Compulsory passages for comment will be set from the whole book; passages set from 62–105 will be accompanied by the English translation of M. Hammond (World's Classic, OUP, 2009). Candidates will also be expected to be familiar with Thucydides VII and Plutarch, *Nicias*.

2. *Aristophanes' Political Comedy*

The prescribed plays are *Knights, Wasps* and *Lysistrata*. Compulsory passages for translation will be set from *Wasps* 1–728 and from *Lysistrata* 980–1220. Compulsory passages for commentary will be set from *Wasps* and from *Lysistrata* 387–613 and 980–1220; those from *Wasps* 729–1537 and *Lysistrata* 387–613 will be accompanied by the English translation of A.H. Sommerstein (Aris & Phillips). Candidates will also be expected to be familiar with the 'Old Oligarch'.

D.

1. *Cicero and Catiline* [Course IA, paper VI D (1)]
2. *Tacitus and Tiberius* [Course IA, paper VI D (2)]

E.

1. *Homeric Archaeology and Early Greece from 1550 BC to 700 BC* [Course IA, paper VI E(1)]
2. *Greek Vases* [Course IA, paper VI E(2)]
3. *Greek Sculpture* [Course IA, paper VI E(3)]
4. *Roman Architecture* [Course IA, paper VI E(4)]

F.

I. *Historical Linguistics and Comparative Philology* [Course IA, paper VI F(1)]

VII. UNPREPARED TRANSLATION FROM GREEK

One paper (3 hours).

VIII. UNPREPARED TRANSLATION FROM LATIN [Course IA, Paper VIII]   5

IX. GREEK LANGUAGE

One paper (3 hours). The paper will be divided into two main sections.
Candidates are required to offer *either* (*a*) *or* (*b*):

(*a*) a selection of passages from D. A Russell, *An Anthology of Greek Prose* (OUP,
 1991), on which questions on accidence, syntax and style will be set (for   10
 the prescribed passages see the Mods Handbook) AND a short passage for
 translation into Greek prose;

(*b*) a passage for translation into Greek prose.

X. LATIN LANGUAGE [Course IA, paper X].

XI. (OPTIONAL PAPER) VERSE COMPOSITION *OR* ADDITIONAL TRANSLATION *OR* A   15
TRANSLATION AND METRE (Course IA, Paper XI).

Course IC

The examination will consist of the following papers.

I. HOMER, *ILIAD* [Course IA, Paper I].

II. VIRGIL, *AENEID*   20

One paper (3 hours) of translation and questions. Compulsory passages for translation and commentary will be set from *Aeneid* I, IV and VI. Candidates will be
expected to have knowledge of the whole poem. They will also be required to scan a
short passage.

III, IV. TEXTS AND CONTEXTS   25

An essay paper and a translation paper (each 3 hours). Candidates are expected to
have considered the general topics as well as the particular texts and archaeological
material specified. In the essay paper they will be required to answer a compulsory
picture question, and three essay questions. A syllabus of images from which items
will be selected for the picture question will be posted on WebLearn under 'Texts and   30
Contexts'. In the translation paper candidates will be required to translate six
passages, three Greek and three Latin, set from the texts listed under α for each topic.

I. *The Persian Wars and Cultural Identities*

 α Herodotus 7.1–53; 8.56–110
 β Aeschylus, *Persians*   35
  Herodotus 1.1–32, 131–40; 3.61–88, 150–160; 7.54–239; 8.1–55
  Bisitun Inscription of Darius 1–15, 51–76
 Archaeological material: Identities in Greek and Persian art

2. *Dionysus, Drama, and Athens*

 α Euripides, *Bacchae* 1–1167   40
  Aristophanes, *Frogs* 1–459, 830–1533
 β Remainder of *Bacchae*
  Remainder of *Frogs*
 Archaeological material: Theatres, theatre images, and Dionysian iconography

3. *Love and Luxury*

α Cicero, *pro Caelio* 30 (*sunt autem*)–50
Catullus 1–8, 10–13, 31, 34, 36, 44–5, 48–51, 69–70, 76, 79, 85, 95, 101
Propertius 1.1, 3, 6, 14
β Remainder of *pro Caelio*   5
Catullus 9, 14–16, 32–3, 35, 37, 42–43, 53, 64.31–266, 75, 83–4, 86, 99–100, 116
Remainder of Propertius 1
Archaeological material: Love pictures and Vesuvian villas

4. *Class*

α Petronius, *Cena Trimalchionis* 26.7–36, 64.2–67, 74.6–78   10
Juvenal 3
β Remainder of *Cena Trimalchionis*
Juvenal 1, 4, 5, 6, 7, 9
Pliny, *Epistulae* 7.29, 8.6
Tacitus, *Annals* 14.42–5   15
Archaeological material: Houses, tombs, and the archaeology of public entertainment.

V. Philosophy Special Subject

All candidates must offer one Philosophy Special Subject, chosen from either Group A or Group B. Candidates may not combine a subject from Group B with   20 a Classical Special Subject (VI) from Group E. One three-hour paper will be set in each subject.

A.
1. *Early Greek Philosophy* [Course IA, paper V A(1)]
2. Plato, *Meno* and *Euthyphro* [Course IA, paper V A(2)]   25
3. Lucretius, *De Rerum Natura* IV [Course IB, paper V A(2)]

B.
1. *General Philosophy* [Course IA, paper V B(1)]
2. *Moral Philosophy* [Course IA, paper V B(2)]
3. *Introduction to Logic* [Course IA, paper V B(3)]   30

VI. Classical Special Subject

All candidates must offer one Classical Special Subject, chosen from one of the groups C–F. Candidates may not combine a subject from Group E with a Philosophy Special Subject (V) from Group B. One three-hour paper will be set in each subject.

C.   35
1. *Thucydides and the West* [Course IA, paper VI C(1)]
2. *Aristophanes' Political Comedy* [Course IA, paper VI C(2)]

D.
1. *Cicero and Catiline* [Course IIA, paper V D(1)]
2. *Tacitus and Tiberius* [Course IIA, paper V D(2)]   40

E.
1. *Homeric Archaeology and Early Greece from 1550 BC to 700 BC* [Course IA, paper VI E(1)]
2. *Greek Vases* [Course IA, paper VI E(2)]
3. *Greek Sculpture* [Course IA, paper VI E(3)]   45
4. *Roman Architecture* [Course IA, paper VI E(4)]

F.

I. *Historical Linguistics and Comparative Philology* [Course IA, paper VI F(I)]

VII. UNPREPARED TRANSLATION FROM GREEK [Course IA, paper VII]

VIII. UNPREPARED TRANSLATION FROM LATIN [Course IIA, paper VI]

IX. GREEK LANGUAGE [Course IA, paper IX]

X. LATIN LANGUAGE [Course IIA, paper VII]

XI. (OPTIONAL PAPER) VERSE COMPOSITION *OR* ADDITIONAL TRANSLATION *OR* ADDITIONAL TRANSLATION AND METRE [Course IA, paper XI]

Course IIA

The examination will consist of the following papers.

I. VIRGIL, *AENEID*

One paper (3 hours) of translation and questions.
Compulsory passages for translation and commentary will be set from *Aeneid* I, II, IV, VI, and XII. Candidates will be expected to have knowledge of the whole poem. They will also be required to scan a short passage.

II, III. TEXTS AND CONTEXTS

An essay paper and a translation paper (each 3 hours). Candidates are expected to have considered the general topics as well as the particular texts and archaeological material specified. In the essay paper they will be required to answer a compulsory picture question, and three essay questions. A syllabus of images from which items will be selected for the picture question will be posted on WebLearn under 'Texts and Contexts'. In the translation paper candidates will be required to translate six passages, set from the Latin texts listed under α for topics 3 and 4.

1. *The Persian Wars and Cultural Identities*

   β Aeschylus, *Persians*
      Herodotus 1.1–32, 131–40; 3.61–88, 150–160; 7.1–239; 8.1–110
      Bisitun Inscription of Darius 1–15, 51–76
   Archaeological material: Identities in Greek and Persian art

2. *Dionysus, Drama, and Athens*

   β Euripides, *Bacchae*
      Aristophanes, *Frogs*
   Archaeological material: Theatres, theatre images, and Dionysian iconography

3. *Love and Luxury*

   α Cicero, *pro Caelio* 30 (*sunt autem*)-50
      Catullus 1–8, 10–13, 31, 34, 36, 44–5, 48–51, 69–70, 76, 79, 85, 95, 101
      Propertius 1.1, 3, 6, 14
   β Remainder of *pro Caelio*
      Catullus 9, 14–16, 32–3, 35, 37, 42–43, 53, 64.31–266, 75, 83–4, 86, 99–100, 116
      Remainder of Propertius 1
   Archaeological material: Love pictures and Vesuvian villas

4. *Class*

   α Petronius, *Cena Trimalchionis* 26.7–36, 64.2–67, 74.6–78
      Juvenal 3
   β Remainder of *Cena Trimalchionis*
      Juvenal 1, 4, 5, 6, 7, 9
      Pliny, *Epistulae* 7.29, 8.6
      Tacitus, *Annals* 14.42–5

Archaeological material: Houses, tombs, and the archaeology of public entertainment.

IV. PHILOSOPHY SPECIAL SUBJECT

All candidates must offer one Philosophy Special Subject. One three-hour paper will be set in each subject.

1. Lucretius, *De Rerum Natura* IV [Course IB paper V A(2)]   5
2. *Early Greek Philosophy*

Candidates will be expected to have studied:

(*a*) Heraclitus, Parmenides, Empedocles, and Anaxagoras; and **any one** of the following:
(*b*) Early Ionian Philosophy;
(*c*) Zeno;   10
(*d*) Early Atomism.

A general knowledge of pre-Socratic philosophy will also be expected.
This subject shall be studied in (i) Aristotle, *Metaphysics* A 1–8; (ii) G.S. Kirk, J.E. Raven, and M. Schofield, *The Presocratic Philosophers* (second edition, Cambridge, 1981); and (iii) a Faculty Supplement (available on WebLearn). The prescribed texts   15
under (ii) and (iii) are as follows:

(*a*) Heraclitus Diels–Kranz B 1, 2, 10, 12, 17, 18, 21, 26, 28–32, 40, 41, 45, 50–62, 64, 67, 78–80, 88, 90, 93, 94, 101, 101a, 102, 103, 107, 108, 111, 113–15, 117–19, 123–6, and the first part of A 22 (Aristotle *Eudemian Ethics* 1235^a25–7); Parmenides Diels–Kranz B 1–9, 19; Empedocles Diels–Kranz B 6, 8, 11–13, 17,   20
28–30, 35, 112, 115, 117, 134, 146; Anaxagoras Diels–Kranz B 1–17, 21, 21a;

(*b*) early Ionian philosophy: Anaximander Diels–Kranz A 9 and B 1; Anaximenes Diels–Kranz B 2; Aristotle *Metaphysics* A 3.983^a24–984^a18, *Physics* III 4.203^a16–18 and 203^b3–15; Xenophanes Diels–Kranz B 1, 7, 10–12, 14–16, 18, 23–9, 32, 34–6, 38; Aristotle *Metaphysics* A 5.986^b10–27;   25

(2) Zeno: Zeno Diels–Kranz B 1–4; Plato *Parmenides* 127a7-128e4; Aristotle *Physics* VI 2.233^a21–31 and 9.239^b5–240^a18;

(3) early atomists: Leucippus Diels–Kranz B 2; Democritus Diels–Kranz B 4, 6–8, 9, 10, 11, 117, 118, 125, 156, 164, 167; Aristotle *De Generatione et Corruptione* I 8.324^b35–325^a36, Metaphysics A 4.985^b3–22.   30

There will be a compulsory question containing passages for comment from Aristotle, *Metaphysics* A 1–8. The passages will be given in translation (to be taken from J. Barnes (ed.), *The Complete Works of Aristotle: The Revised Oxford Translation*, Volume II (Princeton NJ, 1984). A second compulsory question will contain passages for comment. At least one passage will be taken from (*a*), and at least one from each of   35
(*b*)–(*d*); all the passages for this question will be given in translation (to be taken from Kirk, Raven, and Schofield (eds), and/or the Faculty Supplement). Essay questions will also be set which will include questions on (*a*) and on each of (*b*)–(*d*).

3. Plato, *Euthyphro* and *Meno*

To be studied in *The Last Days of Socrates*, tr. Tredennick & Tarrant (Penguin,   40
revised 1993) and *Meno*, tr. Sharples (Aris & Phillips). The paper will include questions on the philosophical topics discussed in the dialogues. There will be a compulsory question containing passages for comment.

4. *General Philosophy* [Course IA, paper V B(1)]
5. *Moral Philosophy* [Course IA, paper V B(2)]   45
6. *Introduction to Logic* [Course IA, paper V B(3)]

V. Classical Special Subject

All candidates must offer one Classical Special Subject, chosen from Group D, E, or F. One three-hour paper will be set in each subject.

D.

1. *Cicero and Catiline*   5

The prescribed texts, from which compulsory passages for comment will be set, are Sallust, *Catiline*; Cicero, *In Catilinam* I-IV, *Pro Sulla*; Asconius, *In orationem in toga candida*. Compulsory passages for translation will be set only from Sallust, *Catiline* and Cicero, *In Catilinam* IV. Passages for comment from Cicero, *In Catilinam* I-III and *Pro Sulla* will be accompanied by the English translation of C. Macdonald (Loeb, 1977)   10 and from Asconius, *In orationem in toga candida* by the English translation of R.G. Lewis (ed.), *Asconius: Commentaries on Speeches by Cicero* (Oxford, 2006).

2. *Tacitus and Tiberius*

The prescribed text is Tacitus, *Annals* I and III. Compulsory passages for translation will be set only from *Annals* I. Compulsory passages for comment will be set   15 from *Annals* I and III; passages set from *Annals* III will be accompanied by the English translation of A.J. Woodman, *Tacitus Annals*, (Indianapolis, Hackett, 2004). Candidates will also be expected to be familiar with *Annals* II and IV–VI.

E.

1. *Homeric Archaeology and Early Greece from 1550 BC to 700 BC* [Course IA,   20 paper VI E(1)]
2. *Greek Vases* [Course IA, paper VI E(2)]
3. *Greek Sculpture* [Course IA, paper VI E(3)]
4. *Roman Architecture* [Course IA, paper VI E(4)]

F.   25

1. *Historical Linguistics and Comparative Philology* [Course IA, paper VI F(1)]

VI. Unprepared Translation from Latin
One paper (3 hours).

VII. Latin Language

One paper (3 hours). The paper will be divided into two main sections.   30
Candidates are required to offer *either* (*a*) *or* (*b*):

(*a*) a selection of passages from D. A Russell, *An Anthology of Latin Prose* (OUP, 1990), on which questions on accidence, syntax and style will be set (for the prescribed passages see the Mods Handbook) AND a short passage for translation into Latin prose;   35
(*b*) a passage for translation into Latin prose.

VIII. (Optional Paper) Verse Composition *or* Additional Translation *or* Additional Translation and Metre [Course IA, paper XI]

Course IIB
The examination will consist of the following papers.   40

I. Homer, *Iliad*

One paper (3 hours) of translation and questions. Compulsory passages for translation and commentary will be set from *Iliad* I, VI, IX, XXII, XXIV. Candidates will be expected to have knowledge of the whole poem. They will also be required to scan a short passage.   45

II, III. Texts and Contexts

An essay paper and a translation paper (each 3 hours). Candidates are expected to have considered the general topics as well as the particular texts and archaeological material specified. In the essay paper they will be required to answer a compulsory picture question, and three essay questions. A syllabus of images from which items will be selected for the picture question will be posted on WebLearn under "Texts and Contexts". In the translation paper candidates will be required to translate six passages, set from the Greek texts listed under α for topics 1 and 2.

1. *The Persian Wars and Cultural Identities*

 α Herodotus 8.56–110
 β Aeschylus, *Persians*
  Herodotus 1.1–32, 131–40; 3.61–88, 150–160; 7.1–239; 8.1–55
  Bisitun Inscription of Darius 1–15, 51–76
 Archaeological material: Identities in Greek and Persian art

2. *Dionysus, Drama, and Athens*

 α Euripides, *Bacchae* 1–169, 370–518, 643–976
  Aristophanes, *Frogs* 1–459, 1004–98, 1378–1481
 β Remainder of *Bacchae*
  Remainder of *Frogs*
 Archaeological material: Theatres, theatre images, and Dionysian iconography

3. *Love and Luxury*

 β Cicero, *pro Caelio*
  Catullus 1–16, 31–7, 42–5, 48–51, 53, 64.31–266, 69–70, 75–6, 79, 83–6, 95, 99–101, 116
  Propertius 1
 Archaeological material: Love pictures and Vesuvian villas

4. *Class*

 β Petronius, *Cena Trimalchionis*
  Juvenal 1, 3, 4, 5, 6, 7, 9
  Pliny, *Epistulae* 7.29, 8.6
  Tacitus, *Annals* 14.42–5
 Archaeological material: Houses, tombs, and the archaeology of public entertainment.

IV. Philosophy Special Subject

All candidates must offer one Philosophy Special Subject. One three-hour paper will be set in each subject.

 1. *Early Greek Philosophy* [Course IB, Paper V A (1)]
 2. *Plato, Meno and Euthyphro* [Course IB, Paper V A (2)]
 3. *General Philosophy* [Course IA, Paper V B (1)]
 4. *Moral Philosophy* [Course IA, Paper V B (2)]
 5. *Introduction to Logic* [Course IA, Paper V B (3)]

V. Classical Special Subject

All candidates must offer one Classical Special Subject, chosen from Group C, E, or F. One three-hour paper will be set in each subject.

C.

 1. *Thucydides and the West* [Course IB, paper VI C(1)]
 2. *Aristophanes' Political Comedy* [Course IB, paper VI C(2)]

E.

1. *Homeric Archaeology and Early Greece from 1550 BC to 700 BC* [Course IA, paper VI E(1)]
2. *Greek Vases* [Course IA, paper VI E(2)]
3. *Greek Sculpture* [Course IA, paper VI E(3)]
4. *Roman Architecture* [Course IA, paper VI E(4)]

F.

1. *Historical Linguistics and Comparative Philology* [Course IA, paper VI F(1)]

VI. UNPREPARED TRANSLATION FROM GREEK [Course IB, paper VII]

VII. GREEK LANGUAGE

One paper (3 hours). The paper will be divided into two main sections. Candidates are required to offer *either* (*a*) *or* (*b*):

(*a*) a selection of passages from D. A Russell, *An Anthology of Greek Prose* (OUP, 1991), on which questions on accidence, syntax and style will be set (for the prescribed passages see the Honour Moderations Handbook) AND a short passage for translation into Greek prose;

(*b*) a passage for translation into Greek prose.

VIII. (OPTIONAL PAPER) VERSE COMPOSITION *OR* ADDITIONAL TRANSLATION *OR* ADDITIONAL TRANSLATION AND METRE [Course IA, paper XI]

N.B. For prescribed editions in all forms of Classics Moderations, see Mods Handbook.

Special Regulations for Law Moderations

A

1. The subjects of Law Moderations shall be:
   (1) A Roman Introduction to Private Law.
   (2) Criminal Law.
   (3) Constitutional Law.
2. Every candidate who has passed in three subjects shall be deemed to have satisfied the Moderators, provided that
   (*a*) he or she shall have passed in not less than two subjects at one and the same time, and
   (*b*) he or she shall not be permitted to count any pass obtained in any subject before he or she satisfied the provision in (*a*).
3. Any candidate may offer himself or herself for examination in one, two, or three subjects. Except as provided in clause 2 hereof, a candidate who has passed a subject in one examination may not offer himself or herself for that subject again in a later examination. No candidate may re-enter the examination on more than one occasion after their first attempt, other than in exceptional circumstances and with the permission of the University Education Committee.

4. The Moderators may award a Distinction to any candidate of special merit who passes in three subjects at any one examination.

B

Every candidate who wishes to pass Law Moderations must offer Criminal Law and   5
Constitutional Law and A Roman Introduction to Private Law.

The individual specifications for Law Moderations subjects will be published in the Law Faculty Student Handbook for the academic year ahead by Monday of noughth week of Michaelmas Term each year.

Statutes and other source material   10

Details of the statutes and other sources of material which will be available to candidates in the examination room will be notified to candidates in Michaelmas Term, and any subsequent changes notified in the moderators' edict.

Special Regulations for the Preliminary Examination in Ancient and Modern History   15

A

The Preliminary Examination in Ancient and Modern History shall be under the joint supervision of the Boards of the Faculties of Classics and History and shall consist of such subjects as they shall jointly by regulation prescribe.   20

B

Every candidate shall offer four papers, as follows:

1. General History: any one of the following period papers I: 370–900 (*The Transformation of the Ancient World*), II: 1000–1300 (*Medieval Christendom and its neighbours*); III: 1400–1650 (*Renaissance, Recovery, and Reform*), and IV: 1815–1914   25
(*Society, Nation, and Empire*).

2. *Either* Greek History 650–479 BC: The Archaic Greek World *or* Roman History 241–146 BC : Rome and the Mediterranean.

3. *Either The World of Homer and Hesiod* (Homer, *Iliad, Odyssey* (tr. Lattimore); Hesiod, *Works and Days* (tr. M. L. West, Oxford 1988)); *or Augustan Rome* (as   30
specified in the Handbook for the Preliminary Examination in History); *or* any other Optional Subject specified for the Preliminary Examination in History.

4. *Either* Approaches to History, as specified for the Preliminary Examination in History; *or* Historiography: Tacitus to Weber, as specified for the Preliminary Examination in History; *or* Herodotus, V. 26-VI. 131, to be read in Greek, ed. C. Hude   35
(Oxford Classical Texts, 3rd edn., 1927); *or* Sallust, *Jugurtha,* to be read in Latin, ed. L. Reynolds (OCT, 1991) (for Herodotus and Sallust, candidates will be required to illustrate their answers by reference to the specified texts); *or* Beginning Ancient Greek *or* Beginning Latin *or* Intermediate Ancient Greek *or* Intermediate Latin.

Any candidate whose native language is not English may bring a bilingual (native   40
language to English) dictionary for use in any examination paper where candidates are required to translate Ancient Greek and/or Latin texts into English.

The individual specifications and prescribed texts for Optional Subjects, Approaches to History, and Historiography: Tacitus to Weber as specified for the Preliminary

Examination in History will be published for candidates in the Handbook for the Preliminary Examination in History by Monday of Week Nought of Michaelmas Term each year for the academic year ahead. The individual specifications and prescribed texts for the Optional Subject *Augustan Rome* will be published for candidates in the Handbook for the Preliminary Examination in History by Monday of Week Nought of Michaelmas Term each year for the academic year ahead. Depending on the availability of teaching resources, with the exception of Optional Subject 1, not all the Optional Subjects listed in the Handbook will be available to candidates in any given year. Candidates may obtain details of the choice for that year by consulting the Definitive List of Optional Subjects posted at the beginning of the first week of Michaelmas Full Term in the History Faculty and circulated to Ancient and Modern History Tutors. The individual specifications and prescribed texts for *Beginning Ancient Greek, Beginning Latin, Intermediate Ancient Greek* and *Intermediate Latin* will be published for candidates in the Ancient and Modern History Handbook by Monday of Week Nought of Michaelmas Term each year for the academic year ahead.

Candidates who fail one or more of papers 1, 2, 3, or 4 above may resit that subject or subjects at a subsequent examination.

Special Regulations for the Preliminary Examination in Archaeology and Anthropology

A

1. The Preliminary Examination in Archaeology and Anthropology shall be under the supervision of the Social Sciences Board, and shall consist of such subjects as it shall by regulation prescribe.

2. The Chair of the Moderators for the Honour Moderations in Archaeology and Anthropology shall designate such of their number as may be required for the Preliminary Examination in Archaeology and Anthropology.

B

Paper (1) Introduction to world archaeology;
Paper (2) Introduction to anthropological theory;
Paper (3) Perspectives of human evolution;
Paper (4) The nature of the archaeological enquiry.

Special Regulations for the Preliminary Examination in Biological Sciences

A

The subjects of the Preliminary Examination in Biological Sciences, the examination, the syllabus, and the number of papers shall be as prescribed by regulation from time to time by the Mathematical, Physical and Life Sciences Board.

B

1. The Biological Sciences Steering Committee shall publish the First Year Biology Handbook not later than the beginning of Michaelmas Full Term before the examination in the following Trinity Term. Further details of the papers, data handling course, and practical requirements shall be set out in that Handbook.   5

2. Candidates will be required to offer three papers, each lasting three hours, as follows:

Paper 1: Organisms
Paper 2: Cells and Genes
Paper 3: Ecology   10

3. All candidates will be required to undertake a course of practical work, including laboratory exercises and the first year field course. Practical Class co-ordinators and the convenor for the field course shall make available to the chair of the examiners records showing the extent to which each candidate has pursued an adequate course of practical work. The Moderators may request coursework from   15
any candidate; such candidates will be named in a list posted one week before the day of the first written paper. Each notebook submitted shall be accompanied by a certificate signed by the candidate indicating that the notebook is the candidate's own work. Failure to complete the coursework to the satisfaction of the Moderators, in the absence of appropriate documentary evidence, will normally constitute failure   20
of the Preliminary Examination. Coursework cannot normally be retaken. Exceptionally a candidate who has failed the coursework may be permitted jointly by the Moderators and the candidate's college to retake the entire academic year.

4. Candidates shall be deemed to have passed the examination if they have satisfied the Moderators in all three papers detailed in clause 2, and in the practical   25
work requirements as outlined in clause 3, either at a single examination, or at two examinations, as set out in clause 5.

5. A candidate who fails in any one of the papers listed in clause 2 must re-sit that paper at one, and only one, subsequent examination. A candidate who fails two or more papers listed in clause 2 must re-sit all three papers at one, and only one,   30
subsequent examination.

6. The Moderators will not provide calculators, but will permit the use of any handheld calculator subject to the conditions set out under the heading 'Use of calculators in examinations' in the Special Regulations concerning Examinations.

Special Regulations for the Preliminary Examination   35
in Biomedical Sciences

A

1. The subjects of the Preliminary Examination in Biomedical Sciences shall be:

(1) Body, Brain and Behaviour   40
(2) Cells, Molecules and Genes
(3) Mathematics and Statistics

2. Candidates shall be deemed to have passed the examination if they satisfy the Moderators in all three subjects.

3. Candidates must offer all three subjects at their first examination attempt.

4. A candidate who fails one subject will be permitted one further attempt at this failed subject, at the first available opportunity.

5. A candidate who fails two or three subjects shall be deemed to have failed the examination. He or she will be permitted one further attempt at the whole examination, at the first available opportunity.

6. The Moderators may award a Distinction to candidates of special merit who satisfy them in all three subjects at their first examination attempt.

B

One written paper will be set in each subject. The duration of the written papers will be three hours for subjects 1 and 2, and two hours for subject 3.

The Moderators will permit the use of hand-held pocket calculators subject to the conditions set out under the heading 'Use of calculators' in the *Regulations for the Conduct of University Examinations*. A list of recommended calculators will be provided by the Chair of the Moderators not later than the Wednesday of the fourth week of the Michaelmas Full Term preceding the examination. The use of calculators may not be permitted in certain papers.

All candidates shall be assessed as to their practical ability in coursework under the following provisions:

(a) The Course Director, or a deputy, shall make available to the Moderators, at the end of the fifth week of the term in which the examinations are held, evidence showing the extent and the standard to which each candidate has completed the prescribed coursework.

(b) Coursework cannot normally be retaken. Candidates whose attendance or performance is deemed unsatisfactory may be required by the Moderators to submit to further examination. Failure to satisfy the Moderators in the coursework associated with an examination paper will normally constitute failure of that examination paper.

Schedule

1. Body, Brain and Behaviour
   a. Body: cardiovascular; respiratory; renal and gastrointestinal systems
   b. Brain: introduction to neuroscience; neuroanatomy overview; sensory; motor; neural development; learning and memory; sleep, dreams, and consciousness
   c. Behaviour: memory; language; awareness and attention; decision-making and rationality; disorders; social; genetics of diseases

2. Cells, Molecules and Genes
   a. Cells: cell division and cell cycle; inter- and intra-cellular signalling; excitable tissues; membrane transport; general principles of pharmacology
   b. Molecules: DNA/RNA structure; protein structure; lipids and membrane structure; energy metabolism
   c. Genes: fundamentals of genes; molecular biology techniques

3. Mathematics and Statistics

Special Regulations for the Preliminary Examination in Chemistry

A

1. The subjects of the Preliminary Examination in Chemistry shall be Chemistry (comprising Inorganic, Organic, and Physical Chemistry) and Mathematics for Chemistry.

2. The number of papers and other general requirements of the Preliminary Examination in Chemistry shall be prescribed by regulation from time to time by the Mathematical, Physical and Life Sciences Board.

B

1. Candidates in the Preliminary Examination in Chemistry must offer four subjects at one examination, provided that a candidate who has failed in one or two subjects may offer that number of subjects at a subsequent examination.

2. The subjects shall be as follows:
(1) Inorganic Chemistry
(2) Organic Chemistry
(3) Physical Chemistry
(4) Mathematics for Chemistry

One two-and-a-half-hour paper will be set for each of subjects (1), (3) and (4); one three-hour paper will be set for subject (2).

3. Candidates shall be deemed to have passed the examination if they have satisfied the Moderators in all four subjects *either* at a single examination *or* at two examinations in accordance with the proviso to clause 1, and provided further that the same subjects as were failed at the first sitting have been passed at the same attempt at a subsequent examination.

4. The Moderators may award a distinction to candidates of special merit who have satisfied them in all four subjects at a single examination.

5. The Moderators will not provide calculators but unless otherwise specified will permit the use of any hand-held pocket calculator subject to the conditions set out under the heading 'Use of calculators in examinations' in the *Regulations for the Conduct of University Examinations* and further elaborated in the Course Handbook.

6. Candidates are required to complete an adequate course of laboratory work as specified in the Course Handbook. Heads of laboratories, or their deputies, and the IT Training Officer, shall make available to the Moderators records showing the extent to which each candidate has pursued an adequate course of laboratory work. Only work completed and marked by 5 p.m. on the Friday of the sixth week of Trinity Term will be taken into account.

Special Regulations for the Preliminary Examination in Classical Archaeology and Ancient History

A

The subjects of the examination shall be under the joint supervision of the Board of the Faculty of Classics and the Social Sciences Board.

B

Every candidate shall offer four papers [of three hours each] as follows:

I. *Aristocracy and democracy in the Greek world, 550–450 BC*

The paper studies the history and archaeology of the changing culture of the Greek *polis* states between the aristocracies in the later sixth century and the emergence of the new demos culture in the first half of the fifth century. Areas of emphasis will include: aristocracy, tyranny, and the history of the interacting archaic states; Achaemenids and the Greek collision with Persia; competing models of social and political culture after the Persian invasion; the archaeology of sanctuaries and cities; and the visual revolution in art and representation.

II. *Republic to Empire: Rome, 50 BC to AD 50*

The paper studies the impact of the first emperors on the history and archaeology of Rome and its subject states in the period from Late Republic to Early Empire. Areas of emphasis will include: Roman political culture from the Republican war-lords to Augustan *princeps*; emperor, senate, and the evolving administration; the Julio-Claudian dynasty and court culture: wallpainting, marbles, gardens and suburban parks; municipal culture: houses, tombs, and freedman art; land and countryside: estates, *vici*, and centuriated settlement; manufacture, trade, and natural resources; the archaeology of the frontier armies; traditional religion and emperor cult.

III, IV. Two papers from the following groups, provided that not more than one paper may be chosen from any one group:

A. Special subjects in archaeology:

1. *Homeric archaeology and early Greece, 1550–700 BC*
   Evidence on the composition and history of the poems provided by extant archaeological remains, with special emphasis on burial practices, architecture, metals, and the world outside the Aegean. An overall knowledge will be required of the archaeological evidence for the Late Bronze Age and Early Iron Age of the Aegean from 1550 BC to 700 BC. The examination will consist of one picture question and three essay questions.

2. *Greek vases*
   The study of the general history of Greek decorated pottery from c.800 BC to c.300 BC, including study of the Attic black-figure and red-figure styles and of South Italian Greek vase painting. Knowledge will be required of the techniques used in making Greek pottery and in drawing on vases, also of the ancient names for vases and the shapes to which they refer. Candidates should in addition study the subjects of the paintings and their treatment by painters as compared with their treatment by writers and should be familiar with actual vases, for example those in the Ashmolean Museum. The examination will consist of one picture question and three essay questions.

3. *Greek sculpture, c.600–300 BC*
   The major monuments of archaic and classical Greek sculpture—their context and purpose as well as their subjects, styles, and techniques. Candidates will be expected to show some knowledge of the external documentary evidence, such as literary and epigraphic texts, on which the framework of the subject depends, and to be acquainted with the major sculptures of the period represented in the Ashmolean Cast Gallery. The examination will consist of one picture question and three essay questions.

4. *Roman architecture*
The subject comprises the study of Roman architecture from the Republic to the Tetrarchy in Italy and in the provinces, looking at public buildings, private housing, and imperial palaces. Particular attention is paid to developments in building materials and techniques, the evolution of architectural styles and ideas, and the ways in which different provinces show variations on a common theme as Roman influences interacted with local culture. The examination will consist of one picture question and three essay questions.

B. Special subjects in Ancient History:

Note: All texts are studied in translation (see Course Handbook for details of the prescribed translation).

1. *Thucydides and the west*
The prescribed text is Thucydides VI and VII. Compulsory passages for comment will be set from these books (from S. Lattimore (ed), *The Peloponnesian War* (Indianapolis, Hackett, 1998). Candidates will also be expected to be familiar with Plutarch, *Nicias*.

2. *Aristophanes' political comedy*
The prescribed plays are *Knights*, *Wasps* and *Lysistrata*. Compulsory passages for comment will be set from *Wasps* and *Knights*. Candidates will also be expected to be familiar with *Lysistrata* and the '*Old Oligarch*'.

3. *Cicero and Catiline*
The prescribed texts are Sallust, *Catiline*: Cicero, In *Catilinam* I–IV, *Pro Sulla*; Asconius, *In orationem in toga candida* (in Asconius, *Commentaries on Five Speeches of Cicero*, ed. S. Squires, Bristol Classical Press, 1990). Compulsory passages for comment will be set from these.

4. *Tacitus and Tiberius*
The prescribed text is Tacitus, *Annals* I and III. Compulsory passages for comment will be set from these books (see Course Handbook for details of the prescribed text). Candidates will also be expected to be familiar with *Annals* II and IV–VI.

C. Ancient languages:

1. *Beginning Ancient Greek*
(This subject is not available to candidates with a qualification in ancient Greek above GCSE-level or equivalent.)

Candidates will be required to show knowledge of some of the main grammatical structures of ancient Greek and of a small basic vocabulary. The paper will consist of prepared and unprepared translations, with grammatical questions on the prepared texts.

2. *Beginning Latin*
(This subject is not available to candidates with a qualification in Latin above GCSE-level or equivalent.)

Candidates will be required to show knowledge of some of the main grammatical structures of Latin and of a small basic vocabulary. The paper will consist of prepared and unprepared translations, with grammatical questions on the prepared texts.

3. *Intermediate Ancient Greek*
(This subject is not available to candidates with a qualification in ancient Greek above AS-level or equivalent.)

Candidates will be required to show an intermediate level knowledge of Greek grammar and vocabulary. The set texts for the course are: Xenophon, *Hellenica* I (Oxford Classical Text) and *Lysias* I (Oxford Classical Text). The paper will consist of a passage of unseen translation, three further passages for translation from the two prescribed texts, and grammatical questions on the prescribed texts.

4. *Intermediate Latin*
(This subject is not available to candidates with a qualification in Latin above AS-level or equivalent.)

Candidates will be required to show an intermediate level knowledge of Latin grammar and vocabulary (including all syntax and morphology). The set texts for the course are: Cicero, letters in D.R. Shackleton Bailey, *Cicero: Select Letters* (Cambridge, 1980), nos. 9, 17, 23, 27, 39, 42-3, 45; Tacitus, Agricola (Oxford Classical Text); Pliny, letters in A.N. Sherwin-White, *Fifty Letters of Pliny*, second edition (Oxford, 1969), nos. 25, 29. The paper will consist of a passage of unseen prose translation, three further passages for translation from the prescribed texts, and grammatical questions on the prescribed texts.

Candidates who fail one or two of papers I, II, III, and IV above may resit only that subject or subjects at a subsequent examination; candidates who fail three or four papers will be required to resit all four papers at a subsequent examination.

Special Regulations for the Preliminary Examination in Classics

A

1. The subjects of the examination shall be as prescribed by regulation from time to time by the Board of the Faculty of Classics and the Board of the Faculty of Philosophy.

2. A candidate shall be deemed to have passed the examination if he or she shall have satisfied the Moderators in all four subjects: provided that he or she shall have passed in not less than three of the four subjects at one and the same examination.

3. A candidate shall be allowed to offer himself or herself for examination in one or four subjects: provided that no candidate may offer a single subject unless he or she has already satisfied the Moderators in three subjects.

4. The Moderators shall not publish the name of any candidate as having satisfied them in only one subject, unless that subject shall have been offered by the candidate as a single subject.

5. In the case of candidates who have satisfied the Moderators in four subjects at a single examination, the Moderators may award a Distinction to those of special merit.

B

Any candidate whose native language is not English may bring a bilingual (native language to English) dictionary for use in any examination paper where candidates are required to translate Ancient Greek and/or Latin texts into English.

Candidates shall take one of the following courses: IA, IB, IC, IIA, IIB.   5

Course IA

The examination will consist of the following papers.

I–II. *Texts and Contexts*

All candidates must offer 'Texts and Contexts' listed under Honour Moderations in Classics Course IA, papers III and IV.   10

III. *Special Subject*

All candidates must offer one of the Special Subjects listed under Honour Moderations in Classics Course IA, papers V and VI.

IV. *Unprepared Translation from Greek and Latin*

One paper (3 hours).   15

Course IB

The examination will consist of the following papers.

I–II. *Text and Contexts*

All candidates must offer 'Texts and Contexts' listed under Honour Moderations in Classics Course IB, papers III and IV.   20

III. *Special Subject*

All candidates must offer one of the Special Subjects listed under Honour Moderations in Classics Course IB, papers V and VI.

IV. *Unprepared Translation from Latin, with simpler Unprepared Translation from Greek*   25

One paper (3 hours).

Course IC

The examination will consist of the following papers.

I–II. *Text and Contexts*

All candidates must offer 'Texts and Contexts' listed under Honour Moderations   30
in Classics Course IC, papers III and IV.

III. *Special Subject*

All candidates must offer one of the Special Subjects listed under Honour Moderations in Classics Course IC, papers V and VI.

IV. *Unprepared Translation from Greek, with simpler Unprepared Translation from*   35
Latin

One paper (3 hours).

Course IIA

The examination will consist of the following papers.

I–II. *Texts and Contexts*   40

All candidates must offer 'Texts and Contexts' listed under Honour Moderations in Classics Course IIA, papers II and III.

III. *Special Subject*

All candidates must offer one of the Special Subjects listed under Honour Moderations in Classics Course IIA, papers IV and V.

IV. *Unprepared Translation from Latin*

One paper (3 hours), as specified for Honour Moderations in Classics Course IIA, paper VI.

Course IIB

The examination will consist of the following papers.

I–II. *Text and Contexts*

All candidates must offer 'Texts and Contexts' listed under Honour Moderations in Classics Course IIB, papers II and III.

III. *Special Subject*

All candidates must offer one of the Special Subjects listed under Honour Moderations in Classics Course IIB, papers IV and V.

IV. *Unprepared Translation from Greek*

One paper (3 hours), as specified for Honour Moderations in Classics Course IB, paper VII.

Special Regulations for the Preliminary Examination in Classics and English

A

1. The Preliminary Examination in Classics and English shall be under the joint supervision of the Boards of the Faculties of Classics and English Language and Literature and shall consist of such subjects as they shall jointly by regulation prescribe.

2. The Chair of Examiners for the Preliminary Examination in English Language and Literature shall designate such of the number of examiners as may be required for the English subjects of the examination for the Preliminary Examination in Classics and English, and the nominating committee for examiners appointed by the Board of the Faculty of Classics shall nominate such of the number of examiners as may be required for the Classics subjects of the examination. When these appointments shall have been made the number of examiners shall be deemed to be complete.

B

The committee appointed by the Boards of the Faculties of English Language and Literature and Classics to advise on the examination for the Honour School of Classics and English shall make proposals to the two boards for regulations for this examination.

Any candidate whose native language is not English may bring a bilingual (native language to English) dictionary for use in any examination paper where candidates are required to translate Ancient Greek and/or Latin texts into English.

Candidates shall take one of the following courses:

I. *Course I*

Each candidate shall offer five papers, each of three hours duration except where specified, as follows:

1. *Introduction to English Language and Literature* (a portfolio submitted in Trinity Term year 1)   5

The paper will be examined by a portfolio of work, comprising one commentary answer and one discursive essay, of not fewer than 1,500 and not more than 2,000 words each. Footnotes will be included in the total word count, but bibliographies do not count towards the limit. The list of questions for this paper will be divided into Section A (Language) and B (Literature) and will be published on Monday of the   10
fourth week of the Trinity Term of the first year. Candidates must select one question from Section A and one question from section B.

Questions in Section A (Language) invite candidates to make their own selection of texts or passages of texts for commentary, in accordance with the terms of the particular question chosen. Copies of the texts or passages used must be included   15
as an appendix to the portfolio. The combined length of all texts or passages chosen must not exceed 70 lines. The texts or passages used will not count towards the word limit for the commentary answer.

Two typed copies of the portfolio must be delivered to the Chair of Examiners for the Preliminary Examinations in English Language and Literature, Examination   20
Schools, High Street, by noon on Thursday of the fifth week of the same Trinity Term. A certificate, signed by the candidate to the effect that each answer is the candidate's own work, and that the candidate has read the Faculty guidelines on plagiarism, must be presented together with each portfolio.

Following the publication of themes for this subject on Monday of the fourth week   25
of Trinity Term, the candidate must neither discuss his or her choice of themes nor the method of handling them with any tutor. Every portfolio must be the work of the candidate alone, but he or she may discuss with his or her tutor the subjects and approach to the essays up until the stated publication date of the portfolio themes.

Portfolios previously submitted for the First Public Examination in English   30
Language and Literature may be resubmitted. No answer will be accepted that has already been submitted, wholly or substantially, for a final honour school or any other degree of this University, or degree of any other institution.

Work deemed to be either too short or of excessive length may be penalised.

Candidates must avoid duplicating material used in this paper when answering   35
other papers. In addition, candidates are not permitted to duplicate material between Section A and Section B of the portfolio.

2. *Literature in English 1550–1660* (excluding the works of Shakespeare)

3. *Unseen translation from Greek and Latin*

Candidates may offer either Latin or Greek or both. Two passages must be offered   40
and in each language one prose passage and one verse passage will be set.

4, 5. *Greek and Latin Literature*

Candidates must offer two of the following.
They must offer either (*a*) or (*b*), but may not offer both.

(*a*) Homer, *Iliad*, I, VI, IX, XVI, XVIII, XXII–XXIV;*   45

(*b*) Virgil, *Aeneid*, I, II, IV, VI;*

(*c*) Euripides, *Bacchae* 1–1167; Aristophanes, *Frogs* 1–459, 830–1533; Herodotus 7.1–53; 8.56–110;**

(*d*) Cicero, *Pro Caelio* 17–53 (*...dedisti.*); Catullus 1–16, 31–7, 42–5, 48–51, 53, 69–70, 75–6, 79, 83–6, 95, 99–101, 116; Propertius I.1–3, 6, 11, 14; Petronius, *Cena Trimalchionis* 26.7–36, 47–78; Juvenal 3, 5.***   5

Paper 4 will consist of essay questions; all candidates will be required to answer questions on each of: Homer or Virgil; other texts; general topics. Paper 5 will comprise passages for translation and comment; all candidates will be required to answer on three passages, at least once passage of Homer or Virgil and at least one from the other texts.   10

The Examiners shall publish the names of candidates who have satisfied them in all five papers, or all of papers 1 and 2 or all of papers 3, 4 and 5.

N.B For prescribed editions, see the Classics and English handbook .

* For the purposes of the essay paper (paper 4), candidates who offer these texts will be expected to have knowledge of the whole work and not merely the prescribed   15
portions.

** For the purposes of the essay paper (paper 4), candidates who offer these texts will be expected to have knowledge of the whole of *Bacchae, Frogs*, and Herodotus 7–8 and not merely the prescribed portions.

*** For the purposes of the essay paper (paper 4), candidates who offer these texts   20
will be expected to have knowledge of the whole of *Pro Caelio*, Propertius I, and the *Cena Trimalchionis* and not merely the prescribed portions.

II. *Course II*

Candidates for Course II shall be required:

(*a*) during their first year of study to have passed an examination under the auspices   25
of the Board of the Faculty of Classics during the Trinity Term. This examination is also available for appropriate candidates intending to offer papers in the Preliminary Examination for Modern Languages in their second year of study. Candidates who fail to satisfy the examiners shall be permitted to offer themselves for re-examination during the following September. Each candidate shall offer two papers, each of three   30
hours' duration, as follows:

1. Greek or Latin texts. Candidates must offer either (*a*) or (*b*):

(*a*) Homer, *Iliad* 24; Lysias 1 and 3; Euripides, *Bacchae* 1–63, 180–369, 434–518.
(*b*) Virgil, *Aeneid* 6; Seneca, *Epistles* 54, 57, 79, 114 and 122; Catullus 1–16, 31–4.

For a list of prescribed texts, see the Classics and English handbook. The paper will   35
comprise passages from these texts for translation and comment.

2. Greek or Latin Language. The paper will consist of passages for unseen translation out of Greek or Latin and sentences for translation from English into Latin or Greek.

(*b*) during their second year of study, to offer papers as for Course I.   40

Special Regulations for the Preliminary Examination in Computer Science

A

1. The subject of the examination shall be Computer Science.

2. The syllabus and number of papers shall be prescribed by regulation from time to time by the Mathematical, Physical and Life Sciences Board.

B

1. The Preliminary Examination in Computer Science shall comprise four compulsory written papers plus compulsory Computer Science practicals equivalent to one written paper:

CS1 Functional Programming, and Design and Analysis of Algorithms
CS2 Imperative Programming
CS3 Discrete Mathematics, Probability and Continuous Mathematics
CS4 Digital Systems, Linear Algebra, and Introduction to Formal Proof
Computer Science Practicals

2. The syllabus for each paper will be published by the Department of Computer Science in a handbook for candidates by the beginning of the Michaelmas Full Term in the academic year of the examination, after consultation with the Faculty of Computer Science (for papers CS1, CS2, CS3, and CS4) and the Faculty of Mathematics (for paper CS3). Each paper will contain questions of a straightforward character.

3. All candidates will be assessed as to their practical ability under the following provisions:

(a) The Head of the Department of Computer Science, or a deputy, shall make available to the examiners evidence showing the extent to which each candidate has pursued an adequate course of practical work. Only that work completed and marked by noon on Monday of the fifth week of the Trinity Term in which the candidate takes the examination shall be included in these records.

(b) Candidates shall submit to the Chair of the Moderators for the Preliminary Examination in Computer Science, c/o the Academic Administrator, Oxford University Department of Computer Science, Oxford, by noon on Monday of the fifth week of the Trinity Term in which the examination is being held, their reports of practical exercises completed during their course of study. For a report on a practical exercise to be considered by the moderators, it must have been marked by a demonstrator and must be accompanied by a statement that it is the candidate's own work except where otherwise indicated.

(c) The moderators shall take the evidence (a) and the reports (b) into account in assessing a candidate's performance.

(d) Candidates whose overall performance on practical work is not satisfactory may be deemed to have failed the examination.

4. Candidates shall be deemed to have passed the examination if they have satisfied the Moderators in the five papers in clause 1 either at a single examination or at two examinations in accordance with clause 6 or clause 7.

5. The Moderators may award a distinction to candidates of special merit who have satisfied them in all five papers in clause 1 in one examination.

6. Candidates who fail one or two written papers listed in clause 1 may offer those papers at one, but no more than one, subsequent examination.

7. Candidates who fail three or more written papers may enter the written part of the examination on one, but no more than one, subsequent examination.

8. The use of calculators is generally not permitted but certain kinds may be allowed for certain papers. Specifications of which papers and which types of calculators are permitted for those exceptional papers will be announced by the examiners in the Hilary Term preceding the examination.

Special Regulations for the Preliminary Examination in Computer Science and Philosophy

A

1. The subject of the examination shall be (a) Computer Science and (b) Philosophy.

2. All candidates must offer both (a) and (b).

3. The Examinations shall be under the joint supervision of the Divisional Board of Mathematical, Physical and Life Sciences and the Board of the Faculty of Philosophy, which shall appoint a joint supervisory committee to make regulations concerning it, subject always to the preceding clauses of this subsection.

B

1. The Preliminary Examination in Computer Science and Philosophy shall comprise five compulsory written papers plus compulsory Computer Science practicals equivalent to one written paper:

CS1 Functional Programming, and Design and Analysis of Algorithms
CS2 Imperative Programming
CSP3 Discrete Mathematics and Probability
P1 Introduction to Philosophy
P2 Elements of Deductive Logic
Computer Science Practicals

2. The syllabus for papers CS1, CS2 and CSP3 will be published by the Joint Supervisory Committee in a handbook for candidates by the beginning of the Michaelmas Full Term in the academic year of the examination, after consultation with the Faculty of Computer Science (for papers CS1, CS2 and CSP3) and the Faculty of Mathematics (for paper CSP3). The syllabus for paper P1 will be as stated below. The syllabus for paper P2 will be as stated for the Elements of Deductive Logic paper in the regulations for the Preliminary Examination in Mathematics and Philosophy.

3. Papers CS1, CS2 and CSP3 will contain questions of a straightforward character.

4. All candidates will be assessed as to their practical ability in Computer Science under the following provisions:

(a) The Head of the Department of Computer Science, or a deputy, shall make available to the examiners evidence showing the extent to which each candidate has pursued an adequate course of practical work. Only that work completed and marked by noon on Monday of the fifth week of the Trinity Term in which the candidate takes the examination shall be included in these records.

(b) Candidates shall submit to the Chair of the Moderators for the Preliminary Examination in Computer Science and Philosophy, c/o the Academic Administrator, Oxford University Department of Computer Science, Oxford, by noon on Monday of the fifth week of the Trinity Term in which the examination is being held, their reports of practical exercises completed during their course of study. For a report on a practical exercise to be considered by the Moderators, it must have been marked by a demonstrator and must be accompanied by a statement that it is the candidate's own work except where otherwise indicated.

(*c*) The Moderators shall take the evidence (*a*) and the reports (*b*) into account in assessing a candidate's performance.

(*d*) Candidates whose overall performance on practical work is not satisfactory may be deemed to have failed the examination.

5. Candidates shall be deemed to have passed the examination if they have satisfied the Moderators in all six papers in clause 1 either at a single examination or at two examinations in accordance with clause 7 or clause 8.

6. The Moderators may award a distinction to candidates of special merit who have satisfied them in all six papers in clause 1 in one examination.

7. Candidates who fail one or two written papers listed in clause 1 may offer those papers at one, but no more than one, subsequent examination.

8. Candidates who fail three or more papers may enter the written part of the examination on one, but no more than one, subsequent examination.

9. The use of calculators is generally not permitted but certain kinds may be allowed for certain papers. Specifications of which papers and which types of calculators are permitted for those exceptional papers will be announced by the examiners in the Hilary Term preceding the examination.

Paper P1, Introduction to Philosophy
The paper shall consist of two parts:

A. *General Philosophy* as stated in the regulations for the Preliminary Examination in Mathematics and Philosophy.

B. *Turing: Computability and Intelligence* This section shall be studied in connection with Alan Turing's papers 'On Computable Numbers, with an Application to the *Entscheidungsproblem*' (reprinted and explained in Charles Petzold's *The Annotated Turing*, Wiley, 2008) and 'Computing Machinery and Intelligence' (*Mind*, 1950). While not being confined to Turing's views, these questions will be satisfactorily answerable by a candidate who has made a critical study of the texts. There will not be a compulsory question containing passages for comment.

Candidates will be required to attempt four questions, including at least one question from Part A and at least one question from Part B.

Special Regulations for the Preliminary Examination in Earth Sciences

A

1. The subject of the Preliminary Examination in Earth Sciences shall be Earth Sciences, including supporting practical techniques and physics, chemistry, mathematics and biology.

2. The number of papers and other general requirements of the Preliminary Examination in Earth Sciences shall be prescribed by regulation from time to time by the Mathematical, Physical and Life Sciences Board.

B

1. The Preliminary Examination in Earth Sciences shall consist of 5 compulsory papers taken at one examination, subject to the conditions of cl. 5 below:

(*a*) Paper 1: Planet Earth

(*b*) Paper 2: Fundamentals of Geology (Theory)

(*c*) Paper 3: Fundamentals of Geology (Practical)

(*d*) Paper 4: Chemistry, Physics and Biology for Earth Sciences

(*e*) Paper 5: an approved paper in Mathematics

The syllabus for these papers shall be published annually in the course handbook, not later than the beginning of Michaelmas Full Term for examination three terms thence.

2. In addition to the above five papers a candidate in Earth Sciences shall be required to submit to the examiners such evidence as they require of the successful completion of field work normally pursued during the three terms preceding the examination. Candidates who fail to satisfy the examiners in this regard will be required to sit a further paper, which may only be taken once.

3. Candidates shall be deemed to have passed the examination if they have:

(*a*) satisfied the Examiners in the five papers in clause 1 either at a single examination or at two examinations in accordance with clause 5, and

(*b*) satisfied the additional requirements in clause 2.

4. The Examiners may award a distinction to candidates of special merit who have satisfied them in all five papers in clause 1 in one examination and in the requirements of clause 2.

5. Candidates who fail in one or two papers listed in clause 1 may offer that number of papers at a subsequent examination. Candidates who fail more than two papers must resit all five papers at a subsequent examination.

6. The examination conventions of each examination paper listed in clause 1 will be published annually in the course handbook.

Special Regulations for the Preliminary Examination in Economics and Management

A

1. The subjects of the Preliminary Examination in Economics and Management shall be:

(1) Introductory Economics

(2) Financial Management

(3) General Management.

2. A candidate shall be allowed to offer himself or herself for examination in one, two, or three subjects.

3. A candidate shall be deemed to have passed the examination if he or she shall have satisfied the Moderators in three subjects.

4. The Moderators may award a distinction to candidates of special merit who have passed all three subjects at a single examination.

B

Three three-hour papers will be set as follows:

Introductory Economics

As specified in the regulation relating to the Introductory Economics paper of the Philosophy, Politics, and Economics Preliminary Examination.

Financial Management

Financial reporting and analysis of company accounts; management accounting, including cost behaviours, capital budgeting, budgetary planning and control; discounting and net present value; internal rates of return; measurement and evaluation of risk; capital asset pricing; investment appraisal; sources of funds; capital budgeting and implementation.

General Management

Historical context; organisational behaviour; human resources; strategic management; technology and operations management; marketing; international business.

Special Regulations for the Preliminary Examination in Engineering Science

A

The subjects of the examination, the syllabus, and the number of papers shall be as prescribed by regulation from time to time by the Divisional Board of Mathematical, Physical and Life Sciences.

B

1. Candidates shall take four written papers of three hours each:

Paper P1 Mathematics
Paper P2 Electronic and Information Engineering
Paper P3 Structures and Mechanics
Paper P4 Energy and the Environment.

The syllabus for Papers P1-P4 will be published annually by the Faculty of Engineering Science in the Engineering Science Undergraduate Course Handbook.

In addition Engineering Coursework (P5) shall be considered by the Moderators as equivalent to half of a three hour written paper.

2. Candidates must offer all subjects at one examination provided that: (i) a candidate who fails in one or two written papers may offer those written subjects at one subsequent examination; (ii) a candidate who fails three or four written papers must offer all four written subjects at one subsequent examination.

3. Candidates shall be deemed to have passed the examination if they shall have satisfied the Moderators in all four written papers and in the engineering coursework either at a single examination or at two examinations in accordance with the proviso to clause 2. Any written subjects retaken must be passed at the same attempt at a subsequent examination.

4. All candidates shall be assessed as to their practical ability in engineering coursework under the following provisions:

(*a*) The Chair of the Faculty, or a deputy, shall make available to the Moderators, by the date of the first written paper, evidence showing the extent to which each candidate has completed coursework.

(*b*) Candidates will not normally be required to submit their coursework. The Moderators may request coursework from some candidates. Such candidates will be named in a list posted by the day of the last written examination.

(*c*) Engineering coursework cannot be retaken. Failure of coursework will normally constitute failure of the examination.

5. In the case of candidates who offer all four written papers, the Moderators shall publish the name of candidates who have satisfied them either in the whole examination or in any written paper. In the case of candidates who, in accordance with the proviso of clause 2, offer one, two, or four written papers at the second attempt, the Moderators shall publish the names only of those candidates who have satisfied them in each of the papers offered.

6. The Moderators may award a distinction to candidates of special merit who have passed all four written subjects and the engineering coursework at a single examination.

7. The Moderators will not provide calculators, but will permit the use of one hand-held pocket calculator from a list of permitted calculators published by the Chair of the Faculty not later than the end of the fourth week of the Trinity Full Term in the academic year preceding the examination.

Special Regulations for the Preliminary Examination in English and Modern Languages

A

1. Candidates in this Preliminary Examination shall be examined in English and one Modern Language. The modern languages that may be offered shall be those which may be offered in the Honour School of Modern Languages.

2. The subjects of the examination, the syllabus, and the number of papers shall be as prescribed by regulation from time to time by the Boards of the Faculties of English Language and Literature and Medieval and Modern Languages.

3. It shall be the duty (a) of the Chair of the Examiners for the Preliminary Examination in English Language and Literature to designate such of their number as may be required for English in the Preliminary Examination in English and Modern Languages, and when this has been done the number of examiners in English shall be deemed to be complete; and (b) of the Chair of the Examiners for the Preliminary Examination for Modern Languages to designate such of their number as may be required for Modern Languages in the Preliminary Examination in English and Modern Languages, and when this has been done, the number of examiners in Modern Languages shall be deemed to be complete.

B

The Boards of the Faculties of English Language and Literature and of Medieval and Modern Languages shall appoint a joint standing committee to make, and to submit to the two faculty boards, proposals for regulations for this examination.

A candidate shall be deemed to have passed the examination if he or she shall have satisfied the Examiners in Part 1 (a Modern Language) and Part 2 (English).

The examiners may award distinctions in Part 1 or in Part 2 or in both to candidates who have done work of special merit in the part or parts concerned.

A candidate who has failed a subject or both the subjects in Part 1 will be allowed to resit the subject or subjects in which he or she has failed at a subsequent examination in accordance with the regulations for the Preliminary Examination for Modern Languages. A candidate who has failed one or both of the papers in Part 2 will be allowed to resit the paper or papers in accordance with the appropriate regulations for the First Public Examinations in English Language and Literature.

Part 1: A Modern Language
Each candidate shall offer the following two subjects in the modern language:

(1) Language papers (one paper of three hours and two papers each of one-and-a-half hours including in French certification of attendance and participation in oral classes, as specified for the Preliminary Examination in Modern Languages). As specified for papers I, IIA, and IIB in the regulations for the Preliminary Examination for Modern Languages.

(2) Literature papers (two papers, each of three hours). As specified for papers III and IV in the regulations for the Preliminary Examination for Modern Languages.

Part 2: English
Each candidate shall offer the following papers, as specified in the regulations for subjects 1 to 4 of the Preliminary Examination in English Language and Literature:

(1) Introduction to English Language and Literature [as specified for the Preliminary Examination in English Language and Literature, subject 1].

(2) *Either* (*a*) Literature in English 650–1350 [as specified for the Preliminary Examination in English Language and Literature, subject 2].

or (*b*) Literature in English 1830–1910 [as specified for the Preliminary Examination in English Language and Literature, subject 3].

or (*c*) Literature in English 1910–present day [as specified for the Preliminary Examination in English Language and Literature, subject 4].

Special Regulations for the Preliminary Examination in English Language and Literature

A

1. The subjects of the examination, the syllabus, and the number of papers shall be as prescribed by regulation from time to time by the Board of the Faculty of English Language and Literature.

2. A Candidate shall be deemed to have passed the examination when he or she shall have satisfied the Examiners in all the papers specified in the regulations.

3. Candidates must offer all the papers at a single examination, provided that: (i) a candidate who fails to satisfy the Examiners in one or two papers may offer those subjects at one subsequent examination, and (ii) a candidate who fails to satisfy the Examiners in three or four papers must offer all four subjects at one subsequent examination.

4. The Examiners may award a distinction to any candidate of special merit who has satisfied the Examiners in all the papers at a single examination.

B

Each candidate shall offer four papers, as set out below. Paper 1 shall be examined by portfolio submission in the third term. Papers 2, 3 and 4 shall be examined by written examinations of three hours' duration.

1. *Introduction to English Language and Literature*   5

The paper will be examined by a portfolio of work, comprising one commentary answer and one discursive essay, of not fewer than 1,500 and not more than 2,000 words each. Footnotes will be included in the total word count, but bibliographies do not count towards the limit. The list of questions for this paper will be divided into Section A (Language) and B (Literature) and will be published on Monday of the   10 fourth week of the Trinity Term of the first year. Candidates must select one question from Section A and one question from Section B.

Questions in Section A (Language) invite candidates to make their own selection of texts or passages of texts for commentary, in accordance with the terms of the particular question chosen. Copies of the texts or passages used must be included   15 as an appendix to the portfolio. The combined length of all texts or passages chosen must not exceed 70 lines. The texts or passages used will not count towards the word limit for the commentary answer.

Two typed copies of the portfolio must be delivered to the Chair of Examiners for the Preliminary Examination in English Language and Literature, Examination   20 Schools, High Street, by noon on Thursday of the fifth week of the same Trinity Term. A certificate, signed by the candidate to the effect that each answer is the candidate's own work, and that the candidate has read the Faculty guidelines on plagiarism, must be presented together with each portfolio.

Following the publication of themes for this subject on Monday of the fourth week   25 of Trinity Term, the candidate must neither discuss his or her choice of themes nor the method of handling them with any tutor. Every portfolio must be the work of the candidate alone, but he or she may discuss with his or her tutor the subjects and approach to the essays up until the stated publication date of the portfolio themes.

Portfolios previously submitted for the First Public Examination in English   30 Language and Literature may be resubmitted. No answer will be accepted that has already been submitted, wholly or substantially, for a final honour school or any other degree of this University, or degree of any other institution.

Work deemed to be either too short or of excessive length may be penalised.

Candidates must avoid duplicating material used in this paper when answering   35 other papers. In addition, candidates are not permitted to duplicate material between Section A and Section B of the portfolio.

2. *Early Medieval Literature 650–1350*

The examination for paper 2 will be divided into Section A and Section B.

(*a*) Section A will consist of four passages for critical commentary: two passages   40 from Old English texts and two passages from Early Middle English texts. Candidates should write on *one* passage only.

Passages will be set from texts specified in the English Preliminary Examination Handbook for the year of examination.

(*b*) Section B will consist of essay questions that are thematic in nature and may be   45 applied to any texts from the period. Candidates should answer *two* questions from section B.

3. *Literature in English 1830–1910*

4. *Literature in English 1910–present day*

Special Regulations for the Preliminary Examination in European and Middle Eastern Languages

A

1. The Preliminary Examination in European and Middle Eastern Languages shall be under the joint supervision of the Boards of the Faculties of Medieval and Modern Languages and Oriental Studies and shall consist of such subjects as they shall jointly by regulation prescribe.

2. Candidates in this Preliminary Examination shall be examined (*a*) in one language from among those which may be offered in the Honour School of Modern Languages, and (*b*) in Arabic or in Hebrew or in Persian or in Turkish.

3. It shall be the duty (*a*) of the Chair of the Examiners for the Preliminary Examination for Modern Languages to designate such of their number as may be required for European Languages in the Preliminary Examination in European and Middle Eastern Languages, and when this has been done the number of examiners in European Languages shall be deemed to be complete; and (*b*) of the Chair of the Moderators for the Preliminary Examination in Oriental Studies to designate such of their number as may be required for Arabic, Hebrew, Persian, and Turkish in the Preliminary Examination in European and Middle Eastern Languages, and when this has been done the number of examiners in Middle Eastern Languages shall be deemed to be complete.

B

There shall be two subjects in the examination.

(1) *The European Language*

Candidates will be required to offer:

(i) Language papers in the European Language (one paper of three hours and two papers each of one-and-a-half hours including in French certification of attendance and participation in oral classes, as specified for the Preliminary Examination in Modern Languages).

As specified for Papers I, IIA, and IIB in the regulations for the Preliminary Examination for Modern Languages.

(ii) Literature paper in the European Language (one paper of three hours).

As specified *either* for Paper III *or* for Paper IV in the regulations for the Preliminary Examination in Modern Languages (Candidates offering French *must* offer Paper IV).

(2) *Language papers in the Middle Eastern Language*

Candidates will be required to offer two three-hour papers and, in the case of Arabic, an oral/aural examination.

Arabic

(i) Translation and precis into English.
(ii) Comprehension, composition, and grammar.
(iii) Oral/aural examination.

Hebrew 5

(i) Biblical and Modern Texts (copies of texts available from the Oriental Institute).
(ii) Grammar and Translation into Hebrew.

Persian

(i) Prepared and unprepared texts for translation from Persian.
(ii) Grammar and translation into Persian. 10

Turkish

(i) Prepared texts and unseen translation from Turkish. (The list of texts to be prepared is published in the current issue of the Islamic Studies handbook.)
(ii) Turkish grammar and translation into Turkish.

Candidates shall be deemed to have passed the examination if they shall have 15 satisfied the examiners in subject (1) (The European Language) and subject (2) (Language papers in the Middle Eastern Language).

The examiners may award distinctions in either or both subjects to candidates who have done work of special merit in the subject or subjects concerned.

A candidate who has failed (i) or (ii) of subject (1) may resit the paper or papers at 20 a subsequent examination in accordance with the regulations for the Preliminary Examination in Modern Languages. A candidate who has failed a paper or papers in subject (2) may resit that paper or papers at a subsequent examination.

Special Regulations for the Preliminary Examination in Fine Art

A 25

1. No person who is not a member of the University may be admitted to the Preliminary Examination in Fine Art.

2. A candidate may enter his or her name for the examination not earlier than the third term from his matriculation.

3. The subjects of the examination shall be 30

(1) Drawing;

(2) Practical Studio-based Work;

(3) History and Theory of Visual Culture;

(4) Human Anatomy.

4. Candidates must offer all four subjects of the examination at 35 the same time, provided that a candidate who has passed in at least two of the subjects but failed in the other subjects (or subject) of the examination may offer at a subsequent examination the subjects (or subject) in which he or she has failed.

5. The examination shall be under the supervision of the 40 Committee for the Ruskin School of Art, which shall make regulations for the examination.

6. The examiners may award a distinction in the examination to any candidate.

B

1. The examination shall include both practical and written work.
2. Every candidate will be required in respect of:

(1) *Drawing*

to submit a portfolio of not less than twelve and no more than twenty drawings in any medium;

(2) *Practical Studio-based Work*

    (*a*) to produce an exhibition of current work or work constructed especially for assessment; and

    (*b*) to submit a portfolio of work made during the course preceding the examination in any medium or media agreed by the candidate and their tutor. This should include at least six and no more than twenty original works; in the case of time-based work, candidates should make a submission of works, or excerpts of works, of no more than a total of twenty minutes' duration. Work which, in the judgement of the candidate's tutor, cannot be submitted for examination for practical reasons, may be represented by documentation.

(3) *History and Theory of Visual Culture*

    (*a*) to submit three essays of no more than 2,000 words each (including footnotes) on aspects of the history and theory of visual culture in accordance with the provisions of clause 3 of these regulations;

    (*b*) to offer a paper on history and theory of visual culture;

(4) *Human Anatomy*

    (*a*) to offer a paper on form and function in human anatomy.

    (*b*) to submit notebooks and a portfolio of not less than six and no more than twenty examples of supporting visual material on the candidate's work in human anatomy.

The work required by (1), (2), and (4) (*b*) above must be submitted to the Chair of Examiners, Preliminary Examination in Fine Art, Ruskin School of Art, 74 High Street, in the case of the examination held in Trinity Term not later than noon on Thursday of the sixth week of that term, and in the case of the examination held in the vacation preceding Michaelmas Term not later than noon on Wednesday in the week before Michaelmas Full Term.

3. Of the essays required by the provisions of clause (3) (*a*) of these regulations, one must be submitted not later than noon on the Friday of the ninth week of the Michaelmas Full Term preceding the examination, one must be submitted not later than noon on the Monday of the first week of Hilary Full Term preceding the examination and one must be submitted not later than noon on the Friday of the ninth week of the Hilary Full Term preceding the examination. One copy of these essays, which may be either typed or in manuscript, must be delivered to the Chair of Examiners, Preliminary Examination in Fine Art, Examination Schools. Each essay must be accompanied by a certificate signed by the candidate that the essay has not been submitted for any previous examination, and that the essay is the candidate's own unaided work save for advice on the choice and scope of the subject, the provision of a

reading list, and guidance on matters of presentation. This certificate must be submitted separately in a sealed envelope addressed to the chair of examiners. The chair of the examiners will announce the list of subjects on which the essays may be submitted by the end of the first week of the Michaelmas Full Term preceding the examination.

Special Regulations for the Preliminary Examination in Geography

A

The Preliminary Examination in Geography shall be under the supervision of the Divisional Board of Social Sciences and shall consist of such subjects as it shall prescribe by regulation.

B

1. Each candidate shall offer four papers as follows:
   * Earth Systems Processes
   * Human Geography
   * Geographical Techniques
   * Geographical Controversies

Each paper will be of three hours' duration.

2. All candidates will be assessed as to their practical ability under the following provisions:

   (*a*) Fieldwork. Candidates shall submit to the Chair of Moderators not later than noon on the Monday of the sixth week of Trinity Full Term a fieldwork folder containing accounts of fieldwork exercises. The requirements for this folder will be published by the Geography Undergraduate Teaching and Examining Committee at the beginning of the Michaelmas Full Term in the academic year of the examination.

   (*b*) Geographical Techniques. The Chair of the Undergraduate Teaching and Examining Committee, or a deputy, shall make available to the Moderators, by the date of the first written paper, evidence showing the extent to which each candidate has pursued an adequate course of practical work for Geographical Techniques.

   (*c*) Geographical Controversies. Candidates shall submit to the Chair of Moderators not later than noon on the Monday of the sixth week of Trinity Full Term a folder of practical work for the Geographical Controversies paper. The requirements for this folder will be published by the Geography Undergraduate Teaching and Examining Committee at the beginning of the Michaelmas Full Term in the academic year of the examination.

In assessing the candidate's performance in the examination, the moderators shall take this evidence into account.

3. Candidates shall be deemed to have passed if they have satisfied the examiners in all four subjects and in the practical work requirements as outlined in section 2.

4. A candidate who fails in one or more subjects may offer that subject or subjects at one, and only one, subsequent examination. A candidate who fails in three or four subjects is required to re-sit all four papers. A candidate who fails to satisfy the practical requirements as outlined in section 2 will be allowed one opportunity to resubmit this work.

5. Examiners may award a distinction to candidates of special merit who have passed all four subjects and satisfied the requirements for practical work outlined in section 2.

6. The examiners will not provide calculators but will permit the use of any handheld calculator subject to the conditions set out under the heading 'Use of calculators in examinations' in the Regulations for the Conduct of University examinations.

Papers for the Preliminary Examination in Geography

1. *Earth Systems Processes*

The paper will require an understanding of the physical geography of the Earth, based around core concepts and principles. Candidates should be able to display familiarity with mechanisms and processes under the headings of atmosphere, biosphere, and lithosphere, and a grasp of linkages between topics taught under these headings.

2. *Human Geography*

The paper will examine the following themes and the relationships between them at a variety of scales Economy and Transformation, Territories and Identities, Culture and Society.

3. *Geographical Controversies*

The paper will require an understanding of geographical controversies past and present. Candidates will be expected to demonstrate critical understanding of the use of evidence and data in geographical argument. Details of the materials to be covered for this course will be published by the Geography Undergraduate Teaching and Examining Committee at the beginning of the Michaelmas Full Term in the academic year of the examination

4. *Geographical Techniques*

The subject will comprise theoretical and practical aspects of geographical techniques. Candidates will be expected to be conversant with problem-solving in both human and physical branches of the discipline. Details of the areas to be covered will be published by the Geography Undergraduate Teaching and Examining Committee at the beginning of the Michaelmas Full Term in the academic year of the examination.

Special Regulations for the Preliminary Examination in History

A

The subjects of the examination, the syllabus, and the number of papers shall be as prescribed by regulation from time to time by the Board of the Faculty of History.

B

Each candidate shall offer four papers, as follows:

1. History of the British Isles: any one of the following periods:.

(I) *c.*300–1087; (II) 1042–1330; (III) 1330–1550; (IV) 1500–1700; (V) 1685–1830; (VI) 1815–1924; (VII) since 1900.

2. General History: any one of the period papers I: 370–900 (*The Transformation of the Ancient World*), II: 1000–1300 (*Medieval Christendom and its neighbours*), III: 1400–1650 (*Renaissance, Recovery, and Reform*), and IV: 1815–1914 (*Society, Nation, and Empire*). Candidates will be given a wide choice of questions relating to themes in

the history of the period and they are advised not to concentrate narrowly on a particular period or topic.

3. Optional Subject: any one of an approved list of subjects, examples of which are given below. A detailed list of Optional Subjects, including the prescribed texts, will be published in the Handbook for Preliminary Examination in History by the Board of the Faculty of History by Monday of noughth week of Michaelmas Term each year for the academic year ahead. Depending on the availability of teaching resources, with the exception of Optional Subject 1, not all the Optional Subjects listed in the Handbook will be available to all candidates in any given year. Candidates may obtain details of the choice of options for that year by consulting the Definitive List of Optional Subjects posted at the beginning of the first week of Michaelmas Full Term in the History Faculty and circulated to History Tutors.

1. Theories of the State (Aristotle, Hobbes, Rousseau, Marx).
2. The Age of Bede *c.*660–*c.*740.
3. Early Gothic France *c.*1100–*c.*1150.
4. Conquest and Frontiers: England and the Celtic Peoples 1150–1220.
5. English Chivalry and the French War *c.*1330–*c.*1400.
6. Nature and Art in the Renaissance.
7. Witch-craft and witch-hunting in early modern Europe.
8. Nobility and Gentry in England 1560–1660.
9. Conquest and Colonization: Spain and America in the Sixteenth Century.
10. Revolution and Empire in France 1789–1815.
11. Women, Gender and the Nation: Britain, 1789–1825.
12. The Romance of the People: The Folk Revival from 1760 to 1914.
13. The American Empire: 1823–1904.
14. The Rise and Crises of European Socialisms: 1881–1921.
15. Theories of War and Peace in Europe 1890–1914.
16. Working-Class Life and Industrial Work in Britain 1870–1914.
17. The World of Homer and Hesiod, as specified for Preliminary Examination in Ancient and Modern History.
18. Augustan Rome, as specified for Preliminary Examination in Ancient and Modern History.

4. *Either* (*a*) Approaches to History *or* (*b*) Historiography: Tacitus to Weber *or* (*c*) Foreign Texts *or* (*d*) Quantification in History, as specified in the Handbook for the Preliminary Examination in History.

Candidates who fail one or more of papers 1, 2, 3, or 4 above may resit that subject or subjects at a subsequent examination.

Special Regulations for the Preliminary Examination in History and Economics

A

The Preliminary Examination in History and Economics shall be under the joint supervision of the Divisional Board of Social Studies, and the Board of the Faculty of History and shall consist of such subjects as they shall jointly by regulation prescribe.

B

Every candidate shall offer four papers, as follows:

1. Introductory Economics, as specified for the Preliminary Examination in Philosophy, Politics, and Economics.

2. General History: any one of the periods specified for the Preliminary Examination in History.

3. Optional Subject: any one of an approved list of subjects, as specified for the Preliminary Examination in History.

or

Industrialization in Britain and France 1750–1870, which is available only for candidates for this examination.

4. *Either* (*a*) Approaches to History *or* (*b*) Historiography: Tacitus to Weber *or* (*c*) Foreign Texts, as specified for the Preliminary Examination in History.

The individual specifications and prescribed texts for papers 3 and 4 above will be published in the Handbook for the Preliminary Examination in History by Monday of noughth week of Michaelmas Term each year for the academic year ahead. Depending on the availability of teaching resources, with the exception of Optional Subject 1, not all the Optional Subjects listed in the Handbook will be available to candidates in any given year. Candidates may obtain details of the choice of options for that year by consulting the Definitive List of Optional Subjects posted at the beginning of the first week of Michaelmas Full Term in the History Faculty and circulated to tutors.

Schedule

Note. The letter c against a text indicates that it is available as a photocopy from the History Faculty Library. The letter t against a text indicates that it is to be read in specially prepared translation.

INDUSTRIALIZATION IN BRITAIN AND FRANCE 1750–1870

This is a paper in comparative economic history and is concerned with the main relationships involved in the industrialization of these two countries.

The texts have been selected to exemplify British commentaries on economic developments in France and French perceptions of Britain's economic progress from 1750 to 1870.

A. Texts by British Authors:

A. Young, *Travels in France During the Years 1787, 1788 and 1789,* ed. Constantia Maxwell (Cambridge, 1950), pp. 279–300, 312–13. (Available in the History Faculty Library.)

c   M. Birkbeck, *Notes on a Journey Through France in 1814,* 3rd edn. (London, 1815), pp. 99–115. (Bodleian reference 8 R 88 BS.)

E. Baines, *History of the Cotton Manufacture in Great Britain* (London, 1835), pp. 512–26. (Bodleian reference 35. 734.)

c   H. Colman, *The Agricultural and Rural Economy of France, Belgium, Holland and Switzerland* (London, 1848), pp. 20–40. (Bodleian reference 48. 105.)

c   Great Exhibition, *The Industry of Nations as Exemplified in the Great Exhibition of 1851* (London, 1852), pp. 223–7. (Bodleian reference 177e. 15.)

c   A. B. Reach, *Claret and Olives* (London, 1852), pp. 256–63. (Bodleian reference 203. b. 301.)

c   F. Marshall, *Population and Trade in France in 1861–2* (London, 1862), pp. 156–207. (Bodleian reference 232. b. 61.)

T. E. Cliffe Leslie, 'The Land System in France', in *Systems of Land Tenure in Various Countries* (London, 1881), ed. J. W. Probyn, pp. 291–312. (Bodleian reference 24754. e. 174.)

B. Texts by French Authors (translated into English):

Leon Faucher, *Manchester in 1844: Its Present Condition and Future Prospects* (London, 1844), pp. 1–20 and 85–152. (Bodleian reference Gough Adds. Lancs., 817.)

c A. P. A. Ledru-Rollin, *The Decline of England* (London, 1850), pp. 19–27, 27–32, 189–225, 249–62, 282–91, 328–47. (Bodleian reference 24712 f.43 [R].)

c H. A. Taine, *Notes on England* (London, 1872), pp. 153–75 and 272–99. (Bodleian reference 226. j. 172.)

c La Rochefoucauld, F. de, *A Frenchman in England* (Cambridge, 1933), pp. 157–242.

c Nickolls, Sir J., pseud. (i.e. R. B. Plumard de Danguel), *Remarks on the advantages and disadvantages of France and of Great Britain* (London, 1754), pp. 1–48.

ct F. Chaumont, *Mémoire sur la France et l'Angleterre* (1769).

D'Eichthal, G., *A French sociologist looks at Britain*, tr. and ed. B. M. Ratcliffe and W. H. Chaloner (Manchester, 1977), pp. 13–108.

Candidates who fail one or more of papers 1, 2, 3, or 4 above may resit that subject or subjects at a subsequent examination.

Special Regulations for the Preliminary Examination in History and English

A

1. The Preliminary Examination in History and English shall be under the joint supervision of the Boards of the Faculties of History and English Language and Literature and shall consist of such subjects as they shall jointly by regulation prescribe.

2. The Chairs of the Examiners for the Preliminary Examination in History and of the Examiners for the Preliminary Examination in English Language and Literature shall consult together and designate such of their number as may be required for the examination for the Preliminary Examination in History and English, whereupon the number of examiners shall be deemed to be complete.

B

Each candidate shall offer four papers as set out below. The papers will be of three hours' duration, except where otherwise specified. The Examiners shall publish the names of candidates who have satisfied them in the whole of the examination, or in papers 1 and 2 only, or in papers 3 and 4 only.

1. *The History of the British Isles* (any one of the periods specified for the Preliminary Examination in History).

2. *One* of the following:

(*a*) One of the Optional Subjects as specified for the Preliminary Examination in History.

(*b*) *Approaches to History* (as specified for the Preliminary Examination in History).

(*c*) *Historiography: Tacitus to Weber* (as specified for the Preliminary Examination in History).

The individual specifications and prescribed texts for these papers will be published in the Handbook for the Preliminary Examination in History by Monday of noughth week of Michaelmas Term each year for the academic year ahead. Depending on the availability of teaching resources, with the exception of Optional Subject 1, not all the Optional Subjects listed in the Handbook will be available to candidates in any given year. Candidates may obtain details of the choice of options for that year by consulting the Definitive List of Optional Subjects posted at the beginning of the first week of Michaelmas Full Term in the History Faculty and circulated to tutors.

3. *Introduction to English Language and Literature.*

The paper will be examined by a portfolio of work, comprising one commentary answer and one discursive essay, of not fewer than 1,500 and not more than 2,000 words each. Footnotes will be included in the total word count, but bibliographies do not count towards the limit. The list of questions for this paper will be divided into Section A (Language) and B (Literature) and will be published on Monday of the fourth week of the Trinity Term of the first year. Candidates must select one question from Section A and one question from Section B.

Questions in Section A (Language) invite candidates to make their own selection of texts or passages of texts for commentary, in accordance with the terms of the particular question chosen. Copies of the texts or passages used must be included as an appendix to the portfolio. The combined length of all texts or passages chosen must not exceed 70 lines. The texts or passages used will not count towards the word limit for the commentary answer.

Two typed copies of the portfolio must be delivered to the Chair of the Examiners for the Preliminary Examination in English Language and Literature, Examination Schools, High Street, by noon on Wednesday of the sixth week of the same Trinity Term. A certificate, signed by the candidate to the effect that each answer is the candidate's own work, and that the candidate has read the Faculty guidelines on plagiarism, must be presented together with each portfolio.

Following the publication of themes for this subject on Monday of the fourth week of Trinity Term, the candidate must neither discuss his or her choice of themes nor the method of handling them with any tutor. Every portfolio must be the work of the candidate alone, but he or she may discuss with his or her tutor the subjects and approach to the essays up until the stated publication date of the portfolio themes.

Portfolios previously submitted for the First Public Examination in English Language and Literature may be resubmitted. No answer will be accepted that has already been submitted, wholly or substantially, for a final honour school or any other degree of this University, or degree of any other institution.

Work deemed to be either too short or of excessive length may be penalised.

Candidates must avoid duplicating material used in this paper when answering other papers. In addition, candidates are not permitted to duplicate material between Section A and Section B of the portfolio.

4. *One* of the following:

(*a*) *Literature in English 650–1350* (as specified in the regulations for the Preliminary Examination in English Language and Literature, subject 2).

(*b*) *Literature in English 1830–1910* (as specified in the regulations for the Preliminary Examination in English Language and Literature, subject 3).

(*c*) *Literature in English 1910–present day* (as specified in the regulations for the Preliminary Examination in English Language and Literature, subject 4).

Candidates who fail one or more of papers 1, 2, 3, or 4 above may resit that subject or subjects at a subsequent examination.

Special Regulations for the Preliminary Examination in History and Modern Languages

A

1. The Preliminary Examination in History and Modern Languages shall be under the joint supervision of the Boards of the Faculties of History and Medieval and Modern Languages and shall consist of such subjects as they shall jointly by regulation prescribe.

2. The chairs of the examiners for the Preliminary Examination in History and for the Preliminary Examination in Modern Languages shall respectively designate such of their number as may be required for History and for Modern Languages in this examination.

B

Candidates are required to offer History and any one of the languages that may be offered in the Honour School of Modern Languages. The examination shall be in two parts, as follows:

Part 1

Each candidate shall offer the following two subjects in the language:

1. *Language papers* (one paper of three hours and two papers each of one and a half hours including in French certification of attendance and participation in oral classes, as specified for the Preliminary Examination in Modern Languages).

As specified for papers I, IIA, and IIB in the regulations for the Preliminary Examination for Modern Languages.

2. *Literature papers* (two papers, each of three hours).

As specified for papers III and IV in the regulations for the Preliminary Examination in Modern Languages.

Part 2

Each candidate shall offer subject 3 and any one of the subdivisions of subject 4.

3. General History: any one of the periods specified for the Preliminary Examination in History.

4. (*a*) A period of The History of the British Isles as specified for the Preliminary Examination in History;
   (*b*) An Optional Subject as specified for the Preliminary Examination in History;
   (*c*) Approaches to History *or* Historiography: Tacitus to Weber *or* Foreign Texts as specified for the Preliminary Examination in History.

The individual specifications and prescribed texts for (*b*) and (*c*) above will be published in the Handbook for the Preliminary Examination in History by Monday of noughth week of Michaelmas Term each year for the academic year ahead. Depending on the availability of teaching resources, with the exception of Optional Subject 1, not all the Optional Subjects listed in the Handbook will be available to candidates in any given year. Candidates may obtain details of the choice of options for that year by consulting the Definitive List of Optional Subjects posted at the beginning of the first week of Michaelmas Full Term in the History Faculty and circulated to tutors.

Candidates who have satisfied the Examiners in both parts shall be deemed to have passed the examination. The Examiners may award distinctions in either or both parts to candidates who have done work of special merit in the part or parts concerned.

Candidates who fail one or both subjects of part 1 may resit that subject or those subjects at a subsequent examination. Candidates who fail one or two subjects of part 2 may resit that subject or subjects at a subsequent examination.

Special Regulations for the Preliminary Examination in History and Politics

A

1. The Preliminary Examination in History and Politics shall be under the joint supervision of the Board of the Faculty of History and the Social Sciences Board and shall consist of such subjects as they shall jointly prescribe.

2. The Chair of the Examiners for the Preliminary Examination in History and the Chair of the Examiners for the Preliminary Examination in Philosophy, Politics, and Economics shall consult together and designate such of their number as may be required for the examination for the Preliminary Examination in History and Politics, whereupon the number of examiners shall be deemed to be complete.

B

Every candidate shall offer four papers as follows:

1. *Either* (*a*) any one of the periods in the History of the British Isles specified for the Preliminary Examination in History *or* (*b*) any one of the four periods in General History specified for the Preliminary Examination in History. For the First or Second Public Examination candidates are required to choose *at least one* paper—whether in General History or the History of the British Isles—covering a period before the nineteenth century. The list of papers satisfying this provision is given in the Handbook for History and Politics. Candidates who take British History paper VII for the Preliminary Examination or the Final Honour School may not also take Politics core paper 202 for the Final Honour School.

2. Theorizing the Democratic State, as specified in section (*a*) of Introduction to Politics: the Theory and Practice of Democracy, for the Preliminary Examination for Philosophy, Politics and Economics.

OR candidates may substitute Optional Subject 1, 'Theories of the State (Aristotle, Hobbes, Rousseau, Marx)' as specified for the Preliminary Examination in History.

3. Any *one* of the following, as specified for the Preliminary Examination in History: (*a*) Quantification in History *or* (*b*) any of the Optional Subjects except No. 1 (Theories of the State), *or* (*c*) Approaches to History, *or* (*d*) Historiography: Tacitus to Weber, *or* (*e*) any one of the seven Foreign Texts.

4. *Introduction to Politics: Analysis of Democratic Institutions*

Candidates will be required to answer *three* questions drawn from section (*b*) of the paper Introduction to Politics: The Theory and Practice of Democracy as specified for the Preliminary Examination in Philosophy, Politics and Economics.

Candidates may choose to answer any combination of questions in section (*b*), but each part (*b-ii*) question chosen must relate to a different country (so answers must be on *two* different countries if *two* answers are chosen from (*b-ii*) and *three* countries if *three* answers). Candidates may, where appropriate, answer questions from part (*b-i*) exclusively in relation to one of the named countries, but any question chosen from part (*b-ii*) should not then be on that same country.

Candidates are expected, where appropriate, to show knowledge of the methodological issues involved in both normative and empirical political research.

The individual specifications and prescribed texts for papers 2 and 3 above will be published in the Handbook for the Preliminary Examination in History by Monday of noughth week of Michaelmas Term each year for the academic year ahead. Depending on the availability of teaching resources, with the exception of the Optional Subject 1, not all the Optional Subjects listed in the Handbook will be available to candidates in any given year. Candidates may obtain details of the choice of options for that year by consulting the Definitive List of Optional Subjects posted at the beginning of the first week of Michaelmas Full Term in the History Faculty and circulated to tutors.

Candidates who fail one or more of papers 1, 2, 3, or 4 above may resit that subject or subjects at a subsequent examination.

Special Regulations for the Preliminary Examination in History of Art

A

The Preliminary Examination in History of Art shall be under the supervision of the Board of the Faculty of History. The subjects of the examination, the syllabus, and the number of papers shall be as prescribed by regulation from time to time by the Board of the Faculty of History.

B

The History Faculty Board shall issue annually the Handbook for the Preliminary Examination in History of Art by Monday of noughth week of Michaelmas Term for the academic year ahead.

Each candidate shall offer four papers as follows:

I. *Introduction to the History of Art*

Candidates will be examined by three-hour unseen examination.

II. *Antiquity after Antiquity*

Candidates will be examined by three-hour unseen examination.

III. *European Art 1400–1800: Meaning and Interpretation*

Candidates will be examined by three-hour unseen examination.

IV. *Objects, Images and Buildings in Oxford*

Candidates will be examined by a 5,000 word extended essay, including footnotes but excluding bibliography. A candidate may propose to study any object, but this object must be approved by the appointed extended essay adviser, and the

Preliminary Extended Essay Co-ordinator. Approval will depend on the object's accessibility and the availability of source material and curatorial expertise. Candidates will have no more than the equivalent of five one-hour meetings with their assigned extended essay advisor. A first draft of the extended essay may be commented on by the extended essay adviser during one of these meetings. Candidates must submit the title of the extended essay to the Chair of Examiners, Preliminary Examination in History of Art, Department of History of Art, Littlegate House, St. Ebbes, Oxford, by midday on Monday of the fifth week of the Hilary Term preceding the examination. Any subsequent changes to title require formal application to the Chair of Examiners not later than noon on Monday of second week of the Hilary term preceding the examination and subsequent approval. Essays should be typed or word-processed in double spacing and should conform to the standards of academic presentation prescribed in the course handbook. Essays must be delivered by hand to the Examination Schools (addressed to the Chair of Examiners, Preliminary Examination in History of Art, Examination Schools, Oxford) not later than noon on Monday of sixth week of the Trinity Term in the academic year in which the candidate is presenting himself or herself for examination. Candidates delivering essays will be required to complete a receipt form, which will only be accepted as proof of receipt if it is counter-signed by a member of the Examination Schools staff. Each essay must be accompanied by a sealed envelope (bearing only the candidate's examination number) containing a formal declaration signed by the candidate that the essay is his or her own work. The University's regulations on *Late Entries* will apply.

Candidates who fail one or two of papers I, II, III or IV above may resit only that paper or papers at a subsequent examination. Candidates who fail three of papers I, II, III or IV above will be asked to resit all papers, including the one they passed, unless the paper they passed is the essay, in which case they will resit only the three written examination papers. Candidates who fail all four of papers I, II, III and IV will be required to resit all four at a subsequent examination. In the case of failure to reach the required standard in the Preliminary Extended Essay, candidates must resubmit the essay by Monday of noughth week of Michaelmas Term of the second year. Candidates are entitled to one further meeting with their extended essay adviser.

Special Regulations for the Preliminary Examination in Human Sciences

A

The examination shall be under the supervision of the Social Sciences Board in accordance with the same arrangements as those established under clause 3 of the decree concerning the Honour School of Human Sciences.

B

1. The subjects of the examination shall be the five subjects listed below.

2. All candidates must offer all five subjects at one examination:
Provided that a candidate who has passed in two (or more) subjects but failed in the other subject (or subjects) may offer at a subsequent examination the subjects (or subject) in which he or she has failed.

3. A candidate shall be deemed to have passed the examination if he or she shall have satisfied the Moderators in all five subjects *either* at one and the same examination *or* at two examinations in accordance with the proviso to cl. 2.

4. In the case of candidates who have satisfied the Moderators in all five subjects in a single examination, the Moderators may award a distinction to those of special merit.

5. The examiners will permit the use of any hand-held pocket calculator subject to the conditions set out under the heading 'Use of calculators in examinations' in the *Special Regulations concerning Examinations.* 5

Subject 1. The Biology of Organisms including Humans

Principles of mammalian physiology: the cell, body fluids, the cardiovascular and respiratory systems, reproduction, hunger and thirst, movement, the senses, and the integrative organization of the central nervous system.

Principles of ecology: ecosystems, plant and animal communities and numbers, 10 biotic interaction, the impact of man on the environment.

One three-hour paper will be set.

Subject 2. Genetics and Evolution

Principles of genetics and evolution illustrated by examples from human and other organisms. 15

Mechanisms of evolutionary change: selection and adaptation, evolution of sex, altruism, kin selection and co-operation. Alternative models of evolution.

The genetic material—its nature, mode of action, and manipulation: the chromosomal basis of heredity; molecular genetics; mapping the human genome; sex determination; mutation at the level of the gene and the chromosome. 20

Mendelian inheritance; genetic variation in populations and its maintenance; quantitative variation and its genetic basis.

One three-hour paper will be set. Candidates shall submit notebooks containing reports, initialled by the demonstrators, of practical work completed during their course of study. These notebooks shall be available to the examiners at any time after 25 the end of the first week of the term in which the examination is held, and shall be taken into consideration by the examiners. A practical examination may be set for candidates whose record of practical work is not satisfactory.

Subject 3. Society, Culture, and Environment

Social and Cultural Anthropology: the comparative study of the world's civilisa- 30 tions and peoples, including cross-cultural, power-based and gender perspectives upon social practice and theories of human life. Specific topics will include production and consumption; transactions and modes of exchange; elementary aspects of kinship and marriage; belief systems and social control; political and social organization; classification; technology and social change; material culture and 35 ethnographic resources; the impact of colonialism; space, place and culture; environment and cultural landscapes in transition; land and property rights. Candidates will be expected to be familiar with appropriate ethnographic monographs.

Human Geography: Approaches to understanding contemporary international migration—from neo-classical to post-structuralist; forced migration, changing 40 international, regional and national legislation and policy; diasporas and transnationalism, especially issues of identity, home and belonging; social divisions and the experience of migration and integration addressing gender, class and ethnicity; cosmopolitan or 'subdiverse' cities; and state policy and the influence of nationalism; xenophobia, economics and ethics. 45

One three-hour paper will be set, on which candidates will be required to answer four questions. The paper will be divided into two sections: (A) Social and Cultural Anthropology, and (B) Human Geography. Candidates will be required to display knowledge of both sections, and will be required to answer at least two questions from section (A) and at least one question from section (B).

Subject 4. Sociology and Demography

Sociology: Current and classic discussions of explanatory strategies and social mechanisms, models of individual action and the consequences of aggregation. Empirical research involving these approaches in areas of substantive sociological interest such as social class, ethnicity, religion, the family, politics.

Demography: Elementary aspects of population analysis. Comparative study of fertility, mortality and family systems in selected human societies. The long-term development of human population and its relation to habitat and resources. The demographic transition.

One three hour paper will be set. The paper will be divided into two sections: (A) Sociology and (B) Demography. Candidates will be required to display knowledge of both sections.

Subject 5. Quantitative Methods for the Human Sciences

The use and importance of statistics and quantitative methods in the human sciences. Graphs, scales, indices, and transformations. Frequency distributions and their parameters, including the binomial, normal, and Poisson distributions. Notions of probability and risk. Problems of sampling. Tests of statistical significance including t-tests, χ^2, and confidence intervals. Elementary analysis of variance, correlation, and regression.

One three-hour paper will be set, consisting mostly of examples taken from the human sciences. Graded questions will be set, not all of which will require numerical answers.

Preliminary Examination in Materials Science

A

1. The subject of the Preliminary Examination in Materials Science shall be Materials Science, including basic practical and mathematical techniques.

2. The number of papers and other general requirements of the examination shall be as prescribed by regulation from time to time by the Mathematical, Physical and Life Sciences Board.

B

In the following, 'the Course Handbook' refers to the Materials Science 'Prelims Course Handbook', published annually at the start of Michaelmas Term by the Faculty of Materials, and also posted on the website at: www.materials.ox.ac.uk/teaching/ug/ughandbooks.html.

1. The Preliminary Examination in Materials Science shall comprise four compulsory written examination papers plus compulsory Materials coursework equivalent to one written examination paper:

    (*a*) Materials Science 1: Structure of Materials

    (*b*) Materials Science 2: Properties of Materials

    (*c*) Materials Science 3: Transforming Materials

    (*d*) Mathematics for Materials and Earth Sciences

    (*e*) Materials Coursework

The syllabuses for the written papers shall be published annually in the Course Handbook, not later than the beginning of Michaelmas Full Term for examination in the Trinity Term immediately following this.

2. In the assessment of the Materials coursework, the Moderators shall take into consideration the requirement for a candidate to complete the coursework to a satisfactory level as defined from time to time by the Faculty of Materials and published in the Course Handbook. Materials Science Coursework shall comprise practical work and work carried out in crystallography classes, as described in the Course Handbook, and it shall be assessed under the following provisions:

(*a*) Candidates will be required to submit the Materials Practical Class reports to the Chair of the Moderators in the Preliminary Examination in Materials Science, c/o the Deputy Administrator (Academic) in the Department of Materials, not later than 10 a.m. on Friday of the sixth week of Trinity Full Term.

(*b*) The Chair of Faculty, or deputy, shall make available to the Moderators, not later than the end of the first week of Trinity Full Term, evidence showing the extent to which each candidate has completed the Crystallography coursework normally pursued during the first two terms preceding the examination.

(*c*) Failure of the coursework normally will constitute failure of the Preliminary Examination. Materials Coursework normally cannot be retaken. Exceptionally a candidate who has failed the coursework may be permitted jointly by the Moderators and the candidate's college to retake the entire academic year.

3. Candidates shall be deemed to have passed the examination if they have satisfied the Moderators in the five papers in clause 1 either at a single examination or at two examinations in accordance with either clause 5 or clause 6, and provided further that the same number of papers as were failed in the first sitting have been passed at the same attempt at a subsequent examination. The Moderators will be guided by the provisions of clause 2 when considering the Materials Coursework paper.

4. The Moderators may award a distinction to candidates of special merit who have satisfied them in all five papers in clause 1 in one examination.

5. Candidates who have passed the coursework paper and fail one or two written papers listed in clause 1 may offer that number of papers at one, but no more than one, subsequent examination.

6. In the case of candidates who offer all four written papers of clause 1, the Moderators shall publish the names only of those who have satisfied them in the coursework paper and in two or more written papers. Candidates whose names do not appear on the Results List but who have passed the coursework paper may enter the written part of the examination on one, but no more than one, subsequent occasion: such candidates must resit all four written papers of clause 1. In the case of candidates who, in accordance with clause 5, offer one or two written papers, the Moderators shall publish the names of only those who have satisfied them in each of the written papers offered.

7. The use of calculators in the papers listed in clause 1 is restricted to those models published annually in the Course Handbook.

8. The examination conventions for the written papers and the coursework listed in clause 1 shall be published annually in the Course Handbook and posted online at the following website: www.materials.ox.ac.uk/teaching/ug/ugexamconventions.html.

Special Regulations for the Preliminary Examination in Mathematics

A

The subject of the examination shall be mathematics and its applications. The syllabus and number of papers shall be prescribed by regulation from time to time by the Mathematical, Physical and Life Sciences Board.

B

1. Candidates shall take five written papers. The titles of the papers shall be:

A. Mathematics I
B. Mathematics II
C. Mathematics III
D. Mathematics IV
E. Mathematics V

2. In addition to the five papers in cl 1, a candidate must also offer a practical work assessment.

3. Candidates shall be deemed to have passed the examination if they have satisfied the Moderators in all five papers and the practical assessment at a single examination or passed all five papers and the practical assessment in accordance with the proviso of cl 4.

4. A candidate who fails to satisfy the Moderators in one or two of papers A-E may offer those papers on one subsequent occasion; a candidate who fails to satisfy the Moderators in three or more of papers A-E may offer all five papers on one subsequent occasion; a candidate who fails to satisfy the Moderators in the practical work assessment may also offer the assessment on one subsequent occasion.

5. The Moderators may award a distinction to candidates of special merit who have passed all five written papers and the practical work assessment at a single examination.

6. The syllabus for each paper shall be published by the Mathematical Institute in a handbook for candidates by the beginning of the Michaelmas Full Term in the academic year of the examination, after consultation with the Mathematics Teaching Committee. Each paper will contain questions of a straightforward character.

7. The Chair of Mathematics, or a deputy, shall make available to the Moderators evidence showing the extent to which each candidate has pursued an adequate course of practical work. In assessing a candidate's performance in the examination the Moderators shall take this evidence into account. Deadlines for handing in practical work will be published in a handbook for candidates by the beginning of Michaelmas Full Term in the academic year of the examination.

Candidates are usually required to submit such practical work electronically; details shall be given in the handbook for the practical course. Any candidate who is unable for some reason to submit work electronically must apply to the Academic Administrator, Mathematical Institute, for permission to submit the work in paper form. Such applications must reach the Academic Administrator two weeks before the deadline for submitting the practical work.

8. The use of hand held pocket calculators is generally not permitted but certain kinds may be permitted for some papers. Specifications of which papers and which types of calculator are permitted for those exceptional papers will be announced by the Moderators in the Hilary Term preceding the examination.

Special Regulations for the Preliminary
Examination in Mathematics and Computer Science
A

The subject of the examination shall be Mathematics and Computer Science. The syllabus and number of papers shall be prescribed by regulation from time to time by the Mathematical, Physical and Life Sciences Board.

B

1. The Preliminary Examination in Mathematics and Computer Science shall comprise five compulsory written papers plus compulsory Computer Science practicals equivalent to one written paper:

CS1   Functional Programming, and Design and Analysis of Algorithms
CS2   Imperative Programming
MCS3 Continuous Mathematics and Probability
M1   Mathematics I (as specified for the Preliminary Examination in Mathematics)
M2   Mathematics II (as specified for the Preliminary Examination in Mathematics)
Computer Science Practicals

2. The syllabus for each paper will be published by the Department of Computer Science in a handbook for candidates by the beginning of the Michaelmas Full Term in the academic year of the examination, after consultation with the Faculty of Computer Science (for papers CS1, CS2 and MCS3) and the Faculty of Mathematics (for papers M1, M2 and MCS3). Each paper will contain questions of a straightforward character.

3. All candidates will be assessed as to their practical ability in Computer Science under the following provisions:

(*a*) The Head of the Department of Computer Science, or a deputy, shall make available to the examiners evidence showing the extent to which each candidate has pursued an adequate course of practical work. Only that work completed and marked by noon on Monday of the fifth week of the Trinity Term in which the candidate takes the examination shall be included in these records.

(*b*) Candidates shall submit to the Chair of the Moderators for the Preliminary Examination in Mathematics and Computer Science, c/o the Academic Administrator, Oxford University Department of Computer Science, Oxford, by noon on Monday of the fifth week of the Trinity Term in which the examination is being held, their reports of practical exercises completed during their course of study. For a report on a practical exercise to be considered by the moderators, it must have been marked by a demonstrator and must be accompanied by a statement that it is the candidate's own work except where otherwise indicated.

(*c*) The moderators shall take the evidence (*a*) and the reports (*b*) into account in assessing a candidate's performance.

(*d*) Candidates whose overall performance on practical work is not satisfactory may be deemed to have failed the examination.

4. Candidates shall be deemed to have passed the examination if they have satisfied the Moderators in the six papers in clause 1 either at a single examination or at two examinations in accordance with clause 6 or clause 7.

5. The Moderators may award a distinction to candidates of special merit who have satisfied them in all six papers in clause 1 in one examination.

6. Candidates who fail one or two written papers listed in clause 1 may offer those papers at one, but no more than one, subsequent examination.

7. Candidates who fail three or more papers may enter the written part of the examination on one, but no more than one, subsequent examination.

8. The use of calculators is generally not permitted but certain kinds may be allowed for certain papers. Specifications of which papers and which types of calculators are permitted for those exceptional papers will be announced by the examiners in the Hilary Term preceding the examination.

Special Regulations for the Preliminary Examination in Mathematics and Philosophy

A

1. The subject of the examination shall be (a) Mathematics, and (b) Philosophy. The syllabus and number of papers shall be prescribed by regulation from time to time by the Mathematical, Physical and Life Sciences Board and the Board of the Faculty of Philosophy.

2. A candidate shall offer both subjects for examination.

3. The Moderators for Mathematics shall include at least two of the Moderators for the Preliminary Examination in Mathematics; the Moderators for Philosophy shall include at least two Moderators nominated by a committee of the Faculty of Philosophy.

4. It shall be the duty of the Chair of Moderators for the Preliminary Examination in Mathematics to nominate such of their number as shall be required to act as Moderators for the Preliminary Examination in Mathematics and Philosophy.

B

1. Candidates shall take five written papers. The titles of the papers shall be:
A. Mathematics I (as specified by the Preliminary Examination in Mathematics)
B. Mathematics II (as specified by the Preliminary Examination in Mathematics)
C. Mathematics III(P)
D. Elements of Deductive Logic
    Subjects to be studied include: propositional and predicate languages; truth tables; Natural Deduction; relations; the critical application of formal logic to the analysis of English sentences and inferences (problems of symbolization; scope, truth-functionality, quantification, identity, descriptions); elementary metatheorems about propositional calculus (including the following topics: expressive adequacy, duality, substitution, interpolation, compactness, consistency, soundness and completeness). Some questions of a mathematical nature will be set.
    These subjects shall be studied in conjunction with Volker Halbach's *Introduction to Logic* manual, published by Oxford University Press. The logical symbols to be used are those found in this publication. Philosophical questions about logic may be studied by reading Mark Sainsbury, *Logical Forms*, 1st or 2nd edition (Blackwell), Chapters 1–2.
E. Introduction to Philosophy
    The paper shall consist of two parts:

1. *General Philosophy* Subjects to be studied include: knowledge and scepticism, induction, mind and body, personal identity, free will, and God and evil. Candidates will have the opportunity, but will not be required, to show first-hand knowledge of Descartes' *Meditations* and Hume's *An Enquiry concerning Human Understanding.*

2. *Frege* This section shall be studied in connection with Frege *Foundations of Arithmetic*, trans. J. L. Austin, Blackwell, 1980. This section, while not being confined to the detailed views of the author of the set text, will be satisfactorily answerable by a candidate who has made a critical study of the text. There will not be a compulsory question containing passages for comment.

Candidates will be required to attempt four questions, and answer at least one question from Part 1 and at least one question from Part 2.

2. Candidates shall be deemed to have passed the examination if they have satisfied the Moderators in all five papers A-E *either* at a single examination *or* at two examinations in accordance with the proviso of cl 3.

3. A candidate who fails to satisfy the Moderators in one or two of papers A-E may offer the papers failed on one, and only one, subsequent occasion. A candidate who fails to satisfy the Moderators in three or more of papers A-E may offer all five papers on one, and only one, subsequent occasion, *except that* a candidate who fails to satisfy the Moderators in all of papers A-C, but who has satisfied the Moderators in papers D and E, may offer papers A-C only on one, and only one, subsequent occasion.

4. The Moderators may award a distinction to candidates of special merit who have passed all five written papers at a single examination.

5. The syllabus for each paper in Mathematics shall be published by the Mathematical Institute in a handbook for candidates by the beginning of the Michaelmas Full Term in the academic year of the examination, after consultation with the Mathematics Teaching Committee.

6. The use of hand held pocket calculators is generally not permitted but certain kinds may be permitted for some papers. Specifications of which papers and which types of calculator are permitted for those papers will be announced by the Moderators in the Hilary Term preceding the examination.

Special Regulations for the Preliminary Examination for Modern Languages

A

The languages, subjects, and papers in the examination shall be as prescribed by regulation from time to time by the Board of the Faculty of Medieval and Modern Languages.

B

Not more than two languages may be offered.

1. The languages which may be offered shall be Latin and Greek and those languages which may be offered in the Final Honour School of Modern Languages.* **Candidates who offer both Latin and Ancient Greek shall be deemed to be offering one ancient language. Candidates for whom it is appropriate shall pass at the**

---

* Czech (with Slovak) and Celtic may not be available in given years. Notice that these subjects will not be available will be given in the *Gazette* in the Trinity Term but one before the examination concerned.

end of their first year of study the examination in Greek or Latin prescribed for first-year candidates in Course II of Honour Moderations in Classics and English, before proceeding to offer papers in the Preliminary Examination for Modern Languages in accordance with the following regulations in their second year of study.

2. The subjects of the examination shall be:

(*a*) Language papers (including in French certification of attendance and participation in oral classes†);

(*b*) Literature papers;

(*c*) Classics and Modern Languages

(*d*) Linguistics;

(*e*) Further Topics (for candidates taking French sole or German sole only);

(*f*) Russian Course B (*ab initio*).

3. A candidate shall be deemed to have passed the examination if he or she shall have satisfied the Examiners

either (i) in all papers in both subjects (*a*) Language and (*b*) Literature in each of two languages, at least one of the languages being modern;

or   (ii) in all papers in both subjects (*a*) Language and (*b*) Literature in one modern language (other than Czech (with Slovak) or Celtic) and in all papers in subject (*c*) Linguistics;

or   (iii) in all papers in both subjects (*a*) Language and (*b*) Literature in *either* French or German and in all three papers in subject (*d*) Further Topics in the same language;

or   (iv) in all papers in both subjects (*a*) Language and (*b*) Literature in one modern language and in all papers in subject (*e*) Russian Course B (*ab initio*).

Candidates must offer all the papers at one examination, provided that a candidate who has previously failed to satisfy the examiners in any paper or papers shall not be required to resit any paper or papers in which he or she has already satisfied the examiners. The pair of papers IIA and IIB (and BIIA and BIIB) counts as a single paper.

4. To a candidate who has done work of special merit in the papers concerned, the Moderators may award a mark of distinction in a language, and in Further Topics, and in Linguistics. A candidate may be awarded either one or two distinctions.

5. Candidates must offer:

Either: I, IIA, IIB, III, IV in two modern languages:

Or: I, IIA, IIB, III, IV in a modern language together with V, VI, and VII in Latin and/or Ancient Greek;

Or: I, IIA, IIB, III, IV in a modern language together with VIII, IX, and X in Linguistics.

Or: I, IIA, IIB III, IV in either French or German together with XI, XII, and XIII in the same language. (For candidates offering French sole or German sole.)

Or: I, IIA, IIB, III, IV in a modern language together with BI, BIIA, BIIB, BIII; and BIV Oral Test (for candidates admitted to Russian Course B).

6. *a. Language papers*

---

† Colleges will submit to the Examiners via the Examination Schools by noon on Friday of Week 5 of Trinity Term a certificate stating that their candidates have attended and participated in at least eight oral classes, consisting of reading aloud in French with attention to pronunciation and intonation, and discussion in French of passages dealing with issues in French contemporary culture.

I. Language I.   3 hours.

French:	The paper will consist of: (*a*) French grammar (20 short sentences for translation into French); (*b*) A prose passage for translation into French; (*c*) A summary in French of a passage of analytical or critical writing in French.
German:	'Deutsche Gesellschaft und Kultur seit 1890.' Reading comprehension (in German) on a passage which relates to the theme of the paper. One essay in German on a topic relating to the theme of the paper.
Italian:	The paper will consist of: (*a*) audio or video listening comprehension exercises; (*b*) reading comprehension exercises; (*c*) one guided essay in Italian.
Spanish:	The paper will consist of: (*a*) translation into Spanish: a set of grammatical sentences. 1½ hours will be allowed for each part.
Portuguese:	The paper will consist of: (*a*) audio or visual listening comprehension exercises; (*b*) translation into Portuguese; (*c*) a guided composition; (*d*) linguistic tests.
Russian:	Translation into Russian and/or exercises in Russian.
Modern Greek:	Translation into Modern Greek and exercises in Modern Greek.
Czech (with Slovak):	(*a*) a modern English prose passage; and (*b*) English sentences testing basic grammar, both to be translated into *either* Czech *or* Slovak.
Celtic:	(*a*) a modern English prose passage; and (*b*) English sentences testing basic grammar, both to be translated into Welsh.

II. Language II.   The paper will be in two parts of 1½ hours each.

French:	Unprepared translation: Translation into English of a prose passage in French.
	Prepared translation: Translation into English of a passage from one of the texts prescribed for French paper IV, excluding *La Chastelaine de Vergi.*
German:	IIA. Translation into German of a prose passage.
	IIB. Translation from German of a prose passage in a modern literary register
Italian:	IIA. Translation into Italian of a prose passage *or* sentences.
	IIB. Translation from Italian. A passage of modern prose will be set.
Spanish:	IIA. Translation from Spanish of a prose passage in a modern literary register.
	IIB. Translation from Spanish of a prose passage in an informal register such as journalism.
Portuguese:	IIA. Translation from Portuguese of a prose passage in a modern literary register.

5

10

15

20

25

30

35

40

IIB. Translation from Portuguese of a prose passage in an informal register such as journalism, and an exercise or exercises in reading comprehension.

Russian: IIA. Translation from Russian. A passage of modern prose will be set.

IIB. Comprehension exercise. A modern passage in the language will be set to test comprehension. All answers in this paper will be in English.

Modern Greek: IIA. Translation from Modern Greek. A passage of modern prose will be set.

IIB. Comprehension exercises. A modern passage or passages in the language will be set to test comprehension. All answers in this paper will be in English.

Czech (with   IIA and IIB. One passage of modern prose in each paper for
Slovak):   translation from Czech into English.

Celtic: IIA. A passage of Middle Welsh prose to be translated into English.

IIB. A passage of Old Irish prose *or* a passage of Modern Welsh prose to be translated into English.

b. Literature papers

III. Literature I. 3 hours.

French: Short texts. Candidates will be required to study six brief but self-contained works arranged in three contrasting pairs:
A Montaigne, 'Des coches' from the *Essais*
Graffigny, *Lettres d'une Péruvienne.*
B Baudelaire, *'Spleen et Idéal'* from *Les Fleurs du Mal*, with 30 poems to be identified for detailed study
Aimé Césaire, *Cahier d'un retour au pays natal*
C Racine, *Phèdre*
Beckett, *En attendant Godot*
The paper will be examined by commentary only, with all texts set, and candidates required to offer three passages, one from each of sections A, B and C.

German: Commentary. Two commentaries on a choice of poems taken from an anthology, which will include some medieval poems. One commentary on an extract from one of the set texts listed under paper IV. Each year two such texts will be designated as the ones from which an extract for commentary may be taken. Texts to be studied for commentary in any given year will be published in the *University Gazette* during noughth week of Michaelmas Term each year.

Italian: Aspects of Italian lyric poetry. Compulsory passages for explanation and detailed comment will be set.
The sonnet from the Middle Ages to the present. (Copies of the list of sonnets for the examinations in the academic year concerned will be available in the Modern Languages Faculty Office, 41 Wellington Square, from the beginning of the Michaelmas Full Term of the year).

Ungaretti, Selections from *L'Allegria* and *Sentimento del tempo* (in Giuseppe Ungaretti, *Vita d'un uomo, 106 poesie 1914–1960,* Mondadori Oscar).

Spanish: Prescribed texts to be studied in relation to various possible approaches to literature. One compulsory passage will be set for translation into English and one for commentary. Candidates will also be required to undertake two essays, to be written on texts other than the one from which the passage chosen for commentary was taken.

M. Vargas Llosa, *La fiesta del Chivo.*

Antonio Machado, *Campos de Castilla* (excluding 'La tierra de Alvargonzález', but including 'Elogios': in *Poesías completas,* Selecciones Austral).

Calderón de la Barca, *El médico du su honra* (ed. D. W. Cruickshank, Clásicos Castalia).

Cervantes, 'Rinconete y Cortadillo', from vol. 1 of *Novelas ejemplares,* ed. H. Sieber, 2 vols. (Madrid: Cátedra, 1989).

Portuguese: Prescribed texts to be studied in relation to various possible approaches to literature. Compulsory passages for explanation and detailed comment will be set. There will be a compulsory essay or commentary question on each of the set texts.

Lídia Jorge, *O vale da paixão*

Mia Couto, *Vinte e Zinco*

Manuel Bandeira, *Libertinagem*

Russian: Poetry. The examination will consist of three commentaries, each on a different author, on the set works by five authors detailed below. One commentary passage will be compulsory.

Derzhavin, *Felitsa*

Pushkin, *Mednyi vsadnik*

Lermontov, *Mtsyri*

Blok, *Na pole Kulikovom* and *Dvenadtsat'*

Akhmatova, *Rekviem*

Examiners may give some guidance to candidates about how to approach the passages set for commentary; they may also require candidates to translate some portion of the passages set for commentary into English.

Modern Greek: Modern Greek poetry and prose. Compulsory passages for explanation and detailed comment will be set. The syllabus will consist of a selection of poems and short stories by a variety of authors. (A list of the selection for the examinations in the academic year concerned will be available in the Modern Languages Faculty Office, 41 Wellington Square, from the beginning of the Michaelmas Full Term of that year).

The examination paper will be divided into two sections. Section A will consist of two compulsory commentary passages from prescribed texts (one poetry passage and one prose passage). Section B will consist of a choice of essay questions, from which each candidate must choose one.

Czech (with   Prescribed texts to be studied as literature. Three compulsory
Slovak):   passages for commentary will be set.

Short stories:

Milan Kundera, *Falešný autostop*

Bohumil Hrabal, *Pábitelé*

Ota Pavel, *Zlatí úhoři*

Jan Neruda, *Doktor Kazisvět*

Celtic: Prescribed texts to be studied as literature. Commentary. One commentary on a poem taken from an anthology. Poems will be set from:
Oxford Book of Welsh Verse, ed. T. Parry (Oxford: Oxford University Press, 1962), nos. 31, 40, 78, 298, 318.
Early Irish Lyrics, ed. G. Murphy (Oxford: Oxford University Press, 1956; repr. Dublin: Four Courts Press, 1998), nos. 5, 7, 11, 35, 36.
and Two commentaries on extracts from the texts listed under paper IV.

IV. Literature II: Prescribed texts. 3 hours.

French: French narrative fiction:
La Chastelaine de Vergi
Laclos, *Les Liaisons dangereuses*
Balzac, *La Peau de chagrin*
Proust, *Combray*
The paper will be examined entirely by essay, with candidates required to answer on *three* texts. There will be a choice of questions on each text.

German: Three essays from a choice of questions on the set texts covering genre, themes and period:
Prose:
Fontane, *Effi Briest*
Kafka, *Die Verwandlung*
Thomas Mann, *Mario und der Zauberer*
Remarque, *Im Westen nichts Neues*
Drama:
Wedekind, *Frühlings Erwachen*
Schnitzler, *Leibelei*
Kaiser, *Von morgens bis mitternachts*
Brecht, *Die Maßnahme*, edition suhrkamp 2058 (Frankfurt a. M.: Suhrkamp, 1998), in the version of 1931

Italian: Candidates will be expected to show knowledge of three of the five works listed below. Candidates will be expected to have such knowledge of the literary, intellectual, and historical background as is necessary for the understanding of these texts. Compulsory passages for commentary will not be set in the examination.
Modern Italian Narrative and Cinema
Primo Levi, *Se questo è un uomo*
Italo Calvino, *Il barone rampante*
Anna Maria Ortese, *Il mare non bagna Napoli*
Natalia Ginzburg, *Lessico famigliare*

Spanish: Prescribed texts to be studied in relation to general trends in literature or thought or to historical background. Compulsory passages for explanation and detailed comment will *not* be set.
The Spanish Ballad Tradition:

Traditional romances:
El romancero viejo (ed. M. Díaz Roig, Cátedra, Madrid, 1979),
poems Nos. 1–3, 5–6, 8–9, 11, 13–14, 23–4, 29–32, 38–59, 63–6,
68, 71–3, 76, 78, 83, 85–6, 88, 91, 94, 96–9, 101, 104, 111, 115–9,
121, 125–8. 5
Golden Age:
Lope de Vega, *Lírica* (ed. J. M. Blecua, Clásicos Castalia), poems
Nos. 1–2, 6–10, 125, and 126.
Góngora, *Romances* (ed. Antonio Carreño, Cátedra, Madrid,
1982), poems Nos. 3, 10–11, 15–16, 18, 23, 27, 48, 52, 58, and 79. 10
Francisco de Quevedo, *Poemas escogidos* (ed. J. M. Blecua,
Clásicos Castallia, Madrid), poems Nos. 155, 160, 165, 167,
and 172.
Nineteenth and Twentieth Centuries:
Duque de Rivas, *El conde de Villamediana; El Alcázar de Sevilla;* 15
El fratricidio; Bailén (from *Romances históricos,* ed. S. García,
Cátedra).
Antonio Machado, 'La tierra de Alvargonzález' (from *Poesías*
completas, Selecciones Austral).
F. García Lorca, *Romancero gitano* (ed. Mario Hernández, Alianza). 20

Portuguese: The examination will consist of:
(*a*) a commentary on passages chosen from two of the set texts
given below; (*b*) an essay, on one of the remaining three texts;
(*c*) an essay on the historical development of the *auto.*
Candidates will be expected to show knowledge of at least 25
one text from each of groups A, B, and C below.
A Gil Vicente *Auto da Barca do Inferno*
Auto da India
B Ana Luísa Amaral *Próspero Morreu*
C Suassuna *Auto da Compadecida* 30
Cabral de Melo Neto *Vida e Morte Severina*

Russian: The paper will consist of: (*a*) one compulsory commentary; and
(*b*) two essays each from a choice of two covering the other two
set authors. Examiners may give some guidance to candidates
about how to approach the passage set for commentary; they 35
may also require candidates to translate some portion of the
passage set for commentary into English.
Pushkin, *Pikovaya dama*
Chekhov, *Sluchai iz praktiki; Anna na shee; Dom s mezoninom*
Dovlatov, *Chemodan* 40

Modern Greek: Twentieth-century Greek prose in context. Candidates will be
expected to have and to be able to demonstrate such knowledge
of the literary, intellectual, cultural and historical background
as is necessary for the understanding of these texts.
Compulsory passages for commentary will not be set in the 45
examination. Angelopoulos's O Θίασος will be taught with an
emphasis on the script, but aspects of the film will also be
discussed.Candidates will be encouraged to make connections
and comparisons between texts where appropriate.

Prescribed texts

Στρατής Δούκας, Ιστορία ευός
αιχμαλώτου
Δινημήτρης Χατζής, Το τέλος
της μικρής μας πόλης
Κώστας Ταχτσής, Το τρίτο
στεφάυι
Θόδωρος Αγγελόπουλος, Ο Θίασος
Παύλος Μάτεσις, Η μητέρα
του σκύλου
Αλέξανδρος Κοπζιάς,
Ιαγουάρος'

Czech (with   Prescribed texts to be studied as literature. Essay-type questions
Slovak):   will be set on the plays, and a compulsory passage for com-
               mentary from the poem. Candidates will be required to answer
               on all three texts.
               Čapek, *R.U.R.*
               Havel, *Vyrozumění*
               Mácha, *Máj*

Celtic: Prescribed texts. Three essays from a choice of questions on the
               following set texts:
               Pwyll Pendefig Dyfed, ed. R. L. Thomson (Dublin, 1957);
               Branwen ferch Lyr, ed. D. Thomson (Dublin, 1961);
               Saunders Lewis, *Brandwen*, in Saunders Lewis, *Dramâu'r Parlwr:
               Branwen a Dwy Briodas Ann* (Llandybïe: Christopher Davies,
               1975);
               Poems of the Cywyddwyr, ed. E. I. Rowlands (Dublin, 1976);
               Scéla Muicce Meic Dathó, ed. R. Thurneysen (Dublin, 1976),
               pp. 33–41;
               Longes Mac n-Uislenn, ed. V. Hull (New York: Modern
               Language Association of America, 1949).

c. Classical and Modern Languages Paper

Latin and Ancient Greek
*Any candidate whose native language is not English may bring a bilingual (native
language to English) dictionary for use in any examination paper where candidates are
required to translate Ancient Greek and/or Latin texts into English.*

1. *Course I.*

Papers V, VI and VII: Candidates will be required to take papers identical with
papers 3, 4, and 5 for the Preliminary Examination in Classics and English, *Course I.*

For prescribed editions of texts, see the Classics and Modern Languages Handbook.

2. *Course II.*

Candidates for Course II shall be required:
(a) to pass at the end of their first year of study the examination in Greek and
Latin prescribed for first-year candidates in Course II of the Preliminary
Examination in Classics and English.
(b) during their second year of study, to offer papers as for Course I.

d. Linguistics

VIII. General Linguistics. 3 hours.
Candidates will be expected to be familiar with the development of contemporary
linguistic theory, both synchronic and historical, and be able to discuss problems and
issues in areas including semantics, pragmatics, sociolinguistics, psycholinguistics,
language acquisition and language change.

IX. Phonetics and Phonology. 3 hours.
Candidates will be expected to be familiar with principles and practice in the
analysis, classification, and transcription of speech, as applied to languages in general, but with an emphasis on European languages.

X. Grammatical Analysis. 3 hours.
Candidates will be expected to be familiar with modern grammatical theory, in
particular as applied to the analysis of European languages.

e. Further Topics

XI. Further Topics I

French: Introduction to French Film Studies:
Candidates must write three essays, each on a different film. There will be a choice
of two questions on each film.
Jean Vigo: L'Atalante (1934)
Jacques Becker: Casque d'Or (1952)
Jean-Luc Godard: A bout de souffle (1960)
Bertrand Blier: Les valseuses (1974)

German: Introduction to German Film Studies:
The paper will consist of one commentary and two essays from a choice of
questions. The commentary will be on a set of stills from one of the films.
Metropolis (dir. Fritz Lang, 1925/26. Eureka edition EKA40321)
Die Abenteuer des Prinzen Achmed (dir. Lotte Reiniger, 1923/26)
Der blaue Engel (dir. Josef von Sternberg, 1929/1930)
Kameradschaft (dir. G. W. Pabst, 1931)

XII. Further Topics II

French: Introduction to French Literary Theory:
Candidates must write three essays, each on a different author. There will be a
choice of two questions on each author.
Valéry, 'Questions de poésie' and 'Poésie et pensée abstraite', in *Théorie poétique et
esthétique*, in *Oeuvres*, I, ed. J. Hytier, Bibliothèque de la Pléiade (Gallimard, 1957),
pp. 1280–94; pp. 1314–39
Sartre, *Qu'est-ce que la littérature?* (Folio) [Sections I and II only]
Barthes, *Critique et vérité* (Seuil)
Todorov, 'La notion de littérature', 'L'origine des genres', 'Les deux principes du
récit', 'Introduction au vraisemblable' in *La notion de littérature et autres essais* (Seuil)

German: Introduction to German Medieval Studies:
The paper will consist of one commentary, one question consisting of several
questions on a passage, and one essay from a choice of questions.
Close study of a single text: Hartmann von Aue, *Gregorius* (Reclam edition Middle
High German text with a facing page translation in modern German).

XIII. Further Topics III

French: Key Texts in French Thought:
Candidates must answer three questions (one commentary and two essays), each
on a different text. There will be a choice of one commentary passage and one essay
question on each text.

Descartes, *Discours de la méthode* (Garnier-Flammarion)

Rousseau, *Discours sur l'inégalité* (Folio)

Bergson, *Essai sur les données immédiates de la conscience* (PUF) [Chapters I and II only]

Beauvoir, *Le Deuxième Sexe* (Folio). I: Introduction, 'Mythes'; II: 'La femme mariée', 'La mère'

German: Key Texts in German Thought:

Kant, *Idee zu einer allgemeinen Geschichte in weltbürgerlicher Absicht*

Marx und Engels, *Das kommunistische Manifest*

Nietzsche, 'Zur Naturgeschichte der Moral' in *Jenseits vom Gut und Böse*

Freud, *Warum Krieg?*

Candidates will be permitted to use translations alongside, but not instead of, the original texts.

f. *Russian Course B: for students who enter Oxford without A level or equivalent level knowledge of Russian*

BI Translation from English into Russian and Russian grammar exercises.

BIIA Translation from Russian into English.

BIIB Comprehension of a passage of written Russian.

BIII Dictation and Aural Comprehension.

BIV Oral Test.

Special Regulations for the Preliminary Examination in Molecular and Cellular Biochemistry

A

1. The subjects of the Preliminary Examination in Molecular and Cellular Biochemistry shall be:

(1) Molecular Cell Biology

(2) Biological Chemistry

(3) Biophysical Chemistry

(4) Organic Chemistry

(5) Mathematics and Statistics for Biochemists.

2. Candidates shall be deemed to have passed the examination if they satisfy the Moderators in all five subjects.

3. Candidates must offer all five subjects at their first examination attempt.

4. A candidate who fails one or two subjects will be permitted one further attempt at the failed subject/s, at the first available opportunity.

5. A candidate who fails three or more subjects shall be deemed to have failed the examination. He or she will be permitted one further attempt at the whole examination, at the first available opportunity.

6. The Moderators may award a Distinction to candidates of special merit who satisfy them in all five subjects at their first examination attempt.

B

One written paper will be set in each subject. The duration of the written papers will be three hours for subjects 1, 2, and 3, and two hours for subjects 4 and 5. The syllabus for each subject will be that set out in the schedule below.

The Moderators will permit the use of hand-held pocket calculators subject to the 5 conditions set out under the heading 'Use of Calculators in examinations' in the *Regulations for the Conduct of University Examinations*. A list of recommended calculators will be provided by the Chair of the Moderators not later than the Wednesday of the fourth week of the Michaelmas Full Term preceding the examination. The use of calculators may not be permitted in certain papers. 10

All candidates shall be assessed as to their practical ability in coursework under the following provisions:

(*a*) The Chair of the Teaching Committee, or a deputy, shall make available to the Moderators, at the end of the fifth week of the term in which the examinations are first held, evidence showing the extent to which each candidate has completed the 15 prescribed coursework.

(*b*) The Moderators may request coursework from any candidate. Such candidates will be named in a list posted by the day of the first written paper.

(*c*) Coursework cannot normally be retaken. Failure to complete the coursework to the satisfaction of the Moderators, in the absence of appropriate documentary 20 evidence (e.g. a signed medical certificate), will normally constitute failure of the examination.

Schedule
(1) *Molecular Cell Biology*

Classification, evolution and structure of bacterial, archeal, and eukaryotic cells; 25 structure of subcellular organelles and the cytoskeleton of eukaryotes. Multicellularity and cell specialization. Differences between plant and animal cells. Nuclear and cell division in plants, animals, and bacteria. Intra- and intercellular signalling.

Chromosomes and genes. Transmission of information between generations. Mitosis and meiosis. Evidence for DNA as the genetic material. The nature of the 30 gene. Organisation and expression of genetic information: mechanism of DNA replication; mechanism and control of transcription; mechanisms and structures involved in protein synthesis; the genetic code; phages, plasmids, and hosts. Gene cloning and mapping techniques.

Major metabolic pathways—chemical and thermodynamic principles. ATP. 35 Oxidation of fuels: glycogen, sugars, amino acids, fats. The TCA cycle. Synthesis of carbohydrates and fats. The glyoxylate cycle. Photosynthesis. Urea cycle.

Structure and properties of biological membranes. Membrane potentials and ion channels. Membrane transport; biological pumps. Bioenergetics; electron transfer, oxidative and photophosphorylation. 40

(2) *Biological Chemistry*

Chemical constraints on biology. Energy transformations. Biological polymers. Polysaccharides: amylose and cellulose. Membranes. Lipid and protein components of membranes.

Structure and properties of proteins: amino acids, peptide bonds, conformational 45 preferences, α-helices, β-sheets, stabilisation by non-covalent interactions; protein sequences and amino acid modification; glycoproteins.

Tertiary structure and protein folding. Structural proteins. Myoglobin and haemoglobin.

Principles of enzyme catalysis—acid-base and nucleophilic catalysis. Proteases and other enzymes.

Organic chemistry of enzyme reactions, particularly those in glycolysis.

Biological aspects of sulphur, iron, and phosphorus chemistry.

Organic chemistry of sugars and other heterocyclic compounds.   5

Structure and properties of nucleic acids; ribose and deoxyribose, keto-enol tautomerism and H-bonding in purines and pyrimidines, phosphate as linking group; nucleotides; polymeric chains of nucleotides; differences in stability between RNA and DNA; the double helix; DNA damage and mutation.

Techniques in molecular biology: purification of DNA and proteins.   10
Electrophoresis. DNA sequencing, cloning, blotting.

(3) *Biophysical Chemistry*

Principles of Newtonian mechanics and electrostatics. Quantum theory: concepts of quantum mechanics in terms of energy levels. Boltzmann distribution. Atomic and molecular structure, atomic orbitals: crystal field theory; LCAO approach to molecular orbitals.   15

Electromagnetic radiation and its interaction with matter. Light absorption. Spectroscopy, Beer's Law. Diffraction; Bragg's Law. X-ray diffraction by crystals. Modern optical microscopy. Electron microscopy.

Thermodynamics of solutions: introduction to First and Second Laws. Gibbs function, chemical potential and electrochemical potential. Osmotic equilibria; chemical equilibria; redox equilibria. Buffer solutions and pH. Non-ideal solutions: activity coefficients. Debye-Huckel theory. Solubility of proteins and other compounds.   20

Kinetics: order and molecularity; first, second, and pseudo-first order kinetics, steady state. Half lives. Theories of reaction rates; collision theory, transition state theory. Activation energy and the Arrhenius equation. Isotope effects, acid-base catalysis. Radioactive decay as a first order process. Biological effects of radiation.   25

Enzyme kinetics, Michaelis-Menten equation and the steady state derivation. Irreversible and reversible inhibitors of enzymes. Classification of reversible inhibitors. Allostery.   30

Non-covalent interactions. Electrostatic forces and dipoles. Electronegativity. Lennard-Jones potential and van der Waal's radii. Hydrogen bonding in proteins, DNA and oligosaccharides. The hydrophobic effect; role of entropy. Accessible surface area and solubility. Protein folding—thermodynamic and kinetic aspects. Co-operativity of folding. Protein denaturation and misfolding.   35

(4) *Organic Chemistry*

Structure: Elementary atomic and molecular orbital theory. Bonding and molecular geometry. Methods for structure determination (e.g. spectroscopy, mass spectrometry, nmr). Stereochemistry: Absolute configuration. Cis-trans and other isomerisations.

Reactivity: Electronegativity; inductive, mesomeric and stereoelectronic effects.   40
Lowry-Bronsted acidity and basicity of organic compounds. Nucleophilicity and electrophilicity. Simple molecular orbital theory as unifying concept.

Mechanism: Classification of reactions proceeding via intermediates and transition states. Substitution, elimination and addition processes. Rate determining steps; kinetic and thermodynamic control. Carbocation, carbanion, carbene and radical   45
intermediates.

Functional group chemistry: Characteristic chemistry of carbonyl groups. Structure, properties and reactions of carbonyls.

(5) *Mathematics and Statistics for Biochemists*

An elementary treatment of the following topics will be expected: 50

Mathematics

Indices, logarithms and exponential functions. Graphs and graphical representation of simple equations, slopes, inflexion points. Partial fractions. Basic trigonometric functions: sine and cosine functions, representation of waves. Differentiation: maxima and minima; rates of progress, use of Product and Chain rules. Partial differentiation. Integration: of powers of x including x^{-1}; by substitution, by parts and using partial fractions. Introduction to Complex numbers. Simple separable differential equations and their solution. Zeroth, first and second order processes. Permutations and combinations. Factorials and the Binomial Theorem. Binomial and Poisson distributions.

Statistics

Mean, median and mode—measures of central tendency. Normal, unimodal and bimodal distributions. Standard deviation, standard error and coefficient of variance. Confidence limits. Experimental errors and biological variation. Relationships between variables—line fitting. Accuracy and precision. Experimental design. Significance testing; t-tests and non-parametric tests. Conditional probabilities and expectation.

Special Regulations for the Preliminary Examination in Music

A

1. The subjects of the examination and the number of papers shall be as prescribed by regulation from time to time by the Board of the Faculty of Music.

2. In the case of candidates who have satisfied the Moderators in all the written and practical subjects, the Moderators may award a distinction to those of special merit.

B

Each candidate will be required to offer papers 1-3 and two of the options in paper 4.

1. *Special Topics*

A three-hour paper in which candidates should attempt to answer three questions.

2. *Musical Analysis*

A three-hour paper in which candidates should attempt to answer one question from a choice of two.

3. *Techniques of Composition and Keyboard Skills*

The paper shall consist of two parts:

A. Techniques of Composition: Studies in Harmony and Counterpoint

A seven-day take-away paper in which candidates should attempt three questions: the two compulsory questions and one other. The examination paper will be available for collection in the Music Faculty Library from noon on Friday of the fifth week in the Trinity Term in which candidates are presenting themselves for examination. Completed papers must be submitted to the Chair of Moderators in Music, Examination Schools, High Street, Oxford, not later than noon on Friday of the sixth week of the same term. Each paper must be accompanied by a declaration, in a sealed envelope bearing the candidate's examination number, in the form prescribed for the portfolio of compositions and the extended essay.

B. Keyboard Skills

A practical examination in which candidates will be asked to: (a) realise a figured bass line at the keyboard or, where appropriate, on another continuo instrument (e.g. lute); (b) read at the keyboard three- or four-part writing in three different clefs. Preparation time for candidates in the examination will be 30 minutes.

4. *Options*

Candidates must choose two from the following:

(*a*) *Issues in the Study of Music*

A two-hour paper in which candidates should attempt to answer two questions.

(*b*) *Composition*

Candidates will be required to submit a portfolio of compositions and to take a listening examination. The specifications for the portfolio are as published in the Faculty Undergraduate Handbook relating to the examination.

(*c*) *Performance*

A solo performance, vocal or instrumental, of some 10-12 minutes in length. Instrumental candidates may choose to perform a single work, a movement from a longer work, or two pieces in contrasting style. The choice of instrument is limited to related families of instruments. Singers may choose to perform up to four pieces. Programmes must be submitted to the Chair of Moderators in Music, Faculty of Music, St Aldate's, not later than noon on Friday of the sixth week in the Hilary Term of the academic year in which the candidates are presenting themselves for examination.

(*d*) *Extended Essay*

An essay of 4,000–5,000 words on a subject to be chosen in consultation with the candidate's tutor.

Each portfolio submitted for the subjects of Portfolio of Compositions and Extended Essay must be accompanied by a declaration placed in a sealed envelope bearing the candidate's examination number and in the following prescribed form.

Form of Declaration

I, ..., hereby declare that this submission is my own work, except where otherwise stated, and that it has not previously been submitted, either wholly or in part, for any other examination.

Signed..

.... College

Date..

Candidates who fail one or two of papers 1,2,3 or 4 above may resit only that paper or papers at a subsequent examination; candidates who fail three or four papers will be required to resit all four papers at a subsequent examination.

Special Regulations for the Preliminary Examination in Oriental Studies

A

1. The languages, subjects, and papers in the examination shall be as prescribed by regulation from time to time by the Board of the Faculty of Oriental Studies.

2. A candidate shall be deemed to have passed the examination when he or she shall have satisfied the Moderators in all the papers associated with one of the languages specified in the regulations.

3. Candidates must offer all subjects at one examination provided that: (i) in languages for which four papers are required, a candidate who fails in one or two papers may offer those subjects at one subsequent examination, and a candidate who fails three or four papers must offer all four subjects at one subsequent examination; and (ii) in languages for which three papers are required, a candidate who fails in one paper may offer that subject at one subsequent examination, and a candidate who fails two or three papers must offer all three subjects at one subsequent examination.

4. In the case of candidates who have satisfied the Moderators in all the papers at a single examination, the Moderators may award a distinction to those of special merit.

B

The languages which may be offered shall be Arabic, Chinese, Egyptology and Ancient Near Eastern Studies, Hebrew, Japanese, Persian, Sanskrit, and Turkish.

Arabic

Candidates will be required to offer three three-hour papers (papers (i), (ii), and (iv) below), plus an oral/aural examination as specified under (iii) below.

   (i) Translation and precis into English.
   (ii) Comprehension, composition, and grammar.
   (iii) Oral/aural examination (to be done at the Oriental Institute)[†]
   (iv) Islamic history and culture.

Chinese

Candidates will be required to offer three three-hour papers.

   (i) Modern.
   (ii) Classical.
   (iii) East Asia Survey: China.

Egyptology and Ancient Near Eastern Studies

Candidates offering Egyptology and Ancient Near Eastern Studies are required to offer four three-hour papers:

1, 2 *Either* Akkadian texts. (Lists are available from the Oriental Institute)
and
Akkadian grammar and unprepared translation.
Or
Egyptian texts: *Middle Egyptian texts*, ed. Baines and Smith. (Copies are available from the Oriental Institute)
and
Middle Egyptian grammar and unprepared translation.

3. Civilizations of the Ancient Near East.

---

† Details of the areas in which candidates will be expected to show competence are provided in the examination conventions and in the handbook.

4. History of the Ancient Near East to 30 BCE.

Hebrew and Jewish Studies

Candidates will be required to offer four three-hour papers.

(i) Hebrew Texts I: Biblical and Rabbinic Hebrew.
(ii) Hebrew Texts II: Medieval and Modern Hebrew.   5

Copies of texts for papers (i) and (ii) are available from the Oriental Institute.

(iii) Grammar and Translation into Hebrew.
(iv) General Paper.

Japanese

Candidates will be required to offer three three-hour papers.   1C

(i) Modern Japanese.
(ii) Modern and Classical Japanese.
(iii) East Asia Survey: Japan.

Persian

Candidates will be required to offer three three-hour papers.   1⁵

(i) Prepared and unprepared texts for translation from Persian.
(ii) Grammar and translation into Persian.
(iii) Islamic History and Culture.

Sanskrit

Candidates will be required to offer three three-hour papers.   2C

(i) Texts: C. R. Lanman, *Sanskrit Reader,* pp. 1–34, l. 11. *Bhagavad-Gītā* (ed. Belvalkar), Books II, IV, VI, and XI.
(ii) Grammar: the subject will be studied from M. A. Coulson, *Teach Yourself Sanskrit*; A. A. Macdonell, *Sanskrit Grammar for Students.*
(iii) General paper.   2⁵

Turkish

Candidates will be required to offer three three-hour papers.

(i) Prepared texts and unseen translation from Turkish. (The list of texts to be prepared is published in the current issue of the Islamic Studies handbook.)
(ii) Turkish grammar and translation into Turkish.   3C
(iii) Islamic history and culture.

Special Regulations for the Preliminary Examination in Philosophy and Modern Languages

A

1. Candidates in this Preliminary Examination shall be examined   3⁵
in Philosophy and one Modern Language. The languages that may
be offered shall be those languages which may be offered in the
Final Honour School of Modern Languages.

2. The subjects of the examination shall be:

In Philosophy,   4C

(1) Introduction to Philosophy

and, in the Modern Language offered

(2) Language papers

(3) Literature papers.

3. Candidates must offer all three subjects at one examination provided that

(*a*) a candidate who fails in either two subjects or one subject may in a subsequent examination offer the two subjects or the one subject only; 5

(*b*) a candidate who has offered two subjects at a subsequent examination under (*a*) above and has failed in one subject may offer in a subsequent examination that subject only.

Provided that a candidate who fails one only of the papers in 2(1) above may offer, in a subsequent examination or subsequent examinations, the paper in which he or she has failed. 10

4. A candidate shall be deemed to have passed the examination if he shall have satisfied the Examiners in all three subjects.

5. In the case of candidates who have satisfied the Examiners in three subjects at a single examination the Examiners may award a distinction either in Philosophy or in the Modern Language or in both to those who have done work of special merit. 15

6. This Preliminary Examination shall be under the joint supervision of the Boards of the Faculties of Philosophy and of Medieval and Modern European Languages and Literature, which shall appoint a standing joint committee to make regulations concerning it, subject always to the preceding clauses of this subsection. 20

7. It shall be the duty of the chair of the Examiners for the Preliminary Examination for Modern Languages to designate such of their number as may be required for Modern Languages in the Preliminary Examination in Philosophy and Modern Languages, and when this has been done and the Examiner for Philosophy has been nominated, the number of the examiners in Philosophy and Modern Languages shall be deemed to be complete. 25

30

B

There shall be three subjects in the examination.

(1) *Introduction to Philosophy* (two papers of three hours each).

I. *General Philosophy*

As defined in the regulations for Preliminary Examination in Philosophy, Politics and Economics. Candidates will be required to answer four questions. 35

II. (*a*) *Moral Philosophy* and (*b*) *Logic*

As defined in the regulations for the Preliminary Examination in Philosophy, Politics and Economics. Candidates will be required to answer four questions, including at least one from each section. 40

(2) *Language papers* (one paper of three hours and two papers each of one and a half hours including in French certification of attendance and participation in oral classes, as specified for the Preliminary Examination in Modern Languages).

As specified for Papers I, IIA, and IIB in the regulations for the Preliminary Examination for Modern Languages.

(3) *Literature papers* (two papers, each of three hours).

As specified for Papers III and IV in the regulations for the Preliminary Examination for Modern Languages.

Special Regulations for the Preliminary Examination for Philosophy, Politics, and Economics

A

1. The subjects of the Preliminary Examination for Philosophy, Politics, and Economics shall be:

(1) Introductory Economics

(2) Introduction to Philosophy

(3) Introduction to Politics: The Theory and Practice of Democracy.

2. A candidate shall be allowed to offer himself or herself for examination in one, two, or three subjects.

3. A candidate shall be deemed to have passed the examination if he or she shall have satisfied the Moderators in three subjects.

4. The Moderators may award a distinction to candidates of special merit who have passed all three subjects at a single examination.

B

Three three-hour papers will be set as follows.

Introductory Economics

Elementary economics including: consumer theory; producer theory; market equilibrium with perfect competition, monopoly and imperfect competition; factor markets; partial equilibrium analysis of welfare, market failure and externalities; national income accounting; the determination of national income and employment; monetary institutions and the money supply; inflation; balance of payments and exchange rates. Elementary mathematical economics; application of functions and graphs, differentiation, partial differentiation, maxima and minima, optimization subject to contraints.

Calculators may be used in the examination room subject to the conditions set out under the heading 'Use of calculators in examinations' in the *Special Regulations concerning Examinations.*

Introduction to Philosophy

The paper shall consist of three sections: (I) General Philosophy, (II) Moral Philosophy, (III) Logic. Each candidate will be required to show adequate knowledge in each of the three sections.

I. *General Philosophy*

Subjects to be studied include: knowledge and scepticism, induction, mind and body, personal identity, free will, and God and evil. The candidates will have the opportunity, but will not be required, to show first-hand knowledge of Descartes' *Meditations* and Hume's *An Enquiry concerning Human Understanding.* 5

II. *Moral Philosophy*

This section shall be studied in connection with Mill's *Utilitarianism.* While not being confined to the detailed views of the author of the set text, the section will be satisfactorily answerable by a candidate who has made a critical study of the text. Questions will normally be set on the following topics: pleasure, happiness and well- 10 being; forms of consequentialism; alternatives to consequentialism; ethical truth, ethical realism and the 'Proof' of Utilitarianism; justice and rights; virtue, character and integrity.

III. *Logic*

Subjects to be studied include: syntax and semantics of propositional and predicate 15 logic, identity and definite descriptions, proofs in Natural Deduction, and the critical application of formal logic to the analysis of English sentences and arguments.

These topics shall be studied in conjunction with Volker Halbach's *Introduction to Logic* manual, published by Oxford University Press. The logical symbols to be used are those found in this publication. The first question in this section of the paper will 20 be a question of an elementary and straightforward nature.

Introduction to Politics: the Theory and Practice of Democracy

The paper will be divided into two sections. Candidates are required to answer *four* questions, of which at least one must be from section (*a*) and two from section (*b*). Section (*b*) will be in two parts. Part (*b-i*) will contain questions on topics set out in 25 para 2, below. Part (*b-ii*) will contain questions on the political history of the United States of America, the United Kingdom, France, and Germany.

Candidates may choose to answer any combination of questions in section (*b*), but each part (*b-ii*) question chosen must relate to a different country (so answers must be on *two* different countries if *two* answers are chosen from (*b-ii*) and *three* countries if 30 *three* answers). Candidates may, where appropriate, answer questions from part (*b-i*) exclusively in relation to one of the named countries, but any question chosen from part (*b-ii*) should not then be on that same country.

Candidates are expected, where appropriate, to show knowledge of the methodo- logical issues involved in both normative and empirical political research. 35

(*a*) *Theorizing the Democratic State*

Questions will be set on the following topics: the nature and grounds of democracy; power and influence in the democratic state; ideology; civil society; public choice approaches to democracy; the nature and limits of liberty. Questions will also be set on the following texts: J. J. Rousseau, *The Social Contract*; J. S. Mill, *On Liberty*; 40 Alexis de Toqueville, *Democracy in America*; Karl Marx and Freidrich Engels, *The Communist Manifesto, Eighteenth Brumaire of Louis Napoleon, Preface to a Critique of Political Economy, Critique of the Gotha Programme*, plus readings 14, 37, 39 in David McLellan, ed., *Karl Marx: Selected Writings*, Second Edition (Oxford University Press, 2000). 45

(*b*) *Analysis of Democratic Institutions*

Questions in part (*b-i*) will be set on the following topics: the state and its institu- tions (executives, legislatures, parties and party systems, courts, constitutions and centre-periphery relations); political representation; the politics of instability;

policy continuity and policy change; democratic transitions and consolidation. Questions in part (*b-ii*) will be set on these topics with reference to the political history of the United States of America since 1932, the United Kingdom since 1945, France since 1946, and Germany since 1932, as outlined in the department's official reading list.   5

Special Regulations for the Preliminary Examination in Physics

A

1. The subject of the Preliminary Examination in Physics shall be Physics, including basic practical and mathematical techniques.

2. The number of papers and other general requirements of the   10
Preliminary Examination in Physics shall be as prescribed by regulation from time to time by the Mathematical, Physical and Life Sciences Board.

B

1. Candidates in Physics must offer four Compulsory Papers at one examination,   15
provided that a candidate who has failed in one or two papers may offer that number of papers at a subsequent examination. The titles of the papers shall be:

CP1: Physics 1
CP2: Physics 2
CP3: Mathematical Methods 1   20
CP4: Mathematical Methods 2.

. Their syllabuses shall be approved by the Faculty of Physics and shall be published in the Physics Course Handbook by the Faculty of Physics not later than the beginning of Michaelmas Full Term for examination three terms thence.

2. In addition to the four papers of cl. 1, a candidate in Physics shall be required   25
   (i) to submit to the Moderators such evidence as they require of the successful completion of practical work normally pursued during the three terms preceding the examination, *and*
   (ii) to offer a written paper on one Short Option.

3. Candidates shall be deemed to have passed the examination if they have   30
satisfied the Moderators in the four Compulsory Papers either at a single examination or at two examinations in accordance with the proviso to cl. 1, and provided further that the same number of papers as were failed at the first sitting have been passed at the same attempt at a subsequent examination.

4. In the case of candidates who offer all four papers of cl. 1, the Moderators shall   35
publish the names only of those who have satisfied them in two or more papers. Candidates whose names do not appear on the pass list must offer four papers at a subsequent examination. In the case of candidates who, in accordance with the proviso to cl. 1, offer one or two papers, the Moderators shall publish the names only to those who have satisfied them in each of the papers offered.   40

5. The Moderators may award a distinction to candidates of special merit who have satisfied them in all four papers of cl. 1 at the single examination and in the requirements of cl. 2.

6. Failure to complete practical work under cl. 2(i), without good reason, will be deemed by the Moderators as failure in the Preliminary Examination and the candi-   45
date will be required to complete the outstanding practicals either by examination or

by completing them alongside second year study, before entry to the Part A examination will be permitted. In these circumstances, distinction at the Preliminary Examination will not be possible.

7. The list of Short Option subjects in cl. 2(ii) and their syllabuses shall be approved by the Faculty of Physics and shall be published in the Physics Course Handbook by the Faculty of Physics not later than the beginning of Michaelmas Full Term for examination three terms thence.

8. With respect to subjects under cl. 2(ii) a candidate may propose to the Head of the Teaching Faculty of Physics or deputy, not later than the last week of Michaelmas Full Term preceding the examination, another subject paper. Candidates shall be advised of the decision by the end of the first week of the subsequent Hilary Full Term.

9. Except for papers for which their use is forbidden, the Moderators will permit the use of any hand-held calculator subject to the conditions set out under the heading 'Use of calculators in examinations' in the *Regulations for the Conduct of University Examinations* and further elaborated in the Course Handbook.

Special Regulations for the Preliminary Examination in Physics and Philosophy

A

1. The subjects of the Examination shall be (a) Physics and Mathematics, (b) Philosophy.

2. All candidates must offer both (a) and (b).

3. The Examiners shall indicate on the pass list each candidate who has not passed the examination, but who has passed in one subject, and shall indicate in which subject the candidate has passed.

4. The Examination shall be under the joint supervision of the Board of the Faculty of Philosophy and the Mathematical, Physical and Life Sciences Board, which shall appoint a standing joint committee to make regulations concerning it, subject always to the preceding clauses of this sub-section.

5. (i) The Examiners for Physics and Mathematics shall be such of the Examiners in the Preliminary Examination in Physics as may be designated by the Chair of Examiners for the Preliminary Examination in Physics.

   (ii) The Examiners for Philosophy shall be nominated by a committee of which the three elected members shall be appointed by the Board of the Faculty of Philosophy.

6. Candidates who do not pass the examination at their first sitting may re-enter on one subsequent occasion as follows:

   (i) Candidates must re-take any papers failed at the first attempt, and

   (ii) Candidates who fail two or more papers in Physics and Mathematics must retake all the papers in that subject.

B

Distinction can be obtained by excellence either in Physics and Mathematics or in Philosophy provided that adequate knowledge is shown in the other subject of the examination.

Candidates will be required to take five papers, as follows:

(*a*) three papers in Physics and Mathematics;

(*b*) two papers in Philosophy.

(*a*) *Physics and Mathematics*

Candidates will be required to take the following three papers:

(1) CP1 Physics 1
(2) CP3 Mathematical Methods 1
(3) CP4 Mathematical Methods 2.

Their syllabuses shall be approved by the Faculty of Physics and published in the Physics Course Handbook not later than the beginning of Michaelmas Full Term for examination three terms thence. Except for papers for which their use is forbidden, the Moderators will permit the use of any hand-held calculator subject to the conditions set out under the heading 'Use of calculators in examinations' in the Regulations for the Conduct of University Examinations and further elaborated in the Physics Course Handbook.

(*b*) *Philosophy*

Candidates will be required to take two papers:

(1) *Elements of Deductive Logic*

As specified for the Preliminary Examination in Mathematics and Philosophy.

(2) *Introduction to Philosophy*

The paper shall consist of two parts:

A. *General Philosophy*

As specified for the Preliminary Examination in Mathematics and Philosophy.

B. *Leibniz-Clarke*

This section shall be studied principally as an introduction to the philosophy of space and time in connection with *The Leibniz-Clarke Correspondence*, ed. H. G. Alexander, Manchester University Press, 1956. This section, while not being confined to the detailed views of the author of the set text, will be satisfactorily answerable by a candidate who has made a critical study of the text. There will not be a compulsory question containing passages for comment.

Candidates will be required to attempt four questions, and answer at least one question from Part A and at least one question from Part B.

Special Regulations for the Preliminary Examination in Psychology, Philosophy, and Linguistics

A

1. The subjects of the examination shall be:

(1) Introduction to Psychology

(2) Introduction to Philosophy

(3) Introduction to Linguistics

(4) Introduction to Neurophysiology

(5) Introduction to Probability Theory and Statistics

2. Candidates shall be deemed to have passed the examination if they satisfy the Moderators in three subjects.

3. Candidates must offer three subjects at their first examination attempt.

4. A candidate who fails one subject will be permitted one further attempt at this failed subject, at the first available opportunity.

5. A candidate who fails two or three subjects shall be deemed to have failed the examination. He or she will be permitted one further attempt at the whole examination, at the first available opportunity.

6. The Moderators may award a Distinction to candidates of special merit who satisfy them in three subjects at their first examination attempt.

B

(1) *Introduction to Psychology*

Methods and topics in: development; individual differences; social behaviour; animal behaviour; the neural basis of behaviour; perception; learning; memory; language; cognition; skills; abnormal behaviour.

One three-hour paper will be set.

(2) *Introduction to Philosophy*

As specified for the Preliminary Examination for Philosophy, Politics, and Economics.

(3) *Introduction to Linguistics*

Provides a foundation in phonetics, phonology, morphology, syntax, and semantics, with an introduction to linguistic theory and the connections between linguistics and other subjects such as philosophy of language, sociology and psychology.

One three-hour paper will be set.

(4) *Introduction to Neurophysiology*

Excitable Tissues. Membrane potential, ion pumps. Action potential, refractory period. Receptor potentials. Neuromuscular transmission. Synaptic mechanisms.

Chemical Transmitters. Storage and release of transmitter. Removal and synthesis of transmitter. Selected drugs acting on the nervous system.

Efferent Mechanisms. Muscle contraction. Muscle receptors. Spinal reflexes. Higher motor centres. Autonomic nervous system.

Afferent Mechanisms. Hearing. Vision. Somaesthetic system, including pain.

One three-hour paper will be set.

(5) *Introduction to Probability Theory and Statistics*

This examination is intended to test the candidate's understanding of the elements of probability theory and of the principles of statistics as applied to the design and analysis of surveys and experiments and to the interpretation of the results of such investigations. The topics below are more fully detailed in *Definitions and Formulae with Statistical Tables for Elementary Statistics and Quantitative Methods Courses,* which is prepared by the Department of Statistics. Copies of this will be available at the examination.

Descriptive statistics and statistical presentation using graphs and simple measures of central tendency and dispersion. Frequency distributions. Samples and populations. The addition and multiplication laws of probability; conditional probability and Bayes' Rule. The binomial, Poisson and normal distributions: their properties and uses and the relationships between them. Statistical inference using sampling distributions, standard errors and confidence limits. Common uses of z, t, chi-square and F tests and nonparametric tests including tests of hypothesis for the mean, median or proportion of a single population or for the difference between two or more populations, goodness-of-fit tests and tests of difference between two population distributions.

Parametric one-way Analysis of variance. Kruskal-Wallis non-Parametric analysis of variance. The analysis of 2-way contingency tables using chi-square tests. Linear regression and correlation.

A comprehensive list of formulae together with statistical tables will be available at the examination.

One three-hour paper will be set.

For papers (1) and (5) only, examiners will permit the use of any hand-held pocket calculator subject to the conditions set out under the heading 'Use of calculators' in the *Regulations for the Conduct of University Examinations*.

Special Regulations for the Preliminary Examination for Theology and Religion

A

1. The subjects of the Preliminary Examination for Theology and Religion shall be:

(1) The Christian Doctrine of Creation

(2) The Study of Old Testament set texts

(3) Introducing the New Testament with special reference to the Gospel of Mark

(4) The History of the Church from Nero to Constantine

(5) Introduction to the Study of Religions

(6) Introduction to Philosophy

(7) New Testament Greek

(8) Biblical Hebrew

(9) Classical Arabic

(10) Pali

(11) Sanskrit.

2. Candidates must offer at least one from amongst papers (6), (7), (8), (9), (10) and (11).

3. Candidates intending to progress to the Honour School of Theology and Religion must satisfy a language requirement for the degree via his or her Preliminary Examination, or will be required to

indicate how he or she will attempt to do so via his or her Second Public Examination. Candidates in the Final Honours School of Theology and Religion will be deemed to have satisfied a language requirement for their degree if they have passed one of Papers 7 (New Testament Greek), 8 (Biblical Hebrew), 9 (Classical Arabic), 10 (Pali), or 11 (Sanskrit) in their Preliminary Examination.

4. A candidate shall be deemed to have passed the examination if he shall have satisfied the Moderators in three of the subjects from the Preliminary Examination:

Provided that he shall have passed in not less than two subjects at one and the same examination and in the third subject at that or a subsequent examination.

5. Candidates may offer an additional subject if they so wish.

6. All candidates must offer at least three subjects in one examination:

Provided that a candidate who has failed in one subject (or in two subjects if he has offered four) but has passed in the other subjects offered may offer at a subsequent examination the subject or subjects in which he or she failed.

7. In the case of candidates who have satisfied the Moderators in at least three subjects in a single examination, the Moderators may award a mark of distinction to those of special merit.

B

Candidates must offer at least one from amongst papers 6, 7, 8, 9, 10 or 11.

1. *The Christian Doctrine of Creation*

This paper will serve as an introduction to Systematic Theology through the critical examination of different aspects of one basic Christian doctrine, the doctrine of Creation.

2. *The Study of Old Testament set texts: Genesis 1–11 and Amos*

Candidates will be expected to comment on passages from the set texts and will be expected to show a general knowledge of their historical, literary, and theological background.*

3. *Introducing the New Testament with special reference to the Gospel of Mark*

Candidates will be expected to show a general knowledge of the contents and background of the New Testament and to answer questions on historical and theological issues which are raised by the Gospel of Mark.

4. *The History of the Church from Nero to Constantine*

Candidates will be expected to show a general knowledge of the history of the Church, and its relations to the Roman empire, from the late first century to the death of Constantine in 337 AD. Questions will be set on some but not necessarily all of the following topics: the growth of the church and the meaning of

---

* The texts will be studied in English in the New Revised Standard Version.

conversion; the causes, scope, and effects of persecution; patterns of ministry and the threefold hierarchy; ecclesiastical discipline and the beginnings of monasticism; schisms caused by Judaizers, Gnostics, Montanists, Novatianists, and Donatists; the development of orthodoxy and synodical government; the evolution of the Biblical canon; the role of Christianity in the Constantinian Empire.   5

5. *Introduction to the Study of Religions*

The principal aim of this paper is to introduce the Study of Religions through the critical study of some different approaches. Candidates will be expected to understand the main attempts to define 'religion' and the problems associated with such definitions, and to have acquired a preliminary insight into the variety of religions,   10
both those that are traditional and new religious movements through the world.

6. *Introduction to Philosophy*

As specified for the Preliminary Examination for Philosophy, Politics, and Economics.

7. *New Testament Greek*[†]   15

Candidates will be expected to show a knowledge of Greek grammar, syntax, and vocabulary (as set out in J. Duff, *The Elements of New Testament Greek*) and its importance for the exegesis of the New Testament, with particular reference to Mark 14:1–16:8 and John 6 and 9, from which passages will be chosen for translation and grammatical comment.   20

8. *Biblical Hebrew*[*]

The paper will include questions on elementary Hebrew grammar (to include only the topics covered in J. Weingreen, *Practical Grammar of Classical Hebrew*, 2nd edn., pp. 1–123), and short passages will be set for translation and grammatical comment from Genesis 1–2.   25

9. *Classical Arabic*

Candidates will be expected to show knowledge of Classical Arabic grammar, syntax and vocabulary (as set out in André d'Alverny, *Cours de langue arabe*). Passages from the Qu'ran, the Hadith, or other theological Islamic literature will be chosen for translation and grammatical comment.   30

10. *Pali*

Candidates will be expected to show knowledge of Pali grammar, syntax and vocabulary (as set out in A. K. Warder: *Introduction to Pali*). Passages from the Pali Canon will be chosen for translation and grammatical comment.

11. *Sanskrit*   35

Candidates will be expected to show knowledge of basic Sanskrit grammar, syntax and vocabulary. The course book will be Walter Maurer's *The Sanskrit Language* and the texts for study will be *Bhagabad Gita* chapter 2 and *Nala* chapter 1. Passages from these texts will be chosen for translation and grammatical comment.

[†] The Greek text will be the text of the United Bible Societies, 4th edition.
[*] The Hebrew text will be the *Biblia Hebraica Stuttgartensia* (Stuttgart, 1977).

SPECIAL REGULATIONS FOR HONOUR SCHOOLS

SPECIAL REGULATIONS FOR THE HONOUR SCHOOL OF ANCIENT AND MODERN HISTORY

A

1. The examination in the Honour School of Ancient and Modern History shall consist of such subjects in Ancient and Modern History as the Boards of the Faculties of Classics and History from time to time shall in consultation prescribe by regulation.

2. No candidate shall be admitted to the examination in this school unless he or she has either passed or been exempted from the First Public Examination.

3. The examination shall be under the joint supervision of the Boards of the Faculties of Classics and History. They shall appoint a standing joint committee to consider any matters concerning the examination which cannot expeditiously be settled by direct consultation between them. Whenever any matter cannot otherwise be resolved they shall themselves hold a joint meeting and resolve it by majority vote.

B

Each candidate shall offer the following subjects:

I. A PERIOD OF ANCIENT HISTORY (ONE PAPER).
  One of the following:
  (*a*) Greek History 478–403 BC;
  (*b*) Greek History 403–336 BC;
  (*c*) Roman History 146–46 BC;
  (*d*) Roman History 46 BC–AD 54.

II. A PERIOD OF MODERN HISTORY (ONE PAPER).
  Either (*a*) Any one of the periods of General History specified for the Honour School of History;
  or (*b*) Any one of the periods of the History of the British Isles specified for the Honour School of History except any such period that has already been offered on passing the First Public Examination.

Students participating in the academic exchange scheme with Princeton University will substitute the courses taken at Princeton for either a General History or History of the British Isles paper. The Princeton courses will be examined at Princeton, and the grades awarded will be reviewed and moderated by the Examiners to produce a single University standard mark, according to procedures laid down in the Handbook and Examining Conventions.

III. FURTHER SUBJECTS

Either, (*a*) (i) any one of the Further Subjects as specified for the Honour School of History (one paper);

or, (*b*) any one of the following Further Subjects in Ancient History (one paper) provided that any candidate who offers alternative IV (*a*) below may only offer alternative III (*b*):
5

(i) *Athenian democracy in the Classical Age* (as specified for the Honour School of Literae Humaniores I. 7).

(ii) *Politics, Society and Culture from Nero to Hadrian* (as specified for the Honour School of Literae Humaniores I. 11).
10

(iii) *Religions in the Greek and Roman World, c.31* BC–AD 312 (as specified for the Honour School of Literae Humaniores I. 12).

(iv) *The Greeks and the Mediterranean World 950–500* BC, (IV.1 as specified for the Honour School of Literae Humaniores).

(v) *Art under the Roman Empire,* AD *14–337,* (IV.4 as specified for the Honour School of Literae Humaniores).
15

IV. SPECIAL SUBJECTS

Either, (*a*) any one of the Special Subjects as specified for the Honour School of History (one paper and one extended essay);

or, (*b*) any one of the following Special Subjects in Ancient History (two papers), provided that any candidate who offers alternative III (*a*) above may only offer alternative IV (*b*)
20

(i) *Alexander the Great and his Early Successors (336–302 BC)* (as specified for the Honour School of Literae Humaniores I. 8).

(ii) *Cicero: Politics and Thought in the Late Republic* (as specified for the Honour School of Literae Humaniores I. 9).
25

The individual detailed specifications and prescribed texts for the Further and Special subjects as specified for the Honour School of History will be given in the Handbook for the Honour School of History. This will be published by the History Board by Monday of Week 1 of the first Michaelmas Full Term of candidates' work for the Honour School.
30

Depending on the availability of teaching resources, not all Further and Special Subjects will be available to all candidates in every year. Candidates and Ancient and Modern History tutors will be circulated by the beginning of the fourth week of the first Hilary Full Term of their work for the Honour School with (i) details of any Further and Special Subjects which will not be available for the following year, (ii) the supplement to the Handbook for the Honour School of History. This book will contain full specifications and prescribed texts for any Further or Special Subjects specified for Modern History introduced for the following year, and any amendments to the specifications and prescribed texts for existing Further and Special Subjects approved by the History Board by its first meeting of the preceding Hilary Term.
35

40

V. DISCIPLINES OF HISTORY

Each candidate shall be examined in the *Disciplines of History* in accordance with regulation V of the Honour School of History.

VI. A THESIS FROM ORIGINAL RESEARCH
45

Regulation VI of the Honour School of History applies with the following modifications:

Cl. 3.(a) (For the avoidance of doubt) the Arnold Ancient History Prize and the Barclay Head Prize in Numismatics are to be read with the schedule.

Cl. 5. For 'Honour School of History' read 'Honour School of Ancient and Modern History'. For theses concerning the years before AD 285 read 'Chair of Examiners, Honour School of Ancient and Modern History' for 'Chair of the Examiners, Honour School of History'.

Cl. 8. For 'Chair of Examiners, Honour School of History' read 'Chair of Examiners, Honour School of Ancient and Modern History'.

VII. AN OPTIONAL ADDITIONAL THESIS

Regulation VII *An Optional Additional Thesis* of the Honour School of History shall apply with the following modifications:

Cl. 4. For dissertations concerning the years before AD 285 read 'Chair of Examiners, Honour School of Ancient and Modern History' for 'Chair of the Examiners, Honour School of History'.

Cl. 7. For 'Chair of Examiners, Honour School of History' read 'Chair of Examiners, Honours School of Ancient and Modern History'.

VIII. AN OPTIONAL LANGUAGE PAPER

Intermediate Ancient Greek *or* Intermediate Latin.

The individual specifications and prescribed texts for *Intermediate Ancient Greek* and *Intermediate Latin* will be published for candidates in the Ancient and Modern History Handbook by Monday of Week 0 of Michaelmas Term each year for the academic year ahead.

Any candidate whose native language is not English may bring a bilingual (native language to English) dictionary for use in either of the Intermediate Ancient Greek or Intermediate Latin papers.

SPECIAL REGULATIONS FOR THE HONOUR SCHOOL OF ARCHAEOLOGY AND ANTHROPOLOGY

A

1. The examination in the Honour School of Archaeology and Anthropology shall consist of such subjects in Archaeology and Anthropology as the Social Sciences Board shall prescribe by regulation from time to time.

2. No candidate shall be admitted to the examination in this school unless he or she has either passed or been exempted from the First Public Examination.

3. The examination shall be under the supervision of the Social Sciences Board. Under the overall direction of the board, the examination shall be administered by the School of Archaeology and the School of Anthropology, which shall jointly appoint a standing committee to advise the board as necessary in respect of this examination, and of Honour Moderations and the Preliminary Examination in Archaeology and Anthropology.

4. Candidates will be required to take part in approved fieldwork as an integral part of their course. The fieldwork requirement will normally have been discharged before the Long Vacation of the second year of the course.

B

Candidates are required to offer the following subjects:
1. Social analysis and interpretation.
2. Cultural representations, beliefs, and practices.
3. Landscape and Ecology.
4. Urbanisation and change in complex societies: comparative approaches.
5., 6. and 7. An approved combination of three optional subjects, from Schedule A (Anthropology) and Schedule B (Archaeology) [see below] or any other optional subject approved by the Committee for the School of Archaeology or the Committee for the School of Anthropology. To encourage a wide-ranging understanding of archaeology and anthropology, options shall be chosen in such a way that they constitute three independent, non-overlapping subjects.
8. A thesis, of not more than 15,000 words, which may be based on research in either archaeology or anthropology or on an interdisciplinary topic.
Candidates may be examined *viva voce*.

Schedule A (Anthropology)

(*a*) Culture and Society of West Africa
(*b*) South Asia
(*c*) Lowland South America

(*d*) Gender theories and realities cross cultural perspectives
(*e*) Understanding Museums and Collections
(*f*) Japanese society
(*g*) The anthropology of medicine
(*h*) Anthropology of Europe   5

Schedule B (Archaeology)

(*a*) The Later Prehistory of Europe
(*b*) Archaeology of Southern African Hunter-Gatherers
(*c*) Farming and early states in Sub-Saharan Africa
(*d*) Mesopotamia and Egypt from the emergence of complex society to *c.*2000 BC   10
(*e*) Mesopotamia and Egypt 1000–500 BC
(*f*) The Late Bronze Age and Early Iron Age Aegean
(*g*) The Greeks and the Mediterranean World *c.*950–500 BC
(*h*) Greek archaeology and art *c.*500–323 BC
(*i*) Roman Archaeology: Cities and settlement under the Empire   15
(*j*) Art under the Roman Empire, AD 14–336
(*k*) The emergence of Medieval Europe AD 400–900
(*l*) Byzantium: the transition from Antiquity to the Middle Ages, AD 500–1100
(*m*) Science-based methods in Archaeology
(*n*) Archaeology of Modern Human Origins   20
(*o*) Anglo-Saxon Society and Economy in the Early Christian Period
(*p*) Archaeology and Geographical Information Systems
(*q*) Landscape Archaeology
(*r*) Biological Techniques in Environmental Archaeology
(*s*) From hunting and gathering to states and empires in South-west Asia   25
(*t*) Physical Anthropology and Human Osteoarchaeology
(*u*) Minoan Crete
(*v*) Hellenistic Art and Archaeology, 330–30 BC

Because of the potential overlap in subject matter, approval will not be given to candidates who wish to select from Schedule B (Archaeology) either two of papers (*f*),   30
(*g*) or (*j*), or both papers (*k*) and (*l*).

Some options may not be available in every year. Candidates will be circulated a list of options offered for examination in the following two years of study by Friday of the eighth week of the Michaelmas Full Term.

Notice of the options to be offered by candidates must be submitted not later than   35
the Friday in the fourth week of the Michaelmas Full Term immediately preceding the examination.

Thesis

1. (*a*) The subject of every thesis shall to the satisfaction of the regulating authority concerned fall within the field of Archaeology or Anthropology or both.   40
   (*b*) The subject of the thesis may, but need not, overlap a subject or period on
   which the candidate offers papers. Candidates are warned, however, that
   they must avoid repetition in the papers of material used in their thesis, and
   that they will not be given credit for material extensively repeated.
   (*c*) Candidates must submit through their college, to the Chair of the   45
   Standing Committee for the Undergraduate Degree in Archaeology and
   Anthropology (c/o the Secretary of the Standing Committee, Institute of
   Archaeology, Beaumont Street), the title of the proposed thesis, together
   with (*a*) a synopsis of the subject in about 100 words; and (*b*) a letter of
   support from the tutor who will supervise the thesis, not later than Monday   50

of the noughth week of the Trinity Full Term preceding that in which the examination is held.

(*d*) The Standing Committee for the Undergraduate Degree in Archaeology and Anthropology will decide as soon as possible, and in every case by the end of the fifth week of the Michaelmas Full Term preceding the examination, whether or not to approve the title, and will advise candidates of its decision forthwith.

2. Every thesis must be the candidate's own work, although it is expected that tutors will discuss with candidates the proposed field of study, the sources available, and the method of presentation. Tutors may also read and comment on a first draft.

Candidates must sign a certificate stating that the thesis is their own work, and their tutors shall countersign the certificate affirming that they have assisted the candidate no more than these regulations allow. This certificate must be presented at the same time that the thesis is submitted, but in a separate sealed envelope addressed to the Chair of the Examiners.

3. Theses previously submitted for the Honour School of Archaeology and Anthropology may be resubmitted. No thesis will be accepted if it has already been submitted, wholly or substantially, for another final honour school or degree of this University or a degree of any other institution. The certificate must also contain confirmation that the thesis has not already been so submitted.

4. No thesis shall be ineligible because it has been submitted, in whole or in part, for any scholarship or prize of this University advertised in the *Oxford University Gazette*.

5. No thesis shall exceed 15,000 words in length, that limit to include all notes but not bibliographies, catalogues of material evidence, gazetteers or technical appendices.

All theses must be typed in double-spacing on one side of A4 paper, and must be bound or held firmly in a stiff cover. Two copies must be submitted to the chair of the examiners, and a third copy must be retained by the candidate. All copies must bear the candidate's examination number but not his or her name.

6. The thesis must be sent, not later than noon on Friday of the ninth week of Hilary Full Term preceding the examination, to the Chair of the Examiners, Honour School of Archaeology and Anthropology, Examination Schools, High Street, Oxford.

Candidates may be examined viva voce.

SPECIAL REGULATIONS FOR THE HONOUR SCHOOL OF BIOLOGICAL SCIENCES

A

1. The subject of the Honour School of Biological Sciences shall be the study of Biological Sciences.

2. No candidate shall be admitted to examination in this school unless he or she has either passed or been exempted from the First Public Examination.

3. The examination in this school shall be under the supervision of the Mathematical, Physical and Life Sciences Board, which shall prescribe the necessary regulations.

4. The examination in Biological Sciences shall consist of Part I (taken at a time not less than two terms after passing the First Public Examination) and Part II (taken at a time not less than five terms after passing the First Public Examination).

5. The name of a candidate shall not be published in a Results List until he or she has completed all parts of the examination. The examiners shall give due consideration to the performance in all parts of the respective examinations.

6. Candidates will be expected to show knowledge based on practical work. This requirement shall normally be satisfied by the examiners' assessment of the practical work done by candidates in Part I and Quantitative Methods, based on attendance records and/or marks awarded. Exceptionally, the examiners may require a candidate to submit a practical notebook. The penalties for unsatisfactory practical performance are given in detail below.

7. Part I may only be taken once, but no candidate who has completed the examination may be deemed to have failed. In Part II, a candidate who obtains only a pass, or fails to satisfy the examiners, may enter again for Part II of the examination on one, but no more than one, subsequent occasion.

B

1. The subjects of the examination shall be those prescribed in Parts I and II below.

2. The examination for Part I shall be taken at the start of Trinity Term of the candidate's second year. The examination for Part II shall be taken during Trinity Term of the candidate's third year. The dates of submission for the Part I practical work, Part II project work and Part II course assignments are those prescribed in Parts I and II below.

3. In the following, 'the FHS Handbook' refers to the Final Honour School Handbook, published annually at the start of Michaelmas Term of the candidate's second year. The 'Guidelines on Projects and Course Assignments' is published annually at the start of Trinity Term of the candidate's second year. Further details of the requirements for Parts I and II shall be set out in the Handbook and Guidelines.

4. The examiners will permit the use of any hand-held calculator subject to the conditions set out under the heading 'Use of calculators in examinations' in the Regulations for the Conduct of University Examinations.

5. *Supplementary Subjects*

(*a*) Candidates may, in addition to any one or more of the below-mentioned subjects, offer themselves for examination in one or more Supplementary Subjects.

(*b*) Candidates for Supplementary Subjects may offer themselves for examination in the academic year preceding that in which they take the Final Honour School.

(*c*) Candidates awarded a pass in a Supplementary Subject examination may not retake the same Supplementary Subject examination.

(*d*) The Supplementary Subjects available in any year will be published, together with the term in which each subject will be examined, in the *University Gazette* not later than the end of the Trinity Term of the academic year prior to delivery of the courses. Regulations governing the use of calculators in individual Supplementary Subjects will be notified when the availability of these subjects is published in the *Gazette*.

Part I

Assessment in Part I will consist of three written papers that will be taken at the start of Trinity Term in the second year as follows:

Paper 1: Evolution
Paper 2: Quantitative Methods
Paper 3: Essay Paper

In Paper 3, candidates will be required to answer four questions, with no more than one from each of the following themes: (i) Animal Behaviour; (ii) Adaptations to the Environment; (iii) Cell and Developmental Biology; (iv) Disease; (v) Ecology; (vi) Plants and People. Knowledge of first year coursework will be assumed.

The written papers for Part I may be taken only once.

Satisfactory performance in three practical blocks will also be required.

The examiners will issue a list of candidates deemed to have completed Part I of the examination, in the form of the completion of the three written papers, and satisfactory performance in the three practical blocks.

Under exceptional circumstances, candidates who have not been able to complete sufficient practicals may be allowed to fulfill the practical requirement in their third year.

Part II

In Part II, Candidates will select from a number of Options, and complete a research project and two course assignments. The Options may be varied from time to time by the Biological Science Steering Committee, and such variations shall be notified by publication in Part II of the FHS Handbook by the end of Week 8 of Hilary Term of the academic year preceding the first examination of the changed options. Each candidate will be expected to have studied at least six Options in order to address the synoptic questions of Paper 4, and to have prepared sufficient of those Options in depth to be able to address the requirements of Papers 5–7.

Assessment in Part II will consist of four written papers, each of three hours' duration, submission of a research project dissertation, and two course assignments, one of which will be examined as an oral presentation.

1. *Written papers*

Four written papers, each of three hours, will be set during Trinity Term of the   5
third year. The papers will be as follows:

Paper 4: General Paper
Paper 5: Long Essay Paper
Paper 6: Short Essay Paper
Paper 7: Data Interpretation Paper   10

In the General Paper, candidates will be required to answer two questions and will be expected to bring together knowledge of the different areas of Biology covered in the Options. In the Long Essay Paper, candidates will be required to answer three questions, with no more than one from any specific Option. In the Short Essay Paper, candidates will be required to answer six questions, with no more than one from any   15
specific Option. In the Data Interpretation Paper, candidates will be required to answer four questions.

2. *Project dissertation*

(i) *Form and subject of the project*

The project shall consist in original experiments, fieldwork or computer-based   20
research project in any area of biology done by the candidate alone or in collaboration with others (where such collaboration is, for instance, needed to produce results in the time available). When choosing a research project, candidates must bear in mind the prohibition on duplicating material in different parts of the examination.

(ii) *Registration*   25

Candidates must register the provisional title of their project and the name of their supervisor to the Examinations Co-ordinator no later than noon on Friday of Week 8 of Hilary Term of their second year. Candidates must submit their completed safety registration form to the appropriate Departmental Safety Officer by the same deadline.   30

(iii) *Residence*

Candidates undertaking project work outside of Oxford will be permitted by the Chair of the Teaching Steering Committee, subject to the written approval also of the Senior Tutor of the candidate's college, to spend a maximum of two weeks outside of Oxford during Trinity Term of their second year working at a supervised field site or   35
another university / institution in the UK or overseas, in accordance with clause 2.8 of the First and Second Public Examination regulations pertaining to residence. Candidates will still be liable for their College battels, if applicable, during this time.

(iv) *Examination*

Candidates shall submit to the examiners a dissertation based on their project   40
according to guidelines that will be published by the Biological Sciences Steering Committee in Week 1 of Trinity Term in the academic year preceding the examination. The project dissertation shall be of not more than 7,000 words, excluding any tables, figures, or references, and must be prefaced by an Abstract of not more than 250 words, to be included within the word limit.   45

(v) *Submission and assessment of project-based written work*

The project report (two copies) must be legibly typed or word-processed (double line spacing to be used throughout) on one side only of A4 paper, held firmly in a stiff cover, and submitted on or before 12 noon on the Thursday of Week 2 of Hilary Full Term of the academic year in which Part II of the examination is taken. It must be   50 addressed to the Examination Schools, High Street, Oxford, for the Chair of Examiners for the Final Honour School of Biological Sciences. Each project report shall be accompanied by a certificate signed by the candidate indicating that the project report is the candidate's own work. This certificate shall be submitted separately in a sealed envelope addressed to the Chair of Examiners. No report will be accepted if it has already been submitted, wholly or substantially, for another Honour School or degree of this University, or for a degree of any other institution.

In all cases, the examiners shall obtain and consider a written report from each supervisor indicating the extent of the input made by the candidate to the outcome of the project and also any unforeseen difficulties associated with the project (e.g. unexpected technical issues or problems in the availability of materials, equipment, or literature or other published data). Material in a candidate's dissertation must not duplicate material that has been included in the submitted course assignments.

3. *Course assignments*

(i) *Form and subject of the Course assignments*

Each candidate must complete two course assignments. One assignment shall be examined by means of a written essay, and one shall be examined by means of an oral presentation as set out below. The precise format of the course assignment may vary between Options and will be specified by the Biological Sciences Steering Committee.

The written essay shall be of not more than 3,000 words, excluding any tables, figures, or references, and must be prefaced by an Abstract of not more than 250 words, to be included within the word limit. All sources used in the essay must be fully documented. The written essay (two copies) must be legibly typed or word-processed on one side only of A4 paper, held firmly in a stiff cover. The oral presentation shall be a maximum of fifteen minutes in duration, followed by ten minutes of questions. The oral presentation should use appropriate audio-visual aids as specified in the Guidelines on Projects and Course Assignments. Candidates shall also submit an Abstract of the oral presentation of not more than 500 words. The Abstract (two copies) must be legibly typed or word-processed on one side only of A4 paper.

Candidates may discuss the proposed topic for both the written essay and the oral presentation, the sources available, and the method of presentation with an adviser. The adviser for the written essay must also read and comment on a first draft. Candidates shall not deal with substantially the same material in their course assignments as is covered in their project report.

(ii) *Registration*

Each assignment will be on a topic proposed by the student and approved by the Chair of the Biological Sciences Steering Committee. The approval of assignments shall be given not later than Friday of the seventh week of the Michaelmas Full Term of the academic year in which the examination is taken.

(iii) *Authorship*

For each assignment, candidates must sign a certificate stating that the assignment is their own work. This certificate must be submitted at the same time as the essay and abstract in a sealed envelope addressed to the Chair of Examiners.

(iv) *Submission*

The written course assignment (two copies), the abstract for the oral presentation (two copies) and the sealed envelope containing the certificate of authorship, should be submitted in an envelope clearly labelled with the candidate's number by noon on Friday of oth week of the Trinity Term of the academic year in which the examination is taken. The envelope should be addressed to the Examination Schools, High Street, Oxford for the Chair of the Examiners in the Final Honour School of

Biological Sciences. Assignments previously submitted for the Honour School of
Biological Sciences may be resubmitted. No assignment will be accepted if it has
already been submitted, wholly or substantially, for another degree in the University
or elsewhere; and each certificate must also contain a confirmation that the assignment has not already been so submitted. An assignment remains eligible even if it has
been submitted, in whole or in part, for any scholarship or prize in this University.
Each essay and each abstract shall clearly indicate on the first page the part of the
examination and the subject under which the assignment is submitted. Further
guidance on the essay and oral presentation will be published in the FHS Handbook.

PART I AND II

Practical Coursework
   All candidates shall be assessed as to their practical ability through coursework.
Coursework includes a range of laboratory practicals, computer-based exercises or
field work, as set out by the Biological Sciences Steering Committee. The following
provisions apply:
   (*a*) The Chair of the Steering Committee, or a deputy, shall make available to the
examiners, at the end of the first week of the term in which the written examinations
in Part II are held, records showing the extent to which each candidate has completed
the prescribed coursework in Part I to a satisfactory standard.
   (*b*) The examiners may request coursework from any candidate. Such candidates
will be named in a list posted by the day of the first written paper in Part II of the
examination. Each notebook submitted shall be accompanied by a certificate signed
by the candidate indicating that the notebook is the candidate's own work.
   (*c*) In assessing the record of coursework undertaken, the examiners shall have
regard to the attendance record of the candidates at the classes provided, and to the
marks awarded for the classes provided. Candidates whose overall coursework
performance is not satisfactory may have their degree class reduced. If the work is
judged by the examiners to be insufficient to warrant the award of Honours they
may either be deemed to have failed the examination, or may, at the discretion of the
examiners, be awarded a Pass.

SPECIAL REGULATIONS FOR THE HONOUR SCHOOL OF CELL AND SYSTEMS BIOLOGY

A

1. The subject of the Honour School of Cell and Systems Biology shall be all aspects of the scientific study of the development and functioning of living organisms with particular but not exclusive reference to mammals.

2. No candidate shall be admitted to examination in this school unless he or she has either passed or been exempted from the First Public Examination.

3. The examination in this school shall be under the supervision of the Medical Sciences Board, which shall make regulations concerning it.

4. The examination in Cell and Systems Biology shall consist of two parts: Part I and Part II.

5. No candidate shall be admitted to the Part II examination in this school unless he or she has passed the Part I examination in this school.

6. The examination for Part I will take place during Week 0 or 1 in Trinity Term of the candidate's second year. The examination for Part II will take place during Trinity Term of the candidate's third year.

7. For the Part I options provided by the Department of Experimental Psychology, candidates shall be examined by such of the Public Examiners in the Honour School of Experimental Psychology as may be required. For the written papers in Part II which are as specified for the Honour School of Medical Sciences, and the Research Project, candidates shall be examined by such of the Public Examiners in the Honour School of Medical Sciences as may be required.

8. In addition to the form of examination prescribed below, candidates may be examined viva voce in either part of the examination.

9. Candidates for Part II may offer themselves for examination in one or more of the *Supplementary Subjects*. The *Supplementary Subjects* available in any year will be notified to students annually during Trinity Term. Account shall be taken of a candidate's results in any such subject in the candidate's overall classification in the

Honour School of Cell and Systems Biology. Candidates awarded a pass in a Supplementary Subject examination may not retake the same Supplementary Subject examination.

B

PART I

1. Candidates will attend lectures and practicals in options selected from a list published in the Medical Sciences Teaching Centre by the end of Week 8 of Hilary Term in the year preceding the examination. Each option will have a number of units ascribed to it. Candidates will be required to study options totalling ten units. The list published in the Medical Sciences Teaching Centre and the handbook for the course will specify how many units are assigned to each option, and which options are recommended to proceed to particular advanced options in Part II.

2. Two written papers will be set:
   (i) Paper I will be a three-hour examination comprising a selection of questions requiring short answers. Candidates will be required to answer those questions relating to their chosen options.
   (ii) Paper II will be a two-hour essay paper. Candidates will be required to answer questions from a selection relating to the different options that they have studied.

3. If, in Paper II of the Part I Examination, a candidate presents essentially the same information on more than one occasion, then credit will be given in only the first instance.

4. Candidates will be required to undertake practical work as specified in the course handbook which will constitute part of the examination. The Course Director, or a deputy, shall make available to the Examiners, at the end of Week 0 of Trinity Term in which the examinations are held, evidence showing the extent and the standard to which each candidate has completed the prescribed practical work. Practical work cannot normally be retaken. Candidates whose attendance or performance is deemed unsatisfactory will forfeit one quarter of the marks in the Part I examination, the outcome of which will be carried forward to the Part II Examination.

PART II

1. Each candidate must offer timed written examination papers and a project report based on a research project.

2. The options of the school shall be:
   A Neuroscience
   B Molecular Medicine
   C Cardiovascular, Renal and Respiratory Biology
   D Infection and Immunity
   E Cellular Physiology and Pharmacology
   as specified for the Honour School of Medical Sciences.

3. Each candidate must offer 4 written papers: Paper 1 for *two* chosen options, Paper 2, and Paper 3 as specified for the Honour School of Medical Sciences, except that Paper 1 for the second chosen option will require candidates to answer 2 questions in 2 hours.

4. The Research Project

The research project will normally be carried out in the Trinity Term of the candidate's second year and the Michaelmas Term of the candidate's third year.

(i) *Form, subject and approval of the project*

The project shall consist of original experiments done by the candidate alone or in collaboration with others (where such collaboration is, for instance, needed to produce results in the time available).

A list of potential supervisors and their research interests shall be published no later than the end of Week 6 of Hilary Term in the academic year preceding the examination. Candidates should normally discuss their intended project with the potential supervisor and their tutor before submitting a project outline to the course administrator no later than noon, Friday of Week 0 of Trinity Term of the academic year preceding the examination. Decision on the application shall be made by the Course Director, or a deputy, and communicated to candidates by Friday of Week 1 of the same term.

(ii) *Submission of the Project Report*

The length and format of the Project Report based on the project shall be according to guidelines published by the Medical Sciences Board in Week 6 of Hilary Term of the academic year preceding the year of examination. Material in a candidate's Project Report must not be duplicated in any answer given in a written examination paper. Project Reports previously submitted for the Honour School of Cell and Systems Biology may be resubmitted. No Project Report will be accepted if it has already been submitted, wholly or substantially, for another Honour School or degree of this University, or for a degree of any other institution.

Project Reports (three copies) must be sent to the Chair of Examiners, Honour School of Cell and Systems Biology, Examination Schools, High Street, Oxford, not later than noon on the Friday of Week 8 of Hilary Term in the academic year in which the candidate intends to take the examination. The copies shall be accompanied (in a separate sealed envelope) by a certificate signed by each candidate indicating that the research project is the candidate's own work and that the supervisor has commented on at least one draft of the Project Report. In the case of laboratory-based work that has been produced in collaboration, the certificate shall indicate the extent of the candidate's own contribution. Each candidate will be required to submit a draft of their Project Report to their supervisor no later than two weeks before the specified deadline for submission to Schools.

In exceptional cases, where through unforeseen circumstances a laboratory-based project produces no useable results (i.e. not even negative or ambiguous results), the candidate may apply through his or her college to the Course Director, or a deputy, for permission to submit a concise review of the scientific context and the aims of the work that was attempted in place of the normal Project Report. Such an application must be accompanied by supporting evidence from the supervisor of the project. The concise review to be submitted in such circumstances should be comparable in length to the Report of a successful laboratory-based project and will be presented orally to the examiners and be examined viva voce in the usual way for a research project. The examiners will be advised that substantive results could not be produced.

In all cases, the examiners shall obtain and consider a written report from each supervisor indicating the extent of the input made by the candidate to the outcome of the project and also any unforeseen difficulties associated with the project (e.g. unexpected technical issues or problems in the availability of materials, equipment, or literature or other published data).

(iii) *Oral Assessment of Project-based Written Work*

In addition, each candidate shall make a brief oral presentation of their project to a group of two examiners (or examiners and assessors appointed to ensure an adequate representation of expertise), after which, the candidate shall be examined viva voce on the project. The form of the presentation to the examiners shall be specified in guidelines published by the Medical Sciences Board.

5. If, in the Part II Examination, a candidate presents essentially the same information on more than one occasion, then credit will be given in only the first instance.

6. The weighting of marks for the five exercises required of each candidate shall be 25 per cent for the Project Report based on the research project, 15 per cent for Papers 1, 2 and 3, except that Paper 1 for the second chosen option will carry 10 per cent of the marks. Marks carried forward from the Part I examination will account for the remaining 20 per cent for the candidate's overall result for the Honour School of Cell and Systems Biology.

SPECIAL REGULATIONS FOR THE HONOUR SCHOOL OF CHEMISTRY

For candidates embarking on the Honour School in or after October 2010, taking Part IA in or after 2011, Part IB in or after 2012, and Part II in or after 2013

A

1. The subject of the Honour School of Chemistry shall be the study of Chemistry.

2. No candidate shall be admitted to examination in this school unless he or she has either passed or been exempted from the First Public Examination.

3. The examination in this school shall be under the supervision of the Mathematical, Physical and Life Sciences Board, which shall prescribe the necessary regulations.

4. The examination in Chemistry shall consist of three parts: IA, IB, II.

5. No candidate may present him or herself for examination in Part II unless he or she has been adjudged worthy of honours by the examiners in Part I (Part IA and Part IB).

6. A candidate shall not be awarded a classified degree until he or she has completed all parts of the examination, and has been adjudged worthy of honours by the examiners in Part I (Part IA and Part IB) and Part II of the examination in consecutive years. The Examiners shall give due consideration to the performance in all parts of the respective examinations.

7. The examiners shall be entitled to award a Pass to candidates in Part I (Part IA and Part IB) who have reached a standard considered adequate but who have not been adjudged worthy of honours.

8. Part IA and Part II shall be entered on one occasion only. Marks obtained at Part IA will be carried over to Part IB. A candidate who obtains only a pass, or fails to satisfy the examiners, may enter again for Part IB of the examination on one, but no more than one, subsequent occasion subject to the following limitations. Part IB consists of two parts, a set of written examinations and the practical course. A candidate may fail to be awarded honours at Part I for any of the following reasons:

(i) The overall mark at Part I is insufficient for honours, but the honours practical requirement set out in cl. 11 below is complete and the practical mark is sufficient for honours. In this case the candidate will only be permitted to re-enter the Part IB written examinations, and the Practical mark will be carried forward.

(ii) The overall mark at Part I is insufficient for honours, and although the marks for the Part I written examination are sufficient for honours and sufficient practicals have been completed to fulfil the requirement set out in cl. 11 below, the marks for the practical course are not sufficient for honours. In this case the candidate will only be permitted to re-enter to repeat failed practicals. The marks for the written examination will be carried forward.

(iii) The overall mark at Part I is insufficient for honours, and although sufficient practicals have been completed to fulfil the requirement set out in cl. 11 below, the marks for both the written examination and the practical course are insufficient for honours. In this case, the candidate must re-enter both the Part IB written examinations and repeat failed practicals.

(iv) The practical requirement set out in cl. 11 below is incomplete, but the marks in the Part I written examination are sufficient for honours. In this case the candidate will only be permitted to re-enter to complete the practical requirement to honours standard. The written examination marks will be carried forward.

9. A candidate adjudged worthy of Honours in Part I (Parts IA and IB) and worthy of Honours in Part II may supplicate for the Degree of Master of Chemistry, provided that the candidate has fulfilled all the conditions for admission to a degree of the University.

10. A candidate who passes Part I (Parts IA and IB) or who is adjudged worthy of Honours in Part I (Parts IA and IB), but who does not enter Part II, or fails to obtain Honours in Part II, is permitted to supplicate for the degree of Bachelor of Arts in Chemistry (pass or unclassified Honours, as appropriate); provided that no such candidate may later enter or re-enter the Part II year or supplicate for the degree of Master of Chemistry; and provided in each case that the candidate has fulfilled all the conditions for admission to a degree of the University.

11. Candidates will be required to complete a core practical requirement: provided that this requirement may be reduced for candidates who have passed one or more supplementary subjects. Details of the requirements and the eligible Supplementary Subjects shall be prescribed in the Course Handbook. Exceptionally, the examiners may require a candidate to take a practical examination.

B

1. In the following, 'the Course Handbook' refers to the Chemistry Undergraduate Course Handbook, posted annually at the start of Michaelmas Term by the Faculty of Chemistry on the website at: www.chem.ox.ac.uk/teaching/ UndergradHandbook.pdf

2. The examiners will permit the use of any hand-held calculator subject to the conditions set out under the heading 'Use of calculators in examinations' in the *Regulations for the Conduct of University Examinations* and further elaborated in the Course Handbook.

3. The syllabus for Parts IA and IB shall be published in the Course Handbook.

4. *Supplementary Subjects*

   (i) Candidates may offer themselves for examination in one or more Supplementary Subjects, provided that no more than three Supplementary Subjects may be offered in total.

   (ii) Candidates awarded a pass in a Supplementary Subject examination may not retake the same Supplementary Subject examination.

   (iii) Supplementary Subjects may be offered in all or any of the years in which candidates take any Part of the Second Public Examination.

   (iv) The Supplementary Subjects available in any year will be published, together with the term in which each subject will be examined, in the Course Handbook in the academic year in which the courses are delivered. Regulations governing the use of calculators in individual Supplementary Subjects will be notified in the Course Handbook.

   (v) Where a Language Supplementary Subject is available, entry of candidates for examination in Language Supplementary Subjects shall require the approval of the Chair of the Chemistry Academic Board and the Director of the Language Centre or their deputies. Approval shall not be given to candidates who have, at the start of the course, already acquired demonstrable skills exceeding the target learning outcomes in the chosen language.

   (vi) In determining the place of candidates in the Results List the Examiners shall take account of distinction in any Supplementary Subjects which have been offered.

Parts IA and IB

In the Part IA examination, one compulsory two and a half hour paper will be set in each of Inorganic, Organic, and Physical Chemistry, covering the fundamental aspects of material from Years 1 and 2.

In the Part IB examination, there will be two compulsory two and a half hour papers in each of Inorganic, Organic, and Physical Chemistry, covering material in the core courses of Years 1-3. In addition, there will one three-hour Option Paper, which will examine the content of the Option courses, but will also require knowledge of core course material. The Option Paper will offer a choice of three questions from at least twelve, and ten minutes reading time will be allowed.

Heads of the three main Sections of the Chemistry Department, or their deputies, and the IT Training Officer, shall make available to the Examiners records showing the extent to which each candidate has pursued an adequate course in laboratory work and in IT. Only that work completed and marked by 5 p.m. of the Friday of the fourth week of the Trinity Term in which the candidate takes Part IB shall be included in these records. The Examiners will require evidence of satisfactory completion of the core practical requirement, or the reduced requirement in the case of candidates who have passed one or more Supplementary Subjects. In determining the place of candidates in the Results List the Examiners shall take account of the marks reported for the core practical requirement.

Satisfactory completion of the prescribed core practical requirement, (or of a reduced core requirement if a Supplementary Subject is passed), is an absolute requirement for the award of Honours at Part IB and for progression to Part II. Satisfactory completion of a smaller core practical requirement will be required for the award of a Pass degree at Part I. The details of these threshold requirements shall be published in the Course Handbook.

Candidates may be examined viva voce at the Examiners' discretion in Part IB, but not in Part IA.

Candidates are not permitted to enter their names for examination in Part IA until they have entered upon the fifth term from their matriculation.

Candidates are not permitted to enter their names for examination in Part IB until they have entered upon the eighth term from their matriculation, or before sitting all the papers set for Part IA in a previous year.

PART II

Candidates, who must have been judged worthy of Honours by the Examiners in Part I (Part IA and Part IB) in a previous year, must present a record of investigations carried out under the supervision of one of the following:

(i) any professor, reader, university lecturer, departmental demonstrator, or senior research officer who is also an official member of the Faculty of Chemistry;

(ii) any other person approved by the Chemistry Academic Board.

In case (ii), a co-supervisor as defined under (i) must also be approved, and so must the proposed project. Applications for project approval, including the names of the supervisor and a co-supervisor and a short project summary (not more than 250 words), should be sent by the student to the Chemistry Academic Board, c/o Chemistry Faculty Office, Inorganic Chemistry Laboratory, South Parks Road, by Friday of the first week of Hilary Full Term preceding the intended Part II year. Students who are uncertain whether their intended Part II supervision is in category (ii) above should consult their College Tutor or the Chemistry Faculty Office.

Candidates shall be examined viva voce, and, if the Examiners think fit, in writing, on their investigations and matters relevant thereto. The Examiners may obtain a report on the work of each candidate from the supervisor concerned.

Heads of the three main Sections of the Chemistry Department, or their deputies, shall make available to the Chemistry Faculty office not later than the Friday of the fourth week of the Hilary Full Term records giving notice of the subject of investigations for each candidate working in their section, together with evidence (a) that the subject has been approved by the candidate's supervisor and (b), if it is to be carried out in a laboratory, that the person in charge of the laboratory considers that it is suitable for investigation in that laboratory. Candidates doing their project outside the Chemistry Department are responsible for ensuring that the subject of their investigations is submitted to the Chemistry Faculty office not later than the Friday of the fourth week of the Hilary Full Term.

A candidate for Part II is required to send in, not later than noon on the Friday of the seventh week of the Trinity Full Term, a record of the investigations which he or she has carried out under the direction of his or her supervisor. Such record, which should conform in length and format with guidance which the examiners may give, should be addressed 'The Examination Schools, Oxford, for the Chair of the Examiners in Part II of the Final Honour School of Chemistry' and should have included a Declaration of Authorship signed by the candidate that it is his or her own work.

Candidates for Part II are required to keep statutory residence and pursue their investigations in Oxford during a period of at least thirty-eight weeks in three terms, i.e. from the third Thursday before Michaelmas Full Term to the third Tuesday after Michaelmas Full Term; from the second Tuesday before Hilary Full Term to the Wednesday following Palm Sunday (i.e. the Sunday before Easter Day); and from the Monday following Easter Monday to the third Saturday after Trinity Full Term; provided that the divisional board shall have power to permit candidates to vary the dates of their residence so long as the overall programme requirement is met.

SPECIAL REGULATIONS FOR THE HONOUR SCHOOL OF CLASSICAL ARCHAEOLOGY AND ANCIENT HISTORY

A

1. The Honour School of Classical Archaeology and Ancient History shall consist of such subjects as the Social Sciences Board and the Board of the Faculty of Classics shall jointly prescribe by regulation from time to time.

2. No candidate shall be admitted to the examination in this school without either having passed, or having been exempted from, the First Public Examination.

3. The examination shall be under the joint supervision of the Board of the Faculty of Classics and the Committee for the School of Archaeology, and they shall appoint a joint standing committee, consisting of three representatives of each body, to consider matters relating to the examination and to Honour Moderations and the Preliminary Examination in Classical Archaeology and Ancient History. Whenever any matter cannot be resolved, the Committee for the School of Archaeology and the Board of the Faculty of Classics shall themselves hold a joint meeting and resolve it by majority vote.

4. Candidates shall be required to take part in approved fieldwork as an integral part of the course. The fieldwork requirement shall normally have been discharged before the Long Vacation following the second year of the course.

Note: It cannot be guaranteed that university lectures or classes or college teaching will be available in all subjects in every academic year. Candidates are advised to consult their tutors about the availability of teaching when selecting their subjects.

B

1. Each candidate shall offer the following elements:

I-VI Six papers from the following options, of which at least one must be taken from each of A, B and C, and no more than one from F. At least two of the six papers must be archaeological (from B and D), and at least two must be historical (from C and E), unless a language paper is taken, as this can replace one of the archaeological or historical requirements.

Any candidate whose native language is not English may bring a bilingual (native language to English) dictionary for use in any examination paper where candidates are required to translate Ancient Greek and/or Latin texts into English.

A. Integrated Classes

> **[Until 1 October 2014**: i. *Early Greece and the Mediterranean, c. 950–550 BC: archaeology and history*

Candidates will be expected to show knowledge of the material and written evidence for the Greek world and the areas of contact between Greek and other   5
Mediterranean peoples. Areas of emphasis will include the development of Athens and Attica; the non-Greek states bordering the Mediterranean; the relationships between them and the Greeks; Greek settlement overseas; trade and coinage; problems of method in history and archaeology; and problems of chronology.]

> **[From 1 October 2014**: i. *Rome, Italy and the Hellenistic East c. 300–100 BC:*   10
> *archaeology and history*

The course studies the political and cultural interaction and conflict between the Hellenistic East and Roman Italy. Candidates will be expected to show knowledge of the material, visual, and written evidence of the period and to show ability in interpreting it in its archaeological and historical contexts. Candidates should be   15
familiar with the relevant archaeology of the following cities and sites: Pella, Alexandria, Pergamon, Ai Khanoum, Athens, Priene, Delos, Praeneste, Pompeii, Rome.]

> **[Until 1 October 2014**: ii. *Rome, Italy and the Hellenistic East c. 300–100 BC:*
> *archaeology and history*   20

The course studies the political and cultural interaction and conflict between the Hellenistic East and Roman Italy. Candidates will be expected to show knowledge of the material, visual, and written evidence of the period and to show ability in interpreting it in its archaeological and historical contexts. Candidates should be familiar with the relevant archaeology of the following cities and   25
sites Pella, Alexandria, Pergamon, Ai Khanoum, Athens, Priene, Delos, Praeneste, Pompeii, Rome.]

> **[From 1 October 2014**: ii. *Imperial Culture and Society, c. AD 50–150: archaeology*
> *and history*

The course studies the complex social history and political culture of Rome and   30
leading cities under the Empire, from the last Julio-Claudians to the Antonines, through the rich and diverse body of written and material evidence that survives from this period – monuments, art, inscriptions, and literary texts from a wide variety of genres.

Candidates should be familiar with the archaeology and major monuments of the   35
period at the following sites and cities: Rome, Pompeii, Ostia, Beneventum, Tivoli; Fishbourne, Vindolanda, Hadrian's Wall; Timgad, Djemila; Athens, Aphrodisias, Ephesos, Masada. They should also show knowledge of written texts as specified for this course in the handbook for the Honour School of Classical Archaeology and Ancient History.]   40

B. Core Papers: Classical Archaeology

> **[From 1 October 2014**: i. *The Greeks and the Mediterranean World,*
> *c. 950–500 BC*

As specified for the Honour School of Literae Humaniores, subject IV.1.]
i. [ii.] *Greek Art and Archaeology c. 500–300 BC*   45
   As specified for the Honour School of Literae Humaniores, subject IV.2.
ii. [iii.] *Cities and Settlement under the Empire*
   As specified for the Honour School of Literae Humaniores, subject IV.4.

iii. [iv.] *Art under the Roman Empire, 14–337*
    As specified for the Honour School of Literae Humaniores, subject IV.4
    [Until 1 October 2014: iv. *The Archaeology of the Late Roman Empire, AD 284–641*

The paper studies the archaeology and art of the Roman Empire from Diocletian through the death of Heraclius. Subjects include urban change; development of the countryside in the east; industry; patterns of trade; persistence of pagan art; and the impact of Christianity (church building, pilgrimage, monasticism) on architecture and art. The main sites to be studied are Rome, Constantinople, Trier, Verulamium, Ravenna, Justiniana Prima, Caesarea Maritima, Scythopolis, Jerusalem, and sites in the Roman provinces of Syria and Palestine.]

C. Core Papers: Ancient History
  i. *Thucydides and the Greek World 479–403 BC*
    As specified for the Honour School of Literae Humaniores, subject 1.2, except that candidates in Classical Archaeology and Ancient History will answer four questions.
 ii. *Alexander the Great and his Early Successors*
    As specified for the Honour School of Literae Humaniores, subject I. 8.
iii. *Roman History 146–46 BC*
    As specified for the Honour School of Literae Humaniores, subject I.5; candidates in Classical Archaeology and Ancient History will answer four questions.
    [Until 1 October 2014: iv. *Politics, Culture and Society from Nero to Hadrian*

    As specified for the Honour School of Literae Humaniores, subject I. 11.]

D. Further Papers: Classical Archaeology
  i. *Egyptian Art and Architecture*
 ii. *The Archaeology of Minoan Crete, 3200–1000 BC*
iii. *The Formation of the Islamic World, AD 550–950*
 iv. *Science-Based Methods in Archaeology*
  v. *Greek and Roman Coins*

Candidates will be expected to show knowledge of the principal developments in coinage from its beginnings c.600 BC until the reign of Diocletian (AD 284–305). Emphasis will be placed on the ways in which numismatic evidence may be used to address questions of historical and archaeological interest.

 vi. *Mediterranean Maritime Archaeology*
    [From 1 October 2014: vii. *The Archaeology of the Late Roman Empire, AD 284–641*
The paper studies the archaeology and art of the Roman Empire from Diocletian through the death of Heraclius. Subjects include urban change; development of the countryside in the east; industry; patterns of trade; persistence of pagan art; and the impact of Christianity (church building, pilgrimage, monasticism) on architecture and art. The main sites to be studied are Rome, Constantinople, Trier, Verulamium, Ravenna, Justiniana Prima, Caesarea Maritima, Scythopolis, Jerusalem and sites in the Roman provinces of Syria and Palestine.]

E. Further Papers: Ancient History
  i. *Epigraphy of the Greek and/or Roman World*
    The course focuses on the inscribed text, mainly on stone and bronze, as monument, physical object and medium of information, and it explores the evidence of particular inscriptions, or groups of inscriptions, for the political, social, and economic history of communities in the ancient world. Candidates may show knowledge

of either Archaic-Classical Greek, or Hellenistic, or Republican Roman or Imperial Roman inscriptions. They will be expected to show knowledge of epigraphic texts in Greek and/or in Latin (though all texts will be accompanied by translations).

   ii. *Athenian Democracy in the Classical Age*
     As specified for the Honour School of Literae Humaniores, subject I. 7.

   iii. *Sexuality and Gender in Greece and Rome*
     As specified for the Honour School of Literae Humaniores, subject I. 13.

   iv. *Cicero: Politics and Thought in the Late Republic*
     As specified for the Honour School of Literae Humaniores, subject I. 10.

   v. *Religions in the Greek and Roman World, 31 BC–AD 312*
     As specified for the Honour School of Literae Humaniores, subject I.12.

   vi. *St Augustine and the Last Days of Rome, 370–430*
     Examined by a single 3-hour written paper combining passages for comment and essay questions.

Augustine, *Against the Academics* 2.2.4–6, 3.18–19, tr. J. O'Meara, *Ancient Christian Writers* 23 (Washington, DC, 1951).

  Confessions, Books I–X, tr. H. Chadwick (Oxford, 1991), pp. 1–220 (recommended to buy)

  City of God, Books XIV, XIX tr. H. Bettenson (Harmondsworth, 1972), pp. 547–94; 842–94

  Letters 10, 15, 16, 17, 188, 209, 262, tr. E. Hill *The Works of St Augustine* (New York, 2003–04), II/1, 33–5, 45–50; II/3, 252–59, 394–97; II/4, 203–09

  Letters 10*, 12*, 20*, 24*, tr. R. Eno, *Saint Augustine: Letters 1*–29** (Washington, DC, 1989), pp. 75–80, 100–08, 133–49, 172–4 (Also online via Questia)

  Sermons 198 (Dolbeau 26), 355, 356, tr. E. Hill (New York, 1997) III/11, 180–228, III/10, 166–84

  Sermon on the Sack of Rome, tr. M. O'Reilly (Washington, DC 1955)

Ammianus Marcellinus, *The Later Roman Empire* [*Res Gestae*], Book 14.6 27.3, 6–7, 9, 11 28.1, 4 29. 2; 30. 5–9, 31.1–2, 12–14, tr. J. C. Rolfe, Loeb Classical Library 3 vols. (Cambridge, MA, 1935). I, 35–53, III, 13–21, 45–51, 57–63, 73–77, 87–123, 137–61, 215–33, 335–73, 377–409, 463–89 (Also online at http://penelope.uchicago.edu)

Ausonius, *The Professors of Bordeaux*, tr. H.G. Evelyn White, Loeb Classical Library 2 vols. (Cambridge Mass., 1921), I, 97–139.

  Letters 12 and 22, tr. White, II, 33–41, 71–8 (Also online at http://www.archive.org)

Symmachus, *Letters*, Book I. 3, 10, 12, 14, 20, 23, 32, 43, 47–9, 51–3, 58–9, 61, 99; Book III. 36; Book VI. 67 (special translation)

  Relatio 3, tr. B. Croke & J. Harries, *Religious Conflict in Fourth-Century Rome* (Sydney, 1982), Document 40, pp. 35–40

  Relationes 10–12, tr. R.H. Barrow, *Prefect and Emperor* (Oxford, 1973), pp. 73–81

Ambrose, *Letters* 17 and 18 (now known as 72 and 73), tr. Croke & Harries, *Religious Conflict*, Documents 39 and 41, pp. 30–35, 40–50

  Letters 75, 75a, 76, 77, tr. W. Liebeschuetz *Ambrose of Milan : political letters and speeches* (Liverpool, 2005/2010), pp.124–73

Jerome, Letters 22, 45, 107, tr. F.A. Wright, *Jerome: Select Letters* Loeb Classical Library (London, 1933), pp. 531–59, 177–79, 229–65 (online at http://www.archive.org)

  Letter 130, tr. *Nicene and Post Nicene* Fathers, II.6, 261–272 (Online at http://www.ccel.org)

Pelagius, *Letter to Demetrias*, tr. B. R. Rees (Woodbridge, 1991), pp. 29–70

  The Life of Melania the Younger, tr. E. Clark (Lewiston, NY, 1984), pp. 25–82

The Theodosian Code, tr. C. Pharr (Princeton, 1952), Book IX. Title 16. paras 4–11
IX. 17.6–7 XII.1 56, 63, 77, 87, 98, 104, 110, 112, 116, 122 XIII. 3, 6–12 XIV. 9.1 XVI.
1.2, 4 XVI. 2.20 XVI. 5.3, 6–7, 9 XVI. 10.4–13

Dessau, *Inscriptiones Latinae Selectae*, nos. 754, 1256, 1258–61, 1265, 294–67, 2951
Diehl, *Inscriptiones Latinae Christianae Veteres*, nos. 63, 104 and 1700   5
Monica's epitaph

F. Classical Languages
i. *Intermediate Ancient Greek*
(This paper is available only to those undergraduates who offered Mods Paper
III–IV C.I and, with the permission of the Standing Committee, to others with   10
equivalent knowledge of Ancient Greek. It is not normally available to candidates
with a qualification in Ancient Greek above AS-level or equivalent, nor to those who
took paper C3 Intermediate Greek in Mods.)
The set texts for the course are: Xenophon, *Hellenica* I-II.3.10 (Oxford Classical
Text) and Lysias I (Oxford Classical Text).   15

ii. *Intermediate Latin*
(This paper is available only to those undergraduates who offered Mods Paper
III–IV C.2 and, with the permission of the Standing Committee, to others with
equivalent knowledge of Latin. It is not normally available to candidates with a
qualification in Latin above AS-level or equivalent, nor to those who took paper C3   20
Intermediate Latin in Mods.)
The set texts for the course are: Cicero, letters in D. R. Shackleton- Bailey, *Cicero:
Select Letters* (Cambridge 1980), nos. 9, 17, 23, 27, 39. 42–3, 45, 48, 52, 58, 63–4,
70–1, 79; Tacitus, *Agricola* (Oxford Classical Text); Pliny, letters in A N. Sherwin-
White, *Fifty Letters of Pliny*, second edn. (Oxford, 1969), nos. 1–3, 6–7, 9, 15–20, 25,   25
27, 29, 33–4, 36, 38–40, 47–48.
VII *A Site or Museum report*, prepared in accordance with Regulation 3 below.
The report must be on

Either

   A. an excavation or archaeological site, based as far as possible on participation   30
      or autopsy and on a consideration of all relevant historical and archaeological
      sources;

Or

   B. a coherent body of finds from one site or of one category, based as far as
      possible on autopsy and on a consideration of all relevant historical and   35
      archaeological sources.

VIII An optional *Additional Thesis*, prepared in accordance with Regulation 3
below.

  2. Candidates may also be examined viva voce.

  3. Theses.   40

    (*a*) This regulation governs theses submitted under Regulation 1.VIII, and the
       Site or Museum report submitted under 1.VII.

    (*b*) The subjects for all theses and for the Site or Museum report must, to the
       satisfaction of the Standing Committee, fall within the scope of the Honour
       School of Classical Archaeology and Ancient History. The subject may, but   45
       need not, overlap any subject on which the candidate offers papers.
       Candidates are warned that they should avoid repetition in papers of mate-
       rials used in their theses, and that substantial repetition may be penalised.

    (*c*) Candidates proposing to offer a thesis must submit the following through
       their college, to the Secretary of the Standing Committee not later than the   50
       Friday of the second week of Trinity Full Term preceding the year of the
       final examination: (i) the title of the proposed thesis or report, together with

(ii) a synopsis of the subject in about 100 words and (iii) a letter of approval from their tutor. The Standing Committee shall decide as soon as possible whether or not to approve the title and shall advise the candidate immediately. No decision shall be deferred beyond the end of the sixth week of the Trinity Full Term preceding the year of the final examination.

(*d*) Every thesis or report shall be the candidate's own work. Tutors may, however, discuss with candidates the field of study, the sources available, and the method of presentation, and may also read and comment on a first draft. The amount of assistance a candidate may receive shall not exceed an amount equivalent to the teaching of a normal paper. Candidates shall make a declaration that the thesis or report is their own work, and their tutors shall countersign the declaration confirming that, to the best of their knowledge and belief, this is so. This declaration must be placed in a sealed envelope bearing the candidate's examination number and presented together with the thesis or report.

(*e*) Theses and reports previously submitted for the Honour School of Classical Archaeology and Ancient History may be resubmitted. No thesis or report shall be accepted which has already been submitted, wholly or substantially, for another Honour School or degree of this or any other institution, and the certificate shall also state that the thesis or report has not been so submitted. No thesis or report shall, however, be ineligible because it has been or is being submitted for any prize of this university.

(*f*) Candidates should aim at a length of 10,000 words but must not exceed 15,000 words (both figures inclusive of notes and appendices but excluding bibliography). No person or body shall have authority to permit the limit of 15,000 words to be exceeded. Where appropriate, there shall be a select bibliography and a list of sources.

(*g*) All theses and reports must be typed in double spacing on one side only of quarto or A4 paper with any notes and references at the foot of each page, and must be bound or held firmly in a stiff cover and identified by the candidate's examination number only. Two copies of each thesis or report shall be submitted to the examiners. Any candidate wishing to have one copy of his or her thesis or report returned must enclose with it, in an envelope bearing only his or her candidate number, a self-addressed sticky label.

(*h*) Candidates wishing to change the title of a thesis or report after it has been approved may apply for permission for the change to be granted by the Chair of the Standing Committee (if the application is made before the first day of Hilary Full Term preceding the examination) or (if later) the Chair of the Examiners, Honour School of Classical Archaeology and Ancient History.

(*i*) Candidates shall submit any thesis or report, identified by the candidates' examination number only, not later than noon on Friday of the week after the Hilary Full Term preceding the examination to the Examination Schools, High Street, Oxford, addressed to the Chair of the Examiners, Honour School of Classical Archaeology and Ancient History.

SPECIAL REGULATIONS FOR THE HONOUR SCHOOL OF CLASSICS AND ENGLISH

For students commencing the Honour School on or before 1 October 2012

A

1. The Honour School of Classics and English shall be under the joint supervision of the Boards of the Faculties of Classics and English Language and Literature and shall consist of such subjects as they shall jointly by regulation prescribe. The boards shall establish a joint committee consisting of three representatives of each faculty, of whom at least one on each side shall be a member of the respective faculty board, to advise them as necessary in respect of the examination and of the Preliminary Examination in Classics and English.

2. No candidate shall be admitted to the examination in this school unless he has either passed or been exempted from the First Public Examination.

3. Candidates who have been adjudged worthy of Honours or who have satisfied the moderators in Honour Moderations in Classics will not be permitted to enter their names for the examination.

4. The Chair of the Examiners for the Honour School of English Language and Literature shall designate such of the number of the examiners as may be required for the English subjects of the examination for the Honour School of Classics and English, and the nominating committee for examiners appointed by the Board of the Faculty of Classics shall nominate such of the number of examiners as may be required for the Classics subjects of the examination. When these appointments shall have been made the number of examiners shall be deemed to be complete.

B

Candidates who have been adjudged worthy of Honours or have satisfied the examiners in Honour Moderations in Classics will *not* be permitted to offer the course.

With the exception of those taking Paper 4.(xxi), all candidates must take seven papers: A, two in English, B, two in Classics; and C, three linking both sides of the school. Candidates taking Paper 4. (xxi) must take two papers in English, two in Classics and two linking both sides of the School including Paper 5. Epic. Candidates may offer in addition *either* an eighth paper selected from papers 2 and 4 (subject to the groupings there set out and the restrictions there placed upon choice of subjects), *or* a thesis, provided that a candidate may not offer more than one option from either

2(*d*) or 2(*e*). Each paper will be of three hours' duration except where otherwise indicated. Candidates must not offer two or more options which are assessed by an extended essay written concurrently.

A. ENGLISH

    1. One of the following periods of English literature: 5

    (*a*) English Literature from 1100–1509 (two papers) [As specified for the Honour School of English Language and Literature Course I Paper 3]

    (*b*) English Literature from 1509–1642 (one paper) [As specified for the Honour School of English Language and Literature Course I Paper 4]

    (*c*) English Literature from 1642–1740 (one paper) [As specified for the Honour   1 School of English Language and Literature Course I Paper 5]

    (*d*) English Literature from 1740–1832 (one paper) [As specified for the Honour School of English Language and Literature Course I Paper 6]

    (*e*) English Literature from 1832–1900 (one paper) [As specified for the Honour School of English Language and Literature Course I Paper 4(a)]   1

    (*f*) English Literature from 1900 to the present day (one paper) [As specified for the Honour School of English Language and Literature Course I Paper 4(b)]

Candidates who have passed the First Public Examination in English Language and Literature, or any subject and English, may not offer whichever of the periods 1832–1900 or 1900–present day they have already offered in that Examination.   2

    2. One of the following as specified for the Honour School of English Language and Literature:

    (*a*) a second of the periods specified in 1 above;

    (*b*) Shakespeare (Course I, Subject 2);

    (*c*) The English Language (Course I, Subject 1);   2

    (*d*) any of the Special Authors from the list for the year concerned which will be published in the *University Gazette* by the beginning of the fifth week of the Trinity Term two years before the examination (Course I, Subject 7) (extended essay);

    (*e*) Special topics subjects (an extended essay unless otherwise specified) under the Honour School of English Language and Literature Course I Subject 8(*a*), (*b*) i. to vi.,   3 (*c*), (*d*), (*e*). Candidates may not offer Course I Papers 8(*d*) or 8(*e*) if they are offering this paper under Papers 1, or 2(*a*);

    (*f*) The History of the English Language to *c.*1750 (Course II, A.5 (examined by portfolio submitted in the second year));

    (*g*) English Literature, 600–1100 (Course II, A1);   3

    (*h*) Old English Philology (Course II, B1);

    (*i*) Middle English Dialectology (Course II, B2);

    (*j*) Modern English Philology (Course II, B3);

    (*k*) Linguistic Theory (Course II, B4);

    (*l*) The Archaeology of Anglo-Saxon England, seventh to ninth centuries AD   4 (Course II, B10);

    (*m*) Gothic (Course II, B11);

    (*n*) Old Saxon (Course II, B12);

    (*o*) Old High German (Course II, B13);

    (*p*) Middle High German (Course II, B14);   4

    (*q*) Old Norse (Course II, B15);

    (*r*) Old Norse Texts (Course II, B16);

    (*s*) Old French Language 1150–1250 (Course II, B18);

    (*t*) Medieval French Literature 1100–1300 (Course II, B19) *or* Medieval French Literature 1300–1500 (Course II, B20);   5

    (*u*) Medieval Welsh Language and Literature I (Course II, B21) *or* Medieval Welsh Language and Literature II (Course II, B22);

(*v*) Old and Early Middle Irish Language and Literature (Course II, B23);
(*w*) Medieval and Renaissance Romance (Course II, B7(*a*));
(*x*) Scottish Literature pre-1600 (Course II, B7(*b*));

provided that candidates who offer Shakespeare or Special Authors will not be permitted to answer in other papers questions on the authors chosen.   5

B. CLASSICS

Any candidate whose native language is not English may bring a bilingual (native language to English) dictionary for use in any examination paper where candidates are required to translate Ancient Greek and/or Latin texts into English.

3. *Either* (*a*) Greek Literature of the Fifth Century BC (one paper of three hours   10
(commentary and essay) with an additional paper (one-and-a-half hours) of translation) [Honour School of Literae Humaniores, subject III.1(*a*)].

or   (*b*) Latin Literature of the First Century BC (one paper of three hours
(commentary and essay) with an additional paper (one-and-a-half   15
hours) of translation) [Honour School of Literae Humaniores, subject III.2(*a*)].

4. One of the following. *Note*: (*a*) Subject (xxi), Second Classical Language counts as two subjects; candidates offering it therefore need only offer two link papers from section C, one of which must be Paper 5. Epic. *Note*: (*b*) Each of the subjects (ii)   20
Historiography, (iii) Lyric Poetry, and (vi) Comedy will be examined by an extended essay of up to 6,000 words and a one and a half hour translation paper, as specified in the Regulations for the Honour School of Literae Humaniores. *Note*: (*c*) It cannot be guaranteed that university lectures or classes or college teaching will be available on all subjects in every academic year. Candidates are advised to consult their tutors   25
about the availability of teaching when selecting their subjects.

(i) *Either* (*a*) Greek Literature of the Fifth Century BC
or   (*b*) Latin Literature of the First Century BC (whichever is not offered under 3 above).

Candidates taking 4 (xxi) Second Classical Language in Greek may if they wish   30
offer Literae Humaniores Subject III.1(*b*) at this point; those offering Second Classical Language in Latin may offer Literae Humaniores subject III.2(*b*).

(ii) [Honour School of Literae Humaniores, subject III.3] *Historiography*
(iii) [Honour School of Literae Humaniores, subject III.4] *Lyric Poetry*
(iv) [Honour School of Literae Humaniores, subject III.6] *Greek Tragedy*   35
(v) [Honour School of Literae Humaniores, subject III.7] *Comedy*
(vi) [Honour School of Literae Humaniores, subject III.8] *Hellenistic Poetry*
(vii) [Honour School of Literae Humaniores, subject III.9] *Cicero*
(viii) [Honour School of Literae Humaniores, subject III.10] *Ovid*
(ix) [Honour School of Literae Humaniores, subject III.11] *Latin Didactic*   40
(x) [Honour School of Literae Humaniores, subject III.12] *Neronian Literature*
(xi) [Honour School of Literae Humaniores, subject III.13] *Euripides*, Orestes: *papyri, manuscripts, text*
(xii) [Honour School of Literae Humaniores, subject III.14]
Either (a) Seneca, Agamemnon: *manuscripts, text, interpretation*   45
or (b) Catullus: manuscripts, text, interpretation.
Note: University classes will be given for only one of these options each year.
(xiii) [Honour School of Literae Humaniores, subject III.15]
One of the following:
(*a*) *The Conversion of Augustine*   50
(*b*) *Byzantine Literature*
(*c*) *Modern Greek Poetry*

(xiv) [Honour School of Literae Humaniores, subject III.16] Thesis in Literature

(xv) Greek Historical Linguistics [Honour School of Literae Humaniores, subject V.1]

(xvi) Latin Historical Linguistics [Honour School of Literae Humaniores, subject V.2]

(xvii) Comparative Philology: Indo-European, Greek and Latin [Honour School of Literae Humaniores, subject V.4]

(xviii) General Linguistics and Comparative Philology [Honour School of Literae Humaniores, subject V.3]. (Candidates offering section (a), General Linguistics, may not also offer the English subject *Linguistic Theory*.)

(xix) Ancient and Medieval Philosophy. Any one of subjects 110 (Aquinas), 111 (Duns Scotus, Ockham), 115 (Plato, *Republic*, in translation), 116 (Aristotle, *Nicomachean Ethics*, in translation), 130 (Plato, *Republic*, in Greek), 131 (Plato, *Theaetetus* and *Sophist*), 132 (Aristotle, *Nicomachean Ethics*, in Greek), 133 (Aristotle, *Physics*), 134 (Sextus Empiricus, *Outlines of Pyrrhonism*), 135 (Latin Philosophy), as specified in Regulations for Philosophy in all Honour Schools including Philosophy.

(xx) Either (a) The Early Greek World and Herodotus' Histories: 650 to 479 BC [Honour School of Literae Humaniores, subject I. 1]

or (b) Thucydides and the Greek World: 479 to 403 BC [Honour School of Literae Humaniores, subject I. 2]

or (c) The End of the Peloponnesian War to the Death of Philip II of Macedon: 403 to 336 BC [Honour School of Literae Humaniores, subject I. 3]

or (d) Polybius, Rome and the Mediterranean: 241–146 BC [Honour School of Literae Humaniores, subject I. 4]

or (e) Republic in Crisis: 146–46 BC [Honour School of Literae Humaniores, subject I. 5]

or (f) Rome, Italy and Empire from Caesar to Claudius: 46 BC to AD 54 [Honour School of Literae Humaniores, subject I. 6]

or (g) Athenian Democracy in the Classical Age [Honour School of Literae Humaniores, subject I. 7]

or (h) Alexander the Great and his Early Successors [Honour School of Literae Humaniores, subject I. 8]

or (i) The Hellenistic World: Societies and Cultures c.300–100 BC [Honour School of Literae Humaniores, subject I. 9]

or (j) Cicero: Politics and Thought in the Late Republic [Honour School of Literae Humaniores, subject I. 10]

or (k) Politics, Society and Culture from Nero to Hadrian [Honour School of Literae Humaniores, subject I. 11]

or (l) Religions in the Greek and Roman World, c.31 BC-AD 312 [Honour School of Literae Humaniores, subject I. 12]

or (m) Sexuality and Gender in Greece and Rome [Honour School of Literae Humaniores, subject I. 13]

Note: Candidates offering any of subjects (xx) *(a)-(f)* must also offer the associated translation paper set in the Honour School of Literae Humaniores.

(xxi) *Second Classical Language*

As specified for the Honour School of Literae Humaniores (VI)

Candidates who offer a Second Classical Language must offer *either both* subjects in Greek *or both* subjects in Latin, and may not offer either subject in the same language as that in which they satisfied the Moderators in Honour Moderations in Classics and English or the Preliminary Examination in Classics and English.

C. LINK PAPERS

For Paper 5 *Epic* and Papers 6, 7 (*a*), (*b*), (*c*), and (*d*) *Tragedy, Comedy, Satire,* and *Pastoral*: Candidates will be expected to be familiar with the texts specified. Opportunities will, however, be given to show knowledge of authors and texts beyond those prescribed. Candidates must answer at least one question that relates Classical and English Literature. 5

5. *Epic* (one paper of three hours plus 15 minutes reading time)
With special reference to Homer, Virgil, Lucan, Milton, Dryden, Pope.

There will be a compulsory question requiring candidates to comment on and bring out points of comparison between *either* (*a*) a passage of Homer and one or more English translations *or* (*b*) a passage of Virgil and one or more English translations. The passages will be drawn from (*a*) *Odyssey*, Books 6 and 9–12, (*b*) *Aeneid*, Books 7, 8 and 12. There will also be a passage for compulsory comment from Milton, *Paradise Lost*. 10

6, 7. Two of the following papers of which at least one must be from (*a*), (*b*), (*c*), and (*d*). Course II candidates may not offer a paper which they have previously offered in their first year of study. 15

(*a*) *Tragedy* [Candidates who offer paper B. 4(iv) *Greek Tragedy* may not also offer this paper]

With special reference to:

Aeschylus, *Agamemnon* 20
Sophocles, *Oedipus the King*
Euripides, *Medea, Hecuba*
Seneca, *Medea, Thyestes*
Kyd, *The Spanish Tragedy*
Marlowe, *Tamburlaine the Great* (Parts I and II), *Edward II, Dr Faustus, Dido Queen* 25
of Carthage
Shakespeare
Jonson, *Sejanus, Catiline*
Webster, *The White Devil, The Duchess of Malfi*
Middleton, *The Changeling, Women Beware Women* 30
Ford, *'Tis Pity She's a Whore*
Milton, *Samson Agonistes*
There will be an optional commentary question with passages drawn from Aeschylus, *Agamemnon*, and Seneca, *Medea*

(*b*) *Comedy* [Candidates who offer paper B. 4 (v) *Comedy* may not also offer this paper] 35

With special reference to:

Aristophanes, *Birds*
Menander, *Dyscolus*
Plautus, *Amphitryo* and *Menaechmi*. 40
Terence, *Adelphoe*
Gascoigne, *Supposes*
Lyly, *Campaspe, Mother Bombie*.
Shakespeare
Jonson, *Every Man in his Humour, Volpone, Epicoene, The Alchemist, Bartholomew Fair* 45
Wycherley, *The Country Wife*
Vanbrugh, *The Relapse*
Congreve, *The Double Dealer, The Way of the World*
Sheridan, *The Rivals, The School for Scandal, The Critic*
There will be an optional commentary question with passages drawn from 50
Aristophanes, *Birds*, and Terence, *Adelphoe*

(c) *Satire*

With special reference to Horace, *Satires,* Book I, 1, 4–6, 9–10, and Book II, 1, 6; Persius 1 and 5; Juvenal 1, 3, 6, and 10; and the satires of Wyatt, Donne, Marston, Dryden, Johnson, Pope.

There will be an optional commentary question with passages drawn from Juvenal, *Satires,* 1, 3, 6, 10.

(d) *Pastoral*

With special reference to Theocritus, *Idylls,* 1, 3, 4, 6, 7, 10, 11; Bion, *Adonidis Epitaphium*; [Moschus], *Epitaphium Bionis*; Virgil, *Eclogues*; Mantuan 1; Tasso, *Aminta*; Guarini, *Il Pastor Fido*; Spenser, *Astrophel* and *The Shepheardes Calendar, Faerie Queen* VI ix–xii; Fletcher, *The Faithful Shepherdess*; Milton, *Lycidas* and *Epitaphium Damonis*; Pope, *Windsor Forest, Pastorals*; Shelley, *Adonais*; Arnold, *Thyrsis.*

There will be an optional commentary question with passages drawn from Theocritus, *Idylls* 1, 3, 4, 6, 7, 10, 11, and Virgil, *Eclogues.*

(e) *The Reception of Classical Literature in Poetry in English since 1900*

Authors in English for study will include Auden, H. D., Eliot, Frost, Longley, Lowell, MacNeice, Carson, Harrison, Heaney, Hughes and Walcott. This paper will be examined only by extended essay of up to 6,000 words. Essay topics set by the examiners will be released on Monday of Week 6 of Hilary Term and essays should be submitted by Monday of Week 10 of the same term (12 noon) to the Examination Schools. Candidates will be required to use at least three authors in their essays, at least one of which must be a classical author.

This subject may NOT be combined with any of the specified Special Topics subjects in English (paper A.2(e)). Candidates must avoid repetition in this paper of material used in Paper 2(d).

Thesis

1. Any candidate who does not offer an eighth paper may offer a thesis, subject to the following provisions:

(i) The subject of an optional thesis must be substantially connected with any subject area currently available in those parts of the Honour School of Literae Humaniores and Course I or Course II of the Honour School of English Language and Literature which are available to candidates for the Honour School.

(ii) The subject of the thesis may, but need not, overlap any subject or period on which the candidates offer papers. But candidates are warned that they must avoid repetition in their papers of material used in their theses, and that they will not be given credit for material extensively repeated.

(iii) Candidates proposing to offer a thesis must submit, through their college, to the Chair of the Joint Standing Committee for Classics and English (care of the English Faculty Office), the title of the proposed thesis, together with (a) a synopsis of the subject in about 100 words; and (b) a letter of support from a tutor, between Monday of the second week of the Trinity Term of the year preceding that in which the examination is held and Wednesday of the second week of the Michaelmas Term preceding the examination.

(iv) The Chair of the Joint Standing Committee for Classics and English will decide as soon as possible, and in every case by the end of the fifth week of the Michaelmas Full Term preceding the examination, whether or not to approve the title, and will advise candidates of its decision forthwith.

(v) Candidates must give notice of withdrawal of submission of a thesis to the chair of examiners not later than the end of the eighth week of the Hilary Full Term preceding the examination.

2. Every thesis must be the candidate's own work. Tutors may, however, advise on the choice and scope of the subject, provide a reading list, and read and comment on a first draft.

Candidates must sign a certificate stating that the thesis is their own work, and that the candidate has read the Joint School guidelines on plagiarism. This certificate must be placed in a sealed envelope bearing the candidate's examination number and presented together with the thesis.

3. No thesis will be accepted if it has already been submitted, wholly or substantially, for a degree of this or any other university; and the certificate must also contain confirmation that the thesis has not already been so submitted.

4. No thesis shall be ineligible because it has been submitted, in whole or in part, for any scholarship or prize of this University advertised in the *University Gazette.*

5. The thesis shall not exceed 6,000 words in length. In the case of a commentary on a text, and at the discretion of the chair of the examiners, any substantial quoting of that text need not be included in the word limit. Where appropriate, there must be a select bibliography and a list of sources.

6. Any candidate proposing to submit a thesis shall give notice of this to the Registrar on the examination entry form not later than Friday of the fourth week of the Michaelmas Full Term preceding the examination (this in addition to seeking approval for the thesis as stipulated in clause I (iii) above). Two copies of the thesis itself, identified by the candidate's examination number only, must be sent, not later than noon on the first Monday of the Trinity Full Term in which the examination will be held, to the Chair of the Examiners, Honour School of Classics and English, Examination Schools, High Street, Oxford.

Texts of Greek and Latin authors

Passages from Aristophanes, *Birds* will be set from the edition of N. Dunbar (Oxford, Student Edition). Passages from Terence, *Adelphoe* will be set from the edition of R. H. Martin (Cambridge University Press). The texts of other Greek and Latin authors used in the examination will be as prescribed by the regulations for the Honour School of Literae Humaniores.

SPECIAL REGULATIONS FOR THE HONOUR SCHOOL OF CLASSICS AND ENGLISH

For students commencing the Honour School on or after 1 October 2013

A

1. The Honour School of Classics and English shall be under the joint supervision of the Boards of the Faculties of Classics and English Language and Literature, and shall consist of such subjects as they shall jointly by regulation prescribe. The boards shall establish a joint committee consisting of three representatives of each faculty, of whom at least one on each side shall be a member of the respective faculty board, to advise them as necessary in respect of the examination and of the First Public Examination in Classics and English.

2. No candidate shall be admitted to the examination in this school unless he or she has either passed or been exempted from the First Public Examination.

3. No candidate shall be permitted to enter his or her name for the examination who has been adjudged worthy of Honours in Honour Moderations in Classics, or who has there satisfied the Moderators.

4. The Chair of Examiners for the Honour School of English Language and Literature shall designate such of the number of the examiners as may be required for the English subjects of the examination for the Honour School of Classics and English, and the nominating committee for examiners appointed by the Board of the Faculty of Classics shall nominate such of the number of examiners as may be required for the Classics subjects of the examination. When these appointments have been made the number of examiners shall be deemed to be complete.

B

All candidates must take seven subjects. All candidates not taking subject 4(xx), Second Classical Language, must offer A, two subjects in English, B, two subjects in Classics, C, two subjects linking both sides of the school, and D, a dissertation. The dissertation may be concentrated on English or on Classics, or may link both sides of the school.

Candidates who under B take 3 (*a*) or (*b*) (Greek or Latin Core) and 4(xx) (Second Classical Language) will under C take only one subject, either subject 5 or one of the subjects under 6. The subjects will be examined by written examinations of three hours' duration, unless otherwise specified.

The texts of Greek and Latin works used in the examination will be as specified each year in the Handbook for the Honour School of Classics and English.

A: ENGLISH

1. One of the following periods of English literature:

   (*a*) Literature in English 1350–1550 (one paper) [As specified for the Honour School of English Language and Literature Course I Subject 2]

   (*b*) Literature in English 1660–1760 (one paper) [As specified for the Honour School of English Language and Literature Course I Subject 4]

   (*c*) Literature in English 1760–1830 (one paper) [As specified for the Honour School of English Language and Literature Course I Subject 5]

2. One of the following as specified for the Honour School of English Language and Literature:

   (*a*) a second of the periods specified in 1 above;

   (*b*) Shakespeare (portfolio) [As specified for the Honour School of English Language and Literature Course I, Subject 1];

   (*c*) The Material Text (portfolio) [As specified for the Honour School of English Language and Literature Course II, Subject 5(a)];

   (*d*) any of the Special Options subjects from the list for the year concerned, which will be published by the English Faculty Office in the year preceding the examination (extended essay) [As specified for the Honour School of English Language and Literature Course I, Subject 6];

   (*e*) any of the Special Options subjects for English Course II, Medieval Literature and Language, from the list for the year concerned [As specified for the Honour School of English Language and Literature Course II, Subject 6];

provided that candidates who offer (*b*), (*c*), (*d*) and (*e*) avoid duplicating, in their answers to one paper, material that they have already used in answering another paper.

B: CLASSICS

Any candidate whose native language is not English may bring a bilingual (native language to English) dictionary for use in any examination paper where candidates are required to translate Ancient Greek and/or Latin texts into English.

3. *Either* (*a*) Greek Literature of the Fifth Century BC (one paper of three hours (commentary and essay) with an additional paper (one-and-a-half hours) of translation) [Honour School of Literae Humaniores, subject III.1(*a*)].

    or   (*b*) Latin Literature of the First Century BC (one paper of three hours (commentary and essay) with an additional paper (one-and-a-half hours) of translation) [Honour School of Literae Humaniores, subject III.2(*a*)].

4. One of the following. *Note*: (*a*) Subject (xxi), Second Classical Language, counts as two subjects; hence candidates offering it should offer only one subject under section C. *Note*: (*b*) Each of the subjects (ii) Historiography, (iii) Lyric Poetry, and (vi) Comedy will be examined by an extended essay of 5,000–6,000 words and a one-and-a-half-hour translation paper, as specified in the Regulations for the Honour School of Literae Humaniores. *Note*: (*c*) It cannot be guaranteed that university lectures or classes or college teaching will be available on all subjects in every academic year. Candidates are advised to consult their tutors about the availability of teaching when selecting their subjects.

  (i) *Either* (*a*) Greek Literature of the Fifth Century BC
      or   (*b*) Latin Literature of the First Century BC (whichever is not offered under 3 above).
  (ii) [Honour School of Literae Humaniores, subject III.3] *Historiography*
  (iii) [Honour School of Literae Humaniores, subject III.4] *Lyric Poetry*
  (iv) [Honour School of Literae Humaniores, subject III.6] *Greek Tragedy*
  (v) [Honour School of Literae Humaniores, subject III.7] *Comedy*
  (vi) [Honour School of Literae Humaniores, subject III.8] *Hellenistic Poetry*
  (vii) [Honour School of Literae Humaniores, subject III.9] *Cicero*
 (viii) [Honour School of Literae Humaniores, subject III.10] *Ovid*
  (ix) [Honour School of Literae Humaniores, subject III.11] *Latin Didactic*
  (x) [Honour School of Literae Humaniores, subject III.12] *Neronian Literature*
  (xi) [Honour School of Literae Humaniores, subject III.13] *Euripides, Orestes: papyri, manuscripts, text*
  (xii) [Honour School of Literae Humaniores, subject III.14]

Either (*a*) Seneca, Agamemnon: *manuscripts, text, interpretation*
or   (*b*) Catullus: *manuscripts, text, interpretation.*
Note: University classes will be given for only one of these options each year.

  (xiii) [Honour School of Literae Humaniores, subject III.15]
One of the following:
    (*a*) *The Conversion of Augustine*
    (*b*) *Byzantine Literature*
    (*c*) *Modern Greek Poetry*
  (xiv) [Honour School of Literae Humaniores, subject III.16] Thesis in Literature
  (xv) Greek Historical Linguistics [Honour School of Literae Humaniores, subject V.1]
  (xvi) Latin Historical Linguistics [Honour School of Literae Humaniores, subject V.2]
  (xvii) Comparative Philology: Indo-European, Greek and Latin [Honour School of Literae Humaniores, subject V.4]

(xviii) General Linguistics and Comparative Philology [Honour School of Literae Humaniores, subject V.3].

(xix) Ancient and Medieval Philosophy. Any one of subjects 110 (Aquinas), 111 (Duns Scotus, Ockham), 115 (Plato, *Republic*, in translation), 116 (Aristotle, *Nicomachean Ethics*, in translation), 130 (Plato, *Republic*, in Greek), 131 (Plato, *Theaetetus* and *Sophist*), 132 (Aristotle, *Nicomachean Ethics*, in Greek), 133 (Aristotle, *Physics*), 134 (Sextus Empiricus, *Outlines of Pyrrhonism*), 135 (Latin Philosophy), as specified in Regulations for Philosophy in all Honour Schools including Philosophy.

(xx) *Either*

        (*a*) The Early Greek World and Herodotus' *Histories*: 650 to 479 BC [Honour School of Literae Humaniores, subject I. 1]

or   (*b*) Thucydides and the Greek World: 479 to 403 BC [Honour School of Literae Humaniores, subject I. 2]

or   (*c*) The End of the Peloponnesian War to the Death of Philip II of Macedon: 403 to 336 BC [Honour School of Literae Humaniores, subject I. 3]

or   (*d*) Polybius, Rome and the Mediterranean: 241–146 BC [Honour School of Literae Humaniores, subject I. 4]

or   (*e*) Republic in Crisis: 146–46 BC [Honour School of Literae Humaniores, subject I. 5]

or   (*f*) Rome, Italy and Empire from Caesar to Claudius: 46 BC to AD 54 [Honour School of Literae Humaniores, subject I. 6]

or   (*g*) Athenian Democracy in the Classical Age [Honour School of Literae Humaniores, subject I. 7]

or   (*h*) Alexander the Great and his Early Successors [Honour School of Literae Humaniores, subject I. 8]

or   (*i*) The Hellenistic World: Societies and Cultures c.300–100 BC [Honour School of Literae Humaniores, subject I. 9]

or   (*j*) Cicero: Politics and Thought in the Late Republic [Honour School of Literae Humaniores, subject I. 10 ; may not be combined with (vii) Cicero above]

or   (*k*) Politics, Society and Culture from Nero to Hadrian [Honour School of Literae Humaniores, subject I. 11]

or   (*l*) Religions in the Greek and Roman World, c.31 BC–AD 312 [Honour School of Literae Humaniores, subject I. 12]

or   (*m*) Sexuality and Gender in Greece and Rome [Honour School of Literae Humaniores, subject I. 13]

Note: Candidates offering any of subjects (xix) (*a*)-(*f*) must also offer the associated translation paper set in the Honour School of Literae Humaniores.

(xxi) Second Classical Language.

As specified for the Honour School of Literae Humaniores (VI).

Candidates who offer a Second Classical Language must offer *either* both subjects in Greek *or both* subjects in Latin, and may not offer either subject in a language in which they satisfied the Moderators in Honour Moderations in Classics and English or the Preliminary Examination in Classics and English.

C. LINK PAPERS

For Paper 5 *Epic* and Paper 6 (*a*) *Tragedy* and (*b*) *Comedy*: while candidates will be expected to be familiar with the texts specified, opportunities will be given to show knowledge of authors and texts beyond those prescribed. Candidates must answer at least one question that relates Classical and English Literature.

5. *Epic* (one paper of three hours plus 15 minutes' reading time)
With special reference to Homer, Virgil, Lucan, Milton, Dryden, Pope.

There will be a compulsory question requiring candidates to comment on and bring out points of comparison between *either* (*a*) a passage of Homer and one or more English translations *or* (*b*) a passage of Virgil and one or more English translations. The passages will be drawn from (*a*) *Odyssey*, Books 6 and 9–12, (*b*) *Aeneid*, Books 7, 8 and 12. There will also be a passage for compulsory comment from Milton, *Paradise Lost*.

6. One of the following:

(*a*) *Tragedy* [Candidates who offer paper B. 4 (iv) *Greek Tragedy* may not also offer this paper].

With special reference to:
Aeschylus, *Agamemnon*.
Sophocles, *Oedipus the King*.
Euripides, *Medea, Hecuba*.
Seneca, *Medea, Thyestes*.
Kyd, *The Spanish Tragedy*.
Marlowe, *Tamburlaine the Great* (Parts I and II).
Edward II, Dr Faustus, Dido Queen of Carthage.
Shakespeare.
Jonson, *Sejanus, Catiline*.
Webster, *The White Devil, The Duchess of Malfi*.
Middleton, *The Changeling, Women Beware Women*.
Ford, *'Tis Pity She's a Whore*.
Milton, *Samson Agonistes*.
There will be an optional commentary question with passages drawn from Aeschylus, *Agamemnon*, and Seneca, *Medea*.

(*b*) *Comedy* [Candidates who offer paper B. 4 (v) Comedy may not also offer this paper].

With special reference to:
Aristophanes, *Birds*.
Menander, *Dyscolus*.
Plautus, *Amphitryo* and *Menaechmi*.
Terence, *Adelphoe*.
Gascoigne, *Supposes*.
Lyly, *Campaspe, Mother Bombie*.
Shakespeare.
Jonson, *Every Man in his Humour, Volpone, Epicoene, The Alchemist, Bartholomew Fair*.
Wycherley, *The Country Wife*.
Vanbrugh, *The Relapse*.
Congreve, *The Double Dealer, The Way of the World*.
Sheridan, *The Rivals, The School for Scandal, The Critic*.
There will be an optional commentary question with passages drawn from Aristophanes, *Birds*, and Terence, *Adelphoe*.

(*c*) *The Reception of Classical Literature in Poetry in English since 1900*
Authors in English for study will include Auden, H. D., Eliot, Frost, Longley, Lowell, MacNeice, Carson, Harrison, Heaney, Hughes and Walcott. This paper will be examined by an extended essay of 5,000–6,000 words. Essay topics set by the examiners will be released on Monday of Week 6 of the Hilary Term preceding the final examination and essays should be submitted by Monday of Week 10 of the same term (12 noon) to the Examination Schools, High Street. Candidates will be required to use at least three authors in their essays, at least one of whom must be a classical author.

This subject may NOT be combined with options in Classics examined by extended essay (4 (ii), (iii), (v)). Candidates must avoid repetition in this paper of material used in Paper 2(*d*).

D: DISSERTATION

1. All candidates for the Honour School of Classics and English must offer a dissertation.

    (i) The subject of the dissertation must be substantially connected with any subject area in those parts of the Honour School of Literae Humaniores and Course I or Course II of the Honour School of English Language and Literature which are available to candidates for the Honour School of Classics and English. The subject may, but need not, be one that connects the two sides of the School.

    (ii) The subject of the dissertation may, but need not, overlap any subject or period on which the candidate offers papers. Candidates are warned, however, that they must avoid repetition in their papers of materials used in their dissertation, and that they will not be given credit for material extensively repeated.

    (iii) Candidates must submit a dissertation abstract of no more than 100 words, to the Chair of Examiners in Classics and English, care of the English Faculty Office, by Friday of the fourth week of the Michaelmas term preceding the examination.

    (iv) The Chair of Examiners in Classics and English will decide as soon as possible, and in every case by the end of the sixth week of the Michaelmas Term preceding the examination, whether or not to approve the abstract, and will advise candidates of the decision forthwith.

2. Every dissertation must be the candidate's own work. Tutors may, however, advise on the choice and scope of the subject, provide a reading list, and read and comment on a first draft.

Candidates must sign a certificate stating that the dissertation is their own work, and that they have read the Joint School guidelines on plagiarism (see also 3 below). This certificate must be placed in a sealed envelope bearing the candidate's examination number and presented together with the dissertation.

3. Dissertations previously submitted for the Honour School of Classics and English may be re-submitted. No dissertation will be accepted if it has already been submitted, wholly or substantially, for any other degree of this or any other university; and the certificate must also contain confirmation that the dissertation has not already been so submitted.

4. No dissertation shall be ineligible because it has been submitted, in whole or in part, for any scholarship or prize of this University advertised in the *University Gazette*.

5. The dissertation shall be of 7,000-8,000 words; failure to keep to these limits is liable to be penalized. In the case of a commentary on a text, and at the discretion of the Chair of the Examiners, any substantial quoting of that text need not be included in the word-count. There must be a select bibliography and, if appropriate, list of sources.

6. Two typed copies of the dissertation must be delivered to the Chair of Examiners, Honour School of Classics and English, Examination Schools, High Street, by noon on Thursday of the eighth week of Hilary Term preceding the examination.

SPECIAL REGULATIONS FOR THE
HONOUR SCHOOL OF CLASSICS
AND MODERN LANGUAGES

A

1. The subjects of the examination in the Honour School of Classics and Modern Languages shall be (*a*) the Greek and Latin languages and literatures and the thought and civilisation of the Ancient World and (*b*) those modern European languages and literatures studied in the Honour School of Modern Languages.

2. No candidate shall be admitted to the examination in this School unless he or she has either passed or been exempted from the First Public Examination.

3. The examiners shall indicate in the lists issued by them the language offered by each candidate obtaining honours or satisfying the examiners under the appropriate regulation.

4. The examination in the Honour School shall be under the joint supervision of the Boards of the Faculties of Classics and of Modern Languages, which shall appoint a standing joint committee to make, and to submit to the two boards, proposals for regulations concerning the examination.

5. (i) The Public Examiners for Classics in this school shall be such of the Public Examiners in the Honour School of Literae Humaniores as may be required, together with one or two additional examiners, if required, who shall be nominated by the committee for the nomination of Public Examiners in the Honour School of Literae Humaniores; those for Modern Languages shall be such of the Public Examiners in the Honour School of Modern Languages as shall be required.

(ii) It shall be the duty of the chair of the Public Examiners in the Honour School of Modern Languages to designate such of their number as may be required for Modern Languages in the Honour School of Classics and Modern Languages, and when this has been done, and the examiners for Classics have been nominated, the number of the examiners in Classics and Modern Languages shall be deemed to be complete.

B

Candidates will be examined in accordance with the examination regulations set out below.

They will also be required to spend, after their matriculation, a year of residence in an appropriate country or countries, and to provide on their entry form for the examination a certificate that they have done this, signed by the Head or by a tutor of their society. Candidates wishing to be dispensed from the requirement to undertake a year of residence abroad must apply in writing to the Chair of the Medieval and Modern Languages Board, 41 Wellington Square, Oxford, OX1 2JF, stating their reasons for requesting dispensation and enclosing a letter of support from their society.

Candidates will be expected to carry out during this year abroad such work as their society may require. It is strongly recommended that candidates should apply through the Central Bureau for Educational Visits and Exchanges for an Assistantship, where these are available, and should accept one if offered. Candidates who are not able to obtain an Assistantship should during their year abroad follow a course or courses in an institution or institutions approved by their society, or should spend their time in such other circumstances as are acceptable to their society. Candidates will agree with their College Tutor in advance of their year abroad an independent course of study to be followed during that period.

Except in a Special Subject or an alternative to a Special Subject, a candidate shall offer one modern language and its literature only except that candidates offering Ancient Greek may offer the subject Modern Greek Poetry, and all candidates may offer the subject Byzantine Literature as specified in the regulations below, if and only if they are not offering Medieval and Modern Greek as their modern language.

Any candidate may be examined viva voce.

Oral Examination: as specified for the Honour School of Modern Languages.

In every case where, under the regulations for the school, candidates have any choice between one or more papers or subjects, every candidate shall give notice to the Registrar not later than the Friday in the fourth week of Michaelmas Full Term preceding the examination of all the papers and subjects being so offered.

Candidates offering two papers both of which involve the study of the same author or authors, may not make the same text or texts the principal subject of an answer in both the papers.

All candidates must offer eight subjects as specified below and may also offer an Additional Subject as specified at no.9.

   1. Honour School of Modern Languages, Paper I.

Any candidate whose native language is not English may bring a bilingual (native language to English) dictionary for use in any examination paper where candidates are required to translate Ancient Greek and/or Latin texts into English.

   2. Honour School of Modern Languages, Papers IIA and IIB.

   3. Honour School of Modern Languages, *one* paper chosen from Papers VI, VII or VIII.

   4. Honour School of Modern Languages, *one* paper chosen from Papers IV, V, IX, X, XI or XII.

   5. *Either* (*a*) Greek Literature of the fifth century BC (one paper of three hours (commentary and essay) with an additional paper (one-and-a-half hours) of translation) [Honour School of Literae Humaniores, subject III.1(*a*)].

     or   (*b*) Latin Literature of the first century BC (one paper of three hours (commentary and essay) with an additional paper (one-and-a-half hours) of translation) [Honour School of Literae Humaniores, subject III.2(*a*)].

   6, 7. Two of the following subjects (i) to (xxv). Candidates not offering (xxiv), (xxv), Second Classical Language must include at least one of the subjects (i)-(xvi).

Note: (*a*) Subject (xxiv), (xxv), Second Classical Language counts as two subjects. It may not be offered by candidates who have satisfied the Moderators in Course IA, IB or IC of Honour Moderations in Classics or of the Preliminary Examination in Classics, or who offered both Greek and Latin in the Preliminary Examination for Modern Languages. Candidates offering it must also offer at least one of subjects 6, 7 (i)-(xxi) under 8 or 9 below. If they offer Second Classical Language in Greek they may if they wish offer Literae Humaniores subject III.1(*b*) at this point; if they offer it in Latin they may offer Literae Humaniores subject III.2(*b*).

Note: (*b*) Each of the subjects (ii) Historiography, (iii) Lyric Poetry and (iv) Comedy (of which candidates may offer only one) will be examined by an extended essay of up to 6,000 words and a one-and-a-half-hour translation paper, as specified in the Regulations for the Honour School of Literae Humaniores. For each of the subjects (ii), (iii), and (iv), version (i) (as specified for the Honour School of Literae Humaniores) is the only version available to candidates who have satisfied the Moderators in Course IA, IB, or IC of Honour Moderations in Classics or of the Preliminary Examination in Classics, or who offered both Ancient Greek and Latin in the Preliminary Examination for Modern Languages.

Note: (*c*) It cannot be guaranteed that university lectures or classes or college teaching will be available on all subjects in every academic year. Candidates are advised to consult their tutors about the availability of teaching when selecting their subjects.

    (i) *Either* (*a*) Greek Literature of the 5th Century BC
       or   (*b*) Latin Literature of the 1st Century BC (whichever is not offered under 5 above).

(ii)-(iv) *Either* (ii) Historiography [Honour School of Literae Humaniores, subject III.3] (**see introductory note 6, 7 (*b*) above**)
       or   (iii) Lyric Poetry [Honour School of Literae Humaniores, subject III.4] (**see introductory note 6, 7 (*b*) above**) *or* (iv) Comedy [Honour School of Literae Humaniores, subject III.7] (**see introductory note 6, 7 (*b*) above**).

    (v) Early Greek Hexameter Poetry [Honour School of Literae Humaniores, subject III.5].

    (vi) Greek Tragedy [Honour School of Literae Humaniores, subject III.6] (not to be offered in combination with subject 8 (iii), Ancient and French Classical Tragedy or 8 (iv), The Creative Reception of Greek Tragedy in German).

    (vii) Hellenistic Poetry [Honour School of Literae Humaniores, subject III.8].

    (viii) Cicero [Honour School of Literae Humaniores, subject III.9].

    (ix) Ovid [Honour School of Literae Humaniores, subject III.10].

    (x) Latin Didactic [Honour School of Literae Humaniores, subject III.11].

    (xi) Neronian Literature [Honour School of Literae Humaniores, subject III.12].

    (xii) Euripides, *Orestes*: papyri, manuscripts, text [Honour School of Literae Humaniores, subject III.13].

    (xiii) [Honour School of Literae Humaniores, subject III.14]
       Either (*a*) Seneca, *Agamemnon*: manuscripts, text, interpretation
       or   (*b*) *Catullus*: manuscripts, text, interpretation

Note: University classes will be given for only one of these options each year.

    (xiv) *Either* (*a*) The Conversion of Augustine [Honour School of Literae Humaniores, subject III.15(*a*)]
       or   (*b*) Byzantine Literature [Honour School of Literae Humaniores, subject III.15(*b*)] (This subject is not available to candidates offering Medieval and Modern Greek as their modern language.)
       or   (*c*) The Latin Works of Petrarch, with special study of *Africa* (ed. N. Festa, Florence, 1926), Books, I, II, V, VII, IX. Candidates will also be expected to have read *Vita Scipionis* (in *La vita di Scipione*

l'Africano, ed. G. Martellotti, Milano-Napoli, 1954), and to show acquaintance with Petrarch's major Latin works (e.g. *Rerum memorandarum libri* (ed. G. Billanovich, Florence, 1945), *De secreto conflictu curarum mearum, De vita solitaria, Epistolae familiares* (in F. Petrarca, *Prose*, ed. G. Martellotti, P.G. Ricci,   5
E. Carrara, E. Bianchi, Milano-Napoli, 1955)).

(xv) Greek Historical Linguistics [Honour School of Literae Humaniores, subject V.1]. (This subject may be combined with one but not more than one of (xvi), (xvii) and (xviii).)

(xvi) Latin Historical Linguistics [Honour School of Literae Humaniores, subject   10
V.2]. (This subject may be combined with one but not more than one of (xv), (xvii) and (xviii).)

(xvii) Comparative Philology: Indo-European, Greek and Latin [Honour School of Literae Humaniores, subject V.4]. (This subject may not be offered by candidates who offered the paper VI F(1) Historical Linguistics and   15
Comparative Philology in Honour Moderations in Classics or in the Preliminary Examination in Classics. It may be combined with one but not more than one of (xv), (xvi) and (xviii).)

(xviii) General Linguistics and Comparative Philology [Honour School of Literae Humaniores, subject V.3]. (This subject may be combined with one but not   20
more than one of (xv), (xvi) and (xvii). Candidates offering section (a), General Linguistics, may not also offer the Modern Languages Special Subject General Linguistics.)

(xix) *Either* (a) The Early Greek World and Herodotus' Histories: 650 to 479 BC [Honour School of Literae Humaniores, subject I. 1].   25

or (b) Thucydides and the Greek World: 479 to 403 BC [Honour School of Literae Humaniores, subject I. 2].

or (c) The End of the Peloponnesian War to the Death of Philip II of Macedon: 403 to 336 BC [Honour School of Literae Humaniores, subject I. 3].   30

or (d) Polybius, Rome and the Mediterranean: 241–146 BC [Honour School of Literae Humaniores, subject I. 4].

or (e) Republic in Crisis: 146-46 BC [Honour School of Literae Humaniores, subject I. 5].

or (f) Rome, Italy and Empire from Caesar to Claudius: 46 BC to AD   35
54 [Honour School of Literae Humaniores, subject I. 6].

or (g) Athenian Democracy in the Classical Age [Honour School of Literae Humaniores, subject I. 7].

or (h) Alexander the Great and his Early Successors [Honour School of Literae Humaniores, subject I. 8].   40

or (i) The Hellenistic World: Societies and Cultures c.300–100 BC [Honour School of Literae Humaniores, subject I. 9].

or (j) Cicero: Politics and Thought in the Late Republic [Honour School of Literae Humaniores, subject I. 10].

or (k) Politics, Society and Culture from Nero to Hadrian [Honour   45
School of Literae Humaniores, subject I. 11].

or (l) Religions in the Greek and Roman World, c.31 BC–AD 312 [Honour School of Literae Humaniores, subject I. 12].

or (m) Sexuality and Gender in Greece and Rome [Honour School of Literae Humaniores, subject I. 13].   50

Note: Candidates offering any of subjects (xix) (a)-(f) must also offer the associated translation paper set in the Honour School of Literae Humaniores.

(xx) *Either* (*a*)   The Greeks and the Mediterranean World c.950–500 BC [Honour School of Literae Humaniores, subject IV. 1].

or   (*b*)   Greek Art and Archaeology c.500–300 BC [Honour School of Literae Humaniores, subject IV. 2].

or   (*c*)   Hellenistic Art and Archaeology, 330–30 BC [Honour School of Literae Humaniores, subject IV.3].

or   (*d*)   Art under the Roman Empire, AD 14–337 [Honour School of Literae Humaniores, subject IV. 4].

or   (*e*)   Roman Archaeology: Cities and Settlement under the Empire [Honour School of Literae Humaniores, subject IV. 5].

(xxi) Ancient and Medieval Philosophy. Any one of subjects 110 (Aquinas), 111 (Duns Scotus, Ockham), 115 (Plato, *Republic*, in translation), 116 (Aristotle, *Nicomachean Ethics*, in translation), 130 (Plato, *Republic*, in Greek), 131 (Plato, *Theaetetus* and *Sophist*), 132 (Aristotle, *Nicomachean Ethics*, in Greek), 133 (Aristotle, *Physics*), 134 (Sextus Empiricus, *Outlines of Pyrrhonism*), 135 (Latin Philosophy), as specified in Regulations for Philosophy in all Honour Schools including Philosophy.

(xxii) Modern Greek Poetry [Honour School of Literae Humaniores, subject III.15(d)]. (This subject is available only to candidates offering Greek Literature of the Fifth Century BC under 5 above who are neither offering Medieval and Modern Greek as their modern language nor offering III.15 (*b*) Byzantine Literature or (xxiv), (xxv), Second Classical Language.)

(xxiii) Thesis. Any candidate may offer a thesis in Classics, or in a subject linking Classics and Modern Languages, in accordance with the Regulation on Theses in the regulations for the Honour School of Literae Humaniores.

(xxiv), (xxv) **(see introductory note 6, 7 (*a*))** Second Classical Language [Honour School of Literae Humaniores, subject VI.1 and VI.2]. (Candidates who offer Second Classical Language must offer either both subjects in Greek or both subjects in Latin, and may not offer either subject in the same language as they offered in Course IIA or IIB of Honour Moderations or the Preliminary Examination in Classics or in the Preliminary Examination for Modern Languages.)

8. One of the following:

(i) A second subject chosen from those listed under 4 above.

(ii) A third subject chosen from those listed under 6, 7 above, subject to the groupings there set out and the restrictions there placed upon choice of subjects.

(iii) Ancient and French Classical Tragedy (not to be offered in combination with any of the following: Greek Tragedy (subject 6, 7(v)); Racine [Honour School of Modern Languages, paper X(5)]; Dramatic Theory and Practice in France 1605–60 with special reference to Corneille [Honour School of Modern Languages, paper XII Special Subject]).

Candidates must make a special study of either of the following pairs of texts, on which a compulsory comparative commentary question will be set: *either* (*a*) Seneca, *Phaedra* and Racine, *Phèdre*, or (*b*) Euripides, *Medea* and Corneille, *Médée*. In addition, essay questions will be set with special reference to the following texts:

Aeschylus, *Agamemnon*
Sophocles, *Oedipus the King*
Euripides, *Hippolytus, Andromache, The Phoenician Women, Iphigenia at Aulis*
Seneca, *Medea*
Corneille, *Discours, Horace, Oedipe, Suréna*
Racine, *La Thébaïde, Andromaque, Iphigénie.*

Candidates will be required to answer two essay questions, one from a choice of questions specifically on the authors and texts prescribed above, the other from a choice of questions requiring a comparative or generic approach. The following editions will be used in the case of the texts prescribed for commentary: Euripides, J. Diggle (Oxford Classical Text); Seneca, *Phaedra*, M. Coffey and R. Mayer (Cambridge University Press); Corneille, A. Stegmann (L'Intégrale); Racine, J. Morela and A. Viala (Classiques Garnier).

(iv) The Creative Reception of Greek Tragedy in German.

Candidates must make a special study of Sophocles, *Antigone* and Hölderlin, *Antigone*, on each of which a compulsory commentary question will be set. In addition, they will be required to answer two essay questions, one from a choice of questions specifically on the authors and texts listed below, the other from a choice of questions requiring a comparative or generic approach.

Sophocles, *Oedipus Tyrannus*
Euripides, *Medea, Iphigenia in Tauris*
Plato, *Republic* II, III, X
Aristotle, *Poetics*
Goethe, *Iphigenie auf Tauris*
Kleist, *Penthesilea*
Nietzsche, *Die Geburt der Tragödie*
Brecht, *Antigone*
Christa Wolf, *Medea: Stimmen*

The following editions will be used in the case of the texts prescribed for commentary: Sophocles, Lloyd-Jones and Wilson (Oxford Classical Text); Hölderlin, Frankfurt edition.

9. Additional Subject.

Good performance in such subjects will be taken in account in allocating all classes. Candidates wishing to offer an Additional Subject may offer one of the following.

(i) A further subject chosen from the list prescribed under 4 above.

(ii) A further subject chosen from the list prescribed under 6, 7 (i)-(xxii) above, subject to the groupings there set out and the restrictions there placed upon choice of subjects.

(iii) Greek Prose Composition. (This subject may not be offered by candidates who have satisfied the Moderators in Course IA or IC of Honour Moderations in Classics.)

(iv) Latin Prose Composition. (This subject may not be offered by candidates who have satisfied the Moderators in Course IA or IB of Honour Moderations in Classics.)

(v) An extended essay on a topic in the modern language or combining the modern language and Classics (to be examined under the regulations for the Honour School of Modern Languages).

(vi) A Special Thesis on a topic in Classics (to be examined under the regulations for the Honour School of Literae Humaniores).

Candidates shall submit two copies of their thesis not later than noon on Friday of the week before the Trinity Full Term of the examination to the Examination Schools, High Street, Oxford, addressed to the Chair of the Examiners, Honour School of Literae Humaniores.

SPECIAL REGULATIONS FOR THE HONOUR SCHOOL OF CLASSICS AND ORIENTAL STUDIES

A

1. The Honour School of Classics and Oriental Studies shall be under the joint supervision of the Boards of the Faculties of Classics and of Oriental Studies, which shall appoint a standing joint committee to make, and to submit to the two boards, proposals for regulations concerning the examination.

2. No candidate shall be admitted to the examination in this School unless he or she has either passed or been exempted from the First Public Examination.

3. The Public Examiners in this School shall be such of the Public Examiners in the Honour Schools of Literae Humaniores and of Oriental Studies as may be required, together with any additional examiners who may be required who shall be nominated by the committee for the nomination of Public Examiners in one or both of those Honour Schools as appropriate.

4. In the Class List issued by the examiners the Main Subject and Additional Language offered by each candidate shall be indicated.

B

Candidates must offer one Main Subject and one Additional Language, of which one must be Classics and the other a subject or language in Oriental Studies as specified below. In addition they may offer, but are not required to offer, a Special Thesis in Classics, or in Oriental Studies, or in a subject linking Classics and Oriental Studies, in accordance with the Regulation on Theses in the Regulations for the Honour School of Literae Humaniores, save that references there to the Honour School of Literae Humaniores shall be deemed to be references to the Honour School of Classics and Oriental Studies, the competent authority for dealing with proposals shall be the standing joint committee for Classics and Oriental Studies, and proposals should be submitted to the chair of that committee. Candidates offering a Special Thesis may not also offer an additional optional special subject where that is allowed under the Regulations for Oriental Studies.

Classics may be offered either as a Main Subject or as an Additional Language, save that those who have satisfied the Moderators in Honour Moderations or the Preliminary Examination in Classics may not offer Classics as an Additional Language without permission from the standing joint committee for Classics and Oriental Studies; such permission must be sought if possible no later than the beginning of the term following that in which the candidate sat the First Public Examination, and in any case no later than noon on the Friday of the first week of Michaelmas Term before the examination.

In Oriental Studies, the following may be offered either as a Main Subject or as an Additional Language: Arabic, Hebrew, Persian, Sanskrit, Turkish.

Egyptology and Ancient Near Eastern Studies may be offered only as a Main Subject.

Any candidate whose native language is not English may bring a bilingual (native language to English) dictionary for use in any examination paper where candidates are required to translate Ancient Greek and/or Latin texts into English.

The following may be offered only as an Additional Language: Akkadian, Aramaic and Syriac, Armenian, Coptic, Egyptology, Old Iranian, Pali.

All Subjects and Languages other than Classics will be examined in accordance with the Regulations for the Honour School of Oriental Studies.

The subjects available in Classics are listed below. Those offering Classics as their Main Subject must offer **five** of these, of which at least two (or, in the case of those offering (xlvii), (xlviii) Greek or Latin for Beginners, at least one) must be drawn from nos (i)–(xx), (xxviii), (xxix) and (xli)–(xlvi); those offering Classics as their Additional Language must offer **three**, of which at least one must be drawn from nos (i)–(xx), (xxviii), (xxix) and (xli)–(xlviii) [on which, see note (*f*) below].

NOTE: (*a*) Subjects in Greek and Latin Literature, nos (i)–(xiv): candidates offering more than one of these subjects must offer (i) or (ii), and may offer both.

NOTE: (*b*) Each of the subjects (iii)(a) Historiography, (iii)(b) Lyric Poetry and (iii)(c) Comedy (of which candidates may offer only one) will be examined by an extended essay of up to 6,000 words and a one-and-a-half hour paper, as specified in the Regulations for the Honour School of Literae Humaniores. For each of the subjects in (iii), version (i) (as specified for the Honour School of Literae Humaniores) is the only version available to candidates who have satisfied the Moderators in Course IA, IB or IC of Honour Moderations in Classics or of the Preliminary Examination in Classics. **Candidates offering one of these subjects who are also offering a dissertation on a topic in their Oriental language should consult the chair of the standing joint committee for Classics and Oriental Studies about the timing of submission of the dissertation.**

NOTE: (*c*) Subjects in Greek and Roman History, nos (xv)–(xxvii): candidates offering more than one of these subjects must offer at least one of (xv)–(xx); candidates offering more than three of these subjects must offer at least two of (xv)–(xx) and may not offer more than two of (xxi)–(xxvii). Candidates offering any of subjects (xv)–(xx) must also offer the associated translation paper(s) set in the Honour School of Literae Humaniores, though candidates without competence in the relevant language may apply for dispensation from this requirement by application to the chair of the standing joint committee by noon on the Friday of the first week of Michaelmas Term before the examination, setting out the full range of their intended options and stating why they think it educationally desirable to offer them.

NOTE: (*d*) Subjects in Philology and Linguistics, nos (xxviii)–(xxxi): candidates may not offer more than two of these subjects.

NOTE: (*e*) Subjects in Greek and Roman Archaeology, nos (xxxii)–(xxxvi): candidates may not offer more than two of these subjects.

NOTE: (*f*) Subject (xlvii), (xlviii), Greek or Latin for Beginners counts as *two* subjects. It may not be offered by candidates who have satisfied the Moderators in Course IA, IB or IC of Honour Moderations in Classics or of the Preliminary Examination in Classics. Candidates who offer Greek or Latin for Beginners must offer *either* both subjects in Greek *or* both subjects in Latin, and may not offer either subject in the same language as they offered in Course IIA or IIB of Honour Moderations or the Preliminary Examination in Classics, if they sat either of those examinations. If they offer Greek for Beginners they may if they wish offer Literae Humaniores subject III.1(*b*) as subject (i); in that case, they must also offer at least one of subjects (ii)-(xx), (xxviii), (xxix) and (xli)–(xlvi) if they are offering Classics as their main subject. If they offer Latin for Beginners they may if they wish offer Literae Humaniores subject III.2(*b*) as subject (ii); in that case, they must also offer at least one of subjects (i), (iii)–(xx), (xxviii), (xxix) and (xli)-(xlvi) if they are offering Classics as their main subject.

NOTE: (*g*) It cannot be guaranteed that university lectures or classes or college teaching will be available on all subjects in every academic year. Candidates are advised to consult their tutors about the availability of teaching when selecting their subjects.

A. Subjects in Greek and Latin Literature (see note (*a*) above)

(i) Greek Literature of the 5th Century BC (one paper of three hours (commentary and essay) with an additional paper (one-and-a-half hours) of translation. [Honour School of Literae Humaniores, subject III. 1]

(ii) Latin Literature of the 1st Century BC (one paper of three hours (commentary and essay) with an additional paper (one-and-a-half hours) of translation) [Honour School of Literae Humaniores, subject III. 2]

(iii) **(See note (*b*) above)** *Either* (*a*) Historiography [Honour School of Literae Humaniores, subject III. 3] *or* (*b*) Lyric Poetry [Honour School of Literae Humaniores, subject III. 4] *or* (*c*) Comedy [Honour School of Literae Humaniores, subject III. 7].

(iv) *Either* (*a*) Early Greek Hexameter Poetry [Honour School of Literae Humaniores, subject III. 5] *or* (*b*) Homer, *Iliad* [Honour Moderations in Classics, Course IA, paper 1; this option may not be offered by candidates who have satisfied the Moderators in Course IA, IB, IC or IIB of Honour Moderations in Classics]

(v) Greek Tragedy [Honour School of Literae Humaniores, subject III. 6]

(vi) Hellenistic Poetry [Honour School of Literae Humaniores, subject III. 8]

(vii) Cicero [Honour School of Literae Humaniores, subject III. 9]

(viii) Ovid [Honour School of Literae Humaniores, subject III. 10]

(ix) Latin Didactic [Honour School of Literae Humaniores, subject III. 11]

(x) Neronian Literature [Honour School of Literae Humaniores, subject III. 12]

(xi) Euripides, *Orestes*: papyri, manuscripts, text [Honour School of Literae Humaniores, subject III. 13]

(xii) *Either* (*a*) Seneca, *Agamemnon*: manuscripts, text, interpretation *or* (*b*) Catullus: manuscripts, text, interpretation [Honour School of Literae Humaniores, subject III. 14] University classes will be given for only one of these options each year.

(xiii) Virgil, *Aeneid* [Honour Moderations in Classics, Course IA, paper 2; this option may not be offered by candidates who have satisfied the Moderators in Course IA, IB, IC or IIA of Honour Moderations in Classics]

(xiv) *Either* (*a*) The Conversion of Augustine [Honour School of Literae Humaniores, subject III. 15 (*a*)]

Or   (*b*) Byzantine Literature [Honour School of Literae Humaniores, subject III. 15 (*c*)]

Or   (*c*) The Latin Works of Petrarch [Honour School of Classics and Modern Languages, subject 6,7 (xiv) (*d*)]

Or   (*d*) Modern Greek Poetry [Honour School of Literae Humaniores, subject III. 15 (*c*) This subject is available only to candidates offering subject (i) Greek Literature of the 5th Century BC who are not offering (xxxviii), (xxxix) Greek or Latin for Beginners.

B. Subjects in Greek and Roman History (see note (*c*) above)

(xv) The Early Greek World and Herodotus' Histories: 650 to 479 BC [Honour School of Literae Humaniores, subject I. 1]

(xvi) Thucydides and the Greek World: 479 to 403 BC [Honour School of Literae Humaniores, subject I. 2]

(xvii) The End of the Peloponnesian War to the Death of Philip II of Macedon: 403 to 336 BC [Honour School of Literae Humaniores, subject I. 3]

(xviii) Polybius, Rome and the Mediterranean: 241–146 BC [Honour School of Literae Humaniores, subject I. 4]

(xix) Republic in Crisis: 146–46 BC [Honour School of Literae Humaniores, subject I. 5]

(xx) Rome, Italy and Empire from Caesar to Claudius: 46 BC to AD 54 [Honour School of Literae Humaniores, subject I. 6]

(xxi) Athenian Democracy in the Classical Age [Honour School of Literae Humaniores, subject I. 7]

(xxii) Alexander the Great and his Early Successors (336 BC–302 BC) [Honour School of Literae Humaniores, subject I. 8]

(xxiii) The Hellenistic World: Societies and Cultures c.300–100 BC [Honour School of Literae Humaniores, subject I. 9]

(xxiv) Cicero: Politics and Thought in the Late Republic [Honour School of Literae Humaniores, subject I. 10]

(xxv) Politics, Society and Culture from Nero to Hadrian [Honour School of Literae Humaniores, subject I. 11]

(xxvi) Religions in the Greek and Roman World (c.31 BC–AD 312) [Honour School of Literae Humaniores, subject I. 12]

(xxvii) Sexuality and Gender in Greece and Rome [Honour School of Literae Humaniores, subject I. 13]

C. Subjects in Philology and Linguistics (see note (*d*) above)

(xxviii) Greek Historical Linguistics [Honour School of Literae Humaniores, subject V. 1].

(xxix) Latin Historical Linguistics [Honour School of Literae Humaniores, subject V. 2].

(xxx) General Linguistics and Comparative Philology [Honour School of Literae Humaniores, subject V. 3].

(xxxi) Comparative Philology: Indo–European, Greek and Latin [Honour School of Literae Humaniores, subject V. 4]. This subject may not be offered by candidates who offered the paper Historical Linguistics and Comparative Philology (paper VI. F. 1 under Honour Moderation in Classics, Course IA) for their First Public Examination.

D. Subjects in Greek and Roman Archaeology (see note (*e*) above)

(xxxii) The Greeks and the Mediterranean World c.950 BC–500 BC [Honour School of Literae Humaniores, subject IV. 1]

(xxxiii) Greek Art and Archaeology, c.500–300 BC [Honour School of Literae Humaniores, subject IV. 2]

(xxxiv) Hellenistic Art and Archaeology, 330–30 BC [Honour School of Literae Humaniores, subject IV. 3]

(xxxv) Art under the Roman Empire, AD 14–337 [Honour School of Literae Humaniores, subject IV. 4]

(xxxvi) Roman Archaeology: Cities and Settlement under the Empire [Honour School of Literae Humaniores, subject IV. 5]

E. Subjects in Ancient and Medieval Philosophy

These subjects are specified in Regulations for Philosophy in all Honour Schools including Philosophy. One or two subjects may be offered. 110 may not be combined with 111. 115 may not be combined with 130. 116 may not be combined with 132.

(xxxvii) 110 (Aquinas)

(xxxviii) 111 (Duns Scotus, Ockham)

(xxxix) 115 (Plato, *Republic*, in translation)

(xl) 116 (Aristotle, *Nicomachean Ethics*, in translation)

   (xli) 130 (Plato, *Republic*, in Greek)
  (xlii) 131 (Plato, *Theaetetus* and *Sophist*)
 (xliii) 132 (Aristotle, *Nicomachean Ethics*, in Greek)
 (xliv) 133 (Aristotle, *Physics*)
  (xlv) 134 (Sextus Empiricus, *Outlines of Pyrrhonism*)   5
 (xlvi) 135 (Latin Philosophy)

F. Other subjects

  (xlvii), (xlviii) Greek or Latin for Beginners [Honour School of Literae Humaniores, subject VI. 1 and VI. 2, Second Classical Language] **(see note (f) above)**.

  (xlix) Thesis. Any candidate may offer a thesis in Classics, or in a subject 10 linking Classics and their Main Subject or Additional Language, in accordance with the Regulation on Theses in the Regulations for the Honour School of Literae Humaniores, save that references there to the Honour School of Literae Humaniores shall be deemed to be references to the Honour School of Classics and Oriental Studies, the competent authority for dealing with proposals shall be the standing 15 joint committee for Classics and Oriental Studies, and proposals should be submitted to the chair of that committee.

SPECIAL REGULATIONS FOR THE HONOUR SCHOOL OF COMPUTER SCIENCE

A

In the following, 'the Course Handbook' refers to the Computer Science Undergraduate Course Handbook and supplements to this published by the Computer Science Teaching Committee and also posted on the website at http://www.cs.ox.ac.uk/currentstudents/

1. The subject of the Honour School of Computer Science shall be the theory and practice of Computer Science.

2. No candidate shall be admitted to examination in this School unless he or she has either passed or been exempted from the First Public Examination.

3. The Examination in Computer Science shall be under the supervision of the Mathematical, Physical and Life Sciences Board. The Board shall have the power from time to time to frame and vary regulations for the different parts and subjects of the examination.

4. (*a*) The examination in Computer Science shall consist of three parts (A, B, C) for the four-year course, and of two parts (A, B) for the three-year course.

   (*b*) Parts A, B, and C shall be taken at times not less than three, six, and nine terms, respectively, after passing or being exempted from the First Public Examination.

5. The Examiners shall classify and publish the combined results of the examinations in Part A and Part B, and in respect of candidates taking the four-year course shall separately classify and publish results in Part C.

6. (*a*) Part A shall be taken on one occasion only. No candidate shall enter for Part B until he or she has completed Part A of the examination.

   (*b*) In order to proceed to Part C, a candidate must achieve upper second class Honours or higher in Parts A & B together.

   (*c*) A candidate on the three-year course who obtains only a Pass or fails to satisfy the Examiners in Part B may retake Part B on at most one subsequent occasion; a candidate on the four-year course who obtains only a Pass or fails to satisfy the Examiners in Part C may retake Part C on at most one subsequent occasion. A candidate on the four-year course shall take Part B on one occasion only.

7. A candidate adjudged worthy of Honours on both Parts A and B together, and on Part C may supplicate for the degree of Master of Computer Science provided that the candidate has fulfilled all the conditions for admission to a degree of the University.

8. A candidate in the final year of the four-year course, adjudged worthy of Honours in both Parts A and B together, but who does not enter Part C, or who fails to obtain Honours in Part C, is permitted to supplicate for the Honours degree of Bachelor of Arts in Computer Science with the classification obtained in Parts A and B together; provided that no such candidate may later enter or re-enter the Part C year or supplicate for the degree of Master of Computer Science; and provided in each case that the candidate has fulfilled all the conditions for admission to a degree of the University.

9. All candidates will be assessed as to their practical ability under the following provisions:

(a) The Head of the Department of Computer Science, or a deputy, shall make available to the examiners evidence showing the extent to which each candidate has pursued an adequate course of practical work. Only that work completed and marked by noon on Monday of the fifth week of the Trinity Term in which the candidate takes the examination shall be included in these records.

(b) Candidates for each part of the examination shall submit to the Chair of the Examiners, Honour School of Computer Science, c/o the Academic Administrator, Oxford University Department of Computer Science, Oxford, by noon on Monday of the fifth week of the Trinity Term in which the examination is being held, their reports of practical exercises completed during their course of study. For a report on a practical exercise to be considered by the examiners, it must have been marked by a demonstrator and must be accompanied by a statement that it is the candidate's own work except where otherwise indicated.

(c) The examiners shall take the evidence (a) and the report (b) into account in assessing a candidate's performance.

(d) Candidates whose overall performance on practical work is not satisfactory may be deemed to have failed the examination or may have their overall classification reduced.

B

The syllabus for each of Parts A, B, and C will be published by the Department of Computer Science in a handbook for candidates by the beginning of Michaelmas Full Term in the academic year of the examination concerned. The duration of each optional paper will be specified in the Course Handbook.

The use of calculators is generally not permitted but certain kinds may be allowed for certain papers. Specifications of which papers and which types of calculators are permitted for those exceptional papers will be announced by the examiners in the Hilary Term preceding the examination.

1. In Part A of the examination, candidates shall be required to offer four core subjects and four optional subjects from Schedule A in the Course Handbook.

Each subject shall be examined by means of a written examination with the exception of Object Oriented Programming, which shall be examined by means of a mini project or a written examination, the details of which are set out in the Course Handbook.

2. In Part B of the examination, each candidate shall be required to offer six optional subjects from Schedules B1, B2, and B4 in the Course Handbook, subject to the conditions that

> (*a*) no candidate shall offer any subject from Schedule B1 that he or she has already offered in Part A of the examination.
>
> (*b*) each candidate shall offer no more than two subjects from Schedule B1.
>
> (*c*) each candidate shall offer no more than two subjects from Schedule B4.

Each optional subject shall be examined by a written paper or by a mini-project. In addition, each candidate in Part B of the examination shall also submit a project report.

3. In Part C of the examination, each candidate shall be required to offer five optional subjects from Schedule C1 in the Course Handbook, subject to the condition that no candidate shall offer any subject that he or she has already offered in Part B of the examination. Each optional subject shall be examined by a written paper or by a mini-project. In addition, each candidate in Part C of the examination shall submit a project report.

4. The schedules of core and optional subjects for Parts A, B, and C of the examination shall be approved by the Faculty of Computer Science, and shall be published in the Course Handbook.

5. The examiners shall have the power to combine two papers on related optional subjects into a single paper for those candidates who offer both the optional subjects concerned.

6. In Part B and in Part C of the examination, each candidate shall carry out a project on a topic in Computer Science approved by the Teaching Committee of the Department of Computer Science. Each project will be supervised by a member of the Faculty of Computer Science, the Faculty of Mathematics or the Faculty of Engineering Science, or by some other person of equivalent seniority approved by the Teaching Committee. Two copies of a report of the project shall be submitted to the Chair of the Examiners, Honour School of Computer Science, c/o the Examination Schools, Oxford, by noon on Monday of the fifth week of the Trinity Term in which the relevant Part of the examination is held. The Part B report must not exceed 10,000 words plus forty pages of additional material (e.g. diagrams, program text). The Part C report must not exceed 10,000 words plus forty pages of additional material (e.g. diagrams, program text).

In retaking Part of an examination, projects previously submitted for Part B or for Part C of the examination may be submitted, but for that Part only. No project may be resubmitted if it has already been submitted, wholly or substantially, for another honour school or degree of the University, or of any other institution.

SPECIAL REGULATIONS FOR THE HONOUR SCHOOL OF COMPUTER SCIENCE AND PHILOSOPHY

A

In the following, 'the Course Handbook' refers to the Computer Science and Philosophy Undergraduate Course Handbook and supplements to this published by the joint supervisory committee and also posted on the website at http://www.cs.ox.ac.uk/teaching/csp

1. All candidates shall be examined in Computer Science and in Philosophy.

2. No candidate shall be admitted to the examination in this School unless he or she has either passed or been exempted from the First Public Examination.

3. The examinations in this school shall be under the joint supervision of the Divisional Board of Mathematical, Physical and Life Sciences and the Board of the Faculty of Philosophy, which shall appoint a joint supervisory committee to make regulations concerning it, subject in all cases to the preceding clauses of this subsection.

4. (*a*) The examination in Computer Science and Philosophy shall consist of three parts (A, B, C) for the four-year course, and of two parts (A, B) for the three-year course.

   (*b*) Parts A, B and C shall be taken at times not less than three, six, and nine terms, respectively, after passing or being exempted from the First Public Examination.

5. The Examiners shall classify and publish the combined results of the examinations in Part A and Part B, and in respect of candidates taking the four-year course shall separately classify and publish results in Part C.

6. (*a*) Part A shall be taken on one occasion only. No candidate shall enter for Part B until he or she has completed Part A of the examination.

   (*b*) In order to proceed to Part C, a candidate must achieve upper second class Honours or higher in Parts A and B together.

   (*c*) A candidate on the three-year course who obtains only a Pass or fails to satisfy the Examiners in Part B may retake Part B on at most one subsequent occasion; a candidate on the four-year course who obtains only a Pass or fails to satisfy the Examiners in Part C may retake Part C on at most one subsequent occasion. A candidate on the four-year course shall take Part B on one occasion only.

7. A candidate adjudged worthy of Honours on both Parts A and B together, and on Part C may supplicate for the degree of Master of Computer Science and Philosophy provided that the candidate has fulfilled all the conditions for admission to a degree of the University.

8. A candidate in the final year of the four-year course, adjudged worthy of Honours in both Parts A and B together, but who does not enter Part C, or who fails to obtain Honours in Part C, is permitted to supplicate for the Honours degree of Bachelor of Arts in Computer Science and Philosophy with the classification obtained in Parts A and B together; provided that no such candidate may later enter or re-enter the Part C year or supplicate for the degree of Master of Computer Science and Philosophy; and provided in each case that the candidate has fulfilled all the conditions for admission to a degree of the University.

B

1. In Part A of the examination, candidates shall be required to offer four Computer Science subjects from Schedule A(CS&P) in the Course Handbook, to include *Models of Computation*.

2. The examination for Part B shall consist of subjects in Computer Science and Philosophy.

The subjects in Computer Science shall be published in three schedules, B1(CS&P), B2(CS&P) and B4(CS&P), in a supplement to the Course Handbook by the beginning of the Michaelmas Full Term in the academic year of the examination concerned. Each Computer Science subject shall be examined by a written paper or by a mini-project.

The subjects in Philosophy shall be subjects 101–120, 122, 124 and 125 from the list given in Special Regulations for All Honour Schools Including Philosophy, and subject to the regulations therein. Each subject in Philosophy shall be assessed by a 3-hour written examination.

Each candidate shall offer:

(*a*) two, four or six Computer Science subjects, and
(*b*) five, four or three Philosophy subjects, respectively,
subject to the following constraints:

   (i) No candidate shall offer any subject from Schedule B1(CS&P) that he or she has already offered in Part A(CS&P) of the examination;
   (ii) Each candidate shall offer no more than two subjects from Schedule B1(CS&P);
   (iii) Each candidate shall offer no more than two subjects from Schedule B4(CS&P);
   (iv) Each candidate shall offer at least two Philosophy subjects from 101, 102, 104, 108, 122, 124 and 125.

3. In Part C each candidate shall offer a total of between 24 and 26 units chosen in any combination from the lists of taught courses for Computer Science and for Philosophy, a Computer Science project or a Philosophy thesis subject to the following constraints:

- No candidate may take more than six Computer Science taught subjects;
- No candidate may offer both a Computer Science project and a Philosophy thesis.

The taught subjects in Computer Science shall be published in a schedule, C (CS&P), in a supplement to the Course Handbook by the beginning of the Michaelmas Full Term in the academic year of the examination concerned. Each such subject shall be examined by a written paper or by a mini-project and shall count as three units.

Each taught Philosophy subject shall be one of the subjects 101–120, 122, 124, 125 and 180 from the list given in Special Regulations for All Honour Schools Including Philosophy, and subject to the regulations therein. Each such subject shall be assessed by a 3-hour written examination together with an essay of at most 5,000 words, conforming to the rules given in the Course Handbook. Each such subject shall count as eight units.

No candidate shall offer any taught subject that he or she has already offered in Part B of the examination.

A Computer Science project shall be as specified for the Honour School of Computer Science, and shall count as nine units. A Philosophy thesis shall be as specified in the Regulations for Philosophy in all Honour Schools including Philosophy (subject 199) except that the thesis shall not exceed 20,000 words, and shall count as eight units.

4. The use of calculators is generally not permitted but certain kinds may be allowed for certain papers. Specifications of which papers and which types of calculators are permitted for those exceptional papers will be announced by the Examiners in the Hilary Term preceding the examination.

5. All candidates will be assessed as to their practical ability in Computer Science under the following provisions:

(*a*) The Head of the Department of Computer Science, or a deputy, shall make available to the Examiners evidence showing the extent to which each candidate has pursued an adequate course of practical work. Only that work completed and marked by noon on Monday of the fifth week of the Trinity Term in which the candidate takes the examination shall be included in these records.

(*b*) Candidates for each part of the examination shall submit to the Chair of the Examiners, Honour School of Computer Science and Philosophy, c/o the Academic Administrator, Oxford University Department of Computer Science, Oxford, by noon on Monday of the fifth week of the Trinity Term in which the examination is being held, their reports of practical exercises completed during their course of study. For a report on a practical exercise to be considered by the Examiners, it must have been marked by a demonstrator and must be accompanied by a statement that it is the candidate's own work except where otherwise indicated.

(*c*) The Examiners shall take the evidence (a) and the report (b) into account in assessing a candidate's performance. Candidates whose overall performance on practical work is not satisfactory may be deemed to have failed the examination or may have their overall classification reduced.

SPECIAL REGULATIONS FOR THE HONOUR SCHOOL OF ECONOMICS AND MANAGEMENT

A

1. The examination in the Honour School of Economics and Management shall include, as stated subjects to be offered by all candidates:

  (i) Macroeconomics

  (ii) Microeconomics

  (iii) Quantitative Economics

2. Candidates shall be required to offer, in addition to the above subjects, at least two subjects from Schedule A and a further three subjects from Schedules A and B.

3. No candidate shall be admitted to examination in this school unless he or she has either passed or been exempted from the First Public Examination.

4. The examination in this school shall be under the supervision of the Social Sciences Board, which shall appoint a standing committee to make regulations concerning it, subject always to the preceding clauses of this sub-section.

B

All candidates will be required to take *eight* subjects in all.

On entering his or her name for the examination by the date prescribed, each candidate must give notice to the Registrar of the papers being offered.

Candidates are permitted the use of one hand-held pocket calculator from a list of permitted calculators published by the Department of Economics on its Undergraduate website, which will be updated annually in the week prior to the first full week of Michaelmas Term.

All candidates will be required to offer the following subjects:

  (i) *Macroeconomics*

As specified for the Honour School of Philosophy, Politics, and Economics.

  (ii) *Microeconomics*

As specified for the Honour School of Philosophy, Politics, and Economics.

  (iii) *Quantitative Economics*

As specified for the Honour School of Philosophy, Politics, and Economics.

  (iv) *Two* subjects selected from Schedule A.

  (v) *Three* optional subjects selected from Schedule A, except that a candidate cannot offer a subject selected from Schedule A offered under (iv), and Schedule B.

Depending on the availability of teaching resources, not all Management Options will be available to all candidates in every year. Candidates and Management tutors will be circulated in Trinity Term with details of all Options which will be available for the following year. The list, from which papers in Schedule A may be selected, and the syllabus for each, shall be approved by the Faculty of Management Studies and published on the Saïd Business School Undergraduate Website by the Chair of the Standing Committee not later than the end of the Trinity Full Term of the academic year preceding the year of the examination.

Not all Economics subjects may be available in any particular year. There may also be restrictions on numbers permitted to offer some Economics subjects in any particular year.

Economics subjects available to candidates in any particular year will depend on the availability of teaching resources. Details of the choices available for the following year will be announced at the Economics Department's 'Option Fair' at the beginning of the fourth week of the first Hilary Full Term of candidates' work for the Honour School, and will be posted on the Department's Undergraduate website at the same time.

Schedule A

(1) *Accounting*

Nature and regulation of financial reporting, analysis of company accounts. Nature of management accounting, including: cost behaviour, budgetary planning and control, capital budgeting, divisional performance.

(2) *Organisational Behaviour and Analysis*

The individual in the organisation; motivation and job satisfaction; groups at work; decision making; gender; organisational strategy and structure; the organisational environment; managerial work and behaviour; leadership; culture; power, conflict and change; contemporary and comparative approaches.

(3) *Employment Relations*

The structure and management of the employment relationship, including its environment, and economic and social consequences; human resource strategy and style; systems of collective representation; trade union objectives and organisation; pay systems and performance appraisal; explicit and psychological contracts; the management of co-operation and conflict; employee involvement, participation and team working; technology, work design and work organisation; job regulation; the utilisation of human resources; training and performance; contemporary and comparative approaches to the management of employees.

(4) *Finance*

Investment appraisal under conditions of certainty/uncertainty. Portfolio theory and capital asset pricing model. Sources of finance, debt capacity, dividends, and cost of capital. Financial market efficiency. Emerging issues in finance. Takeovers and mergers.

(5) *Strategic Management*

Theoretical foundations of strategic management. Structural analysis of industries and industry dynamics. The resource and capability based view of the firm. Strategy and Organization. Nature and sources of competitive advantage and patterns of competition. Competitive and co-operative strategies. Corporate strategy and competitive advantage. International strategy. Strategic management in the public sector and not-for-profit organisations. Current issues in strategic management.

(6) *Marketing*

Exchange in a modern economy. The marketing concept; the marketing mix, its formulation and common components; the product life-cycle and new product development; segmentation and positioning. Buyer behaviour. Marketing information and the analysis of markets and competitors. Marketing planning and marketing strategies. Models for evaluating strategic marketing opportunities.

(7) *Technology and Operations Management*

Goods and service operations. Vertical integration, facilities location and capacity, volume/mix and process relationships, scale economies, automation. Goods/service design, facilities, process planning, aggregate capacity decisions, resource scheduling. Product/service quality assurance, facilities maintenance.

(8) *International Business*

Theoretical foundations of international business strategy. Definition and historical underpinnings of globalisation. Global value chains. Market entry strategies. Institutional analysis and economic theory. Institutional voids. Theories of competitive and comparative advantage. Global culture and marketing. Ethical supply chains. Contemporary theories and controversies in international business.

Schedule B

Subjects (1) to (15) are as specified in the Honour School of Philosophy, Politics, and Economics.

    (1) *Microeconomic Theory*
    (2) *Money and Banking*
    (3) *Public Economics*
    (4) *Economics of Industry*
    (5) *Labour Economics and Industrial Relations (222)*
    (6) *International Economics*
    (7) *Command and Transitional Economies*
    (8) *Economics of Developing Countries*
    (9) *British Economic History since 1870*
    (10) *Econometrics*
    (11) *Comparative Demographic Systems*
    (12) *Economics of OECD Countries*
    (13) *Economic Decisions within the Firm*
    (14) *Game Theory*
    (15) *Mathematical Methods*

(v) *Thesis*

Any candidate may offer a thesis instead of a subject from Schedule A or Schedule B under (v) above, subject to the following provisions:

(a) *Subject*

The subject of every thesis should fall within the scope of the honour school. The subject may, but need not, overlap any subject on which the candidate offers papers. Candidates are warned that they should avoid repetition in papers of materials used in their theses and that substantial repetition may be penalised.

Every candidate shall submit through his or her college for approval to the Chair of the Standing Committee for Economics and Management the title he or she proposes together with

    (i) an indication as to the branch of the school in which the subject falls, i.e. Economics or Management;
    (ii) an explanation of the subject in about 100 words;
    (iii) a letter of approval from his or her tutor,

not earlier than the first day of the Trinity Full Term of the year before that in which he or she is to be examined and not later than the date prescribed for entry to the examination. The standing committee shall decide as soon as possible whether or not to approve the title and shall advise the candidate immediately. No decision shall be deferred beyond the end of the fifth week of Michaelmas Full Term.

(*b*) *Authorship and origin*

Every thesis shall be the candidate's own work. His or her tutor may, however, discuss with him or her the field of study, the sources available, and the method of presentation; the tutor may also read and comment on a first draft. Theses previously submitted for the Honour School of Economics and Management may be resub-   5
mitted. No thesis will be accepted if it has already been submitted, wholly or substantially, for another Honour School or degree of this University, or for a degree of any other institution. Every candidate shall sign a certificate to the effect that the thesis is his or her own work and that it has not already been submitted for a degree of this or any other university and his or her tutor shall countersign the certificate   10
confirming that, to the best of his or her knowledge and belief, these statements are true. This certificate shall be submitted separately in a sealed envelope addressed to the chair of examiners. No thesis shall, however, be ineligible because it has been or is being submitted for any prize of this University.

(*c*) *Length and format*   15

No thesis shall exceed 15,000 words, the limit to include all notes, appendices, but not bibliographies; no person or body shall have authority to permit any excess. There shall be a select bibliography or a list of sources. All theses must be typed in double spacing on one side of quarto or A4 paper. Any notes and references may be placed *either* at the bottom of the relevant pages *or* all together at the end of the   20
thesis, but in the latter case two loose copies of the notes and references must be supplied. The thesis must be bound or held firmly in a stiff cover. *Two* copies shall be submitted to the examiners; they shall be returned to the Saïd Business School library after the examination.

(*d*) *Submission of thesis*   25

Every candidate who wishes to submit a thesis shall give notice of his or her intention to do so on his or her examination entry form (in addition to seeking approval of the subject from the Chair of the Standing Committee for Economics and Management under (*a*) above); and shall submit his or her thesis not later than noon on Monday of the first week of the Trinity Full Term of the examination to the Chair   30
of the Examiners, Honour School of Economics and Management, Examination Schools, High Street, Oxford.

SPECIAL REGULATIONS FOR THE HONOUR SCHOOL OF ENGINEERING SCIENCE

For candidates embarking on the Honour School in October 2009, October 2010, and October 2011

A

1. No candidate shall be admitted to examination in this school unless he or she has either passed or been exempted from the First Public Examination.

2. The subject of the examination shall be Engineering Science.

3. The examination in this school shall be under the supervision of the Divisional Board of Mathematical, Physical and Life Sciences, which will make regulations concerning it, subject always to the provision of this subsection.

4. (*a*) The examination shall consist of three parts: A, B and C.

   (*b*) Parts A, B and C shall be taken at times not less than three, six and nine terms, respectively, after passing or being exempted from the First Public Examination.

   (*c*) Parts B and C shall be taken in consecutive years, save where approval has been given by the Board for an intercalated year of study or industrial attachment between Parts B and C.

5. No candidate may present him or herself for examination in Part C unless he or she has been adjudged worthy of Honours by the examiners in both Parts A and B together.

6. The name of a candidate shall not be published in a class list until he or she has completed all parts of the examination, and has been adjudged worthy of Honours by the examiners in Parts A, B and C of the examination. The Examiners shall give due consideration to the performance in all parts of the respective examinations.

7. The examiners shall be entitled to award a Pass to candidates on Parts A and B who have reached a standard considered adequate but who have not been adjudged worthy of honours.

8. A candidate who obtains only a pass, or fails to satisfy the examiners, may enter again for Part B of the examination on one, but no more than one, subsequent occasion. Parts A and C shall be entered on one occasion only.

9. A candidate adjudged worthy of Honours on both Parts A and B together, and on Part C may supplicate for the Degree of Master of

Engineering in Engineering Science, provided he or she has fulfilled all the conditions for admission to a degree of the University.

10. A candidate who passes both Parts A and B or who is adjudged worthy of Honours in Parts A and B together, but who does not enter Part C, or fails to obtain classified Honours in Part C, may be permitted to supplicate for the degree of Bachelor of Arts in Engineering Science (pass or unclassified Honours, as appropriate); provided that no such candidate may later enter or re-enter the Part C year or supplicate for the degree of Master of Engineering in Engineering Science; and provided in each case that the candidate has fulfilled all the conditions for admission to a degree of the University.

*For candidates embarking on the Honour School in or
after October 2012, taking Part A in or after 2013, taking
Part B in or after 2014, and taking Part C in or after 2015*

A

1. No candidate shall be admitted to the examination in this school unless he or she has either passed or been exempted from the First Public Examination.

2. The subject of the examination shall be Engineering Science.

3. The examination in this school shall be under the supervision of the Divisional Board of Mathematical, Physical and Life Sciences, which shall make regulations concerning it, subject always to the provisions of this subsection.

4. (*a*) The examination shall consist of three parts (A, B, C).

(*b*) Parts A, B and C shall be taken at times not less than three, six and nine terms, respectively, after passing or being exempted from the First Public Examination.

(*c*) Parts B and C shall be taken in consecutive years save where approval has been given by the Board for an intercalated year of study or industrial attachment between Parts B and C.

(*d*) A candidate who obtains only a pass, or fails to satisfy the examiners, may enter again for Part B of the examination on one, but no more than one, subsequent occasion; Part A shall be entered on one occasion only. Part C shall be entered on one occasion only.

5. No candidate may present him or herself for examination in Part C unless he or she has been adjudged worthy of at least second class honours by the examiners in Parts A and B together at the first attempt.

6. (*a*) A candidate adjudged worthy of at least second class honours in Parts A and B together at the first attempt and worthy of Honours in Part C in Engineering Science may supplicate for the Degree of Master of Engineering in Engineering Science provided that the candidate has fulfilled all the conditions for admission to a degree of the University.

(*b*) A candidate who passes Parts A and B together but fails to be adjudged worthy of at least second class honours at the first attempt, or who is adjudged worthy of at least second class honours in Parts A and B together, but who does not enter, or withdraws from, Part C, is permitted to supplicate for the Degree of Bachelor of Arts in Engineering Science (Pass, or Honours with the classification obtained in Parts A and B together, as appropriate); provided that no such candidate may later enter or re-enter the Part C year or supplicate for the degree of Master of Engineering in Engineering Science; and provided in each case that the candidate has fulfilled all the conditions for admission to a degree of the University.

(*c*) The Examiners shall give due consideration to the performance in all parts of the respective examinations.

7. The name of a candidate shall not be published in a class list until he or she has completed all parts of the respective examination (Parts A, B, and C for the Master of Engineering in Engineering Science or Parts A and B for students exiting with a Bachelor of Arts in Engineering Science) in accordance with cl. 6 above.

B

In the following 'the Course Handbook' refers to the Engineering Science Undergraduate Course Handbook, published annually at the start of Michaelmas Term by the Faculty of Engineering Science.

The syllabus for each of Parts A, B and C will be published by the Faculty of Engineering Science in the Course Handbook, together with the relative weighting of each paper and the duration of all written papers.

The examiners will not provide calculators, but will permit the use of one hand-held pocket calculator from a list of permitted calculators published by the Chair of the Faculty not later than the end of the Trinity Full Term in the academic year preceding the examination.

1. In Part A of the examination, candidates will be required to take four written papers, as follows:

A1 Mathematics
A2 Electronic and Information Engineering
A3 Structures, Materials and Dynamics
A4 Energy Systems

In addition, they will be required to take Paper A5 Engineering Practical Work, which will be examined by continuous assessment. Candidates will not normally be required to submit their Engineering Practical Work. However, the examiners may request practical work from some candidates. Such candidates will be named in a list posted by the day of the last written examination.

2. In Part B of the examination, candidates will be required to take five optional written papers from Schedule B papers in the Course Handbook and, in addition, Paper B2 Engineering in Society.

Candidates will also be required to take three coursework subjects, as follows:
B1 Engineering Computation
B3 Group Design Project
B4 Engineering Practical Work
Paper B4 will be examined through continuous assessment. Candidates will not normally be required to submit their Engineering Practical Work. However, the examiners may request practical work from some candidates. Such candidates will be named in a list posted by the day of the last written examination.

3. Candidates shall submit to the examiners reports on the Group Design Project (Paper B3) completed as a part of their course of study. The subject of the project shall be approved by the Projects Committee of the Faculty of Engineering Science and three copies of the report shall be submitted to the Chair of the Examiners, Honour School of Engineering Science, c/o Examination Schools, High Street, Oxford, by noon on Friday of the fourth week of Trinity Term in the year of the Part B examination. The project report must not exceed thirty pages (including all diagrams, photographs, references and appendices). All pages must be numbered, have margins of not less than 20mm all round and type face of Arial 11 pt font with double-line spacing. The report must be the candidate's own work and should include a signed statement to this effect. Project reports previously submitted for the Honour School of Engineering Science may be resubmitted. No project report will be accepted if it has already been submitted wholly or substantially for another honour school or degree of this University, or for a degree at any other institution. Resubmitted work must be physically presented at the time and in the manner prescribed for submission.

4. In Part C a candidate shall be required to offer six written papers from Schedule C in the Course Handbook or an equivalent approved collection of course options if taking part in an exchange scheme. Candidates taking part in an exchange scheme shall have the proposed set of papers to be taken in the host institution approved by the faculty by the end of Trinity full term before going on the exchange.

5. In Part C of the examination, each candidate shall carry out a project on a topic of Engineering Science approved by the Projects Committee of the Faculty of Engineering Science. Each candidate shall submit three copies of his or her own report of the project to the Chair of the Examiners, Honour School of Engineering Science, c/o Examination Schools, High Street, Oxford, by noon on Friday of the fourth week of Trinity Term. The report must not exceed fifty pages (including all diagrams, photographs, references and appendices). All pages must be numbered, have margins of not less than 20mm all round, and type face of Arial 11 pt font with double-line spacing. The report must be the candidate's own work and should include a signed statement to this effect. Reports previously submitted for Part C for the Honour School of Engineering Science may be resubmitted. No work will be accepted if it has already been submitted, wholly or substantially, for Part B or for another honour school or degree of this University, or for a degree of any other institution. Resubmitted work must be physically presented at the time and in the manner prescribed for submission.

6. Each individual candidate taking part in a full year exchange at a host institution approved by the University will provide a collated set of coursework to the Exchange Coordinator of the Faculty of Engineering Science. The Exchange Coordinator will ensure that the host institution forwards a full transcript of the courses taken certified by the host institution. The Exchange Coordinator will also ensure that the host institution retains the examination papers for the approved courses undertaken and that these are submitted under seal, together with the collated coursework and transcript of courses taken, to the Chair of Examiners, Honour School of Engineering Science, c/o Examination Schools, High Street, Oxford by noon on Friday of the sixth week of Trinity Term.

Exceptionally, and with the approval of the Chair of the Faculty of Engineering Science, candidates may undertake their Project during a twenty-four week placement and take a specified equivalent of six papers from Schedule C in the Course Handbook. The placement shall always include the period from the fifth Friday before to the first Saturday after the end of Michaelmas Full Term.

7. Candidates may be examined viva voce at the examiners' discretion.

SPECIAL REGULATIONS FOR THE HONOUR SCHOOL OF ENGINEERING, ECONOMICS, AND MANAGEMENT

A

1. No candidate shall be admitted to examination in this school unless he or she has either passed or been exempted from the First Public Examination.

2. The examination in this school shall be under the joint supervision of the Mathematical, Physical and Life Sciences Board and the Social Sciences Board, which shall appoint a standing joint committee to make regulations concerning it, subject always to the preceding clauses of this subsection.

3. (*a*) The examination shall consist of three parts: A, B and C.

   (*b*) Parts A, B and C shall be taken at times not less than three, six and nine terms, respectively, after passing or being exempted from the First Public Examination.

   (*c*) Parts B and C shall be taken in consecutive years, save where approval has been given by the committee for an intercalated year of study or industrial attachment between Parts B and C.

4. No candidate may present him or herself for examination in Part C unless he or she has been adjudged worthy of Honours by the examiners in both Parts A and B together.

5. The name of a candidate shall not be published in a class list until he or she has completed all parts of the examination, and has been adjudged worthy of Honours by the examiners in Parts A, B and C of the examination. The Examiners shall give due consideration to the performance in all parts of the respective examinations.

6. The examiners shall be entitled to award a Pass to candidates on Parts A and B who have reached a standard considered adequate but who have not been adjudged worthy of Honours.

7. A candidate who obtains only a pass, or fails to satisfy the examiners, may enter again for Part B of the examination on one, but no more than one, subsequent occasion. Parts A and C shall be entered on one occasion only.

8. A candidate adjudged worthy of Honours on both Parts A and B together, and on Part C may supplicate for the Degree of Master of Engineering in Engineering, Economics, and

Management, provided he or she has fulfilled all the conditions for admission to a degree of the University.

9. A candidate who passes both Parts A and B or who is adjudged worthy of Honours in Parts A and B together, but who does not enter Part C, or fails to obtain classified Honours in Part C, may be permitted to supplicate for the degree of Bachelor of Arts in Engineering, Economics, and Management (pass or unclassified Honours, as appropriate); provided that no such candidate may later enter or re-enter the Part C year or supplicate for the degree of Master of Engineering in Engineering, Economics, and Management; and provided in each case that the candidate has fulfilled all the conditions for admission to a degree of the University.

10. The examiners for Engineering Science shall be appointed by the committee for the nomination of examiners in Engineering Science; those for Economics shall be appointed by the committee for the nomination of examiners in Economics in the Honour School of Philosophy, Politics, and Economics; those for Management shall be appointed by the committee for the nomination of examiners in Management Studies.

B

In the following 'the Course Handbook' refers to the Engineering, Economics, and Management Undergraduate Course Handbook, published annually at the start of Michaelmas Term by the committee.

The syllabus for each of Parts A, B and C will be published by the committee in the Course Handbook, together with the relative weighting of each paper and the duration of all written papers.

The examiners will not provide calculators, but will permit the use of one hand-held pocket calculator as specified in the Honour School of Engineering Science.

1. In Part A of the examination, candidates will be required to take four written papers:

Paper A1 Mathematics (as specified in the Honour School of Engineering Science)

Paper M1 General Management (as specified in the regulation relating to the General Management paper of the Economics and Management Preliminary Examination).

Two papers from:

Paper A2 Electronic and Information Engineering (as specified in the Honour School of Engineering Science)

Paper A3 Structures, Materials and Dynamics (as specified in the Honour School of Engineering Science)

Paper A4 Energy Systems (as specified in the Honour School of Engineering Science)

In addition, they will be required to take Paper A5E Engineering Practical Work (a shortened version of the Honour School of Engineering Science Paper A5), which will be examined by continuous assessment of practical work. Candidates will not normally be required to submit their Engineering Practical Work. However, the examiners may request practical work from some candidates. Such candidates will be named in a list posted by the day of the last written examination.

2. In Part B of the examination, candidates will be required to take:

Three optional Engineering written papers from Schedule B of the Honour School of Engineering Science.

Paper B2 Engineering in Society (as specified in the Honour School of Engineering Science)

Paper Ec1 Introductory Economics (as specified in the regulation relating to the Introductory Economics paper of the Economics and Management Preliminary Examination).

Candidates will also be required to take three Engineering coursework subjects:

Paper B1 Engineering Computation (as specified in the Honour School of Engineering Science)

Paper B3 Group Design Project (as specified in the Honour School of Engineering Science)

Paper B4E Engineering Practical Work (a shortened version of the Honour School of Engineering Science Paper B4)

Paper B4E will be examined by continuous assessment. Candidates will not normally be required to submit their Engineering Practical Work. However, the examiners may request practical work from some candidates. Such candidates will be named in a list posted by the day of the last written examination.

3. Candidates shall submit to the examiners reports on the Group Design Project (Paper B3) completed as a part of their course of study. The subject of the project shall be approved by the Projects Committee of the Faculty of Engineering Science and three copies of the report shall be submitted to the Chair of the Examiners, Honour School of Engineering, Economics, and Management, c/o Examination Schools, High Street, Oxford, by noon on Friday of the fourth week of Trinity Term in the year of the Part B examination. The project report must not exceed thirty pages (including all diagrams, photographs, references and appendices); all pages must be numbered, have margins of not less than 20mm all round and type face of Arial 11 pt font with double-line spacing. The report must be the candidate's own work and should include a signed statement to this effect. Project reports previously submitted for the Honour School of Engineering, Economics, and Management may be resubmitted. No project report will be accepted if it has already been submitted wholly or substantially for another honour school or degree of this University, or for a degree at any other institution. Resubmitted work must be physically presented at the time and in the manner prescribed for submission.

4. In Part C a candidate shall be required to offer:

Two written Engineering papers from Schedule C in the Course Handbook.

Two papers from the list of optional Management and Economics papers published annually.

5. Candidates will also be required to undertake either a twenty-four week external project attached to an industrial firm, or a twenty-four week internal university project. The former will be undertaken between the end of Trinity Full Term in the year in which the Part B examination is held and the beginning of Hilary Full Term in the year in which the Part C examination is held. The latter will run from the beginning of Michaelmas Term to the beginning of Trinity Term in the year in which the Part C examination is held. The project will be carried out under the supervision of a person or persons approved by the Project Co-ordinator in Management or Engineering as appropriate. All projects and industrial attachments will normally be arranged by, and must be approved by, the project co-ordinators in Management and/or Engineering. The report shall be on a topic, approved by the standing committee, normally in Management or Engineering. Topics in Economics may be

approved, but the project co-ordinators cannot undertake to arrange projects in the field of Economics.

Candidates undertaking a management project will be required to keep statutory residence for workshops, as specified by the Course Director, in the year in which the Part B examination is taken in order to prepare for the project to be carried out as part of the Part C examination.

Candidates will be required to present, as part of the Part C examination, a report on the project carried out during this period. In the case of a management report, the report shall not exceed 20,000 words including appendices and tables, but excluding references. For an engineering project, the report must not exceed fifty pages (including all diagrams, photographs, references and appendices); all pages should be numbered, have margins of not less than 20mm all round, and type face not less than eleven font with line spacing of no less than 8mm.

6. External project reports must be submitted by noon on Friday of the week before the start of Hilary Full Term in the year in which the Part C examination is held. Internal projects must be submitted by noon on Friday of the fourth week of Trinity Term of the year in which the Part C examination is held. They must be addressed to 'The Examination Schools, High Street, Oxford OX1 4BG, for the Chair of Examiners in Part C of the examination for the Honour School of Engineering, Economics, and Management'. Reports must be accompanied by a signed statement by the candidate that it is his or her own work. Candidates must submit two copies of each project report. Successful candidates will be required to deposit one of these copies in the library of the Department of Engineering Science and the other in the library of the School of Management.

7. Candidates may be examined viva voce on any part of their course of study, including their industrial project.

SPECIAL REGULATIONS FOR THE HONOUR SCHOOL OF ENGLISH AND MODERN LANGUAGES

For students commencing the Honour School on or before 1 October 2012

A

1. The subjects of the examination in the Honour School of English and Modern Languages shall be (*a*) English Language and Literature in English and (*b*) those modern languages and literatures studied in the Honour School of Modern Languages.

2. All candidates must offer both (*a*) and one of the languages in (*b*) with its literature.

3. No candidate shall be admitted to the examination in this school unless he or she has either passed or been exempted from the First Public Examination.

4. The examiners shall indicate in the lists issued by them the language offered by each candidate obtaining honours or satisfying the examiners under the appropriate regulation.

5. The examination in this school shall be under the joint supervision of the Boards of the Faculties of English Language and Literature and of Medieval and Modern Languages, which shall appoint a standing joint committee to make, and to submit to the two faculty boards, proposals for regulations for this examination and for the Preliminary Examination in English and Modern Languages.

6. (i) The examiners in the honour school shall be such of the Public Examiners in the Honour Schools of English and Modern Languages as shall be required.

(ii) It shall be the duty of the chairs of examiners in the Honour School of English and in the Honour School of Modern Languages to consult together and designate such examiners as shall be required for the honour school, whereupon the number of the examiners shall be deemed to be complete.

B

Candidates will be examined in accordance with the examination regulations set out below.

They will also be required to spend, after their matriculation, a year of residence in an appropriate country or countries, and to provide on their entry form for the examination a certificate that they have done this, signed by the Head or by a tutor of their society. Candidates wishing to be dispensed from the requirement to undertake a year of residence abroad must apply in writing to the Chair of the Medieval and Modern Languages Board, 41 Wellington Square, Oxford, OX1 2JF, stating their reasons for requesting dispensation and enclosing a letter of support from their society.

Candidates will be expected to carry out during this year abroad such work as their society may require. It is strongly recommended that candidates should apply through the Central Bureau for Educational Visits and Exchanges for an Assistantship, where these are available, and should accept one if offered. Candidates who are not able to obtain an Assistantship should during their year abroad follow a course or courses in an institution or institutions approved by their society, or should spend their time in such other circumstances as are acceptable to their society. Candidates will agree with their College Tutor in advance of their year abroad an independent course of study to be followed during that period.

The papers and choices of options available to candidates for each of the two courses will be the same.

Each candidate shall offer Part I and either Part II or Part III as prescribed below. Except in a Special Subject or an alternative to a Special Subject, a candidate shall offer (in addition to English) one modern language and its literature only.

In every case where, under the regulations for the school, candidates have a choice between one or more papers or subjects, every candidate shall give notice to the Registrar not later than Friday in the fourth week of the Michaelmas Full Term preceding the examination of all the papers and subjects being so offered.

Candidates are warned that they must avoid duplicating in their answers to one part of the examination material that they have used in another part of the examination.

New optional subjects may be added to those parts of the syllabus for both Part II and Part III where options are already provided by regulation published in the *Gazette* by the beginning of the fifth week of Trinity Full Term of the year before the year of the examination in which the subjects will first be available.

Oral examination

As specified for the Honour School of Modern Languages.

Part I
1. Honour School of Modern Languages, Papers I.
2. Honour School of Modern Languages, Papers IIA and IIB.
3. Honour School of Modern Languages, *one* paper chosen from Papers VI, VII, or VIII.
4. Honour School of Modern Languages, *one* paper chosen from Papers IV, V, IX, X, XI, or XII.

Either
Part II
5. Shakespeare (one paper) [Honour School of English Language and Literature, Course I, Subject 2].
6, 7. *Two* of the following periods of English Literature:
   (i) Introduction to Medieval Studies: Old English Literature (one paper) [Honour School of English Language and Literature, Course I, Subject 9]. Candidates who have satisfied the Examiners in this paper in a First Public Examination may not offer this paper.
   (ii) English Literature from 1100 to 1509 (two papers) [Honour School of English Language and Literature, Course I, Subject 3 (*a*) and (*b*)].
   (iii) English Literature from 1509 to 1642 (one paper) [Honour School of English Language and Literature, Course I, Subject 4].
Candidates who have satisfied the Moderators in Honour Moderations in Classics and English may not offer this paper.

(iv) English Literature from 1642 to 1740 (one paper) [Honour School of English Language and Literature, Course I, Subject 5].

(v) English Literature from 1740 to 1832 (one paper) [Honour School of English Language and Literature, Course I, Subject 6].

(vi) Victorian Literature (1832–1900) (one paper) [Honour School of English Language and Literature, Course I, Subject 4(*a*)]. Candidates who have satisfied the Examiners in this paper in a First Public Examination may not offer this paper.

(vii) Modern Literature (1900 to the present day) (one paper) [Honour School of English Language and Literature, Course I, Subject 4(*b*)]. Candidates who have satisfied the Examiners in this paper in a First Public Examination may not offer this paper.

8. *One* of the following:

(i) The English Language (a portfolio submitted in year 2) [Honour School of English Language and Literature, Course I, Subject 1].

(ii) Special Authors (an extended essay of not fewer than 5,000 nor more than 6,000 words) [Honour School of English Language and Literature, Course I, Subject 7].

Within the confines of the themes set for the paper, candidates may write on a topic combining the modern language with English as long as the modern language element takes up no more than half the essay.

Each candidate must inform the Head of Examinations and Assessment, Examinations School, through the Senior Tutor of his or her college or society by the Friday of the second week of Michaelmas Full Term preceding the examination, of the author on which he or she proposes to offer the essay.

(iii) Special topics [Honour School of English Language and Literature, Course I, Subject 8] (*a*), (*b*), *i.* (may not be taken by candidates offering linguistics options under Part I. 4), *ii.*, *iii.*, *iv.* (may not be taken by candidates offering 'Old Norse' under Part I. 4, (vi)), *vi.* (may not be taken by candidates offering Welsh options under Part I. 4(vi)), *vii.*, *viii.*, (*c*).

With the exception of those Paper 8 options for which a timed examination is the prescribed mode of assessment, and within the confines of the themes set for the paper, candidates may write on a topic combining the modern language with English as long as the modern language element takes up no more than half the essay.

(iv) One subject, not already selected, from among those listed under 4, 6, 7.

(v) An extended essay on a topic combining the modern language and English (to be examined under the regulations for the Honour School of Modern Languages).

9. In addition a candidate may offer one of the following:

either

(i) One subject not already selected from amongst those listed under 4, 6, 7, 8.*

or

(ii) An Extended Essay on a topic in the modern language (to be examined under the regulations for the Honour School of Modern Languages).

or

Part III

5. English Literature 1100–1530 (one paper) [Honour School of English Language and Literature, Course II, Subject A2]

---

* No candidate may offer an extended essay for both 8(ii) and 8(iii) in his or her selection of options for the honour school.

6, 7. *Two* papers chosen from the Honour School of English Language and Literature Course II, Subjects A: 1, 3–5, B: 1–4, 7, provided that a candidate who has not taken paper 3(*c*) in part 2 of the Preliminary Examination must offer Subject A1. Subject B7 will be examined by extended essay. This is with the exception of Course II papers available under B7 (*h*) for which the Course II regulations specify that these shall be assessed by written examination.

Candidates taking subject B7 may write on a topic combining the modern language with English as long as the modern language element takes up no more than half of the essay.

8. *Either*

   (*a*) One subject, not already selected, from among those listed under 4, 6, 7 of this course.

or

   (*b*) One subject chosen from English Course II Subjects B6, 8–9, 15, 21–25, provided that no candidate may offer (i) both B15 and Modern Languages paper XII Special Subject 'Old Norse', or (ii) both B21 or 22 and Modern Languages paper XII Special Subject 'Medieval Welsh Tales and Romances, the Poets of the Welsh Princes and the Poetry of Dafydd ap Gwilym'. Subject B6 will be examined by extended essay (as specified in the regulations for the Honour School of English Language and Literature). Within the confines of the themes set for the paper, candidates taking subject B6 may write on a topic combining the modern language with English as long as the modern language element takes up no more than half the essay.

or

   (*c*) An extended essay on a topic combining the modern language and English (to be examined under the regulations for the Honour School of Modern Languages).

9. In addition a candidate may offer one of the following:

either

   (i) One subject not already selected from among those listed under 4, 6, 7, 8 of this course subject to the restrictions listed under 8 above.

or

   (ii) English Course II Subject B16, provided this paper may only be offered by a candidate who also offers English Course II Subject B15.

or

   (iii) An Extended Essay on a topic in the modern language (to be examined under the regulations for the Honour School of Modern Languages).

SPECIAL REGULATIONS FOR THE HONOUR SCHOOL OF ENGLISH AND MODERN LANGUAGES

*For students commencing the Honour School
on or after 1 October 2013*

A

1. The subjects of the examination in the Honour School of English and Modern Languages shall be (a) English Language and Literature in English and (b) those modern languages and literatures studied in the Honour School of Modern Languages.

2. All candidates must offer both (a) and one of the languages in (b) with its literature.

3. No candidate shall be admitted to the examination in this school unless he or she has either passed or been exempted from the First Public Examination.

4. The examiners shall indicate in the lists issued by them the language offered by each candidate obtaining honours or satisfying the examiners under the appropriate regulation.

5. The examination in this school shall be under the joint supervision of the Boards of the Faculties of English Language and Literature and of Medieval and Modern Languages, which shall appoint a standing joint committee to make, and to submit to the two faculty boards, proposals for regulations for this examination and for the Preliminary Examination in English and Modern Languages.

6. (i) The examiners in the honour school shall be such of the Public Examiners in the Honour Schools of English and Modern Languages as shall be required.

   (ii) It shall be the duty of the chairs of examiners in the Honour School of English and in the Honour School of Modern Languages to consult together and designate such examiners as shall be required for the honour school, whereupon the number of the examiners shall be deemed to be complete.

B

1. The Year Abroad

Candidates will be examined in accordance with the examination regulations set out below. In addition, every candidate shall be required to spend, after their matriculation, a year of residence in an appropriate country or countries, and to provide on their entry form for the examination a certificate confirming that they have done this, signed by the Head or by a tutor of their college or society.

Candidates wishing to be dispensed from the requirement to undertake a year of residence abroad must apply in writing to the Chair of the Medieval and Modern Languages Board, 41 Wellington Square, Oxford, OX1 2JF, stating their reasons for requesting dispensation and enclosing a letter of support from their college or society. Candidates will be expected to carry out during this year abroad such work as their college or society may require. It is strongly recommended that candidates should apply through the Central Bureau for Educational Visits and Exchanges for an Assistantship, where these are available, and should accept one if offered. Candidates who are not able to obtain an Assistantship should during their year abroad follow a course or courses in an institution or institutions approved by their society, or should spend their time in such other circumstances as are acceptable to their society. Candidates will agree with their College Tutor in advance of their year abroad an independent course of study to be followed during that period.

2. English and Modern Languages Papers

Each candidate shall offer Part I and *either* Part II *or* Part III as prescribed below. Except in a Special Subject or an alternative to a Special Subject, a candidate shall offer (in addition to English) one modern language and its literature only.

Candidates are warned that they must avoid duplicating in their answers to one part of the examination material that they have used in another part of the examination.

Part I

The regulations for these subjects shall be those specified in the regulations for the Honour School of Modern Languages.

1. Honour School of Modern Languages, Paper I.
2. Honour School of Modern Languages, Papers IIA and IIB.
3. Honour School of Modern Languages, one paper chosen from Papers VI, VII, or VIII.
4. Honour School of Modern Languages, one paper chosen from Papers IV, V, IX, X, XI, or XII.
5. Oral examination.

EITHER: *Part II*

6, 7, 8. Three papers chosen from Course I, Subjects 1 to 6 of the Honour School of English Language and Literature. A maximum of two of the three papers may be examined by submission. The papers will be written examinations of three hours' duration, unless otherwise specified. Candidates shall choose three from:

(i) *Shakespeare* (a portfolio of 3 essays, each of not fewer than 1,500 and not more than 1,800 words in length) [as specified for the Honour School of English Language and Literature, Course I, Subject 1]. See in addition the regulations in 3. for 'Submitted work'.

(ii) *Literature in English 1350–1550* [as specified for the Honour School of English Language and Literature, Course I, Subject 2].

(iii) *Literature in English 1550 to 1660* [as specified for the Honour School of English Language and Literature, Course I, Subject 3]. Candidates who have satisfied the Examiners for the Preliminary Examination in Classics and English may not offer this paper.

(iv) *Literature in English 1660 to 1760* [as specified for the Honour School of English Language and Literature, Course I, Subject 4].

(v) *Literature in English 1760 to 1830* [as specified for the Honour School of English Language and Literature, Course I, Subject 5].

(vi) *Special Options* (an extended essay of not fewer than 5,000 and not more than 6,000 words in length) [as specified for the Honour School of English Language and Literature, Course I, Subject 6]. See in addition the regulations in 3. for 'Submitted work'.

9. *Dissertation* (an extended essay of not fewer than 7,000 and not more than 8,000 words in length). See in addition the regulations in 3. for 'Submitted work'.

Candidates may offer an extended essay in any subject area of English Language or Literature in English, or combining English and their Modern Language. Candidates should show such historical and/or contextual knowledge as is necessary for the profitable study of the topic concerned.

Candidates should submit to the Chair of Examiners, care of the English Faculty Office, by 5 p.m. on Thursday of the eighth week of the Michaelmas Term preceding the examination, an abstract of no more than 100 words, describing their area of study. Confirmation of the abstract will be received from the Chair of Examiners by Thursday of the first week of the Hilary Term preceding the examination.

The candidate may not discuss with any tutor either his or her choice of content or the method of handling it after Friday of the sixth week of the Hilary Term preceding the examination.

Two typed copies of the essay shall be delivered to the Chair of Examiners, Honour School of English Language and Literature, Examination Schools, High Street, by noon on Tuesday of the ninth week after the commencement of Hilary Full Term. A certificate, signed by the candidate to the effect that each essay is the candidate's own work, and that the candidate has read the Faculty guidelines on plagiarism, must be presented together with the submission (see in addition the regulations in 3. for 'Submitted work').

OR: *Part III*

6, 7, 8. Three papers chosen from Course II, Subjects 1 to 6 of the Honour School of English Language and Literature. A maximum of two of the three papers may be examined by submission. The papers will be written examinations of three hours' duration, unless otherwise specified. Candidates shall choose three from:

  (i) *Literature in English 650–1100* [Honour School of English Language and Literature, Course II, Subject 1].

  (ii) *Medieval English and Related Literatures 1066 to 1550* [Honour School of English Language and Literature, Course II, Subject 2].

  (iii) *Literature in English 1350–1550* [Honour School of English Language and Literature, Course II, Subject 3].

  (iv) *The History of the English Language to c.1800* (a portfolio of two essays of no more than 2,500 words each) [Honour School of English Language and Literature, Course II, Subject 4].

  (v) EITHER *The Material Text* (a portfolio of one essay and one commentary, each of not fewer than 2,000 and not more than 2,500 words in length) [Honour School of English Language and Literature, Course II, Subject 5 (a)]. See in addition the introductory regulations for 'Submitted work' for the Honour School of English and Modern Languages.

OR *Shakespeare* (a portfolio of three essays, each of not fewer than 1,300 and not more than 1,500 words in length) [Honour School of English Language and Literature, Course I, Subject 1/Course II, Subject 5(b)]. See in addition the regulations in 3. for 'Submitted work'.

  (vi) *Special Options* (an extended essay of not fewer than 5,000 and not more than 6,000 words in length) [Honour School of English Language and Literature, Course I & II, Subject 6]. See in addition the regulations in 3. for 'Submitted work'.

9. *Dissertation* (an extended essay of not fewer than 7,000 and not more than 8,000 words in length). See the regulations above for Part II, subject 9. See in addition the regulations in 3. for 'Submitted work'.

3. Submitted Work for Part II and Part III

(*a*) Two typed copies of each extended essay or portfolio essay must be delivered to the Chair of Examiners, Honour School of English Language and Literature, Examination Schools, High Street, according to the deadlines specified in the regulations for each subject. It is additionally strongly recommended that the candidate keep a third copy of his or her submission. A certificate signed by the candidate to the effect that each extended essay or portfolio is the candidate's own work, and that the candidate has read the Faculty guidelines on plagiarism, must be presented together with each submission (see (*b*) below).

(*b*) Every submission must be the work of the candidate alone, and he or she may not discuss with any tutor either his or her choice of content or the method of handling it after the last date indicated in the regulations for each subject.

(*c*) Essays previously submitted for the Honour School of English and Modern Languages may be re-submitted. No essay will be accepted if it has already been submitted, wholly or substantially, for a final honour school or other degree of this University, or degree of any other institution.

(*d*) Essays may be penalised that are deemed to be either too short or of excessive length in relation to the word limits specified in the regulations for each subject.

SPECIAL REGULATIONS FOR
THE HONOUR SCHOOL OF ENGLISH
LANGUAGE AND LITERATURE

For students commencing the Honour School
on or before 1 October 2012

A

1. The subjects of examination in the School of English Language and Literature shall be the English Language and Literature in English, together with such texts or authors as may from time to time be prescribed by the Board of the Faculty of English Language and Literature for special study.

Candidates shall be permitted to offer, in addition, Special Subjects forming a part of or connected with the study of English Language and Literature in English.

2. No candidate shall be admitted to examination in this school unless he or she either (*a*) has passed or been exempted from the First Public Examination or (*b*) has successfully completed the Foundation Course in English Language and Literature at the Department for Continuing Education.

3. The board of the faculty shall by notice from time to time make regulations respecting the examination, and shall have power:

(1) To prescribe authors or portions of authors.

(2) To specify one or more related languages or dialects to be offered either as a necessary or as an optional part of the examination.

(3) To name periods of the history of English Literature and to fix their limits.

(4) To issue lists of Special Subjects in connection either with English Language or with Literature in English, or with both; and to prescribe authors and texts.

B

Candidates shall offer either Course I (a general course in English Language and Literature) or Course II (a special course in English Language and early English Literature). Each course shall consist of eight subjects, as prescribed below.

Every candidate shall, not later than the Friday in the second week of the Michaelmas Full Term preceding the examination, send to the Examination Schools, High Street, Oxford OX1 4BG, through the Senior Tutor of his or her college or society, a statement to say:

(i) whether he or she offers Course I or Course II;

(ii) if he or she offers Course I, which subjects he or she offers under the options provided for Subject 7 (Special Authors) and Subject 8 (Special Topics)

(iii) if he or she offers Course II, which subjects he or she offers from List B, and, in the case of B1, B2, and B3, whether he or she intends to offer (an) extended essay(s) or sit (the) three-hour paper(s);

New optional subjects may be added to those parts of the syllabus for both Course I and Course II where options are already provided, by regulation published in the *Gazette* by the beginning of the fifth week of Trinity Term of the year before the year of the examination in which the subjects will first be available.

COURSE I: GENERAL COURSE IN ENGLISH LANGUAGE AND LITERATURE

Each candidate for Course I shall offer, from the list below, Subjects 1 to 7, and one further subject chosen from Subjects 8 and 9. Candidates may not offer any period of English literature in which they have already satisfied Examiners in a First Public Examination in English. The papers will be of three hours' duration, unless otherwise specified.

Extended essays

(*a*) Subjects 7 and 8 shall be examined by extended essay except in the case of specified Course II options , and centrally-taught Special Topics on Subject 8.

(*b*) An extended essay shall contain no fewer than 5,000 nor more than 6,000 words.

(*c*) The list of themes for the extended essay for Subject 7 will be published on Thursday of the fifth week of Michaelmas Term preceding the examination. The Paper 8 abstracts must be submitted for approval to the Chair of Examiners, care of the English Faculty Office, by 5 p.m. on Thursday of the fourth week of the Hilary Term preceding the examination; approval of abstracts shall be communicated to candidates on Thursday of the sixth week of that term.

(*d*) Two typed copies of each essay for Subject 7 must be delivered to the Chair of Examiners, Honour School of English Language and Literature, Examination Schools, Oxford, by noon on Thursday of the eighth week of Michaelmas Term; and each essay for Subject 8 by noon on Tuesday of the ninth week after the commencement of Hilary Full Term. A certificate signed by the candidate to the effect that each essay is the candidate's own work, and that the candidate has read the Faculty guidelines on plagiarism, must be presented together with each essay (see (*e*) below).

(*e*) Every extended essay for Subject 7 must be the work of the candidate alone, and he or she must not discuss with any tutor either his or her choice of theme or the method of handling it. Every extended essay for Subject 8 must be the work of the candidate alone, but he or she may discuss with his or her tutor both the subject and abstract of the essay up until Thursday of sixth week of Hilary Term preceding the examination.

(*f*) Essays previously submitted for the Honour School of English Language and Literature may be re-submitted. No essay will be accepted if it has already been submitted, wholly or substantially, for a final honour school or other degree of this University, or degree of any other institution.

(*g*) Essays deemed to be either too short or of excessive length may be penalised. Candidates are warned (i) that in the papers for Subjects 3–6 they must not answer questions on individual authors of whom they offer a special study for Subject 7, (ii) that they must avoid duplicating, in their answers to one paper, material that they have already used in answering another paper or in the extended essay under Subject 7 or Subject 8 and must show knowledge, in each of the papers for Subjects 3–6, of other literary genres than that of which they offer a special study for Subject 8.

1. *The English Language* (a portfolio submitted in year two)

The paper will cover the history, use, and theory of the English language, with special reference to literary language.

It will consist of two sections: Section A will contain essay questions on a range of topics relating to literary and sociocultural aspects of the English Language past and present. Section B will require candidates to produce detailed, historically and linguistically informed commentary comparing two or more related texts (which may include both literary and non-literary examples) from different periods, styles, or genres. Candidates will be expected to demonstrate their ability to select suitable textual examples and to analyse the language of the examples closely, making use where appropriate of standard reference tools such as the *Oxford English Dictionary*.

The paper will be examined on a portfolio of work, comprising two essays of no more than 2,500 words each. The list of themes for these essays will be divided into Section A and B and will be published on Tuesday of the seventh week of the Trinity Term preceding the examination. Candidates must write on one theme from each section, and two typed copies of each essay must be delivered to the Chair of Examiners, Honour School of English Language and Literature, Examination Schools by noon on Thursday of the ninth week of the same Trinity Term. A certificate, signed by the candidate to the effect that each essay is the candidate's own work, and that the candidate has read the Faculty guidelines on plagiarism, must be presented together with each essay.

Once submitted, the essays will then be held over until the following Trinity Term, when they will be examined at the same time as Papers 2–9.

Every essay must be the work of the candidate alone. Candidates may consult tutors after the themes have been circulated, but may not submit draft essays to tutors for detailed feedback. Essays previously submitted for the Honour School of English Language and Literature may be resubmitted.

Apart from the above exception, no essay will be accepted if it has already been submitted, wholly or substantially, for a final honour school or other degree of this University, or degree of any other institution.

Essays deemed to be either too short or of excessive length may be penalised. Candidates must avoid duplicating material used in this paper when answering other papers.

2. *Shakespeare* (one paper)

The paper will include questions on Shakespeare's relation to contemporary dramatists. Candidates must address more than one work by Shakespeare in at least two of their answers.

3. *English Literature from 1100 to 1509* (two papers)

    (*a*) A three-hour paper of questions on Medieval English Literature;
    (*b*) A two-hour paper consisting of passages for critical comment, to be set from the following texts:
        (*a*) Chaucer, *Troilus and Criseyde* (ed. L. D. Benson)
        (*b*) *Ancrene Wisse*, Books 6 and 7 (ed. Shepherd)
        (*c*) Langland, *Piers Plowman,* B Text, Passus XVI–XX (ed. A. V. C. Schmidt)
        (*d*) *Pearl* (ed. E. V. Gordon)
        (*e*) Malory, *Morte Darthur,* Books XVIII–XXI (ed. E. Vinaver)
        (*f*) Henryson, *Fables* (ed. D. Fox)

(A passage or passages will be set from each of the specific texts. Candidates will be required to write on two passages, one from *Troilus and Criseyde,* and one from one of the other texts.)

4. *English Literature from 1509 to 1642* (one paper)

Candidates who have satisfied the Moderators in Honour Moderations in Classics and English may not offer this paper. They may offer instead one of the following:

(*a*) English Literature from 1832–1900;

(*b*) English Literature from 1900 to the present day.

5. *English Literature from 1642 to 1740* (one paper)

6. *English Literature from 1740 to 1832* (one paper)

7. *Special Authors* (an extended essay of not fewer than 5,000 nor more than 6,000 words) (see introduction to regulations for Course I)

Candidates may offer any *one* of the following, provided that they may not offer in the Final Honour School any authors they offered in options (*c*), (*h*), (*i*), (*j*), (*k*), or (*l*) of Paper 4 of Moderations in English Language and Literature.

(*a*) (i) The *Beowulf* Poet, or (ii) Alfred, or (iii) *The Exeter Book*.

(*b*) (i) Chaucer, or (ii) Langland, or (iii) the N-Town Cycle.

(*c*) (i) Spenser, or (ii) Milton, or (iii) Jonson.

(*d*) (i) Marvell, or (ii) Dryden, or (iii) Eliza Haywood.

(*e*) (i) Wordsworth, or (ii) Austen, or (iii) Byron.

(*f*) (i) Tennyson, or (ii) Dickens, or (iii) Wilde.

(*g*) (i) Conrad, or (ii) Yeats, or (iii) Woolf.

(*h*) (i) Walcott, or (ii) Roth, or (iii) Friel.

(*i*) (i) Emerson, or (ii) Dickinson, or (iii) Faulkner.

Named authors will be reviewed in cycles of three years. Notice of new named authors will be published in the *University Gazette* by the beginning of the fifth week of Trinity Term two years before first examination.

8. *Special Topics*

Candidates may offer any one of the following (to be assessed by an extended essay of not fewer than 5,000 nor more than 6,000 words unless otherwise specified. For all extended essays candidates should submit to the Chair of Examiners by 5 p.m. on Thursday of the fourth week of Hilary Term preceding the examination an abstract describing their area of study, of no more than 100 words.)

(*a*) An extended essay in any subject area of English Language or Literature in English. Candidates should show such historical and/or contextual knowledge as is necessary for the profitable study of the topic concerned. Candidates should show knowledge of more than one author.

(*b*) Any one of the following Course II options:

i. Linguistic Theory (one paper; as specified for Course II paper B4)

ii. Medieval and Renaissance Romance (extended essay; as specified for Course II paper B7*a*)

iii. Scottish Literature pre-1600 (extended essay; as specified for Course II paper B7*b*)

iv. Old Norse (one paper, as specified in Course II paper B15)

v. Medieval French Literature 1100–1300 *or* Medieval French Literature 1300–1500 (one paper, as specified for Course II papers B19 and B20)

vi. Medieval Welsh Language and Literature I *or* Medieval Welsh Language and Literature II (one paper, as specified for Course II papers B21 and B22)

vii. Classical Literature (extended essay, as specified for Course II paper B24).

(*c*) An extended essay, unless otherwise stipulated, on any one of the centrally-taught Special Topics from the list for the year concerned which will be published by the English Faculty Office by the beginning of the fifth week of the Trinity Term one year before the examination.

(*d*) Victorian Literature (1832–1900) (one paper of three hours' duration as specified under 4(*a*).

(*e*) Modern Literature (1900 to the present day) (one paper of three hours' duration as specified under 4(*b*).

9. *Introduction to Medieval Studies: Old English Literature* (one paper as specified for Course II, Subject B25)

COURSE II: SPECIAL COURSE IN ENGLISH LANGUAGE AND EARLY ENGLISH LITERATURE

Each candidate shall offer the five subjects of List A below, and three subjects chosen from List B, subject to the restrictions set out below. Candidates may not offer more than two papers as extended essays.

Extended essays

(*a*) The following subjects will be assessed by extended essay only: B5 *Old English Special Authors*, B6 *Medieval and Renaissance Special Authors*, B7 *Special Topics*, B17 *Old Norse-Icelandic Literature*, and B24 *Classical Literature.*

(*b*) The following subjects will be assessed by extended essay or examination: B1 *Old English Philology*, B2 *Middle English Dialectology*, B3 *Modern English Philology.* Candidates will be required to specify their chosen mode of examination for these papers on their registration form and may not revert from this choice.

(*c*) Subjects B1 and B2 shall require two essays, each not exceeding 3,000 words. Subjects B3, B5, B6, B7, B17 and B24 shall require an extended essay which shall contain no fewer than 5,000 nor more than 6,000 words. Extended essays for subjects B1, B2, B3, B5 and B6 shall be on a theme chosen from a list published by the examiners. The titles of extended essays for subjects B7, B17, and B24 shall be devised by the candidates themselves.

(*d*) The list of themes for subjects B1, B3, B5, and B6 shall be published on Thursday of the fifth week of Michaelmas Term next before the examination. The list of themes for B2 shall be published on Thursday of the sixth week of Hilary Term next before the examination. The titles of subjects B7, B17, and B24 shall be devised by the candidates themselves, but must be submitted for approval to the Chair of Examiners, care of the English Faculty Office, by 5 p.m. on Thursday of the fourth week of the Hilary Term preceding the examination; approval of abstracts and titles shall be communicated to candidates on Thursday of the sixth week of that term.

(*e*) Two typed copies of each essay for B1, B3, B5, and B6 must be delivered to the Chair of Examiners, Honour School of English Language and Literature (Course II), Examination Schools, Oxford, by noon on Thursday of the eighth week of Michaelmas Term; and those for B2, B7, B17 and B24 by noon on Tuesday of the ninth week after the commencement of Hilary Full Term. A certificate signed by the candidate to the effect that each essay is the candidate's own work, and that the candidate has read the Faculty guidelines on plagiarism, must be presented together with each essay (see (*f*) below).

(*f*) Every extended essay for subjects B1, B2, B3, B5, and B6 shall be the candidate's own work. Every extended essay must be the work of the candidate alone, and he or she must not discuss with any tutor either his or her choice of theme or the method of handling it. Every extended essay for subjects B7, B17, and B24 must be the work of the candidate alone, but he or she may discuss with his or her tutor both the subject and proposed abstract or title of the essay up until Thursday of sixth week of Hilary Term preceding the examination.

(*g*) Essays previously submitted for the Honour School of English Language and Literature may be resubmitted. No essay will be accepted if it has already been submitted, wholly or substantially, for another Honour School or degree of this University, or for a degree of any other institution.

(*h*) Essays deemed to be either too short or of excessive length may be penalised.

List A: English Language and Literature (compulsory subjects)

1. *English Literature 600–1100* (one paper)

Candidates will be expected to show knowledge of a wide range of Old English literature and should show an awareness of the historical and cultural contexts of the period.

2. *English Literature 1100–1530* (one paper)

Candidates will be expected to show knowledge of a wide range of Middle English literature, and should show an awareness of the historical and cultural contexts of the literature of the period. Candidates should not answer on this paper on works by Chaucer on which they intend to answer on paper A3(*a*); candidates should not write on this paper on Langland and/or Gower if they are answering on those authors on paper A3(*b*).

3. *Chaucer, Langland, and Gower* (two papers)

Candidates will be required to take *two* papers as follows:

(*a*) A three-hour paper of questions on Chaucer.

Questions will be set that require a wide knowledge of Chaucer's writings. Candidates will be required to answer two questions.

(*b*) A two-hour paper of questions on Langland and Gower and on comparative studies of the three authors. Candidates will be required to write one essay.

4. *Introduction to Textual Criticism* (one paper 'of three hours' duration with an additional 15 minutes reading time)

Candidates will study Old and Middle English texts as specified in the Handbook for Final Honour Students, where further detailed discussion of the scope of the paper can be found. Question 1, which will be compulsory, will consist of a choice of directed commentaries on passages from the specified texts. Candidates must select three commentary exercises. Rubrics will direct candidates towards specific aspects of textual criticism. Candidates must answer one further essay question.

5. *The History of the English Language to c.1750* (a portfolio submitted in year two)

This paper will cover the development of the written language from the earliest records to c.1750, with particular attention to the emergence of a standard form.

The paper will be examined on a portfolio of work, comprising two essays of no more than 2,500 words each. The list of themes for these essays will be divided into Section A and B and will be published on Tuesday of the seventh week of the Trinity Term preceding the examination.

Candidates will be required to submit two pieces of work, each one of between 2,000–2,500 words. They will be required to submit one piece of work in response to discursive essay questions (Section A) and one piece of close commentary work in response to directed questions (Section B). Candidates will be required to demonstrate knowledge of the language of two consecutive periods from those covered in the paper. The essay questions in Section A will cover subjects such as phonology, morphology, syntax and word order. Broader questions will also be set, but with the understanding that candidates will use detailed linguistic knowledge as the basis of their answer. The commentary questions in Section B will require students to find their own passages for analysis. Credit will be given for the choice of material as well as the quality of its analysis. Passages must not exceed 100 lines in total (i.e. 100 lines altogether, not separately).

Candidates must write on one theme from each section, and two typed copies of each essay must be delivered to the Chair of Examiners, Honour School of English Language and Literature, Examination Schools by noon on Thursday of the ninth week of the same Trinity Term. A certificate, signed by the candidate to the effect that each essay is the candidate's own work, and that the candidate has read the Faculty guidelines on plagiarism, must be presented together with each essay.

Once submitted, the essays will then be held over until the following Trinity Term, when they will be examined at the same time as papers for subjects A1–4 and B1–26.

Every essay must be the work of the candidate alone. Candidates may not consult tutors after the paper have been circulated. Essays previously submitted for the Honour School of English Language and Literature may be resubmitted.

Apart from the above exception, no essay will be accepted if it has already been submitted, wholly or substantially, for a final honour school or other degree of this University, or degree of any other institution.

Essays deemed to be either too short or of excessive length may be penalised. Candidates must avoid duplicating material used in this paper when answering other papers.

List B: English Language and Literature and Subsidiary Languages (optional subjects)

Candidates are required to note that the availability of options is subject to the provision of teaching in the year in question.

1. *Old English Philology* (extended essay or one paper)

Candidates should have made a study of the Old English language in its various dialects up to c.1100, paying particular attention to the evidence available from primary materials; they will be expected to have such awareness of Germanic philology as is necessary for an understanding of the background to Old English. All aspects of the language are included: its orthography, phonology, morphology, syntax, lexis. No texts are prescribed, but those in Sweet's *Anglo-Saxon Reader* (rev. Whitelock, 1967), nos ii, vi-viii, xiv, xvi, xxxii-xxxviii, indicate the range of dialects to be covered. In the three-hour paper the first question (which will be compulsory) will require comment on passages set from texts in these dialects.

Candidates taking the paper by extended essay will be required to write two extended essays, each a maximum of 3,000 and a minimum of 2,500 words in length, on topics from a list to be published by the examiners in the fifth week of Michaelmas Term next preceding the examination.

2. *Middle English Dialectology* (extended essay or one paper)

Candidates will be expected to have made a study of a wide range of Middle English and Middle Scots dialects from c.1100 to c.1500, paying particular attention to the evidence available from primary materials. All aspects of the language are included: its orthography, phonology, morphology, syntax, lexis. No texts are prescribed, but those in Burrow and Turville-Petre (eds), *A Book of Middle English*, nos 2–4, 8–9, 11, 14, and Sisam (ed.), *Fourteenth-Century Verse and Prose* no. 10, indicate the range of dialects to be covered. In the three-hour paper the first question, which will be compulsory, will require comment on passages set from texts in these dialects.

Candidates taking the paper by extended essay will be required to write two extended essays, each a maximum of 3,000 and a minimum of 2,500 words in length, on topics from a list to be published by the examiners in sixth week of Hilary Term preceding the examination.

3. *Modern English Philology* (extended essay or one paper)

Candidates will be expected to show an understanding of developments in the written and spoken language with reference to the period from c.1500 to the present day, paying particular attention to the evidence available from primary materials. The paper involves the consideration of all aspects of the language, including orthography, phonology, morphology, syntax, and lexis. There are no prescribed texts, but candidates are expected to read a range of writings in the language in this period. Candidates must answer questions from both Section A, texts for comment and transcription, and Section B, questions on the history and development of the language in the period in question.

Candidates taking the paper by extended essay will be required to write one extended essay of between 5,000 and 6,000 words in length, on topics from a list to be published by the examiners in the fifth week of Michaelmas Term preceding the examination.

4. *Linguistic Theory* (one paper)

Candidates will be expected to show a general knowledge of theoretical linguistics with special reference to phonology, phonetics, grammar, lexis, semantics, and discourse structure and pragmatics. Opportunities will be given to answer questions on major developments in linguistic theory since 1800.

5. *Old English Special Authors* (extended essay)

Candidates must answer on any one of the *Beowulf* poet, Alfred, or *The Exeter Book*. Candidates answering substantially on any of these writers in paper A1, *English Literature 600–1100* may not offer the same writer in this paper. Candidates answering on Aelfric on paper A4 should not discuss the same texts in detail in this paper.

6. *Medieval and Renaissance Special Authors* (extended essay)

As defined in Course I Subject 7 (*b*) and (*c*) for the year concerned, except that candidates may not answer on any author made the focus of an answer elsewhere in the examination.

7. *Special Topics* (extended essay)

Candidates may choose one of the following:
(*a*) Medieval and Renaissance Romance
(*b*) Scottish Literature pre-1600
(*c*) An extended essay of not fewer than 5,000 nor more than 6,000 words, in any subject area of English Language, or Literature in English. [Course I Subject 8a] Candidates should show such historical and/or contextual knowledge as is necessary for the profitable study of the topic concerned. Candidates should show knowledge of more than one author.

Candidates should submit to the Chair of Examiners by 5 p.m. on Thursday of the fourth week of Hilary Term preceding the examination an abstract describing their area of study, of no more than 100 words.

(*d*) Any one of the Special Topics for the year concerned, as published in the *University Gazette* by the beginning of the fifth week of the Trinity Term one year before the examination.

8. *English Literature from 1509 to 1642* (one paper)

The paper will be the same as that set for Course I (Subject 4), but candidates who offer Course II must not answer questions on authors on whom they have answered questions in paper A2, or on whom they offer an optional subject.

Candidates who have satisfied the Moderators in Honour Moderations in Classics and English may not offer this option.

9. *Shakespeare* (one paper)

The paper will be the same as that set for Course I (Subject 2).

10. *The Archaeology of Anglo-Saxon England, seventh to ninth centuries AD* (one paper)

Questions will be set on such topics as the archaeology of kingship; Celtic influence on Anglo-Saxon material culture; rural settlement and landscape; the archaeology of the Conversion; the emergence of towns; and the 'Golden Age' of Northumbria. The identification, description and discussion of artefacts will be compulsory.

11. *Gothic* (one paper)

Candidates will be expected to show a knowledge of the elements of Gothic phonology, morphology, syntax, and lexicology, and to show special knowledge of the Gospels in Gothic. Three questions must be answered, including a compulsory translation set from passages from the surviving parts of the translation of St Mark's gospel and of II Timothy, as printed in J. Wright, *Grammar of the Gothic Language* (2nd edn. rev. O. L. Sayce, 1954); linguistic commentary may be required.

12. *Old Saxon* (one paper)   5

Candidates will be expected to show a knowledge of the elements of Old Saxon phonology, morphology, syntax, and lexicology. They will be expected to have made special study of the language of the *Heliand*, and to show detailed knowledge of its text from l. 3516 to the end (l. 5983) as edited by O. Behagel (9th edn. rev. B. Taeger, 1984), and of the *Genesis* fragments, as edited by A. N. Doane (1991). Three ques-   10
tions must be answered, including a compulsory translation and comment question.

13. *Old High German* (one paper)

Candidates will be expected to show a detailed knowledge of the elements of Old High German phonology, morphology, syntax, and lexicology, and to have made a special study of the texts set for Paper V (I): German in the Honour School of   15
Modern Languages.

Passages for translation and linguistic commentary, general linguistic questions, and literary questions on these texts will be set. Three questions must be answered, including a compulsory translation and commentary question.

14. *Middle High German* (one paper)   20

Candidates will be expected to study the texts prescribed for Paper IX: German, of the Honour School of Modern Languages, and to show detailed knowledge of three of them.

Passages for translation and literary commentary, and general literary questions on these texts will be set. Three questions must be answered, including a compulsory   25
translation and commentary question.

15. *Old Norse* (one paper)

Three questions must be answered, including one compulsory translation and commentary question from passages from *Íslendingabók; Hrafnkels saga Freysgoða; Skírnismál; Hamðismál;* Snorri's *Edda* (ed. Faulkes, Oxford, 1982): *Gylfaginning,*   30
ch. 43 to end. Literary questions on these texts will be set and candidates will also be given an opportunity to show a knowledge of the elements of Old Norse phonology, morphology, syntax, and lexicology.

16. *Old Norse Texts* (one paper)

Candidates will be expected to have made a special study of the following: *Auðunar*   35
þáttr; Víga Glúms saga; Völundarkviða; Atlakviða. They will be expected to have read but not to have studied in detail, *Fóstbræðra saga; Gísla saga Súrssonar; Hervarar saga; Gylfaginning; Völuspá; Hávamál.* Three questions must be answered, including one compulsory translation and commentary question from passages from the texts set for special study. Literary questions will be set on all the set texts.   40
This subject may be offered only by candidates who also offer Subject B15.

17. *Old Norse-Icelandic Literature* (extended essay)

Candidates will be expected to have read widely, especially in Old Icelandic prose. This subject may be offered only by candidates who also offer either Subject B15 or Subjects B15 and B16.   45

18. *Old French Language 1150–1250* (one paper)

Candidates will be expected to show a knowledge of the elements of Old French (including Anglo-Norman) orthography, morphology, phonology, syntax, and lex-icology, paying particular attention to the evidence available from primary materials. Three questions must be answered, including one compulsory translation and   50 commentary question on passages set from *La Vie de S. Alexis*, ed. C. Storey; *La Chanson de Roland*, ll. 1–660, ed. F. Whitehead; *Piramus et Tisbé*, ed. C. de Boer; *La folie Tristan d'Oxford*, ed. E. Hoepffner (2nd edn.), *Aucassin et Nicolette*, ed. M. Roques; *La Seinte Resureccion* (ANTS 4).

19. *Medieval French Literature 1100–1300* (one paper)

Candidates will be expected to have made a special study of at least two of the following: *La Chanson de Roland*, Chrétien de Troyes, *Yvain; La Mort le roi Artu; Le Roman de la Rose*, ll. 1–4058. Candidates will also be expected to have read, but not to have studied in detail, *either Le Roman de La Rose*, ll. 4059–21780 *or* at least three of the following: Béroul, *Tristan*; Marie de France, *Lais; Charroi de Nîmes; Aucassin et Nicolette*; Jean Renart, *La Lai de l'ombre;* Wace, *Roman de Brut*, 9005–13298; Jean Bodel, *Le Jeu de Saint Nicolas*, and Villehardouin, *La Conquête de Constantinople, Le Roman de Renart*, ed. M. Roques, ll. 3733–4796. Three questions must be answered, including one requiring literary commentary on passages from the set texts, of which candidates must answer **one**. Translation will not be required.

20. *Medieval French Literature 1300–1500* (one paper)

Candidates will be expected to have made a special study of the following: Guillaume de Machaut, *Le Jugement du roy de Behaigne*; Christine de Pisan, *Epistre au dieu d'amours*; François Villon, *Le Testament*. Candidates will also be expected to have read at least three of the following: Machaut, *La Fonteine amoureuse*, Machaut, *Le Livre du Voir-Dit*; Alain Chartier, *La Belle Dame sans Mercy*; Alain Chartier, *La Quadrilogue invectif*, Charles d'Orléans, *Ballades et rondeaux; Les Quinze Joies de mariage*. Three questions must be answered, including one requiring literary commentary on passages from the set texts, of which candidates must answer **one**. Translation will not be required.

21. *Medieval Welsh Language and Literature I* (one paper)

Candidates will be expected to show a knowledge of the elements of Medieval Welsh phonology, morphology, syntax, and lexicology. Opportunities will be provided to discuss the literary qualities of texts. Three questions must be answered, including one compulsory translation and commentary question from passages from *Pwyll Pendeuic Dyuet*, ed. R. L. Thomson (1957, repr. 1972), *Branwen Uerch Lyr*, ed. D. S. Thomson (1961, repr. 1968), *Poems of the Cywyddwyr*, ed. E. I. Rowlands (1976) nos 1, 2, 4, 7, 13, 19, 21–4, *Gwaith Dafydd ap Gwilym*, ed. T. Parry (1979), nos 2, 23, 26, 27, 42, 48, 84, 87, 114, 117, 122, 124. This paper may not be taken by candidates offering B22 *Medieval Welsh Language and Literature II*.

22. *Medieval Welsh Language and Literature II* (one paper)

Candidates will be expected to show a knowledge of the elements of Old and Middle Welsh phonology, morphology, syntax, and lexicology. Opportunities will be provided to discuss the literary qualities of the prescribed texts. Three questions must be answered, including one compulsory translation and commentary question from passages from *Pedeir Keinc y Mabinogi*, ed. I. Williams (1930), *Culhwch and Olwen*, ed. R. Bromwich and D. S. Evans (1992), 'The Juvencus Poems', ed. I. Williams, *The Beginnings of Welsh Poetry* (1980, 1990) *Gwaith Llywelyn Fardd I ac Eraill o Feirdd y Ddeuddegfed Ganrif*, ed. M. E. Owen *et al.* (1994), nos 6-15, 18–21, *Poems of the Cywyddwyr*, ed. E. I. Rowlands (1976), nos 1, 2, 4, 7, 13, 19, 21–4, *Gwaith Dafydd ap Gwilym*, ed. T. Parry (1979), nos 2, 13, 23, 26, 27, 28, 42, 48, 84, 87, 114, 117, 122, 124. They will be expected to have read but not to have studied in detail *Breudwyt Ronabwy*, ed. M. Richards (1984), *Peredur*, ed. G. Goetinck (1976), *Gwaith Iolo Goch*, ed. D. R. Johnston (1988). This paper may not be taken by candidates offering B21 *Medieval Welsh Language and Literature I*.

23. *Old and Early Middle Irish Language and Literature* (one paper)

Candidates will be expected to show a knowledge of the elements of Old Irish phonology, morphology, syntax, and lexicology. They will be given an opportunity to comment on the literary qualities of the prescribed texts. Three questions must be answered, including one compulsory translation and commentary question from passages from *Stories from the Táin*, ed. J. Strachan and O. Bergin (1944), *Scéla Mucce Meic Dathó*, ed. R. Thurneysen (1951), *Longes mac nUislenn*, ed. V. Hull (1949), *Early Irish Lyrics*, ed. G. Murphy (1956), nos 1–3, 5.

24. *Classical Literature* (extended essay)

Candidates will be expected to have studied one of the forms specified below in Greek and/or Latin Literature (and should specify their choice on their entry form).

   (i) Epic

   (ii) Tragedy

25. *Introduction to Medieval Studies: Old English Literature*

Three questions must be answered, including one compulsory question of either translation or commentary. Commentary passages will be taken from *The Dream of the Rood, The Wanderer, The Battle of Maldon,* Aelfric's life of St Edmund, Bede's account of the poet Caedmon and from *Beowulf,* Beowulf's fight with Grendel (ll. 702–897). Literary questions will cover these texts, but candidates will also be given an opportunity to show a knowledge of a wider range of Old English literature, and of aspects of Old English history, culture, and language. Candidates may not offer this paper if it is one in which they have previously satisfied Examiners in any First Public Examination in English.

SPECIAL REGULATIONS FOR THE HONOUR SCHOOL OF ENGLISH LANGUAGE AND LITERATURE

For students commencing the Honour School on or after 1 October 2013

A

1. The subjects of examination in the School of English Language and Literature shall be the English Language and Literature in English, together with such Special Options, texts or authors as may from time to time be prescribed by the Board of the Faculty of English Language and Literature.

2. No candidate shall be admitted to examination in this school unless he or she either (a) has passed or been exempted from the First Public Examination or (b) has successfully completed the Foundation Course in English Language and Literature at the Department for Continuing Education.

3. The Board of the Faculty shall by notice from time to time make regulations respecting the examination, and shall have power:

(1) To prescribe authors or portions of authors.

(2) To specify one or more related languages or dialects to be offered either as a necessary or as an optional part of the examination.

(3) To name periods of the history of English Literature and to fix their limits.

(4) To issue lists of Special Options in connection either with English Language or with Literature in English, or with both; and to prescribe authors and texts.

B

Candidates shall offer either Course I (a general course in English Language and Literature) or Course II (a special course in English Language and early English Literature). Each course shall consist of seven subjects, as prescribed below.

1. Submitted work

(a) Subjects 1, 6 and 7 in Course I, and Subjects 4, 5, 6 and 7 in Course II, shall be examined by submission.

(b) Two typed copies of each extended essay or portfolio essay must be delivered to the Chair of Examiners, Honour School of English Language and Literature, Examination Schools, High Street, according to the deadlines specified in the regulations for each subject. It is additionally strongly recommended that the candidate keep a third copy of his or her submission. A certificate signed by the candidate to the effect that each extended essay or portfolio is the candidate's own work, and that the candidate has read the Faculty guidelines on plagiarism, and observed the specific requirements in (c) below, must be presented together with each submission.

(c) Every extended essay and portfolio must be the work of the candidate alone, and he or she may not discuss with any tutor either his or her choice of content or the method of handling it after the last date indicated in the regulations for each subject.

(d) Essays previously submitted for the Honour School of English Language and Literature may be re-submitted. No essay will be accepted if it has already been submitted, wholly or substantially, for a final honour school or other degree of this University, or degree of any other institution.

(e) Essays may be penalised that are deemed to be either too short or of excessive length in relation to the word limits specified in the regulations for each subject.

2. Course I: General Course in English Language and Literature

Each candidate for Course I shall offer all subjects from the list below. Candidates may not offer any period of English literature in which they have already satisfied Examiners in a First Public Examination in English. The subjects will be examined by written examinations of three hours' duration, unless otherwise specified. Examinations will be held in the Trinity Term of the final year of the Honour School.

Candidates are warned (i) that in the papers for Subjects 1–5 they must not answer questions on any topics of which they offer a special study for Subject 6 or Subject 7 and (ii) that they must avoid duplicating, in their answers to one paper, material that they have already used in answering another paper or in the extended essay under Subject 6 or Subject 7.

1. *Shakespeare* (a portfolio submitted in year 3)

The portfolio will consist of three essays of not fewer than 1,500 and not more than 1,800 words each. Footnotes will be included in the total word count, but bibliographies do not count towards the limit. Candidates must address more than one work by Shakespeare in at least two of their portfolio essays.

The three essays may be selected from tutorial work or can be written specially for the portfolio. The candidate may revise tutorial essays for portfolio submission in light of feedback from his or her tutor; however the tutor may not mark or discuss the revised version. If an essay is written specially for the portfolio it will not be read or marked by a tutor prior to submission.

Every portfolio essay produced for the Shakespeare paper must be the work of the candidate alone, but he or she may discuss with his or her tutor the subjects and approach to the essays up until the Friday of the eighth week of the Michaelmas Term preceding the examination.

The candidate must deliver two typed copies of each portfolio essay to the Chair of Examiners, Honour School of English Language and Literature, Examination Schools, High Street by noon on Thursday of the fourth week of the Hilary Term preceding the examination. A certificate, signed by the candidate to the effect that each essay is the candidate's own work, and that the candidate has read the Faculty guidelines on plagiarism, must be presented together with the submission (see the introductory regulations for 'submitted work' for the Honour School of English Language and Literature).

2. *Literature in English from 1350–1550*

Candidates must answer two essay questions and one commentary question, as indicated in the rubric for the examination. Passages for commentary will be taken from Chaucer, *Troilus and Criseyde* (ed. L.D. Benson). The paper will be shared with Course II candidates [see Course II, subject 3 below].

3. *Literature in English from 1550 to 1660, excluding the works of Shakespeare*

Candidates who have satisfied the Examiners in the First Public Examination in Classics and English may not offer this paper, and instead must offer Literature in English 650 – 1100 [see Course II, subject 1 below].

4. *Literature in English from 1660 to 1760*

5. *Literature in English from 1760 to 1830*

6. *Special Options* (an extended essay of not fewer than 5,000 and not more than 6,000 words) (see the introductory regulations for 'submitted work' for Course I).

All Special Options shall be centrally taught. A list of available Special Options shall be published to candidates by the end of the seventh week of the Hilary Term preceding the year of examination. Enrolment to Special Options will be administered by the English Faculty Office and will take place in the Trinity Term in the first year of the Honour School. Confirmation of the Special Option shall be provided to candidates by the end of the sixth week of the same Trinity Term.

Examination for this paper shall be by an extended essay of not fewer than 5,000 and not more than 6,000 words. Footnotes will be included in the total word count, but bibliographies do not count towards the limit. The theme for the essay shall be formulated by the student in discussion with the option convenors. The candidate may not discuss with any tutor either his or her choice of content or the method of handling it after the conclusion of teaching for the Special Options paper on Friday of the fifth week of the Michaelmas Term preceding the examination.

Two typed copies of the extended essay must be delivered to the Chair of Examiners, Honour School of English Language and Literature, Examination Schools, High Street, by noon on Thursday of the eighth week of Michaelmas

Term. A certificate, signed by the candidate to the effect that each essay is the candidate's own work, and that the candidate has read the Faculty guidelines on plagiarism, must be presented together with the submission (see the introductory regulations for 'submitted work' for the Honour School of English Language and Literature).

7. Dissertation (an extended essay of not fewer than 7,000 nor more than 8,000 words) (see the introductory regulations for 'submitted work' for the Honour School of English Language and Literature).

Footnotes will be included in the total word count, but bibliographies do not count towards the limit. Candidates may offer an extended essay in any subject area of English Language or Literature in English. Candidates should show such historical and/or contextual knowledge as is necessary for the profitable study of the topic concerned.

Candidates should submit to the Chair of Examiners, care of the English Faculty Office, by 5p.m. on Thursday of the eighth week of the Michaelmas Term preceding the examination, an abstract of no more than 100 words, describing their area of study. Confirmation of his or her abstract will be received from the Chair of Examiners by Thursday of the first week of the Hilary Term preceding the examination.

The candidate may not discuss with any tutor either his or her choice of content or the method of handling it after Friday of the sixth week of the Hilary Term preceding the examination.

Two typed copies of the essay shall be delivered to the Chair of Examiners, Honour School of English Language and Literature, Examination Schools, High Street, by noon on Tuesday of the ninth week after the commencement of Hilary Full Term. A certificate, signed by the candidate to the effect that each essay is the candidate's own work, and that the candidate has read the Faculty guidelines on plagiarism, must be presented together with the submission (see the introductory regulations for 'submitted work' for the Honour School of English Language and Literature).

3. Course II: Special Course in English Language and Early English Literature

Each candidate shall offer Subjects 1 to 4 and Subjects 6 and 7 below, and may choose between Subject 5 (The Material Text) or Course I Subject 1 (Shakespeare). Candidates may not offer any period of English literature in which they have already satisfied Examiners in a First Public Examination in English. The papers will be written examinations of three hours' duration, unless otherwise specified. Written examinations will be held in the Trinity Term of the final year of the Honour School.

Candidates are warned (i) that in the papers for Subjects 1-5 they must not answer questions on any topics of which they offer a special study for Subject 6 or Subject 7 and (ii) that they must avoid duplicating, in their answers to one paper, material that they have already used in answering another paper or in the extended essay under Subject 6 or Subject 7.

1. *Literature in English 650–1100*
Candidates will be expected to show knowledge of a wide range of Old English literature and should show an awareness of the historical and cultural contexts of the period.

2. *Medieval English and Related Literatures 1066–1550*
A paper on a specified genre or theme. The paper shall be examined by a written examination of three hours' duration, in which candidates shall write two essays of equal weighting. Across the paper as a whole, candidates must demonstrate (a) knowledge of literature written before 1350; and (b) knowledge of writing in insular or European languages other than English, which are expected to have been studied in translation.

The genre or theme for the paper shall be published in the Handbook for the Honour School of English Language and Literature by noughth week of Michaelmas Full Term in the first year of study for the Honour School. The specified genre or theme may be subject to periodic review.

3. *Literature in English 1350–1550* (shared with Course I) [as specified for the Honour School of English Language and Literature, Course I, Subject 2].

4. *The History of the English Language to c.1800*

This paper will cover the development of the written language from the earliest records to c.1800, with particular attention to the emergence of a standard form. The paper will be examined on a portfolio of work, comprising two essays of no more than 2,500 words each. Footnotes will be included in the total word count, but bibliographies do not count towards the limit. The list of themes for these essays will be divided into Section A and B and will be published on Tuesday of the seventh week of the Trinity Term preceding the examination. Candidates may not consult tutors after the list of themes has been circulated.

Candidates will be required to submit two pieces of work, each one of between 2,000–2,500 words. They will be required to submit one piece of work in response to discursive essay questions (Section A) and one piece of close commentary work in response to directed questions (Section B). The commentary questions in Section B will require students to find their own passages for analysis. Passages must not exceed 100 lines in total (i.e. 100 lines altogether, not separately). Copies of the texts or passages used in Section B must be included as an appendix to the portfolio.

Two typed copies of the portfolio must be delivered to the Chair of Examiners, Honour School of English Language and Literature, Examination Schools, High Street, by noon on Thursday of the ninth week of the same Trinity Term. A certificate, signed by the candidate to the effect that each essay is the candidate's own work, and that the candidate has read the Faculty guidelines on plagiarism, must be presented together with the submission (see the introductory regulations for 'submitted work' for the Honour School of English Language and Literature).

Once submitted, the essays will then be held over until the following Trinity Term, when they will be examined at the same time as papers for Course II subjects 1–3 and 5–7.

5. *One* of the following:

(a) *The Material Text* (a portfolio submitted in year three)

Candidates will study Old and Middle English texts in their original manuscript context.

The portfolio will consist of one commentary answer and one essay, of not fewer than 2,000 and not more than 2,500 words each. Footnotes will be included in the total word count, but bibliographies do not count towards the limit. Themes for the portfolio commentary and essay will be published on Monday of the second week of the Hilary Term preceding the examination. Following their publication, the candidate must not discuss his or her choice of themes with any tutor, nor the method of handling the themes. Every portfolio commentary and essay produced for the Material Text paper must be the work of the candidate alone, but he or she may discuss with his or her tutor the subjects and approach to the essays up until the stated publication date of the portfolio themes.

The candidate must deliver two typed copies of the portfolio to the Chair of Examiners, Honour School of English Language and Literature, Examination Schools, High Street, by noon on Thursday of the fourth week of the Hilary Term preceding the examination. A certificate, signed by the candidate to the effect that each essay is the candidate's own work, and that the candidate has read the Faculty guidelines on plagiarism, must be presented together with the submission (see the introductory regulations for 'submitted work' for the Honour School of English Language and Literature).

    (*b*) *Shakespeare* (a portfolio submitted in year three) [as specified for the Honour School of English Language and Literature, Course I, Subject 1].

6. *Special Options*

For this paper Course II candidates may choose ONE of the following:

    (*a*) Literature in English 1550–1660 [as specified for the Honour School of English Language and Literature, Course I, Subject 3];

    (*b*) any Special Option from the list published for Course I candidates [as specified for the Honour School of English Language and Literature, Course I, Subject 6];

    (*c*) any Special Option from the list published for Course II candidates.

Option (*a*) will be examined by an examination of three hours' duration in Trinity Term of the final year.

A list of available Special Options for (*b*) and (*c*) shall be published to Course II candidates by the end of the seventh week of the Hilary Term in the first year of the Honour School. Enrolment to Special Options will be administered by the English Faculty Office and will take place in the Trinity Term in the first year of the Honour School. Confirmation of the Special Option shall be provided to candidates by the end of the sixth week of the same Trinity Term.

Examination for options (*b*) and (*c*) shall be by an extended essay of not fewer than 5,000 and not more than 6,000 words, except where specified in the published list of options. Footnotes will be included in the total word count, but bibliographies do not count towards the limit. The theme for the essay shall be formulated by the student in discussion with the option convenors. The candidate may not discuss with any tutor either his or her choice of content or the method of handling it after the conclusion of teaching for the Special Options paper on Friday of the fifth week of the Michaelmas Term preceding the examination.

Two typed copies of the extended essay must be delivered to the Chair of Examiners, Honour School of English Language and Literature, Examination Schools, High Street, by noon on Thursday of the eighth week of Michaelmas Term preceding the examination. A certificate, signed by the candidate to the effect that each essay is the candidate's own work, and that the candidate has read the Faculty guidelines on plagiarism, must be presented together with the submission (see the introductory regulations for 'submitted work' for the Honour School of English Language and Literature).

    7. *Dissertation* (an extended essay of not fewer than 7,000 nor more than 8,000 words) [as specified for the Honour School of English Language and Literature, Course I, Subject 7].

SPECIAL REGULATIONS FOR
THE HONOUR SCHOOL OF EUROPEAN
AND MIDDLE EASTERN LANGUAGES

A

1. The subjects of the examination in the Honour School of European and Middle Eastern Languages shall be (*a*) those modern languages and literatures studied in the Honour School of Modern Languages, and (*b*) Arabic, Hebrew, Persian, and Turkish.

2. All candidates must offer (*a*) one of the languages which may be studied in the Honour School of Modern Languages, with its literature, and (*b*) one of the languages specified in clause 1(*b*) above.

3. No candidate shall be admitted to the examination in this school unless he or she has either passed or been exempted from the first Public Examination.

4. The examiners shall indicate in the lists issued by them the languages offered by each candidate obtaining Honours or satisfying the examiners under the appropriate regulation.

5. The examination in this school shall be under the joint supervision of the Boards of the Faculties of Medieval and Modern Languages and Oriental Studies, which shall appoint a standing joint committee to make, and to submit to the two faculty boards, proposals for regulations for this examination and for the Preliminary Examination in European and Middle Eastern Languages.

6. (i) The examiners in the Honour School shall be such of the Public Examiners in the Honour Schools of Modern Languages and Oriental Studies as shall be required.

(ii) It shall be the duty of the Chair of Examiners in the Honour School of Modern Languages and in the Honour School of Oriental Studies to consult together and designate such examiners as shall be required for the Honour School, whereupon the number of the examiners shall be deemed to be complete.

B

Candidates will be examined in accordance with the examination regulations set out below.

They will also be required to spend, after their matriculation, a year of residence in an appropriate country or countries, and to provide on their entry form for the examination a certificate that they have done this, signed by the Head or by a tutor of their society. Candidates wishing to be dispensed from the requirement to undertake a year of residence abroad must apply in writing to the Chair of the Medieval and Modern Languages Board, 41 Wellington Square, Oxford, OX1 2JF, stating their reasons for requesting dispensation and enclosing a letter of support from their society.

Candidates will be expected to carry out during this year abroad such work as their society may require. Candidates will agree with their College Tutor in advance of their year abroad an independent course of study to be followed during that period.

Each candidate shall offer the oral examination in the European language.

Except in a Special Subject or an alternative to a Special Subject, a candidate shall offer one European language and its literature only.

In every case where, under the regulations for the school, candidates have a choice between one or more papers or subjects, every candidate shall give notice to the Registrar not later than Friday in the fourth week of the Michaelmas Full Term preceding the examination of all the papers and subjects being so offered.

Candidates are warned that they must avoid duplicating in their answers to one part of the examination material that they have used in another part of the examination.

For those papers in the Middle Eastern language where a selection of unspecified texts is to be examined, the selection of texts will be determined by the Oriental Studies Board in Hilary Term for the examination in the next academic year, and copies of the list of selected texts will be available for candidates no later than Friday of the third week of the same term.

Oral examination in the European language

As specified for the Honour School of Modern Languages.
1. Honour School of Modern Languages, Paper I.
2. Honour School of Modern Languages, Papers IIA and IIB.
3. Honour School of Modern Languages, *one* paper chosen from Papers VI, VII or VIII.
4. Honour School of Modern Languages, *one* paper chosen from IV, V, IX, X, XI, or XII.
5. An extended essay on a topic bridging the European and the Middle Eastern language.

Arabic

6A. Arabic unprepared translation into English (half paper) and 6B. Prose composition in Arabic (half paper).]
  7. Spoken Arabic.
  8. Arabic literature.
  9. Islamic religion.
  10. One of the following:
   (i) Islamic history, AD 570–1500.
   (ii) Classical Arabic literary texts.
   (iii) Modern Arabic literature.
   (iv) Arabic vernacular literature ad 1900 to the present day.
   (v) History of the Middle East in the late Ottoman age, 1750–1882.
   (vi) A modern Islamic thinker (e. g. Sayyid Qutb, Mohamed Talbi, Rashid Rida).
   (vii) Society and Culture in the Modern Arab World.
   (viii) A short-term Further Subject, as approved by the Board of the Faculty of Oriental Studies and publicised in the Arabic Handbook.

Paper 6A. is identical with the first half of paper 1 for Arabic and Islamic Studies, and paper 6B. is identical with the first half of paper 2 for Arabic and Islamic Studies in the Final Honour School of Oriental Studies. Papers 7–9 are identical with papers of the same title for Arabic and Islamic Studies in the same degree. The options under paper 10 are also identical with papers and options of the same titles for Arabic and

Islamic Studies. The set texts will be those specified in the Arabic Handbook, available from the Oriental Institute.

Hebrew

Candidates must take paper 6. and paper 10. and two of papers 7., 8. and 9.
    6. Hebrew composition and unprepared translation.
    7. Prepared texts I: Biblical texts:
       the texts will be those specified for Hebrew only, paper 2.
    8. Prepared texts II: Rabbinic and Medieval Hebrew Texts:
       the texts will be those specified for Hebrew only, paper 3.
    9. Prepared texts III: Modern Hebrew literature:
       the texts will be those specified for Hebrew only, paper 4.
   10. General paper: language, history, religion, and culture or one of the papers in Jewish Studies Paper b.

Persian

    6. Persian prose composition and unprepared translation.
    7. and 8. Two papers as prescribed for subsidiary Persian, papers 2 and 3.
    9. General questions on one of the following periods of history:
    (*a*) The transition from Sasanian to Islamic Persia (up to the tenth century AD).
    (*b*) The Safavids from 1501 to 1722.
    (*c*) The rise of the Qajars to the end of the Constitutional Revolution.
    (*d*) The Pahlavis from 1926 to 1979.
    (*e*) A short-term Further Subject, as approved by the Board of the Faculty of Oriental Studies and publicised in the Islamic Studies Handbook.
   10. Oral examination (as specified for the Honour School of Oriental Studies).

Turkish

6A. Unprepared translation from modern Turkish (*half paper*) and 6B. Translation into Turkish (*half paper*).
    7. Spoken Turkish.
    8. Turkish political and cultural texts, 1860 to the present.
    9. Modern Turkish literary texts.
   10. One of the following:
    (*a*) Ottoman historical texts.
    (*b*) Turkish and Ottoman literary texts, 1300–1900.
    (*c*) Turkish language reform and language politics from 1850 to the present day.
    (*d*) The Ottoman Empire and the Republic of Turkey, 1807–1980.
Papers 7–9 are identical with papers 3, 5 and 6 for Turkish in the Honour School of Oriental Studies. The options under paper 10 are identical with papers 4, 7(*a*), 7(*c*) and 7(*g*) of the same degree. The set texts will be those specified in the Turkish Handbook, available on the Web site of the Faculty of Oriental Studies.

Extended Essay

   1. The Extended Essay shall be subject to the following provisions:
    (i) The subject of every essay shall, to the satisfaction of the boards of the faculties, fall within the scope of the Honour Schools of Modern Languages and of Oriental Studies.
    (ii) Candidates proposing to offer an essay must submit, through their college, to the Chair of the Board of the Faculty of Medieval and Modern Languages (on a form obtainable from the Modern Languages Faculty Office, 41 Wellington Square) a statement of their name, college, the academic year in which they intend to take the examination, and the title of the proposed essay together with (*a*) a statement in about fifty words of how the subject is to be treated, (*b*) a statement signed by a supervisor or tutor, that he or she considers the subject

suitable, and suggesting a person or persons who might be invited to be an examiner or assessor (the boards will not approve the title unless they are satisfied that a suitably qualified examiner or assessor based in Oxford will be available), and (*c*) a statement by a college tutor that he or she approves the candidate's application, not later than the Wednesday of the second week of the Michaelmas Full Term preceding the examination.

(iii) The faculty boards will decide by the end of the third week of the Michaelmas Full Term preceding the examination whether the proposed essay title is approved. Approval may be granted on condition that the candidate agrees to amend details of the title to the satisfaction of the boards and submits the required amendments to the Modern Languages Faculty Office by the Friday of sixth week of the Michaelmas Full Term preceding the examination.

(iv) A candidate may seek approval after Friday of sixth week of the Michaelmas Full Term preceding the examination for an amendment of detail in an approved title, by application to the Modern Languages Faculty Office. The Chair of Examiners and the chairmen of the boards, acting together, will decide whether or not a proposed amendment shall be approved.

2. While the topic of the essay may be taught by a series of tutorials, candidates will be solely responsible for the final draft, which will not be read by the supervisor or tutor. Candidates must sign a certificate stating that the essay is their own work and that it has not already been submitted, wholly or substantially, for any honour school or degree of this university or a degree of any other institution. This certificate must be sent at the same time as the essay, but under separate cover, addressed to the chair of examiners.

3. No essay shall exceed 10,000 words, exclusive of notes, appendices, and bibliographies. The examiners will not take account of such parts of the essay as are beyond this limit. When appropriate, there must be a select bibliography and a list of sources.

Essays must be typed in double-spacing on one side only of quarto or A4 paper, and must be firmly held in a stiff cover. Two copies must be submitted to the chair of examiners, and a third copy should be kept by the candidate.

4. The two copies of the essay must be sent, not later than noon on the second Friday after the Hilary Full Term of the year in which the examination will be held, to the Chair of Examiners, Honour School of European and Middle Eastern Languages, Examination Schools, High Street, Oxford.

SPECIAL REGULATIONS FOR THE HONOUR SCHOOL OF EXPERIMENTAL PSYCHOLOGY

A

1. The subject of the Honour School of Experimental Psychology shall be the study of psychology as an experimental science.

2. The examination in Experimental Psychology shall consist of two parts. In Part I candidates shall be examined in the subjects prescribed by the Medical Sciences Board. In Part II candidates shall be examined in the subjects prescribed by the Medical Sciences Board and shall also present, as part of the examination, a project report based on work carried out under supervision prescribed by the Board.

3. No candidate shall be admitted for the Part I examination in this school unless he or she has either passed or been exempted from the First Public Examination.

4. No candidate shall be admitted for the Part II examination in this school unless

(*a*) he or she has passed the Part I examination for Experimental Psychology; and

(*b*) he or she has satisfied the Moderators for the Preliminary Examination for Psychology and Philosophy in the subject *Introduction to Probability Theory and Statistics* or has passed the Qualifying Examination in Statistics for this School.

The Head of the Department of Experimental Psychology may dispense a candidate from the Qualifying Examination in Statistics in cases where it is clear that the candidate has reached an adequate standard in Statistics by virtue of previous study and qualification.

5. The examinations in the school shall be under the supervision of the Medical Sciences Board, which shall make regulations concerning them, subject always to the preceding clauses of this sub-section.

B

1. GENERAL

Decree (7) of 3 June 1947 permits the number of candidates offering Psychology to be limited, if necessary.

2. The subjects of the examination shall be those prescribed in Parts I and II below.

3. The examination for Part I shall be taken during Week 0 and 1 of Trinity Term of the candidate's second year. The examination for Part II shall be taken during Trinity Term of the candidate's third year. The dates of submission for the Part I practical work and Part II project work and library dissertation are those prescribed in Parts I and II below.

4. Every candidate shall give notice of all papers being offered not later than Friday in the eighth week of Michaelmas Full Term preceding the examination.

PART I

1. Five written papers will be set:

Paper I Biological Bases of Behaviour.

    Components: (i) Cognitive Neuroscience, (ii) Behavioural Neuroscience.

Paper II Human Experimental Psychology 1.

    Components: (i) Perception, (ii) Memory, Attention, and Information Processing.

Paper III Human Experimental Psychology 2.

    Components: (i) Language and Cognition, (ii) Developmental Psychology.

Paper IV Social Psychology, and Personality, Individual Differences and Psychological Disorders.

    Components: (i) Social Psychology, (ii) Personality, Individual Differences and Psychological Disorders.

In papers I-IV candidates will be required to answer essay and short answer questions from each of the components.

Paper V Experimental Design and Statistics.

2. Candidates will be required to undertake practical work, as specified by the Head of Department of Experimental Psychology, and this will constitute a part of the examination. In exceptional circumstances, the Proctors may dispense a candidate from the specified requirements on the recommendation of the Head of Department, or Deputy.

3. Reports of practical work completed during the course of study for Part I and submitted for marking shall constitute a portfolio which shall be available to examiners as part of the examination. Every report submitted for marking must be accompanied by a statement indicating that the work submitted is the candidate's own work. Where the work submitted has been produced in collaboration the candidates shall indicate the extent of their own contributions. Reports of practical work previously submitted for the Honour School of Experimental Psychology may be resubmitted, but reports will not be accepted if they have already been submitted, wholly or substantially, for another Honour School or degree of this University, or for a degree of any other institution. The Head of Department or deputy shall inform the examiners by the end of Week 0 of the Trinity Term in which the Part I examination is to be held as to which candidates have (a) failed to satisfy the requirement to undertake practical work or (b) failed to submit a portfolio. Candidates in category (a) will be deemed to have failed Paper V. Candidates in category (b) will be deemed to have failed the entire Part I examination. The Head of Department or deputy shall also make available to the examiners records showing the extent to which each candidate has adequately pursued a course of practical work. The examiners shall take this evidence into consideration along with evidence of unsatisfactory or distinguished performance in each portfolio of practical work.

For all papers in Psychology and for the Qualifying Examination in Statistics but not for papers taken from the Honour School of Medical Sciences, the examiners will permit the use of any hand-held pocket calculators subject to the conditions set out under the heading *Regulations for the Conduct of University Examinations*, Part 13.

4. A candidate who fails the Part I examination may retake the examination once only, in the Long Vacation of the same academic year as the original examination. The highest mark that can be awarded to a candidate retaking the examination is a Pass.

Part II

Part II will consist of a research project and *either* three written papers each of 3 hours duration, *or* two written papers, each of 3 hours duration, and a Library Dissertation.

The written papers will be selected from the list of at least 12 options approved by the Medical Sciences Board and published by the Department of Experimental Psychology. A list of options will be posted in the Department of Experimental Psychology not later than noon on Friday of the fifth week of Hilary Term in the year preceding that in which the examination is taken.

If a Library Dissertation is not chosen, candidates may substitute either one or two papers from the list below in place of one or two of the Psychology Advanced Options. If a Library Dissertation is chosen, candidates may substitute one paper from the list below in place of one of the Psychology Advanced Options:

General Linguistics
Phonetics and Phonology

A Paper 1 in the Honour School of Medical Sciences
One or two papers in Philosophy.

1. *Research Project*

The research project will normally be carried out in the Trinity Term and the following Michaelmas Term in the year preceding the Part II examinations.

Candidates will be required to do project work under the supervision of one of the following:

(i) any member of the Faculty of Psychological Studies.
(ii) any other person approved by the Divisional Board provided that such approval shall be applied for not later than Friday of fourth week of Michaelmas Full Term in the year preceding the Part II examinations.

The subject of the library dissertation and the research project should not overlap to the extent that they should not draw on substantially the same literature. Candidates are warned that they should avoid repetition in examination papers of material used in the research project or library dissertation and that substantial repetition may be penalised.

All proposed research projects or library dissertations must be approved in advance by the Head of the Department of Experimental Psychology. The procedures for obtaining this approval will be notified to students by the Head of Department of Experimental Psychology.

Two copies of completed projects and library dissertations must be submitted to the Chair of Examiners, Honour School of Experimental Psychology, Examination Schools, Oxford, not later than noon on Friday of the eighth week and tenth week of Hilary Term respectively, in the year of the examination. A certificate signed by the candidate indicating that the work submitted is the candidate's own work, and a statement of the number of words in the project or dissertation, must be submitted separately in respect of each research project and library dissertation in a sealed envelope addressed to the Chair of Examiners. Research projects and library dissertations previously submitted for the Honour School of Experimental Psychology may be resubmitted. No project or dissertation will be accepted if it has already been submitted wholly or substantially, for another Honour School or degree of this University, or for a degree of any other institution.

2. Candidates will be required to undertake practical work, as specified by the Head of Department of Experimental Psychology, and this will constitute a part of the examination. In exceptional circumstances the Proctors may exempt a candidate from the specified requirements on the recommendation of the Head of Department or deputy.

3. Reports of practical work completed during the course of study for Part II and submitted for marking shall constitute a portfolio which shall be available to examiners as part of the examination. Every report submitted for marking must be accompanied by a statement indicating that the work submitted is the candidate's own work. Reports of practical work previously submitted for the Honour School of Experimental Psychology may be resubmitted but reports will not be accepted if they have been submitted, wholly or substantially, for another Honour School or degree of this University, or for a degree of any other institution. The Head of Department or deputy shall inform the examiners by the end of Week o of the Trinity Term in which the Part II examination is to be held as to which candidates have failed to satisfy the requirement to undertake practical work. Failure to satisfy the requirement to undertake practical work will result in the candidate's final degree classification being lowered by one class. Candidates who fail to submit a portfolio will be deemed to have failed the entire Part II examination. The Head of Department, or deputy, shall make available to the examiners records showing the extent to which candidates have adequately pursued a course of practical work. The examiners shall take this evidence into consideration along with evidence of unsatisfactory or distinguished performance in each portfolio of practical work.

SPECIAL REGULATIONS FOR THE FINAL EXAMINATION IN FINE ART

A

1. No person who is not a member of the University may be admitted to the Final Examination in Fine Art.

2. No member of the University shall be admitted to the Final Examination in Fine Art unless they have either passed or been exempted from the Preliminary Examination in Fine Art.

3. (*a*) No one shall be admitted as a candidate for the examination unless by the end of the term in which the examination is held they shall have kept statutable residence for nine terms, except that a candidate who is a Senior Student may be admitted as a candidate if by the end of the term in which the examination is held they shall have kept statutable residence for six terms.

(*b*) Time spent outside Oxford as part of an academic programme approved by Council shall count towards residence for the purposes of this clause.

(*c*) The Proctors shall have power to excuse from one term of statutable residence any member of the University who shall have been duly certified by them to have been prevented by illness or other reasonable cause from keeping such residence for one or more terms, subject to the conditions set out in the appropriate regulation. Application shall be made through the college or other society or approved institution to which the member belongs. The student, or his or her society, may within fourteen days of the date of the Proctors' decision appeal in writing to the Chair of the Education Committee (who may nominate another member of the committee, other than one of the Proctors, to adjudicate the appeal).

(*d*) The Proctors shall have power to dispense, subject to such conditions as it may from time to time determine, from up to three terms of statutable residence any member of the University who has not completed such residence for any reason which the Proctors shall judge to be sufficient. Application shall be made through the college or other society or approved institution to which the member belongs. The student, or his or her society, may within fourteen days of the date of the Proctors' decision appeal in writing to the Chair of the Education Committee (who may nominate another member of the committee, other than one of the Proctors, to adjudicate the appeal).

(*e*) The candidate's college or other society or approved institution shall be required to certify on the entry form, by the time determined for entry, whether or not the candidate will have met the requirement for statutable residence by the end of the term in which the examination is held, and to notify the University of any change in the candidate's status in this respect between entry and the date of the examination.

(*f*) Nothing in this clause shall affect the conditions required for admission to degrees set out in the appropriate regulations.

4. No one shall be admitted as a candidate for the examination after the lapse of twelve terms from the term of their matriculation inclusively, except that a candidate who has been prevented by urgent cause from offering himself or herself for examination may offer himself or herself as a candidate at the next ensuing examination provided that he or she has satisfied the conditions of the relevant regulations.

5. The examination shall be under the supervision of the Committee for the Ruskin School of Art, which shall make regulations for the examination.

B

1. The examination shall include both practical and written work. Candidates will also be examined viva voce, except that the examiners may dispense from the viva voce examination any candidate concerning whom they shall have decided that performance in the viva voce examination could not properly be allowed to affect the result.

2. Every candidate will be required to

(*a*) Produce a selection of work completed throughout the course preceding the examination in each of the categories scheduled below:

(i) An exhibition of current work or work constructed especially for assessment.

(ii) A portfolio of work made during the course preceding the examination in any medium or media agreed by the candidate and their tutor. This should include at least twelve original works; in the case of time-based work, candidates should make a submission of work, or excerpts of work, of no more than a total of twenty minutes' duration. Work which, in the judgement of the candidate's tutor, cannot be submitted for examination for practical reasons, may be represented by documentation.

(*b*) Submit an essay of no more than 6,000 words (including footnotes), which shall normally be on some aspect of visual culture since 1900, in accordance with the provisions of clause 3 of these regulations.

(*c*) Satisfy the examiners in a paper on the history and theory of visual culture since 1900.

3. (*a*) The work required by the provisions of clause 2 must be submitted to the Chair of Examiners, Final Examination in Fine Art, Ruskin School of Art, 74 High Street, Oxford by noon on Tuesday in the eighth week of Trinity Full Term in which the examination is taken.

(*b*) A candidate submitting an essay in accordance with the provisions of clause 2 (*b*) of these regulations must apply for the approval of the Head of School not later than Friday in the fourth week of the Michaelmas Full Term preceding the examination. Such application shall include the title of the proposed essay and a synopsis of not more than 100 words setting out the manner in which it is proposed to treat the subject. One typed copy of the essay must be delivered to the Chair of Examiners, Final Examination in Fine Art, Examination Schools not later than noon on the Monday of the eighth week of the Hilary Full Term preceding the examination. Each essay must be accompanied by a certificate signed by the candidate that the essay has not been submitted for any previous examination, and that the essay is his or her own unaided work. Tutors may provide advice on the choice and scope of the subject, the sources available, and the method of presentation. They may also read and comment on a first draft of the essay. This certificate must be submitted separately in a sealed envelope addressed to the chair of examiners.

SPECIAL REGULATIONS FOR
THE HONOUR SCHOOL OF GEOGRAPHY

A

1. The examination in the Honour School of Geography shall always include, as stated subjects to be offered by all candidates: 5

Geographical Research

2. Candidates shall be required to offer, in addition to the above subject, two foundational courses chosen from the following list:

(i) Earth Systems Dynamics

(ii) Space, Place and Society   1

(iii) Environmental Geography

3. Candidates shall be required to offer, in addition to the above subjects, and after giving due notice of the subjects they select, three Optional Subjects chosen under arrangements determined by the board by regulation.   1

4. The examination shall be partly practical.

5. No candidate shall be admitted to the examination in the Honour School unless *either*

(*a*) he or she is a Senior Student, *or*

(*b*) he or she has passed or been exempted from the First Public   2
Examination.

6. The examination in the Honour School shall be under the supervision of the Social Sciences Board.

B

1. All candidates will be required to offer the following subjects: 2

i. Geographical Research

ii. Two foundational courses chosen from the following list: Earth Systems Dynamics; Space, Place and Society; Environmental Geography

iii. Three Optional Subjects to be chosen from a list published by the department (3 papers). Submitted work will also be required in three subjects.   3

iv. A Geographical Dissertation in accordance with the detailed regulations given below. The Dissertation will be treated as the equivalent of two papers.

v. A fieldwork report in accordance with the detailed regulations below.

2. Candidates are required to have undertaken field-work as an integral part of their course. Candidates may be examined viva voce.   3

Theses, practical notebooks or extended essays previously submitted for the Honour School of Geography may be resubmitted. No thesis, practical notebook or extended essay will be accepted if it has already been submitted, wholly or substantially, for another final honour school or degree of this University, or a degree of any other institution.

3. The requirements for each subject are as follows:

I. *Geographical Research* A course on the practice of human, physical and environmental geographical research. Emphasis will be placed on the provi- 5 sion of research skills and the relation between conceptual and methodological issues and the practice of research.

II. *Earth Systems Dynamics* The dynamics of climatic, ecological and geomor- phological systems, studied over a wide range of timescales and covering past, present and future changes. Emphasis will also be given to interactions be- 10 tween these components of the earth's system.

III. *Space, Place and Society* A human geographical perspective on space, place and society, taking account of relevant and major concepts in geographical thought, and acknowledging differing theoretical approaches. Specific cases and practices will be introduced at a range of geographical scales. 15

IV. *Environmental Geography* The nature of environmental issues, their causes and consequences, and the development of policies to manage the environment. A range of case studies will be used across various geographical scales.

V. Candidates must offer three Optional Subjects to be chosen from a list to be published by the Head of the School not later than the end of the Trinity Full 20 Term preceding the candidate's admission to the Final Honour School. One paper of three hours will be set on each subject. Each candidate must also submit an individual piece of work (as specified on the rubrics for each optional subject) for all three Optional Subjects to the Chair of Examiners in the Final Honour School of Geography, c/o the Examination Schools, High 25 Street not later than 12 noon on the Monday of the first week of the Trinity Term in which they present themselves for examination. The submitted work should not duplicate material in the candidate's dissertation. Instructions for the submitted work will be published by the Chair of the Undergraduate Teaching and Examination Committee not later than the end of the Trinity 30 Full Term preceding the candidate's admission to the Final Honour School. Information about the Optional Subjects and submitted work will be pub- lished on the departmental website by early October.

Each candidate will submit:

1. A fieldwork report of 4,500 words based on research undertaken as part of 35 the fieldcourse during Trinity Term of the year in which a candidate is admitted to the Honour School. The requirements for the fieldwork report will be published on the departmental website at the beginning of Michaelmas Full Term in the year in which the candidate is admitted to the Honour School. The fieldwork report must be submitted no later than 12 noon on the Friday in the eighth week of Trinity Term 40 in the year preceding that in which they propose to take the examination.

2. A Geographical Dissertation on a Selected Topic.

The Dissertation, exclusive of bibliography, maps and statistical appendices, must not be more than 12,000 words. The attention of candidates is drawn to the fact that limited rather than large areas are more likely to allow for adequate depth of study. 45 The Dissertation should embody original practical work based on primary data (e.g. data collected in the field, archival materials, census data, etc.), and not be based on secondary material (e.g. text books, published local histories, published papers in learned journals, government or local government reports).

Candidates having first secured the approval of their tutors are required to submit 50 to the Head of the School for approval, not later than noon on Friday at the end of the fourth week of the Trinity Full Term in the year preceding that in which they propose to take the examination, an outline of approximately 500 words of the proposed Dissertation. Special permission must also be sought from the Head of the School for any substantive change in the original proposal.

The Dissertation must be firmly bound. It must be the work of the author alone and aid from others must be limited to prior discussion as to the subject and sources   5
and advice on presentation. Every candidate shall sign a certificate to the effect that the Dissertation is his or her own work, and this certificate shall be presented with the Dissertation.

Candidates must submit two copies of their Dissertation not later than 12 noon on the Monday in the first week of the following Hilary Term, to the Chair of Examiners   10
in the Final Honour School of Geography c/o Examination Schools, High Street, Oxford OX1 4BG.

3. The Examiners will require evidence of a candidate's satisfactory attendance at two of the departmental skills workshops.

SPECIAL REGULATIONS FOR
THE HONOUR SCHOOL OF
GEOLOGY/EARTH SCIENCES

A

1. The subject of the Honour School of Geology/Earth Sciences shall be the study of the natural science of the Earth in space and time.

2. No candidate shall be admitted to examination in this school unless he or she has either passed or been exempted from the First Public Examination.

3. The examination in this school shall be under the supervision of the Mathematical, Physical and Life Sciences Board, which shall prescribe the necessary regulations. Details of the conventions used by the examiners can be found in the Undergraduate Course Handbook (see B1 below).

4. The examination shall consist of one part for the three-year course in Geology (Part A) and two parts for the four-year course in Earth Sciences (A, B). Part A shall be subdivided into Part A1 (examinations taking place three terms after the candidate has passed the First Public Examination) and Part A2 (examinations taking place six terms after the candidate has passed the First Public Examination).

5. No candidate may present him or herself for examination in Part B unless he or she has been adjudged worthy of at least second class honours by the examiners in Part A.

6. The name of a candidate in either the three-year course or the four-year course shall not be published in a class list until he or she has completed all parts of the respective examination; and in the case of the four-year course, has been adjudged worthy of honours by the examiners in Part A and Part B of the examination. The Examiners shall give due consideration to the performance in all parts of the respective examinations.

7. Part A1 may only be taken once, but no candidate shall be deemed to have failed. The second year mapping project should be submitted at the beginning of the fifth term after the candidate has passed the First Public Examination, and may not subsequently be modified. A candidate who obtains only a pass, or fails to satisfy the examiners in Part A, may enter again for Part A2 of the

examination on one, but no more than one, subsequent occasion. Where a candidate retakes the whole year, the candidate will submit a new third-year essay on a subject approved by the Chair of the Faculty of Earth Sciences or deputy as set out in section B, Geology (three year course), (ii), below. Where a candidate resits only the examinations, the third-year essay may be resubmitted by the deadline given in the Undergraduate Course Handbook. A candidate who fails to satisfy the examiners in Part A who subsequently enters a second time may not proceed to the fourth year. The fourth-year project should be submitted in the ninth term after the candidate has passed the First Public Examination, and may not subsequently be modified. The rules for handling the fourth-year project are to be found in the departmental Undergraduate Course Handbook. A candidate who obtains only a pass, or fails to satisfy the examiners in Part B, may not enter again for Part B.

8. A candidate adjudged worthy of Honours in the Second Public Examination for the four-year course may supplicate for the Degree of Master of Earth Sciences, provided that the candidate has fulfilled all the conditions for admission to a degree of the University.

9. A candidate in the final year of the four-year course, adjudged worthy of Honours in Part A, but who does not enter Part B, or who fails to obtain Honours in Part B, is permitted to supplicate for the Honours degree of Bachelor of Arts in Geology with the classification obtained in Part A; provided that no such candidate may later enter or re-enter the Part B year or supplicate for the degree of Master of Earth Sciences; and provided in each case that the candidate has fulfilled all the conditions for admission to a degree of the University.

10. Candidates will be expected to show skills and knowledge based upon practical work. The examiners will assess practical skills and knowledge by means of practical examinations, and by assessment of practical work done by candidates during their course of study.

B

1. In the following, 'the Course Handbook' refers to the Geology/Earth Sciences Undergraduate Course Handbook, published annually at the start of Michaelmas Term by the Faculty of Earth Sciences and also posted on the website at www.earth.ox.ac.uk/undergraduate_course.

2. The examiners will permit the use of any hand-held calculator, subject to the conditions set out under the heading 'Use of calculators in examinations' in the Regulations for the Conduct of University Examinations and further elaborated in the Course Handbook.

GEOLOGY (THREE-YEAR COURSE)
A candidate shall be required to offer:
  (i) Five papers (Part A1), including practical elements, to be taken in Weeks 7
      and 8 of Trinity Term, in the third term after the candidate has passed the
      First Public Examination; and
 (ii) a report on an individual mapping or practical project, prepared according to
      the guidelines set out in the Course Handbook, the report to be submitted by
      Thursday of Week 0 of Hilary Term in the fifth term after the candidate has
      passed the First Public Examination; and
(iii) an extended essay, prepared according to the guidelines set out in the Course
      Handbook, the work to be undertaken in Hilary Term in the fifth term after
      the candidate has passed the First Public Examination, and the essay to be
      submitted by the Thursday of Week 0 of Trinity Term in the sixth term after
      the candidate has passed the First Public Examination. The subject of the
      essay must have been approved by the Chair of the Faculty of Earth Sciences
      or deputy no later than the end of Michaelmas Full Term in the fourth term
      after the candidate has passed the First Public Examination; and
 (iv) seven papers (Part A2), including practical elements, to be taken in Week 5 of
      Trinity Term in the sixth term after the candidate has passed the First Public
      Examination.
The list of subjects and syllabuses available will be published in the Course
Handbook.
The Head of Department of Earth Sciences or deputy shall provide the examiners
with information showing the extent to which each candidate has satisfactorily
completed the practicals and field courses. In addition, practical notebooks containing records of both field and laboratory courses must also be made available to the
examiners.
Examiners may take into account these records of practical and fieldwork, in
particular with regard to the attendance record of the candidates, and to any marks
awarded for assignments, when awarding classes. Material handed in from practical
classes will be taken as evidence of attendance.
For candidates whose attendance record is deemed unsatisfactory, the examiners
have the discretion to reduce the final degree class of the candidate. Examiners may
also take into account evidence of excellent performance in field or practical work
when drawing up class boundaries.
Candidates may be examined viva voce at the examiners' discretion.

EARTH SCIENCES (FOUR-YEAR COURSE)
  1. The examination shall be in two parts.
  2. Part A of the examination shall be the same as the requirements for the three-
year course in Geology, and the same conditions, arrangements and examination
timings shall apply.
  3. Part B of the examination shall be taken at a time not less than three terms after
Part A. In Part B a candidate shall be required to offer:
  (i) written papers on four subjects, chosen from a list published by the Faculty of
      Earth Sciences as set out in (4) below, for examination in Trinity Term in the
      ninth term after the candidate has passed the First Public Examination, and
 (ii) either an extended essay, or a report on an advanced practical project or other
      advanced work, prepared according to the guidelines set out in the Course
      Handbook, the work to be undertaken in Michaelmas, Hilary, and Trinity
      Terms in the seventh, eighth and ninth terms respectively after the candidate
      has passed the First Public Examination, and the essay or report to be sub-
      mitted by Thursday of Week 3 of Trinity Term in the ninth term after the

candidate has passed the First Public Examination. The proposed nature and duration of the practical or other advanced work shall be submitted for approval, by no later than the end of Trinity Full Term in the sixth term after the candidate has passed the First Public Examination, to the Chair of the Faculty of Earth Sciences or deputy with the agreement of the Head of the Department of Earth Sciences or deputy.

4. The list of subjects and syllabuses for the written papers in 3(i) will be published in the Course Handbook for the academic year in which they are examined. The subjects and syllabuses shall be approved by the Faculty of Earth Sciences with the agreement of the Head of the Department of Earth Sciences or deputy.

5. Candidates may be examined viva voce at the examiners' discretion.

SPECIAL REGULATIONS FOR
THE HONOUR SCHOOL OF HISTORY

A

1. The examination in the School of History shall be under the supervision of the Board of the Faculty of History, and shall always include:

(1) The History of the British Isles (including the History of Scotland, Ireland, and Wales; and of British India and of British Colonies and Dependencies as far as they are connected with the History of the British Isles);

(2) General History during some period, selected by the candidate from periods to be named from time to time by the Board of the Faculty;

(3) A Special Historical subject, studied with reference to original authorities.

2. No candidate shall be admitted to examination in this school unless he or she has *either* passed or been exempted from the First Public Examination *or* has successfully completed the Foundation Course in History at the Department for Continuing Education.

3. The Board of the Faculty of History shall, by notice from time to time, make regulations respecting the above-named branches of examination, and shall have power

(1) To name certain periods of General History, and to fix their limits;

(2) To issue lists of Special Historical subjects, prescribing particular authorities where they think it desirable.

4. The examination in the Special Historical subject may be omitted by candidates, but such candidates shall not be placed in the Class List.

5. The Board of the Faculty may include in the examination, either as necessary or as optional, other subjects which they may deem suitable to be studied in connection with History, including translation from foreign languages of passages not specially prepared, and may prescribe books or portions of books in any language.

B

The History Board shall issue annually the Handbook for the Honour School of History by Monday of Week 1 of the first Michaelmas Full Term of candidates' work for the Honour School. A supplement to the handbook shall be issued to candidates at the beginning of Week 4 of the first Hilary Full Term of their work for the Honour School, and posted in the History Faculty Building and circulated to tutors.

All candidates are required to offer Subjects I, II, III, V and VI, below. No candidate may be placed in the Class List unless he or she also offers Special Subject IV, below.

Candidates who have taken the Foundation Course in History rather than the Preliminary Examination are required to offer at least one paper from either Subject I or Subject II which relates to a period between 285 and 1550 (this may be taken to include Periods (I), (II), or (III) of the History of the British Isles, or Periods (i), (ii), (iii), (iv), (v), (vi) or (vii) of General History).

Students participating in the academic exchange scheme with Princeton University will substitute the courses taken at Princeton for either a General History or History of the British Isles paper. The Princeton courses will be examined at Princeton, and the grades awarded will be reviewed and moderated by the Examiners to produce a single University standard mark, according to procedures laid down in the Handbook and Examining Conventions.

I. History of the British Isles: any one of the following periods:
    (I) *c.*300–1087;
    (II) 1042–1330;
    (III) 1330–1550;
    (IV) 1500–1700;
    (V) 1685–1830;
    (VI) 1815–1924;
    (VII) since 1900.

No candidate may offer a period offered when passing the First Public Examination.

The History of the British Isles is taken to include the history of the Irish Republic in the twentieth century, and of British India and British Colonies and Dependencies as far as they are connected with the History of Britain.

II. General History: any one of the listed periods:

    (i) 285–476; (ii) 476–750; (iii) 700–900; (iv) 900–1150; (v) 1100–1273; (vi) 1273–1409; (vii) 1409–1525; (viii) 1500–1618; (ix) 1600–1715; (x) 1715–1799; (xi) 1789–1871; (xii) 1856–1914; (xiii) 1914–1945; (xiv) 1941–1973; (xv) Britain's North American Colonies: from settlement to independence, 1600–1812, (xvi) From Colonies to Nation: the History of the United States 1776–1877, (xvii) The History of the United States since 1863, (xviii) Imperial and Global History 1750–1914.

The four periods of British and General History offered by a candidate in the First Public Examination and the Honour School must include at least one from the following groups:

1. Medieval History

    (I) c.300–1087; (II) 1042–1330; General History (taken in the First Public Examination): I: 370–900, II: 1000–1300; (taken in the Final Honour School). (i) 285–476, (ii) 476–750, (iii) 700–900, (iv) 900–1150, (v) 1100–1273, (vi) 1273–1409.

2. Early Modern History

    (III) 1330–1550, (IV) 1500–1700; General History (taken in the First Public Examination): III: 1400–1650; (taken in the Final Honour School): (vii) 1409–1525; (viii) 1500–1618; (ix) 1600–1715.

3. Modern History

    (V) British History 1685–1830; (VI) 1815–1924; (VII) since 1900, General History (taken in the First Public Examination): IV: 1815–1914; (taken in the Final Honour School): (x) 1715–1799; (xi) 1789–1871; (xii) 1856–1914; (xiii) 1914–1945; (xiv) 1941–1973; (xv) Britain's North American Colonies: from settlement to independence, 1600–1812; (xvi) From Colonies to Nation: the History of the United States 1776–1877; (xvii) The History of the United States since 1863; (xviii) Imperial and Global History 1750–1914.

Candidates with Senior Student status, and candidates who have passed the First Public Examination in a course other than Modern History are required to offer one paper in British History and one in General History, to be taken from two out of the three period groups (1. Medieval History, 2. Early Modern History, 3. Modern History).

Candidates who participate in the Princeton Exchange are required to offer one period in the History of the British Isles or General History, so chosen that the periods offered in the First Public Examination and the Honour School are taken from at least two out of the three period groups. This requirement shall also apply to candidates who participate in the Princeton Exchange having taken the First Public Examination in a joint school involving History papers.

III. Further Subject: any one of an approved list of Further Subjects, as detailed in the Handbook for the Final Honour School in History published by the Board of the Faculty of History by Monday of first week of Michaelmas Term each year for the academic year ahead.

Candidates will be examined by means of a timed paper, except in the following case(s):

Further Subject, "Britain at the Movies: Film and National Identity since 1914".

Candidates taking the Further Subject paper(s) listed above will be examined by means of an essay, which shall not exceed 5,000 words (including footnotes but excluding bibliography), and shall be on a topic or theme selected by the candidate from a question paper published by the examiners on the Monday of the seventh week of Hilary Term in the year preceding final examination. Essays should be typed or word-processed in double spacing and should conform to the standards of academic presentation prescribed in the course handbook. Essays (two copies) will be completed during the eighth week of the Hilary Term in the year preceding final examination, and must be delivered by hand to the Examination Schools (addressed to the Chair of Examiners, Honour School of History, Examination Schools, High Street, Oxford) not later than 12 noon on the Friday of the eighth week of the Hilary Term of the year preceding final examination. Candidates delivering essays will be required to complete a receipt form, which will only be accepted as proof of receipt if it is counter-signed by a member of the Examination Schools staff. Each essay must be accompanied by a sealed envelope (bearing only the candidate's examination number) containing a formal declaration signed by the candidate that the essay is his or her own work. The University's regulations on Late Submission of Work will apply.

Further Subjects "Representing the City 1558–1640" and "Post-Colonial Historiography: writing the Indian nation"

Candidates taking the Further Subject paper(s) listed above will be examined by means of an essay, which shall be between 5,000 and 6,000 words (including footnotes but excluding bibliography), and shall be on an interdisciplinary topic relevant to the Further Subject concerned. Candidates must submit their proposed essay title to the Chair of Examiners for History, care of the History Faculty Office, not later than Friday of the eighth week of Hilary Term in the first year of study for the Honour School. Approval of the title may be assumed unless the Chair of Examiners contacts a candidate's tutor by Monday of the second week of the Trinity Term.

The candidate must deliver two copies of the essay by hand to the Examination Schools (addressed to the Chair of Examiners, Honour School of History, Examination Schools, High Street, Oxford) not later than 12 noon on the Thursday of the eighth week of Trinity Term in the first year of study for the Honour School. A certificate, signed by the candidate to the effect that each essay is the candidate's own work, and that the candidate has read the Faculty's guidelines on plagiarism, must be presented together with the submission. Candidates delivering essays will be required to complete a receipt form, which will only be accepted as proof of receipt if it is counter-signed by a member of the Examination Schools staff. The University's regulations on *Late Submission of Work* will apply.

IV. The Special Subjects available in any given year, as approved by the Board of the Faculty of History, will be publicised in the list posted by the Faculty of History in the Hilary Term of the preceding year.

Candidates will be examined by means of a timed paper including compulsory passages for comment, and by means of an extended essay, which shall not exceed 6,000 words (including footnotes but excluding bibliography), and shall be on a topic or theme selected by the candidate from a question paper published by the examiners on the Friday of the fourth week of Michaelmas Term in the year of examination.

Essays should be typed or word-processed in double spacing and should conform to the standards of academic presentation prescribed in the course handbook.

Essays (two copies) shall normally be written during the Michaelmas Term in the year of examination and must be delivered by hand to the Examination Schools (addressed to the Chair of Examiners, Honour School of History, Examination Schools, High Street, Oxford) not later than 12 noon on the Friday before the beginning of Hilary Full Term of the year of examination. Candidates delivering essays will be required to complete a receipt form, which will only be accepted as proof of receipt if it is counter-signed by a member of the Examination Schools staff. Each essay must be accompanied by a sealed envelope (bearing only the candidate's examination number) containing a formal declaration signed by the candidate that the essay is his or her own work. The University's regulations on *Late Submission of Work* will apply.

Depending on the availability of teaching resources, not all Further and Special Subjects will be available to all candidates in every year. Candidates may obtain details of the choice of options for the following year by consulting lists posted at the beginning of the Week Four of Hilary Full Term in the History Faculty, on WebLearn and circulated to History Tutors.

V. *Disciplines of History*

Candidates will be expected to answer two examination questions selected from a paper divided into two sections. One question should be answered from each section.

The sections are:

1. Making Historical Comparisons;
2. Making Historical Arguments.

VI. *A thesis from original research*

1. Candidates must submit a thesis as part of the fulfilment of their final examination.

2. Theses shall normally be written during the Hilary Term of the final year. All theses must be submitted not later than noon on Friday of eighth week of the Hilary Term of the final year.

3. A candidate may submit

   (*a*) any essay or part of any essay which the candidate has submitted or intends to submit for any university essay prize; or

   (*b*) any other work provided in either case that (i) no thesis will be accepted if it has already been submitted, wholly or substantially, for a final honour school other than one involving History, or another degree of this University, or a degree of any other university, and (ii) the candidate submits a statement to that effect, and (iii) the subject is approved by the Chair of the Examiners for the Honour School of History.

4. The provisos in cl. 3 above shall not debar any candidate from submitting work based on a previous submission towards the requirements for a degree of any other university provided that

   (i) the work is substantially new;

   (ii) the candidate also submits both the original work itself and a statement specifying the extent of what is new. The examiners shall have sole authority to decide in every case whether proviso (i) to this clause has been met.

5. Every candidate must submit the title proposed together with a typed synopsis of the thesis topic and proposed method of investigation (no more than 250 words) and the written approval of their College History Tutor to the Chair of the Examiners for the Honour School of History, the History Faculty, George Street, Oxford, not earlier than the beginning of Trinity Full Term in the year preceding that in which the candidate takes the examination and not later than the Friday of sixth week of Michaelmas Term in the final year. If no notification is received from the Chair of Examiners by the first Monday of Hilary Full Term of the final year, the title shall be deemed to be approved. Any subsequent changes to title require formal application to the Chair of Examiners by the Friday of Week 4 of the Hilary Term of the final year and subsequent approval.

6. Theses should normally include an investigation of relevant printed or unprinted primary historical sources, and must include proper footnotes and a bibliography. They must be the work of the author alone. In all cases, the candidate's tutor or thesis adviser shall discuss with the candidate the field of study, the sources available, and the methods of presentation. Candidates shall be expected to have had a formal meeting or meetings with their College History Tutor, and, if necessary, an additional meeting or meetings with a specialised thesis adviser in the Trinity Term of their second year, as well as a second formal meeting or meetings with their thesis adviser in the Michaelmas Term of their final year, prior to submitting the title of their thesis. While writing the thesis, candidates are permitted to have further advisory sessions at which bibliographical, structural, and other problems can be discussed. The total time spent in all meetings with the College History Tutor and/or the specialised thesis adviser must not exceed five hours. A first draft of the thesis may be commented on, but not corrected in matters of detail and presentation, by the thesis adviser.

7. No thesis shall exceed 12,000 words in length (including footnotes, but excluding bibliography and, in cases for which specific permission has been obtained from the Chair of Examiners, appendices), except in the case that a candidate is submitting a thesis as a critical edition of a text, in which case the regulations on word length in VI 10, sections iii and x, below, apply. All theses must be typed or word-processed in double spacing on one side of A4 paper with the notes and references at the foot of each page, with a left-hand margin of one-and-a-half inches and all other margins of at least one inch. The thesis should conform to the standards of academic presentation prescribed in the course handbook. Failure to conform to such standards may incur penalties as outlined in the course handbook.

8. All candidates must submit two copies of their thesis, addressed to the Chair of Examiners, Honour School of History, Examination Schools, High Street, Oxford, not later than noon on Friday of eighth week of the Hilary Term of the year in which they are presenting themselves for examination. The University's regulations on *Late Submission of Work* will apply. Every candidate shall present a certificate, signed by him or herself, in a separate envelope bearing the candidate's examination number, addressed to the Chair of Examiners. The certificate (forms are available from the History Faculty Office) should declare that (*a*) the thesis is the candidate's own work, (*b*) that no substantial portion of it has been presented for any other degree course or examination, (*c*) that is does not exceed 12,000 words in length, except in the case that a candidate is submitting a thesis as a critical edition of a text, in which case the regulations on word length in VI 10, sections iii and x, below, apply, (*d*) that no more than five hours have been spent in preparatory or advisory meetings between the candidate and his or her College History Tutor or thesis adviser, and (*e*) that only the first draft of the thesis has been seen by the thesis adviser. Candidates delivering theses will be required to complete a receipt form, which will only be accepted as proof of receipt if it is countersigned by a member of the Examination Schools staff.

9. Candidates shall not answer in any other paper, with the exception of Disciplines of History (V), questions which fall very largely within the scope of their thesis. Candidates should not choose a thesis that substantially reworks material

studied in the Further or Special Subjects, and should demonstrate familiarity with and use of substantially different and additional primary sources.

10. As an alternative route to fulfilling the requirement for the compulsory thesis, or to submitting an optional one, a candidate may prepare an edition of a short historical text with appropriate textual apparatus, historical annotation and introduction. This exercise, which is different in kind from the writing of a normal dissertation, is governed by the following additional regulations:

i. The original work selected for editing may be a narrative, literary, or archival text of any kind, and may be of any period and in any language. It must be susceptible to historical analysis and commentary, and of a kind that requires the application of editorial and historical skills and techniques, including linguistic and palaeographical skills where appropriate.

ii. The choice of text must be approved by the submission to the Chair of the FHS in History, with the support of a supervisor, of a 250-word outline of the text and its context, and specifying its length. This submission must be made by Friday of noughth week of the Michaelmas Term of the candidate's final year, but candidates are advised to seek permission well before this. The Chair must consult appropriate colleagues before approving the project: they will need to be satisfied that it provides scope for displaying appropriate levels of knowledge and expertise.

iii. The length of the chosen text will depend upon the linguistic and technical challenges which it poses, and the scope it offers for historical analysis and commentary; the advice of the supervisor will be essential. A complex text in a difficult language may only run to a few thousand words. The absolute maxima are 15,000 words for a non-English text, and 30,000 for one in English; but these are not norms or targets. An extract from a longer text is permissible, so long as the selection is rationally justified, and the extract can stand on its own for purposes of historical commentary.

iv. A text in a language other than English must be accompanied by an English translation.

v. The examiners must be provided with a facsimile of no less than 30 per cent of the text in its primary manuscript or printed form. Where there are several versions, the most important should be chosen.

vi. A textual introduction should state how many versions (whether manuscript or printed) there are to the text, how they relate to each other, and what editorial principles have been employed.

vii. A textual apparatus should list variant readings, emendations and textual problems in accordance with normal editorial practice.

viii. Historical notes to the text should comment as appropriate on people, places, events and other references, and should draw out points of wider historical interest.

ix. A historical introduction should discuss the immediate context of the work, including its author or the record-creating system that produced it, and should explain its wider historical context and significance.

x. The textual and historical introductions and the historical notes should not exceed 8,000 words (for an English text) or 6,000 (for a translated one).

xi. The dissertation should be arranged and bound in the following order: historical introduction; textual introduction; text, with textual notes (keyed to the text in the sequence *a, b, c* etc.) at the foot of the page; historical notes (keyed to the text in the sequence 1, 2, 3 etc.) on separate pages; sample facsimile.

VII. *An optional additional thesis*

1. Any candidate may offer an optional additional thesis.
2. Regulation VI 3. above applies.
3. Regulation VI 4. above applies.

4. Every candidate intending to offer an optional thesis except as defined in VI 3 (*a*) above must submit the title proposed together with the written approval of a thesis adviser or College History Tutor to the Chair of the Examiners for the Honour School of History, the History Faculty, George Street, Oxford, not earlier than the beginning of Trinity Full Term in the year preceding that in which the candidate takes the examination and not later than Friday of the first week of the following Hilary Full Term. The Chair shall decide whether or not to approve the title, consulting the Faculty Board if so desired, and shall advise the candidate as soon as possible.

5. Optional additional theses should normally include an investigation of relevant printed or unprinted historical sources, and must include proper footnotes and a bibliography. They must be the work of the author alone. In all cases, the candidate's College History Tutor or thesis adviser shall discuss with the candidate the field of study, the sources available, and the methods of presentation (which should conform to the standards of academic presentation described in the course handbook). The College History Tutor or thesis adviser may comment on the first draft.

6. No optional additional thesis shall exceed 12,000 words in length (including footnotes but excluding bibliographies), except in the case that a candidate is submitting a thesis as a critical edition of a text, in which case the regulations on word length in regulation VI 10, sections iii and x, above, apply. All theses must be typed or word-processed in double spacing on one side of A4 paper with the notes and references at the foot of each page, with a left-hand margin of one-and-a-half inches and all other margins of at least one inch.

7. Candidates must submit two copies of their theses, addressed to the Chair of Examiners, Honour School of History, Examination Schools, High Street, Oxford, not later than noon on Friday of eighth week of the Hilary Term of the year in which they are presenting themselves for examination. Every candidate shall present a certificate signed by him or herself and by a College History Tutor or thesis adviser, in a separate envelope bearing the candidate's examination number, addressed to the Chair of Examiners. The certificate (forms are available from the Faculty Office) should declare that (*a*) the thesis is the candidate's own work, (*b*) that no substantial portion of it has been presented for any other degree course or examination, (*c*) that is does not exceed 12,000 words in length.

8. Candidates shall not answer in any other paper, with the exception of Disciplines of History (V), questions which fall very largely within the scope of their optional additional thesis.

9. Candidates may submit an optional additional thesis in the form of an edition of a short historical text with accompanying scholarly apparatus, in which case the requirements detailed in regulation VI 10, above, apply.

10. The Final Honour School Examiners will arrive at a formal degree result for candidates who submit an Optional Additional Thesis by inclusion of the 7 highest marks awarded for the 8 papers submitted, except that the mark awarded for the Optional Additional Thesis may not substitute for a mark lower than 50. Thus, the papers to be included are determined by the following procedures:

   (i) In the event that the Optional Additional Thesis is awarded a mark below 50, it will be disregarded and the formal degree result will be determined solely by the marks awarded for the compulsory papers.

   (ii) In the event that the Optional Additional Thesis is awarded a mark of 50 or above, the paper awarded the lowest mark of 50 or above (which may be the Optional Additional Thesis) will be disregarded. All other papers awarded a mark of 50 or above, and all papers awarded a mark below 50 will be included.

SPECIAL REGULATIONS FOR THE HONOUR SCHOOL OF HISTORY AND ECONOMICS

A

1. The examination in the Honour School of History and Economics shall consist of such subjects in History and Economics as the Board of the Faculty of History and Division of Social Sciences from time to time shall in consultation prescribe by regulation.

2. No candidate shall be admitted to examination in this School unless he or she has either passed or been exempted from the First Public Examination.

3. The examination in the Honour School shall be under the joint supervision of the Board of the Faculty of History and the Social Sciences Divisional Board, which shall appoint a standing joint committee to make proposals for regulations concerning the examination. Such proposals shall be submitted to the boards of the two faculties which shall make regulations concerning the examination and which, in the case of difference of opinion, shall hold a joint meeting at which the matter in dispute shall be resolved by the vote of the majority.

4. The Chairs of Examiners for the Honour School of History and for the Honour School of Philosophy, Politics, and Economics shall consult together and designate such of their number as may be required for the examination for the Honour School of History and Economics, whereupon the number of examiners shall be deemed to be complete.

B

Each candidate shall offer:
1. *Macroeconomics.*
   As specified for the Honour School of Philosophy, Politics and Economics.
2. *Microeconomics.*
   As specified for the Honour School of Philosophy, Politics and Economics.
3. *Quantitative Economics.*
   As specified for the Honour School of Philosophy, Politics and Economics.
4. *British Economic History since 1870.*
   As specified for the Honour School of Philosophy, Politics and Economics.
5. *Either* one period of General History *or* one period of The History of the British Isles.
6. *Either*
   (*a*) two Further Subjects in History;
   or
   (*b*) (i) one Further Subject in History and (ii) either one period of General History or one period of The History of the British Isles, except any such period offered under paper 5, above.

or

(*c*) (i) one Further Subject in History and (ii) one Further Subject in Economics.

7. *A thesis from original research*

Regulation VI of the Honour School of History applies with the following modifications:

Cl. 1 For 'Candidates must submit a thesis as part of the fulfilment of their final examination' read 'Candidates must submit a thesis—normally, but not necessarily in economic history—as part of the fulfilment of their final examination'.

Cl. 2 For 'Theses shall normally be written during the Hilary Term of the final year' read 'Theses shall normally be written during the Michaelmas and/or Hilary Term of the final year'.

Cl. 3(b) (iii) For 'Chair of the Examiners for the Honour School of History' read 'Chair of the Examiners, Honour School of History and Economics'.

Cl. 5 For 'Honour School of History' read 'Honour School of History and Economics'.

Cl. 6 For 'primary historical sources' read 'primary historical sources or economic data'; for 'College History Tutor' read 'College History Tutor' or Economics Tutor'.

Cl. 8 For 'Chair of Examiners, Honour School of History' read 'Chair of Examiners, Honour School of History and Economics'.

Cl. 9 For 'Candidates shall not answer in any other paper, with the exception of Disciplines of History (V), questions which fall very largely within the scope of their thesis' read 'Candidates shall not answer in any other paper questions which fall very largely within the scope of their thesis.'

Cl. 10ii For 'Chair of the FHS in History 'read 'Chair of the FHS in History and Economics'.

The syllabus for sections 1–4, 6(*b*) and 6(*c*) (ii) is as specified in the Honour School of Philosophy, Politics, and Economics and for sections 5, 6(*a*) and 6(*c*) (i) as specified for the Honour School of History.

The individual detailed specifications and prescribed texts for the Further Subjects as specified for the Honour School of History will be given in the Handbook for the Honour School of History. This will be published by the History Board by Monday of Week 1 of the first Michaelmas Full Term of candidates' work for the Honour School.

Depending on the availability of teaching resources, not all Further Subjects will be available to all candidates in every year. Candidates may obtain details of the choice of Further Subjects in History available for the following year by consulting the supplement to the Handbook for the Honour School of History. This will be issued by the beginning of the fourth week of the first Hilary Full Term of candidates' work for the Honour School and will contain full specifications and prescribed texts for any Further Subjects specified for History introduced for the following year, and any amendments to the specifications and prescribed texts of existing Further Subjects approved by the History Board by its first meeting of the preceding Hilary Term.

Not all Economics subjects may be offered in any particular year. There may also be restrictions on numbers permitted to offer some Economics subjects in any particular year.

Economics subjects available to candidates in any particular year will depend on the availability of teaching resources. Details of the choices available for the following year will be announced at the Economics Department's 'Options Fair' at the beginning of the fourth week of this first Hilary Term of the candidates' work for the Honour School, and will be posted on the Department's undergraduate WebLearn at the same time.

No candidate may offer the same subject twice.

For all Economics papers (which shall be taken to include British Economic History since 1870 but not other papers in Economic History) candidates are permitted the use of one hand-held pocket calculator from a list of permitted calculators published annually by the Department of Economics on its Undergraduate website, which will be updated annually in the week prior to the first full week of Michaelmas Term.

In every case where, under the regulations for this Honour School, candidates have any choice between one or more papers or subjects, every candidate shall give notice not later than Friday in the fourth week of Michaelmas Full Term preceding the examination of all the papers and subjects being so offered.

A second thesis, in addition to the papers listed under sections 1 to 6 may be offered in accordance with the Regulation VII. *An Optional Additional Thesis* of the Honour School of History, q. v. modified as follows:

(*a*) the subject shall, to the satisfaction of the examiners, fall within the scope of the Honour School of History and Economics; or

(*b*) the prizes listed in that regulation with the addition of the Webb Medley Essay Prize and the Sir John Rhys Prize;

(*c*) theses must be submitted to the Chair of the Examiners, Honour School of History and Economics, Examination Schools, High Street, Oxford. In the assignment of honours, attention will be paid to the merits of any such thesis;

(*d*) not more than two theses may be offered.

(*e*) Cl.10 For 'The Final Honour School Examiners will arrive at a formal degree result for candidates who submit an Optional Additional Thesis by taking the highest seven marks of 50 or above, out of the eight papers submitted, except that the Optional Additional Thesis may not substitute for any paper awarded a mark below 50' read 'The Final Honour School Examiners will arrive at a formal degree result for candidates who submit an Optional Additional Thesis by taking the highest eight marks of 50 or above, out of the nine papers submitted, except that the Optional Additional Thesis may not substitute for any paper awarded a mark below 50'.

SPECIAL REGULATIONS FOR THE HONOUR SCHOOL OF HISTORY AND ENGLISH

For students commencing the Honour School on or after 1 Octber 2012

A

1. The Honour School of History and English shall be under the joint supervision of the Boards of the Faculties of History and English Language and Literature and shall consist of such subjects as they shall jointly by regulation prescribe. The boards shall establish a joint committee consisting of three representatives of each faculty, of whom at least one of each side shall be a member of the respective faculty board, to advise them as necessary in respect of the Honour School of, and Honour Moderations in, and of the Preliminary Examination in History and English.

2. No candidate shall be admitted to the examination in this school unless he or she has either passed or been exempted from the First Public Examination.

3. The Chairs of Examiners for the Honour School of History and for the Honour School of English Language and Literature shall consult together and designate such of their number as may be required for the examination for the Honour School of History and English, whereupon the number of examiners shall be deemed to be complete.

B

Each candidate shall offer seven papers as set out below. Papers will be of three hours' duration, except where otherwise indicated.

The subjects of the examination in the Honour School shall be:

(i) and (ii) Two compulsory interdisciplinary papers which are examined by extended essay. The list of papers will be published in the *University Gazette* by the beginning of the first week of the Trinity Term one year before the examination, and which will be available thereafter from the English Faculty Office and the History Faculty Office.

Further details of the interdisciplinary papers will be available from the English Faculty Office and History Faculty Office.

Candidates should note that no more than three out of the total of seven Final Honour School papers can be extended essays. Candidates should also note that some English and History papers are examined *only* by extended essay and should bear this restriction in mind when making their choices.

(iii) A period of British History not taken in the First Public Examination.

(iv) and (v) Two subjects from Course I or Course II of the Honour School of English Language and Literature. Candidates may offer papers 8(*d*), Victorian Literature (1832–1900), 8(*e*), Modern Literature (1900 to the present day) or 9, Introduction to Medieval Studies: Old English Literature, so long as they have not offered equivalent papers in a First Public Examination in English or its joint schools.

(vi) and (vii) *Either* two papers from the Honour School of History, consisting of *either* (*a*) Special Subject (which comprises a three hour paper and an extended essay),

or   (*b*) Two of the following:

1. a Further Subject,
2. a General History Period.
3. an additional British History period not taken in the First Public Examination.

or one additional subject from the Honour School of English Language and Literature, plus one subject from the Honour School of History which shall be either a Further Subject, a General History period or an additional British History period.

The individual detailed specifications and prescribed texts for the Further and Special Subjects as specified for the Honour School of History will be given in the Handbook for the Honour School of History. This will be published by the History Board by Monday of Week 1 of the first Michaelmas Full Term of candidates' work for the Honour School.

Depending on the availability of teaching resources, not all Further and Special Subjects will be available to all candidates in every year. Candidates may obtain details of the choice of Further and Special Subjects available for the following year by consulting the supplement to the Handbook for the Honour School of History. This will be issued by the beginning of the fourth week of the first Hilary Full Term of candidates' work for the Honour School and will contain full specifications and prescribed texts for any Further or Special Subjects specified for History introduced for the following year, and any amendments to the specifications and prescribed texts of existing Further and Special Subjects approved by the History Board.

An extended essay shall not exceed 6,000 words including footnotes and notes but *excluding* bibliography and should conform to the standards of academic presentation prescribed in the course handbook. For interdisciplinary extended essays the candidate should obtain written approval from the course convener for the proposed essay title, not later than Friday of the fourth week of the Michaelmas Full Term immediately preceding the examination. Notification of whether or not approval is forthcoming will be given by the Friday of Week Six of that term. Essays on approved interdisciplinary titles, should be submitted to the Chair of the Examiners for the Joint School of History and English at the Examination Schools, Oxford, by the Friday of eighth week of the Hilary Full Term preceding the examination.

An optional additional thesis may also be offered providing that no more than one thesis can be submitted if extended essays are offered.

The optional additional thesis shall be as under the regulations of the History syllabus *except that* it shall not be less than 8,000 words and shall not exceed 10,000 words, including footnotes and notes, but excluding the bibliography, and shall be on an interdisciplinary theme. For regulations VII 4 and 7 of the History syllabus regulations read 'Honour School of History and English' instead of 'History'.

SPECIAL REGULATIONS FOR THE HONOUR SCHOOL OF HISTORY AND ENGLISH

For students commencing the Honour School on or after 1 October 2013

A

1. The Honour School of History and English shall be under the joint supervision of the Boards of the Faculties of History and English Language and Literature and shall consist of such subjects as they shall jointly by regulation prescribe. The boards shall establish a joint committee consisting of three representatives of each faculty, of whom at least one of each side shall be a member of the respective faculty board, to advise them as necessary in respect of the Honour School and of the Preliminary Examination in History and English.

2. No candidate shall be admitted to the examination in this school unless he or she has either passed or been exempted from the First Public Examination.

3. The Chairs of Examiners for the Honour School of History and for the Honour School of English Language and Literature shall consult together and designate such of their number as may be required for the examination for the Honour School of History and English, whereupon the number of examiners shall be deemed to be complete.

B

Each candidate shall offer seven subjects as set out below. The subjects will be examined by written examinations of three hours' duration, unless otherwise specified.

1. Submitted work

(*a*) Candidates should note that no more than four out of the total of seven Final Honour School papers can be examined by submission. Candidates should also note that some English and History papers are examined only by submission and should bear this restriction in mind when making their choices.

(*b*) Two typed copies of each extended essay or portfolio must be delivered by hand to the relevant Chair of Examiners, Examination Schools, High Street, according to the deadlines specified in the regulations for each subject. It is additionally strongly recommended that the candidate keep a third copy of his or her submission. A certificate signed by the candidate to the effect that each extended essay or portfolio is the candidate's own work, and that the candidate has read the History Faculty and English Language and Literature Faculty guidelines on plagiarism, must be presented together with each submission (see (*d*) below). Certificates will be circulated to candidates for completion by the History Faculty Office and the English Faculty Office.

(*c*) Every submission must be the work of the candidate alone, and he or she may not discuss with any tutor either his or her choice of content or the method of handling it after the last date indicated in the regulations for each subject.

(*d*) Essays previously submitted for the Honour School of History and English may be re-submitted. No essay will be accepted if it has already been submitted, wholly or substantially, for a final honour school or other degree of this University, or degree of any other institution.

(*e*) Essays may be penalised that are deemed to be either too short or of excessive length in relation to the word limits specified in the regulations for each subject.

2. History and English papers

(i) One compulsory interdisciplinary bridge paper, which shall be examined by an extended essay of between 5,000 and 6,000 words, including footnotes and notes but excluding bibliography. The list of topics for this paper shall be published to candidates by the beginning of the first week of the Michaelmas Term in the year preceding the final examination, and shall be available thereafter from the English Faculty Office and the History Faculty Office.

Candidates must obtain written approval from the Chair of Examiners for the Honour school of History and English for the proposed essay title, not later than Friday of the eighth week of the Hilary Term in the year preceding the final examination.

The candidate must deliver two typed copies of the bridge paper essay by hand to the Chair of Examiners for the Joint School of History and English, at the Examination Schools, High Street, by noon on Thursday of the eighth week of the Trinity Term in the year preceding the final examination. A certificate, signed by the candidate to the effect that each essay is the candidate's own work, and that the candidate has read the History Faculty and English Language and Literature Faculty guidelines on plagiarism, must be presented together with the submission (see the introductory regulations for 'submitted work' for the Honour School of History and English).

(ii) One period of British History not taken in the First Public Examination (as specified in the regulations for History).

(iii) and (iv) Two subjects chosen from subjects 1 to 6 of Course I or Course II of the Honour School of English Language and Literature (as specified in the regulations for the Honour School of English Language and Literature).

(v) and (vi) Two subjects from the Honour School of History, consisting of either (a) Special Subject (which comprises a three hour paper and an extended essay, constituting two papers), or (b) Two of the following:

1. One General History paper from the Honour School of History;
2. One Further Subject from the Honour School of History;
3. One additional British History period not taken in the First Public Examination;
4. One additional subject chosen from papers 1 to 6 of Course I or Course II of the Honour School of English Language and Literature.

See the regulations for History and for English Language and Literature. The individual detailed specifications and prescribed texts for the Further and Special Subjects as specified for the Honour School of History will be given in the Handbook for the Honour School of History. This will be published by the History Board by Monday of Week 1 of the first Michaelmas Full Term of candidates' work for the Honour School.

Depending on the availability of teaching resources, not all Further and Special Subjects will be available to all candidates in every year. Candidates may obtain details of the choice of Further and Special Subjects available for the following year by consulting the supplement to the Handbook for the Honour School of History. This will be issued by the beginning of the fourth week of the first Hilary Full Term of candidates' work for the Honour School and will contain full specifications and prescribed texts for any Further or Special Subjects specified for History introduced for the following year, and any amendments to the specifications and prescribed texts of existing Further and Special Subjects approved by the History Board.

(vii) One compulsory interdisciplinary dissertation, which shall be examined by an extended essay of not more than 10,000 words, including notes and source material but excluding bibliography.

Candidates must submit to the Chair of Examiners for the Joint School of History and English, care of the History Faculty Office, not later than 5p.m. on Friday of the sixth week of the Michaelmas Term preceding the examination, a title and abstract of not more than 200 words detailing the proposed dissertation topic.

The candidate must deliver two typed copies of the dissertation by hand to the Chair of Examiners for the Joint School of History and English, at the Examination Schools, High Street, by noon on Thursday of the eighth week of the Hilary Term preceding the examination. A certificate, signed by the candidate to the effect that each essay is the candidate's own work, and that the candidate has read the History Faculty and English Language and Literature Faculty guidelines on plagiarism, must be presented together with the submission (see the introductory regulations for 'submitted work' for the Honour School of History and English).

SPECIAL REGULATIONS FOR THE HONOUR SCHOOL OF HISTORY AND MODERN LANGUAGES

A

1. The subjects of the examination in the Honour School of History and Modern Languages shall be (*a*) History, and (*b*) those modern European languages and literatures studied in the Honour School of Modern Languages.

2. All candidates must offer both (*a*) and one of the languages in (*b*) with its literature.

3. No candidate shall be admitted to examination in the School unless he or she has either passed or been exempted from the First Public Examination.

4. The examination shall always include a period of General History selected by the candidate from periods to be named from time to time in the Regulations of the Honour School.

5. The examiners shall indicate in the lists issued by them the language offered by each candidate obtaining Honours or satisfying the examiners under the appropriate regulation.

6. The examiners in the Honour School shall be under the joint supervision of the Boards of the Faculties of History and Modern Languages, which shall appoint a standing joint committee to make proposals for regulations concerning the examination. Such proposals shall be submitted to the boards of the two faculties which shall make regulations concerning the examination and which, in case of difference of opinion, shall hold a joint meeting at which the matter in dispute shall be resolved by the vote of the majority.

7. (i) The examiners in the Honour School shall be such of the Public Examiners in the Honour Schools of History and Modern Languages as shall be required.

    (ii) It shall be the duty of the Chair of Examiners in the Honour Schools of History and Modern Languages to consult together and designate such examiners as shall be required for the Honour School, whereupon the number of examiners shall be deemed to be complete.

B

Candidates will be examined in accordance with the examination regulations set out below.

They will also be required to spend, after their matriculation, a year of residence in an appropriate country or countries, and to provide on their entry form for the examination a certificate that they have done this, signed by the Head or by a tutor of their society. Candidates wishing to be dispensed from the requirement to undertake a year of residence abroad must apply in writing to the Chair of the Medieval and Modern Languages Board, 41 Wellington Square, Oxford, OX1 2JF, stating their reasons for requesting dispensation and enclosing a letter of support from their society.

Candidates will be expected to carry out during this year abroad such work as their society may require. It is strongly recommended that candidates should apply through the Central Bureau for Educational Visits and Exchanges for an Assistantship, where these are available, and should accept one if offered. Candidates who are not able to obtain an Assistantship should during their year abroad follow a course or courses in an institution or institutions approved by their society, or should spend their time in such other circumstances as are acceptable to their society. Candidates will agree with their College Tutor in advance of their year abroad an independent course of study to be followed during that period.

Save in a Special Subject, each candidate shall offer in his or her language and literature papers one language and literature only.

Oral Examination: as specified for the Honour School of Modern Languages. Candidates are advised, where possible, to ensure that their choice of options provides some chronological overlap between their history and literature papers.

In addition to the compulsory papers listed below, candidates who so desire may offer an optional additional thesis in accordance with Regulation VII. *An Optional Additional Thesis* of the Honour School of History *q.v.,* modified as follows:

(*a*) the subject shall, to the satisfaction of the examiners, fall within the scope of the Honour School of History and Modern Languages; or

(*b*) the prizes listed in that regulation with the addition of the Sir John Rhys Prize;

(*c*) theses must be submitted to the Chair of the Examiners, Honour School of History and Modern Languages, Examination Schools, High Street, Oxford.

(*d*) Cl.10 For 10. The Final Honour School Examiners will arrive at a formal degree result [...] all papers awarded a mark below 50 will be included.' read 'The Final Honour School Examiners will arrive at a formal degree result for candidates who submit an Optional Additional Thesis by taking the marks awarded for the 2 language papers and the oral examination, together with the highest seven marks out of the eight content papers submitted, except that the Optional Additional Thesis may not substitute for a mark lower than 50. Thus, the papers to be included are determined by the following procedures:

(i) In the event that the Optional Additional Thesis is awarded a mark below 50, it will be disregarded and the formal degree result will be determined solely by the marks awarded for the compulsory papers.

(ii) In the event that the Optional Additional Thesis is awarded a mark of 50 or above, the content paper awarded the lowest mark of 50 or above (which may be the Optional Additional Thesis) will be disregarded. All other content papers awarded a mark of 50 or above, and all content papers awarded a mark below 50, together with the marks awarded for the 2 language papers and the oral examination, will be included.

Every candidate shall offer:

1. One period of General History as specified for the Honour School of History (except for candidates offering Celtic, who shall offer one period of The History of the British Isles as specified for the Honour School of History).

2. A bridge essay of 7,500 words on an interdisciplinary topic, designed to draw together interests and develop skills from both sides of the course. The limit of 7,500 words includes footnotes, but excludes bibliography, and, in cases for which specific permission has been obtained from the convenor of the joint school, appendices. Candidates must follow the guidelines on word count, presentation and referencing as outlined in the course handbook.

The candidate will submit a title and short statement of up to fifty words on the manner in which he/she proposes to treat the topic, together with a note from his/her tutor approving the topic, addressed to the convener of the Joint School of History and Modern Languages, c/o the History Faculty, no later than Monday of sixth week of Trinity Term of his/her second year. Titles will be approved by the convener and one other member of the Standing Committee of the Joint School of History and Modern Languages. Notification of whether or not approval is forthcoming will be given by eighth week of Trinity Term.

Changes to the title must be submitted to the convener of the joint school at the latest by the Friday of second week of the Michaelmas Term of the candidate's final year. Notification of whether or not approval is forthcoming will be given no later than fourth week of the Michaelmas Term of the candidate's final year. Bridge essays on approved titles should be submitted to the Chair of the Examiners for the Joint School of History and Modern Languages at the Examination Schools, High Street, Oxford, by noon on the Friday of noughth week in the Hilary Term preceding the examination. Every candidate shall present a certificate, signed by him or herself and by his or her College History Tutor, in a separate envelope bearing the candidate's examination number. The certificate should declare (using a specified form available from the History Faculty Office and Faculty website) that (*a*) the bridge essay is the candidate's own work, (*b*) that it does not exceed 7,500 words in length (including footnotes but not including bibliography and translations from quotations), (*c*) that no more than the specified maximum amount of advice and assistance (no more than three hours of preparatory or advisory meetings) from college or external advisers has been received. In the rare cases when a candidate is dispensed from the requirement to spend a year abroad after their second year, that candidate shall not be required to submit their Bridge Essay until noon on Friday of eighth week of the Hilary Term preceding the examination. Any changes in title for such candidates should be submitted to the convenor of the joint school by the second week of Hilary Term of the final year. Notification of whether approval is forthcoming will be given no later than fourth week of Hilary Term of the final year.

A first draft of the bridge essay may be read and commented on, but not corrected in matters of detail and presentation, by the bridge essay adviser.

3. Honour School of Modern Languages, Paper I.

4. Honour School of Modern Languages, Papers IIA and IIB.

5. Honour School of Modern Languages, *one* paper chosen from Papers VI, VII, or VIII.

6. Honour School of Modern Languages, *one* paper chosen from Papers IV, V, IX, X, XI, or XII.

7, 8, 9. *Either* (*a*) a Special Subject as specified for the Honour School of History (two papers, paper (*b*) of which shall be by extended essay) and one of the items (*b*), (i), (ii), (iii), or (iv) below.

or (*b*) any three of the following four items:

(i) Any period of The History of the British Isles as specified for the Honour School of History; (except for candidates offering Celtic, who may offer one period of General History as specified for the Honour School of History)

(ii) A Further Subject as specified for the Honour School of History;

(iii) Any one of the Papers IV, V, IX, X, XI, XII not already offered, as specified for the Honour School of Modern Languages;

(iv) An Extended Essay as specified for the Honour School of Modern Languages *or* a thesis based on original research as specified in Regulation VI for the Honour School of History, *except* Cl. 4. of that regulation should read 'beginning of Trinity Full Term of the academic year preceding that in which the candidate spends a year abroad'.

The individual detailed specifications and prescribed texts for the Further and Special Subjects as specified for the Honour School of History will be given in the Handbook for the Honour School of History. This will be published by the History Board by Monday of Week 1 of the first Michaelmas Full Term of candidates' work for the Honour School.

Depending on the availability of teaching resources, not all Further and Special Subjects will be available to all candidates in every year. Candidates may obtain details of the choice of Further and Special Subjects available for the following year by consulting the supplement to the Handbook for the Honour School of History. This will be issued by the beginning of the fourth week of the first Hilary Full Term of candidates' work for the Honour School and will contain full specifications and prescribed texts for any Further or Special Subjects specified for History introduced for the following year, and any amendments to the specifications and prescribed texts of existing Further and Special Subjects approved by the History Board by its first meeting of the preceding Hilary Term.

Mutual exclusions and other restrictions

No candidate may offer a period of British History which he or she has offered as a successful candidate in the First Public Examination.

Candidates may offer both the History Further Subject *Culture and Society in Early Renaissance Italy 1290–1348* and the Modern Languages Early Texts paper in Italian. Where candidates offer both the Further Subject and Early Texts papers, they may not answer on Dante in the Further Subject paper.

Candidates offering a paper from the Honour School of Modern Languages and a paper from the Honour School of History, both of which involve the study of the same author or authors, may not make the same text or texts the principal subject of an answer in both the papers. The same regulation applies to the use of material in the Bridge essay and any other papers.

SPECIAL REGULATIONS FOR THE HONOUR SCHOOL OF HISTORY AND POLITICS

A

1. The examination in the Honour School of History and Politics shall consist of such subjects in History and Politics as the Board of   5
the Faculty of History and the Social Sciences Board shall from time to time in consultation prescribe by regulation.

2. No candidate shall be admitted to examination in this School unless he or she has either passed or been exempted from the First Public Examination.   10

3. The examination in the Honour School shall be under the joint supervision of the Board of the Faculty of History and the Social Sciences Board, which shall appoint a standing joint committee to make proposals for regulations concerning the examination. Such proposals shall be submitted to the boards which shall   15
make regulations concerning the examination and which, in the case of difference of opinion, shall hold a joint meeting at which the matter in dispute shall be resolved by the vote of the majority.

4. The Chairs of Examiners for the Honour School of History and for the Honour School of Philosophy, Politics, and Economics shall   20
consult together and designate such of their number as may be required for the examination for the Honour School of History and Politics, whereupon the number of examiners shall be deemed to be complete.

B

1. Except where indicated a paper cannot be substituted. Candidates shall offer   25
seven papers from the following options, which must include the compulsory substitute thesis based on original research, as specified under Regulation 6 below.

Candidates shall offer either one British History paper and one General History paper as specified under sections 2 and 3, or two British History papers or two General History papers.   30

2. Paper 1. Each candidate may offer one or two papers in a period of the *History of the British Isles*, as specified for the Honour School of History, provided that:

(*a*) one paper may be replaced by a compulsory thesis in History;
(*b*) no candidate may offer a period of British History already offered in the First Public Examination;   35
(*c*) candidates who have not offered a period of British or General History before the nineteenth century in the First Public Examination are required to choose at least one such period in the Honour School of History and Politics. The list of papers satisfying this provision is given in the Handbook for History and Politics;   40

(*d*) candidates who have taken or are taking British History VII (since 1900) cannot also take Politics paper 202 (British Politics and Government since 1900); and candidates taking British History VI (1815–1924) in the Honour School of History and Politics and who are also taking Politics Paper 202 must not substantially duplicate material in the two papers.

3. Paper 2. Each candidate may offer one or two papers in a period of General History, as specified for the Honour School of History, provided that:

(*a*) one paper may be replaced by a compulsory thesis in History;

(*b*) candidates who have not offered a period of British or General History before the nineteenth century in the First Public Examination are required to choose at least one such period in the Honour School of History and Politics. The list of papers satisfying this provision is given in the Handbook for History and Politics;

(*c*) candidates taking Politics Paper 212 (International Relations in the era of the Two World Wars) cannot also take General History XIII (1914–45); candidates taking Politics Paper 213 (International Relations in the era of the Cold War) cannot also take General History XIV (1945–73).

4. Papers 3 and 4. Each candidate shall offer any two of the five "core subjects" in Politics, as specified for the Honour School of Philosophy, Politics and Economics (i.e. 201, 202, 203, 214, and 220). A thesis as specified in Regulation 6 below may not be substituted for a Politics core subject.

5. Papers 5, 6, and 7. Each candidate shall offer one of the following combinations:

(i) one Special Subject in History (examined in two papers) and one of subjects 201–228 in Politics which is not offered under Regulation 4 above;

(ii) one Further Subject in History and two of subjects 201–228 in Politics which are not offered under Regulation 4 above;

(iii) one Further Subject in History, one of subjects 201–228 in Politics which are not offered under Regulation 4 above, and one Special Subject in Politics.

Provided that:

(*a*) one of the optional papers in Politics in any of these combinations may be substituted by a compulsory thesis from the Honour School of Philosophy, Politics, and Economics;

(*b*) Candidates who choose Politics Further Subject 215 (Political Thought: Plato to Rousseau) cannot also take History Further Subjects *Scholasticism and Humanism* and *The Science of Society*. Candidates who choose Politics Further Subject 216 (Political Thought: Bentham to Weber) cannot also take History Further Subject *Political Theory and Social Science*. Candidates who choose the Politics Further Subject 221 (British Society in the Twentieth Century) cannot also take the History Further Subject British Society in the 20th Century.

6. Paper 8. Each candidate must offer a thesis, which must be offered in place of either a period of the *History of the British Isles*, as specified under Regulation 2 above, or a period of *General History*, as specified under Regulation 3 above, or a Politics option in any of the combinations as specified under Regulation 5 above. A thesis offered in place of a Politics optional paper shall be either a substitute thesis or a supervised dissertation submitted in accordance with the regulations prescribed for Politics in the Honour School of Philosophy, Politics, and Economics.

(*a*) A thesis in History submitted in accordance with the Regulation VI, *A thesis based on original research*, for the Final Honour School of History may be offered in place of a paper in the History of the British Isles or General History and the candidate (unless he or she is a Senior Student, as defined by decree of

Council, or has passed the First Public Examination in a course other than History and Politics, History, or any other joint school with History) must also offer a paper satisfying those requirements specified in Regulations 1(c) above which have not been satisfied in the First Public Examination.

(*b*) A thesis or supervised dissertation in Politics submitted in accordance with the regulations prescribed for Politics in the Honour School of Philosophy, Politics, and Economics may be offered in place of any one of subjects 201–228 in Politics (as specified for the Honour School of Philosophy, Politics, and Economics) which is not offered under Regulation 4 above.

7. All candidates must offer a substitute thesis or supervised dissertation, but may not offer more than one substitute thesis or supervised dissertation in place of a paper.

8. In every case where, under the regulations for this honour school, candidates have any choice between one or more papers or subjects, every candidate shall give notice to the Registrar not later than Friday in the fourth week of Michaelmas Full Term preceding the examination of all the papers and subjects being offered.

SPECIAL REGULATIONS FOR THE HONOUR SCHOOL OF HISTORY OF ART

A

1. The examination in the School of History of Art shall be under the supervision of the Board of the Faculty of History.

2. No candidate shall be admitted to the examination in this school unless he or she has passed or been exempted from the First Public Examination.

3. The Board of the Faculty of History shall, by notice from time to time, make regulations respecting the examination.

4. The Board of the Faculty of History may include in the examination, either as necessary or optional, other subjects which they may deem suitable to be studied in connection with History of Art.

B

The History Board shall issue annually the Handbook for the Honour School of History of Art by Monday of first week of the first Michaelmas Full Term of candidates' work for the Honour School.

All candidates are required to offer Subjects I, II, III, IV, V and VI below.

I. *Approaches to the History of Art*

II. *A Further Subject in Art History*
Any one of the Further Subjects listed below, as specified for the Honour School of History:
1. Anglo-Saxon Archaeology of the Early Christian Period
2. The Carolingian Renaissance
3. Northern European Portraiture 1400–1800
4. Culture and Society in Early Renaissance Italy 1290–1348
5. Flanders and Italy in the Quattrocento 1420–1480
6. Court Culture and Art in Early Modern Europe
7. Intellect and Culture in Victorian Britain

III. *Classical, Pre-Modern or Non-Western Art Option*
Any one of the options below:
1. Greek Art and Archaeology c.500–300 BC (as specified for the Honour School of Literae Humaniores, Greek and Roman Archaeology).
2. Art under the Roman Empire AD 14–337 (as specified for the Honour School of Literae Humaniores, Greek and Roman Archaeology).
[From 1 October 2014: 3. Hellenistic Art and Archaeology, 330–30 BC.]
3. [4.] The formation of the Islamic World, AD 550–950 (as specified for the Honour Schools of Archaeology and Anthropology, and of Classical Archaeology and Ancient History).
4. [5.] Byzantine Art: the transition from Antiquity to the Middle Ages, AD 500–1100.
5. [6.] Gothic Art through Medieval Eyes.

6. [7.] Art in China since 1911.

7. [8.] **[Until 1 October 2014:** Material culture studies][**From 1 October 2014:** Understanding Museums and Collections] (as specified for the Honour School of Archaeology and Anthropology), if not taken under IV below.

8. [9.] Egyptian Art and Architecture (as specified for the Honour School of Oriental Studies, Egyptology and Ancient Near Eastern Studies with Archaeology and Anthropology).

IV. *Modern Art Option*

Any one of the options below:

1. Literature and the Visual Arts in France (as specified for the Honour School of Modern Languages, Special Subjects).

2. German Expressionism in literature and the visual arts (as specified for the Honour School of Modern Languages, Special Subjects).

3. European Cinema (as specified for the Honour School of Modern Languages, Special Subjects).

4. Modernism and After: **[Until 1 October 2014:** History of Art option.] **[From 1 October 2014:** (as specified for the Final Examination in Fine Art; paper on the history and theory of visual culture since 1900 (Modernism and After)).]

5. **[Until 1 October 2014:** Material culture studies] **[From 1 October 2014:** Understanding Museums and Collections] (as specified for the Honour School of Archaeology and Anthropology), if not taken under III above.

6. The Experience of Modernity: Visual Culture, 1880–1925

7. Art in China since 1911, if not taken under III above.

In the case of Modern Art options 1-3 above, the relevant regulation for the Honour School of Modern Languages, XII Special Subjects, Section B, is modified (modification in italics) for History of Art students to read: An essay or portfolio of essays (the number of essays to be shown in parentheses) aggregating to about 6,000 words and not exceeding 8,000 words, to be submitted by hand to the Examination Schools, High Street, Oxford by noon on the Friday of ninth week of the Hilary Term in *the year prior to examination (i.e. the student's second year of study)*, together with a statement certifying that the essay(s) are the candidate's own work and that they have not already been submitted, either wholly or substantially, for a degree in this university or elsewhere.

[From 1 October 2014: In the case of Modern Art option 4, History of Art students are assessed based on an examination taken in Week 9 of the Michaelmas Term of their final year.]

V. *Special Subject in Art History*, consisting of

(*a*) a paper including compulsory passages and/or images for comment; (*b*) an extended essay.

Any one of the Special Subjects listed below, as specified for the Honour School of History:

1. Royal Art and Architecture in Norman Sicily, 1130–1194.

2. Painting and Culture in Ming China.

3. Politics, Art and Culture in the Italian Renaissance: Venice and Florence, *c*.1475–1525.

4. The Dutch Golden Age: 1618–1672.

5. English Architecture 1660–1720.

6. Art and its Public in France 1815–67.

Depending on the availability of teaching resources in the different Faculties, not all of the options listed under II, III, IV and V will be available to all candidates in every year. Candidates should refer to the course handbook for details about availability and registration for individual options.

VI. *A thesis from original research*

1. Candidates must submit a thesis as part of the fulfilment of their Final Examination.

2. Theses shall normally be written during the Hilary Term of the final year. All theses must be submitted not later than noon on Friday of eighth week of the Hilary Term of the academic year in which the candidate is presenting himself or herself for examination.

3. A candidate may submit:

(*a*) any essay or part of any essay which he or she has submitted or intends to submit for any university essay prize; or

(*b*) any other work provided in either case that (i) no thesis will be accepted if it has already been submitted, wholly or substantially, for a final honour school other than one involving Modern History or History of Art, or another degree of this University, or a degree of any other university, and (ii) the candidate submits a statement to that effect, and (iii) the subject is approved by the Chair of the Examiners for the Honour School of History of Art.

4. The provisos in cl. 3 above shall not debar any candidate from submitting work based on a previous submission towards the requirements for a degree of any other university provided that

(i) the work is substantially new;

(ii) the candidate also submits both the original work itself and a statement specifying the extent of what is new. The examiners shall have sole authority to decide in every case whether proviso (i) has been met.

5. Every candidate except when offering a thesis as defined in cl. 3 (*a*) must submit a proposed preliminary title to the Department of History of Art, St Ebbes, Oxford together with a typed synopsis of the thesis topic and proposed method of investigation (no more than 250 words) and the written approval of their College History of Art Co-ordinator, not later than Friday of eighth week of Michaelmas Term in the year of the examination. The Chair of Examiners shall give notification whether or not the title is approved by the first Monday of Hilary Full Term of the same year. Any subsequent changes to title require formal application to the Chair of Examiners by the Friday of Week 4 of the Hilary Term of the final year and subsequent approval.

6. Theses should normally include an investigation of visual and material culture (broadly defined), with references made to relevant images and printed and/or unprinted primary written sources, and must include proper footnotes and a bibliography. They must be the work of the author alone. In all cases, the candidate's Undergraduate Thesis Adviser shall discuss with the candidate the field of study, the sources available, and the methods of presentation. Candidates shall be expected to have attended a class on choosing a thesis topic, led by the Undergraduate Thesis Co-ordinator, and to have discussed their choice of topic with their College History of Art Co-ordinator during the Trinity Term of the year prior to examination and Michaelmas Term of the year of examination. Details of arrangements are given in the course handbook. The Undergraduate Thesis Co-ordinator will appoint an appropriate expert thesis adviser for each candidate. Candidates shall have meetings with their Undergraduate Thesis Adviser lasting no more than five hours in total. These hours of meetings shall be normally distributed as follows: one hour in total in Trinity Term of the year prior to the examination; one hour in total in the Michaelmas Term of the year of examination; three hours in total in Hilary Term of the year of examination. A first draft of the thesis may be commented on, but not corrected in matters of detail and presentation, by the Undergraduate Thesis Adviser.

7. No thesis shall exceed 12,000 words in length (including footnotes, but excluding bibliography, and, in cases for which specific permission has been obtained from

the Chair of Examiners, appendices). All theses must be typed or word-processed in double spacing on one side of A4 paper with the notes and references at the foot of each page, with a left-hand margin of one-and-a-half inches and all other margins of at least one inch. The thesis should conform to the standards of academic presentation prescribed in the course handbook. Failure to conform to such standards may incur penalties as outlined in the course handbook.

8. All candidates must submit two copies of their thesis, addressed to the Chair of Examiners, Honour School of History of Art, Examination Schools, High Street, Oxford, not later than noon on Friday of eighth week of the Hilary Term of the year in which they are presenting themselves for examination. The University's regulations on late submission of work will apply. Every candidate shall present a certificate, signed by him or herself and by his or her College History of Art Co-ordinator in a separate envelope bearing the candidate's examination number, addressed to the Chair of Examiners. The certificate (forms are available from the History of Art Department) should declare that (*a*) the thesis is the candidate's own work, (*b*) that no substantial portion of it has been presented for any other degree course or examination, (*c*) that it does not exceed 12,000 words in length, (*d*) that no more than five hours have been spent in preparatory or advisory meetings between the candidate and his or her Undergraduate Thesis Adviser, and (*e*) that only the first draft of the thesis has been seen by the Undergraduate Thesis Adviser. Candidates delivering theses will be required to complete a receipt form, which will only be accepted as proof of receipt if it is countersigned by a member of the Examination Schools staff.

9. Candidates shall not answer in any other paper questions which fall very largely within the scope of their thesis nor choose a Special Subject extended essay topic related to their thesis. Candidates should not choose a thesis that only substantially reworks material studied in the Further Subject in Art History, in the Classical, Pre-Modern or non-Western art option, in the Modern art option, or in the Special Subject, and should demonstrate familiarity with and use of substantially different and additional primary sources and visual material.

SPECIAL REGULATIONS FOR THE HONOUR SCHOOL OF HUMAN SCIENCES

A

1. The subject of the Honour School of Human Sciences shall be the biological and social aspects of the study of human beings.

2. No candidate shall be admitted for examination in this school unless he or she has either passed or been exempted from the First Public Examination.

3. The examination shall be under the supervision of the Social Sciences Board, which shall appoint a Teaching Committee for Human Sciences to supervise the arrangements for this examination and the Preliminary Examination in Human Sciences, to consult as necessary with contributing teachers and others; and to carry out such other functions as may be laid down by the Divisional Board by standing order. The committee shall be recognised as having an interest in appointments specifically concerned with the Honour School, and the bodies responsible for such appointments shall ensure that the selection committees for such posts include at least one member appointed in consultation with the committee. It shall be responsible for such funds as the Divisional Board may place at its disposal for general purposes connected with Human Sciences.

B

The Honour School is divided into two sections. All candidates will be required to offer papers: 1, 2, 3, 4, 5(*a*) or 5(*b*), and a dissertation (paper 6):

1. Behaviour and its Evolution: Animal and Human
2. Human Genetics and Evolution
3. Human Ecology
4. Demography and Population

The examiners will permit the use of any hand-held pocket calculator subject to the conditions set out under the heading 'Use of calculators in examinations' in the Special Regulations concerning Examinations.

5(*a*). Anthropological analysis and Interpretation *or* 5(*b*). Sociological Theory

The date by which students must make their choice will be stated in the course handbook.

6. Dissertation

Candidates will also be required to offer any two optional subjects from a list posted in the Human Sciences Centre at the beginning of the first week of Hilary Full Term in the year preceding the final examination. These lists will also be circulated to College Tutors. The date by which students must make their choice will be stated in the course handbook.

Schedule of Subjects

1. *Behaviour and its Evolution: Animal and Human*

Introduction to the study of behaviour including the evolution of behavioural interactions within groups. Behavioural strategies that have evolved in humans and other animals. The use of models to understand complex behaviour. Advanced ethology and cognition, including learning. Perception and decision-making. Primate behaviour and evolutionary ecology, including the development of primate social systems and the evolution of cognition.

2. *Human Genetics and Evolution*

The nature and structure of the human genome, including single gene traits, gene function, and assessment of social implications. Population genetics of humans and primates. Quantitative genetics and complex trait analysis in humans. Genomic complexity as illustrated by the genetic basis for immune response. Molecular evolution, human genetic diversity and the genetic basis of human evolution. Genetic basis of common complex diseases. Human behaviour, cognition and cultural transmission in the context of six million years of physiological evolution and ecological change.

3. *Human Ecology*

Human ecology of disease, emphasising diseases that significantly contribute to the global burden of mortality and cultural change. Diet and nutrition anthropology of human societies. Socio-cultural systems in their environmental context, including philosophical and religious values, differences in ecological perception, and the development of viable conservation strategies, including the impact of humans on other species, the biosphere and climate. Ecology of human reproduction, including cultural differences in reproductive strategies.

4. *Demography and Population*

Candidates will be expected to show knowledge of the major features of past and present population trends, the socio-economic, environmental and biomedical factors affecting fertility, mortality and migration; the social, economic and political consequences of population growth, decline and ageing; and major controversies in demographic theory.

Specific topics will include traditional and transitional population systems in historical and contemporary societies; demographic transitions and their interpretation; demographic processes in post-transitional societies (modern Europe and other industrial areas) including very low fertility, longer life, international migration and new patterns of marriage and family; the changing position of women in the workforce; ethnic dimensions of demographic change; and policy interventions.

The paper will also test knowledge of demographic analysis and techniques including data sources, the quantitative analysis of fertility and mortality, the life table, the stable population and other population models, population dynamics and projections, and limits to fertility and the lifespan. The paper will contain essay questions and questions involving computation. Candidates will be required to answer three questions, two of the former and one of the latter.

5(*a*). *Anthropological analysis and interpretation*

The comparative study of social and cultural forms in the global context: to include economics and exchange, domestic structures and their reproduction, personal and collective identity, language and religion, states and conflict, understanding of biology and environment, historical perspectives on the social world and upon practice in anthropology.

5(*b*). *Sociological Theory*

Theoretical perspectives including rational choice; evolutionary psychology; interpersonal interaction; social integration and networks; functionalism. Substantive problems including stratification; gender; race and ethnicity; collective action; norms; ideology. Candidates will be expected to use theories to explain substantive problems.

6. *Dissertation*

(*a*) *Subject*

In the dissertation the candidate will be required to focus on material from within   5
the Honour School, and must show knowledge of more than one of the basic approaches to the study of Human Sciences. The subject may, but need not, overlap any subject on which the candidate offers papers. Candidates are warned that they should avoid repetition in papers of material used in their dissertation and that substantial repetition may be penalised.   10

Every candidate shall deliver for approval to the Chair of the Human Sciences Teaching Committee c/o the Academic Administrator, Institute of Human Sciences, The Pauling Centre, 58a Banbury Road, the title he or she proposes together with:

  (i) an explanation of the subject in about 100 words explicitly mentioning the two or more basic approaches to the study of Human Sciences that will be   15 incorporated in the dissertation.

  (ii) a letter of approval from his or her tutor **and** the name(s) of the advisor(s) who will supervise the dissertation.

This should not be earlier than the first day of Trinity Full Term of the year before that in which the candidate is to be examined and not later than 12 midday on Friday   20 of the fifth week of the same term.

The Chair of the Teaching Committee, in consultation with the Chair of Examiners and other Senior Members if necessary, shall as soon as possible decide whether or not to approve the title and shall advise the candidate through his or her college. No decision shall normally be deferred beyond the end of the eighth week of the relevant Trinity Term.   25

Proposals to change the title of the dissertation may be made in exceptional circumstances and will be considered by the Chair of the Teaching Committee until the first day of Hilary Full Term of the year in which the student is to be examined, or only by the Chair of Examiners thereafter, but not later than the last day of the same term. Proposals to change the title of the dissertation should be made through the   30 candidate's college via the Academic Administrator, Institute of Human Sciences, The Pauling Centre, 58a Banbury Road.

(*b*) *Authorship and origin*

The dissertation must be the candidates' own work. Tutors may, however, discuss with candidates the proposed field of study, the sources available and the method of   35 presentation. They may also read and comment on a first draft. Every candidate shall sign a certificate to the effect that the thesis is his or her own work and that it has not already been submitted, wholly or substantially, for another Honour School or degree of this University, or for a degree of any other institution. This certificate shall be submitted separately in a sealed envelope addressed to the chair of examiners.   40 No dissertation shall, however, be ineligible because it has been or is being submitted for any prize of this University.

(*c*) *Length and format*

No dissertation shall be less than 5,000 words nor exceed 10,000 words; no person or body shall have authority to permit any excess. Candidates may include appen-   45 dices which will not count towards the word limit. However the examiners are not bound to read the appendices and they shall not be taken into consideration when marking the dissertation. There shall be a select bibliography or a list of sources; this shall not be included in the word count*. All dissertations must be typed on A4 paper

---

* Each dissertation shall be prefaced by an abstract of not more than 350 words which shall not be included in the overall word count.

and be held firmly in a cover. Two copies of the dissertation shall be submitted to the examiners.

(*d*) *Submissions of dissertation*

Every candidate shall deliver two copies of the dissertation to the Chair of Examiners, Honour School of Human Sciences, Examination Schools, High Street, Oxford, not later than noon on Friday of the week preceding Trinity Full Term in the year of the examination.

(*e*) *Resubmission of dissertation*

Dissertations previously submitted for the Honour School of Human Sciences may be resubmitted. No dissertation will be accepted if it has already been submitted, wholly or substantially, for another Honour School or degree of this University, or for a degree of any other institution.

SPECIAL REGULATIONS FOR THE HONOUR SCHOOL OF JURISPRUDENCE

A

1. Candidates in the School of Jurisprudence shall be examined in subjects from such branches of the law and of philosophy as may be prescribed by regulation.

2. No candidate shall be admitted to examination in this school unless he has either passed or been exempted from the First Public Examination.

3. The examination in this school shall be under the supervision of the Board of the Faculty of Law, which shall make regulations concerning it, subject always to the preceding clauses of this sub-section and to the concurrence of the Divisional Board of Humanities in respect of regulations concerning philosophy.

Candidates shall take one of the following courses.

Course 1. Candidates shall be examined in nine standard subjects. Candidates will be examined in accordance with the Examination Regulations set out below.

Course 2. Candidates shall be examined in nine standard subjects. Candidates will be examined in accordance with the Examination Regulations set out below. They will also be required to spend, after their matriculation, an academic year of residence in a European university approved in accordance with these regulations, and to have attended such courses at the approved university as are approved in accordance with these regulations, and to have completed such examinations at the approved university as the faculty board may specify.

B

Regulations applying to Course 2

1. The Law Board will approve courses at certain European universities. The list of approved courses will be available at the Institute of European and Comparative Law, St Cross Building, Manor Road.

2. Candidates may proceed to an academic year of residence at an approved university only if so permitted by the Board of the Faculty of Law. The board shall not give such permission unless the candidate presents (*a*) a certificate of linguistic competence relevant to the proposed year of residence and (*b*) a certificate from his or her society stating that he or she will have resided in Oxford for six terms (or three terms in the case of an applicant with senior status) since matriculation before proceeding to such residence, and (*c*) a statement in support from the head or a tutor of the candidate's society.

3. The certificate of linguistic competence may be provided only by a member of the University approved by the board.

4. Candidates will be required to take certain examinations at the approved universities. Details will be available from the Institute of European and Comparative Law.

5. The Institute of European and Comparative Law will certify to the chair of the examiners for the Honour School of Jurisprudence the names of candidates who have satisfied the requirements for the year abroad.

6. The board may amend or add to any provision in Regulations 1, 4, and 5 by regulation published in the *Gazette* at any time before the commencement of the academic year to which such addition or amendment applies.

Regulations applying to both Course 1 and Course 2:
Candidates shall be examined in the following seven standard subjects
1. Jurisprudence
2. Contract
3. Tort
4. Land Law
5. European Union Law
6. Trusts
7. Administrative Law

and in two further standard optional subjects, and must have satisfactorily completed the Legal Research and Mooting Skills Programme. A list of standard optional subjects approved by the Board of the Faculty of Law for the following academic year shall be posted in the Law Faculty Office and sent to college tutors, together with individual specifications and examination methods, not later than the beginning of the fifth week of the Hilary Term in the year before the Honour School examination will be held. Depending on the availability of teaching resources, not all standard optional subjects will be available to all candidates in every given year. If any such subject has to be withdrawn after it has appeared on the lists approved by the Board of the Faculty of Law, notice will be given in the Law Faculty Handbook for Undergraduate Students for the relevant year, which will be published and made available on the Faculty website by Monday of noughth week of Michaelmas Term that year.

Candidates who have been awarded the Diploma in Legal Studies shall be examined in the same number of subjects as other candidates but shall not be required to repeat in the Final Honour School papers taken for the Diploma which would otherwise be compulsory.

The following further regulations shall apply to the undermentioned Standard Subjects:

1. JURISPRUDENCE
Candidates offering Jurisprudence will be examined in that subject by:
(a) a two hour closed book examination at the end of a student's final year of the Final Honours School, in which students answer two questions from a selection of ten, and
(b) a single essay of 3,000–4,000 words to be written during the summer vacation between the end of Year 2 and commencement of Year 3 of the Final Honour School. Essay questions will be published by the Board of Examiners at noon on the Friday of the seventh week of the Trinity Term preceding the examination. Candidates will be contacted with details of how to collect or access the questions. Two copies of each essay submitted must be delivered to the Chair of the BA Jurisprudence Final Honours School Examiners, Examination Schools, High Street, Oxford OX1 4BG, by noon on the Friday of noughth week preceding the beginning of the Michaelmas Full Term immediately

following. The essays must bear the candidate's examination number, but not his or her name or the name of his or her college. Every candidate shall sign a Declaration of Authorship to the effect that the essay is his or her own work. Candidates shall further state the total number of words used in their essays. This certificate shall be presented together with the essays. To ensure anonymity the certificate must be placed in a sealed envelope. The change to the method of examination by long essay under (b) will apply in the following manner:

(i) All Year 2 students in 2012–13 will undertake the long essay in the summer of 2013;

(ii) Year 3 students. Course 1 in 2012–13 will have been taught the traditional Jurisprudence course in 2011–12 (Year 2), and will sit an unseen written examination in 2012–13;

(iii) Year 3 students, Course 2 in 2012–13 will also have been taught the traditional Jurisprudence course in 2011–12 (Year 2), and will spend the academic year abroad in 2012–13. These students will sit an unseen written examination in 2013–14.

2. CONTRACT

Candidates will be required to show a knowledge of such parts of the law of restitution as are directly relevant to the law of contract. Questions may be set in this paper requiring knowledge of the law of tort.

3. TORT

Questions may be set in this paper requiring knowledge of the law of contract.

4. LAND LAW

5. EUROPEAN UNION LAW

Comprises:

A. The basic structure and functions of the institutions; the aims of the EU; law-making; the composition and jurisdiction of the Court of Justice; the penetration of EU law into national legal orders.

B. Free movement of persons and services.

C. Free movement of goods.

6. TRUSTS

7. ADMINISTRATIVE LAW

Questions will not be set on the law of local government or of public corporations except as illustrating general principles of administrative law.

Candidates will be required to show a sufficient knowledge of such parts of the general law of the constitution as are necessary for a proper understanding of this subject.

Statutes and other source material

Details of the statutes and other sources of material which will be available to candidates in the examination room for certain papers will be given in the teaching conventions and in examiners' edicts circulated to candidates.

Legal Research and Mooting Skills Programme

The Law Board offers a Legal Research and Mooting Skills Programme, which provides training in the use of legal information resources (both paper and electronic), legal research, and team-working. The programme will also check students' competence in the use of Information Technology. Students are required to undertake this programme and to complete the assessments which form part of it, to the satisfaction of the Programme Co-ordinator appointed by the Law Board. The Programme Co-ordinator will certify to the Chair of Examiners for the Honour School of Jurisprudence the names of those students who have done so.

[FROM 1 OCTOBER 2014: SPECIAL REGULATIONS FOR LINGUISTICS IN ALL HONOUR SCHOOLS INCLUDING LINGUISTICS

Candidates offering Linguistics papers in any Honour School must conform to the General Regulations below, and to those for their particular school, as specified elsewhere.

Subjects in Linguistics

The subjects in Linguistics are specified below. Paper A will be examined by three-hour examination. The mode of assessment for B1–6 and F will be specified in the Faculty Handbook.

A General Linguistics

B1 Phonetics and Phonology
B2 Syntax
B3 Semantics
B4 Psycholinguistics
B5 Sociolinguistics
B6 Historical Linguistics

C Linguistic Project

D Thesis

E1 Linguistic Studies I (=Paper IV of the Honour School of Modern Languages)
E2 Linguistic Studies II (=Paper V of the Honour School of Modern Languages)

F A Special Subject in Linguistics

Linguistic Project

The Linguistic Project will consist of a project report of between 8,000 and 10,000 words. Projects should be submitted by hand to the Examination Schools and addressed to the Chair of Examiners in the candidate's Honour School, by noon on the Friday of the ninth week of Hilary Term in the year of the examination, together with a statement, sent under separate cover, certifying that the project is the candidate's own work and has not already been submitted, either wholly or substantially, for a degree in this university or elsewhere.

Candidates proposing to offer a Linguistic Project must submit, through their college, to the Director of Undergraduate Studies of the Faculty of Linguistics, Philology and Phonetics (on a form obtainable from the Linguistics Faculty Office) a statement of their name, college, the Honour School they intend to offer, the academic year in which they intend to take the examination, and the title of the proposed project together with:

    (*a*) a statement of approximately fifty words of how the subject is to be treated,

    (*b*) a statement signed by a supervisor or tutor that he or she considers the subject suitable, and suggesting a person or persons who might be invited to be an examiner or an assessor (the Board will not approve a title unless it is satisfied that a suitably qualified examiner or assessor based in Oxford will be available), (*c*) a statement by a college tutor that he or she approves the candidate's application, and

    (*d*) confirmation that relevant CUREC approval has been obtained no later than the Wednesday of the second week of the Michaelmas Full Term preceding the examination. 5

Thesis

  1. Candidates may offer a Thesis, subject to the following provisions:

    (i) The subject of every thesis shall, to the satisfaction of the Board of the Faculty, fall within the scope of Linguistics.

    (ii) The subject of a thesis may, but need not, overlap any subject on which the 10 candidate offers a paper, but candidates should avoid repetition of material presented in the extended essay in other parts of the examination.

    (iii) Candidates proposing to offer a thesis must submit, through their college, to the Director of Undergraduate Studies of the Faculty of Linguistics, Philology and Phonetics (on a form obtainable from the Linguistics Faculty Office) a 15 statement of their name, college, the Honour School they intend to offer, the academic year in which they intend to take the examination, and the title of the proposed thesis together with (*a*) a statement of approximately fifty words of how the subject is to be treated, (*b*) a statement signed by a supervisor or tutor, preferably in the language or in one of the languages or in the field of 20 study with which the thesis is concerned, that he or she considers the subject suitable, and suggesting a person or persons who might be invited to be an examiner or an assessor (the Board will not approve a title unless it is satisfied that a suitably qualified examiner or assessor based in Oxford will be available), and (*c*) a statement by a college tutor that he or she approves the 25 candidate's application, not later than the Wednesday of the second week of the Michaelmas Full Term preceding the examination.

    (iv) The Board of the Faculty will decide by the end of the third week of the Michaelmas Full Term preceding the examination whether the candidate has permission to offer a thesis. Permission may be granted on the condition that 30 the candidate agrees to amend details of the title to the satisfaction of the Board, and submits the required amendments to the Faculty Office for the Board's approval by Friday of the sixth week of the Michaelmas Full Term preceding the examination. If the proposed title is approved, this will be notified by the Administration and Faculty Office, together with any condi- 35 tions attached to the approval, to the candidate and to the Chair of the Examiners for the candidate's Honour School.

    (v) A candidate may seek approval after Friday of the sixth week of the Michaelmas Full Term preceding the examination for an amendment of detail in an approved title, by application to the Faculty Office. The Chair of the 40 Examiners and the Chair of the Board, acting together, will decide whether or not a proposed amendment shall be approved.

  2. Every thesis must be the candidate's own work. Tutors may, however, discuss with candidates the proposed field of study, the sources available, and the method of presentation. Tutors may also read and comment on a first draft. All quotations, 45 whether direct or indirect, from primary or secondary sources must be explicitly acknowledged. The use of unacknowledged quotations will be penalized. Candidates must sign a certificate stating that the thesis is their own work and this certificate must be sent at the same time as the thesis, but under separate cover, to the Examination Schools, Oxford, addressed to the Chair of the Examiners in the 50 candidate's Honour School.

3. No thesis shall be ineligible because it has been submitted, in whole or in part, for any scholarship or prize in this university.

4. Candidates shall present a one-page summary of the arguments at the beginning of their thesis. Theses shall be in the range 10,000–12,000 words (exclusive of the footnotes, the bibliography, any appendices, and summary (where this applies)). No person or body shall have authority to permit the limit of 12,000 words to be exceeded, except that, in the case of a commentary on a text, and at the discretion of the Chair of the Examiners, any substantial quoting of that text need not be included in the word limit. The examiners will not take account of such parts of an essay as are beyond these limits. There must be a select bibliography, listing all primary and secondary sources cited in the thesis, and full details must be given of all citations at the end of the thesis. All theses must be typed in double-spacing on A4 paper, and must be bound or held firmly in a stiff cover. Two copies must be submitted to the Chair of the Examiners, and a third copy must be retained by the candidate.

5. The candidate shall submit two copies of the thesis, identified by the candidate's examination number only, not later than noon on Friday of the week before the Trinity Full Term of the examination, to the Examination Schools, Oxford, addressed to the Chair of the Examiners in the candidate's Honour School.

Special Subjects

Special Subjects available in Linguistics will be published in the *Gazette* and on-line by the beginning of the fifth week of the Trinity Term preceding the year of examination. Candidates in the Joint Schools involving Linguistics may offer any of the special subjects for paper XII in the Honour School of Modern Languages, provided they are marked with the Linguistics identifier L.

The method of assessment for each subject will be published in the *Gazette* and on-line by the beginning of the fifth week of the Trinity Term preceding the year of examination, according to the following key:

A: Three-hour unseen written paper. N.B. For the option paper in Phonetics and Phonology, candidates must also offer either a 30 minute Phonetics Transcription aural test or a Laboratory Report of a Phonetics experiment.

B: An essay or portfolio of essays (the number of essays required to be shown in parentheses) aggregating to approximately 6,000 words and not exceeding 8,000 words, to be submitted by hand to the Examinations Schools, High Street, Oxford by noon on the Friday of the ninth week of Hilary Term in the year of the examination, together with a statement certifying that the essay(s) are the candidate's own work and that they have not already been submitted, either wholly or substantially, for a degree in this university or elsewhere.

C: An essay or portfolio of essays (the number of essays required to be shown in parentheses) aggregating to approximately 6,000 words and not exceeding 8,000 words written as answers to an examination paper to be collected from the Examination Schools, and signed for by candidates, on the Friday of the fifth week of the Hilary Term next before the examination. Completed essay(s) should be submitted by hand to the Examination Schools by noon on the Friday of the ninth week of Hilary Term in the year of the examination, together with a statement certifying that the essay(s) are the candidate's own work and that they have not already been submitted, either wholly or substantially, for a degree in this university or elsewhere.

General Regulations

Candidates in the Honour School of Psychology, Philosophy, and Linguistics may offer paper E1 or E2 only with the agreement of the Board of the Faculty of Linguistics, Philology and Phonetics.

No candidate may offer more than one special subject F. Candidates may not be permitted to offer certain special subjects in combination with certain other subjects, or may be permitted to do so only on condition that in the papers on the other subjects they will not be permitted to answer certain questions.

Regulations for Particular Honour Schools

Psychology, Philosophy, and Linguistics

Candidates may take at most five subjects in Linguistics. All candidates must take eight subjects in total. Candidates may only take subjects in Psychology if they offer Psychology Parts I and II.

Candidates may take no more than one paper from group F.

All candidates in Linguistics must take paper A.

Candidates who take **two** subjects in Linguistics must take paper A and one of papers B1-B6.

Candidates who take **three** subjects in Linguistics must take (1) paper A, (2) one of papers B1, B2, B3, and (3) one of papers B1–6, C, D, F.

Candidates who take **four** subjects in Linguistics must take (1) paper A, (2) one of papers B1, B2, B3, and (3) two of papers B1–6, C *or* D, E1 *or* E2, F.

Candidates who take **five** subjects in Linguistics must take (1) paper A, (2) one of papers B1, B2, B3, and (3) three of papers B1–6, C, D, E1 *or* E2, F.]

SPECIAL REGULATIONS FOR THE HONOUR
SCHOOL OF LITERAE HUMANIORES

A

1. The Branches of the Honour School of Literae Humaniores shall be (I) Greek and Roman History, (II) Philosophy, (III) Greek and Latin Literature, (IV) Greek and Roman Archaeology, (V) Philology and Linguistics, (VI) Second Classical Language.

2. Each candidate must offer at least two of Branches (I)–(V).

3. No candidate shall be admitted to the examination in this school unless he or she has either passed or been exempted from the First Public Examination.

4. The examination in this school shall be under the joint supervision of the Boards of the Faculties of Classics and Philosophy, which shall appoint a joint standing committee to make regulations concerning it and review its operation, subject always to the preceding clauses of this subsection.

B

1. Candidates shall take either Course I or Course II. Persons who have satisfied the Moderators in Course IA, IB, or IC of Honour Moderations in Classics or of the Preliminary Examination in Classics may not enter for the Honour School of Literae Humaniores Course II without permission from the Board of the Faculty of Classics after consultation where appropriate with the Board of the Faculty of Philosophy. Such permission, which will be given only for special reasons, must be sought as early as possible, and in no case later than noon on the Friday of the first week of Michaelmas Term before the examination, by writing to the Chair of the Board of the Faculty of Classics, c/o 66 St Giles'. Applications must be accompanied by a letter of support from the applicant's society.

2. Candidates must offer eight subjects (and any associated papers of translation), which may include: up to five subjects in Greek and Roman History; up to five subjects in Philosophy; up to five subjects in Greek and Latin Literature; up to two subjects (or up to three, if one is a thesis [IV.6]) in Greek and Roman Archaeology; up to two subjects (or up to three, if one is a thesis [V. 5]) in Philology and Linguistics; two subjects in Second Classical Language; except that (i) candidates in Course I may not offer Second Classical Language and (ii) candidates in Course II who offer Second Classical Language may not offer more than four subjects in any one of Greek and Roman History, Philosophy, and Greek and Latin Literature. The combinations of subjects permitted are set out in I–VI below. Candidates may offer a thesis as one of their subjects, with the proviso that those offering a thesis in Philosophy must offer at least three other subjects in Philosophy. No candidate may offer more than one thesis, except that a Special Thesis may be offered in addition to one other thesis.

3. All candidates must offer at least four text-based subjects, except that candidates in Course II who offer Second Classical Language must offer at least

three text-based subjects. All candidates in Course I must offer at least one text-based
subject in each of (1) Greek and (2) Latin. Some subjects (III. 3, III. 4, III. 7) may
count as text-based subjects in either Greek or Latin. The text-based subjects are as
follows:

(1) in Greek	I. 1: *Greek History* 1	5
	I. 2: *Greek History* 2	
	I. 3: *Greek History* 3	
	I. 4: *Roman History* 4	
	II. 130: *Plato*, Republic	
	II. 131: *Plato*, Theaetetus and Sophist	10
	II. 132: *Aristotle*, Nicomachean Ethics	
	II. 133: *Aristotle*, Physics	
	II. 134: *Sextus Empiricus*	
	III. 1: *Greek Literature of the 5th Century BC*, if	
	offered in version (*a*)	15
	III. 3: *Historiography*	
	III. 4: *Lyric Poetry*	
	III. 5: *Early Greek Hexameter Poetry*	
	III. 6: *Greek Tragedy*	
	III. 7: *Comedy*	20
	III. 8: *Hellenistic Poetry*	
	III. 13: *Euripides*, Orestes	
	III. 15(*b*): *Byzantine Literature*	
	III. 15(*c*): *Modern Greek Poetry*	
	V. 1: *Greek Historical Linguistics*	25
(2) in Latin	I. 5: *Roman History* 5	
	I. 6: *Roman History* 6	
	II. 135: *Latin Philosophy*	
	III. 2: *Latin Literature of the 1st Century BC*, if	
	offered in version (*a*)	30
	III. 3: *Historiography*	
	III. 4: *Lyric Poetry*	
	III. 7: *Comedy*	
	III. 9: *Cicero*	
	III. 10: *Ovid*	35
	III. 11: *Latin Didactic*	
	III. 12: *Neronian Literature*	
	III. 14(*a*): *Seneca*, Agamemnon	
	III. 14(*b*): *Catullus*	
	III. 15(*a*): *The Conversion of Augustine*	40
	V. 2: *Latin Historical Linguistics*	

4. In the assignment of honours all eight subjects offered by a candidate shall
count equally. In assessing a candidate's performance in a subject, the examiners shall
have regard to performance in any associated translation papers.

5. In addition to their eight subjects candidates may also offer, but are not
required to offer, a Special Thesis in accordance with VII below.

6. Any candidate whose native language is not English may bring a
bilingual (native language to English) dictionary for use in any examination paper
where candidates are required to translate Ancient Greek and/or Latin texts into
English.

45

50

I. *Greek and Roman History*

Familiarity with the epigraphical material and awareness of the geography, topography, and physical and visual environment of the relevant parts of the ancient world during the periods under study are required.

Candidates may offer up to five subjects (or up to four if they are offering Second Classical Language in Course II). If they offer more than one subject, at least one must be taken from A below; if they offer more than three subjects, at least two must be taken from A; if they offer five subjects, at least three must be taken from A. Subjects from A must be taken with the associated translation papers from D below.

A. GREEK AND ROMAN HISTORY PERIODS

In Course I all period subjects must be offered as text-based. Course II candidates who are taking period subjects must offer at least one as text-based.

I.1. *The Early Greek World and Herodotus' Histories: 650 to 479 BC*

For those offering this period as a text-based subject, passages for compulsory comment and translation will be set from Herodotus I. 141–77, III. 39–60, V. 28–VI end; Aristotle, *Athenaion Politeia* i-xxiv.

I.2. *Thucydides and the Greek World: 479 to 403 BC*

For those offering this period as a text-based subject, passages for compulsory comment and translation will be set from:

Thucydides, *Histories*: Book I. 89-II. 54; book III. 20–85; book VIII. 45–98.
Xenophon, *Hellenica*: book II. 2–4.

I.3. *The End of the Peloponnesian War to the Death of Philip II of Macedon: 403 to 336 BC*

For those offering this period as a text-based subject, passages for compulsory comment and translation will be set from:

Xenophon, *Hellenica*, Books III and V
Xenophon, *Constitution of the Spartans*
Plutarch, *Life of Pelopidas*
Demosthenes, *Philippic I, On the Peace, Philippic III*.

I.4. *Polybius, Rome and the Mediterranean: 241–146 BC*

For those offering this period as a text-based subject, passages for compulsory comment and translation will be set from the following sections of Polybius: I. 1–4, 62–65; II. 1–13, 21–4; III. 1–34; V. 101–10; VI. 3–18; VII. 9; XI. 4–6; XVI. 24–35; XVIII. 1–12; 34–52; XXI. 29–32, 41–6; XXIII. 1–5, 9, 17; XXIV. 8–13; XXX. 1–5, 30–1; XXXI. 21–30; XXXVI. 1–6, 9, 17; XXXVIII. 1–18.

I.5. *Republic in Crisis: 146–46 BC*

For those offering this period as a text-based subject, passages for compulsory comment and translation will be set from:

Sallust, *Histories* the following fragments:

　1.55 = 1.48 McG (Speech of Lepidus)
　1.77 = 1.67 McG (Speech of Philippus)
　2.47 = 2.44 McG (Speech of Cotta)
　2.98 = 2.82 McG (Letter of Pompey)
　3.48 = 3.34 McG (Speech of Macer)
　4.69 = 4.67 McG (Letter of Mithridates)

(first number that in the OCT, second that in the translation and commentary of P. McGushin (Oxford 1992 and 1994))

Cicero, *Verrines* I, *De imperio Cn. Pompei*
Cicero, Letters: *Ad fam.* I. 2, 9; V. 7; VI. 6; VII. 5; VIII. 1, 4, 8, 13, 14; XIII. 9; XV. 2

Ad Att. I. 1, 13, 14, 19; II. 16, 18, 19, 24; IV. 1, 3, 5; V. 16; VI. 2; VII. 5, 7, 10, 11; VIII. 3, 11, 12D, 13; IX. 6A, 9, 10, 11A; X. 8; XI. 6; XII. 2 *Ad Qu. f.* I. 2; II. 3, 4; III. 6.

I.6. *Rome, Italy and Empire from Caesar to Claudius: 46 BC to AD 54*

For those offering this period as a text-based subject, passages for compulsory comment and translation will be set from:
   Res Gestae Divi Augusti ed. P. A. Brunt and J. M. Moore (1967)
   Suetonius *Life of Augustus*
   Tacitus *Annals* I, XI-XII

B. GREEK AND ROMAN HISTORY TOPICS

Note: It cannot be guaranteed that university lectures or classes or college teaching will be available in all subjects in this section in every academic year. Candidates are advised to consult their tutors about the availability of teaching when selecting their subjects.

I.7 *Athenian Democracy in the Classical Age*

Candidates will be required to study the social, administrative, and constitutional developments in Athens from 462 BC to 321 BC, and will only be required to show such knowledge of external affairs as is necessary for an understanding of Athenian democracy. The following texts are prescribed for study in translation; although compulsory passages for comment will not be set, candidates will be expected to show knowledge of these texts in their answers.

   Aristotle, *Constitution of Athens* (tr. P. J. Rhodes, Penguin Classics),
   Herodotus III.80–82 (Loeb),
   Thucydides I.31–44, 66-79, 140–5; II.35–65; III.35–50, 82–3; V.43–6; VI.8–29; VIII.47-97 (tr. M. Hammond, OUP: Oxford World's Classics, 2009),
   Xenophon, *Hellenica* I.6 and 7; II.3 and 4 (Loeb),
      Memorabilia I.1 and 2; III.6 (Loeb),
         Revenues (Loeb),
   [Xenophon], *Constitution of Athens* (Loeb),
   Andocides I (Loeb, *Attic Minor Orators* I),
   Lysias XXII, XXV (Loeb),
   Aeschines II (Loeb),
   Demosthenes VI, XIX, LIX (Loeb),
   Aristophanes, *Wasps, Clouds, Ecclesiazusae, Acharnians* 1–173, *Thesmophoriazusae* 295–530 (Penguin Classics),
   Plato, *Apology, Gorgias, Protagoras* 309–28 (Penguin Classics),
   Aeschylus, *Eumenides*; Sophocles, *Antigone*; Euripides, *Supplices* (*The Complete Greek Tragedies*, ed. R. Lattimore, D. Grene, Chicago 1958–9),
   C. W. Fornara, *Translated Documents of Greece and Rome 1: Archaic Times to the End of the Peloponnesian War* (Cambridge, 1983) nos. 15, 68, 75, 97, 100, 103, 106, 114, 119, 120, 128, 134, 140, 147, 155, 160, 166,
   P. Harding, *Translated Documents of Greece and Rome 2: From the End of the Peloponnesian War to the Battle of Ipsus* (Cambridge, 1985) nos. 3, 5, 9, 45, 47, 54, 55, 56, 66, 78, 82, 101, 108, 111, 121.
   Optional passages for comment will be set from these texts in translation.
   Opportunity will be given to show knowledge of the archaeology of Classical Athens.

I.8 *Alexander the Great and his Early Successors (336 BC–302 BC)*

The following texts are prescribed for study in translation; although compulsory passages for comment will not be set, candidates will be expected to show knowledge of these texts in their answers.
   Arrian, *Anabasis* (Loeb, Brunt),

[Demosthenes] XVII (Loeb),

Diodorus Siculus, XVI.89, 91–5; XVII.5–7, 16–21, 32, 47–8, 62–3, 69–73, 76–7, 93–5, 100–1, 108–11, 113–15, 117–18; XVIII, the whole; XIX.12–64, 66–8, 77–100, 105; XX.19–21, 27–8, 37, 45–53, 81–99, 100–3, 106–13 (Loeb), Plutarch, *Lives of Alexander, Eumenes and Demetrios* 1–27 (Loeb), the inscriptions translated in a dossier available on WebLearn and the texts in P. Harding, *Translated Documents of Greece and Rome 2: From the End of the Peloponnesian War to the Battle of Ipsus* (Cambridge, 1989) Nos. 123, 125, 126, 128, 129, 132, 133, 136, 138.

Optional passages for comment will be set from these texts in translation and from Arrian, *Anabasis* VII (Loeb, Brunt) in Greek only.

I.9 *The Hellenistic World: Societies and Cultures, c.300–100 BC*

Candidates will be required to study the history, culture, and society of the Hellenistic world, based on the detailed and integrated case study of primary evidence—literary, epigraphical, archaeological. A knowledge of political history is expected, but the main focus is on social and cultural history. Close familiarity with the epigraphical material and awareness of the geography, topography, and physical and visual environment of the Hellenistic world are required. The following texts are prescribed for study in translation. Compulsory passages for comment will not be set, but candidates will be expected to show knowledge of these texts in their answers:

Plutarch, *Demetrios, Philopoimen, Agis-Kleomenes*; Polybius, 4–5; 21.18 to end; 22.3–14; 23.1–4; 29–30 all frgs; 31.1–15; Appian, *Syriaca, Mithridatica*; Theokritos, 2, 14, 15, 17; Callimachus, *Hymn to Delos*; Herodas, *Mimiamboi* 1 and 4.

Special attention will be given to the following cities, sites and monuments:

Ai Khanum, Alexandria, Athens, Delos, Pella, Pergamon, Priene.

I.10 *Cicero: Politics and Thought in the Late Republic*

The following texts are prescribed for study in translation; although compulsory passages for comment will not be set, candidates will be expected to show knowledge of these texts in their answers:

Sallust, *Catilina* (Loeb),

Cicero, *In Verrem* (Actio I) (Loeb),

De Imperio Cn. Pompei (Loeb),

Pro Sestio 97–137 (Loeb),

In M. Antonium Philippica XI (Loeb),

Pro Murena (Loeb),

In Catilinam IV (Loeb),

Epistulae ad Atticum I.1, 2, 13, 14, 16, 17, 19; II.1, 3, 16, 18; IV.1, 3, 5; V.16 and 21; VI.1 and 2; VII.7, 9, 11; VIII.3 and 11; IX. 6A, 10, 11A, 18; X.8 (incl. A and B); XI.6; XII.21 and 40; XIII.19 and 52; XIV.1, 12, 13, 13A and B; XV.1A and 11; XVI.7, 8 and 11 (Loeb),

Epistulae ad Familiares I.1, 8, 9; II.12; III.6 and 7; IV.4, 5; V.1, 2, 7, 12; VI.6; VII.3, 5, 30; VIII.1, 5, 6, 8, 13, 14, 16; IX.16 and 17; X.24 and 28; XI.3, 20, 27, 28; XII.3 and 5; XIII.1, and 9; XIV.4; XV.1, 4, 5, 6, 16, 19; XVI.12 (Loeb),

Epistulae ad Quintum fratrem II.3, 15; III.5 and 6 (Loeb),

Epistulae ad M. Brutum 17, 25 (Loeb),

Brutus 301–33 (Loeb),

De Oratore I.137–59, 185–203; II.30–8 (Loeb),

Orator 113–20, 140–6 (Loeb),

De Re Publica I.1–18, 58–71 (Loeb),

De Legibus II.1–33; III. 1–49 (Loeb),

Tusculanae Disputationes I.1–8 (Loeb),

De Divinatione II.1–24; 136–50 (Loeb),

De Natura Deorum I.1–13; III.1–10 (Loeb),

De Officiis I.1–60; II.1–29, 44–60, 73–89 trans. Griffin and Atkins (Cambridge), Cornelius Nepos, *Atticus* (Loeb).

Optional passages for comment will be set from these texts in translation, and from *In Catilinam I* (Loeb) and *De Finibus I.1–12* (OCT) in Latin only.

This subject may not be combined with III.9, *Cicero*.   5

I.11 *Politics, Society and Culture from Nero to Hadrian*

Candidates will be required to study the political, social, economic and cultural history of the Roman empire in the period AD 54–138. The following texts are prescribed for study in translation. Compulsory passages for comment will not be set, but candidates will be expected to show knowledge of these texts in their answers.   10

Tacitus, *Annals* XIII–XVI, *Histories*, I, IV, *Agricola*
Suetonius, *Lives of Nero, Vespasian, Domitian*
Josephus, *Jewish War* II, VII (Loeb)
Pliny, *Letters* I–X, *Panegyricus*
Dio Chrysostom, *Orations* 38–51 (Loeb)   15
Juvenal, *Satires* VII, VIII, XI, XIV, XVI
Historia Augusta, *Life of Hadrian*
R. K. Sherk, *The Roman Empire: Augustus to Hadrian* (Translated Documents of Greece and Rome 6), nos. 61–200

Attention will be given to relevant archaeological sites and monuments including   20
the following:

Nero's Domus Aurea, the Colosseum, the Templum Pacis, The Arch of Titus, Domitian's Palace, Trajan's Forum, the Arch of Trajan at Beneventum, Trajan's Column, the Great Trajanic Frieze, Hadrian's Villa at Tivoli.

I.12 *Religions in the Greek and Roman World* (c.*31 BC-AD 312*)   25

Candidates will be required to study the workings of Greek and Roman religions, including relevant aspects of Judaism and Christianity and other elective cults, between around 30 BC and AD 312. They will be encouraged to display an understanding of relevant modern theories of religious practice, and to be familiar with the relevant literary, epigraphic and archaeological evidence contained in the following   30
texts prescribed for study in translation; although compulsory passages for comment will not be set, candidates will be expected to show knowledge of these texts in their answers.

Ovid, *Fasti* IV (Loeb),
Acts of the Apostles (New English Bible),   35
Josephus, *Against Apion* II (Loeb),
Plutarch, *Decline of Oracles* (Loeb),
Lucian, *Alexander; Peregrinus* (Loeb),
Aelius Aristides, *Oration* XLVIII (=*Sacred Tales* II) (tr. C. A. Behr),
Pausanias I.1–38 (Loeb),   40
Apuleius, *Metamorphoses* XI (Hanson, Loeb),
Minucius Felix, *Octavius* (Loeb, with Tertullian),
H. A. Musurillo, *Acts of the Christian Martyrs* (1972) nos. 1, 6, 8, 10,
Eusebius, *Ecclesiastical History* VIII-X (Penguin),
M. Beard, J. A. North & S. R. F. Price, *Religions of Rome* vol. 2 (Cambridge 1998).   45

I.13 *Sexuality and Gender in Greece and Rome*

The following texts are prescribed for study in translation; although compulsory passages for comment will not be set, candidates will be expected to show knowledge of these texts in their answers.

M. R. Lefkowitz and M. B. Fant, *Women's Life in Greece and Rome*, 2nd edn.   50
(London, 1992), nos. 1–27, 36–50, 168, 176, 178–9, 181–207, 273–337, 369–440

Semonides fr. 7 (*Greek Iambic Poetry*, Loeb)
Theognis II (lines 1231–1389) (*Greek Elegiac Poetry*, Loeb)
Anacreon fr. 358 (*Greek Lyric II*, Loeb)
Aeschylus, *Agamemnon*, Sophocles, *Philoctetes*, Euripides, *Medea* (in D. Grene
  and R. Lattimore eds, *The Complete Greek Tragedies in Translation* (Chicago,   5
  1957–9)
Aristophanes, *Lysistrata, Thesmophoriazusae, Ecclesiazusae* (Penguin)
Lysias I (Loeb)
Xenophon, *Oeconomicus* (ed. and tr. S. Pomeroy, Oxford, 1992)
Aeschines I *Against Timarchus* (Loeb)   10
Senatusconsultum de Bacchanalibus, in M. Beard, J. North and S. Price, *Religions
  of Rome* (Cambridge, 1998) 2, pp. 290–1
Ovid, *Ars Amatoria* (Loeb)
Musonius Rufus (tr. C. E. Lutz, *Yale Classical Studies* 10 [1947], 39–49, 89–91)
Pliny, *Letters* III. 11, 16; IV. 10, 19; V. 16; VI. 33; VII. 19, 24; X. 120   15
Juvenal VI
Soranus, *Gynaecology* (tr. O. Temkin, Baltimore 1956)
The Forgotten Desert Mothers: Sayings, Lives, and Stories of Early Christian Women
  (tr. L. Swan, New York, 2001), lives of Amma Sarah, Syncletica and Theodora,
  Melania the Elder, Melania the Younger, Macrina the Younger, and Marcella   20
Pelagius, *Letter to Demetrias* in *Pelagius: Life and Letters* (tr. B. R. Rees,
  Woodbridge, 1998)
Jerome, *Letters* 22, 77, 107, 108, 117, 127, 128 (Loeb)
Opportunity will also be given to show knowledge of the artistic and archaeologi-
cal evidence.   25

C.

I.14 *Thesis in Ancient History*

Any candidate who is not offering a thesis in any other branch of the examination
may offer a thesis in Ancient History in accordance with the Regulations on Theses
below.   30

D. *Translation*

Six papers, each of one-and-a-half hours, will be set. Candidates are required to
offer translation from the texts prescribed for all the period subjects which they offer
under A as text-based.

II. *Philosophy*   35

Candidates may offer up to five subjects in Philosophy, from the list below.
Candidates offering one Philosophy subject only may offer any of the subjects listed
below except 199. Those offering at least two Philosophy subjects must select at least
one subject in ancient philosophy, i.e. one of 115, 116, 130, 131, 132, 133, 134 and
135. Those offering three or more subjects must also select one subject from 101, 102,   40
103 and 108. Candidates offering subject 199 (Thesis in Philosophy) must offer at
least three other subjects in Philosophy. The syllabus for each subject, including
thesis regulations, is specified in **Regulations for Philosophy in all Honour Schools
including Philosophy**. In the list below, numbers in parenthesis after a subject's title
indicate other subjects with which it may not be combined.   45

   101 Early Modern Philosophy
   102 Knowledge and Reality
   103 Ethics
   104 Philosophy of Mind
   106 Philosophy of Science and Social Science (**124**)   50

107 Philosophy of Religion
108 The Philosophy of Logic and Language
109 Aesthetics and the Philosophy of Criticism
110 Medieval Philosophy: Aquinas (**111**)
111 Medieval Philosophy: Duns Scotus, Ockham (**110**)   5
112 The Philosophy of Kant
113 Post-Kantian Philosophy
114 Theory of Politics
115 Plato: *Republic* (in translation) (**130**)
116 Aristotle: *Nicomachean Ethics* (in translation) (**132**)   10
117 Frege, Russell, and Wittgenstein (**118**)
118 The Later Philosophy of Wittgenstein (**117**)
119 Formal Logic
120 Intermediate Philosophy of Physics
122 Philosophy of Mathematics   15
124 Philosophy of Science (**106**)
125 Philosophy of Cognitive Science
130 Plato: *Republic* (in Greek) (**115**)
131 Plato: *Theaetetus* and *Sophist* (in Greek)
132 Aristotle: *Nicomachean Ethics* (in Greek) (**116**)   20
133 Aristotle: *Physics* (in Greek)
134 Sextus Empiricus: *Outlines of Pyrrhonism* (in Greek)
135 Latin Philosophy (in Latin)
199 Thesis in Philosophy (I.14, III.12, IV.5, V.5)

III. *Greek and Latin Literature*   25

Course I: Candidates may offer up to a maximum of five subjects from 1-16 below. Candidates offering more than three subjects must offer both III.1 and III.2; candidates offering more than one must offer III.1 or III.2, and may offer both. Only one of papers III.3, 4, 7 and 15(*d*) may be offered.

Course II: Candidates may offer up to a maximum of five subjects from 1-16 below,   30 or four if they take VI, Second Classical Language. Candidates offering more than one subject must offer III.1 or III.2, and may offer both. Only one of papers III.3, 4, 7 and 15(*d*) may be offered.

One paper will be set on each subject except III.3, 4, 7, 15(*d*) and 16. Each of subjects III.3, 4, and 7 will be examined by a one-and-a-half hour paper of transla-   35 tion, and an extended essay of up to 6,000 words. Additional translation papers (one-and-a-half hours each) will be set on III.1 and III.2.

In all subjects credit will be given for showing wider knowledge of Greek and Roman culture.

Note: It cannot be guaranteed that university lectures or classes or college teaching   40 will be available in all subjects in every academic year. Candidates are advised to consult their tutors about the availability of teaching when selecting their subjects.

III.1 *Greek Literature of the 5th Century BC*

(*a*) One paper of three hours (commentary and essay) with an additional paper (one-and-a-half hours) of translation.   45

(*b*) Those taking VI. Second Classical Language in Greek may if they wish offer only the three-hour commentary and essay paper, and in that case they will be given translations of the passages set for commentary. **This version of the subject will not count as text-based.**

For both (*a*) and (*b*) the subject is to be studied with special reference to the   50 following texts, from which the passages for translation and comment will be set.

Pindar, *Olympian* 1, *Pythians* 1 and 9

Sophocles, *Ajax*
Euripides, *Hippolytus*
Aristophanes, *Thesmophoriazusae*
Herodotus I.1-94

III.2 *Latin Literature of the 1st Century* BC

(*a*) One paper of three hours (commentary and essay) with an additional paper (one-and-a-half hours) of translation.

(*b*) Those taking VI. Second Classical Language in Latin may if they wish offer only the three-hour commentary and essay paper, and in that case they will be given translations of the passages set for commentary. **This version of the subject will not count as text-based.**

For both (*a*) and (*b*) the subject is to be studied with special reference to the following texts, from which the passages for translation and comment will be set.

Lucretius I
Catullus 64 and 68
Cicero, *Pro Archia*
Virgil, *Eclogues*
Horace, *Odes* III
Propertius IV

III.3 *Historiography* with special reference to the following texts.

For all candidates, this subject will be examined by a one-and-a-half hour paper of passages for translation taken from the texts in list α, and an extended essay of up to 6,000 words. Essay topics set by the examiners will be released on Monday of Week 6 of Hilary Term immediately preceding the examination and essays should be submitted to the Examination Schools by Monday of Week 10 of the same term (12 noon); at the same time candidates should submit a searchable electronic version to the Academic Administrative Officer of the Faculty of Classics. Every extended essay must be the work of the candidate alone, and he or she must not discuss with any tutor either his or her choice of theme or the method of handling it. This subject may not be combined with III.4, 7 or 15(*d*).

One of the following:

(i) For Course I candidates:

α Herodotus III.1-38, 61-88, 97-119
Thucydides III.1-19, 37-48, 69-85, 94-114
Claudius Quadrigarius fr. 10b Peter
Livy, preface, I.1-16, 39-60, VII.9.6-10
Tacitus, *Annals* XV.23-74

β Rest of Herodotus III
Rest of Thucydides III
Xenophon, *Anabasis* I-IV
Caesar, *De Bello Gallico* VI-VII
Sallust, *Bellum Iugurthinum*
Rest of Livy I

(ii) For Course II candidates or single-language Classics & English, Classics & Modern Languages and Classics & Oriental Studies candidates offering Greek:

α Herodotus III.1-38, 61-88, 97-119
Thucydides III.1-19, 37-48, 69-85, 94-114
Xenophon, *Anabasis* I.7-III.2

β Rest of Herodotus III
Rest of Thucydides III
Rest of Xenophon, *Anabasis* I-IV

Claudius Quadrigarius fr. 10b Peter
Caesar, *De Bello Gallico* VI–VII
Sallust, *Bellum Iugurthinum*
Livy preface, I, VII.9.6–10
Tacitus, *Annals* XV.23–74   5

(iii) For Course II candidates or single-language Classics & English, Classics &
Modern Languages and Classics & Oriental Studies candidates offering Latin:
α Claudius Quadrigarius fr. 10b Peter
Caesar, *De Bello Gallico* VI
Livy, preface, I.1–16, 39–60, VII.9.6–10   10
Sallust, *Bellum Iugurthinum* 1–10, 20–31, 77–101, 107–14
Tacitus, *Annals* XV.23–74
β Herodotus III
Thucydides III
Xenophon, *Anabasis* I–IV   15
Caesar, *De Bello Gallico* VII
Rest of Sallust, *Bellum Iugurthinum*
Rest of Livy I

III.4 *Lyric Poetry*, with special reference to the following texts.

For all candidates, this subject will be examined by a one-and-a-half hour paper of   20
passages for translation taken from the texts in list α, and an extended essay of up
to 6,000 words. Essay topics set by the examiners will be released on Monday of
Week 6 of Hilary Term immediately preceding the examination and essays should
be submitted to the Examination Schools by Monday of Week 10 of the same term
(12 noon); at the same time candidates should submit a searchable electronic version   25
to the Academic Administrative Officer of the Faculty of Classics. Every extended
essay must be the work of the candidate alone, and he or she must not discuss with
any tutor either his or her choice of theme or the method of handling it. This subject
may not be combined with III.3, 7 or 15(*d*).

One of the following: 30
(i) For Course I candidates:
α All of (1) to (4) below:
(1) G. O. Hutchinson, *Greek Lyric Poetry* (Oxford): all texts, except Sophocles
and Euripides.
(2) D. A. Campbell, *Greek Lyric Poetry* (2nd edition, Bristol), including the   35
appendix: all texts by Archilochus, Semonides, Mimnermus, Solon,
Sappho, Alcaeus, Ibycus, Anacreon, Theognis, and Bacchylides. Where
texts overlap with Hutchinson's, the latter's edition should be used.
(3) M. M. Willcock, *Pindar: Victory Odes* (Cambridge): all seven texts.
(4) Catullus 11, 17, 34, 51, 61; Horace, *Odes* I.   40

β All of (5) to (8) below:
(5) M. L. West, *Greek Lyric Poetry: a new translation* (Oxford): all texts that
are not α texts.
(6) Pindar: the remainder of the *Olympians*; all *Pythians; Paeans* 2, 4, 6;
Partheneion 2.   45
(7) Timotheus 788–91; Callimachus, *Iambi* 1, 4, 5, 13, and *Ektheosis Arsinoes*;
Theocritus 29 and 30.
(8) Catullus 4, 16, 21–6, 29–30, 38, 40–3, 52–60, 63; Horace, *Odes* II and IV,
Carmen Saeculare, Epodes.
(ii) For Course II candidates or single-language candidates in Classics & English,   50
Classics & Modern Languages and Classics & Oriental Studies offering Greek:

      α (1), (2), (3), and (6) (except Pindar, *Pythians* and *Paeans* 4 and 6) from (i)
above.

      β (4), (5), (7), and (8) from (i) above, as well as Pindar, *Pythians* and *Paeans* 4 and 6.

  (iii) For Course II candidates or single-language candidates in Classics & English,
Classics & Modern Languages and Classics & Oriental Studies offering Latin: 5
      α (4) and (8) from (i) above.
      β (1), (2), (3), (5), (6) and (7) from (i) above.

III.5 *Early Greek Hexameter Poetry*, with special reference to the following texts.
Compulsory passages for translation and comment will be set from those in list α.

    α Homer, *Odyssey* I, V. 1-XIII. 92   1C
      Hesiod, *Works and Days* (including the bracketed portions)
      Homeric Hymns 2 (*Demeter*), 5 (*Aphrodite*)
    β Homer, *Odyssey* II-IV, XIII. 93-XXIV. 548
      Hesiod, *Theogony*
      Fragments of the Epic Cycle (in M. L. West, *Greek Epic Fragments* (Loeb,   1⸱
      2003), pp. 38–171)
      Candidates will also be expected to be familiar with the *Iliad*.

III.6 *Greek Tragedy*, with special reference to the following texts.
Compulsory passages for translation and comment will be set from those in list α.

    α Aeschylus, *Agamemnon*   2C
      Sophocles, *Oedipus Tyrannus*
      Euripides, *Medea*
    β Aeschylus, *Choephori, Eumenides*
      Sophocles, *Electra, Oedipus Coloneus*
      Euripides, *Electra, Helen, Ion*   2⸱
      Aristophanes, *Frogs*

III.7 *Comedy*, with special reference to the following texts.
  For all candidates, this subject will be examined by a one-and-a-half hour paper of
passages for translation taken from the texts in list α, and an extended essay of up to
6,000 words. Essay topics set by the examiners will be released on Monday of Week 6   3C
of Hilary Term immediately preceding the examination and essays should be
submitted to the Examination Schools by Monday of Week 10 of the same term
(12 noon); at the same time candidates should submit a searchable electronic version
to the Academic Administrative Officer of the Faculty of Classics. Every extended
essay must be the work of the candidate alone, and he or she must not discuss with   3⸱
any tutor either his or her choice of theme or the method of handling it. This subject
may not be combined with III.3, 4 or 15(*d*).

  One of the following:

  (i) For Course I candidates:
    α Aristophanes, *Birds* 1–684, 956–1765   4⸱
      Menander, *Dyskolos*
      Plautus, *Pseudolus*
      Terence, *Eunuchus*
    β Aristophanes, *Birds* 685–955, *Ekklesiazousai*
      Menander, *Aspis, Dis Exapaton, Epitrepontes, Kolax, Misoumenos,*   4
      Perikeiromene, Samia, Sikyonios
      Plautus, *Bacchides*
      Terence, *Adelphoe*
  (ii) For Course II candidates or single-language Classics & English, Classics &
    Modern Languages and Classics & Oriental Studies candidates offering Greek: 5⸱

α Aristophanes, *Birds* 1–684, 956–1765, *Ekklesiazousai*
   Menander, *Dyskolos, Samia, Epitrepontes* 218–581, 853–922, 1062–1131
β Aristophanes, *Birds* 685–955
   Menander, *Aspis, Dis Exapaton,* rest of *Epitrepontes, Kolax, Misoumenos,*
   Perikeiromene, Sikyonios
   Plautus, *Bacchides, Pseudolus*
   Terence, *Adelphoe, Eunuchus*
(iii) For Course II candidates or single-language Classics & English, Classics &
   Modern Languages and Classics & Oriental Studies candidates offering Latin:
   α Plautus, *Bacchides, Pseudolus*
      Terence, *Eunuchus, Adelphoe*
   β Aristophanes, *Birds, Ekklesiazousai*
      Menander, *Aspis, Dis Exapaton, Dyskolos, Epitrepontes, Kolax,*
      Misoumenos, Perikeiromene, Samia, Sikyonios

III.8 *Hellenistic Poetry*, with special reference to the following texts. Compulsory
passages for translation and comment will be set from those in list α
   α Theocritus 1, 2, 7, 11, 13, 15, 17, 28
      Callimachus, *Hymns* 1, 5, 6; frr. 1, 67–75, 110, 178, 191, 194, 260 Pfeiffer (this
      last fr. to be read in Callimachus, *Hecale* (ed. A. S. Hollis) frr. 69–74); epigrams
      2, 4, 8, 13, 16, 19, 21, 25, 27, 28, 29, 30, 41, 43, 46, 50 Pf.
      Posidippus, *Epigrams* 1–20 Austin-Bastianini
      Apollonius, *Argonautica* III. 439–1162
      Asclepiades 1, 2, 3, 10, 11, 12, 16, 18, 25, 26, 28, 32 Page
   β Apollonius *Argonautica* III. 1–438, 1163–IV. 481
      Theocritus 3
      Moschus, *Europa*
      Herodas, 2, 4, 6
      Callimachus, *Hymn* 2

III.9 *Cicero*, with special reference to the following texts. Compulsory passages for
translation and comment will be set from those in list α.
   α *Pro S. Roscio Amerino*
      Pro Sulla
      In Pisonem
      Pro Milone
      Pro Marcello
   β *Auctor ad Herennium* I; II. 1–12, 47–50; IV. 11–16
      Verrine V
      Philippics III and IV
      De Oratore II. 71–216, 290–349
   This subject may not be combined with I.10, *Cicero: Politics and Thought in the
Late Republic.*

III.10 *Ovid*, with special reference to the following texts. Compulsory passages for
translation and comment will be set from those in list α.
   α *Amores* II
      Metamorphoses I–IV
      Fasti IV
      Tristia I
   β *Heroides* 18–21
      Ars Amatoria I
      Metamorphoses XIII–XV

III.11 *Latin Didactic*, with special reference to the following texts. Compulsory passages for translation and comment will be set from those in list α.

α Lucretius III and VI
   Virgil, *Georgics*
   Ovid, *Ars Amatoria* III
β Hesiod, *Works and Days*
   Aratus, *Phaenomena* 1–136, 733–1154
   Lucretius I

III.12 *Neronian Literature*, with special reference to the following texts. Compulsory passages for translation and comment will be set from those in list α.

α Lucan I, VII
   Seneca, *Thyestes*
   Seneca, *Epistles* 28, 47, 53, 56, 63, 77
   Seneca, *De Brevitate Vitae*
   Seneca, *Apocolocyntosis*
   Petronius, *Satyrica* 1–26.6, 81–90, 114–124.3
   Persius 1
β Seneca, *Medea*
   Petronius, *Satyrica* 79–80, 91–113, 124.4-end
   Calpurnius Siculus 1, 4, 7
   Suetonius, *Nero*
   Tacitus, *Annals* XIII-XVI
   Seneca, *Naturales Quaestiones* I *praefatio*, 16, III *praefatio*, 17–18, IVb.13, VI.1–3, 32

III.13 *Euripides*, Orestes: *papyri, manuscripts, text*
   The paper will consist of: (i) transcription of short passages from both (*a*) a papyrus of Greek poetry and (*b*) a medieval manuscript of the *Orestes*; (ii) textual and interpretative commentary on a choice of passages (with apparatus criticus), from Euripides, *Orestes* 1–347 and 1246–1693. Both (i) and (ii) are to be attempted. Candidates will be expected to show appropriate knowledge of the history of transmission and the principles of textual criticism; they will also be expected to show, as appropriate, knowledge of the whole play.

III.14 *Either*

   (*a*) *Seneca*, Agamemnon: *manuscripts, text, interpretation*
   The paper will consist of (i) a compulsory transcription from a manuscript of a passage of the play and (ii) textual and interpretative commentary on a choice of passages (with apparatus criticus). Candidates will be expected to show appropriate knowledge of the history of transmission and the principles of textual criticism.*

   or

   (*b*) Catullus: *manuscripts, text, interpretation*
   The paper will consist of (i) a compulsory transcription from a manuscript of Catullus and (ii) textual and interpretative commentary on a choice of passages (with apparatus criticus). Candidates will be expected to show appropriate knowledge of the history of transmission and the principles of textual criticism. Passages for commentary will be drawn from the following portions of the text: 1–14, 27–39, 44–51, 65–7, 69–76, 95–101, 114–116.*

---

* University classes will be given for only one of these options each year.

III.15 One of the following:

(a) *The Conversion of Augustine.* Compulsory passages for translation and comment will be set from Augustine, *Confessions* V–IX; Symmachus, *Relationes* III; Ambrose, *Epist.* 17–18; Jerome, *Epist.* 22, 38, 45, 107, 127.

(b) *Byzantine Literature.* Compulsory passages for translation and comment will be set; candidates will be required to take all the passages they offer either from (i) below or from (ii). In their essays, candidates will be expected to show knowledge of both (i) and (ii). Texts will be available in a leaflet from the Classics Office, Classics Centre, 66, St Giles'.

    (i) [sixth century AD]. Romanos the Melodist, Kontakia 1, 17, and 54, from *Sancti Romani Melodi Cantica: Cantica Genuina*, ed. C. A. Trypanis and P. Maas (Oxford, 1963); Procopius, *Persian Wars* 1.24, 2.22–23, *Gothic Wars* 4.20, *Secret History* 6–12, from *Opera omnia*, ed. J. Haury, rev. P. Wirth (Leipzig, 1962–4); Agathias, Book 1, from *Historiarum libri quinque*, ed. R. Keydell (Berlin, 1967); Agathias, Epigrams 1–24, 66–75, from G. Viansino, *Epigrammi* (Milan, 1967).

    (ii) [twelfth century AD]. Anna Komnene, *Alexias*, Book 1, ed. D.-R. Reinsch (Berlin, 2001); Niketas Choniates, *Historia*, Book 4, ed. J.-L. van Dieten (Berlin, 1975); *Digenis Akritis*, Grottaferrata version Book 4, from *Digenis Akritis*, ed. E. M. Jeffreys (Cambridge, 1998); Theodore Prodromos, Poems 3, 4, and 6, from *Historische Gedichte*, ed. W. Hörandner (Vienna, 1974).

(c) *Modern Greek Poetry.* Candidates will be expected to have read Kavafis, *Poiemata*, and G. Seferis, *Mythistorema, Gymnopaidia, Hemerologio Katastromatos* I-III and *Kichle*. Compulsory passages for translation and comment will be set.

(d) *The Reception of Classical Literature in Poetry in English since 1900.* Authors in English for study will include Auden, H. D., Eliot, Frost, Longley, Lowell, MacNeice, Carson, Harrison, Heaney, Hughes and Walcott. This paper will be examined only by extended essay of up to 6,000 words. Essay topics set by the examiners will be released on Monday of Week 6 of Hilary Term and essays should be submitted by Monday of Week 10 of the same term (12 noon) to the Examination Schools; at the same time candidates should submit a searchable electronic version to the Academic Administrative Officer of the Faculty of Classics. Candidates will be required to use at least three authors in their essays, at least one of which must be a classical author. Every extended essay must be the work of the candidate alone, and he or she must not discuss with any tutor either his or her choice of theme or the method of handling it. This subject may not be combined with III.3, 4, or 7.

III.16 Thesis in Literature

Any candidate may offer a thesis in Greek and Latin Literature in accordance with the Regulation on Theses below. This subject may not be combined with any of I.14, II.199, IV.5 or V.5.

IV. *Greek and Roman Archaeology*

Course I and *Course II*: Candidates may offer *one* or *two* of the following subjects 1–5, and may, if they wish, offer subject 5 as well. Each of subjects 1–5 will be examined in one paper (3 hours).

They may also offer subject 6 as their sole Archaeology subject.

IV.1 *The Greeks and the Mediterranean World* c.950 BC–500 BC

Candidates will be expected to show knowledge of the material evidence from the Greek world and the areas of contact between Greek and other Mediterranean peoples. Areas of emphasis will include Athens and Attica; the non-Greek states bordering the Mediterranean and their reciprocal relationships with the Greeks; Greek colonial settlements; trade and coinage; problems of method and chronology. Knowledge of the principal series of artefacts of the period, their development and problems of method and chronology will be examined. In the examination candidates will be required to answer one picture question and three others.

IV.2 *Greek art and archaeology, c.500–300 BC*

Candidates will be expected to show knowledge of the architecture, sculpture, and other representational arts of the classical Greek city. Areas of emphasis will include the city of Athens and the historical context and significance of the art and monuments of the period. In the examination candidates will be required to answer one picture question and three others, one each from the following sections: (*a*) architecture, buildings, and urbanism, (*b*) statues, reliefs, temple sculptures, (*c*) painting, painted pottery, and other figured artefacts. Credit will be given for knowledge of relevant material in the Ashmolean Museum and Cast Gallery.

IV.3 *Hellenistic Art and Archaeology, 330–30 BC*

The paper studies major themes, contexts, and media of Hellenistic art, set against the archaeology of the best-preserved cities and sites of the period – from Macedonia to Bactria, from the Aegean to central Italy. The material includes distinctive categories of object, such as bronzeware, clay seals, gems, glassware, grave stelai, jewellery, mosaics, silverware, statues in bronze, statues in marble, terracottas, and wallpaintings. The contexts are cities, sanctuaries, tombs, palaces, villas, and houses. The period extends from Alexander's conquest of Asia to the adoption of Hellenistic art and material technology in Italy and the end of the Ptolemaic dynasty in Alexandria.

IV.4 *Art under the Roman Empire AD 14–337*

The art and visual culture of the Roman empire is studied in its physical, social, and historical contexts. Candidates will be expected to be familiar with major monuments in Rome and Italy and other leading centres of the empire (such as Aphrodisias, Athens, Ephesus, and Lepcis Magna) and with the main strands and contexts of representation in the eastern and western provinces. They will be expected to show knowledge of written evidence where relevant as well as of the main media and categories of surviving images—statues, portrait busts, historical reliefs, funerary monuments, cameos, wallpaintings, mosaics, silverware, and coins. In the examination candidates will be required to answer one picture question and three others.

IV.5 *Roman Archaeology: Cities and Settlement under the Empire*

The subject comprises the study of the Roman city from Augustus to the Tetrarchy placed in the broader context of patterns of rural settlement, agricultural production, transport, and trade. Areas of emphasis include selected key sites (Ostia, Pompeii, Corinth, Caesarea Maritima, Palmyra, Lepcis Magna, and Silchester) and major landscape studies in Italy, Greece, and North Africa. Particular attention is paid to problems and biases in assessing the character of the surviving evidence and in testing theoretical models against physical data. Candidates will be expected to show knowledge of written evidence where relevant as well as of the main categories of surviving ancient material evidence. In the examination candidates will be required to answer one picture question and three others.

IV.6 *Thesis in Greek and Roman Archaeology*

Any candidate may offer a thesis in Greek or Roman Archaeology in accordance with the Regulation on Theses below. This subject may not be combined with any of I.14, II.199, III.16, or V.5.

V. *Philology and Linguistics*

Course I and *Course II*: Candidates may offer *one* or *two* of the following subjects 1–4, and may if they wish offer subject 5 as well. They may also offer subject 5 as their sole Philology and Linguistics subject. Each of subjects 1–4 will be examined in one paper (3 hours).

V.1 *Greek Historical Linguistics*

The paper will consist of two sections: (*a*) the dialects of Greek poetry; Greek dialect inscriptions; Linear B; (*b*) the history of the Greek language with special reference to the development of the literary languages. Candidates must answer questions from both sections. In (*a*) compulsory passages will be set for translation and linguistic commentary. All candidates must answer from two of the three parts of (*a*).

V.2 *Latin Historical Linguistics*

The paper will consist of two sections: (*a*) Oscan and Umbrian; Archaic Latin; the language of Plautus; Imperial and Late Latin; (*b*) the history of the Latin language with special reference to the development of the literary language. Candidates must answer questions from both sections. In (*a*) compulsory passages will be set for translation and linguistic commentary. All candidates must answer from two of the four parts of (*a*).

V.3 *General Linguistics and Comparative Philology*

This paper will be divided into three sections: (*a*) General Linguistics; (*b*) synchronic/descriptive analysis of *either* the Greek language *or* the Latin language; (*c*) the reconstruction of Indo-European. Candidates must answer questions from two sections.

V.4 *Comparative Philology: Indo-European, Greek and Latin*

The paper will consist of two sections: (*a*) the methods and aims of historical and comparative linguistics, the reconstruction of the Indo-European protolanguage and its development into Latin and Greek (the questions set will require specific competence in one of the two classical languages, but not necessarily both); (*b*) linguistic commentary on passages of Greek or Latin. Candidates must answer questions from both sections.

This subject may not be offered by any candidate who offered the Special Subject *Historical Linguistics and Comparative Philology* in Honour Moderations in Classics or in the Preliminary Examination in Classics.

V.5 *Thesis in Philology and Linguistics*

Any candidate may offer a thesis in Philology and Linguistics in accordance with the Regulation on Theses below. This subject may not be combined with any of I.14, II.199, III.16, or IV.6.

VI. *Second Classical Language*

Second Classical Language is available only in Course II. Candidates offering Second Classical Language who satisfied the Moderators in Course IIA of Honour Moderations in Classics or of Preliminary Examination in Classics must offer VI.1(*a*) and VI.2(*a*). Candidates offering Second Classical Language who satisfied the

Moderators in Course IIB of Honour Moderations in Classics or of Preliminary Examination in Classics must offer VI.1(*b*) and VI.2(*b*). Each subject will be examined in one three-hour paper. In each paper candidates will be required (i) to translate and comment on two passages, one from each of the prescribed texts in the language they offer, and (ii) to translate into English one unseen passage from the language they offer.

VI.1 *Verse*

> *Either* (*a*) Homer, *Iliad* XXIV
> Euripides, *Bacchae*.
> *or* (*b*) Virgil, *Aeneid* VI
> Ovid, *Metamorphoses* VIII.

VI.2 *Prose*

> *Either* (*a*) Plato, *Symposium* 189c-end
> Herodotus I.1–94.
> *or* (*b*) Cicero, *In Catilinam* I, *Pro Archia*
> Seneca, *Epistles* 28, 47, 53, 56, 57, 63, 77, 108, 114, 122.

VII. *Special Theses*

Candidates may offer, but are not required to offer, a Special Thesis in addition to the eight subjects required above, in accordance with the Regulations on Theses below.

Regulation on Theses

1. This regulation governs theses in Ancient History (subject I.14), Literature (III.12), Archaeology (IV.6), Philology and Linguistics (V.5) and Special Thesis (VII), with the exception of Special Theses on subjects relating to Philosophy. For theses in Philosophy (II.199) and Special Theses (VII) on Philosophy subjects, see **Regulations for Philosophy in all Honour Schools including Philosophy.**

2. The subject of every thesis shall, to the satisfaction of the joint Standing Committee for Mods and Greats, fall within the scope of the Honour School of Literae Humaniores. The subject may but need not overlap any subject or period on which the candidate offers papers. Candidates are warned that they should avoid repetition in examination essays of material used in their theses and that substantial repetition may be penalised. Candidates who offer a Special Thesis and another thesis must avoid all overlap between them.

3. Candidates proposing to offer a thesis must submit to the Academic Administrative Officer of the Faculty of Classics, on a form obtainable from the Classics Office which must be countersigned by their tutor and (if different) by their proposed supervisor, the title of the proposed thesis, together with a synopsis of the subject in about 100 words, not later than the Wednesday of the first week of the Michaelmas Full Term preceding the examination. The joint Standing Committee for Mods and Greats shall decide as soon as possible whether or not to approve the title and shall advise the candidate immediately. No decision shall be deferred beyond the end of the third week of Michaelmas Full Term.

4. Every thesis shall be the candidate's own work. Tutors may, however, assist candidates by discussing with them, for example, the field of study, the sources available, bibliography, and the method of presentation, and may also read and comment on drafts. The amount of assistance a candidate may receive shall not exceed an amount equivalent to the teaching of a normal paper. All quotations from primary or secondary sources, and all reporting or appropriation of material from those sources, must be explicitly acknowledged. Each candidate must sign a certificate to the effect that the thesis is the candidate's own work, and that the candidate

has read the Faculty's guidelines on plagiarism. This declaration must be placed in a sealed envelope bearing the candidate's examination number and presented together with the thesis.

5. Theses previously submitted for the Honour School of Literae Humaniores may be resubmitted. No thesis shall be accepted which has already been submitted, wholly or substantially, for another Honour School or degree of this or any other institution, and the certificate shall also state that the thesis has not been so submitted. No thesis shall, however, be ineligible because it has been or is being submitted for any prize of this university.

6. No thesis shall exceed 10,000 words (the limit to include all notes and appendices but not including the bibliography). No person or body shall have authority to permit the limit of 10,000 words to be exceeded, except that, in the case of a commentary on a text and at the discretion of the chair of examiners, any substantial quoting of that text or of any translation of that text need not be included in the word limit. Where appropriate, there shall be a select bibliography and a list of sources.

7. All theses must be typed in double spacing on one side only of A4 paper, with any notes and references at the foot of each page, and must be firmly bound and identified by the candidate's examination number only.

8. Candidates wishing to change the title of their thesis after it has been approved may apply for permission for the change to be granted by the Chair of the Joint Standing Committee for Mods and Greats (if the application is made before the first day of Hilary Full Term preceding the examination) or (if later) the Chair of the Examiners, Honour School of Literae Humaniores.

9. Candidates shall submit two copies of their thesis not later than noon on Friday of the week before the Trinity Full Term of the examination to the Examination Schools, High Street, Oxford, addressed to the Chair of the Examiners, Honour School of Literae Humaniores. At the same time they shall submit a searchable electronic version to the Academic Administrative Officer of the Faculty of Classics. *N.B. For prescribed editions in all forms of the Honour School of Literae Humaniores, see the Greats Handbook*

[UNTIL 1 OCTOBER 2015: SPECIAL REGULATIONS FOR THE HONOUR SCHOOL OF MATERIALS SCIENCE

A

1. The subject of the Honour School of Materials Science shall be the study of Materials Science.

2. No candidate shall be admitted to the examination in this school unless he or she has either passed or been exempted from the First Public Examination.

3. The examination in this school shall be under the supervision of the Mathematical, Physical and Life Sciences Board, which shall prescribe the necessary regulations.

4. The examination in Materials Science shall consist of Part I and Part II, and shall be partly of a practical nature. Candidates will be expected to show knowledge based on practical work: this requirement shall normally be satisfied by the Examiners' assessment of the practical work done by candidates during their course of study.

5. No candidate may present him or herself for examination in Part II unless he or she has been adjudged worthy of Honours by the examiners in Part I.

6. The name of a candidate shall not be published in a class list until he or she has completed all parts of the examination and has been adjudged worthy of Honours by the examiners in Part I and Part II of the examination in consecutive years. The examiners shall give due consideration to the performance in all parts of the respective examinations.

7. The examiners shall be entitled to award a pass to candidates in Part I who have reached a standard considered adequate but who have not been adjudged worthy of Honours.

To achieve Honours at Part I normally a candidate must fulfil all of the requirements under (a), (b) & (c) of this clause. (a) Obtain a minimum mark of 40% averaged over all elements of assessment for the Part I Examination, (b) obtain a minimum mark of 40% in each of at least four of the six written papers sat in Trinity Term of the year of Part I of the Second Public Examination, and (c) satisfy the coursework requirements set out in Section B, Part I below.

8. A candidate who obtains only a pass, or fails to satisfy the examiners, may enter again for Part I of the examination on one, but no more than one, subsequent occasion. Part II shall be entered on one occasion only.

9. A candidate adjudged worthy of Honours in Part I and worthy of Honours in Part II may supplicate for the Degree of Master of Engineering in Materials Science, provided that the candidate has fulfilled all the conditions for admission to a degree of the University.

10. A candidate who passes Part I or who is adjudged worthy of Honours in Part I, but who does not enter Part II, or fails to obtain Honours in Part II, is permitted to supplicate for the degree of Bachelor of Arts in Materials Science (pass or unclassified Honours, as appropriate); provided that no such candidate may later enter or re-enter the Part II year or supplicate for the degree of Master of Engineering in Materials Science; and provided in each case that the candidate has fulfilled all the conditions for admission to a degree of the University.

B

1. In the following, 'the Course Handbook' refers to the Materials Science and Materials, Economics & Management Final Honours School Course Handbook, published annually at the start of Michaelmas Term by the Faculty of Materials and also posted on the website at: http://www.materials.ox.ac.uk/teaching/ug/ughandbooks.html

2. Candidates are restricted to models of calculators included in the Course Handbook published in the academic year preceding the Part I examination.

3. Supplementary subjects or the completion of an approved course of instruction in a foreign language

(*a*) As an alternative to offering Engineering and Society coursework, candidates may either offer themselves for examination in a Supplementary Subject or complete an approved, assessed course of instruction in a foreign language, as permitted under clause 3.(*c*) of the regulations for Materials Science Part I. A candidate who wishes to offer a Supplementary Subject must have the proposal approved by the Chair of the Faculty of Materials or deputy. Where an approved course of instruction in a foreign language is available (including a Supplementary Subject in a foreign language), entry of candidates for such examinations shall require the approval of the Chair of the Faculty of Materials and the Director of the Language Centre or their deputies. Approval shall not be given to candidates who have, at the start of the course, already acquired demonstrable skills exceeding the target learning outcomes in the chosen language.

(*b*) Candidates for Supplementary Subjects or a Foreign Language course may offer themselves for examination in the academic year preceding that in which they take Part I.

(*c*) The Supplementary Subjects available in any year will be published, together with the term in which each subject will be examined, in the Course Handbook in the academic year in which the courses are delivered. Regulations governing the use of calculators in individual Supplementary Subjects will be notified when the availability of these subjects is published in the Course Handbook.

PART I

The examination will consist of:

1. Four general papers of three hours each on the fundamental principles and engineering applications of the subject in accordance with the schedule below. The questions set in these papers will be normally such that candidates may reasonably be expected to answer a high proportion of them.

2. Two options papers, each of three hours, containing a wide choice of questions in accordance with the schedule below.

3. In addition to the written papers, the Examiners shall require evidence of satisfactory completion, over a period of five terms subsequent to the sitting of the First Public Examination, of each element of coursework in Materials, as detailed below. In the assessment of the Materials coursework, the Examiners shall take into consideration the requirement for a candidate to complete satisfactorily the coursework to a level prescribed from time to time by the Faculty of Materials and published in the Course Handbook. The coursework elements shall be:

(*a*) *Materials Practical Classes*

Candidates shall be required to submit detailed reports of the practical work completed over a period of three terms subsequent to the sitting of the First Public Examination. Such reports should be delivered to the Chair of the Examiners in the Honour School of Materials Science, Part I, c/o the Deputy Administrator (Academic) in the Department of Materials (or their deputy as nominated in the Course handbook), not later than 5 p.m. on Friday of the first week of Michaelmas Full Term in the year of the Second Public Examination. The Examiners shall have the power to require a practical examination of any candidate or to require further evidence, of any kind that they deem appropriate, of a candidate's practical work and ability.

(*b*) *Reports on Industrial Visits*

Candidates shall be required to submit to the Department (to the person specified in the Course Handbook) reports on a number of industrial visits undertaken over a period of five terms subsequent to the sitting of the First Public Examination. The required number of visits, types of visits allowed, the nature of the reports, and deadlines for submission shall be specified in the Course Handbook.

(*c*) *Engineering and Society Coursework*

Candidates shall be required to submit one piece of Engineering and Society Coursework, the details of which shall be stated in the Course Handbook. Three copies of the coursework shall be submitted to the Chair of Examiners in Materials, c/o Examination Schools, High Street, Oxford, not later than noon on the Monday following the end of Hilary Full Term in the year preceding the Part I examination. The work must be the candidate's own and the candidate shall sign and present with the work a detachable certificate to this effect.

As an alternative to offering Engineering and Society coursework, candidates may either offer themselves for examination in a Supplementary Subject or complete an approved, assessed course of instruction in a foreign language.

(*d*) *Team Design Project*

Candidates shall be required to complete a team design project in the first two weeks of Michaelmas Full Term in the year of the Second Public Examination, and subsequently (i) to submit to the Department (to the person specified in the Course Handbook) three copies of a report on the project and (ii) to deliver to the Examiners an oral presentation on the project, both as detailed in the Course Handbook. The work must be the candidate's own and the candidate shall sign and present with the written report a detachable certificate to that effect.

(*e*) *Characterisation of Materials Coursework or Introduction to Modelling in Materials Coursework*

Candidates shall be required to complete **either** a Characterisation of Materials course **or** an Introduction to Modelling in Materials course in the first two weeks of Hilary Full Term in the year of the Second Public Examination, and subsequently to submit to the Department (to the person specified in the Course Handbook) three copies of a portfolio of work from the course, as detailed in the Course Handbook. The work must be the candidate's own and the candidate shall sign and present with the written report a detachable certificate to that effect.

Essays or reports previously submitted for the Honour School of Materials Science may be resubmitted. No essay or report will be accepted if it has already been submitted wholly or substantially for another honour school or degree of this University, or for a degree at any other institution. Resubmitted work must be physically presented at the time and in the manner prescribed for submission.

Schedule

(*a*) *General papers*

All candidates will be expected to have such knowledge of mathematics as is required for the study of the subjects of the examination.

General Paper 1: Structure and Transformations
General Paper 2: Electronic Properties of Materials
General Paper 3: Mechanical Properties
General Paper 4: Engineering Applications of Materials

(*b*) *Materials Options Papers 1 and 2*

The subjects for these papers will be published annually in the Course Handbook.

PART II

Candidates offering Part II of the examination will be expected to carry out investigations in Materials Science or in related subjects under the supervision of one of the following:

(i) any professor who is a member of one of the Faculties in the Physical Sciences;

(ii) a reader or university lecturer or senior research officer who is a member of one of the Faculties of Physical Sciences;

(iii) a tutor or lecturer in any society who is a member of one of the Faculties of Physical Sciences;

(iv) any other person listed in a Register of Part II Supervisors to be maintained by the Faculty of Materials.

Each candidate shall be examined viva voce, and, if the examiners think fit, in writing, on the subject of his or her work and on matters relevant thereto. The Examiners shall obtain a report on the work of each candidate from the supervisor concerned.

A candidate intending to offer Part II shall give notice to the Registrar not later than Friday in the fourth week of Michaelmas Full Term in the year in which he or she satisfied the examiners in Part I. Such notice must be given on a form to be obtained from the Registrar, University Offices.

Every candidate for Part II is required to submit three copies of a report on the investigations which he or she has carried out under the direction of his or her supervisor. The report on the investigations shall also include an abstract, a literature survey, a brief account of the project management aspects of the investigation, and a description of the engineering context of the investigation and should be accompanied by a signed statement by the candidate that it is his or her own work. The copies should be handed in to the Chair of the Examiners in the Honour School of Materials

Science, Part II, c/o Examination Schools, High Street, Oxford, not later than noon on the Wednesday of the seventh week of Trinity Full Term. The report shall be word-processed or typewritten on A4 paper (within a page area of 247 mm x 160 mm, using double line-spaced type of at least 11pt font size, printed on one side only of each sheet, with a left hand margin of at least 30mm) and presented in a binder. The main report should not normally exceed **12,000 words** together with a maximum of a further **1,500** words for the reflective account of the project management aspects of the investigation that must be included in the final chapter. These word counts exclude references, title page, acknowledgements, table of contents and the three Project Management Forms. All other text is included in the word count, including the abstract and the figure captions. Additionally, the main report should not normally exceed **100 pages** in length (including an abstract, the text as defined above for the word limits, the three Project Management Forms, computer programs, graphs, diagrams, photographs, tables, and similar material). All pages of the report should be numbered sequentially. The report must be accompanied by a signed declaration that it is within the allowed word and page limits. Candidates seeking permission to exceed the word and/or page limits should apply to the Chair of Examiners at an early stage. Further detailed data, computer programs and similar material may be included in one or more appendices at the end of the main report, but appendices are not included within the limits of the word or page counts of the thesis and, entirely at the discretion of the Examiners for each report, may or may not be read.

Candidates for Part II will be required to keep statutory residence and pursue their investigations at Oxford during a period of thirty-seven weeks between the dates specified below, except that the Divisional Board of Mathematical, Physical and Life Sciences shall have power to permit candidates to vary the period of their residence so long as the overall programme requirement is met. The divisional board may, on the recommendation of the Department of Materials, permit candidates to carry out their investigations for the required period at an approved institution outside Oxford; the board shall determine the conditions upon which applications for such permission may be approved and will require to be satisfied in each case (*a*) that adequate arrangements are made for the candidate's supervision and (*b*) that the proposals for the investigations are agreed in advance between the Department of Materials and the host institution.

Periods of required residence for Part II

From the fifth Friday before to the first Saturday following Michaelmas Full Term.

From the second Friday before Hilary Full Term to the Saturday before Palm Sunday.

From the Friday following Easter to the second Saturday following Trinity Full Term.]

[FROM 1 OCTOBER 2015: SPECIAL REGULATIONS FOR THE HONOUR SCHOOL OF MATERIALS SCIENCE

*New Regulations for candidates who embark on the
Final Honour School on or after 1st October 2015*

A

1. The subject of the Honour School of Materials Science shall be the study of Materials Science.

2. No candidate shall be admitted to the examination in this school unless he or she has either passed or been exempted from the First Public Examination.

3. The examination in this school shall be under the supervision of the Mathematical, Physical and Life Sciences Board, which shall prescribe the necessary regulations.

4. A candidate registered on the four year Master of Engineering in Materials Science degree programme is permitted, at a date no later than Friday of the 3rd week of Michaelmas Term in the year of Part I of the Second Public Examination, to transfer to the three year Bachelor of Arts in Materials Science Programme, provided no such candidate may later enter the Part II year or supplicate for the degree of Master of Engineering in Materials Science.

5. Following Friday of the 3rd week of Michaelmas Term in the year of Part I of the Second Public Examination a candidate registered on the four year Master of Engineering in Materials Science degree programme is permitted, at a date no later than Friday of the 8th week of Trinity Term in the year of Part I of the Second Public Examination, to transfer to the three year Bachelor of Arts in Materials Science Programme, provided no such candidate may later enter the Part II year or supplicate for the degree of Master of Engineering in Materials Science. In such cases the candidate will complete the Part I Examination as specified for the Master of Engineering programme and will in addition be required to complete during a specified period of the Long Vacation immediately following Trinity Term of the year of Part I of the Second Public Examination the extended essay specified in the programme for the degree of Bachelor of Arts in Materials Science. The Examiners will consider the outcome for such a candidate at the classification

meeting held soon after the end of Trinity full term in the year following that of Part I of the Second Public Examination.

6. The examination for the Master of Engineering degree in Materials Science shall consist of Part I and Part II, and shall be partly of a practical nature. Candidates will be expected to show knowledge based on practical work: normally this requirement shall be satisfied by the Examiners' assessment of the practical work done by candidates during their course of study.

7. The examination for the Bachelor of Arts degree in Materials Science shall consist of one Part only, and shall be partly of a practical nature. Candidates will be expected to show knowledge based on practical work: normally this requirement shall be satisfied by the Examiners' assessment of the practical work done by candidates during their course of study.

8. No candidate for the degree of Master of Engineering in Materials Science may present him or herself for examination in Part II unless he or she has (a) been adjudged worthy of Honours by the examiners in Part I and (b) normally obtained a minimum mark of 50% averaged over all elements of assessment for the Part I Examination.

9. The name of a candidate for the degree of Master of Engineering in Materials Science shall not be published in a class list until he or she has completed all parts of the examination and has been adjudged worthy of Honours by the examiners in Part I and Part II of the examination in consecutive years. The examiners shall give due consideration to the performance in all elements of the respective examinations.

10. The name of a candidate for the degree of Bachelor of Arts in Materials Science shall not be published in a class list until he or she has completed the examination and has been adjudged worthy of Honours by the examiners. The examiners shall give due consideration to the performance in all elements of the examination.

11. For candidates for the degree of Master of Engineering in Materials Science the examiners shall be entitled to award (i) unclassified Honours to candidates in Part I who have been adjudged worthy of Honours but have obtained a mark of less than 50% averaged over all elements of assessment for the Part I Examination or (ii) a pass to candidates in Part I who have reached a standard considered adequate but who have not been adjudged worthy of Honours. To achieve Honours at Part I normally a candidate must fulfil all of the requirements under (a), (b) & (c) of this clause. (a) Obtain a minimum mark of 40% averaged over all elements of

assessment for the Part I Examination, (b) obtain a minimum mark of 40% in each of at least four of the six written papers sat in Trinity Term of the year of Part I of the Second Public Examination, and (c) satisfy the coursework requirements set out in Section B, Part I below.

12. For candidates for the degree of Bachelor of Arts in Materials Science the examiners shall be entitled to award a pass to candidates who have reached a standard considered adequate but who have not been adjudged worthy of Honours. To achieve Honours normally a candidate must fulfil all of the requirements under (a), (b) & (c) of this clause. (a) Obtain a minimum mark of 40% averaged over all elements of assessment for the Examination, (b) obtain a minimum mark of 40% in each of at least four of the six written papers sat in Trinity Term of the year of the Second Public Examination, and (c) satisfy the coursework requirements set out in Section B, below.

13. A candidate for the degree of Master of Engineering in Materials Science who obtains a mark of less than 50% averaged over all elements of assessment for the Part I Examination or who fails to satisfy the examiners may enter again for the whole of Part I of the examination on one, but no more than one, subsequent occasion. Normally (i) this subsequent occasion shall be during the academic year immediately following the first decision of the examiners and (ii) the examination will be identical to that taken by the other Part I candidates in said academic year. A candidate who is adjudged worthy of Honours and obtains a mark of 50% or more averaged over all elements of assessment on the occasion of this resit may progress to Part II in the academic year following that of the resit examination; such a candidate will carry forward a Part I mark of 50% only. Part II shall be entered on one occasion only.

14. A candidate for the degree of Bachelor of Arts in Materials Science who obtains only a pass, or fails to satisfy the examiners may enter again for the examination on one, but no more than one, subsequent occasion. Normally (i) this subsequent occasion shall be during the academic year immediately following the first decision of the examiners and (ii) the examination will be identical to that taken by the other candidates for the BA in Materials Science in said academic year. The examiners shall be entitled to award a 3rd class Honours classification to a candidate who is adjudged worthy of Honours and obtains a mark of 40% or more averaged over all elements of assessment on the occasion of this resit. The examiners shall be entitled to award a Pass to a candidate who has reached a

standard considered adequate but who has not been adjudged worthy of Honours on the occasion of this resit.

15. A candidate for the degree of Master of Engineering in Materials Science adjudged worthy of Honours in Part I and worthy of Honours in Part II may supplicate for the Degree of Master of Engineering in Materials Science, provided that the candidate has fulfilled all the conditions for admission to a degree of the University.

16. A candidate for the degree of Bachelor of Arts in Materials Science adjudged worthy of Honours may supplicate for the Degree of Bachelor of Arts in Material Science, provided that the candidate has fulfilled all the conditions for admission to a degree of the University.

17. A candidate for the degree of Master of Engineering in Materials Science who fails to obtain Honours in Part II, or who is adjudged worthy of Honours in Part I and who obtains a minimum mark of 50% averaged over all elements of assessment for the Part I Examination but who does not enter Part II, or who is adjudged worthy of Honours in Part I but who obtains a mark of less than 50% averaged over all elements of assessment for the Part I Examination, or who passes Part I is permitted to supplicate for the degree of Bachelor of Arts in Materials Science (unclassified Honours or pass, as appropriate); provided that no such candidate may later enter or re-enter the Part II year or supplicate for the degree of Master of Engineering in Materials Science or supplicate for the degree of Bachelor of Arts in Materials Science (classified Honours); and provided in each case that the candidate has fulfilled all the conditions for admission to a degree of the University.

18. A candidate for the degree of Bachelor of Arts in Materials Science who passes the second public examination but is not adjudged worthy of Honours is permitted to supplicate for the degree of Bachelor of Arts in Materials Science (pass); provided that no such candidate may later supplicate for the degree of Bachelor of Arts (classified or unclassified honours) in Materials Science; and provided in each case that the candidate has fulfilled all the conditions for admission to a degree of the University.

B

1. In the following, 'the Course Handbook' refers to the Materials Science and Materials, Economics & Management Final Honours School Course Handbook, published annually at the start of Michaelmas Term by the Faculty of Materials and also posted on the website at: http://www.materials.ox.ac.uk/teaching/ug/ughandbooks.html

2. Candidates are restricted to models of calculators included in the Course Handbook published in the academic year preceding either Part I of the Second Public Examination for the degree of Master of Engineering in Materials Science or the Second Public Examination for the degree of Bachelor of Arts in Materials Science.

3. Supplementary subjects or the completion of an approved course of instruction in a foreign language

(*a*) As an alternative to offering Engineering and Society coursework, candidates may either offer themselves for examination in a Supplementary Subject or complete an approved, assessed course of instruction in a foreign language, as permitted under clause 3.(*c*) of the regulations for Materials Science Part I. A candidate who wishes to offer a Supplementary Subject must have the proposal approved by the Chair of the Faculty of Materials or deputy. Where an approved course of instruction in a foreign language is available (including a Supplementary Subject in a foreign language), entry of candidates for such examinations shall require the approval of the Chair of the Faculty of Materials and the Director of the Language Centre or their deputies. Approval shall not be given to candidates who have, at the start of the course, already acquired demonstrable skills exceeding the target learning outcomes in the chosen language.

(*b*) Candidates for Supplementary Subjects or a Foreign Language course may offer themselves for examination in the academic year preceding that in which they take either Part I of the Second Public Examination for the degree of Master of Engineering in Materials Science or the Second Public Examination for the degree of Bachelor of Arts in Materials Science.

(*c*) The Supplementary Subjects available in any year will be published, together with the term in which each subject will be examined, in the Course Handbook in the academic year in which the courses are delivered. Regulations governing the use of calculators in individual Supplementary Subjects will be notified when the availability of these subjects is published in the Course Handbook.

PART I OF THE EXAMINATION FOR THE DEGREE OF MASTER OF ENGINEERING IN MATERIALS SCIENCE

The examination will consist of:

1. Four general papers of three hours each on the fundamental principles and engineering applications of the subject in accordance with the schedule below. The questions set in these papers will be normally such that candidates may reasonably be expected to answer a high proportion of them.

2. Two Materials Options papers, each of three hours, containing a wide choice of questions in accordance with the schedule below.

3. In addition to the written papers, the Examiners shall require evidence of satisfactory completion, over a period of five terms subsequent to the sitting of the First Public Examination, of each element of coursework in Materials, as detailed below. In the assessment of the Materials coursework, the Examiners shall take into consideration the requirement for a candidate to complete satisfactorily the coursework to a level prescribed from time to time by the Faculty of Materials and published in the Course Handbook. Failure of the coursework will normally constitute failure of Part I of the Second Public Examination. The coursework elements shall be:

(*a*) *Materials Practical Classes*

Candidates shall be required to submit detailed reports of the practical work completed over a period of three terms subsequent to the sitting of the First Public Examination. Such reports should be delivered to the Chair of the Examiners in the Honour School of Materials Science, c/o the Deputy Administrator (Academic) in the Department of Materials (or their deputy as nominated in the Course handbook), not later than 5 p.m. on Friday of the first week of Michaelmas Full Term in the year of the Second Public Examination. The Examiners shall have the power to require a practical examination of any candidate or to require further evidence, of any kind that they deem appropriate, of a candidate's practical work and ability.

(*b*) *Reports on Industrial Visits*

Candidates shall be required to submit to the Department (to the person specified in the Course Handbook) reports on a number of industrial visits normally undertaken over a period of five terms subsequent to the sitting of the First Public Examination. The required number of visits, types of visits allowed, the nature of the reports, and deadlines for submission shall be specified in the Course Handbook.

(*c*) *Engineering and Society Coursework*

Candidates shall be required to submit one piece of Engineering and Society Coursework, the details of which shall be stated in the Course Handbook. Three copies of the coursework shall be submitted to the Chair of Examiners in Materials, c/o Examination Schools, High Street, Oxford, not later than noon on the Monday following the end of Hilary Full Term in the year preceding the Part I examination. The work must be the candidate's own and the candidate shall sign and present with the work a detachable certificate to this effect.

As an alternative to offering Engineering and Society coursework, candidates may either offer themselves for examination in a Supplementary Subject or complete an approved, assessed course of instruction in a foreign language.

(*d*) *Team Design Project*

Candidates shall be required to complete a team design project in the first two weeks of Michaelmas Full Term in the year of the Second Public Examination, and subsequently (i) to submit to the Department (to the person specified in the Course Handbook) three copies of a report on the project and (ii) to deliver to the Examiners an oral presentation on the project, both as detailed in the Course Handbook. The work must be the candidate's own and the candidate shall sign and present with the written report a detachable certificate to that effect.

(*e*) *Characterisation of Materials Coursework or Introduction to Modelling in Materials Coursework*

Candidates shall be required to complete **either** a Characterisation of Materials course **or** an Introduction to Modelling in Materials course in the first two weeks of Hilary Full Term in the year of the Second Public Examination, and subsequently to submit to the Department (to the person specified in the Course Handbook) three copies of a portfolio of work from the course, as detailed in the Course Handbook. The work must be the candidate's own and the candidate shall sign and present with the written report a detachable certificate to that effect.

Essays or reports previously submitted for the Honour School of Materials Science may be resubmitted. No essay or report will be accepted if it has already been submitted wholly or substantially for another honour school or degree of this University, or for a degree at any other institution. Resubmitted work must be physically presented at the time and in the manner prescribed for submission.

EXAMINATION FOR THE DEGREE OF BACHELOR OF ARTS
IN MATERIALS SCIENCE

For a candidate under clause (4) of Part A of the special regulations for the Honour School of Materials Science the examination will consist of:

All elements described in clauses one, two and three under PART I of the Examination for the degree of Master of Engineering in Materials Science, excepting that:

1. The two Materials Options papers of clause two will be each of 1.5 hours duration.
2. An additional element of coursework is included under clause three:
   (*f*) *An Extended Essay on an approved topic in Materials Science*

Candidates shall be required to complete an extended essay, as detailed in the Course Handbook, in the year of the Second Public Examination, under the guidance of an advisor appointed by the Chair of Faculty or his/her deputy. Every candidate is required to submit three copies of their essay. The Examiners shall obtain a report on the work of each candidate from the advisor concerned. The essay shall also include an abstract and should be accompanied by a signed statement by the candidate that it is his or her own work. The copies should be handed in to the Chair of the Examiners in the Honour School of Materials Science, c/o Examination Schools, High Street, Oxford, not later than noon on the second Friday following the end of Hilary Full Term. The essay shall be word-processed or typewritten on A4 paper (within a page area of 247 mm x 160 mm, using double line-spaced type of at least 11pt font size, printed on one side only of each sheet, with a left hand margin of at least 30mm) and presented in a binder. The essay should not exceed 4,000 words. This word count excludes references, title page, acknowledgements and table of contents. All other text is included in the word count, including the abstract and the figure captions.

Essays or reports previously submitted for the Honour School of Materials Science may be resubmitted. No essay or report will be accepted if it has already been submitted wholly or substantially for another honour school or degree of this University, or for a degree at any other institution. Resubmitted work must be physically presented at the time and in the manner prescribed for submission.

For a candidate under clause (5) of Part A of the special regulations for the Honour School of Materials Science the examination will consist of:

All elements described in clauses one, two and three under PART I of the Examination for the degree of Master of Engineering in Materials Science, excepting that:

1. An additional element of coursework is included under clause three:
   (*f*) *An Extended Essay on an approved topic in Materials Science*

As for a candidate under clause (4) of Part A of the special regulations for the Honour School of Materials Science excepting that, as specified in the Course Handbook, (i) candidates shall be required to complete the extended essay during the Long Vacation immediately following the year of the Second Public Examination and (ii) submission to the Chair of the Examiners in the Honour School of Materials Science, c/o Examination Schools, High Street, Oxford, shall be no later than noon on a day to be specified by the Chair of Faculty or his/her deputy and in any case shall be no later than the last Friday of the Long Vacation immediately following the year of the Second Public Examination.

Schedule

(a) *General papers*

All candidates will be expected to have such knowledge of mathematics as is required for the study of the subjects of the examination.

General Paper 1: Structure and Transformations   5
General Paper 2: Electronic Properties of Materials
General Paper 3: Mechanical Properties
General Paper 4: Engineering Applications of Materials

(b) *Materials Options Papers 1 and 2*

The subjects for these papers will be published annually in the Course   10
Handbook.

PART II OF THE EXAMINATION FOR THE DEGREE OF MASTER
OF ENGINEERING IN MATERIALS SCIENCE

Candidates offering Part II of the examination will be expected to carry out investigations in Materials Science or in related subjects under the supervision of one of the   15
following:
  (i) any professor who is a member of one of the Faculties in the Physical Sciences;
  (ii) a reader or university lecturer or senior research officer who is a member of
        one of the Faculties of Physical Sciences;
  (iii) a tutor or lecturer in any society who is a member of one of the Faculties of   20
        Physical Sciences;
  (iv) any other person listed in a Register of Part II Supervisors to be maintained by
        the Faculty of Materials.

Each candidate shall be examined viva voce, and, if the examiners think fit, in
writing, on the subject of his or her work and on matters relevant thereto. The   25
Examiners shall obtain a report on the work of each candidate from the supervisor
concerned.

A candidate intending to offer Part II shall give notice to the Registrar not later
than Friday in the fourth week of Michaelmas Full Term in the year in which he or
she satisfied the examiners in Part I. Such notice must be given on a form to be   30
obtained from the Registrar, University Offices.

Every candidate for Part II is required to submit three copies of a report on the
investigations which he or she has carried out under the direction of his or her
supervisor. The report on the investigations shall also include an abstract, a literature
survey, a brief account of the project management aspects of the investigation, and a   35
description of the engineering context of the investigation and should be accompanied by a signed statement by the candidate that it is his or her own work. The copies
should be handed in to the Chair of the Examiners in the Honour School of Materials
Science, Part II, c/o Examination Schools, High Street, Oxford, not later than noon
on the Wednesday of the seventh week of Trinity Full Term. The report shall be   40
word-processed or typewritten on A4 paper (within a page area of 247 mm x 160 mm,
using double line-spaced type of at least 11pt font size, printed on one side only of
each sheet, with a left hand margin of at least 30mm) and presented in a binder. The
main report should not normally exceed **12,000 words** together with a maximum of a
further **1,500** words for the reflective account of the project management aspects of   45
the investigation that must be included in the final chapter. These word counts
exclude references, title page, acknowledgements, table of contents and the three
Project Management Forms. All other text is included in the word count, including
the abstract and the figure captions. Additionally, the main report should not
normally exceed **100 pages** in length (including an abstract, the text as defined   50

above for the word limits, the three Project Management Forms, computer programs, graphs, diagrams, photographs, tables, and similar material). All pages of the report should be numbered sequentially. The report must be accompanied by a signed declaration that it is within the allowed word and page limits. Candidates seeking permission to exceed the word and/or page limits should apply to the Chair of 5 Examiners at an early stage. Further detailed data, computer programs and similar material may be included in one or more appendices at the end of the main report, but appendices are not included within the limits of the word or page counts of the thesis and, entirely at the discretion of the Examiners for each report, may or may not be read. 10

Candidates for Part II will be required to keep statutory residence and pursue their investigations at Oxford during a period of thirty-seven weeks between the dates specified below, except that the Divisional Board of Mathematical, Physical and Life Sciences shall have power to permit candidates to vary the period of their residence so long as the overall programme requirement is met. The divisional board may, on the 15 recommendation of the Department of Materials, permit candidates to carry out their investigations for the required period at an approved institution outside Oxford; the board shall determine the conditions upon which applications for such permission may be approved and will require to be satisfied in each case (*a*) that adequate arrangements are made for the candidate's supervision and (*b*) that the proposals 20 for the investigations are agreed in advance between the Department of Materials and the host institution.

Periods of required residence for Part II

From the fifth Friday before to the first Saturday following Michaelmas Full Term.
From the second Friday before Hilary Full Term to the Saturday before Palm 25 Sunday.
From the Friday following Easter to the second Saturday following Trinity Full Term.]

SPECIAL REGULATIONS FOR THE HONOUR SCHOOL OF MATERIALS, ECONOMICS, AND MANAGEMENT

A

1. The subjects of the Honour School shall be (*a*) Materials, (*b*) Economics, and (*c*) Management.

2. All candidates must offer (*a*), (*b*), and (*c*). The examination in all three subjects may be partly practical.

3. No candidate shall be admitted to examination in this school unless he or she has either passed or been exempted from the First Public Examination.

4. The examination in this school shall be under the joint supervision of the Mathematical, Physical and Life Sciences Board and the Social Sciences Board. The standing joint committee set up in accordance with the sub-section relating to the Honour School of Engineering, Economics, and Management shall have power to make regulations concerning this school, subject always to the preceding clauses of this sub-section.

5. The examination shall consist of Part I and Part II. In both parts candidates shall be examined in the subjects prescribed by the committee set up in accordance with the provisions of clause 4 above. In Part II candidates shall also present, as part of the examination, a report on either a project carried out during a period of attachment to an industrial firm, or an industrially-related internal university project.

6. The name of a candidate in this school shall not be published in a class list unless he or she has been adjudged worthy of Honours by the examiners in Part I and in Part II of the respective examinations in consecutive years, and no candidate may present himself or herself for examination in Part II unless he or she has been adjudged worthy of Honours by the examiners in Part I.

7. The examiners shall be entitled to award a pass to candidates in Part I who have reached a standard considered adequate but who have not been adjudged worthy of Honours. To achieve Honours at Part I normally a candidate must fulfil all of the

requirements under (a), (b) & (c) of this clause. (a) Obtain a minimum mark of 40% averaged over all elements of assessment for the Part I Examination, (b) obtain a minimum mark of 40% in each of at least four of the six written papers sat in Trinity Term of the year of Part I of the Second Public Examination, and (c) 5
satisfy the coursework requirements set out in Section B, Part I below.

8. A candidate who obtains only a pass, or fails to satisfy the examiners, may enter again for Part I of the examination on one, but no more than one, subsequent occasion. Part II shall be entered 10
on one occasion only.

9. A candidate adjudged worthy of Honours in Part I and Part II may supplicate for the Degree of Master of Engineering in Materials, Economics, and Management provided that the candidate has fulfilled all the conditions for admission to a degree of the 15
University.

10. A candidate who passes Part I or who is adjudged worthy of Honours in Part I, but who does not enter Part II, or fails to obtain Honours in Part II, is permitted to supplicate for the degree of Bachelor of Arts in Materials, Economics, and Management (pass 20
or unclassified Honours, as appropriate); provided that no such candidate may later enter or re-enter the Part II year or supplicate for the degree of Master of Engineering in Materials, Economics, and Management; and provided in each case that the candidate has fulfilled all the conditions for admission to a degree of the 25
University.

11. The examiners for Materials shall be appointed by the committee for the nomination of Public Examiners in Materials Science in the Honour School of Materials; those for Economics shall be appointed by the committee for the nomination of examiners in 30
Economics in the Honour School of Philosophy, Politics, and Economics; those for Management shall be appointed by the committee for the nomination of examiners in Management Studies for the Degree of Master of Philosophy.

B 35

In the following, 'the Course Handbook' refers to the Materials Science and Materials, Economics & Management Final Honours School Course Handbook, published annually at the start of Michaelmas Term by the Faculty of Materials and also posted on the website at http://www.materials.ox.ac.uk/teaching/ug/ ughandbooks.html 40

PART I

Candidates will be required to take seven papers as follows:

(*a*) *Materials*

The four general papers of three hours each on the fundamental principles and engineering applications of the subject as specified for Part I of the Honour School of Materials Science.

(*b*) *Economics*

Two papers: Ec1—Introductory Economics (as specified in the regulation relating to the Introductory Economics paper of the Economics and Management Preliminary Examination). Microeconomics (as specified for the Honour School of Philosophy, Politics, and Economics).

(*c*) *Management*

One paper: M1—General Management (as specified in the regulation relating to the General Management paper of the Economics and Management Preliminary Examination).

Candidates will take paper Ec1 in the third term after passing the First Public Examination and the remaining papers in the sixth term after passing the First Public Examination.

For all written papers, candidates are restricted to models of hand-held calculators as specified for the Honour School of Materials and published in the Course Handbook.

In addition to the written papers, the Examiners shall require evidence of satisfactory completion, over a period of five terms subsequent to the sitting of the First Public Examination, of each element of coursework in Materials, as detailed below. In the assessment of the Materials coursework, the Examiners shall take into consideration the requirement for a candidate to complete satisfactorily the coursework to a level prescribed from time to time by the Faculty of Materials and published in the Course Handbook.

The coursework elements shall be:

(*a*) *Materials Practical Classes*

Candidates shall be required to submit detailed reports of the practical work completed over a period of five terms subsequent to the sitting of the First Public Examination. Such reports should be handed in to the Chair of the Examiners in the Honour School of Materials Science, Part I, c/o the Deputy Administrator (Academic) in the Department of Materials (or their deputy as nominated in the Course handbook), not later than 5 p.m. on Friday of the first week of Trinity Full Term in the year of the Second Public Examination. The Examiners shall have the power to require a practical examination of any candidate or to require further evidence, of any kind that they deem appropriate, of a candidate's practical work and ability.

(*b*) *Reports on Industrial Visits*

Candidates shall be required to submit to the Department (to the person specified in the Course Handbook) reports on a number of industrial visits undertaken over a period of five terms subsequent to the sitting of the First Public Examination. The required number of visits, types of visits allowed, the nature of the reports, and deadlines for submission shall be specified in the Course Handbook.

(*c*) *Team Design Project*

Candidates shall be required to complete a team design project in the first two weeks of Michaelmas Full Term in the year of the Second Public Examination, and subsequently (i) to submit to the Department (to the person specified in the Course Handbook) three copies of a report on the project and (ii) to deliver to the Examiners an oral presentation on the project, both as detailed in the Course Handbook. The work must be the candidate's own and the candidate shall sign and present with the written report a detachable certificate to that effect.

Reports previously submitted for the Honour School of Materials, Economics and Management may be resubmitted. No report will be accepted if it has already been submitted wholly or substantially for another honour school or degree of this University, or for a degree at any other institution. Resubmitted work must be physically presented at the time and in the manner prescribed for submission.

Schedule
Part II

Candidates will be required to present a report on either a project carried out during a twenty-four week period of attachment to an industrial firm, or an industrially-related university project, and to take two papers. One paper must be from (*a*), and the other may be from (*b*) or (*c*). The papers are described as:

(*a*) *Materials*

Materials Options Paper 2, as specified for Part I of the Honour School of Materials Science. The subjects for this paper will be published annually in the Course Handbook.

(*b*) *Economics*
(*c*) *Management*
Optional papers:

The list from which papers in (b) may be selected shall be published annually by the Faculty of Economics no later than the end of Trinity Full Term of the academic year preceding the Part II examination. The list from which papers in (c) may be selected shall be published annually by the Faculty of Management Studies no later than the end of Trinity Full Term of the academic year preceding the Part II examination.

The regulations on the use of calculators in Part I also apply in Part II.

Candidates will be required to undertake either a twenty-four week period attached to an industrial firm, or a twenty-four week internal university project. The former will be undertaken between the end of the Trinity Full Term in the year in which the Part I examination is held and the beginning of Hilary Full Term in the year in which the Part II examination is held. The latter will run from the beginning of Michaelmas Term to the beginning of Trinity Term in the year in which the Part II examination is held. Candidates will be required to present, as part of the Part II examination, a report on a project carried out during this period under the supervision of a person approved by the standing committee for the school.

The industrial or industrially-related attachment and project required for the course will normally be arranged by, and must be approved by, the Management Project Co-ordinator.

The report shall not exceed 20,000 words.

Two copies of External project reports must be submitted by noon on the Friday of the week before the start of Hilary Full Term in the year following the year in which the Part I examination is held. Two copies of Internal project reports must be submitted by noon on Friday of the fourth week of Trinity Term of that year. Reports must be addressed 'Examination Schools, High Street, Oxford, OX1 4BG, for the Chair of the Examiners in the Honour School of Materials, Economics, and Management', and should be accompanied by a signed statement by the candidate that it is his or her own work. Successful candidates will be required to deposit one copy of the report in the library of the Department of Materials and the other in the library of the Business School. Project reports previously submitted for the Honour School of Materials, Economics, and Management may be resubmitted. No project report will be accepted if it has already been submitted, wholly or substantially, for another Honour School or degree of this University, or for a degree of any other institution.

Periods of required residence in addition to full term

For the purpose of sitting the written examination paper Ec1 – Introductory Economics. In the academic year preceding Part I of the Second Public Examination, from the first Monday following Trinity Full Term to the first Saturday following Trinity Full Term.

For the purpose of sitting the written examination paper General Management. In the academic year of Part I of the Second Public Examination, from the first Monday following Trinity Full Term to the first Saturday following Trinity Full Term.

Candidates undertaking management projects will be required to keep statutory residence for workshops, as specified by the Course Director, in the year in which the Part I examination is taken in order to prepare for the projects to be carried out as part of the Part II examination.

SPECIAL REGULATIONS FOR THE HONOUR SCHOOL OF MATHEMATICS

A

In the following 'the Course Handbook' refers to the Mathematics Undergraduate Handbook and supplements to this published by the Mathematics Teaching Committee and also posted on the website at: http://www.maths.ox.ac.uk/current-students/undergraduates/handbooks-synopses.

1. The subject of the Honour School of Mathematics shall be Mathematics, its applications and related subjects.

2. No candidate shall be admitted to examination in this School unless he or she has either passed or been exempted from the First Public Examination.

3. The Examination in Mathematics shall be under the supervision of the Mathematical, Physical and Life Sciences Board. The Board shall have the power, subject to this decree, from time to time to frame and vary regulations for the different parts and subjects of the examination.

4. (*a*) The examination in Mathematics shall consist of three parts (A, B, C) for the four-year course, and of two parts (A, B) for the three-year course.

   (*b*) Parts A, B, and C shall be taken at times not less than three, six, and nine terms, respectively, after passing or being exempted from the First Public Examination.

5. The Examiners shall classify and publish the combined results of the examinations in Part A and Part B, and in respect of candidates taking the four-year course shall separately classify and publish results in Part C.

6. (*a*) Part A shall be taken on one occasion only. No candidate shall enter for Part B until he or she has completed Part A of the examination.

   (*b*) In order to proceed to Part C, a candidate must achieve upper second class Honours or higher in Parts A and B together.

   (*c*) A candidate on the three-year course who obtains only a Pass or fails to satisfy the Examiners in Part B may retake Part B on at most one subsequent occasion; a candidate on the four-year course who fails to satisfy the Examiners in Part C may retake Part C on at most one subsequent occasion. A candidate on the four-year course shall take Part B on one occasion only.

7. A candidate adjudged worthy of Honours on both Parts A and B together, and on Part C may supplicate for the degree of Master of Mathematics provided that the candidate has fulfilled all the conditions for admission to a degree of the University.

8. A candidate in the final year of the four-year course, adjudged worthy of Honours in both Parts A and B together, but who does not enter Part C, or who fails to obtain Honours in Part C, is permitted to supplicate for the Honours degree of Bachelor of Arts in Mathematics with the classification obtained in Parts A and B together; provided that no such candidate may later enter or re-enter the Part C year or supplicate for the degree of Master of Mathematics; and provided in each case that the candidate has fulfilled all the conditions for admission to a degree of the University.

Transfer to the Honour School of Mathematical and Theoretical Physics

9. Subject to the regulations for the Honour School in Mathematical and Theoretical Physics, candidates on the four-year course in Mathematics may apply to the Supervisory Committee for Mathematics and Physics to transfer, after their Part B examination, to the Honour School of Mathematical and Theoretical Physics for their Part C examination. Such a candidate will need to achieve at least an upper second class or higher at the end of Part B, and be accepted by the Supervisory Committee for Mathematics and Physics under the procedures referred to in the regulations for the Master of Mathematical and Theoretical Physics and set out in the course handbook for that degree. Acceptance is not automatic. As specified in the regulations for that degree, Part C in Mathematical and Theoretical Physics must be taken in the academic year following the candidate's Part B examination, and on successful completion of Part C of the Honour School of Mathematical and Theoretical Physics candidates will be awarded the Master of Mathematics and Physics in Mathematical and Theoretical Physics.

10. The Handbook for Mathematical and Theoretical Physics shall set out the options that candidates should follow to maximize their chances of being accepted for transfer to Mathematical and Theoretical Physics for their Part C examination. This Handbook shall be available by the start of Michaelmas Term in the year in which a candidate starts Part A in Mathematics.

11. A candidate who has transferred from the Honour School of Mathematics to the Honour School of Mathematical and Theoretical Physics for their Part C examination in accordance with cl.9 above is permitted transfer to the Honour School of Mathematics for their Part C examination up to the end of Week 5 4 of the Michaelmas Term in which he or she first registered for Part C in the Honour School of Mathematical and Theoretical Physics, so long as that candidate has not opted to supplicate for the degree of Bachelor of Arts in Mathematics under the regulations for the Honour School of Mathematical and Theoretical Physics. 10

12. The regulations for the Honour School of Mathematical and Theoretical Physics set out how the results obtained in Parts A and B in the Honour School of Mathematics are published for candidates who transfer to the Honour School of Mathematical and Theoretical Physics for their Part C examination. 15

B

1. In Part A each candidate shall be required to offer A1, A2, ASO and five papers from A3–A11 from the schedule of papers for Part A (see 'Schedule' below).

2. In Part B each candidate shall offer a total of eight units from the schedule of units for Part B (see below). 20

    (*a*) A total of at least six units offered should be from the schedule of Mathematics Department units.

    (*b*) Candidates may offer a double unit which is an Extended Essay or a Structured Project.

3. In Part C each candidate shall offer a total of eight units from the schedule of 25 units for Part C (see below).

    (*a*) All eight units offered should be from those designated as M level.

    (*b*) A total of at least six of the units offered should be from the schedule of Mathematics Department units.

    (*c*) Candidates may offer either one unit or one double unit which is a 30 Dissertation. If the Dissertation is a mathematical topic this would be offered under the schedule of Mathematics Department units. If the Dissertation is on a mathematics-related topic, this would be offered under the schedule of 'other units'.

4. No candidate shall offer any unit for Part C that he or she has also offered in 35 Part B.

5. The use of calculators is generally not permitted for written papers. However, their use may be permitted for certain exceptional examinations. The specification of calculators permitted for these exceptional examinations will be announced by the Examiners in the Hilary Term preceding the examination. 40

Schedule
Papers in Part A
  A1 Algebra 1 and Differential Equations 1
  A2 Metric Spaces and Complex Analysis
  A3 Algebra 2 45
  A4 Integration

A5 Topology
A6 Differential Equations 2
A7 Numerical Analysis
A8 Probability
A9 Statistics
A10 Waves and Fluids
A11 Quantum Theory
ASO Short Options

Syllabus details will be published in the Course Handbook by the beginning of the Michaelmas Full Term in the academic year of the examination for Part A.

Units for Part B and Part C

The final list of units will be published in the Course Handbook by the beginning of the Michaelmas Full Term in the academic year of the examination concerned, together with the following details.

1. Designation as either 'H' level or 'M' level.

2. 'Weight' as either a unit or double unit.

3. Method of assessment. Details of methods of assessment for Other Mathematics or Other Non-Mathematical units will be given elsewhere. Some options may require assessment by oral presentation. The Course handbook will indicate where such details will be specified.

4. Rules governing submission of any extended essay, dissertation or mini-project, including deadlines, provided that these shall always be submitted to the Chair of Examiners, Honour School of Mathematics, c/o Examination Schools, High Street, Oxford. In addition an electronic copy must be submitted to the Mathematical Institute's website, details will be included in the relevant Notice to Candidates. No part of any extended essay, dissertation or mini-project submitted may include work previously submitted for this or any other degree.

5. Syllabus content.

6. Whether there is a requirement to register or apply for a place to take a unit, and details of any registration or application procedure.

SPECIAL REGULATIONS FOR
THE HONOUR SCHOOL OF MATHEMATICS
AND COMPUTER SCIENCE

A

In the following, 'the Course Handbook' refers to the Mathematics and Computer Science Undergraduate Course Handbook and supplements to this published by the Teaching Committee and also posted on the website at http://www.cs.ox.ac.uk/currentstudents/

1. The subject of the Honour School of Mathematics and Computer Science shall be Mathematics and the theory and practice of Computer Science.

2. No candidate shall be admitted to examination in this School unless he or she has either passed or been exempted from the First Public Examination.

3. The Examination in Mathematics and Computer Science shall be under the supervision of the Mathematical, Physical and Life Sciences Board. The Board shall have the power from time to time to frame and vary regulations for the different parts and subjects of the examination.

4. (*a*) The examination in Mathematics and Computer Science shall consist of three parts (A, B, C) for the four-year course, and of two parts (A, B) for the three-year course.

   (*b*) Parts A, B, and C shall be taken at times not less than three, six, and nine terms, respectively, after passing or being exempted from the First Public Examination.

5. The Examiners shall classify and publish the combined results of the examinations in Part A and Part B, and in respect of candidates taking the four-year course shall separately classify and publish results in Part C.

6. (*a*) Part A shall be taken on one occasion only.

   (*b*) In order to proceed to Part C, a candidate must achieve upper second class Honours or higher in Parts A & B together.

   (*c*) A candidate on the three-year course who obtains only a Pass or fails to satisfy the Examiners in Part B may retake Part B on at most one subsequent occasion; a candidate on the four-year course who obtains only a Pass or fails to satisfy the Examiners in Part C may retake Part C on at most one subsequent occasion. A candidate on the four-year course shall take Part B on one occasion only.

7. A candidate adjudged worthy of Honours on both Parts A and B together, and on Part C may supplicate for the degree of Master of Mathematics and Computer Science provided that the candidate has fulfilled all the conditions for admission to a degree of the University.

8. A candidate in the final year of the four-year course, adjudged worthy of Honours in both Parts A and B together, but who does not enter Part C, or who fails to obtain Honours in Part C, is permitted to supplicate for the Honours degree of Bachelor of Arts in Mathematics and Computer Science with the classification obtained in Parts A and B together; provided that no such candidate may later enter or re-enter the Part C year or supplicate for the degree of Master of Mathematics and Computer Science; and provided in each case that the candidate has fulfilled all the conditions for admission to a degree of the University.

9. All candidates will be assessed as to their practical ability under the following provisions:

(a) The Head of the Department of Computer Science, or a deputy, shall make available to the examiners evidence showing the extent to which each candidate has pursued an adequate course of practical work. Only that work completed and marked by noon on Monday of the fifth week of the Trinity Term in which the candidate takes the examination shall be included in these records.

(b) Candidates for each part of the examination shall submit to the Chair of the Examiners, Honour School of Mathematics and Computer Science, c/o the Academic Administrator, Oxford University Department of Computer Science, Oxford, by noon on Monday of the fifth week of the Trinity Term in which the examination is being held, their reports of practical exercises completed during their course of study. For a report on a practical exercise to be considered by the examiners, it must have been marked by a demonstrator and must be accompanied by a statement that it is the candidate's own work except where otherwise indicated.

(c) The examiners shall take the evidence (a) and the report (b) into account in assessing a candidate's performance.

(d) Candidates whose overall performance on practical work is not satisfactory may be deemed to have failed the examination or may have their overall classification reduced.

B

The syllabus for each of Parts A, B, and C will be published by the Department of Computer Science in a handbook for candidates by the beginning of Michaelmas Full Term in the academic year of the examination concerned. The duration of each optional paper will be specified in the Course Handbook.

The use of calculators is generally not permitted but certain kinds may be allowed for certain papers. Specifications of which papers and which types of calculators are permitted for those exceptional papers will be announced by the examiners in the Hilary Term preceding the examination.

1. In Part A of the examination, candidates shall be required to offer, from the Mathematics Schedule, papers A1(CP), A2, and either two papers from papers A3–A5, A7–A11 or one paper from A3–A5, A7–A11 and paper ASO:

A1 (CP) Algebra 1 and Differential Equations 1
A2 Metric Spaces and Complex Analysis
A3 Algebra 2
A4 Integration
A5 Topology
A7 Numerical Analysis
A8 Probability
A9 Statistics
A10 Waves and Fluids
A11 Quantum Theory
ASO Short Options

Candidates shall also be required to offer four subjects from Schedule A (MC) in the Course Handbook. The manner of examining the subjects in Schedule A (MC) shall be the same as that prescribed for the same subject in the Honour School of Computer Science.

2. In Part B of the examination, each candidate shall be required to offer eight optional subjects from Schedules B1-B5 in the Course Handbook, subject to the conditions that:

(*a*) no candidate shall offer any subject from Schedule B1 that he or she has already offered in Part A of the examination.
(*b*) each candidate shall offer no more than two subjects from Schedule B1.
(*c*) each candidate shall offer no more than two subjects from Schedules B4 and B5.
(*d*) each candidate shall offer at least two subjects from Schedules B1 and B2.
(*e*) each candidate shall offer at least two subjects from Schedule B3.

Each optional subject in Schedules B1, B2 and B4 shall be examined by a written paper or by a mini-project. The manner of examining each subject in Schedules B3 and B5 shall be the same as that prescribed for the same subject in the Honour School of Mathematics. Each 'unit' in schedules B3 and B5 shall be regarded as equivalent to one subject in the examination, and each 'double unit' shall be regarded as equivalent to two subjects.

3. In Part C of the examination, each candidate shall be required to *either* offer six optional subjects from Schedules C1 and C2 in the Course Handbook and submit a Mathematics dissertation, or offer five optional subjects from Schedules C1 and C2 in the Course Handbook and submit a report on a Computer Science project, subject to the condition that no candidate shall offer any subject that he or she has already offered in Part B of the examination. Each optional subject in Schedule C1 shall be examined by a written paper or by a mini-project. The manner of examining each subject in Schedule C2 shall be the same as that prescribed for the same subject in the Honour School of Mathematics. Each 'unit' in Schedule C2 shall be regarded as equivalent to one subject in the examination, and each 'double unit' shall be regarded as equivalent to two subjects.

4. The schedules of optional subjects for Parts A, B, and C of the examination shall be approved by the Faculty of Mathematics and the Faculty of Computer Science, and shall be published in the Course Handbook.

5. The examiners shall have power to combine two papers on related optional subjects into a single paper for those candidates who offer both the optional subjects concerned.

6. In Part C of the examination, each candidate shall carry out a Computer Science project or a Mathematics dissertation on a topic approved by the Teaching Committee. Each project or dissertation will be supervised by a member of the Faculty of Computer Science, the Faculty of Mathematics or the Faculty of Engineering Science, or by some other person of equivalent seniority approved by the Teaching Committee. Two copies of a report of the project or dissertation shall be submitted to the Chair of the Examiners, Honour School of Mathematics and Computer Science, c/o Examination Schools, Oxford, by the date given in the Course Handbook. In addition for the Mathematics dissertations an electronic copy must be submitted to the Mathematical Institute's website, details will be included in the relevant Notice to Candidates. Rules concerning the form of the report will be published in the Course Handbook.

In retaking Part C of the examination, projects previously submitted for the examination may be resubmitted. No project may be resubmitted if it has already been submitted, wholly or substantially, for another honour school or degree of the University, or of any other institution.

SPECIAL REGULATIONS FOR THE HONOUR SCHOOL OF MATHEMATICS AND PHILOSOPHY

A

In the following 'the Mathematics Course Handbook' refers to the Mathematics Undergraduate Handbook and supplements to this published by the Teaching Committee of the Department of Mathematics and also posted on the website at http://www.maths. ox.ac.uk/current-students/undergraduates/handbooks-synopses/.

1. All candidates shall be examined in Mathematics and in Philosophy.

2. No candidate shall be admitted to the examination in this School unless he or she has either passed or been exempted from the First Public Examination.

3. (*a*) The examination in Mathematics and Philosophy shall consist of three parts: Part A, Part B and Part C.

    (*b*) Parts A, B and C shall be taken at times not less than three, six, and nine terms, respectively, after passing or being exempted from the First Public Examination.

    (*c*) Part A shall be taken on one occasion only. No candidate shall enter for Part B until he or she has completed Part A of the examination.

4. (*a*) In order to proceed to Part C, a candidate must achieve upper second class Honours or higher in Parts A and B together.

    (*b*) A candidate who fails to satisfy the Examiners in Part C may enter again for Part C on at most one subsequent occasion.

    (c) A candidate who has obtained Honours in Parts A and B together or has satisfied the examiners but has not obtained Honours in Parts A and B together is permitted to supplicate for the degree of Bachelor of Arts in Mathematics and Philosophy. A candidate who has achieved upper second class Honours or higher in Parts A and B together and who takes the examination in Part C and fails to obtain Honours in Part C, is permitted to supplicate for the Honours degree of Bachelor of Arts in Mathematics and Philosophy with the classification obtained in Parts A and B together; provided that no such candidate may later enter or re-enter the Part C year or supplicate for the degree of Master of Mathematics and Philosophy; and provided in each case that the candidate has fulfilled all the conditions for admission to a degree of the University.

(*d*) A candidate who has achieved upper second class Honours or higher in Parts A and B together, and achieves Honours in Part C may supplicate for the degree of Master of Mathematics and Philosophy provided that the candidate has fulfilled all the conditions for admission to a degree of the University.

5. The Examiners shall classify and publish the combined results of the examinations in Part A and Part B, and in respect of candidates taking the four-year course shall separately classify and publish results in Part C.

6. The examinations in this school shall be under the joint supervision of the Divisional Board of Mathematical, Physical and Life Sciences and the Board of the Faculty of Philosophy, which shall appoint a standing joint committee to make regulations concerning it, subject in all cases to clauses 1-4 above.

7. (*a*) The Public Examiners for Mathematics in this school shall be such of the Public Examiners in the Honour School of Mathematics as may be required, not being less than three; those for Philosophy shall be appointed by a committee whose three elected members shall be appointed by the Board of the Faculty of Philosophy.

(*b*) It shall be the duty of the chairs of the Public Examiners in Parts A, B and C of the Honour School of Mathematics to designate such of their number as may be required for Mathematics in the Honour School of Mathematics and Philosophy, and when this has been done and the examiners for Philosophy have been nominated, the number of the examiners in Mathematics and Philosophy shall be deemed to be complete. No examiners for Philosophy will be required in Part A of the examination.

B

1. In **Part A**, each candidate shall be required to offer, from the Mathematics Part A Schedule (see below), papers A1(CP), A2, and *either* two papers from papers A3, A4, A5, A8 *or* one paper from papers A3, A4, A5, A8 and paper ASO.

2. The examination for **Part B** shall consist of units in Mathematics and subjects in Philosophy. The schedule of units in *Mathematics* shall be published in Mathematics and Philosophy Synopses of lecture courses supplement to the Mathematics Course Handbook by the beginning of the Michaelmas Full Term in the academic year of the examination concerned. The schedule shall be in two parts: Schedule 1 (standard units) and Schedule 2 (additional units). In *Philosophy* the subjects shall be subjects 101–118, 120, 122, 124, 125 and 199 from the list given in *Special Regulations for All*

Honour Schools Including Philosophy. Each subject in Philosophy other than a Thesis shall be examined in one 3-hour paper. Each candidate shall offer:

- (i) Four units of *Mathematics* from Schedule 1, two of which shall be B1a *Logic* and B1b *Set Theory*.
- (ii) Three subjects in *Philosophy* from 101–118, 120, 122, 124 and 125, of which two must be 122 and **either** 101 **or** 102, and
- (iii) **Either** two further units in *Mathematics* drawn from Schedule 1 and 2 combined **or** one further subject in *Philosophy* from subjects 101–118, 120, 124 and 199: *Thesis.*

3. In **Part C** each candidate shall offer one of the following:
- (i) Six units in Mathematics;
- (ii) Four units in Mathematics and one unit in Philosophy;
- (iii) Two units in Mathematics and two units in Philosophy;
- (iv) Three units in Philosophy;

from the lists for Mathematics and for Philosophy.

The schedule of units in Mathematics shall be published in the Mathematics and Philosophy Synopses of lecture courses supplement to the Mathematics Course Handbook by the beginning of the Michaelmas Full Term in the academic year of the examination concerned. No unit in Mathematics, and no subject in Philosophy, may be offered in both Part B and Part C. A unit in Philosophy consists of one of the subjects 101–18, 120, 124, 125 and 180 as specified in the Regulations for Philosophy in all Honour Schools including Philosophy, or a Special Subject in Philosophy as approved by the Joint Committee for Mathematics and Philosophy by regulations published in the *University Gazette* and communicated to college tutors by the end of the fifth week of Trinity Term in the year before the Part C examination in which it will be examined, or a Thesis as specified below. No candidate may offer more than one Special Subject in Philosophy in Part C. In approving a Special Subject in Philosophy for Part C, the Joint Committee for Mathematics and Philosophy may specify that candidates will not be permitted to offer certain special subjects in combination with certain other subjects, or will be permitted to do so only on condition that in the papers on the other subjects they will not be permitted to answer certain questions. Subject to these qualifications, any candidate may offer any special subject. Each unit in Philosophy other than a Thesis shall be examined by a three-hour written paper together with an essay of at most 5,000 words. The relative weight of the essay to the three-hour exam shall be 1 to 3, i.e. the essay shall count for 25% of the mark in that subject. No essay shall exceed this word limit, which includes all notes and appendices, but not the bibliography. The word count should be indicated on the front of the essay. There shall be a select bibliography or a list of sources. All essays must be typed in double spacing on one side of quarto or A4 paper, with footnotes rather than endnotes. Candidates should avoid any substantial repetition of material between examination scripts and examination essays.The topic for a Philosophy examination essay in a given subject can be any question set for the most recent examination of that subject in Honour Schools with Philosophy, with the exception of questions for Plato *Republic* (115) and Aristotle *Nicomachean Ethics* (116) consisting of multiple passages for comment. Candidates may apply for approval of other essay topics by writing to the Chair of the Board, c/o the Administrator, Philosophy Centre, Radcliffe Humanities Building, Woodstock Road, giving the title he or she proposes, together with an explanation of the subject in about 100 words and enclosing a letter from their tutor attesting to the suitability of this topic for the candidate. Any such application must be received no later than Friday of the sixth week of the Hilary Term preceding the Part C examination for which the essay is to be submitted. Late applications will not be considered. Any such application shall be accepted or rejected by the Board within two weeks of its being received.

Each essay shall be the candidate's own work, though it should show knowledge of relevant literature in the subject and may include passages of quotation or paraphrase so long as these passages are clearly indicated as such and the source properly attributed. The candidate may discuss a first draft of the essay with his or her tutor for that subject. The amount of assistance the tutor may give shall be limited to what can be provided in one of the candidate's tutorials for their study of that subject. For each essay the candidate shall sign a statement to the effect that the essay is his or her own work and the tutor shall also sign a statement confirming that, to the best of his or her knowledge and belief, this is so. These statements shall be placed in a sealed envelope bearing the candidate's examination number and the name of the subject for which the essay has been written and presented with two copies of each essay. Each copy of an essay shall be identified only by the candidate's examination number and bear the name of the Philosophy subject for which the essay is being submitted and must be submitted not later than noon on Friday of the first week of the Trinity Full Term of the examination to the Examination Schools, Oxford, addressed to the Chair of the Examiners for Part C of the Final Honour School of Mathematics and Philosophy.

Philosophy Thesis

1. *Subject*

The subject of every thesis should fall within the scope of philosophy. The subject may but need not overlap any subject on which the candidate offers papers. Candidates should avoid substantial repetition in examination scripts or examination essays of material from their theses. Every candidate shall submit through his or her college for approval by the Board of the Faculty of Philosophy the title he or she proposes, together with an explanation of the subject in about 100 words; and a letter of approval from his or her tutor, not earlier than the first day of Trinity Full Term of the year before that in which he or she is to be examined and not later than Friday of the third week of the Michaelmas Full Term preceding his or her examination. Applications for approval of subject should be directed to the Chair of the Board, c/o The Administrator, Philosophy Centre, Radcliffe Humanities Building, Woodstock Road. The Board shall decide as soon as possible whether or not to approve the title and shall advise the candidate immediately. No decision shall be deferred beyond the end of the fourth week of Michaelmas Full Term. If a candidate wishes to change the title of his or her thesis after a title has already been approved by the Board, he or she may apply for such permission to be granted by the Board. Applications should be directed to the Chair of the Board (if the application is made before the first day of Hilary Full Term preceding the examination). If later than the first day of Hilary Full Term preceding the examination application for change of title should be made to the Chair of Examiners for Part C of the Final Honour School of Mathematics and Philosophy.

2. *Authorship and origin*

Every thesis shall be the candidate's own work. A candidate's tutor may, however, discuss with the candidate the field of study, the sources available, and the method of presentation; the tutor may also read and comment on drafts. The amount of assistance the tutor may give is equivalent to the teaching of a normal paper. Every candidate shall sign a certificate to the effect that the thesis is his or her own work and the tutor shall countersign the certificate confirming, to the best of his or her knowledge and belief, that this is so. This certificate shall be placed in a sealed envelope bearing the candidate's examination number presented together with the thesis. No thesis shall be accepted which has already been submitted for a degree of this or any other university, and the certificate shall also state that the thesis has not been so submitted. No thesis shall, however, be ineligible because it has been or is being submitted for any prize of this university.

3. *Length and format*

No thesis shall exceed 20,000 words, the limit to include all notes and appendices, but not including the bibliography; no person or body shall have authority to permit any excess. The word count should be indicated on the front of the thesis. There shall be a select bibliography or a list of sources. All theses must be typed in double spacing on one side of quarto or A4 paper, with any notes and references at the foot of each page. Two copies of the thesis shall be submitted to the examiners.

4. *Submission of thesis*

Every candidate shall submit two copies of their thesis, identified by the candidate's examination number only, not later than noon on Friday of the week before the Trinity Full Term of the examination to the Examination Schools, Oxford, addressed to the Chair of the Examiners for Part C of the Final Honour School of Mathematics and Philosophy.

5. For the award of the highest honours it is not necessary to perform with excellence in each of *Mathematics* and *Philosophy* separately.

6. The use of calculators is generally not permitted for written papers. However, their use may be permitted for certain exceptional examinations. The specification of calculators permitted for these exceptional examinations will be announced by the Examiners in the Hilary Term preceding the examination.

Schedule

Papers in Part A

A1 (CP) Algebra 1
A2 Metric Spaces and Complex Analysis
A3 Algebra 2
A4 Integration
A5 Topology
A8 Probability
ASO Short Options

Syllabus details will be published in the Mathematics Course Handbook by the beginning of the Michaelmas Full Term in the academic year of the examination for Part A.

Units in Mathematics for Part B and Part C

The list of units along with synopses and other details, will be approved by the Mathematics Teaching Committee and published in the Mathematics Course Handbook by the beginning of Michaelmas Full Term in the academic year of the examination concerned.

The list of units for Part C shall include units in Mathematical Logic as specified by the Joint Committee for Mathematics and Philosophy.

SPECIAL REGULATIONS FOR THE HONOUR SCHOOL OF MATHEMATICAL AND THEORETICAL PHYSICS

A

In the following 'the Course Handbook' refers to the Mathematical and Theoretical Physics Handbook and supplements to this published by the Joint Supervisory Committee for Mathematical and Theoretical Physics and also posted on the website at https://www.maths.ox.ac.uk/current-students/undergraduates/handbooks-synopses/.

The Divisional Board of Mathematical, Physical and Life Sciences shall appoint for the supervision of the course a supervisory committee, which shall have the power to approve lectures and other instruction. The committee shall appoint a Director of Studies who will be responsible for ensuring that the programme is set up and the decisions of the committee are carried out.

1. The subject of Honour School of Mathematical and Theoretical Physics shall be Mathematical and Theoretical Physics and related subjects.

2. The Examination in the Honour School of Mathematical and Theoretical Physics shall be under the supervision of the Mathematical, Physical and Life Sciences Board. The Board shall have power from time to time to frame and vary regulations for different parts and subjects of the examination.

3. The examination in the Honour School of Mathematical and Theoretical Physics shall consist of one Part only, namely Part C, and each candidate shall follow a course of study in Mathematical and Theoretical Physics for three terms.

4. A candidate may only be admitted to the examination in this School if he or she:

(*a*) was, at the time of taking their Part B examinations, registered for the four year course in one of the following Honour Schools: Mathematics, Physics, or Physics and Philosophy;

(*b*) has achieved an upper second class Honours or higher in their Part B examinations referred to in (a) above;

(c) has applied for and been accepted for entry to Part C in Mathematical and Theoretical Physics in accordance with the procedure set out in the Handbook for Mathematical and Theoretical Physics;

(*d*) enters the Mathematical and Theoretical Physics Part C examinations in the academic year after taking their Part B examinations.

(a) and (b) above are necessary minimum conditions of eligibility to transfer to Part C in Mathematical and Theoretical Physics after the Part B examinations. Candidates wishing to transfer will also have to apply to transfer as stated in (c) above by the end of week 1 of Hilary Term of their third year. To be accepted they will have to satisfy the other requirements set out in the Handbook for Mathematical and Theoretical Physics from time to time. These requirements may specify the subject matter of the papers chosen for their Part A and Part B examinations (where relevant), the marks achieved in those papers, the overall mark achieved in their Part A and Part B examinations, and an assessment of their overall aptitude for Mathematical and Theoretical Physics. The Handbook for Mathematical and Theoretical Physics shall set out the subject matter of optional papers that candidates should follow in Part A or Part B to maximize their chances of being accepted for transfer to Mathematical and Theoretical Physics at Part C. For this purpose, this Handbook shall be available by the start of Michaelmas Term in the year in which a candidate starts Part A in Mathematics, Physics, or Physics and Philosophy.

5. A candidate who has transferred to Part C in Mathematical and Theoretical Physics in accordance with cl.4 above is permitted transfer to Part C of the Honour School in which he or she was registered at the time of his or her Part B examination up to the end of Week 4 of the Michaelmas Term in which he or she first registered for Part C in Mathematical and Theoretical Physics, so long as that candidate has not opted to supplicate for the degree of Bachelor of Arts under cl.7 below.

6. The result of the Mathematical and Theoretical Physics Part C examination will be published in terms of Distinction, Pass, or Fail.

7. (*a*) A candidate who obtains a Distinction or Pass in the Mathematical and Theoretical Physics Part C may supplicate for the degree of Master in Mathematical and Theoretical Physics provided that the candidate has fulfilled all the conditions for admission to a degree of the University.

(*b*) For such a candidate, the Examiners of the Honours School in which the candidate sat Parts A and B shall classify and publish the combined results of the examinations in Part A and Part B, and the examiners for the Honour School of Mathematical and Theoretical Physics shall separately assess and publish the results in Part C.

(*c*) Such a candidate will receive a classification for Parts A and B in the subject in which he or she sat those Parts, and a separate result for Part C in Mathematical and Theoretical Physics.

8. A candidate in the final year of a four-year course, registered for Part C in Mathematical and Theoretical Physics, but who does not enter Part C, or who fails to obtain a Distinction or Pass in Part C, is permitted to supplicate for the Honours degree in the subject in which he or she sat Parts A and B (namely the Bachelor of Arts in Mathematics, Physics, or Physics and Philosophy respectively), with the classification he or she obtained in Parts A and B together; provided that no such candidate may later enter or re-enter the Part C year or supplicate for the degree of Master of Mathematics, Master of Physics, Master of Physics and Philosophy or Master of Mathematics and Physics; and provided in each case that the candidate has fulfilled all the conditions for admission to a degree of the University.

9. A candidate on the four-year course who fails to satisfy the Examiners in Part C may retake Part C on at most one subsequent occasion, not later than one year after the initial attempt. In such a case the examiners will specify at the time of failure which components of the examination may or must be redone.

B

1. Candidates will complete and be assessed on the following parts:

(i) Candidates will offer 10 units with one unit corresponding to a 16 hour lecture course.

(ii) At least four units will be assessed by written examination.

(iii) The other units will be assessed by marked course work, take-home papers or mini-projects. The Course Handbook will specify which units will be assessed by each method mentioned above.

(iv) Candidates may offer one unit which is a dissertation. The dissertation will follow the guidelines and procedures of the Part C Mathematics course outlined in the Special Regulations for the Honour School of Mathematics.

(v) Candidates will be required to attend an oral examination at the end of the course of studies.

The examiners may award a distinction for excellence in the whole examination.

2. Syllabus and examination details will be published each year in the Course Handbook and on the course web pages by the beginning of Michaelmas Full Term in the academic year of the examination.

SPECIAL REGULATIONS FOR THE HONOUR SCHOOL OF MATHEMATICS AND STATISTICS

A

In the following 'the Course Handbook' refers to the Mathematics and Statistics Undergraduate Handbook and supplements to this published by the Statistics Academic Committee.

1. The subjects of the Honour School of Mathematics and Statistics shall be Mathematics and its applications, and Statistics.

2. No candidate shall be admitted to examination in this School unless he or she has either passed or been exempted from the First Public Examination.

3. The Examinations in Mathematics and Statistics shall be under the supervision of the Mathematical, Physical and Life Sciences Board. The Board shall have the power, subject to this decree, from time to time to frame and vary regulations for the different parts and subjects of the examination.

4. (*a*) The examination in Mathematics and Statistics shall consist of three parts (A, B, C) for the four-year course, and of two parts (A, B) for the three-year course.

(*b*) Parts A, B, and C shall be taken at times not less than three, six, and nine terms, respectively, after passing or being exempted from the First Public Examination.

5. The Examiners shall classify and publish the combined results of the examinations in Part A and Part B, and in respect of candidates taking the four-year course shall separately classify and publish results in Part C.

6. (*a*) Part A shall be taken on one occasion only. No candidate shall enter for Part B until he or she has completed Part A of the examination.

(*b*) In order to proceed to Part C, a candidate must achieve upper second class Honours or higher in Parts A and B together.

(*c*) A candidate on the three-year course who obtains only a Pass or fails to satisfy the Examiners in Part B may retake Part B on at most one subsequent occasion; a candidate on the four-year course who fails to satisfy the Examiners in Part C may retake Part C on at most one subsequent occasion. A candidate on the four-year course shall take Part B on one occasion only.

7. A candidate adjudged worthy of Honours on both Parts A and B together, and on Part C may supplicate for the degree of Master of Mathematics in Mathematics and Statistics provided that the candidate has fulfilled all the conditions for admission to a degree of the University.   5

8. A candidate in the final year of the four-year course, adjudged worthy of Honours in both Parts A and B together, but who does not enter Part C, or who fails to obtain Honours in Part C, is permitted to supplicate for the Honours degree of Bachelor of Arts in Mathematics and Statistics with the classification obtained   10
in Parts A and B together; provided that no such candidate may later enter or re-enter the Part C year or supplicate for the degree of Master of Mathematics in Mathematics and Statistics; and provided in each case that the candidate has fulfilled all the conditions for admission to a degree of the University.   15

B

1. **In Part A** each candidate shall be required to offer Papers A1, A2, A8, A9, ASO and three papers from A3-A7 and A10-A12 (see 'Schedule' below).

2. **In Part B** each candidate shall offer a total of eight units from the schedule of units for Part B (see below).   20

   (*a*) Each candidate shall offer the double unit BS1.
   (*b*) Each candidate shall offer a total of at least two units from BS2 and BS3.
   (*c*) Each candidate may offer a total of at most two units from BS4 and the schedule of 'Other units':
   (*d*) Each candidate may offer at most one double unit which is an Extended Essay   25
   or Structured Project.

3. **In Part C** each candidate shall offer a total of five units from the schedule of units for Part C (see below), and each candidate shall also offer a dissertation on a statistics project.
   (*a*) The five units offered should be from those designated as M level.   30
   (*b*) At least one unit should be offered from the schedule of 'Statistics' units.

4. No candidate shall offer any unit for Part C that he or she has also offered in Part B.

5. The use of calculators is generally not permitted for written papers. However, their use may be permitted for certain exceptional examinations. The specification of   35
calculators permitted for these exceptional examinations will be announced by the Examiners in the Hilary Term preceding the examination.

Schedule

Papers in Part A

A1 Algebra 1 and Differential Equations 1   40
A2 Metric Spaces and Complex Analysis
A3 Algebra 2
A4 Integration
A5 Topology
A6 Differential Equations 2   45
A7 Numerical Analysis
A8 Probability

A9 Statistics
A10 Waves and Fluids
A11 Quantum Theory
A12 Simulation and Statistical Programming
ASO Short Options   5
Syllabus details will be published in the Course Handbook by the beginning of the
Michaelmas Full Term in the academic year of the examination for Part A.

Units for Part B and Part C

The final list of units will be published in the Course Handbook by the beginning of
Michaelmas Full Term in the academic year of the examination concerned, together   10
with the following details.

1. Designation as either 'H' level or 'M' level.
2. 'Weight' as either a unit or double unit.
3. Method of assessment. Details of methods of assessment for units delivered by
other departments will be given elsewhere. Some options may require assessment   15
by oral presentation. The Course handbook will indicate where such details will be
specified.
4. Rules governing submission of any extended essay, dissertation or mini-project,
including deadlines, provided that these shall always be submitted to the Chair of
Examiners, Honour School of Mathematics and Statistics, c/o Examination Schools,   20
High Street, Oxford. When submitting their Part C dissertation, candidates must
submit both paper and electronic versions which must be identical. The latter may be
used by the examiners to check for plagiarism. See the Course Handbook for further
details. In addition any submission on a mathematical unit must also be submitted to
the Mathematical Institute's website, details will be included in the relevant Notice   25
to Candidates.
5. Syllabus content.
6. Whether there is a requirement to register or apply for a place to take a unit or
double unit, and details of any registration or application procedure.

SPECIAL REGULATIONS FOR THE HONOUR SCHOOL OF MEDICAL SCIENCES

A

1. The subject of the Honour School of Medical Sciences shall be the sciences basic to medicine.

2. No candidate shall be admitted for examination in this school unless he or she has passed Part I of the First Examination for the Degree of Bachelor of Medicine.

3. The examination in this school shall be under the supervision of the Medical Sciences Board, which shall prescribe the necessary regulations.

4. Any candidate offering an optional subject based on courses provided within the Honour School of Experimental Psychology shall be examined in that subject by the Public Examiners in Experimental Psychology.

5. Candidates may offer themselves for examination in one or more *Supplementary Subjects*. The Supplementary Subjects available in any year will be notified to students annually during Trinity Term. A candidate's results in any such subject shall be published, and account shall be taken of those results in the production of the class list. Candidates awarded a pass in a Supplementary Subject examination may not retake the same Supplementary Subject examination.

6. Every candidate shall give notice of all papers being offered not later than Friday in the eighth week of Michaelmas Term in the academic year in which the candidate intends to sit the examination.

B

1. The options of the school shall be:
   A Neuroscience
   B Molecular Medicine
   C Cardiovascular, Renal and Respiratory Biology
   D Infection and immunity
   E Cellular Physiology and Pharmacology

This list may be varied from time to time by the Medical Sciences Board, and such variations shall be published in the *University Gazette* by the end of Week 8 of Trinity Term of the academic year two years preceding the first examination of the changed options.

Minor variations, including changes of nomenclature, and/or changes of content to one or two themes within an option, shall be published by the end of Week 8 of

Hilary Term of the academic year one year preceding the first examination of the changed options.

Each option shall be divided into themes that will be taught starting in Michaelmas Term. The list of themes shall be published no later than 0th week of Michaelmas Term in the academic year in which the themes will be examined. Most themes will be specific each to a single option, but some may be shared. The total number of themes comprising each option shall be at least 8 and no more than 11 (taking account of shared themes). Each candidate will be expected to have studied 8 themes in order to address the synoptic questions of Paper 2, and to have prepared sufficient of those themes in depth to be able to address the requirements of Paper 1 (see paras 2, 3, and 5 below).

2. The following written papers shall be set:

Paper 1 One separate paper for each option (Paper 1A to 1E)
Paper 2 One paper consisting of synoptic questions from each option
Paper 3 Critical reading, data analysis and experimental design

Each Paper 1 shall be of three hours duration and shall contain a choice of questions addressing in-depth knowledge and understanding within individual specified themes of the option. Each Paper 1 will require candidates to answer questions on three different themes.

Paper 2 shall be of three hours duration and shall contain a choice of questions from each option. Each question will require a synoptic approach across several themes of an option. Candidates shall be required to answer any two questions from this paper.

Paper 3 shall be of three hours duration and shall have questions relating to pieces of primary literature relevant to each of the options individually.

3. Each candidate must offer three written papers:

Paper 1 for *one* chosen option, Paper 2 and Paper 3.
In addition, each candidate must both:
  (i) undertake and be examined in a research project
and
  (ii) either submit an Extended Essay; or offer a fourth written paper based on courses provided within Parts I and II of the Honour School of Experimental Psychology. The subjects of the papers to be available for this purpose shall be published no later than the end of Week 5 of Hilary Term in the academic year preceding that in which the examination is taken.

If, in any part of the examination, a candidate presents essentially the same information on more than one occasion, then credit will be given in only the first instance.

4. *Research project*

(i) *Form and subject of the project*

The project shall be classified either as 'laboratory-based' or as 'library-based'. A laboratory-based project shall consist of original experiments and/or data analysis carried out by the candidate alone or in collaboration with others (where such collaboration is, for instance, needed to produce results in the time available). A library-based project shall consist of the candidate undertaking critical appraisal of the relevant literature.

Every project shall be supervised, and the topic and supervisor shall be approved on behalf of the Medical Sciences Board by the Director of Preclinical Studies or his or her deputy. A list of recent project titles registered by students will be made available no later than Friday of Week 8 of Hilary Term of the academic year preceding the examination, to assist candidates in the choice of topic or general field for the research project.

(ii) *Approval*

No later than Friday of Week 2 of Trinity Term in the academic year preceding the examination, every candidate must submit as instructed the title of their proposed research project, provide a brief outline of the subject matter and supply details of supervision arrangements. Decision on the proposal shall be made by the Director of Preclinical Studies or his or her deputy and shall be communicated to the candidate as soon as possible, and work should not start on the project until approval has been given. Candidates should allow at least one week for the process of approval, and should bear in mind that an application may be referred for clarification or may be refused.

When choosing a research project, candidates must bear in mind the prohibition on duplicating material in different parts of the examination (see para 3).

(iii) *Pre-submission Confirmation*

Candidates must provide final confirmation of the details of their project (including title of project and name of supervisor) to the Examiners through the Faculty of Physiological Sciences Undergraduate Studies Office no later than noon on Friday of Week 8 of Michaelmas Term in the academic year in which they intend taking the examination.

(iv) *Examination*

(*a*) Laboratory-based projects

Candidates shall submit a brief Project Report according to guidelines that will be published by the Medical Sciences Board in Week 1 of Trinity Term in the academic year preceding the examination.

(*b*) Library-based projects

Candidates shall submit to the examiners a Project Dissertation not exceeding 10,000 words in all according to guidelines that will be published by the Medical Sciences Board in Week 1 of Trinity Term in the academic year preceding the examination.

In the case of either type of project, each candidate shall make a brief oral presentation of their project to a group of two examiners (or examiners and assessors appointed to ensure an adequate representation of expertise), after which, the candidate shall be examined *viva voce* on the project. The form of the presentation to the examiners shall be specified in guidelines published by the Medical Sciences Board in Week 1 of Trinity Term in the academic year preceding the examination.

(v) *Submission and assessment of project-based written work*

Project Reports (three copies) must be sent to the Chair of Examiners in Medical Sciences, c/o Examination Schools, High Street, Oxford, not later than noon on the Friday of Week 8 in Hilary Term in the academic year in which the candidate intends to take the examination. The copies shall be accompanied (in a separate sealed envelope) by a certificate signed by each candidate indicating that the research project is the candidate's own work. In the case of laboratory-based projects, the certificate shall certify that the supervisor has commented on at least one draft of the written submission. In the case of laboratory-based work that has been produced in collaboration, the certificate shall indicate the extent of the candidate's own contribution. In the case of library-based projects, the certificate shall certify that the supervisor commented on no more than the first draft of the written submission. For both types of project, each candidate will be required to submit a draft of their Project Report to their supervisor no later than Friday of Week 6 (two weeks before submission to Schools).

In all cases, the examiners shall obtain and consider a written report from each supervisor indicating the extent of the input made by the candidate to the outcome of the project and also any unforeseen difficulties associated with the project (e.g. unexpected technical issues or problems in the availability of materials, equipment, or literature or other published data).

In exceptional cases, where through unforeseen circumstances a laboratory-based project produces no useable results (i.e. not even negative or ambiguous results), the candidate may apply through his or her college to the Director of Preclinical Studies or his or her deputy for permission to submit a concise review of the scientific context and the aims of the work that was attempted in place of the normal Project Report. Such an application must be accompanied by supporting evidence from the supervisor of the project. The concise review to be submitted in such circumstances should be comparable in length to the Report of a successful laboratory-based project and will be presented orally to the examiners and be examined viva voce in the usual way for a research project. The examiners will be advised that substantive results could not be produced.

When submitting a Project Report, candidates must bear in mind the prohibition on duplicating material in different parts of the examination (see para 3).

Project Reports previously submitted for the Honour School of Medical Sciences may be resubmitted. No Project Report will be accepted if it has already been submitted, wholly or substantially, for another Honour School or degree of this University, or for a degree of any other institution.

5. *The Extended Essay*
(i) *Form and subject of the essay*

The Extended Essay shall be of not more than 3,000 words, including figure legends but excluding references. It must be typed and bound according to guidelines that will be published by the Medical Sciences Board in Week 5 of Trinity Term in the academic year preceding the examination.

The subject matter of a candidate's essay shall be within the scope of the school. The essay may relate to any of the themes taught in the options of the school, regardless of the candidate's chosen option for Paper 1. However, when choosing an Extended Essay, candidates must bear in mind the prohibition on duplicating material in different parts of the examination (see para 3).

A list of essay titles registered by students in previous academic years will be made available by Week 5 of the Trinity Term of the academic year preceding that of the examination, to assist candidates in the choice of topic or general field for the essay.

(ii) *Registration*

No later than Friday of Week 8 of Michaelmas Term in the academic year of the examination, every candidate must register through the Faculty of Physiological Sciences Undergraduate Studies Office the title of their essay, provide a brief outline of the subject matter, and confirm the main themes to which it relates. Decision on the application shall be made by the Director of Preclinical Studies or his or her deputy and shall be communicated to the candidate not later than Week 4 of Hilary Term in the academic year of the examination.

(iii) *Authorship*

The essay must be the candidate's own work. Candidates' tutors, or their deputies nominated to act as advisors, may discuss with candidates the proposed field of study, the sources available, and the method of treatment, but on no account may they read or comment on any written draft. Every candidate shall sign a certificate to the effect that this rule has been observed and that the essay is their own work; and the candidate's tutor or adviser shall countersign the certificate confirming that, to the best of their knowledge and belief, this is so.

(iv) *Submission*

Essays (two copies) must be submitted to the Chair of Examiners in Medical Sciences, c/o Examination Schools, High Street, Oxford, not later than noon on the Friday of Week 0 of the Trinity Term in which the candidate intends to take the examination. Each essay shall be accompanied (in a separate sealed envelope addressed to the Chair of Examiners) by certification of authorship as specified in the preceding paragraph and an electronic copy of the text of the essay.

6. Should any one option of the school be oversubscribed and the supply of suitable teaching in that option is unable to meet the demand, then the Medical Sciences Board may impose a limit on the number of candidates that may enter for that option. Such regulation of numbers may be achieved by the allocation of places in the option to specified students provided that these allocations are published by 0th week of Michaelmas Term of the academic year in which the candidates are to sit the examination. The board shall make arrangements to allow subsequently for regulated migration between options on receipt of written applications from candidates to the Director of Preclinical Studies or his or her deputy. Such migration will be permitted provided a sufficient supply of suitable teaching can be maintained.

7. Candidates may be examined *viva voce*, the topics may include the subject of any written paper taken by the candidate, or the research project or Extended Essay.

SPECIAL REGULATIONS FOR THE HONOUR SCHOOL OF MODERN LANGUAGES

A

1. The subjects of examination in the Honour School of Modern Languages shall be the French, German, Italian, Spanish, Portuguese, Russian, Medieval and Modern Greek, Czech (with Slovak),* and Celtic* languages and the literatures associated with them, and Linguistics. Save in the case of the subjects Czech (with Slovak) and Celtic, which may be offered only with another of the languages, a candidate may offer one or two languages, or one language and Linguistics. The standard of competence required of a candidate shall be the same in any language which he or she offers whether it be his or her sole language or one of two languages.

2. Every candidate shall be required to show, in the case of any language which he or she offers, a competent knowledge

(1) of the language as it is spoken and written at the present day, such knowledge to be tested by oral and written examination;

(2) of at least one specified period in its literature;

(3) of the history, thought, and civilization of the country necessary for the understanding of the language and literature.

3. A candidate offering one language shall be required to show a competent philological knowledge of the language he or she is offering. A candidate offering two languages shall be permitted to offer a paper or papers on philological topics.

4. Candidates offering the subject Linguistics shall be required to show a competent knowledge of analytical techniques and problems in descriptive and theoretical linguistics and the application of these to the language they are offering.

5. No candidate shall be admitted to examination in this School unless he or she has either passed or been exempted from the First Public Examination.

6. The examiners shall indicate in the lists issued by them the subject or subjects offered by each candidate obtaining honours or satisfying the examiners under the appropriate regulation. In draw-

---

* Czech (with Slovak) and Celtic may not be available in every year. Notice that these subjects, or a particular paper or particular papers, will not be available in a given year will be published in the *University Gazette* in the Trinity Term three years before the examination concerned.

ing up the Class List the examiners shall satisfy themselves that each candidate has shown an appropriate level of competence both in literature (and linguistic studies where this applies) and in language.

7. The board of the faculty shall by notice from time to time make regulations concerning the examination; and shall have power in respect of each subject included in the examination

(1) to determine, within the limits of this decree, the form and content of the individual papers of the examination, and

(2) to issue a list of Special Subjects, prescribing books or authorities where they think it desirable. Such books or authorities may be in other languages than that to which the Special Subject is related. A Special Subject may be concerned with a language or literature not specified in clause 1 of this Regulation.

8. A candidate whose name has been placed in the Class List upon the result of the examination in any one or more of the subjects included in the examination shall be permitted to offer himself or herself for examination in any of the other subjects so included at the examination in either the next year or the next year but one, provided that no such candidate shall offer any of the languages or subjects already offered by him or her in the Honour School of Modern Languages or in the Honour Schools of History and Modern Languages, Philosophy and Modern Languages, Classics and Modern Languages, or English and Modern Languages, or European and Middle Eastern Languages, and provided always that he or she has not exceeded six terms from the date on which he or she first obtained Honours in a Final Honour School.

B

Candidates will be examined in accordance with the examination regulations set out below.

They will also be required to spend, after their matriculation, a year of residence in an appropriate country or countries, and to provide on their entry form for the examination a certificate that they have done this, signed by the Head or by a tutor of their society. Candidates wishing to be dispensed from the requirement to undertake a year of residence abroad must apply in writing to the Chair of the Medieval and Modern Languages Board, 41 Wellington Square, Oxford OX1 2JF, stating their reasons for requesting dispensation and enclosing a letter of support from their society.

Candidates will be expected to carry out during this year abroad such work as their society may require. It is strongly recommended that candidates should apply through the Central Bureau for Educational Visits and Exchanges for an Assistantship, where these are available, and should accept one if offered. Candidates who are not able to obtain an Assistantship should during their year abroad follow a course or courses in an institution or institutions approved by their society, or should spend their time in such other circumstances as are acceptable to their society. Candidates will agree with their College Tutor in advance of their year abroad an independent course of study to be followed during that period.

It is strongly recommended that candidates offering two languages who spend their year abroad in a country or countries of one of the languages only should in addition 5 spend between their matriculation and examination at least four weeks in a country of the other language.

Candidates may offer either one or two languages. The standard of competence shall be as high for candidates who offer two languages as for those who offer only one. A candidate offering one language may also offer Linguistics. The papers and choices of 10 options available to candidates for each of the two courses will be the same.

Candidates may additionally offer an Extended Essay, good performance in which will be taken into account in allocating all classes.

The following is the general scheme of papers in Modern Languages:

I, II, III	Language papers	15
IV, V	Linguistic Studies	
VI, VII, VIII	Period of Literature or Period Topics	
IX	Early Texts	
X, XI	Prescribed Authors (German XI: Early Modern Texts or Goethe)	
XII	Special Subjects	20
XIII	General Linguistics	
XIV	Extended Essay	

Candidates must take one of the schedules of papers listed in 1 below, subject to the general and specific conditions listed in 2, and the special regulations concerning Paper XII Special Subjects listed in 3. 25

1. Combinations of Papers

I. A candidate who offers two languages must take the written papers listed below, and oral examinations in both languages:

Five papers in language A
    Two language papers I, II(A+B)
    One of VI, VII, VIII 30
    Two of IV, V, IX, X, XI, XII

Four papers in language B
    Two language papers I, II(A+B)
    One of VI, VII, VIII 35
    One of IV, V, IX, X, XI, XII
    Optionally, XIV Extended Essay

II. A candidate who offers one language only must take the written papers listed below, and the oral examination in the language:

(*a*) French: 40
    Three language papers I, II(A+B), III
    One of VI, VII, VIII
    Five of IV, V, VI, VII, VIII, IX, X, XI, XII, XIII
    Optionally, XIV Extended Essay

(*b*) Spanish: 45
    Three language papers I, II(A+B), III
    Paper IX
    Two of VI, VII, VIII, XIII
    Three of IV, V, X, XI, XII, XII (Modern Galician *or* Modern Catalan) of which
    at least one must be IV or V 50
    Optionally, XIV Extended Essay

(*c*) All other languages:
    Three language papers I, II(A+B), III
    Paper IX
    Two of VI, VII, VIII, XIII
    Three of IV, V, X, XI, XII, of which at least one must be IV or V
    Optionally, XIV Extended Essay

III. Candidates offering one language and Linguistics must take eight [old regulations, nine] papers as listed below, and the oral examination in the language.
    Three [old regulations, four] papers in the language:
    Two language papers I, II(A+B)
    One of VI, VII, VIII [old regulations, *one* of IX, X, XI]

Four papers in Linguistics:
    IV and V (in the language)
    XII (drawn from Special Subjects bearing the Linguistics identifier)
    XIII

One paper, from IX, X, XI, or XII (whether in the language or Linguistics)
Optionally, XIV Extended Essay

Candidates must avoid substantial overlap between Paper XII Special Subjects and other Linguistics Papers.

IV. Candidates offering one language with Polish must offer:
    Three papers in Polish: II(A+B), IV *or* V, VII
    Six papers in the other language, as specified below
    Oral examination in the other language
    Optionally, XIV Extended Essay

In French
    Two language papers I, II(A+B)
    One of VI,VII,VIII
    Three of IV, V, VI, VII, VIII, IX, X, XI, XII, XIII

In German
    Two language papers I, II(A+B)
    One of VI, VII, VIII, XIII
    Three of IV, V, VI, VII, VIII, IX, X, XI, XII (provided that no more than two of IV, V, IX are taken)

In Italian
    Two language papers I, II(A+B)
    One of VI, VII, VIII
    One of IV, V

    Paper IX
    One of IV *or* V, VI, VII, VIII, X, XI, XII, XIII

In Spanish
    Two language papers I, II(A+B)
    One of VI, VII, VIII, XIII

    Paper IX
    Two of IV *or* V, VI, VII, VIII, X, XI, XII, XII (Modern Galician *or* Modern Catalan)

In Russian
    Two language papers I, II(A+B)
    One of VII, VIII

    Paper IX
    Two of IV *or* V, VI, VII, VIII, X, XI, XII, XIII

In Portuguese
> *Two* language papers I, II(A+B)
> *One* of Papers VI, VII, VIII
> *Three* of IV *or* V, VI, VII, VIII, IX, X, XI, XII

In Medieval and Modern Greek
> *Two* language papers I, II(A+B)
> *Two* of VI, VII, VIII, XIII
> *Two* of IX, X, XI, XII

Examination answers must be written in English, except when directions are given to the contrary.

Candidates will be required to attend for an oral examination in each language they offer. A candidate failing to appear for the oral examination, without good cause shown, will be deemed to have withdrawn from the whole examination.

In the oral examination a candidate will be required to show in each language he offers competence in the following:

(i) Comprehension of a passage or passages of text;

(ii) A short discourse;

(iii) Conversation. Reading aloud may be required of candidates as a further test of their pronunciation.

2. Special Provisions

i. All candidates offering Italian must offer at least one of IV, V, IX in Italian

ii. A candidate offering two languages is required to offer, in one language,
> *either* at least one of papers IV,V
> *or* at least one pre-Modern paper as designated below:
> French VI, VII, IX, X
> German VI, VII, IX, XI(A)
> Italian VI, VII, IX, X
> Spanish VI, VII, IX, X
> Portuguese VI, VII, IX, X
> Russian VI, VII, IX
> Medieval and Modern Greek VI, VII, IX, X
> Celtic VI, IX, X
> Czech IX
> *or* one Paper XII designated as pre-Modern.

Details of Paper XII Special Subjects which have been designated as pre-Modern will be provided in the list of Special Subjects published by the Faculty by the beginning of the fifth week of the Trinity Term one year before the examination.

3. Paper XII Special Subjects

Candidates may offer only one Paper XII, with the following exceptions:

(*a*) Candidates offering Spanish as a sole language or as one of two languages may offer two Paper XII Special Subjects in total, provided that one is either Modern Catalan or Modern Galician;

(*b*) Candidates offering Linguistics may offer either one or two Paper XII Special Subjects. Where one Special Subject is offered, it must bear the appropriate Linguistics identifier. Where two Special Subjects are offered, one must bear the appropriate Linguistics identifier.

Candidates offering a Paper XII Special Subject in the second of two languages (Language B) may choose only a Special Subject bearing the appropriate language identifier.

Candidates offering Spanish as a sole language or in combination with any language other than Portuguese may offer one of the following papers in

Portuguese as a Paper XII Special Subject: Paper X, Paper XI, half of the period covered in Paper VII or Paper VIII.

Candidates offering Portuguese as a sole language or in combination with any language other than Spanish may offer one of the following papers in Spanish as a Paper XII Special Subject: Paper X, Paper XI, half of the period covered in Paper VII or Paper VIII.   5

4. Detailed specifications of papers I to XIV

I, II, III Language Papers

French
I	Essay in French	10
IIA	Translation from Modern French	
IIB	Translation into Modern French	
III	Translation from pre-Modern French	

German
I	Translation into German and Essay in German	15
IIA	Translation from Modern German	
IIB	Translation from Modern German	
III	Translation from pre-Modern German	

Italian
I	Essay in Italian	20
IIA	Translation from Italian	
IIB	Translation into Italian	
III	Translation from pre-Modern Italian	

Spanish
I	Prose translation from English into Spanish and an essay in Spanish	25
IIA	Translation from Modern Spanish	
IIB	Translation from Modern Spanish	
III	Prose translation from English into Spanish and a translation from Spanish into English (medieval or golden age)	

Portuguese
I	Prose composition and essay	30
IIA	Translation from Modern Portuguese (European)	
IIB	Translation from Modern Portuguese (Brazilian)	
III	(A) Translation from pre-Modern Portuguese and (B) a Year Abroad Essay	35

Russian
I	Translation into Russian and essay in Russian with further specifications	
IIA	Translation from Modern Russian	
IIB	Translation from Modern Russian	40
III	Translation from pre-Modern Russian with further specifications	

Czech (with Slovak)
I	Translation into Czech or Slovak and essay in Czech or Slovak	
IIA	Translation from Modern Czech	
IIB	Translation from Modern Slovak	45

Medieval and Modern Greek
I	Translation into Modern Greek and essay in Modern Greek
IIA	Translation from Modern Greek

IIB   Translation from Modern Greek
III   Translation of a prose text in kathareuousa into English
Polish
  IIA   Translation from Modern Polish
  IIB   Translation into Modern Polish
Celtic
  I   Translation into Irish or Welsh and essay in Irish or Welsh
  IIA   Translation from Modern Irish or Modern Welsh
  IIB   Translation from Irish from the period up to 1200 or Welsh from the
    period up to 1400.

IV. Linguistic Studies I.

French:

The History of the French language up to the mid-twentieth century.

The paper will consist of two sections as follows. Candidates must answer questions from both sections.

(1) The history of the language (phonetics, phonology, grammar, vocabulary, semantics, sociolinguistics, external history).

(2) The description of the language of literary and non-literary texts from past periods. Candidates may confine their answer(s) to *one* of the following sub-sections:

(*a*) From Latin to Early Old French: Before 1150;
(*b*) Old and Middle French: 1100–1530;
(*c*) Renaissance and Classical French: 1530–1715;
(*d*) Into Modern French: 1715–1940.

Optional passages from texts for linguistic and stylistic commentary will be set for each period. The following are suggested as illustrative texts:

(*a*) Studer and Waters, *Historical French Reader*, 1, 6, 7, 10, 11, 13.
(*b*) Studer and Waters, *Historical French Reader*, 20, 26, 34, 40, 41, 45, 46, 47, 65.

Passages for commentary will be selected from the texts listed above.

In (*c*) and (*d*) the texts will be selected from appropriate literary and non-literary works.

German:

The development of the German language from 1170 to the present, with a special study of:

Werner der Gärtner, *Helmbrecht* (Reclam edn.).

Martin Luther, *Sendbrief vom Dolmetschen*, ed. K. Bischoff, pp. 6/7–28, l. 21/29, l. 22, and pp. 36–57.

Italian:

The history of the Italian language from the earliest times to the twentieth century.

Spanish:

The history of the Spanish language to 1700. The paper will be divided into three sections, and candidates must answer from two: (*a*) to 1250; (*b*) 1250–1500; (*c*) 1500–1700.

Portuguese:

The history and structure of the Portuguese language. Candidates will be required to show knowledge of the descriptive analysis of the contemporary language, as used in Portugal and Brazil, and of its historical development.

Russian:

The history of the Russian language with the following texts prescribed:

(1) for linguistic comment:

(a) Marginalia to Novgorod service books (V. V. Ivanov *et al.*, *Khrestomatiya po istorii russkogo yazyka*, Moscow, 1990, pp. 26–7).   5

[**Until 1 October 2014:** Novgorod birchbark texts nos. 247, 644, 605, 424, 724, 717, 731, 531, 705, 142, 370, 363, 361, 125, 43, 49, 154, (A. A. Zaliznyak, *Drevnenovgorodskii dialekt*, Moscow, 1995, pp. 223–4, 244–5, 246–8, 295–300, 325–9, 344–7, 349–51, 440–1, 494–5, 508–9, 514, 536, 542–3, 562–4).]

[**From 1 October 2014:** Novgorod birchbark texts, nos. 247, 752, 644, 605, 424, 776,   10
724, 717, 725, 531, 705, 765, 142, 370, 363, 364, 361, 43, 49, 154 (A. A. Zaliznyak, *Drevnenovgorodskii dialekt*, Moscow, 2004, pp. 239–40, 249–54, 267–8, 271–2, 307–9, 350–4, 396–7, 415–20, 422–4, 480–1, 536–8, 588–90, 606–7, 614, 651–2, 672–3).]

Vkladnaya Varlaama (Zaliznyak, pp. 548–60).

Treaty of Alexander Nevsky and Novgorod with the Germans, 1262–3 (S. P.   15
Obnorsky and S. G. Barkhudarov, *Khrestomatiya po istorii russkogo yazyka*, part 1, 2nd edn., Moscow, 1952, pp. 51–2).

Novgorod First Chronicle, *s.a.* 6738–9 (ed. A. N. Nasonov, *Novgorodskaya Pervaya letopis' starshego i mladshego izvoda*, Moscow-Leningrad, 1950, pp. 69–71).

(b) Afanasy Nikitin, *Khozhenie za tri morya* (Ivanov *et al.*, pp. 322–5).   20

Dukhovnaya gramota I. Yu. Gryaznogo (Ivanov *et al.*, pp. 279–80).

Letter of T. I. Golitsyna to V. V. Golitsyn (S. I. Kotkov *et al.*, *Moskovskaya delovaya i bytovaya pis'mennost' XVII veka*, Moscow, 1968, p. 20).

Letters of D. V. Mikhalkov to M. I. Mikhalkova and P. D. Mikhalkov (Kotkov *et al.*, pp. 39–40 (17b–v), 41 (18b)).   25

Letters of U. S. Pazukhina to S. I. Pazukhin and E. Klement'ev to F. M. Chelishchev (S. I. Kotkov and N. P. Pankratova, *istochniki po istorii narodno-razgovornogo yazyka XVII-nachala XVIII veka*, Moscow, 1964, pp. 169–70, 233).

[**Until 1 October 2014:** Letters of Peter I to Tsaritsa Natal'ya Kirillovna, to F. M. Apraksin, to B. P. Sheremetev (S. P. Obnorsky and S. G. Barkhudarov, *Khrestomatiya*   30
po istorii russkogo yazyka, part 2:1, Moscow, 1949, pp. 83, 96–7, 99–100).]

[**From 1 October 2014:** Letters of Peter I to Tsaritsa Natal'ya Kirillovna, to F. M. Apraksin, to B. P. Sheremetev (*Pis'ma i bumagi Petra Velikago*, vol. 1 (1688–1701), St Petersburg, 1887, No. 6, p. 11, No. 14, pp. 15–16; vol. 5 (1707), St Petersburg, 1907, No. 1695, pp. 221–2; vol. 7(i) (1708), St Petersburg, 1918, No. 2186, pp. 35–6).]   35

Evidence of A. Turcheninov on fire of 29 May 1737 (A. I. Sumkina and S. I. Kotkov, *Pamyatniki moskovskoi delovoi pis'mennosti XVIII veka*, Moscow, 1981, pp. 159–60).

Letters of V. B. Golitsyn to Vl. B. Golitsyn, M. D. Kurakina to B. I. Kurakin, M. M. Shcherbatov to D. M. Shcherbatov (Sumkina and Kotkov, pp. 24–6, 49–50   40
(50), 73–4).

(2) for translation and linguistic comment:

(a) Colophon to Ostromir Codex (Ivanov *et al.*, pp. 15–16).

Mstislavova gramota (Ivanov *et al.*, pp. 39–41). Colophon to Mstislav's Gospel Book (Ivanov *et al.*, pp. 49–50).   45

[**Until 1 October 2014:** Treaty of Novgorod with Grand Prince Yaroslav Yaroslavich, 1264 or 1265 (Obnorsky and Barkhudarov, part 1, pp. 52–4).]

[**From 1 October 2014:** *Spisok ubytkov novgorodtsev*, 1412 (Zaliznyak, pp. 686–692).]

Russkaya Pravda (Ivanov, *et al.*, pp. 67–73).   50

Novgorod First Chronicle, *s.a.* 6633–8, 6675–7, 6700, 6712, 6777–80 (Nasonov, pp. 21–2, 32–3, 40, 46–9, 87–90).

[**Until 1 October 2014:** (*b*) *Sudebnik* of 1497 (Ivanov *et al.*, 169–72).
Domostroi (Ivanov *et al.*, 255–60).]
[**From 1 October 2014:** (*b*) *Statejnyi spisok G. I. Mikulina* (D. S. Likhachev,
Puteshestviya russkikh poslov XVI–XVII vv., Moscow – Leningrad, 1954, p. 178,
4th paragraph – p. 181, 2nd paragraph).
Domostroi (Obnorsky and Barkhudarov, part I, pp. 236–241).]
Ulozhenie Alekseya Mikhailovicha, Chapter 10 (Ivanov *et al.*, pp. 380–1).
G. Kotoshikhin, O Rossii v tsarstvovanie Alekseya Mikhailovicha, Chapter
4, Section 24, Chapter 13, Sections 1–4 (ed. A. E. Pennington, Oxford, 1980,
pp. 65–7, 159–63).
Stateinyi spisok P. A. Tolstogo (Obnorsky and Barkhudarov, part 2:1, 1949, pp. 72–5).
Candidates will be required to show knowledge *either* of the texts listed under (1)
(*a*)-(*b*), *of* those listed under (1) (*a*) and (2) (*a*), *or* of those listed under (1) (*b*) and (2) (*b*).

Medieval and Modern Greek:
The History of Modern Greek Language. The paper will study the development of
Greek language from Koine to Standard Modern Greek. A discussion of the
Language Debate will be included in this paper.

Czech (with Slovak):
The history of Czech and Slovak. Passages for commentary and translation will be
taken from Porák, *Chrestomatie k vývoji českého jazyka* (1979), pp. 31–40, 54–64, 72–
88, 115–18, 126–31, 383–7. Candidates will be required to write one translation, one
commentary, and two essay-type questions.

Celtic:
Comparative and Historic Celtic Linguistics. Passages will be set for linguistic
commentary on *one* of (*a*) The history of Welsh *or* of Irish and Scottish Gaelic *or*
(*b*) Comparative Celtic Linguistics*

V. Linguistic Studies II.
French:
Modern French. Candidates will be required to show knowledge of the descriptive
analysis of the contemporary language, and will have the opportunity of discussing
the historical development of the language where this illuminates present-day usage.
The paper will contain optional questions on the principles of descriptive linguistics
to be answered with particular reference to French.

German:
Either
(1) Old High German, with the following texts prescribed for study: W. Braune,
Althochdeutsches Lesebuch (17th edn., by E. A. Ebbinghaus): V *Gespräche*; VIII
Isidor, cap. iii; XX Tatian, subsections 2, 4, and 7; XXIII Notker, subsections 1
and 13; XXVIII *Hildebrandslied*; XXIX *Wessobrunner Gebet*; XXX *Muspilli*; XXXII
Otfrid, subsections 7 (*Missus est Gabrihel angelus*) and 21 (*De die judicii*); XXXVI
Ludwigslied; XLIII *Ezzos Gesang*, Strasbourg version only.
Or
(2) Descriptive analysis of German as spoken and written at the present day
(phonetics, phonology, grammar, vocabulary, semantics, style). The paper will contain optional questions on the principles of descriptive linguistics to be answered with
particular reference to German.

---

* It is possible to do this paper with a knowledge of either Irish (with Scottish
Gaelic) or Welsh, together with some Continental Celtic, or with a knowledge of both
Irish and Welsh. Details of the passages for translation and comment are available
from the Modern Languages Faculty Office.

Italian:
Modern Italian. Candidates will be required to show knowledge of the descriptive analysis of the contemporary language, and will have the opportunity of discussing the historical development of the language where this illuminates present-day usage. The paper will contain optional questions on the principles of descriptive linguistics to be answered with particular reference to Italian.

Spanish:
Modern Spanish. Candidates will be required to show knowledge of the descriptive analysis of the structure of the contemporary language, as used in Spain and in the Americas.

Portuguese:
Varieties of Portuguese. Candidates will be required to apply the principles of descriptive linguistics to the analysis of regional and social varieties of the Portuguese of Portugal, Brazil, and Africa, and to Portuguese-based creoles. This paper will include commentaries on linguistic samples.

Russian:
Either
(1) The development of the Church Slavonic language, with the following texts prescribed:
(*a*) for linguistic comment:
Kiev Missal and *Euchologium Sinaticum* (R. Auty, *Handbook of Old Church Slavonic*, London, 1968 and subsequent reprints, Pt. ii, Texts and Glossary, passages IV, pp. 52–7, and VI, pp. 64–9).
Luke x: 25–37 (Auty, passage XIV, pp. 97–106: ed. L. P. Zhukovskaya *et al.*, *Aprakos Mstislava Velikogo*, Moscow, 1983, p. 131).
Psalm liv (ed. S. Sever'yanov, *Sinaiskaya Psaltyr'*, Petrograd, 1922, pp. 67–9; ed. E. V. Cheshko *et al.*, *Norovskaya psaltyr'. Srednebolgarskaya rukopis' XIV veka*, Sofia, 1989, Pt. ii, pp. 387–91; *Psaltir s posljedovanjem Đurd~a Crnojevića 1494*, reprinted Cetinje, 1986; the Synodal Bible of 1751 and subsequent editions, e.g. Moscow, 1815, St Petersburg, 1820).
(*b*) for translation and linguistic comment:
Vita Constantini, xiv–xv, xvii–xviii, *Vita Methodii*, v–xvii, the Treatise on Letters, the Acrostich Prayer (A. Vaillant, *Textes vieux-slaves*, Paris, 1968, Pt. i, Textes et glossaire, passages I, pp. 30–3, 37–40, II, pp. 46–55, III, pp. 57–61, IV C. pp. 68–70).
[**Until 1 October 2014:** *Kniga Konstantina filosofa i grammatika o pismenex*, sections 4–9 (V. Jagić, *Codex slovenicus rerum grammaticarum*, Berlin, 1896, reprinted Munich, 1968, V, pp. 108–13).]
[**From 1 October 2014:** *Povest' vremennykh let, s.a. 6406* (D. S. Likhachev, *Povest' vremennykh let*, part I, Moscow – Leningrad, 1950, pp. 21–23).]
Zhitie sv. Stefana episkopa Permskogo (ed. V. Druzhinin, St Petersburg, 1897, reprinted The Hague, 1959, pp. 69–74).
V. F. Burstov's *Bukvar'* (V. V. Ivanov *et al.*, *Khrestomatiya po istorii russkogo yazyka*, Moscow, 1990, pp. 369–74).
Candidates will be required to show knowledge of the texts listed under (1) (*a*) and (1) (*b*).
Or
(2) Descriptive analysis of Russian as spoken and written at the present day (phonetics, phonology, grammar, vocabulary, semantics, style). The paper will contain optional questions on the principles of descriptive linguistics to be answered with particular reference to Russian.

Medieval and Modern Greek:
The structure of the standard language as spoken and written at the present day (phonetics, phonology, grammar, vocabulary, semantics, style). The paper will contain optional questions on the principles of descriptive linguistics to be answered with particular reference to Modern Greek.

VI. Topics in the period of literature (*French only*) or Period of literature (i):

French: to 1530.
German: Medieval German Culture (to 1450): Texts, Contexts, and Issues.
Italian: 1220–1430.
Spanish: to 1499.
Portuguese: to 1540.*
Medieval and Modern Greek: Byzantine Greek to 1453.

Celtic: Medieval Irish up to 1600 and Medieval Welsh up to 1500. [Candidates will be able to confine their answers to questions on *either* Irish *or* Welsh topics.]

VII. Topics in the period of literature (*French only*) or Period of literature (ii):
French: 1530–1800†
German: Early Modern German Culture (1450–1730): Texts, Contexts, and Issues.
Italian: 1430–1635
Spanish: 1543–1695
Portuguese: 1500–1697‡
Russian: 1100–1700
Medieval and Modern Greek: Medieval Greek to 1669

VIII. Topics in the period of literature (*French only*) or Period of literature (iii):
French: 1715 to the present.†
German: Modern German Literature (1730 to the present): Texts, Contexts, and Issues.
Italian: Modern Italian Literature (1750 to the present) and Cinema
Spanish: The literature of Spain and of Spanish America: 1811 to the present.
Candidates may offer themselves for examination *either* in the literature of both Spain and Spanish America, *or* in the literature of Spain only, *or* in the literature of Spanish America only.
Portuguese: The literature of Portugal and Brazil: 1761 to the present.
Candidates may offer themselves for examination *either* in the literature of both Portugal and Brazil, *or* in the literature of Portugal only, *or* in the literature of Brazil only.
Russian: 1820–1953
Medieval and Modern Greek: Modern Greek, 1821 to the present.
Czech (with Slovak): Czech and Slovak literature, 1774 to the present.
Candidates will be required to answer three questions.

---

* Candidates offering both Portuguese paper VI and Portuguese paper VII may answer questions on the period 1500–40 in one of the two papers only. In papers VI and VII the questions affected by this provision will be indicated by an asterisk.
† (*a*) Candidates offering both French paper VII and French paper VIII may answer questions on the period 1715–1800 in *one* of the two papers only. In both papers, the questions most obviously affected by this provision will be indicated by an asterisk. (*b*) Candidates offering subject 8(iii), Ancient and French Classical Tragedy, in the Honour School of Classics and Modern Languages will not be permitted to discuss the work of Corneille and Racine in French paper VII.

§IX. **Enlightenment Texts (Russian only) or Early texts prescribed for study as examples of literature:**

French:

In French paper IX, the commentary section of the paper will include compulsory passages for translation.　　5

La Chanson de Roland, ed. Whitehead (Blackwell).

Béroul, *The Romance of Tristran,* ed. Ewert (Blackwell).

Villon, *Œuvres,* ed. Longnon-Foulet, 4th edn., with a special study of *Le Testament,* 1–909, 1660-end, and *Poésies Diverses* IX–XVI.

Candidates will be required to translate from one or more passages set for comment.　　1

German:

Das Nibelungenlied, ed. K. Bartsch *et al.* (Reclam 1997), avent. 1, 14–17, 23–30, 36–9.

Wolfram von Eschenbach, *Parzival,* books 3, 5, and 9.

Heinrich von Morungen, *Lieder,* ed. H. Tervooren (Reclam 1986)

Das Osterspiel von Muri and Das Innsbrucker Osterspiel　　1

Italian:

Dante, *La divina commedia,* with a special study of two of the three *Cantiche.*

Spanish:

Poema de mio Cid, ed. Michael (Clásicos Castalia).

Juan Ruiz, *Libro de Buen Amor,* ed. Gybbon-Monypenny (Clásicos Castalia).　　2

Comedia o tragicomedia de Calisto y Melibea, ed. P. E. Russell (Clásicos Castalia).

Portuguese:

E. Gonçalves and M. A. Ramos, *A Lírica Galego-Portuguesa* (Comunicação).

Alfonso X of Castile, *Cantigas de Santa Maria,* ed. W. Mettmann (Clásicos Castalia, vol. I, 1986).　　2

Fernão Lopes, *Crónica de D. João* I (textos escolhidos), ed. T. Amado (Comunicação).

Zurara, *Crónica dos feitos de Guiné* (chs. 1-25). (Candidates are advised also to read Zurara, *Chronique de Guinée,* ed. L. Bourdon (Ifan-Dakar, 1960)).

Russian:　　3

The syllabus will consist of the following texts with passages for commentary eligible to be set from those marked with an *:

Avvakum, *Zhitie**

'Povest' o Savve Grudtsyne'; 'Povest' o Frole Skobeeve'; 'Povest' o Bove Koroleviche'　　3

Antiokh Kantemir *Satires* I*, II, IV, VII, IX

Mikhailo Lomonosov: 'Oda na vzyatie Khotina'; 'Pis'mo o pol'ze stekla', 'Oda torzhestvennaya (1747)*; 'Oda torzhestvennaya (1762)*; 'Utrennee razmyshlenie o bozhiem velichestve'*, 'Vechernee ramyshlenie'*.

Aleksandr Sumarokov, 'Epistola o stikhotvorstve'; 'Lyubovnye elegii' [extracts]*　　4

Denis Fonvizin, *Brigadir, Nedorosl'*;

Vassily Kapnist, *Yabeda*

Ippolit Bogdanovich, *Dushen'ka*

N.I. Novikov, *Satiricheskie zhurnaly.* Excerpts.

M. Chulkov, *Prigozhaya povarikha**　　4

Alexander Radishchev, *Puteshestvie iz Peterburga v Moskvu* [3 chapters to be prescribed*]

§ Each paper will be divided into two sections, one containing questions on the general aspects of the books and authors, and the other containing passages for explanation and comment. Both sections will be compulsory.

Gavriil Derzhavin: 'Bog'*; 'Pamyatnik geroyu'; 'Vel'mozha'; 'Vlastitelyam i sud'yam'; 'Russkie devushki'; 'Evgeniyu. Zhizn' zvanskaya'*; 'Solovey vo sne'; 'Na smert' knyazya Meshcherskogo'*, 'Priglashenie k obedu'; 'Pamyatnik'; 'Moi istukan'; 'Reka vremen v svoem stremlenii'.

Nikolai Karamzin, Bednaya Liza*, *Ostrov Borngol'm; Pis'ma russkogo puteshes-*   5
vennika [extracts]

Vassily Zhukovsky, *Svetlana*; 'Sel'skoe kladbishche'*

Ivan Krylov, 'Pis'mo o pol'ze zhelanii'; 'Strekoza i muravei', 'Vorona i lisitsa', 'Lebed' rak i shchuka', 'Volk i iagnionok', 'Volk na psarne', 'Kvartet', 'Ryb'i pliaski'

Konstantin Batiushkov, 'Moi Penaty'*; 'Moi genii'; Elegiia; Na razvalnyakh   10
zamke v Shvetsii;

Alexandr Pushkin, *Ruslan i Liudmila*; selected lyrics*

Medieval and Modern Greek:

Candidates may choose one of either A or B:*
The commentary section of the paper will include compulsory passages for translation.   15

A: Byzantine texts:

Paul the Silentiary, *Ekphrasis* of Haghia Sophia (ed. Friedlander).
Christ and Paranikas, *Anthologia graeca carminum Christianorum*, pp. 147–236 and 247–52.
The Life of St Andreas Salos (ed. L. Ryden).   20
Michael Psellos, *Chronographia*, bk. VI (ed. S. Impellizzeri, vol. 1, pp. 246–320, and vol. 2, pp. 8–152).

B: Medieval vernacular texts:

Digenis Akritis: the Grottaferrata and Escorial Versions (ed. E. M. Jeffreys).
Livistros kai Rodamni (ed. P. A. Agapitos).   25
Ptochoprodromos (ed. H. Eideneier).

Passages will *not* be set from:

Digenis Akritis, Grottaferrata version, book V.
Ptochoprodromus, poem IV.

Czech (with Slovak):   30

Dalimilova kronika, chs. 1–32, 41, 66–70, 102–6.
Život svaté Kateřiny.
Tkadleček.
Candidates will be required to answer one question on each of the three texts, including one commentary. They will also be required to translate a passage.   35

Celtic:

Any four of the following: Early Texts (commentary section of the paper will include compulsory passages for translation).
Togail Bruidne Da Derga, ed. E. Knott (Dublin, 1936)
Fingal Rónáin and Other Stories, ed. D. Greene (Dublin, 1955).   40
Scéla Cano meic Gartnáin, ed. D. A. Binchy (Dublin, 1963).
Serglige Con Culainn, ed. M. Dillon (Dublin, 1953).
Cath Almaine, ed. P. O. Riain (Dublin, 1978).
The Irish Adam and Eve Story from Saltair na Rann, ed. D. Greene and F. Kelly (Dublin, 1976).   45
Canu Aneirin, ed. I. Williams (Cardiff, 1938).
Canu Llywarch Hen, ed. I. Williams (Cardiff, 1935).
Armes Prydein, ed. I. Williams (Cardiff, 1955; or Dublin, 1972).

---

* Those who offer B may not offer options (1) and (2) in Paper X.

M. Haycock, *Blodeugerdd Barddas o Ganu Crefyddol Cynnar* (Y Bala: Barddas, 1994).
Culhwch ac Olwen, ed. R. Bromwich and D. Simon Evans (Cardiff, 1992).
Selection from the series: R. Geraint Gruffydd (gen. ed.), Cyfres Beirdd y Tywysogion vols. I, II, V–VII (Cardiff, 1991–6).   5

†**X. Modern Prescribed Authors (i):** ‡Passages for explanation and comment will be taken from the works prescribed for special study. Candidates will be expected to have read works by their chosen authors other than those prescribed for special study.

French: 1(

Any two of the following:

(1) Rabelais, with a special study of *Gargantua* and *Le Quart Livre*.
(2) Montaigne, with a special study of *Essais*, I. 20 (Que philosopher, c'est apprendre à mourir), I. 23 (De la coutume et de ne changer aisément une loi reçue), I. 26 (De l'institution des enfants), II. 17 (De la praesumption), II. 6 (De l'exercitation), III. 2 (Du repentir), III. 5 (Sur des vers de Virgile), III. 13 (De l'expérience).   1‹
(3) Pascal, *Les Provinciales, Pensées et opuscules divers*, éd. G. Ferreyrolles et P. Sellier, in *La Pochothéque* (Livres de poche/Classiques Garnier), with a special study of *Pensées*, 1–414; 419–671; 680–690; 694–695; 697–717; 742–769; *De l'esprit géométrique et de l'art de persuader*.   2(
(4) Molière, with a special study of *L'École des femmes, Les Fourberies de Scapin, Le Tartuffe, Dom Juan, Le Misanthrope, Le Malade Imaginaire*.
(5) Racine, with a special study of: *Andromaque, Britannicus, Bérénice, Bajazet, Iphigénie, Athalie* in *Théâtre complet*, ed. J. Rohou (Pochothèque, Livre de Poche, 1998).   2‹
(6) Voltaire, with a special study of *Romans et contes*, ed. E. Guitton (Pochothèque, Livre de Poche, 1994): the following works: *Zadig, Paméla* (pp. 138–96), *Candide, contes de Guillaume Vadé* (pp. 339–453), *La Princesse de Babylone, Les Lettres d'Amabed, Le Taureau blanc; Lettres philosophiques*, ed. F. Deloffre, Folio.   3(
(7) Diderot, with a special study of *Le Rêve d'Alembert*, ed. Chouillet, Livre de Poche, *Jacques le fataliste*, ed. Belaval, Folio *Le Neveu de Rameau*, ed. Varloot, Folio, *Le Salon de 1765*, ed. Bukdahl and Lorenceau, Hermann.

German: 3‹

Any two of the following:

(1) Luther, with a special study of *Von der Freyheyt eyni Christenmenschen* (http://luther.chadwyck.co.uk).
(2) Gryphius, with a special study of *Gedichte*, ed. Elschenbroich (Reclam). Candidates will further be expected to have studied a representative selection of Gryphius's drama.   4(
(3) Grimmelshausen, with a special study of *Simplicissimus (Teutsch)*. Candidates will further be expected to have studied others of the 'Simplizianische Schriften'.
(4) Goethe as dramatist, with a special study of *Faust*, part I. Candidates will further be expected to have studied at least three other dramatic works by Goethe.   4‹

---

† Each paper will be divided into two sections, one containing questions on the general aspects of the books and authors, and the other containing passages for explanation and comment. Both sections will be compulsory.
‡ Except in the case of Medieval and Modern Greek.

(5) Schiller, with a special study of *Wallenstein*. Candidates will further be expected to have studied other works representative of Schiller's development as a dramatist.

(6) Hölderlin, with a special study of Friedrich Hölderlin, *Gedichte*, ed. Gerhard Kurz and Wolfgang Braungart, Reihe Reclam, the poetry 1798–1806.   5

(7) Kleist, with a special study of *Prinz Friedrich von Homburg*. Candidates will further be expected to have studied a representative selection of Kleist's plays and prose works.

(8) Hoffmann, with a special study of *Der Sandmann* and *Der goldne Topf*. Candidates will further be expected to have studied at least one of the novels   10 and a representative selection of the shorter fiction.

(9) Heine, with a special study of *Atta Troll* and *Deutschland, ein Wintermärchen*. Candidates will further be expected to have studied a representative selection of Heine's poetry and prose, the latter to include the *Reisebilder*.

(10) Rilke, with a special study of *Neue Gedichte*. Candidates will further be   15 expected to have studied a representative selection of Rilke's other writings.

(11) Thomas Mann, with a special study of *Bekenntnisse des Hochstaplers Felix Krull*. Candidates will further be expected to have studied at least one of the novels and a representative selection of the shorter fiction.

(12) Kafka, with a special study of *Der Proce: Roman in der Fassung der*   20 *Handschrift*, ed. Malcolm Pasley (Fischer Taschenbuch Verlag, No. 114123). Candidates will further be expected to have studied a representative selection of Kafka's other fiction.

(13) Brecht, with a special study of *Leben des Galilei*. Candidates will further be expected to have studied other works representative of Brecht's development   25 as dramatist and poet.

(14) Grass, with a special study of *Die Blechtrommel*. Candidates will further be expected to have studied a representative selection of Grass's prose fiction.

(15) Christa Wolf, with a special study of *Nachdenken über Christa T*. Candidates will further be expected to have studied a representative selection of Christa   30 Wolf's prose works.

(16) W. G. Sebald, with special study of *Austerlitz*. Candidates will further be expected to have studied a representative selection of Sebald's other works.

(17) Rainer Werner Fassbinder, with special study of the film *Katzelmacher*. Candidates will further be expected to have studied a representative selection   35 of Fassbinder's other films and plays.

(18) Elfriede Jelinek, with special study of *Die Klavierspielerin*. Candidates will further be expected to have studied a representative selection of Jelinek's other works.

Note. The paper will contain questions of a general nature, and questions on specific   40 texts. Candidates will not be allowed to make any one text the principal subject of more than one answer.

Italian:

Any two of the following:

(1) Petrarch, with a special study of the *Canzoniere,* Nos. 1–12; 16–24; 30; 34–7;   45 50–4; 60–2; 70; 72; 77; 80–1; 90–2; 102; 119; 125–6; 128–9; 132–4; 136; 142; 145; 148; 159–60; 164; 197; 211; 219; 263–4; 268; 272; 279–80; 287–92; 302–4; 310–11; 315; 327; 353; 359–60; 364–6. Candidates will further be expected to have studied a representative selection of Petrarch's other Italian poems and of works originally written in Latin.   50

(2) Boccaccio, with a special study of the *Decameron*, I. 1–3; II, 2, 5, 10; III, 2; IV, 1, 2, 5, 7, 9; V, 6, 8, 9; VI, 1, 9, 10; VII, 4, 9; VIII, 3, 8; IX, 1, 2; X, 2, 9, 10. Candidates will further be expected to have studied a representative selection of other parts of the *Decameron* and of other works by Boccaccio.

(3) Machiavelli, with a special study of *Il Principe*. Candidates will further be   5
expected to have studied a representative selection of Machiavelli's other works, including *I discorsi* and *La mandragola*.

(4) Ariosto, with a special study of *Orlando Furioso*, cantos I-XIII.45; XVIII.146-XXIV; XXVIII-XXX; XXXIV; XLV-XLVI. Candidates will further be ex-pected to have studied other parts of the *Orlando Furioso* and a selection of the   10
Satire.

(5) Tasso, with a special study of *Gerusalemme Liberata*, cantos I-VII, XI-XVI; XIX-XX, and *Aminta*. Candidates will further be expected to have studied other parts of the *Gerusalemme Liberata*.

Spanish: 15
Any two of the following:

(1) Garcilaso de la Vega,*Obra poética y textos en prosa* (ed. B. Morros, Crítica) (not including the Latin poetry and the prose texts).

(2) Cervantes, with a special study of *El ingenioso hidalgo don Quijote de la Mancha*. (Passages for commentary will be set from the Second Part only.)   20

(3) Góngora, with a special study of *Soledad primera* (from *Soledades*, ed. R. Jammes, Castalia), *Fábula de Polifemo y Galatea* (ed. J. Ponce Cárdenas, Cátedra), *Sonnets* (in *Poems of Góngora*, ed. R. O. Jones, pp. 87–92). Candidates will be expected to have read *Soledad segunda*, but passages for commentary will not be set from it.   25

(4) Quevedo, with a special study of 'Infierno', 'El mundo por de dentro', 'Sueño de la muerte', in *Sueños y discursos* (ed. J. O. Crosby, Castalia); *La cuna y la sepultura*, and *España defendida* (Preliminaries and Chapter 5 only), in *Obras completas, I: Prosa* (ed. F. Buendía, Aguilar); *Poesía varia* (ed. J. O. Crosby, Cátedra), nos. 16-30, 35–53, 71–83, 87–106, 128–33, 160–1; *El buscón* (ed.   30
D. Ynduráin, Cátedra).

(5) Calderón, with a special study of *La vida es sueño* (ed. C. Morón, Cátedra) (candidates will be expected to have read the *auto* of the same name, but passages for commentary will be not be set from it). *El pintor de su deshonra* (ed. Ruiz Lagos, Colección Aula Magna), *El mágico prodigioso*,   35
and *El Alcalde de Zalamea* (both Clásicos castellanos), *El gran teatro del mundo* (ed. B. W. Wardropper, Cátedra), *El alcalde de Zalamea* (ed. J. Ma. Díez Borque, Castalia), and *El gran teatro del mundo* (ed. E. Frutos Cortés, Cátedra).

Portuguese: 40
Any two of the following:

(1) Gil Vicente, with a special study of *Auto da Alma, Auto da Feira, Farsa de Inês Pereira, Farsa dos Almocreves, O Triunfo do Inverno, Dom Duardos*.

(2) João de Barros, with a special study of *Rópica Pnefma* (ed. I. S. Révah, Lisbon, 1955) and *Décadas*, vol. I (ed. A. Baião, Sá da Costa, Lisbon, 1945).   45

(3) Camões, with a special study of *Os Lusíadas* (ed. F. Pierce) and *Líricas* (ed. Rodrigues Lapa, 1970 or later).

(4) Francisco Manuel de Melo, with a special study of *Epanáfora política, Relógios falantes, Hospital das Letras, Carta de Guía de Casados, O Fidalgo Aprendiz*.

(5) António Ferreira, *Bristo, Cioso, Poemas Lusitanos* (including *A Castro*).   50

Russian:
Any two of the following:
   (1) Pushkin, with a special study of *Tsygany, Evgeny Onegin, Povesti Belkina,* Selected lyrics (copies of the list of prescribed poems are available from the Slavonic Library, 47 Wellington Square).   5
   (2) Gogol, with a special study of *Mirgorod,* (excluding *Taras Bul'ba) Shinel', Zapiski sumasshedshego, Nevsky Prospekt, Portret, Nos, Mertvye dushi* Part I, *Revizor.*
   (3) Mandel'shtam. Selected lyrics (copies of the prescribed poems are available from the Slavonic Library, 47 Wellington Square). Candidates will also be   10 expected to have read a representative selection of Mandel'shtam's artistic prose and articles on literary topics.
   (4) Mayakovsky, with a special study of *Oblako v shtanakh, Pro eto, Lyublyu, Klop,* and selected lyrics (copies of the prescribed poems are available from the Slavonic Library, 47 Wellington Square). Candidates will also be expected to   15 have read *Kak delat' stikhi* and a representative selection of Mayakovsky's other works.
   (5) Bulgakov, with a special study of *Beelaya gvardiya, Sobach'e serdtse, Beg, Master i Margarita.*

Medieval and Modern Greek: 20
Any two of the following:
   (1) *Digenis Akritis: the Grottaferrata and Escorial Versions* (ed. E. M. Jeffreys).
   (2) The vernacular verse romances.
   (3) Cretan drama, with a special study of Chortatsis' *Erophile, Katzourbos,* and *Panoria* (ed. R. Bancroft-Marcus).   25
   (4) *Erotokritos.*
   (5) Greek oral poetry.

Czech (with Slovak):
Any three of the following:
   (1) Comenius, with a special study of *Labyrint světa a ráj srdce.*   30
   (2) Hrabal, with a special study of *Obsluhoval jsem anglického krále.*
   (3) Hodrová, with a special study of *Podobojí.*
   (4) Holan, with a special study of *Terezka Planetová.*
   (5) Johanides, with a special study of *Marek koniar a uhorský pápež.*
   (6) Mitana, with a special study of the volume *Prievan.*   35
Candidates will be required to answer questions on each of their three authors, including one commentary.

Celtic:
Any two of the following:
   (1) *Gwaith Guto'r Glyn,* ed. I. Williams and J. Llywelyn Williams (Cardiff, 1939).   40
   (2) *Gwaith Tudur Aled,* ed. T. Gwynn Jones (Cardiff, 1926).
   (3) *Gwaith Iorwerth Fynglwyd,* ed. H. Ll. Jones and E. I. Rowlands (Cardiff, 1973).
   (4) *Gramadegau'r Penceirddiaid,* ed. G. J. Williams and E. J. Jones (Cardiff, 1934), Texts A and C (pp. 1–18, 39–58).
   (5) *Acallam na Senórach* (in the selection ed. M. Dillon, *Stories from the Acallam*   45 [Dublin, 1970]).
   (6) *Caithréim Cellaig,* ed. K. Mulchrone, 2nd edn. (Dublin, 1971).
   (7) *Buile Shuibne,* ed. J. G. O'Keefe (Dublin, 1931).
   (8) *Tóruigheacht Dhiarmada agus Ghráinne,* ed. N. Ní Sheaghdha, Irish Texts Society 48 (Dublin, 1967).   50
   (9) *Dánta Grádha,* ed. T. F. O'Rahilly, 2nd edn. (Cork: Cork University Press, 1926).

§**XI. Early Modern Literary Texts *or* Goethe (*German only*) or**
§**Modern Prescribed Authors (ii):**
    Passages for explanation and comment will be taken from the works prescribed for special study. Candidates will be expected to have read works by their chosen authors other than those prescribed for special study.   5

French:
    Any two of the following:
    (1) Stendhal, with a special study of *Le Rouge et le Noir* and *La Chartreuse de Parme.*
    (2) Baudelaire, with a special study of *Les Fleurs du Mal* and the *Petits Poèmes en*   10
        prose.
    (3) Flaubert, with a special study of *Madame Bovary, Trois Contes* and
        L'Éducation sentimentale.
    (4) Mallarmé, with a special study of *Poésies* (edition Deman), ed. Bertrand
        Marchal (Gallimard, Collection Poésie, 1992, pp. 1–74), and *Igitur,*   15
        Divagations, Un coup de dés, ed. Bertrand Marchal (Gallimard, Collection
        Poésie, 2003), omitting *Igitur, Quelques médaillons et portraits en pied* and
        Pages diverses.
    (5) Gide, with a special study of *L'Immoraliste, La Porte étroite, Si le grain ne*
        meurt and *Les Faux-Monnayeurs.*   20
    (6) Sartre, with a special study of *La Nausée, Les Mouches, Les Séquestrés*
        d'Altona and *Les Mots.*
    (7) Duras, with a special study of *Un barrage contre le Pacifique, Le Ravissement de*
        Lol V. Stein, L'Amant, and *Hiroshima, mon amour* (film script).
    (8) Barthes, with a special study of *L'Empire des signes, Le Plaisir du texte, Roland*   25
        Barthes par Roland Barthes, and *La Chambre claire.*

German:
    Either A : Early Modern Literary Texts
    Any four out of the following six topics:
    (1) Luther: *Von der Freyheyt eyni Christenmenschen* and *Von weltlicher Obrigkeit*   30
        (http://luther.chadwyck.co.uk).
    (2) Reformation controversy: Hans Sachs, *Die Wittenbergisch Nachtigall* (Reclam
        edition), and Caritas Pirckheimer, *Denkwürdigkeiten* (http://sophie.byu.edu).
    (3) Religious poetry: Andreas Gryphius, *Gedichte* (Reclam edition) and Catharina
        Regina von Greiffenberg, *Gedichte* (www.wortblume.de).   35
    (4) Secular poetry: Paul Fleming, *Gedichte* (Reclam edition) and Sybille Schwarz,
        Gedichte (www.wortblume.de).
    (5) The novel: *Historia von D. Johann Fausten* (Reclam edition) and
        Grimmelshausen: *Courasche* (Reclam edition).
    (6) Baroque tragedy: Daniel Casper von Lohenstein, *Cleopatra* (Reclam edition)   40
        and *Sophonisbe* (Reclam edition).
Note. This paper will require candidates to attempt a commentary and two essay
questions.
Or B: Goethe. Candidates will be required to read a selection of Goethe's works in
        more than one genre. Candidates for this paper may not offer Goethe as   45
        dramatist as one of their authors on Paper X.

---

    § Each paper will be divided into two sections, one containing questions on the
general aspects of the books and authors, and the other containing passages for
explanation and comment. Both sections will be compulsory.

Italian:
Any two of the following:
(1) Manzoni, with a special study of *I promessi sposi*. Candidates will further be expected to have studied Manzoni's tragedies and a selection of his other works.
(2) Leopardi, with a special study of *I Canti*. Candidates will further be expected to have studied the *Operette morali* and a selection of Leopardi's other writings.
(3) D'Annunzio, with a special study of *Alcyone*. Candidates will further be expected to have studied a selection of D'Annunzio's other works in verse and prose.
(4) Verga, with a special study of *I Malavoglia* and *Mastro-don Gesualdo*. Candidates will further be expected to have studied a selection of Verga's other fiction.
(5) Pirandello, with a special study of *Il fu Mattia Pascal, Sei personaggi in cerca d'autore* and *I giganti della montagna*. Candidates will further be expected to have studied a representative selection of Pirandello's drama and prose work.
(6) Montale, with a special study of 'Ossi di seppia' in *Ossi di seppia*, Section IV of *Le occasioni*, 'Finisterre' in *La bufera e altro* and 'Xenia I' in *Satura*. Candidates will further be expected to have studied a representative selection of Montale's other poems.
(7) Calvino, with a special study of *Il cavaliere inesistente* and *Se una notte d'inverno un viaggiatore*. Candidates will further be expected to have studied other works representative of Calvino's development as a writer.

Spanish:
Any two of the following:
(1) Pérez Galdós, with a special study of *Juan Martín el Empecinado, El amigo Manso, Miau, Nazarín*.
(2) Leopoldo Alas, with a special study of *La Regenta* (ed. Gonzalo Sobejano, Clásicos Castalia), and *Cuentos escogidos* (ed. G. G. Brown, Oxford, 1964).
(3) Valle-Inclán, with a special study of *Sonatas*; *Águila de blasón*; *Romance de lobos*; *Divinas palabras*; *Luces de Bohemia* (ed. A. Zamora Vicente, Clásicos castellanos); *Martes de carnaval*; *Tirano Banderas* (ed. A. Zamora Vicente, Clásicos castellanos). Candidates will also be expected to have read *La lámpara maravillosa* and *La corte de los milagros*.
(4) Federico García Lorca, with a special study of *Amor de Don Perlimplín con Belisa en su jardín, Así que pasen cinco años, Bodas de sangre, Canciones, Divan del Tamarit, Llanto por Ignacio Sánchez Mejías, Mariana Pineda, Poeta en Nueva York* (ed. Millán), *El público, La zapatera prodigiosa*.
(5) Neruda, with a special study of *Veinte poemas de amor y una canción desesperada* (ed. Montes, Clásicos Castalia, Madrid, 1987); *Canto general* (I, II, XIV, XV); *Memorial de Isla Negra* (I, IV) (Seix Barral, Barcelona, 1976); *Pablo Neruda: A Basic Anthology* (ed. Pring-Mill, Dolphin, Oxford, 1975), pp. 8–42 and 80–109, and those poems included in the *Basic Anthology* from the following collections: *Estravagario, Plenos poderes, Jardín de invierno*, and *El mar y las campanas*.
(6) Borges, with a special study of *Ficciones* (ed. either Emecé or Alianza-Emecé); *El aleph*; *El informe de Brodie*; *Obra poética 1923–1976* (ed. Alianza-Emecé, sections entitled *El hacedor* and *El otro, el mismo*).

Portuguese:
Any two of the following:
(1) Almeida Garrett, with a special study of *Portugal na balança da Europa, Frei Luís de Sousa, O Arco de Sant' Ana, Viagens na Minha Terra, Folhas Caídas*.

(2) Eça de Queirós, with a special study of *O Crime do Padre Amaro, Os Maias,* and *A Cidade e as Serras.*

(3) Machado de Assis, with a special study of *Memórias póstumas de Brás Cubas, Dom Casmurro,* and *Quincas Borba.*

(4) Fernando Pessoa, with a special study of *Obras completas,* vol. I (Ática)   5
Mensagem and Poesia de Alvaro de Campos.

(5) Graciliano Ramos, with a special study of *Caetés, Angústia, Vidas Secas, Infância.*

(6) Clarice Lispector, with a special study of *Perto do Coração Selvagem, A Paixão segundo G. H., A Hora da Estrela.*   1(

(7) Mia Couto, with special study of *Vozes anoitecidas, Terra sonâmbula, A varanda do frangipani.*

Russian:
Any two of the following:

(1) Dostoevsky, with a special study of *Prestuplenie i nakazanie, Brat'ya*   1
Karamazovy, Zapiski iz podpol'ya.

(2) Tolstoy, with a special study of *Anna Karenina, Voyna i mir.*

(3) Chekhov, with a special study of *Palata No. 6, Poprygun'ya, Moya zhizn, Muzhiki, Dama s sobachkoy, V ovrage, Dushechka, Arkkhierey,* and *Nevesta,* as well as *Chayka, Dyadya Vanya, Tri sestry, Vishnevi sad.*   2(

(4) Solzhenitsyn, with a special study of *Odin den' Ivana Denisovicha, V kruge pervom* (candidates are expected to be familiar with the 96-chapter version of the novel first published in 1978), *Rakovy korpus.*

(5) Nabokov, with a special study of *Otchayanie, Priglashenie na kazn', Dar.*

Medieval and Modern Greek: 2
Any two of the following:

(1) Solomos, with a special study of the poems composed between 1825 and 1849 (*Apanta,* ed. L. Politis (Athens, 1961), pp. 139–255), the *Dialogos,* and the *Gynaika tes Zakythos.*

(2) Palamas, with a special study of *O dodekalogos tou Gyftou, Oi khairetismoi tes*   3(
Eliogennetes and the following sections of *E asalefte zoe: Patrides, Foinikia, Askraios, Alysides.*

(3) Kavafis, with a special study of *Poiemata,* vols. i and ii, ed. G. P. Savidis (Ikaros, Athens, 1963, or later).

(4) Seferis, with a special study of *Poiemata* (Athens, 1972, or later).   3

(5) Tsirkas, with a special study of the trilogy *Akyvernetes politeies (E leskhe, Ariagne,* and *E nykhterida)*

(6) The novels of Kazantzakis, with a special study of *Vios kai politeia tou Alexe Zorba* and *O Khristos xanastavronetai.*

(7) Melipoiemene Poiese, with special study of Nikos Gatsos, *Amorgos* and   4
Collected Versus (Ikaros); Dionysis Savvopoulos, *He Souma* (Ianos, 2004).

XII. Special Subjects.

1. A candidate may offer one or two (depending on the regulations outlined above) of the Special Subjects from the list circulated in the Trinity Term one year before the examination. The list of options available in that year will be publicised on   4
the Faculty's internal website (and circulated to all students and tutors by e-mail) by the beginning of fifth week of Trinity Term.

Methods of assessment:
The method of assessment for each subject will be published with the list of options by the beginning of the fifth week of the Trinity Term one year before the examina-   5
tion, according to the following key:

A: Three-hour unseen written paper.

B: An essay or portfolio of essays (the number of essays required to be shown in parentheses) aggregating to about 6,000 words and not exceeding 8,000 words, to be submitted by hand to the Examinations Schools, High Street, Oxford by noon on the Friday of the ninth week of Hilary Term in the year of the examination, together with a statement certifying that the essay (s) are the candidate's own work and that they have not already been submitted, either wholly or substantially, for a degree in this university or elsewhere. 5

C: An essay or portfolio of essays (the number of essays required to be shown in parentheses) aggregating to about 6,000 words and not exceeding 8,000 words (except that the Linguistic Project shall be in the range 8,000-10,000 words), written as answers to an examination paper to be collected from the Examination Schools, and signed for by candidates, on the Friday of the fifth week of the Hilary Term next before the examination. Completed essay(s) should be submitted by hand to the Examinations Schools by noon on the Friday of the ninth week of Hilary Term in the year of the examination, together with a statement certifying that the essays are the candidate's own work and that they have not already been submitted, either wholly or substantially, for a degree in this university or elsewhere. 10 15 20

2. Candidates may not be permitted to offer certain Special Subjects in combination with certain other papers. Candidates offering a Special Subject and another paper both of which involve the study of the same author or authors, may not make the same texts the principal subject of an answer in both the papers. 25

3. Instead of a Special Subject from the list for the year concerned, a candidate may follow the directions under **Section 3**. Paper XII. Special Subjects.

XIII. General Linguistics.

Candidates will be required to show knowledge of analytic techniques and problems in contemporary syntax and semantic theory, phonetics, and phonology, and their relation to issues of linguistic variation, language acquisition, and language change. 30

XIV. Extended Essay (*optional*).

1. Candidates may offer an Extended Essay, subject to the following provisions: 35
   (i) The subject of every essay shall, to the satisfaction of the board of the faculty, fall within the scope of the Honour School of Modern Languages.
   (ii) The subject of an essay may, but need not, overlap any subject or period on which the candidate offers a paper, but candidates should avoid repetition of material presented in the extended essay in other parts of the examination. Candidates should not offer a title involving the reading of works only or mainly in translation from the original. 40
   (iii) Candidates are prohibited from making the same *text or texts* the principal subject of their Special Subject or Extended Essay and of an answer or essay in papers VI-XI but they are *not* prohibited from making an *author* the focus of their Special Subject or Extended Essay on whom they also intend to write in another part of the examination, as long as they make use of different texts and have due regard to the need to avoid repetition of the same material. 45

(iv) Candidates proposing to offer an essay must submit, through their college, to the Chair of the Board of the Faculty of Medieval and Modern Languages (on a form obtainable from the Modern Languages Administration and Faculty Office, 41 Wellington Square) a statement of their name, college, the honour school they intend to offer, the academic year in which they intend to take the examination, and the title of the proposed essay together with (*a*) a statement in about fifty words of how the subject is to be treated, (*b*) a statement signed by a supervisor or tutor, preferably in the language or in one of the languages or in the field of study with which the extended essay is concerned, that he or she considers the subject suitable, and suggesting a person or persons who might be invited to be an examiner or an assessor (the board will not approve a title unless it is satisfied that a suitably qualified examiner or assessor based in Oxford will be available), and (*c*) a statement by a college tutor that he or she approves the candidate's application, not later than the Wednesday of the second week of the Michaelmas Full Term preceding the examination.

(v) Subject to the agreement of the faculty board, candidates may offer an essay written in the language or one of the languages they are offering in the Honour School; application, with a letter of support from a college tutor, should be made at the same time as the proposed title of the essay is submitted for approval. (*This provision is not available in the case of Russian*).

(vi) The faculty board will decide by the end of the third week of the Michaelmas Full Term preceding the examination whether the candidate has permission to offer an essay. Permission may be granted on the condition that the candidate agrees to amend details of the title to the satisfaction of the board, and submits the required amendments to the Administration and Faculty Office for the board's approval by Friday of the sixth week of the Michaelmas Full Term preceding the examination. If the proposed title is approved, this will be notified by the Administration and Faculty Office, together with any conditions attached to the approval, to the candidate and to the Chair of the Examiners for the Honour School.

(vii) A candidate may seek approval after Friday of the sixth week of the Michaelmas Full Term preceding the examination for an amendment of detail in an approved title, by application to the Administration and Faculty Office. The Chair of the Examiners and the Chair of the Board, acting together, will decide whether or not a proposed amendment shall be approved.

2. Every essay must be the candidate's own work. Tutors may, however, discuss with candidates the proposed field of study, the sources available, and the method of presentation. Tutors may also read and comment on a first draft.

All quotations, whether direct or indirect, from primary or secondary sources must be explicitly acknowledged. The use of unacknowledged quotations will be penalized.

Candidates must sign a certificate stating that the essay is their own work and this certificate must be sent at the same time as the essay, but under separate cover, addressed to: The Chair of the Examiners, Honour School of Modern Languages, Examination Schools, High Street, Oxford.

3. Essays previously submitted for the Honour School of Modern Languages may be resubmitted. No essay will be accepted if it has already been submitted, wholly or substantially, for another Honour School or degree of this University or a degree of any other institute. The certificate must contain a confirmation that the essay has not already been so submitted.

4. No essay shall be ineligible because it has been submitted, in whole or in part, for any scholarship or prize in this university.

5. Candidates shall present a one-page summary of the arguments in English at the beginning of their essay; essays shall be in the range 6,000–8,000 words (exclusive of the footnotes, the bibliography, any appendices, and summary (where this applies)). No person or body shall have authority to permit the limit of 8,000 words to be exceeded, except that, in the case of a commentary on a text, and at the discretion of the chair of the examiners, any substantial quoting of that text need not be included in the word limit. The examiners will not take account of such parts of an essay as are beyond these limits. There must be a select bibliography, listing all primary and secondary sources consulted when writing the essay, and full details must be given of all citations (either in the text, or in footnotes).

All essays must be typed in double-spacing on one side only of A4 paper, and must be bound or held firmly in a stiff cover. Two copies must be submitted to the chair of the examiners, and a third copy must be retained by the candidate.

6. The two copies of the essay must be sent, not later than noon on the first Friday after the Hilary Full Term of the year in which the examination will be held, to: The Chair of the Examiners, Honour School of Modern Languages, Examination Schools, High Street, Oxford.

SPECIAL REGULATIONS FOR THE HONOUR SCHOOL OF MOLECULAR AND CELLULAR BIOCHEMISTRY

A

1. The subject of the Honour School of Molecular and Cellular   5
Biochemistry shall be the study of Molecular and Cellular aspects of
the structure and behaviour of biological molecules.

2. No candidate shall be admitted to examination in this school
unless he or she has either passed or been exempted from the First
Public Examination.   1

3. The examination in this school shall be under the supervision
of the Medical Sciences Board, which shall prescribe the necessary
regulations.

4. The examination in Molecular and Cellular Biochemistry shall
consist of two parts: Part I and Part II.   1

5. No candidate may present him or herself for examination in
Part II unless he or she has been adjudged worthy of Honours by
the examiners in Part I.

6. A candidate will not be classified for Honours until he or she
has completed all parts of the examination and has been adjudged   2
worthy of Honours by the examiners in Part I and Part II of the
examination in consecutive years. The examiners shall give due
consideration to the performance in all parts of the respective
examinations.

7. A candidate who obtains only a pass, or fails to satisfy the   2
examiners, may enter again for Part I of the examination on one,
but no more than one, subsequent occasion. Part II shall be entered
on one occasion only.

8. A candidate adjudged worthy of Honours in Part I and Part II
may supplicate for the Degree of Master of Biochemistry, provided   3
he or she has fulfilled all the conditions for admission to a degree of
the University.

9. A candidate who passes Part I or who is adjudged worthy of
Honours in Part I of the examination, but who does not enter Part
II of the examination, or who fails to obtain honours in Part II, may   3
be allowed to supplicate for the degree of Bachelor of Arts (pass or
unclassified Honours as appropriate), provided he or she has fulfilled all the conditions for admission to a degree of the University;

but such a candidate may not later enter or re-enter Part II or supplicate for the degree of Master of Biochemistry.

10. Candidates will be expected to show knowledge based on practical work. The examination shall be partly practical: this requirement shall normally be satisfied by the examiners' assessment of the practical work done by candidates during their course of study.

B

1. The examiners will permit the use of any hand-held calculator subject to the conditions set out under the heading 'Use of calculators in examinations' in the *Regulations for the Conduct of University Examinations*.

2. *Supplementary Subjects*

(*a*) Candidates may, in addition to any one or more of the below-mentioned subjects, offer themselves for examination in one or more Supplementary Subjects.

(*b*) Candidates for Supplementary Subjects may offer themselves for examination in the academic year preceding that in which they take the Final Honour School; they may also offer themselves for examination in the year in which they take the Final Honour School, Part I or Part II. No more than one Supplementary Subject may be offered in any one year.

(*c*) The Supplementary Subjects available in any year will be published, together with the term in which each subject will be examined, in the *University Gazette* not later than the end of the Trinity Term of the academic year prior to delivery of the courses. Regulations governing the use of calculators in individual Supplementary Subjects will be notified when the availability of these subjects is published in the *Gazette*.

(*d*) In determining the place of candidates in the Class List the examiners shall take account of good performance in any Supplementary Subjects which have been offered.

(*e*) Candidates awarded a pass in a Supplementary Subject examination may not retake the same Supplementary Subject examination.

PART I

Six written papers will be set:

Paper I Structure and Function of Macromolecules;
Paper II Energetics and Metabolic Processes;
Paper III Genetics and Molecular Biology;
Paper IV Cell Biology and the Integration of Function;
Paper V General Paper;
Paper VI Data Analysis and Interpretation.

Candidates will be required to show knowledge of the fundamental biochemistry of animals, plants, and micro-organisms. This will include the chemical and physical basis of the subject, its relevance to living systems; structure, function, and metabolism of viruses, cells and subcellular components, organs and organisms; biochemical aspects of nutrition, differentiation, genetics, absorption, secretion, biosynthesis, and maintenance of a dynamic state. In the general paper, candidates will be expected to bring together a knowledge of these disparate areas of Biochemistry. The data analysis and interpretation paper will consist of questions designed to examine candidates' skills in data handling and the interpretation of experimental data; relevant tables and formulae will be supplied.

Except with the express permission of the Head of the Department of Biochemistry, no one shall be admitted to the Final Honour School of Molecular and Cellular Biochemistry course of practical work and exercises in biochemical reasoning who has not passed, or been exempted from, the First Public Examination.

Heads of laboratories, or their deputies, shall make available to the examiners records showing the extent to which each candidate has adequately pursued a course of laboratory work and exercises in biochemical reasoning. In assessing the record of practical work and exercises in data handling, the examiners shall have regard to the attendance record of the candidates at each and every class provided, and to the marks recorded for each and every class provided. Candidates whose overall performance in either the written papers or in practical work and data handling is judged by the examiners to be insufficient to warrant the award of Honours may either be deemed to have failed the examination, or may be awarded a Pass. Candidates in either category will not be allowed to proceed to Part II. The examiners will issue a list of candidates who are allowed to proceed to Part II.

If requested by the examiners, candidates shall submit notebooks containing reports, initialled by the demonstrators, of practical work and exercises in biochemical reasoning completed during their course of study for Part I. These notebooks shall be available to the examiners at any time after the end of the first week of the term in which the examination is held. Each notebook shall be accompanied by a certificate signed by the candidate indicating that the notebook submitted is the candidate's own work.

Candidates may be examined viva voce.

PART II

Part II will consist of project work and two written papers, each of three hours duration.

Candidates will be required to pursue their investigations during a period of twenty-eight weeks including an extended Michaelmas Term which will begin on the fourth Friday before the stated Full Term and extend until the first Saturday following it, provided that the divisional board shall have power to permit candidates to vary the dates of their residence so long as the overall requirement is met.

Project work: The project will normally be carried out in the extended Michaelmas Term plus the first six weeks in Hilary Term.

Candidates will be required to do project work under the supervision of any person approved by the Biochemistry Steering Committee provided that such approval shall be applied for not later than Friday in the second week of Trinity Full Term in the year preceding the Part II examination.

Candidates will be required to present an account of such work in the form of a dissertation (not more than 8,000 words excluding tables, figures, reference list and abstract). Dissertations (two copies) must be legibly typed on one side only of A4 paper and must be held in a stiff cover. An electronic copy (ideally on CD) including this, and only this material, should also be provided. Each dissertation must begin with an abstract of not more than 300 words, which should include a brief statement of the aims of the project and a summary of its important findings. The two typed copies, and the electronic copy, of the dissertation must be submitted by noon on Friday of the first week of the Trinity Full Term of the examination, addressed to the Chair of Examiners in the Final Honour School of Molecular and Cellular Biochemistry, Part II, c/o the Examination Schools, High Street, Oxford. Each candidate must submit, together with his or her project, a statement to the effect that the project is the candidate's own work or indicating where the work of others has been used, save that supervisors should give advice on the choice and scope of the project, provide a reading list, and comment on the first draft. This statement must be submitted at the same time as the project in a sealed envelope addressed to the Chair of Examiners. Each project, and the envelope containing the statement, must be clearly labelled with the candidate's number. The name and college of the candidate must not appear on the project or on the envelope. The examiners may obtain a written report on the work of each candidate from the supervisor concerned.

Candidates will be required to present a brief oral report of their research project in the first half of Trinity Full Term to a group of two examiners (or examiner(s) and assessor appointed to ensure an adequate representation of expertise), after which the candidate shall be examined viva voce on the project. The form of the presentation to examiners shall be specified in guidelines published by the Department of Biochemistry in Week 8 of Trinity Full Term in the academic year preceding the examination.

Dissertations previously submitted for the Honour School of Molecular and Cellular Biochemistry may be resubmitted. No dissertation will be accepted if it has already been submitted, wholly or substantially, for an Honour School other than Molecular and Cellular Biochemistry, or for another degree of this University, or for a degree of any other institution.

Written papers: Each candidate will sit written examinations in two areas of Biochemistry, each selected from a list of options approved by the Biochemistry Steering Committee, and published by the Department of Biochemistry. Two lists (A and B) of three options will be published and one option must be chosen from each list. The list of options will be posted in the Department of Biochemistry and sent to Senior Tutors of all colleges not later than noon on Friday of the seventh week of Trinity Term in the year preceding that in which the examination is taken.

One paper of three hours' duration will be set for each option, and candidates will be required to take two papers.

Each candidate may be examined viva voce.

SPECIAL REGULATIONS FOR THE
HONOUR SCHOOL OF MUSIC

A

1. The subject of the Honour School of Music shall be the study of the history, criticism, theory, composition, performance, and practice of music.

2. No candidate shall be admitted to examination in this school, unless he has either passed or been exempted from the First Public Examination.

3. The examination in this faculty shall be under the supervision of the Board of the Faculty of Music which shall make regulations concerning it subject always to the preceding clauses of this subsection.

B

Each candidate will be required to offer papers (1) and (2) from List A, any two of papers (3), (4), and (5) in that list, and four other papers, always provided that of these four at least one is from List B, one is from List C, one is from either List B or C, and one is from List B, C or D. Candidates may always offer both List A (3) and B (1); but certain other combinations of papers may from time to time be disallowed, always provided that notice of such disallowance be communicated to candidates not later than the third week of Michaelmas Full Term in the academic year preceding that of examination.

Candidates must indicate, not later than Friday of the fourth week of Michaelmas Full Term in the academic year of examination, of the eight papers they propose to offer.

Candidates may also be examined viva voce.

List A (core subjects)

(1) Topics in Music History before 1750 (one three-hour paper)

(2) Topics in Music after 1700 (one three-hour paper)

The Board of the Faculty of Music shall approve, and publish each year by notice in the Faculty of Music, not later than the eighth week of Trinity Full Term, a list of specified areas of study in (1) and (2) above for the examination six terms thence.

(3) **Either** *Techniques of Composition I* (one three-hour paper)

Candidates will be required to complete or continue in the appropriate style a piece of music from which at least one part will be given. One question must be answered from four set as follows:

(*a*) later sixteenth-century continental vocal polyphony in four parts;

(*b*) aria in three parts (voice, obbligato instrument, and basso continuo) from the period *c.* 1700–*c.* 1760;

(*c*) four-part texture, of the period *c.* 1760–*c.* 1830;

(*d*) nineteenth-century song accompaniment for piano, in the Austro-Germanic tradition.

Or *Techniques of Composition II* (portfolio submission): see under List B (1)

(4) *Musical Analysis and Criticism* (one three-hour paper)
Analytical and critical comment on one musical work (or movement of a work), normally from the late eighteenth or nineteenth century. The score will be provided but the music will not be heard in performance.

(5) *Musical Thought and Scholarship* (one three-hour paper)
A paper on the history, criticism, and philosophy of music. Candidates may choose to answer either one or two questions.

Lists B, C, and D (optional subjects)
List B (Portfolio and performance options)

(1) *Techniques of Composition II* (portfolio submission)
Candidates will be required to write, at their choice and on material set by the examiners in the eighth week of Hilary Full Term in the academic year of examination, one of the following:

(*a*) a fugue;
(*b*) a sixteenth-century motet or Mass movement in five parts;
(*c*) an eighteenth-century (Baroque style) aria or other ritornello-based movement;
(*d*) a sonata movement (not necessarily the first) from the period from Haydn to Brahms;
(*e*) a movement in a twentieth-century idiom (questions requiring familiarity with indeterminate or electronic techniques will not be set);
(*f*) such other form of music as the examiners may offer,
provided that the examiners shall always offer material on each of (*a*)-(*e*).

Papers will be available for collection in the Music Faculty Library from 12 noon on Friday in the eighth week of Hilary Full Term in the academic year of examination. Two copies of the portfolio, accompanied by a declaration in a sealed envelope in the form prescribed within the Faculty Undergraduate Handbook relating to the examination, must be submitted by candidates not later than noon on Friday of the first week of Trinity Full Term in the academic year of examination, to the Chair of the Examiners, Honour School of Music, Examination Schools, High Street, Oxford.
This option may not be selected under List B(1) if it has already been selected under list A(3).

(2) *Orchestration* (portfolio submission)
Candidates will be required to submit two copies of a piece of orchestration, the style and technique of the orchestration being appropriate to the material set. A choice of pieces, taken from the period 1750 to the present day, will be set. Papers will be available for collection in the Music Faculty Library from 12 noon on Friday in the seventh week of Hilary Full Term in the academic year of examination. The copies, accompanied by a declaration in a sealed envelope in the form prescribed within the Faculty Undergraduate Handbook relating to the examination, must be submitted by candidates not later than noon on Friday of the third week of Trinity Full Term in the academic year of examination, to the Chair of the Examiners, Honour School of Music, Examination Schools, High Street, Oxford.

(3) *Solo Performance, instrumental or vocal* (practical test)
Candidates shall prepare a programme of works in varying styles and submit it for the approval of the examiners, not later than Friday in the fourth week of Hilary Full Term in the academic year of examination, addressed to the Chair of the Examiners, Honour School of Music, Faculty of Music, St Aldate's. They may indicate a single work or a complete movement which they would like to play in full. The time each piece takes to play must be stated. The programme shall be timed to last between 35-40 minutes, including breaks and pauses. If the programme significantly exceeds 40 minutes the examiners are entitled to curtail or interrupt the performance. Candidates must provide for accompaniment, where required.

Candidates may offer self-accompanied vocal performance, which will be judged on both the singing and playing elements. They may not, however, propose a programme on more than one instrument in turn (such as violin and cello), other than such as might occur in the context of normal recital convention. Any candidate contemplating such a proposal should seek early advice from the Chair of the Faculty Board, whose decision on behalf of the Board will be final.

Candidates are required to provide for the examiners two copies of each piece to be performed, in the edition used. The copies shall be presented to the examiners at the beginning of the examination and collected from them at the end.

(4) *Composition* (portfolio submission)

Candidates will be required to submit two copies of a portfolio of four original compositions as follows:

(*a*) one work (or set of pieces) of approximately 5 minutes duration for one of the following mediums:

(i) solo piano;

(ii) solo instrument and piano;

(*b*) and three of the following options (the three pieces to make up a minimum duration of 24 minutes):

(i) a work of 6-10 minutes duration for orchestra;

(ii) a work of 6-10 minutes duration for mixed ensemble of between five and fourteen players;

(iii) a work of 6-10 minutes duration for string quartet;

(iv) a work of 6-10 minutes duration for SATB chorus in up to eight parts;

(v) an electroacoustic composition of no more than 6 minutes, submitted alongside the source materials upon which the work is based;

(vi) a work of the candidate's choice.

Each of these categories may be scored with amplification, live electronics or with an electroacoustic backing track.

Candidates intending to use the electronic studio in connection with this option are required to have attended the preliminary courses offered to undergraduates in their first year. Details relating to submission are given in the general note below.

(5) *Dissertation* (portfolio submission)

Candidates must submit two copies of a dissertation of between 8,000 and 10,000 words (exclusive of bibliography) which has not been previously submitted for a degree of another university. The subject and title must be approved by the Board of the Faculty of Music. Details relating to approval and submission are given in the general note below.

(6) *Edition with commentary* (portfolio submission)

Candidates must submit two copies of an edition with commentary. Editions previously submitted for the Honour School of Music may be resubmitted. No edition will be accepted if it has already been submitted, wholly or substantially, for another Honour School or degree of this University, or a degree of any other institution. The work or works to be edited must be approved by the Board of the Faculty of Music. Details relating to approval and submission are given in the general note below.

(7) *Analysis* (portfolio submission)

Candidates must submit two copies of an analytical study of not more than 10,000 words which has not been previously submitted for a degree of another university. The subject and title must be approved by the Board of the Faculty of Music. Details relating to approval and submission are given in the general note below.

(8) *Music Ethnography* (portfolio submission)

Candidates must submit two copies of a portfolio of essays and ethnographic work to a total of around 10,000 words (or equivalent). This may be submitted in a variety of formats, including recordings with commentary, video, photography, transcription and analysis. The subject and title must be approved by the Board of the Faculty of Music. Details relating to approval and submission are given in the general note below.

General Note on approval of subjects for List B(5), (6), (7) and (8); and the submission of written work for List B(4)–(8).

(*a*) *Approval of subjects*

Candidates intending to submit any of *B(5), (6), (7)*, or *(8)* must obtain prior approval of the subject and title from the Board of the Faculty of Music. They are urged to seek early guidance from their college tutor on whether the subject is likely to be acceptable and must submit the proposed subject and title, together with the signed approval of the tutor, to the Chair of the Board of the Faculty of Music, Faculty of Music, St Aldates, not earlier than the beginning of and not later than the end of Trinity Full Term in the academic year preceding that of examination. The faculty board shall decide whether or not to approve the subject and title and shall advise the candidate as soon as possible.

(*b*) *Submission of written work*

Candidates must also submit two copies of the written work related to the examination of subjects B(4)–(8) by noon on Friday of the second week of Trinity Full Term in the academic year of examination. It must be addressed to the Chair of the Examiners, Honour School of Music, Examination Schools, High Street, Oxford. Each submission (but not each copy) must be accompanied by a declaration in a sealed envelope in the form prescribed within the Music Faculty Undergraduate Handbook relating to the examination. In the case of B(5-7) and for any essay component in B(8) the text of the work must be presented in typescript.

Each portfolio submitted for the subjects of Techniques of Composition II and Orchestration must be accompanied by a signed form of declaration placed in a sealed envelope bearing the candidate's examination number and in the following prescribed form.

List C (three-hour paper options) and *List D* (practical options)

The Board of the Faculty of Music shall approve, and publish each year by notice in the Faculty of Music, not later than the eight week of Trinity Full Term, a list of subjects for the examination six terms hence.

List C consists of special topics, each examined by written paper or by a portfolio of coursework, as specified in the Music Faculty Undergraduate Handbook relating to the examination. List D options combine a practical element with an extended essay (two copies of which must be submitted). Approval and submission details for List D are as published within the Faculty Undergraduate Handbook relating to the examination.

SPECIAL REGULATIONS FOR THE HONOUR SCHOOL OF NEUROSCIENCE

A

1. The subject of the Honour School of Neuroscience shall be all aspects of the scientific study of the nervous system.

2. No candidate shall be admitted to examination in this school unless he or she has either passed or been exempted from the First Public Examination.

3. The examination in this school shall be under the supervision of the Medical Sciences Board, which shall make regulations concerning it.

4. The examination in Neuroscience shall consist of two parts: Part I and Part II.

5. No candidate shall be admitted to the Part II examination in this school unless he or she has passed the Part I examination in this school.

6. The examination for Part I will take place during Week 0 or 1 in Trinity Term of the candidate's second year. The examination for Part II will take place during Trinity Term of the candidate's third year.

7. For the Part I options provided by the Department of Experimental Psychology, and the Part II advanced options which are as specified for Part II of the Honour School of Experimental Psychology, candidates shall be examined by such of the Public Examiners in the Honour School of Experimental Psychology as may be required. For the written papers in Part II which are as specified for the Honour School of Medical Sciences, and the Research Project, candidates shall be examined by such of the Public Examiners in the Honour School of Medical Sciences as may be required.

8. In addition to the form of examination prescribed below, candidates may be examined viva voce in either part of the examination.

9. Candidates for Part II may offer themselves for examination in one or more of the *Supplementary Subjects*. The *Supplementary Subjects* available in any year will be notified to students annually during Trinity Term. Account shall be taken of a candidate's results in any such subject in the candidate's overall classification in the Honour School of Neuroscience. Candidates awarded a pass in a Supplementary Subject examination may not retake the same Supplementary Subject examination.

B

Part I

1. Candidates will attend lectures and practicals in options selected from a list published in the Medical Sciences Teaching Centre by the end of Week 8 of Hilary Term in the year preceding the examination. Each option will have a number of units ascribed to it. Candidates will be required to study options totalling ten units. The list published in the Medical Sciences Teaching Centre and the handbook for the course will specify how many units are assigned to each option, and which options are recommended to proceed to particular advanced options in Part II.

2. Two written papers will be set:
  (i) Paper I will be a three-hour examination comprising a selection of questions requiring short answers. Candidates will be required to answer those questions relating to their chosen options.
  (ii) Paper II will be a two-hour essay paper. Candidates will be required to answer questions from a selection relating to the different options that they have studied.

3. If, in Paper II of the Part I Examination, a candidate presents essentially the same information on more than one occasion, then credit will be given in only the first instance.

4. Candidates will be required to undertake practical work as specified in the course handbook which will constitute part of the examination. The Course Director, or a deputy, shall make available to the Examiners, at the end of Week 0 of Trinity Term in which the examinations are held, evidence showing the extent and the standard to which each candidate has completed the prescribed practical work. Practical work cannot normally be retaken. Candidates whose attendance or performance is deemed unsatisfactory will forfeit one quarter of the marks in the Part I examination, the outcome of which will be carried forward to the Part II Examination.

Part II

1. Each candidate must offer timed written examination papers and a project report based on a research project.

2. Each candidate must offer 4 written papers: Paper 1A, Neuroscience, and Paper 2 as specified for the Honour School of Medical Sciences; two advanced options as specified for the Honour School of Experimental Psychology Part II.

3. The Research Project
The research project will normally be carried out in the Trinity Term of the candidate's second year and the Michaelmas Term of the candidate's third year.
  (i) *Form, Subject and Approval of the Project*
The project shall consist of original experiments done by the candidate alone or in collaboration with others (where such collaboration is, for instance, needed to produce results in the time available).
A list of potential supervisors and their research interests shall be published no later than the end of Week 6 of Hilary Term in the academic year preceding the examination. Candidates should normally discuss their intended project with the potential supervisor and their tutor before submitting a project outline to the course administrator no later than noon, Friday of Week 0 of Trinity Term of the academic year preceding the examination. Decision on the application shall be made by the Course Director, or a deputy, and communicated to candidates by Friday of Week 1 of the same term.
  (ii) *Submission of the Project Report*
The length and format of the Project Report based on the project shall be according to guidelines published by the Medical Sciences Board in Week 6 of Hilary Term

of the academic year preceding the year of examination. Material in a candidate's Project Report must not be duplicated in any answer given in a written examination paper. Project Reports previously submitted for the Honour School of Neuroscience may be resubmitted. No Project Report will be accepted if it has already been submitted, wholly or substantially, for another Honour School or degree of this University, or for a degree of any other institution.

Project Reports (three copies) must be sent to the Chair of Examiners, Honour School of Neuroscience, Examination Schools, High Street, Oxford, not later than noon on the Friday of Week 8 of Hilary Term in the academic year in which the candidate intends to take the examination. The copies shall be accompanied (in a separate sealed envelope) by a certificate signed by each candidate indicating that the research project is the candidate's own work and that the supervisor has commented on at least one draft of the Project Report. In the case of laboratory-based work that has been produced in collaboration, the certificate shall indicate the extent of the candidate's own contribution. Each candidate will be required to submit a draft of their Project Report to their supervisor no later than two weeks before the specified deadline for submission to Schools.

In exceptional cases, where through unforeseen circumstances a laboratory-based project produces no useable results (i.e. not even negative or ambiguous results), the candidate may apply through his or her college to the Course Director, or a deputy, for permission to submit a concise review of the scientific context and the aims of the work that was attempted in place of the normal Project Report. Such an application must be accompanied by supporting evidence from the supervisor of the project. The concise review to be submitted in such circumstances should be comparable in length to the Report of a successful laboratory-based project and will be presented orally to the examiners and be examined viva voce in the usual way for a research project. The examiners will be advised that substantive results could not be produced.

In all cases, the examiners shall obtain and consider a written report from each supervisor indicating the extent of the input made by the candidate to the outcome of the project and also any unforeseen difficulties associated with the project (e.g. unexpected technical issues or problems in the availability of materials, equipment, or literature or other published data).

(iii) *Oral Assessment of Project-based Written Work*

In addition, each candidate shall make a brief oral presentation of their project to a group of two examiners (or examiners and assessors appointed to ensure an adequate representation of expertise), after which, the candidate shall be examined viva voce on the project. The form of the presentation to the examiners shall be specified in guidelines published by the Medical Sciences Board.

4. If, in the Part II Examination, a candidate presents essentially the same information on more than one occasion, then credit will be given in only the first instance.

5. The weighting of marks for the five exercises required of each candidate shall be 25 per cent for the Project Report based on the research project and 55 per cent in total for the four written papers. Marks carried forward from the Part I examination will account for the remaining 20 per cent for the candidate's overall result for the Honour School of Neuroscience.

SPECIAL REGULATIONS FOR THE HONOUR SCHOOL OF ORIENTAL STUDIES

A

1. The main subjects of the examination in the Honour School of Oriental Studies shall be Arabic, Chinese, Egyptology and Ancient Near Eastern Studies, Hebrew, Japanese, Jewish Studies, Persian, Sanskrit, and Turkish, together with such other subjects as may be determined by the Board of the Faculty of Oriental Studies.

2. Every candidate in the examination shall be required to offer one of the main subjects listed above: candidates offering one of the above languages shall also be required to show an adequate knowledge of the literature and history of the civilization concerned, and candidates offering a history subject listed above shall also be required to show an adequate knowledge of the language concerned.

3. No candidate shall be admitted to examination in this school unless he or she has either passed or been exempted from the First Public Examination.

4. In the Class List issued by the examiners in the Honour School of Oriental Studies the main subject and (where appropriate) additional language offered by each candidate who obtains Honours shall be indicated.

5. Any candidate whose name has been placed in the Class List, upon the result of the examination in any one of the subjects mentioned in clause 1, shall be permitted to offer himself or herself for examination in any other of the subjects mentioned in the same clause at the examination in either the next year or the next year but one, provided always that he or she has not exceeded six terms from the date on which he or she first obtained Honours in a Final Honour School, and provided that no such candidate shall offer any of the main subjects already offered by him or her in the School of Oriental Studies.

6. The examination in this school shall be under the supervision of the Board of the Faculty of Oriental Studies, which shall make regulations concerning it subject always to the preceding clauses of this sub-section.

B

Candidates, except in the case of Arabic, proposing to offer a Special Subject not included in the lists below must obtain the approval of the board both for their subject and for the treatises or documents (if any) which they propose to offer with it.

Except in the case of Arabic, Chinese and Japanese, if the candidate so desires and the board thinks it appropriate, such a Special Subject may be examined in the form of a dissertation.

For the submission of all dissertations, two copies must be sent to the Chair of Examiners, Honour School of Oriental Studies, c/o Examination Schools, High Street, Oxford, not later than 12 noon on Friday of the tenth week of the Hilary Term preceding the examination. The dissertation must not bear the candidate's name, but only the examination number. A signed statement that the dissertation is the candidate's own work should be submitted separately in a sealed envelope, to the Chair of Examiners (forms are available from the Faculty Office, Oriental Institute). Theses previously submitted for the Honour School of Oriental Studies may be resubmitted. No thesis will be accepted if it has already been submitted, wholly or substantially, for another Honour School or degree of this University, or for a degree of any other institution. It is recommended that the dissertation shall not exceed 15,000 words.

All applications for approval by the board must be sent to the Secretary of the Board of the Faculty of Oriental Studies, Oriental Institute, on or before the Monday in the second week of the Michaelmas Full Term preceding the examination, and must be accompanied by two copies of a list of the treatises or documents (if any) offered.

All candidates must give notice, on their examination entry forms, of their Special Subjects and choice of books or subjects, where alternatives exist, to the Registrar on or before the Friday in the fourth week of the Michaelmas Full Term preceding the examination. The notice must specify the subject so offered, and, if a subject specially approved by the board, also the treatises or original documents (if any) which it has approved.

Any candidate may be examined viva voce.

The editions of texts specified in the course handbooks are the ones which will be used for the reproduction of material for examination purposes, not necessarily the ones which provide the most useful material for the study of the texts concerned.

For those papers where a selection of unspecified texts is to be examined, the selection of texts will be reported to the Undergraduate Studies Committee of the board at its first meeting in Hilary Term for the examination in the next academic year, and copies of the lists of selected texts will be available for candidates not later than Friday of the third week of the same term in the course handbook.

Oral examinations for Arabic, Chinese, Hebrew (Course II) Japanese, Persian, and Turkish will be held in the week before Trinity Full Term in the year in which the Honour School examination is taken.

The subjects of the school are arranged below in two sections: (i) main subjects; (ii) additional languages. Within each section subjects are listed in alphabetical order as follows:

Main Subjects	*Additional Languages*	
Arabic	Akkadian	Egyptology
Chinese	Arabic	Hebrew
Egyptology and Ancient	Aramaic and Syriac	Hindi
Near Eastern Studies	Armenian	Hittite
Hebrew	Chinese	Japanese
Japanese	Coptic	Korean
Jewish Studies	Persian	Old Iranian
Persian	Prakrit	Pali
Sanskrit	Sanskrit	Tibetan
Turkish	Sumerian	Turkish

In addition, candidates may offer Classics either as a main subject or as an additional language in the Honour School of Classics and Oriental Studies.

Candidates offering Arabic, Chinese, Hebrew, [**From 1 October 2014:** Japanese,] Persian or Turkish as their main subject *may* offer an additional language as specified below; candidates offering Sanskrit *must* offer an additional language as specified below; and candidates offering Egyptology and Ancient Near Eastern Studies *must* offer either an additional language or Archaeology and Anthropology as specified below.

Candidates offering Arabic or Turkish or Persian as their main subject will be required to spend a period of at least one academic year on an approved course of language study in the Middle East.

Candidates offering Chinese [**From 1 October 2014:** or Japanese] as their main subject are required to spend a period of at least one academic year on an approved course of language study in East Asia.

Candidates offering Hebrew shall take one of the following courses:

Course I: Candidates will be examined in accordance with the regulations set out below.

Course II: Candidates will be examined in accordance with the regulations set out below. Candidates offering Hebrew **Course II** as their main subject will be required to spend a period of at least one academic year on an approved course of study in Israel.

Candidates taking Turkish or Persian with Islamic Art and Archaeology will also be required to participate in one or more approved projects of fieldwork or museum-based study normally to be completed in year 2 in a country within the historic *Dār al-Islām*.

References to Classics in the following Regulations are to the syllabus in Classics for the Honour School of Classics and Oriental Studies.

MAIN SUBJECTS

Arabic

Arabic Handbook. The Board of the Faculty of Oriental Studies shall issue annually the Handbook for the Honour Schools of Oriental Studies (Arabic) and Oriental Studies (Arabic with a Subsidiary Language) by Monday of Week 1 of the first Hilary Full Term of candidates' work for the Honour Schools. The Handbook will include, amongst other things, lists of set texts.

Choice and availability of options. It cannot be guaranteed that teaching will be available on all Further and Special Subjects in every academic year. Similarly, the choice of subject for the Thesis will necessarily depend upon availability of a suitable supervisor. Candidates should therefore consult with their tutors about the availability of teaching when selecting their optional and thesis subjects.   5

Either, for Arabic and Islamic Studies

1. Arabic unprepared translation into English and comprehension.
2. Composition in Arabic.
3. Spoken Arabic*
4. Arabic literature.   1
5. Islamic history, 570–1500.
6. Islamic religion.
7. A Further Subject, chosen from the following list:
     i. Ḥadīth
    ii. Early Islamic monetary history   1
   iii. Classical Arabic literary texts
    iv. The ethos of the *jāhilīya* in the *Muᶜallaqa* of Imruʾal-Qays
     v. Early Islamic historiography
    vi. Aspects of Islamic art, architecture and archaeology
   vii. The rise of the Sufi orders in the Islamic world, 1200–1500   2
  viii. Sufism
    ix. al-Ghazālī
     x. Ibn Ṭufayl, *Ḥayy ibn Yaqẓān*
    xi. Ibn al-Arabī, *Fuṣūṣ al-Ḥikam*
   xii. Religion and politics during the Mongol period   2
  xiii. Ottoman State and Society 1566–1700
   xiv. History of the Middle East in the late Ottoman age, 1750–1882
    xv. A modern Islamic thinker (e.g. Sayyid Qutb, Mohamed Talbi, Rashid
          Rida)
   xvi. Modern Arabic literature   3
  xvii. Arabic vernacular literature 1900 to the present day
 xviii. Society and Culture in the Modern Arab World
   xix. The biography of Mohammad
    xx. A short-term Further Subject, as approved by the Board of the Faculty of
          Oriental Studies and publicised in the Arabic Handbook.   3

8 and 9. A Special Subject (to be examined in two papers), chosen from the following list:
     i. Qurʾan
    ii. Themes in classical Arabic literature
   iii. The transformation of ideas from the *jāhilīya* to early Islam in early Arabic   4
          poetry†
    iv. Topics in Islamic law
     v. Learning and culture in Baghdad, 800–900
    vi. Theology and Philosophy in the Islamic World
   vii. Medieval Sufi thought   4
  viii. Ibn al-ᶜArabī
    ix. 'Slave dynasties' in Islam: from the Ghaznavids to the Mamlūk Sultanate

---

* Details of the oral examination and of the areas in which candidates will be expected to show competence are provided in the examination conventions and in the handbook.

† Only available to candidates who have taken the Further Subject 'iv. The ethos of the *jāhilīya* in the *Muᶜallaqa* of Imrual-Qays'.

    x. Royal art and architecture in Norman Sicily
    xi. Islamic Art and Archaeology, *c.* 550–*c.* 1900
    xii. Writing Islamic history, 1250–1500: from palaeography to historiography
    xiii. The Ottomans, Islam and the Arab World 1300–1566
    xiv. History of the Middle East in the age of empire, 1882–1971   5
    xv. Arabic linguistics
    xvi. Themes in Modern Arabic literature
    xvii. Modern Islamic thought in the Middle East
    xviii. Popular culture and mass media, 1930 to the present
    xix. A Short-Term Special Subject, as approved by the Board of the Faculty of   10
    Oriental Studies and publicised in the Arabic Handbook.

Candidates for all Special Subjects will be examined by means of a timed paper, and by means of an extended essay, which shall not exceed 6,000 words (including footnotes but excluding bibliography), and shall be on a topic or theme selected by the candidate from a question paper published by the examiners on the Friday of the 15 fourth week of Michaelmas Term in the year of examination available for collection from the Oriental Institute Faculty Office. Essays should be typed or word-processed in double-spacing and should conform to the standards of academic presentation prescribed in the "Guidelines for writers of Theses" in the course handbook. Essays (two copies) shall normally be written during the Michaelmas Term in the year of 20 examination and must be delivered by hand to the Examination Schools (addressed to the Chair of Examiners, Honour School of Oriental Studies, Examination Schools, High Street, Oxford) not later than 12 noon on the Friday before the beginning of Hilary Full Term of the year of examination. Candidates delivering essays will be required to complete a receipt form, which will only be accepted as proof of receipt if 25 it is countersigned by a member of the Examination Schools staff. Each essay must be accompanied by a sealed envelope (bearing only the candidate's examination number) containing a formal declaration signed by the candidate that the essay is his or her own work. The University's regulations on Late Submission of Work will apply. Any candidate may be examined viva voce. 30

    10. A thesis.
    Submitting the thesis. All candidates must submit two copies of their thesis, addressed to the Chair of Examiners, Honour School of Oriental Studies, Examination Schools, High Street, Oxford, not later than 12 noon on Friday of the tenth week of the Hilary Term preceding the examination. The thesis must not bear 35 the candidate's name, but only the candidate number. A signed statement that the thesis is the candidate's own work should be submitted separately in a sealed envelope to the Chair of Examiners (forms are available from the Faculty Office, Oriental Institute). Theses previously submitted for the Honour School of Oriental Studies may be resubmitted. No thesis will be accepted if it has already been 40 submitted, wholly or substantially, for another Honour School or degree of this University, or for a degree of any other institution.

or, for Arabic with a Subsidiary Language, Papers 1-6 above and

11, 12, and 13. Three papers from one of the following:
Akkadian.
Aramaic and Syriac. 45
Armenian.
Classics (in the Honour School of Classics and Oriental Studies).
Hebrew.
Hindi/Urdu.
Persian. 50
Turkish.

14. An *optional* thesis to be approved by the Board. See under Arabic and Islamic Studies above for notes concerning the choice and approval of options and the preparation and submission of theses.

Chinese

The Board of the Faculty of Oriental Studies shall issue the handbook for the Honour School of Oriental Studies (Chinese and Chinese with a subsidiary language) no later than the Monday of first week of the Hilary full-term prior to the year in which candidates shall sit their Final Honour School examinations. The handbook shall include, amongst other information, course details, lists of set texts and regulations regarding the submission of dissertations and long-essays.

All candidates must have fulfilled attendance requirements (as set out in the handbook) on a designated course at Peking University, unless given exemption by the Board of the Faculty.

Either, for Chinese only,
The following papers will be set:
 1. Modern Chinese I.
 2. Modern Chinese II.
 3. Oral.
 4. Classical I.
 5. Classical II.
 6. Modern China.
 7. Dissertation on a subject approved by the Board of the Faculty.
 8. Special Option I: Texts
The subjects available together with the relevant texts will be set out in the handbook for the year prior to year of the examinations.
 9. Special Option II: Essays
These will be in the same area as that chosen under 8.
 10. Special Option III: Extended Essay
This will be in the same area as that chosen under 8 and 9 or Linguistics (if available).
Or Chinese with a subsidiary language, Papers 1-7 above and papers 11, 12 and 13 below in Japanese, Korean or Tibetan.
 11. Japanese, Korean or Tibetan Texts (Subsidiary).
 12. Japanese, Korean or Tibetan History and Culture (Subsidiary).
 13. Japanese, Korean or Tibetan Language (Subsidiary).

Egyptology and Ancient Near Eastern Studies
Either, for Egyptology and Ancient Near Eastern Studies with a subsidiary language
The languages which may be offered shall be:
As first language: Akkadian or Egyptian
Candidates offering one of the following as second language (which must be different from the first language):
Akkadian
Egyptian
Coptic
Hittite (may not be available every year)
Sumerian
will be required to offer the following papers:
 1. Translation paper (first language).
 2. Translation paper (second language).
 3, 4. Literary and historical topics including prepared translation from first language.

5, 6. Literary and historical topics including prepared translation from second language.

For papers 4 and 6, in each case four passages from a list of prescribed texts will be set for examination by essay. For each paper, candidates must present a translation of and essay on one passage. Papers should be typed and provided with proper scholarly apparatus. The passages for paper 4 will be assigned in the Oriental Institute at 10 a.m. on Monday of first week in Full Term in the term in which the final examination is to be offered, and must be handed in to the Examination Schools, High Street, Oxford no later than 12 noon on Monday of second week. A signed statement that the essay is the candidate's own work should be submitted separately in a sealed envelope bearing his or her candidate number, to the Chair of examiners (forms are available from the Faculty Office, Oriental Institute). The passages for paper 6 will be assigned in the Oriental Institute at 10 a.m. on Monday of third week in Full Term in the term in which the final examination is to be offered, and must be handed in to the Examination Schools, High Street, Oxford no later than 12 noon on Monday of fourth week. Essays should not exceed 3,500 words. A signed statement that the essay is the candidate's own work should be submitted separately in a sealed envelope bearing his or her candidate number, to the Chair of examiners (forms are available from the Faculty Office, Oriental Institute).

Candidates offering one of the following as the second language in the above papers follow the regulations for 'Additional Languages' in the Honour School of Oriental Studies:

Arabic
Aramaic and Syriac
Classics (in the Honour School of Classics and Oriental Studies)
Hebrew (Biblical and Rabbinic)
Old Iranian.

Candidates offering Classics as an Additional Language in the Honour School of Classics and Oriental Studies must offer in place of papers 2, 5 and 6 three subjects in Classics according to the conditions specified in the syllabus for that School.

7. A field of concentration to be chosen from a list of topics published at the beginning of Michaelmas Term each year by the Oriental Studies Faculty Board for examination in the following academic year. Candidates may propose their own field of concentration. The choice must be approved by the Board in each case.

8. Selected Egyptian and/or Ancient Near Eastern artefacts together with essay questions on material culture.

9. General paper, including questions on Egyptology and Ancient Near Eastern Studies today.

10. A dissertation on a topic to be approved by the Faculty Board, of a different character from that chosen for paper 7.

11. Egyptian art and architecture. This paper is optional and may be taken in substitution for 7. or 10. above. Selection of this paper is subject to approval by the Board of the Faculty of Oriental Studies.

Or, for Egyptology and Ancient Near Eastern Studies with Archaeology and Anthropology, candidates will be required to offer papers 1, 3-4, and 7-10 above, **and** the following papers:

12. Anthropological theory and archaeological enquiry.

13. Urbanisation and change in complex societies: comparative approaches **or** From Hunting and Gathering to States and Empires in South-West Asia.

14. Social analysis and interpretation **or** Cultural representations, beliefs and practices.

All candidates will be required to undertake a course of practical work, including laboratory work.

Candidates will be assessed, at the end of the sixth term from matriculation, on their practical ability, under the provisions for Honour Moderations in Archaeology and Anthropology.

Candidates will be required to take part in approved fieldwork as an integral part of their course. The fieldwork requirement will normally have been discharged before the Long Vacation of six terms from matriculation.

Hebrew
Either, for Hebrew only,

Candidates for **Course I** will be required to offer seven papers and a dissertation. Candidates for **Course II** will be required to offer seven papers and a dissertation, and an oral examination. They will be expected to carry out during their year abroad such work as the Board of the Faculty of Oriental Studies may require.

1. (for **Course I**): Hebrew composition and unprepared translation.
   (for **Course II**): Essay in modern Hebrew and unprepared translation.
2. Prepared texts I: Biblical texts (lists of texts are available in the course handbook).
3. Prepared texts II: Rabbinic and Medieval Hebrew texts (lists of texts are available in the course handbook).
4. Prepared texts III: Modern Hebrew literature (lists of texts are available in the course handbook).
5. General paper; language, history, religion, and culture.
6. Prepared texts IV:
   (*a*) Jewish Aramaic and *either* (*b*) Biblical Hebrew *or* (*c*) Rabbinic and Medieval Hebrew *or* (*d*) Modern Hebrew (lists of texts are availablein the course handbook).
7. One of the papers in Jewish Studies paper *b*.
8. Candidates who so desire may offer any special subject as may be approved by the Board of the Faculty of Oriental Studies. Applications for the approval of options must be submitted to the Board not later than Monday of the second week of the Michaelmas Term preceding the examination.
9. (for **Course II**) Spoken Hebrew.*

Or, for Hebrew with a subsidiary language, Papers 1-5 above, and three papers from one of the following additional subjects: Akkadian, Arabic, Aramaic and Syriac, Classics (in the Honour School of Classics and Oriental Studies), Egyptology. Candidates who so desire may offer a special subject as specified in 8.

Japanese
[Until 1 October 2014: The following papers will be set:

Either, for Japanese only,
1. Japanese prose composition.
2. Japanese unprepared translation I: classical and modern literature (there will be one compulsory classical question).
3. Japanese unprepared translation II: modern non-fiction.
4. Spoken Japanese.*
5. Special Texts 1. Translation from texts in *any one* of the following sections:
   (*a*) Classical literature
   (*b*) Theatre
   (*c*) Modern literature
   (*d*) Politics

---

* Details of the oral examination and of the areas in which candidates will be expected to show competence are provided in the examination conventions and in the handbook.

(*e*) Society and social history
(*f*) Economics
(*g*) Linguistics
Lists of the texts specified will be available in the course handbook.
6. Special texts II. Essay questions on the background to the texts studied under 5 above.
7. General questions.
8. A special subject from among the following, or such other special subject as may be approved by the Board of the Faculty:
    (*a*) Japanese art.
    (*b*) Japanese history I: to 1185.
    (*c*) Japanese history II: feudal Japan.
    (*d*) Japanese history III: the emergence of modern Japan, 1868–1972.
    (*e*) The government and politics of Japan.
    (*f*) The intellectual history of the Tokugawa period.
    (*g*) The history of Japanese literature to the end of the Tokugawa period.
    (*h*) The history of modern Japanese literature (from the beginning of the Meiji period).
    (*i*) Modern Japanese economic history.
    (*j*) The modern Japanese economy.
    (*k*) Japanese theatre.
    (*l*) Classical Chinese.
    (*m*) Modern Chinese.
    (*n*) Japanese Linguistics.
    (*o*) Korean Language.
    (*p*) Korean History.
Note: Options in the history of Japanese-Korean relations may be available, by arrangement with the University Lecturer in Korean History.

9. A dissertation on a subject approved by the Board of the Faculty.
Or, for Japanese with a subsidiary language, Papers 1, 4-6, and 9 above; **and**
10. One paper in Japanese: Unprepared translation; **and**
11., 12., and 13. Three papers in Chinese, Korean or Tibetan.]
[**From 1 October 2014:** The Board of the Faculty of Oriental Studies shall issue the handbook for the Honour School of Oriental Studies (Japanese and Japanese with a subsidiary language) no later than the Monday of first week of the Hilary Full Term prior to the year in which candidates shall sit their Final Honour School examinations. The handbook shall include, amongst other information, course details, lists of set texts and regulations regarding the submission of dissertations and long-essays.
All candidates must have fulfilled attendance requirements (as set out in the handbook) on a designated course at an agreed University, unless given exemption by the Board of the Faculty.

Either, for Japanese only,
The following papers will be set:
    1. Modern Japanese I.
    2. Modern Japanese II.
    3. Spoken Japanese.*
    4. Classical Japanese.
    5. Dissertation on a subject approved by the Board of the Faculty.

---

* Details of the oral examination and of the areas in which candidates will be expected to show competence are provided in the examination conventions and in the handbook.

6. Special text option I.†
7. Special subject option I.†
8. Special text option II.†
9. Special subject option II.†
10. Either Special Text option III or Special subject option III.†   5

Or, for Japanese with a subsidiary language, Papers 1-7 above and papers 11, 12 and 13 below in Chinese, Korean or Tibetan.
11. Chinese, Korean or Tibetan Texts (Subsidiary).
12. Chinese, Korean or Tibetan History and Culture (Subsidiary).
13. Chinese, Korean or Tibetan Language (Subsidiary).]   1

Jewish Studies
The following papers will be set.
  a. Jewish History, Religion and Culture
  b. Five of the following, of which at least one must be chosen from each of sections I, II, and III. At least two must be chosen from papers which require study of set texts   1
in the original language. Not more than one paper may be chosen from section V.

Section I	(*a*) Biblical History[1]
	(*b*) Biblical Archaeology
	(*c*) Biblical Narrative[1]
	(*d*) Biblical Prophecy[1] 2
Section II	(*e*) Second Temple Judaism[1]
	(*f*) Second Temple History
	(*g*) History of the Talmudic Period
	(*h*) Medieval Jewish History[1]
	(*i*) Jewish Aramaic Literature[1,2] 2
Section III	(*j*) Haskalah[1]
	(*k*) Modern Jewish Society
	(*l*) Israel: History, Politics and Society
	(*m*) Modern Hebrew Literature[1]
	(*n*) Yiddish Literature[1,2] 3
Section IV	(*o*) History of Jewish-Christian Relations
	(*p*) History of Jewish-Muslim Relations
	(*q*) History of Jewish Bible Interpretation[1]
	(*r*) Hebrew Texts for Jewish Studies[1]
Section V	(*s*) Biblical Religion 3
	(*t*) Medieval Jewish Thought[1]
	(*u*) Modern Jewish History
	(*v*) Modern Judaism

Papers in section V will be examined in the form of two essays (one compulsory, the other from a choice of two) not exceeding 5,000 words in total. The subjects will   4
be assigned in the Oriental Institute at 10 a.m. on Monday of second week in the term in which the final examination is to be offered, and must be handed in to the Examination Schools, High Street, Oxford no later than 12 noon on Monday of third week. A signed statement that the essays are the candidate's own work should

---

[From **1 October 2014:** † Available options will be published in the course handbook.]
  1 List of texts in the course handbook.
  2 These courses are available only to students with adequate knowledge of the relevant language.

be submitted separately in a sealed envelope bearing his or her candidate number, to the Chair of Examiners (forms are available from the Faculty Office, Oriental Institute).

c. A dissertation (see the regulations for dissertations set out under B, SPECIAL REGULATIONS FOR THE HONOUR SCHOOL OF ORIENTAL STUDIES).

Special subjects may be offered subject to the approval of the Oriental Studies Board.

Some options may not be available in every year.

Candidates may obtain from the Oriental Institute information about which options may be offered for examination the first Monday of Michaelmas Full Term of the academic year preceding that in which the papers will be set.

Applications for the approval of options must be submitted not later than Monday of the second week of the Michaelmas Term preceding the examination.

Persian

Candidates taking Persian with Islamic Art and Archaeology will be required to have satisfied the faculty board, by means of written testimonials and a written report upon the project(s) completed in Year 2, as to their active and useful participation in the approved project(s).

The following papers will be set. Candidates will be required to offer nine papers.
Either, for Persian with a subsidiary language,
1. Persian prose composition and unprepared translation.
2. Spoken Persian.*
3., 4., and 5. Three papers from the following:
(*a*) Classical Poetry: Lyric Genres
(*b*) Classical Poetry: Narrative Genres
(*c*) Classical Prose
(*d*) Modern Literature
(*e*) Modern social and political writing
Lists of texts are available in the course handbook.
6. General questions: the transition from Sasanian to Islamic Persia (up to the tenth century AD); or one of the options (i), (ii) or (iii) in papers 11 and 12 below.
7. A special subject, to be approved by the Board of the Faulty of Oriental Studies.
8., 9., and 10. Subsidiary language. Three papers on one of the following languages:
Arabic, Armenian, Old Iranian, Classics (in the Honour School of Classics and Oriental Studies), Hindi/Urdu, and Turkish.

  or, for Persian with Islamic Studies/History,
Papers 1-7 above *and*
  11. and 12. Two papers from the following:
    (i) Iranian history from 1501 to 1722.
    (ii) Iranian history from the rise of the Qajars to the end of the Constitutional Revolution.
    (iii) Iranian history from 1921 to 1979.
    (iv) The development of Shi'ism up to the late nineteenth century.
    (v) Modern Shi'ism.
    (vi) Any one paper under 7 ii, v-viii, xii-xiv, xviii and xix of the syllabus for Arabic and Islamic Studies.

---

* Details of the oral examination and of the areas in which candidates will be expected to show competence are provided in the examination conventions and in the handbook.

13. A further special subject, to be approved by the Board of the Faculty of Oriental Studies.

Applications for the approval of options in papers, 6, 10, 11, and 12 must be submitted not later than Monday of the second week of the Michaelmas Term preceding the examination.

*or, for **Persian with Islamic Art and Archaeology**,* candidates shall be required to offer nine papers.

1. Persian prose composition and unprepared translation.
2. Spoken Persian.
3. and 4. Two papers from the following:
   (*a*) Classical poetry.
   (*b*) Classical prose.
   (*c*) Selected modern texts.
5. Islamic Art and Archaeology, *c.* 550–*c.* 1900 (identical to Paper 8 xi of the syllabus for Arabic and Islamic Studies).
6. and 7. Topics in Islamic Art and Architecture, *c.* 1000–*c.* 1900], to be examined by means of a timed paper, and by means of an extended essay, which shall not exceed 6,000 words (including footnotes but excluding bibliography), and shall be on a topic or theme selected by the candidate from a question paper published by the examiners on or before the Friday of the fourth week of Michaelmas Term in the year of examination available for collection from the Oriental Institute Faculty Office. Essays should be typed or word-processed in double-spacing and should conform to the standards of academic presentation prescribed in the "Guidelines for Writers of Theses" in the course handbook. Essays shall normally be written during the Michaelmas Term in the year of examination and must be delivered by hand to the Examination Schools (addressed to the Chair of Examiners, Honour School of Oriental Studies, Examination Schools, High Street, Oxford) not later than 12 noon on the Friday before the beginning of Hilary Full Term of the year of examination. Candidates delivering essays will be required to complete a receipt form, which will only be accepted as proof of receipt if it is countersigned by a member of the Examination Schools staff. The essay must be accompanied by a sealed envelope (bearing only the candidate's examination number) containing a formal declaration signed by the candidate that the essay is his or her own work. The University's regulations on Late Submission of Work apply. Any candidate may be examined viva voce.
8. One paper in history under 11 and 12 of the syllabus for Persian with Islamic Studies/History, except 7 vi of the syllabus for Arabic and Islamic Studies, Aspects of Islamic art, architecture and archaeology.
9. Thesis.

Some options and special subjects may not be available in every year. Candidates may obtain from the Oriental Institute information about which options may be offered for examination the following year at the beginning of Trinity Term of the preceding year.

Applications for the approval of options in paper 8 and of the special subjects in paper 9 must be submitted to the Oriental Studies Board by Monday of the second week of Michaelmas Term preceding the examination.

Sanskrit

The following papers will be set:

1. Sanskrit unprepared translation.
2. Essay questions on the history of classical Indian literature and civilization. This paper may include questions on the visual arts in ancient India.
3. Indian linguistics.

Candidates will be examined on their general knowledge and understanding of *vyākaraṇa śāstra,* with particular reference to Pāṇini, *Aṣṭādhyāyi* (ed. Böhtlingk, 1,1,1-1,3,16; 1,4-2,2 (inclusive); and 3,1,91-132).

4. For candidates offering Hindi, Old Iranian, Pali, Prakrit, or Tibetan as additional language: The historical philology of Old Indo-Aryan, with particular reference to:

(*a*) Selected *sūktas* from the *Ṛg Veda* (ed. Müller). A list of *sūktas* is available in the course handbook.

(*b*) Selected passages of prose from the Yajurveda Samhitâ and Brahmanas, and from the early Upanisads. A list of passages is available in the course handbook.

For papers 5 and 6, two papers in a chosen area of Sanskrit studies approved by the Board of the Faculty. Applications for approval must be submitted by the Monday of the sixth week of the Trinity Term of the academic year preceding the examination. (*Note*: These papers are intended to allow candidates to specialise in a particular area of Sanskrit studies such as *kāvya, dharmaśāstra,* philosophy, grammar, or religion.)

5. Unprepared translation from Sanskrit texts.

6. Essay questions on the chosen area.

7. A special subject from among the following, or such other special subjects as may be approved by the board of the faculty:

(*a*) Comparative grammar of Sanskrit and Old Iranian.

(*b*) Indian art and archaeology.

(*c*) Composition in Sanskrit prose and/or verse.

(*d*) Practical criticism and appreciation, including translation from the Sanskrit.

Either

8. and 9. Two papers on one of the following additional languages: Hindi, Old Iranian, Pali, Prakrit, Tibetan.

Or 8, 9, 10. Three papers on Classics (in the Honour School of Classics and Oriental Studies) as an additional language.

Turkish

Turkish Handbook. The Board of the Faculty of Oriental Studies shall issue annually the Handbook for the Honour Schools of Oriental Studies (Turkish, Turkish with a Subsidiary Language, and Turkish with Islamic Art and Archaeology) by Monday of Week 1 of the first Hilary Term of candidates' work for the Honour School. The Handbook will include, amongst other things, lists of the set texts prescribed for particular papers.

Candidates for entry to the Final Honour School of Turkish with Islamic Art and Archaeology will be required to have satisfied the faculty board, by means of written testimonials and a written report on the project(s) completed in Year 2, as to their active and useful participation in the approved project(s).

The following papers will be set:

Either, for Turkish only,

1. Unprepared translation from Ottoman and modern Turkish.

2. Translation into Turkish and essay in Turkish.

3. Spoken Turkish.*

4. Ottoman historical texts.

5. Turkish political and cultural texts, 1860 to the present.

---

* Details of the oral examination and of the areas in which candidates will be expected to show competence are provided in the examination conventions and in the handbook.

6. Modern Turkish literary texts.

7, 8, 9. Three papers from the following:

(*a*) Turkish and Ottoman literary texts, 1300–1900.

(*b*) Turkish literature: general questions. (Only available to candidates taking option (*a*).)

(*c*) Turkish language reform and language politics from 1850 to the present day.

(*d*) Islamic History, 570–1500.

(*e*) The Ottoman Empire, 1300–1566.

(*f*) The Ottoman Empire, 1566–1807.

(*g*) The Ottoman Empire and the Republic of Turkey, 1807–1980.

(*h*) Any one paper under 7 ii, v–viii, xii, xiv, xviii and xix of the syllabus for Arabic and Islamic Studies.

10. A special subject, to be approved by the Board of the Faculty of Oriental Studies.

or, for Turkish with a subsidiary language, Papers 1-6 above **and**

7, 8, 9. Three papers on one of the following languages: Arabic, Armenian, Classics (in the Honour School of Classics and Oriental Studies), Hindi/Urdu, Persian.

10. An *optional* special subject, to be approved by the Board of the Faculty of Oriental Studies.

or, for Turkish with Islamic Art and Archaeology, candidates will be required to offer nine papers.

1. Turkish prose composition and unprepared translation.

2. Spoken Turkish.[†]

3. Ottoman texts.

4. Modern Turkish texts.

5. Islamic Art and Archaeology, *c.* 550–*c.* 1900 (identical to Paper 8 xi of the syllabus for Arabic and Islamic Studies).

6. and 7. Topics in Islamic Art and Architecture, *c.* 1000–*c.* 1900], to be examined by means of a timed paper , and by means of an extended essay, which shall not exceed 6,000 words (including footnotes but excluding bibliography), and shall be on a topic or theme selected by the candidate from a question paper published by the examiners on or before the Friday of the fourth week of Michaelmas Term in the year of examination available for collection from the Oriental Institute Faculty Office. Essays should be typed or word-processed in double-spacing and should conform to the standards of academic presentation pre-scribed in the "Guidelines for Writers of Theses" in the course handbook. Essays shall normally be written during the Michaelmas Term in the year of examina-tion and must be delivered by hand to the Examination Schools (addressed to the Chair of Examiners, Honour School of Oriental Studies, Examination Schools, High Street, Oxford) not later than 12 noon on the Friday before the beginning of Hilary Full Term of the year of examination. Candidates delivering essays will be required to complete a receipt form, which will only be accepted as proof of receipt if it is countersigned by a member of the Examination Schools staff. The essay must be accompanied by a sealed envelope (bearing only the candidate's examination number) containing a formal declaration signed by the candidate that the essay is his or her own work. The University's regulations on Late Submission of Work apply. Any candidate may be examined viva voce.

---

* Details of the oral examination and of the areas in which candidates will be expected to show competence are provided in the examination conventions and in the handbook.

8. One paper in history under 7, 8, 9 of the syllabus for Turkish, except 7vi of the syllabus for Arabic and Islamic Studies, Aspects of Islamic art, architecture and archaeology.

9. Thesis.

ADDITIONAL LANGUAGES

Akkadian (for candidates offering Arabic, Classics (in the Honour School of Classics and Oriental Studies) or Hebrew as main subject).

The following papers will be set:

1, 2, 3 = Papers 2, 5, and 6 as specified for Akkadian in the Honour School of Oriental Studies (Egyptology and Ancient Near Eastern Studies). (Instead of either paper 5 or paper 6, candidates may offer one of papers 7, 9 or 10 as specified for the Honour School of Oriental Studies (Egyptology and Ancient Near Eastern Studies).

Arabic (for candidates offering Classics (in the Honour School of Classics and Oriental Studies), Egyptology and Ancient Near Eastern Studies, Hebrew, Persian, or Turkish as main subject).

The following papers will be set:

1. Arabic prose composition and unprepared translation.

2. Additional Arabic: literary texts.

Selected classical and modern Arabic prose texts (lists available in the course handbook).

3. Additional Arabic: Islamic texts.

Selected Arabic religious texts (list available in the course handbook).

Papers 2 and 3 *may* contain general and linguistic questions.

Aramaic and Syriac (for candidates offering Arabic, Classics (in the Honour School of Classics and Oriental Studies), Egyptology and Ancient Near Eastern Studies, Hebrew or Persian as main subject).

The following papers will be set:

1. Syriac prose composition and Aramaic and Syriac unprepared translation.

2. Aramaic prepared texts.*

3. Syriac prepared texts.*

Papers 2 and 3 may contain general and grammatical questions.

Armenian

The following papers will be set:

either

A. Classical Armenian†

1. Classical Armenian prose composition and unprepared translation.

2. Prepared religious texts*

3. Prepared historical and other texts*

or

B. Modern Armenian‡

1. Modern Armenian prose composition and unprepared translation.

2. Prepared texts from the sixteenth to nineteenth centuries*.

3. Prepared texts from the twentieth and twenty-first centuries*.

Papers 2 and 3 will include questions on the subject-matter and grammar of the texts offered, and Paper 3 will also include questions on Armenian language, literature, and history.

---

* Lists of texts are available in the course handbook.

† For candidates offering Arabic, Classics (in the Honour School of Classics and Oriental Studies), Persian or Turkish as main subject.

‡ For candidates offering Arabic, Persian or Turkish as main subject.

Chinese (for candidates offering Japanese as main subject)
The following papers will be set:

1. Chinese Prescribed Texts. (Lists of texts will be available in the course handbook.)
2. *Either* (*a*) Unprepared translation and prose composition, *or* (*b*) Classical Chinese. (Texts will be as prescribed for paper 3, 'Classical texts' of Moderations in Oriental Studies (Chinese).)
3. History and Culture of China.

Coptic (for candidates offering Classics (in the Honour School of Classics and Oriental Studies) or Egyptology as main subject).
The following papers will be set:

1. Coptic unprepared translation and grammar.
2. Prepared texts I*
3. Prepared texts II, with general questions*

Egyptology (for candidates offering Classics (in the Honour School of Classics and Oriental Studies) or Hebrew as main subject).
The following papers will be set:

1, 2, 3 = Papers 2, 5, and 6 as specified for Egyptian in the Honour School of Oriental Studies (Egyptology and Ancient Near Eastern Studies). (Instead of either paper 5 or paper 6, candidates may offer one of papers 7, 9 or 10 as specified for the Honour School of Oriental Studies (Egyptology and Ancient Near Eastern Studies).

Hebrew (for candidates offering Arabic, Classics (in the Honour School of Classics and Oriental Studies) or Egyptology and Ancient Near Eastern Studies as main subject).

Candidates taking Arabic may offer *either* (*a*) Biblical and Rabbinic *or* (*b*) Medieval *or* (*c*) Modern Hebrew. Candidates taking Classics (in the Honour School of Classics and Oriental Studies) may offer *either* (*a*) Biblical and Rabbinic or (*b*) Medieval Hebrew. Candidates taking Egyptology may offer only Biblical and Rabbinic Hebrew. Biblical texts will be set from *Biblia Hebraica Stuttgartensia* (ed. Elliger and Rudolph).

The following papers will be set:
(*a*) Biblical and Rabbinic Hebrew:

1. Prose composition and unprepared translation.
2. Prepared texts I: Biblical texts*
3. Prepared texts II: Biblical and Rabbinic texts*

Papers 2 and 3 may contain general and grammatical questions.
(*b*) Medieval Hebrew:

1. Unprepared translation.
2. Prepared texts I*
3. Prepared texts II*

Papers 2 and 3 may contain general and grammatical questions.
(*c*) Modern Hebrew:

1. Prose composition and unprepared translation.
2. Prepared texts I*
3. Prepared texts II*

Papers 2 and 3 may contain general and grammatical questions.

Hindi (for candidates offering Sanskrit as main subject)
The following papers will be set:

1. Hindi unprepared translation.
2. Prepared texts, with questions on Hindi language and literature.

---

* Lists of texts are available in the course handbook.

Hindi/Urdu (For candidates offering Arabic, Persian or Turkish as main subject)
The following papers will be set
   (1) Hindi and Urdu prose composition and unprepared translation;
   (2) Hindi prepared texts with questions on language and literature;
   (3) Urdu prepared texts with questions on language and literature.   5

Japanese (for candidates offering Chinese as main subject)

The following papers will be set:
   1. *Japanese Prescribed Texts.**
   2. *Either* Unprepared translation, Prose Composition, and Grammatical Questions, *or* any Special Subject set for paper 8 of the syllabus in Japanese only   10
[see the list of Special Subjects for Paper 8 set out under SPECIAL REGULATIONS FOR THE HONOUR SCHOOL OF ORIENTAL STUDIES, REGULATIONS CONCERNING INDIVIDUAL SUBJECTS, MAIN SUBJECTS, **Japanese, Japanese only**]
   3. Essay questions on Japanese Culture.   15

Korean (for candidates offering Chinese and Japanese as main subject)

The following papers will be set:
   1. Korean Texts.*
   2. Korean History and Culture.
   3. Korean Language.   20

Old Iranian (for candidates offering Classics (in the Honour School of Classics and Oriental Studies), Egyptology and Ancient Near Eastern Studies or Persian as main subject).
The following papers will be set:
   1. Avestan Texts*
   2. (i) Old Persian texts*   25
   (ii) *either* (*a*) Questions on the content of the Old Persian texts and their historical background *or* (*b*) Questions on the history of the Persian language.
   3. Questions on Avestan and Old Persian language, and on pre-Islamic Iranian history, religion, and literature.

Old Iranian (for candidates offering Sanskrit as main subject).   30

The following papers will be set:
   1. Old Persian and Avestan Texts*
   2. Questions on Old Persian and Avestan language and literature, and on the religious and historical background to the texts studied for Paper 1.

Pali (for candidates offering Sanskrit as main subject).   35

The following papers will be set:
   1. Pali unprepared translation.
   2. Questions on Pali language and literature, on Theravāda Buddhist doctrine, and on the early history of Buddhism in South Asia.

Pali (for candidates offering Classics (in the Honour School of Classics and Oriental   40 Studies) as main subject).
The following papers will be set:
   1. Pali unprepared translation.
   2. Questions on Pali language and literature, on Theravāda Buddhist doctrine, and on the early history of Buddhism in South Asia.   45
   3. Prepared texts, with questions on contents.

---

* Lists of texts are available in the course handbook.

Persian (for candidates offering Arabic, Classics (in the Honour School of Classics and Oriental Studies) or Turkish as main subject).

The following papers will be set:

   1. Persian prose composition and unprepared translation.

   2 and 3. Two papers from the following:

(*a*) Classical Poetry.

(*b*) Classical Prose.

(*c*) Modern Literature.

(*d*) Modern social and political writing.*

Prakrit (for candidates offering Sanskrit as main subject).

The following papers will be set:

   1. Prakrit unprepared translation.

   2. Questions on Prakrit language and literature and on the doctrine and early history of the Jains.

Sanskrit (for candidates offering Classics (in the Honour School of Classics and Oriental Studies) as main subject.)

The following papers will be set:

   1. Sanskrit unprepared translation.

   2. Questions on Sanskrit language and literature.

   3. Prepared texts.

Tibetan (for candidates offering Chinese or Japanese as main subject)

   1. Tibetan prose composition and unprepared translation.

   2. Prepared texts, with questions.*

   3. Questions on Tibetan culture and history.

Tibetan (for candidates offering Sanskrit as main subject).

The following papers will be set:

   1. Tibetan prose composition and unprepared translation.

   2. Prepared texts, with questions on Tibetan culture and history.

Turkish (for candidates offering Arabic, Classics (in the Honour School of Classics and Oriental Studies) or Persian as main subject).

The following papers will be set:

   1. Turkish prose composition and unprepared translation.

   2. *Either* (*a*) Additional Turkish: Late Ottoman and modern Turkish literary texts*

Or (*b*) Additional Turkish: Modern Turkish literary texts:*

Either (*a*) Additional Turkish: Political and cultural texts, 1860 to the present.*

Or (*b*) Additional Turkish: Political and cultural texts, 1920 to the present.*

---

* Lists of texts are available in the course handbook.

SPECIAL REGULATIONS FOR PHILOSOPHY IN ALL HONOUR SCHOOLS INCLUDING PHILOSOPHY

Candidates offering Philosophy papers* in any honour school must conform to the General Regulations below, and to those for their particular school, as specified elsewhere.

Subjects in Philosophy

The syllabuses of the subjects in Philosophy are specified below. A three hour written examination paper will be set in each subject except 199.

101. *Early Modern Philosophy*

Candidates will be expected to show critical appreciation of the main philosophical ideas of the period. The subject will be studied in connection with the following texts: Descartes, *Meditations, Objections and Replies;* Spinoza, *Ethics*; Leibniz, *Monadology, Discourse on Metaphysics*; Locke, *Essay Concerning Human Understanding*; Berkeley, *Principles of Human Knowledge, Three Dialogues Between Hylas and Philonous*; Hume, *Treatise of Human Nature*. The paper will consist of three sections; Section A will include questions about Descartes, Spinoza, and Leibniz; Section B will include questions about Locke, Berkeley and Hume. Candidates will be required to answer three questions, with at least one question from Section A and at least one question from Section B.

102. *Knowledge and Reality*

Candidates will be expected to show knowledge in some of the following areas: knowledge and justification; perception; memory; induction; other minds; *a priori* knowledge; necessity and possibility; reference; truth; facts and propositions; definition; existence; identity, including personal identity; substances, change, events; properties; causation; space; time; essence; natural kinds; realism and idealism; primary and secondary qualities.

103. *Ethics*

Candidates will be given an opportunity to show some first-hand knowledge of some principal historical writings on this subject, including those of Aristotle, Hume, and Kant, but will not be required to do so. Questions will normally be set on the following topics:

1. The Metaphysics of Ethics: including the nature of morality and moral properties, the truth-aptness of moral judgements, moral knowledge and moral relativism.

2. Value and Normativity: including good and right, reasons, rationality, motivation, moral dilemmas.

3. Self-interest, Altruism, and Amoralism.

4. Ethical Theories: including consequentialism, utilitarianism, and contractualism.

5. Specific Moral Concepts: including happiness, well-being, rights, virtue, fairness, equality, and desert.

---

* The paper for the supplementary subject "History and Philosophy of Science" is not here counted as a Philosophy paper, since it is a joint paper in both History and Philosophy.

6. Moral Psychology: including conscience, guilt and shame, freedom and responsibility.

7. Applied Ethics, including medical ethics.

104. *Philosophy of Mind*

Topics to be studied include the nature of persons, the relation of mind and body, self-knowledge, knowledge of other persons, consciousness, perception, memory, imagination, thinking, belief, feeling and emotion, desire, action, the explanation of action, subconscious and unconscious mental processes.

106. *Philosophy of Science and Social Science*

The paper will include such topics as:

Part A: the nature of theories; scientific observation and method; scientific explanation; the interpretation of laws and probability; rationality and scientific change; major schools of philosophy of science.

Part B: social meaning; individualism; rationality; rational choice theory; prediction and explanation in economics; the explanation of social action; historical explanation, ideology.

Candidates will be required to answer at least one question from each part of the paper.

107. *Philosophy of Religion*

The subject will include an examination of claims about the existence of God, and God's relation to the world; their meaning, the possibility of their truth, and the kind of justification which can or needs to be provided for them; and the philosophical problems raised by the existence of different religions. One or two questions may also be set on central claims peculiar to Christianity, such as the doctrines of the Trinity, Incarnation, and Atonement.

108. *The Philosophy of Logic and Language*

The subject will include questions on such topics as: meaning, truth, logical form, necessity, existence, entailment, proper and general names, pronouns, definite descriptions, intensional contexts, adjectives and nominalization, adverbs, metaphor, and pragmatics. Some questions will be set which allow candidates to make use of knowledge of linguistics.

109. *Aesthetics and the Philosophy of Criticism*

Candidates will have the opportunity to show first-hand knowledge of some principal authorities on the subject, including Plato, *Ion* and *Republic*; Aristotle, *Poetics*; Hume, *Of the Standard of Taste*; Kant, *Critique of Aesthetic Judgement*. Questions will normally be set on the following topics: the nature of aesthetic value; the definition of art; art, society, and morality; criticism and interpretation; metaphor; expression; pictorial representation.

110. *Medieval Philosophy: Aquinas*

The subject will be studied in the following text (The Fathers of the English Dominican Province edition, 1911, rev. 1920):

Aquinas, *Summa Theologiae*, Ia, 2–11, 75–89 (God, Metaphysics, and Mind); *or* Aquinas, *Summa Theologiae*, Ia IIae qq. 1–10, 90–97 (Action and Will; Natural Law). This paper will include an optional question containing passages for comment. This subject may not be combined with subject 111.

111. *Medieval Philosophy: Duns Scotus, Ockham*

The subject will be studied in the following texts:

Duns Scotus, *Philosophical Writings*, tr. Wolter (Hackett) pp. 13–95 (chapters II-IV); Spade, *Five Texts*, pp. 57–113. Ockham, *Philosophical Writings*, tr. Boehner

(Hackett), pp. 17–27, 96–126 (chapters II §1–2, chapters VIII-IX); Spade, *Five Texts*, pp. 114–231. This paper will include an optional question containing passages for comment. This subject may not be combined with subject 110.

112. *The Philosophy of Kant*
  Critique of Pure Reason, Groundwork of the Metaphysic of Morals. The editions to   5
  be used are *Critique of Pure Reason*, ed. and trans. by P. Guyer and A. Wood
  (Cambridge University Press, 1998) and *Groundwork of the Metaphysic of Morals*,
  ed. and trans. by M. Gregor (Cambridge University Press, 1997).
  Candidates may answer no more than one question on Kant's moral philosophy.

113. *Post-Kantian Philosophy*   10
  The main developments of philosophy in Continental Europe after Kant, excluding Marxism and analytical philosophy. Questions on the following authors will
  regularly be set: Hegel, Schopenhauer, Nietzsche, Husserl, Heidegger, Sartre,
  Merleau-Ponty. There will be some general and/or comparative questions, and questions on other authors may be set from time to time. Candidates will be required to   15
  show adequate first-hand knowledge of works of at least two authors (who may be
  studied in translation).

114. *Theory of Politics*
  The critical study of political values and of the concepts used in political analysis:
  the concept of the political; power, authority, and related concepts; the state; law;   20
  liberty and rights; justice and equality; public interest and common good; democracy
  and representation; political obligation and civil disobedience; ideology; liberalism,
  socialism, and conservatism.

115. Plato: *Republic*, tr. Grube, revised Reeve (Hackett).
  There will be a compulsory question containing passages for comment.   25

116. Aristotle: *Nicomachean Ethics*, tr. Irwin (Hackett, second edition).
  There will be a compulsory question containing passages for comment.

117. *Frege, Russell, and Wittgenstein*
  Works principally to be studied are:
  Frege, *Foundations of Arithmetic*, trans. Austin; *Begriffsschrift* ch. 1, 'Function and   30
  Concept', 'Sense and Meaning', 'Concept and Object', and 'Frege on Russell's
  Paradox', in Geach and Black, eds. *Translations from the Philosophical Writings of
  Gottlob Frege*;
  Russell, 'On Denoting', 'Mathematical Logic as Based on the theory of Types', and
  'On the Nature of Acquaintance', in Marsh, ed., *Logic and Knowledge*; 'The Ultimate   35
  Constituents of Matter', 'The Relation of Sense-Data to Physics', and 'Knowledge by
  Acquaintance and Knowledge by Description', in *Mysticism and Logic; Our
  Knowledge of the External World*, chs. I-IV; **either** *Introduction to Mathematical
  Philosophy*, chs. 1-3 and 12-18, **or** 'The Philosophy of Logical Atomism', in Marsh,
  ed., *Logic and Knowledge*;   40
  Wittgenstein, *Tractatus Logico-Philosophicus*.
  Candidates will be required to show adequate knowledge of at least two authors.

118. *The Later Philosophy of Wittgenstein*
  Works principally to be studied are *Philosophical Investigations* and *The Blue and
  Brown Books*.   45

119. *Formal Logic*

The paper will consist of three sections:

(i) Propositional and Predicate Logic

Formal languages of propositional logic, adequate sets of connectives, conjunctive and disjunctive normal form, tautologies, logical consequence; formal languages of predicate logic, satisfaction, truth, validity, logical consequence. Deductive systems of propositional and predicate calculus; proofs and theorems; prenex normal forms; the soundness and completeness theorems. Derivation of the compactness theorem, simple applications of the compactness theorem. Predicate calculus with identity, normal models. Elementariness. The Löwenheim-Skolem theorems. First-order theories and their properties: completeness, categoricity. Differences between first-order and second-order logic.

(ii) Set Theory

Basic axioms of set theory. Cartesian products, relations and functions. Axiom of infinity and the construction of the natural numbers; induction and the recursion theorem. Cardinality: finite, countable and uncountable sets; Cantor's theorem; the Schröder-Bernstein theorem. Linear orders and well-orders; order isomorphism, dense linear order. Transfinite induction and recursion. Comparability of well-orders. Ordinals, and their arithmetic. Equivalence of the axiom of choice, Zorn's lemma, the well-ordering principle, and cardinal comparability. Cardinals, and their arithmetic.

(iii) Metamathematics

Primitive recursion and general recursion. Total and partial functions. Computability: Turing machines or register machines; existence of a universal machine; the s-m-n theorem. Decision problems; undecidability of the halting problem. Church's thesis. Formal systems of arithmetic; representability of sets and functions. Undefinability of truth. Gödel's first incompleteness theorem; Rosser's theorem; Löb's theorem; the Hilbert-Bernays adequacy conditions on a provability predicate; Gödel's second incompleteness theorem. No decision procedure for first-order logical validity; no complete proof procedure for second-order logical validity.

120. *Intermediate Philosophy of Physics*

The paper will consist of two sections. Section A will include philosophical problems associated with classical physics and some basic philosophical issues raised by the Special Theory of Relativity. Section B will be concerned with introductory philosophical problems related to the interpretation of quantum mechanics. Candidates will be required to answer at least one question from each section.

121. *Advanced Philosophy of Physics*

The subject will include advanced topics in the philosophy of space, time, and relativity and in the philosophical foundations of quantum mechanics. It will also include some philosophical issues raised by thermodynamics and statistical mechanics.

122. *Philosophy of Mathematics*

Questions may be set which relate to the following issues: Incommensurables in the development of Greek geometry. Comparisons between geometry and other branches of mathematics. The significance of non-Euclidean geometry. The problem of mathematical rigour in the development of the calculus. The place of intuition in mathematics (Kant, Poincaré). The idea that mathematics needs foundations. The role of logic and set theory (Dedekind, Cantor, Frege, Russell). The claim that mathematics must be constructive (Brouwer). The finitary study of formal systems as a means of justifying infinitary mathematics (Hilbert). Limits to the formalization of mathematics (Gödel). Anti-foundational views of mathematics. Mathematical objects and structures. The nature of infinity. The applicability of mathematics.

124. *Philosophy of Science*

This paper will include such topics as: scientific method, including induction, confirmation, corroboration, and explanation; the structure of scientific theories, including syntactic and semantic approaches, the nature of scientific laws, the theory-observation distinction, inter-theory reduction, theory unification, and 5 emergence; debates over realism, including the aims of science, the underdetermination of theory by data, and structuralism; and scientific rationality, including theory change, epistemological naturalism, and Bayesian epistemology. Questions will also be set on historical schools in the philosophy of science, in particular logical positivism and logical empiricism, on aspects of the history 10 of science, and on the philosophy of probability, including the nature of probabilistic laws.

125. *Philosophy of Cognitive Science*

Topics to be studied include: levels of description, including personal and subpersonal levels, and relationships between levels; the nature of cognitive scientific theories; 15 information and representation, including representational format, the language of thought, and connectionist alternatives; information processing, including algorithms, and tacit knowledge of rules; cognitive architecture, including modularity, and homuncular functionalism; explanation in cognitive science, including functional explanation and mechanistic explanation; methods in cognitive science, including cognitive 20 neuropsychology, computational modelling, and experimental cognitive psychology; the scientific study of consciousness, including the status of introspective reports and non-verbal measures, and the notion of a neural and computational correlate of consciousness. Questions will also be set on philosophical issues arising from aspects of the history of cognitive science and from areas of active research in cognitive 25 science.

126. *The Philosophy and Economics of the Environment*[†]

Philosophical foundations: justice and goodness, theories of value; decision-making under uncertainty. Economic foundations: externalities, public goods, international environmental agreements. Politics and the environment. Intergenerational ethics, 30 discounting. The choice of instruments: taxes, permits and command-and-control; environmental instruments in practice. Valuing human life. Valuing nature. Cost-benefit analysis: foundations and critiques; valuation methods.

130. Plato, *Republic*

Candidates will be expected to have read books I, IV-VII, X in Greek 35 (Slings Oxford Classical Text), and books II-III, VIII-IX in translation (Grube, revised Reeve, Hackett). There will be a compulsory question containing passages for translation and comment from the books read in Greek; any passages for comment from the remaining books will be accompanied by a translation. 40

131. Plato, *Theaetetus* and *Sophist*

Candidates will be expected to have read both dialogues in Greek (Duke *et al.*, Oxford Classical Text). There will be a compulsory question containing passages for translation and comment.

---

† This paper is only available in the Honour School of Philosophy, Politics and Economics (where it can be offered alternatively as Economics paper 321).

132. Aristotle, *Nicomachean Ethics*

Candidates will be expected to have read books I-III, VI-VII, X in Greek (Bywater, Oxford Classical Text), and books IV-V, VIII-IX in translation (Irwin, Hackett second edition). There will be a compulsory question containing passages for translation and comment from the books read in Greek; any passages for comment from the   5
remaining books will be accompanied by a translation.

133. Aristotle, *Physics*

Candidates will be expected to have read books I-IV and VIII in Greek (Ross, Oxford Classical Texts), and books V-VII in translation (in Barnes, ed., *The Complete Works of Aristotle: The Revised Oxford Translation* (Princeton), vol. I).   10
There will be a compulsory question containing passages for translation and comment from the books read in Greek; any passages for comment from the remaining books will be accompanied by a translation.

134. Sextus Empiricus: *Outlines of Pyrrhonism* (Bury, Loeb)

There will be a compulsory question containing passages for translation and   15
comment.

135. *Latin Philosophy*

Cicero: *De Finibus* III (Reynolds, Oxford Classical Text), *De Officiis* I in translation (Griffin and Atkins, *Cicero, On Duties*, Cambridge); Seneca, *Epistulae Morales* 92, 95, 121, *De Constantia, De Vita Beata* (Reynolds, Oxford Classical Text).   20
There will be a compulsory question containing passages for translation and comment from the texts read in Latin; any passages for comment from Cicero, *De Officiis* I will be accompanied by a translation.

150. *Jurisprudence*

As specified in the regulations for the Honour School of Jurisprudence. This   25
subject may be offered only by candidates in PPE, and cannot be combined with either subject 114 or subject 203. Tutorial provision will be subject to the availability of Law tutors and will normally take place in either Hilary or Trinity Term.

180. *The Rise of Modern Logic*

The original authorities for the Rise of Modern Logic. The period of scientific   30
thought to be covered is from 1879 to 1931 and includes principally the logical and foundational works of Frege, Russell, Hilbert, Brouwer, and Gödel that fall within this period. Questions may also be asked concerning Cantor, Dedekind, Poincaré, Zermelo, Skolem, Wittgenstein (Tractatus only), and Ramsey.

198. *Special Subjects*   35

From time to time special subjects may be approved by the Undergraduate Studies Committee of the Faculty of Philosophy. Special subjects will be communicated to college tutors and to undergraduates by the end of the fifth week of Hilary Term one year before examination. The Undergraduate Studies Committee will (a) agree the method of assessment for each special subject offered, which may be by written   40
paper, submitted essay and/or other method (b) forbid, where it sees fit, a combination of a special subject with other subjects (c) forbid, where it sees fit, candidates taking any particular special subject to answer certain questions on the papers for other subjects (d) place restrictions, where it sees fit, on the number of candidates that may take any special subject in any year. No candidate may offer more than one   45
special subject. Subject to these qualifications, any candidate may offer any special subject.

199. *Thesis*:

1. *Subject*

The subject of every thesis should fall within the scope of philosophy. The subject may but need not overlap any subject on which the candidate offers papers. Candidates are warned that they should avoid repetition in papers of material used 5 in their theses and that substantial repetition may be penalised. Every candidate shall submit for approval by the Director of Undergraduate Studies of the Faculty of Philosophy, c/o the Undergraduate Studies Administrator at Philosophy Centre, Radcliffe Humanities Building, Woodstock Road, Oxford OX2 6GG, the title he or she proposes, together with (*a*) an explanation of the subject in about 100 words; 10 and (*b*) a letter of approval from his or her tutor, not earlier than the first day of the Trinity Full Term of the year before that in which he or she is to be examined and not later than Friday of the fourth week of the Michaelmas Full Term preceding his or her examination. (The date before which a proposal cannot be submitted is different in certain circumstances in the case of the Honour School of Philosophy and Modern Languages. 15 See the regulations below for that honour school.) The Director of Undergraduate Studies of the Faculty of Philosophy shall decide as soon as possible whether or not to approve the title and shall advise the candidate immediately. No decision shall be deferred beyond the end of the fifth week of Michaelmas Full Term. If a candidate wishes to change the title, subject or focus of his or her thesis after his or her thesis proposal has already 20 been approved by the body responsible: he or she should write to the Director of Undergraduate Studies of the Faculty of Philosophy, c/o the Undergraduate Studies Administrator, to seek approval. The Undergraduate Studies Administrator will inform the candidate whether the change to the thesis has been approved, and communicate any change, where approved, to the appropriate chair of examiners. 25

2. *Authorship and origin*

Every thesis shall be the candidate's own work. A candidate's tutor may, however, discuss with the candidate the field of study, the sources available, and the method of presentation; the tutor may also read and comment on drafts. The amount of assistance the tutor may give is equivalent to the teaching of a normal paper. Every 30 candidate shall sign a certificate to the effect that the thesis is his or her own work and the tutor shall countersign the certificate confirming, to the best of his or her knowledge and belief, that this is so. This certificate shall be placed in a sealed envelope bearing the candidate's examination number presented together with the thesis. No thesis shall be accepted which has already been submitted for a degree of this or any 35 other university, and the certificate shall also state that the thesis has not been so submitted. No thesis shall, however, be ineligible because it has been or is being submitted for any prize of this university.

3. *Length and format*

No thesis shall exceed 15,000 words, the limit to include all notes and appendices 40 but not including the bibliography; no person or body shall have authority to permit any excess, except that in Literae Humaniores, in a thesis consisting in commentary on a text, quotation from the text will not be counted towards the word limit. The word count should be indicated at the front of the thesis. There shall be a select bibliography or a list of sources. All theses must be typed in double spacing on one 45 side of quarto or A4 paper with any notes and references at the foot of each page. *Two* copies of the thesis shall be submitted to the examiners.

4. *Submission of thesis*

Every candidate shall submit the thesis, identified by the candidate's examination number only, not later than noon on Friday of the week before the Trinity Full Term 50 of the examination to the Examination Schools, Oxford, addressed to the Chair of the Examiners in the candidate's honour school.

General Regulations

The following restrictions on combinations apply to candidates whatever their honour school:

(i) A candidate may not take both of subjects 106 and 124.

(ii) A candidate may not take both of subjects 115 and 130.

(iii) A candidate may not take both of subjects 116 and 132.

(iv) Both of subjects 117 and 118 may be offered *only* by candidates in *Mathematics and Philosophy* and *Computer Science and Philosophy*.

(v) A candidate may not take subject 199 unless he or she also takes three other philosophy subjects.

(vi) Notwithstanding any contrary indication in these regulations, subjects 130, 131, 132, 133, 134, and 135 may be offered *only* by candidates in *Classics and English, Classics and Modern Languages, Classics and Oriental Studies, Literae Humaniores,* and *Oriental Studies.*

(vii) A candidate may not take both of subjects 110 and 111.

(viii) Jurisprudence (subject 150) may be offered only by candidates in PPE, and cannot be combined with either subject 114 or subject 203.

(ix) The Rise of Modern Logic (180) may only be offered by candidates in Part C of the Honour Schools in Mathematics and Philosophy, Physics and Philosophy, and Computer Science and Philosophy.

Whichever a candidate's honour school, where it is prescribed that he or she must take one or other of certain specified subjects and must take in addition some further subjects, a subject that is not chosen from among the specified ones may be chosen as a further subject.

Regulations for Particular Honour Schools

Computer Science and Philosophy

In Part B candidates are required to take at least three subjects in Philosophy from subjects 101–120, 122, 124 and 125, and including at least two from 101, 102, 104, 108, 122, 124 and 125.

In Part C each candidate shall offer a total of three units chosen in any combination from the lists for Computer Science and for Philosophy. A unit in Philosophy consists of one of the subjects 101–120, 122, 124, 125 and 180 as specified above, or a Thesis as specified in 199 above except that the thesis shall not exceed 20,000 words. No subject in Philosophy may be offered in both Part B and Part C. Each unit in Philosophy other than a Thesis shall be examined by a three-hour written paper together with an essay of at most 5,000 words conforming to the rules given in the Course Handbook.

Literae Humaniores

The Honour School is divided into two Courses; for restrictions on entry to Course II, see the regulations under *Honour School of Literae Humaniores.* Candidates in either Course may offer any number of subjects in Philosophy up to five, or up to four if they are offering Second Classical Language in Course II. Any selection is permitted which conforms to the General Regulations above and also to (i)-(v) following:

(i) candidates offering one Philosophy subject only may offer any of the subjects listed above except 121 and 199.

(ii) candidates offering at least two Philosophy subjects must select at least one subject in ancient philosophy, i.e., one of 115, 116, 130, 131, 132, 133, 134, and 135. Those offering three or more subjects must also select one subject from 101, 102, 103, and 108.

(iii) candidates offering subject 199, Thesis in Philosophy, may not offer any other thesis except a Special Thesis;

(iv) all candidates must offer at least four text-based subjects, not necessarily in Philosophy (or three if offering Second Classical Language in Course II);

(v) all candidates in Course I must offer at least one text-based subject in each of classical Greek texts and classical Latin texts, not necessarily in Philosophy.

The text-based subjects in Philosophy are 130 (Greek), 131 (Greek), 132 (Greek), 133 (Greek), 134 (Greek), 135 (Latin).

Candidates may also offer a Special Thesis, which may be in Philosophy, in accordance with the regulations under Honour School of Literae Humaniores.

Mathematics and Philosophy

See SPECIAL REGULATIONS FOR THE HONOUR SCHOOL OF MATHEMATICS AND PHILOSOPHY.

Philosophy and Modern Languages

Candidates are required to take **one** of the following subjects: 101, 115, 116. In addition to this subject, they must take two or three or four further subjects in Philosophy, depending upon whether the number of subjects they take in part II in Modern Languages is three or two or one. Further subjects in Philosophy must be chosen in conformity with the General Regulations.

Where subject 199 is taken, every candidate shall submit his or her application for approval of the subject not earlier than the first day of Trinity Full Term two years before the term of the written examination in the case of candidates planning to spend a year abroad.

Philosophy, Politics and Economics

Any candidate in this school offers *either* Philosophy Politics and Economics *or* Philosophy and Politics *or* Philosophy and Economics *or* Politics and Economics; and takes eight subjects in all. Subjects in Philosophy must be chosen in conformity with the regulations for the honour school and with the General Regulations above; and subject 114 may not be offered by any candidate who takes subject 203 in Politics.

Candidates offering Philosophy Politics and Economics are required to take (i) *either* subject 101, *or* subject 102, *or* subject 115, *or* subject 116, and (ii) subject 103. In addition to these subjects, they may take one or two further subjects in Philosophy.

Candidates offering Philosophy and Politics are required to take (i) *either* subject 101, *or* subject 102, *or* subject 115, *or* subject 116, and (ii) subject 103. In addition to these two, they must take one, and they may take two or three, further subjects in Philosophy.

Candidates offering Philosophy and Economics are required to take (i) *either* subject 101 , *or* subject 102, *or* subject 115, *or* subject 116, and (ii) subject 103. In addition to these two, they must take one, and they may take two or three, further subjects in Philosophy.

Candidates offering Politics and Economics may take any one subject in Philosophy.

Philosophy and Theology

Candidates are required to take (i) subject 107, (ii) **one** of the subjects 101, 115, and 116, and (iii) *either* subject 102 *or* subject 103. In addition to these three, they may take one or two further subjects in Philosophy, depending upon whether they take five or four or three subjects in all in Theology. Further subjects in Philosophy must be chosen in conformity with the General Regulations.

Candidates taking subject 199 who wish to write their thesis during the Long Vacation may submit titles for approval before noon on Friday of the fourth week of the Trinity Term in the year preceding the examination, and approval will be notified before the end of that term.

Physics and Philosophy

Part B: candidates are required to take (i) subject 101 or 102; (ii) one of subjects 106, or 124; and (iii) subject 120. Candidates offering a further subject in Philosophy must select one from the list of subjects 101–122 and 125 above, in accordance with the General Regulations.

Part C: those candidates offering one or more further Philosophy subjects must choose them from the subjects 101–4, 107–22, 125, and 180 as specified above, or a Thesis as specified in 199 above, save that the thesis shall not exceed 20,000 words.

Each subject in Philosophy other than a Thesis shall be examined by a three-hour written paper together with an essay of at most 5,000 words. See Special Regulations for the Honour School of Physics and Philosophy for regulations concerning the examination essays.

The same Philosophy subject may not be taken in more than one part of the final examination.

[Until 1 October 2015: *Psychology and Philosophy*

Candidates may take at most five subjects in Philosophy. All candidates must take eight subjects in total. Candidates may only take subjects in Psychology if they offer Psychology Parts I and II.

Candidates who take one subject in Philosophy may take any subject, except 121, in conformity with the General Regulations. Candidates who take two subjects in Philosophy must take at least one of 101, 102, 104, or 125. Those offering three or more Philosophy subjects must choose at least two from the above list. Their further subjects taken in Philosophy must be chosen in conformity with the General Regulations.]

[From 1 October 2014: *Psychology, Philosophy, and Linguistics*

Candidates may take at most five subjects in Philosophy. All candidates must take eight subjects in total. Candidates may only take subjects in Psychology if they offer Psychology Parts I and II.

Candidates who take one subject in Philosophy may take any subject, except 121, in conformity with the General Regulations. Candidates who take two subjects in Philosophy must take at least one of 101, 102, 104, 108, 124 or 125. Those offering three or more Philosophy subjects must choose at least two from the above list. Their further subjects taken in Philosophy must be chosen in conformity with the General Regulations.]

[Until 1 October 2014: *Psychology, Philosophy, and Physiology*

Candidates may take at most five subjects in Philosophy. All candidates must take eight subjects in total. Candidates may only take subjects in Psychology if they offer Psychology Parts I and II.

Candidates who take one subject in Philosophy may take any subject, except 121, in conformity with the General Regulations. Candidates who take two subjects in Philosophy must take at least one of 101, 102, 104, or 125. Those offering three or more Philosophy subjects must choose at least two from the above list. Their further subjects taken in Philosophy must be chosen in conformity with the General Regulations.]

SPECIAL REGULATIONS FOR
THE HONOUR SCHOOL OF PHILOSOPHY
AND MODERN LANGUAGES

A

1. The subjects of the examination in the Honour School of Philosophy and Modern Languages shall be (*a*) Philosophy and (*b*) those modern European languages and literatures studied in the Honour School of Modern Languages.

2. All candidates must offer both (*a*) and one of the languages in (*b*) with its literature.

3. No candidate shall be admitted to examination in this school unless he or she has either passed or been exempted from the First Public Examination.

4. The examiners shall indicate in the lists issued by them the language offered by each candidate obtaining honours or satisfying the examiners under the appropriate regulation.

5. The examination in this school shall be under the joint supervision of the Boards of the Faculties of Philosophy and of Medieval and Modern European Languages and Literature, which shall appoint a standing joint committee to make regulations concerning it, subject always to the preceding clauses of this subsection.

6. The examiners for Philosophy shall be nominated by a committee of which the three elected members shall be appointed by the Board of the Faculty of Philosophy. It shall be the duty of the chair of the examiners for the Honour School of Modern Languages to designate such of their number as may be required for Modern Languages in the Honour School of Philosophy and Modern Languages, and when this has been done and the examiners for Philosophy have been nominated, the number of examiners in Philosophy and Modern Languages shall be deemed to be complete.

B

Candidates will be examined in accordance with the examination regulations set out below.

They will also be required to spend, after their matriculation, an academic year of approved residence in an appropriate country or appropriate countries, and to provide on their entry form for the examination a certificate that they have done this, signed by the Head or by a tutor of their society. Candidates wishing to be dispensed from the requirement to undertake a year of residence abroad must apply in writing to the Chair of the Medieval and Modern Languages Board, 41 Wellington

Square, Oxford, OX1 2JF, stating their reasons for requesting dispensation and enclosing a letter of support from their society.

Candidates will be expected to carry out during this year abroad such work as their society may require. It is strongly recommended that candidates should apply through the Central Bureau for Educational Visits and Exchanges for an Assistantship, where these are available, and should accept one if offered. Candidates who are not able to obtain an Assistantship should during their year abroad follow a course or courses in an institution or institutions approved by their society, or should spend their time in such other circumstances as are acceptable to their society. Candidates will agree with their College Tutor in advance of their year abroad an independent course of study to be followed during that period.

A candidate shall offer in his or her language and literature papers one modern language and its literature only, except in a Special Subject or an alternative to a Special Subject (Honour School of Modern Languages, paper XII).

No candidate will be examined viva voce unless the examiners elect to do so and have been given leave by the Proctors to take into account illness or other urgent and reasonable cause that may have affected the candidate's performance in any part of the examination.

Oral Examination: as specified for the Honour School of Modern Languages.

In the assignment of honours, in the case of a candidate who offers four Philosophy subjects, Philosophy shall count for the same as the Modern Language and, in the case of a candidate who offers three or five Philosophy subjects, it shall count for correspondingly less or more, provided in each case that the highest honours can be obtained by marked excellence in either Philosophy or the Modern Language subject to an adequate standard being shown in the other branch.

In every case where, under the regulations for the school, candidates have any choice between one or more papers or subjects, every candidate shall give notice to the Registrar not later than the Friday in the fourth week of Michaelmas Full Term preceding the examination of all the papers and subjects being so offered.

Candidates must take eight subjects in all. They must take three subjects in Philosophy of which one shall be either 101, 115, or 116 and they must take three subjects in Modern Languages of which two must be 1. and 2. prescribed in part I of Modern Languages. Candidates take *either* one subject in part II of Modern Languages and five subjects in all in Philosophy *or* two subjects in part II of Modern Languages and four subjects in all in Philosophy *or* three subjects in part II of Modern Languages and three subjects in all in Philosophy.

Candidates offering a paper from the Honour School of Modern Languages and a paper in Philosophy, both of which involve the study of the same author or authors, may not make the same text or texts the principal subject of an answer in both the papers.

Philosophy

Subjects as specified in **Regulations for Philosophy in all Honour Schools including Philosophy**.

Modern Languages

There are nine subjects in Modern Languages, specified below. They are divided between Part I and Part II. The language papers (*a*) and (*b*) in 1 in Part I constitute one subject. Subject 9 (an extended essay) may not be offered as an additional optional subject.

1. Three papers as follows:

(*a*) Honour School of Modern Languages Paper I.

(*b*) Honour School of Modern Languages, Papers IIA and IIB.

2. Honour School of Modern Languages, *one* paper chosen from VI, VII or VIII.   5

3. Honour School of Modern Languages Paper IV.

4. Honour School of Modern Languages Paper V.

5. Honour School of Modern Languages Paper IX.

6. Honour School of Modern Languages Paper X.   10

7. Honour School of Modern Languages Paper XI.

8. Honour School of Modern Languages Paper XII.

9. An extended essay as specified for the Honour School of Modern Languages. Candidates may not offer a Special Topic from Course I for the Honour School of English Language and Literature. They also may not offer an extended essay as well   15 as subject 199 in Philosophy.

Candidates who are offering one subject only from Part II may not offer Subject 9 as that subject.

SPECIAL REGULATIONS FOR THE HONOUR SCHOOL OF PHILOSOPHY, POLITICS, AND ECONOMICS

A

1. The subject of the Honour School of Philosophy, Politics, and Economics shall be the study of modern philosophy, and of the political and economic principles and structure of modern society.

2. Candidates must offer Philosophy, Politics, and Economics or such combination of these subjects as may be determined by the Division of Social Sciences.

3. No candidate shall be admitted to examination in this school unless he or she either (*a*) has passed or been exempted from the first Public Examination or (*b*) has successfully completed the Foundation Course in Social and Political Science at the Department for Continuing Education.

4. The examination for this school shall be under the joint supervision of the Social Sciences Board and the Humanities Board which shall appoint a standing joint committee to make regulations concerning it subject always to the preceding clauses of this subsection.

B

Candidates may offer *either* Philosophy, Politics, and Economics *or* Philosophy and Politics *or* Politics and Economics *or* Philosophy and Economics.

The highest Honours can be obtained by excellence in a minority of subjects offered provided that adequate knowledge is shown throughout the examination.

Candidates must take *eight* subjects in all, and must satisfy requirements of particular branches of the school, including, in Philosophy, those set out in the *Regulations for Philosophy in all Honour Schools including Philosophy*, and, in Politics and Economics, requirements to take core subjects. In Politics, the core subjects are any two of 201, 202, 203, 214 and 220; in Economics the core subjects are 300, 301 and 302. In Politics, any of 201, 202, 203, 214 and 220 which are not offered as core subjects may be offered as further subjects.

On entering his or her name for the examination by the date prescribed, each candidate must give notice to the Registrar of the papers being offered.

For all Economics papers candidates are permitted the use of one hand-held pocket calculator from a list of permitted calculators published annually by the Department of Economics on its undergraduate website, which will be updated annually in the week prior to the first full week of Michaelmas Term.

A. *Philosophy, Politics, and Economics.*

Candidates must take (i) **one** of subjects 101, 102, 115, and 116, and (ii) subject 103, any two of subjects 300, 301 and 302 and any two of 201, 202, 203, 214 and 220.

Their other two subjects may be chosen freely from those listed under Philosophy and under Politics and under Economics, except that (i) if any subjects in Economics are chosen they must include the third core subject; (ii)certain combinations of subjects may not be offered (see List of Subjects below); and (iii) not all Economics subjects may be available in any particular year (see below for details). There may also be restrictions on numbers permitted to offer some Economics subjects in any particular year.

B. *Philosophy and Politics.*

Candidates must take (i) **one** of subjects 101, 102, 115, and 116, and (ii) subject 103, and any two of 201, 202, 203, 214 and 220.

Their other four subjects may be chosen freely from those listed under Philosophy and under Politics, except that (i) at least one must be a subject in Philosophy and the *Regulations for Philosophy in all Honour Schools including Philosophy* must be adhered to; (ii) at least one must be a further subject in Politics (other than the thesis (or the supervised dissertation) if offered); (iii) certain combinations of subjects may **not** be offered (see List of Subjects below).

C. *Politics and Economics.*

Candidates must take subjects 300, 301 and 302 and any two of 201, 202, 203, 214 and 220.

Their other three subjects may be chosen freely from those listed under Politics and under Economics except that (i) at least one must be a further subject in Politics (other than the thesis (or the supervised dissertation) if offered); (ii) one but only one may be a subject in Philosophy; (iii) certain combinations of subjects may **not** be offered (see List of Subjects below); (iv) not all Economics subjects may be available in any particular year (see below for details). There may also be restrictions on numbers permitted to offer some Economics subjects in any particular year.

D. *Philosophy and Economics.*

Candidates must take (i) **one** of subjects 101, 102, 115, and 116, and (ii) subjects 103, 300, 301 and 302.

Their other three subjects may be chosen freely from those listed under Philosophy and under Economics, except that (i) at least one must be a subject in Philosophy and the *Regulations for Philosophy in all Honour Schools including Philosophy* must be adhered to; (ii) one but only one may be a subject in Politics, selected from the following list: 201, 202, 214, 215, 216, 220; (iii) certain combinations of subjects may **not** be offered (see List of Subjects below); (iv) not all Economics may be available in any particular year (see below for details). There may also be restrictions on numbers permitted to offer some Economics subjects in any particular year.

List of Subjects

Certain combinations of further subjects may not be offered: in parentheses after the title of each further subject is the number of any other subject or subjects with which it may *not* be combined. The syllabuses for the subjects in this List are given in *Regulations for Philosophy in all Honour Schools including Philosophy* or in the schedule below.

Philosophy
    101. Early Modern Philosophy
    102. Knowledge and Reality
    103. Ethics
    104. Philosophy of Mind
    106. Philosophy of Science and Social Science (105, 124)
    107. Philosophy of Religion

108. The Philosophy of Logic and Language
109. Aesthetics and the Philosophy of Criticism
110. Medieval Philosophy: Aquinas (111)
111. Medieval Philosophy: Duns Scotus, Ockham (110)
112. The Philosophy of Kant
113. Post-Kantian Philosophy
114. Theory of Politics (203)
115. Plato *Republic*
116. Aristotle *Nicomachean Ethics*
117. Frege, Russell, and Wittgenstein (118)
118. The Later Philosophy of Wittgenstein (117)
120. Intermediate Philosophy of Physics
122. Philosophy of Mathematics
124. Philosophy of Science (105, 106)
125. Philosophy of Cognitive Science
126. The Philosophy and Economics of the Environment (321)
150. Jurisprudence (*The change to the method of examination by long essay under (b) as specified in the regulations for the Honour School of Jurisprudence, will apply to PPE candidates in the following manner:*
   i) *All Year 2 students in 2013–14 will undertake the long essay in the summer of 2014;*
   ii) *Year 3 students in 2013–14 will have been taught the traditional Jurisprudence course in 2012–13 (Year 2), and will sit an unseen written examination in 2013–14)* (114, 203)
198. Special Subjects
199. Thesis (298, 299, 399)

Politics (including Sociology)

Candidates should note that the Politics subjects available in any particular year will depend on the availability of teaching resources. Not all subjects will be available in every year and restrictions may be placed on the number of candidates permitted to offer certain subjects in any particular year.

201. Comparative Government
202. British Politics and Government since 1900
203. Theory of Politics (114)
204. Modern British Government and Politics
205. Government and Politics of the United States
206. Politics in Europe
207. Politics in Russia and the Former Soviet Union
208. Politics in Sub-Saharan Africa
209. Politics in Latin America
210. Politics in South Asia
211. Politics in the Middle East
212. International Relations in the Era of Two World Wars
213. International Relations in the Era of the Cold War
214. International Relations
215. Political Thought: Plato to Rousseau
216. Political Thought: Bentham to Weber
217. Marx and Marxism
218. Sociological Theory
219. The Sociology of Post-Industrial Societies
220. Political Sociology
222. Labour Economics and Industrial Relations (307)

223. The Government and Politics of Japan
224. Social Policy
225. Comparative Demographic Systems (315)
226. Quantitative Methods in Politics and Sociology (313)
227. Politics in China
228. The Politics of the European Union
297. Special subject in Politics (199, 298, 299, 399)
298. Supervised dissertation (199, 297, 299, 399)
299. Thesis (199, 298, 399)

Economics

Not all Economics subjects may be offered in any particular year. There may also be restrictions on numbers permitted to offer some Economics subjects in any particular year.

Economics subjects available to candidates in any particular year will depend on the availability of teaching resources. Details of the choices available for the following year will be announced at the Economics Department's 'Options Fair' at the beginning of the fourth week of the first Hilary Full Term of candidates' work for the Honour School, and will be posted on the Department's undergraduate web-site at the same time.

300. Quantitative Economics
301. Macroeconomics
302. Microeconomics
303. Microeconomic Theory
304. Money and Banking
305. Public Economics
306. Economics of Industry
307. Labour Economics and Industrial Relations (222)
308. International Economics
309. Command and Transitional Economies
310. Economics of Developing Countries
311. British Economic History since 1870
314. Econometrics
315. Comparative Demographic Systems (225)
316. Economics of OECD Countries
317. Economic Decisions within the Firm
318. Finance
319. Game Theory
320. Mathematical Methods
321. The Philosophy and Economics of the Environment (126)
399. Thesis (199, 298, 299)

The Department of Economics should be consulted to confirm numbering and titles in the above list.

Schedule

The schedule of subjects in Philosophy is given in the *Regulations for Philosophy in all Honour Schools including Philosophy*

201. *Comparative Government*

Candidates may be expected to show knowledge of the following topics: political parties and party systems; electoral systems; political executives; legislatures; bureaucracies; federalism and other forms of territorial decentralisation; judiciaries; interest groups; forms of government and the constitutional allocation of power between institutions; democratisation. Questions may be set regarding the nature, origins, and political effects of the individual institutions in the preceding list. Candidates should answer all questions comparatively. They should show knowledge of relevant empirical material, and use evidence, comparative methods, and theoretical perspectives appropriately.

202. *British Politics and Government since 1900*

British politics (including the major domestic political crises, ideologies and political issues) and the evolution of the British political and constitutional system (including elections and the electoral system, political parties, parliament, the cabinet system, and machinery of government). 'Political issues' will be taken to include the political implications of social and economic development and the domestic implications of foreign and imperial policy. Candidates will be expected to show knowledge of developments both before and since 1951.

203. *Theory of Politics**

The critical study of political values and of the concepts used in political analysis: the concept of the political; power, authority, and related concepts; the state; law; liberty and rights; justice and equality; public interest and common good; democracy and representation; political obligation and civil disobedience; ideology; liberalism, socialism, and conservatism.

204. *Modern British Government and Politics*

A study of the structure, powers, and operations of modern British Government, including its interaction with the European Union: the Crown, Ministers, Parliament, elections, parties and pressure groups, the legislative process; Government departments, agencies, and regulatory bodies; local authorities; administrative jurisdiction and the Courts. Candidates will be expected to show familiarity with certain prescribed documents, a schedule of which may be revised annually. Any revisions to the schedule shall apply only to candidates taking the Final Honour School five terms hence, and if no proposals for revising the schedule have been received by noon on Friday of Week One of Hilary Term, the previous year's list shall stand. The revised schedule will be displayed on the PPE syllabus notice-board at the Department of Politics and International Relations, Manor Road Building, and on the Department's website.

205. *Government and Politics of the United States*

The constitution; federalism and separation of powers; the presidency; congress; the federal courts; the federal bureaucracy; parties and the party system; electoral politics; mass media; interest groups; state and local politics; processes of policy-formation and implementation; political culture.

206. *Politics in Europe*

This paper is a comparative study of the national party and institutional systems of Europe, and of comparative issues in European politics, including democratisation, institutional relations, political economy and party politics. Candidates are expected to show a broad knowledge of European politics, and may where appropriate include reference to the UK in answers, but should not answer any question mainly or exclusively with reference to the UK.

207. *Politics in Russia and the Former Soviet Union*

Candidates will be required to show knowledge of the transformation of the Soviet system from 1985, and an understanding of the politics of countries of the former Soviet Union with respect to their formation, post-Soviet transitions, regime types,

---

* May be offered alternatively as a further subject in Philosophy as 114.

institutional arrangements, party systems, electoral processes, ethnic and clan composition, political economy, corruption, and the influence of external factors.

208. *Politics in Sub-Saharan Africa*

Candidates will be required to show knowledge of the politics of the countries of sub-Saharan Africa with respect to their political institutions, political sociology, and political economy. The following topics may be considered: nationalism; forms of government, civilian and military; parties and elections; conditions for democracy; class, ethnicity, religion, and gender; business, labour, and peasantries; structural adjustment and agricultural policies; the influence of external agencies.

209. *Politics in Latin America*

Candidates will be required to show knowledge of politics in Latin America; of the structure of government of the major states of the area; and of their political sociology and political economy. The following topics may be considered: presidential systems; the role of congress; public administration; party and electoral systems; the politics of major groups such as the military, trade unions and business groups, and the churches; political ideologies; political movements; the politics of economic stabilization; the politics of gender; theories of regime breakdown, and of democratic transition and consolidation; the influence of external factors.

210. *Politics in South Asia*

Candidates will be expected to show knowledge of political developments in South Asian countries since their independence, with regard to their political institutions, political sociology, and political economy. The following topics may be considered: the nature of the state; government and political institutions; party and electoral systems; politics in the provinces or states of a federation; the evolution of political ideologies; the politics of gender, caste, religion, language, ethnic regionalism, and national integration; the political economy of development, social change, and class relations; 'New' social movements and Left politics; regional conflicts in South Asia and the influence of external factors on South Asian politics. South Asia is taken to include India, Pakistan, Sri Lanka, and Bangladesh.

211. *Politics in the Middle East*

Candidates will be expected to show knowledge of the politics of the Middle East with regard to their political institutions, political sociology, and political economy. The following topics may be considered: the emergence of the state system in the modern Middle East; the influence of colonialism and nationalism in its development; the military in state and politics; party systems and the growth of democratic politics; the politics of religion; women in the political sphere; the influence of major inter-state conflicts and external factors on internal politics. The Middle East is taken to comprise Iran, Israel, Turkey, and the Arab States.

212. *International Relations in the Era of Two World Wars*

The relations between the major powers; the twentieth-century origins of the First World War and the origins of the Second World War; war aims, strategies, and peace-making; the disintegration of war-time alliances; the League of Nations and the establishment of the United Nations; the impact of major political movements (Communism, Fascism, nationalism) on international society; monetary and economic developments as they affected international politics.

Knowledge of events before 1900 and after 1947 will not be demanded, nor will questions be set on extra-European developments before 1914.

213. *International Relations in the Era of the Cold War*

The relations among the major powers, 1945-91, including domestic and external factors shaping foreign policy; the origins and course of the cold war, including detente and the end of the cold war; East-West relations in Europe with particular reference to the foreign policies of France and the Federal Republic of Germany; European integration; the external relations of China and Japan, particularly with the Soviet Union and the United States; the Soviet Union's relations with Eastern Europe; decolonization and conflict in the developing world.   5

214. *International Relations*

The primary topics will be: the competing approaches to the study of international relations; the principal institutions of international politics; contemporary patterns of war and peace; globalization. Other topics will include: foreign-policy analysis; international law; regional organizations; international political economy; ethnic,   10 national, and cultural sources of insecurity; power, interdependence, and dependency. Candidates will be required to illustrate their answers with contemporary or historical material. They will be expected to know the major developments in international affairs from 1990 onwards, and to cite these wherever appropriate. They may also be given the opportunity to show knowledge of earlier developments; but   15 questions referring specifically to events before 1990 will not be set.

215. *Political Thought: Plato to Rousseau*

The critical study of political thought from Plato to Rousseau. Candidates will be expected to show knowledge of at least three of the following authors, with a primary though not necessarily exclusive focus on the following texts: Plato, *The Republic*;   20 Aristotle, *Politics*; Aquinas: *Political Writings*, ed. R. W. Dyson 2002; Machiavelli, *The Prince, The Discourses* ed. Plamenatz 1972; Hobbes *Leviathan* Parts I and II; Locke, *Second Treatise of Civil Government*; Montesquieu, *The Spirit of the Laws*, Books I-VIII, XI, XII, XIX; Hume, *Moral and Political Writings* ed. Aiken 1948; Rousseau, *Discourse on the Origin of Inequality, The Social Contract*. Questions will   25 also be set on the following topics: theories of political stability and civic virtue; the relationship between the personal and the political; utopian political thought; theories of natural law and justice. In answering examination questions, candidates are expected to discuss the primary texts identified in this rubric, but may also draw on their knowledge of a range of other primary texts from the canon of political thought   30 to the end of the eighteenth century, as indicated in the bibliography issued by the Department of Politics and International Relations.

216. *Political Thought: Bentham to Weber*

The critical study of political and social thought from Bentham to Weber. Candidates will be expected to show knowledge of at least three of the following   35 authors, with a primary though not necessarily exclusive focus on the following texts: Bentham, *Political Thought* ed. Parekh; J. S. Mill, *On Liberty*, essays 'The Spirit of the Age', 'Civilization', 'Bentham', 'Coleridge'; Hegel, *The Philosophy of Right, Lectures on the Philosophy of World History* (Introduction) (CUP edn.); Saint-Simon, *Selected Writings 1760–1825*, ed. Taylor 1975; Tocqueville, *Democracy in*   40 *America* - Everyman edition (Vol. I: Introduction, chapters 2-6, the last section of chapter 8, chapters 11, 12, the first section of chapter 13, chapters 14-17; Vol II: Book II, chapters 1-8, 16-20, Book III, chapters 1, 2, 13-21, Book IV, chapters 1-8); Marx, *Selected Writings*, ed. McLellan, nos. 6–8, 13, 14, 18, 19, 22, 23, 25, 30, 32, 37–40; Weber, *From Max Weber*, eds. Gerth and Mills; Durkheim, *The Division of Labour in*   45 *Society* (Prefaces, Introduction, Book I, chapters 1–3, 7; Book 2, chapters 1, 3; Book 3, chapters 1, 2; Conclusion), *Professional Ethics and Civic Morals*, chapters 4–9. Questions will also be set on the following topics: state, society, and the family; individual and community; history and social change; science and religion. In answering examination questions candidates are expected to discuss the primary texts   50 identified in this rubric, but may also draw on their knowledge of other primary texts from the canon of modern social and political thought, as indicated in the bibliography issued by the Department of Politics and International Relations.

217. *Marx and Marxism*

The study of the ideas of Marx and Engels, of later Marxists and critics of Marxism. Candidates will be expected to study Marxism as an explanatory theory, and also to examine its political consequences. They will be required to show knowledge of the relevant primary texts as specified in the bibliography issued by the Department of Politics and International Relations. Questions will also be set on some later Marxists, as indicated in the bibliography.

218. *Sociological Theory*

Theoretical perspectives including rational choice; evolutionary psychology; interpersonal interaction; social integration and networks; functionalism. Substantive problems including stratification; gender; race and ethnicity; collective action; norms; ideology. Candidates will be expected to use theories to explain substantive problems.

219. *The Sociology of Post-Industrial Societies*

Candidates will be expected to show knowledge of the following aspects of the social structure of urban-industrial societies: occupation and economic structure; social stratification and mobility; education; the social significance of gender and ethnicity; demography and the family; the social structure of religion; and the impact on society of the state and politics. They must show knowledge of modern Britain and at least one other industrial society, and of the main general theories of industrial society.

220. *Political Sociology*

The study of the social basis of political competition (including social cleavages and identities), social and political attitudes (including political culture), processes of political engagement and competition (including elections, protest politics, elite formation and the mass media), the social basis for the formation, change, and maintenance of political institutions (including democracy and welfare states). Candidates must show knowledge based on the study of at least three major industrial countries.

222. *Labour Economics and Industrial Relations*

As specified for 307 below.

223. *The Government and Politics of Japan*

The constitutional framework and structure of government; parliamentary and local politics; the electoral and party systems; the role of corporate interests and pressure groups; the bureaucracy; foreign policy. Candidates will be expected to show knowledge of Japanese political history since 1945 and of the social context of Japanese political institutions and policy-making.

224. *Social Policy*

The nature and development of social policy and welfare states. Public, private and informal systems of welfare. Alternative definitions and explanations of poverty and deprivation. The sources, growth, organisation and outcomes of British social policy with special reference to health, housing, social security, and education.

225. *Comparative Demographic Systems*

As specified for 315 below.

226. *Quantitative Methods in Politics and Sociology*

Candidates will be expected to show an understanding of applications of quantitative methods in politics and sociology including the following: the principles of research design in social science: data collection, the logic of casual inference, and comparative method; major statistical methods and concepts: types of random variables, independence, correlation and association, sampling theory, hypothesis testing, linear and non-linear regression models, event-history analysis, and time-series. Candidates will also be expected to interpret information and show familiarity with major methodological debates in politics and sociology.

227. *Politics in China*

Candidates will be required to show knowledge of the government and politics of China since 1949, and with particular reference to the period since 1978, with respect to its political institutions, political sociology, and political economy. The following topics may be considered: the Communist party and its structure, urban and rural reform since 1978, foreign relations, nationalism, elite politics, gender, legal culture, and the politics of Hong Kong and Taiwan.

228. *The Politics of the European Union*

This paper focuses on the study of the history, institutions, and policy processes of the European Union. It includes analysis of the history and theories of the European integration process. Candidates are expected to show knowledge of politics of the European Union, including the main institutions of the EU, decision making procedures and specific policies, as well as relations between the EU and the rest of the world. The paper also focuses on democracy in the European Union and the impact of European integration on the domestic politics and policies of the member states.

297. *Special Subject in Politics* (199, 298, 299, 399)

Special Subjects will be examined by examination paper. No candidate may offer more than one Special Subject. A Special Subject may not be offered by candidates also offering a thesis (199, 299, 399) or Supervised dissertation (298). Depending on the availability of teaching resources, not all Special Subjects will be available to all candidates in every year. Candidates may obtain details of the choice of Special Subjects for the following year by consulting lists posted at the beginning of the fourth week of Hilary Term in the Department of Politics and International Relations and circulated to Politics tutors at colleges admitting undergraduates.

298. *Supervised dissertation**

With the approval of the Politics sub-faculty, members of staff willing to supervise a research topic shall through the Administrator of the Department of Politics and International Relations place on the noticeboard of that Department not later than Friday of fourth week of Hilary Term a short description of an area of politics (including international relations and sociology) in which they have a special interest, a list of possible dissertation topics lying within that area, an introductory reading list, and a time and place at which they will meet those interested in writing a dissertation under their supervision for assessment in the following year's examination. Members of staff agreeing to supervise an undergraduate shall provide him or her with tutorials or intercollegiate classes equivalent to a term's teaching for a normal paper, the cost of such tutorials or classes to be met by the college. They shall notify the colleges of the undergraduates involved and the Administrator of the Department of Politics and International Relations. Candidates offering a thesis (199, 299, or 399) or a Special Subject in Politics (297) may not also offer a supervised dissertation. The regulations governing the length, the format, and the time, date and place of submission of a supervised dissertation shall be the same as those for the thesis. Every candidate who wishes to submit a supervised dissertation shall give notice of his or her intention to do so to the Registrar on his or her examination entry

---

* This option may not be available every year.

form. Every candidate shall sign a certificate to the effect that the supervised dissertation is his or her own work and that it has not already been submitted, wholly or substantially, for another Honour School of this University or for a degree of any other institution. The supervisor(s) shall countersign the certificate confirming that to the best of his, her or their knowledge and belief these statements are true, and shall also submit a short statement of the supervision provided, together with the original specification of the research topic and any other course material provided. The candidate's certificate and the supervisor's or supervisors' statements shall be presented together with the supervised dissertation. Candidates are warned that they should avoid repetition in papers of material in their supervised dissertation and that substantial repetition may be penalized. Every candidate who wishes to have his or her supervised dissertation returned is required to enclose with the thesis, in an envelope bearing only his or her candidate number, a self-addressed sticky label.

299. *Thesis*

As specified for 399 below.

300. *Quantitative Economics*

Unconditional Modelling: Descriptive statistics, basic statistical distributions and applications to economic data, sampling and hypothesis testing.

Conditional Modelling: Binary data with regressors, regression analysis with two and three variables, testing and interpretation of regression results.

Time series Modelling: introduction to issues of temporal correlation and regression analysis.

Empirical applications in micro and macroeconomics: Interpretation of current literature in two areas of microeconomics and two areas of macroeconomics. Topics will be announced at the beginning of Michaelmas Term for examination in Trinity Term two years later.

The examination will include questions covering theoretical issues and interpretation of econometric results.

301. *Macroeconomics*

Macroeconomic theories and their policy implications; macroeconomic shocks and fluctuations; unemployment and inflation; exchange rates; interest rates and the current account; intertemporal adjustment, growth theory; monetary and fiscal policy.

The paper will be set in two parts. Candidates will be required to answer questions from both parts. Part A will consist of short questions and Part B will consist of longer questions.

302. *Microeconomics*

Risk, expected utility theory; welfare economics and general equilibrium, public goods and externalities; game theory and industrial organisation; information economics; applications of microeconomics.

The paper will be set in two parts. Candidates will be required to answer questions from both parts. Part A will consist of short questions and Part B will consist of longer questions.

303. *Microeconomic Theory*

Rigorous study of core elements of microeconomic theory. Topics may (but not necessarily) include: decision making under risk and uncertainty; theory of search under uncertainty; models of contracting under asymmetric information; theory of general economic equilibrium; theory of social choice. A descriptive list of the topics will be published on the Economics website before the beginning of the year in which the course is taught and examined.

Questions will be set requiring candidates to solve problems and demonstrate conceptual understanding of core elements of microeconomic theory.

304. *Money and Banking*

The role of money in general equilibrium models. Aggregate models of price and output fluctuations. The role of banks and other financial intermediaries. Models of monetary policy. Inflation targeting and other policy regimes. Money and public finance. The transmission of monetary policy to asset prices and exchange rates.

The paper will be set in two parts. Candidates will be required to show knowledge on both parts of the paper. Part A will comprise questions requiring analysis of specific models. Part B will comprise essay questions requiring discussion of the theoretical and empirical literature.

305. *Public Economics*

Welfare measurement and cost-benefit analysis, with applications to healthcare and the environment; taxes and transfers; optimal income and commodity taxation, and intertemporal public finance including pensions provision; government expenditure, including healthcare and education; political economics.

306. *Economics of Industry*

Market structures, costs and scale economies, oligopoly and the theory of games, entry, empirical studies of pricing and profitability, advertising, product differentiation, managerial theories of the firm, mergers and vertical integration, innovation, public policy towards market structure and conduct, regulation.

Candidates will be expected to show knowledge of empirical studies relating to one or more of the advanced industrial economies, but questions relating to specific industrial economies will not be set.

307. *Labour Economics and Industrial Relations**

Employer-employee relations; human resource management including the role of government; trade unions and other collective groupings; the theory and practice of collective bargaining; the application of economic analysis to labour markets; economic aspects of trade unions; the economics of labour policy; factors affecting the distribution of earnings.

308. *International Economics*

Theories of international trade and factor movements, positive and normative, and their application to economic policy and current problems. Theory and practice of economic integration. Current problems of the international trading system. Methods of balance of payments adjustment and financing; policies for attaining internal and external balance. Behaviour of floating exchange rates: theory and evidence. Optimum Currency Areas and Exchange Rate Regimes. International Policy Co-ordination and the International Monetary System.

309. *Command and Transitional Economies*

This paper covers the traditional command economy, attempts to reform it in the direction of market socialism, and transition to a market economy. Candidates will be expected first to be familiar with the evolution of the command economy in the pre-war USSR (War Communism, New Economic Policy, Stalinist central planning) and in the post-war period in the USSR, Eastern Europe and China. But emphasis is placed on knowledge of the features and policies of the main variants of the command system (e.g. central planning, performance of state enterprises, fiscal and monetary policies, foreign trade), rather than of the details of economic history or

---

* May be offered alternatively as a subject in Politics as 222.

experiences of countries. The second area includes the 1965 reform and perestroika in the USSR, the New Economic Mechanism in Hungary, self-management in Yugoslavia, and post-1978 reforms in China. The third area comprises the theory of the transition from command to market systems, as well as policies and economic developments in the major countries after 1989. Although most questions will deal with the Soviet Union and Eastern Europe, at least two will relate fully or partially to the economy of China.

310. *Economics of Developing Countries*

Theories of growth and development. Poverty and income distribution. Human resources. Labour markets and employment. Industrialisation and technology. Agriculture and rural development. Monetary and fiscal issues; inflation. Foreign trade and payments. Foreign and domestic capital; economic aid. The role of government in development; the operation of markets.

Where appropriate, candidates will be expected to illustrate their answers with knowledge of actual situations.

311. *British Economic History since 1870*

Trends and cycles in national income, factor supplies, and productivity; changes in the structure of output, employment, and capital; management and entrepreneurship; the location of industries, industrial concentration, and the growth of large firms; prices, interest rates, money, and public finance; wages, unemployment, trade unions, and the working of the labour market; the distribution of incomes, poverty, and living standards; foreign trade, tariffs, international capital movements, and sterling; Government economic policy in peace and war.

Questions concerned *exclusively* with the periods before 1900 or after 1973 will not be set.

314. *Econometrics*

The paper will be set in two parts. Candidates will be required to show knowledge of both parts.

I Multiple regression: interpretation, estimation, inference, prediction.

Both cross-sectional and time series implementations will be discussed.

A variety of econometric topics will be considered drawn from the following list: maximum likelihood, endogeneity and instrumental variables, unit roots and cointegration, limited dependent variable models, duration models and panel data models.

II Application of the introduced econometric methods to economic problems.

A descriptive list of the topics will be published on the Economics website before the beginning of the year in which the course is taught and examined.

315. *Comparative Demographic Systems**

Candidates will be expected to show knowledge of controversies in demographic theory (Malthus and his critics, Easterlin, Caldwell, the New Home Economics school and others) and to illustrate their answers with varied and specific examples. The paper will contain essay questions and questions involving computation. Candidates will be required to answer three questions, two of the former and one of the latter.

I Demographic analysis and techniques: data sources, adequacy and remedies. Statistical analysis of fertility, mortality, and other demographic phenomena. The life table, stable population, and other models of population structure and growth. Population dynamics, projections and simulations.

---

* May be offered alternatively as a subject in Politics as 225.

II Limits to fertility and the lifespan. Contrasts between stable and transitional population systems in historical European and current non-European societies: the decline of mortality, fertility patterns in relation to systems of household formation, kin organization and risk environments, marital fertility decline and the current status of transition theory. Social, economic, and political consequences of rapid population growth at the national level and the local level.

Demographic systems in post-transitional societies (modern Europe and other industrial areas): low fertility, trends in health and survival, and age structure change; their economic and social causes and consequences. New patterns of marriage and family, women in the workforce, labour migration and the demography of ethnic minorities, population policies.

316. *Economics of OECD Countries*

Main phases of development since 1945. Institutional framework of policy formation; conduct of demand management policies; the welfare state and public expenditure; experience of policies and strategies. The behaviour of major macroeconomic aggregates; the labour market and industrial relations. Development of external trade and financial relations; competitiveness and exchange rates; economic integration and the international coordination of economic policies.

Questions will be set requiring knowledge of one or more of the following countries: France, Germany, Italy, Japan, UK, and US. Candidates will be expected to answer at least one question (out of three) from Part A.

Part A. Comparative analysis of the OECD countries
Part B. The Major Areas
Section 1: Western Europe
Section 2: the United States
Section 3: Japan.

317. *Economic Decisions within the Firm*

Linear economics models, simplex method for linear programming, duality and sensitivity analysis. Network models, including the transportation and assignment problems, shortest path problems, project scheduling. Dynamic and integer programming.

Expected utility theory and decision trees. Markov chain models. Queuing systems. Stochastic dynamic programming. Inventory control. Monte Carlo methods and simulation. Two-person, zero-sum games.

318. *Finance*

As specified in Paper 3, *Finance*, in the Honour School of Economics and Management.

319. *Game Theory*

Strategic-form games and extensive-form games. Solution concepts. Games with incomplete information. Applications and topics which may (but not necessarily) include bargaining, auctions, global games, evolutionary games, co-operative games, learning, games in political science.

The paper will be set in two parts. Candidates will be required to show knowledge on both parts of the paper.

Part A. Questions will be set requiring candidates to solve problems involving the core elements of game theory.

Part B. Questions will be set requiring candidates to solve problems in and show knowledge of specific applications and topics in game theory.

320. *Mathematical Methods*

The paper will cover mathematical tools such as Calculus, Linear Algebra, Differential and Difference Equations, Probability and Statistical Inference and their applications to Economics. Applications will not require knowledge of material covered in other optional papers but will assume knowledge of the core first and second year papers. A detailed syllabus will be published every year.

321. *The Philosophy and Economics of the Environment* (126)* **[NB: This paper may not be taken by bipartite Politics and Philosophy candidates.]**

Philosophical foundations: justice and goodness, theories of value; decision-making under uncertainty. Economics foundations: externalities, public goods, international environmental agreements. Politics and the environment. Inter-generational ethics, discounting. The choice of instruments: taxes, permits and command-and-control; environmental instruments in practice. Valuing human life. Valuing nature. Cost-benefit analysis: foundations and critiques; valuation methods.

399. *Thesis*

(*a*) *Subject*

The subject of every thesis should fall within the scope of the Honour School. The subject may but need not overlap any subject on which the candidate offers papers. Candidates are warned that they should avoid repetition in papers of material used in their theses and that substantial repetition may be penalized.

Every candidate shall submit through his or her college for approval to the Director of Undergraduate Studies for Philosophy, Politics and International Relations, or Economics the title he or she proposes together with

(i) an indication as to the branch of the school in which the subject falls, e.g. Economics;

(ii) an explanation of the subject in about 100 words;

(iii) a letter of approval from his or her thesis tutor;

not earlier than the first day of the Trinity Full Term of the year before that in which he or she is to be examined and not later than the date prescribed for entry to the examination. The relevant chair shall decide as soon as possible whether or not to approve the title and shall advise the candidate immediately. No decision shall be deferred beyond the end of the fifth week of Michaelmas Full Term.

Proposals to change the title of the thesis may be made through the college and will be considered by the chair of the relevant sub-faculty until the first day of the Hilary Full Term of the year in which the student is to be examined, and by the chair of the examiners thereafter.

(*b*) *Authorship and origin*

Every thesis shall be the candidate's own work. His or her thesis tutor may, however, discuss with him or her the field of study, the sources available, and the method of presentation; the thesis tutor may also read and comment on a first draft. The amount of assistance that may be given is equivalent to the teaching of a normal paper. Theses previously submitted for the Honour School of Philosophy, Politics, and Economics may be resubmitted. No thesis will be accepted if it has already been submitted, wholly or substantially, for another Honour School or degree of this University, or for a degree of any other institution. Every candidate shall sign a certificate to the effect that the thesis is his or her own work and that it has not already been submitted, wholly or substantially, for another Honour School or degree of this University, or for a degree of any other institution. This certificate

---

* May be offered alternatively as a subject in Philosophy as 126.

shall be presented together with the thesis. No thesis shall, however, be ineligible because it has been or is being submitted for any prize of this University.

(*c*) *Length and format*

No thesis shall exceed 15,000 words, the limit to include all notes and appendices, but not bibliographies; no person or body shall have authority to permit any excess.   5
There shall be a select bibliography or a list of sources. All theses must be typed in double spacing on one side of quarto or A4 paper. Any notes and references may be placed *either* at the bottom of the relevant pages *or* all together at the end of the thesis, but in the latter case two loose copies of the notes and references must be supplied. The thesis must be bound or held firmly in a stiff cover. Two bound   10
copies shall be submitted to the examiners, along with one electronic copy; they shall be returned to the candidate's college after the examination.

(*d*) *Notice of submission of thesis*

Every candidate who wishes to submit a thesis shall give notice of his or her intention to do so on his or her examination entry form (in addition to seeking   15
approval of the subject from the relevant Chair of the sub-faculty or head of department under (*a*) above); and shall submit his or her thesis not later than noon on Friday of the week before the Trinity Full Term of the examination to the Chair of the Examiners, Honour School of Philosophy, Politics, and Economics, Examination Schools, High Street, Oxford. Every candidate who wishes to have his or her thesis   20
returned is required to enclose with the thesis, in an envelope bearing only his or her candidate number, a self-addressed sticky label.

SPECIAL REGULATIONS FOR THE HONOUR SCHOOL OF PHILOSOPHY AND THEOLOGY

A

1. The subjects of the Honour School of Philosophy and Theology shall be (*a*) Philosophy and (*b*) Theology.

2. All candidates must offer both (*a*) and (*b*).

3. No candidate shall be admitted to examination in this school unless he or she has either passed or been exempted from the First Public Examination.

4. The examination in this school shall be under the joint supervision of the Boards of the Faculties of Philosophy and Theology and Religion, which shall appoint a standing joint committee to make regulations concerning it, subject always to the preceding clauses of this subsection.

5. (i) The examiners for Philosophy in this school shall be such of the Public Examiners in Philosophy in the Honour School of Psychology, Philosophy, and Physiology, and those for Theology shall be such of the Public Examiners in the Honour School of Theology, as may in each case be required.

   (ii) It shall be the duty of the chair of the Public Examiners in Psychology, Philosophy, and Physiology to designate such of the examiners in Philosophy as may be required for Philosophy in the Honour School of Philosophy and Theology, and the duty of the chair of the Public Examiners in the Honour School of Theology to designate such of their number as may be required for Theology in the Honour School of Philosophy and Theology, and when this has been done the number of the examiners in Philosophy and Theology shall be deemed to be complete.

B

The highest honours can be obtained by excellence either in Philosophy or in Theology provided that adequate knowledge is shown in the other subject of the examination.

Candidates are required to take *either* four subjects in Philosophy and four in Theology, *or* five in Philosophy and three in Theology, *or* three in Philosophy and five in Theology. A candidate may offer a Philosophy thesis, or a Theology extended essay, but may not offer both. A candidate may offer an extended essay on a topic combining Philosophy and Theology; such an essay is subject to the provisions below regarding the extended essay in Theology, but additionally, approval will be sought by the Faculty of Theology and Religion from the Director of Undergraduate Studies of the Faculty of Philosophy.

(a) **Philosophy** Subjects as specified in **Regulations for Philosophy in all Honour Schools including Philosophy**

(b) **Theology**

All candidates must take papers (i) and (ii) below. In addition they must take either (iii) or (iv) below. Candidates may select their remaining papers from the paper not selected from (iii) and (iv), paper (v) below, and any other papers prescribed for the Honour School of Theology.

(i) *The Gospels and Jesus (with special reference to the gospels of Matthew and John)*. (Paper (2) in the Honour School of Theology)

Questions will be set on the four gospels, their theology and ethics, literary and historical problems associated with the gospels, the historical Jesus, and different approaches to the gospels. Candidates will be required to comment on two passages from Matthew, at least three of which will be printed in English. They will also be required to comment on two passages from John, at least three of which will be printed in English.

(ii) *God, Christ, and Salvation* (Paper (5) in the Honour School of Theology).

(iii) *The Development of Doctrine in the Early Church to 451* (Paper (4) in the Honour School of Theology).

(iv) *Christian Moral Reasoning* (Paper (12) in the Honour School of Theology).

(v) Thesis. A thesis may be offered either in Theology or in Philosophy or in both Philosophy and Theology jointly. A candidate who offers a thesis in Philosophy and Theology cannot also offer any other thesis. The provisions governing theses are the same as those given for theses in Philosophy in this school, as specified in *Regulations for Philosophy in some of the Honour Schools*, except that the provisions in the Regulations for Philosophy for subject 199 that 'The subject of every thesis should fall within the scope of philosophy' does not apply to theses in theology.

Optional translation papers (2 hours each).

The translation components of paper (24), *The Hebrew of the Old Testament*, of the Honour School of Theology may be offered as an optional extra paper by candidates for the Honour School of Philosophy and Theology. Paper (27), *The New Testament in Greek*, of the Honour School of Theology may also be offered as an optional extra paper by candidates for the Honour School of Philosophy and Theology.

No candidate may offer both philosophy paper 110: *Medieval Philosophy*, and Aquinas for study as a major theologian for paper (10) *Further Studies in History and Doctrine* as prescribed for the Honour School of Theology.

SPECIAL REGULATIONS FOR THE HONOUR SCHOOL OF PHYSICS

A

1. (1) The subject of the Honour School in Physics shall be the study of Physics as an experimental science.

   (2) The examination in Physics shall consist respectively of three parts for the four-year course (A, B, C) and of two parts for the three-year course (A, B) as prescribed by regulation by the Mathematical, Physical and Life Sciences Board.

2. (1) The name of a candidate in either the three-year course or the four-year course shall not be published in a Class List until he or she has completed all parts of the respective examinations.

   (2) The Examiners in Physics for the three-year course or the four-year course shall be entitled to award a pass or classified Honours to candidates in the Second Public Examination who have reached a standard considered adequate; the Examiners shall give due consideration to the performance in all parts of the respective examinations.

   (3) (*a*) A candidate who obtains only a pass or fails to satisfy the Examiners may enter again for Part B (three-year course) or Part C (four-year course) of the examination on one, but not more than one, subsequent occasion.

   (*b*) Part A (three-year and four-year courses) and Part B (four-year course) shall be entered on one occasion only.

   (4) A candidate adjudged worthy of Honours in the Second Public Examination for the four-year course in Physics may supplicate for the Degree of Master of Physics provided that the candidate has fulfilled all the conditions for admission to a degree of the University.

   (5) A candidate who has satisfied the requirements for Part A and Part B of the four-year course, but who does not start or enter Part C or who fails to obtain Honours in Part C is permitted to supplicate for the Degree of Bachelor of Arts in Physics (Pass, or Honours with the classification

obtained in Parts A and B together, as appropriate); provided that no such candidate may later enter or re-enter the Part C year, or supplicate for the degree of Master of Physics; and provided in each case that the candidate has fulfilled all the conditions for admission to a degree of the University.

3. The examination shall be partly practical: this requirement shall normally be satisfied by the Examiners' assessment of the practical work done by candidates during their course of study; exceptionally, the Examiners may require a candidate to take a practical examination.

4. No candidate shall be admitted to examination in this school unless he or she has either passed or been exempted from the First Public Examination.

5. (1) The Examination in Physics shall be under the supervision of the Mathematical, Physical and Life Sciences Board.

   (2) The board shall have power, subject to this decree, from time to time to frame and to vary regulations for the different parts and subjects of the examination.

Transfer to the Honour School of Mathematical and Theoretical Physics

6. Subject to the regulations for the Honour School in Mathematical and Theoretical Physics, candidates on the four-year course in Physics may apply to the Supervisory Committee for Mathematics and Physics to transfer, after their Part B examination, to the Honour School of Mathematical and Theoretical Physics for their Part C examination. Such a candidate will need to achieve at least an upper second class or higher at the end of Part B, and be accepted by the Supervisory Committee for Mathematics and Physics under the procedures referred to in the regulations for the Master of Mathematical and Theoretical Physics and set out in the course handbook for that degree. Acceptance is not automatic. As specified in the regulations for that degree, Part C in Mathematical and Theoretical Physics must be taken in the academic year following the candidate's Part B examination, and on successful completion of Part C of the Honour School of Mathematical and Theoretical Physics candidates will be awarded the Master of Mathematics and Physics in Mathematical and Theoretical Physics.

7. The Handbook for Mathematical and Theoretical Physics shall, where relevant, set out the options that candidates should follow to maximize their chances of being accepted for transfer to

Mathematical and Theoretical Physics for their Part C examination. This Handbook shall be available by the start of Michaelmas Term in the year in which a candidate starts Part A in Physics.

8. A candidate who has transferred from the Honour School of Physics to the Honour School of Mathematical and Theoretical Physics for their Part C examination in accordance with cl.9 above is permitted transfer to the Honour School of Physics for their Part C examination up to the end of Week 4 of the Michaelmas Term in which he or she first registered for Part C in the Honour School of Mathematical and Theoretical Physics, so long as that candidate has not opted to supplicate for the degree of Bachelor of Arts in Physics under the regulations for the Honour School of Mathematical and Theoretical Physics.

9. The regulations for the Honour School of Mathematical and Theoretical Physics set out how the results obtained in Parts A and B in the Honour School of Physics are published for candidates who transfer to the Honour School of Mathematical and Theoretical Physics for their Part C examination.

B

In the following 'the Course Handbook' refers to the Physics Undergraduate Course Handbook, published annually at the start of Michaelmas Term by the Faculty of Physics.

Candidates will be expected to show knowledge based on practical work.

The Examiners will permit the use of any hand-held calculator subject to the conditions set out under the heading 'Use of calculators in examinations' in the *Regulations concerning the Conduct of University Examinations* and further elaborated in the Course Handbook.

The various parts of the examinations for the three and four year courses shall take place in Trinity Term of the year in question and, unless otherwise stated, deadlines shall apply to the year in which that part is taken.

Physics (four year course)

1. The examination shall be in three parts, A, B, C, taken at times not less than three, six and nine terms, respectively after passing the First Public Examination.

2. In order to proceed to Parts B and C of the four-year course in physics a minimum standard of achievement in Part A may be required, as determined by the Faculty of Physics from time to time. Any such requirement shall be published in the Course Handbook not later than the beginning of Michaelmas Full Term of the academic year preceding the year of the Part A examination. Names of those satisfying the requirement shall be published by the Examiners.

3. **In Part A**

(*a*) the candidate shall be required

    (i) to offer three written papers on the Fundamental Principles of Physics, *and*

    (ii) to submit to the Examiners such evidence as they require of the successful completion of practical work normally pursued during the three terms preceding the examination, *and*

    (iii) to offer a written paper on one Short Option.

(*b*) A candidate may also offer a written paper on a second Short Option, in which case the candidate need only submit evidence of the successful completion of practical work normally pursued during one and a half terms of the three terms specified in cl. 3(*a*)(ii).

4. **In Part B**

(*a*) the candidate shall be required

    (i) to offer three written papers on Physics, *and*

    (ii) to submit to the Examiners such evidence as they require of the successful completion of practical work normally pursued during the three terms preceding the examination, *and*

    (iii) to offer a written paper on one Short Option.

(*b*) A candidate may also offer a written paper on a second Short Option, in which case the candidate need only submit evidence of the successful completion of practical work normally pursued during one and a half terms of the three terms specified in cl. 4(*a*)(ii).

5. The titles of the written papers of cl. 3(*a*)(i) & cl. 4(*a*)(i) are given in the Schedule below. Their syllabuses shall be approved by the Faculty of Physics and shall be published in the Course Handbook not later than the beginning of Michaelmas Full Term for the examination three terms thence.

6. The list of Short Option subjects in cls 3(*a*)(iii), 3(*b*), 4(*a*)(iii), 4(*b*) and their syllabuses shall be approved by the Faculty of Physics and shall be published in the Course Handbook not later than the beginning of Michaelmas Full Term for the examination three terms thence. One of the short options included in the list shall be S07, Classical Mechanics.

7. In cl. 4(*a*)(ii), practical work may be replaced by project work, if an appropriate supervisor is available. The subject, duration, and replacement value shall be approved by the Head of the Teaching Faculty of Physics or deputy, by the end of Michaelmas Full Term.

8. With respect to cl. 3(*a*)(iii) or cl. 4(*a*)(iii) a candidate may take, as alternative to the written examination, an assessed course of instruction in a foreign language. A candidate proposing to take this alternative must have the proposal approved by the Head of the Teaching Faculty of Physics or deputy and by the Director of the Language Centre or deputy, by the end of the first week of Hilary Full Term preceding the examination. Approval shall not be given to candidates who have, at the start of the course, already acquired demonstrable skills exceeding the target learning outcomes in the chosen language.

9. With respect to subjects under cl. 3(*a*)(iii) or cl. 4(*a*)(iii) a candidate may propose to the Head of the Teaching Faculty of Physics or deputy, not later than the fourth week of Michaelmas Full Term preceding the examination, either to offer another subject paper, *or* to offer instead a written account of extended practical work, in addition to that specified in cl.3(*a*)(ii) or cl.4(*a*)(ii). Candidates will be advised of the decision by the end of eighth week of that term.

10. **In Part C** the candidate shall be required to offer

(*a*) written papers on each of two Major Options, *and*

(*b*) a project report on *either* advanced practical work, *or* other advanced work. Candidates may also be examined viva voce.

11. In cl. 10(*a*), the Major Options and their syllabuses shall be approved by the Faculty of Physics and the Physics Academic Committee. The titles of the Major Options are given in the Schedule below and the syllabuses shall be published in the Course Handbook not later than the beginning of Michaelmas Full Term for the examination three terms thence.

12. With respect to subjects under cl. 10(*a*) a candidate may propose to the Head of the Teaching Faculty of Physics or deputy, not later than the fourth week of Trinity Full Term in the academic year preceding the examination, another subject paper or papers. Candidates will be advised of the decision by the end of eighth week of that term.   5

13. In cl. 10(*b*), the proposed nature of the practical or other advanced work and its duration shall be submitted for approval to the Head of the Teaching Faculty of Physics or deputy with the agreement of the Physics Academic Committee.

Schedule

Fundamental Principles (Part A)   10
  A1: *Thermal Physics*
  A2: *Electromagnetism and Optics*
  A3: *Quantum Physics*

Physics (Part B)
  Three papers, B1 to B3, each of three hours, each consisting of two subjects, as   15
  follows:
  B1: I. *Flows, Fluctuations and Complexity*, and II. *Symmetry and Relativity*
  B2: III. *Quantum, Atomic and Molecular Physics*, and IV. *Sub-Atomic Physics*
  B3: V. *General Relativity and Cosmology*, and VI. *Condensed-Matter Physics*

Major Options (Part C)   20
  C1: *Astrophysics*
  C2: *Laser Science and Quantum Information Processing*
  C3: *Condensed Matter Physics*
  C4: *Particle Physics*
  C5: *Physics of Atmospheres and Oceans*   25
  C6: *Theoretical Physics*
  C7: *Biological Physics*

Physics (three year course)

1. The examination shall be in two parts, A and B, taken at times not less than three and six terms, respectively, after passing the First Public Examination.   30

2. **Part A** of the examination shall be the same as the Part A of the examination of the four-year course in Physics and the same conditions, arrangements and examination timings shall apply.

3. **In Part B**
  (*a*) the candidate shall be required   35
    (i) to offer four of the subjects I-VI specified for papers B1 to B3 in the Schedule of the four-year course (Part B), each subject having the weight of half a paper, *and*
    (ii) to submit to the Examiners such evidence as they require of the successful completion of practical work normally pursued during one and a half   40
        terms in the academic year of the examination, *and*
    (iii) to offer a written paper on one Short Option.
  (*b*) to offer a project report in the form of *either* an extended essay on a subject approved by the Head of the Teaching Faculty of Physics or deputy (by the end of sixth week of Hilary Full Term), *or* an account of extended practical work   45
    undertaken in the academic year in which the examination takes place.
  (*c*) candidates may be examined by viva voce.

4. With respect to cl. 3(*a*)(ii) a candidate may offer instead a written paper on a second Short Option.

5. The Short Options of cl. 3(*a*)(iii) and cl. 5 are those specified in cl. 6 of the   50
four-year course.

6. In cl. 3(*a*)(ii), practical work may be replaced by project work, if an appropriate supervisor is available. The subject, duration, and replacement value shall be approved by the Head of the Teaching Faculty of Physics or deputy, by the end of Michaelmas Full Term.

7. With respect to cl. 3(*a*)(iii) a candidate may take, as alternative to the written examination, an assessed course of instruction in a foreign language. A candidate proposing to take this alternative must have the proposal approved by the Head of the Teaching Faculty of Physics or deputy and by the Director of the Language Centre or deputy, by the end of the first week of Hilary Full Term. Approval shall not be given to candidates who have, at the start of the course, already acquired demonstrable skills exceeding the target learning outcomes in the chosen language.

8. With respect to subjects under cl. 3(*a*)(iii) a candidate may propose to the Head of the Teaching Faculty of Physics or deputy, not later than the fourth week of Michaelmas Full Term preceding the examination, another subject paper. Candidates shall be advised of the decision by the end of eighth week of that term.

SPECIAL REGULATIONS FOR THE HONOUR SCHOOL OF PHYSICS AND PHILOSOPHY

A

In the following 'the Physics Course Handbook' refers to the Physics Undergraduate Handbook, published annually at the start of Michaelmas Term by the faculty of Physics. The Physics and Philosophy Course Handbook is published annually at the start of Michaelmas Term by the Faculty of Philosophy.

1. All candidates shall be examined in Physics and in Philosophy.

2. No candidate shall be admitted to examination in this school unless he or she has either passed or been exempted from the First Public Examination.

3. (*a*) The examination in Physics and Philosophy shall consist of three parts: Part A, Part B and Part C.

   (*b*) Parts A, B and C shall be taken at times not less than three, six, and nine terms, respectively, after passing or being exempted from the First Public Examination.

4. (*a*) In order to proceed to Part C a minimum standard of achievement in *either* Part A in physics *or* in Part B in philosophy may be required, as determined by the Faculty of Physics or the Faculty of Philosophy from time to time. Any such requirement shall be published in the Physics and Philosophy Course Handbook not later than the beginning of the Michaelmas Full Term of the academic year preceding the year of the Part A examination. Names of those satisfying the requirement shall be published by the Examiners.

   (*b*) A candidate who obtains only a Pass or fails to satisfy the Examiners in Part C may enter again for Part C on at most one subsequent occasion; Parts A and B shall be entered on one occasion only.

   (c) A candidate in the final year of the four-year course, adjudged worthy of Honours in both Parts A and B together, but who does not enter Part C, or who fails to obtain Honours in Part C, is permitted to supplicate for the Honours degree of Bachelor of Arts in Physics and Philosophy with the classification obtained in Parts A and

B together; provided that no such candidate may later enter or re-enter the Part C year or supplicate for the degree of Master of Physics and Philosophy; and provided in each case that the candidate has fulfilled all the conditions for admission to a degree of the University.

(*d*) A candidate who is adjudged worthy of Honours on Parts A and B together, and on Part C, may supplicate for the degree of Master of Physics and Philosphy provided that the candidate has fulfilled all the conditions for admission to a degree of the University.

5. The examination in this school shall be under the joint supervision of the Board of the Faculty of Philosophy and the Mathematical, Physical and Life Sciences Board, which shall appoint a standing joint committee to make regulations concerning it, subject in all cases to clauses 1-4 above.

6. (*a*) The examiners for Physics shall be such of the Public Examiners in Physics in the Honour School of Physics as may be required; those for Philosophy shall be nominated by a committee of which three elected members shall be appointed by the Board of the Faculty of Philosophy.

(*b*) It shall be the duty of the Chair of the Public Examiners in Physics in the Honour School of Physics to designate such of their number as may be required for Physics and Philosophy, and when this has been done and the Examiners for Philosophy have been nominated, the number of the Examiners in Physics and Philosophy shall be deemed to be complete.

Transfer to the Honour School of Mathematical and Theoretical Physics

7. Subject to the regulations for the Honour School in Mathematical and Theoretical Physics, candidates on the four-year course in Physics and Philosophy may apply to the Supervisory Committee for Mathematics and Physics to transfer, after their Part B examination, to the Honour School of Mathematical and Theoretical Physics for their Part C examination. Such a candidate will need to achieve at least an upper second class or higher at the end of Part B, and be accepted by the Supervisory Committee for Mathematics and Physics under the procedures referred to in the regulations for the Master of Mathematical and Theoretical Physics and set out in the course handbook for that degree. Acceptance is not automatic. As specified in the regulations for that degree, Part C in Mathematical and Theoretical Physics must be taken in the academic

year following the candidate's Part B examination, and on successful completion of Part C of the Honour School of Mathematical and Theoretical Physics candidates will be awarded the Master of Mathematics and Physics in Mathematical and Theoretical Physics.

8. The Handbook for Mathematical and Theoretical Physics shall set out the options that candidates should follow to maximize their chances of being accepted for transfer to Mathematical and Theoretical Physics for their Part C examination. This Handbook shall be available by the start of Michaelmas Term in the year in which a candidate starts Part A in Mathematics.

9. A candidate who has transferred from the Honour School of Physics and Philosophy to the Honour School of Mathematical and Theoretical Physics for their Part C examination in accordance with cl.9 above is permitted transfer to the Honour School of Physics and Philosophy for their Part C examination up to the end of Week 4 of the Michaelmas Term in which he or she first registered for Part C in the Honour School of Mathematical and Theoretical Physics, so long as that candidate has not opted to supplicate for the degree of Bachelor of Arts in Physics and Philosophy under the regulations for the Honour School of Mathematical and Theoretical Physics.

10. The regulations for the Honour School of Mathematical and Theoretical Physics set out how the results obtained in Parts A and B in the Honour School of Physics and Philosophy are published for candidates who transfer to the Honour School of Mathematical and Theoretical Physics for their Part C examination.

B

1. For the Physics papers, the Examiners will permit the use of any hand-held calculator subject to the conditions set out under the heading 'Use of calculators in examinations' in the *Regulations concerning the Conduct of University Examinations* and further elaborated in the Physics Course Handbook, save that candidates taking part in an exchange scheme shall be subject to the provisions of the host institution in this regard.

2. The requirements for Parts A, B and C are specified in the *Schedule* below.

3. The highest honours can be obtained by excellence either in Physics or Philosophy, providing that adequate knowledge is shown in the other subject areas. An honours classification will be awarded only if performance in both Physics and Philosophy is of honours standard in Parts A and B taken together, or in Part C.

4. Candidates for Part B must give to the Registrar notice of their choice of papers not later than Friday in the eighth week of the Michaelmas Full Term preceding that part of the examination. Candidates for Part C must give to the Registrar notice of their choice of written papers not later than Friday in the eighth week of the Michaelmas Full Term preceding that part of the examination, or, if taking part in an exchange scheme, shall have the proposed set of papers to be taken in the host institution approved by the standing joint committee by the beginning of the Michaelmas Full Term preceding that part of the examination.

Schedule

Part A

Physics

Candidates are required to

(i) offer three written papers on Fundamental Principles of Physics, *and*

(ii) submit to the Examiners such evidence as they require of the successful completion of practical work normally pursued during the three terms preceding the examination.

The titles of the written papers under (i) are given below. Their syllabuses shall be approved by the Faculty of Physics and shall be published in the Physics Course Handbook not later than the beginning of Michaelmas Full Term for the examination three terms thence.

Fundamental Principles of Physics:

A1: *Thermal Physics*

A2P: *Electromagnetism*

A3: *Quantum Physics*

Part B

Candidates are required to offer either (a) three subjects in Physics (each having the weight of half a paper) and four subjects in Philosophy (each having the weight of a full paper), or (b) five subjects in Physics (each having the weight of half a paper) and three subjects in Philosophy (each having the weight of a full paper).

Candidates may choose their three or five subjects from the following list:

Paper B1: *I. Flows, Fluctuations and Complexity*

Paper B1: *II. Symmetry and Relativity*

Paper B2: *III. Quantum, Atomic and Molecular Physics*

Paper B2: *IV. Sub-Atomic Physics*

Paper B3: *V. General Relativity and Cosmology*

Paper B3: *VI. Condensed-Matter Physics*

Paper BT: *VII. Classical Mechanics*

Candidates must choose at least two of subjects *II*, *V*, and *VII*.

The syllabuses for the above Physics subjects shall be approved by the Faculty of Physics and published in the Physics Course Handbook not later than the beginning of the Michaelmas Full Term preceding the examination.

Philosophy

Candidates are required to take (i) subject 101 or 102; (ii) one of subjects 106 and 124; and (iii) subject 120 as specified in the Regulations for Philosophy in all Honour Schools including Philosophy. Candidates who offer a fourth subject in Philosophy must select one from the list of subjects 101–122 and 125 as specified in the Regulations for Philosophy in all Honour Schools including Philosophy, and in accordance with the General Regulations therein.

Part C

Candidates not on an exchange scheme shall offer a total of three units chosen in any combination from the lists for Physics and for Philosophy, or an approved collection of course options if taking part in an exchange scheme.

A unit in Physics consists of either a written paper on a Major Option, or a project report on either advanced practical work or other advanced work, as specified for Part C of the Honour School of Physics. Candidates may be examined viva voce. A unit in Philosophy consists of one of the subjects 101–104, 107–122, 125 and 180 as specified in the Regulations for Philosophy in all Honours Schools including

Philosophy, or a Thesis as specified below. No subject in Philosophy may be offered in both Part B and Part C.

Each unit in Philosophy other than a Thesis shall be examined by a three-hour written paper together with an essay of at most 5,000 words. No essay shall exceed this word limit, which includes all notes and appendices, but not the bibliography. The word count should be indicated on the front of the essay. There shall be a select bibliography or a list of sources. All essays must be typed in double spacing on one side of quarto or A4 paper, with footnotes rather than endnotes. Candidates should avoid any substantial repetition of material between examination scripts and examination essays. The topic for a Philosophy examination essay in a given subject can be any question set for the most recent examination of that subject in Honour Schools with Philosophy, with the exception of questions for Plato: *Republic* (115) and Aristotle: *Nicomachean Ethics* (116) consisting of multiple passages for comment, and the questions for Formal Logic (119) consisting of formal exercises. Candidates may apply for approval of other essay topics by writing to the Chair of the Board, c/o The Administrator, Philosophy Centre, Radcliffe Humanities Building, Woodstock Road, giving the title he or she proposes, together with an explanation of the subject in about 100 words and enclosing a letter from their tutor attesting to the suitability of this topic for the candidate. Any such application must be received no later than Friday of the sixth week of the Hilary Term preceding the Part C examination for which the essay is to be submitted. Late applications will not be considered. Any such application shall be accepted or rejected by the Board within two weeks of its being received.

Each essay shall be the candidate's own work, though it should show knowledge of relevant literature in the subject and may include passages of quotation or paraphrase so long as these passages are clearly indicated as such and the source properly attributed. The candidate may discuss a first draft of the essay with his or her tutor for that subject. The amount of assistance the tutor may give shall be limited to what can be provided in one of the candidate's tutorials for their study of that subject. For each essay the candidate shall sign a statement to the effect that the essay is his or her own work and the tutor shall also sign a statement confirming that, to the best of his or her knowledge and belief, this is so. These statements shall be placed in a sealed envelope bearing the candidate's examination number and the name of the subject for which the essay has been written, and presented with two copies of each essay. Each copy of an essay shall be identified only by the candidate's examination number and bear the name of the Philosophy subject for which the essay is being submitted and must be submitted not later than noon on Friday of the first week of the Trinity Full Term of the examination to the Examination Schools, High Street, Oxford, addressed to the Chair of the Examiners for Part C of the Final Honour School of Physics and Philosophy.

PHILOSOPHY THESIS

(*a*) *Subject*

The subject of every thesis should fall within the scope of philosophy. The subject may but need not overlap any subject on which the candidate offers papers. Candidates should avoid substantial repetition in examination scripts or examination essays of material from their theses. No part of a Philosophy thesis submitted for Part C may include work submitted for this or any other degree. Every candidate shall submit through his or her college for approval by the Board of the Faculty of Philosophy the title he or she proposes, together with an explanation of the subject in about 100 words; and a letter of approval from his or her tutor, not earlier than the first day of Trinity Full Term of the year before that in which he or she is to be examined and not later than Friday of the fourth week of the Michaelmas Full Term preceding his or her examination. Applications for approval of subject should be directed to the Chair of the Board, c/o The Administrator, Philosophy Centre, Radcliffe Humanities Building, Woodstock Road, Oxford OX2 6GG. The Board shall decide as soon as possible whether or not to approve the title and shall advise the candidate immediately. No decision shall be deferred beyond the end of the fifth week of Michaelmas Full Term. If a candidate wishes to change the title of his or her thesis after a title has already been approved by the Board, he or she may apply for such permission to be granted by the Board. Applications should be directed to the Chair of the Board (if the application is made before the first day of Hilary Full Term preceding the examination). If later than the first day of Hilary Full Term preceding the examination application for change of title should be made to the Chair of Examiners for Part C of the Final Honour School of Physics and Philosophy.

(*b*) *Authorship and origin*

Every thesis shall be the candidate's own work. A candidate's tutor may, however, discuss with the candidate the field of study, the sources available, and the method of presentation; the tutor may also read and comment on drafts. The amount of assistance the tutor may give is equivalent to the teaching of a normal paper. Every candidate shall sign a certificate to the effect that the thesis is his or her own work and the tutor shall countersign the certificate confirming, to the best of his or her knowledge and belief, that this is so. This certificate shall be placed in a sealed envelope bearing the candidate's examination number presented together with the thesis. No thesis shall be accepted which has already been submitted for a degree of this or any other university, and the certificate shall also state that the thesis has not been so submitted. No thesis shall, however, be ineligible because it has been or is being submitted for any prize of this university.

(*c*) *Length and format*

No thesis shall exceed 20,000 words, the limit to include all notes and appendices, but not including the bibliography; no person or body shall have authority to permit any excess. The word count should be indicated on the front of the thesis. There shall be a select bibliography or a list of sources. All theses must be typed in double spacing on one side of quarto or A4 paper, with any notes and references at the foot of each page. Two copies of the thesis shall be submitted to the examiners.

(*d*) *Submission of thesis*

Every candidate shall submit two copies of their thesis, identified by the candidate's examination number only, not later than noon on Friday of the week before the Trinity Full Term of the examination to the Examination Schools, Oxford, addressed to the Chair of the Examiners for Part C of the Final Honour School of Physics and Philosophy.

EXCHANGE SCHEME

Each individual candidate taking part in a full-year exchange at a host institution approved by the University will provide a collated set of coursework to the standing joint committee. Each individual candidate will ensure that the host institution forwards a full transcript of the courses taken certified by the host institution. Each individual candidate will ensure that the host institution retains the examination papers and scripts for the approved courses undertaken and that these are submitted under seal, together with the collated coursework and transcript of courses taken, to the Chair of Examiners, Honour School of Physics and Philosophy, c/o Examination Schools, High Street, Oxford by noon on Friday of the sixth week of Trinity Term.

[UNTIL 1 OCTOBER 2014: SPECIAL REGULATIONS FOR THE HONOUR SCHOOL OF PHYSIOLOGICAL SCIENCES

A

1. The subject of the Honour School of Physiological Sciences shall be all aspects of the scientific study of the development and functioning of living organisms with particular but not exclusive reference to mammals.

2. No candidate shall be admitted for examination in this school unless he or she has either passed or been exempted from the First Public Examination.

3. The examination in this school shall be under the supervision of the Medical Sciences Board, which shall prescribe the necessary regulations.

4. The examiners shall be the Public Examiners for the Final Honour School of Medical Sciences.

5. Any candidate offering an optional subject based on courses provided within the Honour School of Experimental Psychology shall be examined in that subject by the Public Examiners in Experimental Psychology.

6. Candidates may offer themselves for examination in one or more *Supplementary Subjects*. The Supplementary Subjects available in any year will be notified to students annually during Trinity Term. A candidate's results in any such subject shall be published, and account shall be taken of those results in the production of the class list for the Honour School of Physiological Sciences. Candidates awarded a pass in a Supplementary Subject examination may not retake the same Supplementary Subject examination.

7. With the exception of the Extended Essay, for which candidates will be entered automatically, every candidate shall give notice to the Registrar of all papers being offered not later than Friday in the eighth week of Michaelmas Term in the academic year in which the candidate intends to sit the examination.

B

1. The options of the school shall be as specified for the Honour School of Medical Sciences. This list may be varied from time to time by the Medical Sciences Board, and such variations shall be notified by publication in the *University Gazette* by the end of Week 8 of Trinity Term of the academic year two years preceding the first

examination of the changed options. Each option shall be divided into themes that will be taught starting in Michaelmas Term. The list of themes to be taught in each option in any one academic year shall be published no later than Week 0 of Michaelmas Term of that academic year. Most themes will be specific each to a single option, but some may be shared. The total number of themes to be examined in each option shall be at least 8 and no more than 11, taking account of shared and changed themes (see para. 2 below). Each candidate will be expected to have studied 8 themes in order to address the synoptic questions of Paper 2, and to have prepared sufficient of those themes in depth to be able to address the requirements of Paper 1 (see paras 2, 3, and 5 of Part B of the Special Regulations for the Honour School of Medical Sciences).

2. The written papers of the school shall be as specified for the Honour School of Medical Sciences. To account for any minor change from year to year to the academic material taught within each option, the question papers for the Final Honour School of Physiological Sciences shall be set so as to include the material taught within the options both in the academic year of the examination and in the preceding academic year.

3. Each candidate must offer four written papers:
Paper 1 for two chosen options, Paper 2 and Paper 3.

In place of one Paper 1, candidates may offer a written paper based on courses provided within Parts I and II of the Final Honour School of Experimental Psychology. The subjects of the papers to be available for this purpose shall be published no later than the end of Week 5 of Hilary Term in the year preceding the examination.

In addition, each candidate must both:
 (i) undertake and be examined in a research project, and
 (ii) submit an Extended Essay.

The weighting of marks for the six exercises required of each candidate shall be 25 per cent for the research project and 15 per cent for each of the other five exercises. If, in any part of the examination, a candidate presents essentially the same information on more than one occasion, then credit will be given in only the first instance.

4. *Research project*
(i) *Form and subject of the project*
The project shall consist of original experiments and/or data analysis done by the candidate alone or in collaboration with others (where such collaboration is, for instance, needed to produce results in the time available).

The subject of the project shall be approved and the work shall be supervised as specified for the Honour School of Medical Sciences (see para. 4.i of Part B of the Special Regulations for the Honour School of Medical Sciences). A list of recent project titles registered by students will be made available no later than Friday of Week 8 of Hilary Term of the academic year preceding the examination, to assist candidates in the choice of topic or general field for the research project.

(ii) *Approval*
No later than Friday of Week 2 of Trinity Term in the academic year preceding the examination, every candidate must submit as instructed the title of their proposed research project, provide a brief outline of the subject matter and supply details of supervision arrangements. Decision on the proposal shall be made by the Director of Preclinical Studies or his or her deputy and shall be communicated to the candidate as soon as possible, and work should not start on the project until approval has been given. Candidates should allow at least one week for the process of approval, and should bear in mind that an application may be referred for clarification or may be

refused. When choosing a research project, candidates must bear in mind the prohibition on duplicating material in different parts of the examination (see para. 3).

(iii) *Pre-submission Confirmation*

Candidates must provide final confirmation of the details of their project (including title of project and name of supervisor) to the Examiners through the Faculty of Physiological Sciences Undergraduate Studies Office no later than noon on Friday of Week 8 of Michaelmas Term in the academic year in which they intend taking the examination.

(iv) *Examination*

Candidates shall submit to the examiners a Project Report according to guidelines that will be published by the Medical Sciences Board in Week 1 of Trinity Term in the academic year preceding the examination. The length of the Project Report excluding tables, figures, diagrams, and references shall not exceed 10,000 words.

In addition, each candidate shall make a brief oral presentation of their project to a group of two examiners (or examiners and assessors appointed to ensure an adequate representation of expertise), after which, the candidate shall be examined *viva voce* on the project. The form of the presentation to the examiners shall be specified in guidelines published by the Medical Sciences Board in Week 1 of Trinity Term in the academic year preceding the examination.

(v) *Submission and assessment of project-based written work*

Project Reports (three copies) must be sent to the Chair of Examiners, Honour School of Physiological Sciences, c/o Examination Schools, High Street, Oxford, not later than noon on the Friday of Week 8 in Hilary Term of the academic year in which the candidate intends to take the examination. The copies shall be accompanied (in a separate sealed envelope) by a certificate signed by each candidate indicating that the research project is the candidate's own work. The certificate shall certify that the supervisor has commented on at least one draft of the written submission. Each candidate will be required to submit a draft of their Project Report to their supervisor no later than Friday of Week 6 (two weeks before submission to Schools). In the case of laboratory-based work that has been done in collaboration, the certificate shall indicate the extent of the candidate's own contribution.

In all cases, the examiners shall obtain and consider a written report from each supervisor indicating the extent of the input made by the candidate to the outcome of the project and also any unforeseen difficulties associated with the project (e.g. unexpected technical issues or problems in the availability of materials, equipment, or literature or other published data). In exceptional cases, where through unforeseen circumstances a laboratory-based project produces no useable results (i.e. not even negative or ambiguous results), the candidate may apply through his or her college to the Director of Preclinical Studies or his or her deputy for permission to submit a concise review of the scientific context and the aims of the work that was attempted in place of the normal Project Report. Such an application must be accompanied by supporting evidence from the supervisor of the project. The concise review to be submitted in such circumstances should be comparable in length to the Report of a successful laboratory-based project and will be presented orally to the examiners and be examined viva voce in the usual way for a research project. The examiners will be advised that substantive results could not be produced. When submitting a Project Report, candidates must bear in mind the prohibition on duplicating material in different parts of the examination (see para. 3).

Project Reports previously submitted for the Honour School of Physiological Sciences may be resubmitted. No Project Report will be accepted if it has already been submitted, wholly or substantially, for another Honour School or degree of this University, or for a degree of any other institution.

5. *The Extended Essay*

(i) *Form and subject of the essay*

The Extended Essay shall be of not more than 3,000 words, including figure legends but excluding references. It must be typed and bound according to guidelines that will be published by the Medical Sciences Board in Week 0 of Michaelmas Term in the academic year preceding the year of examination.

The subject matter of a candidate's essay shall be within the scope of the school. The essay may relate to any of the themes taught in the options of the school, regardless of the candidate's chosen options for Paper 1. However, when choosing an Extended Essay, candidates must bear in mind the prohibition on duplicating material in different parts of the examination (see para. 3). Likewise, the Project Report on the research project may not duplicate material in the Extended Essay.

A list of essay titles registered by students in previous years will be made available by Week 0 of the Michaelmas Term of the academic year preceding that of the examination, to assist candidates in the choice of topic or general field for the essay. Application shall be made via the Faculty of Physiological Sciences Undergraduate Studies Office and shall include the proposed title, a brief outline of the subject matter, and the main themes to which it relates. Decision on the application shall be made by the Chair of Examiners in consultation with the option organisers and shall be communicated to the candidate as soon as possible and in any case not later than Week 0 of Trinity Term in the academic year preceding the examination.

(ii) *Registration*

No later than Friday of Week 8 of Hilary Term in the academic year preceding the year of examination, every candidate must register through the Faculty of Physiological Sciences Undergraduate Studies Office the title of their essay, provide a brief outline of the subject matter, and confirm the main themes to which it relates. Decision on the application shall be made by the Director of Preclinical Studies or his or her deputy and shall be communicated to the candidate not later than Week 0 of Trinity Term in the academic year preceding the year of examination.

(iii) *Authorship*

The essay must be the candidate's own work. Candidates' tutors, or their deputies nominated to act as advisors, may discuss with candidates the proposed field of study, the sources available, and the method of treatment, but on no account may they read or comment on any written draft. Every candidate shall sign a certificate to the effect that this rule has been observed and that the essay is their own work; and the candidate's tutor or advisor shall countersign the certificate confirming that, to the best of their knowledge and belief, this is so.

(iv) *Submission*

Essays (two copies) must be submitted to the Chair of Examiners in Physiological Sciences, c/o Examination Schools, High Street, Oxford, not later than noon on the Friday of Week 8 of the Trinity Term in the academic year preceding the year of examination. Each essay shall be accompanied (in a separate sealed envelope addressed to the Chair of Examiners) by certification of authorship as specified in the preceding paragraph and an electronic copy of the text of the essay.

6. Candidates may be examined viva voce; the topics may include the subject of any written paper taken by the candidate, or the research project or Extended Essay.]

[UNTIL 1 OCTOBER 2015: SPECIAL REGULATIONS FOR THE HONOUR SCHOOL OF PSYCHOLOGY AND PHILOSOPHY

A

1. All candidates shall be examined in Psychology and Philosophy.

2. No candidate shall be admitted to the examination in this school unless

   (*a*) he or she has either passed or been exempted from the First Public Examination; and

   (*b*) he or she has satisfied the Moderators for the Preliminary Examination in Psychology and Philosophy in the subject *Introduction to Probability Theory and Statistics* or has passed the Qualifying Examination in Statistics for this school.

The Head of the Department of Experimental Psychology may dispense a candidate from the Qualifying Examination in Statistics in cases where it is clear that the candidate has reached an adequate standard in Statistics by virtue of previous study and qualification.

3. The examination shall consist of two parts. Part I shall consist of papers in Psychology. Part II shall consist of papers in Psychology and Philosophy.

4. No candidate shall be admitted for the Part II examination in this school unless he or she has passed the Part I examination.

5. The Examination Board shall comprise such of the Public Examiners in the Honour School of Experimental Psychology as may be required, and such examiners in Philosophy as are nominated by a committee of which the two elected members shall be appointed by the Board of the Faculty of Philosophy.

6. The examinations in this school shall be under the joint supervision of the Medical Sciences Board and the Philosophy Faculty Board which shall make regulations concerning them subject always to the preceding clauses of this sub-section.

B

Candidates must take five papers for Part I and six papers for Part II. The five papers for Psychology Part I shall count as two papers for the Final Honour School.

The examination for Psychology Part I shall be taken during Weeks 0 and 1 of Trinity Term of the candidate's second year. The examination for Psychology Part II and for Philosophy shall be held during Trinity Term of the candidate's third year. The dates of submission for assessed work are those prescribed in sections 1-2 below.

The subjects in Psychology shall be those specified in 1. *Psychology* below; and in Philosophy those listed in the *Special Regulations for Philosophy in all Honour Schools including Philosophy*.

Candidates may offer *either* a research project *or* a library dissertation in Psychology, *or* a thesis in Philosophy.

There are further restrictions on the choice of subjects and requirements to be satisfied which are set out below.

The highest honours can be obtained by excellence in either branch of the School, provided that the candidate has taken sufficient subjects in the branch and that adequate knowledge is shown in the other branch of examination.

Every candidate shall give notice to the Registrar of all papers being offered not later than Friday in Week 8 of Michaelmas Full Term preceding the examination.

1. Psychology

PART I

1. The five written papers as specified for Part I of the Honour School of Experimental Psychology will be set:

Paper I Biological Bases of Behaviour
Component parts: (i) Cognitive Neuroscience, (ii) Behavioural Neuroscience.

Paper II Human Experimental Psychology 1
Component parts: (i) Perception, (ii) Memory, Attention, and Information Processing.

Paper III Human Experimental Psychology 2
Component parts: (i) Language and Cognition, (ii) Developmental Psychology.

Paper IV Social Psychology, and Personality, Individual Differences and Psychological Disorders.
Component parts: (i) Social Psychology, (ii) Personality, Individual Differences and Psychological Disorders.

Paper V Experimental Design and Statistics
Candidates will be required to answer essays and short answer questions in *four* of the eight components of Papers I-IV. All candidates are required to offer Paper V.

Candidates who wish to be deemed eligible for Graduate Basis for Chartered Membership (GBC) of the British Psychological Society (BPS) must ensure that the components they select provide coverage of all five of the areas defined in the GBC curriculum. In order to achieve this, candidates must offer one component from each of four areas, chosen from the five areas prescribed below:

1. Cognitive Neuroscience *or* Behavioural Neuroscience from Paper I
2. Perception; *or* Memory, Attention and Information Processing; *or* Language and Cognition from Papers II and III;
3. Developmental Psychology from Paper III;
4. Social Psychology from Paper IV;
5. Personality, Individual Differences and Psychological Disorders from paper IV.

In addition, candidates must sit additional short answer questions covering one component from the remaining fifth area.

The other requirements for BPS Graduate Basis for Chartered Membership are set out in Part II below.

Qualifying Examination in Statistics
Any candidate who has not satisfied the Moderators for the Preliminary Examination for Psychology and Philosophy in the subject *Introduction to Probability Theory and Statistics* must pass a Qualifying Examination in Statistics before being admitted for examination in the Honour School. The Head of the Department of Experimental

Psychology shall have the capacity to dispense a candidate from the examination in cases where it is clear that an individual has reached an adequate standard by virtue of previous study and qualification.

The syllabus and paper set for the examination shall be that for the subject *Introduction to Probability Theory and Statistics* in the *Preliminary Examination in* 5 *Psychology and Philosophy*.

For all papers in Psychology and for the Qualifying Examination in Statistics, the examiners will permit the use of any hand-held pocket calculator subject to the conditions set out under the heading 'Use of calculators in examinations' in the *Regulations for the Conduct of University Examinations*. 10

Practical work

Candidates will be required to undertake practical work, as specified by the Head of the Department of Experimental Psychology, and this will constitute a part of the examination. In exceptional circumstances the Proctors may dispense a candidate from the specified requirements on the recommendation of the Head of Department 15 or deputy.

Reports of practical work completed during the course of study for Part I and submitted for marking shall constitute a portfolio which shall be available to examiners as part of the examination. Every report submitted for marking must be accompanied by a statement indicating that the work submitted is the candidate's 20 own work. Where the work submitted has been produced in collaboration the candidates shall indicate the extent of their own contributions. Reports of practical work previously submitted for the Honour School of Psychology and Philosophy, may be resubmitted, but reports will not be accepted if they have already been submitted, wholly or substantially, for another Honour School or degree of this 25 University, or for a degree of any other institution. The Head of Department or deputy shall inform the examiners by the end of Week 0 of the Trinity Term in which the Part I examination is to be held as to which candidates have (a) failed to satisfy the requirement to undertake practical work or (b) failed to submit a portfolio. Candidates in category (a) will be deemed to have failed Paper V. Candidates in 30 category (b) will be deemed to have failed the entire Part I examination. The Head of Department or deputy shall also make available to the examiners records showing the extent to which each candidate has adequately pursued a course of practical work. The examiners shall take this evidence into consideration along with evidence of unsatisfactory or distinguished performance in each portfolio of 35 practical work.

A candidate who fails the Part I examination may retake the examination once only, in the Long Vacation of the same academic year as the original examination. The highest mark that can be awarded to a candidate retaking the examination is a Pass. 40

PART II

Candidates must offer six papers for Part II. At least one and at most three of the papers must be in Psychology, the others to be chosen from those available in Philosophy below. Candidates taking three papers in Psychology may offer a Research Project or a Library Dissertation in place of one of the three Psychology 45 papers. Candidates may substitute one paper from the list below in place of one of the Psychology Advanced Options:

General Linguistics

Phonetics and Phonology.

In order to be deemed eligible for Graduate Basis for Chartered Membership of the 50 BPS, candidates must take at least two subjects in Part II Psychology.

Written papers, research project, and Library Dissertation:

Each candidate will be examined in either one, two or three areas of Psychology by means of one, two or three written papers, each of three hours *or* two written papers, each of three hours, and *either* a research project *or* a Library Dissertation. The written papers will be selected from the list of at least 12 options approved by the Medical Sciences Division and published at the Department of Experimental Psychology. A list of options will be posted in the Department of Experimental Psychology not later than noon on Friday of Week 5 of Hilary Term in the year preceding that in which the examination is taken.

Research Project

As specified for the Honour School of Experimental Psychology.

Library Dissertation

As specified for the Honour School of Experimental Psychology.

Reports of practical work completed during the course of study for Part II and submitted for marking shall constitute a portfolio which shall be available to examiners as part of the examination. Every report submitted for marking must be accompanied by a statement indicating that the work submitted is the candidate's own work. Reports of practical work previously submitted for the Honour School of Psychology and Philosophy may be resubmitted but reports will not be accepted if they have been submitted, wholly or substantially, for another Honour School or degree of this University, or for a degree of any other institution. The Head of Department or deputy shall inform the examiners by the end of Week 0 of the Trinity Term in which the Part II examination is to be held as to which candidates have failed to satisfy the requirement to undertake practical work. Failure to satisfy the requirement to undertake practical work will result in the candidate's final degree classification being lowered by one class. Candidates who fail to submit a portfolio will be deemed to have failed the entire Part II examination. The Head of Department, or deputy, shall make available to the examiners records showing the extent to which candidates have adequately pursued a course of practical work. The examiners shall take this evidence into consideration along with evidence of unsatisfactory or distinguished performance in each portfolio of practical work.

2. PHILOSOPHY

Candidates must satisfy both the General Regulations, and those relating specifically to Psychology and Philosophy in the *Special Regulations for Philosophy in all Honour Schools including Philosophy.*]

[FROM 1 OCTOBER 2014: SPECIAL REGULATIONS
FOR THE HONOUR SCHOOL OF PSYCHOLOGY,
PHILOSOPHY, AND LINGUISTICS

A

1. The branches of the Honour School of Psychology, Philosophy, and Linguistics shall be Psychology, Philosophy, and Linguistics. Candidates must offer two or three branches.

2. No candidate shall be admitted to the examination in this school unless he or she has either passed or been exempted from the First Public Examination.

3. For candidates offering Psychology, the examination shall consist of two parts. Part I shall consist of the one subject area, Psychology. Part II shall consist of two or three subject areas: Psychology, and one or both of Philosophy and Linguistics. For candidates not taking Psychology Parts I and II, the examination shall consist only of papers in Philosophy and Linguistics.

4. No candidate who offers Psychology shall be admitted for the Part II examination in this school unless

   (*a*) he or she has passed the Part I examination specified for this school; and

   (*b*) he or she has satisfied the Moderators for the Preliminary Examination for Psychology, Philosophy, and Linguistics, in the subject *Introduction to Probability Theory and Statistics* or has passed the Qualifying Examination in Statistics for this school.

The Head of the Department of Experimental Psychology may dispense a candidate from the Qualifying Examination in Statistics in cases where it is clear that the candidate has reached an adequate standard in Statistics by virtue of previous study and qualification.

5. Candidates offering Psychology shall be examined by such of the Public Examiners in the Honour School of Experimental Psychology as may be required; candidates offering Philosophy shall be examined by such examiners as are nominated by a committee of which the two elected members shall be appointed by the Board of the Faculty of Philosophy; and candidates offering Linguistics shall be examined by such examiners as are nominated by the Board of the Faculty of Linguistics, Philology and Phonetics.

6. The examinations in this school shall be under the joint supervision of the Medical Sciences Board and the Faculty Boards of Philosophy and of Linguistics, Philology and Phonetics, which shall make regulations concerning them subject always to the preceding clauses of this sub-section.

B

Candidates may offer *either* Psychology, Philosophy, and Linguistics *or* Psychology and Philosophy *or* Psychology and Linguistics *or* Philosophy and Linguistics.

For candidates offering Psychology, the examination shall consist of two parts. The five papers for Psychology Part I shall count as two papers for the Final Honour School. Part II will consist of six papers covering two or three subject areas; Psychology, and one or both of Philosophy and Linguistics.

For candidates not offering Psychology, the examination shall consist of eight papers in Philosophy and Linguistics.

No candidate who offers Psychology shall be admitted for the Part II examination in this school unless he or she has passed the Part I examination specified for this school.

The examination for Psychology Part I shall be taken during Weeks 0 and 1 of Trinity Term of the candidate's second year. The examination for Psychology Part II and for Philosophy and Linguistics shall be held during Trinity Term of the candidate's third year. The dates of submission for assessed work are those prescribed in sections 1–3 below.

The subjects in Psychology shall be those specified in *1. Psychology* below; in Philosophy those listed in the *Special Regulations for Philosophy in all Honour Schools including Philosophy*, and in Linguistics those specified in the *Special Regulations for Linguistics in all Honour Schools including Linguistics*.

Candidates may offer *either* a research project or a library dissertation in Psychology, *or* a thesis in Philosophy, *or either* a thesis *or* project in Linguistics.

There are further restrictions on the choice of subjects and requirements to be satisfied within each branch, which are set out below.

The highest honours can be obtained by excellence in any of the branches offered, provided that the candidate has taken sufficient subjects in the branch and that adequate knowledge is shown in the other branch(es) of examination.

Every candidate shall give notice to the Registrar of all papers being offered not later than Friday in Week 8 of Michaelmas Full Term preceding the examination.

1. PSYCHOLOGY

PART I

The five written papers as specified for Part I of the Honour School of Experimental Psychology will be set:

Paper I Biological Bases of Behaviour

Component parts: (i) Cognitive Neuroscience, (ii) Behavioural Neuroscience.

Paper II Human Experimental Psychology 1

Component parts: (i) Perception, (ii) Memory, Attention, and Information Processing.

Paper III Human Experimental Psychology 2

Component parts: (i) Language and Cognition, (ii) Developmental Psychology.

Paper IV Social Psychology, and Personality, Individual Differences and Psychological Disorders

Component parts: (i) Social Psychology, (ii) Personality, Individual Differences and Psychological Disorders.

Paper V Experimental Design and Statistics

Candidates will be required to answer essays and short answer questions in *four* of the eight components of Papers I-IV. All candidates are required to offer Paper V.

Candidates who wish to be deemed eligible for Graduate Basis for Chartered Membership (GBC) of the British Psychological Society (BPS) must ensure that the components they select provide coverage of all five of the areas defined in the GBC curriculum. In order to achieve this, candidates must offer one component from each of four areas, chosen from the five areas prescribed below:

1. Cognitive Neuroscience or Behavioural Neuroscience from Paper I;
2. Perception; *or* Memory, Attention and Information Processing; *or* Language and Cognition from Papers II and III;
3. Developmental Psychology from Paper III;
4. Social Psychology from Paper IV;
5. Personality, Individual Differences and Psychological Disorders from Paper IV.

In addition, candidates must sit additional short answer questions covering one component from the remaining fifth area.

The other requirements for BPS Graduate Basis for Chartered Membership are set out in Part II below.

Qualifying Examination in Statistics

Any candidate who has not satisfied the Moderators for the Preliminary Examination for Psychology, Philosophy, and Linguistics in the subject *Introduction to Probability Theory and Statistics* must pass a Qualifying Examination in Statistics before being admitted for examination in the Honour School. The Head of the Department of Experimental Psychology shall have the capacity to dispense a candidate from the examination in cases where it is clear that an individual has reached an adequate standard by virtue of previous study and qualification.

The syllabus and paper set for the examination shall be that for the subject *Introduction to Probability Theory and Statistics* in the Preliminary Examination in Psychology, Philosophy, and Linguistics.

For all papers in Psychology and for the Qualifying Examination in Statistics, the examiners will permit the use of any hand-held pocket calculator subject to the conditions set out under the heading 'Use of calculators' in the *Regulations for the Conduct of University Examinations*.

Practical work

Candidates will be required to undertake practical work, as specified by the Head of the Department of Experimental Psychology, and this will constitute a part of the examination. In exceptional circumstances the Proctors may dispense a candidate from the specified requirements on the recommendation of the Head of Department or deputy.

Reports of practical work completed during the course of study for Part I and submitted for marking shall constitute a portfolio which shall be available to examiners as part of the examination. Every report submitted for marking must be accompanied by a statement indicating that the work submitted is the candidate's own work. Where the work submitted has been produced in collaboration the candidates shall indicate the extent of their own contributions. Reports of practical work previously submitted for the Honour School of Psychology, Philosophy, and Linguistics may be resubmitted, but reports will not be accepted if they have already been submitted, wholly or substantially, for another Honour School or degree of this University, or for a degree of any other institution. The Head of Department or deputy shall inform the examiners by the end of Week 0 of the Trinity Term in which the Part I examination is to be held as to which candidates have (a) failed to satisfy the requirement to undertake practical work or (b) failed to submit a portfolio.

Candidates in category (a) will be deemed to have failed Paper V. Candidates in category (b) will be deemed to have failed the entire Part I examination. The Head of Department or deputy shall also make available to the examiners records showing the extent to which each candidate has adequately pursued a course of practical work. The examiners shall take this evidence into consideration along with evidence of   5
unsatisfactory or distinguished performance in each portfolio of practical work.

A candidate who fails the Part I examination may retake the examination once only, in the Long Vacation of the same academic year as the original examination. The highest mark that can be awarded to a candidate retaking the examination is a Pass.   10

PART II

Candidates must offer six papers for Part II. At least one and at most three of the papers must be in Psychology, the others to be chosen from those available in Philosophy and/or Linguistics below. Candidates taking three papers in Psychology may offer a Research Project or a Library Dissertation in place of one of the three   15
Psychology papers.

In order to be deemed eligible for Graduate Basis for Chartered Membership of the British Psychological Society, candidates must take at least two subjects in Part II Psychology.

Written papers, Research Project, and Library Dissertation: 20

Each candidate will be examined in either one, two or three areas of Psychology by means of one, two or three written papers, each of three hours *or* two written papers, each of three hours, and *either* a Research Project or a Library Dissertation. The written papers will be selected from the list of at least 12 options approved by the Medical Sciences Division and published at the Department of Experimental   25
Psychology. A list of options will be posted in the Department of Experimental Psychology not later than noon on Friday of Week 5 of Hilary Term in the year preceding that in which the examination is taken.

Research Project

As specified for the Honour School of Experimental Psychology.   30

Library Dissertation

As specified for the Honour School of Experimental Psychology.

Reports of practical work completed during the course of study for Part II and submitted for marking shall constitute a portfolio which shall be available to examiners as part of the examination. Every report submitted for marking must be   35
accompanied by a statement indicating that the work submitted is the candidate's own work. Reports of practical work previously submitted for the Honour School of Psychology, Philosophy, and Linguistics may be resubmitted but reports will not be accepted if they have been submitted, wholly or substantially, for another Honour School or degree of this University, or for a degree of any other institution. The Head   40
of Department or deputy shall inform the examiners by the end of Week 0 of the Trinity Term in which the Part II examination is to be held as to which candidates have failed to satisfy the requirement to undertake practical work. Failure to satisfy the requirement to undertake practical work will result in the candidate's final degree classification being lowered by one class. Candidates who fail to submit a   45
portfolio will be deemed to have failed the entire Part II examination. The Head of Department, or deputy, shall make available to the examiners records showing the extent to which candidates have adequately pursued a course of practical work. The examiners shall take this evidence into consideration along with evidence of unsatisfactory or distinguished performance in each portfolio of practical work.   50

2. PHILOSOPHY

Candidates must satisfy both the General Regulations, and those relating specifically to Psychology, Philosophy, and Linguistics in the *Special Regulations for Philosophy in all Honour Schools including Philosophy.*

3. LINGUISTICS

Candidates must satisfy both the General Regulations, and those relating specifically to Psychology, Philosophy, and Linguistics in the *Special Regulations for Linguistics in all Honour Schools including Linguistics.*]

[UNTIL 1 OCTOBER 2014: SPECIAL REGULATIONS FOR THE HONOUR SCHOOL OF PSYCHOLOGY, PHILOSOPHY, AND PHYSIOLOGY

A

1. The branches of the Honour School of Psychology, Philosophy, and Physiology shall be Psychology, Philosophy, and Physiology. Candidates must offer two or three branches.

2. The examiners shall indicate in the class list issued by them the name(s) of the branch(es) in which each candidate has taken three papers or more for the Final Honour School.

3. No candidate shall be admitted to the examination in this school unless he or she has either passed or been exempted from the First Public Examination.

4. For candidates offering Psychology, the examination shall consist of two parts. Part I shall consist of the one subject area, Psychology. Part II shall consist of two or three subject areas: Psychology, and one or both of Philosophy and Physiology. For candidates not taking Psychology Parts I and II, the examination shall consist only of papers in Physiology and Philosophy.

5. No candidate who offers Psychology shall be admitted for the Part II examination in this school unless

  (*a*) he or she has passed the Part I examination specified for this school; and

  (*b*) he or she has satisfied the Moderators for the Preliminary Examination for Psychology, Philosophy, and Physiology in the subject *Introduction to Probability Theory and Statistics* or has passed the Qualifying Examination in Statistics for this school.

The Head of the Department of Experimental Psychology may dispense a candidate from the Qualifying Examination in Statistics in cases where it is clear that the candidate has reached an adequate standard in Statistics by virtue of previous study and qualification.

6. Candidates offering Psychology shall be examined by such of the Public Examiners in the Honour School of Experimental Psychology as may be required; candidates offering Physiology shall be examined by such of the Public Examiners in Medical Sciences in the Honour School of Medical Sciences as may be

required; and candidates offering Philosophy shall be examined by such examiners as are nominated by a committee of which the two elected members shall be appointed by the Board of the Faculty of Philosophy.

7. The examinations in this school shall be under the supervision joint of the Medical Sciences Board and the Philosophy Faculty Board which shall make regulations concerning them subject always to the preceding clauses of this sub-section.

B

1. Decree (7) of 3 June 1947 permits the number of candidates offering Psychology to be limited, if necessary.

For candidates offering Psychology, the examination shall consist of two parts. Part I will consist of one subject area, Psychology, which shall count as two papers for the Final Honour School. Part II will consist of six papers covering two or three subject areas; Psychology, and one or both of Philosophy and Physiology.

For candidates not offering Psychology, the examination shall consist of eight papers in Philosophy and Physiology.

No candidate who offers Psychology shall be admitted for the Part II examination in this school unless he or she has passed the Part I examination specified for this school.

The examination for Psychology Part I shall be taken during Weeks 0 and 1 of Trinity Term of the candidate's second year. The examination for Psychology Part II and for Philosophy and Physiology shall be held during Trinity Term of the candidate's third year. The dates of submission for assessed work are those prescribed in sections 2–4 below.

The subjects in Psychology shall be those specified in *2. Psychology* below; in Philosophy those listed in the *Special Regulations for Philosophy in all Honour Schools including Philosophy*, and in Physiology those specified in *4. Physiology* below.

Candidates may offer *either* a research project *or* a library dissertation in Psychology, *or* a thesis in Philosophy, *or* a laboratory-based research project in Physiology.

There are further restrictions on the choice of subjects and requirements to be satisfied within each branch, which are set out below.

The highest honours can be obtained by excellence in any of the branches offered, provided that the candidate has taken sufficient subjects in the branch and that adequate knowledge is shown in the other branch(es) of examination.

Every candidate shall give notice to the Registrar of all papers being offered not later than Friday in eighth week of Michaelmas Full Term preceding the examination.

2. PSYCHOLOGY

PART I

1. The five written papers as specified for Part I of the Honour School of Experimental Psychology will be set:

Paper I Biological Bases of Behaviour
Component parts: (i) Cognitive Neuroscience, (ii) Behavioural Neuroscience.

Paper II Human Experimental Psychology 1
Component parts:(i) Perception, (ii) Memory, Attention, and Information Processing.

Paper III Human Experimental Psychology 2
        Component parts: (i) Language and Cognition,(ii) Developmental Psychology.
Paper IV Social Psychology, and Personality, Individual Differences and Psychological Disorders.
        Component parts: (i) Social Psychology, (ii) Personality, Individual Differences and Psychological Disorders.
Paper V Experimental Design and Statistics

Candidates will be required to answer essays and short answer questions in *four* of the eight components of Papers I–IV. All candidates are required to offer Paper V.

Candidates who wish to be deemed eligible for Graduate Basis for Chartered Membership (GBC) of the British Psychological Society (BPS) must ensure that the components they select provide coverage of all five of the areas defined in the GBC curriculum. In order to achieve this candidates must offer one component from each of four areas chosen from the five areas prescribed below:

1. Cognitive Neuroscience *or* Behavioural Neuroscience from Paper I;
2. Perception; *or* Memory, Attention and Information Processing; *or* Language and Cognition from Papers II and III;
3. Developmental Psychology from Paper III;
4. Social Psychology from Paper IV;
5. Personality, Individual Differences and Psychological Disorders from Paper IV.

In addition, candidates must sit additional short answers questions covering one component from the remaining fifth area.
The other requirements for BPS Graduate Basis for Chartered Membership are set out in Part II below.

Qualifying Examination in Statistics

Any candidate offering Psychology who has not satisfied the Moderators for the Preliminary Examination for Psychology, Philosophy, and Physiology in the subject *Introduction to Probability Theory and Statistics* must pass a Qualifying Examination in Statistics before being admitted for examination in the Honour School. The Head of Department of Experimental Psychology shall have the capacity to dispense a candidate from the examination in cases where it is clear that an individual has reached an adequate standard by virtue of previous study and qualification.
The syllabus and paper set for the examination shall be that for the subject *Introduction to Probability Theory and Statistics* in the *Preliminary Examination for Psychology, Philosophy, and Physiology*.
For all papers in Psychology and for the Qualifying Examination in Statistics, the examiners will permit the use of any hand-held pocket calculator subject to the conditions set out under the heading *Regulations for the Conduct of University Examinations*, Part 13.

Practical work

Candidates will be required to undertake practical work, as specified by the Head of Department of Experimental Psychology, and this will constitute a part of the examination. In exceptional circumstances the Proctors may dispense a candidate from the specified requirements on the recommendation of the Head of Department or deputy.
Reports of practical work completed during the course of study for Part I and submitted for marking shall constitute a portfolio which shall be available to examiners as part of the examination. Every report submitted for marking must be accompanied by a statement indicating that the work submitted is the candidate's

own work. Where the work submitted has been produced in collaboration the candidates shall indicate the extent of their own contributions. Reports of practical work previously submitted for the Honour School of Psychology, Philosophy, and Physiology may be resubmitted, but reports will not be accepted if they have already been submitted, wholly or substantially, for another Honour School or degree of this University, or for a degree of any other institution. The Head of Department or deputy shall inform the examiners by the end of Week 0 of the Trinity Term in which the Part I examination is to be held as to which candidates have (a) failed to satisfy the requirement to undertake practical work or (b) failed to submit a portfolio. Candidates in category (a) will be deemed to have failed Paper V. Candidates in category (b) will be deemed to have failed the entire Part I examination. The Head of Department or deputy shall also make available to the examiners records showing the extent to which each candidate has adequately pursued a course of practical work. The examiners shall take this evidence into consideration along with evidence of unsatisfactory or distinguished performance in each portfolio of practical work.

A candidate who fails the Part I examination may retake the examination once only, in the Long Vacation of the same academic year as the original examination. The highest mark that can be awarded to a candidate retaking the examination is a Pass.

PART II

(*a*) Candidates taking Psychology must offer six papers for Part II. At least one and at most three of the papers must be in Psychology, the others to be chosen from those available in Philosophy and/or Physiology below. Candidates taking three papers in Psychology may offer a Research Project or a Library Dissertation in place of one of the three Psychology papers. Candidates may substitute one paper from the list below in place of one of the Psychology Advanced Options:

General Linguistics

Phonetics and Phonology.

In order to be deemed eligible for Graduate Basis for Chartered Membership of the BPS, candidates must take at least two subjects in Part II Psychology.

(*b*) Candidates not taking papers in Psychology. Candidates must offer eight papers.

Written papers, research project, and Library Dissertation:

Each candidate will be examined in either one, two or three areas of Psychology by means of one, two or three written papers, each of three hours *or* two written papers, each of three hours, and *either* a Research Project *or* a Library Dissertation. The written papers will be selected from the list of at least 12 options approved by the Medical Sciences Division and published at the Department of Experimental Psychology. A list of options will be posted in the Department of Experimental Psychology not later than noon on Friday of the fifth week of Hilary Term in the year preceding that in which the examination is taken.

Research Project

As specified for the Honour School of Experimental Psychology.

Library Dissertation

As specified for the Honour School of Experimental Psychology.

Candidates will be required to undertake practical work, as specified by the Head of Department of Experimental Psychology, and this will constitute a part of the examination. In exceptional circumstances the Proctors may dispense a candidate from the specified requirements on the recommendation of the Head of Department or deputy. Reports of practical work completed during the course of study for Part II and submitted for marking shall constitute a portfolio which shall be available to examiners as part of the examination. Every report submitted for marking must be accompanied by a statement indicating that the work submitted is the candidate's own work. Reports of practical work previously submitted for the Honour School of Psychology, Philosophy, and Physiology may be resubmitted but reports will not be accepted if they have been submitted, wholly or substantially, for another Honour School or degree of this University, or for a degree of any other institution. The Head of Department or deputy shall inform the examiners by the end of Week 0 of the Trinity Term in which the Part II examination is to be held as to which candidates have failed to satisfy the requirement to undertake practical work. Failure to satisfy the requirement to undertake practical work will result in the candidate's final degree classification being lowered by one class. Candidates who fail to submit a portfolio will be deemed to have failed the entire Part II examination. The Head of Department, or deputy, shall make available to the examiners records showing the extent to which candidates have adequately pursued a course of practical work. The examiners shall take this evidence into consideration along with evidence of unsatisfactory or distinguished performance in each portfolio of practical work.

3. PHILOSOPHY

Candidates must satisfy both the General Regulations, and those relating specifically to Psychology, Philosophy, and Physiology, in the *Special Regulations for Philosophy in all Honour Schools including Philosophy.*

4. PHYSIOLOGY

Candidates taking papers in physiology may offer a minimum of three and a maximum of five components from the Honour School of Medical Sciences and this must include Paper 1 for any one of the options (A) to (E), Paper 2, and an Extended Essay. In addition, as a fourth component in Physiology, a candidate may offer a laboratory-based research project on a topic within the scope of the Honour School of Medical Sciences as approved by or on behalf of the Medical Sciences Board. As a fifth component in Physiology, a candidate may offer Paper 1 in a second of the options (A) to (E).

Each of the exercises undertaken by each candidate in Physiology shall be given equal weight in assessment, each carrying one eighth of the total credit for the examination. If, in any part of the examination, a candidate presents essentially the same information on more than one occasion, then credit will be given in only the first instance.

The Extended Essay

The form of the Extended Essay, the approval of its subject, and the procedures for registration of the title, for certification of authorship, and for submission are as set out in the Special Regulations for the Honour School of Medical Sciences.

Research Project

The form of the project, which must be laboratory-based, the approval of its subject, and the procedures for confirmation of the title and for examination, including the submission of written work, are as set out in the Special Regulations for the Honour School of Physiological Sciences.

Examination viva voce

In addition to examination *viva voce* of the research project, candidates may be also examined *viva voce* in other components of the examination that may include the subject of any written paper taken by the candidate, or the Extended Essay.]

SPECIAL REGULATIONS FOR THE HONOUR SCHOOL OF THEOLOGY

A

1. The examination in the Honour School of Theology shall include:

(1) Biblical Studies including such sections of the New Testament in Greek as the Board of the Faculty of Theology and Religion shall from time to time prescribe by regulation.

(2) Christian Doctrine and its Historical Context.

(3) The study of a variety of religions.

(4) Such other subjects as the Board of the Faculty of Theology and Religion shall from time to time prescribe by regulation.

2. No candidate shall be admitted to examination in this school unless he or she has either passed or been exempted from the First Public Examination.

3. No candidate shall be admitted to examination in this Honour School unless he or she has satisfied a language requirement for the degree.

4. No candidate shall be admitted to examination in this school unless he or she has satisfied a language requirement for the degree via his or her Preliminary Examination or has indicated how he or she will attempt to do so via his or her Second Public Examination.

5. The examination in this school shall be under the supervision of the Board of the Faculty of Theology and Religion, which shall prescribe the necessary regulations.

B

1. All candidates will be required to offer eight papers, as specified below, from the Schedule of Papers. There shall be four compulsory papers, taken by all candidates, covering the Old and New Testaments and the development of Christian Doctrine in its historical context. In addition to these compulsory papers, candidates will be required to offer four further papers chosen according to the schedules in either Track I, Track II, or Track III.

Examination regulations applying to all Tracks

2. With the permission of the Board of the Faculty of Theology and Religion, any candidate may offer an essay *either* in place of one of the eight papers, *or* in addition to the eight required papers. The regulations governing essays are set out below.

3. Candidates not offering the full Hebrew paper (24) as one of their eight papers may, in addition to their eight papers, offer the Hebrew translation component of paper 24 as an optional extra paper. All candidates may, in addition to their eight

papers, offer the optional translation paper in New Testament Greek (paper 27). Candidates who so wish may offer both the Hebrew paper (whether as a full paper or as an optional translation paper) and the optional translation paper in New Testament.

4. In papers (7) to (36), teaching may not be available every year on every subject.   5

5. Any candidate may be examined *viva voce*.

6. Candidates in the Final Honours School of Theology will be deemed to have satisfied a language requirement for their degree if they have passed one of Papers 7 (New Testament Greek), 8 (Biblical Hebrew), 9 (Classical Arabic), 10 (Pali), or 11 (Sanskrit) in their Preliminary Examination.   10

Candidates in the Final Honours School of Theology who have not passed one of Papers 7, 8, 9, 10, or 11 in their Preliminary Examination can still satisfy a language requirement by demonstrating a familiarity in their Second Public Examination with either Biblical Hebrew in Paper 1 or New Testament Greek in Paper 2.

Candidates on Track I of the Single Honours School of Theology may also   15 satisfy a requirement to be familiar with Biblical Hebrew by passing one of Papers 22, 23, or 24.

7. In the following regulations, the English version of the Bible used will be the New Revised Standard Version. The Greek text used will be the text of the United Bible Societies, 4th edn.   20

All candidates must offer eight subjects, as specified below, from the Schedule of Papers.

TRACK I
    (i) Paper (1)
    (ii) Paper (2)   25
    (iii) Paper (3)
    (iv) Paper (4)
    (v) Paper (5)
    (vi) One paper chosen from Papers (22), (23), (24), (25), (26) or (29)
    (vii) One further paper   30
    (viii) One further paper.

TRACK II
    (i) Paper (1)
    (ii) Paper (2)
    (iii) Paper (4)   35
    (iv) Paper (5)
    (v) One paper chosen from Papers (7), (8) or (9)
    (vi) Paper (10)
    (vii) One further paper
    (viii) One further paper.   40

TRACK III
    (i) Paper (1)
    (ii) Paper (2)
    (iii) Paper (4)
    (iv) Paper (5)   45
    (v) Paper (13)
    (vi) and (vii)
        either Papers (14) and (15) OR Papers (16) and (17) *or* Papers (18) and (19) *or* Papers (20) and (21)
    (viii) One further paper.   50

Regulations concerning language requirements

Candidates for the Final Honours School of Theology will be deemed to have satisfied a language requirement for their degree if they have passed one of Papers 7 (New Testament Greek), 8 (Biblical Hebrew), 9 (Classical Arabic), 10 (Pali), or 11 (Sanskrit) in their Preliminary Examination. Candidates in the Final Honours School of Theology who have not passed one of Papers 7, 8, 9, 10, or 11 in their Preliminary Examination can still satisfy a language requirement by demonstrating a familiarity in their Second Public Examination with either Biblical Hebrew in Paper 1 or New Testament Greek in Paper 2. Candidates on Track I of the Single Honours School of Theology may also satisfy a requirement to be familiar with Biblical Hebrew by passing one of Papers 22, 23 or 24. Failure to attempt to demonstrate knowledge of a biblical language ('language requirement') in the paper through which a candidate has stated he or she will do so, will result in a failure of the examination. Inadequate demonstration of knowledge or understanding of the language concerned may result in the reduction of the mark for the paper by one class (i.e. normally 10 marks).

Regulations concerning essays

1. Candidates may offer an extended essay *either* in place of the paper to be chosen under clause (viii) of Tracks I–III, *or* in addition to the eight required papers. Candidates should in general aim at a length of 10,000 words, but must not exceed 15,000 words (both figures inclusive of notes and appendices, but excluding bibliography).

2. Prior approval of the subject of the essay must be obtained from the Board of the Faculty of Theology and Religion. Such approval must be sought not later than Friday in the third week of Trinity Full Term in the year preceding the examination. The request for approval should be addressed to the Secretary of the Board of the Faculty of Theology and Religion, Theology Faculty Centre, 34 St Giles', Oxford OX1 3LW. The request must be accompanied by a letter from the tutor stating that this subject has his or her approval. The application should include, in about 100 words, an explanation as to how the topic will be treated, and a brief bibliography.

3. The candidate's application for approval of title should be submitted through and with the support of his or her college tutor or the tutor with overall responsibility for his or her studies, from whom he or she should seek guidance on whether the subject is likely to be acceptable to the Board.

4. The candidate is advised to have an initial discussion with his or her supervisor regarding the proposed field of study, the sources available, and the method of presentation. He or she should have further discussions with his or her supervisor during the preparation of the essay. His or her supervisor may read and comment on drafts of the essay.

5. The subject of the essay need not fall within the areas covered by the papers listed in the Honour School of Theology. It may overlap any subject or period on which the candidate offers papers, but the candidate is warned against reproducing the content of his or her essay in any answer to a question in the examination. Subject to the provision of cl. 4 above, every candidate shall sign a letter declaring the essay to be his or her own work and that it has not already been submitted (wholly or substantially) for a final honour school other than one involving Theology, or another degree of this University, or a degree of any other institution. This letter, which can be found in the Handbook or collected from the Theology and Religion Faculty Office, 34 St Giles', Oxford OX1 3LW, shall be presented together with the essay. No essay shall, however, be ineligible because it has been or is being submitted for any prize of this University.

6. The candidate must submit two typed copies of the essay (bound or held firmly in a stiff cover), addressed to the Chair of the Examiners, Honour School of

Theology, Examination Schools, High Street, Oxford not later than noon on the Friday of the eighth week of Hilary Term in the academic year in which he or she is presenting himself or herself for examination. The letter signed by the candidate in accordance with cl. 5 above must be submitted separately in a sealed envelope addressed to the Chair of the Examiners at the above address at the same time as the copies are submitted.

7. The provisions of clauses 3–4 and clause 6 of these regulations will also apply to candidates submitting an extended essay as part of papers 6 and 34. (39).

Schedule of papers

(1) *God and Israel in the Old Testament*

The paper will include questions on such topics as the origins and purpose of Deuteronomy; the development of Israelite law; the theology and setting of Isaiah of Jerusalem; Deutero-Isaiah; psalmody and the Psalms; worship and festivals; the history of Israel; pentateuchal issues; the covenant; prophecy and particular prophets; wisdom; apocalyptic; the fate of the individual; creation; the Torah in post-exilic Judaism; method in Old Testament study; Old Testament ethics; Israel within its ancient Near Eastern Environment; God in history; king and messiah; divine grace and human freedom; Israel and the nations.

Candidates will be required to comment on passages from the following texts in English:

(*a*) Deuteronomy 5–15; 26–8.

(*b*) Isaiah 1–11; 28–31; 40–5.

(*c*) Psalms 1, 2, 8, 15, 19, 46–9, 51, 72–4, 89, 96–9, 104 and 118.

There will be an opportunity to comment on passages in Hebrew from:

Deuteronomy 5; 12; 26.

Isaiah 1: 6; 40.

Psalms 1, 2, 8, 48 and 96.

Candidates who choose to comment on Hebrew passages must also translate them. Credit will be given to candidates demonstrating competence in Biblical Hebrew.

(2) *The Gospels and Jesus (with special reference to the gospels of Matthew and John)*

Questions will be set on the four gospels, their theology and ethics, literary and historical problems associated with the gospels, the historical Jesus, and different approaches to the gospels.

Candidates will be required to comment on two passages from Matthew, at least three of which will be printed in English. They will also be required to comment on two passages from John, at least three of which will be printed in English.

(3) *Pauline Literature*

Candidates will be expected to show a knowledge of the theological, ethical, literary and historical issues posed by study of the Pauline corpus of letters in the New Testament.

Candidates will be required to comment on two passages from 1 Corinthians, and on two passages from Romans. Candidates for Track 1 will be required to comment on at least one passage from 1 Corinthians in Greek, and at least one passage from Romans in Greek. Of the passages printed in Greek only, at least one will be taken from 1 Corinthians 1–7, 15, and at least one from Romans 3–8. Of the passages printed in English only, at least one will be taken from 1 Corinthians 1–7, 15, and at least one from Romans 3–8; however, candidates from Track I may restrict their comment to texts printed in English if their other papers include translation and/or comment on at least two passages of Hebrew. Candidates for Track II or Track III or for the Joint School of Philosophy and Theology may restrict their comment to passages printed in English.

(4) *The Development of Doctrine in the Early Church to AD 451*

Candidates will be expected to explain how early Christian thinkers undertook to clarify the teachings of the primitive Church and formulate a coherent system of thought in their cultural context. The paper will not only concern itself with formal pronouncements on the doctrines of the Trinity and Incarnation, but also with other controversies and the contributions of particular theologians.

Questions relevant to the Gnostic, Arian, Nestorian and Pelagian controversies will always be set; other questions may relate, wholly or partly, to such topics as anthropology, soteriology, hermeneutics, ecclesiology, political theology, and the doctrine of creation and the fall. Candidates will be required to comment on a passage from one of the following texts or group of texts:

The Nicene Definition, Arius' Letter to Eusebius, Arius' Letter to Alexander (from E. R. Hardy, *Christology of the Later Fathers*, Library of Christian Classics).

Gregory of Nyssa, *That there are not Three Gods* (in Hardy, *op. cit.*).

Cyril's Second Letter to Nestorius (in R. A. Norris, *The Christological Controversy*, Philadelphia: Fortress Press).

The tome of Leo and the Chalcedonian Definition (in Norris *op. cit.*).

Credit will be given to candidates who show knowledge (where appropriate) of the other texts contained in Norris.

(5) *God, Christ, and Salvation*

Candidates will be expected to answer questions on topics in modern theology, from the early twentieth century through to the present, with particular reference to the doctrine of God, Christology, and soteriology. Special emphasis will be placed on the interrelationship between these three topics and on the way in which their treatment is affected by differing understandings of the nature, the sources, and the practice of theology. Candidates will be expected to be aware of the interplay of tradition, innovation and confessional context in the work of major systematic theologians of the twentieth century. All candidates should be able to use prescribed texts in an appropriate manner.

(6) *Further Studies in New Testament and Christian Origins*

Candidates will be expected to study one particular subject area concerned with New Testament texts and/or related literature. In the Michaelmas Term of each year, the Board of the Faculty of Theology will publish a list of options on which teaching will be provided in the following academic year and on which the examination will be based. The options offered may vary from year to year and will be related to the research interests of the teachers concerned.

(7) *The History and Theology of Western Christianity, 1050–1350*

The paper will consist of questions on the thought of the leading theologians (especially Anselm, Peter Abelard, Aquinas, Duns Scotus, and William of Ockham), and of questions on the main developments in the western church. It will be so set that any period of 150 years, with its theological writers, will provide sufficient coverage.

(8) *The History and Theology of Western Christianity, 1500–1648*

The subject includes the work and thought of the leading mainstream Protestant reformers, especially Luther, Zwingli, and Calvin, together with the radicals, and the development of the Reformation in European society. Questions will be set both on renewal in the Roman Catholic Church throughout Europe, the confessional tensions which led to the Thirty Years' War (1618-48) and on religious change in the kingdom of England from the Henrician reforms through to the reign of Charles I and the downfall of his government and Church.

(9) EITHER

A. *Christian Life and Thought in Europe and the English-Speaking World, 1789–1921*

Candidates will be expected to show knowledge of the life and thought of the Christian churches of Europe and North America in their social and political context (with special reference to Britain) and the development and influence of Roman Catholic and Protestant theology in the context of Europe (including Britain) and North America. Candidates may approach the topic through the works of theologically important writers of the period, as well as other historical materials. Such writers might typically include S.T. Coleridge, J.H. Newman, F.D. Maurice, G. Tyrrell, E. Underhill and P.T. Forsyth in Britain; R.W. Emerson, W. James, H. Bushnell, and W. Rauschenbusch in the USA; and F.D.E. Schleiermacher, G.W.F. Hegel, K. Marx, L. Feuerbach, S. Kierkegaard, F.R. de Lamennais, A. Harnack, A. Loisy and K. Barth in Europe.

OR

B. *Issues in Theology, 1789–1921*

The paper addresses key issues in theological thinking in Britain and Europe during the long nineteenth century. These include biblical interpretation, the nature of authority, reason and faith, ecclesiology, Christology, romanticism, literature and imagination, spirit and history, reductionism, religious experience, and the encounter with world religions. The topics will be addressed through seminal or representative texts. Kant, Hegel, Schleiermacher, Kierkegaard, Nietzsche, Newman and Coleridge are especially significant thinkers whose work or influence will normally be represented in the paper. Four main topics with prescribed texts will be published for each year.

(10) *Further Studies in History and Doctrine*

Candidates will be expected to study one major theologian in relation to the situation and problems of the time, with special attention to certain texts. In the Michaelmas Term of the year preceding the year of examination the Board of the Faculty of Theology and Religion will publish a list of theologians (with texts) on which teaching will be provided in the following academic year and on which the examination will be based. In the event of a candidate's opting to take a year out after having studied a chosen theologian, the examiners will set questions on that theologian in the year of that candidate's examination, even if that theologian is not available for study that year. Texts will be studied in English. One or two optional questions may be set which will require knowledge of the texts in original languages when these are other than English.

A candidate may offer a second major theologian from amongst those available in the year of his or her examination. In the event that a candidate does choose to offer a second major theologian, that candidate will offer paper 10 as two papers. To facilitate this, separate papers (10(*a*), 10(*b*) etc.) will be set for each major theologian.

(11) *Philosophy of Religion*

The subject will include an examination of claims about the existence of God, and God's relation to the world: their meaning, the possibility of their truth, and the kind of justification which can or needs to be provided for them, and the philosophical problems raised by the existence of different religions. One or two questions may also be set on central claims peculiar to Christianity, such as the doctrines of the Trinity, Incarnation, and Atonement.

(12) *Christian Moral Reasoning*

Candidates will be expected to elucidate and assess themes in Christian traditions of moral reasoning in relation to major ethical writings and contemporary moral and social debates. The paper will consist of three sections: (A) Christian Moral Concepts; (B) Prescribed Texts; (C) Concrete Moral Issues.

Candidates will be required to answer one question from each section.

A. *Christian Moral Concepts*

Methodological issues such as the moral roles of Scripture, and the relation of Scripture to other moral sources (e.g., reason, theological and philosophical traditions, experience); and basic concepts such as the good, worship, sanctification, freedom, natural law, divine command, discipleship, virtue, love, justice, and double effect.

B. *Prescribed Texts*

Augustine, *On Christian Doctrine*, bk.1 (trans. R.P.H. Green, Oxford University Press)

Thomas Aquinas, *Summa Theologiae*, Ia IIae, pp.91–4 (trans. Thomas Gilby, Blackfriars ed., vol.28, Eyre & Spottiswood)

Martin Luther, "The Freedom of a Christian" (trans. W.A. Lambert, Harold J. Grimm, *Luther's Works*, vol.31, Fortress Press)

Dietrich Bonhoeffer, "Christ, Reality and Good", in *Ethics* (*Works*, vol. 6, ed. C. Green, Fortress Press).

C. *Concrete Moral Issues*

Sexual, medical, and political.

(13) *The Nature of Religion*

The paper will consist of questions on the main classical and contemporary approaches to the Study of Religions. It includes an overview of methods of both the humanities and the social sciences, essentialist approaches as well as historical and social scientific approaches. Candidates should be aware of the main debates in the Study of Religions, from the debate concerning the definition of 'Religion' to post-modern topics of gender and post-colonialism. The course addresses issues involved in claims for religious truth and rationality, of 20th century discussions of religious conflict and diversity, and of inter-religious dialogue. It focuses on phenomenological descriptive studies as well as studies in explaining religion.

(14) *The Formation of Rabbinic Judaism (Judaism I)*

This paper examines the history of rabbinic Judaism from the first century CE to the Renaissance against the background of the societies in which it flourished. Candidates will be required to comment on passages from the prescribed texts in English, and will be given an opportunity to comment upon the Hebrew text of certain selected passages. Also, discussion of the relation of Judaism to other religious traditions may be included.

(15) *Judaism in History and Society (Judaism II)*

This paper examines the nature of modern Judaism against the background of recent history, including such topics as: the impact on Jewish thought and society of the Enlightenment and the Emancipation; the growth of Hasidism in the eighteenth and Reform in the nineteenth century; responses to the Holocaust, to the establishment of the State of Israel, and to the women's movement. Also, discussion of the relation of Judaism to other religious traditions may be included.

(16) *The Classical Period of Islam (Islam I)*

The paper covers the historical origins and development of the theology, law and mysticism of Islam, from the seventh to the fifteenth centuries. It will consist of questions on the Prophethood of Muhammad; the Quran; the Hadith; Shiism; the theologies of the Mutazilis, Asharis, and Hanbalis; Sufism (*tasawwuf*) and the major

Sufi orders; and classical Muslim authorities. Candidates should be aware of the various interpretative methods relating to Muslim Scripture, the main debates and historical controversies of the Islamic tradition, and of contemporary methodologies in philosophy of religion. References to other religious traditions may be included.

(17) *Islam in the Modern World (Islam II)*

The paper examines Islam against the background of recent history, including such topics as: Islamic reformism in the nineteenth to the twenty-first centuries; various Islamic movements including the anti-Hadith faction and Wahhabism; women and Islam; democracy and Islam; violence and war in Islam; and various modern Muslim thinkers.

(18) *Early Buddhist Doctrine and Practice (Buddhism I)*

The earliest Buddhist doctrine is studied against the background of the early Upanishads and other religious movements in north-east India about the fifth century BC. Practice includes both meditation and monastic life. The primary source is the Pali Canon supplemented by the commentarial literature of the Theravadin tradition.

(19) *Buddhism in History and Society (Buddhism II)*

The paper falls into two main parts. The first part covers the history of Buddhism's diffusion through Asia, beginning with the emperor Asoka (third century BC); what forms of Buddhism have dominated which states and societies (and when), and their main similarities and differences; the development of Buddhist institutions. The second part deals with Buddhism in modern Asia.

(20) *Hinduism I: Sources and Development*

This paper offers a thematic and historical introduction to the sources and early development of "Hindu" traditions from their early formation to the early medieval period. We will explore the formation of Hindu traditions through textual sources, such as the Vedas, Upaniṣads and Bhagavad Gītā, along with the practices and social institutions that formed classical Hindu traditions. The lectures will include an introduction to Hindu philosophy.

(21) *Hinduism II: Hindu Traditions*

Beginning with the early medieval period, this paper traces the development of Hinduism in devotional (bhakti) and tantric traditions. The paper examines the development of Śaiva, Śākta, and Vaiṣṇava traditions along with ideas about liberation, ritual, asceticism, yoga and devotion. There will be some exploration of Hinduism and Modernity and there may also be reference to major schools of Hindu philosophy such as Vedānta.

(22) *Selected topics (Old Testament) I*

Candidates will be required to show detailed knowledge of one of the following topics. They will be required to comment on passages from the prescribed texts in English (New Revised Standard Version), and will be given an opportunity to comment upon the Hebrew text of certain specified chapters and sections.

  (i) *Prophecy*
    1 Samuel 9; 10
    2 Samuel 7
    1 Kings 13; 18; 22
    Isaiah 1; 5–8; 10; 40; 42–4; 49; 51–3; 55
    Jeremiah 1–5; 7–9; 11; 12; 26–8; 31
    Ezekiel 1–4; 8–11; 14; 18; 20; 23; 36; 37
    Amos 1–5; 6–9
    Zechariah 1–8; 13

Among these the following may be offered in Hebrew:
> 1 Kings 13; 18; 22
> Isaiah 42–4
> Amos 1–5

(ii) *Apocalyptic*
> Isaiah 24–7
> Daniel
> Zechariah
> 1 Enoch 1–16 (ed. H. F. D. Sparks, *The Apocryphal Old Testament*, OUP, 1984)
> 2 Esdras 3–14
> Revelation
> Among these the following may be offered in Hebrew:
> Isaiah 24–7
> Zechariah 9–14

(23) *Selected topics (Old Testament) II*

Candidates will be required to show detailed knowledge of one of the following topics. They will be required to comment on passages from the prescribed texts in English (New Revised Standard Version), and will be given an opportunity to comment upon the Hebrew text of certain selected chapters and sections.

(1) *Wisdom*
> Proverbs 1–9; 22:17–31:31
> Job 1–19; 38–42
> Ecclesiastes
> Wisdom of Solomon 1–9
> Ecclesiasticus (Sirach) Prologue; 1:1–25:12; 36:18–43:33; 51
> Among these the following may be offered in Hebrew:
> Proverbs 1–9

(ii) *Worship and Liturgy*
> Exodus 12–15; 19; 20; 24
> Leviticus 1–7; 16
> Deuteronomy 12–18
> 1 Kings 5–8
> 1 Chronicles 16
> Psalms 2; 18; 24; 27; 47–51; 68; 72; 78; 89; 95–100; 110; 113–18; 122; 124; 126; 128; 130–2
> A. E. Cowley, *Aramaic Papyri of the Fifth Century BC* (OUP, 1923), nos. 21; 30–4
> Among these the following may be offered in Hebrew:
> Exodus 19; 20; 24
> Leviticus 16
> Psalms 24; 95–100

(24) *The Hebrew of the Old Testament*

Candidates will be required to show a general knowledge of the language, with a special study of the following prose texts from which passages will be set for translation and comment:
> Genesis 6–9
> Deuteronomy 5–6; 12; 26
> 2 Samuel 11–14
> 1 Kings 17–19
> Jonah

Candidates will also be given an opportunity to show knowledge of Hebrew verse, and especially of the following texts, from which passages will be set for translation and comment:

Psalms 1; 2; 8; 45–48; 96
Proverbs 7–9
Isaiah 1–2; 6; 40–42

Candidates who do not offer Hebrew verse will not thereby be penalized.

(25) *Archaeology in relation to the Old Testament*

The subject includes the geography of Palestine and of the neighbouring lands; the history of the development of Canaanite, Hebrew and Jewish social life and culture; the history of places of worship and their furniture; and the general results of recent archaeological research in the Ancient Near East, insofar as they throw light on these subjects.

(26) *Religions and Mythology of the Ancient Near East*

The paper will include a wide range of questions. The following texts are prescribed for special study:

(a) Akkadian Myths and Epics: The Epic of Creation, in B.R. Foster, *Before the Muses: An Anthology of Akkadian Literature* (3rd edition, Bethesda: CDL Press, 2005), pp. 439–85, and The Epic of Gilgamesh (standard version), in A. George, *The Epic of Gilgamesh* (revised edition, London: Penguin, 2003), pp. 1–100, 191–5.

(b) Egyptian Myths, Hymns and Prayers: in M. Lichtheim, *Ancient Egyptian Literature* (Berkeley: University of California Press, 1973–1980; republished 2006), vol. I, pp. 51–7, 131–3; vol. II, pp. 81–132, 197–9, 203–23.

(c) Hittite Myths: The Disappearance of Telipinu (version 1) and The Song of Kumarbi, in H.A. Hoffner, *Hittite Myths* (2nd edition, Atlanta: Scholars Press, 1998), pp. 15–18, 42–5.

(d) Ugaritic Myths: The Baal Cycle, in W.W. Hallo (ed.), *The Context of Scripture* (Leiden: Brill, 1997; republished 2003), vol. I, pp. 243–73, 'The Ba'lu Myth' (trans. D. Pardee).

(e) Philo of Byblos' Phoenician History, in H.W. Attridge and R.A. Oden, *Philo of Byblos: The Phoenician History* (Washington: Catholic Biblical Association of America, 1981), pp. 29–71.

(f) The Sefire Inscriptions, in W.W. Hallo (ed.), *The Context of Scripture* (Leiden: Brill, 2000; republished 2003), vol. II, pp. 213–17, 'The Inscriptions of Bar-Ga'yah and Mati'el from Sefire' (trans. J.A. Fitzmyer).

(27) *The New Testament in Greek*

Candidates will choose passages for translation from amongst a number taken from the Greek New Testament. The text used will be that of the United Bible Societies, 4th edn. The selection of passages will allow candidates to select passages for translation from the following texts and chapters: Acts 20–6, Colossians, 1 and 2 Thessalonians, Hebrews 7–10, James, 1 and 2 Peter, Revelation 1–12. There will also be opportunity to translate passages from outside these specified chapters.

NB. This paper is not available as a full paper but only as an optional extra translation paper.

(28) *Varieties of Judaism 100 BC–AD 100*

The paper will include a number of general questions and the following texts are prescribed for special study:

Set texts in English:

Qumran Community Rule, MMT (Miqsat Ma'ase Ha-Torah) (Some Observances of the Law) and *Commentary on Habakkuk*, in G. Vermes, *The Complete Dead Sea Scrolls in English* (Allen Lane/Penguin, 1997).

Josephus, *Jewish War* II (Loeb, 1956); *Antiquities* XVIII, 1–119 (Loeb, 1965); *Against Apion* II, 145–296 (Loeb, 1956).

IV Ezra, ed. B. M. Metzger, in J. H. Charlesworth, ed., *The Old Testament Pesudepigrapha* (2 vols., DLT, 1983–5).

Wisdom of Solomon (New Revised Standard Version).   5

Philo, *Migration of Abraham; Life of Moses* I, 1–84 (Loeb, 1958).

Mishnah, Berakoth, Bikkurim, and Aboth, chapter 1 (translated Danby, OUP, 1933).

Psalms of Solomon XVII, tr. S. P. Brock, in H. F. D. Sparks, ed., *The Apocryphal Old Testament* (OUP, 1984).   10

I Enoch 92–105, tr. M. A. Knibb, in Sparks, *op. cit.*

Any or all of the following texts may be offered in the original languages. Such questions will only be set when a candidate or candidates have given notice on the entry form of an intention to comment on texts in Hebrew and/or Greek.

Qumran Community Rule 1–4, in E. Lohse (ed.), *Die Texte aus Qumran, Hebräisch*   15
und Deutsch (2nd edn., Darmstadt, Wissenschaftliche Buchgesellschaft, 1971).

Qumran Commentary on Habakkuk, ed. E. Lohse, *op. cit.*

Josephus, *Antiquities* XVIII, 1–28, 63–4, 109–19 (Loeb, 1965).

Philo, *Life of Moses* I, 1–44 (Loeb, 1958).

(29) *Christian Liturgy*   20

Candidates will be expected to study the rites of initiation and the eucharist up to AD 451, the relationship between liturgy and theology and the influence of early Christian worship on contemporary liturgical revision.

Candidates will be expected to have studied the following texts. Texts shown in square brackets will not be examined by gobbets.   25

E. C. Whitaker (ed. M.E. Johnson), *Documents of the Baptismal Liturgy* (3rd edn., SPCK, 2003) pp.1–11, [11–13], 14–21, 40–50, 124–7, 176–83.

R. C. D. Jasper and G.J. Cuming, *Prayers of the Eucharist: Early and Reformed* (3rd edn., Pueblo, 1987) pp.7–12, 20–44, [52–66], 67–81, 88–99, 114–23, 129–37, 143–6, 159–67.   30

E. J. Yarnold, *The Awe-Inspiring Rites of Initiation* (2nd edn., T. & T. Clark. 1994) pp. [70–5], 76–97.

[Church of England, *Common Worship* (Church House Publishing, 2000), Eucharistic Prayers B & F, 188–90, 198–200].

[Church of England, *Common Worship: Initiation Services* (Church House   35
Publishing, 2005)].

[Methodist Church, *Methodist Worship Book* (Methodist Publishing House, 1999), The Baptism of those who are able to answer for themselves, and of Young Children, with Confirmation and Reception into Membership, 62–75; Eucharistic Prayer for Ordinary Seasons (3), 215–17].   40

[Roman Catholic Church, *The Roman Missal* (ICEL, 1973), Eucharistic Prayers 2 & 4]

[Roman Catholic Church, *The Rite of Christian Initiation of Adults* (ICEL, 1985)]

[M. Thurian and G. Wainwright (eds.), *Baptism and Eucharist: Ecumenical Texts in Convergence* (WCC Publications, 1983), Eucharistic Prayer from the Eucharistic   45
Liturgy of Lima, 252–4].

(30) *Early Syriac Christianity*

Candidates will be expected to show a general knowledge of symbolism in the theology of the early Syriac Church.

The following texts are prescribed for special study: 50

Odes of Solomon 6, 11, 17, 19, 21, 24, 30, 36, 42, tr. J. A. Emerton in H. F. D. Sparks. *The Apocryphal Old Testament* (OUP, 1984).

Acts of Thomas, secs. 1–29, 108–14, tr. A. F. J. Klijn (E. J. Brill, 1962).

Aphrahat, *Demonstrations* 1, 4, 6, 12 (*Dem.* 1 and 6 tr. in J. Gwynn, ed. *Select Library of Nicene and Post-Nicene Fathers* II.13 [1898, repr. W. B. Eerdmans, 1956], Dem. 4, tr. S. P. Brock, *The Syriac Fathers on Prayer and the Spiritual Life* [1987], ch. 1; *Dem.* 12, tr. in J. Neusner, *Aphrahat and Judaism* [E. J. Brill, 1971]).

Ephrem, *Sermon on Our Lord*, tr. in E. Mathews and J. Amar, *St Ephrem the Syrian. Selected Prose Works* (1994); *Hymns on the Nativity*, nos. 1 and 2, tr. K. McVey, *St Ephrem the Syrian*. Hymns (*Classics of Western Spirituality*, 1989); *Hymns on Faith*, no. 10, *Hymns on the Church*, no. 36, *Hymns on Epiphany*, nos. 1 and 6, tr. S. P. Brock in T. Finn, *Early Christian Baptism and the Catechumenate* (1992). The Hymns, tr. S. P. Brock, *The Harp of the Spirit: Eighteen Poems of St Ephrem* (Fellowship of St Alban and St Sergius, 2nd edn. 1983). *Letter to Publius*, tr. S. P. Brock, *Le Muséon* (1976). *Book of Steps*, Homily 12, tr. R. Murray, *Symbols of Church and Kingdom* (CUP, 1975).

(31) *History and Theology of the Church in the Byzantine Empire from AD 1000 to AD 1453*

Candidates will be expected to show knowledge of the constitution and worship of the Church; monasticism; the development of mystical theology; the relations between Church and state and with the Western Church.

(32) *Science and Religion*

Candidates will be expected to have an understanding of the richness and diversity of the relations between science and religion as they have been constructed in western cultures. They should be able to analyse the simplistic models of conflict and harmony, which have so often served ideological purposes. Questions will be set on the role of religious belief in the rise of modern science and on the challenge to religious orthodoxies from new forms of science. There will be questions on the religious beliefs of major scientists, such as Newton and Darwin, on the responses of theologians to major paradigm shifts within the sciences, and on the interplay between natural theology and the natural sciences. The examination will also provide an opportunity for candidates to discuss current issues such as the most appropriate response theologians might make to contemporary neuroscience and genetic reductionism. Questions may also be set on recurrent issues such as the presumed existence of extraterrestrial life.

(33) *The Sociology of Religion*

The paper will consist of two parts. Candidates will be expected to answer at least one question from each part.

(a) *Texts*

Candidates will be expected to know at least one of the following in detail:

    (i) Karl Marx, *Marx on Religion*, ed. John Raines, Temple University Press, 2002 together with *Capital*, chapters 1 and 13 (Penguin Books, 1990).

    (ii) E. Durkheim, *The Elementary Forms of the Religious Life* (Allen and Unwin, 1976).

    (iii) M. Weber, *The Protestant Ethic and the Spirit of Capitalism* (Harper Collins, 1991).

    (iv) E. Troeltsch, *The Social Teaching of the Christian Churches* (2 vols., J. Knox, 1992).

    (v) Talcott Parsons, *Action Theory and the Human Condition* (New York, 1978).

(*b*) *Themes*

Candidates will be expected to show an understanding of some of the following issues in sociology of religion: secularization, fundamentalism, church and sect, new religious movements, civil religion. Questions will also be set on issues relating to class, race, legitimation, power and violence in religion and religious organization; and sociological readings of other parts of the Theology syllabus, including Biblical studies, doctrine and Church history. Familiarity with contemporary sociological discussion will be assumed.

(34) *Mysticism*

Candidates will be expected to show knowledge of theoretical issues relating to the definition and interpretation of mysticism as well as important examples of mystical literature and traditions. The paper will be examined by two 5000 word essays: one essay, chosen from a list of prescribed titles, will address theoretical issues; the other will relate to a special topic. The subject of the second essay will be chosen by candidates in consultation with tutors. Prior approval of the subject of the second essay must be obtained in advance from the Faculty Board. Titles, abstracts and bibliographies should reach the Faculty Board Secretary not later than the beginning of fifth week in Trinity Term of the candidate's second year.

Possible subjects for essays include, but will not be limited to: Neoplatonism, hermetic and alchemical speculations, the Origenist tradition in Christianity, the Dionysian tradition, Rhineland mystics, medieval English mystics, Counter-Reformation mystics, Merkabah mysticism, Hekhalot mysticism, Ismaili and Sufi traditions, Upanishadic thought, Vedanta philosophy, Tantric traditions, Buddhist traditions.

(35) *Psychology of Religion*

Psychology of religion is concerned with human experience and behaviour associated with religion in general. Psychological explanations of religion are based on empirical research of human behaviour (cognitive, emotional, and social) through life span and across different cultures.

The paper will cover theories about aspects of behaviour or experiences relevant to religion and the empirical evidence on these theories: psychological research of different aspects of religion such as conversion, prayer, mysticism; cognitive and affective (i.e. psychoanalytic) accounts of religion; origin and development of religious concepts; normal and abnormal religious experience and behaviour; religious and secular moral behaviour; applications of psychology to religious education and health.

(36) *English Church and Mission* 597–754

Candidates will be expected to study the main lines of the history of the English Church in this period, and some aspects of its theology. There will also be an opportunity to study works of art. Candidates will be expected to have studied the texts in Group I, on which alone gobbets will be set, and in at least one of sections (*a*), (*b*), (*c*) in Group II.

Group I

(*a*) Bede, *Ecclesiastical History of the English People*, Preface, Books I, 23–26; II; III; IV; V, 9–10, 19 (trans. B. Colgrave, in: *Bede: the Ecclesiastical History of the English People*; *The Greater Chronicle*; *Bede's Letter to Egbert*, ed. Judith McClure and Roger Collins, OUP, 1994) pp. 37–41, 63–233, 247–51, 267–74.

(*b*) Bede's *Letter to Egbert*, trans. D. H. Farmer, ibid., pp. 337–51.

(*c*) Bede, *On the Temple*, trans. S. Connolly, in J. O'Reilly (Liverpool University Press: *Translated Texts for Historians* 21, 1995), Prologue and Book I to I, 8.4, pp. 1–33; Book II, 18.8 to 20.9, pp. 76–100.

(*d*) Eddius Stephanus, *Life of Wilfrid in The Age of Bede* (ed. D. H. Farmer, trans. J. Webb, Penguin Classics, 1988) pp. 105–82.

(*e*) 'The Dream of the Rood', in *A Choice of Anglo-Saxon Verse*, ed. and trans. R. Hamer (Faber, 1970), pp. 161–71.

Group II

(*a*) Adomnan of Iona, *Life of St Columba*, ed. and trans. R. Sharpe (Penguin Classics, 1995).

(*b*) Bede, *Life of Cuthbert*, in *The Age of Bede* (Penguin Classics, 1988), pp. 41–102, Bede, *Lives of the Abbots of Wearmouth and Jarrow*, ibid., pp. 185–208.

Bede's *Homily on the Gospel for the Feast of St Benedict Biscop*, in Bede, *Homilies on the Gospels*, trans. L. T. Martin and D. Hurst, Preface by B. Ward (Cistercian Studies Series, 110, 1991), pp. 125–32.

Letters of Aldhelm, in Aldhelm, *The Prose Works*, trans. M. Lapidge and M. Herren (Boydell and Brewer, 1979), pp. 152–70.

(*c*) Willibald's *Life of St Boniface* and *The Correspondence of St Boniface*, in C. H. Talbot, *The Anglo-Saxon Missionaries in Germany* (Stead and Ward, 1954), pp. 25–62, 65–149.

(37) Any other subject that may be approved by the Board of the Faculty of Theology from time to time by regulation published in the Gazette and communicated to college tutors by the end of the first week of the Trinity Full Term in the academic year preceding the examination in which the option will be available.

Optional translation papers (2 hours each)

The translation component of paper (24), *The Hebrew of the Old Testament*, may be offered as an optional extra paper by candidates who are not taking the full paper. Paper (27), *The New Testament in Greek*, may also be offered as an optional extra translation paper.

SPECIAL REGULATIONS FOR THE HONOUR SCHOOL OF THEOLOGY AND ORIENTAL STUDIES

A

1. The subjects of the Honour School of Theology and Oriental Studies shall be 1 Theology and 2 Oriental Studies. All candidates must offer both 1 and 2.

2. The Honour School of Theology and Oriental Studies shall be under the joint supervision of the Boards of the Faculties of Theology and Religion, and of Oriental Studies, which shall appoint a standing joint committee to make, and to submit to the two boards, proposals for regulations concerning the examination.

3. No candidate shall be admitted to the examination in this School unless he or she has either passed or been exempted from the First Public Examination.

4. The Public Examiners in this School shall be such of the Public Examiners in the Honour Schools of Theology and of Oriental Studies as may be required, together with any additional examiners who may be required who shall be nominated by the committee for the nomination of Public Examiners in one or both of those Honour Schools as appropriate.

B

1. In the Honour School candidates will take eight papers, of which at least three and not more than five must be taken in Theology, and at least three and not more than five must be taken in Oriental Studies. One paper will be examined in the form of a dissertation. Completion of an application form will be required for the approval of the subject of the dissertation, indicating the paper for which it is substituting. In all cases the regulations that apply to the dissertation will be the Theology and Religion regulations, except for the date for submission of the title for approval, which will be sixth week in Hilary Term of Year 2. The request for approval should be addressed to the relevant Faculty Board Secretary using the application form available from the relevant Faculty Office. The application should include, in about 100 words, an explanation as to how the topic will be treated, and a brief bibliography.

Candidates should in general aim at a length of 10,000 words, but must not exceed 15,000 words (both figures inclusive of notes and appendices, but excluding bibliography). The candidate is advised to have an initial discussion with his or her supervisor regarding the proposed field of study, the sources available, and the method of presentation. He or she should have further discussions with his or her supervisor during the preparation of the dissertation. His or her supervisor may read and comment on drafts of the dissertation.

Every candidate shall sign a letter declaring the dissertation to be his or her own work and that it has not already been submitted (wholly or substantially) for a final honour school other than one involving Theology or Oriental Studies, or another degree of this University, or a degree of any other institution. This letter, which can be found in the Course Handbook or collected from the relevant Faculty Office, shall be presented together with the dissertation. No dissertation shall, however, be ineligible because it has been or is being submitted for any prize of this University.

The candidate must submit two typed copies of the dissertation (bound or held firmly in a stiff cover), addressed to the Chair of the Examiners, Honour School of Theology and Oriental Studies, Examination Schools, High Street, Oxford not later than noon on the Friday of the eighth week of Hilary Term in the academic year in which he or she is presenting himself or herself for examination. The letter of declaration signed by the candidate must be submitted separately in a sealed envelope addressed to the Chair of the Examiners at the above address at the same time as the copies are submitted.

2. Candidates who offer some papers in Oriental Studies will be precluded from taking papers in Theology that have a similar content. A list of combinations of papers that are not permitted will be published in the course handbook two years before the examination.

1. Theology

Candidates will be required to offer *either*: God and Israel in the Old Testament (as for the Honour School of Theology Paper 1)

or The Gospels and Jesus (with special reference to the gospels of Matthew and John) (as for the Honour School of Theology Paper 2)

and either: The Development of Doctrine in the Early Church to AD 451 (as for the Honour School of Theology Paper 4)

or God, Christ and Salvation (as for the Honour School of Theology Paper 5) and may take up to three other papers chosen from the Theology FHS.

2. Oriental Studies

The Oriental Studies papers may be chosen from any one of the following sections: 1 Buddhism, 2 Eastern Christianity, 3 Hinduism, 4 Islam, and 5 Judaism.

Choice and availability of options. It cannot be guaranteed that teaching will be available on all papers in every academic year. Similarly, the choice of subject for the dissertation will necessarily depend upon availability of a suitable supervisor. Candidates should therefore consult with their tutors about the availability of teaching when selecting their optional and dissertation subjects.

Approval of choice of options. Applications for the approval of all options and papers must be submitted to the Undergraduate Studies Committee of the Faculty Board of Oriental Studies by Monday of the sixth week of Hilary Term in the academic year preceding that in which the examination is taken.

1. *Buddhism*

1. Pali, Sanskrit, *or* Tibetan language
  either (*a*) A Buddhist canonical language: Pali
  or   (*b*) A Buddhist canonical language: Tibetan
  or   (*c*) A Buddhist canonical language: Sanskrit
2. Pali texts, Sanskrit texts, *or* second Tibetan language paper
  either (*a*) Set texts in a Buddhist canonical language: Pali
  or   (*b*) Set texts in a Buddhist canonical language: Tibetan
  or   (*c*) Set texts in a Buddhist canonical language: Sanskrit
3. Early Buddhist Doctrine and Practice (Buddhism I) (as for the Honour School of Theology Paper 18)
4. Buddhism in History and Society (Buddhism II) (as for the Honour School of Theology Paper 19)

5. Further Buddhist texts
either (*a*) Further Buddhist texts: Pali
or   (*b*) Further Buddhist Texts: Tibetan
or   (*c*) Further Buddhist Texts: Sanskrit
Candidates will be required to take paper 1 and up to four other papers. Students
must choose the same language in papers 1, 2 and 5.

2. *Eastern Christianity*
   1. Armenian *or* Syriac language
   2. Early Armenian theological and ecclesiastical texts *or* Early Syriac Christianity
      (Armenian as for the Honour School of Oriental Studies, ADDITIONAL
      LANGUAGES, Armenian, A. Classical Armenian, Paper 2. Prepared religions
      texts; Early Syriac Christianity as for FHS Theology Paper 32)
   3. Armenian historical texts *or* Syriac biblical and exegetical texts (Armenian as
      for FHS Oriental Studies, ADDITIONAL LANGUAGES, Armenian, A.
      Classical Armenian, Paper 3. Prepared historical and other texts, but excluding
      essay questions on literature, etc.)
   4. Armenian *or* Syriac poetry (Armenian as for FHS Oriental Studies, ADDITIONAL
      LANGUAGES, Armenian, A. Classical Armenian, Paper 3. Prepared historical
      and other texts, but excluding essay questions on literature, etc.)
   5. Armenian Christology and the development of doctrine *or* Syriac theology and
      mystical texts.
Candidates will be required to take paper 1 and up to four other papers.

3. *Hinduism*
   1. Sanskrit language and texts I
   2. Sanskrit language and texts II
   3. Hinduism I: Sources and Development (as for the Honour School of Theology
      Paper 20)
   4. Texts on the nature of dharma
   5. Vedic religion and Brahmanism
   6. Shaiva Doctrine and Practice
Candidates will be required to take papers 1, 2 and 3, and up to two other papers.

4. *Islam*
   1. Translation from Classical Arabic
   2. Islamic Texts (as for the Honour School of Oriental Studies, ADDITIONAL
      LANGUAGES, Arabic Paper 3. Additional Arabic: Islamic texts)
   3. Hadith (as for the Honour School of Oriental Studies, Arabic and Islamic
      Studies, Paper 7. i.)
   4. Medieval Sufi thought (as for the Honour School of Oriental Studies, Arabic
      and Islamic Studies, Paper 7. ix.)
   5. A modern Islamic thinker (as for the Honour School of Oriental Studies, Arabic
      and Islamic Studies, Paper 7. xvi.)
   6. Topics in Islamic Law (The Honour School of Oriental Studies, Arabic and
      Islamic Studies, Paper 9 iv.)
Candidates will be required to take papers 1 and 2 and may take up to three other
papers. Teaching may not be available for all of papers 3–6 in every year.

5. *Judaism*
   1. Classical Jewish Texts and Language
   2. Second Temple Judaism (as for the Honour School of Oriental Studies, Jewish
      Studies, b. Section II. (e))
   3. The Formation of Rabbinic Judaism (as for the Honour School of Theology,
      The Formation of Rabbinic Judaism (Judaism 1), Paper 14)

4. History of Jewish-Christian Relations (as for the Honour School of Oriental Studies, Jewish Studies, b. Section IV. (o))

5. History of Jewish-Muslim Relations (as for the Honour School of Oriental Studies, Jewish Studies, b. Section IV. (p))

6. History of Jewish Bible Interpretation (as for the Honour School of Oriental Studies, Jewish Studies, b. Section IV. (q))

7. Modern Judaism (as for the Honour School of Oriental Studies, Jewish Studies, b. Section V. (v)).

Candidates will be required to take paper 1 and up to four other papers. Lists of set texts will be published in the handbook.

3

REGULATIONS FOR THE DEGREE OF
BACHELOR OF THEOLOGY

General Regulations

1. The examination for the Degree of Bachelor of Theology shall be under the supervision of the Board of Faculty of Theology and Religion which shall have power to make regulations governing the examination.

2. Any person who has been admitted under the provisions of this section as a Student for the Degree of Bachelor of Theology, who has satisfied the conditions prescribed in this section, and who has satisfied the examiners for the degree may supplicate for the Degree of Bachelor of Theology.

3. No full-time student for the Degree of Bachelor of Theology shall be granted leave to supplicate unless, after admission, he or she has kept statutory residence and pursued his or her course of study at Oxford for at least nine terms. Time spent outside Oxford as part of an academic programme approved by the faculty board shall count towards residence for the purposes of this clause.

4. No full-time student for the Degree of Bachelor of Theology shall retain that status for more than twelve terms in all.

5. Part-time students for the Degree of Bachelor of Theology shall in each case be required to pursue their course of study for twice the number of terms required of an equivalent full-time student. A student who takes the degree by two years full-time and the rest part-time shall retain the status of Student for the Degree of Bachelor of Theology for no more than fifteen terms. A student who takes the degree by one year full-time and the rest part-time shall retain that status for no more than eighteen terms. A student who takes the degree wholly part-time shall retain that status for no more than twenty-one terms. A student may transfer from full-time to part-time status or vice-versa with the approval of the B.Th. Supervisory Committee.

6. Part-time students shall not be required to keep statutory residence, but must attend for such instruction at their college for such times during full term as shall be required by the faculty board concerned, and must also attend at least one week's residential course each year, the total hours of attendance in each year of the course being as prescribed by the faculty board concerned.

7. Students for the Degree of Bachelor of Theology may transfer to the Certificate in Theology with the approval of the B.Th. Supervisory Committee.

8. The B.Th. Supervisory Committee will supervise arrangements for the Bachelor of Theology, the Certificate in Theology and the Certificate for Theology Graduates. This committee will elect its Chair, Secretary, and Treasurer. The Chair and Secretary will form a Standing Committee together with the Chair of Examiners for these courses. In addition to these officers, the committee will consist of two representatives of the Board of the Faculty of Theology and one representative of each of the participating institutions. The committee will have such powers and duties as may from time to time be prescribed by the Board of the Faculty of Theology and Religion.

9. Candidates for this degree may be admitted by Blackfriars; Campion Hall; Harris Manchester College; Mansfield College; Regent's Park College; Ripon College, Cuddesdon; St Benet's Hall; St Stephen's House; and Wycliffe Hall.

10. The Registrar shall keep a register of all candidates so admitted.

Special Regulations

A. REGULATIONS FOR THE COURSE OF INSTRUCTION AT BLACKFRIARS; CAMPION HALL; HARRIS MANCHESTER COLLEGE; MANSFIELD COLLEGE; REGENT'S PARK COLLEGE; RIPON COLLEGE, CUDDESDON; ST BENET'S HALL; ST STEPHEN'S HOUSE; AND WYCLIFFE HALL.

A.1 *Course requirements*

Candidates must take at least *twelve* papers. In Part 1 candidates must take all four papers. In Part 2 they must take at least: one paper from section B; either C1 or C4; and one paper from section D. Candidates, including those who take E9 twice, may take a maximum of four papers from section E. Only one paper may be taken from section F. The B.Th. Supervisory Committee may dispense a candidate from individual compulsory papers on the basis of previous academic work, but not from the total number of papers required.

Details of which subjects may or must be taken by two short essays or one long essay in place of written examination papers are given in the syllabus in section B below.

A.2 *Examinations*

Candidates will be examined at the end of each academic year of their course of study. Examination will be held in April or May, beginning on the Monday of the second week of Trinity Term, and in September or October, at the end of the second week before Michaelmas Full Term.

Every candidate shall send through his or her college an entry form, showing the subject he or she intends to take in that year, to the Examination Schools, High Street, Oxford OX1 4BG, by noon on Friday of the second week of Hilary Term for the May examination, and by noon on Friday of the seventh week of Trinity Term for the Autumn examination. All entries shall be accompanied by certification of college approval and by the examination fee prescribed in the appropriate regulation.

The examiners may examine the candidate viva voce, no candidate who has passed in a subject may sit that examination again.

A candidate who has failed in more than two subjects in an examination shall be deemed to have failed in all the subjects offered at that examination. A candidate may offer at a subsequent examination a subject or subjects in which he or she has failed. Normally only one resit will be allowed in each subject, provided that the B.Th. Supervisory Committee shall have power in exceptional circumstances and on submission of a case by a candidate's college to approve a second resit.

A.3 *Long Essays*

Approval for the subjects proposed for long essays must be obtained from the B.Th. Supervisory Committee by completing a Long Essay Title Form and submitting it to the Supervisory Committee by noon on the Friday of: Week Four of Michaelmas Term, Week Four of Hilary Term, or Week Six of Trinity Term.

A proposed title must cover a theme within the rubric of the paper. Candidates are advised to seek approval for titles as early as practicable in advance of the examination. After the Long Essay Title Form is returned with dated approval, it must be retained for submission with the completed work.

Long essays must be entirely the candidate's own work. Candidates may receive tutorial guidance in the early stages of composition, and tutors may read and comment on a first draft.

Candidates must submit two copies of each essay (marked A and B), which must be printed on a single side of paper. Each copy must have a standard title sheet, indicating essay title and candidate number (but not name or college) and word count (including footnotes but not bibliography). Candidates must also submit the approved Long Essay Title Form, with its final section now completed to confirm that the essay is entirely the candidate's own work and that a course of instruction covering the syllabus has been satisfactorily completed. These documents must be placed together in a sealed envelope, marked with the number and title of the paper and the candidate's examination number and addressed to the Chair of Examiners, Bachelor of Theology, Examination Schools, High Street, Oxford OX1 4BG. Long essays must be submitted by noon on the first Monday of Trinity Full Term for the Trinity Term examination, or the second Monday before Michaelmas Full Term for the Long Vacation examination.

Note. All communications for the Supervisory Committee for the Degree of Bachelor of Theology should be addressed to the Secretary of the B.Th. Supervisory Committee, whose address may be obtained from each college's B.Th. course director or from the Theology and Religion Faculty Centre, 34 St Giles', Oxford OX1 3LD.

B. THE SYLLABUS

† assessed by three-hour written examination

‡ assessed in Part I by two essays of 2,500 words (± 10%), whose titles are to be drawn from a list agreed by tutors and approved by the Supervisory Committee; and in Part II by a long essay of 5,000 words (± 10%), the title of which must be submitted to the Supervisory Committee for approval. Candidates must sign a declaration supported by their society that they have attended an appropriate course of instruction and have adequately covered the syllabus of the paper or, where specified, of the option(s) selected.

§ assessed by other means, as noted in the rubric.

Note that most papers may be examined by more than one means.

Full-time candidates must attempt all Part 1 papers in their first year. They may attempt Part 2 papers at any examination session following the first Trinity Term. Part-time candidates must attempt all Part 1 papers in their first two years. They may attempt Part 2 papers at any examination session after their first year, provided they have completed Part 1 or are completing it in the same session. Any candidate who withdraws from a Part I paper must also withdraw from all Part II papers entered in the same session.

Part 1 papers will be assessed at first year level, and will be given reduced weighting in considering a candidate's degree classification or certificate award.

In all written examinations candidates will be provided with a copy of the New Revised Standard Version with the Apocrypha (Anglicized Edition), except when they are answering questions on Hebrew or Greek texts. Those who wish to answer questions on Hebrew or Greek texts must specify this on their entry forms. The texts used in these cases will be: *The Greek New Testament* (United Bible Societies, 4th edn. 1993); *Biblia Hebraica Stuttgartensia* (Stuttgart, 1977).

PART 1

This part addresses fundamental issues of Biblical Study, Christian Thought and Christian Ministry, laying a foundation for further study.

SECTION A. Foundation Studies

†A.1—Old Testament A

Candidates will study the Pentateuch and the Prophetic Books, with particular reference to Genesis, Deuteronomy and Isaiah. They will study specific texts: *either* Genesis 1-3, 15-17, Deuteronomy 5-7, 12, 15-16 and Isaiah 5-11, 49-53 in English; *or* Genesis 1-4 or Jonah in Hebrew. Candidates who wish to prepare for assessment in Hebrew must enter for the written examination with texts in Hebrew. However, in the examination itself they may transfer to texts in English without penalty.

† A.2—New Testament A

Candidates will study Matthew and 1 Corinthians, and may also study Mark, addressing such issues as methodology in New Testament study, the person and ministry of Jesus, the context and theology of the authors, and ecclesiological issues. They will also study in detail *either* Matthew 9-10, 26-8 (with the option of Markan parallels) and 1 Corinthians 7-11 in English, *or* Matthew 9-10 in Greek, *or* 1 Corinthians 7-8 in Greek. Candidates who wish to prepare for assessment in Greek must enter for the written examination with texts in Greek. However, in the examination itself they may transfer to texts in English without penalty.

‡ A.3—Christian Life and Thought

Foundation studies in this discipline can take different routes:

Either ‡ A.3.A—Foundations of Christian Thought

Candidates will study some of the foundational issues involved in the study of Christian theology including faith, revelation, Scripture, authority, tradition, development, religious language, and the relationship of Christian theology to other disciplines.

Or ‡ A.3.B—Development of Christian Life and Thought

Candidates will study the development of Christian life and thought in its cultural and historical context, including issues of authority, spirituality and ministry within Christian communities; and sources and forms of theological reflection and conflict. They should demonstrate some awareness of primary sources (in translation).

Candidates will study the following foundational period:

(*a*) First to fifth centuries.

They may also study one of the following periods:

(*b*) Sixth to eleventh centuries;

(*c*) Eleventh to fourteenth centuries;

(*d*) Fifteenth and sixteenth centuries.

Candidates must specify the period within which the subject of their essay falls on their examination entrance forms; they cannot subsequently be assessed on these periods in Paper C.2.

‡ **A.4—Christian Witness and the Contemporary World**

Candidates will study the relationship between Christian faith and contemporary culture, including religious and secular understandings of society, environment, personhood, and faith. Candidates will be expected to reflect on the practice of mission and pastoral care.

PART 2

SECTION B. BIBLICAL STUDIES
†‡ B.1—Old Testament B
Candidates will study the Historical Books (Joshua, Judges, 1 and 2 Samuel, 1 and 2 Kings, 1 and 2 Chronicles, Ezra, Nehemiah) and the other Writings (Psalms, Proverbs, Job, Ecclesiastes, Song of Songs, Lamentations, Ruth, Esther, Daniel).

They will also study at least one of the following set texts:

(i) 2 Samuel 1-12 or 2 Kings 17-25 in English;

(ii) Psalms 42-49, 84-89 or Job 1-5, 38–42 in English;

(iii) 2 Kings 21-23 in Hebrew;

(iv) Ruth in Hebrew.

Candidates who wish to prepare for assessment in Hebrew must enter for the written examination with texts in Hebrew. However, in the examination itself they may transfer to texts in English without penalty.

†‡ B.2—New Testament B
Candidates will study issues of New Testament theology, ethics and interpretation, and at least two of the following books: John, Romans, Hebrews. They may also study the Pastoral Epistles and Revelation. They will study in detail texts from John 1-6, 9-12, 17-20, Romans 1-12, and Hebrews in English; and they may study John 1-3, 6, 17 *and/or* Romans 5-8 in Greek. Candidates being assessed by long essay may write on any New Testament text (except those texts listed in the rubric for paper A.2), so long as they have adequately covered the syllabus of the paper in their course of instruction. Candidates who wish to prepare for assessment in Greek must enter for the written examination with texts in Greek. However, in the examination itself they may transfer to texts in English without penalty.

†‡ B.3—Biblical Interpretation
Candidates will study Part A or Part B or both.

Part A: Candidates will study: central themes in both testaments such as God, creation, the people of God, redemption, messiah, community, worship, hope; and the methodological issues of constructing biblical theology.

Part B: Candidates will study the history and practice of biblical interpretation, including major contemporary trends.

SECTION C. DOCTRINE AND HISTORY
†‡ C.1—Christian Doctrine
Candidates will study the central doctrines of the Christian church, as set out in the historic creeds and formulae, including critical reflection on traditional

and recent expositions of these doctrines and engagement with contemporary theological discussion.

†‡ C.2—Church History

Candidates will study the development of Christian life and thought in its cultural and historical context, including issues of authority, spirituality, and ministry within Christian communities; and sources and forms of theological reflection and conflict. They should demonstrate some awareness of primary sources (in translation).

Candidates must specify one period for assessment by written exam or long essay, which must not be one on which they were assessed in Paper A.3.B:

(*a*) First to fifth centuries;
(*b*) Sixth to eleventh centuries;
(*c*) Eleventh to fourteenth centuries;
(*d*) Fifteenth and sixteenth centuries;
(*e*) Seventeenth and eighteenth centuries;
(*f*) Nineteenth and twentieth centuries.

†‡ C.3—Ecclesiology

Candidates will study the theology of the church, including ministry and the sacraments, in its historical development and contemporary practice.

†‡ C.4—Study of Theology

(Candidates who have taken A.3.A may not take this paper.)

Candidates will study some of the major issues involved in the study of Christian theology, including faith, revelation, reason, Scripture, authority, tradition, development, religious language, and the relationship of Christian thought to other disciplines and other religions.

SECTION D. PRACTICAL THEOLOGY

§ D.1—Mission and Ministry

This paper will be assessed by an essay of 5,000 words (± 10%), which must be based on a supervised placement of at least twenty-one days in a church or secular setting in which the candidate shares in the experiences of those involved, and must be accompanied by a declaration supported by the student's society that the placement has been undertaken. The essay may be accompanied by additional documentation on the nature of the placement that would not otherwise be available to the examiner, which must not exceed ten A4 pages in total and must not identify the candidate. The essay should contain theological reflection on the placement with the help of the candidate's study of issues of mission and ministry and, as appropriate, of contributory disciplines.

§ D.2—Christian Ethics

This paper consists of two parts, (*a*) and (*b*):

(*a*) Ethics and Faith (three hour examination or long essay)

Candidates will study the foundations of Christian moral thought and practice; contemporary moral and social problems; and the relation of Christian moral life to faith, witness, and worship. This part of the paper will be assessed either by a long essay of 4,000 words (± 10%), the title of which must be submitted for approval to the Supervisory Committee, or by a three-hour written examination.

(*b*) Ethics and Ministry (two hour examination)

This part of the paper will be assessed by a two-hour written examination. Candidates should demonstrate ethical and pastoral competence in analysis of, reflection on, and response to a particular situation. This will be a situation relating to sexuality, marriage, and the family, unless the Supervisory Committee gives notice otherwise.

†‡ D.3—Christian Worship

Candidates will study the history and theology of Christian initiation, the Eucharist, the daily worship; the place of prayer in worship; non-verbal aspects of liturgy and their cultural factors; relevant insights from the human sciences; word and sacrament, liturgical symbolism, and the place of preaching; worship and the Church's mission; other forms of corporate worship.

†‡ D.4—Christian Spirituality

Candidates will study the history and theology of Christian spirituality including major traditions and figures; and the relationship of spirituality to: scripture, liturgy, hymnody, doctrine, and current trends.

SECTION E. OTHER SUBJECTS

†‡ E.1—Christian Mission

Candidates will study the following: the biblical and theological foundations of mission; the relationship of the Church to the *missio Dei*; factors in the contemporary world affecting mission, such as industrialisation, urbanisation, secularism, pluralism, and new forms of imperialism. These subjects may be focused through the study of: the history of Christian mission; the distinction between mission and evangelism; the encounter with other faiths; issues of contextualisation; apologetics; liberation movements; and the work of significant missiologists.

†‡ E.2—Christian Faith and Other Religions

Candidates will study methodology in the study of religion; Christian approaches to other religions; and one religion other than Christianity, chosen from (and to be specified on the entry form): Hinduism, Buddhism, post-Biblical Judaism, Islam, or a religion proposed by the candidate and approved by the Supervisory Committee.

†‡ E.3—Christian Faith and Philosophy

Candidates will study the relationship between Christianity and the Western philosophical tradition. They will also study relevant issues including: the relation between reason and revelation; the existence of God; the problem of evil; non-objective theism; religious language; religious experience; resurrection and the immortality of the soul.

†‡ E.4—Christian Faith and Science

Candidates will study the relationship between Christian theology and the development of modern science, including: methodology and epistemology in science and theology; the origin of the universe and humanity; the quantum world; the biosphere and ecosystems; and ethical issues of scientific research and development.

†‡ E.5—Christian Faith and Social Sciences   Candidates will study the relationship between Christian theology and the social sciences, including such areas as methodology in both disciplines; sociological and anthropological interpretations of religion; theological and sociological understandings of social phenomena; sociological understandings of religious organisation; and theological critiques of social sciences.

†‡ E.6—Christian Faith and Psychology

Candidates will study the contribution of psychological theory to pastoral theology and pastoral care, in areas such as: developmental theory and the life cycle; human sexuality; love and attachment; and mental health. They will also study: major psychological theories and their critique of religious systems; the counselling movement; the role of the pastor; the nature of pastoral ministry in relation to birth, marriage, and death.

†‡ E.7—Canon Law

Candidates will study the sources, history, and theology of Western canon law or the Eastern canonical tradition or both (to be specified on the entry form); and current systems of canons, e.g. the Roman Catholic *Code of Canon Law* and the *Canons of the Church of England*, including an introduction to comparative issues.   5

‡ E.8—Confessional Study

Candidates will study the tradition of a Christian denomination as expressed in its formularies, liturgy, spirituality, and ethics.

§ †‡ E.9—Translation Paper

Candidates may propose texts for approval by the Supervisory Committee, from   10
which passages will be set for translation and comment in a three-hour written examination. The texts must be in a language relevant to theological study, such as Biblical Hebrew, New Testament Greek or Ecclesiastical Latin.

A candidate may offer Paper E.9 twice, so as to be examined on texts in two different languages.   15

SECTION F. DISSERTATION OR PROJECT

Candidates may either write a dissertation or undertake a project capable of suitable assessment. In either case, it is expected that no college-assessed formative pieces of work will be required.

§ F.1—Dissertation   20

Candidates may propose a topic for approval by the Supervisory Committee, a topic which will involve some research and/or interdisciplinary study leading to the composition of a dissertation of 10,000 words (± 10%).

The proposal should include the title, a brief description of the subject and approach envisaged, and a preliminary bibliography.   25

§ F.2—Project

Candidates may propose a project for approval by the Supervisory Committee.

The proposal should include the title, a brief description of the subject and approach envisaged, a preliminary bibliography and details of the proposed assessment method.   30

4

REGULATIONS FOR THE DEGREE OF MASTER OF ARTS

1. A Bachelor of Arts (other than one covered by the provisions of clause 2 below) or a Bachelor of Fine Art may, with the approval of his or her society, supplicate for the Degree of Master of Arts in or after the twenty-first term from his or her matriculation.

2. A Bachelor of Arts whose qualification for admission to a Final Honour School was the successful completion of a Foundation Course at the Department for Continuing Education may, with the approval of his or her society, supplicate for the Degree of Master of Arts in or after the eighteenth term from his or her matriculation.

3. A Bachelor of Arts or a Bachelor of Fine Art who has been admitted to the Degree of Doctor of Philosophy may supplicate for admission to the Degree of Master of Arts, provided that he or she has satisfied all other necessary conditions, at any time after his or her admission to the Degree of Doctor of Philosophy.

4. If a Bachelor of Civil Law or a Bachelor of Medicine shall first have been admitted to the Degree of Bachelor of Arts, he or she may supplicate for the Degree of Master of Arts with the approval of his or her society in or after the nineteenth term from his or her matriculation, and may retain the Degree of Bachelor of Civil Law or of Medicine, as the case may be.

NOTES

5

REGULATIONS FOR DEGREES IN MUSIC

GENERAL REGULATIONS

§1. Qualifications of Candidates for the Degree of Bachelor of Music

Any persons who have been admitted to the Degree of Bachelor of Arts and have been placed in the First or Second Class (Division 1) in the Final Honour School of Music may apply to the Board of the Faculty of Music for the appointment of examiners and for leave to supplicate for the Degree of Bachelor of Music.

§2. Musical Exercise for the Degree of Bachelor of Music

1. Candidates shall submit to the Board of the Faculty of Music through the Registrar a Musical Exercise of their own unaided composition. The board shall make and publish regulations concerning the type and content of the Exercise.

2. The Exercise shall be accompanied by:

(1) a statement signed by the candidate that the whole of the Exercise is his or her own unaided work and has not been submitted to any other person for advice, assistance, or revision or presented for examination in whole or in part in the Final Honour School of Music;

(2) a certificate signed by an officer of, or person deputed by, the society to which the candidate belongs, showing that the entry is made with the approval of such society and that he or she has paid the fee prescribed in the appropriate regulation (see Appendix I).

3. The Musical Exercise shall be examined by at least two examiners appointed by the Board of the Faculty of Music. The examiners shall report to the board, and it shall be the duty of the

board to decide whether leave to supplicate for the degree should be granted to the candidate, provided that such leave shall in no case be granted unless the examiners have reported that the Exercise submitted by the candidate is of a high standard of merit such as to entitle him or her to supplicate for the Degree of Bachelor of Music.

4. Candidates shall not be permitted to submit their Exercise for approval earlier than the third term after that in which they have passed the examination in the Final Honour School of Music.

5. No candidate shall be permitted to supplicate for the Degree of Bachelor of Music who has not delivered his or her Exercise in a form approved by the examiners to the Registrar, who shall deposit it in the Bodleian Library.

§3. Degree of Doctor of Music

1. Any person belonging to one of the following classes may apply to the Board of the Faculty of Music for leave to supplicate for the Degree of Doctor of Music:

(a) Persons who have been admitted to the Degree of Bachelor of Music at this University; provided that no Bachelor of Music may submit evidence for approval until he or she has entered upon the ninth term after that in which he or she was admitted to the Degree of Bachelor of Music;

(b) Masters of Arts who have incepted in this University and have entered upon the thirtieth term from their matriculation;

(c) Masters of Arts of the University of Cambridge or Dublin who have been incorporated in this University and have entered upon the thirtieth term from their matriculation at Cambridge or Dublin;

(d) Undergraduates or Bachelors of Arts of the University of Cambridge or Dublin who have been incorporated and have incepted in the Faculty of Arts in this University and have entered upon the thirtieth term from their matriculation at Cambridge or Dublin;

(e) Persons on whom the Degree of Master of Arts has been conferred by decree or special resolution, other than a degree *honoris causa,* and who have entered upon the ninth term from their admission to that degree.

Candidates intending to submit for the Degree of Doctor of Music are strongly advised to consult the Chair of the Faculty Board who will arrange, free of charge, for an advisory consultation on one or more of the works intended for submission, prior to their formal submission.

2. A candidate for the Degree of Doctor of Music shall be required to submit through the Registrar two copies of a portfolio for approval by the Board of the Faculty of Music. The portfolio shall normally consist of between five and seven compositions which, taken together, demonstrate originality and high level of technical and aesthetic distinction, significantly in advance of what is required for a D.Phil. in composition. Each portfolio shall include a copy of any recordings of the compositions. The portfolio should demonstrate an ability to handle varied musical forces and large-scale structures. Where the composer is predominantly concerned with acoustic instrumental music, there should be evidence of extended structures such as symphonic work and carefully wrought music such as that associated with the string quartet medium, amongst contrasting work. Where the composer has concentrated on the development of other areas, such as mixed media, studio, ethnic or community approaches, the work should be of comparable quality in its field. No work so submitted shall have previously been submitted for examination purposes, but it may previously have been published in any of the forms indicated in (3) below. The application shall be accompanied by:

(1) evidence that the candidate's application has the approval of his or her society;

(2) the fee prescribed in the appropriate regulation (see Appendix I).

(3) A list of publications where publication is understood to take place by any or all means including public performance, CD recording, broadcast etc. and not solely or necessarily by commercial printing of the score.

(4) A *curriculum vitae* (including main landmarks in career, full list of significant published works with full details of principal performances, esteem indicators such as prizes, bursaries, composer-in-residence posts, honours).

(5) A declaration that the portfolio is the candidate's own unaided work.

3. On receipt of an application under clause 2 above, the Registrar shall submit it to the Board of the Faculty of Music as soon as may be, for approval. The board shall appoint two external assessors to consider the portfolio and present an agreed joint report to the board. The report should be sufficiently comprehensive and detailed to enable the board to assess the work submitted

by the candidate, and should make a clear recommendation as to whether the degree is to be awarded. The board shall decide whether the evidence submitted by the candidate is of sufficient merit to entitle him or her to supplicate for the Degree of Doctor of Music.

4. If the board approves the evidence as of sufficient merit it shall give leave to the candidate to supplicate for the degree, and shall notify its decision in the *University Gazette*. One copy of each musical work so approved shall remain in the possession of the University for deposit in the Bodleian Library.

SPECIAL REGULATIONS

DEGREE OF BACHELOR OF MUSIC

1. *The Exercise for the Degree of Bachelor of Music*

(*a*) The Exercise shall consist of a portfolio of three or more original musical compositions of varied character, lasting in total at least thirty minutes. Music for any combination of three or more of the categories specified below will be acceptable, provided that the portfolio includes some purely instrumental music and some vocal music with words. Candidates may also submit recordings of any of their works, and shall submit recordings of electro-acoustic compositions and of any pieces whose ordering or content is not fixed by the notation. The categories are (i) music for one or two instruments, or instrument and voice; (ii) music for choral or solo vocal ensemble, accompanied or unaccompanied; (iii) music for chamber ensemble, with or without voice or voices; (iv) music for larger forces than the above; (v) music involving electro-acoustic composition, accompanied by a commentary describing the technical procedures.

(*b*) A viva-voce examination may be held unless candidates are individually dispensed by the examiners.

2. *General Regulations about the Exercise*

(*a*) The score of each work must be written out so as to accord with the standards and methods that a professional performer, copyist, or publisher would expect, with rehearsal letters and/or regular bar-numbering. The pages should be numbered consecutively throughout the portfolio.

(*b*) **The Exercise must be accompanied by a declaration on a prescribed form, which must be obtained beforehand by application to the Examination Schools, High Street, Oxford. It must be sent in by the Friday in Trinity Term in the fifth week.**

FORM OF DECLARATION

I,...
....

hereby declare that these compositions are entirely my own unaided work and that no
part of them has been presented for examination on any previous occasion.

Signed... 5

.... College,

in the presence of

....

Witnesses' ....

names and 10

addresses ....

in full. ....

Date ....

The Exercise must show the private address as well as the name and college of the
composer. 15

It must be strongly bound and paged, and lettered (with clearly stamped lettering)
up the spine with title and composer's name, and also on the outside cover with title,
name, and college, and the words 'B.Mus. Exercise'.

Any electronic tape submitted in addition to the Exercise must be in a box on
which the title, the composer's name and college, and the words 'B.Mus. Exercise' are 20
again clearly shown.

DEGREE OF DOCTOR OF MUSIC

A candidate is required to submit for approval by the board of the faculty a major
musical work or works of his own composition and of outstanding merit. Two copies
of each work must be submitted 25

Evidence submitted for the Degree of Doctor of Music

The work or works submitted must show the private address as well as the name
and college of the composer. The work or works must be strongly bound and paged,
and lettered (with clearly stamped lettering) up the spine with title and composer's
name, and also on the outside cover with title, name, and college, and the degree for 30
which it was composed.

NOTES

6

REGULATIONS FOR THE DEGREE OF BACHELOR OF PHILOSOPHY OR MASTER OF PHILOSOPHY

§1. Degrees of Bachelor and Master of Philosophy

1. Any person who has kept six terms of statutory residence after admission as a student for the Degree of Bachelor or Master of Philosophy (or, in the case of a Student for the Degree of Doctor of Philosophy or Student for the Degree of Master of Letters or Student for the Degree of Master of Studies who has transferred to the Degree of Bachelor or Master of Philosophy, after his or her admission as a Student for the Degree of Doctor of Philosophy or Student for the Degree of Master of Letters or Student for the Degree of Master of Studies, as the case may be), and who has satisfied the examiners in one of the examinations hereinafter provided may supplicate for the Degree of Bachelor or Master of Philosophy as appropriate; provided that the board or other authority specified in cl. 3 of §2 below may dispense a student on application through his or her college and with the support of his or her supervisor from not more than two terms of such statutory residence if he or she has been granted leave to pursue his or her course of study at some other place than Oxford for those terms under the provisions of cl. 2(*c*) of §3 hereof.

2. A Student for the Degree of Bachelor or Master of Philosophy who is not a graduate of the University may wear the same gown as that worn by Students for the Degree of Doctor of Philosophy.

§2. Examinations for the Degrees of Bachelor and Master of Philosophy

1. For the Degree of Bachelor of Philosophy there shall be an examination in Philosophy.

For the Degree of Master of Philosophy there shall be examinations in Archaeology, Celtic Studies, Classical Archaeology, Comparative Social Policy, Criminology and Criminal Justice, Development

Studies, Eastern Christian Studies, Economic and Social History, Economics, English Studies (Medieval Period), Evidence-Based Social Intervention, General Linguistics and Comparative Philology, Geography and the Environment, Greek and Latin Languages and Literature, Greek and/or Roman History, History of Science, Medicine, and Technology, International Relations, Judaism and Christianity in the Graeco-Roman World, Late Antique and Byzantine Studies, Latin American Studies, Medical Anthropology, Modern British and European History, Modern Japanese Studies, Modern Languages, Music, Oriental Studies, Philosophical Theology, Politics (Comparative Government, Political Theory, European Politics and Society), Russian and East European Studies, Slavonic Studies, Social Anthropology, Sociology, Theology, Visual, Material and Museum Anthropology, and such other subjects as the University may hereafter determine.

2. There shall be a Register of students who are studying for the Degrees of Bachelor and Master of Philosophy which shall be entitled the Register of Bachelor and Master of Philosophy Students and the University may from time to time determine by decree the conditions of admission to the Register.

3. Subject to such regulations as the University may make under the provisions of cl. 2, any person who has obtained permission from the board concerned (or other authority as hereinafter specified) may enter for the examinations as follows. The bodies specified below shall be responsible for the examinations as listed.

Archaeology—Social Sciences

Celtic Studies—Modern Languages

Classical Archaeology—Social Sciences

Comparative Social Policy—Social Sciences

Criminology and Criminal Justice—Social Sciences

Development Studies—International Development, Queen Elizabeth House

Eastern Christian Studies—Oriental Studies and Theology

Economic and Social History—History

Economics—Social Sciences

English Studies (Medieval Period)—English Language and Literature

Evidence-Based Social Intervention—Social Sciences

General Linguistics and Comparative Philology—Linguistics, Philology and Phonetics

Geography and the Environment—Social Sciences

Greek and/or Latin Languages and Literature—Classics

Greek and/or Roman History—Classics

History of Science, Medicine, and Technology—History

International Relations—Social Sciences

Judaism and Christianity in the Graeco-Roman World—Oriental Studies and Theology

Late Antique and Byzantine Studies—Classics and History

Latin American Studies—Social Sciences

Law—Law (see SECTION 18: *Regulations for Degrees in Civil Law and for the Degrees of Magister Juris and Master of Philosophy in Law*)

Medical Anthropology—Social Sciences

Modern British and European History—History

Modern Japanese Studies—Social Sciences

Modern Languages—Modern Languages

Music—Music

Oriental Studies—Oriental Studies

Philosophical Theology—Theology

Philosophy (Bachelor of Philosophy)—Philosophy

Politics (Comparative Government, Political Theory, European Politics and Society)—Social Sciences

Russian and East European Studies—Social Sciences

Slavonic Studies—Modern Languages

Social Anthropology—Social Sciences

Sociology—Social Sciences

Theology—Theology

Visual, Material and Museum Anthropology—Social Sciences

The subjects of each examination shall be determined by regulation of the board or other authority concerned, which shall have power to include therein a thesis written by the candidate on a subject approved by the board or other authority or by a person or persons to whom the board or other authority may delegate the function of giving such approval. The thesis submitted shall be wholly or substantially the result of work undertaken while a candidate is studying for the Degree of Bachelor or Master of Philosophy, except that a candidate may make application for dispensation from this requirement to the Education Committee not later than the fourth term after his or her admission to the Register of Bachelor and Master of Philosophy Students.

4. Final examination marks shall be released to candidates at the conclusion of the examination. Exceptions to this may be made where assessment takes place throughout the course. In such cases, examination boards must meet formally, with all members present, at interim points in the year in order to agree final marks for specified assessment components. Marks released as final marks may not subsequently be amended without permission of the Proctors.

5. A candidate who has failed to satisfy the examiners in any one of the examinations for the Degrees of Bachelor or Master of Philosophy may enter again for that examination on one (but not more than one) subsequent occasion.

6. The examiners may award a distinction for excellence in the whole examination. Candidates who have initially failed any element of assessment shall not normally be eligible for the award of distinction.

§3. Register of Students for the Degree

1. The Registrar shall keep a Register of students who are studying for the Degrees of Bachelor or Master of Philosophy. The Register shall be entitled the Register of Bachelor and Master of Philosophy Students.

2. No candidate for the Degree of Bachelor or Master of Philosophy shall be admitted to the examination for the degree unless

(*a*) he or she has applied through the Head or a tutor of his or her college to the Registrar to have his or her name entered by the appropriate board or other authority on the Register of Bachelor and Master of Philosophy Students;

(*b*) his or her name shall have been kept on the Register for at least six terms inclusive of the term in which it was placed on the Register;

(*c*) he or she shall have pursued his or her course of study at Oxford for not less than six terms, except that the board or other authority concerned may grant him or her leave of absence for up to two of these terms if it is desirable in the interests of his or her work that he or she should be allowed to pursue his or her studies at some other place; time spent outside Oxford during term as part of an academic programme approved by Council shall count towards residence for the purpose of this clause:

Provided that

(i) a graduate may be admitted to the examination after his or her name has been on the Register and he or she has pursued his or her course of study at Oxford for only four or five terms if he or she has been given leave by the appropriate board or other authority to enter for the examination;

(ii) a Student for the Degree of Doctor of Philosophy or Student for the Degree of Master of Letters or Student for the Degree of Master of Studies or a Diploma Student may apply through his or her college to the appropriate board or other authority for the transference of his or her name to the Register of Students for the Degrees of Bachelor and Master of Philosophy and, if it is transferred, the number of terms he or she held the status of Student for the Degree of Doctor of Philosophy or Student for the Degree of Master of Letters or Student for the Degree of Master of Studies or Diploma Student shall be reckoned for the purpose of this clause.

3. No person shall attend seminars or advanced classes for Bachelor or Master of Philosophy Students unless his or her name is on the Register of Bachelor and Master of Philosophy Students; provided that the holder of a seminar or advanced class may give leave to a person who is not studying for the Degree of Bachelor or Master of Philosophy to attend his or her seminar or advanced class.

4. Any person shall be entitled to have his name entered on the Register of Bachelor and Master of Philosophy Students if he or she has obtained permission from the appropriate faculty board or other authority under the provisions of the appropriate regulation, provided he or she has matriculated as a member of the University.

5. The name of any Bachelor and Master of Philosophy Student may be removed from the Register by the body which entered it.

6. No name shall remain on the Register for more than twelve terms in all.

7. A Student for the Degree of Master of Philosophy shall cease to hold that status if:

(i) he or she shall have been refused permission to supplicate for the Degree of Master of Philosophy;

(ii) the board concerned shall, in accordance with provisions set down by regulation by the Education Committee, and after consultation with the student's society and supervisor, have deprived the student of such status;

(iii) he or she shall have been transferred under the relevant provisions to another status;

(iv) he or she shall not have entered for the relevant examination within the time specified under this subsection.

§4. Supervision of Students for the Degrees

1. Any board or other authority having power to make regulations for the subjects for the Degrees of Bachelor and Master of Philosophy may place a student for those degrees under the supervision of a graduate member of the University or other competent person selected by it, and it shall have power, for sufficient reason, to change the supervisor of any student. If a student requires special supervision in some branch of his or her studies, the supervisor may give this himself or herself or, with the approval of the board or other authority concerned, arrange for it to be given by some other person or persons.

2. A supervisor shall send a report on the progress of a student to the board at the end of each term (excepting the term in which the student is admitted to the examination) and at any other time when the board so requires or he or she deems it expedient. The supervisor shall communicate the contents of the report to the student on each occasion that a report is made, so that the student is aware of the supervisor's assessment of his or her work during the period in question. In addition he or she shall inform the board if he or she is of the opinion that a student is unlikely to reach the standard required for the Degree of Bachelor or Master of Philosophy.

§5. Examination Regulations

1. *Notice of Options*

In the Trinity Full Term preceding the year in which the examination is to be taken, candidates must give notice to the Registrar of all the subjects and options which they intend to offer, together with the subject of their thesis by the following weeks:

B.Phil. in Philosophy	By Friday in the first week

In the Michaelmas Full Term preceding the examination, candidates must give notice to the Registrar of all the subjects and options which they intend to offer, together with the subject of their thesis (if offered) by the following weeks:

M.Phil. in Archaeology and in Classical Archaeology and M.Phil. in Comparative Social Policy and in Evidence-Based Social Intervention	By Friday in the eighth week
All other M.Phil. courses	By Friday in the second week

2. *Preparation and dispatch of B.Phil. and M.Phil. theses*

The theses (**two copies**) must be typewritten and sent to the Chair of the Examiners for the Degree of B.Phil. [or M.Phil.], c/o the Examination Schools, High Street, Oxford, at least fourteen days before the first day of the examination, **except where stated otherwise in the particular regulations for individual courses in the following pages.**

The parcel should bear the words 'B.PHIL. [or M.PHIL.] THESIS IN [here insert subject]' in **BLOCK CAPITALS** in the bottom left-hand corner. The thesis must be printed or typed with a margin of 3 to 3.5 cms on the left-hand edge of each page (or on the inner edge, whether left-hand or right-hand, in the case of a thesis which is printed on both sides of the paper). Loose-leaf binding is not acceptable.

3. *Deposit of theses or dissertations in a university library*

If the examiners are satisfied that the candidate's thesis or dissertation, as submitted, is of sufficient merit but they consider, nevertheless, that before the thesis is deposited in a university library the candidate should make minor corrections, they may require the candidate to correct the thesis to their satisfaction. The library copy of the thesis must be hard bound.

4. *Submission of theses, dissertations and other material*

Except where otherwise indicated, all material submitted for examination (dissertations, extended essays, etc) shall be accompanied by a statement signed by the candidate indicating that it is the candidate's own work, except where otherwise specified. This statement must be submitted separately in a sealed envelope addressed to the chair of examiners of the degree course in question.

Bachelor of Philosophy

Philosophy

The regulations made by the Board of the Faculty of Philosophy are as follows:

1. Candidates will be required to attend the B.Phil. Pro-seminar in Michaelmas and Hilary Terms of the first year of their studies (i.e. the year in which their names are first entered on the Register of B.Phil. students). In addition, candidates will be required to attend two graduate classes in each of the first four terms of their studies.

2. Candidates will be examined by submitting:

(A) Seven essays of no more than 5,000 words each, in conformity with the following distribution requirement. Each essay will be assigned to a subject; the seven essays must cover at least five subjects, with no more than two essays on any one subject. One essay must be on a subject from Group 1 (Theoretical Philosophy), one on a subject from Group 2 (Practical Philosophy) and two on a subject or subjects from Group 3 (History of Philosophy), of which at least one must be concerned with philosophy written before 1800. The remaining three essays may be assigned to subjects in any of the three Groups, provided that the distribution requirement above is met. The list of approved subjects in each Group will be published at the beginning of each academic year in the Course Handbook. In exceptional circumstances, students may request to have one or more elements of the distribution requirement waived. Candidates wishing to do this must seek approval from the Graduate Studies Committee in Philosophy *as soon as they decide they would like to do so*, and in any case no later than the Friday of the noughth week of the Michaelmas Full Term of their second year of study. Any such application must be supported by the relevant B.Phil. Course Coordinator.

(B) A thesis of not more than 30,000 words, exclusive of bibliographical references, on a subject proposed by the candidate in consultation with his or her supervisor, and approved by the Graduate Studies Committee in Philosophy.

3. Topics for the essays will be chosen by the candidates. Candidates may offer up to two essays on at most one subject not included in the list of approved subjects in the Handbook. Candidates wishing to offer an essay or essays on a subject not on the prescribed list must seek approval for the proposed subject from the Graduate Studies Committee in Philosophy *as soon as they decide they would like to offer it*, and in any case no later than Friday of the fifth week of the Trinity Full Term of the first year of their studies. Any such application must be supported by the relevant B. Phil. Course Coordinator. Where a subject is approved by the Graduate Studies Committee in Philosophy, the Committee will assign it to one of Groups 1–3.

4. Candidates must inform the Graduate Studies Committee in Philosophy of their thesis title and abstract as soon as they have made their decisions and in any case not later than Friday of the eighth week of Trinity Full Term of the first year of their studies. Requests for permission to change the thesis title must be submitted for approval, with the support of the candidate's supervisor, to the Director of Graduate Studies in Philosophy *as soon as the candidate has decided to seek such permission*.

5. Two printed copies of each essay must be delivered to the Examination Schools, High Street, Oxford OX1 4BG, by 10 a.m. on the Wednesdays of the following weeks. In the first year of study, one essay is due in noughth week of Hilary Term and two essays are due in noughth week of Trinity Term. In the second year of study, two essays are due in each of the noughth weeks of Michaelmas and Hilary Terms. Candidates must give notice of the subject of each essay and the Group to which it will be assigned in accordance with the procedures and deadlines specified in the Course Handbook.

6. The thesis must be delivered to the Examination Schools, of the above address, by 10 a.m. on Wednesday of the eighth week of Trinity Full Term in the second year of study. The thesis must be accompanied by a brief abstract and a statement of the number of words it contains (exclusive of bibliographical references). A penalty may be imposed on any thesis that exceeds the word limit. Successful candidates will be required to deposit one copy of the thesis in the Bodleian Library.

7. The examiners may award a distinction for excellence in the whole examination.

8. Candidates who fail up to two essays will be permitted to resubmit those essays at any of the subsequent essay submission dates during the first or second year of their studies, or at the thesis submission date in their second year. A resubmitted essay may be on a new topic, and may be on a new subject, provided that the distribution requirement is met. Candidates who fail the thesis but who receive passing marks on all their essays will be permitted to resubmit an amended or different thesis by 10 a.m. on Wednesday of noughth week of the Hilary Term of the year following the whole examination. Candidates who fail three or more essays or two or more essays and the thesis will be permitted to resubmit work for the failed elements of the examination in the following academic year (or over four terms for candidates who fail more than five essays or more than four essays and the thesis). Candidates need only resubmit work for those elements of the Examination that they failed, but no resubmitted essay or thesis can receive a mark of more than 60. Candidates who fail to satisfy the examiners a second time in any part of the examination may not resubmit work for any part of the examination on any subsequent occasion.

9. Candidates for the MSt in Philosophy of Physics may apply to transfer to the second year of the BPhil in Philosophy. A formal application must be made by Friday of Week 4 of the Trinity Term preceding the Michaelmas Term in which they wish to transfer to the BPhil. Admission of those whose application is approved by the Philosophy Faculty's Graduate Studies Committee shall always be conditional on a level of performance in the examination for the MSt in Philosophy of Physics, as specified in the Student Handbook.

10. Candidates for the MSt in Philosophy of Physics who have successfully transferred to the second year of the BPhil in Philosophy shall be deemed to have completed the first year of the BPhil in Philosophy and the four essays submitted for their MSt examination shall be deemed to replace the first four essays required of candidates for the BPhil in the first year of studies on the BPhil in Philosophy. Such candidates will be required to submit three 5,000 word essays and a 30,000 word thesis, in line with the BPhil assessments schedule specified under paragraphs 5. and 6. above.

11. Candidates for the MSt in Philosophy of Physics who have successfully transferred to the second year of the BPhil in Philosophy, may apply for the award of MSt in Philosophy of Physics only if they fail or withdraw from the second year of the BPhil in Philosophy.

12. Candidates who fail or withdraw from the BPhil but have completed the requirements for the MSt in Philosophy may be permitted to supplicate for that degree.

Master of Philosophy

Archaeology

(*See also the general notice at the commencement of these regulations.*)

Within the Division of Social Sciences, the course shall be administered by the Committee for the School of Archaeology. The regulations made are as follows:

1. Candidates for admission must apply to the Committee for the School of Archaeology. They will be required to produce evidence of their appropriate quali-

fications for the proposed course including their suitable proficiency in relevant ancient or modern languages.

2. Candidates must follow for six terms a course of instruction in Archaeology.

3. The registration of candidates will lapse from the Register of M.Phil students on the last day of the Trinity Full Term in the academic year after that in which their name is first entered in it, unless the committee decides otherwise.

4. All candidates are required:

(*a*) to satisfy the examiners in a Qualifying Examination identical with that for the degree of Master of Studies in Archaeology and governed by regulations 5–9 for that degree, in the Trinity Full Term of the academic year in which their name is first entered on the Register for M.Phil students except that under regulation 5(*b*) of that degree a 10,000 word dissertation may not normally be offered in place of one of the subject options and must be examined by two pre-set essays or by a three-hour written paper. In the case of failure in one part of the Qualifying Examination, the candidate will have the same rights of resubmission as for the Master of Studies and, if successful, will be granted permission to supplicate for the degree of Master of Studies but will not be permitted to proceed to the second year of the M.Phil. Candidates whose work in the Qualifying Examination is judged by the examiners to be of the standard required for the degree of M.St in Archaeology, but not of the standard required to proceed to the second year of the M.Phil in Archaeology, will be granted permission to supplicate for the degree of Master of Studies in Archaeology;

(*b*) to deliver to the Examination Schools, High Street, Oxford, not later than noon on the Friday of the sixth week of Trinity Full Term in the academic year after that in which their name is first entered on the Register for M.Phil students, a thesis of not more than 25,000 words (excluding bibliography and any descriptive catalogue or other factual matter, but including notes and appendices) on the subject approved in accordance with regulations 6 and 10 below;

(*c*) to present themselves for written examination in accordance with regulation 5 below in the Trinity Full Term of the academic year after that in which their name is first entered on the Register for M.Phil students;

(*d*) to present themselves for an oral examination as required by the examiners.

5. The written examination shall comprise one subject chosen from Schedules A-D for the Master of Studies in Archaeology. [Candidates who offered a subject from Schedule C or D in the Qualifying Examination may not normally offer another subject from the same schedule.] The subjects will be examined by two pre-set essays (each of 5,000 words), except that further subjects from Schedule A in the M.St in Archaeology may also be examined by a written paper, and those from Schedule A of the M.St in Classical Archaeology will only be examined by written paper.

6. The choice of subjects for thesis and examination must be approved by the candidate's supervisor and by the committee, having regard to the candidate's previous experience and to the availability of teaching.

7. Candidates will be expected to show sufficient general knowledge of the appropriate history and geography for a proper understanding of their subjects.

8. The subject for examination and the chosen method of examination must be submitted for approval by the committee in time for its meeting in eighth week of the Trinity Full Term of the academic year in which the candidate's name is first entered on the Register for M.Phil students. Notice of the subject must be given to the Registrar no later than Friday of the eighth week of the Michaelmas Full Term preceding the examination.

9. Where options are examined by pre-set essays (as specified in 5 above), candidates will normally select essay topics from a list offered by their supervisors. The proposed essay titles, countersigned by the supervisor, must be submitted for approval to the Chair of Examiners by noon on Friday of the seventh week of the Hilary Full Term preceding the examinations. Candidates must submit two copies of their essays by not later than noon on Friday of the sixth week of Trinity Full Term, to the Examination Schools. Essays must be typed or printed.

10. The proposed thesis title must be submitted for approval by the committee in time for its meeting in the eighth week of the Trinity Full Term of the year in which the candidate's name is first entered on the Register for M.Phil students.

11. Candidates are advised that adequate reading knowledge of an appropriate language or languages (other than English) may be necessary to reach the standard required by the examiners.

12. Candidates will be required to deposit one copy of the thesis with the Examination Schools. Successful candidates will be required to deposit one copy of the thesis in the Sackler Library or the Balfour Library, as directed by the examiners. Such candidates will be required to complete a form stating whether they give permission for their thesis to be consulted.

13. Candidates whose work in the Final Examination is judged by the Examiners not to be of the standard required for the degree of M.Phil in Archaeology but whose work in the Qualifying Examination nevertheless reached the standard required for the degree of M.St in Archaeology, may be offered the option of resitting the M.Phil Examination under the General Regulations § 2, cl. 4, or of being granted permission to supplicate for the degree of Master of Studies in Archaeology.

14. The examiners may award a distinction for excellence in the whole examination.

Celtic Studies

(*See also the general notice at the commencement of these regulations.*)
The regulations made by the Board of the Faculty of Medieval and Modern Languages are as follows:

1. All candidates shall be required at the time of admission to satisfy the Board of Faculty of Medieval and Modern Languages (if necessary, by written test) that they possess the appropriate qualifications for the proposed course, including suitable proficiency in relevant languages. Normally the course will be restricted to candidates who have taken a first degree in a relevant subject area.*

2. All candidates shall be required

(a) To offer themselves for written examination as defined in section 5 below.

(b) To present themselves for viva voce examination at the time appointed by the examiners.

3. The subjects and papers of the examination shall be as follows:

(a) Historical and comparative Celtic linguistics.

(b) Irish literature up to the Cromwellian wars. Candidates will be expected to offer nine texts in all, three from each of the three periods, Old Irish, Middle Irish, and Early Modern Irish. The following are the prescribed texts:

---

* Even though their first degree is considered to have fitted them to pursue a course of study for an M.Phil. in Celtic Studies candidates may be required to take an intensive course in a Modern Celtic language *either* in the long vacation prior to their admission *or* in the long vacation following the third term of their course of instruction.

Old Irish:

Scéla mucce Meic Dathó, ed. R. Thurneysen (Dublin, 1951).

Togail bruidne Dá Derga, ed. E. Knott (Dublin, 1936).

Longes mac n-Uislenn, ed. V. Hull (New York, 1949).

Scéla Cano meic Gartnáin, ed. D. A. Binchy (Dublin, 1963).   5

Fingal Rónáin and Other Stories, ed. D. Greene (Dublin, 1955).

Táin Bó Fraich, ed. W. Meid, rev. edn. (Dublin, 1974).

Selected passages from *Táin Bó Cúailnge*, Recension I, ed. C. O'Rahilly (Dublin, 1976).

Middle Irish:

Stories from the Acallam, ed. M. Dillon (Dublin, 1970).   1◦

Aislinge meic Conglinne, ed. K. H. Jackson (Dublin, 1990).

Caithreim Cellaig, ed. K. Mulchrone (Dublin, 1933).

Cath Almaine, ed. P. Ó Riain (Dublin, 1978).

The Irish Adam and Eve Story from Saltair na Rann, ed. D. Greene and F. Kelly (Dublin, 1976).   1

Buile Shuibne, ed. J. G. O'Keeffe (Dublin, 1931)

Selected passages from *Táin Bó Cúalnge from the Book of Leinster*, ed. C. O'Rahilly (Dublin, 1967).

Early Modern Irish:

An introduction to Irish syllabic poetry of the period 1200-1600, ed. E. Knott (2nd edn., Dublin, 1957).   2◦

Tóruigheacht Dhiarmada agus Ghráinne, ed. Nessa Ni Shéaghdha (Dublin, 1967)

The Bardic poems of Tadhg Dall O Huiginn, ed. E. Knott (2 vols., London, 1922–6).

Sgéalaigheacht Chéitinn, ed. O. Bergin, 3rd edn. (Dublin, 1930).

Cath Muighe Tuireadh, ed. B. Ó Cuív (Dublin, 1945).   2

Nua-Dhuanaire, vol. 1, ed. P. de Brún, B. Ó Buachalla and Tomás Ó Concheanainn (Dublin, 1975).

Dánta Gradha, ed. T. F. O'Rahilly, 2nd edn. (Cork, 1926).

Scottish Poetry from the Book of the Dean of Lismore, ed. W. J. Watson (Edinburgh, 1937).   3◦

(*c*) Welsh literature up to the Reformation. Candidates will be expected to offer nine texts in all, three from each of three periods, Old, Middle and Early Modern Welsh. The following are prescribed texts:

Old Welsh:

Canu Taliesin, ed. I. Williams (Cardiff, 1960).   3

Canu Aneirin, ed. I. Williams (Cardiff, 1938).

Canu Llywarch Hen, ed. I. Williams (Cardiff, 1953).

Armes Prydein, ed. I. Williams, Engl. version by R. Bromwich (Dublin, 1972).

M. Haycock, *Blodeugerdd Barddas o Ganu Crefyddol Cynnar* (Y Bala, 1994), Nos. 1–8, 13–14, 16, 18, 21, 30.   4◦

Middle Welsh:

Pedeir Keinc y Mabinogi, ed. I. Williams (Cardiff, 1951).

Culhwch and Olwen, ed. R. Bromwich and D. Simon Evans (Cardiff, 1992).

Welsh Court Poems, ed. Rhian Andrews (Cardiff: University Wales Press, 2007).

Historia Peredur vab Efrawc (from Llyfr Gwyn Rhydderch: Y Chwedlau a'r Rhamantau, ed. J. Gwenogvryn Evans (Cardiff, 1973).   4:

Brut y Brenhinedd, ed. B. F. Roberts (Dublin, 1971).

The following shorter tales: *Breudwyt Ronabwy*, ed. M.Richards (Cardiff, 1948), *Breudwyt Maxen Wledic*, ed. B. F. Roberts (Dublin, 2005), *Cyfranc Lludd a Llefelys*, ed. B. F. Roberts (Dublin, 1975).

Early Modern Welsh:

Cerddi Dafydd ap Gwilym, ed. D. Johnston et al. (Cardiff, 2010).   5

Poems of the Cywyddwyr, ed. E. I. Rowlands (Dublin, 1976).

Rhagymadroddion 1547-1659, ed. Garfield H. Hughes (Cardiff, 1951).

A Welsh Bestiary of Love, ed. G. C. G. Thomas (Dublin, 1988).

Gwaith Tudur Aled, ed. T. Gwynn Jones (Cardiff, 1926).

Gwaith Guto'r Glyn, ed. I. Williams and J. Ll. Williams (Cardiff, 1939).   10

T. Parry, *Detholion o Destament Newydd* 1567 (Cardiff, 1967).

Llyvyr Iob: Cyvieithad Dr. Morgan 1588, ed. J. Gwenogvryn Evans (Oxford, 1888).

(*d*) Special Subjects

For the special subjects, each candidate may, with the agreement of his/her super-visor, submit an extended essay not exceeding 8,000 words in lieu of a three-hour   15
examination.

    (1) The archaeology of Celtic Society in pre-Christian Europe.

    (2) The Latin Literature of the British Isles.

    (3) The records of Continental Celtic.

    (4) Irish and Welsh origin legends.   20

    (5) The Celtic context of Old and Middle English literature.

    (6) The history of Ireland up to 1216.

    (7) The history of Scotland up to 1153.

    (8) The history of Wales *either* from *c.*550 to 1063 *or* from 1063 to 1415.

    (9) The history of the Celtic peoples from *c.*400 to *c.*900.   25

    (10) The Normans and the Celtic peoples 1066–1216.

    (11) Early Irish Law.

    (12) Medieval Welsh Law.

    (13) The Ulster Cycle of tales.

    (14) The Classical Irish bardic tradition.   30

    (15) *Echtrai* and *immrama*.

    (16) The medieval Welsh Arthurian romances.

    (17) Middle Cornish language and literature.

    (18) Middle Breton language and literature.

    (19) Twentieth-Century Scottish Gaelic literature.   35

    (20) Literature of the modern revival in Irish.

    (21) The Welsh literary renaissance of the twentieth century.

    (22) Language and society in modern Scotland.

    (23) The palaeography of medieval Celtic vernacular manuscripts (candidates may restrict themselves either to Irish or to Welsh manuscripts).   40

    (24) The comparative syntax of modern Celtic languages.

    (25) The Celtic inscriptions of the British Isles before 800.

    (26) The poetry of Cynddelw.

The Special Subjects listed above are not prescriptive: candidates are allowed to offer a Special Subject or Special Subjects of their own devising, provided that these   45 are similar in character and scope to those listed and that they are approved under the arrangements set out in section 6 below.

(*e*) A thesis of approximately 20,000 words and not more than 25,000 words on a subject approved by the board or by a person or persons to whom the board may delegate this function. When seeking approval for the subject of the thesis, every candidate shall submit with the proposed title a written statement of not more than 500 words explaining the scope of the topic and the manner in which it is proposed to treat it.

4. Candidates shall be required to offer three papers and a thesis, as follows:

(*a*) *Either*

    (i) Two papers, one on each of two subjects selected from those described in section 3 (*a*), (*b*), and (*c*) above.

    (ii) One paper on a Special Subject as described in Section 3 (*d*) above.

    Or

    (i) One paper on a subject selected from those described in section 3 (*a*), (*b*), and (*c*) above.

    (ii) Two papers, one on each of two Special Subjects as described in section 3 (*d*) above.

(*b*) A thesis as described in section 3 (*e*) above.

5. Candidates shall seek approval (by application to the Modern Languages Graduate Office, 41 Wellington Square, Oxford) for the proposed subject of their thesis by the end of the fourth week of the second term after that in which their names have been placed on the register of M.Phil. Students, i.e. normally by the end of the fourth week of Trinity Term in their first year.

The thesis (*two copies*) must be typewritten and must be delivered to the Examination Schools, High Street, Oxford, not later than Friday of the first week of the Trinity Full Term in which the examination is to be taken.*

Successful candidates will be required to deposit one copy of their thesis in the Bodleian Library.†

6. Each candidate's choice of papers shall be subject to the approval of the Board of the Faculty of Medieval and Modern Languages or of a person or persons to whom the board may delegate the function of giving such approval. Approval shall be given only if the choice of papers proposed, and any titles of Special Subjects of the candidate's own devising, have the written support of the candidate's supervisor. Approval of the choice of papers proposed will be dependent on the availability of teaching and examining resources at the relevant times. Candidates shall seek approval (by application to the Modern Languages Graduate Office, 41 Wellington Square, Oxford) by the end of the first term after that in which their names have been placed on the register of M.Phil. students, i.e. normally by the end of Hilary Term in their first year.

A proposal for a Special Subject or Special Subjects of the candidate's own devising shall be accompanied by a *brief* statement of the candidate's view of the character and scope of the Special Subject or Special Subjects proposed.

---

* See the general regulation concerning the preparation and dispatch of theses. Candidates are reminded that work submitted for the Degree of M.Phil. may subsequently be incorporated in a thesis submitted for the Degree of D.Phil.

† Such candidates will also be required to sign a form stating whether they give permission for their theses to be consulted.

7. If it is the opinion of the examiners that the work done by a candidate while not of sufficient merit to qualify for the degree of M.Phil. is nevertheless of sufficient merit to qualify for the degree of Master of Studies in Celtic Studies, the candidate shall be given the option of resitting the M.Phil. examination under the appropriate regulation or of being granted permission to supplicate for the Degree of Master of Studies.

8. The examiners may award a distinction for excellence in the whole examination.

Classical Archaeology

Within the Division of Social Sciences, the course shall be administered by the Committee for the School of Archaeology. The regulations made are as follows:

1. Candidates for admission must apply to the Committee for the School of Archaeology. They will be required to produce evidence of their appropriate qualifications for the proposed course, including their suitable proficiency in relevant ancient or modern languages.

2. Candidates must follow for six terms a course of instruction in Classical Archaeology.

3. The registration of candidates shall lapse from the Register of M.Phil. students on the last day of Trinity Term in the academic year after that in which their name is first entered in it, unless the committee decides otherwise.

4. All candidates are required:

   (a) to satisfy the examiners in a Qualifying Examination identical with that for the degree of Master of Studies in Classical Archaeology and governed by regulations 5-9 for that degree, in the Trinity Full Term of the academic year in which their name is first entered on the Register of M.Phil. students except that under regulation 5(b) of that degree a 10,000 word dissertation may not normally be offered in place of one of the subject options (examined by two pre-set essays). In the case of failure in one part of the qualifying examination, the candidate will have the same rights of resubmission as for the M.St in Classical Archaeology and, if successful, will be granted permission to supplicate for the degree of M.St in Classical Archaeology but will not be permitted to proceed to the second year of the M.Phil in Classical Archaeology. Candidates whose work in the Qualifying Examination is judged by the examiners to be of the standard required for the degree of M.St. in Classical Archaeology but not of the standard required to proceed to the second year of the M.Phil. in Classical Archaeology, will be granted permission to supplicate for the degree of Master of Studies in Classical Archaeology;

   (b) to deliver to the Examination Schools, High Street, Oxford, not later than noon on the Friday of the sixth week of Trinity Full Term in the academic year after that in which their name is first entered on the Register for M.Phil. Students, a thesis* of not more than 25,000 words (excluding bibliography and any descriptive catalogue or other factual matter, but including notes and appendices) on the subject approved in accordance with regulations 6 and 10 below; the thesis should bear the candidate's examination number but not his or her name.

---

* See the general regulation concerning the preparation and dispatch of theses. Candidates are reminded (i) that two copies are required but that one of these may be a reproduction or carbon copy of the other, provided that any maps, diagrams, or other illustrations in the second copy are adequately reproduced, (ii) that the copy of the thesis deposited in the Ashmolean Library shall be the one containing the original illustrations, and (iii) that work submitted for the Degree of M.Phil. may be subsequently incorporated in a thesis submitted for the Degree of D.Phil.

(*c*) to present themselves for written examination in accordance with regulation 5 below in the Trinity Full Term of the academic year after that in which their name is first entered on the Register for M.Phil. Students;

(*d*) to present themselves for an oral examination as required by the examiners.

5. The written examination shall comprise one subject chosen from Schedules A-C for the Master of Studies in Classical Archaeology to be examined by two pre-set essays each of 5,000 words. [Candidates who offered a subject from Schedule C in the qualifying examination may not normally offer another subject from Schedule C.]

6. The choice of subjects for thesis and examination must be approved by the candidate's supervisor and by the committee, having regard to the candidate's previous experience and to the availability of teaching.

7. Candidates will be expected to show sufficient general knowledge of Ancient History and Geography for a proper understanding of their periods and subjects.

8. The period or subject for examination must be submitted for approval by the committee in time for its meeting in the eighth week of the Trinity Full Term of the academic year in which the candidate's name is first entered on the Register for M.Phil. Students. Notice of the period or subject to be offered by each candidate must be given not later than Friday of the eighth week of the Michaelmas Term preceding the examination.

9. Where options are being examined by pre-set essays (as specified in 5 above), candidates will normally select essay topics from a list offered by their supervisors. The proposed essay titles, countersigned by the supervisor, must be submitted for approval to the Chair of Examiners by noon on Friday of the eighth week of the term in which the instruction for that subject is given. Candidates must submit two copies of their essays by not later than noon on the Monday of the second week of the term following that in which the instruction for that subject was given to the Examination Schools, High Street, Oxford. Essays must be typed or printed and should bear the candidate's examination number but not his or her name.

10. The proposed thesis title must be submitted for approval by the committee in time for its meeting in the eighth week of the Trinity Term of the year in which the candidate's name is first entered on the Register for M.Phil. Students.

11. Candidates are advised that adequate reading knowledge of an appropriate language or languages (other than English) may be necessary to reach the standard required by the examiners.

12. Candidates will be required to deposit one copy of the thesis with the Examination Schools, High Street, Oxford. Successful candidates will be required to deposit one copy of the thesis in the Sackler Library. Such candidates will be required to complete a form stating whether they give permission for their thesis to be consulted.

13. In the case of failure in just one part of the final examination, the candidate will be permitted to retake that part of the examination on one further occasion, not later than one year after the initial attempt. Written papers would be retaken the following year. A candidate who is not judged to have reached the standard required for the degree of Master of Philosophy in Classical Archaeology but whose examinations fulfil the requirements of the M.St in Classical Archaeology may be granted permission to supplicate for the degree of M.St in Classical Archaeology.

14. The examiners may award a distinction for excellence in the whole examination.

Comparative Social Policy

(*See also the general notice at the commencement of these regulations.*)

The regulations made by the Divisional Board of Social Sciences are as follows:

Qualifying Test

Every candidate must pass a qualifying test at the end of the third term from the beginning of the course in the *two* compulsory papers, *Methods of Social Research*, and *Comparative Social Policy/Welfare States* and *one Optional Paper* from the list of optional papers, specified by the Department of Social Policy and Intervention . This will be from a list published annually by Friday of the sixth week of Michaelmas Full Term in the Department of Social Policy and Intervention. Candidates may, after special permission of the Course Director, offer subjects outside this list. This may also include papers offered in any other relevant master's degree in the University subject to the permission of the relevant Course Director as appropriate. The examiners may examine candidates viva voce. Candidates who fail the qualifying test may, in exceptional circumstances, be allowed to retake the test before the beginning of the first week of the next academic year. The examiners can decide that the retake shall consist of the whole test or parts thereof.

Final Examination

Every candidate must offer:

1. One further optional paper. This will be from a list published annually by Friday of the sixth week of Michaelmas Full Term in the Department of Social Policy and Intervention. Candidates may, after special permission of the Course Director, offer subjects outside this list. This may also include papers offered in any other relevant master's degree in the University subject to the permission of the relevant Graduate Studies Committee as appropriate.

2. A thesis* of not more than 30,000 words to be delivered to the Examination Schools, High Street, Oxford, by noon on Friday of the sixth week of Trinity Full Term in which the examination is to be taken. The thesis should employ comparative method in the study of a social policy topic. Successful candidates will be required to deposit a copy of their thesis in the Social Science Library.

The examiners may examine any candidate viva voce.

The examiners may award a Distinction for excellence in the whole examination on the basis of the material submitted to them in both the qualifying and the final examination.

Compulsory Papers

Methods of Social Research

(*a*) A course of practical work in (i) basic principles of statistical inference, and statistical models for the analysis of quantitative social science data, (ii) the rationale and techniques of qualitative research appropriate to social policy and related social enquiry, and (iii) methods of data collection including research and questionnaire design, interviewing and coding. Such practical course work in social research methods shall be assessed by a series of assignments set during the first two terms of the course. These shall be listed in the Course Handbook and submission dates set for each assignment. Each assignment shall be marked during the course. In the event of any candidate not reaching the pass mark set, one further attempt shall be permitted, though in the event of a successful resubmission only the bare pass mark shall be awarded. The combined set of completed assignments forms the practical research methods workbook. Candidates shall submit this workbook to the Director of Graduate Studies in the Department of Social Policy and Intervention by noon on Friday of the sixth week of the third term of the course, accompanied by a statement that it is the candidate's own work except where otherwise indicated. The practical workbooks shall be available for inspection by the examiners.

---

* See the general regulation concerning the preparation and dispatch of theses.

(*b*) Candidates are required to produce two essays of up to 2,500 words evaluating the research design, methods of data collection and analysis, and any ethical or philosophical issues that arise in a specified research paper. The Director of Graduate Studies shall publish two lists of research papers not later than noon on Monday of the first week of the second term; candidates will be required to select one from both of these lists of papers as the subject for each essay. Candidates shall submit their essay to the Examination Schools by 12 noon on Monday of the first week of the third term of the course, accompanied by a statement that it is the candidate's own work except where otherwise indicated.

Comparative Social Policy/Welfare States

Concepts and typologies of social policies and welfare states. Approaches to the study of social policy. Theories of the origin and growth of the welfare state. Goals and means in social policy. Effectiveness and efficiency in social policy: unintended side effects. Methodological issues in comparative social research.

Optional Papers

These will be from a list published annually by Friday of the sixth week of Michaelmas Full Term in the Department of Social Policy and Intervention. Candidates may, after special permission of the Course Director, offer subjects outside this list. This may also include papers offered in any other relevant master's degree in the University subject to the permission of the relevant Course Director as appropriate.

Criminology and Criminal Justice

(*See also the general notice at the commencement of these regulations.*)

1. Candidates must follow for at least six terms a course of instruction in Criminology and Criminal Justice.

2. There shall be a Board of Studies for the course, to be chaired by the Director of Graduate Studies for Criminology, and also comprising all the members of the Board of Examiners for the Master of Philosophy in Criminology and Criminal Justice for the current year, the Director or Assistant Director of the Centre for Criminology, and a student representative (the latter for open business only).

3. *Admissions*

Candidates may signify their intention to take the M.Phil. in Criminology and Criminal Justice when they apply for the M.Sc. in Criminology and Criminal Justice or the M.Sc. in Criminology and Criminal Justice (Research Methods) or after they have been admitted. In either case, a formal application, the form for which is obtainable from the Graduate Studies Office, must then be made by Friday of Week Four of Trinity Term preceding the Michaelmas Term in which they wish to study for the M.Phil. Admission of those whose thesis topics are approved by the Centre for Criminology's Board of Studies and for whom that Committee certifies the availability of supervision will always be conditional on a specified level of performance in the Part I examination.

4. *Residence*

Candidates must keep six terms statutory residence, which may include periods spent in residence while studying for the M.Sc. in Criminology and Criminal Justice or the M.Sc. in Criminology and Criminal Justice (Research Methods).

5. *Courses and examination*

Candidates for the M.Phil. shall satisfactorily complete Part I and Part 2. Part I and Part 2 shall be taken in that order and shall normally be taken in successive years. A candidate wishing to take Part 2 but not to proceed directly from Part I to Part 2 in successive years must seek permission from the Centre for Criminology's Board of

Studies. Part I shall consist of the courses and examinations as specified for the M.Sc. in Criminology and Criminal Justice or the M.Sc. in Criminology and Criminal Justice (Research Methods).

6. (*a*) *Qualifying Test (Part 1)*

Every candidate must pass a qualifying test by the end of the third term from the beginning of the course, which shall consist of the elements as specified in cll. 3–7 of the examination regulations for the M.Sc. in Criminology and Criminal Justice or cll. 3-7 of the examination regulations for the M.Sc. in Criminology and Criminal Justice (Research Methods).

Candidates who fail the qualifying test may be allowed to be reassessed, as specified in cl. 10 of the examination regulations for the M.Sc. in Criminology and Criminal Justice or cl. 10 of the examination regulations for the M.Sc. in Criminology and Criminal Justice (Research Methods).

6. (*b*) *Final examination (Part 2)*

Candidates shall follow a course of instruction in Empirical Research Methods, satisfy the examiners that they have completed to the required standard such tests or exercises in Research Methods as prescribed as part of such a course of instruction, and be examined by thesis which must not exceed 30,000 words and should not normally be less than 25,000 words. Candidates are required to deliver two typewritten copies of the thesis to the Examination Schools, High Street, Oxford, by noon on Friday of Week Eight of the Trinity Term in which the examination is to be taken.

The course in Empirical Research Methods shall be Research Design and Data Collection, and Social Explanation and Data Analysis, as specified for the M.Sc. in Criminology and Criminal Justice and the M.Sc. in Criminology and Criminal Justice (Research Methods). Where candidates have already taken these courses as part of either M.Sc., they will not be required to take them a second time. Where a candidate has elected to write a thesis that draws significantly on legal research methods, the Director of Graduate Studies (Research) for Criminology, at the suggestion of the prospective thesis supervisor, may grant the candidate exemption from taking Research Design and Data Collection, and Social Explanation and Data Analysis and instruct the candidate to take the Legal Research Method Course, as specified for the M.Phil. in Law.

7. The examiners may award a distinction for excellence in the whole examination.

8. Arrangements for reassessment shall be as follows:

Candidates who fail, or withdraw from, Social Explanation and Data Analysis may resubmit assessments in line with cl. 10 of the examination regulations for the MSc in Criminology and Criminal Justice. Such candidates who have completed successfully all or part of any of the other components may carry forward the marks gained for the successfully completed parts of the degree.

Candidates who fail, or withdraw from, the Legal Research Method course as specified for the M.Phil. in Law (if they have received permission to take this course instead of Research Design and Data Collection and Social Explanation and Data Analysis), may resit course elements according to the standard arrangements for reassessment for that course. Such candidates who have completed successfully all or part of any of the other components may carry forward the marks gained for the successfully completed parts of the degree.

Candidates who fail, or withdraw from, the M.Phil. thesis may resubmit the thesis to the Examination Schools, High Street, Oxford, by noon on Friday Week 8 of the term following publication of their results. Such candidates who have completed successfully all or part of any of the other components may carry forward the marks gained for the successfully completed parts of the degree.

Development Studies

(See also the general notice at the commencement of these regulations.)

The regulations made by the Graduate Studies Committee are as follows:

1. Candidates for admission must apply to the Graduate Studies Committee. They will be required to produce evidence of their appropriate qualifications for the proposed course.

2. Candidates must follow for six terms courses of instruction as laid down for the M.Phil. in Development Studies by the Graduate Studies Committee.

3. Candidates will be admitted to take the examination as defined below in a specific year. In exceptional circumstances candidates may be allowed to take an examination later than the one to which they were admitted. Permission for this must be sought from the Proctors through the candidate's college.

4. The registration of candidates shall lapse from the Register of M.Phil. Students on the last day of Trinity Term of their second academic year.

5. *Qualifying Test*

5.1 Every candidate must pass a qualifying test in two foundation papers to be taken at the start of the Trinity Term of the first year of study.

5.2. The qualifying test will be set and administered by the examiners appointed to examine for the M.Phil. in Development Studies. Candidates must enter themselves for the qualifying test via their Colleges.

5.3. Candidates may select the two foundation papers which they offer from the list set out below except that candidates with a non-economics background are required to include Economics as one of the two papers and candidates are not permitted, except with the permission of the Graduate Studies Committee, to offer a paper in the subject of their bachelor's degree.

   (i) *History and Politics*

      Topics may include the themes of state formation and development; encounters between different civilisations; colonialism, collaboration, and resistance; nationalism, decolonisation; class formation, gender relations, and the formation of political identities; politics and policy. Students will be expected to show knowledge of developments in countries from more than one of the following regions: Africa, Asia, and Latin America.

   (ii) *Economics*

      Topics may include the basic elements of macro- and micro-analysis for open, less developed, economies; national income accounting and analysis; macro-economic policy, theories of inflation and growth; supply and demand; theories of the firm; the functioning of markets, externalities and other market failures; theories of international trade; trade policy, exchange rates, and balance of payments management; the operation of the international monetary system. The emphasis will be on concepts and their application in the context of development.

   (iii) *Social Anthropology*

      Topics may include the perspectives of anthropology upon social change; personhood and well-being; social and personal agency, authority and responsibility in the field of productive activity; marriage, kinship, family and gender in theory and practice; agencies of managed change and their interaction with local communities.

5.4. A candidate who fails to pass the qualifying test may be permitted to retake the test before the beginning of the first week of the next academic year. Candidates shall retake only the failed component of the qualifying test.

5.5. Only candidates who have passed the qualifying test may proceed to the second year of the course.

6. *Core Course in Development Studies*

Candidates must pursue a core course in development studies which runs throughout the two years of the degree. The core course covers the following three aspects: (i) social theory and development theory, (ii) analysis of major interdisciplinary issues, and (iii) international dimensions of development. Issues which may be included are, under (i) the intellectual origins and legacies of development; under (ii) the agrarian question; industrialisation; urbanisation; gender, ethnicity, culture and development and environmental aspects of development; and under (iii) finance, trade, aid, information technology, the United Nations and global governance.

7. *Final Examination*

7.1. The final examination shall consist of the following:

(*a*) One written paper on *Research Methods* which is taken at the end of the Trinity Term of the first year of study. Questions will be set on: Epistemology of social science, social science paradigms; ethics and values; quantitative methods; the presentation of statistical information, hypothesis testing; research design; sampling theory; questionnaire design; the critical reading of documents; participant observation; action research; rapid research; evaluation research.

A candidate who fails to pass the paper in Research Methods may, at the discretion of the Development Studies Committee, be permitted to retake the paper before the beginning of the first week of the next academic year. Only candidates who have passed the paper in Research Methods may proceed to the second year of the course.

(*b*) One research design essay of 3,000-5,000 words, assessed by the examiners appointed to examine for the M.Phil in Development Studies. Candidates are required to submit the essay in Trinity Term of the first year of study. In the event of a candidate's failing the essay, it must be rewritten, resubmitted and a pass mark awarded before the candidate may proceed to the second year of the course. The research design essay and the written paper in (a) above shall each constitute 50 per cent of the marks available for the examination of the candidate's knowledge of research methods.

(*c*) Three core course essays assessed by the examiners appointed to examine for the M.Phil. in Development Studies. Candidates are required to submit these essays at specified intervals over the two years of the course. The topics to be covered in these essays must fall within the three themes (one per essay) included in the core course in development studies: social theory and development; major interdisciplinary issues; and the international dimension of development. Candidates must pass all three essays. In the event of a candidate's failing either or both essays submitted in the first year of the course, either or both must be rewritten, resubmitted and a pass mark awarded before the candidate may proceed to the second year of the course. In the event of a candidate's failing the third essay, submitted in the second year of the course, it must be rewritten, resubmitted and a pass-mark awarded before the candidate can be deemed to have successfully completed the course.

(*d*) A thesis of not more than 30,000 words (excluding bibliography but including footnotes and appendices) on a topic approved by the M.Phil Teaching Committee, to which the Graduate Studies Committee delegates this function.

The thesis must be on a topic in the general field of development studies. The topic of the thesis must be chosen in consultation with and with the approval of the candidate's supervisor. If a separate thesis supervisor is required, he or she must have agreed to undertake the supervision prior to the approval of the topic as specified above.

(*e*) One written paper selected from a range of optional papers. Details of the optional papers available will be notified during the first year of the course. Candidates may include subjects offered in other relevant masters degrees in the University, subject to permission from the relevant graduate studies committee and from the M.Phil Teaching Committee. Applications to do this must normally be made by the first Friday of Trinity Term in the student's first year.

(*f*) One further written paper selected from a range of optional papers, or offered in other relevant masters degrees in the University with the provisos specified in section 7.1 (e) above.

7.2. Theses must be delivered to the Examination Schools, High Street, Oxford not later than the Friday of the first week of the Trinity Full Term in which the examination is to be taken.

7.3. Failure in one or more components of the final examination results in failure of the degree. The examiners may permit candidates to re-take the examination of the failed component(s) in Trinity Term of the following academic year. In the case of a failed dissertation, the dissertation must be re-submitted in Trinity Term of the following year. Viva voce examinations are not used for this course.

7.4. The examiners may award a Distinction for excellence in the whole examination.

Eastern Christian Studies

(*See also the general notice at the commencement of these regulations.*)

The regulations made by the Boards of the Faculties of Oriental Studies and Theology are as follows:

Candidates will be admitted to take the examination as defined below in a specific year. In exceptional circumstances candidates may be allowed to take an examination later than one to which they were admitted. Permission for this must be sought from the faculty board not later than Monday of the week before the first week of the Trinity Term in which the examination was to have been taken. The application must have the support of the candidate's college and be accompanied by a statement from the supervisor.

I. Every candidate shall be required

(*a*) to present himself or herself for a written examination, as prescribed below;

(*b*) to present a thesis of not more than 30,000 words on a subject approved by the faculty boards. Theses should be presented not later than noon on the Friday of the second week of the Trinity Term in which the examination is taken. Successful candidates may be required to deposit one copy of the thesis in the Bodleian;[†]

---

† Candidates will also be required to sign a form stating whether they give permission for the thesis to be consulted.

(*c*) to present himself or herself for a viva voce examination, unless individually dispensed by the examiners.

II. The written examination shall consist of four papers:

(1) A general paper on the development of doctrine and the history of the Church in the Christian East to AD 717.

(2), (3), (4) Three papers on one of the following options.

A. *Greek*

(i) The philosophical background of the Greek Fathers*.

(ii) The history of the Church in the Byzantine Empire, AD 717-886*.

(iii) Byzantine ecclesiastical texts*.

The three papers will include passages for comment as well as general questions relating to the set texts.

B. *Armenian with Greek*

(i) Armenian historical texts*.

(ii) Armenian theological and ecclesiastical texts*.

(iii) A translation paper from Greek ecclesiastical texts. Passages for translation will be set from unspecified texts and set texts*.

Papers (i) and (ii) will include passages for translation and comment as well as general questions relating to the set texts.

C. *Syriac with Greek*

(i) Syriac historical texts*.

(ii) Syriac theological texts*.

(iii) as Paper B (iii) above.

Papers (i) and (ii) will include passages for translation and comment as well as general questions relating to the set texts.

Teaching in all three options (Greek, Armenian with Greek, Syriac with Greek) may not be available every year, and applicants for admission will be advised whether teaching will be available in the option of their choice.

Note. Candidates with sufficient knowledge of Greek may offer Paper A (i) in place of Paper B (iii)/C (iii). Except in the case of Papers A (i) and B (iii)/C (iii), and subject to the approval of the faculty boards, a candidate may offer texts — or, in the case of Paper A (ii), a period of Greek church history — other than those specified in the regulations.

III. The examiners may award a Distinction for excellence in the whole examination.

Economic and Social History

(*See also the general notice at the commencement of these regulations.*)

The regulations of the Board of the Faculty of History are as follows:

1. Every candidate must follow for at least six terms a course of instruction in Economic and Social History and must upon entering for the examination produce from his or her society a certificate to that effect.

2. The examination will consist of the following parts:

---

* Lists of texts are available in the Course Handbook.

Qualifying test

Every candidate must pass a qualifying test. The test shall consist of two courses on
(1) Methodological introduction to research in the social sciences and history.

(2) *Either* Quantitative methods and computer applications for historians

or A paper from another established course within the University where this would
provide a more appropriate training for the candidate's dissertation focus. Such
a choice will need formal approval from both the Course Director and the Chair
of the Graduate Studies Committee of the Board of the Faculty of History.

The methodological introduction course will be assessed by a methodological essay
of up to 4,000 words. Two copies of the essay must be submitted by noon on Monday
of first week of Trinity Term of the candidate's first year to the Chair of Examiners for
the M.Phil. in Economic and Social History, c/o Examination Schools, High Street,
Oxford OX1 4BG. A quantitative methods course is assessed by an assignment to be
completed over the Christmas Vacation; two typewritten copies of the completed
assignment must be submitted by noon on Monday of second week of Hilary Term
of the candidate's first year to the Chair of Examiners for the M.Phil. in Economic and
Social History at the above address. In addition, convenors of qualifying courses will
confirm in writing to the chair of examiners not later than Friday of eighth week of
Hilary Term the candidates' satisfactory participation in their classes, including the
completion of any assignments for the weekly sessions. Any approved alternative
qualifying course will be assessed within the format and timetable of the paper's parent
course. No candidate who has failed the qualifying test of two courses will be permitted
to supplicate for the degree. Candidates who fail a qualifying course once will be
permitted to take it again, not later than one year after the initial attempt.

Final examination

The examination shall consist of four papers and a dissertation.

I. Three advanced papers at least two of which must be selected from Schedule I
below (Advanced Papers for the M.Phil. and M.Sc. in Economic and Social History),
and not more than one from any other M.Phil. the choice of which must be approved
by the chair of the Graduate Studies Committee of the History Board not later than
Monday of the fourth week of the second Michaelmas Term of the course.

Candidates must take at least two of their advanced papers as three-hour written
examinations. For each of their remaining advanced papers candidates must choose
to be assessed either by written examination or by two 5,000 word essays. Essays may
be only submitted in lieu of written papers for subjects in Schedule I or for papers
from other M.Phil.s where similar provision exists in the regulations for those
examinations. The essays must be the work of the candidates alone and they must
not consult any other person including their supervisors in any way concerning the
method of handling the themes chosen. The themes chosen by the candidate must be
submitted for approval by the chair of examiners by the examination entry date.
Candidates will be informed within two weeks, by means of a letter directed to their
colleges, whether the topics they have submitted have been approved. The finished
essays must be delivered by the candidate to the Examination Schools, High Street,
Oxford, by noon on Monday of sixth week of Trinity Full Term. The essays must be
presented in proper scholarly form, and two typed copies of each must be submitted.

II. *Either* (i) one paper in a discipline or skill or sources or methods selected
from Schedule II below.

or (ii) A fourth advanced paper selected from Schedule I or from any
additional list of papers for the M.Phil. and M.Sc. in Economic and
Social History approved by the Graduate Studies Committee of the
Board of the Faculty of History and published in the definitive list
of Advanced Papers as set out in Schedule I.

III. A dissertation of not more than 30,000 words, including appendices but excluding bibliography on a topic approved by the candidate's supervisor. The dissertation must be delivered not later than noon on the Monday of the first week of the Trinity Full Term in which the examination is to be taken to the Examination Schools, High Street, Oxford. Dissertations submitted must not exceed the permitted length. If they do the examiners will reduce the marks awarded. The presentation and footnotes should comply with the requirements specified in the Regulations of the Education Committee for the degree of M.Litt. and D.Phil. and follow the *Conventions for the presentation of dissertations and theses* of the Board of the Faculty of History.

Each dissertation must include a short abstract which concisely summarises its scope and principal arguments, in about 300 words.

Candidates must submit by the specified date three copies of their dissertation. These must be securely and firmly bound in either hard or soft covers. One copy of an M.Phil. dissertation which is approved by the examiners must be deposited in the Bodleian Library. This finalised copy should incorporate any corrections or amendments which the examiners may have requested. It must be in a permanently fixed binding, drilled and sewn, in a stiff board case in library buckram, in a dark colour, and lettered on the spine with the candidate's name and initials, the degree, and the year of submission.

3. Candidates may, if they so wish, be examined in up to two of their four papers (or submit essays in lieu of these papers as provided for above) at the end of their first year.

4. The examiners will permit the use of any hand-held pocket calculator subject to the conditions set out under the heading 'Use of calculators in examinations' in the *Regulations for the conduct of University Examinations.*

5. The examiners may award a distinction for excellence in the whole examination.

6. If it is the opinion of the examiners that the work done by a candidate, while not of sufficient merit to qualify for the degree of M.Phil., is nevertheless of sufficient merit to qualify for the degree of Master of Science in Economic and Social History, the candidate shall be given the option of re-sitting the M.Phil. (as provided under the appropriate regulation) or of being granted leave to supplicate for the degree of Master of Science.

7. A candidate who fails the examination will be permitted to re-take it on one further occasion only, not later than one year after the initial attempt.

Such a candidate whose dissertation has been of a satisfactory standard may re-submit the same piece of work, while a candidate who has reached a satisfactory standard on the written papers will not be required to re-take that part of the examination.

Schedule I
Advanced Papers for the M.Phil. and M.Sc. in Economic and Social History
A broad range of the course resources are shared with the corresponding courses in History of Science, Medicine, and Technology, and Advanced Papers are therefore available in the subject areas listed here.

1. Economic and business history
2. History of science and technology
3. Social history
4. Historical demography
5. History of medicine

A descriptive list of Advanced Papers will be published by the Board of the Faculty of History in September for the academic year ahead (not all options may be available in every year). The definitive list of the titles of Advanced Papers for any one year will be circulated to candidates and their supervisors and posted on the Faculty notice board not later than Friday of third week of Michaelmas Term of the academic year in which the paper is to be taken.

Schedule II

The paper in a relevant discipline or skill may be:

1. One of the papers from the M.Phil. in Economics.

2. One of the papers from the M.Phil. in Sociology or in Comparative Social Policy.

3. One of the papers from the M.Phil. in Russian and East European Studies.

4. One suitable paper from another Master's degree under the auspices of the Faculty of History approved from time to time by the Graduate Studies Committee of the Board of History.

5. One suitable paper from another Master's degree on the recommendation of the candidate's supervisor and endorsed by the Course Director.

Choices under Schedule II have to be approved by the chair of the Graduate Studies Committee of the Board of the Faculty of History not later than Monday of the fourth week of the second Michaelmas Term of the course. Candidates wishing to take a paper under 1, 2, 3, or 5 will also need the approval of the appropriate course convenor and the Graduate Studies Committee of the relevant faculty board or inter-faculty committee who need to be satisfied that each candidate has an adequate background in the subject. Not all options may be available in any one year.

Economics

(*See also the general notice at the commencement of these regulations.*)

The regulations made by the Divisional Board of Social Sciences are as follows:

The examiners will not provide calculators, but will permit the use of any hand-held pocket calculator in the examination room, both for the first year examinations and for the final examination, subject to the conditions set out under the heading 'Use of calculators in examinations' in the *Special Regulations concerning Examinations.*

First-year examinations

There will be three compulsory papers to be taken at the end of the first year of the course.

(*a*) *Macroeconomics*

(*b*) *Microeconomics*

(*c*) *Econometrics*

Details of the content of the three compulsory papers will be published in the Course Booklet distributed to students at the beginning of Michaelmas Term each year.

The Microeconomics and Macroeconomics papers will be set in two parts (A and B). Questions must be selected from both parts. Questions in part A will involve the use of mathematical techniques.

The papers shall be set and administered by the examiners appointed to examine the M.Phil. in Economics. Applications must be made by the Friday of eighth week in Michaelmas Full Term. The examination will be held in the eighth week of Trinity Full Term. The examiners may also examine any candidate viva voce. In exceptional circumstances, the Economics Graduate Studies Committee may give permission for a candidate to defer one of these papers. This paper will then be taken at the same time as the final examination.

Candidates who pass these papers will proceed to the second year of the course and take the Final Examination at the end of the second year. Candidates who fail only one out of the three papers may, by permission of the Economics Graduate Studies Committee, proceed to the second year of the course and resit the one failed paper at the same time as the final examination. Otherwise, candidates who fail the first-year examination will be permitted to resit all three papers at the end of their second year but will not be permitted to enter the final examination at that time. If they then pass the three compulsory papers, they will be permitted to proceed with the course and enter the final examination at the end of their third year. In exceptional cases, the Economics Graduate Studies Committee may permit the deferral of resitting one of the three papers at the end of the second year until the final examination. No candidate will be permitted to resit any of the compulsory papers more than once.

Final Examination

No candidate shall enter the final examination unless he or she has already passed the three compulsory papers in the first-year examinations, save that the Economics Graduate Studies Committee may permit any candidate who has failed one of the compulsory papers to resit that paper at the same time as the final examination.

All candidates must offer five second year papers and submit a thesis.*

Candidates must take at least one starred (*) paper (advanced core subject) and at least one non-starred paper (field subject).

Candidates must deliver two copies of the thesis (clearly marked with the candidate's name, college, and the words 'M.Phil in Economics' and accompanied by a statement signed by the candidate that it is the candidate's own work except where otherwise indicated) to the Examination Schools, High Street, Oxford OX1 4BG, by noon on Wednesday in the third week of Trinity Full Term in which the final examination is to be taken. Successful candidates will be required to deposit one copy of their thesis in the Economics Library.

The Examiners may also examine any candidate viva voce.

Second year papers for the M.Phil. in Economics

Second year papers are normally available in the following subject areas:

1. Advanced Macroeconomics 1*
2. Advanced Macroeconomics 2*
3. Advanced Microeconomics 1*
4. Advanced Microeconomics 2*
5. Advanced Econometrics 1*
6. Advanced Econometrics 2*
7. Advanced Econometrics 3*
8. Behavioural Economics
9. Development Economics 1: The Microeconomics of Development
10. Development Economics 2: Topics in Development Economics

---

* Theses must be of not more than 30,000 words and must be typewritten. The thesis must be accompanied by a statement that it is the candidate's own work except where otherwise indicated. See the general regulation concerning the preparation and dispatch of theses. Candidates are reminded that work submitted for the Degree of M.Phil. may subsequently be incorporated in a thesis submitted for the Degree of D.Phil.

11. Economic History 1: The Great Divergence
12. Economic History 2: Money, Finance and Cycles in History
13. Financial Economics 1
14. Financial Economics 2
15. Industrial Organisation 1: Pricing and Competition Analysis   5
16. Industrial Organisation 2: Market Structure and Industry Performance
17. International Trade 1
18. International Trade 2
19. Labour Economics: The Economics of Pay and Personnel
20. Public Economics.   10

A *descriptive list* of second year papers for an academic year, together with their rubrics, will be published before the beginning of the year by the Department of Economics. Not all second year papers on the descriptive list may be available in that year. The *definitive list* of second year papers together with information on content and structure will be published in the MPhil Economics Handbook published at the   15
beginning of Michaelmas Term of the year in which the exam is to be taken.

For all Economics papers candidates are permitted the use of a hand-held pocket calculator from a list of permitted calculators, which will be updated annually in the week prior to the first full week of Michaelmas Term and published by the Department of Economics on its website.   20

English Studies (Medieval Period)

(*See also the general notice at the commencement of these regulations.*)
The regulations made by the Board of the Faculty of English Language and Literature are as follows:

Every candidate must follow for at least six terms a course of study in English.   25

In the first year candidates must follow the courses and submit the essays and dissertations prescribed for the M.St. in English. Candidates must have achieved a pass mark in the first-year assessments before they are allowed to proceed to the second year.

In the second year candidates must offer three of the following subjects and a   30
dissertation.

Syllabus

1. The History of the Book in Britain before 1550 (Candidates will be required to transcribe from and comment on specimens written in English under examination conditions (1 hour).)   35

2. Old English

3. The Literature of England after the Norman Conquest

4. The Medieval Drama

5. Religious Writing in the Later Middle Ages

6. Medieval Romance   40

7. Old Norse sagas

8. Old Norse poetry

9. Old Norse special topic (only to be taken by candidates offering either paper 7 or paper 8 or both)

10./11. One or two of the C course special options as on offer in any year, as specified by the M.St. English, provided that they may not re-take any option on which they have submitted examined work as part of their M.St. course.

12./13./14./15. Relevant options from other courses as specified in the list for the year concerned which will be published by the Graduate Studies Office before the beginning of MT. The teaching and assessment of these options will follow the provisions and requirements as set by the Faculty offering the option.

Examination

The method of examination for each course will be an essay of 5,000–7,000 words to be submitted to Examination Schools, High Street, Oxford not later than noon on Thursday of the tenth week of Michaelmas Term or Hilary Term (depending on the term in which the course was offered).

Two copies of the dissertation (c.15,000 words) on a subject related to their subject of study should be delivered to Examination Schools, by noon on Monday of the eighth week of Trinity Term. The dissertation must be presented in proper scholarly form. Candidates must gain approval of the topic of their dissertation by writing to the Chair of the M.St./M.Phil. examiners, care of the English Graduate Studies Office, by Friday of sixth week of Hilary Term, providing an outline of the topic of not more than 200 words.

Each candidate's choice of subjects shall require the approval of the Chair of the M.St./M.Phil. examiners, care of the English Graduate Studies Office. Approval must be applied for on or before Saturday of the second week of Michaelmas Term preceding the examination.

Candidates are warned that they must avoid duplicating in their answers to one part of the examination material that they have used in another part of the examination, but the dissertation may incorporate work submitted for the first year dissertation.

No candidate who has failed any of the above subjects will be awarded the degree in that examination. Candidates who fail any one of the three papers or the dissertation may re-submit that element by noon on the last Monday of the Long Vacation; candidates who fail more than one element of the examination (including one element plus the translation paper where applicable) must re-submit those elements (and, where applicable, take the translation paper) according to the timetable for the examination in the following year. A candidate may only resubmit or retake a paper on one occasion.

Evidence-Based Social Intervention

(*See also the general notice at the commencement of these regulations.*)

1. Candidates must follow for at least six terms a course of instruction in Evidence-Based Social Intervention.

2. *Qualifying Test*

Every candidate must pass a qualifying test at the end of the third term from the beginning of the course in the *two* compulsory papers, *Evidence-Based Interventions* and *Research Methods* and one *Optional Paper* from the list of optional papers specified by the Department of Social Policy and Intervention. This will be from a list published annually by Friday of the sixth week of Michaelmas Full Term in the Department of Social Policy and Intervention. The examiners may examine candidates viva voce. Candidates who fail the qualifying test will be allowed to retake the test before the beginning of the first week of the next academic year. The Social Policy and Intervention Graduate Studies Committee can decide that the retake shall consist of the whole test or parts thereof.

3. *Final Examination*

Every candidate must offer:

(i) One further optional paper. This will be from a list published annually by Friday of the sixth week of Michaelmas Full Term in the Department of Social Policy and Intervention.

(ii) A thesis* of not more than 30,000 words , on a topic related to, and attentive to the methods of, Evidence-Based Social Intervention, to be delivered to the Examination Schools, High Street, Oxford, by noon of Friday of the sixth week of Trinity Full Term in which the examination is to be taken. Successful candidates may be required to deposit a copy of their thesis in the Social Science Library.

The examiners may examine any candidate viva voce.

The examiners may award a distinction for excellence in the whole examination on the basis of the material submitted to them in both the qualifying test and the final examination.

Compulsory Papers

Evidence-Based Interventions. As specified for the M.Sc. in Evidence-Based Social Intervention.

Research Methods. As specified for the M.Sc. in Evidence-Based Social Intervention.

Optional Papers

These will be from a list published annually by Friday of the sixth week of Michaelmas Full Term in the Department of Social Policy and Intervention. Not every option will be offered in any one year, and applicants for admission will be advised of this. Areas from which options may be offered include: promoting the welfare of children and families; multicultural mental health interventions; substance misuse and offending; interventions in relation to HIV and AIDS; community analysis and community-based intervention; refugees and asylum seekers. Certain other options from the M.Sc. in Comparative Social Policy may also be available in any one year.

General Linguistics and Comparative Philology

(*See also the general notice at the commencement of these regulations.*)

The regulations made by the Faculty of Linguistics, Philology and Phonetics are as follows:

1. Candidates shall normally have a degree in a subject which has given them at least some experience of linguistic or philological work. Those intending to offer options chosen from C or D below should normally have, and may be required to demonstrate, some knowledge of the chosen (group of) language(s) and those intending to offer options chosen from C will normally be expected to be able to read secondary literature in French and German.

2. Each candidate is required:

(*a*) to present himself or herself for written examination as defined in regulation 2 below;

(*b*) to deliver to the Examination Schools, High Street, Oxford, not later than noon on the Friday of the first week of the Trinity Term in the academic year in which he is examined, two copies of a thesis of not more than 25,000 words on the subject approved in accordance with regulation 5 below. The word limit

---

* See the general regulation concerning the preparation and dispatch of theses.

excludes the bibliography, appendices consisting of a catalogue of data, any extensive text which is specifically the object of a commentary or linguistic analysis, and any translation of that text, but includes quotations and foot-notes.

(*c*) to present himself or herself for an oral examination if and when required by the examiners.

3. The examination shall consist of four parts:

(*a*) One general paper as indicated in A.

(*b*) Three papers which must be chosen from those listed in B or must be those listed in C or those listed in D.

A. Linguistic Theory.

B.   (i) Phonetics and Phonology.

   (ii) Syntax.

   (iii) Semantics.

   (iv) Historical and comparative linguistics.

   (v) Psycholinguistics and Neurolinguistics.

   (vi) History and structure of a language.

   (vii) Experimental Phonetics.

   (viii) Sociolinguistics.

   (ix) Computational Linguistics.

   (x) Any one option from those offered as C options for the M.St. in English Language.

   (xi) Any other subject which, from time to time, the Faculty of Linguistics, Philology and Phonetics at its own discretion may consider suitable.

C.   (i) The comparative grammar of two Indo-European languages or language groups.

   (ii) The historical grammar of the languages or language groups selected.

   (iii) Translation from, and linguistic comment upon, texts in the languages selected.

D.   (i) The history of one or two languages.

   (ii) The structure of the language or languages selected.

   (iii) *Either* (*a*) Translation from, and/or linguistic comment upon, texts in the language or languages selected, *Or* (*b*) Any paper from B above except B (vi).

4. The general paper A and the papers in C and D are each assessed by 3-hour written examination. The papers in B are assessed by one of:

(*a*) 3-hour written examination.

(*b*) An essay of between 5,000 and 7,500 words (these limits to exclude symbols and diacritics, figures, the bibliography, appendices consisting of a catalogue of data, questionnaire, or other research instrument used to gather data, any extensive text which is specifically the object of a commentary or linguistic analysis, and any translation of that text, but include quotations and foot-notes). For all B papers except for B(ix) and B(x), the essay (in two typewritten copies) must be sent in a parcel bearing the words 'Essay for the M.St./M.Phil. in General Linguistics and Comparative Philology' to the Chair of Examiners for the Degree of M.St/M.Phil in General Linguistics, c/o Examination Schools, High Street, Oxford. Work for paper B(ix) is submitted as specified in the regulations for the M.Sc. in Computer Science, and work for papers under B(x) is submitted as specified in the regulations for the M.St. in English Language.

(c) A written report of between 5,000 and 7,500 words on the design and execution of an original research project (these limits exclude symbols and diacritics, figures, the bibliography, appendices consisting of a catalogue of data, questionnaire, or other research instrument used to gather data, any extensive text which is specifically the object of a commentary or linguistic analysis, and any translation of that text, but include quotations and footnotes). The research report (in two typewritten copies) must be sent in a parcel bearing the words 'Written work for the M.St./M.Phil. in General Linguistics and Comparative Philology' to the Chair of Examiners for the Degree of M.St./M.Phil. in General Linguistics, c/o Examination Schools, High Street, Oxford.

In addition, the lecturer on the course of instruction may require:

(a) one or more practical problem set(s), to be completed and submitted at a time specified by the lecturer; and

(b) one or more oral presentation(s) in a public forum.

For each paper in B, the lecturer on the course of instruction shall prescribe a suitable combination of these options, and shall make available to the Chair of Examiners evidence showing the extent to which each candidate has pursued an adequate course of work.

5. Of the two languages or language groups selected by the candidates who wish to offer the papers mentioned in C above, one must be studied in greater depth than the other.

Combinations previously offered under the auspices of the Faculty of Linguistics, Philology and Phonetics are:

(a) Greek with the elements of Sanskrit Philology.

(b) Italic with the elements of Old Irish Philology.

(c) Germanic with the elements of Greek Philology.

(d) Greek with the elements of Anatolian Philology.

(e) Romance with the elements of Italic Philology.

(f) Italic with the elements of Greek Philology.

(g) Sanskrit with the elements of Greek Philology.

(h) Greek with the elements of Slavonic Philology.

(i) Celtic with the elements of Italic Philology.

Other combinations will be allowed subject to the approval of the faculty and the availability of teaching.

6. The language or languages selected by the candidates who wish to offer the papers mentioned in D above may be ancient (e.g. Ancient Greek, Latin, Sanskrit, Akkadian, etc.) or modern (e.g. French, Italian, German, English, Turkish, etc.). Only languages for which teaching is available at the time may be offered.

7. The choice of the subjects for the thesis and examination will be subject to the approval of the candidate's supervisor and the faculty, having regard to the candidate's previous experience and to the availability of teaching. Not all options may be offered every year. The subjects which a candidate wishes to offer for examination must be submitted to the faculty for approval not later than Monday of the first week in Michaelmas Term in the academic year in which the candidate is to be examined.

The subject of the thesis must be submitted for approval by the faculty not later than Monday of the first week in Michaelmas Term in the academic year in which the candidate is to be examined.

8. The examiners may require a successful candidate to deposit one of the submitted copies of his thesis in the Bodleian Library. Such a candidate will be required to complete a form stating whether he gives permission for his thesis to be consulted.

Candidates are reminded that work submitted for the degree of M.Phil. may subsequently be incorporated in a thesis submitted for the degree of D.Phil.

9. The Examiners may award a distinction for excellence in the whole examination.

10. If it is the opinion of the examiners that the work done by a candidate is not of sufficient merit to qualify him for the degree of M.Phil. but is nevertheless of sufficient merit to qualify him for the Degree of Master of Studies in General Linguistics and Comparative Philology, the candidate shall be given the option of resitting the M.Phil. examination under the appropriate regulation or of being granted permission to supplicate for the Degree of Master of Studies.

11. Candidates requesting re-examination should be required to resit or resubmit any paper in which they have failed to achieve a pass mark. The highest mark awarded for a re-examined paper should be the pass mark.

Geography and the Environment

1. The Social Sciences Board shall elect for the supervision of the course a Standing Committee, comprising the Director and Deputy Director of the International Graduate School and the two Course Directors of the M.Sc programmes identified in (2) below. The Director of the International Graduate School shall be the Course Director.

2. During the first year, candidates for the M.Phil will:

   (*a*) follow a course of instruction for three terms under the aegis of the School of Geography and the Environment in one of the three M.Sc. programmes, either Nature, Society and Environmental Policy, or Biodiversity, Conservation and Management, or Water Science Policy and Management. They will be assessed in all aspects of the M.Sc. programme, with the exception of the dissertation.

   (*b*) develop a thesis topic, the title and proposal for which will be submitted for approval to the Course Director by the end of Hilary Term of the first year, on the date specified by the department. Candidates registered for the M.Sc programmes listed in paragraph 2 may petition for transfer to the M.Phil degree by submitting a thesis title and proposal by the deadline stipulated above.

3. Examinations at the end of the first year will serve to qualify for entry into the second year of the M.Phil course. Candidates who fail one or more papers at the end of the first year without compensating strength on other papers will be required to resit and pass the failed paper or papers, as determined by the Standing Committee, by the start of the Michaelmas Term of their second year in order to proceed with the degree.

4. In the second year, candidates for the M.Phil will:

   (*a*) offer a thesis of not more than 30,000 words, excluding footnotes, appendices and the abstract. The thesis shall be accompanied by an abstract not exceeding 150 words. Two typewritten copies of the thesis must be submitted to the Examination Schools and addressed to the Chair of Examiners of the M.Phil in Geography, c/o the Examination Schools, High Street, Oxford, by noon of the first weekday of September at the end of the second year. Successful candidates will be required to deposit one copy of their thesis in the Bodleian Library, and will be required to sign a form stating whether they will permit their thesis to be consulted. The thesis shall be accompanied by a statement certifying that the thesis is the candidate's own work except where otherwise indicated.

(*b*) submit one extended essay based on new work set as part of the assessment of the appropriate SoGE M.Sc elective module not taken in the first year of study. Essays based on an elective taken during Michaelmas Term shall be submitted by noon on the first weekday of Hilary Term. Essays based on an elective taken during Hilary Term, shall be submitted by noon on the first weekday of Trinity Term. Approval for the topic of the essay must have been obtained from the elective leader prior to submission. The extended essay shall be accompanied by a statement certifying that the extended essay is the candidate's own work except where otherwise indicated.

5. Arrangements for reassessment shall be as follows:

Candidates who fail to satisfy the examiners on the thesis and/or the extended essay may resubmit the thesis and/or the extended essay on not more than one occasion, which shall normally be within one year of the original failure.

6. Viva voce examination: Candidates must present themselves for viva voce examination when required to do so by the examiners.

7. The examiners may award a distinction for excellence in the whole examination.

Greek and/or Latin Languages and Literature

(*See also the general notice at the commencement of these regulations.*)
The regulations made by the Board of the Faculty of Classics are as follows:

1. *Qualifications.* Candidates must satisfy the board that they possess the necessary qualifications in Greek and/or Latin to profit by the course.

2. *Course.* Every candidate must follow for at least six terms a course of instruction in Greek and/or Latin Languages and Literature. Candidates will, when they enter for the examination, be required to produce from their society a certificate that they are following such a course.

3. *Options.* See the schedule below. Candidates are required to offer a thesis (C) and any *two* options chosen from A and B.

4. *Approval of Options.* The choice of options will be subject to the approval of the candidate's supervisor and of the Graduate Studies Committee in Classics, having regard to the candidate's previous experience, the range covered by the proposed options, and the availability of teaching and examining resources.

Not all options may be available in any given year.

Candidates must submit their provisional choice of *options* to the Academic Administrative Officer, Ioannou Centre, 66 St. Giles', Oxford OX1 3LU not later than noon on the Monday of the week preceding first week of Hilary Full Term next after the beginning of their course; the proposed *thesis title* not later than Tuesday of first week in the Trinity Full Term next following; and the proposed titles of any *pre-submitted essays* (*see* §§ 5 and 7) as soon as practicable, but in any case no later than noon on the Monday of the week preceding first week of Hilary Full Term of the second year of the course (except that the titles of essays to be examined at the end of the first year of study in accordance with cl. 8 below should be submitted no later than the noon on the Monday of the week preceding first week of Hilary Full Term of the *first* year of the course).

5. *Examination.* Each option in section A will be examined by (i) a written paper (three hours) of passages for translation and comment, in which the passages for comment will be set only from the books listed under α in each case, while passages for translation will be set from the books listed under both α and β in each case, and (ii) by three presubmitted essays (see § 7 below) which between them display knowledge of more than a narrow range of the topic. For the examinations to be set in the options under Section B, see the detailed schedule in the Student Handbook.

6. Any candidate whose native language is not English may bring a bilingual (native language to English) dictionary for use in any examination paper where candidates are required to translate Ancient Greek and/or Latin texts into English.

7. *Presubmitted essays.* Essays should each be of between 5,000 and 7,500 words (these limits to exclude the bibliography, any text that is being edited or annotated, any translation of that text, and any descriptive catalogue or similar factual matter, but to include quotations, notes and appendices). A note of the word-count must be included.

Supervisors or others are permitted to give bibliographical help with, and to discuss a first draft of, such essays.

The essays (two typewritten or printed copies) must be delivered in a parcel bearing the words 'Essays presubmitted for the M.Phil. in Greek and/or Latin Languages and Literature' to the Examination Schools, High Street, Oxford OX1 4BG, to arrive by noon on Thursday of sixth week in the appropriate Trinity Full Term.

8. One of the two options taken from A and B must be completed by the end of the first year of study. If it is an option to be examined by presubmitted essays, these must be delivered as in § 7 above, but to arrive by noon on the Thursday of sixth week in the Trinity Full Term of the first year of study for the M.Phil.

9. In theses and pre-submitted essays all quotations from primary or secondary sources, and all reporting or appropriation of material from those sources, must be explicitly acknowledged. Each candidate must sign a certificate to the effect that the thesis or pre-submitted essay is the candidate's own work, and that the candidate has read the Faculty's guidelines on plagiarism. This declaration must be placed in a sealed envelope bearing the candidate's examination number and presented together with the thesis or pre-submitted essay.

10. *Oral Examination.* Candidates are required to present themselves for oral examination if summoned by the examiners.

11. *Distinction.* The examiners may award a distinction for excellence in the whole examination.

12. A candidate who fails to satisfy the examiners may enter for the examination on one (but not more than one) subsequent occasion (as provided under the appropriate regulation). If it is the opinion of the examiners that the work done by a candidate, while not of sufficient merit to qualify for the degree of M.Phil., is nevertheless of sufficient merit to qualify for the degree of M.St. in Greek and/or Latin Languages and Literature, the candidate shall be given the option of resitting the M.Phil. or of being granted leave to supplicate for the degree of Master of Studies.

SCHEDULE

Section A

1. Historiography
2. Lyric Poetry
3. Early Greek Hexameter Poetry
4. Greek Tragedy
5. Comedy
6. Hellenistic Poetry
7. Cicero
8. Ovid
9. Latin Didactic
10. Neronian Literature

The exact prescribed texts for each of options 1-10 will be as listed in the Student Handbook.

11. Medieval and Renaissance Latin Hexameter Poetry	α	In Latin:

         α In Latin:
          1. Walter of Châtillon, *Alexandreis* Book 10;
          2. Petrarch, *Africa* Book 9; *Bucolicum Carmen* 1 and 3;
          3. Vida, *Ars Poetica* Book 3;
          4. Milton, *In Quintum Novembris, Mansus, Epitaphium Damonis.*

         β In translation:
          1. Walter of Châtillon, *Alexandreis* Books 1–9;
          2. Petrarch, *Africa* Books 1–8;
          3. Vida, *Ars Poetica* Books 1–2.

12. Any other text or combination of texts approved by the Graduate Studies Committee in Classics.

In 1–11 passages for translation and comment will be set from the editions listed in the regulations for the Honour School of Literae Humaniores. The editions to be used for any option approved under 12 will be specified by the Graduate Studies Committee in Classics.

Section B

1. *The transmission of Greek texts, and the elements of palaeography and textual criticism,* with closer study of *Euripides*, Orestes 1-347 and 1246-1693. Candidates will be required (i) to presubmit two essays on some aspect of the transmission of Greek texts or textual criticism, (ii) to transcribe a passage from a medieval manuscript (1 hour), and (iii) to take a paper (Honour School of Literae Humaniores, option III.13: 3 hours) of transcription and of comment on passages in the set text.

2. *The transmission of Latin texts, and the elements of palaeography and textual criticism,* with closer study of either (*a*) Seneca, *Agamemnon* or Catullus 1-14, 27-39, 44-51, 65-7, 69-76, 95-101, 114-16*. Candidates will be required (i) to presubmit two

---

* University classes will be given for only one of these options each year.

essays on some aspect of the transmission of Latin texts or textual criticism, (ii) to transcribe a passage from a medieval manuscript (1 hour), and (iii) to take a paper (Honour School of Literae Humaniores, option III.14: 3 hours) of transcription and of comment on passages in the set text.

3. *Greek and Latin Papyrology, with special reference to literary papyri.* Candidates will be required (i) to submit two essays that between them display more than a narrow range of the topic, and (ii) to undertake a practical test, in their own time, in deciphering and commenting on original papyri. (The examiners, in consultation with the supervisor and/or the teacher of the course, will assign each candidate a papyrus or small group of papyri not later than Saturday of sixth week in the Hilary Full Term preceding the candidate's final term; he or she must prepare an edition of it, in proper scholarly form, and deliver two typed copies of this edition to the Examination Schools not later than noon on Thursday of sixth week in the Trinity Full Term in which the examination will be taken. The copies should be accompanied by a statement signed by the candidate to the effect that they are solely his or her own work. This statement must be placed in a sealed envelope bearing the candidate's examination number and presented together with the copies.)

4. *Comparative Philology, with special reference to the history of the Greek and/or Latin language.* Two papers will be set. Paper (i), Essays, will cover (*a*) basic questions about the comparative and/or historical grammar of Greek and/or Latin, and (*b*) questions about the history of the Greek and/or Latin language. Paper (ii), texts for translation and linguistic commentary, will include a compulsory question with passages from *either* Greek dialect inscriptions *or* Latin archaic inscriptions; other passages will be set from Greek and/or Latin literary texts; there will be an opportunity to show knowledge of Linear B and/or Oscan and Umbrian.

5. *Theory and methodology of classical literary studies.* Candidates will be expected to be familiar with the major theoretical and methodological issues that arise in the study of ancient literature, and with the major positions in contemporary critical theory and their relationship to classical studies. They will be required to show knowledge of a range of issues in these areas. Examination will be by means of four pre-submitted essays.

6. *Intermediate Greek.* Candidates will be expected to be familiar with *An Anthology of Greek Prose*, ed. D. A. Russell (Oxford University Press 1991), nos. 17, 18, 23, 24, 33, 40, 44, 66, 78. There will be one two-hour paper and one three-hour paper. The first paper will include passages for unseen translation and grammatical questions on the Russell selection. In the second paper candidates will be expected to translate from the Russell selection and also from two of the following texts: (i) Herodotus I. 1-94 [ed. Hude, OCT]; (ii) Plutarch, *Life of Antony* 1-9, 23-36, 71-87 [ed. Pelling, CUP]; (iii) Euripides, *Bacchae* [ed. Diggle, OCT]. Alternative texts for translation under this head may be offered by agreement with the Graduate Studies Committee.

7. *Intermediate Latin.* Candidates will be expected to be familiar with *An Anthology of Latin Prose*, ed. D. A. Russell (Oxford University Press 1990), nos. 7, 12, 22, 23, 34, 52, and 63. There will be one two-hour paper and one three-hour paper. The first paper will include passages for unseen translation and grammatical questions on the Russell selection. In the second paper candidates will be expected to translate from the Russell selection and also from two of the following texts: (i) Cicero, *Pro Caelio* [ed. OCT]; (ii) Pliny, *Letters* I. 6, 9, 13, 19; VII. 21, 24, 26, 29; VIII. 16, 17; IX. 6, 12, 15, 27, 33, 39; X. 31, 32, 96, 97 [ed. M. B. Fisher and M. R. Griffin, CUP 1973]; (iii) Ovid, *Metamorphoses* 8 [ed. A. S. Hollis, OUP 1970]. Alternative texts for translation under this head may be offered by agreement with the Graduate Studies Committee.

8. Any other subject approved by the Graduate Studies Committee in Classics, which will determine the method of examination.

Section C

A thesis of up to 25,000 words, on a subject to be proposed by the candidate in consultation with the supervisor, and approved by the Graduate Studies Committee in Classics. (The thesis word limit excludes the bibliography, any text that is being edited or annotated, any translation of that text, and any descriptive catalogue or similar factual matter, but includes quotations, notes and appendices. A note of the word-count must be included.) Supervisors or others are permitted to give bibliographical help and to discuss drafts.

The thesis (two typewritten or printed copies) must be delivered in a parcel bearing the words 'Thesis for the M.Phil. in Greek and/or Latin Languages and Literature' to reach the Examination Schools, High Street, Oxford OX1 4BG, by noon on Thursday of sixth week in the Trinity Full Term in which the examination is to be taken.

The examiners may invite a successful candidate to agree that one copy of his or her thesis be deposited in the Bodleian Library.

Greek and/or Roman History

(See also the general notice at the beginning of these regulations.)

1. Every candidate must follow, for at least six terms, a course of instruction in Greek and/or Roman History. Candidates will, when they enter for the examination, be required to produce from their society a certificate that they are following such a course.

2. Candidates may satisfy the Examiners in not more than three options in the Trinity Term of the first year of their course.

3. (*a*) In the case of options in languages, Schedule A below, candidates will be examined by written examination. Candidates taking options A (iii)–(vi) may bring a dictionary for their use in the examination. Any candidate taking either of options A (i) or A (ii) whose native language is not English may bring a bilingual (native language-English) dictionary for use in the examination.

   (*b*) For options in topics and techniques, Schedules B and C below, candidates will be required to pre-submit two essays of not more than 5,000 words in length, which between them display knowledge of more than a narrow range of the topic covered by the course. (The essay word limit excludes the bibliography, any text that is being edited or annotated, any translation of that text, and any descriptive catalogue or similar factual matter, but includes quotations, notes and appendices.)

   (*c*) For the Graduate Seminars, Schedule E below, candidates will be required to pre-submit one essay of not more than 5,000 words, based on a presentation to the Seminar, and one essay of not more than 5,000 words, based on other work done in connection with the Seminar. (The essay word limit excludes the bibliography, any text that is being edited or annotated, any translations of that text, and any descriptive catalogue or similar factual matter, but includes quotations, notes and appendices.)

Supervisors or others are permitted to give bibliographical help with and to discuss drafts of essays. Such essays (two typewritten or printed copies) must be sent in a parcel bearing the words 'Essays presubmitted for the M.Phil. in Greek and/or Roman History' to the Examination Schools, High Street, Oxford, OX1 4BG by noon on the Thursday of the sixth week of the Trinity Term in which the examination is to be taken.

4. *Oral Examination.* Candidates are required to present themselves for oral examination if summoned by the examiners.

5. If it is the opinion of the examiners that the work done by a candidate, while not of sufficient merit to qualify for the degree of M.Phil., is nevertheless of sufficient merit to qualify for the degree of Master of Studies in Greek and/or Roman History, the candidate shall be given the option of resitting the M.Phil. (as provided under the appropriate regulation) or of being granted leave to supplicate for the degree of Master of Studies.

6. *Syllabus*

Candidates must offer (1) an option from A below, (2) an option from B below (3) an option from B or C below, (4) a dissertation as described in D below, and must take, in the first year of their course, (5) one of the Graduate Seminars in Ancient History as described in E below. The option from A must be (i) or (ii), unless a candidate is dispensed from this requirement by the Graduate Studies Committee for Ancient History.

Not all options may be available in any given year.

A

   (i) Intermediate Greek, as prescribed for the Master of Studies in Greek and/or Roman History. Paper A(ii)

  (ii) Intermediate Latin, as prescribed for the Master of Studies in Greek and/or Roman History, Paper A(iv).

 (iii) French

 (iv) German

  (v) Italian

 (vi) Any other language which the candidate has satisfied the Graduate Studies Committee for Ancient History is relevant to their other papers including any dissertation.

B

   (i) Greek Numismatics

  (ii) Roman Numismatics

 (iii) Greek Epigraphy

 (iv) The Epigraphy of the Roman World

  (v) Documentary Papyrology

 (vi) Any of the following papers on the B list of the M.St. in Greek and/or Latin Language and Literature: (i)–(iv); (vii)

 (vii) Any of the papers from Schedule B of the M.St. in Classical Archaeology

(viii) Any other subject approved by the Graduate Studies Committee for Ancient History.

C

   (i) Greek history to *c.*650 BCE

  (ii) Greek history to *c.*650–479 BCE

 (iii) Greek history to *c.*479–336 BCE

 (iv) Athenian democracy in the Classical age

  (v) Alexander and his successors 336–301 BCE

 (vi) The Hellenistic world 301–*c.*100 BCE

  (vii) Rome and the Mediterranean world 241–146 BCE

 (viii) Roman history 146–46 BCE

   (ix) Cicero

    (x) Roman history 46 BCE–54 CE

   (xi) Roman history 54–138 CE

  (xii) Roman history 138–312 CE

 (xiii) The ecology, agriculture and settlement history of the ancient Mediterranean world

 (xiv) The economy of the Roman Empire

  (xv) The provinces of the Roman Empire

 (xvi) Greek and/or Roman religion

 (xvii) Gender and sexuality in the Greek and/or Roman world

(xviii) Greek and/or Latin historiography

 (xix) Roman law

  (xx) The Church in the Roman Empire from the beginnings to 312 CE

 (xxi) The world of Augustine

 (xxii) The City of Rome. This course is run in collaboration with the British School at Rome, and involves attendance at the residential course organised by the School annually in Rome; only those accepted by the School may take the option.

(xxiii) British School at Athens taught course (title and topic vary from time to time). This option is run in collaboration with the British School at Athens, and involves attendance at the residential course organised by the School in even-numbered years in Athens; only those accepted by the School may take the option.

(xxiv) Any other subject approved by the Graduate Studies Committee for Ancient History.

D

A dissertation of not more than 25,000 words on a subject to be approved by the Graduate Studies Committee for Ancient History. (The dissertation word limit excludes the bibliography, any text that is being edited or annotated, any translation of that text, and any descriptive catalogue or similar factual matter, but includes quotations, notes and appendices.)

The dissertation (two typewritten or printed copies) must be sent in a parcel bearing the words 'Dissertation for the M.Phil. in Greek and/or Roman History' to The Chair of the Examiners, c/o Examination Schools, High Street, Oxford, to arrive no later than noon on the Thursday of the sixth week of the Trinity Full Term in which the examination is to be taken.

E

Graduate Seminars

  (i) Greece and the East

 (ii) Rome and the West

These working seminars, organised by members of the faculty in areas of current interest to them, run fortnightly in Michaelmas and Hilary Terms. The topics of the Seminars will vary from time to time. Details are announced in the Graduate hand-book for the Degrees of M.St. and M.Phil. in Greek and/or Roman History.

7. All options, including the dissertation, require the approval of the candidate's supervisor and the Graduate Studies Committee for Ancient History, having regard to the candidate's previous experience, the range covered by the chosen options, and the availability of teaching and examining resources. The options must be submitted for approval not later than the Friday of the fifth week of Michaelmas Term in the candidate's first academic year. Candidates will not normally be allowed to be examined in languages of which they are native speakers or which they have previously studied in taught courses for more than two years.

History of Science, Medicine, and Technology

(*See also the general notice at the commencement of these regulations.*)
The regulations of the Board of the Faculty of History are as follows:

(1) Every candidate must follow for at least six terms a course of instruction in History of Science, Medicine, and Technology, and must upon entering for the examination produce from his or her society a certificate to that effect.

(2) The examination will consist of the following parts:

Qualifying test

Every candidate must pass a qualifying test. The test shall consist of two courses on

1. Methods and themes in the history of science and technology.

2. Methods and themes in the history of medicine.

Candidates may be advised on the basis of their prospective individual research to substitute one of the following courses from the Master of Philosophy in Economic and Social History for (1) or (2) above:

(i) Methodological introduction to research in the social sciences and history.

(ii) Quantitative Methods and Computer Applications for Historians.

A paper from another established course within the University may be substituted for one of the standard courses where this would provide a more appropriate training for the candidate's dissertation focus. Such a choice will need formal approval from both the Course Director and the Chair of the Graduate Studies Committee of the Board of the Faculty of History.

The two methodological introduction courses will each be assessed by a methodological essay of up to 3,000 words. Two typewritten copies of each of the essays must be submitted by noon on Monday of second week of Hilary Term of the candidate's first year to the Chair of Examiners for the M.Phil. in History of Science, Medicine, and Technology, c/o Examination Schools, High Street, Oxford OX1 4BG. In addition, convenors of qualifying courses will confirm in writing to the chair of examiners not later than Friday of eighth week of Hilary Term the candidates' satisfactory participation in their classes, including the completion of any assignments for the weekly sessions. Any approved alternative qualifying course will be assessed within the format and timetable of the paper's parent course. No candidate who has failed the qualifying test of two courses will be permitted to supplicate for the degree. Candidates who fail a qualifying course once will be permitted to take it again, not later than one year after the initial attempt.

Final Examination

The examination shall consist of four papers and a dissertation.

I. Three advanced papers at least two of which must be selected from Schedule I below ('Advanced Papers for the M.Phil. and M.Sc. in History of Science, Medicine, and Technology'), and not more than one from any other M.Phil., the choice of which must be approved by the chair of the Graduate Studies Committee of the History Board not later than Monday of the fourth week of the second Michaelmas Term of the course.

Candidates must take at least two of their advanced papers as three-hour written examinations. For each of their remaining advanced papers candidates must choose to be assessed either by written examination or by two 5,000-word essays. Essays may only be submitted in lieu of written papers for subjects in Schedule I or for papers from other M.Phil.s where similar provision exists in the regulations for those examinations. The essays must be the work of the candidates alone and they must not consult any other person including their supervisors in any way concerning the method of handling the themes chosen. The themes chosen by the candidate must be submitted for approval by the chair of examiners by the examination entry date. Candidates will be informed within two weeks, by means of a letter directed to their colleges, whether the topics they have submitted have been approved. The finished essays must be delivered by the candidate to the Examination Schools, High Street, Oxford, by noon on Monday the sixth week of Trinity Term. The essays must be presented in proper scholarly form, and two typed copies of each must be submitted.

II. *Either* (i) one paper in a discipline or skill or sources or methods selected from Schedule II below.

or   (ii) A fourth advanced paper selected from Schedule I or from any additional list of papers for the M.Phil. and M.Sc. in History of Science, Medicine, and Technology approved by the Graduate Studies Committee of the Board of the Faculty of History and published in the definitive list of Advanced Papers as set out in Schedule I.

III. A dissertation of not more than 30,000 words, including appendices but excluding bibliography on a topic approved by the candidate's supervisor. The dissertation must be delivered not later than noon on the Monday of the first week of the Trinity Term in which the examination is to be taken to the Examination Schools, High Street, Oxford. Dissertations submitted must not exceed the permitted length. If they do the examiners will reduce the marks awarded. The presentation and footnotes should comply with the requirements specified in the Regulations of the Education Committee for the degree of M.Litt. and D.Phil. and follow the *Conventions for the presentation of dissertations and theses* of the Board of the Faculty of History.

Each dissertation must include a short abstract which concisely summarises its scope and principal arguments, in about 300 words.

Candidates must submit by the specified date three copies of their dissertation. These must be securely and firmly bound in either hard or soft covers. One copy of an M.Phil. dissertation which is approved by the examiners must be deposited in the Bodleian Library. This finalised copy should incorporate any corrections or amendments which the examiners may have requested. It must be in a permanently fixed binding, drilled and sewn, in a stiff board case in library buckram, in a dark colour, and lettered on the spine with the candidate's name and initials, the degree, and the year of submission.

3. Candidates may, if they so wish, be examined in up to two of their four papers (or submit essays in lieu of these papers as provided for above) at the end of their first year.

4. The examiners will permit the use of any hand-held pocket calculator subject to the conditions set out under the heading 'Use of calculators in examinations' in the *Regulations for the Conduct of University Examinations*.

5. The examiners may award a distinction for excellence in the whole examination.

6. If it is the opinion of the examiners that the work done by a candidate, while not of sufficient merit to qualify for the degree of M.Phil., is nevertheless of sufficient merit to qualify for the degree of Master of Science in History of Science, Medicine, and Technology, the candidate shall be given the option of resitting the M.Phil. (as provided under the appropriate regulation) or of being granted leave to supplicate for the degree of Master of Science.

7. A candidate who fails the examination will be permitted to retake it on one further occasion only, not later than one year after the initial attempt.

Such a candidate whose dissertation has been of a satisfactory standard may resubmit the same piece of work, while a candidate who has reached a satisfactory standard on the written papers will not be required to retake that part of the examination.

Schedule I

Advanced Papers for the M.Phil. and M.Sc. in History of Science, Medicine, and Technology

A broad range of the course resources are shared with the corresponding courses in Economic and Social History, and Advanced Papers are therefore available in the subject areas listed here.

1. Economic and business history

2. History of science and technology

3. Social history

4. Historical demography

5. History of medicine

A descriptive list of Advanced Papers will be published by the Board of the Faculty of History in September for the academic year ahead (not all options may be available in every year). The definitive list of the titles of Advanced Papers for any one year will be circulated to candidates and their supervisors and posted on the Faculty notice board not later than Friday of third week of Michaelmas Term.

Schedule II

The paper in a relevant discipline or skill may be:

1. One of the papers from the M.Phil. in Economics.

2. One of the papers from the M.Phil. in Sociology or in Comparative Social Policy.

3. One of the papers from the M.Phil. in Russian and East European Studies.

4. One suitable paper from another Master's degree under the auspices of the Faculty of History approved from time to time by the Graduate Studies Committee of the Board of History.

5. One suitable paper from another Master's degree on the recommendation of the candidate's supervisor and endorsed by the Course Director.

Choices under Schedule II have to be approved by the Chair of the Graduate Studies Committee of the Board of the Faculty of History not later than Monday of the fourth week of the second Michaelmas Term of the course. Candidates wishing to take a paper under 1, 2, 3, or 5 will also need the approval of the appropriate course convenor and the Graduate Studies Committee of the relevant faculty board or interfaculty committee who need to be satisfied that each candidate has an adequate background in the subject. Not all options may be available in any one year.

Insert Rider to pages 560-564 (6 pages)

International Relations

(See also the general notice at the commencement of these regulations.)
The regulations made by the Social Sciences Board are as follows:

Qualifying Test
Every candidate must pass a qualifying test before the end of the third term from
commencement of the course unless given exemption by the International Relations
Graduate Studies Committee. The qualifying test shall be set and administered by the
examiners appointed to examine for the M.Phil. in International Relations. This test
shall consist of three parts, as follows:

1. A formally assessed Research Design Proposal of 4,000 words, excluding bibliography, on the subject of the student's proposed M.Phil. thesis. Two hard copies,
together with a copy on CD, must be submitted to the Examination Schools by noon
on the Monday of sixth week of Trinity Term. It must be accompanied by a separate
signed declaration that it is the candidate's own work except where otherwise indicated and that it has not previously been submitted for assessment, either at Oxford
or at another institution. The scope and the format are as stated in the *Notes of
Guidance for Graduate Students and Supervisors in International Relations.*

2. A single, three-hour examination paper covering material from the core papers
as taught in the first two terms. Details of the scope and coverage are given in the
Notes of Guidance for *Graduate Students and Supervisors in International Relations.*
The examination shall take place on the Thursday of noughth week of Trinity Term,
the exact time to be set by the examiners.

3. The examiners must also be satisfied that candidates have satisfactorily completed their designated course of research training, and candidates must submit to the
examiners all course work completed as a part of their research methods training. The
coursework requirements, including administrative arrangements and dates of submission, are set out in the *Notes of Guidance* for *Graduate Students and Supervisors in
International Relations.* Candidates should note that the *Notes of Guidance* will set
dates for the submission (and, where necessary resubmission) of work for individual
research modules.

Entries for the qualifying test must be made on the appropriate form, obtainable from
the University Offices, by Friday of the fourth week of the Hilary Full Term following
the candidate's admission. Candidates who fail the examination part of the qualifying
test may retake it in the eighth week of the same Trinity Term. Candidates who fail the
Research Design Proposal or the course work submitted for the research modules may
resubmit their work by the last Friday of August following the end of Trinity Full Term.

Final Examination
No candidate shall enter the final examination unless he or she has already passed the
qualifying test or has been granted exemption by the Graduate Studies Committee as
stated above. In the final examination every candidate must offer:

1. A thesis of not more than 30,000 words, excluding bibliography, to be delivered
to the Examination Schools, High Street, Oxford, by noon on Monday in the first
week of the Trinity Full Term in which the examination is to be taken. Two hard
copies of the thesis, together with a copy on CD, must be accompanied by a separate
signed declaration that it is the candidate's own work except where otherwise indicated and that it has not previously been submitted for assessment, either at Oxford
or at another institution. After the examination process is complete, each successful
candidate must deposit one hardbound copy of their thesis in the Bodleian Library.

2. *The Development of the International System since 1900.* The history of the
relations between states in peace and war, and the development of the international
system since 1900. It will include such topics as: the pre-1914 system; the balance of

power and the causes of the First World War; the effects of the peace settlement and
the rise of liberal and realist approaches to international relations; collective security
and the League of Nations system; political and economic co-operation in the
interwar period; the USA, Soviet Union, Middle East, and Far East in the interwar years; the impact of domestic politics and ideology on foreign policy; the causes 5
of the Second World War; the relationship between politics and strategy in the
Second World War; post-war reconstruction and the origins of the Cold War; the
evolution of the Cold War; decolonisation and self-determination; regional conflicts;
integration in Western Europe; détente and the end of the Cold War; the evolution of
international economic institutions; the evolution of security institutions; and inter- 10
national relations in the post Cold War world.

3. *Contemporary Debates in International Relations Theory*: Ideas about, and
explanations of, international relations, concentrating mainly (but not exclusively)
on the major theoretical approaches in the academic study of international relations
since 1945. The key theories and approaches to be examined include: realism and neo- 15
realism; theories about war, security, and the use of force in international relations;
classical liberalism, globalisation, and transformation in world politics; theories
about inter-state co-operation and transnationalism; the concept of international
society; constructivism and the impact of law and norms in international relations;
neo-Marxist and critical theory approaches to international relations; normative 20
theory and international ethics.

4. Two subjects chosen from the following. (Teaching in some options may not be
available every year. Students will be advised during the first year of the course of the
teaching arrangements for the optional subjects.)

(a) *European International History since 1945.* The origins of the Cold War 25
in Europe; institution-formation (including Council of Europe, NATO,
European Communities, CSCE); Europe in East-West relations; Germany,
France, and Britain (impact of war, decolonisation; intra-European relations
and relations with the superpowers; values, priorities, and historical memory);
the emergence and character of European Community/Union external policies; 30
the causes and consequences of the end of the Cold War in Europe.

(b) *The Politics of the United Nations and its Agencies.* Examines the evolving role
of the United Nations in world politics. After a theoretical and historical
introduction, the option examines the role and significance of the United
Nations system in four functional areas: human rights, security, humanitarian 35
action, and refugees/internally displaced persons.

(c) *The USSR and Russia in International Relations since 1945.* The evolution of
Soviet foreign policy under Stalin and Khrushchev; the rise and fall of détente;
the USSR and the Third World; ideology and Soviet foreign policy; the role of
the military and military factors; the emergence of Russian foreign policy; the 40
making of Russian foreign policy and the role of domestic factors; NATO
enlargement and relations with Europe; policy in the 'near abroad', including
Ukraine, Central Asia and the Caucasus.

(d) *Strategic Studies.* The development of strategic thought and practice, and the
place of strategic factors in international relations, since the early nineteenth 45
century, with main emphasis on the period since the First World War. The
course, which is varied from year to year in accordance with the research
interests of the graduate students participating, encompasses the following:
security concerns as motives of state behaviour; the phenomenon of civil war
and international response to it; the military implications of technological 50
changes, including in weapons, delivery systems, information management
and communications; strategic doctrine and practice in specific states, includ-

ing the major powers, and in different regions of the world; the emergence of doctrines of deterrence, limited war, and peacekeeping; the roles of alliances and international organisations (including the United Nations) in the authorisation and management of force; aspects of international law relating to armed conflict; the attempts to develop alternatives to reliance on national armaments; negotiations about, and measures of, arms limitation and disarmament; the role of guerrilla warfare and non-violent forms of pressure in international relations; political assumptions of strategic thought.

(*e*) *The United States in International Relations since 1945.* This course examines the foreign policy of the United States since the end of the Second World War. Special emphasis is placed on the forces and factors that have shaped US foreign policy such as political culture, coalitions, the bureaucracy, and cognitive schemas and on the theories used by political scientists to explain the sources and the making of US foreign policy.

(*f*) *The International Relations of the Middle East.* This course covers the international politics of the Middle East and of the Persian Gulf with an emphasis on the period since 1945. There are three main elements: the foreign policies of the Arab states and the relations between them; the Arab-Israeli conflict; and external involvement in the affairs of the region. The course also examines a number of issue areas such as the impact of economic power, the role of Islam, secular ideologies, security, and the causes and consequences of war.

(*g*) *International Political Economy.* The interrelationship between the world economy and the international political system, including the principal theories regarding international political economy. The course seeks to integrate readings and discussions on theory and methodology and analysis of contemporary issues in IPE. Topics will include: the reconstruction of the international economy after 1945; the role of the US in the post-war period and theories of hegemonic stability; the politics of international trade and the evolution of the GATT/WTO system; the development of regional economic arrangements and the relationship between regionalism, multilateralism and globalisation in the world economy; the political economy of the European Single Market; the European Monetary Union; current issues in transatlantic economic relations.

(*h*) *The Function of Law in the International Community.* This course examines the basic aspects of the international legal system, including the sources of international law, the relationship between national law and international law, jurisdiction, state responsibility, and human rights. A central focus is the role of law in international politics, that is, in the day to day relations between states and international organisations, and between states and individuals. The study of the theoretical and analytical aspects of international law, through the literature, is complemented by a practical focus on current issues, including the use of force, international humanitarian law, dispute management, economic conflict, and the role generally of international organisations, particularly the United Nations. Details of the international law documents that will be available to candidates in the examination room will be specified on the reading list issued by the Department of Politics and International Relations.

(*i*) *The International Relations of East Asia.* The Yalta settlement in 1945 and its contributions to establishing a durable security order in the region; the origins and impact of the Cold War in the region, in particular through an examination of the Korean War, the transformation of the American occupation of Japan, and the onset of the Sino-American hostility; the fracturing of the Cold War system examined via the sub-regional organisation, ASEAN, the onset of the Sino-Soviet and Sino-Vietnamese conflicts, the Sino-American rapprochement;

the features of the post Cold War era, including an examination of newly-established institutions such as the ASEAN regional Forum (ARF) and Asia Pacific Economic Cooperation Forum (APEC). The course also examines a number of issues, such as the international causes and consequences of the economic rise of the regional states, democratisation, and the impact of nuclear weapons. The course content varies to some degree from year to year in accordance with the research interests of those taking this option.

(*j*) *Classical Theories of International Relations.* This option provides an advanced understanding of the history and thought on International Relations in the period of the classical European state system, with particular emphasis on the period 1750-1939. Topics will include: theories of the state and the development of the concept of sovereignty; nationalism and national self-determination; international institutions (including international law, international organisations, the balance of power, and diplomacy); war and the use of force (including the evolution of strategic thought, doctrines of intervention, and ideas arising from the rise of the peace movement); liberal, marxist and mercantilist approaches to international political economy; imperialism and the expansion of international society; revolution and its impact on international relations; theories of progress and of historical change. The works bearing on these subjects by, *inter alia*: Rousseau, Herder, Mill, Mazzini, Hegel, Vattel, Hume, Kant, Burke, Castlereagh, von Gentz, Oppenheim, Clausewitz, Smith, Cobden, Bentham, List, Marx, Lenin, Angell, Wilson, Nietzsche, Carr, Zimmern. Candidates will also be expected to demonstrate knowledge of the principal methodological approaches to the history of political thought.

(*k*) *The International Relations of the Developing and Post-Colonial World.* The paper analyses the international relations of developing and post-colonial countries, primarily in the period since 1945. The focus is on (a) the international political economy of development and underdevelopment; (b) the characteristics of developing states and their interaction with the political, economic and military arrangements in the international system; and (c) the rise of the Third World as a challenge to western dominance and the legacy of anti-western challenges in contemporary world politics. Topics include: international relations theory and the international relations of the developing world; decolonization and the emergence of the Third World; the nature of the state and problems of state building in developing countries; the political and economic forces which have shaped international arrangements for trade and finance since 1944 and the role of developing countries within them; political and economic constraints on growth in the world economy; security, intervention, and conflict; regionalism and 'regimes'; emerging powers, especially China, India and Brazil; South-South coalitional politics; political Islam and the West; Southern social movements in global politics.

(*l*) *The International Relations of Latin America.* The history of US-Latin American relations, including the regional significance of the Cold War, impact of the end of the Cold War, and the making of US policy towards the region. Relations between the major European states and the European Union and the sub-continent. Foreign and security policies of the principal Latin American states, including interstate alliances, rivalries within the region and the international aspects of internal conflicts. Latin American perspectives on non-interventionism, international law, dispute settlements, the international human rights and regional and international organisations. Regional and sub-regional co-operation and integration schemes, including the Andean Community, Mercosur, NAFTA, and the proposed Free Trade Area of the Americas. The political economy of the multi-national corporation, and international flows of capital, of labour (including undocumented migrants' remittances), and narcotics. Theories of dependency and underdevelopment; liberalism; realism and foreign policy making. Interactions between domestic and international policy, including the international dimensions of democratisation.

(m) *International Normative Theory.* An analysis of the role of norms and ethics in international affairs. Topics include: state sovereignty, national self-determination, global society and cultural diversity, just war, humanitarian intervention, human rights, international justice, transnational environmental responsibility, and the interrelationships of common morality, international law, and political effectiveness in the cases of specific norms. Candidates will be expected to demonstrate knowledge of the principal contemporary approaches to the study of ethics and norms in International Relations.

(n) *Global Institutional Design.* The Option examines the question of what analytical approaches best explain global institutional design and change in a broad range of issue-areas, including trade and money, human rights, the environment, and security. The term "institution" is broadly defined here and includes not only governance arrangements but also regulation, policies, and norms. The option will also explore new research findings of interest not only to theorists in international relations but also to policy-makers struggling with the issue of how to design effective and fair transnational institutional arrangements in a wide-range of issue-areas.

(o) *State Failure and State Reconstruction (Post-Conflict State Building).* This course examines the theoretical foundations and practices of post-conflict state building, with an emphasis on the experiences of the post-Cold War period. Among the topics addressed will be the changing strategic context of the 1990s; the debates surrounding international intervention in support of post-conflict state building; strategies for assisting and rebuilding fragile and war-torn states; humanitarian, development and security approaches to state reconstruction; the roles of major states and international and regional organisations; and normative issues arising with respect to post-conflict state building. Candidates will be expected to demonstrate strong knowledge of one or more relevant cases.

(p) *Special Topic in International Relations.* To be decided annually by the International Relations Graduate Studies Committee and, if offered, to be notified to candidates by the end of Hilary Term of their first year.

5. Candidates must present themselves for viva voce examination when requested by the examiners. The examiners shall not normally fail any candidate without inviting him or her to attend such an examination. However, in the case of a failing mark in three or more of a candidate's final examination papers, the examiners shall not be obliged to ask the candidate for a viva. The examiners may award a distinction for excellence in the whole examination.

Judaism and Christianity in the Graeco-Roman World

(*See also the general notice at the commencement of these regulations.*)

The regulations made by the Boards of the Faculties of Oriental Studies and Theology are as follows:

Candidates will be admitted to take the examination as defined below in a specific year. In exceptional circumstances candidates may be allowed to take an examination later than one to which they were admitted. Permission for this must be sought from the Faculty Board not later than Monday of the week before the first week of the Trinity Term in which the examination was to have been taken. The application must have the support of the candidate's college and be accompanied by a statement from the supervisor.

I. All candidates shall be required:

(*a*) To satisfy the boards that they possess the necessary knowledge of Hebrew and Greek to profit by the course.

(*b*) To present themselves for a written examination and to offer a thesis, as specified below.

(*c*) To present themselves for viva voce examination unless individually dispensed by the examiners. (No candidate will be failed without a viva.)

II. Candidates shall offer four papers and a thesis, not to exceed 20,000 words. Two papers must be taken on Judaism and two papers must be taken on Christianity, and A(1) and B(1) must be included, unless the boards shall otherwise determine.

A. Judaism

(1) Judaism from 200 BCE to 200 CE.

(2) Jewish historiography (with prescribed texts).

(3) Jewish Bible interpretation (with prescribed texts).

(4) Jewish eschatology (with prescribed texts).

(5) Jewish wisdom literature (with prescribed texts).

B. Christianity

(1) Christianity to 200 CE.

(2) The Gospels and the historical Jesus (with prescribed texts).

(3) Acts and the Pauline corpus (with prescribed texts).

(4) The Apostolic Fathers (with prescribed texts).

(5) The Apologists (with prescribed texts).

Note: Texts will be reported to the Faculty Board's second meeting of Michaelmas Full Term in the first year of the course.

III. The Examiners may award a Distinction for excellence in the whole examination.

Late Antique and Byzantine Studies

(See also the general notice at the commencement of these regulations.)

1. Each candidate will be required to:

(a) follow for at least six terms a course of instruction in Late Antique and Byzantine Studies. Candidates will, when they enter for the examination, be required to produce from their society a certificate that they are following such a course.

(b) present a thesis of not more than 30,000 words on a subject approved by his/her supervisor; the thesis (three copies) must be typewritten and delivered to the Examination Schools, High Street, Oxford, by Monday of seventh week of Trinity Term of the candidate's second year at the latest.

(c) present himself/herself for a viva voce examination when required to do so by the examiners.

2. Candidates must take four of the following six papers. All candidates take the core paper on History, Art and Archaeology, *or*, if they already have the required linguistic competence, History and Byzantine Literature. For the remainder of their course they choose either the two Language and Literature papers and one other paper (which may be a second single language paper), or, if they already have considerable competence in their chosen language or languages, and their principal interests lie in History, Art and Archaeology, or Religion, they choose Auxiliary Disciplines and two Special Subjects.

I. Compulsory core paper on History, Art and Archaeology, *or* History and Byzantine Literature:

Either

(a) Late Antiquity (covering the Roman Empire and adjoining regions)

or

(b) Byzantium

The core paper will be taught in classes in Michaelmas and Hilary Terms. Examination will be by two 5,000-word essays, to be submitted by Monday of seventh week of Trinity Term of the candidate's first year.

II. and III. Language and Literature (teaching in Greek, Latin, Slavonic, Armenian, Syriac, and Arabic will normally be available)

These papers are taught over three terms in classes, with reference to a selection of texts and/or extracts from texts which may vary from year to year according to the interests of candidates. Examination is by two three-hour papers: (candidates are permitted the use of relevant bilingual dictionaries, which will be provided by the faculty)

(a) translation, and

(b) set texts (with passages for translation and comment).

Candidates who are embarking on the study of one of the above languages will normally be expected to take both examinations in that language, but the Committee for Byzantine Studies may in special circumstances permit them to substitute another paper for one of these examination papers, taken at the end of the candidate's first year. Candidates taking a second language in their second year are only required to enter for examination in a single paper.

IV. Auxiliary Discipline(s):

Either

(*a*) any two of the following: epigraphy, palaeography, numismatics, sigillography

or

(*b*) papyrology: Greek, Coptic or Arabic

or

(*c*) artefact studies: one of ceramics, metalware, ivories, codices, carved marbles.

Paper IV will be taught by lectures/classes/tutorials. Examination will be by a three-hour paper, except for papyrology which is assessed by two 5,000-word essays on distinct aspects of the subject.

V. A Special Subject selected from the subject areas listed under 3. below.

Special Subjects will be taught by lectures/classes/tutorials. Examination will be either by two 5,000-word essays or by a 10,000-word dissertation (to be submitted by Monday of seventh week of Trinity Term of the candidate's first year).

VI. A second Special Subject selected from the subject areas listed under 3. below.

Special Subjects will be taught by lectures/classes/tutorials. Examination will be either by two 5,000-word essays or by a 10,000-word dissertation (to be submitted by Monday of seventh week of Trinity Term of the candidate's second year).

Note: both Special Subjects may be taken from the same section of the list below.

3. Overview of Special Subjects (for details, please consult the Course Handbook)

(*a*) History: Special Subjects on offer deal either with specific periods or with certain aspects of late Roman and Byzantine history (including military, diplomatic, political, social, economic and religious history) between the fourth and fifteenth centuries, as well as important developments in neighbouring regions.

(*b*) Art and Archaeology: Special Subjects on offer cover sculpture, portraiture, minor arts, monumental art and architecture of the late Roman, Byzantine, and Islamic spheres of influence as well as the archaeology of town and country throughout the Mediterranean and Near Eastern worlds.

(*c*) Literature (texts prescribed in translation): Special Subjects on offer range through historiography, hagiography, poetry and popular literature, and scholarship in the languages available for the degree programme.

(*d*) Religion: Special Subjects on offer cover theological debates and practical spirituality in the fields of Judaism, Christianity, and Islam.

(*e*) Such other subjects as may be approved on application to the Committee for Byzantine Studies.

Note: The list of Special Subjects detailed in the Course Handbook reflects the expertises and interests of current postholders. The list may be altered from time to time with developments of expertise and changes of interest on the part of the postholders.

4. Teaching in all the options may not be available each year, and applicants for admission will be advised whether teaching will be available in the options of their choice.

5. The examiners may award a distinction for excellence in the whole examination.

6. If it is the opinion of the examiners that the work done by a candidate, while not of sufficient merit to qualify for the degree of Master of Philosophy, is nevertheless of sufficient merit to qualify for the degree of M.St. in Late Antique and Byzantine Studies, the candidate shall be given the option of resitting the M.Phil. (as provided by the appropriate regulation) or of being granted leave to supplicate for the degree of Master of Studies.

Latin American Studies

(*See also the general notice at the commencement of these regulations.*)

For the purposes of this examination, 'Latin America' will be interpreted as the eighteen Spanish-speaking republics of the Western Hemisphere, plus Brazil, Haiti, and Puerto Rico.

The regulations are as follows:

Year 1:

1. In the first year, candidates for the M.Phil in Latin American Studies will:

(*a*) Follow for three terms a course of instruction in the M.Sc in Latin American Studies with the exception of the extended essay. Candidates will present three qualifying examinations, each of which counts for 16.6 per cent of the final degree mark. Examinations at the end of the first year will serve to qualify for entry onto the second year of the course.

(*b*) Develop a thesis topic, which will be the subject of fieldwork in the long vacation between the first and second year. A draft title for the thesis must be submitted for approval by the Latin American Centre Management Committee by 12:00 noon on the Friday of Week 0 of Hilary Term.

(*c*) Candidates may also be required to present themselves for an oral examination if requested to do so by the examiners. The oral examination will focus on the candidate's examination papers.

2. The list of examination papers will be published on the Latin American Centre website and in the *University Gazette* in Week 0 of Michaelmas Term. Candidates must take the core paper in Economics if they wish to take a further paper in that discipline. Specialisation on a single country or a combination of countries is permitted so long as the choice appears in the list of available papers published.

3. Candidates shall be deemed to have passed the qualifying examination if they have passed all three examination papers.

4. Candidates who fail one of the three papers taken at the end of the first year without compensating strengths on the other papers shall be deemed to have failed the qualifying examination. Such candidates will be required to retake it and pass it by the start of the Michaelmas Term of their second year, on a date stipulated by the Chair of Examiners, in order to continue the course without interruption.

5. Candidates who fail more than one paper shall be deemed to have failed the qualifying examination. Such candidates will be permitted to retake the papers failed on one (but not more than one) subsequent occasion, in Trinity Term, one year after the initial attempt. Such candidates must pass the papers that they have retaken in order to continue onto the second year of the course.

Year 2:

6. In the second year, candidates for the M.Phil in Latin American Studies will:

(*a*) Offer a thesis of not more than 30,000 words, including footnotes and appendices. Two typewritten copies of the thesis must be delivered to the Examination Schools and addressed to the Chair of Examiners for the M.Phil in Latin American Studies, c/o Examination Schools, High Street, Oxford, by 12 noon on the Monday of Week 5 of Trinity Term in the calendar year in which the examination is to be taken. Successful candidates will be required to deposit one copy of their thesis in the Bodleian Library, and will be required to sign a form stating whether they will permit their thesis to be consulted. The thesis will be equivalent to two examination papers, and so will count for 33.3 per cent of the final degree mark.

(*b*) Take another examination paper from the list; or by agreement with the Latin American Centre Director of Graduate Studies and the relevant department, take a methodology or other paper from an appropriate M.Phil elsewhere in the University of Oxford. The examination will count for 16.6 per cent of the final degree mark.

(*c*) Candidates will be required to present themselves for an oral examination. The oral examination may focus on the candidate's examination papers, thesis, or both.

7. Candidates shall be deemed to have passed the examination if they have passed all examination papers and the thesis.

8. Candidates who fail the second year examination paper (without compensating strengths on the thesis) or who fail the thesis shall be deemed to have failed the examination. Such candidates will be permitted to resubmit the thesis or retake the examination paper on one (but not more than one) subsequent occasion, in Trinity Term, one year after the initial attempt. Such candidates must pass the thesis or examination paper in order to pass the examination.

9. Candidates who fail both the thesis and the examination paper shall be deemed to have failed the examination. Such candidates will be permitted to retake the examination and resubmit the thesis on one (but not more than one) subsequent occasion, in Trinity Term, one year after the initial attempt. Such candidates must pass both the thesis and the examination paper in order to pass the examination.

10. The examiners may award a distinction for excellence in the whole examination.

Law

(See the regulations for the Bachelor of Civil Law and Magister Juris)

Medical Anthropology

(*See also the general notice at the commencement of these regulations.*)

Within the Division of Social Sciences, the course shall be administered by the School of Anthropology. The regulations made by the divisional board are as follows:

1. The Division of Social Sciences shall elect for the supervision of the course a Standing Committee, namely the Teaching Committee of the School of Anthropology, which shall have power to arrange lectures and other instruction. The course director shall be responsible to the Standing Committee.

The examination shall consist of the following:

1. *Qualifying Examination*

Every candidate will be required to satisfy the examiners in an examination for which, if he or she passes at the appropriate level, he or she will be allowed to proceed to the second year of the M.Phil. Candidates must follow a course of instruction in Medical Anthropology for at least three terms, and will, when entering for the examinations, be required to produce a certificate from their supervisor to this effect. Every candidate for the M.Phil. qualifying examination will be required to satisfy the examiners in four written papers to be taken in the Trinity Term of the academic year in which the candidate's name is first entered on the Register of M.Phil. Students or, with the approval of the Divisional Board, in a subsequent year. The following four papers shall be taken:

(1) *Concepts of disease, illness, health and medicine in global perspective*

The scope of this paper includes discussion of cross-cultural concepts of health, disease, sickness, pain, illness causation, diagnosis and treatment, from conjoined socio-cultural perspectives and human ecology. It explores metaphor and narrative at the interface of biological and cultural processes, the distribution of disease patterns in the light of environmental change, social inequality, global mobility and marginality, and the co-existence of conventional, alternative and traditional health systems.

(2) *Theory and practice of bio-medicine and of other medical systems*

The scope of this paper includes issues of public health and policy on a comparative and global basis. It draws on ethnographies of particular societies to illustrate and test theoretical claims in medical anthropology. It discusses infectious diseases, specific health campaigns, evolutionary trends and life histories, alongside culturally defined concepts of risk, vulnerability, fate, evil, pollution, divination, religion and shamanism.

(3) *Critical medical anthropology*

The scope of this paper comprises ecological and socio-cultural perspectives, and explores links to other fields and disciplines, including the place of material culture in medicine. It includes a critique of basic assumptions and methods in medical anthropology and consideration of the concept of well-being as being broader than conventional concepts of health. Themes for discussion include the phenomenology of the body, growth and personhood, gender, ageing and dying, notions of resistance and resilience, relationships between biodiversity and adaptability, reproduction and fertility, and nutrition.

(4) *Option paper*

Candidates must select one option paper from those taught each year for the M.Sc in Social Anthropology. Titles of options will be made at the beginning of each academic year, and candidates may select their option from any of Lists A, B or C.

2. *Final Examination*

Candidates must follow a course of instruction in Medical Anthropology for at least three terms, and will, when entering for the final examination, be required to produce a certificate from their supervisor to this effect. The final examination shall be taken in the Trinity Term of the academic year following that in which the candidate's name is first entered on the Register of M.Phil. Students or, with the approval of the Divisional Board, in a subsequent year.

Each candidate shall be required:

(1) to submit evidence of practical work and a research proposal in accordance with I below;

(2) to submit a thesis in accordance with II below;

(3) to present himself or herself for oral examination if required by the examiners. The oral examination may be on the candidate's written assignments, or dissertation, or both.

I. *Methods of fieldwork and social research*

The satisfactory completion of a course of practical work in (i) participant observation, in-depth interviewing, archival research, and qualitative data analysis; (ii) basic principles of statistical inference, and statistical models for the analysis of quantitative social science data, and (iii) methods of data collection, including questionnaire design, interviewing, and coding.

The research proposal should not exceed 2,500 words. It need not be on the theme of the thesis, but should reflect the candidate's competence in conceiving and structuring an independent research project.

Candidates shall submit to the Examination Schools by noon on Tuesday of fifth week of the third term of the second year of the course reports of the practical work completed and the research proposal, accompanied by a statement that they are the candidate's own work except where otherwise indicated.

II. *Thesis*

Each candidate shall be required to submit a thesis of not more than 30,000 words (excluding references and appendices) on a subject approved by the supervisor. He or she shall send to the Teaching Committee of the School of Anthropology, with the written approval of his or her supervisor, the proposed title of the thesis for consideration by the School of Anthropology, by noon on the Monday of second week of Michaelmas Term in the academic year following that in which his or her name was entered on the Register of M.Phil. Students. The thesis (three copies) must be typewritten and delivered to the Examination Schools, High Street, Oxford, not later than noon on Tuesday of the fifth week of Trinity Term in the academic year in which the Final Examination is taken. The word count shall be stated on the outside front cover of the thesis.

The Examiners shall require a successful candidate to deposit a copy of his or her thesis in the Tylor Library. If the thesis is superseded by a D.Phil. thesis by the same student partly using the same material, the Divisional Board of Social Sciences may authorise the withdrawal of the M.Phil. thesis from the Tylor Library. Such candidates will be required to sign a form stating whether they give permission for their thesis to be consulted.

The examiners may award a distinction for excellence in the whole examination.

III. *Resits*

In order to pass the degree, a student must pass all its assessed components. Where one or more components are failed, the student will be given the opportunity to re-sit or re-submit them once, as the case may be. Any subsequent award of the degree on successful completion of all the assessed components may be delayed by up to three terms, i.e. until the Examination Board next meets.

Modern British and European History

(*See also the general notice at the commencement of these regulations.*)
The regulations of the Board of the Faculty of History are as follows:

1. Candidates for the Master of Philosophy in Modern British and European History must follow for at least six terms a course of instruction and directed research and must, upon entering the examination, produce from their society a certificate to that effect.

2. Candidates must attend such lectures, seminars and classes as their supervisor shall determine. In addition to the formally examined programme elements described below, each candidate will be expected to attend and complete in-course requirements for a series of skills and specialist options based on a schedule to be published from year to year by the Faculty's Graduate Studies Committee. The candidate's individual programme, agreed with her/his supervisor, will be subject to approval by the Director of Graduate Studies, in consultation with the programme convenor, by Friday of Week One of Michaelmas Term; subsequent changes must be agreed by the Director of Graduate Studies not later than Friday of Week Three of Hilary Term. Class teachers will report to the Chair of Examiners on the candidate's attendance and participation, and, where appropriate, test results, not later than Monday of Week Nine of Hilary Term, except in the case of three-term language classes where the respective reporting deadline will be Monday of Week Nine of Trinity Term.

3. The final examination shall comprise (i) one extended essay based on the programme's theory component, (ii) one extended essay based on an Advanced Option, (iii) one extended essay based on a class on the writing of History, and (iv) one dissertation proposal in the first year of the programme, and (v) one research methodology essay and (vi) a dissertation of not more than 30,000 words in the final year of the programme.

   I. During Michaelmas Term of the first year each candidate will attend core classes on historical theory and methodological approaches as well as a series of classes on sources and resources. The core classes will be assessed by an extended essay of between 4,000 and 5,000 words (the sources and resources component will feed into the preparation of a dissertation proposal in Trinity Term of the first year). Two copies of the essay, addressed to the Chair of Examiners for the Master of Philosophy in Modern British and European History, must be submitted to the Examination Schools by 12 noon on Monday of Week One of Hilary Term of the candidate's first year.

   II. In Hilary Term of the first year candidates must choose one Advanced Option, either from the joint Advanced Options for the Master of Studies in Modern British and European History and the Master of Philosophy in Modern British and European History, or from the Advanced Options for one of the Faculty of History's other Master's programmes. The choice of Advanced Option will depend on the candidate's training objectives or dissertation project. Details of available Advanced Options are published in course handbooks. Approval of the Advanced Option choice must be obtained from the programme convenor and Director of Graduate Studies by Friday of Week Four of Michaelmas Term. The request for approval must be sent to the History Graduate Office.

On recommendation from the candidate's supervisor, the Director of Graduate Studies, in consultation with the programme convenor, may approve relevant taught papers from Master's programmes offered by faculties other than History, provided that the respective faculty's Graduate Studies Committee is satisfied that the candidate has an adequate background in the subject.

This part of the programme will be assessed by one extended essay of between 6,500 and 7,500 words. Two copies of the essay, addressed to the Chair of Examiners for the Master of Philosophy in Modern British and European History, must be submitted to the Examination Schools by 12 noon on Monday of Week Nine of Hilary Term of the candidate's first year.

Essays should reflect skills and understanding the candidate has developed by following the approved choice of paper. The essay may complement but must not share significant content with the essay submitted under I. above.

Teaching may not be available for all the Advanced Options each year, and restrictions may be imposed on the combination of Advanced Options that may be taken in a particular year.

III. In Trinity Term candidates take a class on Writing History and finalise a proposal for their dissertation research during the Long Vacation and Michaelmas Term of their second year. The Writing History classes will be assessed by an extended essay of between 4,000 and 5,000 words. The essay may complement but must not share significant content with the essays submitted under I. and II. above. Two copies of the extended essay on Writing History, addressed to the Chair of Examiners for the Master of Philosophy in Modern British and European History, must be submitted to the Examination Schools by 12 noon on Monday of Week Nine of Trinity Term of the candidate's first year.

IV. Candidates must prepare an extended dissertation proposal of between 2,000 and 2,500 words. Two copies of the extended dissertation proposal, addressed to the Chair of Examiners for the Master of Philosophy in Modern British and European History, must be submitted to the Examination Schools by 12 noon on Monday of Week Six of Trinity Term of the candidate's first year.

V. Candidates must prepare one methodological essay (of up to 7,000 words) and a seminar presentation for a class on 'Historical concepts and controversies', to be examined in Trinity Term of the candidate's second year. Students may choose a topic for their essay and presentation in an area proximate to their dissertation subject, but may not replicate any other material submitted for examination.

Two typewritten copies of the extended essay, addressed to the Chair of Examiners for the Master of Philosophy in Modern British and European History, must be submitted to the Examination Schools by 12 noon on Monday of first week of Trinity Term of the candidate's second year.

VI. A dissertation of not more than 30,000 words, including footnotes and appendices but excluding bibliography, on a topic approved by the candidate's supervisor and the Programme Convenor of the M.Phil. in Modern British and European History. Candidates must apply in writing to the Programme Convenor for approval of the proposed topic of their dissertation. The application must be submitted to the History Graduate Office by 12 noon on Monday of Week Six of Trinity Term of the candidate's first year. Two copies of the dissertation must be submitted to the Examination Schools by 12 noon on Monday of Week

Six of Trinity Term of the candidate's second year. Dissertations submitted must not exceed the permitted length. If they do the Examiners will reduce the marks awarded. The presentation and footnotes should comply with the requirements specified in the Regulations of the Education Committee for the degrees of M.Litt and D.Phil and follow the *Conventions for the presentation of dissertations and theses* of the Faculty of History.

Each dissertation must include a short abstract which concisely summarises its scope and principal arguments, in about 300 words.

Each copy of the dissertation must be securely and firmly bound in either hard or soft covers. One copy of an M.Phil. dissertation which is approved by the examiners must be deposited in the Bodleian Library. This final copy should incorporate any corrections or amendments which the examiners may have requested. It must be hard bound, in a dark colour, and lettered on the spine with the candidate's name and initials, the degree, and the year of submission.

4. A candidate who, at the end of the first year of the course, is unable to continue on to the second year, may, with the support of his or her college and supervisor, apply to the Director of Graduate Studies in History for permission to transfer to the status of a student for the Master of Studies in Modern British and European History and to enter that examination in the current year.

5. The examiners may award a distinction to candidates who have performed with special merit in all parts of the examination for the Master of Philosophy in Modern British and European History.

6. A candidate who fails the examination will be permitted to retake the examination on one further occasion only, not later than one year after the initial attempt. A candidate whose dissertation has been of satisfactory standard will not be required to resubmit the dissertation. A candidate who has reached a satisfactory standard on the extended essays will not be required to retake those papers. If it is the opinion of the examiners that the work done by a candidate, while not of sufficient merit to qualify for the Degree of Master of Philosophy, is nevertheless of sufficient merit to qualify for the Degree of Master of Studies in Modern British and European History, the candidate shall be given the option of resitting the M.Phil (as provided under the General Regulations § 2, cl. 4, and in accordance with this regulation) or of being granted leave to supplicate for the Degree of Master of Studies.

Modern Japanese Studies

(See also the general notice at the commencement of these regulations.)
The regulations made by the School of Interdisciplinary Area Studies are as follows:

First year examinations
1. Candidates will be required to present themselves for examination EITHER in a compulsory paper in Japanese Language; and in two optional subjects at the end of Trinity Term in the year of registration; OR in three optional subjects at the end of Trinity Term in the year of registration.

2. Candidates taking the examination in Japanese Language will also be required to undertake a series of written tests and essays as specified by the MSc/MPhil Programme in Modern Japanese Studies Committee. The forms of assessment, and the dates and times of submission, where applicable, will be notified to students by not later than Friday of noughth week of Michaelmas Full Term.

3. In addition, all candidates will be required to undertake the following assessment:

(i) Research Methods for Area Studies: a series of assignments and/or an unseen written examination as specified by the MSc/MPhil Programme in Modern Japanese Studies Committee. The forms of assessment, and the dates and times of submission, where applicable, will be notified to students by not later than Friday of noughth week of Michaelmas Full Term.

(ii) One 10,000 word dissertation: the title of the dissertation must be approved by the Director of Graduate Studies by not later than 12 noon on Friday of fourth week of Hilary Full Term in the year in which the examination is taken. The dissertation must be submitted by not later than 12 noon of the weekday on or nearest to 1 September in the year in which the examination is taken. The dissertation must be accompanied by a statement that the dissertation is the candidate's own work except where otherwise indicated.

Two typewritten or word processed copies of the dissertation must be delivered to the Examination Schools, addressed to the Chair of Examiners for the M.Sc. in Modern Japanese Studies, c/o Examination Schools, High Street, Oxford at the times and days specified.

Successful candidates will be required to deposit one copy of the dissertation in the Bodleian Library.

4. Candidates who pass these papers will proceed to the second year of the course and take the final examinations at the end of the second year. Candidates who fail one or more of the examination papers may, by permission of the MSc/MPhil in Japanese Studies Examination Board, proceed to the second year of the course and resit the failed papers during the final examination. Candidates who fail any item of coursework may, at the discretion of the MSc/MPhil in Japanese Studies Examination Board, be allowed to revise and resubmit that work no later than the Friday of sixth week of the Trinity Term in the academic year in which they begin the course.

Schedule

The structure of the first year of the course is as follows:

EITHER Mode A

(a) *Compulsory core course in Japanese Language*

(b) *Research Methods for Area Studies*

(c) *Optional papers:* Candidates must choose two optional papers from a list published annually and distributed to students by Friday of noughth week of Michaelmas Full Term.

OR Mode B

(a) *Research Methods for Area Studies*

(b) *Optional papers:*Candidates must choose three optional papers from a list published annually and distributed to students by Friday of noughth week of Michaelmas Full Term.

Final examination

5. No candidate shall enter the final examination unless he or she has already passed all the elements of the first year examination, save that the MSc/MPhil in Japanese Studies Examination Board may permit any candidates who has failed one or more of these elements to resit the papers at the same time as the final examination. In the final examination, every candidate must offer:

(a) a thesis of not more than 30,000 words on a subject approved by the Director of Graduate Studies not later than fourth week of Michaelmas Full Term in the year in which the examination is to be taken, to be delivered to the Examination Schools, High Street, Oxford, by not later than 12 noon on Friday of the third week of Trinity Term in the year in which the examination is taken. The thesis must be accompanied by a statement that the thesis is the candidate's own work except where otherwise indicated. Successful candidates will be required to deposit one copy of the thesis in the Bodleian Library.

(*b*) Advanced Research Methods: a series of assignments and/or an unseen written examination as specified by the MSc/MPhil Programme in Modern Japanese Studies Committee. The forms of assessment, and the dates and times of submission, where applicable, will be notified to students by Friday of noughth week of Michaelmas Full Term.

(*c*) EITHER Mode A

(i) A compulsory paper in Advanced Japanese Language for candidates successfully passing the compulsory core course in Japanese at Upper Intermediate Level in the first year examinations, or for candidates successfully passing the compulsory core course in Japanese at Advanced Level in the first year examinations, a compulsory paper in Upper Advanced Japanese Language. Candidates taking the examination in Japanese language at either Advanced Level or Upper Advanced Level will also be required to undertake a series of written tests and essays as specified by the MSc/MPhil Programme in Modern Japanese Studies Committee. The forms of assessment, and the dates and times of submission, where applicable, will be notified to students by Friday of noughth week of Michaelmas Full Term.

(ii) One optional paper chosen from a list published annually and distributed to students by Friday of noughth week of Michaelmas Full Term, and taken at the end of Trinity Term of the second year of the course.

OR Mode B

(i) Two optional papers chosen from a list published annually and distributed to students by Friday of noughth week of Michaelmas Full Term, and taken at the end of Trinity Term of the second year of the course.

6. Candidates may be required to attend an oral examination on any part of the examination.

7. Candidates who fail one or more of the elements of the final examination will be permitted to resubmit the relevant work or retake the examination paper or papers, as applicable, on one further occasion only, not later than one year after the first attempt.

8. The examiners may award a distinction for excellence in the whole examination.

Modern Languages

(see also the general notice at the commencement of these regulations)

1. Candidates must follow a Programme chosen from those listed in the 'Handbook for Taught-Course Graduate Students'.

In order to gain admission to the course, applicants must show evidence of linguistic ability compatible with advanced literary study in the language(s) chosen to study. Comparative Literature candidates shall not be required to have reading fluency in more than two languages other than English. Unless otherwise stated, candidates will be expected to write in English unless explicit permission is obtained to write in the language (or one of the languages) studied. In the case of Comparative Literature candidates, writing in more than one language in addition to English will not be authorised.

All candidates must follow a course of instruction in Modern Languages at Oxford for a period of six terms. In exceptional circumstances, the Board of the Faculty of Medieval and Modern Languages may permit an extension of time. Candidates shall, when entering their name for the examination, be required to produce from their society a certificate stating that they are following the course of instruction for the period prescribed.

2. All candidates shall be required:

(a) To offer A, B, C, D, and E as defined in 3 below.

(b) To present themselves for viva voce examination at the time appointed by the examiners.

3. The examination shall consist of the following:

(A) *Either*

(i) Methods of Criticism and the Theory of Literature. All candidates must attend such lectures, seminars, and classes as the course convener shall determine. All candidates must present one seminar paper during their course, and submit a written essay based on some aspect of the work done for the seminar. This essay shall be written in English and must be of between 5,000 and 7,000 words in length, inclusive of a bibliography of works consulted. Candidates must submit three typed copies of the essay to the Head of Examinations and Assessments, Examination Schools, High Street, Oxford, by noon on Thursday of tenth week of Hilary Term of their first year. Each copy must have a cover sheet giving the candidate's name, college, the title of the essay, the name of the candidate's supervisor, and the words 'Methods of Criticism and the Theory of Literature, submitted in partial fulfilment of the requirements of the M.Phil. in Modern Languages'.

Or

(ii) Methods of Criticism and History of Ideas in Germany from the Eighteenth to the Twentieth Centuries. All candidates must attend such lectures, seminars, and classes as the course convener shall determine. All candidates must present one seminar paper during their course, and submit a written essay based on some aspect of the work done for the seminar. This essay may be written in English or German and must be of between 5,000 and 7,000 words in length. Candidates must submit three typed copies of the essay to the Head of Examinations and Assessments, Examination Schools, High Street, Oxford, by noon on Thursday of tenth week of Hilary Term of their first year. Each copy must have a cover sheet giving the candidate's name, college, the title of the essay, the name of the candidate's course convener, and the words 'Methods of Criticism and History of Ideas in Germany, submitted in partial fulfilment of the requirements of the M.Phil. in Modern Languages'.

Or

(iii) Methods of Scholarship. Each candidate shall be required to offer either, (1) the History of the Book, or (2) Palaeography with Textual Criticism. Candidates will be examined on one or two essays on topics agreed by them with their course convener relating either to the history of the book (for (1)) or to palaeography with textual criticism (for (2)). The essay or essays should be between 5,000 and 7,000 words in total. Candidates must submit three typed copies to the Head of Examinations and Assessments, Examination Schools, High Street, Oxford, by noon on Thursday of tenth week of Hilary Term of their first year. Each copy must have a cover sheet giving the candidate's name, college, the title of the essay, the name of the candidate's supervisor, and the words 'Methods of Scholarship, submitted in partial fulfilment of the requirements of the Master of Philosophy in Modern

Languages'. For (2), candidates will in addition be required to undertake a practical transcription test, made without reference to dictionaries or handbooks, on a short manuscript text selected by the course convener, who will also mark, sign, and date the candidate's work. The test should take place by the end of the fourth week of the Trinity Term in which the examination is to be taken. The mark should be sent by the course convener to the Modern Languages Graduate Office.

Or

(iv) A methodological essay of between 5,000 and 7,000 words on a topic or issue related to the candidate's Special Subject or dissertation. It might consist, for example, of a theoretical discussion of the candidate's approach to the material being studied, or a detailed analysis of existing approaches. If candidates choose this option, they will be expected to also attend a set of seminars in (i) or (ii) above, or a set of tutorials in (iii), and to make a presentation. The essay must be typed, and include a bibliography. Candidates must submit three copies to the Head of Examinations and Assessments, Examination Schools, High Street, Oxford, by noon on Thursday of tenth week of Hilary Term of their first year. Each copy must have a cover sheet giving the candidate's name, college, the title of the essay, the name of the candidate's supervisor, and the words 'Essay on Method, submitted in partial fulfilment of the requirements of the M.Phil. in Modern Languages'.

The work submitted under (i) must be written in English; the work submitted under (ii) may be written in English or German; the work submitted under (iii) may be written in English or, subject to the approval of the Medieval and Modern Languages Faculty Board, in a language appropriate to the literature concerned.

Approval must be sought for the choice of options in (A) by the end of the fourth week of Michaelmas Term in the first year.

(B) A thesis, which may be written in English or, with the approval of the Medieval and Modern Languages Faculty Board, in the language appropriate to the literature concerned, of approximately 20,000 words and not more than 25,000 words, on a subject approved by the Board or by a person or persons to whom the Board may delegate this function. The subject of the thesis shall be related either to the fields of study represented by (A) (i), (ii) or (iii) above or to one or more of the candidate's Special Subjects (C). When seeking approval for the subject of the thesis, every candidate shall submit with the proposed title a written statement of not more than 500 words explaining the scope of the topic and the manner in which it is proposed to treat it. Candidates are required to register the subject area or title of their dissertation with the Modern Languages Graduate Office by the end of the fourth week of Hilary Term of their second year. The thesis must be presented in proper scholarly form. Three copies typed in double-spacing on one side only of quarto or A4 paper, each copy bound or held firmly in a stiff cover, must be delivered to the Head of Examinations and Assessments, Examination Schools, High Street, Oxford, by noon on Thursday of the sixth week of Trinity Term of the second year.

Successful candidates will be required to deposit one copy of their thesis in the Bodleian Library.

(C) Three Special Subjects.

(i) and (ii) Candidates must select two Special Subjects from those listed in the 'Graduate Studies in Modern Languages' handbook associated with the programme which they are following; candidates may select a special subject from a different programme with approval from their supervisor; (iii) the third Special Subject must be of the candidate's own devising, worked out under supervisory guidance.

Candidates will normally offer two Special Subjects from the same language and area, or from different areas in the same language. The Comparative Literature

Programme will contain Special Subjects from two different languages, or one at least of the special subjects (C, D and E) is comparative in scope

Approval of Special Subjects (i) and (ii) must be sought, by application to the Modern Language Graduate Office, 41 Wellington Square, Oxford by the end of the fourth week of Michaelmas Term of the first year. Approval of Special Subject (iii)   5
and proposed title of the Dissertation must be sought, by application to the Modern Language Graduate Office, 41 Wellington Square, Oxford by the end of the fourth week of Hilary Term of the second year.

The Special Subjects must have the written support of the candidate's supervisor and be approved by or on behalf of the Medieval and Modern Languages Faculty   10
Board. A proposal for a Special Subject of the candidate's own devising shall be accompanied by a statement (of approximately 100 words) of the character and scope of the subject proposed.

Candidates will be assessed on an essay, or two essays (which may be written in English, or, with the approval of the Medieval and Modern Languages Faculty   15
Board, in the language appropriate to the literature concerned), on the topics they have agreed with the supervisor of each Special Subject.

The essay or essays submitted for each Special Subject should be between 5,000 and 7,000 words in total.

Students are required to submit work for assessment on all four of the non-   20
dissertation components (A, C, D and E). Of these four, the component gaining the lowest passing mark will be discounted in the final assessment. A fail mark must always be included in the final assessment.

The Special Subject essays shall be submitted to the Head of Examinations and Assessments, High Street, Oxford, by noon on Thursday of the first week of Hilary   25
Term. However, candidates are strongly advised to complete their essays for the first two Special Subjects by the end of Hilary Term of their first year.

4. Candidates for Comparative Literature should ensure that either at least one of the special subjects (C, D and E) is comparative in scope or the three special subjects are concerned with different languages. The dissertation must deal explicitly with   30
comparative issues.

5. If it is the opinion of the examiners that the work done by a candidate, while not of sufficient merit to qualify for the degree of M.Phil., is nevertheless of sufficient merit to qualify for the Degree of Master of Studies in Modern Languages, the candidate shall be given the option of re-sitting the M.Phil. examination under the   35
appropriate regulation, or of being granted permission to supplicate for the Degree of Master of Studies.

6. In the case of re-submission, candidates shall be required to submit all the material by noon on Thursday of the sixth week of the first Trinity Term following their first examination. Candidates may resubmit on one occasion only.   40

7. The examiners may award a Distinction for excellence in the whole examination.

Music

(*See also the general notice at the commencement of these regulations.*)
The regulations made by the Board of the Faculty of Music are as follows:
Each candidate will be required: 45

1. To follow for at least six terms a course of study in music. Candidates will, when they enter for the examination, be required to produce from their society a certificate to that effect.

2. To have satisfied the examiners in a Qualifying Examination identical to that for the degree of Master of Studies in Music, and governed by the regulations for that degree, in the Trinity Full Term of the academic year in which their name is entered on the Register of graduate students. Candidates whose work in the Qualifying Examination is judged by the examiners to be of the standard required for the degree of Master of Studies in Music but not of the standard required to proceed to the second year of the M.Phil. in Music may supplicate for the degree of Master of Studies in Music. Candidates whose work in the Qualifying Examination is not judged by the examiners to be of the standard required for the degree of Master of Studies may retake the examination on one occasion only. Only candidates who reach the required standard to proceed to the second year at the first attempt may do so.

3. To take a two-part examination of equally weighted components, as follows:

(a) *either* a dissertation of not more than 30,000 words in musicology or ethnomusicology;

    or   a substantial editorial exercise (edition), with prefatory matter, of comparable length.

The topic for the dissertation or edition must be submitted for approval to the Director of Graduate Studies, Faculty of Music, by noon on Friday of the fourth week of Michaelmas Term. Subject to the approval of the Director of Graduate Studies, a dissertation may be a development of the M.St. dissertation or of a relevant portfolio essay. Two typewritten copies of the dissertation or edition must be submitted, not later than noon on the Friday of the first week of Trinity Term, to the Chair of Examiners for the M.Phil. in Music, c/o Examination Schools, High Street, Oxford. Successful candidates will be required to deposit one copy of the dissertation or edition in the Music Faculty Library; minor corrections, as required by the examiners, must be incorporated prior to deposit in the library.

(b) *either* a portfolio of course-work consisting of two essays in musicology or ethnomusicology, neither of which shall be less than 3,000 words, and both of which taken together shall be not more than 10,000 words. The proposed titles of the portfolio essays must be submitted for approval to the Director of Graduate Studies, Faculty of Music, by Friday of third week of Hilary Term. Two copies of the portfolio of essays must be submitted, not later than noon on Friday of the seventh week of Trinity Term, to the Chair of Examiners for the M.Phil. in Music, c/o Examination Schools, High Street, Oxford;

    or a portfolio of one or two well-contrasted compositions of not more than thirty minutes' duration. The portfolio of compositions must be submitted, not later than noon on Friday of the seventh week of Trinity Term, to the Chair of Examiners for the M.Phil. in Music, c/o Examination Schools, High Street, Oxford;

    or a recital of not more than sixty minutes' duration, vocal or instrumental, of at least two contrasted pieces. Two possible programmes must be submitted for approval to the Director of Graduate Studies, Faculty of Music, by Friday of third week of Hilary Term. Candidates will be informed of the examiners' choice of programme by the Friday of eighth week in the same term.

The selected component in part 3(b) (essays/composition(s)/recital) must correspond to that pursued for the Qualifying Examination, but the subject matter of the essays, composition(s) or recital pieces must be different from those offered for examination in the first year.

4. Each candidate must attend an oral examination when required to do so by the examiners, at which any aspect of the candidate's submissions and course work might be subject to discussion.

5. The examiners may award a distinction for excellence in the whole examination.

6. A candidate who fails the final examination will be permitted to retake it on one further occasion only, not later than one year after the initial attempt. Such a candidate whose work has been of satisfactory standard in one or more elements examined will be required to resubmit for examination the element(s) which fell below the passmark when originally examined.

Oriental Studies

(See also the general notice at the commencement of these regulations.)

The regulations made by the Board of the Faculty of Oriental Studies are as follows:

1. Every candidate must present himself or herself for a written examination in one of the following subjects.

   (i) Cuneiform Studies.

  (ii) Egyptology (including Graeco-Roman and Christian Egypt).

 (iii) Modern Middle Eastern Studies.

 (iv) Classical Indian Religion.

  (v) Modern Jewish Studies.

 (vi) Jewish Studies in the Graeco-Roman Period.

 (vii) Islamic Art and Archaeology.

(viii) Ottoman Turkish Studies.

 (ix) Islamic Studies and History.

  (x) Modern Chinese Studies.

 (xi) Tibetan and Himalayan Studies.

 (xii) Modern South Asian Studies.

(xiii) Traditional East Asia: Classical, Medieval, and Early-Modern.

2. Candidates for subject (i) must satisfy the Oriental Studies Board by the time of their qualifying examination that they possess a working knowledge of French and German; candidates for (ii) must satisfy the Oriental Studies Board by the time of their qualifying examination that they possess a working knowledge of French and German, and candidates who wish to offer Greek papyrology must possess a fluent knowledge of Greek; and for subject (v) candidates must satisfy the person appointed by the board to interview them that they possess a working knowledge of either Hebrew or Yiddish, and a relevant European language. For subject (viii) and the Turkish option in subject (ix) candidates must satisfy the person appointed by the board to interview them that they possess a sound reading knowledge of Modern Turkish or Arabic or Persian. For subject (x) Modern Chinese Studies, candidates will normally have a first degree in a discipline relevant to their elective subject. For subject (xiii) Traditional East Asia: Classical, Medieval, and Early Modern, candidates must satisfy the person appointed by the board to interview them that they possess a good proficiency (normally at least two years' study or equivalent) in modern Chinese, Japanese or Korean.

A candidate who fails any part or parts of the Qualifying Examination may retake such part or parts during the Long Vacation prior to the second year of the course, except in the cases of the M.Phil. in Classical Indian Religion, Modern Middle Eastern Studies, Modern Jewish Studies and Tibetan and Himalayan Studies.

A candidate who fails any part or parts of the Qualifying Examination for these four courses may retake such part or parts during Trinity Term of the first year of study.

3. Subject to such regulations as the board may hereinafter make, every candidate must offer a thesis* on a subject approved by the board (or by a person or persons to whom it may delegate the power of giving such approval), and as far as possible falling within the scope of the subject offered by the candidate in the examination. Applications for approval of the thesis subject must reach the Board of the Faculty of Oriental Studies, Oriental Institute, on or before Monday in the sixth week of Trinity Full Term in the academic year preceding that in which the examination is to be taken except for thesis titles for (iii) and (xii), which must be received by Monday in the second week of Michaelmas Term, in the second year of the course and for (x) which must be received by Friday of the first week of the Hilary Term preceding the examination. A title approval form is available on the Oriental Studies website. The thesis should be presented not later than noon on the Friday of the second week of the Trinity Term in which the examination is taken except in (ii) below, in which the thesis should be presented not later than noon on the Friday of the fourth week of the Trinity Term in which the examination is taken; (v) below, in which the thesis should be presented by noon on Friday of the sixth week of Trinity Term; (vii) below, in which the thesis should be presented at least fourteen days before the first day of the examination; (x) below, in which the thesis should be presented not later than noon of Monday of the second week of Trinity Term in which the examination is taken; and (xiii) below, in which the thesis should be presented not later than noon of Friday of the fifth week of Trinity Term in which the examination is taken.

Successful candidates will be required to deposit one copy of the thesis in the Bodleian.

4. Every candidate will be examined viva voce in the subjects of the school unless he or she shall have been individually excused by the examiners.

5. The examiners may award a distinction for excellence in the whole examination.

Subjects

(i) *Cuneiform Studies*

A. *Qualifying Examination*

Each candidate will be required, unless exempted by the Oriental Studies Board, to pass a qualifying examination in the Sumerian and Akkadian languages not later than the end of the third term after that in which his or her name has been placed on the register.

B. *Final Examination*

Each candidates will be required to offer the following papers:

1. Prepared translations of Sumerian texts and related essay questions (1 paper)

2. Prepared translations of Akkadian texts and related essay questions (1 paper)

A list of prepared texts in the Sumerian and Akkadian languages will be provided to the candidate after he or she has successfully passed the qualifying examination. The list of texts will be reported to the Faculty Board's second meeting of Michaelmas Term in the second year of the course.[†]

---

* See the general regulation concerning the preparation and dispatch of theses. Candidates are reminded that work submitted for the Degree of M.Phil. may subsequently be incorporated in a thesis submitted for the Degree of D.Phil.

† Lists of set texts will be available in the Course Handbook.

3. Unprepared translations of Akkadian (1 paper)

4. History and culture of ancient Mesopotamia (1 paper)

Candidates must demonstrate knowledge of the outlines of major aspects of Mesopotamian history, including political, social, economic, and cultural developments. They will be required to submit two essays each of not more than 5,000 words in length, which display knowledge of more than just a narrow range of the topic.

Candidates are required to collect the subject of the essays from the Faculty Office, Oriental Institute, by noon, Friday of Week 1 of Michaelmas Term of the second year of the course for the first essay and by noon, Friday Week 1 of Hilary Term of the second year of the course for the second essay. The essays must be submitted to the Examination Schools by the end of Weeks 8 of Michaelmas Term and Hilary Term respectively. For each essay two printed copies and a signed form certifying that the essay is the candidate's own work must be delivered in a parcel bearing the words 'Essay presubmitted for the M.Phil. in Cuneiform Studies' to the Examination Schools, High Street, Oxford OX1 4BG.'

5. The cuneiform world in context and approaches to the study of Assyriology;

(*a*) Cuneiform world in context (one half paper)

Candidates must be able to integrate the study of the cuneiform world into the wider context of the Near East. Three approaches may be pursued:

(1) The cuneiform world and the ancient Near East, i.e. the Hittite, Egyptian, or Biblical worlds.

(2) The cuneiform world and the ancient Mediterranean, i.e. Graeco-Roman antiquity.

(3) The cuneiform world and the later Near East, i.e. late antique and medieval periods.

Candidates must specify which of these approaches they will pursue not later than the end of the third term after that in which their name has been placed on the register. Not all options may be available every year.

(*b*) Approaches to the study of Assyriology (one half paper):

Questions will be set on the method, theory, bibliography, and history of Assyriology. Candidates will be expected to demonstrate knowledge of how to research any subject relating to cuneiform studies, and how to evaluate critically the contributions of disciplines, such as anthropology, archaeology, art history, history, and literary criticism, to the study of the cuneiform world.

C. *Thesis*

Each candidate will be required to present a thesis of not more than 20,000 words on a subject approved by the board. The thesis needs to include a substantial cuneiform-related element. The thesis should be presented not later than noon on the Friday of the second week of Trinity Term in which the final examination is taken.*

(ii) *Egyptology*

This course covers topics relating to dynastic, Graeco-Roman, and Christian Egypt.

A. *Qualifying Examination*

Each candidate will be required, unless exempted by the Oriental Studies Board, to pass a qualifying examination in Egyptian and/or Coptic not later than the end of the

---

* See general regulations for theses and special regulations for theses in Oriental Studies.

third term after he or she is admitted. Candidates offering options relating to the Graeco-Roman period may be required to pass a qualifying examination in Greek.

B. *Final Examination*

1. Syllabus A: A candidate who has a first degree in Egyptology or equivalent qualification must offer Section I, *three* papers from Section II, and a thesis of not more than 30,000 words on a subject to be approved by the board.

2. Syllabus B: All other candidates must offer Section I, *two* papers from Section II, Section III, and a thesis of not more than 20,000 words on a subject to be approved by the board.*

3. All applications for approval of options and thesis title must reach the Secretary, Board of the Faculty of Oriental Studies, Oriental Institute, on or before Monday in the sixth week of Trinity Full Term in the academic year preceding that in which the examination is to be taken. For options under Section II applicants must include a detailed definition of the topics offered and a list of primary sources, to be countersigned by their supervisors.

4. For the Final Examination the following papers will be set:

   I. (i) A general paper on Egyptology.

   Questions will be set on method, theory, bibliography, and the history of Egyptology. Candidates will be expected to answer some questions outside the areas of their fields of specialisation.

   (ii) Unprepared translation from Egyptian texts.

   Passages may be set for translation from texts of all periods from the end of the Old Kingdom to the Conquest of Alexander. Texts of other periods may be set with the permission of the board.

   II. *Two* (for candidates under 2 above) or *three* (for candidates under 1 above) papers in a special field selected from the list below, of which one will be on an appropriate category of primary source material.

Since all fields may not be available in every year, candidates must confirm with the Graduate Studies Committee of the Oriental Studies Board that the field they intend to offer is available by the end of the second term after they are admitted. Some related fields (e.g. demotic with Greek papyrology) may be combined with the permission of the board.

One paper in the special field will be set as a take-home examination. The answer or answers for this examination should be typed and presented in proper scholarly form. Candidates will be informed as to which paper is to be examined as a take-home on Friday of eighth week of the Hilary Term preceding the Final examination; conventions for the setting of the paper will be released at the same time. The question paper for the take-home examination will be distributed to candidates in the Oriental Institute at 10 a.m. on Monday of first week in Full Term in the term in which the final examination is to be offered. The completed examination must be handed in to the Examination Schools, High Street, Oxford no later than 12 noon on Monday of second week. The completed paper should not exceed 5,000 words in length.

For a second topic in the special field, candidates will be required to presubmit two essays of not more than 5,000 words each, which between them display command of

---

* See general regulations for theses and special regulations for theses in Oriental Studies.

more than a narrow range of the topic. Supervisors or others are permitted to give bibliographical help and to discuss drafts of essays. Such essays (two printed copies) must be delivered in a parcel bearing the words 'Essays presubmitted for the M.Phil. in Egyptology' to the Examination Schools, High Street, Oxford OX1 4BG by noon on the Thursday of the sixth week of Trinity Term in which the examination is to be taken.

The following fields will normally be available:

Archaeology

Art and iconography

Christian Egypt

Demotic

Egyptian grammar

Graeco-Roman hieroglyphic texts

Greek papyrology

Hieratic texts

Egyptian literary *or* religious texts

Periods of history, from the early dynastic to the Byzantine.

III. Prescribed texts in Middle and Late Egyptian (two papers). The list of texts to be offered will be reported to the Faculty Board's second meeting in Michaelmas Term in the second year of the course and subsequently published in the Course Handbook.

(iii) *Modern Middle Eastern Studies*

A. *Qualifying Examination*

Every candidate must pass a qualifying examination not later than the end of the second term from the commencement of the course. A candidate with an intermediate level of proficiency (the equivalent of 2-3 years of study) in Arabic, Persian or Turkish may offer respectively Advanced Arabic, Advanced Persian or Advanced Turkish. A candidate with native fluency or who has satisfied the examiners in the Second Public Examination in Arabic or Persian or Turkish or Hebrew, or has passed a similar examination in another university, must offer a different language for examination. The examination will consist of two papers:

(i) A language examination in Arabic or Advanced Arabic or Hebrew or Persian or Advanced Persian or Turkish or Advanced Turkish, (subject to the availability of teaching), based on grammar knowledge and reading comprehension.

(ii) A general methodological paper on the Middle East in the twentieth century.

Entries must be made on the appropriate form, obtainable from the University Offices, by Friday in the second week of Hilary Full Term following the candidate's admission. Candidates who fail the Qualifying Examination may at the discretion of the board be allowed to retake it in the first week after the following Full Trinity Term.

B. *Final Examination*

It is strongly recommended that candidates for the Final Examination should, in the course of the Long Vacation preceding the year in which they propose to take the examination, attend a recognised language course in an appropriate Middle Eastern country.

1. All candidates must offer

   (*a*) one language paper in Arabic or Hebrew or Persian or Turkish, subject to the availability of teaching, based on knowledge of grammar, translation from the Oriental language to English, and reading comprehension or, for candidates who offered Advanced Arabic, Advanced Persian or Advanced Turkish for the Qualifying Examination, one language paper in Arabic, Persian or Turkish respectively based on prose composition, translation from the Oriental language to English, and reading comprehension;

   (*b*) a thesis of not more than 30,000 words on a subject to be approved by the board*;

   (*c*) three papers from (1)–(16), provided that instead of one of these papers, a candidate may offer a paper on a subject not included in the list below, with the approval of the board.

      (1) History of the Middle East, 1860–1970.

      (2) Politics of the Middle East.

      (3) Social anthropology of the Middle East.

      (4) International Relations of the Middle East.

      (5) Iranian History from the Constitutional to the Islamic Revolution, 1905–1979.

      (6) History of Turkey, 1908–80.

      (7) History and Politics of the Islamic Republic of Iran, 1979–2005.

      (8) Mass Media and the Middle East.

      (9) Politics of the Maghreb.

      (10) The Maghreb since 1830.

      (11) Israel: History, Politics and Society.

      (12) The Political Economy of the Middle East and North Africa.

      (13) Islam in the West.

      (14) Contemporary Islamic Ethics.

      (15) Political Islam, Islamism and Modern Islamic Movements.

      (16) Modern Turkish Literature: Texts and Contexts.

Teaching for some options may not be available in every year. Applicants for admission will be advised whether teaching will be available in the options of their choice.

2. All applications for approval must reach the Secretary, Board of the Faculty of Oriental Studies, Oriental Institute, on or before the Monday in the second week of the Michaelmas Full Term preceding the examination.

(iv) *Classical Indian Religion*

A. *Qualifying Examination*

Candidates must pass a qualifying examination in Sanskrit not later than the end of the second term of the academic year in which the candidate's name is first entered on the register of M.Phil. students unless exempted by the Board of the Faculty of Oriental Studies.

---

* See general regulations for theses and special regulations for theses in Oriental Studies.

B. *Final Examination*

Candidates will be required to offer the following four papers, but a candidate may submit a thesis of not more than 20,000 words on a subject approved by the board* instead of Paper (iv).

(i) (*a*) Unprepared translation from epic and commentarial Sanskrit.

(*b*) Translation from the set books in two of the sections, as published in the Course Handbook. Lists of set texts will be reported to the Faculty Board's second meeting of Michaelmas Full Term in the second year of the course.

In Papers (ii) and (iii) candidates will be expected to show background knowledge of relevant social and political history. Emphasis will be laid on the study of primary sources, which may, however, be read in translation.

(iv) Approaches to the study of Indian religion:

Candidates will be asked to give a critical appreciation of the contributions of different disciplines (theology, anthropology, philology etc.) and to discuss the application of various theoretical approaches (e.g. evolutionism, diffusionism, dialectical materialism, phenomenology, structuralism) to the subject.

(v) *Modern Jewish Studies*

A. *Qualifying Examination*

Candidates must pass a qualifying examination in Modern Hebrew or Yiddish not later than the end of the second term of the academic year in which the candidate's name is first entered on the Register of M.Phil. students unless exempted by the Board of the Faculty of Oriental Studies. The examination will consist of a language examination in Hebrew based on grammar knowledge and reading comprehension. Candidates who fail the Qualifying Examination may be allowed to retake that part in Trinity Term of the first year of the course.

Candidates, who will submit a take-home essay in their first year of the course to partially fulfil the requirements of (*b*) in the Final Examination, must enter for this paper in their first year. Marks will not be moderated for Final Examination take-home essays taken in the first year of the course until the end of the second year of the course. Any failed Final Examination papers may be retaken on one occasion only, at the same time in the following academic year.

B. *Final Examination*

All candidates must offer

(*a*) one language paper in Modern Hebrew or Yiddish based on grammar knowledge, reading comprehension, and translation into English, at a level equivalent to Intermediate or higher.

(*b*) Four papers from the following list.

Candidates will present themselves for take-home essay examination. Essay examination will consist of the submission of two essays of not more than 2,500 words each for each of the four papers chosen, which must be submitted to the Examination Schools, High Street, Oxford, by 12 noon on the Friday of noughth week of the term following that in which the paper was taught. Candidates will collect the essay topics from the Oriental Institute Faculty Office, on the Friday of eighth week of the term in which the paper is taught. When a paper assessed by take-home essay is taught in the first year of the course, candidates must enter for the paper in the first year. Candidates proposing to offer a paper not included in the list below must obtain

---

* See general regulations for theses and special regulations for theses in Oriental Studies.

the permission of the Board of the Faculty of Oriental Studies. All applications for approval must be sent to the Secretary of the Board on or before the Monday in the second week of the Michaelmas Full Term preceding the examination.

1. Modern Jewish History.
2. Religious movements in Judaism from *c.*1700 to the present day.
3. Modern Jewish thought.
4. Hebrew literature and society (with prescribed texts):
   (*a*) Hebrew literary centres prior to 1948 *or* (*b*) Hebrew literature in Israel from 1948.
5. Modern Jewish politics.
6. Israel: History, Politics and Society.
7. The Holocaust: from History to Memory.
8. Jewish literature in the nineteenth and twentieth centuries.
9. Modern Yiddish literature.

Teaching for some options may not be available in every year. Applicants for admission will be advised whether teaching will be available in the options of their choice. Prescribed texts will be reported to the Faculty Board's second meeting of Michaelmas Full Term in the first year of the course.

C. *Thesis*

A candidate shall submit a thesis of not more than 30,000 words on a topic selected in consultation with his or her supervisor and approved by the faculty Board.* Any failed Final Examination papers or thesis may be retaken on one occasion only, at the same time in the following academic year.

(vi) *Jewish Studies in the Graeco-Roman Period*

A. *Qualifying Examination*

Candidates must pass a qualifying examination in Jewish Studies not later than the end of the third term after that in which the candidate's name is first entered on the register of M.Phil. students unless exempted by the Board of the Faculty of Oriental Studies.

B. *Final Examination*

Every candidate shall submit a thesis of not more than 30,000 words* and present himself for a written examination. The written examination shall consist of Paper 1 and three further papers to be chosen from Papers 2 to 8.

(1) Jewish literature, history, and institutions from 200 BC to AD 425.
(2) Jewish historiography with prescribed texts.
(3) Jewish law with prescribed texts.
(4) Jewish Bible interpretation with prescribed texts.
(5) Jewish eschatology with prescribed texts.
(6) Jewish liturgy with prescribed texts.
(7) Jewish wisdom literature with prescribed texts.
(8) Jewish papyrology and epigraphy with prescribed texts.

Notes. 1. Candidates must satisfy the Board of the Faculty of Oriental Studies before admission to the course that they possess the necessary qualifications in the Hebrew language to profit by the course. Those wishing to take options 2 or 8 must show evidence of their knowledge of Greek.

---

* See general regulations for theses and special regulations for theses in Oriental Studies.

2. Papers 2–8 will contain passages for translation and comment as well as general questions relating to the prescribed texts.

3. Texts will be reported to the Faculty Board's second meeting of Michaelmas Full Term in the first year of the course.

(vii) *Islamic Art and Archaeology*

A. *Qualifying Examination*

Every candidate will be required to satisfy the examiners in a qualifying examination not later than the end of the third term after that in which the candidate's name is first entered on the Register of M.Phil. Students. The examination will include:

(*a*) a three-hour written examination: Introduction to Islamic Art and Archaeology, *c.550–c.1900*.

(*b*) a portfolio, containing reports on the practical work completed during the year (according to the schedule given in the Course Handbook).

(*c*) a language examination in Arabic or Persian or Turkish.

Candidates must submit the portfolio in (*b*) above not later than 12 noon on Monday of 7th Week of Trinity Term. Two printed copies and one digital copy on either a CD-ROM disc or a memory stick must be submitted in a securely sealed parcel clearly addressed to the Chair of Examiners, M. Phil. in Islamic Art and Archaeology (Oriental Studies), Examination Schools, High Street, Oxford. The parcel must bear the words 'QUALIFYING EXAMINATION FOR THE M. PHIL. IN ISLAMIC ART AND ARCHAEOLOGY (PORTFOLIO). The portfolio must bear the candidate's examination number (but not the candidate's name, which must be concealed). Candidates must include a signed declaration sealed in an envelope addressed to the Chair of Examiners that the work is the candidate's own.

B. *Final Examination*

This shall be taken in the Trinity Term of the academic year following that in which the candidate's name is first entered on the Register of M.Phil. Students.

1. Every candidate must follow for at least six terms a course of instruction in Islamic Art and Archaeology.

2. The examination will include:

(*a*) A paper on a topic of Islamic art and archaeology or related fields (e.g. non-Islamic art, architecture and archaeology; Islamic studies; history; museology) to be selected by the candidate in consultation with the candidate's supervisor. This paper will be examined by an extended essay of between 5,000 and 6,000 words. Applications for the approval of the essay topic should be submitted to the Faculty office by Monday of sixth week of Michaelmas Term and will be reported to the Faculty Board's second meeting of Michaelmas Term.

(*b*) Arabic or Persian or Turkish language examination.

(*c*) Arabic or Persian or Turkish prepared texts.

(*d*) A three-hour written examination: Approaches to Islamic Art and Archaeology.

(*e*) A dissertation* of not more than 30,000 words on a subject to be approved by the Faculty Board. Applications for such approval should be submitted to the Faculty office by Monday of sixth week of Michaelmas Term and will be reported to the Faculty Board's second meeting of Michaelmas Term.

3. Candidates must submit the extended essay in (*a*) above not later than noon on the Monday of first week of Trinity Term of the year in which they sit the examination.

---

* See general regulations for theses and special regulations for theses in Oriental Studies.

4. Candidates must submit the dissertation in (*e*) not later than 12 noon on Monday of 7th Week of Trinity Term.

5. Both the extended essay and the dissertation must be submitted in printed form and as a digital copy on either a CD-ROM disc or a memory stick. Two printed copies and one digital copy of each must be submitted in a securely sealed parcel clearly addressed to the Chair of Examiners, M. Phil. in Islamic Art and Archaeology (Oriental Studies), Examination Schools, High Street, Oxford. The parcels must bear the words 'FINAL EXAMINATION FOR THE M.PHIL. IN ISLAMIC ART AND ARCHAEOLOGY (EXTENDED ESSAY [or DISSERTATION]). Each piece of work must bear the candidate's examination number (but not the candidate's name, which must be concealed). Candidates must include a signed declaration sealed in an envelope addressed to the Chair of Examiners that the work is the candidate's own.

If it is the opinion of the examiners that the work which has been required of a candidate is not of sufficient merit to qualify him or her for the Degree of M.Phil., the candidate shall be given the option of resitting the M.Phil. examination under the appropriate regulation, or of being granted permission to supplicate for the Degree of Master of Studies.

(viii) *Ottoman Turkish Studies*

A. *Qualifying Examination*

Every candidate will be required, unless exempted by the Oriental Studies Board, to pass a qualifying examination in Ottoman Turkish not later than the end of the third term after that in which his or her name has been placed on the register.

B. *Final Examination*

Every candidate will be required to offer the following four papers and a thesis* of not more than 30,000 words.

(1) Essay questions on Ottoman history and institutions, 1453–1699.

(2) Ottoman historical texts.

(Set texts will be reported to the Faculty Board's second meeting of Michaelmas Full Term in the second year of the course.)†

(3) Ottoman texts in modern transcription and post-1928 Ottomanising texts.†

(4) Ottoman documents:

Ottoman Documents, ed. Repp (copies are available from the Oriental Institute).

Teaching for the course may not be available in every year: applicants for admission will only be accepted if teaching is available.

(ix) *Islamic Studies and History*

A. *Qualifying Examination*

Each candidate will be required, unless exempted by the Oriental Studies Board, to pass a qualifying examination in Arabic or Persian or Ottoman Turkish or any other language approved by the Faculty Board not later than the end of the third term after that in which his name has been placed on the register. The content of the examination shall be of such nature as to satisfy the board that the candidate is capable of using pre-modern in the respective language.

---

* See general regulations for theses and special regulations for theses in Oriental Studies.

† Lists of texts are available in the Course Handbook.

B. *Final Examination*

1. It is strongly recommended that candidates for the Final Examination attend a recognised language course in an appropriate Middle Eastern country during the long vacation between the third and fourth terms of their study.

2. The examination shall take place not later than the end of the third term of the second year from the candidate's admission to the M.Phil degree programme. Full details of the examination will be provided in the examination conventions, which will be made available to the candidates in the second term of the second year of the course. Candidates must make their entries for the Final Examination by filling out the appropriate examination entry form by Friday of the first week of the second term of the second year from the candidate's admission to the course. The examiners may award a distinction to candidates who have performed with special merit. A candidate who fails this examination will be permitted to retake it on one further occasion only, not later than one year after the initial attempt. Such a candidate whose dissertation has been of a satisfactory standard may resubmit the same piece of work, while a candidate who has reached a satisfactory standard on the written papers will not be required to retake that part of the examination.

3. The Final Examination shall consist of these elements (a–c):

(*a*) All three of the following papers (1–3):

(1) A language examination in Arabic, or Persian, or Ottoman Turkish, or any other language approved by the Faculty Board.[†]

(2) A prescribed take-home essay on methods and research materials which must not exceed 4,000 words (on deadlines see below).

(3) Islamic studies and history, 570–1500.

(*b*) Two of the following papers (5.1–5.22, at least one of which must involve translation into English of excerpts from a set text, or from a selection of set texts). Teaching for some options may not be available in every year. Applicants for admission will be advised whether teaching will be available in the options of their choice. All candidates must obtain the approval of the Board of the Faculty of Oriental Studies for the papers they wish to offer. All applications for approval must reach the Secretary, Board of the Faculty of Oriental Studies, Oriental Institute, not later than the Monday in the second week of Michaelmas Full Term preceding the examination.

5.1 From late antiquity to early Islam

5.2 Religion, politics and culture in the Umayyad period, 661–750

5.3 History, culture and society in the early Abbasid period, 750–925

5.4 Islamic historiography

5.5 The Seljuqs

5.6 Mamluk Egypt

5.7 History and culture during the Mongol Period

5.8 The rise of the Ottomans to 1566

5.9 Mughul India

5.10 Timurid History and Historiography

5.11 Safavid History

5.12 Arabic or Persian or Ottoman Palaeography

5.13 Qur'an

---

* Lists of texts are available in the Course Handbook.

5.14 Hadith

5.15 Islamic law

5.16 Sufism

5.17 Islamic theology

5.18 Muslim/non-Muslim relations

5.19 Arabic or Persian or Ottoman Turkish literature in any period prior to 1500

5.20 Topics in Arabic Philosophy

5.21 A paper chosen from the M.St. in Islamic Art and Archaeology

5.22 Other subject approved by the Board of the Faculty of Oriental Studies

All papers will be examined in the Examination Schools, High Street, Oxford at the end of Trinity Term except the prescribed essay on methods and research materials a (2). The topic of that paper will be announced by noon on Monday of the fifth week of the Trinity Term. The paper must be submitted to the Examination Schools, High Street, Oxford by noon on Monday of the sixth week of the Trinity Term.

(c) A thesis of 25,000 words on a subject approved by the Oriental Studies Faculty Board, of which two typed copies must be delivered to the Examination Schools, High Street, Oxford, by Noon of Monday of the fifth week of Trinity Term of the second year from the candidate's admission to the course. The thesis must be accompanied by a signed statement by the candidate that the thesis is his or her own work except where otherwise indicated.

(x) *Modern Chinese Studies*

Candidates in Modern Chinese Studies must follow EITHER Track A (Social Science) OR Track B (Humanities) throughout the entire course. Candidates are required to spend a period of at least three months on an approved course of language study in China or Taiwan after the qualifying examination at the end of the Trinity Term of the first year, and before the start of the Hilary Term of the second year.

A. *Qualifying Examination*

The examination shall take place not later than the end of the third term from the candidate's admission to the programme. Full details of the Qualifying Examination will be provided in the examination conventions, which will be made available to the candidates from the eighth week of the first term of the candidate's admission. Candidates who fail one or more parts of the Qualifying Examination may be allowed to retake that part or parts once at the end of the Long Vacation of the first year of the course. Candidates who fail the Final Examination elective paper taken with the Qualifying Examination in the first year of the course may be allowed to retake that part with the remainder of the Final Examination papers offered at the end of the second year of the course.

The Qualifying Examination shall consist of three parts for Track A and two parts for Track B, as follows:

(1) *Study of Modern China* Each candidate will be required to follow a course of instruction on modern China. Candidates will present themselves for examination in the core course Study of Modern China at the beginning of Hilary Term of the first year.

(2) *Modern Chinese language (written and oral)*

All candidates must offer one written and one oral Chinese examination. Candidates will be examined in Chinese I or Chinese II. Those who have followed the Chinese II course will not be permitted to enter for the Chinese I examination. Candidates shall present themselves for examination in Chinese language at the end of Trinity Term of the first year.

(3) *Research Methods for Area Studies* (Track A only)

All candidates are required to undertake an assessment in research methods for Asian studies, which is a series of assignments and/or unseen written examinations as specified by the Oriental Studies Faculty Board. The forms of assessment, and the dates and times of submission, where applicable, will be notified to candidates by not later than Friday of noughth week of Michaelmas Full Term.

Candidates shall also be required to offer one Final Examination Elective Paper at the end of Trinity Term of the first year (see below).

B. *Final Examination*

No candidate can pass the Final Examination unless he or she has already passed all parts of the first-year Qualifying Examination. The examination shall take place not later than the end of the third term of the second year from the candidate's admission to the M.Phil. degree programme, with the exception of the first of the two elective papers that shall be taken at the end of the first year of the programme. Full details of the examination will be provided in the examination conventions that will be made available to the candidates in the second term of the second year of the course. (see A. above). In order to pass the degree all parts of the Final Examination must be passed. A candidate who fails the Final Examination will be permitted to retake it on one further occasion in the following year and only have to retake those parts of the examination that were failed.

The Final Examination shall consist of:

(1) *Thesis*

The thesis will not be more than 20,000 words on a subject approved by the Oriental Studies Faculty Board. Applications for approval of the thesis subject must reach the Secretary, Board of the Faculty of Oriental Studies, Oriental Institute, on or before Friday of the first week of the Hilary Term preceding the examination. Two typewritten or word-processed copies of the thesis must be delivered to the Examination Schools, High Street, Oxford, by Noon of Monday of the second week of Trinity Term of the second year from the candidate's admission to the programme. The thesis must be accompanied by a statement that it is the candidate's own work except where otherwise indicated. Successful candidates will be required to deposit one copy of the thesis in the Bodleian Library, and to sign a form stating whether they give permission for it to be consulted.

(2) *Two Elective papers*

Candidates will be required to choose two elective papers offered as option courses under the M.Phil. or M.Sc. in Modern Chinese Studies or under another Master's (M.Phil., M.Sc. or M.St.) degree programme in the University. The latter must be approved by the Board. The first elective paper will be taken at the end of the first year of the course, while the second paper will be taken at the end of the second year of the course. A list of papers approved for this purpose by the Oriental Studies Faculty Board will be available from the Course Director. The paper elected in the second year may not be the same as that taken in the first year. The examiners may, at their discretion, either require candidates to sit the standard examination paper for these elective papers, or offer a paper set specifically for students on the M.Phil. in Modern Chinese Studies.

(3) *Modern Chinese language (written and oral)*

Candidates will be required to take the written examination and an oral examination at the end of the Trinity Term of their final year. Candidates will be examined in Chinese I or Chinese II. Those who have followed the Chinese II course will not be permitted to enter for the Chinese I examination.

(4) *Modern China Humanities* (Track B only)

Candidates will be required to take a final written examination in the study of Modern China.

The examiners may examine any candidate viva voce.

The examiners may award a distinction for excellence in the final examination, but not in the qualifying examination.

(xi) *Tibetan and Himalayan Studies*

A. *Qualifying Examination*

Candidates must pass a qualifying examination in Tibetan language at the end of the Hilary Term of their first year. This will consist of a written and an oral examination.

B. *Final Examination*

1. All candidates will be required to offer the following three papers, to offer a thesis of not more than 30,000 words, and to present themselves for an oral examination.

    (i) Unseen translation both from and into Tibetan.

    (ii) Translation from two set texts, which will include a modern Tibetan work and a classical work. The texts will be reported to the Faculty Board's second meeting of Trinity Full Term in the second year of the course[†].

    (iii) History and civilisation of Tibet and the Himalayas. Topics covered will include the history, politics, religion, and anthropology of the region.

C. *Thesis*

Candidates must submit a thesis of not more than 30,000 words on a topic selected by the candidate in consultation with his or her supervisor and approved by the faculty board.[*]

(xii) *Modern South Asian Studies*

A. *Qualifying Examination*

Candidates must pass a qualifying examination in Modern South Asian Studies not later than the end of the third term after that in which the candidate's name is first entered on the register of M.Phil students. Unless exempted by the Board of the Faculty of Oriental Studies candidates will be required to offer the following papers:

1. Qualifying examination in Hindi (or the substitute core) language, based on knowledge of grammar, translation and reading comprehension.

2. A general methodological paper on the history and culture of South Asia, to be assessed by three-hour examination.

Candidates, who will submit a take-home essay in their first year of the course to partially fulfil the requirements of (*c*) in the Final Examination, must enter for this paper in their first year. The mark for such essays will not be moderated until the candidate's final year of the course. Any failed Final Examination papers may be retaken on one occasion only, at the same time in the following academic year.

B. *Final Examination*

1. All candidates must offer:

(*a*) one of the following language papers in Hindi, Literary Hindi, Bengali Brajbhasha, Sanskrit, Tibetan or Persian, based on knowledge of grammar, translation and reading comprehension. (Teaching for some languages may not be available every year.)

---

† Lists of set texts are available in the Course Handbook.

* See general regulations for theses and special regulations for theses in Oriental Studies.

(*b*) a thesis of not more than 20,000 words on a topic selected by the candidate in consultation with his or her supervisor and approved by the Faculty Board at its second meeting in the Michaelmas Term preceding the term in which the candidate proposes to take the final examination, in the academic year following that in which the candidate's name was entered in the Register of M.Phil. students. Three typewritten copies of the thesis must be delivered to the Examination Schools, High Street, Oxford not later than noon on Friday of the third week of the Trinity Full Term in which the examination is to be taken.

(*c*) three papers from (i)-(xvii) below. Instead of one of these papers, a candidate may offer a paper on a subject not included in the list below, with the approval of the board.

2. Optional Subjects

Courses marked with an asterisk are assessed by three-hour examination at the end of the second year. Others may be assessed either by three-hour examination at the end of the second year or on the basis of two essays of not more than 5,000 words each, on topics selected by the candidate from a list on the take-home examination paper, to be collected from the Faculty Office after 12 noon on the last Friday of term in which teaching for the paper is completed. The essays must be submitted to the Examination Schools, High Street, Oxford, by 12 noon on the Friday of noughth week of the term following that in which formal teaching for the Optional Subject is completed. When a paper assessed by essay is taught in the first year of the course, candidates must enter for the paper in the first year.

The Optional Subjects are:

    (i) Early Hindi Texts*

    (ii) Modern Hindi Texts*

    (iii) Urdu Literary Texts*

    (iv) History and Civilisation of Tibet and the Himalayas (Paper (iii) in the MPhil in Oriental Studies (xi) *Tibetan and Himalayan Studies*)

    (v) The Social Anthropology of a Selected Region: South Asia (Paper (i) in the MPhil in Social Anthropology)

    (vi) Societies and economies in India 1600–1800

    (vii) Aspects of social change in South Asia, c. 1860 to the Present (Advanced Option (ii) in the MSt in Global and Imperial History)

    (viii) Islamic History in South Asia

    (ix) Scientific knowledge systems and their history in India

    (x) History and Politics of South Asia (Paper (e) in the MPhil in Politics)

    (xi) Gender and Society in India, c. 1800 to the present

    (xii) Material and visual culture of South Asia

    (xiii) Approaches to the history of Hinduism in India

    (xiv) Shaivism

    (xv) History of Medicine in South Asia

    (xvi) Gender and experience in Hindi Literature

    (xvii) History of Afghanistan c. 1900 to the present

    (xviii) Any other subject approved by the faculty board

Teaching for some optional subjects may not be available in every year.

---

* See general regulations for theses and special regulations for theses in Oriental Studies.

3. The examiners may award a distinction for excellence in the whole examination.

4. A candidate who fails the examination will be permitted to retake it on one further occasion only, not later than one year after the initial attempt. Such a candidate whose thesis has been of a satisfactory standard may resubmit the same piece of work, while a candidate who has reached a satisfactory standard on the written papers will not be required to retake that part of the examination.

(xiii) *Traditional East Asia: Classical, Medieval, and Early Modern*

A. *Qualifying Examination*

Every candidate will be required, unless exempted by the Board of the Faculty of Oriental Studies, to satisfy the examiners in an examination, to be known as the Qualifying Examination for the M.Phil in Traditional East Asia: Classical, Medieval, and Early Modern, not later than the end of the third term after that in which the candidate's name is first entered on the Register of M.Phil Students. All candidates must offer:

1. A language examination in modern Chinese or modern Japanese or modern Korean

2. A language examination in classical Chinese or classical Japanese or middle Korean

3. A written examination in Traditional East Asia

4. Three submitted essays on traditional East Asia. The essays, which must be of not more than 2,500 words each, must be written by the candidate, one in each of the three terms of the first year, and must be chosen by the candidate to represent the candidate's best written performance in that term. Each essay must be submitted to the Examination Schools, High Street, Oxford, by 12 noon on the Friday of eighth week of the term in which the paper is taught.

B. *Final Examination*

This shall be taken in the Trinity Term of the academic year following that in which the candidate's name is first entered on the Register of M.Phil Students or, with the approval of the faculty board, in a subsequent year. All candidates must offer:

1. Prescribed texts in one of the following: (i) Classical Chinese; (ii) Classical Japanese; (iii) Middle Korean; (iv) Classical Chinese and Classical Japanese; (v) Classical Chinese and Middle Korean.

2. Research Bibliography and Methodology on one of the following: (i) China; (ii) Japan; (iii) Korea. This paper will be set as a take-home examination. The answer or answers should be typed and presented in proper scholarly form. The question paper will be distributed to candidates in the Oriental Institute at 10 a.m. on Monday of eighth week of the Trinity Term in which the Final Examination is to be taken. The completed examination must be handed in to the Examination Schools no later than 12 noon on Friday of the same week.

3. Thesis. Candidates must submit a thesis of not more than 30,000 words on a subject selected by the candidate in consultation with his or her supervisor and approved by the Board of the Faculty of Oriental Studies.*

4. The examiners will also examine every candidate viva voce unless excused.

---

* See general regulations for theses and special regulations for theses in Oriental Studies.

Philosophical Theology

(*See also the general notice at the commencement of these regulations.*)

The regulations made by the Board of the Faculty of Theology and Religion are as follows:

Candidates will be admitted to take the examination as defined below in a specific year. In exceptional circumstances candidates may be allowed to take an examination later than one to which they were admitted. Permission for this must be sought from the faculty board not later than Monday of the week before the first week of the Trinity Term in which the examination was to have been taken. The application must have the support of the candidate's college and be accompanied by a statement from the supervisor.

Candidates shall be required:

(*a*) To present themselves for a written examination in three of the papers prescribed below, the selection to depend on their previous qualifications;

(*b*) to present a thesis* of not more than 30,000 words on a topic in philosophical theology to be approved by the faculty board (the thesis must be accompanied by a signed statement by the candidate that the thesis is his or her own work except where otherwise indicated; successful candidates may be required to deposit one copy of the thesis in the Bodleian and to sign a form stating whether they give permission for the thesis to be consulted);

(*c*) to present themselves for a viva voce examination unless individually dispensed by the examiners (no candidate will be failed without a viva).

1. *Philosophy of Religion*

with syllabus for examination the same as that for essays for the B.Phil. in Philosophy.

2. *Either Moral Philosophy*

or Metaphysics and Theory of Knowledge

or Philosophical Logic and Philosophy of Language

or Philosophy of Science

or Philosophy of Mind and of Action

with syllabus for examination the same as that for essays for the B.Phil. in Philosophy.

3. *History of Philosophical Theology*

The paper will contain questions on philosophical influences on theology during the patristic period, the early medieval period, and the period 1760–1860. Candidates are required to show knowledge of two of the three periods, and, within each of those two periods, of some of the principal relevant writings, viz. for the patristic period of works of Origen and Augustine, for the early medieval period of works of Anselm and Aquinas, and for the period 1760–1860 of works of Kant, Kierkegaard, and Schleiermacher. Study of texts in the original languages will not be required.

4. Either *The Development of Christian Doctrine to* AD *787* or *Theology in Western Europe from Gabriel Biel to Jacob Arminius*

as specified for the M.Phil. in Theology (paper 1 of Section A and paper 1 of Section C of the Christian Doctrine option).

The Examiners may award a Distinction for excellence in the whole examination.

If it is the opinion of the examiners that the work done by a candidate is not of sufficient merit to qualify him or her for the Degree of M.Phil. but is nevertheless of

---

* See general regulations for theses and special regulations for theses in Oriental Studies.

sufficient merit to qualify him or her for the Degree of Master of Studies in Philosophical Theology, the candidate shall be given the option of resitting the M.Phil. examination under the appropriate regulation, or of being granted permission to supplicate for the Degree of Master of Studies.

Politics (Comparative Government, Political Theory, European Politics and Society)

(*See also the general notice at the commencement of these regulations. The current edition of the Notes of Guidance for Graduate Students and Supervisors in Politics contains an elaborated version of these regulations.*)

The regulations made by the Politics Graduate Studies Committee are as follows:

Qualifying Test

Each candidate must pass a Qualifying Test at the end of the third term from the beginning of the course in the two *compulsory* papers specified for their course, unless given exemption by the Politics Graduate Studies Committee.

In *Comparative Government* the two compulsory papers are Comparative Government and Research Methods in Political Science.

In *European Politics and Society* the two compulsory papers are European Governance and Research Methods in Political Science.

In *Political Theory* the two compulsory papers are Theory of Politics and Research Methods in Political Theory.

Candidates who fail the written examination part of the Qualifying Test will normally be allowed to retake it before the beginning of the next academic year.

Compulsory papers:

(*a*) *Research Methods*

  (i) *Research Methods in Political Science* is a compulsory paper for candidates in Comparative Government and in European Politics and Society. Candidates will satisfactorily complete a programme of core and optional research methods training, as specified in the Notes of Guidance for Graduate Students and Supervisors in Politics, and will also produce a Research Design Essay of between 4,000 and 6,000 words, excluding bibliography, on research design as it bears on some aspect of politics. Two hard copies of the Research Design Essay, together with a copy on CD, must be submitted to the Examination Schools by noon on the Friday of sixth week of Trinity Term. It must be accompanied by a separate signed declaration that it is the candidate's own work except where otherwise indicated and that it has not previously been submitted for assessment, either at Oxford or at another institution. The essay will normally be related to the subject of the student's proposed M.Phil. thesis. The Director of Graduate Studies in Politics shall draw the attention of the examiners to the names of any candidates who have failed to complete their research methods training to a satisfactory level of quality, and the examiners may require candidates to retake the course or a specified part thereof.

  (ii) *Research Methods in Political Theory* is a compulsory paper for candidates in Political Theory. Candidates will satisfactorily complete a programme of core and optional research methods training, as specified in the Notes of Guidance for Graduate Students and Supervisors in Politics, and will also produce a Research Design Essay of between 4,000 and 6,000 words, excluding bibliography, on research design as it bears on some aspect of political theory. Two copies of the Research Design Essay, together with a copy on CD, must be submitted to the Examination Schools by noon on the Friday of sixth week of Trinity Term. It must be accompanied by a separate signed declaration that it is the candidate's own work except where otherwise indicated and that it has not previously been submitted for assessment, either at Oxford or at another institution. The essay will normally be related to the subject of the student's proposed M.Phil. thesis.

The Director of Graduate Studies in Politics shall draw the attention of the examiners to the names of any candidates who have failed to complete their research methods training to a satisfactory level of quality, and the examiners may require candidates to retake the course or a specified part thereof.

Candidates in European Politics and Society will be required to have a working (i.e. good reading) knowledge of two of the following languages of the European Union: viz. English, and one of French, German, Italian, Polish, or Spanish. Unless exempted by the Politics Graduate Studies Committee, candidates will be tested in the language or languages they propose to offer by the end of their third term. Candidates who fail the test will normally be allowed to retake the test before the beginning of the next academic year.

(*b*) *Comparative Government*

(Compulsory paper for Comparative Government students only)

The theory and practice of government in modern states.

(*c*) *Theory of Politics*

(Compulsory paper for Political Theory students only)

A critical examination of political concepts and theories, including social concepts and theories with political relevance.

(*d*) *European Governance*

(Compulsory paper for European Politics and Society students only)

The constitutions and formal structure of governments in European states, including the UK, and the theory and practice of integration in Europe.

The marks achieved by candidates in the two compulsory papers of the Qualifying Test will be carried forward to be considered by the examiners in the second year alongside the marks achieved in the Final Examination.

Final examination

No candidate shall enter the final examination unless he or she has already passed the Qualifying Test. In the final examination every candidate must offer:

(1) A thesis* of not more than 30,000 words, excluding bibliography. Two hard copies, together with a copy on CD, must be submitted to the Examination Schools by noon on the Monday of first week of Trinity Term. The thesis must be accompanied by a separate signed declaration that it is the candidate's own work except where otherwise indicated and that it has not previously been submitted for assessment, either at Oxford or at another institution. After the examination process is complete, each successful candidate must deposit one hardbound copy of their thesis in the Bodleian Library.

(2) Two subject papers.

Candidates sitting for the M.Phil. (Comparative Government) may select two papers from the following list: (*e*)–(*y*).

Candidates sitting for the M.Phil. (Political Theory) may select two papers from the following list: (*x*)–(*ag*).

Candidates sitting for the M.Phil. (European Politics and Society) may select two papers from the list: (*e*)–(*ag*).

---

* See the general regulations concerning the preparation and dispatch of theses. Candidates are reminded that if after completing the M.Phil. they are accepted by the Politics Graduate Studies Committee for registration for the D.Phil., work submitted for the Degree of M.Phil. may subsequently be incorporated in a thesis submitted for the Degree of D.Phil.

Candidates may, with the special permission of the Politics Graduate Studies Committee, offer subjects outside this list. Applications must be made by the last Friday of the Trinity Term preceding that in which the examination is to be taken, and must be supported by the student's supervisor. Supervisors should ensure that applications are submitted as early as possible so that if approval is not given, the candidate has sufficient time to choose an alternative. Teaching in some options may not be available each year.

(*e*) *The History and Politics of South Asia*

The political history, political sociology, political institutions, and political economy of South Asia (India, Pakistan, Sri Lanka, and Bangladesh) since 1947; the state, political institutions, party politics, and 'movement' politics; conditions for democracy; the politics of gender, class, caste, religion, and ethnicity; the evolution of political ideologies; social organisation, culture and identities as they bear on politics, the politics of 'development'.

(*f*) *Politics in Africa*

Political action, representation, and institutions in African countries through comparative perspectives: generalisations and exceptionalisms; analytic approaches; forms of colonial rule; African nationalisms; one-party systems; military regimes; multi-party systems; politics of democracy; parties and elections; conditions of democracy; politics of economic reforms; politics of health and HIV/AIDS; land reform and agricultural policies; politics of elites; workers and trade unions; rural societies and politics; ethnicities and politics; religions and politics; gender and politics.

(*g*) *The Politics of Transition in Central and Eastern Europe*

This course chooses a comparative and thematic approach to explore the politics of transition in Central and Eastern Europe (broadly defined). The key themes this course analyses are: the dynamics of the collapse of socialism; theories of transition and consolidation; the role of agency, leadership and institutional design; political and social mobilisation; EU accession and EU conditionality; nation- and state-building (including federal break-up, ethnic conflicts and minority protection); and migration patterns.

(*h*) *Political Sociology*

As specified for the *M.Phil. in Sociology*.

(*i*)–(*p*) *The Politics and Government of Major States*

    (*i*) The Politics and Government of the UK;

    (*j*) The Politics and Government of the USA;

    (*k*) The Politics and Government of France;

    (*l*) The Politics and Government of Russia;

    (*m*) The Politics and Government of Germany;

    (*n*) The Politics and Government of Italy;

    (*o*) The Politics and Government of China;

    (*p*) The Politics and Government of Japan.

Candidates will be expected to show a thorough knowledge of the recent political development of the country chosen, of its political structure, and of the manner in which its system of government operates. They must be able to read the available literature in a language of the country selected, except in the cases of Russia, China and Japan.

(q) The Politics of Democracy in Latin America

Definitions of democracy in Latin America; the conditions for stable democratic regimes; the breakdown of democratic regimes; transitions from authoritarian regimes; parties and electoral systems; political participation; political ideologies; the role of constitutions in theory and practice; public administration; policy making in democratic systems; civil-military relations; the international context of democracy.

(r) Executive Government

Candidates will explore generic and comparative themes in executive government and bureaucracy using a range of analytical perspectives. Candidates are expected to be familiar with the politics of bureaucracy in at least one country and to show awareness of the basic literature in the comparative study of bureaucracy.

(s) European International History since 1945

The origins of the Cold War in Europe; institution-formation (including Council of Europe, NATO, European Communities, CSCE); Europe in East-West relations; Germany, France, and Britain (impact of war, decolonisation; intra-European relations and relations with the superpowers; values, priorities, and historical memory); the emergence and character of European Community/Union external policies; the causes and consequences of the end of the Cold War in Europe.

(t) Comparative Political Economy

Candidates will be introduced to some of the major topics related to the comparative political economy of industrialised democracies and will be encouraged to question whether the political relationships among individuals, institutions and the economy are different in different countries. Topics will include the relationship between social coalitions and politics; the nature of corporatism; the existing diversity among advanced market economies; the influence of unions and wage bargaining institutions; the reasons why some countries have comprehensive welfare states and whether the welfare state is declining; the impact of government partisanship and electoral factors on economic policy; the political causes and effects of inequality; the political and economic importance of globalisation; and the relationship between democracy and economic growth.

(u) The Political Economy of Inequality and Democracy

This course will introduce MPhil students to some of the major topics related to the political economy of inequality, politics, institutions and redistribution. It is organized around a framework that emphasizes the relationship between equality and efficiency, the nature of inequality, the political causes and consequences of redistribution, and the relationship between inequality and democracy. Through reading, writing of discussion papers, and seminar participation, students will develop the relevant analytical skills to understand the relationships affecting individual preferences, political and economic institutions, and policy outcomes.

(v) Comparative European Parliaments

Candidates will explore generic and comparative themes in European legislative politics, at both national and EU level, using a range of analytical perspectives. Candidates are expected to be familiar with legislative politics in at least two European states and the EU level as well as to show awareness of the basic literature in the comparative study of legislatures.

(w) Comparative Presidentialism

This course will introduce students to the leading theoretical, empirical and cross-regional issues that are addressed by comparative studies of presidentialism. Candidates will be required to show knowledge of competing definitions of presidentialism; debates about the contribution of presidentialsm to democratisation and regime stability; the phenomenon of coalitional presidentialism; the impact of presidentialism on legislative politics and cabinet formation; presidentialism and party development; paraconstitutional practices and informal institutions under presidentialsm; and the policy consequences of presidential systems.

(x) Theory of Voting

The properties of majority rule; the Condorcet and Borda rules; the main modern results on majority rule (including the median voter theorem, Arrow's, May's, Sen's, and Gibbard's Theorems); the relationship between majority rule and proportional representation, and between proportional representation and apportionment; normative consequences of the formal results on voting.

(y) Democratization: Theory and Practice

Democratic theory and democratisation; theories of regime change; the establishment, stabilisation, and breakdown of democratic regimes; interactionist, structuralist, and discourse-based interpretations; economic and sociological correlates; issues of comparative methodology; definitions, concepts, and cultural relativism; constitutions, institutional design, and party organisation; democratisation and international politics. Practice. Candidates will be expected to show knowledge of the main analytical issues arising from contemporary democratization experiences in at least two of the following clusters of countries: China (including Hong Kong, Singapore, and Taiwan); East-Central Europe (post-Communist countries excluding the former USSR); Middle America (i.e. Mexico, Central America, and the Caribbean); South America; South Asia; Southern Africa (Angola, Botswana, Mozambique, Namibia, South Africa); Southern Europe (Greece, Italy, Portugal, Spain, Turkey); Sub-Saharan Africa (other than Southern Africa); ex-USSR states. *Note:* Candidates taking options to study the politics of any of these areas, in addition to this paper, will be required to show knowledge of at least one other region.

(z) The Political and Ethical Thought of Plato and Aristotle

Candidates are required to show knowledge of the major writings on ethics and politics in the works of both Plato and Aristotle. Questions may also be asked on the ethical and political thought of the Pre-Socratics.

(aa) Political Theories from Machiavelli to Burke

The authors to be studied will include: Machiavelli, Hobbes, Locke, Hume, Montesquieu, Rousseau, and Burke. Candidates are required to show knowledge of at least three authors.

(ab) Political Theories of Hegel and Marx

In addition to a knowledge of the original texts, candidates will be expected to show some knowledge of later developments in Hegelian and Marxist ideas, and to be able to discuss the theories of Hegel and Marx in the context of contemporary political thought. Candidates are required to show knowledge of the work of both of these authors.

(ac) The History of Liberal Thought in the Nineteenth and Twentieth Centuries

The development of liberal thought in the nineteenth and twentieth centuries, including the study of key thinkers and significant liberal traditions. The paper will include the study of some of the following authors and topics: Bentham and the philosophical radicals, J. S. Mill, the new liberalism, German liberalism (Weber and national liberalism), French solidarism and republicanism, American liberalism (Croly and Dewey), social democracy, Berlin and pluralism, Hayek, and the Rawlsians.

(*ad*) *Issues in Contemporary Continental European Social and Political Thought*

A critical examination of the issues in contemporary European social and political thought: politics and power, state and society, the political subject, ideology and language.

(*ae*) *Ideologies and Political Traditions in Modern Europe*

The conceptual and historical analysis of the principal political ideologies of Europe from the late nineteenth century; theories of ideologies and political traditions; conservatism, liberalism; socialism, communism; anarchism; nationalism; fascism; republicanism.

(*af*) *Contemporary Political Philosophy*

Recent developments in political philosophy. Candidates will be expected to show knowledge of the work of selected authors working within the analytical tradition of political philosophy, as well as critical ability in dealing with political concepts and theories.

(*ag*) *Kant's Political Philosophy*

The course will address all aspects of Kant's political philosophy, including its relation to his moral philosophy. Specifically, it will look at his theory of the formation of the state, the nature of law and constitution, the role of social contract, his rather authoritarian view of political obligation, his conception of citizenship, his theory of property, his theory of international law and international relations, and his cosmopolitanism.

Candidates sitting for the M.Phil. (Comparative Government) and the M.Phil (European Politics and Society) may also select the following paper:

(*ah*) *Comparative Presidentialism*

This course will introduce students to the leading theoretical, empirical and cross-regional issues that are addressed by comparative studies of presidentialism. Candidates will be required to show knowledge of competing definitions of presidentialism; debates about the contribution of presidentialsm to democratisation and regime stability; the phenomenon of coalitional presidentialism; the impact of presidentialism on legislative politics and cabinet formation; presidentialism and party development; paraconstitutional practices and informal institutions under presidentialsm; and the policy consequences of presidential systems.

Candidates must present themselves for *viva voce* examination when requested by the examiners.

The Examiners may award a distinction for excellence in the whole examination on the basis of the work submitted to them in both the Qualifying Test and the Final Examination.

Russian and East European Studies

(*See also the general notice at the commencement of these regulations.*)

The regulations made by the Russian and East European Studies Management Committee are as follows:

First year examinations

There will be three compulsory papers to be taken at the end of the first year of the course.

1. An examination paper on *Twentieth Century Russian, Soviet and East European History.*

2. An examination paper on *Politics, Economics and International Relations of the Former Soviet Union and Eastern Europe.*

3. An examination paper on *Society and Culture in the Former Soviet Union and Eastern Europe.*

The papers shall be set and administered by the examiners appointed to examine the M.Phil in Russian and East European Studies. The examination will be held in the eighth week of Trinity Full Term.

Candidates who pass these qualifying papers may proceed to the second year of the course and take the final examination at the end of the second year. Candidates who fail one or more of the examination papers may, by permission of the Russian and East European Studies Management Committee, proceed to the second year of the course and resit the failed papers during the final examination. All candidates will also be required to have demonstrated competence in Methods and Language as specified in Language Requirement.

Final Examination

In the final examination, every candidate must offer:

(*a*) a thesis of at least 25,000 words but not more than 30,000 words on a subject approved by the Management Committee for Russian and East European Studies, to be delivered to the Examination Schools, High Street, Oxford, by Monday in the fourth week of Trinity Term in which the final examination is taken. The thesis must be accompanied by a statement that the thesis is the candidate's own work except where otherwise indicated.

(*b*) two subjects (optional courses) chosen from a list, which is approved annually by the Russian and East European Studies Management Committee. The selection of subjects have to be approved by the Russian and East European Studies Management Committee in Trinity Term, Year 1.

The examiners may award a distinction for excellence in the whole examination.

Methods Requirement. Each candidate will be required to participate in training in methodology (quantitative and qualitative) and research skills related to Russian and East European Studies and to have achieved pass marks for the assessed components, as specified in the Notes of Guidance of the year of Matriculation of the Candidates.

Language Requirement. Before admission to the final examination all candidates will be required to pass a language qualifying exam on the region, which is usually in Russian. In special circumstances permission may be granted for sitting an exam in another language. The specific arrangements for the provision and methods of assessment of language training are governed by the Examination Conventions and Notes of Guidance of the year of matriculation of the candidates.

Slavonic Studies

(*See also the general notice at the commencement of these regulations.*)

The regulations made by the Board of the Faculty of Medieval and Modern Languages are as follows:

1. Candidates will be required to satisfy the examiners in a Qualifying Examination identical with that for the M.St. in Slavonic Studies, in the academic year in which their names are first entered on the Register of M.Phil. Students, before proceeding to the final examination for the M.Phil. in the following year. Holders of the M.St. in Slavonic Studies are exempt from this Qualifying Examination.

2. In the final examination for the M.Phil. each candidate will be required to take two subjects from the Schedules listed for the M.St., excluding Schedule 2 v. Candidates must take at least one subject from Schedule 2 i–iv, if they have not already done so for the M.St. or for the Qualifying Examination. Candidates may not repeat subjects which they have taken for the M.St. or for the Qualifying Examination, nor take subjects from Schedules from which they have already taken two subjects for the M.St. or for the Qualifying Examination. Candidates may not take subjects which they have already studied in a first degree course.

3. Each candidate will be required to present a thesis of approximately 20,000 words and not more than 25,000 words. Candidates are required to register the subject area or title of their thesis with the Modern Languages Graduate Office by the end of the fourth week of Hilary Term of their second year. The subject of the thesis should fall within the area of Slavonic languages and literatures. Three copies of the M.Phil. thesis must be submitted to the Examination Schools by noon on Thursday of Week 6 of Trinity Term of the second year. Work submitted in the thesis for the Degree of M.Phil. may subsequently be incorporated in a thesis submitted for the Degree of D.Phil.

4. Candidates must present themselves for oral examination unless dispensed by the examiners.

5. Candidates will be expected to be able to read secondary literature in at least one European language other than English and the Slavonic languages, and may be required to demonstrate this ability. Candidates will also be expected to attend a course of lectures on bibliographical, library, and archival resources in the field of Slavonic Studies.

6. If it is the opinion of the examiners that the work done by a candidate is not of sufficient merit to qualify him for the Degree of M.Phil. but that nevertheless his or her work in the Qualifying Examination was of sufficient merit to qualify him or her for the Degree of M.St. in Slavonic Studies, the candidate shall be given the option of resitting the M.Phil. examination under the appropriate regulation or of being granted permission to supplicate for the Degree of Master of Studies.

7. The examiners may award a distinction for excellence in the whole examination.

Social Anthropology

(*See also the general notice at the commencement of these regulations.*)

The Social Sciences Divisional Board shall elect for the supervision of the course a Standing Committee, namely the Teaching Committee of the School of Anthropology, which shall have power to arrange lectures and other instruction. The course director shall be responsible to that committee.

The examination shall consist of the following:

1. *Qualifying Examination*

Every candidate will be required to satisfy the examiners in an examination for which, if he or she passes at the appropriate level, he or she will be allowed to proceed to the second year of the M.Phil. Candidates must follow a course of instruction in Social Anthropology for at least three terms, and will, when entering for the examinations, be required to produce a certificate from their supervisor to this effect. The Qualifying Examination shall be taken in the Trinity Term of the academic year in which the candidate's name is first entered on the Register of M.Phil. students or, with the approval of the divisional board, in a subsequent year.

Each candidate will be required to satisfy the examiners in papers I–IV on the syllabus described in the Schedule for the M.Sc. in Social Anthropology, and governed by regulation 4 for that degree.

2. *Final Examination*

This shall be taken in the Trinity Term of the academic year following that in which the candidate's name is first entered on the Register of M.Phil. Students or, with the approval of the faculty board, in a subsequent year.

Each candidate shall be required: 5

(i) to present himself or herself for written examination in one of the optional areas or topics available for that year, other than that taken by the candidate in the M.Phil. Qualifying Examination the previous year;

(ii) to submit to the Chair of Examiners not later than noon on Tuesday of the fifth week of Trinity Term an essay of 5,000 words (two copies) in the field of 10 general Social Anthropology, on a topic to be selected from a list set by the examiners at the beginning of the third week of Trinity Term;

(iii) to submit a thesis in accordance with the regulations below;

(iv) to present himself or herself for oral examination if required by the examiners.

3. *Thesis** 15

Each candidate shall be required to submit a thesis of not more than 30,000 words (excluding references and appendices) on a subject approved by the supervisor. He or she shall send to the Teaching Committee of the School of Anthropology, with the written approval of his or her supervisor, the proposed title of the thesis, by noon on the Monday of second week of the Michaelmas Term in the academic year following 20 that in which his or her name was entered on the Register of M.Phil. Students. The thesis (three copies) must be typewritten and delivered to the Examination Schools, High Street, Oxford, not later than noon on Tuesday of the second week of the Trinity Term in the academic year in which the Final Examination is taken. The word count shall be stated on the outside front cover of the thesis. 25

The examiners shall require a successful candidate to deposit a copy of his or her thesis in the Tylor Library. If the thesis is superseded by a D.Phil. thesis by the same student partly using the same material, the Teaching Committee of the School of Anthropology may authorise the withdrawal of the M.Phil. thesis from the Tylor Library. Such candidates will be required to sign a form stating whether they give 30 permission for their thesis to be consulted.

The examiners may award a distinction for excellence in the whole examination.

If it is the opinion of the examiners that the work which has been required of a candidate is not of sufficient merit to qualify him or her for the Degree of M.Phil. the candidate shall be given the option of resitting the M.Phil. examination under the 35 appropriate regulation.

4. *Resits*

In order to pass the degree, a student must pass all its assessed components. Where one or more components are failed, the student will be given the opportunity to re-sit or re-submit them once, as the case may be. Any subsequent award of the degree on 40 successful completion of all the assessed components may be delayed by up to three terms, i.e. until the Examination Board next meets.

---

* See the general regulation concerning the preparation and dispatch of theses. Candidates are reminded (i) that two copies are required but that one of these may be a reproduction or carbon copy of the other, provided that any maps, diagrams, or other illustrations in the second copy are adequately reproduced, (ii) that if a copy of the thesis is deposited in the Tylor Library it shall be the one containing the original illustrations, and (iii) that work submitted for the Degree of M.Phil. may be subsequently incorporated in a thesis submitted for the Degree of D.Phil.

Sociology

(See also the general notice at the commencement of these regulations.)
The regulations made by the Board of the Faculty of Social Studies are as follows:

Qualifying test
Every candidate must pass a qualifying test at the end of the third term from the   5
beginning of the course in the *three* compulsory papers, *Methods of Social Research,
Sociological Analysis, Advanced Research Methods* and *one Optional Paper* from the
list of optional papers, specified by the Department of Sociology. This list will be
published annually by Friday of the third week of Michaelmas Full Term in the
Department of Sociology. Where coursework forms a part of the assessment, two   10
typewritten copies must be delivered to the Examination Schools, High Street,
Oxford, by noon on Friday of the eighth week of the Trinity Full Term in which
the examination is to be taken unless otherwise specified in the Graduate Studies
Handbook, or, in the case of options taken outside the Department of Sociology, as
specified by the department or faculty concerned. The examiners may examine   15
candidates viva voce. Candidates who fail the qualifying test are allowed to retake
the test before the beginning of the first week of the next academic year. Such
candidates are required to retake only those elements of the qualifying test that they
have failed. Candidates who fail only one out of the four papers may, by permission of
the Sociology Graduate Studies Committee, proceed to the second year of the course   20
and re-sit the failed paper at the same time as the final examination. No candidate will
be permitted to re-sit any of the compulsory papers more than once.

Final Examination
Every candidate must offer:
    1. One further optional paper from the list of optional papers specified by the   25
Department of Sociology.
    2. A thesis* of not more than 30,000 words on a topic within the subject of the
course, to be specified jointly by supervisor and student; two typewritten copies to be
delivered to the Examination Schools, High St, Oxford, by noon on Friday of the
sixth week of the Trinity Full Term in which the examination is to be taken.   30
Successful candidates will be required to deposit a copy of their thesis in the
Department of Sociology. Candidates are warned that they should avoid repetition
in their theses of material used in their option papers and that substantial repetition
may be penalised.

The examiners may examine any candidate viva voce.   35

The examiners may award a Distinction for excellence in the whole examination on
the basis of the material submitted to them in both the qualifying and the final
examination.

Compulsory Papers

Methods of Social Research   40
    (*a*) The satisfactory completion of a course of practical work including (i) statis-
tical methods; (ii) qualitative methods; (iii) research design.

Candidates shall submit reports of the practical work completed to the
Examination Schools, High Street, Oxford, by the following deadlines: for (i) statistical methods by 12 noon on Friday of the fifth week of the second term of the course;   45
for (ii) qualitative methods, assignment 1 by 12 noon on Friday of the ninth week of
the first term of the course and assignment 2 by 12 noon on the Friday preceding the
first week of the second term of the course; for (iii) research design by 12 noon on

---

* See the general regulations concerning the preparation and dispatch of theses.

Monday of the first week of the third term of the course. The reports must be accompanied by a statement that they are the candidate's own work except where otherwise indicated. For (i) statistical methods, candidates will also be required to take a two-hour in-class test to be held on the Friday preceding the first week of the second term of the course. The Director of Graduate Studies, or a deputy, shall draw 5 to the attention of the examiners the names of any candidates who have failed to complete to a satisfactory level of quality the course of practical work, and the examiners may require candidates to retake the course or a specified part thereof. The reports of practical work shall be available for inspection by the examiners.

Sociological Analysis 10
The object and objective of sociological analysis in relation to other social sciences. The nature of different sociological explanations, their possibilities and methodological implications. The relevance of rationality and of its limits with regard to both individual agents and institutions. The interrelationships between description and explanation, theory and empirical data, macro- and micro-levels of analysis as they 15 emerge from areas of major sociological enquiry.

Advanced Research Methods
The theoretical foundation and practical implementation of the advanced research methods for sociology. This paper also covers the linkage between advanced research methods and substantive debates in sociological research. The specific methods 20 covered in this paper will be revised from time to time. Candidates shall submit research essays or reports as specified in the graduate studies handbook. Submitted work must be accompanied by a statement that it is the candidate's own work expect where otherwise indicated.

Theology 25
(*See also the general notice at the commencement of these regulations.*)
The regulations made by the Board of the Faculty of Theology and Religion are as follows:
Candidates will be admitted to take the examination as defined below in a specific year. In exceptional circumstances candidates may be allowed to take an examination later 30 than one to which they were admitted. Permission for this must be sought from the faculty board not later than Monday of the week before the first week of the Trinity Term in which the examination was to have been taken. The application must have the support of the candidate's college and be accompanied by a statement from the supervisor.
1. Every candidate shall be required: 35

(*a*) to present himself or herself for written examinations and to submit essays in one of the subjects prescribed below;

(*b*) to present a thesis* of not more than 20,000 words in the case of subjects (*a*) and (*b*) or of not more than 30,000 words in the case of subjects (*c*), (*d*), and (*e*). The subject of the thesis must be approved by the faculty board. The candidate 40 should submit to the meeting of the board's Graduate Studies Committee in the first week of Michaelmas Term in his or her second year (submitting the application to the Graduate Studies Assistant for Theology and Religion (Humanities Division, Radcliffe Humanities, Woodstock Road) by Monday of noughth week): the proposed title, a short statement of how the subject will 45 be treated, and the signature of the supervisor indicating his approval. The completed thesis must be accompanied by a signed statement by the candidate that it is his or her own work except where otherwise indicated. Successful

---

* See the general regulation concerning the preparation and dispatch of theses. Candidates are reminded that work submitted for the Degree of M.Phil. may be subsequently incorporated in a thesis submitted for the Degree of D.Phil.

candidates may be required to deposit one copy of the thesis in the Bodleian. Candidates will also be required to sign a form stating whether they give permission for the thesis to be consulted.

(*c*) to present himself or herself for a viva voce examination unless individually dispensed by the examiners.   5

A candidate who fails the examination will be permitted to retake it on one further occasion only, not later than one year after the initial attempt. Such a candidate whose thesis has been of satisfactory standard will not be required to submit the same piece of work, while a candidate who has reached a satisfactory standard on the written papers will not be required to retake that part of the examination.   10

2. The subjects for examination are:

(*a*) Old Testament

(*b*) New Testament

(*c*) Christian Doctrine

(*d*) Ecclesiastical History   15

(*e*) Christian Ethics.

3. Candidates intending to offer a 10,000–15,000 word essay and/or three short essays should make a written application for approval of the essay topic to the Graduate Studies Assistant in Theology and Religion (Humanities Division, Radcliffe Humanities, Woodstock Road) not later than Monday of fifth week in   20 Trinity Term of the candidate's first year (to reach the Graduate Studies Committee in sixth week of the same term). In cases where there is some doubt about the acceptability of the proposal, candidates are asked to submit their applications earlier if possible. All applications should be accompanied by a recommendation from the supervisor. All presubmitted essays must be typewritten and two copies must be sent   25 to the Chair of Examiners for the degree of M.Phil in Theology, c/o Examination Schools, High Street, Oxford, at least fourteen days before the first day of the examination. The essay must be accompanied by a signed statement by the candidate that the essay is his or her own work except where otherwise indicated.

OLD TESTAMENT   30

Candidates will be required to offer papers (i), (ii), and (iii), and *either* paper (iv) *or* paper (v).

One of papers (i), (ii) and (iii) must be examined either by a long essay (10,000–15,000 words) or by three short essays of up to 5000 words each. One or two of the remaining papers (except Paper iv) may be examined by three short essays (up to 5000   35 words each). Titles must be approved by the Graduate Studies Committee not later than sixth week in the candidate's first year of study.

(i) *The Literature of the Old Testament and the Apocrypha in its Historical Setting. Either* (A) a general paper comprising the following two sections: (1) passages for comment from the Old Testament and Apocrypha in English; (2) literary and historical   40 questions; Archaeology and Old Testament study; the canon, text, and versions of the Old Testament. Candidates will be required to answer Section 1 and at least two and not more than three questions from Section 2. *or* (B) a paper on an area for special study approved by the Board of the Faculty of Theology and Religion within the scope of the subject. The choice of area must be submitted to the Graduate Studies Assistant in   45 Theology and Religion, Humanities Division, Radcliffe Humanities, Woodstock Road for approval by the board at its first meeting in the Trinity Term *preceding* the academic year in which the candidate is to be examined.

(ii) *Old Testament Theology.* This paper includes questions on such topics as the nature and method of Old Testament theology; the theological ideas of the Old Testament (e.g. ideas of God, creation, election, covenant, sacrifice, atonement, life after death, etc.); Israelite religion and the religions of the Ancient Near East; the relation between the Old Testament and the New Testament. Candidates will be required to answer three and not more than four questions.

(iii) *Prescribed Hebrew Texts.* This paper includes passages for translation with textual and exegetical comments from each of the following: 2 Samuel 9–20; Isaiah 40–55; Amos; Ecclesiastes. Candidates will be required to attempt four passages.

(iv) *Either* (A) unseen passages for translation from the Hebrew text of the Old Testament; *or* (B) the Aramaic portions of the Old Testament (Daniel 2.4–7.28; Ezra 4.8–6.18; 7.12–26); *or* (C) the Septuagint (Genesis 2–4; Isaiah 42, 52–3; Psalms 2, 21 (MT 22), 109 (MT 110); Proverbs 1, 8, 9). Candidates will be expected to translate and comment on four passages, one from each of the groups of texts, and to answer one question of a general nature on the Septuagint, with reference to the set texts.

(v) *The History and Principles of Biblical Study.* This paper includes questions on such topics as method in biblical study, the history of the interpretation of the Bible, both Jewish and Christian, the use and interpretation of the Bible today.

NEW TESTAMENT

Candidates will be required to offer papers (i) and (ii), and any two out of papers (iii), (iv), and (v).

One of papers (iii), (iv) and (v) must be examined by a long essay (10,000–15,000 words). Another choice from these papers may be examined by three short essays of up to 3000 words each. Titles must be approved by the Graduate Studies Committee not later than sixth week in Trinity Term of the candidate's first year of study.

(i) Religion and Literature of the New Testament: the Four Gospels and Acts in Greek.

Candidates will be required to translate and to comment on matters of literary, historical, and theological importance from a selection of these set texts.

(ii) Religion and Literature of the New Testament: the Epistles and Apocalypse in Greek.

Candidates will be required to translate and to comment on matters of literary, historical, and theological importance from a selection of these set texts.

(iii) New Testament Theology: General Paper.

(iv) Varieties of Judaism: 200 BE–CE 200.

Candidates should be prepared to show knowledge of the following texts (in English):

I Enoch, chs. 6–20, 46–51, 89–94 (tr. M. A. Knibb, in H. F. D. Sparks, *The Apocryphal Old Testament,* OUP, 1984).

Qumran Community Rule, Damascus Rule, Commentary on Habbakuk, Messianic Rule, Midrash on the Last Days (tr. G. Vermes, in *The Dead Sea Scrolls in English,* Pelican Books, 2nd edn., 1975).

Josephus, Jewish War II (Loeb, 1956); Antiquities XVIII (Loeb, 1965); Against Apion II (Loeb, 1956).

IV Ezra (ed. B. M. Metzger, in J. H. Charlesworth, ed., *The Old Testament Pseudepigrapha,* 2 vols., Darton, Longman and Todd, 1983, 1985).

Shemoneh 'Esreh (The Authorised Daily Prayer Book).

Mishnah Tractates Sanhedrin, Aboth, Mikwaoth (tr. H. Danby, *The Mishnah,* OUP, 1933).   5

Targum Neofiti Genesis 1-4, 22 (ed. A. Díez Macho, *Neophyti 1,* Consejo Superior de Investigaciones Científicas, Madrid-Barcelona, 1968).

The Wisdom of Solomon (RSV).

Philo, Migration of Abraham (Loeb, 1958); On Rewards and Punishments; On the Virtues (Loeb, 1960).   10

Joseph and Aseneth (ed. C. Burchard, in Charlesworth, op. cit.).

Sibylline Oracles III (ed. J. J. Collins, in Charlesworth, op. cit.).

Candidates may offer any or all of the following texts in the original languages:

Qumran Community Rule 1-4, in E. Lohse, ed., *Die Texte aus Qumran, Hebräisch und Deutsch* (2nd edn., Darmstadt, Wissenschaftliche Buchgesellschaft, 1971).   15

Qumran Commentary on Habakkuk (ed. E. Lohse, op. cit.).

Philo, *Life of Moses* I, 1-44 (Loeb, 1958).

Josephus, *Antiquities* XVIII, 1-28, 63-4, 109-19 (Loeb, 1965).

Joseph and Aseneth, in M. Philonenko, ed. *Joseph et Aséneth* (E. J. Brill, 1968).

(v) The History and Principles of Biblical Study (= Paper (v) for the Old   20
Testament).

CHRISTIAN DOCTRINE

Candidates will be required to offer one of the following sections:
Section A: History of Doctrine: Patristic Theology
Section B: History of Doctrine: Scholastic Theology   25
Section C: History of Doctrine: Reformation Theology
Section D: Issues in Theology with special reference to Patristic Theology
Section E: Issues in Theology with special reference to Scholastic Theology
Section F: Issues in Theology with special reference to Reformation Theology
Section G: Modern Theology (1780 – the present).   30
Candidates will be expected to offer all the three or four papers prescribed under each section, together with the dissertation. In Sections A-C candidates will not be required to translate passages from the set texts for Paper 2 but will be required to comment on passages given in the original languages.

Section A—History of Doctrine: Patristic Theology   35
Candidates must do Paper 1, Paper 2a or 2b, and paper 3.

1. The Development of Christian Doctrine to AD 787. Candidates will be expected to show knowledge of the main lines of development of Christian Doctrine and to be able to discuss these in relation to the historical conditions which influenced that development.   40

2(*a*). Hellenistic Philosophy and Christian Theology.
An examination consisting of essays and passages for translation and comment will be set. Candidates may choose whether to translate and comment on Greek or on Latin texts. The prescribed texts to be studied in Greek are:

Ps.-Aristotle, *De Mundo* (Loeb)
*Plutarch, *De E apud Delphos* (Loeb)
Albinus, *Epitome* VIII-XI (Budé)
Plotinus, *Enneads* 1.6, V.1 (Loeb or *Oxford Classical Texts*).
Origen, *Contra Celsum* VII (*Sources Chrétiennes* (S.C.))   5
Gregory of Nyssa, *Quod non sint Tres Dii* (Migne, P. G., Vol. 45)
*————*De Hominis Opificio* (Migne, P. G., Vol. 44)
Dionysius the Areopagite, *De Mystica Theologia* (Migne, P. G., Vol. 3).
The prescribed texts to be studied in Latin are:
*Augustine, *Contra Academicos* (Corpus Christianorum Series Latina (C.C.S.L.,   10
Vol. XXIX)
————*Confessions* X-XII (C.C.S.L., Vol. XXVII)
————*De Civitate Dei* VIII-X (C.C.S.L., Vol. XLVII)
————*De Trinitate* XII, XIII (C.C.S.L., Vols. L and LA)
2(*b*). Christology of the Patristic Era   15
An examination containing essays and passages for translation and comment will
be set. Candidates may choose to translate and comment either on Greek or on Latin
texts. The prescribed texts to be studied in Greek are:
*Origen, *Dialogue with Herakleides* 1, 1–8.17 (S.C., Vol. 67)
Athanasius, *De Incarnatione* (S.C., Vol. 199)   20
*Athanasius, *Epistle to Epictetus* (Migne, P. G., Vol. 26)
Gregory of Nazianzus, *Theological Orations* 4 (S.C., Vol. 250)
Theodore of Mopsuestia, *De Incarnatione* VII (ed. H. B. Swete, *Theodore of
Mopsuestia's Commentaries on the Pauline Epistles* (Vol. II, pp. 293–7))
Cyril of Alexandria, 2nd and 3rd letters to Nestorius; 2nd Letter to Succensus   25
(*Oxford Early Christian Texts*); Letter to John of Antioch (ed. T. H. Bindley, *The
Oecumenical Documents of the Faith*)
The Chalcedonian Definition of the Faith (ed. T. H. Bindley, op. cit.).
The prescribed texts to be studied in Latin are:
Tertullian, *Adversus Praxean* (ed. E. Evans)   30
*————*De Carne Christi* (ed. E. Evans)
Hilary, *De Trinitate* X (C.C.S.L., Vol. LXIIA)
Augustine, *De Trinitate* IV (C.C.S.L., Vol. L)
————*Epistle* 137 (*Corpus Scriptorum Ecclesiasticorum Latinorum,* Vol. XXXXIIII)
————*Sermons* 186, 187 (Migne, P. L., Vol. 38)   35
Leo 1, *Tome* (ed. T. H. Bindley, *Oecumenical Documents*)
————*Sermon* 8 (XXVIII) (S.C., Vol. 22)

3. Either one long essay of 10,000–15,000 words or three short essays of up to 5000
words each on (a) topic(s) falling within the patristic era and approved by the
Graduate Studies Committee not later than sixth week of Trinity Term in the   40
candidate's first year of study.

Section B—History of Doctrine: Scholastic Theology
   1. Doctrine and Methods. To be studied in relation to such works as:
Anselm, *Proslogion*
————*Cur Deus Homo*   45
Abelard, *Sic et Non*
The Gloss on Romans
Bernard, *De Gratia et libero arbitrio*

---

  * Copies of a translation of this work are available in the Theology Faculty
Library.

Hugh of St Victor, *De sacramentis christianae fidei*

Peter Lombard, *IV Libri Sententiarum,* Bk. IV

Bonaventure, *De reductione artium ad theologiam*

——*Breviloquium*

Albert, *In librum Dionysii de mystica theologia*   5

Bacon, *Compendium studii theologiae*

Scotus, *Prologue to the Ordinatio.*

2. The Thought of Aquinas.

An examination containing essays and passages for comment will be set. The
prescribed texts for the examination (in Latin) are: 1

Summa Theologiae: Prima Pars, qq. 1–2, 12–13, 43;

Prima Secundae, Prologue, qq. 6–10*, 18–21, 106–14;

Secunda Secundae, qq. 23–7;

Tertia Pars, Prologue*, qq. 7–8*, 46–9, 60–5, 75–6.

3. *Either* one long essay of 10,000–15,000 words *or* three short essays of up to 5000   1
words each on a topic/topics falling within the scholastic era and approved by the
Theology and Religion Graduate Studies Committee not later than sixth week of
Trinity Term in the candidate's first year of study.

Section C—History of Doctrine: Reformation Theology

1. Theology in Western Europe from Gabriel Biel to Jacob Arminius. This will be   2
examined by a set paper. Candidates will be expected to show familiarity with the
tenets of the most seminal theologians of this era and to discuss them in relation to
the political, social and economic tendencies of the age.

2. Protestant and Tridentine Teaching on the Doctrines of Grace, Freewill and
Predestination.   2

An examination containing essays and passages for comment will be set. The
prescribed texts, to be studied in Latin where that was the original language, are:

*Luther, *Lectures on Romans,* chapter 8 (1515–16) (Weimar Ausgabe (W.A.) LVI)
(Scholia)

*——*Disputation against Scholastic Theology* (1517) (W.A. I 221–8).   3

*——*The Heidelberg Disputation* (1518) (W.A. I 350–65).

——*On the Bondage of the Will* (1525) (W.A. XVIII 661–699)

Calvin, *Institutes* (1559), II 1–2; III 11–14, 21, 24.

Council of Trent, *Sessio* V (1546), *Decretum super peccato originali.*

——*Sessio* VI (1547), *Decretum et canones de justificatione.*   3

3. Either one long essay of 10,000–15,000 words or three short essays of up to
5,000 words each on a topic/topics falling within the reformation era and approved
by the Theology and Religion Graduate Studies Committee not later than sixth week
of Trinity Term in the candidate's first year of study.

Section D—Issues in Theology with special reference to Patristic Theology   4
Candidates must take papers (1), (3) and one of papers 2(a), 2(b) and 2(c).

1. A paper on *Methods and Styles in Theology from 1780 to the Present.*
Candidates will be expected to discuss problems of theological method, and to
show a critical understanding of the main themes in systematic theology, taking

---

* Copies of a translation of this work are available in the Theology Faculty
Library.

account of the impact on Christian theology of contemporary philosophy, critical historical studies, the natural and social sciences, and non-Christian religions and ideologies.

2. Candidates will sit an examination in *one of* the following:

(a) The Development of Christian Doctrine to 787 AD, as prescribed for Paper 1 of Section A;

(b) Hellenistic Philosophy and Early Christian Thought, as prescribed for Paper 2a of Section A;

(c) Christology of the Patristic Era, as prescribed for Paper 2b of Section A.

Passages for comment on Papers 2b and 2c in Section D will be chosen from the same prescribed texts but in English only.

3. See regulations for Paper 3 in Section A.

Section E—Issues in Theology with special reference to Scholastic Theology
1. Methods and Styles in Theology from 1780 to the Present (as specified for paper 1 of Section D).

2. *Either* (a) a paper on Doctrine and Methods, as prescribed for Paper 1 of Section B; *or* (b) a paper on the Thought of Aquinas, as prescribed for paper 2 of Section B. The prescribed texts for Paper 2b, to be studied in English, are:

Summa Theologiae
Prima Pars

qq.	1	Theology
	2–11	The God of 'Classical Theism'
	12–13	Knowing and Naming God, Analogy Theory
	27–32	The Doctrine of the Trinity
	43	The Mission of the Divine Persons

Prima Secundae

qq.	6–10	Human Action
	18–21	Principles of Morality
	90–94	Law and Politics
	106–114	Grace and Justification

Secunda Secundae

| qq. | 1–2 | Faith |
| | 23–27 | Charity as Friendship |

Tertia Pars

qq.	1	The Purpose of the Incarnation
	7–15	Christ's Holiness and Knowledge
	46–49	The Passion of Christ
	60–65	The Sacraments
	75–78	The Eucharistic Presence.

in the Blackfriars edition vols. 1, 2, 3, 6, 7, 48, 49, 54, 56, 58.

3. See regulations for Paper 3 in Section B.

Section F—Issues in Theology with special reference to Reformation Theology
1. Methods and Styles in Theology from 1780 to the Present (as specified for paper 1 of Section D).

2. *Either* (a) Theology in Western Europe from Gabriel Biel to Jacob Arminius, as prescribed for Paper 1 of Section C; *or* (b) Protestant and Tridentine Teaching on the Doctrines of Grace, Freewill and Predestination, as prescribed for Paper 2 in Section C. The prescribed texts for Paper 2b, to be studied in English, are:

*Luther, *Lectures on Romans,* chapters 7 and 8 (1515–16) (*Library of Christian   5
Classics,* Vol. XV)

*————*Disputation against Scholastic Theology* (1517) (LCC, Vol. XVI)

*————*The Heidelberg Disputation* (1518) (LCC, Vol. XVI)

————*On the Bondage of Will* (1525), Parts I–III (LCC, Vol. XVII)

Calvin, *Institutes* (1559) II 1–2; III 11–14, 21, 24 (LCC, Vol. XX, pp. 241–89, 725–   10
88; Vol. XXI, pp. 920–32, 964–87).

Council of Trent, Session V (1546) *Decree concerning original sin*

Council of Trent, Session VI (1547) *Decree and canons concerning justification*

(H. J. Schroeder, *Canons and decrees of the Council of Trent: original text with English Translation* (1941, pp. 21–3, 29–46)).   15

3. See regulations for Paper 3 in Section C.

Section G—Modern Theology (1780–the present)
1. Methods and Styles of Theology from 1780 to the Present (as specified for paper 1 of Section D).

2. A set examination on: 20

(a) Modern Theology or

(b) Theology and Modern European Thought from 1780 to the Present or

(c) Theology and Literature from 1780 to the Present.

3. Either an essay of 10,000–15,000 words or three short essays of up to 5,000 words each on a subject falling within one of the three options specified under (2) and   25
approved by the Theology and Religion Graduate Studies Committee not later than sixth week of Trinity Term in the candidate's first year of study.

ECCLESIASTICAL HISTORY

Candidates will be required to offer three papers in addition to the dissertation:
(i) General paper on the Nature and Practice of Ecclesiastical History   30

This paper introduces candidates to the nature of ecclesiastical history as a sub-discipline within History through study of the writing of the History of the Church from the Early Church to the modern day and investigation of shifts in historical method, with particular reference to methodological debates within History since the mid nineteenth century. It aims to introduce students to a range of historiographical   35
approaches to key questions in ecclesiastical history; to foster an awareness of developments in historiography particular over the last 150 years; and to encourage critical reflection on students' own historical research. Classes are organised chronologically and cover the contemporaneous writing of ecclesiastical history within four broad periods (the early Church; the middle ages; the early modern; the late modern   40
era) and the modern historiography of each of those periods. In the examination candidates will be expected to answer questions on the various understandings of history which have been advanced within Christianity at different periods. They will also be expected to show knowledge of the variety of approaches to historical method which have emerged as a result of the modern professionalisation of teaching and   45
research in history.

* Copies of a translation of this work are available in the Theology Faculty Library.

(ii) A general paper on one of the following, assessed either by unseen examination or by three essays of up to 5,000 words each:

(*a*) The Early Church AD 200–476

(*b*) The Western Church AD 476–1050

(*c*) The Western Church AD 1050–1400

(*d*) English Church History AD 1066–1272

(*e*) European Christianity AD 1400–1800

(*f*) European Christianity AD 1800–2000

3. Either one long essay of 10,000–15,000 words or three short essays of up to 5,000 words each on a topic/topics falling within the general description of the course and approved by the Theology and Religion Graduate Studies Committee not later than sixth week of Trinity Term in the candidate's first year of study.

CHRISTIAN ETHICS

All candidates shall offer the following four papers, in addition to the dissertation:

(i) *Christian Moral Concepts and Methodology: Contemporary and Historical Discussions*. Candidates will be expected to show understanding of basic conceptual and methodological issues as these are discussed in relevant classical and contemporary texts. Topics will include: God and the good, natural law, the role of Scripture, divine commands, moral absolutes, consequences and intentions, narrative and virtue, Christian ethics and public discourse.

(ii) *Select Texts in Christian Ethics I*. Candidates will be expected to show careful interpretation of important texts. The selection of texts will vary from year to year and might comprise, e.g. classic expressions of a range of Christian traditions, the works of major theologians, texts on a chosen theme.

(iii) *Select Texts in Christian Ethics II*. Candidates will be expected to show careful interpretation of important texts. The selection of texts will vary from year to year and might comprise, e.g. classic expressions of a range of Christian traditions, the works of major theologians, texts on a chosen theme.

(iv) *Practical Fields of Christian Ethics*: Contemporary and Historical Discussions. Candidates will be expected to show understanding of a range of practical moral issues arising in the following fields: (a) sexual; (b) medical; and (c) political. In any one year only two of (a)–(c) will be studied.

All candidates will be assessed in paper (i) by a written examination; and in each of papers (ii), (iii), and (iv) by one 5,000 word essay. In addition, candidates will be required to write a fourth 5,000 word essay on a topic within the field of any of the papers (i)–(iv). It is expected that students will have identified a subject for their dissertation by the end of Trinity Term in Year 1, and that they will be in a position to submit a title and proposal by the Monday of Week 0 in Michaelmas Term of Year 2. The choice of essay and dissertation topics will be a matter for negotiation between student and supervisor.

Visual, Material, and Museum Anthropology

1. The Social Sciences Board shall elect for the supervision of the course a Standing Committee, namely the Teaching Committee of the School of Anthropology, which shall have power to arrange lectures and other instruction. The course director shall be responsible to that committee.

In order to pass the degree, a student must pass all its assessed components. Where one or more components are failed, the student will be given the opportunity to re-sit or re-submit them once, as the case may be. Any subsequent award of the degree on successful completion of all the assessed components may be delayed by up to three terms, i.e. until the Examination Board next meets.

2. The examinations shall consist of the following:

(*1*) *Qualifying Examination* Every candidate will be required to satisfy the exam-   5
iners in an examination for which, if he or she passes at the appropriate level, he
or she will be allowed to proceed to the second year of the M.Phil. Candidates
must follow a course of instruction in Visual, Material, and Museum
Anthropology for at least three terms, and will, when entering for the examinations, be required to produce a certificate from their supervisor to this effect.   10
The Qualifying Examination shall be taken in the Trinity Term of the academic
year in which the candidate's name is first entered on the Register of M.Phil.
students or, with the approval of the divisional board, in a subsequent year.
Each candidate will be required to satisfy the examiners in papers 1-4 on the
syllabus described in the Schedule for the M.Sc. in Visual, Material, and   15
Museum Anthropology, and governed by regulation 4 for that degree.

(*2*) *Final Examination* This shall be taken in the Trinity Term of the academic year
following that in which the candidate's name is first entered on the register of
M.Phil. students or, with the approval of the divisional board, in a subsequent
year. Each candidate shall be required: 20

(i) to present himself or herself for written examination in one of the
optional areas or topics available for that year in Lists A, B or C, other
than that taken by the candidate in the M.Phil. Qualifying Examination
the previous year;

(ii) to submit to the Chair of Examiners not later than noon on Tuesday of   25
the fifth week of Trinity Term an essay of 5,000 words (three copies) in
the field of Visual, Material, and Museum Anthropology, on a topic to be
selected from a list set by the examiners at the beginning of the third week
of Trinity Term (candidates should not duplicate any material already
used in their submission for paper 2 in the Qualifying Examination in the   30
previous year);

(iii) to submit a thesis in accordance with the regulations below;

(iv) to present himself or herself for oral examination if required by the
examiners.

Thesis   35

3. Each candidate shall be required to submit a thesis of not more than 30,000
words (excluding references and appendices) on a subject approved by the supervisor.
The thesis may be based on the analysis of objects or photographs in the collections
of the Pitt Rivers Museum, or a topic from one of the subject areas covered during
the qualifying year, including option topics. The candidate shall send to the Teaching   40
Committee of the School of Anthropology, with the written approval of his or her
supervisor, the proposed title of the thesis, by noon on Monday of the second week of
Michaelmas Term in the academic year following that in which his or her name was
entered on the register of M.Phil. students. The thesis (three copies) must be typewritten and delivered to the Chair of Examiners, M.Phil. in Visual, Material and   45
Museum Anthropology, c/o Examination Schools, High Street, Oxford, not later
than Tuesday of the second week of Trinity Term in the academic year in which the
Final Examination is taken. The word count shall be stated on the outside front cover
of the thesis.

4. The examiners shall require a successful candidate to deposit a copy of his or   50
her thesis in the Balfour Library. If the thesis is superseded by a D.Phil. thesis by the

same student partly using the same material, the Graduate Studies Committee of the School of Anthropology may authorise the withdrawal of the M.Phil. thesis from the Balfour Library. Such candidates will be required to sign a form stating whether they give permission for their thesis to be consulted.

5. The examiners may award a distinction for excellence in the whole examination.   5

NOTES

7

REGULATIONS FOR THE DEGREE OF MASTER OF STUDIES

GENERAL REGULATIONS

§1. Degree of Master of Studies

1. Any person who has
   (*a*) been admitted as a student for the Degree of Master of Studies under the provisions of this section,
   (*b*) satisfied the examiners in one of the examinations prescribed in this section, and
   (*c*) kept three terms of statutory residence as a matriculated member of the University after admission as a Student for the Degree of Master of Studies,
   may supplicate for the Degree of Master of Studies.

2. For the purpose of this section the words 'board' or 'faculty board' shall include any committee or other body authorised to admit candidates for the Degree of Master of Studies.

§2. Examinations for the Degree of Master of Studies

1. The examinations for the degree and the bodies responsible for the supervision of each examination shall be as listed below.

(Examination)	(Board)
Ancient Philosophy	Philosophy
Archaeological Science	Social Sciences
Archaeology	Social Sciences
Bible Interpretation	Oriental Studies
Celtic Studies	Modern Languages
Chinese Studies	Oriental Studies
Classical Archaeology	Social Sciences
Classical Armenian Studies	Oriental Studies
Classical Hebrew Studies	Oriental Studies
Creative Writing	Continuing Education
Diplomatic Studies	Continuing Education
English	English Language and Literature
English Language	English Language and Literature
Film Aesthetics	Modern Languages

General Linguistics and Comparative Philology — Faculty of Linguistics, Philology and Phonetics

Global and Imperial History — History

Greek and/or Latin Languages and Literature — Classics

Greek and/or Roman History — Classics

History of Art and Visual Culture — History

History of Design — Continuing Education

International Human Rights Law — Continuing Education

Islamic Art and Archaeology — Oriental Studies   1

Japanese Studies — Oriental Studies

Jewish Studies — Oriental Studies

Jewish Studies in the Graeco-Roman Period — Oriental Studies

Korean Studies — Oriental Studies   1

Late Antique and Byzantine Studies — Classics and History

Legal Research/Socio-Legal Research — Law

Literature and Arts — Continuing Education

Medieval History — History   2

Medieval Studies — History

Mindfulness-Based Cognitive Therapy — Continuing Education

Modern British and European History — History   2

Modern Jewish Studies — Oriental Studies

Modern Languages — Modern Languages

Modern South Asian Studies — History and Oriental Studies

Music — Music

Oriental Studies — Oriental Studies   3

Philosophical Theology — Theology

Philosophy — Philosophy

Philosophy of Physics — Philosophy

Psychodynamic Practice — Continuing Education

Slavonic Studies — Modern Languages   3

Social Anthropology — Social Sciences

Study of Religions — Theology

Syriac Studies — Oriental Studies

Theology — Theology

US History — History   4

Women's Studies — Modern Languages

Yiddish Studies — Modern Languages

2. The subjects of each examination shall be determined, subject to the approval of the Education Committee, by regulation of the board concerned, which shall have power to arrange lectures and courses of instruction for the examination.

3. No full-time student shall be admitted as a candidate for examination for the degree until he or she shall have spent at least three terms at work in Oxford after his or her admission as a student for the degree; time spent outside Oxford during term as part of an academic programme approved by Council shall count towards residence for the purpose of this clause.

4. Part-time students for the degree shall in each case be required to pursue their course of study for twice the number of terms required of an equivalent full-time student. Part-time students will not be required to keep statutory residence but must attend for such instruction and undertake such supervised fieldwork as the faculty board or committee concerned shall require. The Director of Graduate Studies of the faculty board concerned, or the director of the department concerned, as the case may be, shall keep a register of attendance of part-time students. No student shall be granted leave to supplicate unless the register shows satisfactory attendance by him or her.

5. Final examination marks shall be released to candidates at the conclusion of the examination. Exceptions to this may be made where assessment takes place throughout the course. In such cases, examination boards must meet formally, with all members present, at interim points in the year in order to agree final marks for specified assessment components. Marks released as final marks may not subsequently be amended without permission of the Proctors.

6. A candidate who has failed to satisfy the examiners in any one of the examinations may enter again for that examination on one, but not more than one, subsequent occasion.

7. The examiners may award a distinction for excellence in the whole examination. Candidates who have initially failed any element of assessment shall not normally be eligible for the award of distinction.

§3. Admission of Candidates

1. Any person may be admitted by the board concerned as a candidate for an examination for the Degree of Master of Studies provided the following conditions have been satisfied:

(*a*) The application must be supported by the candidate's college.

(*b*) A candidate must either (i) have passed all the examinations required for the Degree of Bachelor of Arts and have obtained first or good second class honours in the Second Public Examination, or have obtained such honours in a degree examination of another university, such university having been approved by Council for the purpose of senior status, or (ii) in the opinion of the board, be otherwise adequately qualified to undertake the course.

2. An application for admission of a candidate who has passed the examinations required for the Degree of Bachelor of Arts shall be sent to the Registrar by the head or tutor of his or her college, and shall be accompanied by a statement of the subject which he or she proposes to study and evidence of his or her fitness to undertake a course of study therein.

3. An application for admission by a graduate of another university shall be sent to the Registrar by the head or tutor of the college to which he or she belongs or to which he or she has applied for admission, and shall be accompanied by all the necessary certificates from his or her previous university and by a statement of the subject which he or she proposes to study and evidence of his or her fitness to undertake a course of study therein.

4. An application for admission by any other candidate shall be sent to the Registrar by the head or tutor of the college to which he or she belongs or to which he or she has applied for admission, and shall be accompanied by evidence of his or her previous education and by a statement of the subject which he or she proposes to study and evidence of his or her fitness to undertake a course of study therein.

5. The Registrar shall bring any application submitted under cll. 2, 3, or 4 before the appropriate board for its approval. Such approval shall not be granted unless the board is satisfied that the candidate is well-fitted to enter on the course of study proposed by him or her.

6. A board shall have power to appoint a standing committee of its own members to consider the applications of candidates and to report to the board.

7. It shall be the duty of the Registrar to notify a candidate of the decision of a board as soon as may be.

8. A member of the University who holds the status of Probationer Research Student or the status of student for another higher degree or postgraduate diploma within the University may, with the approval of the board which admitted him or her, transfer to the status of Student for the Degree of Master of Studies, in which case the date of his or her admission as a Probationer Research Student or to the status of student for a higher degree or post-graduate diploma shall then be reckoned, unless the board shall determine otherwise, as the date of his or her admission as a Student for the Degree of Master of Studies.

9. A candidate for the B.Phil. in Philosophy may, with the approval of the Board of the Faculty of Philosophy, transfer to the status of a Student for the Degree of Master of Studies in Philosophy. The application must be submitted not later than Friday of the fourth week of the Hilary Full Term of the year in which he or she wishes to take the examination for the Degree of Master of Studies. The date of the candidate's admission as a B.Phil. Student shall then be reckoned as the date of his or her admission as a Student for the Degree of Master of Studies.

10. A student holding the status of Probationer Research Student may, with the approval of the board which admitted him or her, be admitted as a candidate for an examination for the Degree of Master of Studies. Time spent as a student holding the status of Probationer Research Student shall count as time spent working for the Degree of Master of Studies.

11. A Student for the Degree of Master of Studies who is not a graduate of the University may wear the same gown as that worn by Students for the Degree of Doctor of Philosophy.

12. A Student for the Degree of Master of Studies shall cease to hold such status if

(i) he or she shall have been refused permission to supplicate for the Degree of Master of Studies, or

(ii) the board concerned shall, in accordance with provisions set down by regulation by the Education Committee, and after consultation with the student's society and supervisor, have deprived the student of such status;

(iii) he or she shall have been transferred under the relevant provisions to another status;

(iv) he or she shall not have entered for the relevant examination within six terms for a full-time student and twelve terms for a part-time student.

§4. Supervision of Students

1. Every candidate on admission as a Student for the Degree of Master of Studies shall be placed by the board which admitted him or her under the supervision of a graduate member of the University or other competent person selected by the board, and the board shall have power for sufficient reason to change the supervisor of any student.

2. It shall be the duty of a supervisor of a student to direct and superintend the work of the student for any part of the student's course in which supervision is required and to undertake such duties as shall be from time to time set out in the relevant Policy and Guidance issued by the Education Committee.

3. The supervisor shall send a report on the progress of the student to the board at the end of each term and at any other time when the board so requests, or he or she deems it expedient.

The supervisor shall communicate the contents of the report to the student on each occasion that a report is made, so that the student is aware of the supervisor's assessment of his or her work during the period in question. In addition, he or she shall inform the board at once if he is of the opinion that the student is unlikely to reach the standard required for the Degree of Master of Studies.

The Registrar shall send a copy of each report by the supervisor to the student's society.

§5. Duties of the Registrar

It shall be the duty of the Registrar

(*a*) to keep a record of the names of those candidates who have been admitted as students for each examination for the Degree of Master of Studies and, where they have been examined, of the results of the examination;

(*b*) to publish at the end of the year the names of those persons in that year, to whom permission to supplicate for the Degree of Master of Studies has been granted, together with a statement of the course which each has pursued.

Special Regulations

Except where otherwise indicated, all material submitted for examination (dissertations, extended essays, etc) shall be accompanied by a certificate signed by the candidate indicating that it is the candidate's own work, except where otherwise specified. This certificate must be submitted separately in a sealed envelope addressed to the chair of examiners of the degree course in question.

Ancient Philosophy

1. Every candidate must follow for at least three terms a course of instruction in Ancient Philosophy. Candidates will, when they enter for the examination, be required to produce from their society a certificate that they are following such a course.

2. Every candidate shall be required to offer (i) three essays in Ancient Philosophy: one on the first subject (refer to 4. below) and the other two on the second subject (refer to 5. below); and (ii) a thesis in Ancient Philosophy of 10,000 words.

3. The choice of subjects must be notified on the entry form for the examination, to be submitted by Friday of fourth week of Michaelmas Term.

4. The first subject shall be chosen from the list of undergraduate papers in ancient philosophy 0130–0135, as specified in the special regulations for *Philosophy in all Honour Schools including Philosophy*. The subject will be assessed by one

5,000 word essay on a topic (relevant to the subject) to be chosen by the candidate and approved by the Chair of Examiners no later than Friday of eighth week of Michaelmas Term. Two copies of the essay must be submitted to the Examination Schools, High Street, Oxford OX1 4BG by 10 a.m. on the Friday of nought week of Hilary Term in the year in which the examination is taken. Essays must be typed or printed.

5. The second subject shall be a dedicated class taught across the Michaelmas and Hilary terms of the year of examination. The subject will be assessed by two 5,000 word essays on two topics (relevant to the subject) to be chosen by the candidate and approved by the Chair of Examiners no later than Friday of fifth week of Hilary Term. Two copies of each essay must be submitted to the Examination Schools, High Street, Oxford OX1 4BG, by 10 a.m. on Friday of ninth week of Hilary Term in the year in which the examination is taken. Essays must be typed or printed.

6. Candidates may not be permitted to offer certain combinations of subjects.

7. The reading lists for all subjects will include texts both in the original language and in translation; candidates' readings will be guided by their supervisor(s) according to their level of Ancient Greek. All reading lists will be posted on the Faculty website in Trinity Term preceding the year of examination.

8. Candidates must offer a thesis of no more than 10,000 words, exclusive of bibliographical references, on a subject proposed by the candidate in consultation with his or her supervisor and approved by the Graduate Studies Committee in Philosophy. A subject and thesis title must be submitted to the Committee not later than the fifth week of the Hilary Term of the year in which the examination is to be taken. Requests for permission to make later changes to the thesis title should be submitted, with the support of the candidate's supervisor to the Director of Graduate Studies in Philosophy *as soon as the candidate has decided to seek permission.* Two copies of the thesis must be submitted to the Examination Schools, High Street, Oxford OX1 4BG, by 10 a.m. on Friday of eighth week of Trinity Term in the year in which the examination is taken. The thesis shall be accompanied by a brief abstract and statement of the number of words it contains (exclusive of bibliographical references). Successful candidates will be required to deposit one copy of the thesis in the Bodleian Library (candidates will also be required to sign a form stating that they give permission for the thesis to be consulted).

9. Candidates who have not delivered the essays or the thesis as prescribed by the due date shall, unless they show exceptional cause, be deemed to have withdrawn from the examination.

10. Each essay shall be the candidate's own work. The candidate may discuss a draft (but not more than one) of each essay with his or her supervisor. The candidate's supervisor may provide bibliographical advice on essays throughout.

11. The examiners may award a distinction for excellence in the whole examination. A candidate who fails any one of the four elements of the examination (i.e. one of the three essays or the thesis) may apply to retake that element in the September immediately following the examination. A candidate who fails two or more elements may retake the examination in the year immediately following the failed examination. It is necessary for a candidate to retake only the failed elements of the examination.

Archaeological Science

1. Within the Division of Social Sciences, the course shall be administered by the Committee for the School of Archaeology. The regulations made are as follows:

2. Candidates for admission must apply to the Committee for the School of Archaeology.

3. Candidates must follow a course of instruction in Archaeological Science for at least three terms and for a substantial part of the first two subsequent vacations, as determined by the course timetable.

4. The registration of candidates will lapse at the end of Trinity Term in the academic year of their admission, unless it shall have been extended by the committee.

5. The written examination shall consist of:

(*a*) three papers on the syllabus described in the Schedule, to be taken in the second week of Trinity Term, *and*

(*b*) *either* one pre-set essay of approximately 10,000 words, *or* two pre-set essays of approximately 5,000 words each. The subject and length of each essay must be approved by the examiners before the end of Michaelmas Full Term. Two copies of each essay must be delivered to the Examination Schools by noon on the Friday of first week of Trinity Term. Essays must be typed or printed, must bear the candidate's examination number but not his or her name, and must include a statement of the number of words. Any illustrations must be included in both copies.

(*c*) in lieu of one of the three papers described in the Schedule, candidates may, with the permission of the School of Archaeology Committee for Graduate Studies, take one of the options from the M.St in Archaeology (Schedules A and B) or M.St in Classical Archaeology (Sechedule B only). Candidates taking such an option would only be examined on one pre-set essay of approximately 5,000 words on Archaeological Science in lieu of the requirements laid out in b) above.

6. Each candidate will be required to submit a report of approximately 5,000 words, on a practical project selected in consultation with the supervisor and approved by the Committee for the School of Archaeology.

7. Three typewritten copies of the report on the practical project must be sent, not later than noon on the Friday of ninth week of the Trinity Term in the year in which the examination is taken, to the M.St. Examiners (Archaeological Science), c/o Examination Schools, High Street, Oxford.

8. The examiners may require to see the records of practical work carried out during the first two terms of the course.

9. Candidates must present themselves for an oral examination as required by the examiners. This may be on the candidate's written papers, or practical work, or both.

10. The examiners may award a distinction for excellence in the whole examination.

11. In the case of failure in just one part of the examination, the candidate will be permitted to retake that part of the examination on one further occasion, not later than one year after the initial attempt. Written papers would be retaken the following year.

Schedule

(i) *Principles and practice of scientific dating*

The principles of scientific dating methods including radiocarbon, luminescence, uranium series, and dendro-chronology. The practical aspects of these methods and the problems encountered in their application. The statistical analysis of chronological information in the study of archaeological sites and cultures.

(ii) *Bio-archaeology*

Scientific methods for the study of biological remains from archaeological sites; introduction to the analysis of plant and faunal remains including indicators of disease and artefactual analysis; theoretical and practical aspects of quantitative methods for diet reconstruction by isotopic analysis; introduction to ancient DNA studies; residue analysis.

(iii) *Materials analysis and the study of technological change*

Introduction to the history of technology; theoretical and practical aspects of materials analysis methods-SEM, microprobe, TIMS, ICP, ICP-MS, XRF, XRD, PIXE, FTIR, and NAA; application to analysis to different material types-stone, ceramics, vitreous materials, and metals; provenance of raw materials; case studies of application to archaeological problems.

Archaeology

1. Within the Division of Social Sciences, the course shall be administered by the Committee for the School of Archaeology. The regulations made are as follows:

2. Candidates for admission must apply to the Committee for the School of Archaeology. They will be required to produce evidence of their appropriate qualifications for the proposed course, including their suitable proficiency in relevant ancient or modern languages.

3. Candidates must follow for three terms a course of instruction in Archaeology and must attend the core course component seminars.

4. The registration of candidates will lapse on the last day of the Trinity Full Term in the academic year of their admission, unless it shall have been extended by the committee.

5. The written examination shall comprise three subjects:

(*a*) one subject selected from Schedule A below to be examined by written paper;

(*b*) two further subjects selected from Schedules A–D. [Not more than one subject of the three selected may normally be taken from either one of Schedule C or D.] These subjects will be examined by two pre-set essays (each of 5,000 words) except that further subjects from Schedule A of the M.St in Classical Archaeology will only be examined by written paper.

In lieu of one of the subjects in (*b*) above, M.St (but not normally M.Phil) candidates may offer, with the permission of the committee, a dissertation of not more than 10,000 words (excluding bibliography and descriptive catalogue or similar factual matter, but including notes and appendices).

The topic of the dissertation must be approved by the candidate's supervisor and by the School of Archaeology Committee for Graduate Studies. If the candidate has elected to be examined by pre-set essays in another part of the examination, the topic of the dissertation must be clearly distinct from the pre-set essay titles. The dissertation must be the work of the candidate alone, and aid from others must be limited to prior discussion of the subject, bibliographic advice, help with access to study material and advice on presentation. The dissertation must be a new piece of work, substantially different from any dissertation previously submitted by the candidate for a degree of this or another university. When the dissertation is submitted, it must be accompanied by a statement, signed by the candidate, confirming that these conditions have been met. The proposed title of the dissertation, countersigned by the supervisor, must be submitted for approval by the committee by noon on the Monday of the seventh week of the Michaelmas Full Term preceding the examination. Two copies typed or printed (the second may be a photocopy) in double spacing on one side only of A4 paper and bound simply or filed securely, must be delivered in a parcel bearing the words 'Dissertation for the M. St. in Archaeology' to the

Examination Schools, High Street, Oxford, not later than noon on the Friday of the sixth week of Trinity Full Term and should bear the candidate's examination number but not his or her name. Candidates will be required to deposit one copy of the dissertation with the Examination Schools.

Schedule A: Main Subjects

Aegean Area, 2000–1100 BC
Ancient Maritime Societies
Archaeological Method and Theory
Archaeology of Asia
Archaeology of Colonialism
Archaeology of Early Anglo-Saxon England
Archaeology of Southern African Hunter-gatherers
Chinese Archaeology
Environmental Archaeology
Formation of the Islamic World
Landscape Archaeology and Spatial Technology
Mesolithic and Neolithic Europe
Methods and Techniques in Maritime Archaeology
Neolithic and Bronze Age Europe
Palaeolithic and Mesolithic Europe
Palaeolithic Archaeology
Palaeolithic Asia
Regional studies in Australian and Pacific prehistory
Transformation of the Celtic World 500 BC-AD 100
Visual Cultures of the Ancient World
Western Europe in the Early Middle Ages AD 400–900

Schedule B: Options

Aegean Bronze Age religion
Aegean Bronze Age trade: interaction and identities
Archaeology and Geographical Information Systems
Archaeology and Material Culture
Archaeology of Late Anglo-Saxon England
Body and Adornment Material Culture of Later Medieval Britain, AD 1000–1500
Coinage and Monetary History of the Indian Subcontinent
Coinage and Society in Anglo-Saxon England
Cultural Heritage and Law I: History
Culture and Heritage Law II: Application
Farming and States in Sub-Saharan Africa
Hunter-gatherers in World Perspective
Maritime Archaeology up to AD 1000
Object Analysis and Research Methods
Practical Archaeobotany
Themes in Archaeological Science
Topics in Aegean Prehistory

Schedule C: Archaeological Science

Any subject offered in the M.St in Archaeological Science.

Schedule D: Classical Archaeology

Any subject offered in the M.St in Classical Archaeology.

Candidates may apply for other subjects, to be taken under Schedule B, to be approved by the committee, which shall define their scope and inform both the candidate and the examiners of this definition in writing. Not all course options may be available in any given year.

6. Candidates will be expected to show a general knowledge of the appropriate history and geography, so far as they are concerned with their subjects.

7. Candidates must present themselves for an oral examination as required by the examiners.

8. The subjects to be offered by the candidates and their chosen method of examination, duly approved by their supervisors, must be submitted for approval to the committee in time for its meeting in eighth week of the Michaelmas Full Term preceding the examination. Notice of options to be offered by candidates must be given to the Registrar not later than Friday of the eighth week of that same term.

9. Where options are examined by pre-set essays as specified in 5 above), candidates will normally select essay topics from a list offered by their supervisor. The proposed essay titles, countersigned by the supervisor, must be submitted for approval to the Chair of Examiners by noon on Friday of the seventh week of the Hilary Full Term preceding the examinations. Candidates must submit two copies of their essays by not later than noon on Friday of the sixth week of Trinity Full Term to the Examination Schools. Essays must be typed or printed.

10. The examiners may award a distinction for excellence in the whole examination.

11. In the case of failure in just one part of the examination, the candidate will be permitted to retake that part of the examination on one further occasion, not later than one year after the initial attempt. Written papers would be retaken the following year.

Bible Interpretation

1. Before admission to the course, candidates must satisfy the Board of the Faculty of Oriental Studies that they possess the necessary qualification in Classical Hebrew, Aramaic or Syriac, to profit by the course. Teaching for a second language from these three will be provided during the course if required. Evidence of proficiency in Greek or Latin will be expected if options in either of these languages are chosen.

2. Every candidate must follow for at least three terms a course of study in Bible Interpretation.

3. *Syllabus*

There will be four Units:

Unit (i) Essay questions on general background and methodology.

Unit (ii) Prescribed texts I. Passages for translation and comment, and essay questions on prescribed texts (a passage, or passages, for unprepared translation may also be set).

Unit (iii) Prescribed texts II. Passages for translation and comment, and essay questions on rescribed texts (a passage, or passages, for unprepared translation may also be set).

Units (ii) and (iii) must be chosen from two of the following:

(*a*) Hebrew biblical and exegetical texts

(*b*) Aramaic (Targum) texts

(*c*) Syriac biblical and exegetical texts

(*d*) Greek biblical and exegetical texts

(*e*) Latin biblical and exegetical texts

Unit (iv) A dissertation of not more than 15,000 words (excluding bibliography), on a topic selected in consultation with the candidate's supervisor and approved by the Faculty Board. Applications for such approval should be submitted to the Faculty office by Friday of seventh week of Michaelmas Term and will be reported to the Faculty Board's second meeting of Michaelmas Term. Two typewritten copies of the dissertation must be delivered to the Chair of Examiners, M.St in Bible Interpretation, Examination Schools, High Street, Oxford, not later than 12 noon on Friday of fourth week of Trinity Term.

4. Lists of set texts must be submitted to the Faculty office by Friday of seventh week of Michaelmas Term and will be reported to the Faculty Board's second meeting of Michaelmas Term.

5. All work submitted to the Chair of Examiners must be in typewritten form. Two copies must be submitted, securely sealed and addressed. The work must bear the candidate's examination number (but not the candidate's name, which must be concealed). Candidates must include a signed declaration sealed in an envelope addressed to the Chair of Examiners that the work is the candidate's own.

6. Every candidate will be examined by oral examination unless he or she shall have been individually excused by the examiners.

Teaching for some options may not be available in every year. Applicants for admission will be advised of this.

Celtic Studies

1. All candidates shall be required at the time of admission to satisfy the Board of the Faculty of Medieval and Modern Languages (if necessary, by written test) that they possess the appropriate qualifications for the proposed course, including suitable proficiency in relevant languages. Normally the course will be restricted to candidates who have taken a first degree in a relevant subject area.

2. All candidates must follow a course of instruction in Celtic Studies at Oxford for a period of three terms, unless the Board of the Faculty of Medieval and Modern Languages in exceptional circumstances shall permit an extension of time, and they shall, when they enter their names for the examination, be required to produce from their society a certificate stating that they are following the course of instruction for the period prescribed.

3. Candidates shall be required:

(*a*) to offer themselves for written examination as defined below.

(*b*) to offer themselves for viva voce examination at the time appointed by the examiners.

4. The subjects and papers of the examination shall be as follows:

(*a*) *Either*

(1) Two papers, one on each of two subjects selected from the following:

(i) Historical and comparative Celtic linguistics.

(ii) Irish literature up to the Cromwellian wars (4(*b*) for the M.Phil. in Celtic Studies).

(iii) Welsh literature up to the Reformation (4(*c*) for the M.Phil. in Celtic Studies).

Or

(2) Two papers as follows:

    (i) One paper on a subject selected from those described in section (*a*) (1) above.

    (ii) One paper on a Special Subject to be chosen from the list given in section 4(*d*) of the regulations for the M.Phil. in Celtic Studies. Candidates are allowed to offer a Special Subject of their own devising provided that it is similar in character and scope to those listed for the M.Phil. in Celtic Studies and that it is approved under the arrangements set out in section 7 of the regulations for that M.Phil. (Candidates shall, however, seek approval for their choice of Special Subject, whether it involves a title of their devising or not, by application to the Modern Languages Graduate Office, 41 Wellington Square, Oxford, by the end of the fourth week of their first term as a student for the examination).

(*b*) A dissertation of approximately 8,000 words and not more than 10,000 words on a topic approved by the Board of the Faculty of Medieval and Modern Languages or by a person or persons to whom the board may delegate the function of giving such approval. Candidates shall seek approval (by application to the Modern Languages Graduate Office, 41 Wellington Square, Oxford) for the proposed topic of their dissertation by the end of the fourth week of their second term as a student for the examination.

The dissertation must be the work of the candidate alone and aid from others must be limited to prior discussion as to the subject and advice on presentation. It must be presented in proper scholarly form. Two copies, typed in double-spacing on one side only of quarto or A4 paper, each copy bound or held firmly in a stiff cover, must be delivered to the Chair of the Examiners for the Degree of M.St. in Celtic Studies, c/o Examination Schools, High Street, Oxford, not later than Monday of the fourth week of the Trinity Full Term in which the examination is to be taken.

5. Other arrangements for the above papers and subjects shall be as specified for the M.Phil. in Celtic Studies.

6. The examiners may award a distinction for excellence in the whole examination.

Chinese Studies

1. Before admission to the course, candidates must either have taken a degree in Chinese in the Honour School of Oriental Studies at Oxford or a comparable degree from another university, or must otherwise satisfy the Board of the Faculty of Oriental Studies that they possess the necessary qualifications in the Chinese language to profit by the course.

2. Every candidate must follow for at least three terms a course of instruction in Chinese Studies.

3. *Syllabus*

There will be four Units.

Unit (i) Prescribed texts, with special reference to a subject approved by the Board.

Unit (ii) Either Classical Chinese unprepared translation or Japanese or another Asian language approved by the Board.

Candidates may choose a language other than Classical Chinese only if the Board is satisfied that they possess a good knowledge of Classical Chinese. Candidates who have taken Chinese in the Honour School of Oriental Studies at Oxford are required to take Japanese or another Asian language.

Unit (iii) Bibliography and techniques of sinology, with special reference to the subject chosen in Unit (i).

Exercises will be set after examinations for Units (i) and (ii) have taken place. Each candidate will be assigned one or more exercises set on a topic directly relating to the course of instruction he/she has followed, and will be required to submit a written answer to the Chair of Examiners by a date which the Chair will announce, but which shall, in any case, be not sooner than two days and not later than seven days following the examinations.

Unit (iv) A dissertation of not more than 15,000 words (excluding bibliography) on a topic selected in consultation with the candidate's supervisor and approved by the Faculty Board. Applications for such approval should be submitted to the Faculty office by Friday of seventh week of Michaelmas Term and will be reported to the Faculty Board's second meeting of Michaelmas Term.

The dissertation must be sent to the Chair of Examiners, M.St in Chinese Studies (Oriental Studies), Examination Schools, High Street, Oxford, not later than 12 noon on Friday of fourth week of Trinity Term.

4. Lists of set texts must be submitted to the Faculty office by Friday of seventh week of Michaelmas Term and will be reported to the Faculty Board's second meeting of Michaelmas Term.

5. All work submitted to the Chair of Examiners must be in typewritten form. Two copies must be submitted, securely sealed and addressed. The work must bear the candidate's examination number (but not the candidate's name, which must be concealed). Candidates must include a signed declaration sealed in an envelope addressed to the Chair of Examiners that the work is the candidate's own.

6. Every candidate will be examined by oral examination unless he or she shall have been individually excused by the examiners.

Classical Archaeology

1. Within the Division of Social Sciences, the course shall be administered by the Committee for the School of Archaeology. The regulations made are as follows:

2. Candidates for admission must apply to the Committee for the School of Archaeology. They will be required to produce evidence of their appropriate qualifications for the proposed course, including their suitable proficiency in relevant ancient or modern languages.

3. Candidates must follow for three terms a course of instruction in Classical Archaeology.

4. The registration of candidates will lapse on the last day of the Trinity Term in the academic year of their admission, unless it shall have been extended by the committee.

5. The written examination shall comprise three subjects:

(*a*) one subject on a period selected from Schedule A below, to be examined by written paper;

(*b*) two subjects selected from Schedules A–C [not more than one subject may normally be taken from Schedule C] examined by two pre-set essays (each of 5,000 words).

In lieu of one of the subjects in (*b*) above, M.St. (but not normally M.Phil.) candidates may offer, with the permission of the committee, a dissertation of not more than 10,000 words (excluding bibliography and descriptive catalogue or similar factual matter, but including notes and appendices).

The topic of the dissertation must be approved by the candidate's supervisor and by the School of Archaeology Committee for Graduate Studies. The topic of the dissertation must be clearly distinct from the pre-set essay titles. The dissertation must be the work of the candidate alone, and aid from others must be limited to prior discussion of the subject, bibliographic advice, help with access to study material and advice on presentation. The dissertation must be a new piece of work, substantially different from any dissertation previously submitted by the candidate for a degree of this or another university. When the dissertation is submitted, it must be accompanied by a statement, signed by the candidate, confirming that these conditions have been met. The proposed title of the dissertation, countersigned by the supervisor, must be submitted for approval by the committee by noon on the Monday of the seventh week of the Michaelmas Full Term preceding the examination. Two copies typed or printed (the second may be a photocopy) in double spacing on one side only of A4 paper and bound simply or filed securely, must be delivered in a parcel bearing the words 'Dissertation for the M.St. in Classical Archaeology' to the Examination Schools, High Street, Oxford, not later than noon on the Monday of the fifth week of Trinity Full Term and should bear the candidate's examination number but not his or her name. Candidates will be required to deposit one copy of the dissertation with the Examination Schools.

Schedule A: Periods

Aegean Area, 2000–1100 BC
Early Iron Age Greece, 1200–700 BC
Archaic, 800–480 BC
Classical, 500–300 BC
Hellenistic, 330–30 BC
Late Republican, 200–30 BC
Early Imperial, 30 BC–AD 120
Middle Imperial, AD 70–250
Late Antiquity, AD 280–650
Byzantine, AD 600–1453

Schedule B: Subjects

Aegean Bronze Age trade: interaction and identities
Aegean Bronze Age Scripts
Aegean Bronze Age religion
Topics in Aegean Prehistory
Aegean and the East, 1200–600 BC
Burials, settlements, and society in Early Greece, 1200–650 BC
Archaeology of the Early Greek polis, 800–450 BC
Early Ionia, 1000–450 BC
Greek sculpture
Greek vases
Myth and daily life in Greek art
Archaeology of Athens and Attica, 600–50 BC (This may be taken in conjunction with the British School at Athens taught course only if accepted by the British School at Athens on its programme, and it involves attendance at the residential course organised by the British School at Athens in even-numbered years in Athens.)
The archaeology of ancient Macedonia, 600–100 BC
Greek funerary archaeology, 600–100 BC
Archaeology of Greek women

Greek coinage
Greek and Roman wallpainting
Roman sculpture
Historical narrative in Hellenistic and Roman art
Problems and methods in ancient art-history   5
Roman architecture
Topography of Rome (This may be taken in conjunction with the British School at
    Rome taught course only if accepted by the British School at Rome on its
    programme, and it involves attendance at the residential course organised by
    the British School at Rome in Rome.)   1
Pompeii and Ostia
Greek and Roman housing
Archaeology of the Roman economy
The archaeology of Roman urban systems
Roman North Africa   1
Landscape archaeology in the Greek and Roman world
Maritime archaeology of the Greek and Roman Mediterranean
Roman Britain
Roman coinage
City, country and economy in the Late Roman Empire (fourth-seventh centuries)   2
Byzantine Constantinople
Late Roman and Byzantine mosaics and painting
Late Roman and Byzantine architecture
History of collections: classical art
Roman Portraits   2
Roman Provincial Art

Schedule C: Other subjects

Any subject offered in the M.St in Archaeology, Byzantine Studies, Greek and/or
Latin Languages and Literature, Greek and Roman History, History of Art,
Women's Studies.   3

Candidates may apply for other subjects, to be taken under Schedule B, to be
approved by the committee, which shall define their scope and inform both the
candidate and the examiners of this definition in writing.
Not all subjects may be available in any one year.

6. Candidates will be expected to show a general knowledge of Ancient History   3
and Geography, so far as they are concerned with their periods and subjects.

7. Candidates must present themselves for an oral examination as required by the
examiners.

8. The period and subjects to be offered by candidates and their chosen method of
examination, duly approved by their supervisors, must be submitted for approval to   4
the committee in time for its meeting in eighth week of the Michaelmas Full Term
preceding the examination. Notice of options to be offered by candidates must be
given to the Registrar not later than Friday of the eighth week of that same term.

9. Candidates offering pairs of pre-set essays will select essay topics from a list
offered by their supervisor. The proposed essay titles, countersigned by the super-   4.
visor, must be submitted for approval of the Chair of Examiners by noon on Friday
of the eighth week of the term in which the instruction for that subject is given.
Candidates must deliver to the Examination Schools two copies of their essays not
later than noon on Monday of the second week of the term following that in which
the instruction for that subject was given. Essays must be typed or printed and should   5

bear the candidate's examination number but not his or her name. Any illustrations must be included in both copies.

10. The examiners may award a distinction for excellence in the whole examination.

11. In the case of failure in just one part of the examination, the candidate will be permitted to retake that part of the examination on one further occasion, not later than one year after the initial attempt. Written papers would be retaken the following year.

Classical Armenian Studies

1. Before admission to the course, candidates must satisfy the Board of the Faculty of Oriental Studies that they possess the necessary qualifications to profit by the course.

2. Every candidate must follow for at least three terms a course of instruction in Classical Armenian Studies.

3. *Syllabus*

There will be four Units:

Unit (i). Essay questions on the language, literature, history, and culture of Ancient and Medieval Armenia.

Units (ii), (iii), (iv). Passages for translation and commentary, and essay questions on prescribed texts in Classical and, where relevant, post-Classical Armenian, with special reference to three of the following subjects (passages for unprepared translation from and into Classical Armenian will be set):

(1) Biblical texts.

(2) Homiletic and polemical literature.

(3) Hagiographic texts.

(4) Historical literature of the 5th–9th centuries.

(5) Historical literature of the 10th–14th centuries.

(6) Religious and secular verse.

(7) Any other subject approved by the Board.

4. Lists of set texts must be submitted to the Faculty office by Friday of seventh week of Michaelmas Term and will be reported to the Faculty Board's second meeting of Michaelmas Term.

5. Every candidate will be examined by oral examination unless he or she shall have been individually excused by the examiners.

Teaching for the course may not be available in every year. Applicants for admission will be advised of this.

Classical Hebrew Studies

1. Before admission to the course, candidates must satisfy the Board of the Faculty of Oriental Studies that they possess the appropriate qualifications in Classical Hebrew to profit by the course.

2. Every candidate must follow for at least three terms a course of study in Classical Hebrew Studies.

3. *Syllabus*

There will be four Units:

Unit (i) Essay questions on the history and literature of Israel and Judah in the Biblical period.

Unit (ii) Prepared and unprepared Biblical texts.

Units (iii) and (iv) *Two* of the following:

(1) Classical Hebrew Language;

(2) The principles and practice of textual criticism;

(3) North-west Semitic epigraphy;

(4) Aramaic;

(5) Dead Sea Scrolls;

(6) Any other subject approved by the Board.

4. Lists of set texts must be submitted to the Faculty office by Friday of seventh week of Michaelmas Term and will be reported to the Faculty Board's second meeting of Michaelmas Term.

5. Every candidate will be examined by oral examination unless he or she shall have been individually excused by the examiners.

Teaching for some options may not be available in every year. Applicants for admission will be advised of this.

Creative Writing

1. Every candidate must follow for at least six terms a part-time course of instruction in Creative Writing.

2. The course will consist of lectures, seminars, workshops, individual tutorials, and a placement.

3. The examination will consist of the following parts:

(*a*) Two assignments selected from two of the genres listed in the schedule below. Assignments submitted for 1, 2 or 5 in the schedule should be no more than 2,500 words of prose. Assignments submitted for 3 in the schedule should be no more than 130 lines of poetry. Assignments submitted for 2 in the schedule should be: no more than 15 minutes (or *c*.2500 words) of Radio Drama; between 12 and 15 minutes stage play (no more than 2,500 words); approximately 15 minutes or no more than 2,500 words of screen play.

(*b*) Two critical appraisal assignments of no more than 2,500 words, selected from two of the genres listed in the schedule below.

(*c*) A portfolio of Creative Writing which may be no more than either approximately 7,000 words of prose or approximately 350 lines of poetry; or no more than 40 minutes (or *c*.7,000 words) of radio drama; or a stage play of between 35 and 40 minutes (no more than 7,500 words); or approximately 40 minutes or no more than 7,000 words of screenplay.

(*d*) Two extended critical essays, one of no more than 4,000 words and one of no more than 5,000 words, the latter related to the genre in which the final project is written, and both to be approved by the candidate's supervisor.

(*e*) A report on the candidate's Placement of no more than 2,500 words.

(*f*) A Final Project on a topic selected by the candidate in consultation with his or her supervisor and approved by the examiners. The final project may take the format of one of the following:

(i) a piece of prose fiction or narrative non fiction of approximately 25,000 words;

(ii) one sixty-minute and one thirty-minute radio drama (approximately 12,000 and 6,000 words);

(iii) a 110-minute stage play (23,000–25,000 words);

(iv) a screenplay of up to two hours in length (entire); approximately 110–120 pages (12pt Courier) 25,000 words;

(v) a ninety-minute TV play (approximately 18,000 words);

(vi) a collection of poetry of between 40 and 60 pages *and* between 600 and 1,200 lines.

Candidates may be required to attend a viva voce examination.

The second Extended Essay under 3(*d*) and the Final Project under 3(*f*) must be delivered not later than noon on the third Friday in September of the final year of the course to the Chair of Examiners for the Degree of M.St. in Creative Writing, c/o Examination Schools, High Street, Oxford.

All other elements of assessed work shall be forwarded to the examiners, c/o Registry, Department for Continuing Education, 1 Wellington Square, Oxford for consideration by such dates as the examiners shall determine and shall notify the candidates and tutors at the start of each academic year.

All assessed work (3(*a*) to 3(*f*)) must be accompanied by a statement that it is the candidate's own work.

4. The examiners may award a distinction for excellence in the whole examination.

5. A candidate who fails to satisfy the examiners in 3 may be permitted to resubmit work in respect of part or parts of the examination which they have failed for examination on one further occasion, not later than one year after the initial attempt.

Schedule

1. Prose fiction
2. Drama
3. Poetry
4. Critical reading and analysis
5. Narrative non-fiction
6. Any other option approved by the Board of Study.

The schedule of assessment for any one year will be circulated to candidates and supervisors by the second week of Michaelmas Term.

Diplomatic Studies

1. Candidates for admission will be expected to have satisfactorily completed the Postgraduate Diploma in Diplomatic Studies not more than three terms before admission to the M.St.

2. The course will be taken on a part-time basis over a period of not fewer than three terms and not more than six terms. The total period of study for the Postgraduate Diploma in Diplomatic Studies and the M.St in Diplomatic Studies combined shall be not more than nine terms to be taken over a maximum of eighteen terms from the commencement of the Diploma.

3. In addition to having previously satisfied the examiners in all four modules and in the dissertation specified for the Postgraduate Diploma in Diplomatic Studies, every candidate will be required to satisfy the examiners in the following:

(*a*) participation in on-line dissertation supervisions;

(*b*) submission of a dissertation of no more than 15,000 words. The topic of the dissertation, which should be related to one or more of the subject areas of the four modules in the Postgraduate Diploma, and which should be distinct from, though may be complementary to, the topic of the dissertation examined for the Postgraduate Diploma, must be approved by the course director not later than 12 noon on the Friday of first week of Michaelmas Full Term in the academic year in which the examination is taken. Two typewritten or word processed copies of the dissertation must be delivered to the Registry, Department for Continuing Education, 1 Wellington Square, Oxford not later than 12 noon on Friday of sixth week of Trinity Full Term in the year in which the examination is taken.   5

4. Candidates may be required to attend a viva voce examination at the end of the course of study at the discretion of the examiners.

5. The examiners may award a distinction for excellence in the whole examination.

6. A candidate whose dissertation fails to satisfy the examiner may be permitted to resubmit on one further occasion only not later than one year after the initial failure.   10

7. If any candidate who is successful in the examination for the Degree of Master of Studies in Diplomatic Studies has previously successfully completed the Postgraduate Diploma in Diplomatic Studies, the Master of Studies will subsume his or her Diploma.

English   15

Every candidate must follow for at least three terms a course of study in English.
Syllabus
The following subjects are prescribed:
   A. Literature, Contexts, and Approaches
   B. Bibliography, Palaeography, and Theories of Text   20
   C. Special Options

The Faculty Board shall prescribe from year to year the particular courses which will be offered for each of these subjects. Courses under A will be taught over Michaelmas and Hilary Terms. Courses on bibliography and palaeography will be taught mainly in Michaelmas Term and courses on Theories of Text in Hilary Term.   25
There will be two lists of Special Options, one for Michaelmas Term and one for Hilary Term. Options under C shall include an American Studies option. Entry to this option may be restricted by the faculty board.

Candidates must take A and four other subjects: two in Michaelmas Term (of which one at least must be a Special Option) and two in Hilary Term (of which one at   30
least must be a Special Option). They must also offer a dissertation. Courses under A will be divided according to chronological period and candidates must take the course appropriate to their period of specialisation.

Candidates will be required to attend the lectures and classes prescribed by the Faculty Board for the courses they have chosen, and undertake such written work,   35
exercises or presentations for those courses as the course tutors shall prescribe.

Essays
In Michaelmas Term candidates will be required to submit an essay of 5,000–7,000 words on a topic related to one of the special options taken under C in that term; two copies of the essay must be delivered to the Examination Schools, High Street,   40
Oxford, not later than noon on Thursday of the tenth week of Michaelmas Term.
In Hilary Term, candidates will be required to submit the following:

   1. An essay of 5,000–7,000 words on a topic related to one of the special options taken under C in that term, to be submitted to the Examination Schools, High Street, Oxford, not later than noon on Monday of the tenth week of Hilary Term.   45

   2. An essay of 5,000–7,000 words on a topic related either to an option taken under B (in either term) or to a second special option taken under C in that term, to be submitted to the Examination Schools, High Street, Oxford, not later than noon on Thursday of the tenth week of Hilary Term. Candidates must gain approval of the topic of their essays by writing to the Chair of the M.St. Examiners, care of the English Faculty Office,   50

by Friday of the sixth week of Michaelmas Term (for the first essay) and of Hilary Term (for the second and third essays).

Candidates offering the course in bibliography, palaeography and theories of text in the period up to 1550 under B will be required to pass a test in transcription and dating at the end of Hilary Term. Those who do not achieve a satisfactory mark in the test will be required to retake it at the start of Trinity Term. Any candidate not achieving a satisfactory mark at that stage will be deemed to have failed the whole examination. The test will not contribute to the final marks awarded by the examiners.

Candidates offering the course in bibliography in the period 1550 to the present day under B will be required also to attend a course in manuscript reading and transcription and to pass a test in transcription at the end of Michaelmas Term. Those who do not achieve a satisfactory mark in this test will be required to retake it at the start of Hilary Term. Any candidate not achieving a satisfactory mark at that stage will be deemed to have failed the whole examination. The test will not contribute to the final marks awarded by the examiners.

Not later than noon on Monday on the eighth week of Trinity Term, candidates must deliver to the Examination Schools two copies of a dissertation (about 10,000–11,000 words) on a subject related to their course of study. The dissertation must be presented in proper scholarly form. Candidates must gain approval of the topic of their dissertation by writing to the Chair of the M.St. Examiners, care of the English Graduate Studies Office, by Friday of the sixth week of Hilary Term, providing an outline of the topic of not more than 200 words.

Candidates who fail any part of the examination other than the test in bibliography in the period 1550 to the present day described above may resubmit that part by noon on the last Monday of the following Long Vacation.

Candidates whose course of study includes the American Studies C Special Option and a dissertation on a topic recognised by the Graduate Studies Committee for English as being within the interdisciplinary field of English and American studies shall be awarded, if successful, degree of Master of Studies with the title English (English and American Studies).

Candidates whose course of study includes the World Literatures in English A and B options and a dissertation on a topic recognised by the Graduate Studies Committee for English as being within the field of World Literatures in English shall be awarded, if successful, the degree of Master of Studies with the title English (World Literatures in English).

The examiners may award a distinction for excellence in the whole examination.

English Language

Every candidate must follow for at least three terms a course of study in English Language.

Syllabus

The following subjects are prescribed:

   A. Topics in English Language: History, Structure and Use

   B. Research Methods for English Language

   C. Special Options

The Faculty Board shall prescribe from year to year the particular courses which will be offered for each of these subjects. Courses under A and B will be taught over Michaelmas and Hilary Terms. There will be two lists of Special Options, one for Michaelmas Term and one for Hilary Term. Students will also be able to choose any one option selected from those offered as B courses for the M.St./M.Phil. in General Linguistics and Comparative Philology, subject to the approval of the student's own Course Convener and the tutor for the option. The teaching and assessment of the Linguistics B courses will follow the provisions and requirements as set by the Faculty of Linguistics, Philology and Phonetics.

Candidates must take courses A, B and two C Option courses (one in each term). They must also offer a dissertation.

Candidates will be required to attend the lectures and classes prescribed by the Faculty Board for the courses they have chosen, and undertake such written work, exercises or presentations for those courses as the course tutors shall prescribe.

Assessed written work

In Michaelmas Term candidates will be required to submit a piece of written work of 5,000–7,000 words on a topic related to one of the special options taken under C in that term; two copies must be delivered to the Examination Schools, High Street, Oxford, not later than noon on Thursday of the tenth week of Michaelmas Term.

In Hilary Term, candidates will be required to submit the following:

1. A piece of written work of 5,000–7,000 words on a topic related to one of the special options taken under C in that term, to be submitted to the Examination Schools, High Street, Oxford, not later than noon on Monday of the tenth week of Hilary Term.

2. A piece of written work of 5,000–7,000 words on a topic related to the B course, to be submitted to the Examination Schools, High Street, Oxford, not later than noon on Thursday of the tenth week of Hilary Term.

'Written work' may consist of either an essay or a project which includes an analysis of linguistic data and/or an evaluation of a particular method of analysis. The three pieces of work submitted by candidates must include one piece of each type. Candidates must gain approval of the topic of their written work by writing to the Chair of the M.St. Examiners, care of the English Faculty Office, by Friday of the sixth week of Michaelmas Term (for the first essay) and of Hilary Term (for the second and third essays).

Candidates (as part of the B course) will be required to pass a test in English Language Analysis (assessing their competence in the phonetic transcription and grammatical analysis of English) by the end of Michaelmas Term. Those who do not achieve a satisfactory mark in this test will be required to retake it at the start of Hilary Term. Any candidate not achieving a satisfactory mark at that stage will be deemed to have failed the whole examination. The test will not contribute to the final marks awarded by the examiners.

Not later than noon on Monday on the eighth week of Trinity Term, candidates must deliver to the Examination Schools two copies of a dissertation (about 10,000–11,000 words) on a subject related to their course of study. The dissertation must be presented in proper scholarly form. Candidates must gain approval of the topic of their dissertation by writing to the Chair of the M.St. Examiners, care of the English Graduate Studies Office, by Friday of the sixth week of Hilary Term, providing an outline of the topic of not more than 200 words.

Candidates who fail any part of the examination other than the English language analysis test may resubmit that part by noon on the last Monday of the following Long Vacation.

The examiners may award a distinction for excellence in the whole examination.

Film Aesthetics

1. In order to be considered for admission to the course, applicants must have completed a Bachelors degree, normally in a discipline from the Humanities, Fine Art or the Social Sciences.

2. Candidates must follow a course of instruction in Film Aesthetics at Oxford for a period of three terms, unless the Modern Languages Board in exceptional circumstances shall permit an extension of time, and shall when entering for the examination be required to produce from their society a certificate stating that they are following the course of instruction for the period prescribed.

3. The course shall comprise:

(*a*) A specified film workshop during the week preceding Week 0 of Michaelmas Term.

(*b*) Four classes during Michaelmas Term which explore fundamental aspects of film criticism, film analysis, film theory, film form, and film aesthetics.

(*c*) Four classes during Hilary Term on different, specialised areas of film aesthetics.

(*d*) A specified programme of films, to be screened publicly during Weeks 1–8 of Michaelmas and Hilary Terms.

(*e*) Dissertation supervision and two revision seminars in Trinity Term.

4. Assessment shall comprise two 6,000 word essays, a 10,000 word dissertation, and a three-hour written examination.

5. Each essay topic should bear a clear and identifiable relation to a specified part of the course and there should not be substantial overlap between the two essay topics.

6. The topic for the *first essay* shall be drawn from one or more of the four classes specified for Michaelmas Term. Each candidate shall submit their essay topic, with a supporting letter from a subject tutor, to the Chair of examiners, Modern Languages Faculty Office, 41 Wellington Square, Oxford, for approval by noon on the Friday of Week 7 in Michaelmas Term. Written approval of essay topics will be given to candidates by noon on the Friday of Week 8 in Michaelmas Term. Essays shall be delivered to the Examination Schools, High Street, Oxford, by noon on Monday of Week 1 of Hilary Term. Essays will be marked by subject tutors and returned to candidates with comments by Week 4 of Hilary Term. Candidates may amend their essays in the light of these comments and shall resubmit their essays within the portfolio containing the first essay and the second essay, each clearly marked by 5 p.m. on the Friday of Week 9 in Trinity Term.

7. The topic for the *second essay* shall be drawn from one or more of the four classes specified for Hilary Term. Each candidate shall submit their essay topic, with a supporting letter from a subject tutor, to the chair of examiners, Modern Languages Faculty Office, 41 Wellington Square, Oxford for approval by noon on the Friday of Week 7 in Hilary Term. Written approval of essay topics will be given to candidates by noon on the Friday of Week 8 in Hilary Term. Essays shall be delivered to the Examination Schools, High Street, Oxford, by noon on Monday of Week 1 of Trinity Term. Essays will be marked by subject tutors and returned to candidates with comments by Week 4 of Trinity Term. Candidates may amend their essays in the light of these comments and shall resubmit their essays within the portfolio containing the first essay and the second essay, each clearly marked by 5 p.m. on the Friday of Week 9 in Trinity Term.

8. Each candidate shall submit their *dissertation* topic, with the prior approval of the course coordinator, to the chair of examiners, Modern Languages Faculty Office, 41 Wellington Square, Oxford, for approval by noon on the Friday of Week 4 in Hilary Term. Written approval of dissertation topics will be given to candidates by noon on the Friday of Week 5 in Hilary Term. Dissertations shall be delivered to the Examination Schools, High Street, Oxford, by noon on the Friday of Week 6 in Trinity Term.

9. Candidates shall sit a three-hour written examination on the Friday of Week 9 in Trinity Term.

10. The examiners may award a distinction for excellence in the whole examination.

11. Candidates must present themselves for an oral examination if required to do so by the examiners.

General Linguistics and Comparative Philology

1. Candidates shall normally have a degree in a subject which has given them at least some experience of linguistic or philological work. Those intending to offer options chosen from C or D below should normally have, and may be required to demonstrate, some knowledge of the chosen (group of) language(s) and those intending to offer options chosen from C will normally be expected to be able to read secondary literature in French and German.

2. The names of all candidates for the M.St. must be registered with the Graduate Studies Assistant of the Faculty of Linguistics, Philology and Phonetics.

3. Every candidate shall pursue a course of study in General Linguistics and Comparative Philology for at least one academic year under the supervision of the faculty. Such study shall be pursued at Oxford.

4. Any person may be admitted to a course of study approved by the faculty, provided that he has *either* (*a*) passed the examinations required for the degree of Bachelor of Arts, *or* (*b*) taken a degree at some other university, such degree and such university having been approved by Council, and provided further that he has satisfied the faculty that he is qualified to pursue the study of General Linguistics and Comparative Philology.

5. The faculty shall have power in exceptional circumstances to admit a person not qualified under the provisions of clause 3 above, who has nevertheless satisfied the faculty that he is qualified to pursue the study of General Linguistics and Comparative Philology.

6. The examination shall consist of three parts:

(*a*) one general paper as indicated in A;

(*b*) two papers both of which must be chosen from those listed in B, or those listed in C (except that, at the discretion of the faculty, candidates may submit a paper from list B in place of one of those from list C), or those listed in D.

In lieu of one of the papers in list B or C or D candidates may offer with the permission of the faculty a thesis of no more than 15,000 words to be written on a subject within the field of the M.St. The word limit excludes the bibliography, appendices consisting of a catalogue of data, any extensive text which is specifically the object of a commentary or linguistic analysis, and any translation of that text, but includes quotations and footnotes.

The thesis (in two typewritten copies) must be sent in a parcel bearing the words 'Thesis for the M.St. in General Linguistics and Comparative Philology' to the Examination Schools, High Street, Oxford, not later than noon on the Friday of the first week of the Trinity Term in the academic year in which the examination takes place.

A. Linguistic Theory.

B.   (i) Phonetics and Phonology.

(ii) Syntax.

(iii) Semantics.

(iv) Historical and comparative linguistics.

(v) Psycholinguistics and Neurolinguistics.

(vi) History and structure of a language.

(vii) Experimental Phonetics.

(viii) Sociolinguistics.

(ix) Computational Linguistics.

(x) Any one option from those offered as C options for the M.St. in English Language.

(xi) Any other subject which, from time to time, the Faculty of Linguistics, Philology and Phonetics at its own discretion may consider suitable.

C. (i) The comparative grammar of two Indo-European languages or language-groups.

(ii) The historical grammar of the two languages or language-groups selected.

(iii) Translation from, and linguistic comment upon, texts in the languages selected.

D. (i) The history of one or two languages.

(ii) The structure of the language or languages selected.

(iii) *Either* (*a*) Translation from, and/or linguistic comment upon, texts in the language or languages selected, *Or* (*b*) Any paper from B above except B (vi).

7. The general paper A and the papers in C and D are each assessed by three-hour written examination. The papers in B are assessed by:

Either (*a*) three-hour written examination.

Or (*b*) An essay of between 5,000 and 7,500 words (these limits to exclude symbols and diacritics, figures, the bibliography, appendices consisting of a catalogue of data, questionnaire, or other research instrument used to gather data, any extensive text which is specifically the object of a commentary or linguistic analysis, and any translation of that text, but include quotations and footnotes). For all B papers except for B(ix) and B(x), the essay (in two typewritten copies) must be sent in a parcel bearing the words 'Essay for the M.St./M.Phil. in General Linguistics and Comparative Philology' to the Chair of Examiners for the Degree of M.St/M.Phil in General Linguistics, c/o Examination Schools, High Street, Oxford. Work for paper B(ix) is submitted as specified in the regulations for the M.Sc. in Computer Science, and work for papers under B(x) is submitted as specified in the regulations for the M.St. in English Language.

Or (*c*) A written report of between 5,000 and 7,500 words on the design and execution of an original research project (these limits exclude symbols and diacritics, figures, the bibliography, appendices consisting of a catalogue of data, questionnaire, or other research instrument used to gather data, any extensive text which is specifically the object of a commentary or linguistic analysis, and any translation of that text, but include quotations and footnotes). The research report (in two typewritten copies) must be sent in a parcel bearing the words 'Written work for the M.St./M.Phil. in General Linguistics and Comparative Philology' to the Chair of Examiners for the Degree of M.St./M.Phil. in General Linguistics, c/o Examination Schools, High Street, Oxford.

In addition, the lecturer on the course of instruction may require:

(*a*) one or more practical problem set(s), to be completed and submitted at a time specified by the lecturer; and

(*b*) one or more oral presentation(s) in a public forum.

For each paper in B, the lecturer on the course of instruction shall prescribe a suitable combination of these options, and shall make available to the Chair of Examiners evidence showing the extent to which each candidate has pursued an adequate course of work.

8. Of the two languages or language-groups selected by the candidates who wish to offer the papers listed in C above, one must be studied in greater depth than the other.

Combinations previously offered under the auspices of the Faculty of Linguistics, Philology and Phonetics are:

(*a*) Greek with the elements of Sanskrit Philology.

(*b*) Italic with the elements of Old Irish Philology.

(*c*) Germanic with the elements of Greek Philology.

(*d*) Greek with the elements of Anatolian Philology.

(*e*) Romance with the elements of Italic Philology.

(*f*) Italic with the elements of Greek Philology.

(*g*) Sanskrit with the elements of Greek Philology.

(*h*) Greek with the elements of Slavonic Philology.

(*i*) Celtic with the elements of Italic Philology.

Other combinations are allowed subject to the approval of the faculty and the availability of teaching.

9. The language or languages selected by candidates who wish to offer the papers mentioned in D above may be ancient (e.g. Ancient Greek, Latin, Sanskrit, Akkadian, etc.) or modern (e.g. French, Italian, German, English, Turkish, etc.). Only languages for which teaching is available at the time can be offered.

10. The choice of the subjects for examination will be subject to the approval of the candidate's supervisor and the faculty, having regard to the candidate's previous experience and the availability of teaching. Not all options may be offered every year. The subjects which a candidate wishes to offer for examination must be submitted to the faculty for approval not later than Tuesday of the sixth week of the Michaelmas Term in the academic year in which the candidate is to be examined.

11. If a thesis is offered, the subject must be submitted for approval by the faculty not later than Tuesday of the sixth week of the Michaelmas Term in the academic year in which the candidate is to be examined.

12. Each candidate is required to present himself for an oral examination if and when required by the examiners.

13. The Examiners may award a distinction for excellence in the whole examination.

14. Candidates requesting re-examination should be required to resit or resubmit any paper in which they have failed to achieve a pass mark. The highest mark awarded for a re-examined paper should be the pass mark.

Global and Imperial History

The regulations of the Board of the Faculty of History are as follows:

1. Candidates for this degree must follow for at least three terms a course of instruction and directed research and must, upon entering the examination, produce from their society a certificate to that effect.

2. Candidates must attend such lectures, seminars and classes as their supervisor shall determine. In addition to the formally examined programme elements described below, each candidate will be expected to attend and complete in-course requirements for a series of skills and specialist options based on a schedule to be published from year to year by the Faculty's Graduate Studies Committee.

3. The final examination shall comprise (i) two extended essays of between 4,000 and 5,000 words based on an Advanced Option, (ii) one three-hour examination paper based on the programme's conceptual and methodological component, and (iii) a dissertation of not more than 15,000 words.

I. The programme has three streams, providing the following distinct Advanced Options:

    (i) *Imperial History*: Empires in Global History 1750–2000;

    (ii) *South Asian History*: paper t.b.c.;

    (iii) *East Asian History*: history and historiography of modern China.

Two copies of the two essays, addressed to the Chair of Examiners for the M.St. in Global and Imperial History, must be submitted to the Examination Schools, High Street, Oxford by 12 noon on Monday of Week Nine of Hilary Term. The essays should reflect the skills and understanding acquired by the candidate through attending the Advanced Option classes. One of the essays may complement—but must not share significant content with—the dissertation, and the essays are also expected to be distinct from each other in period or issues covered.

    II. Each candidate must sit a three-hour written examination on conceptual and methodological issues relating to their chosen stream through the course:

        (i) *Imperial History*: concepts and methods of imperial history;

        (ii) *South Asian History*: history and culture of South Asia;

        (iii) *East Asian History*: Research methods (East Asia).

    III. Each candidate must submit a dissertation of not more than 15,000 words on a topic in the candidate's chosen subject area. The dissertation must include a short abstract which concisely summarises in about 300 words its scope and principal arguments.

Two copies of the dissertation, addressed to the Chair of Examiners for the M.St. in Global and Imperial History, must be submitted to the Examination Schools, High Street, Oxford, by 12 noon on Monday of Week Six of Trinity Term. Material submitted under I and II may be summarised or substantially further developed in the dissertation, but no significant part of the dissertation should reproduce or paraphrase other work submitted for examination.

    4. The examiners may award a distinction to candidates who have performed with special merit in the whole examination.

    5. A candidate who fails the examination will be permitted to retake it on one further occasion only, not later than one year after the initial attempt.

Greek and/or Latin Languages and Literature

    1. Candidates must satisfy the board that they possess the necessary qualifications in Greek and/or Latin to profit by the course.

    2. Every candidate must follow for at least three terms a course of instruction in Greek and/or Latin Languages and Literature. Candidates will, when they enter for the examination, be required to produce from their society a certificate that they are following such a course.

    3. *Syllabus*

Candidates must take three options from lists A, B, C, and D below, at least one of which must be drawn from A or B. Not more than one dissertation (D) may be offered. Every candidate must offer at least one option that requires detailed study of Greek or Latin or of texts in those languages. Options which meet this criterion are specified in the Handbook.

A

EITHER (i) Classical Greek: *either*

    (*a*) *Elementary Greek*. There will be one three-hour paper, consisting of passages of Greek which will test knowledge of Attic grammar and competence in translation from Greek into English.

    or

    (*b*) *Intermediate Greek*. Candidates will be expected to be familiar with *An Anthology of Greek Prose* ed. D. A. Russell (Oxford University Press 1991), nos. 17, 18, 23, 24, 33, 40, 44, 66, 78. There will be one two-hour paper and one three-hour paper. The first paper will include passages for unseen translation and grammatical questions on the Russell selection. In the second paper candidates will be expected to translate from the Russell selection and also from TWO of the following texts: (i) Herodotus I. 1–94 [ed. Hude, OCT]; (ii) Plutarch, *Life of Antony* 1–9, 23–36, 71–87 [ed. Pelling, Cambridge University Press 1988]; (iii) Euripides, *Bacchae* [ed. Diggle, OCT]. Alternative texts for translation under this head may be offered by agreement with the Graduate Studies Committee in Classical Languages and Literature.

OR (ii) Latin: *either*

(*a*) *Elementary Latin*. There will be one three-hour paper, consisting of passages of Latin prose which will test knowledge of classical Latin grammar and competence in translation from Latin into English.

or

(*b*) *Intermediate Latin*. Candidates will be expected to be familiar with *An Anthology of Latin Prose* ed. D. A. Russell (Oxford University Press 1990), nos. 7, 12, 22, 23, 34, 52, and 63. There will be one two-hour paper and one three-hour paper. The first paper will include passages for unseen translation and grammatical questions on the Russell selection. In the second paper candidates will be expected to translate from the Russell selection and also from TWO of the following texts:

(i) Cicero, *Pro Caelio* [ed. OCT].

(ii) Pliny, *Letters* 1.6, 9, 13, 19; VII.21, 24, 26, 29; VIII.16, 17; IX.6, 12, 15, 27, 33, 39; X.31, 32, 96, 97 (ed. M. B. Fisher and M. R. Griffin, CUP 1973)

(iii) Ovid, *Metamorphoses* 8 (ed. A. S. Hollis, OUP 1970)

Alternative texts for translation under this head may be offered by agreement with the Graduate Studies Committee in Classical Languages and Literature.

B

(i) *Methods and Techniques of Scholarship*. Candidates are required to offer *two* of the following topics:

(*a*) Greek Literary Papyrology;

(*b*) Greek Palaeography;

(*c*) Latin Palaeography;

(*d*) Greek Metre;

(*e*) Latin Metre.

Each of these options will be examined in one paper of 1½ hours except for Greek Literary Papyrology, which will be examined by a practical test taken in the candidate's own time (as prescribed for Greek and Latin Papyrology in the M.Phil. for Greek and/or Latin Languages and Literature). Option B(i)(a) may not be combined with option B(ix) below.

(ii) Euripides, *Greek textual criticism*: *Orestes* 1–347 and 1246–1693: papyri, manuscripts, text. (Honour School of Literae Humaniores, option III.13).

(iii) *Latin textual criticism*.

Either (*a*) Seneca, *Agamemnon*: manuscripts, text, interpretation*

or (*b*) Catullus 1–14, 27–39, 44–51, 65–7, 69–76, 95–101, 114–16 [Honour School of Literae Humaniores, option III.14].*

(iv) *Historical Linguistics and Comparative Philology*.

Each of options (ii)–(iv) will be examined in one paper of three hours.

(v) Any option available in the M.St. in Classical Archaeology, Schedule B.

---

* University classes will be given for only one of these options each year.

Option (v) will be examined *either* by two presubmitted essays *or* by one written paper of three hours.

(vi) Any option available in the M.St. in Greek and/or Roman History, Lists B and C.

(vii) *Literary Theory for Classical Studies*

Each of options (vi)-(vii) will be examined by two presubmitted essays.

(viii) *Theory and Methods of Reception.* Option (viii) will be examined by two presubmitted essays and requires attendance at the associated classes.

(ix) *Greek and Latin Literary Papyrology.* This option will be examined by one presubmitted essay and by a practical test taken in the candidate's own time (as prescribed for Greek and Latin Papyrology in the M.Phil. for Greek and/or Latin Languages and Literature). This option may not be combined with option B(i)(a) above.

(x) Any other subject proposed with the aim of developing skills needed for future research and approved by the Graduate Studies Committee in Classical Languages and Literature, which will determine the method of examination.

C

Each of the following options will be examined by (*a*) one paper of translation (1½ hours) and (*b*) two pre-submitted essays. The texts listed are those which should be studied in preparation for the pre-submitted essays. Passages will be set for translation only from those texts in section (*α*). Passages for translation will be set from the editions listed in the regulations for the Honour School of Literae Humaniores, whenever applicable. For any option approved under 12 the edition will be specified by the Graduate Studies Committee in Classical Languages and Literature.

1. Historiography
2. Lyric Poetry
3. Early Greek Hexameter Poetry
4. Greek Tragedy
5. Comedy
6. Hellenistic Poetry
7. Cicero
8. Ovid
9. Latin Didactic
10. Neronian Literature.
11. Medieval and Renaissance Latin Hexameter Poetry

α In Latin:

1. Walter of Chtillon, *Alexandreis* Book 10;
2. Petrarch, *Africa* Book 9;
3. Vida, *Ars Poetica* Book 3;
4. Milton, *In Quintum Novembris.*

β In translation:

1. Walter of Chtillon, *Alexandreis* Books 1–9;
2. Petrarch, *Africa* Books 1–8;
3. Vida, *Ars Poetica* Books 1–2.

The exact prescribed texts for options 1–10 will be as listed in the student handbook.

12. Any other text or combination of texts approved by the Graduate Studies Committee for Classical Languages and Literature.

D

A dissertation (if offered) should be of not more than 10,000 words on a subject to be proposed by the candidate in consultation with the overall supervisor or the supervisor for the dissertation, and approved by the Graduate Studies Committee in Classical Languages and Literature. (The dissertation word limit excludes the bibliography, any text that is being edited or annotated, any translation of that text, and any descriptive catalogue or similar factual matter, but includes quotations, notes, and appendices. A note of the word-count must be included.) Supervisors or others are permitted to give bibliographical help and to discuss drafts.

4. The choice of options and/or dissertation will be subject to the approval of the candidate's supervisor and the Graduate Studies Committee in Classical Languages and Literature, having regard to the candidate's previous experience, the range covered by the candidate's choices, and the availability of teaching and examining resources. The options which the candidate wishes to offer must be submitted to the Academic Administrative Officer, Classics Centre, 66 St. Giles', Oxford OX1 3LU, for approval not later than the Wednesday of the first week of Michaelmas Full Term. The candidate should also indicate by this date whether or not he or she wishes to offer a dissertation; the title of the dissertation need not be given until the Friday of the first week of Hilary Term (see under 8(i) below).

Not all options may be available in any given year.

5. In those options for which candidates are examined by presubmitted essays, two essays should be submitted, each of not more than 5,000 words in length, which between them display knowledge of more than a narrow range of the topic. (The essay word limit excludes the bibliography, any text that is being edited or annotated, any translation of that text, and any descriptive catalogue or similar factual matter, but includes quotations, notes, and appendices. A note of the word-count must be included.) Supervisors or others are permitted to give bibliographical help with, and to discuss a first draft of, such essays. Supervisors are also required to certify that, in their tutorial and class work, students have covered a wider range of topics within the overall subject.

6. Candidates are required to present themselves for oral examination if summoned by the examiners.

7. The examiners may award a distinction for excellence in the whole examination.

8. *Submission of proposed titles for essays and dissertations:*

(1) Those submitting two options examined by presubmitted essays must submit the proposed titles of two of those essays through their supervisors to the Academic Administrative Officer, Ioannou Centre, 66 St. Giles', Oxford OX1 3LU, not later than noon on the Monday of the week preceding first week of Hilary Full Term. The proposed dissertation title, for those offering that option, must be submitted by the same date.

(2) Those offering only one option examined by presubmitted essays may submit the proposed titles of their two essays through their supervisors to the Academic Administrative Officer, Ioannou Centre, 66 St. Giles', Oxford OX1 3LU, not later than noon on the Monday of the week preceding first week of Hilary Full Term. Otherwise they must submit the proposed titles of their two essays through their supervisors to the Academic Administrative Officer, Ioannou Centre, 66 St. Giles', Oxford OX1 3LU, not later than Friday of the first week of Trinity Full Term.

(3) Those offering more than two presubmitted essays must offer their proposed titles for the remaining essays by Friday of the first week of Trinity Full Term.

(4) The final confirmation of the title of the dissertation, if different from that submitted under (1) above, must be submitted not later than Friday of the first week of Trinity Full Term.

9. *Delivery of final copies of essays and dissertations:*

(1) Two typewritten or printed copies of each presubmitted essay should be sent in a parcel bearing the words 'Essays presubmitted for the M.St. in Greek and/or Latin Languages and Literature' to the Examination Schools, High Street, Oxford OX1 4BG. If the candidates are offering only one option examined by presubmitted essays, the essays may be sent as above to arrive not later than noon on the Thursday of the fifth week of Hilary Full Term. Otherwise they must be sent as above to arrive not later than noon on the Thursday of the sixth week of Trinity Full Term. If candidates are offering two options examined by presubmitted essays, at least two of the essays must be sent as above to arrive not later than noon on the Thursday of the fifth week of Hilary Full Term; any others must be sent as above to arrive not later than noon on the Thursday of the sixth week of Trinity Full Term.

In theses and pre-submitted essays all quotations from primary or secondary sources, and all reporting or appropriation of material from those sources, must be explicitly acknowledged. Each candidate must sign a certificate to the effect that the thesis or pre-submitted essay is the candidate's own work, and that the candidate has read the Faculty's guidelines on plagiarism. This declaration must be placed in a sealed envelope bearing the candidate's examination number and presented together with the thesis or pre-submitted essay.

(2) Two typewritten or printed copies of dissertations should be delivered in a parcel bearing the words 'Dissertation for the M.St. in Greek and/or Latin Languages and Literature' to the Examination Schools, High Street, Oxford OX1 4BG, to arrive not later than noon on the Thursday of the sixth week of Trinity Full Term in which the examination is to be taken.

10. *Use of bilingual dictionaries in examinations:*

Any candidate whose native language is not English may bring a bilingual (native language to English) dictionary for use in any examination paper where candidates are required to translate Ancient Greek and/or Latin texts into English.

Greek and/or Roman History

1. Every candidate must follow, for at least three terms, a course of instruction in Greek and/or Roman History. Candidates will, when they enter for the examination, be required to produce from their society a certificate that they are following such a course.

2. (*a*) In the case of options in languages, Schedule A below, candidates will be examined by written examination. Candidates taking options A (v)–(viii) may bring a dictionary for their use in the examination. Any candidate taking options A (i)–(iv) whose native language is not English may bring a bilingual (native language-English) dictionary for use in the examination.

(*b*) For options in topics and techniques, Schedules B and C below, candidates will be required to pre-submit two essays of not more than 5,000 words in length, which between them display knowledge of more than a narrow range of the topic covered by the course. (The essay word limit excludes the bibliography, any text that is being edited or annotated, any translation of that text, and any descriptive catalogue or similar factual matter, but includes quotations, notes, and appendices.)

Supervisors or others are permitted to give bibliographical help with and to discuss drafts of essays. Such essays (two typewritten or printed copies) must be sent in a parcel bearing the words 'Essays presubmitted for the M.St. in Greek and/or Roman History' to the Examination Schools, High Street, Oxford, OX1 4BG, to reach there by noon on the Thursday of the sixth week of the Trinity Term in which the examination is to be taken.

3. *Oral Examination.* Candidates are required to present themselves for oral examination if summoned by the examiners.

4. *Syllabus*

Candidates must offer (1) an option from A below, (2) an option from B or C below, and (3) a dissertation as described in D below. The option from A must be (i), (ii), (iii), or (iv), unless a candidate is dispensed from this requirement by the Graduate Studies Committee for Ancient History. In addition, all candidates must attend and participate in one of the Graduate Seminars in Ancient History as described in E below, although this will not be a subject of examination.

A

   (i) *Elementary Greek.* There will be one three-hour paper, consisting of passages of Greek which will test knowledge of Attic grammar and competence in translation from Greek into English.

   (ii) *Intermediate Greek.* There will be one three-hour paper. Candidates will be expected to be familiar with *An Anthology of Greek Prose*, ed. D. A. Russell (Oxford University Press 1991), Nos. 17, 18, 23, 24, 33, 40, 44, 66, 78, from which a selection of passages will be set for translation, in addition to a passage for unseen translation. Candidates will also be expected to translate from (i) Herodotus I. 1–94 (ed. Hude, OCT) and (ii) Plutarch, *Life of Antony* 1–9, 23–36, 71–87 (ed. Pelling, Cambridge University Press 1988). Alternative texts for translation under this head may be offered by agreement with the Graduate Studies Committee for Ancient History.

   (iii) *Elementary Latin.* There will be one three-hour paper, consisting of passages of Latin prose which will test knowledge of classical Latin grammar and competence in translation from Latin into English.

   (iv) *Intermediate Latin.* There will be one three-hour paper. Candidates will be expected to be familiar with *An Anthology of Latin Prose* ed. D. A. Russell (Oxford University Press 1990), nos. 7, 12, 22, 23, 34, 52, 63, from which a selection of passages will be set for translation, in addition to a passage for unseen translation. Candidates will also be expected to translate from (i) Cicero, *Pro Caelio* [ed. Clark OCT] and (ii) Pliny, *Letters*, 1.6, 9, 13, 19; VII.21, 24, 26, 29, VIII.16, 17; IX.6, 12, 15, 27, 33, 39; X.31, 32, 96, 97 (ed. M. B. Fisher and M. R. Griffin, Cambridge University Press 1973). Alternative texts for translation under this head may be offered by agreement with the Graduate Studies Committee for Ancient History.

   (v) French

   (vi) German

   (vii) Italian

   (viii) Any other language which the candidate has satisfied the Graduate Studies Committee for Ancient History is relevant to their other papers including any dissertation.

B

   (i) Greek Numismatics.

   (ii) Roman Numismatics.

   (iii) Greek Epigraphy.

   (iv) The epigraphy of the Roman World.

   (v) Documentary papyrology.

   (vi) any of the following papers on the B list of the M.St. in Greek and/or Latin Language and Literature: (i)–(iv); (vii).

(vii) any of the papers from Schedule B of the M.St. in Classical Archaeology.

(viii) any other subject approved by the Graduate Studies Committee for Ancient History.

C

 (i) Greek history to *c*.650 BCE

 (ii) Greek history *c*.650–479 BCE

 (iii) Greek history 479–336 BCE

 (iv) Athenian democracy in the Classical age

 (v) Alexander and his successors 336–301 BCE

 (vi) The Hellenistic world 301–*c*.100 BCE

 (vii) Rome and the Mediterranean World 241–146 BCE

 (viii) Roman history 146–46 BCE

 (ix) Cicero

 (x) Roman history 46 BCE–54 CE

 (xi) Roman history 54–138 CE

 (xii) Roman history 138–312 CE

 (xiii) The ecology, agriculture, and settlement history of the ancient Mediterranean world

 (xiv) The economy of the Roman Empire

 (xv) The provinces of the Roman Empire

 (xvi) Greek and/or Roman religion

 (xvii) Gender and sexuality in the Greek and/or Roman world

 (xviii) Greek and/or Latin historiography

 (xix) Roman law

 (xx) The Church in the Roman Empire from the beginnings to 312 CE

 (xxi) The world of Augustine

 (xxii) The City of Rome. This course is run in collaboration with the British School at Rome, and involves attendance at the residential course organised by the School annually in Rome; only those accepted by the School may take the option.

 (xxiii) British School at Athens taught course (title and topic varies from time to time). This option is run in collaboration with the British School at Athens, and involves attendance at the residential course organised by the School in even-numbered years in Athens; only those accepted by the School may take the option.

 (xxiv) Any other subject approved by the Graduate Studies Committee for Ancient History.

D

A dissertation of not more than 10,000 words on a subject to be approved by the Graduate Studies Committee for Ancient History. (The dissertation word limit excludes the bibliography, any text that is being edited or annotated, any translation of that text, and any descriptive catalogue or similar factual matter, but includes quotations, notes, and appendices.)

The dissertation (two typewritten or printed copies) must be sent in a parcel bearing the words 'Dissertation for the M.St. in Greek and/or Roman History' to The Chair of the Examiners, c/o Examinations Schools, High Street, Oxford, to arrive no later than noon on the Thursday of the sixth week of the Trinity Full Term in which the examination is to be taken.

E

Graduate Seminars
   (i) Greece and the East
   (ii) Rome and the West
These working seminars, organised by members of the faculty in areas of current interest to them, run fortnightly in Michaelmas and Hilary Terms. The topics of the Seminars will vary from time to time. Details are announced in the Graduate Handbook for the Degrees of Master of Studies and Master of Philosophy in Greek and/or Roman History.

   5. All options, including the dissertation, require the approval of the candidate's supervisor and the Graduate Studies Committee for Ancient History, having regard to the candidate's previous experience, the range covered by the chosen options and the availability of teaching and examining resources. The options must be submitted for approval not later than the Friday of the fifth week of the Michaelmas Term in the academic year in which the candidate intends to be examined. Candidates will not normally be allowed to be examined in languages of which they are native speakers or which they have previously studied in taught courses for more than two years.

History of Art and Visual Culture
   (See also the general notice at the commencement of these regulations.)
   The regulations of the Board of the Faculty of History are as follows:
   1. Every candidate must follow for at least three terms a course of instruction in the History of Art, and must, upon entering for the examination, produce from his or her society a certificate to this effect.

   2. *Syllabus*
   The course shall comprise: I, one compulsory paper; II, one optional paper chosen by the candidate; and III, a dissertation.

   I. The compulsory paper entitled 'Theory and Methods in the History of Art will be assessed by three essays of between 1,200 and 1,500 words each. A choice of topics for these essays as prescribed by the examiners will be published on the WebLearn pages for this degree programme by noon on Monday of Ninth Week of Trinity Term. Two copies of each essay submitted must be delivered to the Examination Schools, High Street, Oxford OX1 4BG, by noon on Thursday of Ninth Week of Trinity Term in the year in which the examination is to be taken.

   II. Optional papers will cover topics and issues of art history and visual culture from the later Middle Ages to the present, as approved from time to time by the Committee of the History of Art. A definitive list of the optional papers available in any one year will be posted on the notice boards of the Faculty of History by Friday of fourth week of Michaelmas Term at the latest. Optional papers will be examined by two extended essays of between 4,000 and 5,000 words.

   III. A dissertation of not more than 15,000 words on a topic in the history of art, to be approved by the candidate's supervisor and the Head of the Department of History of Art prior to the submission of essay and dissertation titles to the Chair of Examiners for the degree.

   3. Candidates shall make written application for the approval of the titles of their extended essays in their optional paper, and also notify the examiners of the title of their dissertation by the examination entry date.

   4. Two typewritten or printed copies of each extended essay for the optional paper must be sent to the Chair of the Examiners for the M.St in History of Art and Visual Culture, c/o Examination Schools, High Street, Oxford OX1 4BG by noon on Monday of Week One of Trinity Term. Two typewritten or printed copies of the

dissertation must be sent to the Chair of Examiners at the same address by noon on Monday of Week Six of Trinity Term. The dissertation must include a short abstract which concisely summarizes its scope and principal arguments, in about 300 words. Both the essays and the dissertations must be (individually) securely and firmly bound in either hard or soft covers; and the presentation and footnotes should comply with the requirements specified in the Regulations of the Education Committee for the degrees of M.Litt. and D.Phil. and follow the *Conventions for the presentation of dissertations and theses* of the Board of the Faculty of History.

5. The examiners may award a distinction for excellence in the whole examination.

6. A candidate who fails the examination will be permitted to re-take the examination on one further occasion only, not later than one year after the initial attempt. Such a candidate whose dissertation has been of satisfactory standard will not be required to re-submit the dissertation, while a candidate who has reached a satisfactory standard on *both* the option and the prescribed theory and methods essays will not be required to re-take those parts of the examination.

History of Design

1. Candidates must follow a course of instruction in the History of Design. The course will be taken on a part-time basis over a period of not fewer than two years and not more than three years within a maximum period of five years.

2. The examination will consist of the following parts:

A Mandatory Course Papers

Every candidate must submit a written assignment for each of the three mandatory course papers taught in Year 1:

    I. Techniques and Materials (Object Case Study: 2,500 words)

    II. Historical Methods (Methodology and Critical Sources Review: 3,000 words)

    III. Research Project (Extended Essay: 5,000 words)

B Advanced Papers

Every candidate must follow two Advanced Papers courses from the options listed in the Schedule below, and submit one written assignment of no more than 5,000 words in length for each paper. Candidates will select two Advanced Papers in Year 2 of the M.St from a list of available options.

C Dissertation

Every candidate must produce a dissertation of not more than 15,000 words, including appendices but excluding bibliography and endnotes, on a topic approved by the Course Director. The dissertation must be delivered not later than noon on the last Monday in September of the second year of the course to the Chair of Examiners for the Degree of M.St in the History of Design, c/o Head of Examinations and Assessment, Examination Schools, High Street, Oxford.

3. Each candidate must attend a viva voce examination when required to do so by the examiners.

4. The examiners may award a distinction for excellence in the whole examination.

5. A candidate who fails a core topic or advanced paper, or whose dissertation fails to satisfy the examiners, may be permitted to retake the paper, or resubmit the dissertation, on one further occasion only, not later than one year after the initial attempt.

Schedule

Advanced Papers are available in the following areas:
* *Decoration in Modern France*
* *The Arts and Crafts Tradition in Modern Britain*

- *Design in the Machine Age*
- *Design, Body, Environment*
- *Visual Cultures of the World Wars*
- *Academic Writing and Contemporary Practice**
- *Medieval Period or Early Modern* Paper Option (shared with the proposed M.St Architectural History)
  - Papers available to be shared with the existing MSc English Local History:
  A.7 *The social history of English architecture, 1870–1940*
  A.8 *The English suburb, 1800–1939*
  A.4 *English architecture 1500–1640*

* This Advanced Paper will be assessed by means of two written assignments: a Documentation Project and a Critical Sources Review; each 1,500 words in length

Not all advanced papers will be available in any one year and the definitive list of advanced papers available in any one year will be circulated to candidates and their supervisors during the second week of Michaelmas Term

A Postgraduate Diploma will be available only to those registered as M.St students but who for whatever reason are not continuing to complete the full M.St. To be awarded the Postgraduate Diploma in the History of Design students must successfully complete the Core papers in 2a(I–III) and the Advanced Papers in 2b.

International Human Rights Law

1. Candidates must follow a course of instruction in International Human Rights Law. The course will be taken on a part-time basis over a period of not fewer than six terms and not more than twelve terms.

2. Every candidate will be required to satisfy the examiners in the following:

    (*a*) i. Attendance at classes, individual tutorials, group seminars, and other teaching sessions as required;

        ii. Participation in all parts of the course to the satisfaction of the Course Director;

        iii. Participation in (electronic) group discussions under the guidance, and to the satisfaction, of the students academic tutor;

    (*b*) four written papers, each of three hours duration, as set out below:

        i. Fundamentals of International Human Rights Law II

        ii. The Implementation and Development of International Human Rights Law I

        iii. The Implementation and Development of International Human Rights Law II

        iv. Populations at Risk

    (*c*) six essays, each of not more than 2,000 words in length, covering the Fundamentals of International Human Rights Law I;

    (*d*) a dissertation prospectus not to exceed 1,500 words in length that identifies the dissertation topic, central question, thesis and methodology; provides a summary of the dissertation; a schedule for completion and a working bibliography. The bibliography will not count towards the word length of the prospectus;

    (*e*) a dissertation of no more than 12,000 words on a topic selected by the student in consultation with the supervisor and agreed by the Board of Examiners.

The assignments under 2(*c-d*) and the dissertation under 2(*e*) will be forwarded to the examiners c/o Registry, Department for Continuing Education, Wellington Square, Oxford OX1 2JA, for receipt by such date as the examiners shall determine and shall notify the candidates and tutors.

3. Candidates may be required to attend a viva voce examination at the end of the course of study at the discretion of the examiners.

4. The examiners may award a distinction for excellence in the whole examination.

5. Candidates who fail to satisfy the examiners in the written examinations under 2 (*b*), the written portfolios under 2(*c-d*) or the dissertation under 2(*e*) may be permitted to resubmit work in respect of the part or parts of the examination which they have failed on not more than one occasion which shall normally be within one year of the original failure.

Islamic Art and Archaeology

1. Before admission to the course, candidates must satisfy the Board of the Faculty of Oriental Studies that they possess the necessary qualifications in Arabic or Persian or Ottoman Turkish to profit by the course.

2. Every candidate must follow for at least three terms a course of instruction in Islamic Art and Archaeology.

3. *Syllabus*

There will be four Units:

Unit (i) A dissertation of not more than 15,000 words (excluding bibliography), on a topic selected in consultation with the candidate's supervisor and approved by the Faculty Board. Applications for such approval should be submitted to the Faculty office by Monday of sixth week of Michaelmas Term and will be reported to the Faculty Board's second meeting of Michaelmas Term.

Unit (ii) A portfolio containing reports on the practical work completed during the course (according to the schedule given in the Course Handbook).

Unit (iii) A three-hour written examination: Introduction to Islamic Art and Archaeology, *c.* 550–*c.* 1900.

Unit (iv) A three-hour written examination: Themes in Islamic Art and Archaeology.

4. Candidates must submit the portfolio in Unit (ii) above not later than 12 noon on the Monday of first week of Trinity Term.

5. The dissertation in Unit (i) above must be submitted not later than 12 noon on Friday of fourth week of Trinity Term.

6. Both the portfolio and the dissertation must be submitted in printed form and as a digital copy on either a CD-ROM disc or a memory stick. Two printed copies and one digital copy of each piece of work must be submitted in a securely sealed parcel clearly addressed to the Chair of Examiners, MSt in Islamic Art and Archaeology (Oriental Studies), Examination Schools, High Street, Oxford. The parcels must bear the words 'EXAMINATION FOR THE M.ST. IN ISLAMIC ART AND ARCHAEOLOGY (PORTFOLIO [or DISSERTATION])'. All work must bear the candidate's examination number (but not the candidate's name, which must be concealed). Candidates must include a signed declaration sealed in an envelope addressed to the Chair of Examiners that the work is the candidate's own.

7. Every candidate will be examined by oral examination unless he or she shall have been individually excused by the examiners.

Japanese Studies

1. Before admission to the course, candidates must *either* have taken Japanese in the Oxford Honour School of Oriental Studies *or* have taken a comparable degree from another university, *or* must satisfy the Board of the Faculty of Oriental Studies that they possess the necessary qualifications in the Japanese language to profit by the course.

2. Every candidate must follow for at least three terms a course of instruction in Japanese Studies with reference to one of the following subjects:

  (i) Japanese Linguistics

  (ii) Modern Japanese Literature

  (iii) Classical Japanese Literature

  (iv) another subject at the discretion of the Board of the Faculty of Oriental Studies.

The availability of subjects in a given year will be subject to the availability of teaching.

3. *Syllabus*

There will be four Units:

Unit (i) Context and Background. The examination will be by two take-home exercises, each comprising an essay of not more than 2,500 words on topics to be issued by the Oriental Institute Faculty Office, related directly to the course of instruction each candidate has followed. The exercises will be set not later than noon on Friday on each of Week 6 of Michaelmas Full Term and Week 6 of Hilary Full Term. At the same time as issuing each exercise, the Faculty Office will announce the date by which it is to be submitted, which shall be at least fourteen days later. The essays must be submitted to the Chair of Examiners, M.St in Japanese Studies, Examination Schools, High Street, Oxford.

Unit (ii) Texts, to be examined by written examination.

Unit (iii) Theory and Methodology, to be examined by written examination.

Unit (iv) A dissertation of not more than 15,000 words (excluding bibliography), on a topic selected in consultation with the candidate's supervisor and approved by the Faculty Board. Applications for such approval should be submitted to the Faculty office by Friday of seventh week of Michaelmas Term and will be reported to the Faculty Board's second meeting of Michaelmas Term.

The dissertation must be sent to the Chair of Examiners, M.St in Japanese Studies (Oriental Studies), Examination Schools, High Street, Oxford, not later than 12 noon on Friday of fourth week of Trinity Term.

4. Lists of set texts must be submitted to the Faculty office by Friday of seventh week of Michaelmas Term and will be reported to the Faculty Board's second meeting of Michaelmas Term.

5. All work submitted to the Chair of Examiners must be in typewritten form. Two copies must be submitted, securely sealed and addressed. The work must bear the candidates examination number (but not the candidates name, which must be concealed). Candidates must include a signed declaration sealed in an envelope addressed to the Chair of Examiners that the work is the candidates own.

6. Every candidate will be examined by oral examination unless he or she shall have been individually excused by the examiners.

Jewish Studies

1. Before admission to the course, candidates must satisfy the Board of the Faculty of Oriental Studies that they possess the necessary qualifications to profit by the course.

2. Every candidate must follow for at least three terms a course of instruction in Jewish Studies.

3. *Syllabus*

There will be four Units:

Unit (i) Three terms of *either* Biblical Hebrew, *or* Modern Hebrew, *or* Yiddish. Written examination will take place at the end of Trinity Term.

Unit (ii) Two options, to be taken in Michaelmas Term.

Unit (iii) Two options, to be taken in Hilary Term.

Unit (iv) A dissertation of not more than 15,000-words (excluding bibliography), on a topic selected in consultation with the candidate's supervisor and approved by the Faculty Board. Applications for such approval should be submitted to the Faculty office by Friday of seventh week of Michaelmas Term and will be reported to the Faculty Board's second meeting of Michaelmas Term.

The dissertation must be sent to the Chair of Examiners, M.St in Jewish Studies (Oriental Studies), Examination Schools, High Street, Oxford, not later than 12 noon on Friday of sixth week of Trinity Term.

A list of options for units (ii) and (iii) will be published in the Course Handbook.

The method of examination will be either by three-hour written examination held at the end of Trinity Term or by essay examination. The method of examination of each option will be determined in advance and will be published in the course handbook. Candidates will collect the essay topics on the Friday of eighth week of the term in which the option is taught, from the Oriental Institute Faculty Office. The essay examination will consist of two essays of not more than 2,500 words each, which must be submitted to the Examination Schools, High Street, Oxford by 12 noon on the Friday of noughth week of the term following that in which the option was taught.

4. Lists of set texts must be submitted to the Faculty office by Friday of seventh week of Michaelmas term and will be reported to the Faculty Board's second meeting of Michaelmas Term.

5. All work submitted to the Chair of Examiners must be in typewritten form. Two copies must be submitted, securely sealed and addressed. The work must bear the candidate's examination number (but not the candidate's name, which must be concealed). Candidates must include a signed declaration sealed in an envelope addressed to the Chair of Examiners that the work is the candidate's own.

6. Every candidate will be examined by oral examination unless he or she shall have been individually excused by the examiners.

Jewish Studies in the Graeco-Roman Period

1. Before admission to the course, candidates must satisfy the Board of the Faculty of Oriental Studies that they possess the necessary qualification in the Hebrew language to profit by the course. Those wishing to take options (*e*) or (*f*) must show evidence of their knowledge of Greek.

2. Every candidate must follow for at least three terms a course of study in Jewish Studies in the Graeco-Roman Period.

3. *Syllabus*

There will be four Units:

Unit (i) Essay questions on Jewish history and institutions from 200 BCE to 135 CE.

Units (ii), (iii) and (iv) Prescribed texts. Select one paper for each unit from the following list:

- (*a*) Dead Sea scrolls
- (*b*) Mishnah
- (*c*) Midrash
- (*d*) Targum
- (*e*) Septuagint
- (*f*) Hellenistic Jewish literature
- (*g*) Any other subject approved by the Board.

4. Lists of set texts must be submitted to the Faculty office by Friday of seventh week of Michaelmas Term and will be reported to the Faculty Board's second meeting of Michaelmas Term.

5. Every candidate will be examined by oral examination unless he or she shall have been individually excused by the examiners.

Teaching for some options may not be available in every year. Applicants for admission will be advised of this.

Korean Studies

1. Before admission to the course, candidates must satisfy the Board of the Faculty of Oriental Studies that they possess the necessary qualification to profit by the course. Candidates must have a knowledge of Korean at least up to the standard of a first degree.

2. Every candidate must follow for at least three terms a course of instruction in Korean Studies.

3. *Syllabus*

There will be four Units:

Unit (i) Set texts.

Unit (ii) *Either* Korean Language

or Classical Chinese

or Modern Japanese

Candidates who already possess a sufficient knowledge of Modern Korean will be required to choose Classical Chinese or Modern Japanese.

Unit (iii) Bibliography and techniques of Koreanology.

The examination will take the form of exercises to be set after examinations for Units (i) and (ii) have taken place. Each candidate will be assigned one or more exercises set on a topic directly relating to the course of instruction he or she has followed, and will be required to submit a written answer to the Chair of Examiners by a date which the Chair will announce at the conclusion of the written papers, but which shall, in any case, be not sooner than two days and not later than seven days from the date of the examination.

Unit (iv) A dissertation of not more than 15,000 words (excluding bibliography), on a topic selected in consultation with the candidate's supervisor and approved by the Faculty Board. Applications for such approval should be submitted to the Faculty office by Friday of seventh week of Michaelmas Term and will be reported to the Faculty Board's second meeting of Michaelmas Term.

The dissertation must be sent to the Chair of Examiners, M.St in Korean Studies (Oriental Studies), Examination Schools, High Street, Oxford, not later than 12 noon on Friday of fourth week of Trinity Full Term.

4. Lists of set texts must be submitted to the Faculty office by Friday of seventh week of Michaelmas Term and will be reported to the Faculty Board's second meeting of Michaelmas Term.

5. All work submitted to the Chair of Examiners must be in typewritten form. Two copies must be submitted, securely sealed and addressed. The work must bear the candidates examination number (but not the candidates name, which must be concealed). Candidates must include a signed declaration sealed in an envelope addressed to the Chair of Examiners that the work is the candidates own.

6. Every candidate will be examined by oral examination unless he or she shall have been individually excused by the examiners.

Late Antique and Byzantine Studies

(See also the general notice at the commencement of these regulations.)

1. Candidates must satisfy the Committee for Byzantine Studies and the appropriate Faculty Boards that they possess the necessary qualifications in Greek (ancient or modern) and/or Latin to profit by the course.

2. Every candidate must follow for at least three terms a course of instruction in Late Antique and Byzantine Studies. Candidates will, when they enter for the examination, be required to produce from their society a certificate that they are following such a course.

3. Candidates must take three of the following five papers. All candidates take the core paper on History, Art and Archaeology, *or*, if they already have the required linguistic competence, History and Byzantine Literature. For the remainder of their course they choose either the two Language and Literature papers, or, Auxiliary Disciplines and one Special Subject.

I. Core paper on History, Art and Archaeology, *or* History and Byzantine Literature:

Either

(*a*) Late Antiquity (covering the Roman Empire and adjoining regions)

or

(*b*) Byzantium

The core paper will be taught in classes in Michaelmas and Hilary Terms. Examination will be by two 5,000 word essays, to be submitted by Monday of seventh week of Trinity Term.

II. and III. Language and Literature (teaching in Greek, Latin, Slavonic, Armenian, Syriac, and Arabic will normally be available)

These papers are taught over three terms in classes, with reference to a selection of texts and/or extracts from texts which may vary from year to year according to the interests of candidates. Examination is by two three-hour papers (candidates are permitted the use of relevant bilingual dictionaries, which will be provided by the faculty):

(*a*) translation, and

(*b*) set texts (with passages for translation and comment).

Candidates who are embarking on the study of one of the above languages will normally be expected to take both examinations in that language, but the Committee for Byzantine Studies may in special circumstances permit them to substitute another paper for one of these examination papers. Candidates cannot normally offer an examination in the language which qualified them for admission to the degree programme in the first instance.

IV. Auxiliary Discipline(s):

Either

(*a*) any two of the following: epigraphy, palaeography, numismatics, sigillography

or

(*b*) papyrology: Greek or Coptic or Arabic

or

(*c*) artefact studies: one of ceramics or metalware or ivories or codices or carved marbles.

Paper IV will be taught by lectures/classes/tutorials. Examination will be by a three-hour paper, except for papyrology which is assessed by two 5,000 word essays on distinct aspects of the subject.

V. A Special Subject selected from the subject areas listed under 4. below.

Special Subjects will be taught by lectures/classes/tutorials. Examination will be either by two 5,000 word essays or by a 10,000 word dissertation (to be submitted by Monday of seventh week of Trinity Term).

4. Overview of Special Subject (for details please consult the Course Handbook)

(*a*) History: Special Subjects on offer deal either with specific periods or with certain aspects of late Roman and Byzantine history (including military, diplomatic, political, social economic and religious history) between the fourth and fifteenth centuries, as well as important developments in neighbouring regions.

(*b*) Art and Archaeology: Special Subjects on offer cover sculpture, portraiture, minor arts, monumental art and architecture of the late Roman, Byzantine and Islamic spheres of influence, as well as the archaeology of town and country throughout the Mediterranean and Near Eastern worlds.

(*c*) Literature (texts prescribed in translation): Special Subjects on offer range through historiography, hagiography, poetry, popular literature and scholarship in the languages available for the degree programme.

(*d*) Religion: Special Subjects on offer cover theological debates and practical spirituality in the fields of Judaism, Christianity, and Islam.

(*e*) Such other subjects as may be approved on application to the Committee for Byzantine Studies.

Note. The list of Special Subjects detailed in the Course Handbook reflects the expertise and interests of current postholders. The list may be altered from time to time with development of expertise and changes of interest on the part of the postholders.

5. Teaching in all the options may not be available each year, and applicants for admission will be advised whether teaching will be available in the options of their choice.

6. The examiners may award a distinction for excellence in the whole examination.

Legal Research/Socio-Legal Research

1. Candidates for admission to the course will be required to produce evidence of their appropriate qualifications for the course.

2. Candidates must follow a course of instruction in Legal Research Method approved by the Law Board, and must satisfy the examiners that they have completed to the required standard such tests or exercises in Legal Research Method as

may be prescribed by the Law Board as part of such a course of instruction. Where the Law Board judges that it has sufficient evidence of a candidate's proficiency in legal research method, it may in exceptional circumstances dispense a candidate from this requirement.

3. Every candidate on admission as a student shall be placed by the board of the Law Faculty under the supervision of a graduate member of the University or other competent person selected by the board, and the board shall have power for sufficient reasons to change the supervisor of any student.

4. Examination for the Degree shall be by thesis, and by oral examination. The thesis must not exceed 30,000 words and should not normally be less than 25,000 words in length (the limit to include all notes but to exclude all tables and bibliography, and the candidate to state the number of words in the thesis to the nearest hundred words). The thesis shall be wholly or substantially the result of work undertaken whilst registered for the degree of M.St. in Legal Research. The required format for this thesis is the common format prescribed for all law theses, which is printed in the Faculty of Law's Graduate Students' Handbook. The examiners must satisfy themselves that the thesis affords evidence of serious study by the candidate and of ability to discuss a difficult problem critically; that the candidate possesses a good general knowledge of the field of learning within which the subject of the thesis falls; that the thesis is presented in a lucid and scholarly manner, and that the candidate has made a worthwhile contribution to knowledge or understanding in the field of learning within which the subject of the thesis falls to the extent that could reasonably be expected within the time normally spent as a student for the Degree.

5. At any time not earlier than the third nor later than the fifth term after the term of admission, a candidate may apply to the Board for examination. Such application shall be made to the Registrar and Secretary of Faculties and shall be accompanied by

(1) a statement as to what part, if any, of his or her thesis has already been accepted, or is being currently submitted, for any degree in this University or elsewhere;

(2) a statement that the thesis is the candidate's own work, except where otherwise indicated;

(3) two copies or, if leave has been obtained from the Board of the Faculty of Law, one copy of his or her thesis either at the same time as his or her application or at such later time as the Education Committee shall by regulation permit. The thesis must be securely and firmly bound in either hard or soft covers. Looseleaf binding is not acceptable.

6. On receipt of any such application the Registrar shall submit it to the Board. The Board shall thereupon appoint two examiners whose duties shall be:

(1) to consider the thesis sent in by the student under the provisions of the preceding clause, provided that they shall exclude from consideration in making their report any part of the thesis which has already been accepted, or is being concurrently submitted, for any degree in this University or elsewhere, and shall have the power to require the candidate to produce for their inspection the complete thesis so accepted or concurrently submitted.

(2) to examine the candidate orally on the subject of his or her thesis and on subjects relevant to his or her field of study, and, if they wish on such matters as will enable them to discharge their duties under sub-paragraph (3) or (4);

(3) to report to the Board whether on the basis of the thesis submitted, the oral examination, and, where applicable, the report referred to in paragraph (7), the candidate:

(i) should be awarded the Degree;

(ii) should be awarded the Degree with Distinction; or

(iii) should be given the opportunity to re-submit for the Degree within a further three terms.

The Education Committee shall have power, on the application of a faculty board in a special case, to authorise the appointment of a third examiner (or an assessor), upon such conditions and to perform such functions as the committee shall approve; any fee paid to such an additional examiner or assessor shall be met from the funds at the disposal of the committee.

The Education Committee shall have power to make regulations concerning the notice to be given of the oral examination and of the time and place at which it may be held.

7. On receipt of the report of the examiners, it shall be the duty of the board to decide whether the candidate is qualified to supplicate for the Degree of Master of Studies, with or without the award of a Distinction, and, if not, to indicate that the candidate should be given the opportunity to apply for re-examination.

The board may not permit the candidate to supplicate for the degree unless and until the Director of the Course in Legal Research Method, failing whom the Director of Graduate Studies (Research), has certified that the candidate has satisfied or been exempted from the requirements of that course.

8. If the board has adopted a recommendation that the candidate be given the opportunity to resubmit, and the candidate indicates the wish to take up that opportunity, the candidate shall retain the status and obligations of a Student for the Degree of Master of Studies and shall be permitted to apply to be re-examined within the period specified in para.6 (3) (iii) above. Upon receiving such an application, the Board may reappoint the previous examiners, or may appoint different examiners instead of any or all of the previous examiners, as it shall judge appropriate.

9. The board may exempt any candidate who has re-submitted for the Degree from oral examination provided that the examiners are satisfied, without examining the candidate orally, that they can recommend to the board that the candidate has reached the standard required for the Degree.

Literature and Arts

(for candidates commencing in MT 2013 and later)

1. Every candidate must follow for at least six terms (and a maximum of eight terms) a part-time course of instruction in interdisciplinary study in the Humanities (Literature, History and History of Art).

2. The course will consist of lectures, seminars, on-line courses and individual tutorials.

3. Every candidate will be required to satisfy the examiners in the following parts:

(*a*) Four essays, each of no more than 5,000 words in length

(*b*) Engagement with the on-line courses to the satisfaction of the Course Director.

(*c*) A dissertation on a topic selected by the candidate in consultation with the Course Director and his or her supervisor and approved by the examiners. The dissertation must be of no more than 11,000 words in length, and will need to demonstrate knowledge and awareness of more than one subject discipline.

Candidates may be required to attend a viva voce examination if the Examiners require further information in order to make a judgement on an individual candidate.

The dissertation under 3(*c*) must be submitted not later than noon on the third Friday in September of the final year of the course to the Chair of Examiners for the Degree of MLA, c/o Registry, 1 Wellington Square, Oxford. All other elements of assessed work shall be forwarded to the examiners, c/o Registry, 1 Wellington Square, Oxford for consideration by such dates as the examiners shall determine and shall notify the candidates and tutors at the start of each academic year.

The assessed work under 3(*a*) and 3(*c*) must be accompanied by a statement that it is the candidate's own work.

4. The examiners may award a Distinction for the MLA.

5. A candidate who fails to satisfy the examiners in 3 may be permitted to resubmit work in respect of part or parts of the examination which they have failed for examination on one further occasion. In the case of 3(*a*), candidates should resubmit work within one year, but normally not later than three months after the initial attempt. In the case of 3(*c*), candidates should resubmit work not later than twelve months after the initial attempt.

Medieval History

The regulations of the Board of the Faculty of History are as follows:

1. Candidates for the M.St in Medieval History must follow for at least three terms a course of instruction and directed research and must, upon entering the examination, produce from their society a certificate to that effect.

2. Candidates must attend such lectures, seminars, classes, and language courses as his or her supervisor shall determine, and undertake any language tests set by language teachers. Language and class teachers will report to the Chair of Examiners on a candidate's attendance and participation, and where appropriate test results, not later than Friday of ninth week of Trinity Term.

3. Candidates will follow a core course in medieval history, focussing on historical methods and the interpretation of historical evidence, during Michaelmas Term. In consultation with the convenor of the core course they will select a historiographical or methodological problem in medieval history for individual in-depth study. On this agreed topic, candidates must submit to the Chair of the Examiners of the M.St in Medieval History, c/o Examination Schools, High Street, Oxford OX1 4BG, by noon on Monday of first week of Trinity Term two typewritten copies of an essay of between 3,000 and 5,000 words.

4. In Hilary Term candidates will be required to choose an option paper of historical study within the field of medieval history, as offered by the History Faculty. A descriptive list of option papers will be published by the Faculty of History in September for the academic year ahead (not all options may be available in every year). The definitive list of option papers for any year will be posted on the Faculty's graduate notice board not later than Friday of third week of Michaelmas Term of the academic year in which the paper is to be taken. Candidates must submit to the Chair of the Examiners of the M.St. in Medieval History, at the address above, by noon on Monday of first week of Trinity Term two typewritten copies of an extended essay (of between 8,000 and 10,000 words) based on an aspect of the chosen option paper.

5. The examiners may make the marks awarded to the candidates for the written work known to the Director of Graduate Studies where necessary for the purpose of grant applications and progression assessments. However, the pass list shall be issued only following the completion of the whole examination, including submission and final assessment of the dissertation.

6. Candidates must choose, after due consultation with their supervisor, a topic for a dissertation based on their individual research. Candidates are required to

submit two typewritten copies of the dissertation, which shall not normally exceed 15,000 words, to the Chair of the Examiners, at the address above, at the latest by 12 noon on the last Friday in August of the academic year in which they are registered for the degree.

7. The examiners may award a distinction to candidates who have performed with special merit in the whole examination.

8. A candidate who fails the examination will be permitted to retake it on one further occasion only, not later than one year after the initial attempt.

Such a candidate whose dissertation has been of satisfactory standard may resubmit the same piece of work, while a candidate who has reached a satisfactory standard on the written work will not be required to retake that part of the examination.

Medieval Studies

The regulations of the Board of the Faculty of History are as follows:

1. Candidates for the M.St. in Medieval Studies must follow for at least three terms a course of instruction and directed research and must, upon entering the examination, produce from their society a certificate to that effect.

2. Candidates must attend such lectures, seminars, classes as his or her supervisor, in consultation with the convenor of the M.St. in Medieval Studies, shall determine. These will include one compulsory language class over three terms, and candidates must attend any language tests set by their language teachers. The choice of languages includes Latin, Old English, Old Norse, Old French, Old High German, Old Irish, Middle Welsh, Greek, Hebrew, and Arabic. Language and class teachers will report to the Chair of Examiners a candidate's attendance and participation, and where appropriate, test results not later than Monday of ninth week of Trinity Term.

3. In Michaelmas Term all candidates will follow, as directed by the programme convenor, a series of classes on research methods relevant to their particular combination of disciplines. In Hilary Term candidates will follow a compulsory interdisciplinary seminar, on a theme chosen by the convenor of the M.St. which will exemplify the different but complementary approaches to medieval sources offered by individual disciplines. Candidates must provide evidence of attendance to the examiners.

4. In each Michaelmas and Hilary Term candidates will take one Option Paper of their choice, from the subject options made available by the participating faculties in any given year and term. A descriptive list of option papers will be published by the Faculty of History in September for the academic year ahead (not all options may be available every year). The definitive list of option papers for any one year will be posted on the History Faculty's graduate notice board not later than Friday of third week of Michaelmas Full Term preceding the examination. For each of the two Option Papers candidates are to be assessed in the format prescribed by the procedures of the host programmes, provided the assessment does not exceed the equivalent of an essay of between 5,000 and 7,000 words. Candidates should consult the convenor of the Option Paper on the modes and timetables of the prescribed assessment. Essay submissions must be addressed to the Chair of Examiners for the M.St in Medieval Studies, c/o Examination Schools, High Street, Oxford OX1 4BG, and handed in no later than 12 noon on Monday of first week of Trinity Term. Where the host programme specifies an earlier deadline that deadline will apply.

5. Candidates will choose a course of palaeography and/or codicology classes in one of the participating faculties. Unless otherwise instructed through the host programme, they must submit two copies of the assessment portfolio prescribed by the host programme no later than 12 noon on Monday of first week of Trinity Term to the Chair of Examiners, at the address above.

6. Candidates must choose, after due consultation with their supervisor, a topic for a dissertation based on their individual research. Candidates are required to submit two typewritten or printed copies of the dissertation, which shall not normally exceed 12,000 words, to the Chair of the Examiners, at the address above, at the latest by 12 noon on Monday of ninth week of Trinity Term. Each dissertation must include a short abstract which concisely summarises its scope and principal arguments, in about 300 words.

7. The examiners may award a distinction to candidates who have performed with special merit in the whole examination.

8. A candidate who fails the examination will be permitted to retake it on one further occasion only, not later than one year after the initial attempt.

Such a candidate whose dissertation has been of satisfactory standard may resubmit the same piece of work, while a candidate who has reached a satisfactory standard on the written work will not be required to retake that part of the examination.

Mindfulness-Based Cognitive Therapy

1. *Course*

(*a*) The course consists of twelve intensive teaching blocks, combining academic teaching, practical skills acquisition, and experiential learning. It is designed to develop knowledge of the theoretical basis of Mindfulness-Based Cognitive Therapy (MBCT) and of related research and clinical principle, and to develop the competencies required in order to become an effective MBCT practitioner. The course may be taken over a period of not less than two years and not more than four years, subject to the Board of Studies being able to approve an extension of time of not more than three terms.

(*b*) The course places equal emphasis on critical understanding of theory, on critical appreciation of research, and on candidates' capacity to demonstrate these through evidence of knowledge, understanding and the ability to apply these in practice (including personal experience of insight meditation as well as instructing others in MBCT). Candidates are expected to engage in independent study, to practise what they have learned between teaching sessions, and to receive feedback on what they have done.

2. Every candidate will be required to satisfy the examiners in the following:

(*a*) attendance at a minimum of 80 per cent of forty-two teaching days, spread across two years, and including two residential training retreats of five and seven days' duration;

(*b*) Written assignments as follows:

(i) two essays of no more than 4,000 words, demonstrating the capacity critically to appraise theory, research and clinical literature relevant to MBCT (Year I);

(ii) one written reflective analysis of personal meditation practice, relating experience to theory, research and clinical principle in no more than 4,000 words (Year I);

(iii) one written assignment describing the development, delivery and evaluation of a programme of MBCT suitable for the student's client group, along with appropriate copies of instructional materials (handouts, guided meditation CDs). This should be of no more than 4,000 words, excluding tables, figures, references, appendices and instructional materials (Year II);

(*c*) one videotape of an MBCT class, evaluated for adherence to protocol and competence as an instructor (Year II);

(*d*) one dissertation of no more than 10,000 words on a topic selected by the student, related to the theory and practice of MBCT and related research, and displaying in depth knowledge and understanding, and capacities for investigation, critical analysis, and independent, creative thought (Year II).

Two printed copies of each written assignment under 2(*b*) and 2(*d*), and one copy of the videotaped MBCT session and accompanying documentation under 2(*c*) shall be forwarded to the examiners for consideration by the examiners by such date as the examiners shall determine and shall notify candidates before the start of the academic year in which the assignment is due.

3. Candidates may be required to attend a viva voce examination at the end of the course of study.

4. Candidates who fail to satisfy the examiners in any of the assignments, including both written assignments under 2(*b*) and 2(*d*) and videotaped performance under 2(*c*), may be permitted to resubmit work in the part or parts of the examination which they have failed for examination on one further occasion only. That is, no assignment may be resubmitted more than once. In addition, candidates may resubmit only two assignments during the course as a whole. Resubmission shall normally be within three months of the original award of marks in Year I, and within one year of the original award of marks for the more substantial assignments in Year II. Approval for deferral must be obtained from the relevant board of studies.

5. The examiners may award a Distinction for the Master of Studies.

Modern British and European History

The regulations of the Board of the Faculty of History are as follows:

1. Candidates for this degree must follow for at least three terms a course of instruction and directed research and must, upon entering the examination, produce from their society a certificate to that effect.

2. Candidates must attend such lectures, seminars and classes as their supervisor shall determine. In addition to the formally examined programme elements described below, each candidate will be expected to attend and complete in-course requirements for a series of skills and specialist options based on a schedule to be published from year to year by the Faculty's Graduate Studies Committee. The candidate's individual programme, agreed with her/his supervisor, will be subject to approval by the Director of Graduate Studies, in consultation with the programme convenor, by Friday of Week One of Michaelmas Term; subsequent changes must be agreed by the Director of Graduate Studies not later than Friday of Week Three of Hilary Term. Class teachers will report to the Chair of Examiners on the candidate's attendance and participation, and, where appropriate, test results, not later than Monday of Week Nine of Hilary Term, except in the case of three-term language classes where the respective reporting deadline will be Monday of Week Nine of Trinity Term.

3. The final examination for candidates in British and European History shall comprise (i) one extended essay based on the programmes theory component, plus one dissertation proposal, (ii) one extended essay based on an Advanced Option, and (iii) a dissertation of not more than 15,000 words.

    I. During Michaelmas Term each candidate will attend core classes on historical theory and methodological approaches as well as a series of classes on sources and resources. The core classes will be assessed by an extended essay of between 4,000 and 5,000 words, and the sources and resources component by a dissertation proposal of between 800 and 1,000 words.

        Two copies of the essay and proposal, addressed to the Chair of Examiners for the M.St. in Modern British and European History, must be submitted to the Examination Schools, High Street, Oxford by 12 noon on Monday of Week One of Hilary Term.

II. In Hilary Term candidates must choose one Advanced Option, either from the joint Advanced Options for the Master of Studies in Modern British and European History and the Master of Philosophy in Modern British and European History, or from the Advanced Options for one of the Faculty of History's other Master's programmes. The choice of Advance Option will depend on the candidate's training objectives or dissertation project. Details of available Advanced Options are published in course handbooks. Approval of the Advanced Option choice must be obtained from the programme convenor and Director of Graduate Studies by Friday of Week Four of Michaelmas Term. The request for approval must be sent to the History Graduate Office.

On recommendation from the candidate's supervisor, the Director of Graduate Studies, in consultation with the programme convenor, may approve relevant taught papers from Master's programmes offered by faculties other than History, provided that the respective faculty's Graduate Studies Committee is satisfied that the candidate has an adequate background in the subject.

This part of the programme will be assessed by one extended essay of between 6,500 and 7,500 words . Two copies of the essay, addressed to the Chair of Examiners for the M.St. in Modern British and European History, must be submitted to the Examination Schools, High Street, Oxford by 12 noon on Monday of Week Nine of Hilary Term.

This essay should reflect skills and understanding the candidate has developed by following the approved choice of Advanced Option paper. This essay may complement but must not share significant content with the essay submitted under II.

Teaching may not be available for all the Advanced Options each year, and restrictions may be imposed on the combination of Advanced Options that may be taken in a particular year.

III. Each candidate must prepare a dissertation of not more than 15,000 words on a topic in his or her chosen subject area. The dissertation must include a short abstract which concisely summarises in about 300 words its scope and principal arguments.

Two copies of the dissertation, addressed to the Chair of Examiners for the Master of Studies in Modern British and European History, must be submitted to the Examination Schools by 12 noon on Monday of Week Six of Trinity Term. Material submitted under I and II may be summarised or substantially further developed in the dissertation, but no significant part of the dissertation should reproduce or paraphrase other work submitted for examination.

4. The examiners may award a distinction to candidates who have performed with special merit in the whole examination.

5. A candidate who fails the examination will be permitted to retake it on one further occasion only, not later than one year after the initial attempt.

Modern Jewish Studies

1. Before admission to the course, candidates must satisfy the Board of the Faculty of Oriental Studies that they possess the necessary qualification in the Hebrew or Yiddish languages to profit by the course.

2. Every candidate must follow for at least three terms a course of instruction in Modern Jewish Studies.

3. *Syllabus*

There will be four Units:

Unit (i) Passages for translation and comment and essay questions on prescribed texts in Hebrew or Yiddish. This paper will be examined by a three-hour written examination.

Units (ii) and (iii) Two papers from the following list, to be examined either by written examination or by take-home essay examination:

(*a*) Hebrew literature 1888–1948.

(*b*) The literature of the State of Israel.

(*c*) Jewish literature of the nineteenth and twentieth centuries.

(*d*) Major trends in Jewish religion and thought since 1789.

(*e*) Modern Jewish History.

(*f*) Israel: History, Politics and Society.

(*g*) Yiddish literature and culture.

(*h*) The Holocaust: from History to Memory.

(*i*) Modern Jewish politics.

(*j*) Any other subject approved by the Board.

Papers will be examined by two take-home essays of not more than 2,500 words each. Candidates will be notified of the essay topics on the Friday of eighth week of the term in which the paper is taught. Essays must be submitted to the Examination Schools, High Street, Oxford, by 12 noon on the Friday of noughth week of the term following that in which the paper was taught.

Unit (iv) A dissertation of not more than 15,000 words (excluding bibliography) on a topic selected in consultation with the candidate's supervisor and approved by the Faculty Board. Applications for such approval should be submitted to the Faculty office by Friday of seventh week of Michaelmas Term and will be reported to the Faculty Board's second meeting of Michaelmas Term.

Two copies of the dissertation must be submitted, to the Chair of Examiners, M.St in Modern Jewish Studies (Oriental Studies), Examination Schools, by 12 noon on Friday of fourth week of Trinity Full Term.

4. Lists of set texts must be submitted to the Faculty office by Friday of seventh week of Michaelmas Term and will be reported to the Faculty Board's second meeting of Michaelmas Term.

5. All work submitted to the Chair of Examiners must be in typewritten form. Two copies must be submitted, securely sealed and addressed. The work must bear the candidates examination number (but not the candidates name, which must be concealed). Candidates must include a signed declaration sealed in an envelope addressed to the Chair of Examiners that the work is the candidates own.

6. Every candidate will be examined by oral examination unless he or she shall have been individually excused by the examiners.

Teaching for some options may not be available in every year. Applicants for admission will be advised of this.

Modern Languages

1. Candidates must follow a Programme chosen from those listed in the Handbook for Taught-Course Graduate Students.

In order to gain admission to the course, applicants must show evidence of linguistic ability compatible with advanced literary study in the language(s) chosen to study. Comparative Literature candidates shall not be required to have reading fluency in more than two languages other than English. Unless otherwise stated, candidates will be expected to write in English unless explicit permission is obtained to write in the language (or one of the languages) studied. In the case of Comparative Literature candidates, writing in more than one language in addition to English will not be authorised.

All candidates must follow a course of instruction in Modern Languages at Oxford for a period of three terms, unless the Board of the Faculty of Medieval and Modern Languages in exceptional circumstances shall permit an extension of time, and candidates shall, when entering their name for the examination, be required to produce from their society a certificate stating that they are following the course of instruction for the period prescribed.

2. All candidates shall be required:

(*a*) To offer A, B, C and D as defined in 3 below.

(*b*) To present themselves for viva voce examination at the time appointed by the examiners.

3. The examination shall consist of the following:

(A) *Either*

(i) Methods of Criticism and the Theory of Literature. All candidates must attend such lectures, seminars, and classes as their course convener shall determine. All candidates must present one seminar paper during their course, and submit a written essay based on some aspect of the work done for the seminar. This essay shall be written in English and must be between 5,000 and 7,000 words in length. Candidates must submit three typed copies of their essay to the Head of Examinations and Assessments, Examination Schools, High Street, Oxford, by noon on Thursday of tenth week of Hilary Term. Each copy must have a cover sheet giving the candidate's name, college, the title of the essay, the name of the candidate's supervisor, and the words 'Methods of Criticism and the Theory of Literature, submitted in partial fulfilment of the requirements of the M.St. in Modern Languages'.

Or

(ii) Methods of Criticism and History of Ideas in Germany from the Eighteenth to the Twentieth Centuries. All candidates must attend such lectures, seminars, and classes as their course convener shall determine. All candidates must present one seminar paper during their course, and submit a written essay based on some aspect of the work done for the seminar. This essay may be written in English or German and must be between 5,000 and 7,000 words in length. Candidates must submit three typed copies to the Head of Examinations and Assessments, Examination Schools, High Street, Oxford, by noon on Thursday of tenth week of Hilary Term. Each copy must have a cover sheet giving the candidate's name, college, the title of the essay, the name of the candidate's supervisor, and the words 'Methods of Criticism and History of Ideas in Germany, submitted in partial fulfilment of the requirements of the M.St. in Modern Languages'.

Or

(iii) Methods of Scholarship. Each candidate shall be required to offer either, (1) the History of the Book, or (2) Palaeography with Textual Criticism. Candidates will be examined on one or two essays on topics agreed by them with the course convener relating either to the history of the book (for (1)) or to palaeography with textual criticism (for (2)). The essay or essays should be between 5,000 and 7,000 words in total. Candidates must submit three typed copies to the Head of Examinations and Assessments, Examination Schools, High Street, Oxford, by noon on Thursday of tenth week of Hilary Term. Each copy must have a cover sheet giving the candidates name, college, the title of the essay, the name of the candidates supervisor, and the words 'Methods of Scholarship, submitted in partial fulfilment of the requirements of the M.St. in Modern Languages'. For (2), candidates will in addition be required to undertake a practical transcription test, made without reference to dictionaries or handbooks, on a short manuscript text selected by the course convener, who will also mark, sign, and date the candidate's work. The test should take place by the end of the fourth week of the Trinity Term in which the examination is to be taken.

Or

(iv) A methodological essay of between 5,000 and 7,000 words in length on a topic or issue related to one of the candidate's Special Subjects or dissertation. It might consist, for example, of a theoretical discussion of the candidate's approach to the material being studied, or a detailed analysis of existing approaches. If candidates choose this option, they will also be expected to attend a set of seminars in (i) or (ii) above, or a set of tutorials in (iii), and to make a presentation. Candidates must submit three copies to the Head of Examinations and Assessments, Examination Schools, High Street, Oxford, by noon on Thursday of tenth week of Hilary Term. Each copy must have a cover sheet giving the candidate's name, college, the title of the essay, the name of the candidate's supervisor, and the words 'Essay on Method, submitted in partial fulfilment of the requirements of the M.St. in Modern Languages'.

The work submitted under (i) must be written in English; the work submitted under (ii) may be written in English or German; the work submitted under (iii) may be written in English or, subject to the approval of the Medieval and Modern Languages Faculty Board, in a language appropriate to the literature concerned.

Approval must be sought for the choice of options in (A) by the end of the fourth week of Michaelmas Term.

(B) A dissertation of between 10,000 and 12,000 words written in English, or, with the approval of the Medieval and Modern Languages Faculty Board, in the language appropriate to the literature concerned, on a topic connected with those offered in (A) (i), (ii) or (iii) above or (C) below, but distinct from those covered by the essays submitted under (A) or (C), and approved by the Modern Languages Board. Candidates are required to register the subject area or title of their dissertation with the Modern Languages Graduate Office by the end of the fourth week of Hilary Term.

The dissertation must be presented in proper scholarly form. Three copies typed in double-spacing on one side only of quarto or A4 paper, each copy bound or held firmly in a cover, must be delivered to the Head of Examinations and Assessments, Examination Schools, High Street, Oxford, by noon on Thursday of the sixth week of Trinity Term.

(C and D) Two Special Subjects

Candidates may select two Special Subjects from those listed in the 'Graduate Studies in Modern Languages' handbook as associated with the programme which they are following; candidates may select a special subject from a different programme with the approval of their supervisor; or candidates may propose Special Subjects of their own devising, provided that each subject has the written support of the candidate's supervisor and is approved by or on behalf of the Medieval and Modern Languages Faculty Board. A proposal for a Special Subject of the candidate's own devising shall be accompanied by a statement (of approximately 100 words) of the character and scope of the subject proposed. Approval of all Special Subjects must be sought, by application to the Modern Languages Graduate Office, 41 Wellington Square, Oxford by end of the fourth week of Michaelmas Term. Approval of Special Subjects proposed will be dependent on the availability of teaching and examining resources at the relevant time.

Candidates will normally offer two Special Subjects from the same language and area or from different areas in the same language. The Comparative Literature Programme will contain Special Subjects from two different languages.

Candidates will be examined on an essay, or two essays (which may be written in English, or, with the approval of the Medieval and Modern Languages Faculty Board, in the language appropriate to the literature concerned), on the topics they have agreed with the supervisor of each Special Subject. The length of the work submitted for each Special Subject should be between 5,000 and 7,000 words in total.

4. Candidates for Comparative Literature should ensure that either at least one of the special subjects (C and D) is comparative in scope or the two special subjects are concerned with different languages. The dissertation must deal explicitly with comparative issues.

5. In addition to submitting the dissertation (B), students are required to submit work for assessment on all three of the non-dissertation components (A, C and D). Of these three, the lowest passing mark will be discounted in the final assessment. A fail mark must always be included in the final assessment.

The Special Subject essays for Michaelmas Term shall be submitted to the Head of Examinations and Assessments, Examination Schools, High Street, Oxford, by noon on Thursday of the tenth week of Michaelmas Term. The Special Subject essays for Hilary Term shall be submitted to the Head of Examinations and Assessments, Examination Schools, High Street, Oxford, by noon on Thursday of the tenth week of Hilary Term.

In the case of resubmission, candidates shall be required to resubmit all the material by noon on Thursday of the sixth week of the first Trinity Term following their first examination. Candidates may resubmit on one occasion only.

6. The examiners may award a Distinction for excellence in the whole examination.

Modern South Asian Studies

The regulations of the Boards of the Faculty of History and of Oriental Studies are as follows:

1. Candidates for the MSt in Modern South Asian Studies must follow for at least three terms a course of instruction and directed research and must, upon entering the examination, produce from their society a certificate to that effect.

2. Candidates must attend such lectures, seminars, classes and language classes as the convenors of the course shall determine, and must undertake any language tests set by the language teachers.

The final examination consists of the following four units, which all candidates must take:

(i) A Language Paper in one of the following languages: Hindi, Literary Hindi, Bengali, Sanskrit, Persian or Tibetan. The examination will be based on knowledge of grammar, translation and reading comprehension. Tuition for the language paper will be through classes, and will continue through all three terms of the academic year. Not all language options may be available every year.

(ii) A General Methodological Paper, The History and Culture of South Asia. Tuition for this paper will be through weekly seminars held during Michaelmas and the first 4 weeks of Hilary Term. A choice of essay questions as prescribed by the examiners will be published on the WebLearn pages for this degree programme by noon on Friday of fourth week of Hilary Term. They will be required to select one question from this paper, and prepare an essay of up to 5,000 words (excluding bibliography). Candidates must submit two typewritten copies of this essay to the Chair of the Examiners of the M.St. in Modern South Asian Studies, c/o Examination Schools, High Street, Oxford OX1 4BG, by noon on Friday of 8th week of the Hilary Term.

(iii) An Optional Paper within the field of Modern South Asian Studies, from a list of options offered by the Faculties of History and Oriental Studies. The definitive list of options for the year ahead, together with short descriptions of each, will be published on Weblearn at the latest by the start of the Michaelmas Term. Tuition for this paper will be through a course of 8 weekly seminars held through the Hilary Term. A list of essay questions as prescribed by the examiners will be published on the WebLearn pages for this degree programme by noon on Friday of eighth week of Hilary Term. Candidates will be required to select one question from this paper, and prepare an essay of up to 5,000 words (excluding bibliography). Candidates must submit two typewritten copies of this essay to the Chair of the Examiners of the M.St. in Modern South Asian Studies, c/o Examination Schools, High Street, Oxford OX1 4BG, by noon on Friday of 4th week of the Trinity Term.

(iv) A Dissertation based on individual research. Candidates will choose their topics after due consultation with their supervisor. Candidates are required to submit two typewritten copies of the dissertation, which shall not normally exceed 15,000 words (excluding bibliography), to the Chair of the Examiners, at the address above, by noon on Friday of eighth week of Trinity Term. Each Dissertation must include a short abstract which concisely summarises its scope and principal arguments, in about 300 words.

3. The examiners may make the marks awarded to the candidates for the written work known to the Director of Graduate Studies where necessary for the purpose of grant applications and progression assessments. However, the pass list will be issued only following completion of the whole examination, including submission and final assessment of the dissertation.

4. The examiners may award a Distinction to candidates who have performed with special merit in the whole examination.

5. A candidate who fails the examination will be permitted to re-take it on one further occasion only, not later than one year after the initial attempt. Such a candidate whose thesis has been of a satisfactory standard may resubmit the same piece of work. A candidate who has reached a satisfactory standard on the written work will not be required to take that part of the examination. Candidates who have failed the language examination, but have otherwise satisfied the Examiners, will be required to re-sit the language examination only.

Music

1. Each candidate will be required:

(*a*) to follow for at least three terms a course of study in music;

(*b*) to specialise in musicology, performance or composition;

(*c*) to take a three-part examination (Part 1a, Part 1b and Part 2).

2. The elements of the examination will be determined by the candidates chosen specialism.

3. Candidates specialising in musicology will be required to submit:

Part 1a: an essay or exercise on issues and methods in musicology of between 5,000 and 6,250 words (or equivalent in notation, visual documentation, or analytical diagrams), two copies of which must be submitted, not later than noon on Monday of the tenth week of Michaelmas Term, to the Chair of Examiners for the M.St. in Music, c/o Examination Schools, High Street, Oxford.

Part 1b: three essays in musicology (broadly conceived), none of which shall be less than 5,000 words, and which taken together shall be not more than 18,750 words; two copies must be submitted, not later than noon on Friday of the seventh week of Trinity Term, to the Chair of Examiners for the M.St. in Music, c/o Examination Schools, High Street, Oxford. A portfolio of appropriately assessed language work that is directly relevant to the candidates intended field of research may substitute for one such essay or exercise with the approval of the Director of Graduate Studies by noon on Friday of the third week of Hilary Term.

Part 2: a dissertation of not more than 13,000 words (this word limit including footnotes but excluding bibliography and appendices) in musicology or ethnomusicology, or an editorial exercise (edition), with prefatory matter, of comparable length. The topic for the dissertation or edition must be submitted for approval to the Director of Graduate Studies, Faculty of Music, by noon on Friday of the third week of Hilary Term. Two typewritten copies of the dissertation or edition must be submitted, not later than noon on the first Monday in July, to the Chair of Examiners for the M.St. in Music, c/o Examination Schools, High Street, Oxford.

4. Candidates specialising in performance will be required to submit:

Part 1a: a performance of not more than ten minutes duration, to be given by the candidate in an examination in noughth week of Hilary Term;

Part 1b: three essays in musicology (broadly conceived), none of which shall be less than 5,000 words, and which taken together shall be not more than 8,750 words; two copies must be submitted, not later than noon on Friday of the seventh week of Trinity Term, to the Chair of Examiners for the M.St. in Music, c/o Examination Schools, High Street, Oxford.

Part 2: a recital of not more than thirty minutes duration, vocal or instrumental, of at least two contrasted pieces, to be performed not later than the tenth week of Trinity Term. Two possible programmes must be submitted for approval to the Director of Graduate Studies, Faculty of Music, by noon on Friday of third week of Hilary Term. Candidates will be informed of the examiners choice of programme by Friday of eighth week in the same term.

5. Candidates specialising in composition will be required to submit:

Part 1a: a musical composition produced in response to techniques presented in composition seminars, two copies of which must be submitted, not later than noon on Monday of the tenth week of Michaelmas Term, to the Chair of Examiners for the M.St. in Music, c/o Examination Schools, High Street, Oxford.

Part 1b: two essays in musicology (broadly conceived), none of which shall be less than 5,000 words, and which taken together shall be not more than 12,500 words, and one musical composition produced in response to techniques presented in composition seminars; two copies must be submitted, not later than noon on Friday of the seventh week of Trinity Term, to the Chair of Examiners for the M.St. in Music, c/o Examination Schools, High Street, Oxford.

Part 2: a musical composition or portfolio of compositions, of not more than fifteen minutes duration in total, two copies of which must be submitted, not later than noon on the first Monday in July, to the Chair of Examiners for the M.St. in Music, c/o Examination Schools, High Street, Oxford.

6. The examiners may award a distinction for excellence in the whole examination. In this case the work will normally display an excellent command of the subject studied, evidence of critical understanding, and some demonstration of an original conceptual approach.

7. A candidate who fails the examination will be permitted to retake it on one further occasion only, not later than one year after the initial attempt. Such a candidate whose work has been of satisfactory standard in one or more elements examined will be required to resubmit for examination the element(s) which fell below the passmark when originally examined.

Oriental Studies

1. Before admission to the course, candidates must satisfy the Board of the Faculty of Oriental Studies that they possess the necessary qualifications to profit by the course. The Board will not permit students to be admitted to the course if an M.St. in a particular subject under the aegis of the Board is considered more appropriate.

2. Candidates shall be required to attend for at least three terms such lecture courses and participate in such seminars as their supervisor shall specify.

3. *Syllabus*

There will be four Units:

Unit (i) Candidates shall submit either (A) two typed copies each of two essays of between 5,000 and 7,000 words in length, or (B) two typed copies of a dissertation (excluding bibliography).

Option (A) may be any two of the following:

a. what might become part of a thesis for the M.Litt or D.Phil;

b. an essay on the theoretical issues raised by the subject which the candidate is proposing for the thesis;

c. an essay on a topic relevant to the subject of the thesis;

d. a discussion of the historical and literary background or of the source material which is relevant to the proposed subject.

Option (B) should be equivalent to a substantial draft chapter or chapters of a proposed thesis for the M.Litt or the D.Phil.

The essays or dissertation must be submitted to the Chair of Examiners, M.St in Oriental Studies, Examination Schools, High Street, Oxford, not later than 12 noon on Friday of fourth week of Trinity Term.

Units (ii) and (iii) Two three-hour examination papers, which may be any combination of language or non-language papers. When the elective papers are shared with another degree, the regulations for the paper follow that of the home degree.

Unit (iv) A prescribed essay, prepared in proper scholarly form, on research methods and materials relating to the area of study chosen under (i) above, of between 5,000 and 7,000 words. The topic of the essay will be set at the conclusion of the two examination papers Units (i) and (ii).The essay must be submitted to the Chair of Examiners, M.St in Oriental Studies, Examination Schools not later than seven days from the date on which the topic was set.

4. Candidates must submit titles for their written work (Unit (i) of the examination, above) and subjects for the two examinations (Units (ii) and (iii) of the examination, above) to the Faculty office by Friday of seventh week of Michaelmas Term. These will be reported to the Faculty Board's second meeting of Michaelmas Term.

5. Candidates must submit titles for their written work (Unit (i) of the examination, above) and subjects for the two examinations (Units (ii) and (iii) of the examination, above) to the Faculty office by Friday of seventh week of Michaelmas Term. These will be reported to the Faculty Board's second meeting of Michaelmas Term.

6. Lists of set texts must be submitted to the Faculty office by Friday of seventh week of Michaelmas term and will be reported to the Faculty Board's second meeting of Michaelmas Term.

7. All work submitted to the Chair of Examiners must be in typewritten form. Two copies must be submitted, securely sealed and addressed. The work must bear the candidates examination number (but not the candidates name, which must be concealed). Candidates must include a signed declaration sealed in an envelope addressed to the Chair of Examiners that the work is the candidates own.

8. Every candidate will be examined by oral examination unless he or she shall have been individually excused by the examiners.

Philosophical Theology

Candidates shall be required:

(*a*) to present themselves for a written examination in two of the papers prescribed below, the selection to depend on their previous qualifications;

(*b*) to present an essay of not more than 15,000 words on a topic in philosophical theology to be approved by the faculty board;

(*c*) to present themselves for a viva voce examination unless individually dispensed by the examiners (no candidate will be failed without a viva).

Candidates must make a written application for approval of the essay topic, to reach the Theology and Religion Graduate Studies Committee not later than Monday of noughth week in Hilary Term. In cases where there is some uncertainty about the acceptability of the proposal, candidates are advised to submit their applications earlier if possible. All applications should be accompanied by a recommendation from the candidates supervisor. Two copies of the dissertation must be sent to the Chair of Examiners for the M.St in Philosophical Theology, c/o the Examination Schools, High Street, Oxford by the Friday of eighth week in Trinity Term of the year in which the examinations are taken. The dissertation must be accompanied by a signed statement by the candidate that the essay is the candidates own work, except where otherwise indicated. The candidates name should not appear on the dissertation itself.

Written examinations will be set in the tenth or eleventh week of Trinity Term.

The examiners may award a distinction to candidates who have performed with special merit in the whole examination.

1. *Philosophy of Religion*

As specified for Part B of the B.Phil. in Philosophy. See also regulations for Paper 1 of the M.Phil in Philosophical Theology in the 'Course Regulations for the M.Phil in Philosophical Theology' section of the course handbook.

2. *History of Philosophical Theology*

The paper will contain questions on philosophical influences on theology during the patristic period, the early medieval period, and the period 1760-1860. Candidates are required to show knowledge of two of the three periods and, within each of those two periods, of some of the principal relevant writings, viz. for the patristic period of works of Origen and Augustine, for the early medieval period of works of Anselm and Aquinas, and for the period 1760-1860 of works of Kant, Kierkegaard, and Schleiermacher. Study of texts in the original languages will not be required. Lectures, tutorials etc.: as for Paper 3 of the M. Phil. in Philosophical Theology.

3. Either *The Development of Christian Doctrine to AD 451*

or *Theology in Western Europe from Gabriel Biel to Jacob Arminus*

See regulations for Paper 1 of Section A and Paper 1 of Section C of the Christian Doctrine option of the M. Phil. in Theology in the 'Course Regulations for the M.Phil in Theology' section of the course handbook.

Philosophy

1. Every candidate must follow for at least three terms a course of instruction in Philosophy. Candidates will, when they enter for the examination, be required to produce from their society a certificate that they are following such a course.

2. Candidates will be required to attend the B.Phil. Pro-seminar in Michaelmas and Hilary terms. In addition, candidates will be required to attend two graduate classes in each of the three terms of their studies.

3. Candidates will be examined by submitting five essays of no more than 5,000 words each, in conformity with the following distribution requirement. Each essay will be assigned to a subject, with no more than two essays assigned to any one subject. One essay must be on a subject from Group 1 (Theoretical Philosophy), one on a subject from Group 2 (Practical Philosophy) and one on a subject from Group 3 (History of Philosophy). The remaining two essays may be assigned to subjects in any of the three Groups. The list of approved subjects in each Group will be the same as the list published in the Course Handbook for the B.Phil. in Philosophy.

4. Topics for the essays will be chosen by the candidates. Candidates may offer up to two essays on at most one subject not included in the list of approved subjects in the Handbook. Candidates wishing to offer an essay or essays on a subject not on the prescribed list must seek approval for the proposed subject from the Graduate Studies Committee in Philosophy *as soon as they decide they would like to offer it*, and in any case no later than the Friday of the fifth week of Trinity Full Term. Any such application must be supported by the relevant Course Coordinator. Where a subject is approved by the Graduate Studies Committee in Philosophy, the Committee will assign it to one of Groups 1–3.

5. Two printed copies of each essay must be delivered to the Examination Schools, High Street, Oxford OX1 4BG, by 10 a.m. on the Wednesdays of the following weeks: one essay is due in noughth week of Hilary Term and two essays are due in noughth week of Trinity Term. The final two essays must be submitted in noughth week of the Michaelmas Term following the year in which candidates are first entered on the Register of M.St. students. Candidates must give notice of the subject of each essay and the Group to which it will be assigned in accordance with the procedures and deadlines specified in the Course Handbook.

6. The examiners may award a distinction for excellence in the whole examination.

7. Candidates who fail up to two essays will be permitted to resubmit those essays; a resubmitted essay may be on a new topic, and may be on a new subject, provided that the distribution requirement is met. Candidates who choose to resubmit one or two failed essays must do so by 10 a.m. on Wednesday of noughth week of the following Michaelmas Term where the failed essay or essays had been submitted during the first year of the degree, or by Wednesday of noughth week of the following Hilary Term where the essay or essays had been submitted in noughth week of Michaelmas Term. Candidates who fail three or more essays will be permitted to resubmit work for the failed elements of the examination during the following academic year. Candidates need only resubmit work for those elements of the examination that they failed. No resubmitted essay can receive a mark of more than 60. Candidates who fail to satisfy the examiners a second time in any part of the examination may not re-submit work for any part of the examination on any subsequent occasion.

Philosophy of Physics

1. Every candidate must follow for at least three terms a course of instruction in Philosophy of Physics. Candidates will, when they enter for the examination, be required to produce from their society a certificate that they are following such a course.

2. Every candidate shall be required to offer the following subjects:

(i) *Philosophy of Physics.*

(ii) *Philosophy of Science.*

(iii) One further subject chosen from the following list: Metaphysics and the Theory of Knowledge; Philosophy of Mind and Action; Philosophical Logic and the Philosophy of Language; Philosophy of Mathematics.

3. The choice of subjects must be notified on the entry form for the examination, to be submitted to the Examination Schools, High Street, Oxford by Friday of seventh week of Hilary Term.

4. Candidates will be examined by submitting:

(i) Two essays of no more than 5,000 words each on topics within the philosophy of physics. At most one essay may fall under each of the following subjects: (a) the philosophy of quantum theory; (b) the philosophy of space, time and symmetry; (c) the philosophy of statistical mechanics and thermodynamics; (d) other topics in the philosophy of physics.

(ii) One essay of no more than 5,000 words on a topic in the philosophy of science (to be understood as excluding topics specifically in the philosophy of physics as specified under 4. (i) above).

(iii) One essay of no more than 5,000 words, falling under one of the following subjects: (a) Metaphysics and the Theory of Knowledge; (b) Philosophy of Mind and Action; (c) Philosophical Logic and the Philosophy of Language; (d) Philosophy of Mathematics.

5. Topics for all essays will be chosen by the candidates.

6. Two printed copies of each of the essays in Philosophy of Physics must be delivered to the Examinations Schools, High Street, Oxford OX1 4BC, by 10am on Wednesday of Week 0 of Trinity Term in the year that the examination is to be taken. Two printed copies of each of the other two essays must be delivered to the same address by 10am on Friday of Week 9 of Trinity Term in the year that the examination is to be taken. Essays must be typed or printed.

7. Candidates who have not delivered essays as prescribed by the due dates above shall, unless they show exceptional cause to the examiners, be deemed to have withdrawn from the examination.

8. The examiners may award a distinction for excellence in the whole examination.

9. A candidate will be deemed to have passed the examination if they obtain a passing mark on all four essays. In addition, a mark for the Philosophy of Science or elective paper (but not both) judged to be narrowly below passing quality may be compensated for by strong performance on the Philosophy of Physics papers, provided that the candidate's average performance remains above the level judged sufficient for a pass by the Examiners.

10. A candidate who fails one element of the examination (i.e. one of the four essays), which has not been compensated in line with the provisions made under paragraph 9., may apply to retake that element in the September immediately following the examination. A candidate who fails two or more elements may retake the examination in the year immediately following the failed examination. It is necessary for a candidate to retake only the failed elements of the examination.

11. In the case of candidates whose formal application to transfer to the second year of the BPhil in Philosophy has been conditionally approved by the Graduate Studies Committee of the Faculty, the Board of Examiners for the MSt in Philosophy of Physics shall assess whether the candidate's overall performance meets the level of performance specified in the Student Handbook as a condition for entrance to the BPhil in Philosophy. If so, the candidate shall be deemed to have withdrawn from the examination for the MSt in Philosophy of Physics, and their MSt essays shall be deemed to have been submitted for the BPhil in Philosophy.

Psychodynamic Practice

1. Candidates will be expected to have satisfactorily completed the Postgraduate Diploma in Psychodynamic Practice.

2. *Course*

The course will consist of Day Workshops, research methodology and application   5
seminars, clinical seminars, individual clinical and research tutorials, and continuing personal therapy and supervised practice. The course will be taken on a part-time basis for a period of one year's duration.

3. Every candidate will be required to satisfy the examiners in the following:

(*a*) attendance at Day Workshops, research methodology and application semi-   10
nars, clinical seminars, individual clinical and research tutorials, and personal therapy and clinical placement sessions;

(*b*) submission of a dissertation of no more than 15,000 words on a topic selected by the student in consultation with the research tutor and course director and agreed by the external examiner. The dissertation must be forwarded to the   15
examiners c/o Registry, Department for Continuing Education, Wellington Square, Oxford, OX1 2JA, for receipt not later than noon on the last Friday of September in the year in which the course is studied. Material already submitted for the Postgraduate Diploma in Psychodynamic Practice may not be included;   20

(*c*) participation in a minimum of 17 placement supervisions and at least 100 hours of client/patient contact, and submission of an end-of-year report by a candidate's placement supervisor;

(*d*) participation in a minimum of 40 hours of personal therapy exceptions may be made for candidates who have had extensive personal therapy previously;   25

(*e*) submission of annual reports from both research and clinical tutors;

(*f*) a viva voce examination at the end of the course of study.

4. The examiners may award a distinction for excellence in the whole examination.

5. A candidate whose dissertation fails to satisfy the examiner may be permitted to resubmit on one further occasion only not later than one year after the initial failure.   30
Approval for deferral must be obtained from the relevant board of studies.

6. If any candidate who is successful in the examination for the Degree of Master of Studies in Psychodynamic Practice has previously successfully completed the Postgraduate Diploma in Psychodynamic Practice, the Master of Studies will subsume his or her diploma.   35

Slavonic Studies

1. Candidates must have taken *either* Russian (as sole language *or* as one of two languages) *or* Czech (with Slovak) in the Oxford Honour School of Modern Languages, *or* have taken a comparable degree in a Slavonic language from another university, *or* must satisfy the committee that they possess the necessary qualifica-   40
tions in a Slavonic language to profit by the course.

2. Candidates must follow for at least three terms a course of instruction in Slavonic Studies.

3. Each candidate will be required to take one language from Schedule 1 and three subjects from Schedules 2-10. Candidates may take no more than two subjects from   45
any one Schedule. Candidates may not take subjects which they have already studied in a first degree course.

4. Candidates will be examined by written examination, except:

  (i) for Schedule 2.iv (Methods of Criticism and the Theory of Literature) which will be examined under the regulations for the M.St./M.Phil. in Modern Languages;

  (ii) for Schedule 6.i-ix which will be examined under the regulations for the M.St./M.Phil. in Modern Languages;

  (iii) that in lieu of written examination in one subject a candidate may elect under Schedule 2.v to submit an essay of 5,000 to 7,000 words on a subject of the candidates choice.

The subject of the essay should fall within the areas of Slavonic languages and literatures. Candidates are required to register the subject area or title of their essay with the Modern Languages Graduate Office by the end of the fourth week of Hilary Term. Three typed copies of the essay must be delivered to the Examination Schools, High Street, Oxford by noon on Thursday of sixth week of Trinity Term. Work submitted in the form of an essay for the Degree of M.St. may subsequently be incorporated in a thesis submitted for the Degree of M.Phil., or may be used as the basis for the piece of written work required for admission to the status of student for the Degrees of M.Litt. or D.Phil.

5. Candidates must present themselves for oral examination unless dispensed by the examiners.

6. The examiners may award a distinction for excellence in the whole examination.

Schedule 1

Unseen translation from any one of the following languages (this must not be a language previously studied by the candidate to degree standard):

    i. Bulgarian

   ii. Croatian

  iii. Czech

   iv. Polish

    v. Russian

   vi. Serbian

  vii. Slovak

 viii. Slovene

   ix. Sorbian

    x. Ukrainian

Schedule 2

    i. Cyrillic Palaeography

   ii. Textual Criticism

  iii. Prague School of Linguistics

   iv. Methods of Criticism and the Theory of Literature (from the M.St. course in Modern Languages)

    v. A subject of the candidate's choice, approved by the committee.

Schedule 3

    i. Comparative Slavonic Philology

   ii. Old Church Slavonic

  iii. History of Church Slavonic

Schedule 4

The History of:
    i. Ukrainian
    ii. Bulgarian *and* Macedonian
    iii. Croatian   5
    iv. Czech *and* Slovak
    v. Polish
    vi. Russian
    vii. Serbian
    viii. Slovene   1(
    ix. Sorbian

Schedule 5

The Structure and Present State of:
    i. Bulgarian
    ii. Croatian   1‹
    iii. Czech
    iv. Polish
    v. Russian
    vi. Serbian
    vii. Slovak   2(
    viii. Slovene
    ix. Sorbian
    x. Ukrainian

Schedule 6

    i. Literature and Culture of the Russian Enlightenment (from the M.St. course   2‹
    in Modern Languages).
    ii. Pushkin and Romanticism (from the M.St. course in Modern Languages).
    iii. Gender and Representation in Russian Culture from 1800 (from the M.St.
    course in Modern Languages).
    iv. Russian Modes of Lyric (1820–1940).   3(
    v. The Rise of the Russian Novel (from the M.St. course in Modern Languages).
    vi. Russian Drama in the 19th and 20th Centuries (from the M.St. course in
    Modern Languages).
    vii. The Russian Experience of Modernity, 1905–1945 (from the M.St. course in
    Modern Languages).   3‹
    viii. The GULag and the Russian Literary Process (from the M.St. course in
    Modern Languages).
    ix. Post-Soviet Russian Literature (from the M.St. course in Modern Languages).

Schedule 7

    i. Czech Poetry since 1774.   4(
    ii. Czech Prose Fiction and Drama since 1774.
    iii. Polish Literature since 1798.
    iv. Slovak Literature since 1783.

Schedule 8

  i. Byzantine Civilization and its Expansion, 913–1204.

  ii. Bohemia from the Hussite Wars to the Battle of the White Mountain (1415–1620).

  iii. The History of Poland and Hungary, 1506 to 1795.

  iv. The Habsburg Monarchy, 1790–1918.

  v. The History of the Balkans, 1774–1918.

Schedule 9

  i. Russian Social and Political Thought, 1825–1917 (M.Phil. in Russian and East European Studies B.1).

  ii. The History of Russia, 1861–1917 (M.Phil. in Russian and East European Studies B.2).

  iii. The History since 1918 of either Poland or Czechoslovakia and its successor states or Yugoslavia and its successor states.

Teaching for some options may not be available in every year. Applicants for admission will be advised whether teaching will be available in the options of their choice.

Social Anthropology

1. The Social Sciences Divisional Board shall elect for the supervision of the course a Standing Committee, namely the Teaching Committee of the School of Anthropology, which shall have power to arrange lectures and other instruction. The course director shall be responsible to that committee.

2. Candidates must follow a course of instruction in Social and Cultural Anthropology for at least three terms, and will, when entering for the examinations, be required to produce a certificate from their supervisors to this effect.

3. Candidates will be required to present themselves for written and (if requested) oral examinations and to submit three copies of a long essay in prescribed form on an approved topic as defined below.

4. The written examination will consist of four papers on the syllabus described in the schedule.

5. Each candidate will be required to submit a long essay of approximately 5,000 words on a topic selected from a list issued by the Chair of Examiners on Monday of the eighth week of Hilary Term.

6. Three typewritten copies of the long essay must be delivered not later than noon on Tuesday of the first week of Trinity Term, to the Chair of Examiners, M.St. in Social Anthropology, c/o Examination Schools, High Street, Oxford.

7. The oral examination (if requested) may be on the candidate's written papers, or long essay, or both.

8. The examiners may award a distinction for excellence in the whole examination.

9. In order to pass the degree, a student must pass all its assessed components. Where one or more components are failed, the student will be given the opportunity to re-sit or re-submit them once, as the case may be. Any subsequent award of the degree on successful completion of all the assessed components may be delayed by up to three terms, i.e. until the Examination Board next meets.

Schedule

Each candidate will also be required to satisfy the examiners in papers I–IV in the syllabus described in the Schedule for the M.Sc. in Social Anthropology, and governed by regulation 4 for that degree.

Study of Religions

1. Each candidate will be required to follow a course of instruction for three terms and present himself or herself for examination in three subjects as set out in the syllabus.

2. A 10,000–15,000 word dissertation must be offered. All candidates must normally make a written application for approval of the topic no later than Monday of noughth week of Hilary Term. The application should be submitted to the Faculty of Theology and Religion for consideration by the Theology and Religion Graduate Studies Committee. In cases where there is some uncertainty about the acceptability of the proposal, candidates are asked to submit their applications earlier if possible. All applications should be accompanied by a recommendation from the candidates supervisor. Two copies of the dissertation must be sent to the Chair of Examiners for the Degree of M.St in the Study of Religion, c/o the Examination Schools, High Street, Oxford before the end of eighth week of Trinity Term in the year of examination.

Titles for the two shorter essays must normally be submitted to the Faculty of Theology and Religion no later than Monday of noughth week of Hilary Term for consideration by the Graduate Studies Committee. Two copies of the essays must be submitted to the Examination Schools by the Friday before the beginning of Trinity Term in the year in which the examination is taken. Decisions on the suitability of titles for both dissertation and essays will be taken in consultation with the Chair of Examiners for that year.

The three-hour examination will be held in tenth or eleventh week of Trinity Term.

3. Each candidate will be required to present himself or herself for an oral (viva voce) examination unless individually dispensed by the examiners. This will take place within a few days of the written examination, and may include discussion of both the examination paper and any pre-submitted work.

4. The examiners may award a distinction to candidates who have performed with special merit in the whole examination.

5. A candidate who fails the examination will be permitted to retake it on one further occasion only, not later than one year after the initial attempt. Such a candidate whose 10,000-15,000 word essay has been of satisfactory standard may resubmit the same piece of work, while a candidate who had reached a satisfactory standard on the written papers will not be required to retake that part of the examination.

Syllabus

Candidates must offer the paper on the Nature of Religion and two papers selected from papers on the major texts and doctrines of (*a*) Buddhism, (*b*) Christianity, (*c*) Islam, (*d*) Judaism, or (*e*) Hinduism, or (*f*) any other paper that may from time to time be approved by the Board of the Faculty of Theology and Religion.

The paper on one of the candidates two chosen religions will consist of a dissertation of 10,000–15,000 words.

The paper on the other religion will consist of two essays of up to 5000 words.

Candidates will not normally be allowed to substitute a long essay or two short essays for the paper on The Nature of Religion. Any candidate who believes that he or she has special grounds for seeking a dispensation must present a case to the Graduate Studies Committee, with the supervisor's approval, before the fifth week of Hilary Term.

The Nature of Religion

The aim of this paper is to examine the main classical and contemporary approaches to the study of religions, the problems involved in comparative study of religions, and the relation between religious belief, theology and the study of religions.

1. Students should know the work of key figures in the study of religions, the main   5
attempts to define religion and the problems of defining religion. The works of J. G. Frazer ('The Golden Bough'), Edward Tylor, Rudolf Otto, Evans-Pritchard, and Cantwell Smith are important in this respect.

2. They should be aware of the differing approaches to the study of religion in phenomenology, anthropology, sociology, psychology, philosophy, and theology. By   10
the use of examples, the strengths and limits of each approach should be investigated.

3. They should be aware of the major explanations that have been offered of religious belief, particularly by Durkheim, Freud, Feuerbach, and Jung, and of the problems in giving such general explanations.

4. They should be aware of some major authors who have attempted comparative   15
studies in religion, and the problems of such comparative studies. They should be aware of some of the issues involved in claims for religious truth and rationality, and attitudes to religious conflict and diversity. Relevant authors for study would be John Bowker, Ninian Smart, John Hick, Paul Knitter, and Max Müller.

They should have sufficient data to take an informed view of the place of religion in   20
the modern world.

Students should refer to the student handbook for a list of the texts to be used in studying the subject.

(*a*) *Buddhism*

The earliest Buddhist doctrine and practice will be studied against the background   25
of the early Upanishads and other religious movements in north-east India round the 5th century BCE. Practice includes both meditation and monastic life. The primary source is the Pali Canon supplemented by the commentarial literature of the Theravadin tradition.

(*b*) *Christianity*   30

This paper will deal with Christian theology and Christian practices, which will be studied in their historical and local contexts. Students will study the Gospels, the figure of Jesus; and they will consider various examples of Christian literature, history and institutions.

(*c*) *Islam*   35

The paper will consist of a broad introduction to Islamic history and religion from the Prophet Muhammad to the modern period, with particular emphasis on the formative period (7th to the 11th century, CE).

Candidates will cover the following topics in lectures and tutorials:

1. Muhammad and the Arabian milieu   40
2. Qur'an
3. Hadith
4. Law
5. Theology
6. Sects   45
7. Sufism
8. Islam and other monotheisms
9. Modern Islam

(*d*) *Judaism*

Jewish religion and thought since 70 CE with reference both to its historical development and to Judaism in the modern world.

Selections from the texts listed in the student handbook will be assigned by the course
tutor by the beginning of Michaelmas Term.

(*e*) *Hinduism*

This paper, for which the source material lies in Sanskrit texts read in English
translation and in the context of reliable secondary sources, will be concerned with
the main components of the brahminical tradition which, though of ancient origin,
are still relevant today. Key areas include Vedic religion, nondualism, and traditional
(smarta) ritual practice. Particular attention will be paid to leading ideas developed in
the listed primary texts read in translation, though the secondary sources provide
necessary context. No attempt will be made to cover later theism or Hindu sects.

Lectures will focus on key primary texts, in translation, and generalize from them
to basic features of brahmanical Hinduism. The paper will also be supported by
tutorials. A thorough reading of the primary texts will give students a good sense of
the tradition in its main lines and its complexity, but what is to be learned may also be
encapsulated with reference to the following concepts: ultimate reality (brahman),
action (karman), liberation (moksa), rites of passage (samskara), renunciation (sam-
nyasa), sacrifice (yajna), primary revelation (sruti), tradition (oral, written) (smrti),
righteousness, right order (dharma), religious class (varna), stages of life (asrama),
impurity (asauca), gift (dana), austerity (tapas), (goddess) power (sakti), yoga, verses
for recitation (mantra), religious competence (adhikara), initiation (diksa).

Syriac Studies

1. Candidates must satisfy the Board of the Faculty of Oriental Studies before
admission to the course that they possess the necessary qualification in the Syriac
language to profit by the course.

2. Every candidate must follow for at least three terms a course of study in Syriac
Studies.

3. *Syllabus*

There will be four Units:

Unit (i) Essay questions on the history, literature, and culture of the Syriac
Churches.

Units (ii), (iii) and (iv) Passages for translation and comment, and essay questions
on prescribed texts in Syriac, with special reference to *three* of the following subjects
(a passage, or passages, for unprepared translation may also be set):

(1) Biblical versions;

(2) Exegetical literature;

(3) Early poetry;

(4) Liturgy;

(5) Historical literature;

(6) Secular literature;

(7) Monastic literature;

(8) Hagiography;

(9) Translations of Greek patristic texts;

(10) Theological texts;

(11) Any other subject approved by the Board.

4. Lists of set texts must be submitted to the Faculty office by Friday of seventh week of Michaelmas Term and will be reported to the Faculty Board's second meeting of Michaelmas Term.

5. Every candidate will be examined by oral examination unless he or she shall have been individually excused by the examiners.

The examiners may award a distinction for excellence in the whole examination.

Teaching for the course may not be available in every year. Applicants for admission will be advised of this.

Theology

1. All candidates will be required to follow a course of instruction and directed research for three terms and present themselves for examination in one of the following subjects: Old Testament; New Testament; Ecclesiastical History (split into 6 subsections, see below); Christian Doctrine (split into 4 subsections, see below); Christian Ethics; Science and Religion; Biblical Interpretation.

2. Candidates will be expected to attend such lectures and seminars as their supervisor shall recommend.

3. The examination shall consist of:

(i) a three-hour examination as prescribed in the regulations for each course;

(ii) two essays of not more than 5,000 words on topics proposed by the candidate and accepted by the Theology and Religion Faculty Board (candidates should be very aware of this word limit when proposing their titles; the most significant cause of rejected essay titles is insufficient focus);

(iii) a dissertation of not more than 15,000 words on a topic proposed by the candidate and accepted by the Theology and Religion Graduate Studies Committee. For candidates intending to proceed to doctoral study, the topic of the thesis should be such as to provide a foundation for future research.

The examiners may award a distinction for excellence in the whole examination.

4. Proposals for titles of essays and dissertations must be submitted to the Theology and Religion Faculty by Monday of Week Nought of Hilary Term for consideration by the Theology and Religion Graduate Studies Committee. These will be considered by the committee in consultation with the examiners. Candidates are advised that some time may be required for communication with the Examiners to take place before permission is granted; permission will normally be granted by Monday of Week 8 of Hilary Term. All proposals should be accompanied by a brief indication of how the subject will be treated and a brief account of the primary and secondary sources used. The titles and contents of essays and the dissertation should not substantially overlap with each other, though they may cover ground included in the scope of examinations as detailed below, and, in the case of Christian Doctrine and Ecclesiastical History, they may fall within the same section.

5. Two copies of essays must be submitted not later than the Friday before the beginning of Trinity Term. Two copies of the dissertation must be submitted at the end of eighth week of Trinity Term. All submitted work must be printed and sent in a parcel bearing the words M.St in Theology to The Chair of Examiners, c/o the Examination Schools, High Street, Oxford. The 3-hour examination will take place in the tenth or eleventh week of Trinity Term. Each candidate will be required to present himself or herself for an oral (viva voce), which will take place within a few days of the written examination, and may include discussion of both the examination paper and any pre-submitted work. Candidates must not put their names on the examination paper or on any pre-submitted work. The dissertation must be accom-

panied by the candidates signed statement that it is entirely his or her own work except where otherwise indicated.

I. *Old Testament*

The examination shall consist of:

(i) A three-hour paper on prescribed Old Testament Texts in Hebrew. The pre-   5
scribed texts for the examination will be published in the *Gazette*by the Board of the Faculty of Theology and Religion before the end of Michaelmas Term.

(ii) Two essays of not more than 5,000 words on topics approved by the Theology and Religion Graduate Studies Committee (see 4 above).

(iii) A dissertation of not more than 15,000 words on a topic approved by the   10
Theology and Religion Graduate Studies Committee (see 4 above).

II. *New Testament*

The examination shall consist of:

(i) a three-hour paper on prescribed texts in Greek, which will be published in the
Gazette by the Board of the Faculty of Theology and Religion before the end   15
of Michaelmas Term.

(ii) Two essays of not more than 5,000 words on topics approved by the Theology and Religion Graduate Studies Committee (see 4 above).

(iii) A dissertation of not more than 15,000 words on a topic approved by the
Theology and Religion Graduate Studies Committee (see 4 above).   20

III. *Ecclesiastical History*

The examination shall consist of:

(i) a three-hour general paper on the nature and practice of ecclesiastical history.
Candidates will be expected to show knowledge of a range of historiographical approaches to key questions in ecclesiastical history and of the variety of   25
approaches to historical method which have emerged as a result of the professionalisation of teaching and research in history and of the introduction of new methods into the writing of history.

(ii) Two essays of not more than 5,000 words on topics approved by the Theology and Religion Graduate Studies Committee (see 4 above).   30

(iii) A dissertation of not more than 15,000 words on a topic approved by the
Theology and Religion Graduate Studies Committee (see 4 above). All work submitted by a candidate under (ii) and (iii) shall lie within one (and only one) of the following sections:

(*a*) The Early Church AD 200–476   35

(*b*) The Western Church AD 476–1050

(*c*) The Western Church AD 1050–1400

(*d*) English Church History AD 1066–1272

(*e*) European Christianity AD 1400–1800

(*f*) European Christianity AD 1800–2000   40

IV. *Christian Doctrine*

Work submitted on Christian doctrine shall lie within one of the following sections:

(*a*) History of Doctrine: Patristic Theology (c.100–787 AD)

(*b*) History of Doctrine: Scholastic Theology (c. 1050–1350 AD)

(*c*) History of Doctrine: Theology of the Reformation period (c. 1500–1650 AD)   45

(*d*) Modern Theology (1780– the present)

The examination shall consist of:

  (i) a three-hour paper. For section (*a*), this will include passages for translation and comment from one or more prescribed texts in Greek or Latin. For section (*b*) it will include passages for translation and comment from prescribed texts in Latin. Prescribed texts will be published in course handbooks.   5

    For section (*c*) it will consist of passages for translation and comment from prescribed texts in Latin, German or French of the Reformation period. The prescribed texts will be approved by the Graduate Studies Committee on the advice of course leaders and ratified by the Faculty Board before the end of Michaelmas Term in the year when the course commences, and will be   10 published in the *Gazette*. Essays will also be set, both on the prescribed texts and on general topics within the stated period. For section (*d*), the examination will be on methods and styles in theology.

  (ii) Two essays of not more than 5,000 words on topics approved by the Theology and Religion Graduate Studies Committee (see 4 above).   15

  (iii) A dissertation of not more than 15,000 words on a topic approved by the Theology and Religion Graduate Studies Committee (see 4 above).

All work submitted by a candidate shall fall within the same section. In proposing titles for essays and the dissertation, candidates in section (*d*) should explain in which pieces of work they will demonstrate competence in (a) exploring the encounter   20 between theology and some non-theological discipline; (b) exploring a modern theological response to some theological reflection of the past.

V. *Christian Ethics*

The examination shall consist of:

  (i) a three-hour paper on Christian Moral Concepts and Methodology: 25 Contemporary and Historical Discussions.

  (ii) Two essays of not more than 5,000 words on topics approved by the Theology and Religion Graduate Studies Committee (see 4 above).

  (iii) A dissertation of not more than 15,000 words on a topic approved by the Theology and Religion Graduate Studies Committee (see 4 above).   30

In proposing titles for essays and the dissertation, candidates should explain in which pieces of work they will demonstrate competence in (a) exploring an ethical question, substantive or conceptual, in relation to contemporary discussion; (b) the interpretation of a Biblical text of moral significance; (c) the discussion of a non-Biblical text of moral significance from some period of history prior to 1900.   35

VI. *Science and Religion*

The examination shall consist of:

  (i) a three-hour paper on topics in Science and Religion.

  (ii) Two essays of not more than 5,000 words on topics approved by the Theology and Religion Graduate Studies Committee (see 4 above).   40

  (iii) A dissertation of not more than 15,000 words on a topic approved by the Theology and Religion Graduate Studies Committee (see 4 above).

In proposing titles for essays and the dissertation, candidates should explain in which pieces of work they will demonstrate competence in (a) exploring a historical debate in which scientific and religious issues are involved; (b) exploring a philoso-   45 phical debate with a bearing on the discussion of science and religion; (c) analysing a contemporary issue on the interface between science and religion.

VII. *Biblical Interpretation*

The examination shall consist of:

  (i) a three-hour paper on the History and Principles of Biblical Study with special   50 reference to a selected period. The period will be selected by the student in consultation with his or her supervisor. Where there is more than one student, each will be able to answer on the period that he or she has selected.

(ii) Two essays of not more than 5,000 words on topics approved by the Theology and Religion Graduate Studies Committee (see 4 above).

(iii) A dissertation of not more than 15,000 words on a topic approved by the Theology and Religion Graduate Studies Committee (see 4 above). Pre-submitted work under (ii) and (iii) shall fall within the period covered by the examined paper (i).

US History

The regulations of the Board of the Faculty of History are as follows:

1. Candidates for this degree must follow for at least three terms a course of instruction and directed research and must, upon entering the examination, produce from their society a certificate to that effect.

2. Candidates must attend such lectures, seminars and classes as their supervisor shall determine. In addition to the formally examined programme elements described below, each candidate will be expected to attend and complete in-course requirements for a series of skills and specialist options based on a schedule to be published from year to year by the Faculty's Graduate Studies Committee.

3. The final examination shall comprise (i) two extended essays of between 4,000 and 5,000 words based on the Advanced Option, (ii) one examination paper based on the programme's conceptual and methodological component, and (iii) a dissertation of not more than 15,000 words.

I. There is currently only one Advanced Option in the 'History of the United States, and the colonies that preceded it, since 1600', which is supplemented by tutorial sessions which enable candidates and supervisors to tailor their studies to individual training needs.

Two copies of the two essays, addressed to the Chair of Examiners for the Master of Studies in US History, must be submitted to the Examination Schools, High Street, Oxford by 12 noon on Monday of Week Nine of Hilary Term. The essays should reflect skills and understanding the candidate has acquired through attending the Advanced Option classes, one of them may complement but must not share significant content with the dissertation, and the essays are also expected to be distinct from each other in period or issues covered.

II. The corresponding examination paper on conceptual and methodological issues is 'Methods and evidence in the History of the United States of America'.

III. Candidates must prepare a dissertation of not more than 15,000 words on a topic in his or her chosen subject area. The dissertation must include a short abstract which concisely summarises in about 300 words its scope and principal arguments.

Two copies of the dissertation, addressed to the Chair of Examiners for the Master of Studies in US History, must be submitted to the Examination Schools by 12 noon on Monday of Week Six of Trinity Term.

Material submitted under I. and II. may be summarised or substantially further developed in the dissertation, but no significant part of the dissertation should reproduce or paraphrase other work submitted for examination.

4. The examiners may award a distinction to candidates who have performed with special merit in the whole examination.

5. A candidate who fails the examination will be permitted to retake it on one further occasion only, not later than one year after the initial attempt.

Women's Studies

1. Every candidate must follow, for at least three terms, a course of instruction in Women's Studies. Candidates will, when they enter for the examination, be required to produce from their society a certificate that they are following such a course.

2. Candidates are required to present themselves for viva voce examination if summoned by the examiners.

3. The examiners may award a distinction for excellence in the whole examination.

4. *Syllabus:*

Candidates must offer A and B below, two options from C, and a dissertation (D).

A. Feminist Theory

B. Approaches to Feminist Research

C. Options. Candidates must follow two of a range of option courses approved by the Joint Standing Committee for Women's Studies. A full list of the options available is given in the course handbook for the academic year in question.

D. A dissertation of up to 12,000 words (and not less than 10,000), including footnotes but excluding bibliography, on a subject proposed by the candidate in consultation with the dissertation supervisor. Appendices should be avoided but must in any case be approved by the Chair of Examiners on an individual basis. Cases must be made on the basis that they are required for the examiners to understand the content of the dissertation. A form detailing the title and subject of the dissertation, countersigned by the dissertation supervisor, must be submitted for approval to the Chair of Examiners (c/o Modern Languages Graduate Studies Office) not later than Friday of fourth week of Hilary Term. The subject matter of the dissertation may be related to that of either or both of the two pieces of written work submitted for the Options courses, but material deployed in such pieces of work may not be repeated in the dissertation.

5. In the case of C candidates will be examined by the submission of written work. The essays submitted under C should be of 6,000–7,000 words, including footnotes and excluding bibliography. Forms detailing the titles and topics of the written work proposed, countersigned by a course convenor and option tutor respectively, must be submitted for approval to the Chair of Examiners (c/o Modern Languages Graduate Studies Office) not later than Friday of fourth week of Hilary Term. The two pieces of written work under C (three typewritten or printed copies of each piece, bearing on the front the candidate's examination number but neither his or her name nor the name of his or her college) must be delivered in envelopes bearing the words: 'Option Essay submitted for the M.St. in Women's Studies to the Examination Schools, High Street, Oxford. The first piece of written work under C must be delivered not later than noon on Friday of eighth week of Hilary Term; the second piece of written work under C must be delivered not later than noon on Friday of first week of Trinity Term. Candidates must themselves retain one typewritten or printed copy of each piece of work. Supervisors or others are permitted to give bibliographical help with and to discuss drafts of written work submitted. Each envelope of written work must be accompanied, under a separate cover, by a signed statement by the candidate that it is his or her own work except where otherwise indicated.

6. In the case of D, the dissertation (three typewritten or printed copies, bearing on the front the candidate's examination number but neither his or her name nor the name of his or her college) must be delivered in an envelope bearing the words: 'Dissertation submitted for the M.St. in Women's Studies' to the Examination

Schools, High Street, Oxford, not later than noon on Friday of eighth week of Trinity Term. Students must also submit three copies of a brief abstract (no more than 500 words) outlining the rationale and approach of the thesis. Candidates must themselves retain one typewritten or printed copy of their dissertation. Supervisors or others are permitted to give bibliographical help with and to discuss drafts of dissertations. The dissertation must be accompanied, under a separate cover, by a signed statement by the candidate that it is his or her own work, except where otherwise indicated.

7. In the case both of the submission of written work under C and of the submission of the dissertation (D), candidates must ensure that a separate receipt for each submission is received from the Examination Schools and is retained for future reference.

8. A candidate who fails to submit any of the three written elements (that is, the two pieces of written work and the dissertation) by the dates specified above shall be deemed to have withdrawn from the examination.

9. If the two pieces of written work, submitted for C and/or the dissertation, submitted for D, fail the examination, the candidate shall not be granted leave to supplicate for the degree of M.St. Such a candidate is permitted to resubmit the elements of the examination which have failed to satisfy the examiners, on one further occasion only. The two pieces of written work submitted for C shall be resubmitted by noon on Friday of first week of the Trinity Term following their first examination. The dissertation (D) shall be resubmitted by not later than noon of Friday of eighth week of the Trinity Term following their first examination.

Yiddish Studies

1. All candidates shall be required at the time of admission to satisfy the board (if necessary, by written and oral tests) that they possess the appropriate qualifications for the proposed course, including suitable proficiency in written and spoken Yiddish. Normally the course will be restricted to candidates who have taken a first degree in a relevant subject area.

2. All candidates must follow a course of instruction in Yiddish Studies at Oxford for a period of three terms, unless the Board of the Faculty of Medieval and Modern Languages in exceptional circumstances shall permit an extension of time and they shall, when they enter their names for the examination, be required to produce from their society a certificate stating that they are following the course of instruction for the period prescribed.

3. *Syllabus*

Candidates must offer both components of A below, one option from B, and a dissertation (C).

A.

   (i) Modern Yiddish Literature (1864–1939).

   (ii) History of the Yiddish Language.

Assessment of these subjects is by take-home examination, one of which must be submitted by Friday of Week 9 of Hilary Term and one by Friday of Week 1 of Trinity Term. The examination papers will be distributed on the Friday of the preceding week.

B.

   (i) Old Yiddish Literature (survey).

   (ii) Old Yiddish Literature: Secular and Religious Trends.

   (iii) Old Yiddish: Between Folklore and Literature.

(iv) Nineteenth-Century Yiddish Literature.

(v) Modern Yiddish Poetry.

(vi) Yiddish Drama and Theatre.

(vii) Twentieth-Century Centres of Yiddish Literature and Culture.

(viii) Sociology of Yiddish.

(ix) History of Yiddish Studies.

(x) Yiddish Stylistics.

(xi) Yiddish Bibliography and Booklore.

(xii) Any other option approved by the board.

Unless the subject is governed by regulations laid down elsewhere, the subject is examined by submission of an essay of 5,000–7,000 words, to be submitted by Friday of Week 1 of Trinity Term.

Candidates shall seek approval (by application to the Modern Languages Graduate Office, 37 Wellington Square, Oxford) of their proposed option by the end of the fourth week of their first term.

Teaching for some options listed under B may not be available in every year. Applicants for admission will be advised of this.

C.

A dissertation of approximately 10,000 words and not more than 12,000 words on a subject proposed by the candidate in consultation with the supervisor and approved by the Board of the Faculty of Medieval and Modern Languages. Candidates shall seek approval (by application to the Modern Languages Graduate Office, 41 Wellington Square, Oxford) for the proposed topic of their dissertation by the end of the fourth week of their second term.

The dissertation must be presented in proper scholarly form. Two copies, typed in double-spacing on one side only of A4 paper, each bound or held firmly in a stiff cover bearing on the front the candidate's examination number but neither his or her name nor the name of his or her college, must be delivered in a parcel bearing the words 'Dissertation submitted for the M.St. in Yiddish Studies' to the Examination Schools, High Street, Oxford, not later than noon on the Friday of the eighth week of Trinity Term. Candidates must themselves retain one copy of the dissertation.

Supervisors or others are permitted to give bibliographical help during the preparation of the dissertation and to discuss drafts.

5. The examiners may award a distinction for excellence in the whole examination.

NOTES

8

REGULATIONS FOR THE DEGREE OF MASTER OF SCIENCE BY COURSEWORK

§1. Degree of Master of Science by Coursework

1. Any person who has been admitted to the status of student for the degree of Master of Science by Coursework, who has satisfied the conditions prescribed by this section, and has satisfied the examiners as required, may supplicate for the Degree of Master of Science by Coursework.

2. The Education Committee shall have power to make and vary such regulations as may be necessary for carrying out the duties laid upon it and upon the Registrar by this section.

3. For the purposes of this section, the words 'board', 'faculty board', or 'board of the faculty' shall include any committee authorised to admit candidates for the Degree of Master of Science by Coursework.

4. A Student for the Degree of Master of Science by Coursework who is not a graduate of the University may wear the same gown as that worn by Students for the Degree of Doctor of Philosophy.

§2. Status of Student for the Degree of Master of Science by Coursework

1. Any person who, in the opinion of the board concerned, is well-qualified and well-fitted to undertake the course of study for which application is made, may be admitted to the status of Student for the Degree of Master of Science by Coursework.

2. It shall be the duty of the Registrar to keep a Register of those admitted to the status of Student for the Degree of Master of Science by Coursework.

§3. Admission of Candidates for the Degree of Master of Science by Coursework

1. A candidate seeking admission as a Student for the Degree of Master of Science by Coursework shall apply to the board under whose aegis the proposed course of study falls. Candidates for admission shall be required to provide such information as the board may determine from time to time by regulation. Applicants shall in addition be required to undertake such other tests and meet such conditions as, subject to the approval of the Education Committee, a board may determine by regulation.

2. Applications shall be made through the Registrar, and it shall be the duty of the Registrar to submit each application to the board concerned and to inform the candidate of the outcome, as soon as may be.

3. No person shall be admitted as a Student for the Degree of Master of Science by Coursework under these provisions unless he or she is also a member of a college, and unless the application for admission as a Student for the Degree of Master of Science by Coursework has the approval of that college. The Registrar shall forward the application to the candidate's college or to the college to which the candidate wishes to apply for membership, as appropriate; and admission by the faculty board shall be conditional upon admission by an approved society.

4. A student registered for any other higher degree or diploma in the University may apply for transfer to the status of Student for the Degree of Master of Science by Coursework*. The board concerned shall have power to make such transfer, provided that it is satisfied that the student is well qualified and well fitted to undertake the course of study for which application is made, and that the application has the support of the candidate's society. A candidate who transfers status in this way shall be reckoned as having held the status of Student for the Degree of Master of Science by Coursework from the time of admission to his or her previous status, unless the board shall determine otherwise.

5. A student holding the status of Probationer Research Student may, with the approval of the board which admitted him or her, be admitted as a candidate for an examination for the Degree of Master of Science by Coursework. Time spent as a student holding

---

* Students applying for the M.Sc in Advanced Cognitive Therapy Studies must commence by studying the Postgraduate Diploma in Advanced Cognitive Therapy Studies.

the status of Probationer Research Student shall count as time spent working for the Degree of Master of Science.

§4. Supervision of Students for the Degree of Master of Science by Coursework

1. Every candidate on admission as a Student for the Degree of Master of Science by Coursework shall be placed by the board concerned under the supervision of a member of the University or other competent person selected by the board, and the board shall have power for sufficient reason to change the supervisor of any student or to arrange for joint supervision by more than one supervisor, if it deems it necessary.

2. It shall be the duty of the supervisor of a student entered upon a course of study to direct and superintend the work of the student, to meet the student regularly, and to undertake such duties as shall from time to time be set out in the relevant Policy and Guidance issued by the Education Committee.

3. The supervisor shall submit a report on the progress of a student to the board three times a year, and at any other time when the board so requests or the supervisor deems it expedient. The supervisor shall communicate the contents of the report to the student on each occasion that a report is made, so that the student is aware of the supervisor's assessment of his or her work during the period in question. In addition, the supervisor shall inform the board at once if he or she is of the opinion the student is unlikely to reach the standard required for the Degree of Master of Science by Coursework.

4. It shall be the duty of every Student for the Degree of Master of Science by Coursework to undertake such guided work and to attend such seminars and lectures as his or her supervisor requests; to attend such meetings with his or her supervisor as the supervisor reasonably arranges; and to fulfil any other requirements of the Education Committee as set out in relevant Policy and Guidance issued by the Education Committee.

§5. Residence and other Requirements for Students for the Degree of Master of Science by Coursework

1. No full-time Student for the Degree of Master of Science by Coursework shall be granted leave to supplicate unless, after admission, he or she has kept statutory residence and pursued his or her course of study at Oxford for at least three terms.

2. No full-time Student for the Degree of Master of Science by Coursework shall retain that status for more than six terms in all, except that any candidate for the Examination in Education may retain that status for nine terms in all.

3. Part-time students for the Degree of Master of Science by Coursework shall in each case be required to pursue their course of study for twice the number of terms required of an equivalent full-time student. Part-time students shall not be required to keep statutory residence but must attend for such instruction and undertake such supervised fieldwork as the faculty concerned shall require. The Director of Graduate Studies of the board concerned, or director of the department concerned, as the case may be, shall keep a register of attendance of part-time students. No student shall be granted leave to supplicate unless the register shows satisfactory attendance by him or her.

4. Part-time students may hold the status of Student for the Degree of Master of Science by Coursework for up to twice the number of terms for which equivalent full-time students may hold that status except where an extension of time is permitted by special regulation.

5. A Student for the Degree of Master of Science by Coursework shall cease to hold that status if:

(i) he or she shall have been refused permission to supplicate for the Degree of Master of Science by Coursework;

(ii) the board concerned shall, in accordance with provisions set down by regulation by the Education Committee, and after consultation with the student's society and supervisor, have deprived the student of such status;

(iii) he or she shall have been transferred under the relevant provisions to another status;

(iv) he or she shall not have entered for the relevant examination within the time specified under this subsection.

§6. Examination of Students

1. The examinations for the Degree of Master of Science by Coursework shall be under the supervision of the boards authorised to admit candidates for the Degree of Master of Science by Coursework. The examinations for the degree and the bodies responsible for the supervision of each examination are listed below.

Examination	*Board*	
African Studies	Social Sciences	
Applied Landscape Archaeology	Continuing Education	
Applied Linguistics and Second Language Acquisition	Social Sciences	5
Applied Statistics	Mathematical, Physical and Life Sciences	
Archaeological Science	Social Sciences	
Biodiversity, Conservation, and Management	Social Sciences	
Biomedical Engineering	Mathematical, Physical and Life Sciences	10
Clinical Embryology	Medical Sciences	
Cognitive and Evolutionary Anthropology	Social Sciences	
Cognitive Behavioural Therapy	Continuing Education	
Comparative Social Policy	Social Sciences	15
Computer Science	Mathematical, Physical and Life Sciences	
Contemporary Chinese Studies	Social Sciences	
Contemporary India	Social Sciences	
Criminology and Criminal Justice	Law	20
Criminology and Criminal Justice (Research Methods)	Law	
Economic and Social History	History	
Economics for Development	Social Sciences	
Education	Social Sciences	25
Endovascular Neurosurgery (Interventional Neuroradiology)	Medical Sciences	
English Local History	Continuing Education	
Environmental Change and Management	Social Sciences	
Evidence-Based Health Care	Medical Sciences/ Continuing Education	30
Evidence-Based Social Intervention	Social Sciences	
Experimental Therapeutics	Medical Sciences/ Continuing Education	
Financial Economics	Social Sciences	35
Global Governance and Diplomacy	Social Sciences	
Global Health Science	Medical Sciences	
History of Science, Medicine, and Technology	History	
Integrated Immunology	Medical Sciences	
Latin American Studies	School of Interdisciplinary Area Studies	40
Law and Finance	Social Sciences	
Learning and Teaching	Social Sciences	
Major Programme Management	Social Sciences	

Management Research	Social Sciences	
Mathematical and Computational Finance	Mathematical, Physical and Life Sciences	
[From 1 October 2015: Mathematical and Theoretical Physics	Mathematical, Physical and Life Sciences]	5
Mathematical Finance	Mathematical, Physical and Life Sciences/ Continuing Education	
Mathematical Modelling and Scientific Computation	Mathematical, Physical and Life Sciences	
Mathematics and Foundations of Computer Science	Mathematical, Physical and Life Sciences	1(
Medical Anthropology	Social Sciences	
Migration Studies	Social Sciences	
Modern Japanese Studies	Social Sciences	
Musculoskeletal Sciences	Medical Sciences	1!
Nature, Society, and Environmental Policy	Social Sciences	
Neuroscience	Medical Sciences	
Pharmacology	Medical Sciences	
Political Theory Research	Social Sciences	
Politics Research	Social Sciences	2(
Professional Archaeology	Continuing Education	
Psychological Research	Medical Sciences	
Public Policy in Latin America	Social Sciences	
Radiation Biology	Medical Sciences	
Refugee and Forced Migration Studies	Social Sciences	2!
Russian and East European Studies	Social Sciences	
Social Anthropology	Social Sciences	
Social Anthropology (Research Methods)	Social Sciences	
Social Science of the Internet	Social Sciences	
Sociology	Social Sciences	3(
Software and Systems Security	Mathematical, Physical and Life Sciences	
Software Engineering	Mathematical, Physical and Life Sciences	
Software Engineering Programme	Mathematical, Physical and Life Sciences	3!
Surgical Science and Practice	Medical Sciences/ Continuing Education	
Sustainable Urban Development	Continuing Education	
Teaching English Language in University Settings	Social Sciences	4(
Theoretical Chemistry	Mathematical, Physical and Life Sciences	
Visual, Material and Museum Anthropology	Social Sciences	
Water Science Policy and Management	Social Sciences	

2. No candidate shall be permitted to take an examination under the preceding clause unless he or she has been admitted as a candidate for the examination in question by the body responsible for the course and has satisfied any other conditions prescribed in the regulations for that course.

3. Final examination marks shall be released to candidates at the conclusion of the examination. Exceptions to this may be made where assessment takes place throughout the course. In such cases, examination boards must meet formally, with all members present, at interim points in the year in order to agree final marks for specified assessment components. Marks released as final marks may not subsequently be amended without permission of the Proctors.

4. A candidate who has failed to satisfy the examiners in the examination may enter again for the examination on one, but not more than one, subsequent occasion.

5. The examiners may award a distinction for excellence in the whole examination. Candidates who have initially failed any element of assessment shall not normally be eligible for the award of distinction.

SPECIAL REGULATIONS

Except where otherwise indicated, all material submitted for examination (dissertations, extended essays, etc) shall be accompanied by a certificate signed by the candidate indicating that it is the candidate's own work, except where otherwise specified. This certificate must be submitted separately in a sealed envelope addressed to the chair of examiners of the degree course in question.

African Studies

1. Each candidate will be required to follow a course of instruction in African Studies for three terms, and will, when they enter their names for the examination, be required to produce a certificate from their supervisors to this effect.

2. Candidates will be required to present themselves for examination in the compulsory paper in Themes in African History and the Social Sciences, and in one optional paper at the end of Trinity Term in the year of registration. In addition, each candidate will be required to submit the following written work:

   (i) One 4,500 word essay for the compulsory core course in Methodology, Ethics and Research Strategies selected from a list of questions approved by the African Studies Teaching Committee and made available to candidates by the last Friday of Michaelmas Term. The essay must be submitted not later than 12 noon on the first Monday of Hilary Term in the year in which the examination is taken.

(ii) One 15,000 word dissertation, which must include discussion of the comparative reading, historiography, or theory relevant to the dissertation. The title of the dissertation must be approved by the African Studies Teaching Committee not later than 12 noon on the last day of eighth week of Michaelmas Full Term in the year in which the examination is taken. The dissertation must be submitted not later than 12 noon on Friday of sixth week of Trinity Full Term in the year in which the examination is taken.

Two typewritten or word processed copies of the written work detailed above must be delivered to the Examination Schools, addressed to the Chair of Examiners for the M.Sc. in African Studies, c/o Examination Schools, High Street, Oxford at the times and days specified.

3. A candidate must pass all components of the examination in order to pass the degree. A candidate who fails any element of the examination will be permitted to retake or resubmit it on one further occasion within six terms of his or her initial registration. A candidate who fails one or more of the compulsory or optional papers will be required to resit both papers. In the case of a failed essay or dissertation, the resubmitted dissertation can be on the same topic and include previously submitted work.

4. Candidates may be required to attend an oral examination on any part of the examination.

5. The examiners may award a distinction for excellence in the whole examination.

Schedule

The structure of the course is as follows:

(*a*) *Compulsory core course in Methodology, Ethics and Research Strategies*: ethics, politics; disciplinary approaches including history, politics, anthropology; conducting interviews: oral traditions, questionnaires, archives on and in Africa; visual materials, photographs and films; practical aspects of research.

(*b*) *Compulsory core course in Themes in African History and the Social Sciences*: key features of African states; social and economic change and the dilemmas of development; globalisation and conflict in the post-colonial era; environmental history and politics.

(*c*) *Optional paper*: Candidates must choose one optional paper from a list published annually and distributed to students by the last day of eighth week of Michaelmas Full Term.

Applied Landscape Archaeology

1. Every candidate must follow for at least six terms a part-time course of instruction in Applied Landscape Archaeology and must upon entering for examination produce from his or her society a certificate to that effect.

2. The examination will consist of the following parts:

A Core Topics

Every candidate must submit two written assignments of no more than 2,500 words in length for each of the two core topic courses on:

(1) Method and Theory in Landscape Archaeology;

(2) Managing Twenty-first Century Landscapes.

One core topic will be taken in each year of the course.

B Advanced Papers

Every candidate must follow four of the six Advanced Paper courses listed in the Schedule below, and submit one written assignment of no more than 5,000 words in length for each paper. Candidates will take two Advanced Papers per year of the M.Sc.

C Dissertation 5

A dissertation of not more than 15,000 words, including appendices but excluding bibliography, on a topic approved by the candidate's supervisor. The dissertation must be delivered not later than noon on the last Monday in September of the second year of the course to the Chair of Examiners for the Degree of M.Sc. in Applied Landscape Archaeology, c/o Examination Schools, High Street, Oxford. 10

3. Candidates must attend one compulsory field training week (or in exceptional circumstances equivalent day or weekend schools) during their registration on the course.

4. Each candidate must attend a viva voce examination when required to do so by the examiners. 15

5. The examiners may award a distinction for excellence in the whole examination.

6. A candidate who fails a core topic or advanced paper, or whose dissertation fails to satisfy the examiners, may be permitted to retake the paper, or resubmit the dissertation, on one further occasion only, not later than one year after the initial attempt.

Schedule 20

Advanced Papers are available in the following areas:

1. Archaeological prospection

2. Reading the historic landscape

3. Artefacts and Ecofacts in the landscape

4. Digital landscapes 25

5. Placement work

6. Geoarchaeology

Not all advanced papers will be available in any one year and the definitive list of advanced papers available in any one year will be circulated to candidates and their supervisors during the second week of Michaelmas Term. 30

Applied Linguistics and Second Language Acquisition

1. Candidates may normally only be admitted to the course if they have successfully obtained an honours degree which contained a substantial element of second language learning and/or linguistics.

2. The course shall consist of eight taught modules (constituting Part 1 of the 35 examination) and a dissertation (constituting Part 2 of the examination). Candidates shall be deemed to have passed the examination if they have satisfied the examiners in both Part 1 and Part 2.

3. Every candidate who is required to complete Part 1 will be required to complete all eight Modules of the course unless they can make a case for prior accreditation (by 40 virtue of having successfully completed the Diploma in Education, Modern Foreign Languages), in which case they will be required to complete six Modules, and this will constitute Part 1 of the examination for these candidates. Candidates must pass Part 1 by examination or by prior accreditation before submitting a dissertation for Part 2. Interim marks for the first four Modules of Part 1 will be released to candidates 45 following the first meeting of the Examination Board. At the close of the examination in Part 1, a list of candidates shall be published who have satisfied the examiners in that part of the examination.

4. Every candidate will be required to satisfy the examiners in the following:

(i) Satisfactory attendance at the appropriate classroom-based courses;

(ii) Satisfactory performance in both Part 1 and Part 2.

5. Three word-processed or printed copies of each of four module assignments must be delivered to the Chair of Examiners, M.Sc. in Applied Linguistics and Second Language Acquisition Examiners, c/o Examination Schools, High Street, Oxford no later than noon on the Monday of Week 1 of Hilary Full Term, and three word-processed or printed copies of each of four further module assignments must be delivered to the same address no later than noon on the Monday of Week 1 of Trinity Full Term. Part-time students must submit assignments for two modules on each of these occasions over a period of two years. Candidates will also be required to submit an electronic copy of each assignment to assignments@education.ox.ac.uk by 15.00 on the same days. Each assignment must be accompanied by a declaration indicating that it is the candidate's own work.

6. Candidates will be required to submit a dissertation of between 15,000 and 20,000 words (including footnotes/endnotes but excluding appendices and references or bibliography) on a subject selected by the candidate in consultation with the supervisor, which must be closely related to one or more of the themes of the course. The subject and title selected by the candidate must be approved by Departmental Board not later than the first day of the fifth week of Hilary Term of the course (for full-time candidates) and of the second year of the course (for part-time candidates).

7. Three word processed or printed copies of the dissertation must be delivered to the Chair of the Examiners, M.Sc. in Applied Linguistics and Second Language Acquisition, c/o Examination Schools, High Street, Oxford, OX2 6PY not later than noon on the last Friday of August of the year in which the final Module examination has been taken. One copy should be hard bound and two soft bound, the latter of which should be anonymous except for the candidate number. The hard bound copy of the dissertation of each candidate who passes the examination shall be retained by the department for deposit in the departmental library. The dissertation must be accompanied by a declaration indicating that it is the candidate's own work. Candidates will also be required to submit an electronic copy of the dissertation to assignments@education.ox.ac.uk by noon on the same day. If Part 1 is failed, the candidate may retake the whole examination of Part 1 one further time on the next occasion when this is examined. If Part 2 is failed the candidate may resubmit the dissertation one further time on the next occasion when it is examined.

8. The candidate may also be examined orally. The oral examination may only be on the candidate's dissertation.

9. The examiners may award a distinction for excellence in the whole examination.

Schedule

Module A First Language Acquisition and Bilingualism

Module B Theories, Progression, and Methods

Module C Individual and Group Differences

Module D Input and Interaction

Module E Accessing Meaning

Module F Producing and Communicating Meaning

Module G Vocabulary Acquisition

Module H Error, Analysis, Interlanguage, and Testing

Optional Double Module: Teaching English as a Foreign Language Certificate.

Applied Statistics

1. The Divisional Board of Mathematical, Physical and Life Sciences shall elect for the supervision of the course a Standing Committee which shall have power to arrange lectures and other instruction.

2. Candidates shall follow for at least three terms a course of instruction in Statistics, and will, when entering their name for the examination, be required to produce from their society a certificate that they are doing so.

3. The examination will consist of:

(i) a written examination consisting of two papers on the syllabus described in the schedule;

(ii) a dissertation on a subject selected in consultation with the supervisor and approved by the chair of the committee.

4. Candidates must submit to the chair of the committee by the end of Hilary Term in the year in which they enter the examination, the title and a brief statement of the form and scope of their dissertation, together with the name of a person who has agreed to act as their supervisor during the preparation of the dissertation.

5. Two typewritten or printed copies of the dissertation must be sent not later than noon on 15 September in the year in which the written examination is taken, to the M.Sc. examiners (Applied Statistics), c/o Examination Schools, High Street, Oxford. The examiners may retain one copy of the dissertation of each candidate who passes the examination for deposit in an appropriate departmental library.

6. Each candidate will be expected to have displayed evidence of the ability to apply statistical methods to real data.

The examiners will take into account the results of an assessment of ability to apply statistical methods to real data organised by the supervisory committee. The supervisory committee will be responsible for notifying the candidates of the arrangements for the assessment, and for forwarding the assessed material to the chair of the examiners before the end of the Trinity Term in the year in which the assessment is made. The supervisory committee may specify that one of the practical assessments will be carried out as group projects, the details of which will be given in the Course Handbook.

7. In the written examination the examiners will permit the use of any hand-held pocket calculators subject to the conditions set out under the heading 'Use of calculators in examinations' in the *Special Regulations concerning Examinations*.

8. In the written examination the examiners will permit the use of bilingual dictionaries.

9. The examiners may also examine any candidate viva voce.

10. The examiners may award a distinction for excellence in the whole examination.

11. If it is the opinion of the examiners that the work done by the candidate is not of sufficient merit to qualify for the Degree of M.Sc., but is nevertheless of sufficient merit to qualify for the Diploma in Applied Statistics, the candidate shall be given the option of retaking the M.Sc. examination on one further occasion, not later than one year after the initial attempt, or of being issued with a diploma. In the event of a candidate's work not being of sufficient merit to qualify for the award of the M.Sc., the examiners will specify which of the components of the course may or must be redone.

Schedule

Paper 1: Principles of statistical analysis
Statistical distribution theory; statistical inference; statistical methods.

Paper 2: Further statistical methodology

Topics in statistical methodology chosen from a list approved by the Standing Committee and published in the Course Handbook by the beginning of Michaelmas Term of the academic year in which the written examination is to be taken.

Archaeological Science

1. Within the Division of Social Sciences, the course shall be administered by the Committee for the School of Archaeology. The regulations made are as follows:

2. Candidates for admission must apply to the Committee for the School of Archaeology.

3. Candidates must follow a course of instruction in Archaeological Science for at least three terms and for a substantial part of the three subsequent vacations, as determined by the course timetable.

4. The written examination shall consist of:

(*a*) three papers on the syllabus described in the Schedule, to be taken in the second week of Trinity Term, *and*

(*b*) *either* one pre-set essay of approximately 10,000 words, *or* two pre-set essays of approximately 5,000 words each. The subject and length of each essay must be approved by the examiners before the end of Michaelmas Full Term. Two copies of each essay must be delivered to the Examination Schools by noon on the Friday of first week of Trinity Term. Essays must be typed or printed, must bear the candidate's examination number but not his or her name, and must include a statement of the number of words. Any illustrations must be included in both copies.

(*c*) in lieu of one of the three papers described in the Schedule, and the extended essay(s), candidates may, with the permission of the School of Archaeology Committee for Graduate Studies, take one of the options from the M.St in Archaeology (Schedules A and B) or M.St in Classical Archaeology (Schedule B only), to be examined by two pre-set essays of approximately 5,000 words.

5. Each candidate will be required to submit a dissertation of approximately 15,000 to 20,000 words, on a research area selected in consultation with the supervisor and approved by a person designated for this purpose by the Committee for the School of Archaeology.

6. Three typewritten copies of the dissertation must be sent, not later than noon on the Friday four weeks and two days before the start of the following Michaelmas Term, to the M.Sc. Examiners (Archaeological Science), c/o Examination Schools, High Street, Oxford. The examiners will retain one copy of the dissertation of each candidate for the departmental library.

7. The examiners may require to see the records of practical work carried out during the course.

8. Candidates must present themselves for an oral examination as required by the examiners. This may be on the candidate's written paper, or dissertation, or both.

9. The examiners may award a distinction for excellence in the whole examination.

10. In the case of failure in just one part of the examination (written papers, extended essay(s), dissertation), the candidate will be permitted to retake that part of the examination on one further occasion, not later than one year after the initial attempt. Written papers would be retaken the following year. Pass or failure in the written papers will be taken as an average of all written papers and in the case of failure all written papers must be retaken. If the candidate passes all parts of the

examination except the dissertation, the dissertation may be considered as a practical report as defined in the schedule for the M.St and, if of a sufficiently high standard, the candidate may be granted permission to supplicate for the degree of M.St.

Schedule

(i) *Principles and practice of scientific dating*

The principles of scientific dating methods including radiocarbon, luminescence, uranium series and dendro-chronology. The practical aspects of these methods and the problems encountered in their application. The statistical analysis of chronological information in the study of archaeological sites and cultures.

(ii) *Bio-archaeology*

Scientific methods for the study of biological remains from archaeological sites; introduction to the analysis of plant and faunal remains including indicators of disease and artefactual analysis; theoretical and practical aspects of quantitative methods for diet reconstruction by isotopic analysis; introduction to ancient DNA studies; residue analysis.

(iii) *Materials analysis and the study of technological change*

Introduction to the history of technology; theoretical and practical aspects of materials analysis methods—SEM, microprobe, TIMS, ICP, ICP-MS, XRF, XRD, PIXE, FTIR and NAA; application of analysis to different material types—stone, ceramics, vitreous materials and metals; provenance of raw materials; case studies of application to archaeological problems.

Biodiversity, Conservation, and Management

1. The Social Sciences Divisional Board shall elect for the supervision of the course a Standing Committee.

2. Candidates must follow a course of instruction in Biodiversity, Conservation, and Management for at least three terms, and will, when entering for the examination, be required to produce a certificate from the Course Director to this effect.

3. The examination will consist of:

   (i) a written examination of three three-hour papers based on core courses as described in the schedule;

   (ii) two assessed essays based on elective courses;

   (iii) a dissertation on a subject selected in consultation with the supervisor and Course Director and approved by the Standing Committee.

4. Candidates must submit to the Course Director by the end of Hilary Term in the year in which they enter the examination, the title and a brief statement of the form and scope of their dissertation, together with the name of a person who has agreed to act as their supervisor during preparation of the dissertation.

5. The dissertation shall be of a maximum length of 15,000 words and accompanied by an abstract not exceeding 150 words. The maximum word count shall exclude appendices, references and the abstract. The detailed format and specification of the dissertation shall be approved by the Standing Committee, and published in the course handbook.

6. The deadline for submission is noon on the first weekday of September in the year in which the written examination is taken. Two copies of the dissertation must be submitted, to the M.Sc examiners (Biodiversity, Conservation, and Management), c/o Examination Schools, High Street, Oxford OX1 4BG. The examiners may retain

one copy of the dissertation of each candidate who passes the examination for deposit in an appropriate library. Both copies must bear the candidate's examination number but not his/her name.

7. All submitted work shall be accompanied by a separate statement certifying that the submitted work is the candidate's own work except where otherwise indicated.   5

8. In the written examination, the examiners will permit the use of hand-held pocket calculators subject to the conditions set out under the heading 'Use of calculators in examinations' in the *Regulations for the Conduct of University Examinations.*

9. The examiners may also examine any candidate viva voce on the candidate's   10
written papers, dissertation, or both.

10. Arrangements for reassessment shall be specified by the Standing Committee and published in the course handbook.

11. The examiners may award a distinction for excellence in the whole examination.

Schedule   15

(*a*) *Core courses*

The core courses will be examined under the following heads:

(i) *Biodiversity science.*

Candidates will be expected to have knowledge of and a critical understanding of the major contemporary themes in biodiversity science and conservation including an   20
appreciation of the various research methods used to collect scientific data.

(ii) *Conservation ethics and values.*

Candidates will be expected to have knowledge of the various ethical frameworks and value systems adopted by conservationists and how differing value systems can influence the development of effective conservation practice and policy.   25

(iii) *Biodiversity policy and management.*

Candidates will be expected to have knowledge of the techniques and conceptual basis of contemporary conservation planning and the international and national legal frameworks for implementing conservation policy.

(*b*) *Elective courses*   30

Candidates will be expected to show advanced knowledge of two of the option elective courses on offer in any one year.

Biomedical Engineering

1. The Divisional Board of Mathematical, Physical and Life Sciences, in consultation with the Faculty of Engineering Science, shall elect for the supervision of the   35
course an Organising Committee which shall have power to arrange lectures and other instruction.

2. Candidates shall follow a course of instruction in Biomedical Engineering for at least three terms and a substantial part of the three subsequent vacations, as determined by the course timetable, and will, when entering their name for the examina-   40
tion, be required to produce a certificate from their society to that effect.

3. The course syllabus shall be published annually in the Course Handbook.

4. The examination shall consist of the following parts:

(*a*) Candidates shall be required to take written papers in Biomedical Engineering
and Applied Biomedical Engineering. The examiners will not provide calculators,   45

but will permit the use of one hand-held pocket calculator from a list of permitted calculators. This list will be published annually in the Course Handbook.

(*b*) Candidates will be required to submit two assignments on subjects selected by the committee in the area of the healthcare industry. Each assignment must be typed and must not exceed 3,000 words, except where specified. Two copies of the healthcare industry assignments must be delivered to the M.Sc. Examiners (Biomedical Engineering), c/o Examination Schools, High Street, Oxford, not later than noon on Friday of the first week of Trinity Term in the year of the examination.

(*c*) Candidates will be required to undertake a prescribed schedule of practical work in computational methods. In the assessment of this paper the examiners will take into consideration the failure of a candidate to complete the practical work to a level prescribed by the committee. The Course Director will provide a list showing the extent to which each candidate has satisfied these requirements.

(*d*) Candidates will be required to undertake a prescribed schedule of practical work in biomedical engineering. In assessing the practical work the examiners will take into consideration the failure of a candidate to complete the practical work to a level prescribed by the committee. The Course Director will provide a list showing the extent to which each candidate has satisfied these requirements.

(*e*) Candidates will be required to carry out a group project and to submit a written report on the project completed as part of the course of study. The subject of the project shall be approved by the Course Director. Candidates shall be required to take part in a presentation of their group project. The project report must be not more than 30 pages (including all diagrams, photographs, references and appendices). All pages should be numbered, have margins of not less than 20mm all round, and type face not less than 11 pt font with line spacing of no less than 8mm. Two copies of the group project report must be delivered to the M.Sc. Examiners (Biomedical Engineering), c/o Examination Schools, High Street, Oxford, not later than noon on Friday of the week before the start of Hilary Term in the year of the examination. The report must be the candidate's own work and should include a signed statement to this effect. No project report will be accepted if it has already been submitted wholly or substantially for another degree of this University, or for a degree at any other institution.

(*f*) Candidates will be required to submit a written report on an individual project completed as part of the course of study. The subject of the project shall be approved by the Course Director. The project report must be not more than 60 pages including all diagrams, photographs, references and appendices). All pages should be numbered, have margins of not less than 20mm round, and type face not less than 11 pt font with line spacing of no less than 8mm. Three copies of the individual project report must be delivered to the M.Sc. Examiners (Biomedical Engineering), c/o Examination Schools, High Street, Oxford, not later than noon on the last Friday in August in the year of the examination. The report must be the candidate's own work and should include a signed statement to this effect. No project report will be accepted if it has already been submitted wholly or substantially for another degree of this University, or for a degree at any other institution.

5. The examiners may award a distinction for excellence in the whole examination.

6. A candidate who fails the examination will be permitted to retake it on one further occasion only, not later than one year after the initial attempt. Such a candidate whose individual or team design project report has been of satisfactory

standard may resubmit the same piece of work. A candidate who has reached a satisfactory standard on any of the written assignments, laboratory reports or practical exercises will not be required to retake that part of the examination.

7. Candidates may be examined viva voce at the examiners' discretion.

Clinical Embryology

The Divisional Board of Medical Sciences shall appoint for the supervision of the course an Organising Committee, which shall have the power to arrange lectures and other instruction.

The Organising Committee shall appoint for each candidate an academic adviser.

Each candidate shall follow a course of study in Clinical Embryology for at least three terms and for a substantial part of the three subsequent vacations, as determined by the course timetable, and will, when entering for the examination, be required to produce a certificate from their academic adviser to this effect.

Candidates shall be examined in all of the following ways:

(i) Each candidate must submit to the Course Director by Monday of Week 8 of Michaelmas Term a skills checklist, initialled by the practical skills tutor, to verify that they have acquired the practical skills associated with the course. This checklist will be made available to the examiners. A candidate who submits an incomplete checklist will be required to undertake remedial training, and to resubmit the checklist by a specified date.

(ii) Each candidate must pass a qualifying examination at the end of Michaelmas Term. The examination shall normally consist of a two-hour computer-based assessment on the topics covered in modules I–V, as set out in the Schedule. Candidates who fail the qualifying examination shall be permitted to take it on one further occasion in Week 0 of Hilary Term. The Organising Committee shall submit to the examiners a list of candidates who have satisfactorily completed the qualifying examination not later than the end of the Hilary Term preceding the examination.

(iii) Each candidate must submit a typewritten or printed essay of between 3,000 and 4,000 words on a topic approved by the Organising Committee. The arrangements for approval will be notified to candidates not later than the start of Michaelmas Term of the academic year in which the examination is taken. The essay must be submitted by noon, Thursday of Week 9 of Hilary Term. In the event that they are deemed not to have achieved the required standard in this element of the examination, candidates will have the opportunity to revise and resubmit their essay by noon, Friday of Week 3 of Trinity Term.

(iv) Each candidate must pass a written examination in Week 0 of Trinity Term. The examination shall consist of a three-hour written paper on the topics covered in modules VI–X, as set out in the Schedule. Candidates who fail the examination shall be permitted to take it on one further occasion, no sooner than three weeks after the first occasion. Candidates must pass this examination in order to proceed with their research project.

(v) Each candidate must submit a typewritten or printed dissertation of not more than 10,000 words (excluding bibliography and appendices) on the research project as set out in the Schedule below. The research project and the subject of the dissertation must have been approved by the Organising Committee. The arrangements for approval will be notified to candidates not later than the start of Michaelmas Term of the academic year in which the examination is taken.

Candidates shall be examined viva voce on their dissertation, or on any other element of the examination, and shall also give poster and oral presentations on their research project. The viva voce examination will normally be conducted in September of the year in which the candidate is examined on dates to be determined by the examiners.

Each written submission (consisting of three hard copies plus an electronic copy) must be sent to the Chair of Examiners, M.Sc. in Clinical Embryology, c/o Examination Schools, High Street, Oxford on the following dates:

(*a*) The dissertation on the research project must be submitted by dates to be specified by the Organising Committee and published in the *University Gazette* not later than the start of Michaelmas Term of the academic year in which the examination is taken.

(*b*) The essay must be submitted by noon on Thursday of Week 9 of Hilary Term.

Each written submission must be accompanied (in a separate sealed envelope addressed to the Chair of Examiners) by a certificate indicating that it is the candidate's own work and a CD containing an electronic copy of each written submission.

The examiners may award a distinction for excellence in the whole examination.

The examiners shall retain one copy of each dissertation of each successful candidate for deposit in the Radcliffe Science library.

Schedule

(A) *Modules*

    I Essential Cellular and Molecular Biology

    II Laboratory Methods and Practical Skills

    III The Mammalian Reproductive System

    IV Fertilisation and Early Embryogenesis

    V Embryonic Development and Pregnancy

    VI Infertility

    VII Assisted Reproductive Technology (ART)

    VIII Assisted Conception: Skills and Techniques

    IX Micromanipulation in ART

    X Infertility and ART: Developments and Current Issues

(B) *Research project*

A research project under the supervision of a research supervisor. Students will undertake reading and research in relation to their research project during Trinity Term and the Long Vacation. The subject of each student's dissertation and the supervision arrangements for each student must be approved by the Organising Committee.

Cognitive and Evolutionary Anthropology

1. Candidates must follow a course of instruction in Cognitive and Evolutionary Anthropology, including training in research, for at least three terms, and will, when entering for the examination, be required to produce a certificate from their supervisor to this effect.

2. Candidates will be required to present themselves for written and (if requested by the examiners) oral examinations and to submit three copies of a dissertation in a prescribed form on an approved topic as defined in (6) and (7) below.

3. The written examination will consist of four papers, one in each of the subjects listed in the Schedule.

4. For Paper 1, candidates will be required to submit three assignments (chosen from a list provided by the course convener not later than the Friday of eighth week of Hilary Term). The assignments must be submitted by the third Tuesday of Trinity

Term to the Chair of Examiners, M.Sc. in Cognitive and Evolutionary Anthropology, c/o Examination Schools, High Street, Oxford.

5. For each of Papers 2, 3 and 4, candidates will be required to sit an examination.

6. Candidates will be required to submit a dissertation of no more than 15,000 words in length, on a topic agreed with their supervisors. Three typewritten copies of the dissertation must be delivered not later than noon on the last Wednesday in August in the year in which the examination is taken, to the Chair of Examiners, M.Sc. in Cognitive and Evolutionary Anthropology, c/o Examination Schools, High Street, Oxford. The word count shall be stated on the outside front cover of the thesis.

7. The four papers will be taken to constitute Part I of the degree and the dissertation to constitute Part II. At the close of the written examinations, the examiners will issue a list of those who have satisfied them in Part I.

8. The oral examination, if held, may be on any or all of the candidate's assessed essays, and/or the dissertation.

9. The examiners may award a distinction for excellence in the whole examination.

10. In order to pass the degree, a student must pass all its assessed components. Where one or more components are failed, the student will be given the opportunity to re-sit or re-submit them once, as the case may be. Any subsequent award of the degree on successful completion of all the assessed components may be delayed by up to three terms, i.e. until the Examination Board next meets.

Schedule

Paper 1. *Quantitative Methods in the Human Sciences*

(*a*) Hypothesis testing

(*b*) Statistical analysis

(*c*) Research design

Paper 2. *Primate Evolution and Behaviour*

(*a*) Primate and hominin phylogeny and evolution

(*b*) Primate and hominin physiology

(*c*) Primate and human diet and substance

(*d*) Reconstructing past behaviour from primatology and archaeology

Paper 3. *Human Evolution and Behaviour*

(*a*) Hominid evolutionary history

(*b*) Human evolutionary psychology

(*c*) Kinship and inheritance

(*d*) Cultural evolutionary processes

Paper 4. *Mind and Culture*

(*a*) Cognitive and evolutionary explanations in anthropology

(*b*) Pan-human cognition: developmental and evolutionary perspectives

(*c*) Cognitive origins of culture

(*d*) Communication and transmission of culture.

Cognitive Behavioural Therapy

1. Candidates will be expected to have satisfactorily completed either the Postgraduate Diploma in Cognitive Behavioural Therapy or the Postgraduate Diploma in Advanced Cognitive Therapy Studies.

2. The course will consist of research seminars and supervision. The course will be taken on a part-time basis over a period of three terms.

3. Candidates may be permitted in certain circumstances to suspend status for a maximum of six terms. Any such period shall not count towards the maximum or minimum period of registration and no fee liability will be incurred against such periods.

4. Every candidate will be required to satisfy the examiners in the following:

(*a*) attendance at appropriate classroom-based courses including small group meetings. 5

(*b*) a research project of no more than 15,000 words on a topic approved by the Course Committee

The research project shall be submitted to The Registry, Department for Continuing Education, 1 Wellington Square, Oxford, OX1 2JD by such dates as the examiners 10 shall determine. Research projects will be forwarded to the examiners for consideration. Students are required to submit both a hard copy and an electronic copy.

5. Candidates may be expected to attend a viva voce examination at the end of the course of studies at the discretion of the examiners.

6. The examiners may award a distinction to candidates for the MSc. 15

7. A candidate whose research project fails to satisfy the examiners may be permitted to resubmit on one further occasion only not later than one year after the initial failure.

8. If any candidate who is successful in the examination for the Degree of Master of Science in Cognitive Behavioural Therapy has previously successfully completed 20 the Postgraduate Diploma in Cognitive Behavioural Therapy or the Postgraduate Diploma in Advanced Cognitive Therapy studies, the Master of Science will subsume his or her diploma.

Comparative Social Policy

Every candidate must follow, for at least three terms, a course of instruction in 25 Comparative Social Policy.

The examination will be in four parts.

A. Two compulsory papers in *Methods of Social Research*. As specified for the M.Phil. in Comparative Social Policy.

B. A compulsory paper in *Comparative Social Policy/Welfare States*. As specified 30 for the M.Phil. in Comparative Social Policy.

C. One optional paper. This may be from the list of optional papers as specified for the M.Phil. in Comparative Social Policy. Teaching in some options may not be available every year. Candidates may, after special permission of the Social Policy and Intervention Graduate Studies Committee, offer subjects outside this list. This 35 may include papers offered in other relevant master's degrees in the University, subject to permission by the relevant Graduate Studies Committee as appropriate.

D. A thesis of not more than 10,000 words on a topic within the subject of the course, to be specified jointly by supervisor and student. The thesis should employ comparative method in the study of a social policy topic. Two typewritten copies of 40 the thesis must be delivered to the Examination Schools, High Street, Oxford, by noon of the weekday on or nearest to 15 August of the year in which the examination is to be taken. Successful candidates will be required to deposit a copy of their thesis in the Social Science Library.

The examiners may examine any candidate viva voce. 45

The examiners may award a Distinction for excellence in the whole examination on the basis of the material submitted to them.

Computer Science

1. The Divisional Board of Mathematical, Physical and Life Sciences, in consultation with the Faculty of Computer Science, shall elect for the supervision of the course an Organising Committee which shall have power to arrange lectures and other instruction.

The committee shall elect a chair from its own members; the chair shall have power to approve applications on behalf of the committee. The committee shall be responsible for appointment of a supervisor for each student.

2. Candidates must follow a course of instruction in Computer Science for at least three terms and a substantial part of the three subsequent vacations, as determined by the course timetable, and will be required to produce a certificate from their supervisors to that effect.

3. The examination shall be in three parts, as follows:

(i) Candidates shall be assessed on at least twenty-eight and no more than thirty-four units of topics chosen from a list of topics approved by the Organising Committee and published in the *University Gazette* by the beginning of Michaelmas Full Term in the academic year of the examination. The mode of assessment shall be either written assignment or written examination, as detailed in the Course Handbook and on the website www.cs.ox.ac.uk/teaching/MSCinCS/. The list of courses shall be divided into three sections: Schedule A, Schedule B and Schedule C, as detailed on the website www.cs.ox.ac.uk/teaching/MSCinCS/.

(ii) Candidates shall submit a dissertation of not more than 30,000 words, plus not more than 30 pages of diagrams, tables, listing etc., on a subject selected by the candidate in consultation with the supervisor and approved by the director of the course.

(iii) There shall be an examination viva voce, unless the candidate shall have been individually dispensed by the examiners, on the dissertation and on any of the topics for which he or she submitted a written assignment or written examination, to take place on the Friday of week minus 1 of Michaelmas Term of the following academic year.

4. Every candidate must submit to the director of the course no later than the first Monday in Trinity Full Term in the year of the examination the title and a brief statement of the form and scope of his or her dissertation, together with an essay of not more than 3,000 words, describing the background of the project, its objectives and its plan of work. The submission must be approved by the person who has agreed to act as supervisor during the preparation of the dissertation.

Candidates will be expected to demonstrate in their dissertation an understanding of the topics studied in the course.

5. Two typewritten or printed copies of the dissertation must be delivered not later than noon on Friday of week minus 5 of Michaelmas Term of the following academic year to the M.Sc. Examiners (Computer Science), c/o Examination Schools, High Street, Oxford.

One copy of the thesis of each successful candidate will normally be presented to the Department of Computer Science.

6. By a date in each term to be specified in the Course Handbook, each candidate in consultation with their supervisor must submit for approval by the director of the course a list of topics which will be taken in that term. At least twenty-eight units of topics must be selected with a maximum of 12 units to be taken from Schedule A; candidates shall be allowed to choose a maximum of thirty-four units of topics. The choice must exclude any topics which substantially overlap the topics of the candidate's undergraduate degree or other recent academic study.

7. For each topic, the lecturer on the course of instruction shall prescribe a schedule of practical work, tutorial exercises and a written assignment or written examination, and shall make available to the Chair of Examiners evidence showing the extent to which each candidate has pursued an adequate course of practical and class work.   5

8. With the permission of the Organising Committee, a candidate may offer up to two alternative topics to replace any of the topics listed in Schedules B and C. An application for such replacement must be made to the director of the course by the end of the first week of the term in which the lecture course on the topic is given; it must be approved by the student's supervisor and by the lecturer on the course, who   10 thereby undertakes to accept appointment as assessor for the topic.

9. Not later than noon on a date in each term to be determined by the examiners, who are responsible for making sure candidates are aware of that date and that the date is announced at the head of the assignment sheet, the completed assignment for each topic must be delivered to the M.Sc. Examiners (Computer Science), c/o   15 Examination Schools, High Street, Oxford. Not later than noon on Wednesday of Week 0 of the following term, practicals for all topics must be delivered to the M.Sc. Examiners (Computer Science), c/o the Post-Graduate Taught Course Administrator, Department of Computer Science, Oxford. Topics to be assessed by written examination will take place in Week 0 of the following term. No candidate   20 shall attend classes or receive any form of individual tuition in the subject of an assignment between the time when the assignment is made available to the candidate and the time fixed for the delivery of the assignment to the examiners.

10. Any candidate who has not achieved an average of at least 50 in 24 units of topics by the beginning of Trinity Term shall be deemed to have failed the degree   25 course and will not be permitted to submit a dissertation.

11. To satisfy the examiners for the degree of MSc in Computer Science, a candidate must attain an average of at least 50 (pass) in the assignments or written examination in their best 28 units of topics, pass in the dissertation, pursue an adequate course of practical work and achieve an overall pass in practicals, and unless dispensed under cl.3   30 (iii) above satisfy the examiners in the viva voce examination.

12. The examiners may award a distinction for excellence in the whole examination.

13. A candidate who fails the examination will be permitted to retake it on one further occasion only, not later than one year after the initial attempt. Such a candidate whose dissertation has been of satisfactory standard may resubmit the   35 same piece of work, while a candidate who has reached a satisfactory standard on the assignments or written examinations will not be required to retake that part of the examination.

Contemporary Chinese Studies

1. Each candidate will be required to follow a course of instruction in   40 Contemporary Chinese Studies for three terms.

2. Candidates will present themselves for examination in the core course Study of Contemporary China at the beginning of Hilary Term. Candidates who satisfy the examiners in this compulsory paper will be permitted to submit a 10,000 word dissertation on an approved topic.   45

3. Candidates will choose two optional papers among the following:

    i. Examination papers as part of option courses from the M.Sc. in Contemporary Chinese Studies or from another Master's (M.Phil., M.Sc., or M.St.) degree programme in the University. A list of papers approved for this purpose by the Contemporary Chinese Studies Management Committee will be available from the Course Director. Students are free to elect any one of these papers in consultation with their supervisor, and must do so by filling out the examination entry form. The examiners may, at their discretion, either require candidates to sit the standard examination paper for this elective paper, or set a paper specifically for students on the M.Sc. in Contemporary Chinese Studies.

  ii. Students may elect a modern Chinese language paper at the appropriate level to be determined by the language teaching staff at the Faculty of Oriental Studies at the start of the academic year. The examination paper will consist of both a written and an oral part.

4. Candidates who have elected the Upper Intermediate Chinese Language option course will be required to submit translation and comprehension course work throughout the academic year. Full details and submission dates will be provided in the course handbook.

  5. In addition, all candidates will be required to undertake the following assessment:

   (i) Research Methods for Area Studies: a series of assignments and/or unseen written examinations as specified by the teaching committee for the M.Sc. in Contemporary Chinese Studies. The forms of assessment, and the dates and times of submission, where applicable, will be notified to students by not later than Friday of noughth week of Michaelmas Full Term.

   (ii) One 10,000 word dissertation: the title of the dissertation must be approved by the Director of Graduate Studies not later than 12 noon on Wednesday of the ninth week of Michaelmas Term in the academic year in which the examination is taken. The dissertation must be submitted not later than 12 noon on Friday of sixth week of Trinity Term in the academic year in which the examination is taken. The dissertation must be accompanied by a statement that the dissertation is the candidate's own work except where otherwise indicated. Two typewritten or word processed copies of each of the items of written work detailed in 5 (i)-(ii) above must be delivered to the Examination School, addressed to the Chair of Examiners for the M.Sc. in Contemporary Chinese Studies, c/o the Examination Schools, High Street, Oxford at the times and days specified.

6. A candidate who fails the examination will be permitted to retake it on one further occasion within six terms of his or her initial registration. The candidate will be permitted to resubmit the same item or items of written work that reached a satisfactory standard.

7. Candidates may be required to attend an oral examination on any part of the examination.

8. The examiners may award a distinction for excellence in the whole examination.

Schedule

The structure of the course is as follows:

  (*a*) Compulsory Core course on The Study of Contemporary China

  (*b*) Compulsory Core course in Research Methods for Area Studies

  (*c*) Elective papers: Candidates must choose two optional papers from a list published annually by the Contemporary Chinese Studies Management Committee. With the permission of the language teaching staff at the Faculty of Oriental Studies, the student can elect an appropriate language option as one of the two optional papers.

Contemporary India

1. Each candidate will be required to follow a course of instruction in Contemporary India for three terms. Candidates must attend and satisfactorily complete the Induction Programme and the designated coursework for each compulsory module, specifically the 2,500 word essay per module. Candidates must also attend the course of lectures and classes for the Research Methods course.

2. Candidates will be required to present themselves for examination in two compulsory papers in Themes in Contemporary India at the end of Trinity Term of the year of registration.

3. In addition, all candidates will be required to undertake the following assessment:

(i) Research Methods a series of assignments and/or unseen written examinations as specified by the teaching committee for the M.Sc. in Contemporary India. The forms of assessment, and the dates and times of submission, where applicable, will be notified to students by not later than Friday of noughth week of Michaelmas Full Term.

(ii) Critical theory of India essay: one 5,000 word essay on a topic in comparative theory, epistemology or historiography to be submitted no later than 12 noon on the Monday of the third week of Trinity Term in the year in which the examination is taken.

(iii) One 10,000 word dissertation: the title of the dissertation must be approved by the Director of Graduate Studies not later than 12 noon on Friday of third week of Hilary Full Term. The dissertation must be submitted not later than 12 noon on Monday of seventh week of Trinity Full Term in the year in which the examination is taken.

Two typewritten or word processed copies of each of the items of written work detailed in 3 (i)-(iii) above must be accompanied by a statement that the submission is the candidate's own work except where otherwise indicated, and be delivered to the Examinations Schools, addressed to the Chair of Examiners for the M.Sc. in Contemporary India, c/o the Examination Schools, High Street, Oxford at the times and days specified.

An identical electronic copy in word format of all submissions must be submitted to the Programme Administrator on or before the deadline.

4. A candidate who fails the examination will be permitted to retake it on one further occasion within six terms of his or her initial registration. The candidate will be permitted to resubmit the same item or items of written work that did not reach a satisfactory standard.

5. The examiners may award a distinction for excellence in the whole examination.

Schedule

The structure of the course is as follows:

(*a*) *Core course in Themes in Contemporary India*

  i. Politics, International Relations and Political Economy

  ii. Society and Culture, Human Development and Environment

(*b*) *Core course in Research Methods*

Criminology and Criminal Justice

1. Every candidate must follow, for at least three terms, a course of instruction in Criminology and Criminal Justice.

2. There shall be a Board of Studies for the course, to be chaired by the Director of Graduate Studies for Criminology and also comprising all the members of the Board of Examiners for the Master of Science in Criminology and Criminal Justice for the current year, the Director or Assistant Director of the Centre for Criminology and a student representative (the latter for open business only).

3. The course will consist of four elements: core course in Explanation and Understanding in Criminology (Michaelmas Term) and Understanding Criminal Justice (Hilary Term); the course Research Design and Data Collection (Michaelmas Term); options; and dissertation. The core course will run for six weeks throughout the first two terms (Michaelmas and Hilary). The Research Design and Data Collection course runs for six weeks in the first term (Michaelmas). Options will run for six weeks in each term (Michaelmas, Hilary and Trinity). Candidates will be required to choose two options in each of the first two terms and one for the final term. The dissertation will be 8,000-10,000 words long on a topic to be agreed by the Board of Studies. The required format for this dissertation is the common format prescribed for all law theses, which is printed in the Faculty of Law's Graduate Students' Handbook.

4. The options are listed in the Schedule below.

5. Not all options will necessarily be taught or examined in any one year. Details of those which are available will be published in the Graduate Student Handbook produced by the Centre for Criminology for the year of the examination, subject to any amendment posted on the designated notice board in the Centre for Criminology by Monday of Week Minus One of the Michaelmas Term before the examination is held.

6. In addition to the options set out in the Schedule, candidates may offer any other option that may be approved from time to time by regulation published in the *Gazette* by the end of Monday of Week Minus One of the Michaelmas Term before the examination is held.

7. The course shall be assessed as follows:

(i) *Core Course*: There shall be a three-hour examination for the core course to be taken in Week Nought of Trinity Term.

(ii) *Options and Research Design and Data Collection*: Courses other than Research Design and Data Collection,Social Explanation and Data Analysis, Statistical Methods for Social Scientists, and Qualitative Methods shall be examined by means of an assessed essay of no less than 3,500 and no more than 5,000 words (inclusive of footnotes, but excluding bibliography and appendices), for which time will be set aside during the last three weeks of each term. A selection of three titles (as determined by the Board of Examiners), shall be posted on the designated noticeboard at the Centre for Criminology by noon on Friday of Week Six of the relevant term. Candidates shall be required to submit two typewritten copies of each essay to the Examination Schools, High Street, Oxford, not later than three weeks after this date, by noon.

Research Design and Data Collection, Social Explanation and Data Analysis, Statistical Methods for Social Scientists, and Qualitative Methods shall be examined by an assessed essay of 2,500 to 3,000 words (inclusive of footnotes, but excluding bibliography and appendices), to be written between Friday of Week Six and Friday of Week Nine of the term in which the course runs. A choice from three titles (as determined by the Board of Examiners) will be posted on the designated noticeboard at the Centre for Criminology by noon on Friday of Week Six of the relevant term. Candidates shall be required to submit two copies of the essay to the Examination Schools, High Street, Oxford, not later than three weeks after this date, by noon. In addition, candidates taking Research Design and Data Collection, and where relevant,

Social Explanation and Data Analysis and/or Statistical Analysis for Social Scientists and/or Qualitative Methods shall be required to complete to the satisfaction of the Course Tutor for the option a form of continuous assessment, which will be approved by the Board of Studies and the details of which will be published in the Graduate Student Handbook for the relevant year.

(iii) *Dissertation*: Two typewritten copies of the dissertation shall be submitted to the Examination Schools by noon on Friday of Week Nine of Trinity Term. One bound copy of the dissertation of each candidate who passes the examination shall be deposited in the Social Science Library, Manor Road.

8. The degree of M.Sc. shall be awarded to any candidate who achieves a mark of at least 50 per cent for (*a*) the five options and the Research Design and Data Collection course, (*b*) the core course paper, and (*c*) the dissertation, as well as satisfactory completion of the continuous assessment element of the Research Design and Data Collection, and, where relevant, those of Social Explanation and Data Analysis, and/or Statistical Methods for Social Scientists and/or Qualitative Methods.

9. The examiners may award a distinction for excellence in the whole examination.

10. Arrangements for reassessment shall be as follows:

(i) *Core Course*: Candidates who fail, or withdraw from, the core course examination may resit the examination in the Trinity Term of the following academic year. Such candidates who have completed successfully either or both of (*a*) the options and Research Design and Data Collection (i.e. have obtained an aggregate mark of 50 per cent or more) and (*b*) the dissertation, may carry forward the marks gained for the successfully completed components. Candidates may also carry forward their certificate of satisfactory completion of the continuous assessment element of Research Design and Data Collection, and, where relevant, those of Social Explanation and Data Analysis, and/or Statistical Methods for Social Scientists and/or Qualitative Methods.

(ii) *Options and Research Design and Data Collection*: Candidates who have failed to obtain an aggregate mark of 50 per cent for all assessments for the options and Research Design and Data Collection together, or who have withdrawn from any assessment, may resubmit assessments for which they obtained a mark of 49 per cent or less. Candidates may resubmit assessed essays in which they have obtained a mark of 49 per cent or less to the Examination Schools, High Street, Oxford, according to the standard timetable for submitting essays in the following academic year. Such candidates who have completed successfully (*a*) the core course examination, (*b*) the dissertation, and (*c*) any assessment for which they have received a mark of 50 per cent or more, may carry forward the marks gained for the successfully completed components. Candidates may also carry forward their certificate of satisfactory completion of the continuous assessment element of Research Design and Data Collection, and, where relevant, that of Social Explanation and Data Analysis, and/or Statistical Methods for Social Scientists and/or Qualitative Methods.

(iii) *Continuous assessment element of Research Design and Data Collection, Social Explanation and Data Analysis, Statistical Methods for Social Scientists and Qualitative Methods:* Candidates who fail to complete an assignment which forms part of the continuous assessment element of Research Design and Data Collection, Social Explanation and Data Analysis and/or Statistical Methods for Social Scientists and/or Qualitative Methods to the satisfaction of the respective Course Tutor may be required to resubmit that assignment once by noon on Friday of Week Nine of the relevant term.

(iv) *Dissertation*: Candidates who fail, or withdraw from, the dissertation may resubmit the dissertation by the required date in Trinity Term of the following academic year. Such candidates who have completed successfully (*a*) the core course and/or (*b*) the options and/or (*c*) Research Design and Data Collection, may carry forward the marks gained for the successfully completed compo-   5 nents. Candidates may also carry forward their certificate of satisfactory completion of the continuous assessment element of Research Design and Data Collection, Social Explanation and Data Analysis and/or Statistical Methods for Social Scientists and/or Qualitative Methods.

Schedule   10

Comparative Criminal Justice
Crime and the Family
Crime, Political Ideologies and Political Culture
Desistance from Crime: The Role of Criminal Justice Agencies
Human Rights and Criminal Justice   15
Law, Economics and Crime
Mafias
News Media, Crime and Policy
Policing Global Insecurities
Prisons   20
Public and Private Policing
Public Opinion, Crime and Criminal Justice
Qualitative Methods
Race and Gender
Research Design and Data Collection   25
Restorative Justice
Risk, Security and Criminal Justice
Sentencing
Social Explanation and Data Analysis
Sociology of Punishment   30
The Death Penalty
Transitional Justice
Victims
Violence and Civilisation
Youth Justice   35

Criminology and Criminal Justice (Research Methods)

1. Every candidate must follow, for at least three terms, a course of instruction in Criminology and Criminal Justice (Research Methods).

2. There shall be a Board of Studies for the course, to be chaired by the Director of Graduate Studies for Criminology and also comprising all the members of the Board of   40 Examiners for the Master of Science in Criminology and Criminal Justice (Research Methods) for the current year, the Director or Assistant Director of the Centre for Criminology and a student representative (the latter for open business only).

3. The course will consist of four components: two compulsory core courses in Explanation and Understanding in Criminology, and in Understanding Criminal Justice; four compulsory core research methods courses in Research Design and Data Collection, Social Explanation and Data Analysis, Statistical Methods for Social Scientists, and Qualitative Methods; three options; and a dissertation. The core courses will run for six weeks throughout the first two terms (Michaelmas and Hilary). Options will run for six weeks in Michaelmas Term and Trinity Term. Candidates will be required to choose one option for the first term and two options for the final term. The dissertation, which must not exceed 15,000 words and should not normally be less than 13,000 words, will be on a topic to be agreed by the Board of Studies. The required format for this dissertation is the common format prescribed for all law theses, which is printed in the Faculty of Law's Graduate Students' Handbook.

4. The options are listed in the Schedule below.

5. Not all options will necessarily be taught or examined in any one year. Details of those which are available will be published in the Graduate Student Handbook produced by the Centre for Criminology for the year of the examination, subject to any amendment posted on the designated notice board in the Centre for Criminology by Monday of Week Minus One of the Michaelmas Term before the examination is held.

6. In addition to the options set out in the Schedule, candidates may offer any other option that may be approved from time to time by regulations published in the *Gazette* by the end of Monday of Week Minus One of the Michaelmas Term before the examination is held.

7. The course shall be assessed as follows:

(i) *Core Courses in Explanation and Understanding in Criminology, and Understanding Criminal Justice*: There shall be a single three-hour examination covering both courses to be taken in Week Nought of Trinity Term.

(ii) *Core courses in Research Design and Data Collection, Social Explanation and Data Analysis, Statistical Methods for Social Scientists and Qualitative Methods*: These courses will each be examined by one written assignment of 2,500–3,000 words to be submitted by noon on Friday of Week Nine of the relevant term. In addition, candidates shall be required to complete to the satisfaction of the respective Course Tutor a form of continuous assessment, which will be approved by the Board of Studies and the details of which will be published in the Graduate Student Handbook for the relevant year.

(iii) *Options*: Each option shall be examined by means of an assessed essay of no less than 3,500 and no more than 5,000 words (inclusive of footnotes, but excluding bibliography and appendices), for which time will be set aside during the last three weeks of term. A selection of three titles (as determined by the Board of Examiners) shall be posted on the designated noticeboard at the Centre for Criminology by noon on Friday of Week Six of the relevant term. Essays should be submitted not later than three weeks after this date, by noon.

(iv) *Dissertation*: Two typewritten copies of the dissertation shall be submitted to the Examination Schools by noon on the Friday nearest to 14th September in the year in which the examination is taken. One bound copy of the dissertation of each candidate who passes the examination shall be deposited in the Bodleian Social Science Library, Manor Road.

Candidates shall be required to submit two typewritten copies of each essay and the dissertation detailed in (ii) to (iv) above to the Examination Schools, High Street, Oxford, on the dates and times specified.

8. The degree of M.Sc. shall be awarded to any candidate who achieves a mark of at least 50 per cent in all four components of the course, namely the Explanation and Understanding in Criminology, and Understanding Criminal Justice Core Courses; the Research Methods courses; the options; and the dissertation.

9. The examiners may award a distinction for excellence in the whole examination.

10. Arrangements for reassessment shall be as follows:

(i) *Core Courses in Explanation and Understanding in Criminology, and Understanding Criminal Justice*: Candidates who fail, or withdraw from, the joint examination may resit the examination in the Trinity Term of the following academic year. Such candidates who have completed successfully all or part of any of the other three components may carry forward the marks gained for the successfully completed parts of the degree.

(ii) *Research Methods courses*: Candidates who fail to obtain an aggregate average mark of 50 per cent for their assessed assignments for the Research Methods coursesin Michaelmas and Hilary Terms, or who withdraw, may resubmit those assignments in which they have received a mark of 49 per cent or less to the Examinations Schools, High Street, Oxford, according to the standard timetable for submitting essays in the following academic year. Candidates who have completed successfully all or part of any of the other three components of the degree may carry forward the marks gained for the successfully completed components.

(iii) *Options*: Candidates who have failed to obtain an aggregate average mark of 50 per cent for their assessed essays, or have withdrawn from any of the assessed essays, may resubmit those essays in which they have received a mark of 49 per cent or less to the Examination Schools, High Street, Oxford, according to the standard timetable for submitting essays in the following academic year. Candidates who have completed successfully all or part of any of the other three components of the degree may carry forward the marks gained for the successfully completed components.

(iv) *Dissertation*: Candidates who fail, or withdraw from, the dissertation may resubmit the dissertation by the required date in the following academic year. Candidates who have completed successfully all or part of any of the other three components of the degree may carry forward the marks gained for the successfully completed components.

Schedule

Comparative Criminal Justice
Crime and the Family
Crime, Political Ideologies and Political Culture
Desistance from Crime: The Role of Criminal Justice Agencies
Human Rights and Criminal Justice
Law, Economics and Crime
Mafias
News Media, Crime and Policy
Policing Global Insecurities
Prisons
Public and Private Policing
Public Opinion, Crime and Criminal Justice
Qualitative Methods
Race and Gender

Research Design and Data Collection
Restorative Justice
Risk, Security and Criminal Justice
Sentencing
Social Explanation and Data Analysis 5
Sociology of Punishment
The Death Penalty
Transitional Justice
Victims
Violence and Civilisation 10
Youth Justice

Economic and Social History

The regulations of the Board of the Faculty of History are as follows:

1. Every candidate must follow for at least three terms a course of instruction in Economic and Social History and must upon entering for the examination produce 15 from his or her society a certificate to that effect.

2. The examination will consist of the following parts:

Qualifying test

Every candidate must pass a qualifying test. The test shall consist of two courses on

(1) Methodological introduction to research in the social sciences and history. 20

(2) *Either* Quantitative methods and computer applications for historians

or A paper from another established course within the University where this would provide a more appropriate training for the candidate's dissertation focus. Such a choice will need formal approval from both the Course Director and the Chair of the Graduate Studies Committee of the Board of the Faculty of History. 25

The methodological introduction course will be assessed by a methodological essay of up to 4,000 words. Two copies of the essay must be submitted by noon on Monday of first week of Trinity Term to the Chair of Examiners for the M.Sc. in Economic and Social History, c/o Examination Schools, High Street, Oxford OX1 4BG. A quantitative methods course is assessed by an assignment to be completed over the 30 Christmas Vacation; two typewritten copies of the completed assignment must be submitted by noon on Monday of second week of Hilary Term to the Chair of Examiners for the M.Sc. in Economic and Social History at the above address. In addition, convenors of qualifying courses will confirm in writing to the Chair of Examiners not later than Friday of eighth week of Hilary Term the candidates' 35 satisfactory participation in their classes, including the completion of any assignments for the weekly sessions. Any approved alternative qualifying course will be assessed within the format and timetable of the paper's parent course. No candidate who has failed the qualifying test of two courses will be permitted to supplicate for the degree. Candidates who fail a qualifying course once will be permitted to take it 40 again, not later than one year after the initial attempt.

Final examination

The examination shall consist of two papers and a dissertation.

Candidates must take at least one of their papers as a three-hour written examination. For the remaining paper candidates must choose to be assessed either by written 45 examination or by two 5,000 word essays. Essays may be only submitted in lieu of written papers for subjects in Schedule I below ('Advanced Papers for M.Phil. and

M.Sc. in Economic and Social History') or for other papers permitted in Schedule II below where similar provision exists in the regulations for those examinations. The essays must be the work of the candidates alone and they must not consult any other person including their supervisors in any way concerning the method of handling the themes chosen. The themes chosen by the candidate must be submitted for approval by the chair of examiners by the examination entry date. Candidates will be informed within two weeks, by means of a letter directed to their colleges, whether the topics they have submitted have been approved. The finished essays must be delivered by the candidate to the Examination Schools, High Street, Oxford, by noon on Monday of sixth week of Trinity Full Term. The essays must be presented in proper scholarly form, and two typed copies of each must be submitted.

I. One advanced paper selected from Schedule I below.

II. *Either* (i) one paper in a relevant discipline or skill or sources or methods selected from Schedule II below;

or (ii) a second advanced paper selected from Schedule I or from any additional list of papers for the M.Phil. and M.Sc. in Economic and Social History approved by the Graduate Studies Committee of the Board of the Faculty of History and published in the definitive list of Advanced Papers as set out in Schedule I.

III. A dissertation of not more than 15,000 words, including appendices but excluding bibliography, on a topic approved by the candidate's supervisor. The dissertation must be delivered not later than noon on the last Monday in September of the year in which the examination is taken to the Examination Schools, High Street, Oxford. Dissertations submitted must not exceed the permitted length. If they do the examiners will reduce the marks awarded. The presentation and footnotes should comply with the requirements specified in the Regulations of the Education Committee for the degrees of M.Litt. and D.Phil. and follow the *Conventions for the presentation of dissertations and theses* of the Board of the Faculty of History.

Each dissertation must include a short abstract which concisely summarises its scope and principal arguments, in about 300 words.

Candidates must submit by the specified date three copies of their dissertation. These must be securely and firmly bound in either hard or soft covers.

3. The examiners will permit the use of any hand-held pocket calculator subject to the conditions set out below under the heading 'Use of calculators in examinations' in the *Regulations for the Conduct of University Examinations*.

4. The examiners may award a distinction for excellence in the whole examination.

5. A candidate who fails the examination will be permitted to re-take it on one further occasion only, not later than one year after the initial attempt.

Such a candidate whose dissertation has been of satisfactory standard may re-submit the same piece of work, while a candidate who has reached a satisfactory standard on the written papers will not be required to re-take that part of the examination.

Schedule I

Advanced Papers for the M.Phil. and M.Sc. in Economic and Social History
A broad range of the course resources are shared with the corresponding courses in History of Science, Medicine, and Technology, and Advanced Papers are therefore available in the subject areas listed here.

1. Economic and business history
2. History of science and technology
3. Social history

4. Historical demography

5. History of medicine

A descriptive list of Advanced Papers will be published by the Board of the Faculty of History in September for the academic year ahead (not all options may be available in every year). The definitive list of the titles of Advanced Papers for any one year will be circulated to candidates and their supervisors and posted on the Faculty notice board not later than Friday of third week of Michaelmas Term.

Schedule II

The paper in a relevant discipline or skill may be:

1. One of the papers from the M.Phil. in Sociology or in Comparative Social Policy.

2. One suitable paper from another Master's degree under the auspices of the Faculty of History approved from time to time by the Graduate Studies Committee of the Board of the Faculty of History.

3. One suitable paper in a related skill or discipline other than those specified in paragraphs 1 to 2 above on the recommendation of the candidate's supervisor and endorsed by the Course Director.

Choices under Schedule II have to be approved by the chair of the Graduate Studies Committee of the Board of the Faculty of History not later than Monday of the fourth week of Michaelmas Term. Candidates wishing to take a paper under 1 or 3 will also need the approval of the appropriate course convenor and the Graduate Studies Committee of the relevant faculty board or inter-faculty committee who need to be satisfied that each candidate has an adequate background in the subject. Not all options may be available in any one year.

Economics for Development

1. Every candidate for the M.Sc. must follow a course of instruction in Economics for Development for at least three terms. Candidates will, when entering for the examination, be required to produce a certificate from their society to this effect.

2. The examination will consist of:

(*a*) the following written papers, the syllabuses for which are given in the schedule:

(i) Economic Theory

(ii) Development Economics

(iii) Quantitative Methods

(*b*) an extended essay.

The extended essay shall be on a topic falling within the general field of development economics. The essay topic shall be selected by the student in consultation with the supervisor, and approved by the Course Director by the end of the first week of the Trinity Full Term in which the examination is taken. The maximum length and form of the extended essay and instructions for submission will be communicated to candidates by the Chair of Examiners.

3. The candidate may also be examined orally.

4. The examiners may award a distinction for excellence in the whole examination.

Schedule

(i) *Economic Theory*

Questions will be set on aspects of microeconomic theory, macroeconomic theory and international trade central to the study of economic development. Full details of course content and structure will be provided in the *M.Sc. Economics for*

Development Handbook published at the beginning of Michaelmas Full Term of the academic year in which the examination is taken.

(ii) *Development Economics*

Questions will be set on topics in development economics from a series of taught modules. The modules offered, which may vary from year to year, will be listed in the *M.Sc. Economics for Development Handbook* issued at the beginning of Michaelmas Full Term of the academic year in which the examination is taken.

(iii) *Quantitative Methods*

Questions will be set on the theory and practice of quantitative methods used in the study of economic development. Full details of course content and structure will be provided in the *M.Sc. Economics for Development Handbook* published at the beginning of Michaelmas Full Term of the academic year in which the examination is taken.

Education

1. Candidates must follow for three terms a course of instruction in Education, specialising in one of the following pathways: Comparative and International Education, Higher Education, Learning and Technology, Child Development and Education, or Research Design and Methodology. The examination shall consist of six one-term papers and a dissertation.

2. Part 1 of the course consists of six papers. Candidates take a combination of required pathway-specific core papers and option papers, as determined in advance by each pathway convenor. Candidates will be informed of the available options, along with the assessment requirement, by Friday of 0th week of Michaelmas Term in the year in which the examination is taken. On some pathways, students are also required to successfully complete a research internship.

3. Exceptionally, candidates may offer one paper from a relevant masters degree in another department in the University, in place of one option paper, subject to permission from the relevant pathway convenor and the Education Graduate Studies Committee. Applications to take such a paper must normally be made by Friday of the fifth week of Michaelmas Term.

4. Papers are normally assessed by one or more coursework assignments totalling no more than 3,000 words (inclusive of footnotes but excluding bibliography and appendices). All such assignments must be uploaded to the Assignments section of the Higher Degrees Weblearn site by the times and dates specified at the start of the course. Each submission must be accompanied by a declaration indicating that it is the candidate's own work. Exceptionally, candidates are assessed by unseen examination.

5. For Part 2 of the course, candidates will be required to submit a dissertation of 15,000–20,000 words (including footnotes/endnotes but excluding appendices and references or bibliography), the title to be selected in consultation with the supervisor, on a topic relevant to the pathway being followed. The subject and title selected by the candidate must be approved by the Departmental Board not later than the first day of the fifth week in Hilary Term in the year in which the written examination is taken.

6. Three word-processed or printed copies of the dissertation must be delivered to the Chair of Examiners, M.Sc. Education, c/o Examination Schools, High Street, Oxford, not later than noon on the second Friday in August in the year in which the written examination is taken. One copy should be hard bound and two soft bound. The two soft bound copies should be anonymous except for the candidate number. The hard bound copy of the dissertation of each candidate who passes the examination shall be retained by the department for deposit in the departmental library. Each

submission must be accompanied by a declaration indicating that it is the candidate's own work. Candidates are also required to upload an electronic copy.

7. Every candidate will be required to satisfy the examiners in the following: (i) Satisfactory attendance at the appropriate classroombased courses; (ii) Satisfactory performance in both Part 1 and Part 2.

8. Candidates may also be required to attend an oral examination. The oral examination may be on the candidate's written papers, dissertation, or both. Candidates shall be deemed to have passed the examination if they have satisfied the examiners in both Part 1 and Part 2. If Part 1 is failed, the candidate may retake the whole examination of Part 1 one further time on the next occasion when this is examined. If Part 2 is failed the candidate may resubmit the dissertation one further time on the next occasion when this is examined.

9. The examiners may award a distinction for excellence in the whole examination.

Endovascular Neurosurgery (Interventional Neuroradiology)

1. The Medical Sciences Board shall elect for the supervision of the course an Organising Committee which shall have the power to arrange lectures and other instruction.

2. Every candidate must follow for at least three terms or, in the case for part-time students, for at least six terms, a course of instruction in Endovascular Neurosurgery (Interventional Neuroradiology).

3. Candidates will be required to present themselves for written and oral examination and to submit a logbook and a dissertation in prescribed form on an approved topic.

4. Candidates will be required to take three papers of three hours each:

Paper 1 Pathology, Physiology and Anatomy relevant to Endovascular Neurosurgery and Interventional Neuroradiology

Paper 2 Diagnosis in Endovascular Neurosurgery and Interventional Neuroradiology

Paper 3 Interventional Neuroradiological Techniques

Examination questions will reflect aspects of the subject as described in the schedule.

5. Candidates must be registered with the General Medical Council, hold an appropriate contract with the National Health Service, and have had appropriate experience in Diagnostic Radiology and/or Neurosurgery.

6. Each candidate will be required to submit a logbook to the Course Director by the end of their second term, or, in the case of part-time students, by the end of their fourth term. The logbook will subsequently be submitted to the examiners as part of the candidate's whole examination.

7. Each candidate will be required to submit a dissertation of no more than 15,000 words on a subject selected in consultation with the candidate's supervisor and approved by the Organising Committee. The dissertation may vary from an account of original research work to a survey of the literature. Dissertations which reproduce substantially work submitted in the other written assignments will not be admissible.

8. Three word-processed and appropriately bound copies of the dissertation must be delivered to the Course Director by a date prescribed by the examiners, together with the logbook as described above. The examiners shall retain two copies of the dissertation of each candidate who passes the examination, for deposit in the departmental library.

9. An oral examination will be held and this may include questions on the candidate's dissertation, logbook, or written papers.

10. The examiners may award a distinction for excellence in the whole examination.

Schedule

Paper 1: Pathology, Physiology, and Anatomy relevant to Endovascular Neurosurgery and Interventional Radiology

Pathology of lesions amenable to interventional neuroradiological techniques. The natural history of such conditions and the indications for interventional measures. Anatomy of the central nervous system with special reference to vascular anatomy including common variations to the normal pattern. The embryology and phylogeny of the blood supply of the head and spine. Vascular physiology with special reference to the cerebral and spinal circulations. Normal and potential sites of collateral circulation. Endovascular routes to lesion of the head and spine.

Paper 2: Diagnosis in Endovascular Neurosurgery and Interventional Neuroradiology

The clinical and radiological diagnosis of conditions amenable to interventional neuroradiological techniques including recognition of common symptoms and signs associated with such conditions.

Radiological and other imaging techniques for localisation and evaluation of cerebral and spinal lesion, including angiography, myelography, CT and MR scanning, Doppler ultrasound (transcranial and intra-operative), and the use of radio-pharmaceuticals. Electrophysiological and cerebral blood flow measurement techniques as well as neurological and cardiovascular monitoring pertinent to interventional neuroradiological procedures.

Paper 3: Interventional Neuroradiological Techniques

Interventional techniques for biopsy, embolisation, thrombolysis, and angioplasty. Delivery systems: their construction and applications. Embolisation materials including balloons, coils, stents, particulate and liquid embolic agents and their advantages and disadvantages for different applications. Pre-and post-procedural precautions, including indications for treatment, informed consent, and the recognition and management of complications.

The official name, constitution pharmacology, modes of administration, clinical agents used in interventional neuroradiological techniques. Sedation and the provision of analgesia during procedures. In particular the use of anticoagulation, fibrinolytic, and anticonvulsant agents.

English Local History

1. Every candidate must follow for at least six terms a part-time course of instruction in English Local History and must upon entering for examination produce from his or her society a certificate to that effect.

2. The examination will consist of the following parts:

Qualifying test

Every candidate must pass a qualifying test. The test shall consist of the satisfactory completion of a course on:

Concepts and methods: an introduction to research in local history

The organisers of the course shall, not later than the end of the Hilary Term in the first year of the course submit to the examiners a list of candidates who have satisfactorily completed the qualifying course. No candidate who has failed the qualifying test will be permitted to supplicate for the degree. Candidates who fail the qualifying course once will be permitted to take it again, not later than one year after the initial attempt.

Final Examinations

The final examination shall consist of three parts:

A. *Skills for local history*

Every candidate must submit two written assignments of no more than 2,500 words in length for each of two courses from the list below:

(1) Sources, Methods and Foundations in Medieval Local History

(2) Sources, Methods and Foundations in Early Modern Local History   5

(3) Sources, Methods and Foundations in Modern Local History

B. *Advanced papers*

Every candidate must follow either

(1) two advanced papers from Schedule A below,

or   10

(2) one advanced paper from Schedule A below and a second paper from Schedule B, which consists of papers also offered as part of the MSc in Economic and Social History. Other Schedule B papers may be added subject to the approval of the Chair of the Graduate Studies Committee of the History Faculty Board and of the Board of Studies of the Committee for Continuing Education.   15

Each candidate will submit two written assignments of not more than 5,000 words in length for each paper. Some Schedule B papers may be assessed by a three hour unseen examination.

C. *Dissertation*

A dissertation of not more than 15,000 words, including appendices but excluding   20
bibliography, on a topic approved by the candidate's supervisor. The dissertation must be delivered not later than noon on the last Monday in September of the second year of the course to the Chair of Examiners for the M.Sc. in Local History, c/o Examination Schools, High Street, Oxford.

Schedule A   25

Advanced Papers are available in the following areas:

1. The development of rural society

2. Social history

3. Urban history

4. History of religion   30

5. Architecture and local society

Schedule B

Advanced Papers are available in the following areas:

1. Economic and business history

2. History of science and technology   35

3. Social history

4. Historical demography

5. History of medicine

A list of Advanced Papers will be published by the Board of Studies for the M.Sc. in English Local History in September for the academic year ahead (not all options   40
may be available in every year). The definitive list of the titles of Advanced Papers for any one year will be circulated to candidates and their supervisors not later than Friday of the third week of Michaelmas Term. Teaching for the Advanced Papers will take place in Hilary Term.

3. The examiners will permit the use of any hand-held pocket calculator subject to   45
the conditions set out in *Regulations for the Conduct of University Examinations*.

4. Each candidate must attend an oral examination when required to do so by the examiners.

5. The examiners may award a distinction for excellence in the whole examination.

6. A candidate who fails an advanced paper, or whose dissertation fails to satisfy the examiners, may be permitted to retake the paper, or resubmit the dissertation, on one further occasion only, not later than one year after the initial attempt.

Environmental Change and Management

1. The Social Sciences Divisional Board shall elect for the supervision of the course a Standing Committee. The Course Director will be responsible to the Standing Committee.

2. Candidates must follow a course of instruction in Environmental Change and Management for at least three terms, and will, when entering for the examination be required to produce a certificate from the Course Director to this effect.

3. The examination will consist of:

   (i) a written examination of three papers on the syllabus described in the schedule:

   (ii) a dissertation on a subject selected in consultation with the supervisor and Course Director and approved by the Standing Committee.

   (iii) two assessed essays based on Elective courses.

4. Candidates must submit to the Course Director by the end of the Hilary Term in the year in which they enter the examination, the title and a brief statement of the form and scope of their dissertation, together with the name of a person who has agreed to act as their supervisor during preparation of the dissertation.

5. The dissertation shall be of maximum length 15,000 words excluding abstract, appendices and references. The dissertation shall be accompanied by an abstract not exceeding 150 words.

6. Two typewritten or printed copies of the dissertation must arrive, not later than noon on the first weekday of September in the year in which the written examination is taken, to the M.Sc. Examiners (Environmental Change and Management), c/o Examination Schools, High Street, Oxford OX1 4BG. The examiners may retain one copy of the dissertation of each candidate who passes the examination for deposit in an appropriate department library.

7. In the written examination the examiners will permit the use of any hand-held pocket calculators subject to the conditions set out under the heading 'Use of calculators in examinations' in the *Regulations for the Conduct of University Examinations*.

8. The examiners may also examine any candidate viva voce on the candidate's written papers, dissertation, or both.

9. Arrangements for reassessment shall be specified by the Standing Committee and published in the course handbook.

10. The examiners may award a distinction for excellence in the whole examination.

Schedule

(i) *Understanding environmental change*. Candidates will be expected to have integrative knowledge of the critical issues in current and future environmental change as applied to terrestrial, aquatic, and atmospheric systems. Forces driving change including resource scarcity, competition, population, land use, pollution, technological change, and climatic factors.

(ii) *Responding to environmental change.* Candidates will be expected to have knowledge of governance, economics, ethics, law, and sociocultural dimensions of mitigating and adapting to environmental change. Strategies appropriate for the management of changing environments.

(iii) *Methods and techniques for environmental management.* Candidates will be expected to have knowledge of methods for environmental appraisal and management. These may include: basic computing and modelling, experimental design, data acquisition and handling; remote sensing and GIS; methods of ecological economic and social analysis.

(iv) *Electives.* Candidates will be expected to show advanced knowledge of two of the elective courses on offer in any one year.

Evidence-Based Health Care

(Old regulations for students registered on the MSc EBHC before 1 October 2012)

1. The Divisional Board of Medical Sciences, jointly with the Continuing Education Board, shall elect for the supervision of the course a Standing Committee, which shall have the power to arrange lectures and other instruction.

2. Every candidate must follow for at least three and at most twelve terms a part-time course of instruction in the theory and practice of Evidence-Based Health Care, which shall normally take place over a period of no more than six years.

3. Every candidate will be required to satisfy the examiners in the following:

(a) attendance at both of the modules listed in Schedule A (below);

(b) attendance at four of the modules listed in Schedule B (below);

(c) six written assignments, usually of no more than 5,000 words, one on each of the modules from 3(a) and 3(b) above;

(d) a dissertation of not more than 30,000 words (including appendices and footnotes but excluding bibliography), on a subject selected by the candidate in consultation with the supervisor and approved by the Standing Committee.

The assessed work set out in clause 3(c) shall be forwarded to the examiners c/o Registry, Department for Continuing Education, 1 Wellington Square, Oxford OX1 2JA, for consideration by such date as the examiners shall determine and of which they shall notify candidates. The dissertation set out in clause 3(d) shall be forwarded to the examiners c/o Examination Schools, High Street, Oxford OX1 4BG for consideration by such date as the examiners shall determine and of which they shall notify candidates.

4. Candidates may be required to attend a viva voce examination at the end of the course of studies at the discretion of the examiners.

5. The examiners may award a distinction to candidates for the M.Sc.

6. Candidates who fail to satisfy the examiners in any of the six assignments under 3(c) may be permitted, normally within one year of the original failure, to resubmit work in respect of the part or parts they have failed on not more than one occasion for each assignment without being required to repeat attendance at the relevant module or modules under 3(a) and/or 3(b). Candidates who fail to satisfy the examiners under 3(d) may be permitted to resubmit work in respect of the part or parts of the examination which they have failed, for examination on not more than one occasion which shall normally be within one year of the original failure.

7. The Standing Committee shall have the discretion to permit any candidate to be exempted, in exceptional circumstances, from attendance at a module under 3(a) or 3(b) and from submitting an assignment required under 3(c) above, provided that the Standing Committee is satisfied that such a candidate has undertaken equivalent study, or has appropriate work experience to an equivalent standard.

Schedule A

M1: Practice of EBHC

M2: Introduction to Study Design and Research Methods

Schedule B

M3: Knowledge into Action

M4: Clinical Epidemiology

M5: Evidence-Based Diagnosis and Screening

M6: Systematic Reviews

M7: Randomised Control Trials

M8: Essential Medical Statistics

M9: Patient-Based Evidence

M10: Ethics in Health Care

M11: Qualitative Research Methods

M12: Evidence-Based Dentistry

M13: Introduction to Statistics in Health Care Research

Any other module as defined by the Programme Director and approved by the Standing Committee.

Postgraduate Programme in Evidence-Based Health Care Studies

Postgraduate Programme in Evidence-Based Health Care Studies (new regulations for students registering on any of the awards listed from 1 October 2012 and available to existing students)

A. Definition of the Programme

1. The Continuing Education Board and the Medical Sciences Board shall jointly offer a Programme in Evidence-Based Health Care Studies at postgraduate level.

2. The Continuing Education Board and the Medical Sciences Board shall jointly elect for the supervision of the Programme a Standing Committee which shall have the power to arrange lectures and other instruction.

3. The subject of the Programme shall be Evidence-Based Health Care Studies.

4. The policy of the Continuing Education Board on variable intensity part-time postgraduate study applies to this Programme.

5. The following awards shall be available within the Programme:
   i. MSc in Evidence-Based Health Care
   ii. Postgraduate Diploma in Evidence-Based Health Care
   iii. Postgraduate Certificate in Evidence-Based Health Care
   iv. Postgraduate Diploma in Health Research
   v. Postgraduate Certificate in Health Research

B. Progression

6. Students admitted to the Programme with the intention of studying towards the award of the M.Sc. are required to matriculate, involving admission by a college of the University. Students admitted to the Programme intending to study towards a Postgraduate Certificate or Postgraduate Diploma who subsequently apply for admission to the M.Sc. will be required at that point to matriculate and to be admitted by a college.

7. Students who have satisfied the requirements for the award of the Postgraduate Certificate or the Postgraduate Diploma and who do not wish to continue their studies may end their registration at that point and be awarded the Postgraduate Certificate or Postgraduate Diploma as the case may be.

C. Duration

8. The minimum period of registration on the Programme shall be three terms.

9. The maximum period of registration shall be six terms for each of the Postgraduate Certificates, nine terms for each of the Postgraduate Diplomas and twelve terms for the MSc.

10. Candidates may be permitted in certain circumstances to suspend status, for a maximum of six terms. Any such period shall not count to the maximum or minimum permitted period of registration and no fee liability will be incurred during such periods.

D. Study criteria for eligibility for awards

11. The modules available in the Programme are specified in the Schedule below. Not all modules are available for each award. Every candidate for a given award will be required to satisfy the examiners in the following:

i. *M.Sc. in Evidence-Based Health Care*
   (i) attendance at both of modules (i) and (ii);
   (ii) attendance at any four of modules (iii) to (xiii) or (xx) of the schedule at H;
   (iii) submission of the required assessed work relating to each of the six modules in (i) and (ii) above, which shall be of not more than 4,000 words per module;
   (iv) submission of a dissertation of not more than 15,000 words (including tables, appendices and footnotes but excluding reference list), on a subject selected by the candidate in consultation with the supervisor and approved by the Standing Committee. Approval must be sought no later than the first day of the ninth term of registration. The dissertation must be submitted within three terms of the date of approval, notwithstanding the maximum permitted period of registration.

ii. *Postgraduate Diploma in Evidence-Based Health Care*
   (i) attendance at both of modules (i) and (ii);
   (ii) attendance at any four of modules (iii) to (xiii) or (xx) of the schedule at H;
   (iii) submission of the required assessed work relating to each of the six modules in (i) and (ii) above, which shall be of not more than 4,000 words per module.

iii. *Postgraduate Certificate in Evidence-Based Health Care*
   (i) attendance at both of modules (i) and (ii);
   (ii) attendance at any one of modules (iii) to (xiii) or(xx) of the schedule at H;
   (iii) submission of the required assessed work relating to each of the three modules in (i) and (ii) above, which shall be of not more than 4,000 words per module.

iv. *Postgraduate Diploma in Health Research*
   (i) attendance at modules (i) and (ii);
   (ii) attendance at any three of modules (iii) to (xi), or (xx) of the schedule at H, or of the modules indicated as available in the regulations for the MSc in Experimental Therapeutics;
   (iii) attendance at one additional module taken from under (ii) above, or (xii) of the schedule at H, or from those indicated in the regulations for the MSc in Surgical Science and Practice;
   (iv) submission of the required assessed work, which shall be of not more than 4,000 words, relating to each of the six modules in (i) and (ii) and (iii) above.

v. *Postgraduate Certificate in Health Research*
   (i) attendance at modules (i) and (ii);

(ii) attendance at one of modules (iii) to(x) in the schedule at H, or one of the modules indicated as available from the regulations for the MSc in Experimental Therapeutics;

(iii) submission of the required assessed work, which shall be of not more than 4,000 words, relating to each of the three modules taken under (i) and (ii) above.

12. Assignments shall be forwarded (usually electronically via a specified online submission system) to the examiners c/o Registry, Department for Continuing Education, 1 Wellington Square, Oxford OX1 2JA, for consideration by such dates as the examiners shall determine and of which they shall notify candidates. Dissertations shall be forwarded to the Examiners c/o Examination Schools High Street Oxford OX1 4BG for consideration by such dates as the examiners shall determine and of which they shall notify candidates.

Assignments and dissertations must be accompanied by a statement that they are the candidate's work except where otherwise indicated.

13. Provided the Standing Committee is satisfied that a student on the Programme has undertaken equivalent study, of an appropriate standard, normally at another institution of higher education, or has appropriate work experience to an equivalent standard, the committee shall have the discretion to permit the candidate to be exempted from attendance and the submission of a written assignment in respect of one module for a Postgraduate Certificate, two modules for a Postgraduate Diploma and three modules for the M.Sc. In exercising this discretion the Standing Committee shall have consideration to the length of time that has elapsed since the study or work experience was undertaken.

E. The Examinations

14. Students on the Register shall enter for the examination for the award of the M.Sc. or the Postgraduate Diploma or the Postgraduate Certificate in Evidence-Based Health Care or the award of the Postgraduate Diploma or the Postgraduate Certificate in Health Research.

15. Candidates are required to attend a viva voce examination at the end of the course of studies leading to each award unless dispensed by the examiners.

16. The examiners may award a distinction for excellence in the overall examination for each award.

17. Candidates who fail to satisfy the examiners in any of the assignments or the dissertation under 11 above may be permitted, normally within one year of the original failure, to resubmit work in respect of the part or parts they have failed on not more than one occasion for each assignment without being required to repeat attendance at the relevant module or modules.

F. Prior Undertaking of modules for credit

18. The Standing Committee shall have the discretion to deem satisfactory completion of a module including the associated assessment prior to registration for an award listed under 5i–v above as having met the attendance and examination requirements in respect of that module under 11 above. Such discretion will normally only be exercised if the time elapsed between commencement of the accredited module concerned and registration for the award is not more than two years.

19. The maximum number of modules taken prior to registration for an award that can contribute to the achievement of the award shall be one for the Postgraduate Certificate, three for either of the Postgraduate Diplomas and three for the MSc.

G. Subsuming of previous modules and awards under the Programme

20. If any student who has previously successfully completed the Postgraduate Certificate and ended their registration on the Programme subsequently is re-admitted to another award listed under 5i–iv, the Standing Committee shall have the

discretion to deem satisfactory completion of modules within the Postgraduate
Certificate as having met the attendance and examination requirements in respect
of the modules under 11 above. Such discretion will normally only be exercised if the
time elapsed between first registration on a module contributing to the Postgraduate
Certificate and registration for the higher award is not more than two years.   5

21. If any student who has previously successfully completed the Postgraduate
Diploma and ended their registration on the Programme subsequently is re-admitted
to the M.Sc., the Standing Committee shall have the discretion to deem satisfactory
completion of modules within the Postgraduate Diploma as having met the attendance and examination requirements in respect of the modules under 11 above. Such   10
discretion will normally only be exercised if the time elapsed between first registration
on a module contributing to the Postgraduate Diploma and registering for the MSc is
not more than two years.

22. If a student who has been awarded a Postgraduate Diploma or Postgraduate
Certificate is subsequently awarded a higher award then the MSc or Postgraduate   15
Diploma will subsume the lower award.

H. Schedule of Modules
    (i) Practice of Evidence-Based Health Care
    (ii) Introduction to Study Design and Research Methods
    (iii) Ethics for Biosciences   20
    (iv) Knowledge into Action
    (v) Clinical Epidemiology
    (vi) Evidence-Based Diagnosis and Screening
    (vii) Introduction to Statistics for Health Care Research
    (viii) Systematic Reviews   25
    (ix) Randomized Control Trials
    (x) Qualitative Research Methods
    (xi) Essential Medical Statistics
    (xii) Teaching Evidence-Based Practice
    (xiii) The History and Philosophy of Evidence-Based Health Care   30
    (xx) Any other module as defined by the Programme Director and approved by
the Standing Committee.
Additional modules available (as specified above) from the regulations for the MSc in
Experimental Therapeutics
Structure of clinical trials and experimental therapeutics   35
Drug development, pharmacokinetics and imaging
Pharmacodynamics, biomarkers and personalised therapy
Adverse drug reactions, drug interactions, and pharmacovigilance
How to do research on therapeutic interventions: protocol preparation
Biological therapeutics   40
Additional modules available (as specified above) from the regulations for the MSc in
Surgical Science and Practice
Human factors, teamwork and communication
Becoming a medical educator
Quality improvement science and systems analysis   45

Evidence-Based Social Intervention
    1. Candidates must follow for at least three terms a course of instruction in
Evidence-Based Social Intervention.

    2. Every candidate will be required to satisfy the examiners in the following:
       (i) A compulsory core paper, Evidence-Based Interventions;   50

   (ii) A compulsory Research Methods paper, for which students will be examined on the basis of a methods work book and an essay of up to 2,500 words;

   (iii) One Option paper;

   (iv) A thesis of not more than 10,000 words, on a topic related to, and attentive to the methods of, Evidence-Based Social Intervention and decided jointly with, and approved by, the supervisor on behalf of the Department.

3. Two printed or word-processed copies of the Research Methods essay must be delivered to the M.Sc. Examiners (Evidence-Based Social Intervention), c/o Examination Schools, High Street, Oxford OX1 4BG, no later than 12 noon on Friday of sixth week of the Trinity Term in which the examination has been taken.

4. Two printed or word-processed copies of the thesis must be delivered to the M.Sc. examiners (Evidence-Based Social Intervention), c/o Examination Schools, High Street, Oxford OX1 4BG, no later than noon on 15 August or the weekday nearest to 15 August of the year in which the examination has been taken. Successful candidates will be required to deposit a copy of their thesis in the Social Science Library.

5. A candidate who fails the examination may enter for one subsequent examination only, provided this is within six terms of his or her initial registration. A candidate who has attained a satisfactory mark in any one of the four components of the examination in 2 above will not be required to retake the component(s) concerned.

6. Each candidate must attend an oral examination when required to do so by the examiners.

7. The examiners may award a distinction for excellence in the whole examination.

Schedule

   (i) *Evidence-Based Intervention* (core course): Candidates will be expected to have a knowledge of major theories underlying evidence-based interventions. The course will introduce students to a comparative perspective and use exemplary intervention research studies to illustrate important theoretical, ethical, methodological, and practice issues.

   (ii) *Research Methods* (core course): Candidates will be expected to have a knowledge of major quantitative and qualitative techniques, and research designs for understanding social problems and evaluating interventions. There will be a particular emphasis on the appraisal and design of randomised controlled trials for evaluating social interventions.

   (iii) *Option course*: This will enable students to link evidence-based solutions to a range of social problems. Not every option will be offered in any one year, and applicants for admission will be advised of this. Areas from which options may be offered include: promoting the welfare of children and families; multicultural mental health interventions; substance misuse and offending; interventions in relation to HIV and AIDS; community work; refugees and asylum seekers; day care for young children and their families.

Experimental Therapeutics (*old regulations for students registered before 1 October 2012*)

1. The Medical Sciences Board, in consultation with the Continuing Education Board, shall elect for the supervision of the course a Standing Committee that shall have the power to arrange lectures and other instruction.

2. Every candidate must follow for at least six terms a part-time course of instruction in the theory and practice of Experimental Therapeutics, which shall normally take place over a period of two years and no more than four years.

3. Every candidate will be required to satisfy the examiners in the following:

(*a*) active participation, to the satisfaction of the Programme Director, in each of the modules listed below.

(*b*) six written assignments of not more than 5,000 words in length, one from each of the six modules specified.

(*c*) a dissertation of not more than 20,000 words (excluding tables, appendices, footnotes and bibliography), on a subject selected by the candidate in consultation with the supervisor and approved by the Standing Committee.

The assessed work set out in cl. 3(*b*) and in 3(*c*) shall be forwarded to the examiners c/o Registry, Department for Continuing Education, 1 Wellington Square, Oxford OX1 2JA, for consideration by such date as the examiners shall determine and of which they shall notify candidates. The assessed work under 3(*b*) will, in normal circumstances, be submitted through an electronic submission system.

4. Candidates may be required to attend a viva voce examination at the end of the course of studies at the discretion of the examiners.

5. The examiners may award a distinction to candidates for the M.Sc.

6. Candidates who fail to satisfy the examiners in any part of the examination may be permitted to resubmit work in respect of the part or parts of the examination that they have failed, for examination on not more than one occasion which shall normally be within one year of the original failure.

7. The Standing Committee shall have the discretion to permit any candidate to be exempted, in exceptional circumstances, from submitting an assignment of the total of six written assignments required under 3(*b*) above, provided that the Standing Committee is satisfied that such a candidate has undertaken equivalent study, or has appropriate work experience to an equivalent standard.

Schedule

(1) Structure of clinical trials and experimental therapeutics

(2) Pharmacokinetics and Drug Therapy

(3) Pharmacodynamics, Biomarkers and Personalised Therapy

(4) Adverse drug reactions, drug interactions, and pharmacovigilance

(5) How to do research on therapeutic interventions: protocol preparation

(6) Biological Therapeutics

(7) Any other module as defined by the Programme Director and approved by the Standing Committee.

Experimental Therapeutics (*new regulations for students registering from 1 October 2012 and available to existing students*)

1. The Medical Sciences Board, in consultation with the Continuing Education Board, shall elect for the supervision of the course a Standing Committee that shall have the power to arrange lectures and other instruction.

2. The course is available on a part time basis only and shall consist of instruction in the theory and practice of Experimental Therapeutics.

3. The policy of the Continuing Education Board on variable intensity part-time postgraduate study shall apply to this award.

4. The minimum period of registration for the M.Sc. course shall be three terms and the maximum period of registration shall be twelve terms.

5. Candidates may be permitted in certain circumstances to suspend status, for a maximum of six terms. Any such period shall not count to the maximum or minimum permitted period of registration and no fee liability will be incurred during such periods.   5

6. Every candidate will be required to satisfy the examiners in the following:
   (*a*) participation, to the satisfaction of the course director, in each of the modules listed below;
   (*b*) six written assignments, each of not more than 4,000 words in length, one from each of the six modules specified;   10
   (*c*) a dissertation of not more than 15,000 words (including tables, appendices, footnotes but excluding reference list) on a subject selected by the candidate in consultation with the supervisor and approved by the Standing Committee. Approval must be sought no later than the first day of the ninth term of registration. The dissertation must be submitted within three terms of the date   15
   of approval, notwithstanding the maximum permitted period of registration.

The assessed work set out in clause 6(*b* and *c*) shall be forwarded to the examiners c/o Registry, Department for Continuing Education, 1 Wellington Square, Oxford OX1 2JA, for consideration by such date as the examiners shall determine and shall notify candidates. The assessed work will, in normal circumstances, be submitted   20
through an electronic submission system.

7. Candidates may be required to attend a viva voce examination at the end of the course of studies at the discretion of the examiners.

8. The examiners may award a distinction to candidates for the M.Sc.

9. Candidates who fail to satisfy the examiners in any of the assignments or the   25
dissertation under 6 above may be permitted to resubmit work in respect of the part or parts they have failed on not more than one occasion for each assignment without being required to repeat attendance at the relevant module or modules. The resubmission shall normally be within one year of the original failure.

10. Provided the Standing Committee is satisfied that a student on the award has   30
undertaken equivalent study, of an appropriate standard, normally at another institution of higher education, or has appropriate work experience to an equivalent standard, the committee may permit the candidate to be exempted from attendance and the submission of a written assignment in respect of up to three modules. In exercising this discretion the Standing Committee shall take into consideration the   35
length of time that has elapsed since the study or work experience was undertaken.

11. The Standing Committee may deem satisfactory completion of a module (including the associated assessment) undertaken prior to registration for the award as having met the attendance and examination requirements in respect of that module. Such discretion will normally only be exercised if the time elapsed between   40
commencement of the accredited module concerned and registration for the award is not more than two years. The maximum number of modules taken prior to registration for the award that may be counted in this way shall be three.

Module Schedule

(1) Structure of clinical trials and experimental therapeutics*   45
(2) Drug development, pharmacokinetics and imaging*
(3) Pharmacodynamics, biomarkers and personalised therapy*
(4) Adverse drug reactions, drug interactions, and pharmacovigilance*
(5) How to do research on therapeutic interventions: protocol preparation*
(6) Biological therapeutics*   50

(7) Any other module as defined by the programme director and approved by the Standing Committee.[1]

* Also available to students on the PG Certificate and Diploma in Health Research

Financial Economics

1. Candidates must follow for at least three terms a course of instruction in Financial Economics. Candidates must complete:

    (*a*) all courses from the Schedule, and satisfy the examiners in the assignment and/or examination associated with each course;

    (*b*) five electives, of which one may be an individual project. Candidates must satisfy the examiners in the assignment/examination/written report associated with each course, the list of electives to be published annually by the MFE Standing Committee before the first Monday of Hilary Term. If chosen, individual project written reports to be of not more than 10,000 words. Such projects must be approved by the MFE Standing Committee;

    (*c*) candidates may be required to attend an oral examination on any of the above.

2. Assignments and written reports on projects must be presented not later than the time and date stipulated for each exercise; these will be published by the MFE Standing Committee before the first Monday of each term in which the assignment or project must be undertaken. The required number of copies must be delivered to the Examination Schools, and addressed to the Chair of Examiners for the M.Sc. in Financial Economics, c/o Examination Schools, High Street, Oxford, except in the case of practical work, which should be submitted to the Saïd Business School, Park End Street, Oxford in the format advised by the MFE Standing Committee.

3. The examiners may award a distinction for excellence in the whole examination to candidates for the Degree.

4. In exceptional circumstances, a candidate wishing to take an examination later than the one to which he or she has been admitted may do so by application to the Chair of Examiners, via his or her College Senior Tutor or Tutor for Graduates.

5. Candidates are permitted on only one occasion to resubmit or retake failed assessment items on any course on which they have failed to achieve the required standard.

Schedule

The following courses are required to be taken during Michaelmas and Hilary Terms. Details can be found in the course handbook:

    (*a*) Corporate Finance
    (*b*) Economics
    (*c*) Asset Pricing
    (*d*) Financial Econometrics.

Global Governance and Diplomacy

1. Each candidate will be required to follow a course of instruction in Global Governance and Diplomacy for three terms, and will, when they enter their names for

---

[1] The Medical Sciences Divisional Board and the Continuing Education Board elect for the supervision of the programme a Standing Committee. The Standing Committee is chaired alternately by the heads of Clinical Pharmacology and Continuing Education and the Programme Director reports to the Standing Committee.

the examination, be required to produce a certificate from their supervisors to this effect. Candidates must offer:

(i) One of two foundation papers from the following list as detailed in the Schedule:

(*a*) Global Governance

(*b*) International Diplomacy

(ii) A mandatory paper in Research Methods as detailed in the Schedule.

(iii) Two option papers to be selected from a list published annually by the Course Director by Monday of Week Nought of Michaelmas Full Term.

(iv) One 10,000–12,000 word dissertation: the title of the dissertation must be submitted to the Course Director for approval not later than 12 noon on Friday of seventh week of Michaelmas Term in the year in which the examination is taken. The dissertation must be submitted not later than 12 noon on Friday of sixth week of Trinity Full Term in the year in which the examination is taken. Two typewritten or word processed copies of the dissertation must be delivered to the Examination Schools, addressed to the Chair of Examiners for the M.Sc. in Global Governance and Diplomacy, c/o Examination Schools, High Street, Oxford at the time and date specified.

2. A candidate who fails the examination will be permitted to retake it on one further occasion within six terms of his or her initial registration. Such a candidate will be permitted to resubmit the same dissertation provided that this reached a satisfactory standard, while a candidate who has reached a satisfactory standard on one or more examination papers will not be required to retake that part of the examination.

3. Candidates may be required to attend an oral examination on any part of the examination.

4. The examiners may award a distinction for excellence in the whole examination.

Schedule

(*a*) *Global Governance*: The sources, mechanisms, processes and practices of global governance at the subnational, national, supranational, international, and public and private transnational levels: at the national, sub-national and transnational levels, the focus is on globalisation; at the supranational level of governance, on literature on regional integration; at the level of international governance, on international organisations, international regimes and multilateralism. The course includes the role of various types of public and private actors - such as states, international organisations, regional blocs, non-governmental organisations (NGOs), civil social organisations (CSOs), transnational corporations (TNCs), business associations, and trans-governmental networks-across areas such as finance, trade, development, environmental protection, and human rights. It assesses the effectiveness, accountability, and legitimacy of governance arrangements;

(*b*) *International Diplomacy*: substantive knowledge and theoretical background concerning the institutions and processes of international diplomacy.

(*c*) *Research Methods*: common research methods in the social sciences including but not limited to the topics of concept formation, social mechanisms and theory building, comparative method, case selection, historiography, ethnography, genealogy, textual content and discourse analysis, qualitative interviewing, and common quantitative analytic methods.

Global Health Science

1. The Divisional Board of Medical Sciences shall appoint for the supervision of the course an Organising Committee, which shall have the power to arrange lectures and other instruction.

2. The Organising Committee shall appoint for each candidate an academic adviser.

3. Each candidate shall follow a course of study in Global Health Science for at least three terms and for a substantial part of the three subsequent vacations, as determined by the course timetable, and will, when entering for the examination, be required to produce a certificate from their academic adviser to this effect.

4. Candidates shall be examined in all of the following ways:

  (i) A written examination paper relating to 1 and 2 of the compulsory modules.

  (ii) A written examination paper relating to 3 and 4 of the compulsory modules.

  (iii) A typewritten or printed essay of 3,000–4,000 (excluding bibliography) words on topics approved by the Organising Committee in each of the two optional modules chosen for study, as set out in the Schedule. The arrangements for approval will be notified to candidates not later than the start of Michaelmas Term of the academic year in which the examination is taken.

  (iv) A typewritten or printed dissertation of not more than 10,000 words (excluding bibliography and appendices) on the research project as set out in the Schedule below. The research project and the subject of the dissertation must have been approved by the Organising Committee. The arrangements for approval will be notified to candidates not later than the start of Michaelmas Term of the academic year in which the examination is taken.

5. Candidates may be examined viva voce and this examination will take place on dates to be determined by the examiners.

6. Three copies of each of the required written submissions must be sent to the Chair of Examiners, M.Sc. in Global Health Science, c/o Examination Schools, High Street, Oxford on the following dates:

  (*a*) The dissertation on the research project must be submitted by dates to be specified by the Organising Committee and published in the *University Gazette* not later than the start of Michaelmas Term of the academic year in which the examination is taken.

  (*b*) The essay must be submitted by dates to be specified by the Organising Committee and published in the *University Gazette* not later than the start of Michaelmas Term of the academic year in which the examination is taken.

Each submission must be accompanied by a certificate indicating that it is the candidate's own work.

The examiners may award a distinction for excellence in the whole examination.

The examiners shall retain one copy of each dissertation of each successful candidate for deposit in the Radcliffe Science library.

Schedule

I. *Compulsory modules*

  1. Challenges in global health

  2. Health policy and public health

  3. Principles of epidemiology

  4. Statistical concepts for global health

II. *Optional modules*

Students will select two modules from the following list:

5. Vaccinology
6. Tropical medicine
7. International development
8. Health economics
9. Maternal and child health
10. Health, environment and development

Modules 5–10 may not all be available every year.

III. *Research project*

A research project under the supervision of a research supervisor. Students will undertake reading and research in relation to their research project during Trinity Term. Students may elect to go on an overseas research placement during Trinity Term and the Long Vacation though this is not a requirement of the course. The subject of each student's dissertation, the overseas placement, and the supervision arrangements for each student must be approved by the Organising Committee.

History of Science, Medicine, and Technology

The regulations of the Board of the Faculty of History are as follows:

1. Every candidate must follow for at least three terms a course of instruction in History of Science, Medicine, and Technology, and must upon entering for the examination produce from his or her society a certificate to that effect.

2. The examination will consist of the following parts:

Qualifying test

Every candidate must pass a qualifying test. The test shall consist of two courses on

1. Methods and themes in the history of science and technology.

2. Methods and themes in the history of medicine.

Candidates may be advised on the basis of their prospective individual research to substitute one of the following courses from the Master of Science in Economic and Social History for (1) or (2) above:

(i) Methodological introduction to research in the social sciences and history.

(ii) Quantitative Methods and Computer Applications for Historians.

A paper from another established course within the University may be substituted for one of the standard courses where this would provide a more appropriate training for the candidate's dissertation focus. Such a choice will need formal approval from both the Course Director and the Chair of the Graduate Studies Committee of the Board of the Faculty of History.

The two methodological introduction courses will each be assessed by a methodological essay of up to 3,000 words. Two typewritten copies of each of the essays must be submitted by noon on Monday of second week of Hilary Term to the Chair of Examiners for the M.Sc. in History of Science, Medicine, and Technology, c/o Examination Schools, High Street, Oxford, OX1 4BG. In addition, convenors of qualifying courses will confirm in writing to the chair of examiners not later than Friday of eighth week of Hilary Term the candidates' satisfactory participation in their classes, including the completion of any assignments for the weekly sessions. Any approved alternative qualifying course will be assessed within the format and timetable of the paper's parent course. No candidate who has failed the qualifying test of two courses will be permitted to supplicate for the degree. Candidates who fail a qualifying course once will be permitted to take it again, not later than one year after the initial attempt.

Final examinations

The examination shall consist of two papers and a dissertation.

Candidates must take at least one of their papers as a three-hour written examination. For the remaining paper candidates must choose to be assessed either by written examination or by two 5,000 word essays. Essays may only be submitted in lieu of written papers for subjects in Schedule I below ('Advanced Papers for M.Phil. and M.Sc. in History of Science, Medicine, and Technology') or for other papers permitted in Schedule II below where similar provision exists in the regulations for those examinations. The essays must be the work of the candidates alone and they must not consult any other person including their supervisors in any way concerning the method of handling the themes chosen. The themes chosen by the candidate must be submitted for approval by the Chair of Examiners by the examination entry date. Candidates will be informed within two weeks, by means of a letter directed to their colleges, whether the topics they have submitted have been approved. The finished essays must be delivered by the candidate to the Examination Schools, High Street, Oxford, by noon on Monday of sixth week of Trinity Full Term. The essays must be presented in proper scholarly form, and two typed copies of each must be submitted.

I. One advanced paper selected from Schedule I below.

II. *Either* (i) one paper in a relevant discipline or skill or sources or methods selected from Schedule II below;

    or   (ii) a second advanced paper selected from Schedule I or from any additional list of papers for the M.Phil. and M.Sc. in History of Science, Medicine, and Technology approved by the Graduate Studies Committee of the Board of the Faculty of History and published in the definitive list of Advanced Papers as set out in Schedule I.

III. A dissertation of not more than 15,000 words, including appendices but excluding bibliography, on a topic approved by the candidate's supervisor. The dissertation must be delivered not later than noon on the last Monday in September of the year in which the examination is taken to the Examination Schools, High Street, Oxford. Dissertations submitted must not exceed the permitted length. If they do the examiners will reduce the marks awarded. The presentation and footnotes should comply with the requirements specified in the Regulations of the Education Committee for the degrees of M.Litt. and D. Phil. and follow the *Conventions for the presentation of dissertations and theses* of the Board of the Faculty of History.

Each dissertation must include a short abstract which concisely summarises its scope and principal arguments, in about 300 words.

Candidates must submit by the specified date three copies of their dissertation. These must be securely and firmly bound in either hard or soft covers.

3. The examiners will permit the use of any hand-held pocket calculator subject to the conditions set out under the heading 'Use of calculators in examinations' in the *Regulations for the Conduct of University Examinations*.

4. The examiners may award a distinction for excellence in the whole examination.

5. A candidate who fails the examination will be permitted to retake it on one further occasion only, not later than one year after the initial attempt.

Such a candidate whose dissertation has been of satisfactory standard may resubmit the same piece of work, while a candidate who has reached a satisfactory standard on the written papers will not be required to retake that part of the examination.

Schedule I

Advanced Papers for the M.Phil. and M.Sc. in History of Science, Medicine, and Technology

A broad range of the course resources are shared with the corresponding courses in Economic and Social History, and Advanced Papers are therefore available in the subject areas listed here.

1. Economic and business history
2. History of science and technology
3. Social history
4. Historical demography
5. History of medicine

A descriptive list of Advanced Papers will be published by the Board of the Faculty of History in September for the academic year ahead (not all options may be available in every year). The definitive list of the titles of Advanced Papers for any one year will be circulated to candidates and their supervisors and posted on the Faculty notice board not later than Friday of third week of Michaelmas Term.

Schedule II

The paper in a relevant discipline or skill may be:

1. One of the papers from the M.Phil. in Sociology or in Comparative Social Policy.

2. One suitable paper from another Master's degree under the auspices of the Faculty of History approved from time to time by the Graduate Studies Committee of the Board of the Faculty of History.

3. One suitable paper in a related skill or discipline other than those specified in paragraphs 1 to 2 above on the recommendation of the candidate's supervisor and endorsed by the Course Director.

Choices under Schedule II have to be approved by the Chair of the Graduate Studies Committee of the Board of the Faculty of History not later than Monday of the fourth week of Michaelmas Term. Candidates wishing to take a paper under 1 or 3 will also need the approval of the appropriate course convenor and the Graduate Studies Committee of the relevant faculty board or inter-faculty committee who need to be satisfied that each candidate has an adequate background in the subject. Not all options may be available in any one year.

Integrated Immunology

1. The Divisional Board of Medical Sciences shall appoint for the supervision of the course an Organising Committee, which shall have the power to arrange the teaching, assessment and other instruction.

2. The Organising Committee shall appoint an academic mentor for each candidate.

3. Each candidate shall:

(*a*) follow a course of study in Integrated Immunology for at least three terms and for a substantial part of the three vacations, as determined by the course timetable;

(*b*) attend all organised sessions including lectures, tutorials, class-directed learning, problem-based learning and continuing professional development sessions which will be compulsory (a record of attendance is kept).

4. Candidates shall be examined in all of the following ways:

(i) At the end of Michaelmas Term (normally in Week 10), each candidate must pass a computer-based examination on the topics in the Schedule for Term 1. Candidates who fail the examination once will be permitted to take it again on one further occasion, in order to proceed with the course.

(ii) At the end of Hilary Term (normally in Week 10), each candidate must pass a computer-based examination on the topics in the Schedule for Term 2. Candidates who fail the examination once will be permitted to take it again on one further occasion, in order to proceed with the course.

(iii) Each candidate will be required to submit to the examiners two copies of a printed essay of between 3,000–4,000 words by noon, Monday of Week 8 of Michaelmas Term. The subject of the essay must have been approved by the Examining Board. Each candidate shall make a public presentation on their essay to the examiners and will be examined viva voce, at the end of Michaelmas Term at a time to be notified by the examiners. Candidates will have the opportunity to revise and re-submit their essay by noon, Friday of the week preceding Week 0 of Hilary Term, in the event that they are deemed not to have passed this element of the examination.

(iv) Each candidate will be required to submit to the examiners two copies each of four clinical commentaries (printed) of 1,000–1,500 words each by noon, Monday of Week 8 of Hilary Term. The subjects of the clinical commentaries must have been approved by the Examining Board. Each candidate will be required to make a public presentation of one of their commentaries and will be examined viva voce, at the end of Hilary Term at a time to be notified by the examiners. Candidates will have the opportunity to revise and re-submit their clinical commentaries by noon, Friday of the week preceding Week 0 of Trinity Term, in the event that they are deemed not to have passed this element of the examination.

(v) Each candidate will be required to submit to the examiners three copies of a printed research dissertation of not more than 10,000 words (excluding bibliography and appendices) on the research project selected for study as set out in the Schedule. The dissertation must be submitted by noon on the last Monday of July in the academic year in which the examination is taken.

(vi) Each candidate shall make a presentation of their research project and will be examined viva voce, normally in the first week of September in the year of examination on a date to be determined by the examiners. Under exceptional circumstances, candidates may be permitted to redo the research project and/ or resubmit the research dissertation to an Examining Board sitting in Michaelmas, Hilary or Trinity Term of the following year (and which will be according to the Examiners' discretion in each case), in the event they are deemed not to have reached the required standard.

5. The examiners may examine any candidate viva voce on any part of the examination.

6. Candidates must pass each element of the examination to pass overall.

7. Candidates must pass each element of the examination in each term before being permitted to progress to the next term.

8. Candidates will be allowed one opportunity to retake or resubmit each of the required elements should they fail to reach the necessary standard. Students failing to pass any element on the second attempt will normally be judged to have failed to reach the necessary standard for the award.

9. The examiners may award a distinction for excellence in the whole examination.

10. The required written submissions must be sent to the Chair of Examiners, M.Sc. in Integrated Immunology, c/o Examination Schools, High Street, Oxford.

11. The examiners shall retain one copy of each dissertation of each successful candidate for deposit in the Radcliffe Science Library.

Schedule

The syllabus for study will be:

Term 1: Fundamental aspects of immunology

The dynamic anatomy of immunity

Innate immunity

Antigen presentation and recognition

Adaptive Immunity

Phylogenetically ancient systems

Term 2: Clinical aspects of immunology

Infection and immunity

Failure of immunity

Aberrant and unwanted immunity

The immunology of cancer

Manipulation of Immunity

Term 3: A basic or clinical research project

The project will be chosen in consultation with the Organising Committee. A research supervisor will be assigned who will provide regular supervision and guidance during the course of the 14-week laboratory-based research project in Oxford.

Latin American Studies

(*See also the the general notice at the commencement of these regulations.*)

For the purposes of this examination, 'Latin America' will be interpreted as the eighteen Spanish-speaking republics of the Western Hemisphere, plus Brazil, Haiti, and Puerto Rico.

The regulations are as follows:

1. Candidates for the M.Sc in Latin American Studies will:

(*a*) Follow a course of instruction for three terms and present three examination papers at the end of Trinity Term in the year of registration. These papers must include at least two of the core papers from among the following five disciplines: Economics, History, International Relations, Politics and Sociology. Each of the examination papers counts for 25 per cent of the final degree mark.

(*b*) Submit an extended essay, not exceeding 10,000 words, including footnotes and appendices. A draft title for the extended essay must be submitted for approval by the Latin American Centre Management Committee by 12:00 noon on the Friday of Week 0 of the Hilary Term preceding the written examination. Two typewritten copies of the extended essay must be delivered to the Examination Schools, addressed to the Chair of Examiners for the M.Sc in Latin American Studies, c/o Examination Schools, High Street, Oxford, by 12:00 noon on the Monday of Week 5 of Trinity Term in the calendar year in which the examination is taken. The extended essay will be equal to one examination paper, i.e. 25 per cent of the final degree mark.

(*c*) Candidates may also be required to present themselves for an oral examination if requested to do so by the examiners. The oral examination may focus on the candidate's examination papers, extended essay, or both.

2. The list of examination papers will be published on the Latin American Centre website and in the *University Gazette* in Week 0 of Michaelmas Term. Candidates must take the core paper in Economics if they wish to take a further paper in that discipline. Specialisation on a single country or a combination of countries is permitted so long as the choice appears in the list of available papers published.

3. Candidates shall be deemed to have passed the examination if they have passed all examination papers and the extended essay.

4. Candidates who fail one of the examination papers or the extended essay (without compensating strengths on the other components) shall be deemed to have failed the examination. They will be permitted to resubmit the extended essay or retake the examination paper on one (but not more than one) subsequent occasion, in Trinity Term, one year after the initial attempt. Such candidates must pass the extended essay or examination paper in order to pass the examination.

5. The examiners may award a distinction for excellence in the whole examination.

Law and Finance

1. Candidates must follow for at least three terms a course of instruction in Law and Finance.

2. Candidates must complete the following courses, and satisfy the examiners in the summative assessment in each case:

(*a*) all courses from Schedule A; *and*

(*b*) either two law electives from Schedule B, *or* one law elective from Schedule B *and* an individual dissertation.

3. Not all electives will necessarily be taught or examined in any one year. Details of those which are available will be published in the M.Sc in Law and Finance Handbook for the year of the examination, subject to any amendment posted on the designated course website by Monday of week minus 1 of the Michaelmas Term before the examination is held.

4. With the consent of the MLF Academic Director and the Subject Group Convener of the Course in question, candidates may offer as an alternative to one or both law electives from Schedule B, any other course listed in Schedule A of the BCL/M.Jur regulations (subject to the same limitations imposed on BCL and M.Jur students).

5. Candidates may offer a dissertation on a subject to be proposed by the candidate in consultation with the supervisor, and approved by the Chair of the Board of Examiners. The dissertation shall be wholly or substantially the result of work undertaken whilst registered for the degree of M.Sc in Law and Finance. The required format for this dissertation is the common format prescribed for all law theses, which is printed in the Law Faculty Graduate Student Handbook and the MSc. in Law and Finance Handbook.

6. Course assignments, where set, must be submitted not later than the time and date stipulated for each exercise; these will be published by the Board of Examiners before the first Monday of each term in which the assignment or project must be undertaken.

7. The degree of M.Sc shall be awarded to any candidate who achieves marks of at least 50 per cent in assessments for all courses (for which purposes a dissertation, if offered, shall count as one course), with satisfactory completion of pass/fail course assessment components where relevant.

8. The Board of Examiners may award a distinction for excellence in the examination.

9. Candidates are permitted on only one occasion to resubmit or retake failed assessment items on any course on which they have failed to achieve the required standard.

Schedule A

Law and Economics of Corporate Transactions
Finance I
Finance II
Microeconomics
First Principles of Financial Economics

Schedule B

Comparative and European Corporate Law
Competition Law
Conflict of Laws
Corporate and Business Taxation
Corporate Finance Law
Corporate Insolvency Law
European Business Regulation
International Intellectual Property Rights
International Economic Law
Principles of Financial Regulation
Regulation
Transnational Commercial Law

Learning and Teaching

1. Candidates for the M.Sc. in Learning and Teaching may only be admitted to the course if they are graduates who have been awarded Qualified Teacher Status in the United Kingdom, or an equivalent overseas award recognised by the Departmental Board. They must also be employed in a teaching post within a school or other educational setting. All candidates will be admitted initially for the Postgraduate Diploma in Learning and Teaching.

2. Every candidate must follow for at least three and at most nine terms a part-time course of instruction in Learning and Teaching.

3. The course will consist of four optional programmes of study and a research and development project. The examination shall be in three parts as follows:

Part I will be examined by two coursework assignments as described in clause 4 below.

Part II will be examined by one coursework assignment as described in clause 5 below.

Part III will be examined by a research and development project report as described in clause 6 below.

Those candidates who meet the criteria set out in clause 7 below will only be required to undertake two optional programmes of study (rather than four) and they will not be required to undertake Part I of the examination.

4. Part I of the M.Sc in Learning and Teaching shall be examined by means of two assignments relating to the content of the first and second options studied by the

candidate. Each assignment must be between 4,000 and 5,000 words in length, or their equivalent. Two printed copies of each assignment and one electronic copy (in a software format available in the department) must be delivered to the Chair of Examiners, M.Sc in Learning and Teaching, c/o Department of Education, 15 Norham Gardens, Oxford OX2 6PY. The deadline for the submission of assignments 1 and 2 will be no later than noon on the first Monday of May.

5. Part II of the M.Sc in Learning and Teaching shall be examined by means of one coursework assignment relating to the content of the third and fourth options studied by the candidate (or their first and second options if the candidate is exempted from Part I). (Candidates may choose, in consultation with their supervisors, whether the assignment should be presented as a single piece of work, drawing explicitly on the learning from the two options, or as two smaller scale pieces each carried out within different options but linked by a reflective introduction that brings the two studies together within the candidate's own practice of professional learning.) The assignment must be between 8,000 and 10,000 words in length, or their equivalent. Two printed copies of the assignment and one electronic copy (in a software format available in the department) must be delivered to the Chair of Examiners, M.Sc in Learning and Teaching, c/o Department of Education, 15 Norham Gardens, Oxford OX2 6PY. The deadline for submission of the assignments will be noon on the first Friday of May of the candidate's second year (or the first year if the candidate is exempted from Part I) as a part-time student on the course.

6. Part III of the M.Sc. in Learning and Teaching shall be examined through a research and development project report, which presents a systematic account of a substantial practitioner research enquiry, focused on the design and implementation of a specific innovation in teaching and learning with a strong emphasis on the choice of appropriate criteria, and relevant evidence for evaluating its impact. The research and development work must involve a significant degree of collaboration with other adults, either engaging others in research; or enabling others to learn from research findings within the candidate's own school or educational setting. The research and development project report must be between 15,000 and 20,000 words in length, or their equivalent. Three printed copies of the project report and one electronic copy (in a software format available in the department) must be delivered to the Chair of Examiners, M.Sc. in Learning and Teaching, c/o Department of Education, 15 Norham Gardens, Oxford OX2 6PY, no later than noon on the third Friday in September of the candidate's third year on the course. One of the printed copies of the report must be hard bound and bear the name of the candidate. The hard bound copy of the research and development project report of each candidate who passes the examination will be retained by the Department of Education for deposit in the departmental library.

7. Those candidates who meet any of the following criteria will only be required to undertake two optional programmes of study (rather than four). Such candidates will also be exempt from Part I of the examination and will only be required to undertake Parts II and III. In such cases the assignment for Part II should relate to the content of the first and second options studied by each candidate.

    (*a*) Those candidates who have, since October 2007, successfully completed the course leading to the award of a Postgraduate Certificate in Education at the University of Oxford (i.e. the Oxford Postgraduate Certificate in Education examined at Master's level)

    (*b*) Those candidates who have successfully completed a Postgraduate Certificate in Education at another university, assessed at Master's level and including an award equivalent to at least one third of a full Master's degree.

    (*c*) Those candidates who have successfully completed the course leading to a Postgraduate Diploma in Educational Studies from the University of Oxford.

8. Candidates who fail to satisfy the examiners in an assignment or in the research and development project may be permitted to resubmit the assignment or project report on one occasion only. In each case the deadline for resubmission is normally the standard submission deadline for the following year.

9. Candidates who fail an assignment within either Part I or Part II of the examination will not normally be permitted to embark on the next year's programme of study within the M.Sc. in Learning and Teaching until they have successfully resubmitted their assignment.

10. The award of Distinction within the M.Sc. in Learning and Teaching is normally reserved for those candidates who receive distinction marks for both the assignment submitted for Part II of the examination, and for the final research and development project report.

11. Candidates may also be examined orally on their final research and development project.

12. Candidates who successfully complete Parts I and II of the M.Sc. in Learning and Teaching (or who are exempt from Part I and successfully complete Part II) and who choose not to continue with their programme of study may be awarded a Postgraduate Diploma in Learning and Teaching.

Schedule

Options

A. *Learners and learning*

Theories of mind and learning

Critical analysis of the most influential theories about learning 'styles' and strategies

Understanding differences in learning, including special educational needs

Students' perspectives: young people's perspectives on learning, teaching, the curriculum and schooling

The diverse purposes and forms of assessment, the nature of progression within subject disciplines, and the use of assessment data with students

Consulting pupils about their learning: critical analysis of research claims and other moral and pragmatic justifications for attending to the 'student voice'; practical strategies for eliciting students' views

B. *Responsive Teaching*

Competing definitions of 'personalised learning' and pedagogical solutions intended to address perceived differences among students

Exploration and critique of approaches to transforming learning capacity

Examination of the role and nature of authority in the classroom

The role of language and classroom talk in relation to learning

Curriculum design and development the tensions between an entitlement curriculum and responsiveness to students' diverse needs and interests

New technologies and their integration into classroom practice as learning tools: exploration and critique of the role of e-learning

C. *Learners, Diversity and Inclusion*

Data analysis in relation to achievement and diversity

Understanding and addressing issues of social justice and inclusion related to differences of gender, class, ethnicity, disability and sexuality

Citizenship and school ethos: the role of democracy in schools and students as partners in change

Building community cohesion: expectations, strategies and challenges

D. *Professional Learning: Communities and Networks*

Mentoring and coaching

Intra/inter-professional collaboration

Roles of parents and carers as co-educators

Subject departments as learning communities

E. *Mathematics Education*

Principles of mathematics teaching:

* The nature of mathematics and mathematics education

* Key research issues in mathematics *teaching*

* *Understanding* mathematics—models and frameworks of understanding and their relationship to curriculum and assessment models

* Theories of *learning* mathematics

* Variation in teaching, learning, interpretation of policy and task design.

Design of teaching and learning in mathematics:

* Histories of curriculum development

* Implications of cognitive and neural science for practice and research in mathematics education

* Critical analysis of approaches to design

* Elements of mathematics lessons

* Effectively combining content, task, examples, questioning, mathematical activity with students' ideas

F. *Science Education*

This follows a similar framework to that outlined for mathematics education with particular emphasis on the nature of scientific knowledge, scientific learning and critical exploration of the underlying rationale and implications of current curriculum reform.

The research and development project

The focus of the final project is rooted in each student's professional practice in school. It includes a collaborative dimension requiring students either to engage colleagues (such as teachers or teaching assistants) or other stakeholders (such as parents) in the research process, or to develop strategies for disseminating the findings of their research in ways that will enable others to engage in further development work.

Core teaching for the project will therefore include two strands:

1. The design and conduct of school-based practitioner research

* The range of methods appropriate to a variety of types of school-based practitioner research and the ethical considerations guiding their use

* Principles for establishing a worthwhile focus and elaborating appropriate criteria for evaluation of educational innovations

* Statistical and qualitative data analysis, including the use of appropriate software packages such as SPSS, NVivo

2. Collaboration and leadership in educational innovation

* Developing expansive learning environments and a culture of enquiry

* Effective dissemination of research findings for practitioners

* Leading professional learning

As part of the work for their research and development project students will be expected to contribute to an annual conference held for course participants and members of the partnership schools within the Oxford Internship Scheme, with a specific emphasis on the presentation and review of the research instruments and strategies used to evaluate the outcomes of the teaching innovations that they implemented.

Major Programme Management

1. Candidates will follow for six terms (part time), a programme of instruction in Major Programme Management and will, when entering for the examination, be required to produce a certificate to this effect from a supervisor of the M.Sc. in Major Programme Management appointed for the purpose.

2. The programme will consist of eight compulsory courses, as prescribed in the schedule, and a dissertation of 10,000 words. Candidates must satisfy the examiners in the assessment (assignment/practical work) associated with each component. Modes of assessment and submission dates will be published by the M.Sc. Director and distributed to all candidates in the first week of the Michaelmas Term of the year in which the assessment takes place. The dissertation should demonstrate an ability to identify, formulate, implement and present a project in the area of Major Programme Management. Two typewritten copies of the dissertation, not exceeding 10,000 words in length (including endnotes, appendices, tables, but excluding references), must be submitted to the Examination Schools and addressed to the Chair of Examiners for the M.Sc. in Major Programme Management, c/o the Examination Schools, High Street, Oxford, by noon on the first Monday of September in the calendar year in which the examination is taken.

3. Candidates who fail to satisfy the Examiners in the assessment of any one of the components may retake/resubmit the failed assessment only once, no more than six months after the release of results for the original piece of assessment. Candidates who fail to satisfy the examiners in the dissertation may resubmit it on one, but no more than one, occasion which shall be by Week 10 of the Hilary Term in the following year.

4. The Examiners may choose to examine any candidate or group viva voce.

5. The Examiners may award a distinction for overall excellence in the examination.

Schedule of Core Courses

(i) Designing and Managing Successful Programmes

(ii) Systems Engineering

(iii) Financial Management

(iv) Contract Management

(v) Major Programme Risk

(vi) Research Methods

(vii) Managing Performance

(viii) Globalisation and Major Programmes

Management Research

1. Candidates must follow for three terms a course of instruction in Management Research and will, when entering for the examination be required to produce a certificate from a supervisor for the M.Sc. in Management Research appointed for the purpose to this effect.

2. The course will consist of two parts and candidates must satisfy the examiners in the assessment (assignment/examination/practical work) associated with each component in Part One and Part Two. Modes of assessment and submission dates will be published by the M.Sc. Director and distributed to all candidates in the first week of the term in which the assessment takes place.

(a) *Part One*

(i) *Introduction to Research Methods*, as prescribed in the Schedule. This course has two components-Management Research Methods, and Statistical Research Methods (both of which are assessed in Part One).

(ii) *Management and Organisational Theory*, (core course in Management Research) as prescribed in the Schedule.

(b) *Part Two*

(i) *Advanced Research Methods*. One of two possible Advanced Research Methods courses (Qualitative or Quantitative).

(ii) *Two elective courses*. Two required specialist elective courses, one elective to be taken and assessed in Hilary Term, and one elective to be taken and assessed in Trinity term, chosen from the list of subjects and rubrics approved by the M.Sc. Director and published in the *Gazette* not later than the end of the Trinity term of the academic year preceding the year of the examination.

(iii) *Dissertation*. Candidates are required to submit a dissertation in an agreed field of management research. The dissertation should demonstrate an ability to identify, formulate, implement and present a research project. Three typewritten copies of the dissertation, not exceeding 15,000 words in length (including endnotes, appendices, tables, but excluding references), must be submitted to the Examination Schools and addressed to the Chair of Examiners for the M.Sc. in Management Research, c/o Examination Schools, High Street, Oxford, by noon on the first Monday of August in the calendar year in which the examination is taken.

3. Candidates who fail to satisfy the Examiners in any one of the *Part One* Introduction to Research Methods components, or the Management and Organisational Theory core course assessment may retake/resubmit the failed assessment only once, by Week 10 of Trinity Term in the year in which the examination is taken. Candidates who fail to satisfy the examiners in *Part Two* the Advanced Research Methods course or in either one of the two required electives my resit or resubmit the failed elective only once, by Week 0 of Hilary Term in the following year. Candidates who fail to satisfy the Examiners in Part Two in the dissertation may resubmit it on one, but no more than one, subsequent occasion, which shall be by Week 0 of Hilary term in the following year.

4. The Examiners may choose to examine any candidate or group viva voce.

5. The Examiners may award a distinction for excellence for the overall examination of the course.

Schedule

(*a*) *Research Methods (Introduction to Research Methods and Advanced Research Methods)*

The two components address and discuss the nature of research in management studies and its relation to other social sciences, epistemology, strategies for literature review, research design, qualitative methods, interviewing, questionnaire design and ethnography, data sources and data collection, statistical methods, statistical and econometric modelling, analysis and interpretation of qualitative and quantitative data and the presentation of research results.

(b) *Management and Organisational Theory*

The course aims to demonstrate and introduce the wide range of social science perspectives which can be brought to bear in the study of management and organisations. It will explore a range of epistemological and ontological interpretations of management in organisations, especially emphasising recent developments in theory. It will do so by treating a series of key substantive issues and topics-for example, trust and accountability; rationality; language and discourse, technology-from each of two broadly contrasting theoretical commitments. The first commitment comprises those perspectives and frameworks that focus on structure and institutionalised arrangements. A second comprises those approaches that emphasise action and process.

By the end of the course students should be equipped to identify and evaluate the relative merits of a diversity of theoretical perspectives. A second and complementary purpose of the course is to provide sufficient understanding of key concepts within management and organisation theory to enable the student to make informed decisions on optional areas of study offered in subsequent terms.

Mathematical and Computational Finance

1. The Divisional Board of Mathematical, Physical and Life Sciences shall appoint for the supervision of the course a supervisory committee, which shall have the power to approve lectures and other instruction. The committee shall appoint a course organiser who will be responsible for ensuring that the programme is set up and the decisions of the committee are carried out.

2. The course organiser shall arrange for the appointment of a supervisor for each candidate.

3. Each candidate shall follow a course of study in Mathematical and Computational Finance for at least three terms and for a substantial part of the intervening vacations.

4. The examination will consist of the following parts:

(i) Four written examinations, each of two hours duration. The written examinations will cover the core courses in mathematical methods and numerical analysis, based on the schedule below. Two of the examinations will be based on Michaelmas Term courses and will be held before the start of Hilary Full Term, the date and time to be specified by the Examiners. Two of the examinations will be based on Hilary Term courses and will be held before the start of Trinity Full Term, the date and time to be specified by the Examiners. The examinations will be organised within the department.

(ii) Two options chosen from a list that will be published by the start of Michaelmas Full Term each year in the Course Handbook. Unless otherwise stated each option will be assessed by a written mini-project. Completed mini-projects shall be submitted electronically. Submission shall be in accordance with both the details given on the Course Website and with the deadlines which the examiners shall determine and notify candidates of. In exceptional cases where a candidate is unable to submit work electronically, he or she must apply to the Standing Committee for permission to submit the work in paper form to the Examiners, c/o the Academic Administrator for Mathematical Finance, Mathematical Institute. Such applications must reach the Mathematical Institute not less than two weeks before the deadline for submitting the work.

(iii) Two courses in Financial Computing which will be assessed by two practical examinations arranged within the Department. One practical examination will normally be held in, or shortly after, Hilary Term; one practical examination will normally be held in, or shortly after, Trinity Term. The details will be specified by the Examiners.

(iv) A dissertation of between twenty-five and forty pages on a topic approved by the examiners.

Candidates must submit a proposal for a dissertation, with the support of their supervisor, to the Chair of Examiners, M.Sc. in Mathematical and Computational Finance, c/o the Course Administrator, M.Sc. in Mathematical and Computational Finance, Mathematical Institute, 24–29 St Giles', Oxford, by a date to be specified by the Examiners.

More detail on these requirements will be set out each year in the Course Handbook.

5. Three copies of the dissertation must be delivered not later than noon on a date to be specified by the examiners which will normally be in late June, to the Examiners, M.Sc. in Mathematical and Computational Finance, c/o Examination Schools, High Street, Oxford OX1 4BG. The examiners may also direct that a copy of the dissertation in pdf or other machine-readable format be made available. Candidates will also be required to give an oral presentation based on their dissertation.

6. The examiners may award a distinction for excellence in the whole course.

7. A candidate who fails the examination will be permitted to retake it on one further occasion only, not later than one year after the initial attempt. In such a case the examiners will specify at the time of failure which components of the examination may or must be redone.

Schedule

Mathematical methods including stochastic analysis, partial differential equations, probability and statistics. Mathematical models of financial markets; associated topics in financial economics. The numerical solution of ordinary, partial and stochastic differential equations. Monte Carlo methods. Numerical methods for optimisation. Programming in appropriate languages, and use of relevant packages.

[From 1 October 2015: Mathematical and Theoretical Physics

1. The Examination in Mathematical and Theoretical Physics shall be under the supervision of the Mathematical, Physical and Life Sciences Board.

2. The Divisional Board of Mathematical, Physical and Life Sciences shall appoint for the supervision of the course a supervisory committee, which shall have the power to approve lectures and other instruction. The committee shall appoint a Director of Studies who will be responsible for ensuring that the programme is set up and the decisions of the committee are carried out.

3. The subject of the MSc of Mathematical and Theoretical Physics shall be Mathematical and Theoretical Physics and related subjects.

4. In the following 'the Course Handbook' refers to the Mathematical and Theoretical Physics Handbook and supplements to this published by the Joint Supervisory Committee for Mathematical and Theoretical Physics and also posted on the website at https://www.maths.ox.ac.uk/current-students/undergraduates/handbooks-synopses/.

5. Each candidate shall follow a course of study in Mathematical and Theoretical Physics for at least three terms.

6. Candidates will complete and be assessed on the following parts:

(i) Candidates will offer 10 units with one unit corresponding to a 16 hour lecture course.

(ii) At least four units will be assessed by written, invigilated examinations which will take place. Examination details will be published in the Course Handbook.

(iii) Candidates may offer one unit which is a dissertation. The dissertation will follow the guidelines and procedures of the Part C Mathematics course outlined in the Special Regulations for the Honour School of Mathematics.

(iv) The other units will be assessed by marked course work, take-home papers or mini-projects. The Course Handbook will specify which units will be assessed by each method mentioned above.

(v) Candidates will be required to attend an oral examination at the end of the course of studies.

7. The examiners may award a distinction for excellence in the whole examination.

8. A candidate who fails to satisfy the Examiners may retake the examination on at most one subsequent occasion, not later than one year after the initial attempt. In such a case the examiners will specify at the time of failure which components of the examination may or must be redone.

9. Syllabus and examination details will be published each year in the Course Handbook and on the course web pages by the beginning of the Michaelmas Full Term in the academic year of the examination.]

Mathematical Finance (*old regulations*)

For students registered on the M.Sc. and PG.Dip. in Mathematical Finance in or before January 2011

1. The Mathematical, Physical and Life Sciences Board, jointly with the Continuing Education Board, shall elect for the supervision of the course a Standing Committee which shall have the power to arrange lectures and other instruction.

2. Every candidate must follow for at least seven and at most twelve terms a part-time course of instruction in the theory and practice of Mathematical Finance.

3. Every candidate must normally:

(*a*) attend four modules from Section A, and three from Section B, of the Schedule below. Candidates may, in exceptional circumstances, and with the permission of the Standing Committee, be exempt from attendance at part of module 1;

(*b*) submit four assignments, one on each of the modules in Section A of the Schedule. These assignments will be assessed formatively and will not contribute towards the final award;

4. Every candidate will be required to satisfy the examiners in the following:

(*a*) two written examinations, covering material relevant to modules 1 to 4 in Section A of the Schedule;

(*b*) three assignments chosen from the advanced modules in Section B of the Schedule. Assignments should be of no more than ten sides of A4 in length (excluding tables, appendices, footnotes and bibliography);

(*c*) a dissertation of not more than fifty sides of A4 in length (excluding tables, appendices, footnotes and bibliography), on a subject selected by the candidate in consultation with the supervisor and approved by the Standing Committee.

The assignments under clause 4(*b*) above and the dissertation under (*c*) above shall be submitted electronically, in accordance with details given in the handbook for the M.Sc, by such date as the examiners shall determine and shall notify candidates. In exceptional cases where a candidate is unable to submit work electronically, he or she must apply to the Standing Committee for permission to submit the work in paper form to the Examiners c/o Registry, Department for Continuing Education, 1 Wellington Square, Oxford OX1 2JA not later than two weeks before the submission date. Such applications must reach the Registry two weeks before the deadline for submitting the work.

5. For candidates who have previously registered for the Postgraduate Diploma in Mathematical Finance, the requirements set out in 4(*a*) and (*b*) above shall be satisfied in part or in total by:

(*a*) the written examination taken under 5(*a*) of the Regulations for the Postgraduate Diploma;

(*b*) the assignments submitted under 5(*b*) of the Regulations for the Postgraduate Diploma;

(*c*) any assignments submitted under 5(*d*) of the Regulations for the Postgraduate Diploma;

provided that normally no more than eighteen months may elapse between the latest deadline for submission of any assignment under this provision and the first day of the first term of admission to M.Sc. status.

6. Candidates may be required to attend a viva voce examination at the end of the course of studies at the discretion of the examiners.

7. The examiners may award a distinction to candidates for the M.Sc.

8. Candidates who fail to satisfy the examiners in the written examinations under 4(*a*), the assignments under 4(*b*) or the dissertation under 4(*c*) may be permitted to resubmit work in respect of the part or parts of the examination which they have failed. In the case of the written examinations, this shall normally be on the occasion of the written examinations next following; in the case of assignments or the dissertation, the work shall normally be resubmitted within one year of the decision of the examiners.

9. If any candidate who is successful in the examination for the M.Sc. in Mathematical Finance has previously successfully completed the Postgraduate Diploma, then the subsequent award will subsume his or her previous award.

Schedule

Section A: Core Modules
Modules 1 to 4 shall be offered each year.
    Module 1. Mathematical and Technical Prerequisites
    Module 2. Black-Scholes Theory
    Module 3. Extensions of the Black-Scholes Framework
    Module 4. Exotic Options and Advanced Modelling Techniques
Section B: Advanced Modules
The Standing Committee shall approve the content of at least three advanced modules to be given each year which shall be made known to students by the end of Week Eight of the Trinity term in the calendar year in which the written examination is held.

Mathematical Finance (*new regulations*)

For students registering on the M.Sc. in Mathematical Finance in or after January 2012 and available to those who enrolled on the M.Sc. or PG.Dip. in Mathematical Finance in or before January 2011 and who have not already been awarded the relevant qualification.

1. Every student must follow a part-time course of instruction in the theory and practice of Mathematical Finance.

2. The Mathematical, Physical and Life Sciences Divisional Board and the Continuing Education Board shall elect for the supervision of the M.Sc. a Standing Committee which shall have the power to arrange lectures and other instruction.

3. The following awards shall be available to students registering on the M.Sc. in Mathematical Finance:
   (i) M.Sc. in Mathematical Finance
   (ii) Postgraduate Diploma in Mathematical Finance

4. Admission is only to the M.Sc. in Mathematical Finance.

5. Exceptionally, a candidate for the M.Sc. in Mathematical Finance may apply to be awarded the Postgraduate Diploma in Mathematical Finance, subject to such a candidate having satisfied the criteria for that award as set out in clauses 7 and 10 below. Candidates so awarded the Postgraduate Diploma cease, at that point, to be registered for the M.Sc. in Mathematical Finance, and may not normally be re-admitted to the M.Sc.

6. To be eligible for the award of an M.Sc., a student must be on the Register for the M.Sc. for at least seven terms.

7. To be eligible for the Postgraduate Diploma, a student must be on the Register for the M.Sc. for at least four terms.

8. A student may apply to extend for five further terms up to a maximum of twelve terms in total.

9. Every candidate will be required to satisfy the examiners in the following:
(*a*) M.Sc. in Mathematical Finance
   (i) attendance at each core module as detailed in Section A, and three advanced modules from Section B, of the Schedule below;
   (ii) two written examinations, covering material relevant to the core modules in Section A of the Schedule;
   (iii) three assignments chosen from the advanced modules in Section B of the Schedule. Assignments should be of no more than ten sides of A4 in length (excluding tables, appendices, footnotes and bibliography);
   (iv) a dissertation of not more than forty five sides of A4 in length (excluding the abstract, tables, appendices, footnotes and bibliography), on a subject selected by the candidate in consultation with the supervisor and approved by the Standing Committee.
(*b*) Postgraduate Diploma in Mathematical Finance
   (i) attendance at each core module as detailed in Section A, and three advanced modules from Section B, of the Schedule below;
   (ii) two written examinations, covering material relevant to the core modules in Section A of the Schedule;
   (iii) three assignments chosen from the advanced modules in Section B of the Schedule. Assignments should be of no more than ten sides of A4 in length (excluding tables, appendices, footnotes and bibliography).

The assignments under (*a*) (iii) and (*b*) (iii) above, and the dissertation under (*a*) (iv) above, shall usually be submitted electronically, in accordance with details given in the handbook, by such date as the examiners shall determine and shall notify candidates.

Any candidate who is unable, for some reason, to submit work electronically must apply to the Standing Committee for permission to submit the work in paper form to the examiners c/o Registry, Department for Continuing Education, 1 Wellington Square, Oxford OX1 2JA. Such applications must reach the Registry two weeks before the deadline for submitting the work.

10. Candidates may be required to attend a viva voce examination at the end of the course of studies (for the M.Sc. or the Postgraduate Diploma) at the discretion of the examiners.

11. The examiners may award a distinction to candidates for the M.Sc. or Postgraduate Diploma.

12. Candidates who fail to satisfy the examiners in the written examinations under 9 (*a*) (ii) or (*b*) (ii), the assignments under 9 (*a*) (iii) or (*b*) (iii), or the dissertation under 9 (*a*) (iv) may be permitted to resubmit work in respect of the part or parts of the examination which they have failed on one further occasion. In the case of the written examinations, this shall normally be on the occasion of the written examinations next following; in the case of assignments or the dissertation, the work shall normally be resubmitted within one year of the decision of the examiners.

13. In the exceptional circumstances that a candidate previously awarded the Postgraduate Diploma is re-admitted to the M.Sc. and is successful in the examination for the M.Sc. having for that examination incorporated the assignments submitted for the Postgraduate Diploma, then the subsequent award will subsume his or her previous award.

Schedule

Section A: Core Modules

The Standing Committee shall approve the content of four core modules to be given each year which shall be published in the handbook. The following components will be covered: Mathematical Techniques; Derivative Pricing; Portfolio Theory and Asset Pricing; Numerical Methods; Interest Rates.

Candidates may, in exceptional circumstances, and with the permission of the Standing Committee, be exempt from attendance at part of the first core module undertaken.

Section B: Advanced Modules

The Standing Committee shall approve the content of at least three advanced modules to be given each year which shall be made known to students by the end of Week Eight of the Trinity term in the calendar year in which the written examination is held.

Mathematical Modelling and Scientific Computing

1. The Divisional Board of Mathematical, Physical and Life Sciences shall appoint for the supervision of the course a supervisory committee, including a member from outside the University, which shall have the power to approve lectures and other instruction. The committee shall appoint a course organiser who will be responsible for ensuring that the programme is set up and the decisions of the committee are carried out.

2. The course organiser shall arrange for the appointment of a supervisor for each candidate.

3. Each candidate shall follow a course of study in Mathematical Modelling and Scientific Computing for three terms and their corresponding vacations.

4. Candidates will complete and be assessed on all the following parts:

(i) Four written examinations on core course material in mathematical methods and numerical analysis. These examinations will be organised within the department [1 unit each];

(ii) Two Special Topics chosen from a list that will be published each year. One special topic should be labelled 'Modelling' and one should be labelled 'Scientific Computing'. These special Topics will be assessed by a written project [1 unit each];

(iii) Case Studies in Mathematical Modelling and Scientific Computing. Students will submit a project on each of these courses for assessment [1 unit each];

(iv) One further Special Topic or one further Case Study in either Mathematical Modelling or Scientific Computing [1 unit];

(v) A dissertation on a topic approved by the examiners. The dissertation need not necessarily contain original research to pass. [4 units]

The detailed requirements will be set out each year on the course website.

5. Three copies of the dissertation must be delivered not later than noon on a date to be specified by the examiners which will normally be a Friday in early September to the Examiners, M.Sc. in Mathematical Modelling and Scientific Computing, c/o Examination Schools, High Street. The examiners may also direct that a copy of the dissertation in pdf or other machine-readable format be made available.

6. Candidates will be required to attend an oral examination at the end of the course of studies.

7. In addition to the academic elements of the course there will be a programme of career development activities requiring participation from each student.

8. The examiners may award a distinction for excellence in the whole course.

9. A candidate who fails the course will be permitted to retake it on one further occasion only, not later than one year after the initial attempt. In such a case the examiners will specify at the time of failure which of the assessed components of the course may or must be redone.

Schedule

Mathematical methods including ordinary and partial differential equations, transforms, applications of complex variable theory, distributions and asymptotics. Mathematical modelling and application of mathematics to problems in physical sciences, biology and medicine, industry and other areas.

The numerical solution of ordinary and partial differential equations. Finite element methods, numerical linear algebra, numerical methods for optimisation and approximation.

Mathematics and Foundations of Computer Science

1. The Divisional Board of Mathematical, Physical and Life Sciences shall elect for the supervision of the course a Standing Committee which shall have power to arrange lectures and other instruction.

2. Candidates shall follow for at least three terms a course of instruction in Mathematics and Foundations of Computer Science.

3. The examination shall be in three parts, as follows:

(a) Candidates shall successfully complete a written assignment on each of five courses chosen from a list of courses approved by the Standing Committee and published in the course handbook. The list of courses shall be divided into two sections: Section A (Mathematical Foundations) and Section B (Applicable Theories). Each section shall be divided into schedule I (basic) and schedule II (advanced). Candidates shall be required to satisfy the examiners in at least two courses taken from Section B and in at least two courses taken from schedule II.

(b) Candidates shall submit a short dissertation on a topic selected by the candidate in consultation with the supervisor and approved by the Standing Committee. The dissertation must bear regard to course material from Sections A or B. Between thirty-five and sixty-five typed pages is the preferred length.

(c) There shall be an oral examination on the dissertation and its background material, and the candidate shall normally be expected to give a short presentation on the dissertation.

4. Candidates must submit to the chair of the Standing Committee by the end of the second week of Trinity Term in the year in which they enter the examination, the title and a brief statement of the form and scope of their dissertation, together with the name of a person who has agreed to act as their supervisor during the preparation of the dissertation.

5. Two typewritten copies of the dissertation must be delivered not later than noon on 1 September in the year in which the examination is taken, to the M.Sc. Examiners (Mathematics and Foundations of Computer Science), c/o Examination Schools, High Street, Oxford. The dissertation must be accompanied by a certificate from the candidate's society to the effect that he or she has followed for three terms a course of instruction in Mathematics and Foundations of Computer Science. The examiners may retain one copy of the dissertation of each candidate who passes the examination for deposit in an appropriate departmental library.

6. Each candidate in consultation with their supervisor shall notify the director of the course of their intention to offer a written assignment for a lecture course not later than the Friday of the third week of each term. No candidate may offer more than four courses in one term. There will be a written assignment for each course. The topics in the assignment will be suggested by the relevant lecturer not later than the Monday of eighth week of the term during which the course is given. These topics will be sufficient to offer options appropriate to the course. The choice of topics will vary from year to year. Completed assignments must be delivered not later than noon on the Monday of the eleventh week of the term during which the course is offered, to the M.Sc. Examiners (Mathematics and Foundations of Computer Science), c/o Examination Schools, High Street, Oxford, together with a signed statement that the work offered for assessment is the candidate's own.

7. A candidate who does not submit a written assignment on a course for which he or she has entered, by noon on the Monday of the eleventh week of the relevant term, shall be deemed to have failed the course in question.

8. If a candidate is deemed to have failed a particular course, he or she shall not be permitted to re-enter for examination in that course in the same year.

Any candidate who has not satisfied the examiners in four courses, at least one of which shall have been taken from schedule II and at least one from Schedule B, by the beginning of the Trinity Term shall be deemed to have failed the degree course.

9. A candidate who has failed to satisfy the examiners in the examination may be admitted to, and examined on, the course as offered in the year subsequent to the initial attempt. No piece of written work shall be submitted for examination on more than one occasion.

10. The examiners may award a distinction for excellence in the whole examination.

Medical Anthropology

1. The Social Sciences Divisional Board shall elect for the supervision of the course a Standing Committee, namely the Teaching Committee of the School of Anthropology, which shall have power to arrange lectures and other instruction. The course director will be responsible to this committee.

2. Candidates must follow a course of instruction in Medical Anthropology for at least three terms, and will, when entering for the examination, be required to produce a certificate from their supervisor to this effect.

3. Candidates will be required to present themselves for written and, where invited, oral examinations, and to submit three copies of a dissertation in prescribed form on an approved topic as defined below.

4. The written examination will consist of four papers on the syllabus described in the Schedule.

5. Each candidate will be required to submit a dissertation of no more than 10,000 words, on a subject selected in consultation with the supervisor and approved by the Chair of Examiners. The proposed title of the dissertation together with a paragraph describing its scope and the supervisor's written endorsement, must be submitted to the Chair of Examiners by Tuesday of the second week of Trinity Term.

6. Three typewritten copies of the dissertation must be delivered not later than noon on the last Wednesday in August in the year in which the examination is taken, to the Chair of the Examiners, M.Sc. in Medical Anthropology, c/o Examination Schools, High Street, Oxford. The word count shall be stated on the outside front cover of the thesis.

7. An oral examination, if held, may be on the candidate's written papers, or dissertation, or both.

8. The examiners may award a distinction for excellence in the whole examination.

The four papers will be taken to constitute Part I of the degree and the dissertation to constitute Part II. At the close of the written examinations, the examiners will publish a list of those who have satisfied them in Part I.

9. In order to pass the degree, a student must pass all its assessed components. Where one or more components are failed, the student will be given the opportunity to re-sit or re-submit them once, as the case may be. Any subsequent award of the degree on successful completion of all the assessed components may be delayed by up to three terms, i.e. until the Examination Board next meets.

Schedule

Every candidate will be required to satisfy the examiners in four papers as follows:

1. *Concepts of disease, illness, health and medicine in global perspective*

The scope of this paper includes discussion of cross-cultural concepts of health, disease, sickness, pain, illness causation, diagnosis and treatment, from conjoined sociocultural perspectives and human ecology. It explores metaphor and narrative at the interface of biological and cultural processes, the distribution of disease patterns in the light of environmental change, social inequality, global mobility and marginality, and the coexistence of conventional, alternative and traditional health systems.

2. *Theory and practice of bio-medicine and of other medical systems*

The scope of this paper includes issues of public health and policy on a comparative and global basis. It draws on ethnographies of particular societies to illustrate and test theoretical claims in medical anthropology. It discusses infectious diseases, specific health campaigns, evolutionary trends and life histories, alongside culturally defined concepts of risk, vulnerability, fate, evil, pollution, divination, religion and shamanism.

3. *Critical medical anthropology*

The scope of this paper comprises ecological and socio-cultural perspectives, and explores links to other fields and disciplines, including the place of material culture in medicine. It includes a critique of basic assumptions and methods in medical anthropology and consideration of the concept of well-being as being broader than conventional concepts of health. Themes for discussion include the phenomenology of the body, growth and personhood, gender, ageing and dying, notions of resistance and resilience, relationships between biodiversity and adaptability, reproduction and fertility, and nutrition.

4. *Option paper*

Candidates must select one option paper from those taught each year for the M.Sc. in Social Anthropology. Titles of options will be made available by the end of the third week of Michaelmas Term at the beginning of each academic year, and candidates may select their option from any of Lists A, B or C.

5

Migration Studies

1. The Social Sciences Board shall elect for the supervision of the course a Standing Committee, which shall consist of the Directors of the Centre on Migration, Policy and Society (COMPAS) and of the International Migration Institute (IMI) ex officio, the course director, and two other members of the teaching staff drawn from the Oxford Department of International Development and the School of Anthropology, which shall have the power to arrange lectures and other instruction. The course director shall be responsible to that committee.

10

2. Candidates must follow a course of instruction in Migration Studies for at least three terms and will, when entering for the examinations, be required to produce a certificate from their supervisor to this effect. Candidates will be expected to attend such lectures and seminars as their supervisor/course director shall recommend.

15

3. The final examination shall be taken in Trinity Term of the academic year in which the candidate's name is first entered on the Register of M.Sc Students or, with the approval of the Board, in a subsequent year.

20

4. The examiners may at their discretion require any candidate to attend for a viva voce examination.

5. Each candidate will be required to satisfy the examiners in five papers in accordance with I, II, III, IV and V below.

I *International Migration in the Social Sciences: An Interdisciplinary Introduction*

25

6. The paper will cover theories and approaches in migration studies; basic concepts in migration studies; types of human migration and mobility; the history and development of migration studies. Assessment of this paper will take place in the form of one written essay of a maximum of 5,000 words (excluding notes and bibliography). This essay will be expected to display an understanding of key concepts and analysis in the economics, politics, sociology and anthropology of migration. Candidates shall submit their essay to the Examination Schools no later than 12 noon on Tuesday of the first week of the Hilary Term of the course, accompanied by a statement that the essay is the candidate's own work except where otherwise indicated.

30

II *Migration, Globalisation and Social Transformation*

35

7. This paper will be examined by means of a three-hour written examination to be taken during Trinity Term. Candidates will be expected to display understanding of the major debates in contemporary migration, including theoretical and practical questions and issues that currently drive research in the field of migration studies. Topics to be covered will vary from year to year, depending on changes in the focus of migration studies.

40

III *Elective paper*

8. Candidates' understanding of the two options they choose will be assessed through two sets of questions in an options paper. A list of papers approved for this purpose by the Standing Committee will be available from the course director by Monday of sixth week of Michaelmas Term. Students are free to elect any one of these papers in consultation with their supervisor. The examiners may, at their discretion, either require candidates to sit the standard examination paper for

45

this elective paper, or else set a paper specifically for students on the M.Sc in Migration Studies.

IV *Methods in Social Research*

9. Each student must display an understanding of research methods relevant to migration studies, which will be assessed by satisfactory completion of a course of practical work. This paper will cover (i) participant observation, in-depth interviewing, archival research, and qualitative data analysis; (ii) basic principles of statistical inference, and statistical models for the analysis of quantitative social science data; (iii) methods of data collection, including questionnaire design, interviewing and coding; and (iv) basic principles of statistical modelling in the social sciences.

10. Assessment of this paper shall take the form of three pieces of coursework, written during Michaelmas Term and Hilary Term. Candidates shall submit a portfolio consisting of copies of all coursework to the Examination Schools no later than 12 noon on Tuesday of noughth week of the Trinity Term of the course, accompanied by a statement that the coursework is the candidate's own work except where otherwise indicated.

V *Dissertation*

11. Each candidate shall be required to submit a dissertation of not more than 15,000 words (excluding references and appendices) on a subject approved by the supervisor. The candidate shall send to the Standing Committee, with the written approval of his or her supervisor, the proposed title of the dissertation for consideration by the Standing Committee, by noon on the Friday of the first week of Hilary Term in the academic year in which his or her name was entered on the Register of M.Sc Students.

12. The dissertation (three copies) must be typewritten and delivered to the Examination Schools, High Street, Oxford, not later than noon on Thursday of eighth week of Trinity Term in the year in which the examination is taken. An electronic copy must also be submitted to the M.Sc in Migration Studies Course Coordinator, again by the date and time specified above. The dissertation must be presented in proper scholarly form, in double-spacing and on one side only of quarto or A4 paper, each copy bound or held firmly in a stiff cover. The dissertation must be marked for the attention of the Chair of Examiners, M.Sc in Migration Studies, c/o Examination Schools, High Street, Oxford. The word count shall be stated on the outside front cover of the dissertation. The examiners shall retain a copy of the dissertation of each candidate who passes the examination for deposit in the Social Sciences Library.

13. The examiners may award a distinction for excellence in the whole examination.

14. If it is the opinion of the examiners that the work done by a candidate is not of sufficient merit to qualify for the degree of M.Sc, the candidate shall be given the option of re-sitting the M.Sc examination on one further occasion only, normally not later than one year after the first attempt.

Modern Japanese Studies

1. Candidates will be required to present themselves for examination EITHER in a compulsory paper in Japanese Language; and in two optional subjects at the end of Trinity Term in the year of registration; OR in three optional subjects at the end of Trinity Term in the year of registration.

2. Candidates taking the examination in Japanese Language will also be required to undertake a series of written tests and essays as specified by the MSc/MPhil Programme in Modern Japanese Studies Committee. The forms of assessment, and

the dates and times of submission, where applicable, will be notified to students not later than Friday of noughth week of Michaelmas Full Term.

3. In addition, all candidates will be required to undertake the following assessment:

(i) Research Methods for Area Studies: a series of assignments and/or an unseen written examination as specified by the MSc/MPhil Programme in Modern Japanese Studies Committee. The forms of assessment, and the dates and times of submission, where applicable, will be notified to students by not later than Friday of noughth week of Michaelmas Full Term.

(ii) One 10,000 word dissertation: the title of the dissertation must be approved by the Director of Graduate Studies by not later than 12 noon on Friday of fourth week of Hilary Full Term in the year in which the examination is taken. The dissertation must be submitted by not later than 12 noon of the weekday on or nearest to 1 September in the year in which the examination is taken. The dissertation must be accompanied by a statement that the dissertation is the candidate's own work except where otherwise indicated.

Two typewritten or word processed copies of the dissertation must be delivered to the Examination Schools, addressed to the Chair of Examiners for the M.Sc. in Modern Japanese Studies, c/o Examination Schools, High Street, Oxford at the times and days specified. Successful candidates will be required to deposit one copy of the dissertation in the Bodleian Library.

4. A candidate who fails the examination will be permitted to retake it on one further occasion within six terms of his or her initial registration. Candidates will be permitted to resubmit the same item or items of written work that reached a satisfactory standard.

5. Candidates may be required to attend an oral examination on any part of the examination.

6. The examiners may award a distinction for excellence in the whole examination.

Schedule

The structure of the course is as follows:

EITHER Mode A

(*a*) *Compulsory core course in Japanese Language*

(*b*) *Research Methods for Area Studies*

(*c*) *Optional papers:* Candidates must choose two optional papers from a list published annually and distributed to students by not later than Friday of noughth week of Michaelmas Full Term.

OR Mode B

(*a*) *Research Methods for Area Studies*

(*b*) *Optional papers:* Candidates must choose three optional papers from a list published annually and distributed to students by not later than Friday of noughth week of Michaelmas Full Term.

Musculoskeletal Sciences

1. The Medical Sciences Board shall elect for the supervision of the course an Organising Committee, which shall have the power to arrange teaching, assessments and other instruction.

2. The Organising Committee shall appoint for each candidate an academic supervisor.

3. Candidates will hold a first degree in medicine, or exceptionally a biomedical science degree.

4. Candidates shall follow a course of study in Musculoskeletal Sciences on a part-time basis for at least six terms, and including vacations, as determined by the course timetable. The course commences every two years in January and runs until December of the following year.

5. Candidates shall be examined in all of the following ways:

(i) Year 1 (January to December)

(*a*) Each candidate shall submit a literature review of no more than 4,000 words on a topic selected by the candidate and approved by the Organising Committee. The review must be submitted during the Long Vacation on a date to be specified in the course handbook.

(*b*) Each candidate must pass an examination in Michaelmas Term. The examination will comprise two elements: the first of these will consist of a one-hour computer-based assessment comprising multiple-choice questions; the second of these will constitute a two-hour written paper. The dates of the examination will be specified in the course handbook.

(ii) Year 2 (January to December)

[**Until 1 October 2014:** (*a*) Each candidate must submit a research proposal of no more than 10,000 words on a topic selected by the candidate and approved by the Organising Committee. The proposal must be submitted in Michaelmas Term on a date to be specified in the course handbook.

(*b*) Each candidate must submit, for assessment of their progress, an outline research proposal. The outline must be submitted in Hilary Term on a date to be specified in the course handbook.

(*c*) Each candidate will be assessed on their presentation skills by means of a public oral presentation on his or her research topic. The presentation must take place in Trinity Term on a date to be specified in the course handbook.

(*d*) Each candidate must pass a written examination in Michaelmas Term on a date to be specified in the course handbook. Part of the written examination will comprise computer-based multiple choice questions.]

[**From 1 October 2014:** (*a*) Each candidate must submit, for assessment of their progress, an outline research proposal. The outline must be submitted in Hilary Term on a date to be specified in the course handbook.

(*b*) Each candidate will be assessed on their presentation skills by means of a public oral presentation on his or her research topic. The presentation must take place in Trinity Term on a date to be specified in the course handbook.

(*c*) Each candidate must submit a written research proposal of no more than 10,000 words on a topic selected by the candidate and approved by the Organising Committee. The proposal must be submitted in Michaelmas Term on a date to be specified in the course handbook.

(*d*) Each candidate must pass an examination in Michaelmas Term. The examination will comprise two elements: the first of these will consist of a one-hour computer-based assessment comprising multiple-choice questions; the second of these will constitute a two-hour written paper. The dates of the examination will be specified in the course handbook.]

6. Candidates may be examined viva voce on their research proposal. The viva voce examination will normally be conducted at the end of the course.

7. Candidates must pass each examination or written assignment in order to pass overall.

8. Candidates will be allowed one opportunity to retake or resubmit each of the required elements, normally within six months of the original failure, should they fail to reach the necessary standard. Candidates failing to pass any element at the second attempt will normally be judged to have failed to reach the necessary standard for the award and will not be permitted to continue.

9. The required written submissions must be sent to the Chair of Examiners, MSc in Musculoskeletal Sciences, c/o Examination Schools, High Street, Oxford. Submissions must be accompanied by a declaration of authorship and originality.

10. The examiners may award a distinction for excellence in part of or in the whole examination.

11. The examiners may award a postgraduate diploma to candidates who have satisfied the requirements for the award of the Postgraduate Diploma **[From 1 October 2014:** (comprising all assessment with the exception of the written research proposal)] and who do not wish to continue their studies, or who fail to meet the required standard for the **[From 1 October 2014:** written] research proposal.

Schedule

The syllabus for study will include the following components:
Core Subjects
Candidates are required to complete all of the following modules:
1. Principles of Musculoskeletal Diseases
2. Research, Statistics and Epidemiology
3. Scientific Aspects of Common Musculoskeletal Diseases

Specialist Subjects
Candidates are required to complete one of the following modules:
1. Advanced Rheumatology
2. Advanced Orthopaedics

Nature, Society, and Environmental Policy

1. The Social Sciences Divisional Board shall elect for the supervision of the course a Standing Committee. The Academic Director(s) and Course Director will be responsible to the Standing Committee.

2. Candidates must follow a course of instruction in Human Geography for at least three terms, and will, when entering for the examination, be required to produce a certificate from the Course Director to this effect.

3. The examination will consist of:
   (i) a written examination of three three-hour papers as described in the schedule;
   (ii) two assessed essays based upon elective courses;
   (iii) a dissertation on a subject selected in consultation with the supervisor and the Course Director and approved by the Standing Committee.

4. Candidates must submit to the Course Director by the end of Hilary Term in the year in which they enter the examination, the title and a brief statement of the form and scope of their dissertation, together with the name of a person who has agreed to act as their supervisor during preparation of the dissertation.

It may be (*a*) a theoretical argument related to themes in contemporary human geography and/or environmental governance, or (*b*) a piece of empirically based research, or (*c*) an extended treatment of an issue which is intended to be the basis for future research for the degree of M.Litt. or D.Phil. In that case (*c*), it may be part of a proposal and/or application for further degree study.

5. The dissertation shall be of a maximum length of 15,000 words and accompanied by an abstract not exceeding 150 words. The maximum word count shall exclude appendices, references and the abstract. The detailed format and specification of the dissertation shall be approved by the Standing Committee, and published in the course handbook.

6. The deadline for submission is noon on the first weekday of September in the year in which the written examination is taken. Two copies of the dissertation must be submitted, to the M.Sc examiners (Nature, Society and Environmental Policy), c/o Examination Schools, High Street, Oxford OX1 4BG. The examiners may retain one copy of the dissertation of each candidate who passes the examination for deposit in an appropriate library. Both copies must bear the candidate's examination number but not his/her name.

7. All submitted work shall be accompanied by a separate statement certifying that the submitted work is the candidate's own work except where otherwise indicated.

8. In the written examination the examiners will permit the use of hand-held pocket calculators subject to the conditions set out under the heading 'Use of calculators in examinations' in the *Regulations for the Conduct of University Examinations.*

9. The examiners may also examine any candidate viva voce on the candidate's written papers, dissertation, or both.

10. Arrangements for reassessment shall be agreed by the Standing Committee and published in the course handbook.

11. The examiners may award a distinction for excellence in the whole examination.

Schedule

(*a*) *Core courses*

The core courses will be examined under the following heads:

1. *Research Skills*

Candidates will be expected to have a knowledge of research methods in social, environmental, and geographical research. These will include qualitative and quantitative methods relevant to contemporary research themes.

2. *Theory and Analysis*

Candidates will be expected to have knowledge of relevant debates in human geography and related disciplines concerning the relations between nature and society, science and environmental politics, and global and local political and economic processes.

3. *Policy and Governance*

Candidates will be expected to have knowledge of relevant debates and issues concerning environmental policy and governance, and corporate environmental management.

(*b*) *Elective courses*

Candidates will be expected to show advanced knowledge of two of the elective courses on offer in any one year.

Neuroscience

1. The Divisional Board of Medical Sciences shall elect for the supervision of the course an Organising Committee which shall have power to arrange lectures and other instruction.

2. The Organising Committee shall appoint for each candidate an academic advisor.

3. Each candidate shall follow a course of study in Neuroscience for at least three terms and for a substantial part of the three subsequent vacations, as determined by the course timetable, and will, when entering for the examination, be required to produce a certificate from the Organising Committee to this effect.

4. Candidates shall be examined in all of the following ways:

   (i) each candidate must pass a qualifying examination at the end of the first term from the beginning of the course. The test shall consist of the satisfactory completion of the Neuroscience Introductory Course and one three-hour written paper on the topics covered in that course, as set out in the Schedule; the Organising Committee shall not later than the end of the Hilary Term preceding the examination submit to the examiners a list of candidates who have satisfactorily completed the qualifying examination. Candidates who fail the qualifying examination once shall be permitted to take it again in the first week of Hilary Term of the year of the final examination;

   (ii) each candidate will be required to submit to the examiners *either* two copies of a typewritten or printed essay of not more than 3,000 words on a topic approved by the Organising Committee in each of the five modules chosen for study, as set out in the Schedule, *or* in the case of the modules specified by the Organising Committee one practical notebook in each module chosen for study; candidates must submit their titles for approval by deadlines determined by the Organising Committee and posted in the *Gazette* no later than the end of the preceding term;

   (iii) each candidate will be required to submit to the examiners three copies of a typewritten or printed dissertation of not more than 10,000 words (excluding bibliography and appendices) on each of the two research projects chosen for study, as set out in the Schedule;

   (iv) each candidate will be required to give a public oral presentation on each of his or her research projects, on dates to be determined by the Organising Committee.

5. Each candidate will be examined viva voce.

6. Before being given leave to supplicate, candidates must have demonstrated understanding of and competence in the topics covered by the professional development programme as set out in the Schedule, to the satisfaction of the programme organisers, who shall submit a ceritificate to the examiners to this effect.

7. The required written submissions must be sent to the Chair of Examiners, M.Sc. in Neuroscience, c/o Examination Schools, High Street, Oxford, on the following dates:

   (*a*) The dissertations on the first and second research projects must be submitted by dates to be specified by the Organising Committee and which will be published in the *University Gazette* not later than the start of Michaelmas Term of the academic year in which the examination is taken.

   (*b*) The essays or the practical notebooks for each module must be submitted by deadlines determined by the Organising Committee and posted in the *Gazette* no later than the end of the preceding term.

Each submission must be accompanied by a certificate indicating that it is the candidate's own work.

8. The viva voce examinations will be conducted in September in the year in which the candidate is examined on dates to be determined by the examiners.

9. The examiners may award a distinction for excellence in the whole examination.

10. The examiners shall retain one copy of each dissertation of each successful candidate for deposit in the most appropriate departmental library.

Schedule

The syllabus for study will include four principal components:

(*a*) *Professional Development Programme for Neuroscientists*

Candidates will be required to follow a programme of Professional Development courses to provide transferable skills for a career in scientific research. The programme will consist of practical exercises and taught classes with interactive discussions and practical assignments in the following areas:

(i) Presentation skills, verbal and written;

(ii) Career planning, assessing personal skills and values, curricula vitae and interview techniques;

(iii) Exploitation of science: patents and intellectual property;

(iv) Ethical and social issues in science.

(*b*) *Introduction to Neuroscience*

Five module introduction to neuroscience, each consisting of lectures and practicals. Candidates who have already received training in neuroscience may, at the discretion of the Organising Committee, be exempted from attendance at one or more of the introductory modules. Such candidates will be required to pass the qualifying examination which will cover the topics covered in the Introduction to Neuroscience. They will be required to follow an alternative course of instruction approved by the Organising Committee.

Module I: Introduction to the brain

Module II: Neuroanatomy

Module III: Neuronal Cell and Molecular Biology

Module IV: Synapses and transduction

Module V: Systems overview.

Candidates will also be required to take courses on experimental design, computing, and statistics, approved by the Organising Committee.

(*c*) *Specialist neuroscience courses*

This will consist of five taught courses consisting of lectures, seminars, practicals, and demonstrations, chosen from a list of courses in neuroscience to be approved annually by the Organising Committee. These will be grouped under three headings: molecular, cellular, and systems, and candidates will be required to choose at least one course under each of the three headings. Details of the courses available in each academic year will be published in the *Gazette* in the preceding Trinity Term.

(*d*) *Laboratory research projects*

Two research projects based on the candidate's laboratory placements, each under the supervision of a research supervisor, on subjects selected in consultation with the Organising Committee. The research projects shall be in separate areas of neuroscience.

Pharmacology

1. The Divisional Board of Medical Sciences shall appoint for the supervision of the course an Organising Committee, which shall have the power to arrange lectures and other instruction.

2. The Organising Committee shall appoint for each candidate an academic advisor (*mentor*).

3. Each candidate shall:

(*a*) follow a course of study in Pharmacology for at least three terms and for a substantial part of the three subsequent vacations, as determined by the course timetable;

(*b*) attend practical classes which will be compulsory (a record of attendance will be kept);

(*c*) when they submit their dissertations in September, produce a certificate from their academic advisor to the effect that they have fulfilled the requirements of (*a*) and (*b*).

4. Candidates shall be examined in all of the following ways:

(i) each candidate must pass a qualifying examination at the end of Michaelmas Term. The test shall consist of one three-hour written paper on the topics covered by the Pharmacology Introductory Course, as set out in the Schedule. The Organising Committee shall not later than the end of the Hilary Term preceding the final examination submit to the examiners a list of candidates who have satisfactorily completed the qualifying examination. Candidates who fail the qualifying examination once shall be permitted to take it again in the first week of the Hilary Term of the year of the final examination.

(ii) each candidate must pass a three-hour data handling and experimental design examination (also known as the quantitative examination) during Hilary Term. Candidates must pass the examination in order to proceed with the course, and those who fail shall be permitted to sit the examination on one further occasion only.

(iii) each candidate must pass an essay examination at the beginning of Trinity Term on the material covered in the Advanced Pharmacology courses. Candidates must pass the examination in order to proceed with the course, and those who fail shall be permitted to sit the examination on one further occasion only.

(iv) each candidate will be required to submit to the examiners two copies of a printed Critical Literature Review of not more than 3,000 words which will be an extended introduction to their approved research project. One practical notebook in which all practical class experiments are recorded will also be submitted.

(v) each candidate will be required to submit to the examiners three copies of a printed dissertation of not more than 10,000 words (excluding bibliography and appendices) on the research project selected for study as set out in the Schedule. The arrangements for approval will be notified to candidates not later than the start of Michaelmas Term of the academic year in which the examination is taken;

(vi) each candidate will be expected to give a public oral presentation on his or her research project, on dates to be determined by the Organising Committee.

5. Each candidate shall be examined viva voce.

6. Before being given leave to supplicate, candidates must have demonstrated understanding of and competence in the topics covered by the professional development programme as set out in the Schedule, to the satisfaction of the programme organisers, who shall submit a certificate to the examiners to this effect.

7. The required written submissions must be sent to the Chair of Examiners, M.Sc. in Pharmacology, c/o Examination Schools, High Street, Oxford on the following dates:

(*a*) The dissertation on the research project must be submitted by dates to be specified by the Organising Committee and which will be published in the *University Gazette* not later than the start of Michaelmas Term of the academic year in which the examination is taken.

(*b*) The essay and the practical notebook must be submitted by deadlines determined by the Organising Committee and posted in the *Gazette* no later than the end of the term preceding submission.

Each submission must be accompanied by a certificate indicating that it is the candidate's own work.

8. The viva voce examination will normally be conducted in September in the year in which the candidate is examined on dates to be determined by the examiners.

9. The examiners may award a distinction for excellence in part of or in the whole examination.

10. The examiners shall retain one copy of each dissertation of each successful candidate for deposit in the Radcliffe Science Library.

Schedule

The syllabus for study will include four principal components:

(*a*) *Professional Development Programme for Pharmacologists*

To provide transferable skills for a career in scientific research, this programme will consist of classes, exercises and interactive discussions in the following areas:

(i) Presentation skills, verbal and written;

(ii) Career planning, assessing personal skills and values, curricula vitae and interview techniques;

(iii) Exploitation of science: getting ideas to the marketplace, patents, intellectual property rights; the relationship between academic and industrial research; government science policy and research funding;

(iv) Ethical and social issues in science.

Creativity and teamwork are integral components of the learning undertaken during the practical classes and research projects. Time management and learning skills are developed as part of the structured timetable of examinations and coursework submission deadlines throughout the year.

(*b*) *Introduction to Pharmacology*

Three module introduction to pharmacology, each consisting of lectures and practical classes. Candidates who have already received training in some of the topic areas covered may, at the discretion of the Organising Committee, be exempted from attendance at one or more of the introductory lecture series. Such candidates will be required to pass the qualifying examination, which will cover the topics covered in the Introduction to Pharmacology.

Module I: Cell & Receptor Pharmacology

Module II: Tissue and Organ Pharmacology

Module III: Neuropharmacology

Candidates will also be required to take courses on experimental design, data interpretation, computing and statistics, approved by the Organising Committee. Candidates will be required to obtain a Home Office licence and will follow the course of study required for modules 1 to 4 of this.

(*c*) *Advanced pharmacology courses*

This will consist of the following five taught courses consisting of lectures, seminars and practical classes: Cardiovascular & Systems Pharmacology, Cell Signalling, Neuropharmacology I, Neuropharmacology II, Drug Discovery & Personalised Medicine.

(*d*) *Research Project Dissertation*

Candidates shall submit a dissertation on a research project undertaken under the supervision of a research supervisor. The subject of each dissertation and the supervision arrangements for each student must be approved by the Organising Committee. The research project will normally be laboratory-based, but in exceptional circumstances students may undertake a library-based project, subject to approval from the Organising Committee.

Political Theory Research

(*See also the general notice at the commencement of these regulations. The current edition of the Notes of Guidance for Graduate Students and Supervisors in Politics contains an elaborated version of these regulations.*)

A candidate for the M.Sc. in Political Theory Research shall follow for twelve months a course of instruction in Political Theory Research. Each candidate must pass the M.Sc. Examination at the end of Trinity Term in the two compulsory papers. Each student must also submit a thesis during the Long Vacation. The two compulsory papers are Theory of Politics and Research Methods in Political Theory.

Compulsory papers:

(*a*) *Theory of Politics*

Compulsory paper taken from the M.Phil. in Politics (Political Theory)

A critical examination of political concepts and theories, including social concepts and theories with political relevance.

(*b*) *Research Methods in Political Theory*

Compulsory paper taken from the M.Phil. in Politics (Political Theory)

Candidates will satisfactorily complete a programme of core and optional research methods training, as specified in the *Notes of Guidance for Graduate Students and Supervisors in Politics*, and will also produce a Research Design Essay of between 4,000 and 6,000 words, excluding bibliography, on research design as it bears on some aspect of political theory. Two hard copies of the Research Design Essay, together with a copy on CD, must be submitted to the Examination Schools by noon on the Friday of sixth week of Trinity Term. It must be accompanied by a separate signed declaration that it is the candidate's own work except where otherwise indicated and that it has not previously been submitted for assessment, either at Oxford or at another institution. The essay will normally be related to the subject of the student's proposed M.Sc. thesis. The Director of Graduate Studies in Politics shall draw the attention of the examiners to the names of any candidates who have failed to complete their research methods training to a satisfactory level of quality, and the examiners may require candidates to retake the course or a specified part thereof.

(*c*) A thesis of not more than 15,000 words, excluding bibliography. Two hard copies, together with a copy on CD, must be submitted to the Examination Schools by noon on the last Friday of August following the end of Trinity Full Term. It must be accompanied by a separate signed declaration that it is the candidate's own work except where otherwise indicated and that it has not previously been submitted for assessment, either at Oxford or at another institution. The thesis must be clearly marked with the candidate's examination number, the title of the thesis and the words M.Sc. in Political Theory Research. After the examination process is complete, each successful candidate must deposit one hardbound copy of their thesis in the Bodleian Library.

The examiners may also examine any candidate viva voce. The examiners may award a distinction for excellence in the whole examination.

Politics Research

(*See also the general notice at the commencement of these regulations. The current edition of the 'Notes of Guidance for Graduate Students and Supervisors' in Politics contains an elaborated version of these regulations.*)

A candidate for the M.Sc. in Politics Research shall follow for twelve months a course of instruction in Politics Research. Each candidate must pass the M.Sc. Examination at the end of Trinity Term in the two compulsory papers. Each student must also submit a thesis during the Long Vacation. The two compulsory papers are Research Methods in Political Science and *either* Comparative Government *or* European Governance.

Compulsory papers:

(*a*) *Comparative Government*

Compulsory paper taken from the M.Phil. in Politics (Comparative Government)

The theory and practice of government in modern states.

Or

(*b*) *European Governance*

Compulsory paper taken from the M.Phil. in Politics (European Politics and Society)

The constitutions and formal structure of governments in European states, including the UK, and the theory and practice of integration in Europe.

and

(*c*) *Research Methods in Political Science*

Compulsory paper taken from the M.Phil. in Politics.

Candidates will satisfactorily complete a programme of core and optional research methods training, as specified in the *Notes of Guidance for Graduate Students and Supervisors in Politics*, and will also produce a Research Design Essay of between 4,000 and 6,000 words, excluding bibliography, on research design as it bears on some aspect of politics. Two hard copies of the Research Design Essay, together with a copy on CD, must be submitted to the Examination Schools by noon on the Friday of sixth week of Trinity Term. It must be accompanied by a separate signed declaration that it is the candidate's own work except where otherwise indicated and that it has not previously been submitted for assessment, either at Oxford or at another institution. The essay will normally be related to the subject of the student's proposed M.Sc. thesis. The Director of Graduate Studies in Politics shall draw the attention of the examiners to the names of any candidates who have failed to complete their research methods training to a satisfactory level of quality, and the examiners may require candidates to retake the course or a specified part thereof.

(*d*) Where necessitated by a candidate's choice of subject the Politics Graduate Studies Committee may require a candidate to pass a test of proficiency in a language other than English. Candidates who fail the test will normally be allowed to retake the test before the beginning of the next academic year.

(*e*) A thesis of not more than 15,000 words, excluding bibliography. Two hard copies, together with a copy on CD, must be submitted to the Examination Schools by noon on the last Friday of August following the end of Trinity Full Term. It must be accompanied by a separate signed declaration that it is the candidate's own work except where otherwise indicated and that it has not previously been submitted for assessment, either at Oxford or at another institution. The thesis must be clearly marked with the candidate's examination number, the title of the thesis and the words 'M.Sc in Politics Research'. After the examination process is complete, each successful candidate must deposit one hardbound copy of their thesis in the Bodleian Library.

The examiners may also examine any candidate viva voce. The examiners may award a distinction for excellence in the whole examination.

Professional Archaeology

1. Every candidate must follow for three terms (full-time) or six terms (part-time) a course of instruction in Professional Archaeology.

2. The course will consist of lectures, seminars, individual tutorials and, in the case of full-time students, three approved placements of approximately ten weeks each, or in the case of part-time students, approved work-place projects undertaken.

3. The examination will consist of the following parts:

(*a*) a portfolio which shall include:

> (i) a written report of 5,000 words maximum of the work undertaken at the first placement;

> (ii) a written report of 5,000 words maximum of the work undertaken at the second placement;

> (iii) a written report of 5,000 words maximum of the work undertaken at the third placement;

(In the case of part-time students, a written report of 15,000 words maximum on work-place projects undertaken with an approved relevant organisation.) The portfolio material for each placement must represent ten weeks of professionally competent work;

> (iv) three written assignments of 2,000–2,500 words each, one during each of the placements on an agreed topic;

> (v) five written reports of 1,000 words maximum each, one on each of the following courses: four optional short courses and a survey week.

The portfolio shall be forwarded to the examiners, c/o Registry, Department for Continuing Education, 1 Wellington Square, Oxford for consideration by such a date as the examiners shall determine and shall notify the candidates and tutors at the start of each academic year.

(*b*) a dissertation (two copies) of not more than 15,000 words on a topic selected by the student in consultation with his or her tutor and approved by the examiners. The dissertation must be delivered not later than noon on the third Friday in September of the final year of the course to the Chair of Examiners for the Degree of M.Sc. in Professional Archaeology, c/o Examination Schools, High Street, Oxford. The dissertation must be accompanied by a statement that it is the candidate's own work;

(*c*) a viva voce examination.

4. The examiners may award a distinction for excellence in the whole examination.

5. With the approval of the Board of Studies in each case, a candidate who has obtained a pass mark on section 3(*a*), but who is prevented by exceptional circumstances from completing section 3(*b*), may be awarded a Postgraduate Diploma in Professional Archaeology.

6. A candidate who fails to satisfy the examiners in 3(*a*) or (*b*) may be permitted to resubmit work in respect of part or parts of the examination which they have failed for examination on one further occasion, not later than one year after the initial attempt.

Psychological Research

1. The Medical Sciences Board shall elect for the supervision of the course a course committee which shall have the power to arrange lectures and other instruction.

2. The course committee shall appoint an academic adviser for each candidate.

3. Each candidate shall follow a course of study in Psychological Research for at least three terms and for a substantial part of the three subsequent vacations, as determined by the course timetable, and shall, when entering for the examination, be required to produce a certificate from their academic adviser to this effect.

4. The syllabus shall include ten principal modules as listed in the schedule below, and candidates shall be examined in accordance with the schedule below. Candidates must achieve a pass in each of the modules in order to pass the examination overall. Candidates who do not achieve a pass mark may submit for assessment on one further occasion only. When the failed assessment is a course assignment, as specified in the Schedule below in sections (*e*), (*i*), and (*j*), the form taken by additional assessment is at the discretion of the Module Coordinator. The Coordinator will make a report to the examiners on the form of the assessment taken in such cases. The marks for each assessed piece of work within each module shall be made available to the examiners.

5. The required written submissions, two copies of each, including the essays, journal article review, literature review, statistical reports, and activities report, but excluding the course assignments, must be sent to the Chair of Examiners, M.Sc. in Psychological Research, c/o Examination Schools, High Street, Oxford, by the times and dates specified at the start of the course. Each submission must be accompanied by a certificate indicating that it is the candidate's own work.

6. Candidates may be required to attend an oral examination at the discretion of the examiners and this may include questions on the candidate's dissertation, assignments, or written papers.

7. The examiners may award a distinction for excellence in the whole examination.

Schedule

(*a*) *Philosophical Foundations of Psychology*

This module begins with historical and foundational issues and progresses to philosophical issues arising from areas of contemporary research in psychology. Topics studied will include some of: the subject matter of psychology; levels of description; the epistemology of psychology; psychological understanding; cognitive science; the study of neuropsychological and psychiatric disorders; the scientific study of consciousness; and philosophical issues arising from areas of contemporary research.

Each candidate shall be required to submit an essay of no more than 3,000 words. Essay topics must be approved by the course committee. The deadline for submission shall be notified to students at the start of the course.

(*b*) *Research Evaluation*

This module is delivered as a series of oral presentations collaboratively prepared by groups of students followed by group discussions. The focus is on research articles that illustrate the use of particular kinds of methodology and/or design.

Each candidate shall be required to submit a 2,000 word review of a journal article assigned by the course committee. Details of this assessment shall be notified to students at the start of the course.

(*c*) *Brain and Cognition*

This module covers methods used in research in cognitive psychology and neuropsychology. It presents foundational knowledge from neuroanatomy, neurological disorders, neurological and psychological assessment and the use of experimental methods, to familiarise students with the diverse methodologies which contribute to cognitive neuropsychology. Methodologies deployed in the investigation of perception and cognition are discussed and evaluated.

Each candidate shall be required to submit an essay of no more than 3,000 words. 5
Essay topics must be approved by the course committee. The deadline for submission shall be notified to students at the start of the course.

(*d*) *Emotion, Personality, and Social Behaviour*

This module provides a critical analysis of the range of methods and approaches used in social psychology and the study of individual differences. 10

Each candidate shall be required to submit an essay of no more than 3,000 words. Essay topics must be approved by the course committee. The deadline for submission shall be notified to students at the start of the course.

(*e*) *Project Design*

This module provides practical instruction in research and presentation skills. 15
Students will undertake detailed planning of the research project to be carried out under (*j*).

Each candidate shall be required to submit a 3,000 word review of relevant literature and methods relating to their research project. The deadline for submission shall be notified to students at the start of the course. In addition each candidate shall 20
be required to give an oral presentation outlining the design of his or her research project and the ideas behind it, but this shall not contribute to the overall result for this module.

(*f*) *Statistical Theory and Methods*

This module comprises a series of statistical lectures and complementary statistical 25
workshops.

Each candidate shall be required to submit a series of reports based on SPSS data analyses carried out during the workshops. Each of the reports will be assessed on a pass/fail basis. The deadline for each submission shall be notified to students at the start of the course. 30

Each candidate shall also be required to sit a two-hour written examination. The examination will be marked on a pass/fail basis and candidates failing to reach the required standard will have one further opportunity to enter for the examination before the end of the academic year.

(*g*) *Mini Project* 35

Small groups of 2–4 students will be assigned to research teams within the Department of Experimental Psychology and guided through research tasks involving, for example, setting up equipment and procedures for a study, collection of pilot data, coding and processing of data, and statistical analysis.

The module will be assessed by a written report of activities conducted in the mini- 40
project. The deadline for submission shall be notified to students at the start of the course.

(*h*) *Language and Development*

This module addresses methods used in selected areas of developmental psychology with a particular emphasis on language. Longitudinal designs, and observational 45
and experimental methods are reviewed and evaluated with examples from recent research. Attention is also given to studies of brain function during development and to the uses of fMRI and EEG data. Particular issues arising from the study of infants lacking verbal skills are identified.

Each candidate shall be required to submit an essay of no more than 3,000 words. Essay topics must be approved by the course committee. The deadline for submission shall be notified to students at the start of the course.

(*i*) *Computational Neuroscience*

This module provides an introduction to the goals and methods of computational modelling in the context of cognitive neuroscience, covering the architecture, function, and properties of a number of basic prototypical classes of neural network. It also looks at how these basic neural networks provide building blocks for larger-scale models of brain function. Lectures will be supplemented by practical sessions providing hands-on experience of computational modelling.

Each candidate shall be required to submit an essay of no more than 3,000 words. Essay topics must be approved by the course committee. The deadline for submission shall be notified to students at the start of the course. In addition, candidates shall be required to complete reports based on practical assignments conducted as part of the module but these shall not contribute to the overall result for this module.

(*j*) *Research Project*

Each student shall carry out a project under the supervision of a research supervisor on a subject selected in consultation with the academic advisor and approved by the course committee. The course committee shall be responsible for the appointment of the research supervisor. The Research Project module shall consist of data collection, analysis of the data, delivering a poster presentation and writing a dissertation on the project.

Candidates shall be required to submit to the examiners not later than noon on the first Monday in September three copies of a typewritten or printed dissertation of not more than 10,000 words in length (excluding bibliography and any appendices) on his or her research project. The cover of the copies must bear the candidate's examination number and name of the examination, but not their name or college, and must be sent in a parcel to, 'The Chair of Examiners: M.Sc. in Psychological Research, c/o Examination Schools, High Street, Oxford'. The dissertation must be accompanied by a signed statement by the candidate that the dissertation is his or her own work.

Candidates shall also be required to deliver a poster presentation based on their research project. However this shall not contribute to the overall result for this module. The date on which candidates are required to deliver their presentations will be in the Long Vacation.

Public Policy in Latin America

(*See also the general notice at the commencement of these regulations.*)

For the purposes of this examination, 'Latin America' will be interpreted as the eighteen Spanish-speaking republics of the Western Hemisphere, plus Brazil, Haiti, and Puerto Rico.

The regulations are as follows:

1. Candidates for the M.Sc in Public Policy in Latin America will:

(*a*) Follow for at least three terms a course of instruction in Public Policy in Latin America.

(*b*) Present a written examination paper from the list to be published on the Latin American Centre website for this degree and in the *University Gazette* in Week 0 of Michaelmas Term. The examination will count for 33.3 per cent of the final degree mark.

(*c*) Submit a dissertation of not more than 15,000 words, including footnotes and appendices. The title of the dissertation must be submitted for approval by the

Latin American Centre Management Committee by 12:00 noon on the Friday of Week 6 of the Michaelmas Term in which they are admitted. Two typewritten copies of the dissertation must be delivered to the Examination Schools, addressed to the Chair of Examiners for the M.Sc in Public Policy in Latin America, c/o Examination Schools, High Street, Oxford, by 12:00 noon on the Monday of Week 5 of Trinity Term in the calendar year in which the examination is taken. The dissertation will count for 66.7 per cent of the final degree mark.

(*d*) Candidates will be required to present themselves for an oral examination. The oral examination will focus on the candidate's examination paper and their dissertation.

2. Candidates who fail the examination paper (without compensating strengths on the dissertation) or who fail the dissertation shall be deemed to have failed the examination. They will be permitted to resubmit the dissertation or retake the examination paper on one (but not more than one) subsequent occasion, in Trinity Term, one year after the initial attempt.

3. Candidates shall be deemed to have passed the examination if they have passed the examination paper and the dissertation.

4. Candidates who fail both the dissertation and the examination paper shall be deemed to have failed the examination. They will be permitted to retake the examination and resubmit the dissertation on one (but not more than one) subsequent occasion, in Trinity Term, one year after the initial attempt.

5. The examiners may award a distinction for excellence in the whole examination.

Radiation Biology

1. The Medical Sciences Board shall elect for the supervision of the course an Organising Committee, which shall have the power to arrange lectures and other instruction.

2. The Organising Committee shall appoint an academic adviser for each candidate.

3. Each candidate shall follow a course of study in Radiation Biology for at least three terms and for a substantial part of the three subsequent vacations, as determined by the course timetable, and produce a certificate from their academic adviser to this effect when they submit their dissertation.

4. Candidates shall be examined in all of the following ways:

 (i) Each candidate must pass a qualifying examination at the end of Michaelmas Term. The examination shall be on modules 1-6 in the Schedule. Candidates who fail the qualifying examination once, shall be permitted to take it again in Week 0 of Hilary Term.

 (ii) Each candidate will be required to submit to the examiners two copies of a typewritten or printed assignment of 3,000 words by noon, Friday of Week 8 of Hilary Term. A choice of assignment titles will be provided to students by Week 8 of Michaelmas Term and will have been approved by the Organising Committee. The assignment will account for 15 per cent of the final marks.

 (iii) Each candidate must pass a three-hour written examination at the end of Hilary Term (normally in Week 9). The examination shall be on the modules set out in the Schedule. Candidates who fail the examination once, will be permitted to take it again in Week 0 of Trinity Term. The examination will account for 25 per cent of the final marks.

(iv) Each candidate shall undertake an original laboratory research project of approximately six months. Candidates will be examined on their project in three ways:

    a. Each candidate will be required to submit to the examiners three copies of a typewritten or printed research dissertation of not more than 10,000 words (excluding bibliography and appendices) based on the research project. The dissertation must be submitted by a date to be specified by the Organising Committee and which will be published in the student handbook not later than the start of Michaelmas Term of the academic year in which the examination is taken.

    b. Each candidate will be expected to give a presentation to the examiners and assessors on his or her research project after submission of the dissertation.

    c. Each candidate will be examined viva voce by the examiners. The dissertation, presentation and viva voce will be given a single grade and account for 60 per cent of the final marks.

5. Candidates must pass the written examination in Hilary Term in order to pass the examination overall. In addition candidates must achieve an overall pass mark on the written assignment and dissertation combined.

6. The examiners may award a distinction for excellence in the whole examination.

7. The required written submissions must be sent to the Chair of Examiners, M.Sc. in Radiation Biology, c/o Examination Schools, High Street, Oxford.

8. The examiners shall retain one copy of each dissertation of each successful candidate for deposit in the Radcliffe Science Library.

Schedule

The modules for study will be:
1. Physics and Chemistry of Radiation Action
2. Molecular Radiation Biology
3. Cellular and Tissue Radiation Biology
4. Whole Body Exposure and Carcinogenesis
5. Radiation Epidemiology
6. Radiation Protection
7. Imaging Technologies
8. Tumour microenvironment
9. Principles of Clinical Radiation Biology
10. Applications of Radiation Therapy
11. Translational Radiation Biology
12. Clinical Radiation Biology.

Refugee and Forced Migration Studies

1. Candidates will be expected to attend such lectures and seminars as their supervisor/course director shall recommend.

2. Candidates will, when they enter for their examination, be required to produce a certificate from their society that they are following a course of study in the field which they have pursued in Oxford for at least three terms.

3. Candidates must present themselves for an oral examination if requested by the examiners.

4. The examiners may award a distinction for excellence in the whole examination. Every candidate will be required to satisfy the examiners in two papers and two essay papers as follows:

Paper I: International Legal and Normative Framework

International legal and normative framework in relation to refugees and displaced persons. International and domestic application of individual and group rights to displaced persons and refugees. Activities and involvement of the relevant international organs, governments, and intergovernmental and non-governmental organisations relevant to forced migration. Concepts of migration and intervention and their justifications. Evolution of humanitarian responses to forced migration. Organisational culture of assistance.

Paper II: Causes and Consequences of Forced Migration

Theories of the causes of forced migration and humanitarian crises. Historical dimensions, political and social dynamics of forced migration. Social, political and cultural constructions of place and space. Impact of forced migration on gender relations and age structures. Coercion and conflict. Implications of forced migrants for conceptualising the modern state and the international order. Security and stability of states. Environmental and development-induced displacement. Poverty and vulnerability. Impact of forced migrants on host populations and governments. Ethical issues raised by migration. Agency, coping mechanisms and survival strategies of affected populations. Nationalism, ethnicity and group identity. Consequences of resettlement programmes for livelihood and economic autonomy. Repatriation and local-level social reconstruction. Institutional responses to forced migrants.

Multidisciplinary Thesis

Each student will be required to write a thesis of not less than 10,000 and not more than 15,000 words on a topic relevant to forced migration. The purpose of this thesis is to ensure that the students have engaged in a multidisciplinary analysis of a single issue in forced migration to gain an awareness of the complex interrelations in the field.

The topic of the thesis will require approval by the chair of examiners. This thesis must be the work of the candidate alone and aid from others must be limited to prior discussion as to the subject and advice on presentation. The thesis (three copies) must be typewritten and delivered to the Examination Schools, High Street, Oxford, not later than noon on Thursday of Week Eight of Trinity Term. An electronic copy must also be submitted to the MSc in Refugee and Forced Migration Studies Coordinator, again by the date and time specified above. The thesis must be presented in proper scholarly form, in double-spacing and on one side only of quarto or A4 paper, each copy bound or held firmly in a stiff cover. The examiners shall retain a copy of the thesis of each candidate who passes the examination for deposit in the Social Sciences Library.

Research Methods Group Essay

Each student must display an understanding of research methods relevant to forced migration. This will be in the form of a group essay of approximately, but no more than 5,000 words, based on directed field research conducted during a four-week period in Hilary Term. The essay will present findings and engage with topics which include: epistemology of social science; social science paradigms; ethics and values; quantitative, qualitative, and participatory methods of data collection; the presentation of statistical information; research design; sampling theory; hypothesis testing; questionnaire design; participant observation; participatory learning and action; and evaluative research.

The essay must be presented in a proper scholarly form and delivered to the Examination Schools, High Street, Oxford, no later than Friday noon in Week Seven of Hilary Term.

A candidate who fails the examination will be permitted to retake it on one further occasion only, not later than one year after the initial attempt. A candidate who has reached a satisfactory standard on any of the three components of the examination: (i) the thesis; (ii) the two written papers; (iii) the research methods group essay, will not be required to retake that part of the examination. Candidates may also be required to attend an oral examination, which may be on one or more of the candidate's written examinations, thesis or group essay. Any candidate who fails a group assignment may be considered for a pass on the basis of an oral examination.

Russian and East European Studies

The regulations made by the Russian and East European Studies Management Committee are as follows.

1. Each candidate will be required to follow a course of instruction for three terms and to present himself or herself for examination in the three compulsory papers in Week Eight of Trinity Term, as well as to present a thesis for examination. In addition, each candidate will be required to participate in training in methodology (quantitative and qualitative) and research skills related to Russian and East European Studies and to have achieved pass marks for the assessed components, as specified in the Notes of Guidance of the year of matriculation of the candidate. Two copies of a thesis should be delivered to the Chair of Examiners for the MSc in Russian and East European Studies, c/o Examination Schools, High Street, Oxford, by noon on the Friday of the sixth week of Trinity Term in the calendar year in which the examination is taken.

2. Candidates who fail a written examination may be allowed to retake it in the following year. In the case of a failed thesis, this may be resubmitted in Trinity Term of the following year. Only one resubmission is permitted. In special circumstances, the Examiners may allow a marginal failure in one component in accordance with the rules outlined in the Examination Conventions.

3. The examiners may award a distinction for excellence in the whole examination.

Schedule of Papers

1. *Twentieth-Century Russian, Soviet and East European History.*

2. *Politics, Economics and International Relations of the Former Soviet Union and Eastern Europe.*

3. *Society and Culture in the Former Soviet Union and Eastern Europe* (compulsory paper Hilary and Trinity Terms).

4. A thesis of at least 12,000 words but not more than 15,000 words.

Social Anthropology

1. The Social Sciences Divisional Board shall elect for the supervision of the course a Standing Committee, namely the Teaching Committee of the School of Anthropology, which shall have power to arrange lectures and other instruction. The course director shall be responsible to that committee.

2. Candidates must follow a course of instruction in Social and Cultural Anthropology for at least three terms, and will, when entering for the examinations, be required to produce a certificate from their supervisor to this effect.

3. Candidates will be required to present themselves for written and (if requested) oral examinations and to submit three copies of a dissertation in prescribed form on an approved topic as defined below.

4. The written examination will consist of four papers on the syllabus described in the Schedule.

5. Each candidate will be required to submit a dissertation of no more than 10,000 words, on a subject selected in consultation with the supervisor and approved by the Chair of Examiners. The proposed title of the dissertation, together with a paragraph describing its scope and the supervisor's written endorsement, must be submitted to the Chair of Examiners by Tuesday of the second week of Trinity Term.

6. Three typewritten copies of the dissertation must be delivered not later than noon on the last Wednesday in August in the year in which the examination is taken, to the Chair of the Examiners, M.Sc. in Social Anthropology, c/o Examination Schools, High Street, Oxford. The word count shall be stated on the outside front cover of the thesis.

7. The oral examination (if requested) may be on the candidate's written papers, or dissertation, or both.

8. The examiners may award a distinction for excellence in the whole examination.

9. If it is the opinion of the examiners that the work done by a candidate is not of sufficient merit to qualify for the Degree of M.Sc. the candidate shall be given the option of resitting the M.Sc. examination.

The four papers will be taken to constitute Part I of the degree and the dissertation to constitute Part II. At the close of the written examinations, the examiners will issue a list of those who have satisfied them in Part I.

10. In order to pass the degree, a student must pass all its assessed components. Where one or more components are failed, the student will be given the opportunity to re-sit or re-submit them once, as the case may be. Any subsequent award of the degree on successful completion of all the assessed components may be delayed by up to three terms, i.e. until the Examination Board next meets.

Schedule

Students must satisfy the examiners in four papers, two of a general nature and two options; one option paper must be selected from List A (below). The syllabuses for the two general papers are as follows:

I. *Culture and Identity*

This paper will focus on the following topics: history and politics of anthropology; anthropology, ethnography and colonialism; gift and exchange; production and consumption; aesthetics, poetics, music and dance; material culture and museums; landscape and the built environment; personhood and the body; identity, ethnicity and nationalism; power, violence, resistance and agency.

II. *Kinship, Power and Charge*

This paper will focus on the following topics: family, kinship and relatedness; gender and age; ritual and religion; myth, history, memory and time; symbolism; representations of misfortune, including witchcraft, possession and healing; politics, law and the state; multiculturalism, migration and globalisation; language and literacy; classification.

The two option papers are as follows:

III. *Option Paper I: The Social Anthropology of a Selected Region*

This option paper must be selected from List A (below).

IV. *Option Paper II: Open Choice*

This option paper must be selected from any of the lists below:

List A. Anthropology of a Selected Region

List B. Topics in Material Anthropology

List C. Anthropology and Topical Issues

Options offered in any of the three lists may vary from year to year. Lists for the current academic year will be issued by the Director of Graduate Studies or his or her delegate by the end of the third week of Michaelmas term.

Social Anthropology (Research Methods)

1. The Social Sciences Divisional Board shall elect for the supervision of the course a Standing Committee, namely the Teaching Committee of the School of Anthropology, which shall have the power to arrange lectures and other instruction. The course director shall be responsible to that committee.

2. Candidates must follow a course of instruction in Social and Cultural Anthropology for at least three terms, and will, when entering for the examinations, be required to produce a certificate from their supervisor to this effect.

3. The final examination shall be taken in the Trinity Term of the academic year in which the candidate's name is first entered on the Register of M.Sc. Students or, with the approval of the Board, in a subsequent year.

4. Each candidate will be required:

(1) To satisfy the examiners in two papers on *Methods of Anthropological and Social Research* by submitting evidence of practical work and two written essays in accordance with I and II below;

(2) To satisfy the examiners in two papers in accordance with III and IV below;

(3) To submit a dissertation in accordance with V below.

I. *Methods of Anthropological and Social Research* (1)

This paper consists of the following components:

(*a*) The satisfactory completion of a course of practical work in (i) participant observation, in-depth interviewing, archival research, and qualitative data analysis; (ii) basic principles of statistical inference, and statistical models for the analysis of quantitative social science data, and (iii) methods of data collection, including questionnaire design, interviewing and coding.

Candidates shall submit to the Examination Schools, High Street, Oxford by noon on Tuesday of fifth week of the third term of the course reports of the practical work completed, accompanied by a statement that they are the candidate's own work except where otherwise indicated.

(*b*) A research proposal of up to 5,000 words, on a topic to be chosen in consultation with the supervisor.

Candidates shall submit their research proposals to the Examination Schools by 12 noon on Tuesday of the second week of the third term of the course, accompanied by a statement that they are the candidate's own work except where otherwise indicated.

II. *Methods of Anthropological and Social Research* (2)

Candidates will be required to produce two essays of up to 2,500 words.

(*a*) The first essay will evaluate the research design, methods of data collection and analysis, and any ethical or philosophical issues that arise in a specified research paper in Social Anthropology. The Director of Graduate Studies of the Institute of Social and Cultural Anthropology shall publish a list of research papers not later than noon on Monday of the first week of the third term; candidates will be required to select one from this list of papers as the subject of their essay.

(*b*) The topic of the second essay will be chosen in consultation with the supervisor and will explore one or more methodological, practical, or ethical issues of anthropological research.

Candidates shall submit their essays to the Examination Schools by 12 noon on Tuesday of the second week of the third term of the course, accompanied by a statement that they are the candidate's own work except where otherwise indicated.

III. *Compulsory Paper*

Every candidate will be required to satisfy the examiners in the following paper:

Social and Cultural Anthropology: Theory and Methods

The scope of this paper includes the following topics: concepts of the individual, society and the person in anthropological perspective; issues of the body, theories of practice, phenomenology; theories of power, order and law; aspects of disorder and violence in society, systems of knowledge and belief; ritual and myth; symbolism and symbolic classification; moral systems and the world religions; oral literature and historical memory; linguistic and artistic modes of communication; aesthetic anthropology, methodological approaches to the study of arts, performance, and material culture; museums, written texts and representation. Fieldwork and data collection methods; quantitative and qualitative techniques; cultural property and indigenous rights; applications of film and sound recording; preparing research proposals; ethical problems; photo- and artefact elicitation, formal analysis of artefacts, archival research, software for material culture analysis and research, and questionnaire surveys.

IV. *Option Paper*

Candidates must choose one option paper. Titles of available options will be made known at the beginning of each academic year. They will be divided into three lists, as follows:

List A: The Social Anthropology of a Selected Region;

List B: Topics in Material Anthropology;

List C: Anthropology and Topical Issues.

Candidates for the degree of M.Sc. in Social Anthropology (Research Methods) must select an option from any of the three lists.

V. *Dissertation*

Each candidate shall be required to submit a dissertation of not more than 10,000 words (excluding references and appendices) on a subject approved by the supervisor. The dissertation shall consist of a critical review of the secondary literature on a specific regional or thematic topic of research. The word count shall be stated on the outside front cover of the thesis.

5. The candidate shall send to the Teaching Committee of the School of Anthropology, with the written approval of his or her supervisor, the proposed title of the dissertation for consideration by the School of Anthropology, by noon on the Tuesday of the second week of Trinity Term in the academic year when his or her name was entered on the Register of M.Sc. Students.

6. The dissertation (three copies) must be typewritten and delivered to the Examination Schools, High Street, Oxford, not later than noon on the last Wednesday of August in the year in which the examination is taken.

7. The oral examination (if requested) may be on the candidate's written papers, or dissertation, or both.

8. The examiners may award a distinction for excellence in the whole examination.

9. If it is the opinion of the examiners that the work done by a candidate is not of sufficient merit to qualify for the Degree of M.Sc. the candidate shall be given the option of re-sitting the M.Sc. examination.

The four papers will be taken to constitute Part I of the degree and the dissertation to constitute Part II. At the close of the written examinations, the examiners will issue a list of those who have satisfied them in Part I.

Social Science of the Internet

1. Candidates must follow for three terms a course of instruction in Social Science of the Internet.

2. The examination will be in seven parts, as follows:

A. Compulsory core paper in Social Dynamics of the Internet, assessed by examination.

B. Compulsory core paper in Internet Technologies and Regulation, assessed by examination.

C. Compulsory core paper in Social Research Methods and the Internet: part I and part II (Methods) assessed by written coursework. Details of and arrangements for submission of the written course work shall be notified to candidates by the first Monday of Michaelmas Term.

D. Compulsory core paper in Social Research Methods and the Internet: part I and part II (Data analysis), consisting of Statistics, and a choice of either Advanced Quantitative Analysis or Advanced Qualitative Analysis, assessed by written coursework and examinations. Details of and arrangements for submission of the written course work shall be notified to candidates by the first Monday of Michaelmas Term.

E. Option paper 1, to be chosen from a list to be published on the Oxford Internet Institute website annually by the first Monday of Michaelmas Term. Not all options may be available every year. The option papers will be assessed by written coursework, details of and arrangements for submission of which shall be notified to candidates by the first Monday of Michaelmas Term.

F. Option paper 2, to be chosen from a list to be published on the Oxford Internet Institute website annually by the first Monday of Michaelmas Term. Not all options may be available every year. The option papers will be assessed by written coursework, details of and arrangements for submission of which shall be notified to candidates by the first Monday of Michaelmas Term. Candidates may, after special permission of the Oxford Internet Institute's Graduate Studies Committee, take this option paper from outside the list of the department's options.

G. A thesis of between 10,000 and 15,000 words on a topic within the subject of the course, to be specified jointly by supervisor and student, and approved by the programme director. Two written copies of the thesis must be delivered to the Examination Schools, High Street, Oxford, by noon of the weekday on or nearest to 1 of August of the year in which the examination is to be taken. Successful candidates will be required to deposit a copy of their thesis in the Oxford Internet Institute Library.

3. The examiners may examine any candidate viva voce.

4. The examiners may award a Distinction for excellence in the whole examination on the basis of the material submitted to them.

Sociology

Every candidate must follow, for at least three terms, a course of instruction in Sociology.

The examination will be in four parts:

A. A compulsory paper in *Methods of Social Research*. As specified for the M.Phil.   5
in Sociology.

B. A compulsory paper in *Sociological Analysis*. As specified for the M.Phil. in Sociology.

C. One optional paper. This will be from a list published annually by Friday of the third week of Michaelmas Full Term in the Department of Sociology.   10

D. A thesis of not more than 10,000 words on a topic within the subject of the course to be specified jointly by supervisor and student. Candidates are warned that they should avoid repetition in their theses of material used in their option papers and that substantial repetition may be penalised. Two typewritten copies of the thesis must be delivered to the Examination Schools, High Street, Oxford, by noon of the   15
weekday on or nearest to 1 September of the year in which the examination is to be taken. Successful candidates will be required to deposit a copy of their thesis in the Department of Sociology.

The examiners may examine any candidate viva voce.

The examiners may award a Distinction for excellence in the whole examination on   20
the basis of the material submitted to them.

Software and Systems Security *(old regulations)*

For students registered on the M.Sc., PG Dip, and PG Cert in Software Engineering; the M.Sc., PG Dip, and PG Cert in Software and Systems Security; or the PG Cert in Object Technology before 1 April 2010.   25

1. The Mathematical, Physical and Life Sciences Divisional Board, in consultation with the Faculty of Computer Science, shall elect for the supervision of the course a Standing Committee which shall have the power to arrange lectures and other instruction.

2. The course will consist of lectures, tutorials, seminars, and classes in the theory and practice of Software and Systems Security. The course may be taken over a   30
period of not less than two years, and not more than four years subject to the Board being able to approve an extension of time of not more than three terms.

3. Every candidate will be required to satisfy the examiners in the following:

(*a*) attendance at twelve modules chosen from those in the Schedules for the M.Sc. in Software and Systems Security below, of which no fewer than seven should   35
come from Schedule A below, and including both from Schedule C below, together comprising a programme of study approved by the Standing Committee;

(*b*) submission of ten written assignments based on the modules chosen from Schedules A and B in cl. 3(*a*) above;

(*c*) submission of written reports following attendance at the modules from   40
Schedule C below, and a dissertation of not more than 20,000 words (including appendices and footnotes but excluding bibliography), all on a subject selected by the candidate in consultation with the supervisor; and

(*d*) a viva voce examination, unless individually dispensed by the examiners.

The assignments under 3(*b*) and two typewritten or printed copies of the disserta-   45
tion shall be forwarded to the examiners for consideration by such dates as the examiners shall determine and shall notify to candidates, supervisors and tutors. The assignments and the dissertation must be accompanied by a statement that it is the candidate's work except where otherwise indicated. In preparation for the dis-

sertation, candidates will be required to submit a project report or proposal following attendance at each of the two modules from Schedule C below.

4. The examiners may award a distinction for excellence in the whole examination.

5. The Standing Committee shall have the discretion to permit any assignments submitted as part of the course for the Postgraduate Certificate in Software Engineering, or the Postgraduate Certificate in Software and Systems Security or the Postgraduate Certificate in Object Technology, or the Postgraduate Diploma in Software Engineering, or the Postgraduate Diploma in Software and Systems Security to be submitted for the examination for the M.Sc., so long as the choice of assignments normally complies with the requirements of cll. 3(*a*) and (*b*) above. No more than one calendar year of study undertaken for the Postgraduate Certificate and/or the Postgraduate Diploma may be counted towards the minimum period of study for the M.Sc.; the entire period of study undertaken for the Postgraduate Certificate and/or the Postgraduate Diploma shall be counted towards the maximum period of study for the M.Sc.

6. If any candidate who is successful in the examination for the M.Sc. in Software and Systems Security has previously successfully completed the Postgraduate Diploma or Certificate in Software and Systems Security, or the Postgraduate Certificate or Postgraduate Diploma in Software Engineering, or the Postgraduate Certificate in Object Technology, and for that examination has incorporated the assignments submitted for the Postgraduate Certificate or Postgraduate Diploma into the M.Sc., then the subsequent award will subsume his or her previous award.

7. The Standing Committee shall have the discretion to permit any candidate to be exempted from submitting up to two of the total of ten written assignments required under 3(*b*) above, provided that the Standing Committee is satisfied that such a candidate has undertaken equivalent study, of an appropriate standard, normally at another institution of higher education.

8. Candidates who fail to satisfy the examiners may re-enter the examination on not more than one occasion which shall normally be within one year of the initial failure. No written assignment shall be submitted to the examiners on more than one occasion.

Schedule A

1. People and Security
2. Safety Critical Systems
3. Security Principles
4. Security Risk Analysis and Management
5. Design for Security
6. Secure and Robust Programming
7. Network Security
8. Trusted Computing Infrastructure
9. Any other module as defined by the course director and approved by the Standing Committee

Schedule B

1. Any module drawn from Schedule A of the M.Sc. in Software Engineering (old regulations)

Schedule C

1. Project and Dissertation I
2. Project and Dissertation II

In June and December each year a list of modules will be published in the *University Gazette*. Each such list, which will have been approved by the Standing Committee and which will be a selection from the full set above, will contain those modules which will be available during the following twelve months.

Software Engineering *(old regulations)*

For students registered on the M.Sc., PG Dip, and PG Cert. in Software Engineering; the M.Sc., PG Dip, and PG Cert in Software and Systems Security; or the PG Cert in Object Technology before 1 April 2010.

1. The Mathematical, Physical and Life Sciences Board, in consultation with the Faculty of Computer Science, shall elect for the supervision of the course a Standing Committee which shall have the power to arrange lectures and other instruction.

2. The course will consist of lectures, tutorials, seminars, and classes in the theory and practice of Software Engineering. The course may be taken over a period of not less than two years, and not more than four years subject to the Board being able to approve an extension of time of not more than three terms.

3. Every candidate will be required to satisfy the examiners in the following:

(*a*) attendance at twelve modules chosen from those in the Schedules for the M.Sc. in Software Engineering below, including both from Schedule C below, comprising a programme of study approved by the Standing Committee;

(*b*) submission of ten written assignments based on the modules chosen from Schedules A and B in cl. 3(*a*) above;

(*c*) submission of written reports following attendance at the modules from Schedule C below, and a dissertation of not more than 20,000 words (including appendices and footnotes but excluding bibliography), all on a subject selected by the candidate in consultation with the supervisor; and

(*d*) a viva voce examination, unless individually dispensed by the examiners.

The assignments under 3(*b*) and two typewritten or printed copies of the dissertation shall be forwarded to the examiners for consideration by such dates as the examiners shall determine and shall notify to candidates, supervisors and tutors. The assignments and the dissertation must be accompanied by a statement that it is the candidate's work except where otherwise indicated. In preparation for the dissertation, candidates will be required to submit a project report or proposal following attendance at each of the two modules from Schedule C below.

4. The examiners may award a distinction for excellence in the whole examination.

5. The Standing Committee shall have the discretion to permit any assignments submitted as part of the course for the Postgraduate Certificate or Postgraduate Diploma in Software Engineering, or the Postgraduate Certificate or Postgraduate Diploma in Software and Systems Security, or the Postgraduate Certificate in Object Technology, to be submitted for the examination for the M.Sc., so long as the choice of assignments normally complies with the requirements of cll. 3(*a*) and (*b*) above. No more than one calendar year of study undertaken for the Postgraduate Certificate and/or the Postgraduate Diploma may be counted towards the minimum period of study for the M.Sc.; the entire period of study undertaken for the Postgraduate Certificate and/or the Postgraduate Diploma shall be counted towards the maximum period of study for the M.Sc.

6. If any candidate who is successful in the examination for the M.Sc. in Software Engineering has previously successfully completed the Postgraduate Diploma, or Certificate in Software Engineering, or the Postgraduate Diploma, or Certificate, in Software and Systems Security, or the Postgraduate Certificate in Object Technology, and for that examination has incorporated the assignments submitted for the Postgraduate Certificate or Postgraduate Diploma into the M.Sc., then the subsequent award will subsume his or her previous award.

7. The Standing Committee shall have the discretion to permit any candidate to be exempted from submitting up to two of the total of ten written assignments required under 3(*b*) above, provided that the Standing Committee is satisfied that such a candidate has undertaken equivalent study, of an appropriate standard, normally at another institution of higher education.

8. Candidates who fail to satisfy the examiners may re-enter the examination on not more than one occasion which shall normally be within one year of the initial failure. No written assignment shall be submitted to the examiners on more than one occasion.

Schedule A

1. Advanced Concurrency Tools
2. Concurrency and Distributed Systems
3. Database Design
4. Design Patterns
5. Distributed Objects
6. Extensible Markup Language
7. Functional Programming
8. Machine-Assisted Software Engineering
9. Management of Risk and Quality
10. Object Orientation
11. Object-Oriented Design
12. Object-Oriented Programming
13. Performance Modelling
14. Process Quality and Improvement
15. Requirements Engineering
16. Software Development Management
17. Software Engineering Mathematics
18. Software Testing
19. Specification and Design
20. Web Services
21. Any other module as defined by the Course Director and approved by the Standing Committee

Schedule B

1. Any module from Schedule A of the M.Sc. in Software and Systems Security (old regulations)

Schedule C

1. Project and Dissertation I
2. Project and Dissertation II

In June and December each year a list of modules will be published in the *University Gazette*. Each such list, which will have been approved by the Standing Committee and which will be a selection from the full set above, will contain those modules which will be available during the following twelve months.

Software Engineering Programme *(new regulations)*   5

For students registering on the M.Sc. in Software Engineering or the M.Sc. in Software and Systems Security on or after 1 April 2010.

A. Definition of the Programme

1. The Mathematical, Physical and Life Sciences Divisional Board shall offer a Programme of Studies in Software Engineering at postgraduate level.   10

2. The subjects of the Programme shall be Software Engineering, Software and Systems Security, and Object Technology.

3. The following awards shall be available within the Programme:

   i. M.Sc. in Software Engineering

   ii. M.Sc. in Software and Systems Security   15

   iii. Postgraduate Diploma in Software Engineering

   iv. Postgraduate Diploma in Software and Systems Security

   v. Postgraduate Certificate in Software Engineering

   vi. Postgraduate Certificate in Software and Systems Security

   vii. Postgraduate Certificate in Object Technology   20

4. The Mathematical, Physical and Life Sciences Divisional Board shall elect for the supervision of the Programme a Supervisory Committee which shall have the power to arrange lectures and other instruction.

B. Progression

5. Entry to the Programme is to the M.Sc. in Software Engineering or the M.Sc. in   25
Software and Systems Security.

6. With the approval of the Programme Director, a candidate may transfer from the M.Sc. in Software Engineering to the M.Sc. in Software and Systems Security, or from the M.Sc. in Software and Systems Security to the M.Sc. in Software Engineering, subject to being eligible to study for the relevant award as set out in   30
sections C and D below.

7. With the approval of the Programme Director, a candidate for the M.Sc. in Software Engineering or for the M.Sc. in Software and Systems Security may be awarded one of the Postgraduate Certificates or Postgraduate Diplomas set out in clause 3 above, subject to such a candidate having satisfied the criteria for the award   35
of the relevant Postgraduate Certificate or Postgraduate Diploma as set out in sections C-D below. Candidates awarded the Postgraduate Certificate or Postgraduate Diploma under this section cease at that point to be registered for the Software Engineering Programme, and may not normally re-enter the Programme.

C. Eligibility for awards: duration of study   40

8. To be eligible for the award of an M.Sc., a student must have been on the Register for the Programme for a period of not less than two years, and not more than four years.

9. To be eligible for the award of a Postgraduate Diploma, a student must have been on the Register for the Programme for a period of not less than one year, and   45
not more than three years.

10. To be eligible for the award of a Postgraduate Certificate, a student must have been on the Register for the Programme for a period of not less than one year, and not more than two years.

11. The Programme Director shall have power

a. to grant suspension from the Register for a period or periods totalling not more than three terms during each of the maximum periods given in clauses 8, 9, and 10 above;

b. to approve an extension of time of not more than three terms to each of the maximum periods given in clauses 8, 9, and 10 above;

subject to the total periods of suspensions and extensions not exceeding six terms overall.

D. Eligibility for awards: study and examinations

12. Students on the Register shall enter for the examination for the award of the M.Sc., unless they have been given approval under clause 7 above to be awarded one of the Postgraduate Certificates or Postgraduate Diplomas.

13. Every candidate will be required to satisfy the examiners in the following:

a. M.Sc. in Software Engineering

(i) attendance at a minimum of twelve modules chosen from those in the Schedule below, including both from Schedule D, comprising a programme of study approved by the Supervisory Committee;

(ii) submission of at least ten written assignments corresponding to those modules attended that were chosen from Schedules A, B, or C below;

(iii) submission of a dissertation of not more than 20,000 words (including appendices and footnotes but excluding bibliography) on a subject selected by the candidate in consultation with the supervisor and approved by the Supervisory Committee;

b. M.Sc. in Software and Systems Security

(i) attendance at a minimum of twelve modules chosen from those in the Schedule below, of which six should come from Schedule C, and including both from Schedule D, together comprising a programme of study approved by the Supervisory Committee;

(ii) submission of at least ten written assignments corresponding to those modules attended that were chosen from Schedules A, B, or C below;

(iii) submission of a dissertation of not more than 20,000 words (including appendices and footnotes but excluding bibliography) on a subject selected by the candidate in consultation with the supervisor and approved by the Supervisory Committee;

(iv) the subject of the projects and dissertation shall relate to software and systems security, and must have been approved as such by the Supervisory Committee.

c. Postgraduate Diploma in Software Engineering

(i) attendance at a minimum of eight modules chosen from those in Schedules A, B, or C below, comprising a programme of study approved by the Supervisory Committee;

(ii) submission of at least eight written assignments corresponding to those modules attended.

d. Postgraduate Diploma in Software and Systems Security

(i) attendance at a minimum of eight modules chosen from those in Schedules A, B, or C below, of which at least five should come from Schedule C, comprising a programme of study approved by the Supervisory Committee;

(ii) submission of at least eight written assignments corresponding to those modules attended.

e. Postgraduate Certificate in Software Engineering

(i) attendance at a minimum of four modules, chosen from Schedules A, B, or C below, together comprising a programme of study approved by the Supervisory Committee;

(ii) submission of at least four written assignments, corresponding to those modules attended.

f. Postgraduate Certificate in Software and Systems Security

(i) attendance at a minimum of four modules, at least three of which chosen from Schedule C below, with the remainder chosen from Schedules A, B, or C below, together comprising a programme of study approved by the Supervisory Committee;

(ii) submission of at least four written assignments, corresponding to those modules attended.

g. Postgraduate Certificate in Object Technology

(i) attendance at a minimum of four modules, at least three of which chosen from Schedule B below, with the remainder chosen from Schedules A, B, or C below, together comprising a programme of study approved by the Supervisory Committee;

(ii) submission of at least four written assignments, corresponding to those modules attended.

The assignments and, for the M.Sc., two typewritten or printed copies of the dissertation, shall be forwarded to the examiners for consideration by such dates as the examiners shall determine and shall notify to candidates, supervisors and tutors. The assignments and the dissertation must be accompanied by a statement that it is the candidate's work except where otherwise indicated. Candidates are usually required to submit the assignments electronically. Details will be given in the programme handbook. Any candidate who is unable, for some reason, to submit practical work electronically must apply to the Programme Director for permission to submit the work in paper form. Such applications must reach the Programme Director two weeks before the deadline for submitting the work. The two copies of the dissertation shall be addressed to the Chair of Examiners, Software Engineering Programme, c/o Examination Schools, High Street, Oxford, OX1 4BG.

In preparation for the dissertation, candidates will be required to submit a project report or proposal following attendance at each of the two modules from Schedule D below.

14. Provided the Supervisory Committee is satisfied that a candidate has undertaken equivalent study, of an appropriate standard, normally at another institution of higher education, the committee shall have the discretion to permit the candidate to be exempted from attending at, and submitting the written assignment for, modules chosen from Schedule A, B, or C below, as required under clause 13 above as follows:

a. For the M.Sc.: up to two of the total of ten modules for which written assignments are required;

b. For the award of the Postgraduate Diploma: up to two of the total of eight modules;

c. For the award of the Postgraduate Certificate: up to one of the total of four modules.

15. Candidates will be expected to attend a viva voce examination as part of the examination for each award unless dispensed by the examiners.

16. The examiners may award a distinction for excellence in the whole examination for each award.

17. Candidates who fail to satisfy the examiners in the assignments under clause 13 above may be permitted to resubmit work in respect of part or parts of the examination which they have failed for examination on not more than one occasion which shall normally be within one year of the initial failure. No written assignment shall be submitted to the examiners on more than one occasion.

E. Subsuming of previous awards under the Programme

18. In the exceptional circumstances that a candidate granted approval under clause 7 above to be awarded of one of the Postgraduate Certificates or Postgraduate Diplomas (set out in clause 3 above) is readmitted to one of the M. Scs (set out in clause 3 above), then the following apply:

a. If any candidate who is successful in the examination for the Postgraduate Diploma has previously successfully completed the Postgraduate Certificate, and for that examination has incorporated the assignments submitted for the Postgraduate Certificate into the Postgraduate Diploma, then the Postgraduate Diploma will subsume his or her Certificate.

b. If any candidate who is successful in the examination for the M.Sc. has previously successfully completed the Postgraduate Diploma or the Postgraduate Certificate, and for that examination has incorporated the assignments submitted for the Postgraduate Certificate or Postgraduate Diploma into the M. Sc., then the subsequent award will subsume his or her previous award.

Schedule of Modules

Schedule A

1. Model Checking
2. Concurrency and Distributed Systems
3. Database Design
4. Extensible Markup Language
5. Functional Programming
6. Management of Risk and Quality
7. Performance Modelling
8. Process Quality and Improvement
9. Requirements Engineering
10. Software Development Management
11. Software Engineering Mathematics
12. Software Testing
13. Specification and Design
14. Agile Methods
15. Mobile and Sensor Networks

16. Software Product Lines

17. Any other module as defined by the course director and approved by the Standing Committee

Schedule B

18. Design Patterns

19. Object Orientation

20. Object-Oriented Design

21. Object-Oriented Programming

22. Service Orientated Architecture

Schedule C

23. People and Security

24. Safety Critical Systems

25. Security Principles

26. Security Risk Analysis and Management

27. Design for Security

28. Secure and Robust Programming

29. Network Security

30. Trusted Computing Infrastructure

Schedule D

31. Project and Dissertation I

32. Project and Dissertation II

The Supervisory Committee shall have the power to add or delete modules from the Schedule. In June and December each year a list of modules will be published in the *University Gazette*. Each such list, which will have been approved by the Supervisory Committee and which will be a selection from the full set above, will contain those modules which will be available during the following twelve months.

Surgical Science and Practice (*old regulations for students registered before 1 October 2012*)

1. The Divisional Board of Medical Sciences, jointly with the Continuing Education Board, shall elect for the supervision of the course a Standing Committee, which shall have the power to arrange lectures and other instruction.

2. Candidates must follow for at least six terms and no more than nine terms, a part-time course of instruction in the theory and practice of Surgical Science and Practice, which shall normally take place over a period of two years and no more than four years.

3. Every candidate will be required to satisfy the examiners in the following:

(*a*) Attendance at the modules in Schedule A and Schedule B below and other teaching sessions as required.

(*b*) Active participation in all parts of the course to the satisfaction of the Course Director.

(*c*) Four written assignments related to the modules in Schedule A, each of not more than 4,000 words in length.

(*d*) Two assignments consisting of multiple choice questions or structured short questions, online project working and practical tests related to the modules in Schedule B.

(*e*) A dissertation of not more than 20,000 words (excluding tables, appendices, footnotes and bibliography), on a subject selected by the candidate in consultation with the supervisor and approved by the Course Director.

The assignments set out in clauses 3(*c-e*) shall be forwarded, usually through a specified electronic submission system, to the examiners c/o Registry, Department for Continuing Education, 1 Wellington Square, Oxford OX1 2JA, for consideration by such date as the examiners shall determine and of which they shall notify candidates.

4. Candidates may be required to attend a viva voce examination at the end of the course of studies at the discretion of the examiners.

5. The examiners may award a distinction to candidates for the MSc.

6. Candidates who fail to satisfy the examiners in any part of the examination may be permitted to resubmit work in respect of the part or parts of the examination that they have failed, for examination on not more than one occasion which shall normally be within one year of the original failure.

7. The Standing Committee shall have the discretion to permit any candidate to be exempted, in exceptional circumstances, from attendance at any module under 3(*a*) and from submitting the associated assignment required under 3(*c*) and 3(*d*) above, provided that the Standing Committee is satisfied that such a candidate has undertaken equivalent study, or has appropriate work experience to an equivalent standard.

Schedule A

The practice of evidence-based health care
Quality improvement science and systems analysis
Introduction to surgical management and leadership
Becoming a medical educator
  Any other module as defined by the Course Director and approved by the Standing Committee.

Schedule B

Human factors, teamwork and communication
Surgical technology and robotics.

Surgical Science and Practice (*new regulations for students registering on any of the awards listed from 1 October 2012 and available to existing students*)

1. The Medical Sciences Board, jointly with the Continuing Education Board, shall elect for the supervision of the course a Standing Committee, which shall have the power to arrange lectures and other instruction.

2. The course is available on a part time basis only and shall consist of instruction in the theory and practice of Surgical Science and Practice.

3. The policy of the Continuing Education Board on variable intensity part time study shall apply to this award.

4. The minimum period of registration on the M.Sc. shall be three terms and the maximum period of registration shall be twelve terms.

5. Candidates may be permitted in certain circumstances to suspend status, for a maximum of six terms. Any such period shall not count to the maximum or minimum permitted period of registration and no fee liability will be incurred during such periods.

6. Every candidate will be required to satisfy the examiners in the following:

(*a*) Attendance at the modules in Schedule A and Schedule B below and other teaching sessions as required.

(*b*) Participation in all parts of the course to the satisfaction of the Course Director.

(*c*) Four written assignments related to the modules in Schedule A, each of not more than 4,000 words in length.

(*d*) Two assignments consisting of multiple choice questions or structured short questions, online project working and practical tests related to the modules in Schedule B.

(*e*) A dissertation of not more than 15,000 words (including tables, appendices and footnotes but excluding reference list), on a subject selected by the candidate in consultation with the supervisor and approved by the Standing Committee. Approval must be sought no later than the first day of the ninth term of registration. The dissertation must be submitted within three terms of the date of approval, notwithstanding the maximum permitted period of registration.

The assignments set out in clauses 6(*c-e*) shall be forwarded, usually through a specified electronic submission system, to the examiners c/o Registry, Department for Continuing Education, 1 Wellington Square, Oxford OX1 2JA, for consideration by such date as the examiners shall determine and shall notify candidates.

7. Candidates may be required to attend a viva voce examination at the end of the course of studies at the discretion of the examiners.

8. The examiners may award a distinction to candidates for the M.Sc.

9. Candidates who fail to satisfy the examiners in any part of the examination under 6 (*c-e*) above may be permitted to resubmit work in respect of the part or parts of the examination that they have failed, on not more than one occasion for each assignment without being required to repeat attendance at the relevant module or modules. The resubmission will normally be within one year of the original failure.

10. Provided the Standing Committee is satisfied that a student on the award has undertaken equivalent study, of an appropriate standard, normally at another institution of higher education, or has appropriate work experience to an equivalent standard, the committee may permit the candidate to be exempted from attendance and the submission of a written assignment in respect of up to three modules. In exercising this discretion the Standing Committee shall take into consideration the length of time that has elapsed since the study or work experience was undertaken.

11. The Standing Committee may deem satisfactory completion of a module (including the associated assessment) prior to registration for the award as having met the attendance and examination requirements in respect of that module. Such discretion will normally only be exercised if the time elapsed between commencement of the accredited module concerned and registration for the award is not more than two years. The maximum number of modules taken prior to registration for the award that may count in this way shall be three.

Schedule A

The practice of evidence-based health care

Quality improvement science and systems analysis*

Introduction to surgical management and leadership

Becoming a medical educator*

Any other module as defined by the Course Director and approved by the Standing Committee.

Schedule B

Human factors, teamwork and communication*

Surgical technology and robotics

* Also available to students registered for the PG Diploma in Health Research

Sustainable Urban Development

1. The Continuing Education Board shall elect for the supervision of the course a course committee that shall have the power to arrange lectures and other instruction.

2. Every candidate must follow for at least six terms a part-time course of instruction in the theory and practice of Sustainable Urban Development, which shall normally take place over a period of two years and no more than four years.

3. Every candidate will be required to satisfy the examiners in the following:

    (*a*) Attendance at classes, tutorials, group seminars and other teaching sessions;

    (*b*) seven written assignments, each being on one of the units listed in the Schedule below, and each of not more than 3000 words in length;

    (*c*) a dissertation of not more than 15,000 words (excluding tables, appendices, footnotes and bibliography), on a subject selected by the candidate in consultation with the supervisor and approved by the course committee.

The assessed work set out in clause 3(*b*) shall be forwarded in normal circumstances through an electronic submission system to the examiners c/o Registry, Department for Continuing Education, 1 Wellington Square, Oxford OX1 2JA, for consideration by such date as the examiners shall determine and of which they shall notify candidates. The assessed work set out in clause 3(*c*) shall be forwarded to the examiners c/o, Examination Schools, High Street, Oxford OX1 4BG for consideration by such date as the examiners shall determine and of which they shall notify candidates.

4. Candidates may be required to attend a viva voce examination at the end of the course of studies at the discretion of the examiners.

5. The examiners may award a distinction to candidates for the MSc.

6. Candidates who fail to satisfy the examiners in any part of the examination may be permitted to resubmit work in respect of the part or parts of the examination that they have failed for examination on not more than one occasion which shall normally be within one year of the original failure.

7. The course committee shall have the discretion to permit any candidate to be exempted, in exceptional circumstances, from submitting an assignment, provided that the committee is satisfied that such a candidate has undertaken equivalent study, or have appropriate work experience to an equivalent standard.

Schedule

Concepts of the City and Environmental Change
Climate Change and the Built Environment
Placemaking
Financing Sustainability
Transportation and Sustainability
Urbanism and the Design Process
The Flexible City? Urban Theory, Practice and Project Management
Urbanisation and the Global South
Any other subject approved by the course committee.
Not all units will be available in any one year.

Teaching English Language in University Settings

1. The part-time course is open only to candidates who are currently enrolled upon the Postgraduate Diploma in Teaching English Language in University Settings (PGDip TELUS), and who have submitted a satisfactory dissertation proposal for approval by the Departmental Board.Candidates will normally apply by Hilary Term   5
of their second PGDip TELUS year; successful candidates will initially be offered a place conditional on passing the PGDip TELUS at an appropriate level (normally a mark of at least 65). Entries will be confirmed after the Examination Board at the beginning of Trinity Term.

2. Candidates will be required to submit a dissertation of between 15,000 and   10
20,000 words (including footnotes/endnotes but excluding appendices and references or bibliography) on a subject selected by the candidate in consultation with the supervisor, which must be closely related to one or more of the themes of the course, and has been approved by the Departmental Board.

3. Three word processed or printed copies of the dissertation must be delivered to   15
the Chair of the Examiners, M.Sc. Teaching English Language in University Settings, c/o Examination Schools, High Street, Oxford, OX2 6PY no later than noon of the last Friday in August of the year in which the examination for the final postgraduate diploma module has been taken.

4. One copy should be hard bound and two soft bound, the latter of which should   20
be anonymous except for the candidate number. The hard bound copy of the dissertation of each candidate who passes the examination shall be retained by the department for deposit in the departmental library. The dissertation must be accompanied by a declaration indicating that it is the candidate's own work.

5. The pass mark for the dissertation will be 50. The examiners may award a   25
distinction for excellence in the examination.

6. The candidate may also be examined orally. The oral examination will only be on the candidate's dissertation.

7. Successful students will be awarded the degree of Master of Science, which will subsume the award of the Diploma.If the dissertation is awarded a failing mark, the   30
candidate may resubmit the dissertation one further time on the next occasion when it is examined.If a failing mark is received, either at the time of the original submission (and the candidate does not wish to re-sit) or after re-submission, students will retain the award of the Diploma.

Theoretical Chemistry   35

1. The course shall be under the supervision of the Coulson Professor of Theoretical Chemistry or an appointed deputy, who shall have power to arrange lectures and other instruction.

2. Candidates shall follow for at least three terms a course of instruction in Theoretical Chemistry.   40

3. The examination shall be in three parts, as follows:

(*a*) Candidates shall successfully complete a written assignment on each of the lecture courses listed below.

(*b*) Candidates shall submit a short dissertation on a topic selected by the candidate in consultation with the supervisor and approved by the Coulson   45
Professor of Theoretical Chemistry or an appointed deputy. Between thirty-five and sixty-five typed pages is the preferred length.

(*c*) There shall be an oral examination on the dissertation and its background material.

4. The Coulson Professor of Theoretical Chemistry or an appointed deputy shall make available to the examiners a certificate showing the extent to which the candidate has an adequate command of (*a*) mathematics and (*b*) computational chemistry. Candidates must submit for approval to the Coulson Professor of Theoretical Chemistry or an appointed deputy by the end of Hilary Term in the year in which they enter the examination the title and brief statement of the form and scope of their dissertation, together with the name of a person who has agreed to act as their supervisor during the preparation of the dissertation. Approval shall normally be given not later than two weeks after submission of a proposal.

5. Two typewritten copies of the dissertation must be delivered, not later than noon on 15 September in the year in which the examination is taken, to the M.Sc. Examiners (Theoretical Chemistry), c/o Examination Schools, High Street, Oxford. The dissertation must be accompanied by a statement that it is the candidate's own work except where otherwise indicated, and a certificate from the candidate's society to the effect that he or she has followed for three terms a course of instruction in Theoretical Chemistry. The examiners may retain one copy of the dissertation of each candidate who passes the examination for deposit in an appropriate departmental library.

6. For each lecture course, an essay topic or problem set shall be prescribed by the relevant lecturer no later than the Monday of the eighth week of the term during which the lectures are given. Completed assignments must be delivered to the M.Sc. Examiners (Theoretical Chemistry), c/o the Examination Schools, High Street, Oxford, not later than noon on the days specified in the following schedule.

Quantum Mechanics	Friday second week of Hilary Term
Statistical Mechanics	Friday second week of Hilary Term
Molecular Electronic Structure	Friday second week of Trinity Term
Applied Statistical Mechanics	Friday second week of Trinity Term
Many-body quantum and statistical mechanics	Friday ninth week of Trinity Term

7. A candidate who does not submit a written assignment on a lecture course by the stated time according to the examination schedule in cl. 6 above shall be deemed to have failed the lecture course in question.

8. A list of those candidates who have satisfied the examiners in particular lecture courses in the relevant term shall be posted in the Physical and Theoretical Chemistry Laboratory, by the Friday preceding the following Full Term.

9. If a candidate is deemed to have failed a particular lecture course, he or she shall not be permitted to re-enter for examination in that lecture course.

Any candidate who has not satisfied the examiners in four lecture courses by the beginning of fifth week of Trinity Term shall be deemed to have failed the degree course.

10. A candidate who has failed to satisfy the examiners in the examination may enter again for the examination on one, but not more than one, subsequent occasion, not later than one year after the initial attempt. No written assignment shall be submitted to the examiners on more than one occasion.

11. The examiners may award a distinction for excellence in the whole examination.

List of lecture courses
   Quantum Mechanics
   Statistical Mechanics
   Molecular Electronic Structure

Applied Statistical Mechanics

Many-body quantum and statistical mechanics.

Instruction will also be provided in mathematics and computational chemistry.
The Coulson Professor of Theoretical Chemistry or an appointed deputy shall have power to delete courses and to add other lecture courses to this list, and shall publish details of the full list including such additional courses in the *University Gazette* by not later than the Friday of the eighth week of the Trinity Term in the year preceding the examination.

Visual, Material, and Museum Anthropology

1. The Social Sciences Divisional Board shall elect for the supervision of the course a Standing Committee, namely the Teaching Committee of the School of Anthropology, which shall have power to arrange lectures and other instruction. The course director will be responsible to that committee.

2. Candidates must follow a course of instruction in Visual, Material and Museum Anthropology for at least three terms, and will, when entering for the examination, be required to produce a certificate from their supervisor to this effect.

3. Candidates will be required to submit three copies of written work required for Papers 2 and 3 comprising an essay for Paper 2 and a portfolio of coursework notes and a research proposal for Paper 3; to present themselves for a written examination for Papers 1 and 4 (where relevant), and to submit three copies of a dissertation in prescribed form on an approved topic as defined below.

4. The assessed written work will consist of:

(i) one essay of no more than 5,000 words for Paper 2 on the syllabus described in the Schedule; for Paper 2 a list of essay titles will be announced no later than Monday of the fourth week of Michaelmas Term. Three typewritten copies of the essay, together with three copies of any associated non-print materials, must be delivered not later than noon of the Tuesday of the first week of Hilary Term to the Chair of the Examiners, M.Sc. in Visual, Material, and Museum Anthropology, c/o Examination Schools, High Street, Oxford. Non-print materials shall not constitute more than fifteen minutes of viewing/reading time in the case of video or multimedia submissions.

(ii) a research proposal relating to the subject of the candidate's intended doctoral research or a general essay on visual, material, or museological anthropological methods and/or ethnographic museological methods of no more than 2,500 words for Paper 3 on the syllabus described in the Schedule. Three typewritten copies of the research proposal or essay, together with three copies of any associated non-print materials, must be delivered not later than noon of the Tuesday of the fifth week of Trinity Term to the Chair of the Examiners, M.Sc. in Visual, Material, and Museum Anthropology, c/o Examination Schools, High Street, Oxford. Non-print materials shall not constitute more than fifteen minutes of viewing/reading time in the case of video or multimedia submissions.

(iii) a portfolio of notes and written exercises of no more than 2,500 words relating to visual and material anthropological methods and/or ethnographic museological methods. The portfolio must be delivered not later than noon on the Tuesday of the fifth week of Trinity Term to the Chair of Examiners, M.Sc. in Visual, Material, and Museum Anthropology, c/o Examination Schools, High Street, Oxford. Non-print materials shall not constitute more than fifteen minutes of viewing/reading time in the case of video or multimedia submissions.

(iv) a dissertation of no more than 10,000 words, on a subject selected in consultation with the supervisor and approved by the Chair of Examiners. The
proposed title of the dissertation together with a paragraph describing its
scope and the supervisor's written endorsement, must be submitted to the
Chair of Examiners by Tuesday of the second week of Trinity Term. Three   5
typewritten copies of the dissertation, together with three copies of any
associated non-print materials, must be delivered not later than noon of the
last Wednesday in August in the year in which the examination is taken to the
Chair of the Examiners, M.Sc. in Visual, Material, and Museum
Anthropology, c/o Examination Schools, High Street, Oxford. The word   10
count shall be stated on the outside front cover of the thesis. Non-print
materials shall not constitute more than fifteen minutes of viewing/reading
time in the case of video or multimedia submissions.

5. The written examination will consist of one three-hour paper for Paper 1 and
one three-hour paper for Paper 4 on the syllabus described in the Schedule.   15

6. There will be no oral examination.

7. The examiners may award a distinction for excellence in the whole examination.

8. A candidate who fails any of the component parts of the examination may retake or re-submit that part of the examination on one occasion only. The four papers
will be taken to constitute Part I of the degree and the dissertation to constitute Part   20
II. At the close of the written examinations, the examiners will issue a list of those
who have satisfied them in Part I.

9. In order to pass the degree, a student must pass all its assessed components.
Where one or more components are failed, the student will be given the opportunity
to re-sit or re-submit them once, as the case may be. Any subsequent award of the   25
degree on successful completion of all the assessed components may be delayed by up
to three terms, i.e. until the Examination Board next meets.

Schedule

Every candidate will be required to satisfy the examiners in four papers as follows:

1. *Fundamental Concepts in Visual, Material, and Museum Anthropology*   30

This paper focuses on anthropology's distinctive contribution to understanding
social and cultural form and process, and the role of human creativity within them,
with particular reference to artefacts of material and visual culture, and to the
collection, display, production, circulation and consumption of such artefacts.
Attention will be paid to the subject's history and its place within broader concerns   35
of politics, colonialism, and culture; issues of power and identity in relation to visual,
material and museum anthropology; the formation of museum collections and visual
archives; and also to the place of the socio-cultural in constituting such 'natural'
phenomena as ecology, landscape, and population. The scope of this paper includes
the following topics: the history and development of anthropological photography   40
and object analysis, of documentary and ethnographic film, and of visual display in
and beyond museums; an introduction to film and photographic theory, to material
culture theory and to anthropological theories of representation, exchange and
consumption; the Colonial archive and Colonial documentary practices; the ethnography of film, photography and other visual representational practices.   45

2. *Contemporary themes in Visual, Material, and Museum Anthropology*

Topics central to this paper include: the changing roles and meanings of artefacts
over time; the legacies of anthropology's history in the present – with special reference to museums and material culture; issues of representation, politics and power;

theoretical and methodological shifts in the analysis of material culture, museums and display; fieldwork, collecting, archival processes and other methodologies central to the production of anthropological knowledge. Case studies may focus on topics such as; visual culture (including photography, the internet, art and aesthetics); music and performance; museum ethics and relationships with 'source communities'; land-scape and the built environment; religion, identity, and material culture; dress and body modification; mass production and trade; debates concerning tradition, mod-ernity and authenticity; transnational cultural flows; the wider issues of cross-cultural investigation; phenomenological, semiotic and post-structuralist approaches to visual media and material culture; time, memory and perception; film and photographs as material culture; social uses and local practices of visual media use, including in-digenous media and indigenous curation; professional visual media production; visual media and contemporary arts practices; image ethics; digital media practice; audience response and reception theory; art, performance and display; detailed study of the work of one or more contemporary ethnographic filmmaker, artist, or photo-grapher. *[Note: some topics may vary slightly from year to year]*.

3. *Research Methods in Visual, and Material Anthropology and Museum Ethnography*

The scope of this paper includes: fieldwork and data collection methods, visual and non-visual, including photo-, object- and film/video-elicitation; qualitative and quantitative techniques; cultural property and indigenous rights; preparing research proposals; museum display and design; ethical problems; curating exhibitions, arte-facts and photographs; working with artists, curators, 'culture brokers' and 'source communities'; elementary still photographic, video and digital multimedia produc-tion; exhibition design, analysis and presentation techniques.

4. *Option paper*

Candidates must select one option paper from those taught each year for M.Sc. candidates at the Institute of Social and Cultural Anthropology. Titles of options will be made known at the beginning of each academic year and candidates may select their option from any of Lists A, B or C.

Water Science Policy and Management

1. The Social Sciences Divisional Board shall elect for the supervision of the course a Standing Committee. The Academic Director and Course Director will be respon-sible to the Standing Committee.

2. Candidates must follow a course of instruction in Water Science, Policy and Management for at least three terms, and will, when entering for the examination, be required to produce a certificate from the Course Director to this effect.

3. The examination will consist of:

(i) a written examination of three three-hour papers based on core courses as described in the schedule;

(ii) two assessed essays based on elective courses;

(iii) a dissertation on a subject selected in consultation with the supervisor and Course Director and approved by the Standing Committee.

4. Candidates must submit to the Course Director by the end of Hilary Term in the year in which they enter the examination, the title and a brief statement of the form and scope of their dissertation, together with the name of a person who has been agreed by the Course Director or Academic Director to act as their supervisor during preparation of the dissertation.

5. The dissertation shall be of a maximum length of 15,000 words and accompanied by an abstract not exceeding 150 words. The word count shall exclude appendices, references and the abstract. The detailed format and specification of the dissertation shall be approved by the Standing Committee, and published in the course handbook.

6. The deadline for submission of the dissertation is noon on the first weekday of September in the year in which the written examination is taken. Two copies of the dissertation must be submitted, to the M.Sc Examiners (Water Science, Policy and Management) c/o Examinations Schools, High Street, Oxford OX1 4BG. The examiners may retain one copy of the dissertation of each candidate who passes the examination for deposit in an appropriate library. Both copies must bear the candidate's examination number but not his/her name.

7. All submitted work shall be accompanied by a separate statement certifying that that the submitted work is the candidate's own work except where otherwise indicated.

8. In the written examination, the examiners will permit the use of hand-held pocket calculators subject to the conditions set out under the heading 'Use of calculators in examinations' in the Special Regulations concerning Examinations.

9. The examiners may also examine any candidate viva voce on the candidate's written papers, dissertation or both.

10. Arrangements for reassessment shall be specified by the Standing Committee and published in the course handbook.

11. The examiners may award a distinction for excellence in the whole examination.

Schedule

(a) Core courses

The core courses will be examined under the following heads:

1. *Water Science*

Candidates will be expected to have knowledge and a critical understanding of the physical, chemical and biological processes, and interactions across the hydrological cycle at the global, basin/catchment and hillslope scale, and of the engineering and technological solutions to water supply and sanitation.

2. *Water and Society*

Candidates will be expected to have knowledge and a critical understanding of the arguments and issues related to the legal, social, political and institutional dimensions of water decision-making.

3. *Water Management*

Candidates will be expected to have knowledge and a critical understanding of the principles of integrated water resource management and policy, along with the economic approaches, modelling tools and analysis techniques that can be used to support water management and policy.

(b) Elective courses

Candidates will be expected to show advanced knowledge of two of the elective courses on offer in any year.

9

REGULATIONS FOR THE DEGREE OF MASTER OF THEOLOGY (IN APPLIED THEOLOGY) AND FOR THE POSTGRADUATE DIPLOMA IN APPLIED THEOLOGY

GENERAL REGULATIONS

1. The Board of the Faculty of Theology and Religion shall have power to award Postgraduate Diplomas in Applied Theology. Any person who has been admitted under the provisions of this section as a Student for the Postgraduate Diploma in Applied Theology, who has satisfied the conditions prescribed in the relevant regulations made by the faculty board under Section B below, and who has satisfied the examiners for the Diploma may be awarded the Postgraduate Diploma in Applied Theology.

2. Any person who has been admitted under the provisions of this section as a Student for the Degree of Master of Theology, who has satisfied the conditions prescribed in the relevant regulations made by the faculty board under Section A below, and who has satisfied the examiners for the degree may supplicate for the Degree of Master of Theology. Alternatively, such persons may be awarded the Postgraduate Diploma in Applied Theology if they have satisfied the conditions prescribed in the relevant regulations made by the faculty board under Section B below and have satisfied the examiners for the Diploma.

3. The examinations for the Degree of Master of Theology and for the Postgraduate Diploma in Applied Theology shall be under the supervision of the Board of the Faculty of Theology and Religion which shall have power to make regulations governing the examinations.

4. There shall be a Committee for the supervision of arrangements for the Degree of Master of Theology and for the Postgraduate Diploma in Applied Theology which shall be called the Master of Theology Studies Committee. This Committee shall consist of two representatives of the Board of the Faculty of Theology and Religion (at least one of whom shall be a member

of the board's Graduate Studies Committee) and one representative of each of the participating institutions, as listed in the Schedule below. The Committee may co-opt up to three additional members. The Committee shall have such powers and duties in respect of the Degree of Master of Theology and the Postgraduate Diploma in Applied Theology as may from time to time be prescribed by the Board of the Faculty of Theology and Religion.

5. The Board of the Faculty of Theology and Religion shall have the power to admit as students for the Degree of Master of Theology and for the Postgraduate Diploma in Applied Theology candidates nominated by the institutions listed in the Schedule below.

6. Each of the institutions listed in the Schedule below shall make a return to the Registrar by the end of the first week of Michaelmas Full Term, showing the names of all persons nominated in that term as Students for the Degree of Master of Theology and for the Postgraduate Diploma in Applied Theology, and the Registrar shall keep a register of such students.

7. The Board of the Faculty of Theology and Religion shall have power, on the advice of a student's society or other institution, to remove temporarily or permanently the name of a student from the register.

Schedule

The participating institutions for the Degree of Master of Theology and for the Postgraduate Diploma in Applied Theology are: Blackfriars; Campion Hall; Harris Manchester College; Mansfield College; Regent's Park College; Ripon College, Cuddesdon; St Benet's Hall; St Stephen's House; and Wycliffe Hall.

SPECIAL REGULATIONS

A. **Regulations for the course of instruction for the Master of Theology (in Applied Theology) at the participating institutions listed in the Schedule.**

1. Candidates, who must be members of the University, shall be graduates in theology, or shall hold an equivalent theological qualification.

2. Full-time residential candidates will complete Part I of the course in *one* year and *one* additional residential year for Part II [dissertation]. Submission of Unit 2 may be delayed until the April submission after the first year of the course.

3. Part-time non-residential candidates will complete Part I of the course in *two* years part-time and *two* additional years for Part II [dissertation].

4. Candidates may change from full-time to part-time after the first year of study.

5. Part-time candidates shall be required to attend courses of instruction organised by the participating institutions equivalent to one day a week over six terms.

6. For part-time students there shall be no residential requirement for Part II.

7. In Part I, all candidates will take the first two units and any two others. All units in Part I are examined by extended essays of not more than 7,000 words. In addition, Unit 2 will normally be supplemented with a portfolio of supporting materials.

8. Part II will consist of a dissertation of between 15,000 and 20,000 words on an aspect of applied theology. All Candidates for Part II are required to present themselves   5
for a viva voce examination unless individually dispensed by the examiners.

9. A request for approval for the specific titles of the extended essays submitted in Part I, written on the appropriate form, must reach the Chair of Examiners for the M.Th. in Applied Theology by the final Friday in February (for essays to be submitted in the following late April), and by the final Friday in June (for essays to   10
be submitted in the following late September). In the case of Unit 2, the application should include a brief description of any portfolio of material to be submitted. Proposed topics for Part II dissertations may be submitted to the M.Th. Studies Committee before the completion of Part 1, and must have been submitted by the final Friday in December (for submissions in the following late April) and by the final   15
Friday in March (for submissions in the following late September).

10. Extended essays must be the candidate's own work, and must be typed or printed on one side of the paper. Essays must include a bibliography and footnotes (only the latter being included in the word count). Candidates may receive tutorial guidance in the preliminary stages of composition; tutors may also read or comment   20
on a first draft, giving the candidate not more than one tutorial session at this further stage. Normal graduate supervision shall be provided for the preparation of the dissertation in Part II. When submitted, the extended essays must be accompanied by a certificate signed by the candidate indicating that it is the candidate's own work. This certificate must be submitted separately in a sealed envelope addressed to the   25
Chair of the Examiners for the M.Th. in Applied Theology at the address below.

11. Extended essays may be submitted to the Chair of the Examiners, M.Th. in Applied Theology, c/o Examination Schools, High Street, Oxford OX1 4BG, by 12 noon on the Friday before 1 May and 1 October in any year, provided that all extended essays must have been submitted by 12 noon on the Friday before 1 October   30
following the third term in which a candidate's name has been on the register if the course is being taken full-time, or the sixth term if part-time. Candidates may delay the submission of their extended essay for Unit 2 until the April following the end of the first year of their course.

12. In Part I, a candidate whose extended essay fails to reach the level which the   35
examiners have determined to be the pass mark (or the required average for passing Part I) may be allowed at the discretion of the examiners to resubmit that work on one further occasion only, within the next two examination periods, provided that (save in the case envisaged in 16. below) no extended essay is submitted later than the submission of the dissertation. Permission to resubmit a unit must be sought in   40
writing from the Chair of Examiners by the final Friday in February (for essays to be submitted in the following late April), and by the final Friday in June (for essays to be submitted in the following late September).

13. In Part II, if the examiners are satisfied that the dissertation has reached the required level for the M.Th., but minor corrections are needed, they shall require the   45
candidate to make these corrections before they submit their report. If the dissertation fails to reach the required level, the examiners may, but are not obliged to, give a candidate permission to revise and resubmit a dissertation at one further examination period, not later than three terms after the first submission.

14. Full-time students for the M.Th. must submit their dissertation within six   50
terms of beginning the course; part-time students must submit their dissertation within twelve terms of beginning the course; students who change from full-time to

part-time status after three terms must submit their dissertation within nine terms of beginning the course. This regulation is not affected by a student's need to resubmit a Part I Unit, except in the case covered by 16. below.

15. No full-time student for the degree shall retain that status for more than nine terms. No part-time student for the degree shall retain that status for more than eighteen terms; and no student who changes from full-time to part-time status after the first year of study shall retain student status for more than fifteen terms.

16. In the event of a full-time student needing to resubmit Unit 2 following a first examination in the Trinity Term of the student's second year of study, the M.Th. Studies Committee will review the case. It may at its absolute discretion grant permission, either for the resubmission to occur after the submission of the dissertation (notwithstanding 12. above), or for the submission of the dissertation to be delayed until the Trinity Term examination in the following academic year.

Part I (and Postgraduate Diploma in Applied Theology)
Candidates will take the first two units and any two others.

1. *Doctrine, Context and Practice*
Candidates will explore the interrelationship between Christian doctrine and Christian practice in historical and social context. They will be able to demonstrate an understanding of Christian doctrine and practice as these have been developed in scripture, tradition and in the modern world.

2. *Experiential project with theological reflection*
Candidates will be expected to offer a theological evaluation of a project undertaken in either a church or secular setting in which the candidate shares in the concerns and experiences of those involved. They should normally submit a portfolio of material which should include relevant documentation and one or more case studies based upon contact made over a period of not less than twenty-one days and should offer a theological reflection based on this evidence. Full-time candidates may delay submission of this unit until the April submission following the end of the first year of their course.

3. *Sociology of Religion*
Candidates will be expected to demonstrate an understanding of the main methods of the study of religion in relation to modern society. They should consider such topics as secularisation, religious organisation, civil religion, and fundamentalism. They may also address the relationship between sociology and the different areas of theological study including biblical studies, doctrine and church history.

4. *Pastoral Psychology*
Candidates will study the contribution of psychological studies to pastoral understanding and practice; the principles of psychological explication with particular reference to the psychology of religious experience; the importance of the psychological dimension in particular areas of pastoral concern, for instance human development, marriage, sickness, death and bereavement.

5. *Science and Faith in the Modern World*
Candidates will explore the interrelationships between Christian theology and the natural sciences, with special reference to the implications for contemporary Christian practice. They will consider methodological issues in their own right, and such specific topics as the implications of evolutionary theory, or developments in fundamental physics, for the Christian doctrine of creation.

6. *The use of the Bible*
Candidates will be expected to study the use of the Bible in preaching, worship, and ethics, the phenomenon of diversity in the Bible; the contribution of hermeneutics to

the use of the Bible in pastoral ministry; and the quest for a critical standpoint in contextual study of the Bible.

7. *Christian Spirituality*

Candidates will explore critically the theological issues raised by selected well-established traditions of Christian prayer and devotion, drawing when appropriate on insights from the human sciences and from other academic disciplines. They should also consider different models of spiritual growth and spiritual guidance, drawing out the theology of ministry implicit within these.

8. *Liturgy and Worship*

Candidates will explore theologically the role of liturgy within Christian life, mission and discipleship, drawing when appropriate on insights from the human sciences and from other academic disciplines. They should consider such topics as the role of symbols, the relationship between the verbal and the non-verbal in worship, the relationship between liturgy and creativity, and the interaction between liturgy and culture.

9. *Christian Ethics*

Candidates will consider the interrelationships between Christianity and the theory and practice of the moral life. They will explore questions of fundamental moral theology, and also address selected specific ethical issues.

10. *Mission in the Modern World*

Candidates will study the mission of the Church in the light of the mission of God and in the context of contemporary societies and cultures. They should consider the inter-relationship of various aspects of mission such as evangelism; social and political action; dialogue with other faiths and ideologies. Candidates should evaluate the implications on mission of issues such as secularisation, urbanisation, post-colonialism and post-modernity.

11. *Inter-Faith Dialogue*

Candidates will study the encounter of faith communities and the development of inter-faith dialogue in plural societies. They will critically examine models of dialogue and may, if they wish, focus on the relationship of Christianity to one other faith tradition.

12. *Ecclesiology in an Ecumenical Context*

Candidates will examine the doctrines of the Church, the ministry and the sacraments in their relationship to the concrete realities of the life of the Church and the nature of its authority. The study will be made in the light of current thought across the Christian traditions.

Part II

1. The title of the proposed dissertation, together with a summary, must be submitted for approval by the Master of Theology Studies Committee in the final term of Part I of the course. The Committee shall approve a supervisor for the writing of the dissertation.

2. The dissertation (two copies) shall be submitted to the Chair of the Examiners, M.Th. in Applied Theology, c/o Examination Schools, High Street, Oxford OX1 4BG, not later than 12 noon on the Friday before 1 October following the ninth term in which a candidate's name has been on the register if the course is being taken full-time, or the twelfth term if part-time.

3. The thesis must be printed or typed on one side of the paper only, with a margin of 3 to 3.5 cms on the left-hand edge of each page, and must be securely and firmly bound in either hard or soft covers. Loose-leaf binding is not acceptable.

4. The completed dissertation must be accompanied by a signed statement by the candidate that it is his or her own work except where otherwise indicated. This statement must be submitted separately in a sealed envelope addressed to the Chair of Examiners for the M.Th. in Applied Theology at the above address.

5. All candidates are required to present themselves for a viva voce examination unless individually dispensed by the examiners.

6. Certain successful theses, on the recommendation of the examiners, should be deposited in the Theology Faculty Library. The library copy of thesis must be in a permanently fixed binding, drilled and sewn, in a stiff board case in library buckram, in a dark colour, and lettered on the spine with the candidate's name and initials, the degree, and the year of submission.

B. Regulations for the course of instruction for the Postgraduate Diploma in Applied Theology at the participating institutions listed in the Schedule.

1. The entry requirements for the course are as prescribed at A.1. above.

2. A candidate may complete the course either in ONE year full-time (residential) *or* TWO years part-time (non-residential).

3. Part-time candidates shall be required to attend courses of instruction organised by the participating institutions for one day a week during six terms, together with one three-day residential study conference organised by the M.Th. Studies Committee in each of the two years of their course.

4. The examination will consist of an extended essay of up to 7,000 words on each of the two compulsory and two optional units of Part I of the M.Th. course as set out above. The regulations concerning extended essays are as prescribed at A.4. above.

5. No full-time student for the Diploma shall retain that status for more than six terms in all, and no part-time student for that award shall retain that status for more than nine terms in all.

6. Candidates who have successfully completed the Diploma at an appropriate level may subsequently proceed to Part II of the M.Th. on the recommendation of the M.Th. Studies Committee. At the discretion of the Committee, transfer of Diploma candidates to Part II of the M.Th. course may be allowed to those candidates who have reached the required standard in the four papers submitted by the end of their first year.

10

REGULATIONS FOR THE DEGREE OF MASTER OF BUSINESS ADMINISTRATION

GENERAL REGULATIONS

§1. Degree of Master of Business Administration (Full-time and Part-time)

1. Any person who has been admitted to the status of student for the Degree of Master of Business Administration, who has satisfied the conditions prescribed by this section, and who has satisfied the examiners as required, may supplicate for the Degree of Master of Business Administration.

2. The Social Sciences Board with the concurrence of the Education Committee shall have power to make and vary such regulations as may be necessary for carrying out the duties laid upon it and upon the Registrar by this section.

3. A Student for the Degree of Master of Business Administration who is not a graduate of the University may wear the same gown as that worn by Students for the Degree of Doctor of Philosophy.

§2. Status of Student for the Degree of Master of Business Administration

1. Any person who, in the opinion of the MBA Committee, is well qualified and well fitted to undertake the course of study for which application is made, may be admitted to the status of Student for the Degree of Master of Business Administration. Decision on entry is made by the Head of MBA programmes or the EMBA Director (for part-time students) following an interview.

2. It shall be the duty of the Registrar to keep a Register of those admitted to the status of Student for the Degree of Master of Business Administration.

§3. **Admission of Candidates**

1. A candidate seeking admission as a Student for the Degree of Master of Business Administration shall apply to the MBA Committee. Candidates for admission shall be required to provide such information as the committee may determine from time to time by regulation. Applicants shall in addition be required to undertake such other tests and meet such conditions as, subject to the approval of the Social Sciences Board, the committee may determine by regulation.

2. No person shall be admitted as a Student for the Degree of Master of Business Administration under these provisions unless he or she is also a member of some college, hall, or other approved society, and unless the application for admission as a Student for the Degree of Master of Business Administration has the approval of that society. The Head of MBA programmes shall forward the application to the candidate's society or to the society to which the candidate wishes to apply for membership, as appropriate; and admission by the committee shall be conditional upon admission by an approved society.

3. A student registered for any other higher degree or diploma in the University may apply for transfer to the status of Student for the Degree of Master of Business Administration. The committee shall have power to make such transfer, provided that it is satisfied that the student is well qualified and well fitted to undertake the course of study for which application is made, and that the application has the support of the candidate's society. A candidate who transfers status in this way shall be reckoned as having held the status of Student for the Degree of Master of Business Administration from the time of admission to his or her previous status, unless the committee shall determine otherwise.

§4. **Supervision of Students**

1. Every candidate on admission as a Student for the Degree of Master of Business Administration shall be placed by the MBA Committee under the supervision of a member of the University or other competent person selected by the committee, and the committee shall have power for sufficient reason to change the supervisor of any student or to arrange for joint supervision by more than one supervisor, if it deems necessary.

2. It shall be the duty of the supervisor of a student entered upon a course of study to direct and superintend the work of the student, to meet the student regularly, and to undertake such duties as shall

be from time to time set out in the Divisional Board's memorandum of guidance for students and supervisors.

3. The supervisor shall submit a report on the progress of a student to the committee three times a year, and at any other time when the committee so requests or the supervisor deems expedient. The supervisor shall communicate the contents of the report to the student on each occasion that a report is made, so that the student is aware of the supervisor's assessment of his or her work during the period in question. In addition, the supervisor shall inform the committee at once if he or she is of the opinion that the student is unlikely to reach the standard required for the Degree of Master of Business Administration.

4. It shall be the duty of every Student for the Degree of Master of Business Administration to undertake such guided work and to attend such seminars and lectures as his or her supervisor requests; to attend such meetings with his or her supervisor as the supervisor reasonably arranges; and to fulfil any other requirements of the Divisional Board as set out in its memorandum of guidance for students and supervisors.

§5. Residence and other Requirements

1. No full-time Student for the Degree of Master of Business Administration shall be granted leave to supplicate unless, after admission, he or she has kept statutory residence and pursued his or her course of study at Oxford for at least thirty-two weeks.

2. No full-time Student for the Degree of Master of Business Administration shall retain that status for more than six terms in all.

3. Part-time students for the Degree of Master of Business Administration shall in each case be required to pursue their course of study over an elapsed time of 21 months. Part-time students shall not be required to keep statutory residence but must attend for such instruction and undertake such supervised coursework as the MBA committee shall require. The part-time MBA Director shall keep a register of attendance of part-time students. No student shall be granted leave to supplicate unless the register shows satisfactory attendance by him or her.

4. Part-time students may hold the status of Student for the Part-time Degree of Master of Business Administration for a period not exceeding 48 months.

5. A Student for the Degree of Master of Business Administration shall cease to hold that status if:

(*a*) he or she shall have been refused permission to supplicate for the Degree of Master of Business Administration;

(*b*) the MBA Committee shall, in accordance with provisions set down by regulation by the Divisional Board, and after consultation with the student's society and supervisor, have deprived the student of such status;

(*c*) he or she shall have been transferred under the relevant provisions to another status; or

(*d*) he or she shall not have entered for the relevant examination within the time specified under this sub-section.

§6. Examination of Students

1. The examination for the Degree of Master of Business Administration shall be under the supervision of the MBA Committee. The subjects of each examination shall be determined by regulation by the committee, which shall have power to arrange lectures and courses of instruction for the assessment. The assessment shall consist of:

(*a*) course assignments;

(*b*) written examinations;

(*c*) written reports on a business project approved by the committee; and

(*d*) an oral examination; provided that the committee shall have power by regulation to authorise the examiners to dispense individual candidates from the oral examination. This provision notwithstanding, the examiners may, if they deem expedient, set a candidate a further written examination after examining the candidate orally.

2. No candidate shall be permitted to take an examination under the preceding clause unless he or she has been admitted as a candidate for the examination in question by the committee and has satisfied any other conditions prescribed in the regulations for that course.

3. Unless otherwise provided in this sub-section, the number and distribution of examiners shall be as set out in the relevant regulation.

4. A candidate who has failed to satisfy the examiners in the examination may enter again on one, but not more than one, subsequent occasion for that part of the examination which he or she failed.

Special Regulations

A. Full-time students

1. Candidates must follow for at least three terms a course of instruction in Management Studies. Candidates must complete the following and may be required to attend an oral examination on any part: 5

(*a*) all courses from Schedule A;

(*b*) seven electives, the list of electives to be published by the MBA Director before the first Monday of the preceding term in which the elective is to be offered;

(*c*) a written report on the Entrepreneurship project of not more than 8,000 words. Such projects must be undertaken in groups and approved by the MBA   10 Director;

(*d*) a written report on a consulting project of not more than 15,000 words. Such projects must be undertaken in groups and approved by the MBA Director; or two further electives, from those available during the summer; or an individual academic thesis of not more than 12,000 words. The titles of such theses must   15 be submitted to the MBA Director by Monday of first week of Trinity Term in the year in which the examination is taken, and must be approved by the MBA Director. Three typewritten copies of the thesis must be submitted to the Examination Schools and addressed to the Chair of Examiners for the MBA, c/o Examination Schools, High Street, Oxford, OX1 4BG, by the date and time   20 advised to candidates in the term preceding that of submission;

2. In order to obtain the degree of Master of Business Administration candidates must complete all the requirements set out in 1 (*a*)-(*d*) above and satisfy the examiners in the assignment and/or examinations associated with:

(i) at least seven core courses;   25

(ii) the Entrepreneurship project;

(iii) at least six electives and a consulting projects/individual thesis, or at least eight electives;

3. Any student wishing to undertake an optional summer internship must submit a proposal to the MBA Committee for approval.   30

4. The examiners may award a distinction for excellence in the whole examination to candidates for the Degree.

5. In exceptional circumstances, a candidate wishing to take an examination later than the one to which he or she has been admitted may do so by application to the Chair of Examiners.   35

B. Part-time students

1. Every candidate wishing to take the course on a part-time basis must follow for not less than 21 months a course of instruction in Management Studies. Candidates must complete:

(*a*) all courses from Schedule B, and satisfy the examiners in the assignment and/or   40 examination associated with at least eight core courses, including Understanding General Management;

(*b*) eight electives, and satisfy the examiners in the assignment and/or examination associated with at least seven electives, the list of electives to be published not later than the first day of the first module of the second year of the programme;   45

(c) a written report on the Entrepreneurship project of not more than 8,000 words. Such projects must be approved by the Director of the part-time MBA;

(d) the Business in Emerging Markets module and satisfy the examiners in the form of an essay submission associated with this module of not more than 5,000 words;   5

(e) candidates may be required to attend an oral examination on any of the above.

2. The MBA Committee shall have the discretion to permit any candidate to be exempted from up to four courses providing that the Committee is satisfied that such a candidate has completed equivalent study of an appropriate standard, and has passed the assessment associated with that equivalent study, on either the   10 Postgraduate Diploma in Financial Strategy, the Postgraduate Diploma in Global Business, the Postgraduate Diploma in Organisational Leadership, or the Postgraduate Diploma in Strategy and Innovation (previously the Postgraduate Diploma in Advanced Strategy) no more than five years before initial registration for the part-time MBA.   15

Schedule A

The following courses are required to be taken during Michaelmas and Hilary Terms for full-time students. Details can be found in the course handbook.

(a) Decision and Data Analytics

(b) Managerial Economics   20

(c) Financial Reporting

(d) Strategy

(e) Finance I

(f) Developing Effective Managers

(g) Operations Management   25

(h) Marketing

Schedule B

The following courses are required to be taken by part-time students. Details can be found in the course handbook.

(a) Understanding General Management   30

(b) Decision and Data Analytics

(c) Strategy

(d) Developing Effective Managers

(e) Marketing

(f) Managerial Economics   35

(g) Financial Reporting

(h) Finance

(i) Operations Management

I I

REGULATIONS FOR THE DEGREE OF MASTER OF FINE ART

GENERAL REGULATIONS

§1. Degree of Master of Fine Art

1. Any person who has been admitted to the status of Student for the Degree of Master of Fine Art, who has satisfied the conditions prescribed by this section, and who has satisfied the examiners as required, may supplicate for the Degree of Master of Fine Art.

2. The Education Committee shall have power to make and vary such regulations as may be necessary for carrying out the duties laid upon it and upon the Registrar by this section.

3. A Student for the Degree of Master of Fine Art who is not a graduate of the University may wear the same gown as that worn by Students for the Degree of Doctor of Philosophy.

§2. Status of Student for the Degree of Master of Fine Art

1. Any person who, in the opinion of the Committee for the Ruskin School of Drawing and Fine Art, is well-qualified and well-fitted to undertake the course of study for which application is made, may be admitted to the status of Student for the Degree of Master of Fine Art.

2. It shall be the duty of the Registrar to keep a Register of those admitted to the status of Student for the Degree of Master of Fine Art.

§3. Admission of Candidates

1. A candidate seeking admission as a Student for the Degree of Master of Fine Art shall apply to the Committee for the Ruskin School of Art. Candidates for admission shall be required to provide such information as the Committee may determine from time to time by regulation. Applicants shall in addition be required to undertake such other tests and meet such conditions as, subject to the approval of the Education Committee, the Committee may determine by regulation.

2. Applications shall be made through the Registrar, and it shall be the duty of the Registrar to submit each application to the Committee and to inform the candidate of the outcome, as soon as may be.

3. No person shall be admitted as a Student for the Degree of Master of Fine Art under these provisions unless he or she is also a member of some college, hall, or other approved society, and unless the application for admission as a Student for the Degree of Master of Fine Art has the approval of that society. The Registrar shall forward the application to the candidate's society or to the society to which the candidate wishes to apply for membership, as appropriate; and admission by the Committee shall be conditional upon admission by an approved society.

4. A student registered for any other higher degree or diploma in the University may apply for transfer to the status of Student for the Degree of Master of Fine Art. The Committee shall have power to make such transfer, provided that it is satisfied that the student is well-qualified and well-fitted to undertake the course of study for which application is made, and that the application has the support of the candidate's society. A candidate who transfers status in this way shall be reckoned as having held the status of Student for the Degree of Master of Fine Art from the time of admission to his or her previous status, unless the Committee shall determine otherwise.

§4. Supervision of Students

1. Every candidate on admission as a Student for the Degree of Master of Fine Art shall be placed by the Committee for the Ruskin School of Art under the supervision of a member of the University or other competent person selected by the Committee, and the Committee shall have power for sufficient reason to change the supervisor of any student or to arrange for joint supervision by more than one supervisor, if it deems necessary.

2. It shall be the duty of the supervisor of a student entered upon a course of study to direct and superintend the work of the student, to meet the student regularly, and to undertake such duties as shall be from time to time set out in the relevant Policy and Guidance issued by the Education Committee.

3. The supervisor shall submit a report on the progress of a student to the Committee three times a year, and at any other time when the Committee so requests or the supervisor deems expedient. The supervisor shall communicate the contents of the

report to the student on each occasion that a report is made, so that the student is aware of the supervisor's assessment of his or her work during the period in question. In addition, the supervisor shall inform the Committee at once if he or she is of the opinion that the student is unlikely to reach the standard required for the Degree of Master of Fine Art.

4. It shall be the duty of every Student for the Degree of Master of Fine Art to undertake such guided work and to attend such seminars and lectures as his or her supervisor requests; to attend such meetings with his or her supervisor as the supervisor reasonably arranges; and to fulfil any other requirements of the relevant Policy and Guidance issued by the Education Committee.

§5. Residence and other Requirements

1. No full-time Student for the Degree of Master of Fine Art shall be granted leave to supplicate unless, after admission, he or she has kept statutory residence and pursued his or her course of study at Oxford for at least forty weeks.

2. No full-time Student for the Degree of Master of Fine Art shall retain that status for more than two years in all.

3. A Student for the Degree of Master of Fine Art shall cease to hold that status if:

(*a*) he or she shall have been refused permission to supplicate for the Degree of Master of Fine Art;

(*b*) the Committee for the Ruskin School of Art shall, in accordance with provisions set down by regulation by the Education Committee, and after consultation with the student's society and supervisor, have deprived the student of such status;

(*c*) he or she shall have been transferred under the relevant provisions to another status; or

(*d*) he or she shall not have entered for the relevant examination within the time specified under this sub-section.

§6. Examination of Students

1. The examination for the Degree of Master of Fine Art shall be under the supervision of the Committee for the Ruskin School of Art. The subjects of each examination shall be determined by regulation by the Committee, which shall have power to arrange lectures and courses of instruction for the examination.

2. No candidate shall be permitted to take an examination under the preceding clause unless he or she has been admitted as a candidate for the examination in question by the Committee and has satisfied any other conditions prescribed in the regulations for that course.

3. Unless otherwise provided in this sub-section, the number and distribution of examiners shall be as set out in the relevant regulation.

4. A candidate who has failed to satisfy the examiners in the examination may enter again on one, but not more than one, subsequent occasion for that part of the examination which he or she failed.

SPECIAL REGULATIONS

1. Applicants will be expected to have completed a good honours degree which should normally be in Fine Art.

2. The examination shall include both practical and written work.

3. Every candidate for the examination must follow for at least two terms a course of study in contemporary art and cultural theory, and must by noon on Friday of the eighth week of the Hilary Term submit to the Chair of the Examiners in Fine Art, Examination Schools, High Street, Oxford OX1 4BG a certificate to that effect from his or her supervisor.

4. Syllabus

(a) Every candidate must submit during the Long Vacation, and not later than noon on the Monday three weeks prior to the start of Michaelmas Full Term, an exhibition of completed projects chosen from one or more of the subjects 1-8.

   1. Drawing
   2. Digital image handling
   3. Sculpture
   4. Painting
   5. Performance
   6. Printmaking
   7. Photography
   8. Video and film

(b) Every candidate must submit full documentation of their studio project. This should be either a carousel of not more than 30×35mm slides or a 10 minute VHS video tape, and it should be accompanied by a brief statement of not more than 500 words.

   This submission must be sent to the Chair of Examiners in Fine Art, Examination Schools, High Street, Oxford not later than noon on the Monday three weeks prior to the start of Michaelmas Full Term.

(c) Every candidate must present one seminar paper of up to 2,500 words during Hilary Term related to his or her studio project. A written version of the paper must be submitted by noon on Friday of the eighth week of the Hilary Term to the Chair of Examiners in Fine Art, Examination Schools. The work done for the seminar paper may form the basis of the extended essay required under (*d*) below.

(*d*) Every candidate must, after consultation with his or her supervisor, submit an extended essay of at least 4,000 words. This may be an account of the methodology used in the studio project, an exposition of its theoretical framework, or an essay on another topic of direct relevance to the project. Notice of the subject of the essay must reach the Chair of the Examiners in Fine Art, Examination Schools, by noon on the Friday of the tenth week of Hilary Term. Three typewritten or printed copies of the essay must be sent to the Chair of the Examiners in Fine Art, Examination Schools, not later than noon on the Friday of the tenth week of Trinity Term.

5. Candidates must present themselves for an oral examination unless individually dispensed from this requirement by the examiners. In this examination the essay referred to in 4(*d*), the submission in 4(*b*) and the candidate's general command of their field will be discussed.

6. A candidate who fails the examination may re-sit at the end of the following Michaelmas Term.

7. The examiners may award a distinction for excellence in the examination.

NOTES

I 2

REGULATIONS FOR THE DEGREE OF MASTER OF PUBLIC POLICY

GENERAL REGULATIONS

§1. Degree of Master of Public Policy

1. Any person who has been admitted to the status of student for the Degree of Master of Public Policy, who has satisfied the conditions prescribed by this section, and who has satisfied the examiners as required, may supplicate for the Degree of Master of Public Policy.

2. The Social Sciences Board with the concurrence of the Education Committee shall have power to make and vary such regulations as may be necessary for carrying out the duties laid upon it and upon the Registrar by this section.

3. A student for the Degree of Master of Public Policy who is not a graduate of the University may wear the same gown as that worn by Students for the Degree of Doctor of Philosophy.

§2. Status of Student for the Degree of Master of Public Policy

1. Any person who, in the opinion of the Blavatnik School of Government (BSG) Graduate Studies Committee, is well qualified and well fitted to undertake the course of study for which application is made, may be admitted to the status of Student for the Degree of Master of Public Policy.

2. It shall be the duty of the Registrar to keep a Register of those admitted to the status of Student for the Degree of Master of Public Policy.

§3. Admission of Candidates

1. A candidate seeking admission as a Student for the Degree of Master of Public Policy shall apply to the BSG Graduate Studies Committee. Candidates for admission shall be required to provide such information as the committee may determine from time to time by regulation. Applicants shall in addition be required to undertake

such other tests and meet such conditions as, subject to the approval of the Social Sciences Board, the committee may determine by regulation.

2. No person shall be admitted as a Student for the Degree of Master of Public Policy under these provisions unless he or she is also a member of some college, hall, or other approved society, and unless the application for admission as a Student for the Degree of Master of Public Policy has the approval of that society. The Academic Director shall forward the application to the candidate's society or to the society to which the candidate wishes to apply for membership, as appropriate; and admission by the committee shall be conditional upon admission by an approved society.

3. A student registered for any other higher degree or diploma in the University may apply for transfer to the status of Student for the Degree of Master of Public Policy. The committee shall have power to make such transfer, provided that it is satisfied that the student is well qualified and well fitted to undertake the course of study for which application is made, and that the application has the support of the candidate's society. A candidate who transfers status in this way shall be reckoned as having held the status of Student for the Degree of Master of Public Policy from the time of admission to his or her previous status, unless the committee shall determine otherwise.

§4. Supervision of Students

1. Every candidate on admission as a Student for the Degree of Master of Public Policy shall be placed by the BSG Graduate Studies Committee under the supervision of a member of the University or other competent person selected by the committee, and the committee shall have power for sufficient reason to change the supervisor of any student or to arrange for joint supervision by more than one supervisor, if it deems necessary.

2. It shall be the duty of the supervisor of a student entered upon a course of study to direct and superintend the work of the student, to meet the student regularly, and to undertake such duties as shall be from time to time set out in the Divisional Board's memorandum of guidance for students and supervisors.

3. The supervisor shall submit a report on the progress of a student to the committee three times a year, and at any other time when the committee so requests or the supervisor deems expedient. The supervisor shall communicate the contents of the report to the student on each occasion that a report is made, so that the student is

aware of the supervisor's assessment of his or her work during the period in question. In addition, the supervisor shall inform the committee at once if he or she is of the opinion that the student is unlikely to reach the standard required for the Degree of Master of Public Policy.

4. It shall be the duty of every Student for the Degree of Master of Public Policy to undertake such guided work and to attend such seminars and lectures as his or her supervisor requests; to attend such meetings with his or her supervisor as the supervisor reasonably arranges; and to fulfil any other requirements of the Divisional Board as set out in its memorandum of guidance for students and supervisors.

§5. Residence and other Requirements

1. No full-time Student for the Degree of Master of Public Policy shall be granted leave to supplicate unless, after admission, he or she has kept statutory residence and pursued his or her course of study at Oxford for at least thirty-two weeks.

2. No full-time Student for the Degree of Master of Public Policy shall retain that status for more than six terms in all.

3. A Student for the Degree of Master of Public Policy shall cease to hold that status if:

(*a*) he or she shall have been refused permission to supplicate for the Degree of Master of Public Policy;

(*b*) the BSG Graduate Studies Committee shall, in accordance with provisions set down by regulation by the Divisional Board, and after consultation with the student's society and supervisor, have deprived the student of such status;

(*c*) he or she shall have been transferred under the relevant provisions to another status; or

(*d*) he or she shall not have entered for the relevant examination within the time specified under this sub-section.

§6. Examination of Students

1. The examination for the Degree of Master of Public Policy shall be under the supervision of the BSG Graduate Studies Committee. The subjects of each examination shall be determined by regulation by the committee, which shall have power to arrange lectures and courses of instruction for the assessment. The assessment shall consist of:

(*a*) course assignments;

(*b*) written examinations;

(*c*) written reports on a summer project approved by the committee; and

(*d*) an oral examination; provided that the committee shall have power by regulation to authorise the examiners to dispense individual candidates from the oral examination. This provision notwithstanding, the examiners may, if they deem expedient, set a candidate a further written examination after examining the candidate orally.

2. No candidate shall be permitted to take an examination under the preceding clause unless he or she has been admitted as a candidate for the examination in question by the committee and has satisfied any other conditions prescribed in the regulations for that course.

3. Unless otherwise provided in this sub-section, the number and distribution of examiners shall be as set out in the relevant regulation.

4. A candidate who has failed to satisfy the examiners in the examination may enter again on one, but not more than one, subsequent occasion for that part of the examination which he or she failed.

SPECIAL REGULATIONS

1. Candidates must follow for at least three terms a course of instruction in Public Policy. Candidates must complete:

(*a*) all courses from the Schedule, and satisfy the examiners in the assignment and/or examination associated with each course;

(*b*) two electives. Candidates must satisfy the examiners in the assignment/examination/written report associated with each course, the list of electives to be published annually by the BSG Graduate Studies Committee before the first Monday of Hilary Term;

(*c*) a summer project. Candidates must satisfy the examiners in the written report associated with the summer project;

(*d*) candidates may be required to attend an oral examination on any of the above.

2. Assignments and written reports on projects must be presented not later than the time and date stipulated for each exercise; these will be published by the BSG Graduate Studies Committee before the first Monday of each term in which the assignment or project must be undertaken. The required number of copies must be delivered to the Examination Schools, and addressed to the Chair of Examiners for the Masters in Public Policy, c/o Examination Schools, High Street, Oxford.

3. The examiners may award a distinction for excellence in the whole examination to candidates for the Degree.

4. In exceptional circumstances, a candidate wishing to take an examination later than the one to which he or she has been admitted may do so by application to the Chair of Examiners, via his or her College Senior Tutor or Tutor for Graduates.

5. Candidates are permitted on only one occasion to resubmit or retake failed assessment items on any course on which they have failed to achieve the required standard.

5

SCHEDULE

The following courses are required to be taken. Details can be found in the course handbook:

1. Major policy challenge introduction   10
2. Core I Foundations
3. Core II Economics
4. Core III The Organization and Practice of Government
5. Core IV Science and Public Policy
6. Practical skills I—Strategy and Communication   15
7. Practical skills II—Public Budgeting and Private Finance
8. Practical skills III—Delivery and Management
9. Practical skills IV—Negotiation
10. Master Classes
11. Decision and Data Analytics   20
12. Evidence and Evaluation in Public Policy

NOTES

13

REGULATIONS FOR ADMISSION AS A PROBATIONER RESEARCH STUDENT*

GENERAL REGULATIONS

§1. Status of Probationer Research Student

1. Any person intending to work for the Degree of Master of Letters or of Master of Science by research or of Doctor of Philosophy must apply in the first instance for admission as a Probationer Research Student, except as provided in the appropriate regulation.

2. The Education Committee shall have power to make and vary such regulations as may be necessary for carrying out the duties laid upon it and upon the Registrar by this section.

3. For the purposes of this section the words 'board', 'faculty board', 'board of the faculty' or 'divisional board' shall include any body with powers to admit students to the status of Probationer Research Student.

4. A Probationer Research Student who is not a graduate of the University may wear the same gown as that worn by Students for the Degree of Doctor of Philosophy.

§2. Admission of Candidates as Probationer Research Students

1. The board to which a prospective student's branch of study belongs may admit any person as a Probationer Research Student provided that the board is satisfied:

(1) that the candidate is well-fitted and well-qualified to conduct work for a research degree,

(2) that the branch of study proposed by the candidate is one which may profitably be pursued under the superintendence of the board,

---

* This general regulation should be read in conjunction with the associated regulations made by the individual faculty or divisional boards.

References within this regulation to part-time students relate to a small number of faculties/departments which have been given permission to admit research students to study on a part-time basis. There is no general provision for the award of research degrees through part-time study within the University.

(3) that supervision will be available, and

(4) that the faculty board or department under whose aegis the research is to be conducted has adequate facilities to enable the research to be undertaken.

2. Applications for admission shall be forwarded to the Registrar, according to such timetables as the Education Committee shall determine. The Registrar shall be responsible for transmitting the candidate's application to the faculty board or department concerned, together with a statement of the branch of study which the candidate intends to pursue, and such evidence of his or her fitness to undertake the proposed study as may be required by the board or department.

3. No person shall be admitted as a Probationer Research Student unless he or she is also a member of a college, and unless the application for admission as a Probationer Research Student has the approval of his or her college. The Registrar shall forward the application to the candidate's college or to the college to which the candidate wishes to apply for membership, as appropriate; and admission by the board shall be conditional upon admission by an approved society.

4. A student already on the register of graduate students and holding the status of student for another degree, and who wishes to read for the M.Sc. by Research, M.Litt., or D.Phil. may apply for transfer to the status of Probationer Research Student, provided that before admitting the student to that status the board concerned shall be satisfied that he or she fulfils the conditions set out in clause I above. Students who transfer in this way shall be reckoned as having been admitted as Probationer Research Students from the time they were admitted to their previous status.

5. It shall be the duty of the Registrar to notify candidates of the decision of the board as soon as may be and to inform a candidate whose application has been approved by the board of the term from which his or her admission as a Probationer Research Student is to be reckoned.

6. It shall be the duty of the Registrar to keep a Register of those admitted to the status of Probationer Research Student.

7. A board may grant a student suspension from the Register or deprive a student of his or her status; and in such cases it shall at all times follow procedures determined by the Education Committee by regulation. A board may also reinstate a student to the Register, provided that the total number of terms a student has spent as a Probationer Research Student has not exceeded five terms in the case of a full-time student, or ten terms in the case of a part-time student.

§3. Supervision of Probationer Research Students

1. Every candidate, on admission as a Probationer Research Student, shall be placed by the board concerned under the supervision of a member of the University or other competent person selected by the board, and the board shall have power for sufficient reason to change the supervisor of any student or to arrange for joint supervision by more than one supervisor, if it deems it necessary.

2. It shall be the duty of a supervisor to advise a student as to the courses of instruction and classes, if any, which he or she should attend, and generally to direct and superintend the student's work. It shall also be the supervisor's duty to assist a student, when satisfied of his or her competence, in the selection of a subject for his or her thesis.

3. The supervisor shall submit a report on the progress of the student to the board three times each year, and at any other time when the board so requests or the supervisor deems it expedient; and shall undertake such other duties as shall be from time to time set out in the relevant Policy and Guidance issued by the Education Committee. The supervisor shall communicate the contents of the report to the student on each occasion that a report is made, so that the student is aware of the supervisor's assessment of his or her work during the period in question. In addition, the supervisor shall inform the board at once if he or she is of the opinion that a student is unlikely to reach the standard required for admission at least to the status of student for the Degree of Master of Letters or of Science.

The Registrar shall send a copy of each report by the supervisor to the student's college, and to the Director of Graduate Studies or other nominated person under the board concerned.

4. It shall be the duty of a Probationer Research Student to pursue any course of study preparatory to research recommended by his or her supervisor, and in particular to attend such courses of instruction as the supervisor may advise or the board concerned may require. A board may award a certificate of graduate attainment at the end of the Trinity Term in the year of the student's admission as Probationer Research Student. Subject to the approval of the Education Committee, each board shall have power to determine by regulation what test or condition, if any, it may require before awarding such a certificate.

§4. Residence and other Requirements of
Probationer Research Students

1. A full-time Probationer Research Student who has been admitted under the provisions of the preceding sub-section shall normally keep statutory residence and pursue his or her course of study at Oxford during the period in which he or she holds the status of Probationer Research Student. Time spent outside Oxford during term as part of an academic programme approved by Council shall count towards residence for the purpose of this clause.

2. A board may, on application from a candidate, and with the support of his or her college and supervisor, grant dispensation from such residence in exceptional circumstances, on the grounds that it is necessary to the student's work that he or she should be allowed to study at some other place than Oxford.

3. Part-time students holding the status of Probationer Research Student shall in each case be required to pursue their course of study for a minimum of four terms, and a maximum of eight terms. (*For students admitted before 1 October 2011*, a minimum of six terms and maximum of twelve terms), prior to an application for transfer of status, save that students who have completed the requirements for the Degrees of Master of Studies or Master of Science (by Coursework) by part-time study may, with the permission of the board or other relevant body, apply for transfer of status after three terms. Part-time students shall not be required to keep statutory residence, but must attend for such instruction as the board or other relevant body shall require, subject to the approval of the Education Committee. No student may apply to the relevant faculty board or other body for the appointment of examiners unless his or her supervisor has certified that the student has fulfilled the requirements for part-time students laid down by the board or other relevant body.

4. Any student may, with the permission of the board, alter the subject of research approved by the board, provided that the conditions of suitability set out in §2, cl. 1 of this section continue to be met. In such cases the date of the student's admission for all the purposes of this section shall remain unchanged, unless the board shall determine otherwise.

For Probationer Research Students admitted before 1 October 2011

5. A full-time student may hold the status of Probationer Research Student for up to six terms, and a part-time student for up to twelve terms, including the term in which he or she was admitted.

6. A Probationer Research Student shall cease to hold such status if:

(i) he or she shall not have gained admission to another status within six terms of admission as a full-time student to the status of Probationer Research Student, or within twelve terms for a part-time student;

(ii) the board concerned shall, in accordance with provisions set down in §2, cl. 7, and after consultation with the student's college and supervisor, have deprived the student of such status.

For Probationer Research students admitted after 1 October 2011

5. A full-time student (other than students registered on a Doctoral Training Centre Programme or the Doctoral Training Partnership Programme under §4, cl. 9) may hold the status of Probationer Research Student for up to four terms and a part-time student for up to eight terms, including the term in which he or she was admitted.

6. A candidate whose first application for transfer to D.Phil. status is not approved shall be permitted to make one further application, following the procedures laid down in clauses 1–4 above, and shall be granted an extension of time for one term if this is necessary for the purposes of making the application.

7. Subject to the approval of the responsible divisional board or the CE Board as appropriate, and for good cause, a full-time student may be permitted to hold the status of PRS (prior to the first application for transfer of status) for a further one or two terms, and a part-time student for a further one to four terms. A first application for transfer of status must take place within the six term limit of PRS status. Any application outside those limits (other than in clause 6 above) must be approved by or on behalf of Education Committee.

8. A Probationer Research Student (other than a student registered on a Doctoral Training Centre Programme or the Doctoral Training Partnership Programme—see §4, cl. 10) shall cease to hold such status if:

(i) (*a*) he or she shall not have gained admission to another status within four terms of admission as a full-time student to the status of Probationer Research Student, or within eight terms for a part-time student, and

(*b*) he or she has not been given approval under clause 6 above to hold Probationer Research Student status for a further one or two terms as a full-time student or one to four terms as a part-time student;

(ii) he or she has failed to gain admission to either doctoral status or to the status of the applicable lower degree after the two transfer applications allowed under clause 7 above;

(iii) the board concerned shall in accordance with provisions set down in chapter 16, section 5, and after consultation with the student's college and supervisor, have deprived the student of such status.

9. For a full-time Probationer Research Student registered on a Doctoral Training Centre Programme or the Doctoral Training Partnership Programme, the maximum number of terms for which he or she may hold that status is as specified in the special regulations governing students on the Doctoral Training Centre Programmes or the Doctoral Training Partnership Programme in the Mathematical, Physical and Life Sciences and the Medical Sciences Divisions.

10. A Probationer Research Student registered on a Doctoral Training Centre Programme or the Doctoral Training Partnership Programme shall cease to hold such status if:

(i) (*a*) he or she shall not have gained admission to another status within the number of terms specified in the special regulations governing Probationer Research Students on the Doctoral Training Centre Programmes or the Doctoral Training Partnership Programme in the Mathematical, Physical and Life Sciences and the Medical Sciences Divisions and

(*b*) he or she has not been given approval under clause 7 above to hold Probationer Research Student status for a further one or two terms as a full-time student or one to four terms as a part-time student;

(ii) he or she has failed to gain admission to either doctoral status or to the status of the applicable lower degree after the two transfer applications allowed under clause 7 above;

(iii) the board concerned shall in accordance with provisions set down in chapter 17, section 5, and after consultation with the student's college and supervisor, have deprived the student of such status.

14

REGULATIONS FOR THE DEGREE OF MASTER OF LETTERS*

GENERAL REGULATIONS

§1. Degree of Master of Letters

1. Any person who has been admitted to the status of Student for the Degree of Master of Letters and who has satisfied the conditions prescribed by this decree may supplicate for the Degree of Master of Letters.

2. The Education Committee shall have power to make and vary such regulations as may be necessary for carrying out the duties laid upon it and upon the Registrar by this section.

3. For the purposes of this section the words 'board', 'faculty board', 'board of the faculty', 'divisional board' shall include any body with powers to admit students to read for the Degree of Master of Letters.

4. A Student for the Degree of Master of Letters who is not a graduate of the University may wear the same gown as that worn by Students for the Degree of Doctor of Philosophy.

§2. Status of Student for the Degree of Master of Letters

1. The following may be admitted to the status of Student for the Degree of Master of Letters:

(i) a member of the University who, having held the status of Probationer Research Student under the provisions of the appropriate regulation has successfully completed the

---

* These general regulations should be read in conjunction with the associated special regulations made by the Education Committee and individual boards. Those provisions of this regulation which govern admission to, and transfer from, one status to another shall apply only to research students first registered from Michaelmas Term 1991 or later. Students first registered for a research degree before that term shall continue to be subject to the relevant sections of the 1990 *Examination Decrees* in this respect.

References within this regulation to part-time students relate to a small number of faculties/departments which have been given permission to admit research students to study on a part-time basis. There is no general provision for the award of research degrees through part-time study within the University.

relevant qualifying test or tests and fulfilled the other requirements for transfer to M.Litt. status prescribed in §3 of this section;

(ii) a member of the University who, having held the status of student for another higher degree within the University, has successfully completed the relevant qualifying test or tests and fulfilled the other requirements for transfer to M.Litt. status prescribed in §3 of this section;

(iii) a member of the University who has successfully completed the examination for the Degree of Bachelor or Master of Philosophy or Master of Science by Coursework or of Bachelor of Civil Law and who has fulfilled the conditions laid down in §3 of this section for applicants in that category.

2. It shall be the duty of the Registrar to keep a register of those admitted to the status of Student for the Degree of Master of Letters.

3. A board may grant a student suspension from the Register or deprive a student of his or her status; and in such cases it shall at all times follow the procedures determined by the Education Committee by regulation. A board may also reinstate a student to the Register, provided that the number of terms a student has spent with the status of Student for the Degree of Master of Letters shall not have exceeded fifteen in all in the case of a full-time student, or eighteen terms in the case of a part-time student.

§3. Admission of Candidates to the Status of Student for the Degree of Master of Letters

1. Candidates qualified under §2 of this section may apply for admission as a Student for the Degree of Master of Letters to the board concerned through the Registrar. Such applications shall be accompanied by:

(i) a statement from the supervisor that he or she approves the proposed subject for a thesis and considers the candidate well qualified to undertake research in that subject;

(ii) a statement of support for the application from the candidate's college;

(iii) a statement of the subject of the thesis and of the manner in which the candidate proposes to treat it.

2. Candidates qualified under §2, cl. 1 (i) and (ii) of this section shall in addition be required to submit written work, the precise manner and form of which shall be determined by regulation by each board. This shall be considered by two assessors appointed by the board, neither of whom shall normally be the candidate's

supervisor, and who shall examine the candidate orally. Upon completion of their examination of the candidate's application, the assessors shall make a recommendation as to whether it should be granted. In each case the assessors shall make a reasoned written report to the board in support of their recommendation. 5

3. The board shall consider the candidate's application together with the material supplied in accordance with clauses 1 and 2 above. No application shall be granted unless the board is satisfied that the candidate is capable of carrying out research, that the subject of the thesis and the manner of its treatment proposed by the candi- 10 date are acceptable, that the subject is one which may profitably be pursued under the superintendence of the board, and that the board or department concerned is satisfied that it has adequate facilities to enable the research to be undertaken.

4. Subject to the approval of the Education Committee, each 15 board may determine by regulation what other test or condition, if any, it requires before admitting a candidate to M.Litt. status. Each board shall be empowered, without further authority, to require from the supervisor any further confidential report on an applicant's suitability to pursue research towards the Degree of 20 Master of Letters.

5. It shall be the duty of the Registrar to submit any application made under these provisions to the board concerned, and to notify the candidate of the outcome as soon as may be.

6. A student qualified under §2, cl. 1 (i) or (ii) of this section 25 whose application for transfer to M.Litt. status is successful shall be reckoned as having been admitted to the status of student for the Degree of Master of Letters with effect from the date of admission to his or her previous status, unless the board determines otherwise.

7. A student qualified under §2, cl. 1 (iii) of this section whose 30 application for admission to M.Litt. status is successful shall be admitted as a Student for the Degree of Master of Letters from the beginning of the term in which admission takes place.

§4. Supervision of Students for the Degree of Master of Letters

1. Every candidate on admission as a Student for the Degree of 35 Master of Letters shall be placed by the board concerned under the supervision of a member of the University or other competent person selected by the board, and the board shall have power for sufficient reason to change the supervisor of any student or to arrange for joint supervision by more than one supervisor, if it 40 deems it necessary.

2. It shall be the duty of a supervisor to direct and superintend the work of the student, to meet the student regularly, and to undertake such duties as shall from time to time be set out in the relevant Policy and Guidance issued by the Education Committee.

3. The supervisor shall submit a report on the progress of the student to the board three times a year, and at any other time when the board so requests or he or she deems it expedient. The supervisor shall communicate the contents of the report to the student on each occasion that a report is made, so that the student is aware of the supervisor's assessment of his or her work during the period in question. In addition, the supervisor shall inform the board at once if he or she is of the opinion that the student is unlikely to reach the standard required for the Degree of Master of Letters.

The Registrar shall send a copy of each report by the supervisor to the student's college, and to the Director or other nominated person under the faculty board concerned.

4. It shall be the duty of every Student for the Degree of Master of Letters to undertake such guided work as his or her supervisor requests; to attend such meetings with his or her supervisor as the latter reasonably arranges; and to fulfil any other requirements of the General Board set out from time to time in the relevant Policy and Guidance issued by the Education Committee.

§5. Residence and other Requirements for Students for the Degree of Master of Letters

1. Except as provided in clause 3 of this sub-section, a Student for the Degree of Master of Letters who has been admitted for full-time study under the provisions of §3 of this section shall be required to be on the Register for at least six terms, and during this period shall keep statutory residence and pursue his or her course of study at Oxford. Time spent outside Oxford during term as part of an academic programme approved by Council shall count towards residence for the purpose of this clause.

2. The board concerned may dispense a student on application through his or her college and with the support of the supervisor from not more than three terms of such residence and study in Oxford, provided that such dispensation shall be granted only on grounds that it is necessary to the student's work that he or she should be allowed to study at some other place than Oxford.

3. A student who has successfully completed the examination for the Degree of Master or Bachelor of Philosophy or of Master of Studies or of Master of Science by Coursework, or a student under

the supervision of the Board of the Faculty of Law admitted under the provisions of §2, cl. 1 (iii) of this section, shall keep statutory residence and pursue his or her course of study at Oxford for not less than three terms after such admission.

4. Any student who, after admission under §3 of this section, has kept statutory residence and studied at Oxford for a period of forty-two days, not necessarily consecutive, but falling within the same academic year, may apply to the board concerned for leave to reckon such period as one term towards the total required under clause 1 of this sub-section. The board shall have power to grant such leave provided that:

(i) no day so reckoned which falls within any term shall also be reckoned for the purpose of keeping that term;

(ii) no student who has kept the Michaelmas, or the Hilary, or the Trinity Term shall be allowed to reckon in this manner any day that falls within the eight weeks beginning on the first day of Full Term in Michaelmas, or Hilary, or Trinity Term, as the case may be;

(iii) no student shall be allowed to reckon in this manner more than one such period in the same academic year;

(iv) no student shall be allowed to reckon more than three terms in the same academic year.

For the purposes of this clause, the academic year shall begin on the first day of Michaelmas Term and end on the day preceding the first day of Michaelmas Term in the following calendar year.

Applications for leave to reckon any period as a term under the provisions of this clause shall be made to the board, through the Registrar, by the student's college.

5. Part-time students holding the status of student for the Degree of Master of Letters shall in each case be required to pursue their course of study for a minimum of twelve terms, subject to the provisions of §3, cl. 6. Part-time students shall not be required to keep statutory residence, but must attend for such instruction as the board or other relevant body shall require, subject to the approval of the Education Committee. No student may apply to the relevant faculty board or other body for the appointment of examiners unless his or her supervisor has certified that the student has fulfilled the requirements for part-time students laid down by the board or other relevant body.

6. Any student may, with the permission of the board, alter the subject of research approved by the board, provided that the conditions of suitability set out in §2 above continue to be met. In such

cases the date of the student's admission for all the purposes of this section shall remain unchanged, unless the board shall determine otherwise.

7. If a full-time Student for the Degree of Master of Letters has held that status for nine terms, or a part-time student for fifteen terms, but has been prevented by exceptional circumstances from completing his or her thesis, the board shall have power to grant an extension of time for a period or periods not exceeding six terms in all for a full-time student, or three terms in all for a part-time student, to be determined by the board. Applications for such extension of time shall be made through the Registrar not later than the term in which the student is due to apply for permission to supplicate, and must be accompanied by statements of support from the student's society and supervisor.

8. A Student for the Degree of Master of Letters shall cease to hold such status if:

(i) he or she shall have been refused permission to supplicate for the Degree of Master of Letters;

(ii) the board concerned shall in accordance with §2 cl. 3 of this section, and with the provisions set down by regulation by the Education Committee, and after consultation with the student's college and supervisor, have deprived the student of such status;

(iii) he or she shall have been transferred under the relevant provisions to another status;

(iv) he or she shall have failed to complete his or her thesis within nine terms for a full-time student, or fifteen terms for a part-time student or within such further extension of time as may have been granted by the board concerned.

§6. Examination of Students for the Degree of Master of Letters

1. A Student for the Degree of Master of Letters who has fulfilled the applicable residence and other requirements set out in §5, and whose status has not expired, may apply for the appointment of examiners and for leave to supplicate for the Degree of Master of Letters.

2. Such applications should be made to the board concerned through the Registrar. They shall include:

(i) a certificate from the student's college that the application has the approval of that college;

   (ii) a certificate from the supervisor that the candidate has pursued his or her course of study in Oxford in accordance with the provisions of §5 of this section;

  (iii) a statement by the candidate of what part, if any, of the thesis has already been accepted, or is being concurrently submitted, for any degree or diploma or certificate or other qualification in this University or elsewhere;

  (iv) a statement by the candidate that the thesis is his or her own work, except where otherwise indicated.

3. The supervisor shall consult with the candidate concerning possible examiners, and forward to the board the names of suggested examiners with details of any special considerations which the candidate wishes to make known about any potential examiners.

4. The student shall also submit for examination, at such time as the Education Committee shall by regulation require:

   (i) two printed or typewritten copies of a thesis;

  (ii) two printed or typewritten copies of an abstract of the thesis, which shall not normally exceed 300 words.

5. On receipt of an application for the appointment of examiners the board concerned shall appoint two examiners, neither of whom shall be the candidate's supervisor, and whose duties shall be:

   (i) to consider the thesis and the abstract of it submitted by the student under the provisions of the preceding clause, provided that they shall exclude from consideration in making their report any part of the thesis which has already been accepted, or is being concurrently submitted, for any degree or other qualification in this University or elsewhere (except for the Degree of Bachelor of Civil Law of this University) and shall have the power to require the candidate to produce for their inspection the complete thesis so accepted or concurrently submitted;

  (ii) to examine the student orally, and also, if they think fit, by a written examination, in the subject of the thesis and in other relevant subjects;

  (iii) to report to the board through the Registrar;

  (iv) to return to the student the copies of the thesis and of the abstract thereof submitted for examination.

The Education Committee shall have power to make regulations concerning the notice to be given of the oral examination and of the time and place at which it may be held. The examination may be attended by any member of the University in academic dress, while non-members may attend only with the consent of the examiners. In the case of theses submitted to the Divisional Boards of Social Sciences, Mathematical, Physical and Life Sciences, and Medical Sciences, the Proctors after consultation with the relevant faculty board may decide (either at their own discretion or at the request of   5 the candidate or the supervisor or department) to forbid the attendance of any person or all persons (other than the examiners and the candidate) or to impose any condition on attendance if and to the extent that such action is in their view necessary to protect the interests of the University or the candidate or both, and the exam-   10 iners shall be informed accordingly and shall include this information in the notice of examination. The student, or his or her college, may within fourteen days of the date of the Proctors' decision appeal in writing to the Chair of the Education Committee (who may nominate another member of the committee, other than one of   15 the Proctors, to adjudicate the appeal).

6. Having completed the examination of a candidate for the first time, the examiners may make recommendation (i) or (ii) below only. Having completed the examination of a candidate who has revised and re-submitted his or her thesis, the examiners may make   20 any one of recommendations (i) to (iii). The recommendations are:

(i) that the candidate should be granted leave to supplicate for the Degree of Master of Letters. In this case the examiners must include in their report statements that:

1. the candidate possesses a good general knowledge of the   25 field of learning within which the subject of the thesis falls;

2. that the candidate has shown competence in investigating the chosen topic;

3. that the candidate has made a worthwhile contribution to knowledge or understanding in the field of learning within   30 which the subject of the thesis falls;

4. that the thesis is presented in a lucid and scholarly manner;

5. that it merits of the award of the Degree of Master of Letters.

Examiners shall bear in mind that their judgement of the extent of the candidate's contribution to knowledge or understanding of the   35 relevant field of learning shall take into account what may reasonably be expected of a capable and diligent student after two years of full-time study in the case of a full-time student, or twelve terms in the case of a part-time student.

If the examiners are satisfied that the candidate's thesis is of   40 sufficient merit for the degree but consider, nevertheless, that before the thesis is deposited the candidate should make minor corrections (which are not sufficiently substantial to justify reference back for re-examination), they must require the candidate to correct the thesis to their satisfaction before they submit their report. If the candidate has not completed these corrections within one calendar month of the date of the oral examination, his or her name shall be removed by the Registrar from the Register of Students for the Degree of Master of Letters, provided that the board may, on good cause shown by the candidate, grant an extension of time of one further calendar month in which the candidate may fulfil this requirement before the removal of his or her name from the Register. No subsequent extension shall be granted, but it shall be open to a candidate who has failed to fulfil this requirement within those one or two months in total, as the case may be, to apply to the board for reinstatement as a Student for the Degree of Master of Letters, with the support of his or her society and supervisor, upon submission to the Registrar of a copy of his or her thesis incorporating the required corrections, and upon payment of such reinstatement fee as may from time to time be prescribed by Council by decree. Permission to supplicate shall not be granted until this fee has been paid;

  (ii) that the board should refer the thesis back to the student in order that he or she may revise it for re-examination. If the examiners so recommend they shall annex to their report to the board a statement (for transmission to the student) setting out the respects in which the thesis falls below the standard required for the degree. If the board adopts this recommendation the student shall retain the status and obligations of a Student for the Degree of Master of Letters, and may apply again for the appointment of examiners, in accordance with the procedure laid down in this subsection, not later than the third term after that in which the board gave permission so to reapply. If such permission shall have been given by a board during a vacation, it shall be deemed to have been given in the term preceding that vacation. On submission of the revised thesis, students should submit a separate report indicating the specific changes made. The word limit for the accompanying report shall be 1000 words;

  (iii) that the board should refuse the candidate's application for leave to supplicate.

7. In each case the examiners must embody in their report, in support of their recommendation, an account of the scope, character, and quality of the candidate's work.

8. On receipt of the examiners' report the board shall reach a decision on whether to accept the examiners' recommendation, provided that no candidate shall be given leave to supplicate unless the examiners have made the statements required in clause 6 (i) above.

9. A candidate who has been granted leave to supplicate by a board shall be required to submit to the Registrar a copy of his or her thesis, incorporating any amendments or corrections required by the examiners and approved by the board. It shall be the duty of the Registrar to deposit this copy of the thesis in the Bodleian or other appropriate university library. Leave to supplicate shall in all cases be conditional upon fulfilment of this requirement.

10. In an exceptional case in which a board is unable to accept the examiners' recommendation, or in which the examiners cannot reach an agreed recommendation, the board shall have power to appoint one or two new examiners as it deems necessary, to conduct such further examination of the candidate as the board may require. The board shall make a report on any such case to the Education Committee.

11. The board may exempt a candidate who is being re-examined under the provisions of clause 6 (ii) above from the oral examination, provided that the examiners are able to certify that they are satisfied, without examining the candidate orally, that they can recommend to the board in the terms required by clause 6 (i) above that he or she be given leave to supplicate for the Degree of Master of Letters.

12. It shall be the duty of the Registrar to notify the candidate of the board's decision as soon as may be. The Registrar shall also be responsible for publishing at the end of each academic year the names of those candidates to whom permission to supplicate has been granted during that year, together with a statement of the subject of the thesis written by each.

13. When, on the conclusion of the investigation of a complaint made by a candidate, the Proctors recommend that a candidate be re-examined, the board shall have power to hold a new examination.

15

REGULATIONS FOR THE DEGREE OF MASTER OF SCIENCE BY RESEARCH*

GENERAL REGULATIONS

§1. Degree of Master of Science by Research

1. Any person who has been admitted to the status of Student for the Degree of Master of Science by Research and who has satisfied the conditions prescribed by this decree, may supplicate for the Degree of Master of Science.

2. The Education Committee shall have power to make and vary such regulations as may be necessary for carrying out the duties laid upon it and upon the Registrar by this section.

3. For the purpose of this section the words 'board', 'faculty board', 'board of the faculty' or 'divisional board' shall include any committee with powers to admit candidates for the Degree of Master of Science by Research.

4. A Student for the Degree of Master of Science by Research who is not a graduate of the University may wear the same gown as that worn by Students for the Degree of Doctor of Philosophy.

§2. Status of Student for the Degree of Master of Science by Research

1. The following may be admitted to the status of Student for the Degree of Master of Science by Research:

(i) a member of the University who, having held the status of Probationer Research Student under the provisions of the

---

* To be read in conjunction with the associated special regulations made by the Education Committee and individual boards. Those provisions of this regulation which govern admission to, and transfer from, one status to another shall apply only to research students first registered from Michaelmas Term 1991 or later. Students first registered for a research degree before that term shall continue to be subject to the relevant sections of the 1990 Examination Decrees in this respect.

References within this regulation to part-time students relate to a small number of faculties/departments which have been given permission to admit research students to study on a part-time basis. There is no general provision for the award of research degrees through part-time study within the University.

appropriate regulation, has successfully completed the relevant qualifying test for transfer to M.Sc. status prescribed in §3 of this section;

(ii) a member of the University who, holding the status of student for another higher degree within the University, has successfully completed the relevant qualifying test for transfer to M.Sc. status prescribed in §3 of this section.

2. It shall be the duty of the Registrar to keep a Register of those admitted to the status of Student for the Degree of Master of Science by Research.

3. A board may grant a student suspension from the Register or deprive a student of his or her status; and in such cases it shall at all times follow procedures determined by the Education Committee by regulation. A board may also reinstate a student to the Register, provided that the number of terms a student has spent as a Student for the Degree of Master of Science shall not have exceeded fifteen in all in the case of a full-time student, or eighteen terms in the case of a part-time student.

§3. Admission of Candidates for the Degree of Master of Science by Research

1. A candidate qualified under §2 of this section may apply for admission as a Student for the Degree of Master of Science by Research to the board under whose aegis the proposed subject of research falls. Such applications should be made through the Registrar, and must be accompanied by:

(i) a statement from the supervisor (where appropriate) that he or she approves the proposed subject for a thesis and considers the candidate well fitted to undertake research;

(ii) a statement of the subject of the proposed thesis and details of the manner in which the candidate proposes to treat it;

(iii) a statement of support for the application from the candidate's society.

2. Applicants shall in addition be required to undertake such other tests and meet such other conditions as, subject to the approval of the Education Committee, a board may determine by regulation.

3. The board shall consider the candidate's application together with the material supplied in accordance with clauses 1 and 2 above. No application shall be granted unless the board is satisfied that the candidate is capable of carrying out research, that the subject of the thesis and the manner of its treatment proposed by the

candidate are acceptable, that the subject is one which may profitably be pursued under the superintendence of the board, and that the board or department concerned is satisfied that it has adequate facilities to enable the research to be undertaken.

4. It shall be the duty of the Registrar to submit any application made under these provisions to the board concerned and to inform a candidate of the outcome as soon as may be.

5. A candidate who is admitted to the status of Student for the Degree of Master of Science by Research shall be reckoned as having held that status from the time of admission to his or her previous status, unless the board shall determine otherwise.

§4. Supervision of Students for the Degree of Master of Science by Research

1. Every candidate on admission as a Student for the Degree of Master of Science by Research shall be placed by the board concerned under the supervision of a member of the University or other competent person selected by the board, and the board shall have power for sufficient reason to change the supervisor of any student or to arrange for joint supervision by more than one supervisor, if it deems it necessary.

2. It shall be the duty of a supervisor to direct and superintend the work of the student, to meet the student regularly, and to undertake such duties as shall be from time to time set out in Policy and Guidance issued by the Education Committee. The supervisor shall submit a report on the progress of the student to the board three times a year, and at any other time when the board so requests or the supervisor deems it expedient; and shall carry out such other duties as are set out in Policy and Guidance issued by the Education Committee. The supervisor shall communicate the contents of the report to the student on each occasion that a report is made, so that the student is aware of the supervisor's assessment of his or her work during the period in question. In addition, the supervisor shall inform the board at once if he or she is of the opinion the student is unlikely to reach the standard required for the Master of Science by Research.

The Registrar shall send a copy of each report by the supervisor to the student's college and to the Director of Graduate Studies or other nominated person under the faculty board concerned.

3. It shall be the duty of every Student for the Degree of Master of Science by Research to undertake such guided work as his or her supervisor requests; to attend such meetings with his or her

supervisor as the latter reasonably arranges; and to fulfil any other requirements set out in Policy and Guidance issued by the Education Committee.

§5. Residence and other Requirements for Students for the Degree of Master of Science by Research

1. A Student for the Degree of Master of Science by Research shall, after admission for full-time study, keep statutory residence and pursue his or her work at Oxford for at least three terms. Time spent outside Oxford during term as part of an academic programme approved by Council shall count towards residence for the purpose of this clause.

2. Any student who, after admission under §3 of this regulation, has kept statutory residence and studied at Oxford for a period of forty-two days, not necessarily consecutive, but falling within the same academic year, may apply to the board concerned for leave to reckon such period as one term towards the total required under the preceding clause. The board shall have power to grant such leave provided that:

(i) no day so reckoned which falls within any term shall also be reckoned for the purpose of keeping that term;

(ii) no student who has kept the Michaelmas, or the Hilary, or the Trinity Term shall be allowed to reckon in this manner any day that falls within the eight weeks beginning on the first day of Full Term in Michaelmas, or Hilary, or Trinity Term, as the case may be;

(iii) no student shall be allowed to reckon in this manner more than one such period in the same academic year;

(iv) no student shall be allowed to reckon more than three terms in the same academic year.

For the purposes of this clause, the academic year shall begin on the first day of Michaelmas Term and end on the day preceding the first day of Michaelmas Term in the following calendar year.

3. Applications for leave to reckon any period as a term under the provisions of the preceding clause shall be made to the board, through the Registrar, by the student's society.

4. Part-time students holding the status of Student for Degree of Master of Science by Research shall in each case be required to pursue their course of study for a minimum of twelve terms, subject to the provisions of § 3, cl. 5. Part-time students shall not be required to keep statutory residence, but must attend for such instruction as the board or other relevant body shall require, subject

to the approval of the Education Committee. No student may apply to the relevant board or other body for the appointment of examiners unless his or her supervisor has certified that the student has fulfilled the requirements for part-time students laid down by the board or other relevant body.

5. Any student may, with the permission of the board, alter the subject of research approved by the board, provided that the conditions of suitability set out in §2 above continue to be met. In such cases the date of the student's admission for all the purposes of this section shall remain unchanged, unless the board shall determine otherwise.

6. If a full-time Student for the Degree of Master of Science by Research has held that status for nine terms, or a part-time student for fifteen terms but has been prevented by exceptional circumstances from completing his or her thesis, the board shall have power to grant an extension of time for a period or periods not exceeding six terms in all for a full-time student, or three terms in all for a part-time student, to be determined by the board. Applications for such an extension of time shall be made through the Registrar not later that the term in which the student is due to apply for permission to supplicate.

7. A Student for the Degree of Master of Science by Research shall cease to hold such status if:

(i) he or she shall have been refused permission to supplicate for the Degree of Master of Science;

(ii) the board concerned shall, in accordance with provisions set down by regulation by the Education Committee, and after consultation with the student's society and supervisor, have deprived the student of such status.

(iii) he or she shall have failed to complete his or her thesis within nine terms for a full-time student, or fifteen terms for a part-time student, or within such further extension of time as may have been granted by the board concerned.

§6. Examination of Students for the Degree of Master of Science by Research

1. Candidates who have fulfilled the applicable residence and other requirements set out in §5 of this section, and whose status has not expired, may apply for the appointment of examiners and for leave to supplicate for the Degree of Master of Science by Research.

2. Applications for the appointment of examiners should be made to the board concerned through the Registrar. They shall include:

    (i) a certificate from the student's society that the application has the approval of that society;

    (ii) a certificate from the supervisor that the candidate has pursued his or her course of study in Oxford in accordance with the provisions of §5 of this section;

    (iii) a statement by the candidate what part, if any, of the thesis has already been accepted, or is being concurrently submitted for any degree or diploma or certificate or other qualification in this University or elsewhere;

    (iv) a statement by the candidate that the thesis is his or her own work, except where otherwise indicated.

3. The supervisor shall consult with the candidate concerning possible examiners, and forward to the board the names of suggested examiners with details of any special considerations which the candidate wishes to make known about any potential examiners.

4. The student shall also submit for examination, at such time as the Education Committee shall by regulation require:

    (i) two printed or typewritten copies of a thesis;

    (ii) two printed or typewritten copies of an abstract of the thesis, which shall not normally exceed 300 words.

5. On receipt of an application for the appointment of examiners the board concerned shall appoint two examiners neither of whom shall be the candidate's supervisor, and whose duties shall be:

    (i) to consider the thesis and the abstract of it submitted by the student under the provisions of the preceding clause, provided that they shall exclude from consideration in making their report any part of the thesis which has already been accepted, or is being concurrently submitted, for any degree or other qualification in this University or elsewhere and shall have the power to require the candidate to produce for their inspection the complete thesis so accepted or concurrently submitted;

    (ii) to examine the student orally, and also, if they think fit, by a written examination, in the subject of the thesis and in other relevant subjects;

    (iii) to report to the board through the Registrar;

    (iv) to return to the student the copies of the thesis and of the abstract thereof submitted for examination.

The Education Committee shall have power to make regulations concerning the notice to be given of the oral examination and of the time and place at which it may be held. The examination may be attended by any member of the University in academic dress, while non-members may attend only with the consent of the examiners. In the case of theses submitted to the Social Sciences, Mathematical, Physical and Life Sciences, and Medical Sciences Boards, the Proctors after consultation with the relevant divisional board may decide (either at their own discretion or at the request of the candidate or the supervisor or department) to forbid the attendance of any person or all persons (other than the examiners and the candidate) or to impose any condition on attendance if and to the extent that such action is in their view necessary to protect the interests of the University or the candidate or both, and the examiners shall be informed accordingly and shall include this information in the notice of examination. The student, or his or her college, may within fourteen days of the date of the Proctors' decision appeal in writing to the Chair of the Education Committee (who may nominate another member of the committee, other than one of the Proctors, to adjudicate the appeal).

6. Having completed the examination of a candidate for the first time, the examiners may make recommendation (i) or (ii) below only. Having completed the examination of a candidate who has revised and re-submitted his or her thesis, the examiners may make any one of recommendations (i) to (iii). The recommendations are:

(i) that the candidate should be granted leave to supplicate for the Degree of Master of Science by Research. In this case the examiners must include in their report statements that:

   1. the candidate possesses a good general knowledge of the field of learning within which the subject of the thesis falls;
   2. that the candidate has shown competence in investigating the chosen topic;
   3. that the candidate has made a worthwhile contribution to knowledge or understanding in the field of learning within which the subject of the thesis falls;
   4. that the thesis is presented in a lucid and scholarly manner;
   5. that it merits of the award of the Degree of Master of Science.

Examiners shall bear in mind that their judgement of the extent of the candidate's contribution to knowledge or understanding of the relevant field of learning shall take into account what may reasonably be expected of a capable and diligent student after two years of full-time study in the case of a full-time student, or twelve terms in the case of a part-time student.

If the examiners are satisfied that the candidate's thesis is of sufficient merit for the degree but consider, nevertheless, that before the thesis is deposited the candidate should make minor corrections (which are not sufficiently substantial to justify reference back for re-examination), they must require the candidate to correct the thesis to their satisfaction before they submit their report. If the candidate has not completed these corrections within one calendar month of the date of the oral examination, his or her name shall be removed by the Registrar from the Register of Students for the Degree of Master of Science by Research, provided that the board may, on good cause shown by the candidate, grant an extension of time of one further calendar month in which the candidate may fulfil this requirement before the removal of his or her name from the Register. No subsequent extension shall be granted, but it shall be open to a candidate who has failed to fulfil this requirement within those one or two months in total, as the case may be, to apply to the board for reinstatement as a Student for the Degree of Master of Science by Research, with the support of his or her society and supervisor, upon submission to the Registrar of a copy of his or her thesis incorporating the required corrections, and upon payment of such reinstatement fee as may from time to time be prescribed by Council by decree. Permission to supplicate shall not be granted until this fee has been paid;

(ii) that the board should refer the thesis back to the student in order that he or she may revise it for re-examination. If the examiners so recommend they shall annexe to their report to the board a statement (for transmission to the student) setting out the respects in which the thesis falls below the standard required for the degree. If the board adopts this recommendation the student shall retain the status and obligations of a Student for the Degree of Master of Science, and may apply again for the appointment of examiners, in accordance with the procedure laid down in this subsection, not later than the third term after that in which the board gave permission so to reapply. If such permission shall have been given by a board during a vacation, it shall be deemed to have been given in the term preceding that vacation. On submission of the revised thesis, students should submit a separate report indicating the specific changes made. For students in the Medical Sciences Division and the Department for Continuing Education, the word limit for the accompanying report shall be 1000 words; for students in the Mathematical, Physical and Life Sciences Division, the word limit shall be 2000 words;

(iii) that the board should refuse the candidate's application for leave to supplicate.

7. In each case the examiners must embody in their report, in support of their recommendation, an account of the scope, character, and quality of the candidate's work.

8. On receipt of the examiners' report the board shall reach a decision on whether to accept the examiners' recommendation, provided that no candidate shall be given leave to supplicate unless the examiners have made the statements required in clause 6 (i) above.

9. A student who has been granted leave to supplicate by the board shall be required to submit to the Examination Schools a copy of his or her thesis, incorporating any amendments or corrections required by the examiners and approved by the board, with a view to deposit in the Bodleian or other appropriate university library. [For candidates supplicating on or after 1 July 2013: candidates are also required to submit to the Examination Schools the library copy of the thesis no later than the end of the fifth day before the date of the degree ceremony booked by the candidate for conferral of their degree.] Permission to supplicate shall in all cases be conditional upon fulfilment of these requirements.

10. In an exceptional case in which a board is unable to accept the examiners' recommendation, or in which the examiners cannot reach an agreed recommendation, the board shall have power to appoint one or two new examiners as it deems necessary, to conduct such further examination of the candidate as the board may require. The board shall make a report on any such case to the Education Committee.

11. The board may exempt a candidate who is being re-examined under the provisions of clause 6 (ii) above from the oral examination, provided that the examiners are able to certify that they are satisfied, without examining the candidate orally, that they can recommend to the board in the terms required by clause 6 (i) above that he or she be given leave to supplicate for the Degree of Master of Science.

12. It shall be the duty of the Registrar to notify the candidate of the board's decision as soon as may be. The Registrar shall also be responsible for publishing at the end of each academic year the names of those candidates to whom permission to supplicate has been granted during that year, together with a statement of the subject of the thesis written by each.

13. When, on the conclusion of the investigation of a complaint made by a candidate, the Proctors recommend that a candidate be re-examined, the board shall have power to hold a new examination.

NOTES

16

REGULATIONS FOR THE DEGREE
OF DOCTOR OF PHILOSOPHY*

A

§1. Degree of Doctor of Philosophy

1. Any member of the University who has been admitted to the status of Student for the Degree of Doctor of Philosophy and who has satisfied the conditions prescribed by this decree may supplicate for the Degree of Doctor of Philosophy. 10

2. The Education Committee shall have power to make and vary such regulations as may be necessary for carrying out the duties laid upon it and upon the Registrar by this section.

3. For the purposes of this section the words 'board', 'faculty board', 'board of the faculty' or 'divisional board' shall include any 15 body which has power to admit students to read for the Degree of Doctor of Philosophy.

4. Students for the Degree of Doctor of Philosophy who are not graduates of the University may wear a long gown of black stuff, whose shape and ornaments shall be in accordance with a pattern 20 approved by the Vice-Chancellor and Proctors and preserved in the University Offices, Wellington Square.

---

* To be read in conjunction with the associated special regulations made by the Education Committee and individual boards. Those provisions of this regulation which govern admission to, and transfer from, one status to another shall apply only to research students first registered from Michaelmas Term 1991 or later. Students first registered for a research degree before that term shall continue to be subject to the relevant sections of the 1990 Examination Decrees in this respect.

References within this regulation to part-time students relate to a small number of faculties/departments which have been given permission to admit research students to study on a part-time basis. There is no general provision for the award of research degrees through part-time study within the University.

§2. Status of Student for the Degree of Doctor of Philosophy

1. The following may be admitted to the status of Student for the Degree of Doctor of Philosophy:

   (i) a member of the University who, having held the status of Probationer Research Student under the provisions of the appropriate regulation, or having held the status of student for another higher degree within the University, or having completed the requirements for another higher degree within the University, has successfully completed the relevant qualifying test for entry to D.Phil. status prescribed in §3 of this section;

   (ii) a member of the University who has been given leave to supplicate for the Degree of Master or Bachelor of Philosophy, or of Master of Science by Research, or of Master of Letters, provided that the subject of the thesis offered by the candidate in the examination for that degree shall be in the broad field of research proposed for the D.Phil.

2. It shall be the duty of the Registrar to keep a Register of those admitted to the status of Student for the Degree of Doctor of Philosophy.

3. A board may grant a student suspension from the Register or deprive a student of his or her status; and in such cases it shall at all times follow procedures determined by the Education Committee by regulation. A board may also reinstate a student to the Register, provided that the number of terms a student has spent with the status of Student for the Degree of Doctor of Philosophy shall not have exceeded twenty-one in all in the case of a full-time student, or twenty-seven terms in the case of a part-time student.

§3. Admission of Candidates to the Status of Student for the Degree of Doctor of Philosophy

1. Candidates qualified under §2 of this section may apply for admission as Student for the Degree of Doctor of Philosophy to the board concerned through the Registrar. Such applications shall be accompanied by:

   (i) a statement from the supervisor that he or she approves the proposed subject for a thesis* and considers the candidate well-fitted to undertake advanced research;

---

* Here and hereafter in these regulations, in the case of Fine Art candidates offering studio practice as part of their submission, and in the case of Music candidates offering a portfolio of musical compositions as part of their submission, 'thesis' shall be understood to include the totality of the candidate's submission.

(ii) a statement of support for the application from the candidate's society;

(iii) a statement of the subject of the proposed thesis and details of the manner in which the candidate proposes to treat it.

2. Save for those applying under the provisions of § 2, cl. 1 (ii) of this section, applicants shall in addition be required to submit written work to the board, which work shall be assessed by two assessors appointed by the board, neither of whom shall normally be the candidate's supervisor. The precise manner and form of the written work shall be determined by regulation by each board. In the case of Fine Art candidates offering studio practice, and in the case of Music candidates offering a portfolio of musical compositions as part of their submissions, this will include such studio or compositional work as the board requires. The process of assessment shall normally include an interview with the applicant; it shall always do so if the assessors are unable to certify that they are satisfied without interviewing the applicant that they can recommend transfer to D.Phil. status. Upon completion of their assessment of the candidate's work, the assessors shall make a recommendation as to whether the application for transfer to D.Phil. status should be granted. In each case the assessors shall make a reasoned written report to the board in support of their recommendation.

3. The board shall consider the candidate's application together with the material supplied in accordance with clauses 1 and 2 above. No application for transfer shall be granted unless the assessors shall have certified and the board is satisfied that the candidate is capable of carrying out advanced research, and that the subject of the thesis and the manner of its treatment proposed by the candidate are acceptable; and unless the board or department under whose aegis the research is to be conducted has adequate facilities to enable the research to be undertaken.

4. Subject to the approval of the Education Committee, each board shall have power to determine by regulation what other test or condition, if any, it may require before approving admission to D.Phil. status. Each board shall be empowered, without further authority, to require from the supervisor any further confidential report on an applicant's suitability to pursue research towards the D.Phil.

5. It shall be the duty of the Registrar to submit any application made under these provisions to the board concerned, and to inform the candidate of the outcome as soon as may be.

6. A candidate whose first application for transfer to D.Phil. status is not approved shall be permitted to make one further application, following the procedures laid down in clauses 1–4 above, and shall be granted an extension of time for one term if this is necessary for the purposes of making the application.

7. An applicant who transfers to the status of Student for the Degree of Doctor of Philosophy shall be reckoned as having held that status from the time he or she was admitted to his or her previous status unless the board shall determine otherwise.

§4. Confirmation of Status as a Student for the Degree of Doctor of Philosophy

1. A candidate who has been admitted to the status of Student for the Degree of Doctor of Philosophy must, not later than the ninth term or normally earlier than the sixth term after that in which he or she was initially admitted to the status of a Probationer Research Student or to the status of a student for another higher degree of the University, or the eighteenth and twelfth terms respectively in the case of a part-time student, apply to the faculty board or committee concerned for confirmation of his or her status as a D.Phil. Student. A board or committee may, for good reason, permit a candidate to defer for a maximum of three terms his or her application for confirmation of status. A student who has been admitted to the status of Student for the Degree of Doctor of Philosophy after successfully completing the requirements for the Degree of Master (or Bachelor) of Philosophy, or having held the status of Student for the M.Litt. or M.Sc. by Research, may be exempted by the board or committee concerned from the requirement for confirmation of status. With the exception of students who have been exempted under this provision, all Students for the Degree of Doctor of Philosophy must have their status confirmed before making an application for the appointment of examiners.

2. Candidates applying for confirmation of their status shall submit their application to the board concerned, through the Registrar; and such applications shall be accompanied by:
    (i) certification from the supervisor that the candidate's progress has been such as to warrant confirmation of status;
    (ii) a statement of support for the application from the candidate's society.

3. Each faculty board shall, subject to the approval of the Education Committee, determine by regulation any other conditions which a student must fulfil before his or her status may be confirmed.

4. A candidate whose first application for confirmation of their status is not approved shall be permitted to make one further application following the procedures laid down in this section normally within one term of the original application, and shall be granted an extension of time for one term if this is necessary for the purposes of making the application. 5

5. A Student for the Degree of Doctor of Philosophy shall cease to hold such status unless it has been confirmed within nine terms of his or her admission to that status (or within a maximum of twelve terms where deferral has been approved in accordance with paragraph 4.1) in the case of a full-time student, or eighteen terms (or a maximum of twenty-four terms where deferral has been approved in accordance with paragraph 4.1) in the case of a part-time student, in accordance with the provisions of this section. 10

6. If, after considering a candidate's second application for confirmation of status, a board concludes that the student's progress does not warrant this, the board may approve his or her transfer to the status of Student for the Degree of Master of Science by Research or of Master of Letters, as appropriate. 15

§5. Supervision of Students for the Degree of Doctor of Philosophy 20

1. Every candidate on admission as a Student for the Degree of Doctor of Philosophy shall be placed by the board which approved his or her application under the supervision of a member of the University or other competent person selected by the board, and the board shall have power for sufficient reason to change the supervisor of any student or to arrange for joint supervision by more than one supervisor, if it deems it necessary. 25

2. It shall be the duty of a supervisor to direct and superintend the work of the student, to meet the student regularly, and to undertake such duties as shall be from time to time set out in Policy and Guidance issued by the Education Committee. The supervisor shall submit a report on the progress of the student to the board three times a year as required, and at any other time when the board so requests or the supervisor deems it expedient; and shall carry out such other duties as are set out in Policy and Guidance issued by the Education Committee. The supervisor shall communicate the contents of the report to the student on each occasion that a report is made, so that the student is aware of the supervisor's assessment of his or her work during the period in question. In addition, the supervisor shall inform the board at once if he or she is 30

35

40

of the opinion the student is unlikely to reach the standard required for the Degree of Doctor of Philosophy.

The Registrar shall send a copy of each report by the supervisor to the student's college, and to the Director of Graduate Studies or other nominated person under the board concerned.

3. It shall be the duty of every Student for the Degree of Doctor of Philosophy to undertake such guided work as his or her supervisor requests; to attend such meetings with his or her supervisor as the latter reasonably arranges; and to fulfil any other requirements of the Education Committee set out in its memorandum of guidance for students and supervisors.

§6. Residence and other Requirements for Students for the Degree of Doctor of Philosophy

1. Except as provided in clause 2 of this subsection, a Student for the Degree of Doctor of Philosophy shall after admission for full-time study keep statutory residence and pursue his or her course of study at Oxford for at least six terms, provided that a Student for the Degree of Doctor of Philosophy who is also a Bachelor or Master of Philosophy or Master of Science or Master of Letters or Master of Studies or Bachelor of Civil Law or Magister Juris or Master of Theology (except for those who hold the degree having studied for it at Westminster College) shall keep statutory residence and pursue his or her course of study at Oxford for at least three terms after admission as a Student for the Degree of Doctor of Philosophy. Time spent outside Oxford during term as part of an academic programme approved by Council shall count towards residence for the purpose of this clause.

2. The board concerned may dispense a student for the Degree of Doctor of Philosophy, on application through his or her society and with the support of his or her supervisor, from not more than three terms of residence and study in Oxford either on the ground that it is necessary to the student's work that he or she should be allowed to pursue his or her course of study at some other place than Oxford, or for other good cause.

3. Students exceptionally permitted to undertake their research in a well-found laboratory outside Oxford shall not be required to keep statutory residence, but must attend for such instruction as the board shall require.

4. Any student who, after admission under §3 of this section, has kept statutory residence and studied at Oxford for a period of forty-two days, not necessarily consecutive, but falling within the

same academic year, may apply to the board concerned for leave to reckon such period as one term towards the total required under the preceding clause. The board shall have power to grant such leave provided that:

(i) no day so reckoned which falls within any term shall also be reckoned for the purpose of keeping that term;

(ii) no student who has kept the Michaelmas, or the Hilary, or the Trinity Term shall be allowed to reckon in this manner any day that falls within the eight weeks beginning on the first day of Full Term in Michaelmas, or Hilary, or Trinity Term, as the case may be;

(iii) no student shall be allowed to reckon in this manner more than one such period in the same academic year;

(iv) no student shall be allowed to reckon more than three terms in the same academic year.

For the purposes of this clause, the academic year shall begin on the first day of Michaelmas Term and end on the day preceding the first day of Michaelmas Term in the following calendar year.

Applications for leave to reckon any period as a term under the provisions of this clause shall be made to the board, through the Registrar, by the student's society.

5. Part-time students holding the status of Student for the Degree of Doctor of Philosophy shall in each case be required to pursue their course of study for a minimum of twelve terms, subject to the provisions of § 3, cl. 6. Part-time students shall not be required to keep statutory residence, but must attend for such instruction as the board or other relevant body shall require, subject to the approval of the Education Committee. No student may apply to the relevant faculty board or other body for the appointment of examiners unless his or her supervisor has certified that the student has fulfilled the requirements for part-time students laid down by the faculty board or other relevant body.

6. Any student may, with the permission of the board alter the subject of the research originally approved provided that the conditions of suitability set out in §3 of this section continue to be met. In such cases the date of the student's admission for all the purposes of this section shall remain unchanged, unless the board shall order otherwise.

7. If a full-time Student for the Degree of Doctor of Philosophy has held that status for twelve terms, or a part-time student for twenty-four terms, but has been prevented by exceptional circumstances from completing his or her thesis, the board shall have

power to grant an extension of time for a period or periods, not exceeding six terms in all for a full-time student, or three terms in all for a part-time student, to be determined by the board. Applications for such extension of time shall be made through the Registrar not later than the term in which the student is due to apply for permission to supplicate.

8. A Student for the Degree of Doctor of Philosophy shall cease to hold that status if:

(i) he or she shall have been refused permission to supplicate for the Degree of Doctor of Philosophy; or

(ii) the board concerned shall in accordance with §2, cl. 3 of this section, and with the provisions set down by regulation by the Education Committee and after consultation with the student's college and supervisor, have deprived the student of such status;

(iii) he or she shall have been transferred under the relevant provisions to another status;

(iv) he or she shall have failed to complete his or her thesis within twelve terms for a full-time student, or twenty-four terms for a part-time student or within such further extension of time as may have been granted by the board concerned.

§7. Examination of Students for the Degree of Doctor of Philosophy

1. A Student for the Degree of Doctor of Philosophy who has fulfilled the applicable residence and other requirements set out in §6 of this section and whose status has not expired, may apply to the board concerned for the appointment of examiners and for leave to supplicate for the Degree of Doctor of Philosophy.

2. Such applications should be made to the board concerned through the Registrar. They shall include:

(i) a certificate from the student's college that the application has the approval of that college;

(ii) a certificate from the supervisor that the student has pursued his or her course of study in Oxford in accordance with the provisions of §6 of this section;

(iii) a statement by the candidate of what part, if any, of the thesis has already been accepted, or is concurrently being submitted, for any degree or diploma or certificate or other qualification in this University or elsewhere;

(iv) a statement by the candidate that the thesis is his or her own work, except where otherwise indicated.

3. The supervisor shall consult with the candidate concerning possible examiners, and forward to the board the names of suggested examiners together with details of any special considerations which the candidate wishes to make known about any potential examiners.

4. The candidate shall also submit for examination, at such time and in such format as the Education Committee shall by regulation permit:

(i) two printed or typewritten copies of a thesis; or (in the case of Fine Art candidates offering studio practice as part of their submission) two printed or typewritten copies of the written portion of the thesis, and a portfolio or exhibition of work, together with documentation of that work;

(ii) two printed or typewritten copies of an abstract of the thesis, which shall not normally exceed 300 words.

5. On receipt of an application the board concerned shall appoint two examiners, neither of whom shall be the candidate's supervisor, and whose duties shall be:

(i) to consider the thesis and the abstract of it submitted by the student, provided that they shall exclude from consideration in making their report any part of the thesis which has already been accepted, or is being concurrently submitted, for any degree or other qualification in this University or elsewhere otherwise than as part of the requirements of this University for the Degree of Bachelor of Philosophy or of Master of Philosophy or of Bachelor of Civil Law, or as part of the dissertation submitted by a Student for the Degree of Master of Science by Coursework or of Master of Studies, and shall have the power to require the candidate to produce for their inspection the complete thesis so accepted or concurrently submitted;

(ii) (in the case of Fine Art candidates offering studio practice as part of their submission) to consider the portfolio or exhibition of work documented under section 4 (i) of these regulations, and presented or mounted by the candidate in partial satisfaction of the examination requirements;

(iii) to examine the student orally in the subject of his or her thesis;

(iv) to satisfy themselves by examination (oral, written, or both) whether the student possesses a good general knowledge of the particular field of learning within which the subject of the thesis falls;

(v) to report to the board through the Registrar on the scope, character, and quality of the work submitted;

(vi) to return to the student the copies of the thesis and the abstracts thereof.

The Education Committee shall have power to make regulations concerning the notice to be given of the oral examination, and of the time and place at which it may be held. The examination may be attended by any member of the University in academic dress, while non-members may attend only with the consent of the examiners. In the case of theses submitted to the Social Sciences, Mathematical, Physical and Life Sciences, and Medical Sciences Boards, the Proctors after consultation with the relevant Divisional Board may decide (either at their own discretion or at the request of the candidate or the supervisor or department) to forbid the attendance of any person or all persons (other than the examiners and the candidate) or to impose any condition on attendance if and to the extent that such action is in their view necessary to protect the interests of the University or the candidate or both, and the examiners shall be informed accordingly and shall include this information in the notice of examination. The student, or his or her college, may within fourteen days of the date of the Proctors' decision appeal in writing to the Chair of the Education Committee (who may nominate another member of the committee, other than one of the Proctors, to adjudicate the appeal).

6. Having completed the examination of a candidate for the first time, the examiners may make any one of recommendations (i), (ii) or (iv) below only. Having completed the examination of a candidate who has revised and re-submitted his or her thesis, the examiners may make any one of recommendations (i)–(vi). The recommendations are:

(i) that the board should grant the candidate leave to supplicate for the Degree of Doctor of Philosophy. In making this recommendation, the examiners must include in their report statements that:

1. the student possesses a good general knowledge of the particular field of learning within which the subject of the thesis falls;

2. the student has made a significant and substantial contribution in the particular field of learning within which the subject of the thesis falls;

3. the thesis is presented in a lucid and scholarly manner;

4. in their opinion the thesis merits the Degree of Doctor of Philosophy;

5. the student has presented a satisfactory abstract of the thesis.

Examiners shall bear in mind that their judgement of the substantial significance of the work should take into account what may reasonably be expected of a capable and diligent student after three or at most four years of full-time study in the case of a full-time student, or eight years in the case of a part-time student.

(i) (*a*) **Minor corrections**

If the examiners are satisfied that the candidate's thesis is of sufficient merit to qualify for the degree but consider, nevertheless, that before the thesis is deposited the candidate should make minor corrections (which are not sufficiently substantial to justify reference back for re-examination and which should be capable of completion within one month), they must require the candidate to correct the thesis to their satisfaction before they submit their report. If the candidate has not completed these corrections within one calendar month of the date of receipt of the list of minor corrections from the examiners, his or her name shall be removed by the Registrar from the Register of Students for the Degree of Doctor of Philosophy, provided that the board may, on good cause shown by the candidate, grant an extension of time of one further calendar month in which the candidate may fulfil this requirement before the removal of his or her name from the Register. No subsequent extension shall be granted, but it shall be open to a candidate who has failed to fulfil this requirement within those one or two months in total, as the case may be, to apply to the board for reinstatement as a Student for the Degree of Doctor of Philosophy, with the support of his or her society and supervisor, upon submission to the Registrar of a copy of his or her thesis incorporating the required corrections, and upon payment of such reinstatement fee as may from time to time be prescribed by Council by decree. Permission to supplicate shall not be granted until this fee has been paid;

(i) (*b*) **Major corrections**

If the examiners are satisfied that the candidate's thesis is of sufficient potential merit to qualify for the degree but consider, nevertheless, that before the thesis is deposited the candidate should make major corrections (which are not sufficiently substantial to justify reference back for re-examination and which should be capable of completion within six months), they should report this preliminary recommendation to the board with a description of the major corrections which they require the candidate to make before they confirm their recommendation.

Where the examiners make this recommendation, and the board, considering the extent and nature of the major corrections, takes the view that the recommendation ought to be reference of the thesis back to the candidate in order that he or she may revise it for re-examination, the board may, exceptionally, ask the examiners to review their recommendation.

If the candidate has not completed these corrections within six calendar months of the date of receipt of the list of major corrections from the examiners, his or her name shall be removed by the Registrar from the Register of Students for the Degree of Doctor of Philosophy. No extension shall be granted, but it shall be open to a candidate who has failed to fulfil this requirement within those six months, to apply to the board for reinstatement as a Student for the Degree of Doctor of Philosophy, with the support of his or her society and supervisor, upon submission to the Registrar of a copy of his or her thesis incorporating the required corrections, and upon payment of such reinstatement fee as may from time to time be prescribed by Council by decree. Permission to supplicate shall not be granted until this fee has been paid.

Where a recommendation of approval subject to major corrections has been made, the examiners, on receipt of the corrected thesis on the first occasion, may conclude and report one of the following:

(*a*) the original recommendation is now fully substantiated;

(*b*) the work as submitted still requires minor corrections prior to confirmation of the original recommendation and a further one month may be allowed for this from that date;

(*c*) the work as now submitted still requires major corrections prior to confirmation of the original recommendation and a further six months may be allowed for this from that date.

Recommendation (*a*) or (*b*) may be made without a further oral examination on condition that both examiners have reviewed and approved the major corrections. A further oral examination must be held if either of the examiners requires it or if the recommendation is likely to be (*c*).

In the exceptional instance where (*c*) applied and the outcome of the second and final submission of corrections still remained unsatisfactory, the examiners will amend their original recommendation to (ii) below.

(ii) that the board should offer the candidate a choice between (a) reference of the thesis back to him or her in order that he or she may revise it for re-examination for the Degree of Doctor of Philosophy, and (b) leave to supplicate for the Degree of Master of Letters or of Master of Science, as appropriate, on the basis that the thesis has not reached the standard required for the Degree of Doctor of Philosophy but has nevertheless reached that required for the Degree of Master of Letters or of Master of Science. If the board adopts this recommendation, and the student chooses to revise the thesis for re-examination for the Degree of Doctor of Philosophy, the student shall retain the status and obligations of a Student for the Degree of Doctor of Philosophy and shall be permitted to apply again for the appointment of examiners, in accordance with the procedure laid down in this sub-section, not later than the sixth term after that in which the board gave permission so to reapply. If such permission shall have been given by a board during a vacation, it shall be deemed to have been given in the term preceding that vacation. Accompanying the revised thesis at re-submission should be a separate report indicating the specific changes made. For students in the Humanities, Medical Sciences and Social Sciences Divisions and the Department for Continuing Education, the word limit for the accompanying report shall be 1000 words; for students in the Mathematical, Physical and Life Sciences Division, the word limit shall be 2000 words.

(iii) that the board should refer the student's thesis back in order that he or she may present it for re-examination for the Degree of Master of Letters or of Master of Science only. If the board adopts the recommendation the student shall be transferred forthwith to the status of Student for the Degree of Master of Letters or Student for the Degree of Master of Science as the case may be, and shall be permitted to apply for permission to supplicate for the Degree of Master of Letters or Master of Science in accordance with the provisions of the appropriate regulation. If such permission shall have been given by a board during a vacation, it shall be deemed to have been given in the term preceding that vacation. The word limit for a thesis resubmitted under this provision shall be that specified by the DPhil regulations under which it was originally submitted;

(iv) that the board should refer the student's thesis back in order that he or she may present it for re-examination either under

(ii) above for the Degree of Doctor of Philosophy or, if the student chooses, under (iii) above for the Degree of Master of Letters or of Master of Science only. The board shall adopt such a recommendation only if it is fully satisfied that the thesis as it stands is not of the standard required for the Degree of Doctor of Philosophy, nor for the Degree of Master of Letters or of Master of Science as the case may be, but that the candidate could reach the standard required for the Degree of Doctor of Philosophy. If such permission shall have been given by a board during a vacation, it shall be deemed to have been given in the term preceding that vacation;

(v) that the thesis has not reached the standard required for the Degree of Doctor of Philosophy but has nevertheless reached that required of the Degree of Master of Letters or of Master of Science, and that the candidate may be granted leave to supplicate for one of the latter degrees on the basis of the thesis as it stands;

(vi) that the student's application for leave to supplicate should be refused.

7. If the examiners recommend reference back of the student's application under clause 6 (ii) or (iii) or (iv) above, they shall annex to their report to the board a statement (for transmission to the candidate) setting out the respects in which the thesis falls below the standard required for the degree in question, and what changes are necessary for it to reach that standard, save that examiners of a thesis submitted for the first time may, in exceptional circumstances, and notwithstanding a recommendation under clause 6 (ii) or (iv) above, certify that they are unable to indicate how the thesis might be changed, within the time allowed, in order to reach the required standard for the degree of Doctor of Philosophy.

8. On receipt of the examiners' report the board shall reach a decision on whether to accept the examiners' recommendation, provided that no candidate shall be given leave to supplicate for the Degree of Doctor of Philosophy unless the examiners have made the statements required in clause 6 (i) above.

9. A candidate who has been granted leave to supplicate by a board shall be required to submit to the Examination Schools a copy of his or her thesis, incorporating any amendments or corrections required by the examiners and approved by the board, with a view to deposit in the Bodleian or other appropriate university library. [For candidates admitted on or after 1 October 2007: candidates are also required to submit an electronic copy of their thesis

to the Oxford Research Archive, unless an exception to this requirement has been granted by the Proctors.] [For candidates supplicating on or after 1 July 2013: candidates are also required to submit
the library copy to the Examination Schools and where applicable
the electronic copy of the thesis to the Oxford Research Archive no
later than the end of the fifth day before the date of the degree
ceremony booked by the candidate for conferral of their degree.]
Permission to supplicate shall in all cases be conditional upon
fulfilment of these requirements.

10. In an exceptional case in which a board is unable to accept
the examiners' recommendation, or in which the examiners cannot
reach an agreed recommendation, the board shall have power to
appoint one or two new examiners as it deems necessary, to conduct
such further examination of the candidate as the board may require.
The board shall make a report on any such case to the Education
Committee.

11. The board may exempt a candidate who is being re-examined
under the provisions of clause 6 (ii)-(v) above from the oral examination, provided that the examiners are able to certify that they are
satisfied without examining the candidate orally that they can recommend to the board in the terms required by clause 6 (i) above
that he or she be given leave to supplicate for the Degree of Doctor
of Philosophy.

12. It shall be the duty of the Registrar to notify the candidate
of the board's decision as soon as may be. The Registrar shall also
be responsible for publishing at the end of each academic year the
names of those candidates to whom permission to supplicate has
been granted during that year, together with a statement of the
subject of the thesis written by each.

13. When, on the conclusion of the investigation of a complaint
made by a candidate, the Proctors recommend that a candidate
be re-examined, the board shall have power to hold a new
examination.

NOTES

17

GENERAL REGULATIONS OF THE EDUCATION COMMITTEE GOVERNING THE EXAMINATION OF STUDENTS FOR THE DEGREES OF M.SC. BY RESEARCH, M.LITT., AND D.PHIL., AND CONCERNING THE MAINTENANCE OF THE REGISTER OF GRADUATE STUDENTS

REGULATIONS

1. Regulations governing the content and length of theses

(i) *Material for transfer or submission*

Material submitted for transfer to, or for the award of, the degrees of M.Litt., M.Sc. by Research, and D.Phil., shall be wholly or substantially the result of work undertaken while the student holds the status of Probationer Research Student or the status of a student for the degree concerned, except that a candidate may make application for a dispensation from this requirement to the Education Committee.

(ii) *Prior publication*

Prior publication of material arising from research undertaken while holding the status of Probationer Research Student or the status of a student for the M.Litt., M.Sc. by Research, or D.Phil., is fully acceptable, but the inclusion of published papers within a thesis may be subject to special regulation by the board concerned. Candidates should note that the acceptance of such material for publication does not of itself constitute proof that the work is of sufficient quality or significance to merit the award of the degree concerned. This remains a judgement of the relevant board on the recommendation of its examiners.

(iii) *Thesis length*

If a thesis exceeds the permitted length, the board concerned may decline to appoint examiners or to forward the thesis to examiners already appointed, and may return it to the candidate for revision. If the examiners find that a thesis which has been forwarded to them exceeds the permitted length, they should report the fact to the relevant board and await further instructions before proceeding with the examination.

2. Preparation and submission of theses for the Degrees of M.Litt., M.Sc. by Research, and D.Phil.

(i) *Text and footnotes*

Candidates should note that the purpose of these regulations is not only to ease the task of the examiners (which is obviously in the candidates' interests), but also to ensure that the copy finally deposited in the Bodleian or other university library is of a standard of legibility which will allow it (subject to applicable copyright rules) to be photocopied or microfilmed if required in future years.

The thesis must be printed or typed with a margin of 3 to 3.5 cm on the left-hand edge of each page (or on the inner edge, whether left-hand or right-hand, in the case of a thesis which is printed on both sides of the paper). Theses in typescript should present the main text in *double spacing* with quotations and footnotes in single spacing. In the case of word-processed or printed theses, where the output resembles that of a typewriter, double spacing should be taken to mean a distance of about 0.33 inch or 8 mm between successive lines of text. Candidates are advised that it is their responsibility to ensure that the print of their thesis is of an adequate definition and standard of legibility.

Footnotes should normally be placed at the bottom of each page. Where they are given at the end of each chapter or at the end of the thesis, two separate unbound copies of footnotes should also be presented, for the convenience of the examiners.

Candidates should carefully note the regulations concerning word limits which individual boards have made. In such cases, candidates should state the approximate number of words in their theses.

Theses must be submitted in English unless for exceptional reasons a board otherwise determines in the term in which the candidate is first admitted as a research student.

The pages of the thesis must be numbered. Each copy should have an abstract included (see below).

(ii) *Examiners' copies: binding and presentation*

At the time of their examination, candidates must submit two copies of their thesis, which must be securely and firmly bound in either hard or soft covers. Loose-leaf binding is not acceptable. Candidates are responsible for ensuring that examiners' copies are securely bound and should note that theses which do not meet this requirement will not be accepted.

Fine Art candidates offering studio practice as part of their submission must submit, together with the written portion of their thesis, documentation in appropriate form of the exhibition or portfolio of works to be examined. Wherever possible, this documentation should be bound with the written portion of the thesis.

Candidates should pack each copy of the thesis intended for the examiners into a separate but *unsealed* parcel or padded envelope, ready in all respects, except the address, to be posted to the examiners when appointed. Each parcel should bear the candidate's name and society and the words 'M.LITT./M.SC./D.PHIL. (as appropriate) THESIS AND ABSTRACT' in BLOCK CAPITALS in the bottom left-hand corner. A slip giving the address to which the examiners should write in order to contact the candidate about arrangements for the oral examination should be enclosed with each copy of the thesis. Candidates are responsible for ensuring that their examiners have no difficulty in communicating with them. The separate copies thus packed should be submitted to the Examination Schools, High Street, Oxford. If sent or posted they should be enclosed in one covering parcel.

The theses of candidates who fail to follow this advice are liable to delay in being forwarded to the examiners.

(iii) *Date of submission of examiners' copies*

Candidates may submit the examiners' copies of their thesis, prepared as described above, at the same time as they apply for the appointment of their examiners. If they intend, however, to submit the examiners' copies at a later date, they will be required to state, at the time of their application for appointment of examiners, the date by which they will submit. This should be as soon as possible after the date of application and may in no case be later than the last day of the vacation immediately following the term in which application for the appointment of examiners has been made.

(iv) *Library copies: binding and presentation*

Once the board has granted a candidate leave to supplicate, he or she must submit a finalised copy of the thesis, as approved by the examiners, to the Examination Schools for deposit in the relevant university library. [For candidates admitted on or after 1 October 2007: The candidate must also submit an electronic copy to the Oxford Research Archive. (Candidates whose thesis has been prepared in non-standard media such as to make electronic submission impracticable may apply to the Proctors for exemption from this requirement.)] These should incorporate any corrections or amendments which the examiners may have requested of the candidate. The examiners must confirm in writing in their report to the board that any corrections required have been made.

The library copy of the thesis must be in a permanently fixed binding, drilled and sewn, in a stiff board case in library buckram, in a dark colour, and lettered on the spine with the candidate's name and initials, the degree, and the year of submission.

Fine Art candidates offering studio practice as part of their submission must submit the written portion of their thesis together with documentation in appropriate form of their exhibition or portfolio of works. Wherever possible, this documentation should be bound with the written portion of the thesis.

Candidates should note that leave to supplicate is conditional upon receipt by the Examination Schools of the library copy of their thesis and [for candidates admitted on or after 1 October 2007, receipt by the Oxford Research Archive of an electronic copy and [for candidates supplicating on or after 1 July 2013] receipt by the Examination Schools of the library copy of the thesis and receipt by the Oxford Research Archive of the electronic copy of the thesis no later than by the end of the fifth day before the date of the degree ceremony booked by the candidate for conferral of their degree and that candidates may not proceed to take their degree until they have fulfilled the requirement [by the stipulated deadline for those supplicating on or after 1 July 2013] to submit a library copy of the thesis and [for candidates admitted on or after 1 October 2007]: an electronic copy (unless an exception to the requirement to submit an electronic copy of the thesis has been granted by the Proctors)].

(v) *Abstracts*

The abstract of the thesis should concisely summarize its scope and principal arguments, in about 300 words. It should be printed or typewritten, on one side only, of A4-sized paper. Each copy of the abstract should be headed with the title of the thesis, the name and college of the candidate, the degree for which it is submitted, and the term and year of submission.

One copy of the abstract prepared at the time of the examination should be bound into each of the examiners' copies of the thesis. Subsequently, when the examination is completed, candidates should also arrange for a copy of the abstract to be bound into the library copy of their thesis, and should submit with the library copy a separate, unbound copy of their abstract which may be despatched to ASLIB and published. The copy of the abstract which is earmarked for dispatch to ASLIB should be presented separately in a form suitable for microfilming, i.e. it should be (1) on one side of a single sheet of A4 paper, (2) a typed, single-spaced top copy, a clear photocopy, or a printed copy (i.e. it should not be a carbon or poor photocopy), and (3) headed up with name, college, year and term of submission and the title of the thesis.

It should be noted that some boards have made regulations requiring the submission of more detailed abstracts in addition to the general requirement of an abstract not normally exceeding 300 words.

3. Conduct of Oral Examinations for the Degrees of M.Litt., M.Sc. by Research, and D.Phil.

(i) The oral examination shall be held at Oxford in a suitable university or college building, unless the Proctors give special permission for it to be held at some other place. In the case of Fine Art candidates offering studio practice as part of their submission, where it does not take place in the presence of the exhibition or portfolio of works, the candidate's supervisor must arrange for the examiners to view this part of the submission prior to the commencement of the oral examination. It shall, except in special circumstances, begin not earlier than 9 a.m. nor later than 5 p.m. and may be held in term or vacation. The student or his or her college, other society, or approved institution, may within fourteen days of the date of the Proctors' decision in respect of the granting of consent, appeal in writing to the Chair of the Education Committee (who may nominate another member of the committee, other than one of the Proctors, to adjudicate the appeal).

(ii) The examination may be attended by any member of the University in academic dress. No person who is not a member of the University may attend it except with the consent of both examiners.

(iii) The place and time of the examination shall be fixed by the examiners, who shall be responsible for informing the candidate of the arrangements made. It shall be the duty of candidates to ensure that any letter addressed to them at their college or any other address which they have given is forwarded to them if necessary. The examiners shall allow reasonable time for receiving an acknowledgement from the candidate of their summons.

(iv) Except as provided in clause (v) below, the day shall be fixed by the examiners to suit their convenience. So that candidates may know what arrangements for absence from Oxford they may safely make, the examiners shall inform candidates within a reasonable time of the date fixed.

(v) Candidates may apply to the board concerned for the oral examination to be held not later than a certain date, provided that this date shall not be earlier than one calendar month after the date on which the thesis has been received at the Examination Schools or after the date on which the examiners have agreed to act, whichever is the later. If the board is satisfied that there are special circumstances justifying this application, it will ask the examiners to make arrangements to enable the oral examination to be held within the period specified.

In such cases the examiners, when invited to act, will be informed that the candidate has asked that the oral examination should be held not later than a certain date, and acceptance of the invitation to examine will be on the understanding that they would seek to meet this request. If is not practicable to meet the student's request, then the board shall decide how to proceed.

(vi) Notice of the examination shall be given in one of the following ways:

1. it may be published in the *University Gazette** not later than the day before it is due to take place;

2. Not later than two days before the examination the examiners may

    (*a*) inform the Graduate Studies Office in writing; and

    (*b*) post a notice in the Examination Schools; and

    (*c*) if the examination is to be held at a place other than the Examination Schools, post a notice also at the place of the examination.

---

* Notice should reach the editor at the Oxford University Press, Great Clarendon Street, not less than six days before publication.

The notice shall state the name of the candidate, the subject of the thesis, the place, day, and hour of the examination, and the names of the examiners.

If an examination is held without the giving of the notice required by this regulation it shall be invalid, unless the Proctors, on receipt of a written application from the examiners, shall determine otherwise. The student or his or her college, other society, or approved institution, may within fourteen days of the date of the Proctors' decision in respect of the granting of consent, appeal in writing to the Chair of the Education Committee (who may nominate another member of the committee, other than one of the Proctors, to adjudicate the appeal).

(vii) If, owing to illness or other urgent and unforeseen cause, an examiner is unable to attend the examination, it shall be postponed to a later date, provided that, if the Proctors are satisfied that postponement would be a serious hardship to the candidate, they may authorize another member of the board concerned to attend the examination as a substitute, but such substitute shall not be required to sign the report. The Proctors shall determine what payment, if any, the substitute examiner shall receive.

(viii) Candidates are strongly recommended to take a copy of their thesis to the examination. In the case of Fine Art candidates offering studio practice as part of their submission, where the oral examination is not taking place in the presence of the exhibition or portfolio of works, it is recommended they attend with the written portion of their thesis together with documentation of the work.

(ix) An oral examination shall be held in Oxford as prescribed in clause (i). In exceptional circumstances, normally affecting the ability of the external examiner to take part in an Oxford-based oral examination, application may be made to the relevant board for special permission to hold the examination using audiovisual electronic communication with the external examiner concerned. The board concerned may approve the application only where:

(i) it accepts that no alternative and timely arrangements may reasonably be put in place;

(ii) the proposed arrangements are acceptable to both examiners and to the candidate;

(iii) it involves remote communication with only one of the examiners (normally the external);

(iv) it is content to bear the additional cost of the necessary arrangements;

(v) an oral examination of this type takes place according to arrangements and in premises approved by the Proctors;

(vi) the oral examination takes place according to the protocol approved by the Education Committee;

(vii) in the event of any technical or other problems, the validity of the process used to conduct the oral examination and to determine the outcome will be decided by the Proctors.

4. Suspension of Graduate Students from the Register

(i) If, for good cause, a student is temporarily unable to carry out his or her research or coursework, the board concerned may grant him or her a request for a temporary suspension of status, for not less than one and not more than three terms at any one time. Applications for suspension of status should be made to the board concerned, c/o the relevant Graduate Studies Assistant; and should be accompanied by statements of support from a student's supervisor and society. No student may be granted more than six terms' suspension of status in this way by a board.

(ii) A board may for sufficient reason, and after consultation with the student's supervisor and college, temporarily suspend him or her from the Register on its own initiative.

5. Removal of Graduate Students from the Register

1. A board which considers that it may be necessary to consider the removal of a student from the Register on academic grounds shall, except in cases requiring immediate action, follow the procedures for counselling and warnings set out in paras. 4–6.

2. A board shall not be required to follow the procedures for the removal of a graduate student from the Register where a student ceases to hold the status of a student for a degree through failure to meet the requirements laid down in the decrees and regulations governing that degree. In particular where a student fails to achieve transfer within the prescribed time his or her status automatically lapses, and his or her name is removed from the Register.

3. A board shall not be required to follow the procedures for counselling and warnings set out below in cases of particular gravity and/or urgency or where it considers, for whatever reason, that immediate action is required, and in such circumstances a board may immediately notify the Education Committee as set out at paragraph 6 below and the matter will proceed as set out in that and subsequent paragraphs. In these circumstances, the board should indicate to the Education Committee why the procedures for counselling and warnings are not to be followed in that instance.

4.1. Subject to para. 3 above, wherever practicable, the formal procedures for the removal of a student from the Register should be preceded by private and informal counselling involving the student's supervisor and college, with the object of establishing the cause of any problem and advising appropriate remedial action.

4.2. If informal means are not effective in producing the necessary improvement, the student will be invited to a formal interview. Written notice of a formal interview should be given at least seven days before it takes place. Such notice will include an indication of the nature and purpose of the interview and the problem or problems that the interview is intended to address. The student will have the right to put his or her case and to be accompanied by a friend. The formal interview will be conducted by the head of department or Director of Graduate Studies who on conclusion of the interview and if further action is considered necessary will issue either (a) a first formal warning, to be confirmed in writing to the student and to his or her supervisor and society, setting out the reason for which it is given, and specifying a period of time for improvement to be made (which period should in no case be less than one month or more than three months); or (b) a final warning as set out in 5 below.

4.3. If the student unreasonably fails to attend the formal interview, a formal warning in writing may be issued without interview, and the student shall be required to acknowledge receipt of the formal warning.

5.1. If the first formal warning issued under 4.2 above is not effective in producing the necessary improvement, the head of department or Director of Graduate Studies shall invite the student to a second formal interview. The procedure will be as for the first formal interview. At the conclusion of the interview the head of department or Director of Graduate Studies shall, if further action is required, issue a final warning, which shall be confirmed in writing to the student and to his or her supervisor and society.

5.2. Where a final warning is issued under 4.2 or 5.1 above the warning itself and the written confirmation should make it clear that if the necessary improvement is not achieved within the specified period, the board may initiate action for the removal of the student from the Register of Graduate Students.

6. Where a final written warning is issued to a graduate student, a copy of the written warning shall be sent to the Education Committee. Where, following a final

written warning, the necessary improvement is not achieved within the specified period and further action is indicated, the Education Committee shall be informed by the Secretary of the board concerned. A full report of the action taken by the board in relation to the student shall be made to the Proctors who shall decide whether further action should be taken and, if so, whether under the relevant disciplinary procedures of the University or under the board's power to remove a student from the Register of Graduate Students on academic grounds. The Proctors' ruling (which may include a decision that no further action is to be taken) shall be taken without reference to the Education Committee, and shall be final.

7.1. Where the Proctors determine that it is appropriate for the matter to be considered under the board's power to initiate action for the removal of a student from the Register of Graduate Students, the board shall seek the approval of the Chair of the Education Committee to undertake any such action. Where such approval is given, the board shall inform the student and the student's college and supervisor, in writing, with a minimum of seven days' notice, of its intention to consider the removal of the student from the Register, set out its reasons and invite comments. In particular the board shall inform the student of his or her right under paragraph 7.3 to present his or her case.

7.2. A board shall delegate the task of hearing the student's case to a panel comprising at least three of its members and shall set out the terms of reference to be followed by the panel. The board shall not appoint any member who has had a previous connection with the student or his or her work.

7.3. The student may be accompanied by a friend and shall have the right to hear and to challenge any evidence presented to the panel. The student may present his or her case in writing or orally, or both, as the student wishes, and the student's society and supervisor shall have the same rights. (All written evidence shall be circulated to the student, the student's supervisor, and the student's college not less than four days before the panel considers the case.) In conducting a hearing, the panel shall ensure that the student has every opportunity to hear and to challenge the case made out by the board for the removal of the student from the Register including any evidence (written or oral) which the panel will consider in reaching a conclusion. Where the student fails to appear without good cause, the panel may proceed in the student's absence.

8. The panel shall then determine its decision as to whether the student's name shall, or shall not, be removed from the Register of Graduate Students. The decision shall be communicated to the student, college, and supervisor. The student shall also be advised in writing of the reasons for the decision and of his or her rights of appeal. The board shall also inform the Education Committee of all cases where the board has decided to deprive a student of his or her status.

9.1. A student or his or her society may appeal in writing against the decision of the faculty board within fourteen days of the date of the letter from the board conveying its decision. The appeal shall be addressed to the Education Committee (c/o the Secretary, Education Committee, University Offices, Wellington Square, Oxford OX1 2JD), which shall appoint a sub-committee to conduct a hearing of the student's appeal.

9.2. The sub-committee shall include a minimum of three members of the Education Committee, which shall appoint one of the chosen members as chair, with the power to cast an additional vote if necessary. The sub-committee may seek such legal advice as it believes to be necessary for the proper conduct of its duties, and shall have power to require any members of the University to assist it in the hearing.

9.3. The sub-committee shall give the board, the student, the student's college, and the student's supervisor, not less than seven days' notice in writing, of the date and time of the hearing, and shall give them the opportunity to make representations to the sub-committee orally and/or in writing. The student may be accompanied by a friend and shall have the right to hear and to challenge any evidence (written or oral) presented to the sub-committee; the student may present his or her case in writing, or orally, or both, as the student wishes: the board, the student's college, and the student's supervisor shall have the same rights. (All written evidence shall be circulated to the faculty board, the student, the student's supervisor, and the student's college not less than four days before the sub-committee considers the case.)

9.4. At the conclusion of a hearing, the sub-committee shall have power to:

(i) confirm the board's decision to remove the student's name from the Register of Graduate Students;

(ii) uphold the student's appeal and direct that the student's name shall remain on the Register of Graduate Students;

(iii) impose such lesser penalty or requirement in place of the removal of the student's name from the Register of Graduate Students as it deems appropriate.

9.5. In reaching its decision, the sub-committee shall have regard to:

(*a*) whether the board correctly followed the required procedures, and, in the case of procedural irregularity or irregularities, whether any irregularity or irregularities were such as to have materially prejudiced the board's inquiry;

(*b*) whether the board's decision could reasonably have been reached on the evidence before it;

(*c*) any evidence presented to the sub-committee which was not available to the board's panel;

(*d*) any mitigating circumstances offered by or on behalf of the student;

(*e*) any other factors which in the opinion of the sub-committee are relevant to a fair consideration of the student's appeal.

9.6. The sub-committee shall communicate its decision to the student, to the student's society and supervisor, and to the board, in writing, within two months of the conclusion of any hearing. The decision of the sub-committee will be final, subject only to a complaint to the Proctors.

6. Reinstatement of Graduate Students to the Registers

A student who has lapsed from the Register or has withdrawn or whose name has been removed from the Register by the board concerned may apply for reinstatement to his or her former status on the Register. Such applications shall be addressed by the student to the board concerned, and shall be accompanied by written statements commenting on the application from the candidate's college and former supervisor. The board shall reach a decision on such applications and shall determine the date from which any reinstatement granted under these provisions shall be effective. No reinstatement may be granted under these provisions if the student's name has been on the Register of students of the relevant status for the maximum number of terms allowed under the decree governing that status.

7. Memorandum of Guidance for Supervisors and Research Students

ACADEMIC RESPONSIBILITIES

Responsibilities of the supervisor

1. In considering an invitation to supervise a research student, the supervisor must recognise and accept the responsibilities both to the student and to the relevant board or committee implicit in the supervisory relationship.

2. Where practicable, the supervisor should assign the student some directed reading before arrival. This might be of a general background nature so as to put the student in a position to discuss the topic with the supervisor soon after arrival, or it might form the start of a survey of current literature. The supervisor is required to meet the new student not later than the second week of Full Term.

3. The supervisor is responsible for giving early advice about the nature of research and the standard expected, and about the planning of the research programme. The supervisor should ensure that, where the student's research forms part of a funded research programme, sufficient financial support will be available for the duration of the student's period of study; if there is any doubt, he or she should agree with the student an alternative fallback project at an early stage. The supervisor is also responsible for advising the student about literature and sources, attendance at classes, and requisite techniques (including helping to arrange instruction where necessary). The supervisor should discuss with the student the lecture list for his or her subject and related lecture lists. The supervisor should identify with the student any subject-specific skills necessary for the proposed research.

4. Where during his or her first year of research a student wishes, in addition to contact with his or her supervisor(s), to have limited consultation with one or two other academics the supervisor should try to identify (in conjunction with the Director of Graduate Studies for the faculty, sub-faculty or department) such colleagues and to arrange for an approach to them by the student.

5. Where a supervisor operates as a co-supervisor or as a part of a supervisory team, it is important to clarify the responsibilities of each supervisor and to co-ordinate advice and guidance.

6. Where the thesis is likely to involve statistical analysis or tabulation of numerical results, the supervisor should arrange for the student to obtain advice, at an early stage, about the design of any experiment or the collection and storage of data, and about its subsequent analysis.

7. The supervisor should ensure that the student works within a planned framework which marks out the stages which the student should be expected to have completed at various points in his or her period of study. The nature of the framework will of course vary widely from subject to subject, but in all subjects the formulation of the topic, planning and management of time should begin at an early stage. Particular attention should be given to the selection and refinement of the research topic, which in the case of the D.Phil. should be one which a diligent student may reasonably be expected to complete within three (or at most four) years of full-time study.

8. The supervisor should meet with the student regularly. Supervisor and student should agree a formal schedule of meetings on a termly or annual basis. The supervisor should also be accessible to the student at other appropriate times when advice is needed. The supervisor should also request written work as appropriate and in accordance with the plan discussed with the student. Such work should be returned with constructive criticism and in reasonable time.

9. The supervisor should tell the student from time to time how well, in the supervisor's opinion, work is getting on, and try to ensure that the student feels properly directed and able to communicate with the supervisor. It is essential that when problems arise, corrective action is clearly identified and full guidance and assistance are given to the student.

10. The supervisor is required to report to the board on the student's work three times a year, once at the end of each term. Each report should state the nature and extent of recent contact with the student, and, if there has been none, state why this is so. The report should also make clear whether the student is making satisfactory

progress, bearing in mind that a D.Phil. thesis should normally be completed within three (or at least four) years of full-time research. Any student who has not satisfied his or her supervisor on at least one occasion in an academic year that he or she is making progress will be liable to have his or her name removed from the register.

11. The supervisor should aim to ensure that by the end of the first year the topic or goal of the student's research is clearly defined, that the student has the necessary background knowledge, and that the required resources are available. The supervisor must have ascertained by then that the student can write a coherent account of his or her work in good English.

12. The supervisor should try to ensure that unnecessary delays do not occur. These have been known to arise, for example, for reasons such as:

(*a*) insufficient effort at the outset in choosing and formulating the research topic;

(*b*) a slow start because of the time taken to adjust to research work;

(*c*) distractions from the main line of inquiry;

(*d*) superfluous attempts to tie up every loose end; and, mainly in the sciences;

(*e*) inadequate and delayed planning and assembly of apparatus and equipment;

(*f*) insufficient collection or recording of data at an early stage, so that work has to be repeated in the later stages.

13. The supervisor should arrange for students to have the opportunity to discuss their research with other staff and students in the subject area (see also (4) above) and to communicate to others in the wider academic community, both orally and in writing, his or her research findings.

14. Where a student undertakes research as part of a team or group the supervisor should ensure that this is in full awareness of the way in which the student's own contribution fits into the work of the remainder of the group.

15. The supervisor should not be absent on leave unless he or she has ensured that appropriate temporary supervision has been arranged for the student.

Responsibilities of the student

1. The student must accept his or her obligation to act as a responsible member of the University's academic community.

2. The student should take ultimate responsibility for his or her research programme and endeavour to develop an appropriate working pattern, including an agreed and professional relationship with the supervisor(s). The student should discuss with the supervisor the type of guidance and comment which he or she finds most helpful, and agree a schedule of meetings.

3. He or she should make appropriate use of the teaching and learning facilities available within the University.

4. It is the student's responsibility to seek out and follow the regulations relevant to his or her course, including faculty/departmental handbooks/notes of guidance, and to seek clarification from supervisors and elsewhere if this is necessary.

5. The student should not hesitate to take the initiative in raising problems or difficulties, however elementary they may seem. He or she should ensure that any problems regarding the project are drawn to the attention of the supervisor so that appropriate guidance may be offered.

6. The student should seek to maintain progress in accordance with the plan of work agreed with the supervisor, including in particular the presentation of the required written material in sufficient time for comment and discussion before proceeding to the next stage. As groundwork for the thesis, the student should as soon as possible write rough drafts of possible chapters. Students in the sciences

should keep a systematic record of all that has been attempted and accomplished. Both the student and the supervisor will want to keep a record of all formal, scheduled meetings. They may well want to agree a record of what has been discussed and decided.

7. The student should recognise that a supervisor may have many competing demands on his or her time. The student should hand in work in good time to the supervisor and give adequate notice of unscheduled meetings. The need for adequate notice also applies to requests for references from the supervisor.

8. The student should be aware that the provision of constructive criticism is central to a satisfactory supervisory relationship, and should always seek a full assessment of the strengths and weaknesses of his or her work.

9. If the student feels that there are good enough grounds for contemplating a change of supervision arrangements, this should first be discussed with the supervisor or, if this seems difficult, with the appropriate head of department, director of graduate studies or their deputies, or the college adviser.

10. Where problems arise, it is essential that a student gives full weight to any guidance and corrective action proposed by the supervisor.

11. The student should provide regular reports on his or her progress to the board in accordance with any requirements of the Education Committee. The student must satisfy the supervisor on his or her progress at least once a year and should inform the supervisor at once of any circumstances that might require his or her mode of study to be modified or his or her registration as a graduate student to be extended, suspended or withdrawn.

12. The student should ensure that the standard of his or her English is sufficient for the presentation of a thesis. Students whose first language is not English should take advice on this.

13. The student should make full use of the facilities for career guidance and development, and should consult their supervisor for advice and encouragement where appropriate.

14. The student should ensure that he or she allows adequate time for writing up the thesis, taking the advice of the supervisor. Particular attention should be paid to final proof-reading.

15. It is the student's responsibility to decide when he or she wishes to submit the thesis for examination, after taking due account of the supervisor's opinion, though this is only advisory. It is in the student's interests to ensure that the final version has been made available to the supervisor in good time before the intended date of submission.

Responsibilities of faculties and/or departments

1. Faculties and/or departments should provide information about:

   (i) any induction provided on a departmental, faculty or University basis;

   (ii) welfare arrangements within the University, e.g. the Counselling Service, Student Hardship and Access funds, the provisions for support offered by the Proctors and the Assessor;

   (iii) any general transferable skills from which the student is likely to profit during the course of his or her research, and the available provision at departmental, faculty and university level.

2. Faculties and/or departments should ensure that there is appropriate monitoring of a student's work and progress and that reports are submitted on a termly basis in accordance with the University's requirements.

3. Faculties and/or departments should endeavour to provide opportunities for a student to:

(i) defend his or her findings to appropriate research seminars and respond to potentially critical questioning;

(ii) at an appropriate stage to present his or her findings to national, and if appropriate, international conferences.

4. *Faculties and/or departments should*

(i) help the student to present work in a clear and professional manner;

(ii) help the student to develop his or her communication skills, especially for different audiences;

(iii) provide some guidance in oral examination techniques.

Safety and Health

Supervisors of all students, whether in the arts or the sciences, should consider carefully the safety implications of their students' research. Those supervising students (particularly those in the sciences) are responsible for all aspects of safety under their control, and in particular for the safe conduct of all experiments carried out in the course of their students' research. In the event of an accident, inadequate supervision may render the supervisor liable to prosecution. Supervisors should also ensure that their students are made aware that in the event of injury to other persons as a result of their negligence, the student could be subject to civil claims for damages. Advice on the legal responsibilities for safety may be obtained from the University Safety Officer. For their part, *students* must carry out research with proper regard to good health and safety practices. Supervisors and students should be aware of the need for adequate health insurance and health precautions when travelling abroad. In case of doubt, reference should be made to the University Occupational Physician.

18

SPECIAL REGULATIONS OF DIVISIONAL AND FACULTY BOARDS CONCERNING THE STATUS OF PROBATIONER RESEARCH STUDENT AND THE DEGREES OF M.LITT., M.SC. BY RESEARCH, AND D.PHIL.

A. HUMANITIES DIVISION

1. TRANSFER OF STATUS AND CONFIRMATION OF STATUS

1. *Transfer of Status*

Purpose and criteria

(i) To assess whether the candidate is capable of carrying out advanced research, and has had suitable preparation in terms of subject-specific research training.

(ii) To assess whether the subject of the thesis and the manner of its treatment as proposed by the candidate are acceptable and potentially of D.Phil quality.

(iii) To assess whether the thesis can reasonably be completed in no more than 6 to 9 terms from transfer.

Applying for transfer of status

(i) Students admitted to Probationer Research Student (PRS) status

Students who have completed a one-year Master's degree at the University of Oxford or elsewhere, or a two-year M.Phil degree at a university other than the University of Oxford are admitted to Probationer Research Student (PRS) status. Transfer of status from PRS to D.Phil must take place in Trinity Term of Year 1 or Michaelmas Term of Year 2 as measured from the admission to PRS status.

(ii) Students admitted to D.Phil status

Students who have completed a two-year M.Phil degree at the University of Oxford and who have already commenced work on their doctoral thesis will be admitted either as a Probationer Research Student or as a student with D.Phil status. The decision will be made by the relevant University Admitting Body based on the proposed doctoral research and on previous qualifications, including research undertaken at Master's level. For students who are admitted to PRS status, transfer of status from PRS to D.Phil must take place in Trinity Term of Year 1 or Michaelmas Term of Year 2 as measured from the admission to PRS status.

The relevant University Admitting Body may only admit students directly to D.Phil status if the Admitting Body is satisfied that the student meets the three conditions described under 'purpose of transfer of status' above. In such cases, the admissions process should follow the same pattern as the transfer of status process, and normally all candidates who are admitted directly to D.Phil status must be interviewed. For students who are admitted directly to D.Phil status, the transfer of status process is waived.

Material normally required for applications for transfer of status

Entries for individual Faculty Boards below indicate exactly which materials students studying for a D.Phil degree in that faculty should submit to apply for transfer of status.

Candidates applying for transfer of status from Probationer Research Student (PRS) to D.Phil should normally submit the following documents:

(i) GSO.2 form: Application to transfer status.

(ii) A detailed outline (not exceeding 1,000 words) of the proposed thesis subject and of the manner in which it will be treated, including a provisional list of chapters and their proposed coverage.

(iii) Written work (or equivalent, e.g. a portfolio, score or CD/DVD), to be specified by the faculty. The submitted work should be on the topic of the proposed thesis, and if this consists of written work, should be about 10,000 words long (usually a draft chapter of the thesis; if the submitted work is not a draft chapter, then the candidate should provide a written explanation of the written work's relationship to the thesis).

(iv) A reference from the supervisor: the supervisor (or supervisors, if there is more than one) must provide a full and detailed assessment of the student and the student's application for transfer in the 'Comment' section of the GSO.2 form. Where there are two supervisors, either each one must submit an assessment report or both must sign a joint assessment.

(v) Information about subject-specific research or other training completed by the student, e.g. proof of linguistic competence. The faculty should specify any research training/research skills (e.g. linguistic competence, ability to use archives, handling of ancient documents) which students are expected to have acquired by this stage of their doctoral studies.

Assessment

(i) Assessors: the faculty must appoint two assessors, neither of whom must be the candidate's supervisor.

(ii) Interview: an interview by both assessors, based on the submitted written materials, is compulsory.

(iii) Report: the assessors must submit a joint written report, making a clear recommendation to the relevant faculty Graduate Studies Committee (or equivalent) of 'transfer' or 'not transfer', and providing reasons for their recommendation. The report should note any subject-specific research training still required by the student successfully to complete their doctorate.

Outcome of assessment

(i) The assessors may recommend that the candidate be transferred to D.Phil status.

(ii) The assessors may judge that the candidate is not (yet) ready to transfer, in which case they may:

(*a*) recommend that the candidate should reapply after undertaking further preparatory work, which should be clearly described in their report, or

(*b*) recommend that the candidate should transfer to a lower level of research degree, such as the Master of Letters (M.Litt).

Unsuccessful applications

(i) A candidate whose first application for transfer to D.Phil status is not approved shall be permitted to make one further application, and will be granted an extension of time for one term if this is necessary for the purposes of making the application. Normally the assessors should be the same as for the original application.

(ii) If, after considering a candidate's second application for transfer of status, the relevant board concludes that the student's progress does not warrant transfer, the board must consider whether to approve his or her transfer to the status of Student for the Degree of Master of Letters (M.Litt).

(iii) Candidates who are transferred to M.Litt. status are permitted one further opportunity to apply for transfer to D.Phil status, provided that (a) not more than three terms have elapsed from the original transfer attempt, and (b) that the candidate's supervisor is prepared to support a further application.

Reporting

The report of the assessors must be considered by the Faculty Graduate Studies Committee (or equivalent), which may delegate authority to the Director of Graduate Studies. Where authority is delegated, the Director of Graduate Studies must report his or her decision to the Faculty Graduate Studies Committee (or equivalent). A copy of the transfer report must also be sent to the student, supervisor and college.

Appeals

Candidates who wish to contest the outcome of the transfer assessment, either on procedural or academic grounds, should first discuss the matter with their Director of Graduate Studies. Where a concern is not satisfactorily settled by that means, the candidate, their supervisor or their college authority may make an appeal directly to the Proctors. In accordance with the University's complaints and appeals processes, the Proctors can only consider whether the procedures for reaching an academic decision were properly followed, and cannot challenge the academic judgement of the assessors.

Loss of Probationer Research Student status

Candidates will lose their Probationer Research Student status if they have not gained admission to another status (e.g. D.Phil or M.Litt) within six terms of admission as a full-time student to the status of Probationer Research Student, or if the faculty board concerned deprives them of such status (after consultation with the college/hall and supervisor). If a candidate loses his or her status as a Probationer Research Student and has not gained admission to another status, the candidate is no longer registered as a student of the University.

2. *Confirmation of Status*

Purpose and criteria

The purpose of confirmation is to:

(i) assess the progress of the student's research, and

(ii) to ensure that the student's research progress is such that the student may reasonably be expected to submit within six months to one year.

Applying for confirmation of status

(i) Candidates who were admitted to Probationer Research Student (PRS) status must apply for confirmation of status between Trinity Term of Year 2 and Trinity Term of Year 3 as measured from their admission to PRS status.

(ii) Application for confirmation of status should be made at least *six months* (i.e. two terms, or Trinity Term plus the summer vacation) prior to submission of the thesis.

Material normally required for applications for confirmation of status

Entries for individual faculty boards below indicate exactly which materials students studying for a D.Phil degree in that faculty should submit to apply for confirmation of status.

Candidates applying for confirmation of D.Phil status should normally submit the following documents:

(i) GSO.14 form: Application to Confirm D.Phil status.

(ii) An abstract of the thesis, a list of chapters with a paragraph describing each chapter, a clear statement indicating which chapters have been written, and a detailed timetable for the completion of the remaining chapters.

(iii) Written work (or equivalent, e.g. a portfolio, score or CD/DVD), to be specified by the faculty. The submitted work should be on the topic of the proposed thesis, and if this consists of written work, should be about 10,000 words long (usually a draft chapter of the thesis including all footnotes, bibliography etc.; if the submitted work is not a draft chapter, then the candidate should provide a written explanation of the written work's relationship to the thesis).

(iv) A reference from the supervisor: the supervisor (or supervisors, if there is more than one) must provide a confidential assessment of the student and their application (this must be in addition to, or instead of, the 'Comment' section of GSO.14). The faculty may specify additional references.

(v) Confirmation material should normally include copies of the report(s) from the transfer process.

Assessment

(i) Assessors: the faculty must appoint at least one assessor, who must not be the candidate's supervisor. Ideally two assessors should be appointed.

(ii) Interview: an interview by at least one assessor who is not the supervisor, based on the submitted written materials, is compulsory.

(iii) Report: the assessor(s) must submit a written report on both the written and interview components of the application, making a clear recommendation to the relevant Faculty Graduate Studies Committee (or equivalent).

Outcome of assessment

(i) The assessor(s) may recommend that the candidate's D.Phil status be confirmed.

(ii) The assessor(s) may judge that the candidate does not (yet) satisfy the purpose of the confirmation process as described above, and may:

(*a*) recommend resubmission of the application at a later date within the normal timetable;

(*b*) recommend that the candidate should transfer to a lower level of research degree, such as the M.Litt.

Unsuccessful applications

If the candidate's first application for confirmation of status is not approved, the candidate is permitted to make one further application, normally within one term of the orginal application. The candidate will be granted an extension of time for one term if this is necessary for the purposes of making the application. If, after considering a candidate's second application for confirmation of status, a board concludes that the student's progress does not warrant confirmation, the board may approve his or her transfer to the status of Student for the Degree of Master of Letters (M.Litt).

Deferral of confirmation

In exceptional circumstances where unforeseen and unavoidable obstacles have arisen since transfer of status so as to delay a student's research progress, the student may apply to their faculty board for deferral of confirmation of status up to a maximum of three terms. An application for deferral must consist of:

(i) a clear and detailed description of the obstacles;

(ii) a statement of support from the student's supervisor;

(iii) a statement of support from the Director of Graduate Studies.

Reporting

The report of the assessor(s) must be considered by the Faculty Graduate Studies Committee (or equivalent), which may delegate authority to the Director of Graduate Studies. Where authority is delegated, the Director of Graduate Studies must report their decisions to the Faculty Graduate Studies Committee (or equivalent). A copy of the transfer report must also be sent to the student, supervisor and college.

2. BOARD OF THE FACULTY OF LINGUISTICS, PHILOLOGY AND PHONETICS

1. *Probationer Research Students*

Candidates for admission will normally be expected to have a first or upper second class degree. They will be required to submit evidence (in the form of essays written in English) of their competence in the broad subject of their intended research and should have a basic knowledge of the language(s) in which the main secondary literature is written.

2. *M.Litt. status*

(i) Candidates for admission must submit a piece of written work, normally of about 5,000 words, in the broad field of their proposed thesis. From time to time the Faculty may make other requirements of candidates in order to ascertain their ability to engage in research.

(ii) Probationer Research Students applying for transfer to M.Litt. status must inform the Faculty in writing of their intention eleven days before the beginning of the Trinity Term of their first year, and should at the same time indicate the subject of their proposed thesis and of the written work which they will submit. The written work and other statements required must be submitted by the Wednesday of the second week of that Trinity Term. In special circumstances (for example, those who entered Probationer Research Student status after taking an M.St.), it will be possible to follow this procedure one term later.

(iii) M.Phil. students applying for admission to M.Litt. status after taking the M.Phil. should do so by the Trinity Term of their second year at the latest, in accordance with the procedure in (ii) above. Acceptance of applications will in all cases be conditional upon a satisfactory result in the M.Phil. examination.

3. *D.Phil. status*

(i) Candidates for admission must submit a piece of written work, normally of about 5,000 words, in the broad field of their proposed thesis.

(ii) Probationer Research Students applying for transfer to D.Phil. status must inform the Faculty in writing of their intentions eleven days before the beginning of the Trinity Term of their first year, and should at the same time indicate the subject of their proposed thesis and of the written work which they will submit. The written work and other statements required must be submitted by the Wednesday of the second week of that Trinity Term. In special circumstances (for example, those who transferred to Probationer Research Student status from M.St. status), it will be possible to follow this procedure one term later.

(iii) M.Phil. students applying for admission to D.Phil. status after taking the M.Phil. should do so by the Trinity Term of their second year at the latest, in accordance with the procedure in (ii) above. Acceptance of applications will in all cases be conditional upon a satisfactory result in the M.Phil. examination.

4. *Confirmation of D.Phil. status*

(i) Candidates for confirmation of D.Phil. status should submit a detailed plan, and a draft chapter, of their proposed thesis.

(ii) The application shall be examined by an assessor appointed by the Faculty, not normally the candidate's supervisor, who shall interview the candidate and make a recommendation to the Faculty. The assessor shall be entitled, if he or she so wishes, to consult with another person (who need not be a member of the University) and who may, but need not, take part in the interview.

5. *Theses*

Theses submitted for the Degree of M.Litt. in Comparative Philology and General Linguistics should not exceed 50,000 words. The word limit excludes the bibliography, appendices consisting of a catalogue of data, any extensive text which is specifically the object of a commentary or linguistic analysis, and any translation of that text, but includes quotations and footnotes.

Theses submitted for the Degree of D.Phil. in Comparative Philology and General Linguistics should not exceed 100,000 words. The word limit excludes the bibliography, appendices consisting of a catalogue of data, any extensive text which is specifically the object of a commentary or linguistic analysis, and any translation of that text, but includes quotations and footnotes.

3. BOARD OF THE FACULTY OF CLASSICS

1. *Admission to M.Litt. status*

Applications from Probationer Research Students for transfer to the status of Student for the Degree of Master of Letters will not normally be considered before the beginning of the candidate's third term as a Probationer Research Student. Transfer will normally take place in the third or fourth term.

The written work to be submitted should be a single essay, preferably typed, on a subject relevant to the candidate's proposed thesis. For candidates in *Languages and Literature* the essay should not be more than 10,000 words in length; for candidates in *Ancient History* it should not be more than 5,000 words in length.

2. *Admission to D.Phil. status*

Applications from Probationer Research Students for transfer to the status of Student for the Degree of Doctor of Philosophy will not normally be considered before the beginning of the candidate's third term as a Probationer Research Student. The board regards the end of the third, or the beginning of the fourth, term as the normal time for this application to be made.

The written work to be submitted should be a single essay, preferably typed, and should be close in content to a chapter or part of a chapter of the candidate's proposed thesis.

For candidates in *Languages and Literature* the essay should not be more than 5,000 words in length; for candidates in *Ancient History* it should not be more than 5,000 words in length.

In *Languages and Literature* candidates will also be required to have attended such classes as the Graduate Studies Committee shall from time to time determine.

3. *Confirmation of D.Phil. status*

Applications from Students for the Degree of Doctor of Philosophy for confirmation of status should be accompanied by a reasoned statement of the nature of the proposed thesis. Candidates in *Ancient History* are required to submit in addition a single essay of between 5,000 and 10,000 words in length, which should be close in content to a chapter or part of a chapter of the proposed thesis; candidates in Languages and Literature should be required to submit an essay, of approximately 5,000 words in length. Candidates may also be required to attend an interview.

In Languages and Literature candidates will also be required to provide evidence of reading competence in German and a second modern language by the time of confirmation. Further details on the modern language policy are set out in the Faculty's D.Phil handbook.

The board regards the end of the sixth, or the beginning of the seventh, term from the candidate's admission as a Probationer Research Student as the normal time for this application to be made except in the case of candidates who have been admitted directly to the status of Student for the Degree of Doctor of Philosophy of Philosophy after taking the M.Phil. and whose admission as Probationer Research Student is thereafter deemed to have begun when they began the M.Phil.: in this case the normal time is the end of the ninth term after admission to the Status of Probationer Research Student.

4. *Theses*

All candidates when they submit their theses must state the approximate number of words therein both (*a*) including citations and, if they have been granted permission to count citations separately, (*b*) excluding citations. Theses exceeding the limit are liable to be returned unexamined for reduction to the proper length. Candidates who have submitted in their final term may be allowed a maximum period of two terms to effect the necessary reduction.

Theses submitted for the Degree of M.Litt. in *Ancient History and Archaeology* should not exceed 50,000 words, and those submitted for the Degree of D.Phil. should not exceed 100,000 words, excluding the bibliography, any text that is being edited or annotated, and any descriptive catalogue, but including footnotes and appendices. Leave to exceed these limits will only be given in exceptional cases, and upon the presentation of a detailed explanation by the candidate, together with a statement of the excess length required and the written support of the supervisor. Such applications should be made immediately it becomes clear that authorisation to exceed the limit will be required, and in any case not later than the Friday of the fifth week of the term before that in which application is made for appointment of examiners. Every candidate submitting a thesis must state the number of words therein.

A thesis submitted for the Degree of M.Litt. in Classical Languages and Literature should not exceed 60,000 words. There is no minimum word limit but approximately 50,000 words would be accepted as a guideline. A thesis submitted for the Degree of D.Phil. should not exceed 100,000 words. There is no minimum word limit but approximately 80,000 words would be accepted as a guideline. The word limit excludes the bibliography, any text that is being edited or annotated, translations of Greek or Latin quoted, and any descriptive catalogue, but includes Greek or Latin quoted, footnotes and appendices.

Candidates submitting archaeological theses incorporating photographs are required to present original photographs in one copy of the thesis only, provided that the copies in the other two are adequately reproduced.

The copy of the thesis containing the original photographs should be the one deposited in the Bodleian Library.

5. *Written Examination for the D.Phil.*

The board recommends that, when a written examination is held, two papers be set, three hours being allowed for each.

Questions should be set testing candidates' knowledge of matters germane to, but not specifically included in, their treatment of the subject of their thesis, and command of the methods appropriate to the handling of them. Where submitted work is professedly based upon evidence, literary, material, or monumental, candidates should be required in the written examination to satisfy the examiners that they have adequately studied the original sources of such evidence.

The examiners are requested to include in their report to the board a statement of their judgement upon the qualifications shown in these regards by candidates.

4. BOARD OF THE FACULTY OF ENGLISH LANGUAGE AND LITERATURE

General

Candidates for admission to D.Phil. and M.Litt. status, must have been interviewed by one of the persons appointed by the board for this purpose, unless the board determines otherwise.

Students admitted prior to 1 OCTOBER 2009 should refer to *Examination Regulations* 2008.

FOR STUDENTS ADMITTED FROM 1 OCTOBER 2009:

1. *Transfer to M.Litt. and D.Phil. status*

  (i) All research candidates are initially registered as Probationer Research Students and will be required to submit an application to transfer to M.Litt or D.Phil status no later than Friday of noughth week in the Trinity Term of their first year as a Probationer Research Student. In exceptional cases the English Graduate Studies Committee may permit the candidate to postpone submission; candidates seeking such postponement must apply to the Director of Graduate Studies well in advance, and no later than Monday of fifth week of Hilary Term.

  (ii) Candidates must write to the English Graduate Office by Friday of the eighth week of Hilary Term of their first year as a Probationer Research Student, giving notice of their intention to apply for transfer to D.Phil status, and providing the title of their proposed thesis.

  (iii) Candidates must submit the following materials: (1) The transfer of status application form, endorsed by the candidate's society and supervisor. (2) Two copies of a detailed outline (not exceeding 1,000 words) of the proposed subject and the manner in which it will be treated, including a provisional list of chapters and their proposed coverage. (3) Two copies of a piece of written work on the topic of their proposed thesis (of about 10,000 words).

  (iv) A confidential report from the supervisor should be sent by the supervisor directly to the English Graduate Office. The Graduate Office shall send the outline, written work and the confidential report to two assessors appointed by the Director of Graduate Studies. The Director of Graduate Studies shall not appoint the candidate's supervisor as an assessor.

(v) The assessors shall then examine the candidate orally and report to the Graduate Studies Committee in writing whether the candidate's subject is satisfactory for the degree in question and whether he or she is competent to undertake it. If they think this is not the case, they may recommend resubmission after a set period of probation; such resubmission will constitute   5
the second attempt at Transfer of Status provided for in the General Regulations for the degree. If the assessors disagree, the Graduate Studies Committee shall decide what should be done.

(vi) Candidates holding the status of M.Litt student may apply for transfer to D.Phil status at any time, with the statutory limit of nine terms. Their Transfer   10
of Status application will be considered according to the procedure laid down for confirmation of D.Phil Status (see below). The assessor appointed by the Director of Graduate Studies shall follow that procedure, except that the assessor will be asked to state explicitly whether in addition to this procedure a subsequent formal confirmation of D.Phil status would be desirable, or not.   15

2. *Confirmation of D.Phil. status*

For students admitted to the D.Phil. in English before 1 October 2010:

(i) Application for confirmation of D.Phil. status shall normally be presented to the English Faculty Graduate Studies Office not later than two weeks before any meeting of the Graduate Studies Committee before the end of the ninth   20
term after the candidate's admission as a Probationer Research Student, or the tenth term after the candidate's admission to M.Phil. student status.

(ii) Application for confirmation of D.Phil. status shall be accompanied by (*a*) a statement giving the title of the thesis, and summarising each component chapter in approximately 100 words per chapter, and (*b*) an overview of the   25
intended thesis, of approximately 1,000 words, stating how much of the thesis is complete and how much remains to be done (with an estimate of the probable date of completion).

(iii) The candidate's supervisor shall provide a confidential report on the candidate's application upon the form provided for this purpose. The report shall   30
comment upon the accuracy of the account and feasibility of the timetable, and upon the candidate's progress, together with an estimate of the probable date of completion.

(iv) The documents under (ii) and (iii) above shall be considered by the Graduate Studies Committee, or by at least two members of that committee to whom   35
power may be delegated. The committee shall have power *either* (*a*) to authorise confirmation of D.Phil. status, *or* (*b*) to call for further examination by two assessors.

(v) If the committee adopts (*b*) under (iv) above, two assessors shall be appointed, one of whom shall, wherever practicable, be one of those who acted at the time   40
of the candidate's transfer to D.Phil. status. The assessors shall have power to call for the submission of written work (which shall normally be of 20,000-30,000 words in length and intended to form part of the thesis) by a date which they shall determine, and shall in any event interview the candidate. The assessors shall jointly report to the Graduate Studies Committee in   45
writing whether they think the status of the candidate should be confirmed. If they do not consider that confirmation should be made, they may recommend *either* (*a*) that the candidate should reapply at a later date, *or* (*b*) that the candidate should be transferred to M.Litt. status. If they cannot agree, the committee shall appoint a third assessor to read the written work.   50

(vi) Any candidate whose first application for confirmation is refused may reapply on one (only) further occasion. This second application should normally be within two terms of the first. The material required will be the same as under (ii) above, and the same procedure as under (iii)–(iv) will be followed.

For students admitted to the D.Phil. in English from 1 October 2010:

(i) Application for confirmation of D.Phil. status, with endorsements by the candidate's society and supervisor, shall normally be presented to the English Faculty's Graduate Office not later than Monday of third week in the eighth term after admission to the D. Phil. programme. In exceptional cases the Graduate Studies Committee may permit the candidate to postpone submission by up to one term: candidates seeking such postponement should apply to the Committee through the Director of Graduate Studies well in advance.

(ii) Application for confirmation of D.Phil. status shall be accompanied by: (1) a full outline of chapters (c.100 words per chapters), summarising the scope of individual chapters and their state of completion, including a timetable for completion of the work which remains to be done before submission of the thesis; (2) a draft abstract of the thesis as a whole, of approximately 1,000 words; (3) a sample chapter, of between 6,000 and 10,000 words; (4) a confidential report from the supervisor which should be sent direct to the English Faculty's Graduate Office. The English Graduate Office will send the written work and the confidential report as well as any previous reports on transfer to the interviewer appointed by the English Graduate Studies Committee on behalf of the English Faculty Board.

(iii) The interviewer shall examine the candidate orally. If the interviewer considers it necessary, a second assessor may be appointed in consultation with the Director of Graduate Studies.

(iv) The interviewer(s) shall report to the English Graduate Studies Committee in writing whether the candidate's subject is satisfactory and whether he or she is competent to tackle it. If confirmation is not recommended the interviewer may (1) recommend reapplication after a further period of study or (2) recommend transfer to M.Litt. status.

(v) Any candidate whose first application for confirmation is refused may reapply on one (only) further occasion, normally within two terms of the first. The material required will be the same as (ii) above.

3. *Theses*

Theses submitted to the Board of the Faculty of English Language and Literature for the Degree of M.Litt. should normally be around 40,000 words in length and should in no case exceed 50,000 words, exclusive of the bibliography and of any text that is being edited but including notes, glossary, appendices, etc. Theses submitted for the Degree of D.Phil. should normally be around 80,000 words in length and should in no case exceed 100,000 words, exclusive of the bibliography and of any text being edited, but including notes, glossary, appendices, etc. Leave to exceed these limits will be given only in exceptional cases (e.g. when the subject of the thesis requires extensive quotation from unpublished or inaccessible material, or where substantial and supplementary bibliographical or biographical listings are essential or helpful for an understanding of the arguments of the thesis) and on the recommendation of the supervisor. Applications to exceed the limit of 50,000 words for the M.Litt. or 100,000 words for the D.Phil. must be made in writing to the board's Graduate Studies Committee in advance of the application for appointment of examiners. Each application should include a detailed explanation, a statement of the excess length requested, and a covering letter from the supervisor.

4. *Written Examination for the D.Phil.*

The board recommends that when a written examination is held, it should consist of not more than two papers for each of which three hours should be allowed. 5

Questions should be set testing candidates' knowledge of matters germane to, or arising out of, their treatment of the subject of their thesis, and command of the methods appropriate to the handling of them. Candidates should be required in the written examination to satisfy the examiners that they have adequately studied the original sources of the evidence upon which the submitted work is based. 10

The examiners should include in their report to the board a statement of the judgement upon the qualifications shown in these regards by candidates.

5. COMMITTEE FOR THE RUSKIN SCHOOL OF ART

1. *Admission*

Candidates may elect to pursue research by thesis alone, or by a combination of 15 thesis and studio practice; where the latter course is proposed, the studio work produced must be original work developed and realised in respect of the stated aims of the research programme, exemplifying and locating the ideas that have been developed in conjunction with the written part of the thesis. Fine Art candidates are initially admitted as Probationer Research Students. Depending on whether they 20 wish to pursue research by thesis alone, or through a combination of thesis and studio practice, candidates should support their application with:

EITHER

(A) 1. a sample of recent written work (4,000–6,000 words), preferably but not necessarily related to the proposed topic or area of research, such as an 25 undergraduate or Master's dissertation (or part of it) or a substantial essay;

2. a proposal for a research topic or area (about 1,000 words), which should include a statement why this work should be carried out at Oxford.

OR

(B) (For those intending to offer studio practice as part of the final submission) 30

1. a sample of written work (2,000–3,000 words);

2. a portfolio of recently completed studio work with slides or other documentation of work not available for inclusion;

3. a plan of work to be completed in Oxford.

All candidates should expect to attend for interview. 35

Part-time study

In assessing applications from candidates seeking to undertake a research degree through part-time study, the Committee for the Ruskin School of Art shall have regard to evidence that:

(i) the candidate is suitable to undertake research at doctoral level; 40

(ii) the candidate's personal and professional circumstances are such that it is both practicable for him or her to fulfil the requirements of the course, and necessary for him or her to study on a part-time basis;

(iii) if appropriate, the candidate has the written support of his or her present employer for his or her proposed course of study and its obligations; 45

(iv) the candidate's proposed topic of research is suitable for part-time study;

(v) the candidate can meet the attendance requirements relating to part-time study.

Attendance requirements for part-time study

Part-time students are required to attend for a minimum of thirty days of university-based work each year, to be arranged with the agreement of their supervisor, for the period that their names remain on the Register of Graduate Students unless individually dispensed by the committee.

2. *Transfer of status to M.Litt. or D.Phil.*

During the first year of study, Probationer Research Students are required to attend lectures, seminars, and classes within the University as directed by their supervisor(s). Students will also undertake foundation work related to their research area.

Applications for transfer to M.Litt. or D.Phil. status should normally be made by the end of the third term, and must be made by the end of the sixth term. Students must satisfy the committee that (*a*) they have followed and completed their prescribed courses of study, (*b*) they have undertaken preparatory research (and, where applicable, studio work) to the satisfaction of their supervisor(s), (*c*) the proposed research topic is acceptable, and that they are competent to undertake it, (*d*) (in the case of those intending to offer studio practice as part of the final submission) the proposed work to be undertaken is of sufficient substance.

In the case of part-time students, applications for transfer should normally be made by the end of the sixth term, and must be made by the end of the twelfth term.

Candidates for transfer should submit a brief statement (1,000 words) on the topic of their research and the manner in which they propose to treat it. This should be accompanied by:

EITHER

(A) an essay of about 5,000 words relevant to the topic proposed for the thesis.

OR

(B) (for those intending to offer studio practice as part of the final submission) a portfolio or exhibition of studio work with slides or other documentation of work not available for inclusion and a related essay of 3,000 words.

Application for transfer (including all the submitted material) should be submitted no later than the third week of the third term and accompanied by a report from the student's supervisor(s). (Upon the recommendation of the supervisor(s), a student may be permitted to submit no later than Monday of the week before full term in the fourth term.) On receiving the submissions the committee shall appoint two assessors, both of whom shall consider the submitted material, and conduct the oral examination. Transfer to D.Phil. student status is dependent on satisfactory reports from assessors and confirmation of (*a*)–(*d*) above.

3. *Confirmation of D.Phil. status*

Applications for confirmation of D.Phil. status should normally be made by the end of the eighth term as a research student at Oxford, and must be made by the end of the ninth term; or, in the case of part-time students, normally by the end of the eighteenth term (and must be made by the end of the twenty-fourth term).

Every student seeking confirmation of status should make a submission consisting of:

EITHER

(A) 1. a thesis title, together with an outline of the thesis, and an essay of about 6,000 words on the current state of the student's research, or a portion of the thesis of comparable length.

OR

(B) 1. a portfolio or exhibition of studio work, accompanied by a statement of future plans;

2. an essay on a related topic (3,000 words).

All candidates will be examined orally by two assessors. In the case of those intending to offer studio practice as part of the final submission, both assessors will view the portfolio or exhibition of studio work prior to the oral examination. Confirmation of status may take place only when the committee has received satisfactory reports from the assessors, and from the student's supervisor(s).

4. *Final submission*

EITHER

(A) For the Degree of M.Litt. a thesis not exceeding 40,000 words, or for the Degree of D.Phil, a thesis not exceeding 80,000 words, including notes, bibliography, glossary, appendices, etc.

OR

(B) For the Degree of M.Litt. an exhibition of studio work and a written thesis of up to 20,000 words. For the Degree of D.Phil. an exhibition of studio work and a written thesis of up to 40,000 words.

In the case of those offering studio practice as part of the final submission, both assessors will view the portfolio or exhibition of studio work prior to the oral examination. The supervisor will ensure that the assessors view the studio work. This may take place in a different venue from, and on a day prior to the oral examination. There should normally be no more than three months between the dates of the viewing and the oral examination. In conducting the oral examination, the assessors will be concerned to establish that the studio work has been clearly presented in relation to the argument of the written thesis, and that it has been set in its relevant theoretical, historical, or critical context.

6. BOARD OF THE FACULTY OF HISTORY

1. Admission/First year course work

In History (which includes medieval history, economic and social history, history of science, and history of art) graduate students are initially admitted *either* as candidates for a taught programme *or* as candidates for a research programme. The requirements for all taught programmes are laid out in detail under their individual regulations above.

Research students are admitted as Probationer D.Phil students, and are required to undertake the following work in their probationary period:

(*a*) attend such lectures, seminars and classes as his or her supervisor shall determine; and

(*b*) present one seminar paper during the first year. Such paper shall normally be assessed by two assessors. Such assessors should not include the candidate's supervisor. The work done for the seminar paper may form the basis of the essay required under (2) below.

Applications for admission/transfer to M.Litt. or D.Phil. status shall be accompanied by:

(1) two copies of a statement (of 500 to 1,000 words) of the subject of the thesis and the manner in which the candidate proposes to treat it; such a statement will also normally include a descriptive title for the research project, an indication of identified or envisaged primary sources, an outline of the time table for background reading, archival or field work, and writing-up; also an account of how the research project relates to work done for any relevant master's dissertation;

(2) two copies of a piece of written work, normally 3,000–5,000 words long, being *either* (*a*) a section of the proposed thesis, *or* (*b*) an essay on a relevant topic, or (*c*) an augmented version of the statement required under (1) above; candidates should note that if they adopt alternative (*c*) they must also submit separately the statement required under (1) above;

(3) two copies of a confidential report from the supervisor, which should be sent by the supervisor directly to the Faculty's Graduate Office.

Successful completion of the work prescribed above is not in itself sufficient qualification for students to advance to M.Litt. or D.Phil. status.

2. *Readmission after completion of a taught programme*

Students who are currently entered as candidates for the examination in the M.St. in Medieval History, M.St. or M.Phil. in Late Antique and Byzantine Studies, M.St. in Medieval Studies, M.St. or M.Phil in Modern British and European History, M.St. in Global and Imperial History, M.St. in US History, M.St. in History of Art and Visual Culture, M.Sc. in English Local History, M.Sc. or M.Phil. in Economic and Social History, M.Sc. or M.Phil. in History of Science, Medicine, and Technology, or another relevant Master's programme may apply for admission to the M.Litt. or D.Phil. programme in the year in which they enter the final examination for their M.Sc., M.St., or M.Phil. programme. Readmission may be made conditional on such requirements as the Graduate Studies Committee may impose, and successful completion of their current degree is not in itself sufficient qualification for students to be admitted to a research programme.

3. *Special provisions for part-time students**

In assessing applications from candidates seeking to undertake a research degree through part-time study, the Graduate Studies Committee of the Board of the Faculty of History shall have regard to evidence that:

(i) the candidate is suitable to undertake research at doctoral level;

(ii) the candidate's proposed topic of research is suitable for part-time study;

(iii) the candidate's personal and professional circumstances are such that it is both practicable for him or her to fulfil the requirements of the course, and necessary for him or her to study on a part-time basis;

(iv) if appropriate, the candidate has the written support of their present employer for their proposed course of study and its obligations;

(v) the candidate can meet the following attendance requirements for their period of part-time study: attendance for a minimum of thirty days of university-based work each year, normally coinciding with the full terms of the academic year, to be arranged with the agreement of their supervisor, for the period that their names remain on the Register of Graduate Students unless individually dispensed by the Graduate Studies Committee on the Board of the Faculty of History. During a candidate's probationary period the attendance arrangements must take account of relevant induction and training events scheduled by the Faculty.

4. *Transfer to full M.Litt. or D.Phil. status*

(i) The application form, endorsed by the candidate's society and supervisor, and the supporting material as outlined under 1. above shall normally be presented to the Faculty's Graduate Office not later than Friday of eighth week in the candidate's first Hilary Term (or Friday of eighth week in the candidate's

---

* It should be noted that admission or change to study on a part-time basis in History is reviewed on an annual basis, and is subject to decisions by the University on the availability of doctoral research by means of part-time study.

second Hilary Term in the case of part-time students). In exceptional cases the Graduate Studies Committee may permit the candidate to postpone submission: candidates seeking such postponement should apply to the Director of Graduate Studies well in advance.

(ii) Two copies of a confidential report from the supervisor should be sent by the supervisor directly to the Faculty's Graduate Office. The Graduate Office shall send both copies of the written work and the confidential report to the candidate's interviewer who will pass on one copy to the second assessor nominated as below.

(iii) The interviewer shall then, together with a second assessor appointed in conjunction with the Director of Graduate Studies, examine the candidate orally. The interviewer shall be entitled, after consultation with the Director of Graduate Studies, to appoint a deputy to act instead. When the interviewer is also the supervisor, the Director of Graduate Studies shall act as if he or she were the interviewer and shall have power to appoint a deputy and the second assessor.

(iv) The assessors shall report to the Graduate Studies Committee in writing whether the candidate's subject is satisfactory for the degree in question and whether he or she is competent to tackle it*. If they think this is not the case, they may recommend resubmission after a set period of further probation; such resubmission will constitute the second attempt at Transfer of Status provided for in the General Regulations for the degree. If the assessors disagree, the Graduate Studies Committee shall decide what should be done.

(v) Candidates holding the status of M.Litt. student may apply for transfer to D.Phil. status at any time, within the statutory limit of nine terms. Their Transfer of Status application will be considered according to the procedure laid down for confirmation of D. Phil. status (see below). The interviewer appointed by the Faculty Board shall follow that procedure, except that the interviewer will be asked to state explicitly whether in addition to this procedure a subsequent formal confirmation of D. Phil. status would be desirable, or not.

5. *Confirmation of D.Phil. status*

(i) Application for confirmation of D. Phil. status, with endorsements by the candidate's society and supervisor, shall normally be presented to the Faculty's Graduate Office not later than Monday of third week in the eighth term after admission to the D. Phil. programme (or in the candidate's twelfth term after transfer to full D.Phil. status in the case of part-time students). In exceptional cases the Graduate Studies Committee may permit

---

* Assessors are asked to note the important distinction in the criteria for the two degrees. In the case of the M.Litt. candidates are required to have made 'a worthwhile contribution to knowledge or understanding in the field of learning within which the subject of the thesis falls', while for the D.Phil. it is necessary to have made 'a significant and substantial contribution in the particular field of learning within which the subject of the thesis falls'. The phrase 'a significant and substantial contribution', in the case of doctoral theses, is interpreted as work that displays stature, judgement, and persuasiveness in historical exposition and the shaping of conclusions. But examiners are explicitly requested to bear in mind that their judgement of the significance of the work submitted should be based on what may reasonably be expected of a capable and diligent graduate student after three or, at most, four years of full-time study. Similarly, the requirement that candidates for the M.Litt. should make 'a worthwhile contribution to knowledge or understanding' in their chosen field is qualified by the request that examiners should take into account what may be expected after two years of full-time study.

the candidate to postpone submission by up to one term: candidates seeking such postponement should apply to the Committee through the Director of Graduate Studies well in advance.

(ii) Application for confirmation of D.Phil status shall be accompanied by: (1) a full outline of chapters (1–2 pages), summarising the scope of individual chapters and their state of completion, including a timetable for completion of the work which remains to be done before submission of the thesis; (2) a draft abstract of the thesis as a whole, of between 1,000 and 2,000 words; (3) a sample chapter, of between 6,000 and 10,000 words; (4) a confidential report from the supervisor which should be sent direct to the Faculty's Graduate Office. The Graduate Office shall send the written work and the confidential report to the interviewer appointed by the Faculty Board.

(iii) The interviewer shall then examine the candidate orally. If the interviewer considers it necessary, a second assessor may be appointed in conjunction with the Director of Graduate Studies. In cases where the interviewer is also the supervisor, the Director of Graduate Studies shall act as if he or she were the interviewer and shall have power to appoint a deputy and, if necessary, a second assessor.

(iv) The interviewer shall report to the Graduate Studies Committee in writing whether the candidate's subject is satisfactory and whether he or she is competent to tackle it. If confirmation is not recommended the interviewer may recommend reapplication after a further period of study (within the timeframe provided for in the General Regulations) or alternatively transfer to M.Litt. status, subject to the general regulations governing confirmation of status.

6. Theses

Theses submitted for the Degree of M.Litt. should not exceed 50,000 words and those submitted for the Degree of D.Phil. should not exceed 100,000 words, *including* all notes, appendices, any source material being edited, and all other parts of the thesis whatsoever, *excluding* only the bibliography; any thesis exceeding these limits is liable to be rejected on that ground. Any application for permission to exceed the limit should be submitted with a detailed explanation and statement of the amount of excess length requested, and with a covering letter from the supervisor. Applications should be made as soon as possible and may not be made later than the last day of the fifth week of the term before that in which application is made for appointment of examiners. The presentation and footnotes should comply with the requirements specified in the Regulations of the Education Committee for the degrees of M.Litt. and D. Phil. and follow the *Conventions for the presentation of essays, dissertations and theses* of the Faculty of History.

All candidates must submit with their thesis two printed or typewritten copies of an abstract of the thesis, which shall not normally exceed 1,500 words for the M.Litt. or 2,500 words for the D. Phil., prepared by the student. This is in addition to the requirement to submit an abstract of not more than 300 words in length required by the Education Committee's regulations. Copies of both abstracts shall be bound into the copy of the thesis which shall be deposited in the Bodleian Library. One loose copy of the 300 words abstract, printed on a single page, must be submitted together with the Library copy to the Examination Schools.

7. BOARD OF THE FACULTY OF MEDIEVAL AND MODERN LANGUAGES

1. *Application for admission as a Probationer Research Student*

General

Applicants from the United Kingdom for admission as Probationer Research Students will normally be expected to attend for interview; other applicants required for interview will be notified as appropriate. The interviews will be conducted by or on behalf of a member of the board or its Graduate Studies Committee.

1. *Transfer to M.Litt. and D.Phil. status*

Unless they have successfully completed the M.Phil. in European Literature or the M.Phil. in Medieval and Modern Languages, research students are normally regis-   5
tered in the first instance for the degree of Master of Studies in Medieval and Modern Languages, and follow the requirements laid down for that degree. Transfer to M.Litt. or D.Phil. status normally takes place at the end of the first year and is dependent on successful completion of the M.St. course though this is in itself not a sufficient condition for transfer.   10

The board may however (i) permit candidates to register in the first instance for another degree of M.St. or for the degree of M.Phil., or (ii) permit those who have already obtained an equivalent qualification to the degree of M.St. in Medieval and Modern Languages to register as Probationer Research Students for the first year, following such courses as the board may require.   15

2. *Admission to M.Litt. status*

Candidates must give notice of intention to apply for transfer in writing to the Modern Languages Graduate Office, 41 Wellington Square, Oxford, by the end of the fourth week of the third term before they seek entry to M.Litt. status, giving the title of the proposed thesis. By Friday of the sixth week they shall submit an   20
application form together with (i) three copies of a statement (not more than 500 words) of the title of the proposed thesis and of the manner in which the subject will be treated, and of the way in which the proposed treatment relates to existing work relevant to the chosen topic, the statement to include a provisional scheme of the contents of the thesis, and (ii) two typed copies of a piece of written   25
work normally not more than about 10,000 words long (which will usually be the same as the dissertation submitted for the degree of M.St. in Medieval and Modern Languages). The material shall be sent to two assessors, neither of whom shall normally be the candidate's supervisor and who, in the case of students for the M.St. in Medieval and Modern Languages, shall normally be acting as assessors   30
in that examination also. The assessors shall examine the candidate orally (if appropriate in the course of the examination for that degree).

The assessors will be asked to report to the Graduate Studies Committee for its meeting in July.

3. *Admission to D.Phil. status*   35

Candidates must give notice of intention to apply for transfer in writing to the Modern Languages Graduate Office, 41 Wellington Square, Oxford, by the end of the fourth week of the third term before they seek entry to D.Phil. status, giving the title of the proposed thesis. By Friday of the sixth week they shall submit an application form together with (i) three copies of a statement (not more than 500   40
words) of the title of the proposed thesis and of the manner in which the subject will be treated, and of the way in which the proposed treatment relates to existing work relevant to the chosen topic, the statement to include a provisional scheme of the contents of the chosen topic, and (ii) two typed copies of a piece of written work normally not more than about 10,000 words long (which will usually be the same as   45
the dissertation submitted for the degree of M.St. in Modern Languages).

No application for admission within the terms of §3 of the general regulations for the Degree of Doctor of Philosophy will normally be considered by the Graduate Studies Committee of the board unless the applicant has previously been interviewed by a member of the Faculty invited to act in this capacity by the   50
committee. The application form must be signed by the person who interviews the candidate.

The material shall be sent to two assessors, neither of whom shall normally be the candidate's supervisor and who, in the case of students for the M.St. in European Literature, shall normally be acting as assessors in that examination also. The assessors shall examine the candidate orally (if appropriate in the course of the examination for that degree).

The assessors will be asked to report to the Graduate Studies Committee for its meeting in July.

The requirements for the submission of a piece of written work at (ii) above and for action by assessors will not apply in the case of candidates who have been given leave to supplicate for the degree of M.Phil. or M.Litt. whose subject of thesis for that degree is in the broad field of research proposed for the D.Phil.

Any candidate whose application for transfer to M.Litt. or D. Phil. Status is refused may reapply on one (only) further occasion.

4. The board will award a Certificate of Graduate Attainment to a Probationer Research Student whose application for transfer to the status of student for the degree of D.Phil. or M.Litt. is approved by the committee. In exceptional circumstances the committee may recommend the award of the certificate to other Probationer Research Students who are strongly supported by their supervisor.

2. *Application for confirmation of status as a student for the Degree of Doctor of Philosophy*

(*a*) **Candidates other than those who have already been given leave to supplicate for the Degree of M.Phil.**

(i) Each applicant for confirmation of D.Phil. status must submit two copies of a piece of written work of 15,000 words in length (except where text is accompanied by graphs or statistical material), being a draft of a chapter or chapters of the thesis (excluding the introductory or concluding chapters and any section submitted for the first transfer examination). The student shall show on a provisional list of the contents of the thesis the place he or she plans for the draft chapter(s). This piece of work must be substantially different from that submitted on application for admission to D.Phil. status. Each applicant must also submit, at the time of application, three copies of a statement (of not more than 1,000 words) of the title of the proposed thesis and of the manner in which the subject will be treated, and of work achieved on other parts of the thesis and work remaining to be done.

(ii) Unless permission is given otherwise by the committee, the application for confirmation of D.Phil. status shall be submitted to the Modern Languages Graduate Office, 41 Wellington Square, Oxford, not later than the Friday of the fourth week of the applicant's ninth term from admission to graduate status, and copies of the written work by not later than 30 June. The written work shall be read by two assessors appointed by the Graduate Studies Committee of the board. Neither of the assessors shall normally be the candidate's supervisor. The assessors shall examine the candidate orally.

(iii) The assessors shall report to the committee in writing whether they recommend that the candidate's status as a D.Phil. student should be confirmed. They shall also make a written report, in support of their recommendation, covering the following points: whether the subject of the thesis and the manner of its treatment proposed by the candidate are acceptable; and whether the thesis can reasonably be completed in three or at most four years of full-time study from the date of the candidate's admission as a research student,

(Note: students reading for the M.St. in Modern Languages are considered to be taught-course students). On receipt of the report, the committee shall decide whether to approve the candidate's application. If it reaches the conclusion that the candidate's subject for a thesis is unsatisfactory and/or that the candidate is unlikely to be able to complete the thesis proposed, it may permit resubmission by a date which the committee shall specify. If, after a second application, the committee continues to be unable to give approval, it will *either* admit the candidate to M.Litt. status *or* take appropriate action under the regulations made by the Education Committee for the removal of a student from the Register.

(*b*) **Candidates who have already been given leave to supplicate for the degree of M.Phil. (Candidates who propose a topic for their D.Phil. which is different from their M.Phil. topic shall be subject to the regulations under (*a*) above).**

Applicants must submit to the Modern Languages Graduate Office, 41 Wellington Square, Oxford with their applications three copies of a statement (of not more than 1,000 words) of the title of the proposed thesis and of the manner in which the subject will be treated, and of the way in which the proposed treatment relates to existing work relevant to the chosen topic, and of work achieved on other parts of the thesis and work remaining to be done. The statement should include a provisional scheme of the contents of the thesis, which identifies the place of the M.Phil. thesis in the scheme. Confirmation will be subject to the Graduate Studies Committee of the board being satisfied, on the evidence of the statement and of the examiners of the M.Phil., that the student is capable of carrying out advanced research; that the M.Phil. thesis is in the field of research proposed for the D.Phil.; that the subject can be profitably pursued under the superintendence of the board; and that the thesis can reasonably be expected to be completed in three or at the most four years of full-time study from the date of the candidate's admission as an M.Phil. student. If the committee is not satisfied, it may permit one further application by a date which it shall specify.

3. *Theses*

Theses submitted for the Degree of M.Litt. should not exceed 50,000 words and those submitted for the Degree of D.Phil. should not exceed 80,000 words, excluding the bibliography and any text that is being edited but including notes, glossary, appendices, etc. Leave to exceed these limits will be given only in exceptional cases. Any application for permission to exceed the limit should be submitted with a detailed explanation and statement of the amount of excess length requested, and with a covering letter from the supervisor. Application must be made immediately it seems clear that authorisation to exceed the limit will be sought and normally not later than six months before the intended date of submission of the thesis.

Every candidate who is editing a text must also state the length of the text being edited.

In addition to the arrangements for an abstract of the thesis set out in the Education Committee's regulations above, three printed or typewritten copies of a fuller abstract of the thesis (which shall not normally exceed 1,500 words for the M.Litt. and 2,500 words for the D.Phil.) prepared by the student is required. A copy of the fuller abstract must be bound into the copy of the thesis which, if the application for leave to supplicate for the degree is successful, will be deposited in the Bodleian Library. The fuller abstract may be bound into the two examiners' copies of the thesis if the candidate so desires.

8. BOARD OF THE FACULTY OF MUSIC

1. *Probationer Research Student*

(*a*) **Admission**

(i) Each candidate for admission as a Probationer Research Student should support the application with:

EITHER

(A) 1. a sample of recent written work (4,000–6,000 words), preferably but not necessarily related to the proposed topic or area of research, such as an undergraduate dissertation (or part of it) or a substantial essay;

2. a proposal for a research topic or area (about 1,000 words), which should include a statement why this work should be carried out at Oxford.

OR

(B) (For those intending to offer compositions as part of the final submission)

1. a sample of written work (2,000–3,000 words);

2. one or two recently completed compositions;

3. a plan of work to be completed in Oxford.

Candidates should expect to attend for interview if required.

(*b*) **Course of study**

Candidates seeking admission in order to read for the M.Litt. or D.Phil. are normally registered as Probationer Research Students and as such, unless specifically exempted by the board must follow the requirements laid down for the Degree of Master of Studies in Music. Such exemption will not normally be granted except to candidates who have already obtained a qualification of equivalent status and breadth elsewhere. Transfer to M.Litt. or D.Phil. status normally takes place at the end of the first year and is dependent on successful completion of the M.St. course (though this in itself is not a sufficient condition of transfer).

Probationer Research Students who have been exempted from the requirements laid down for the Degree of Master of Studies in Music must attend courses as recommended by their supervisors and approved by the Director of Graduate Studies. In most instances these courses of study will be undertaken in the Faculty of Music, but exemptions will be made where more appropriate courses are offered in other faculties.

Students will also undertake foundation work related to their research area or topic under the direction of a supervisor.

A Certificate of Graduate Attainment may be awarded on the basis of satisfactory reports on the work undertaken in the initial year.

(*c*) **Transfer to the status of M.Litt. or D.Phil. Student**

(i) Probationer research students seeking to transfer to the status of M.Litt. or D.Phil. Student must satisfy the Board of the Faculty of Music that (*a*) they have followed and completed their prescribed courses of study, (*b*) they have undertaken preparatory research work to the satisfaction of their supervisor, (*c*) the proposed research topic is acceptable, and (*d*) they are competent to handle the research topic.

A candidate for transfer to the new status must make a submission in the manner prescribed in the University's *Examination Regulations*.

The faculty board requires that the written work submitted shall be:

EITHER

(A) an essay of about 5,000 words relevant to the topic proposed for the thesis, and a bibliographic essay of the same length reviewing the historical and/or theoretical literature relevant to the thesis topic and its field.

OR

(B) (For those intending to offer compositions as part of the final submission) a portfolio of two significantly contrasted compositions (together lasting between ten and fifteen minutes maximum), a proposed work-schedule for the following year, and a related essay of 5,000–10,000 words. 5

Two copies of the thesis title, thesis outline, essays and compositions must be submitted. The essay must be typewritten in double spacing, and placed in a temporary form of binding. The submissions must be made through the Registrar no later than seven days before the second meeting of the Graduate Studies Committee of the board in the student's third term from admission. Upon the recommendation of the supervisor, the board may permit a student to submit no later than seven days before the second meeting in the fourth term of study. 10

(ii) On receiving the submissions the board shall appoint two assessors, both of whom shall read the scripts and conduct the oral examination, provided that the board may appoint additional assessors should the need arise. 15

(iii) Transfer to the new status shall only take place when the board has received satisfactory reports from the assessors, from those who conducted the prescribed courses of study, and from the student's supervisor.

(iv) M.St. students admitted to the status of Probationer Research Students must apply for transfer to M.Litt. or D.Phil. status in their fourth term of graduate study. The submissions required may consist of all or part of the work submitted for the Degree of M.St. provided that it is relevant to the research topic. 20

(v) Students for the M.Phil. who intend to take the degree may seek admittance to the status of M.Litt. or D.Phil. Student, provided that they satisfy the general regulations of the university, and that they submit a provisional thesis title and outline of the manner in which it is intended to treat the research topic which is acceptable to the board. 25

2. *M.Litt. Students*
(*a*) **Admission** 30

The procedure for the admission of a Probationer Research Student to the status of M.Litt. Student is outlined in section (*c*) of the faculty board's regulations for Probationer Research Students in Music.

(*b*) **Supervision**

The Graduate Studies Committee of the board will receive a report on each student's progress from his or her supervisor at the end of each term. The committee may request or receive an additional report at the end of the Long Vacation. 35

3. *D.Phil. Students*
(*a*) **Admission**

The procedure for the admission of a Probationer Research Student to the status of D.Phil. Student is outlined in section (*c*) of the faculty board's regulations for Probationer Research Students in Music. 40

(*b*) **Supervision**

The Graduate Studies Committee of the board will receive a report on each student's progress from his or her supervisor at the end of each term. The committee may request or receive an additional report at the end of the Long Vacation. 45

(*c*) **Confirmation of Status**

The status of D.Phil. Student shall normally be confirmed in the sixth term as a research student at Oxford. In addition to the general requirements of the regulations, the Board of the Faculty of Music requires that every student seeking confirmation of status must make a submission consisting of:

EITHER

(A) 1. thesis title, together with an annotated outline of the thesis (both title and outline may be altered or revised forms of those submitted for the examination for admission to D.Phil. status);   5

  2. an essay of about 6,000 words on the current state of the student's research, or a portion of the thesis of comparable length.

OR

(B) 1. an annotated inventory of the proposed contents of the final portfolio of compositions and title of the supporting dissertation;   10

  2. a portfolio of two or more well-contrasted compositions, with a total duration of approximately 25 minutes;

  3. a critical or analytical essay of 5,000–10,000 words.

   (i) Candidates will be examined orally. Two copies of the thesis title, thesis outline and essay (or thesis extract), or inventory, thesis title, portfolio, and essay must be submitted. The essay (or thesis extract) must be typewritten in double spacing, and placed in a temporary form of binding. The submissions must be made through the Registrar no later than seven days before the second meeting of the Graduate Studies Committee in the student's fifth term from admission. Upon the recommendation of the supervisor, the board may permit a student to submit no later than seven days before the second meeting in a subsequent term of study, provided that this falls within the limits set down in the University's *Examination Regulations*.   15 · 20 · 25

   (ii) On receiving the submissions the board shall appoint two assessors, both of whom shall read the scripts and conduct the examination, provided that the board may appoint additional assessors should the need arise.

   (iii) Confirmation of status may only take place when the board has received satisfactory reports from the assessors, and from the student's supervisor.   30

4. *Final submission for the Degree of M.Litt*

EITHER a thesis of not more than 50,000 words.

OR (Musical Composition) a portfolio of between three and six musical compositions, totalling approximately 45 minutes' duration, and a dissertation of not more than 15,000 words either on the candidate's own music or on some aspect of music related to the candidate's compositional concerns.   35

5. *Final submission for the Degree of D.Phil.*

EITHER a thesis of not more than 100,000 words, exclusive of any text being edited but including notes, bibliography, glossary, appendices, etc.   40

OR (Musical Composition) (*a*) a portfolio of between three and six musical compositions, totalling between 45 and 90 minutes' duration, with at least one composition being of large scale (defined as for large-scale forces, such as orchestra, and/or of more than 30 minutes' duration); and (*b*) a dissertation of between 20,000 and 25,000 words either on the candidate's own music or on some aspect of music related to the candidate's compositional concerns.   45

9. BOARD OF THE FACULTY OF ORIENTAL STUDIES

1. *M.Litt. in Oriental Studies*

The first year of study in the Oriental Studies Faculty will be regarded as a qualifying period, during which the student shall be registered as a Probationer Research Student. (For Chinese, see below.) Application for transfer to M.Litt. status should be made by the end of the third term. All students will normally be expected to submit:

(*a*) a piece of formal written work related to the field of their proposed thesis of approximately 5,000 words in length;

(*b*) a satisfactory outline (of not more than 500 words) of the proposed subject of the thesis.

The written work shall be assessed by two assessors (neither of whom may be the supervisor), appointed by the board, and they shall normally be expected also to discuss the submission with the student in person. They must do so if they are not able to make a positive recommendation. When examiners make a positive recommendation to the board, they shall be required explicitly to state in their report that they have satisfied themselves on the basis of their discussion with the student and/or their consideration of the submitted material that the student has the linguistic competence necessary to carry out the proposed research. If on the basis of the evidence available to them they are not able to make such a statement, they shall recommend to the board that the results of a formal written language test arranged by the board for this purpose should be submitted to them for consideration before their recommendation on the student's application is made.

The course of study for the qualifying examination in the field of Chinese Studies will be that required for the M.St. in Chinese Studies, and the examination will be set and examined by the examiners for the M.St. at the end of each Trinity Term.

On the basis of the results of the examination the faculty board will decide whether the student should be accepted for admission to M.Litt. status.

Candidates who have successfully completed the M.St. in Oriental Studies may be recommended for admission to M.Litt. status on the basis of the results of the examination, subject to the submission of a satisfactory outline (of not more than 500 words) of the proposed subject of the thesis.

2. *D.Phil. in Oriental Studies*

The first year of study in the Oriental Studies Faculty will be regarded as a qualifying period, during which the student shall be registered as a Probationer Research Student. (For Chinese, see below.) Application for transfer to D.Phil. status should be made by the end of the third term. All students will normally be expected to submit:

(*a*) a piece of formal written work related to the field of their proposed thesis of between 5,000 and 10,000 words in length;

(*b*) a satisfactory outline (of not more than 500 words) of the proposed subject of the thesis.

The written work shall be assessed by two assessors (neither of whom may be the supervisor), appointed by the board, and they shall normally be expected also to discuss the submission with the student in person. They must do so if they are not able to make a positive recommendation. When examiners make a positive recommendation to the board, they shall be required explicitly to state in their report that they have satisfied themselves on the basis of their discussion with the student and/or their consideration of the submitted material that the student has the linguistic competence necessary to carry out the proposed research. If on the basis of the evidence available to them they are not able to make such a statement, they shall recommend to the board that the results of a formal written language test arranged by the board for this purpose should be submitted to them for consideration before their recommendation on the student's application is made.

The course of study for the qualifying examination in the field of Chinese Studies will be that required for the M.St. in Chinese Studies, and the examination will be set and examined by the examiners for the M.St. at the end of each Trinity Term. On the basis of the results of the examination the faculty board will decide whether the student should be accepted for admission to D.Phil. status.

Candidates who have successfully completed the M.St. in Oriental Studies may be recommended for admission to D.Phil. status on the basis of the results of the examination, subject to the submission of a satisfactory outline (of not more than 500 words) of the proposed subject of the thesis.

Candidates who have successfully completed the M.Phil. in Oriental Studies may be recommended for admission to D.Phil. status on the basis of the results of the examination, subject to the submission of a satisfactory outline (of not more than 500 words) of the proposed subject of the thesis. In exceptional cases, such candidates may be recommended for admission to confirmed D.Phil. status.

The board requires from each applicant for confirmation of D.Phil. status a written statement of the manner in which he or she proposes to treat the subject. The board will approve such applications only if the assessors appointed by the board shall have certified that a piece of work written by the applicant (of 10,000–15,000 words in length) is of the requisite standard to justify the confirmation. Assessment of the application shall include a viva voce examination of the candidate by two persons appointed by the board.

3. *Theses*

Theses submitted for the Degree of M.Litt. should not exceed 50,000 words and those for the Degree of D.Phil. should not exceed 100,000, exclusive of any text that is being edited, and of bibliography, but including notes, glossary, appendices, etc. Leave to exceed this limit will be given only in exceptional cases.

10. BOARD OF THE FACULTY OF PHILOSOPHY

1. *Admission as Probationer Research Student*

Candidates for admission are required to submit with their application one piece of written work of between 4,500 and 5,000 words, on a subject related to the proposed research topic. The piece must be typed and in English, unless by special permission.

2. *Admission to M.Litt. or D.Phil. status*

Applications from Probationer Research Students for transfer to the status of Student for the Degree of Master of Letters or Doctor of Philosophy will not normally be considered before the beginning of the candidate's third term as a Probationer Research Student. The board regards the third term as the normal time for this application to be made and expects applications to be made by the end of the second week of the third term.

Applications should be accompanied by a thesis outline of about two pages and a piece of written work of approximately 5,000 words in the area and philosophical style of the proposed thesis. The board will appoint two assessors, who will read the submissions and conduct an interview with the candidate.

Candidates admitted as Probationer Research Students after completing the Master of Studies degree in Ancient Philosophy at the University of Oxford must complete all of the following requirements by the end of Week 8 of their third term as a Probationer Research Student:

(*a*) Attend two graduate classes with at least one from the following subject areas: moral philosophy; metaphysics; theory of knowledge; philosophical logic and philosophy of language; philosophy of mind and action.

(*b*) Submit one 5,000 word essay on a topic of the student's choice for one of the above listed classes, the pass mark for which is 68.

(*c*) Submit a thesis outline of about two pages.

(*d*) Submit a piece of written work of approximately 5,000 words in the area and philosophical style of the proposed thesis.

The board will appoint two assessors, who will read the submissions and conduct an interview with the candidate. If the mark for the essay mentioned in (*b*) above is between 60 and 67 (inclusive) then the assessors may, depending on the quality of the candidate's other submitted work, recommend approval or refusal of the Transfer of Status application.

The Philosophy Graduate Studies Committee may, depending on the student's prior experience and education, waive requirements (*a*) and/or (*b*). If it waives both requirements then the student must complete the requirements by the end of Week 2 of their third term as a Probationer Research Student.

Candidates admitted as Probationer Research Students after completing the Master of Studies degree in Philosophy of Physics at the University of Oxford must complete the following requirements by the end of the Week 0 before the start of their fourth term as a Probationer Research Student:

(*a*) Attend two graduate classes (which cannot be in the subject area of their MSt in Philosophy of Physics elective option, Philosophy of Physics or Philosophy of Science) with at least one from the following subject areas: moral philosophy; metaphysics; theory of knowledge; philosophical logic and philosophy of language; philosophy of mind and action.

(*b*) Submit one 5,000 word essay on a topic of the student's choice for one of the above listed classes, the pass mark for which is 68.

(*c*) Submit a thesis outline of about two pages.

(*d*) Submit a 20,000 word dissertation on a topic of their choice, preferably in the area and philosophical style of their thesis.

The board will appoint two assessors, who will read the submissions and conduct an interview with the candidate. If the mark for the essay mentioned in (*b*) above is between 60 and 67 (inclusive) then the assessors may, depending on the quality of the candidate's other submitted work, recommend approval or refusal of the Transfer of Status application.

The Philosophy Graduate Studies Committee may, depending on the student's prior experience and education, waive requirements (*a*) and/or (*b*), and it has the power to replace requirement (*d*) by requirement

(*e*) Submit a piece of written work of approximately 5,000 words in the area and philosophical style of the proposed thesis.

If it waives (*a*) and (*b*) and replaces (*d*) by (*e*) then the student must complete the requirements by the end of Week 2 of their third term as a Probationer Research Student.

3. *Confirmation of D.Phil. status*

Applications from Students for the Degree of Doctor of Philosophy for confirmation of status will not normally be considered before the beginning of the candidate's third term after transfer to D.Phil. status. The board regards the third term after transfer as the normal time for this application to be made and expects applications to be made by the end of the second week of the third term. [*Note: This change applies to students commencing their doctoral degree in or after October 2012.*]; it also expects that students should normally have their D.Phil. status confirmed at least one year before the submission of their thesis.

Applications should be accompanied by a thesis outline of about two pages and a piece of written work of approximately 5,000 words, intended as a part of the thesis, in final or near-final draft. The board will appoint two assessors. The application will be considered, in the first instance, by the first assessor. If the first assessor is satisfied that the application should be approved, then he or she will interview with the candidate and recommend approval to the board. If the first assessor is not satisfied that the application should be approved, the application will be sent to the second assessor. Both assessors will interview the candidate and a joint recommendation will be made. The assessors may not recommend that the application be refused unless they have first interviewed the candidate.

4. *Theses*

M.Litt. theses should not exceed 50,000 words, and D.Phil. theses should not exceed 75,000 words, exclusive of bibliographical references, unless the candidate has, with the support of his or her supervisor, secured the leave of the board to exceed this limit.

All candidates when they submit their theses must state the approximate number of words therein both (*a*) including citations and, if they have been granted permission to count citations separately, (*b*) excluding citations. Theses exceeding the limit are liable to be returned unexamined for reduction to the proper length. Candidates who have submitted in their final term may be allowed a maximum period of two terms to effect the necessary reduction.

11. BOARD OF THE FACULTY OF THEOLOGY AND RELIGION

1. *Admission to the status of Probationer Research Student*

Applicants may be admitted to M.Litt. or D. Phil. student status either (1) from M.St. status; (2) from M.Phil. status; (3) from Probationer Research Student Status. The Board expects most applicants seeking to pursue doctoral research in the Faculty to seek M.St. Student status first.

2. *Admission to M.Litt. or D. Phil. Student status from M.St. or M.Phil. student status*

   (i) Applicants holding M.St. or M.Phil. Student status shall apply for admission to M.Litt. or D.Phil. status in the year of their M.St. or M.Phil. examination at the times announced for graduate admissions applications.

   (ii) In either case the application shall include a description in about 500 words of the research which it is intended to undertake, supported by the proposed supervisor.

   (iii) The Board may indicate a provisional readiness to admit to M.Litt. or D. Phil. Student status, which will then be subject to a report from the Examiners of the M.St. or M.Phil.

3. *Admission by the route of Probationer Research Student*

   (i) Admission to the status of Probationer Research Student will normally be granted only to applicants who have already completed a Master's level graduate degree, including a dissertation or thesis, in a theological subject.

   (ii) Application for admission as a Probationer Research Student, which shall be made at the times and in the manner announced for graduate admissions applications, will normally be accompanied by an interview with a member of the Graduate Studies Committee, though the Board may dispense from this.

(iii) A Probationer Research Student is normally expected to apply for transfer within three terms (or six terms in the case of part–time students). A Probationer Research Student who has not successfully transferred by the end of the six terms for which such status may be held in total (twelve terms in the case of part–time students) shall lapse from the register of Graduate Students.

(iv) The application for transfer must include two typewritten copies of a description in about 500 words of the research which it is intended to undertake and two typewritten copies of a piece of original written work of about 5,000 words relevant to the subject of the proposed research.

(v) There shall be an oral examination with a competent person appointed by the Board as assessor, which may treat of the description of the proposed research, the submitted piece of work and any other aspect of the applicant's progress towards research. The candidate's supervisor may attend this examination. If the candidate fails to satisfy the assessor, the Board may appoint a date by which a further oral examination must be held, with such conditions as it sees fit, and grant extension of Probationer Research Student status up to that date, subject to the overall limit in 1(iii) above.

4. *Admission directly to M.Litt. or D.Phil. Student status by former M.St. or M.Phil. students*

(i) The Board may admit directly to M.Litt. or D. Phil. Student status applicants who within the past five years have received permission from the Board of the Faculty of Theology and Religion to supplicate for the degrees of M.St. or M.Phil.

(ii) Application for admission, which shall be made at the times and in the manner announced for graduate admissions applications, will normally require an interview with a member of the Graduate Studies Committee, though the Board may dispense from this.

(iii) The application shall be accompanied by the dissertation or thesis which formed part of the Master's degree.

5. *Special Provisions for part-time students*

In assessing applications from candidates seeking to undertake a research degree through part-time study, the Graduate Studies Committee of the Board of the Faculty of Theology and Religion shall have regard to evidence that:

(i) the candidate is suitable to undertake research at doctoral level;

(ii) the candidate's personal and professional circumstances are such that it is both practicable for him or her to fulfil the requirements of the course, and necessary for him or her to study on a part-time basis;

(iii) if appropriate, the candidate has the written support of their present employer for their proposed course of study and its obligations;

(iv) the candidate's proposed topic of research is suitable for part-time study;

(v) the candidate can meet the attendance requirements relating to part-time study.

6. *Attendance requirements (for part-time students)*

Part-time students are required to attend for a minimum of thirty days of university-based work each year, to be arranged with the agreement of their supervisor, for the period that their names remain on the Register of Graduate Students unless individually dispensed by the Graduate Studies Committee on the Board of the Faculty of Theology and Religion.

7. *Confirmation of D.Phil. status*

Applications should be accompanied by one short abstract of approximately 300 words and one long abstract of 1500–2000 words, a draft chapter, and an outline of the thesis, indicating what has been completed to date and a timetable for completion. The written work shall be read by two assessors appointed by the Graduate Studies Committee. Neither of the assessors shall normally be the candidate's supervisor. The assessors shall examine the candidate orally.

8. *Preparation of theses for the Degrees of M.Litt. and D.Phil.*

(i) Theses submitted for the Degree of M.Litt. should not exceed 50,000 words, or 100,000 for the D.Phil., excluding only the bibliography in both cases. The faculty board is prepared to consider an application for a relaxation of this limit in special circumstances.

(ii) All candidates must submit an abstract of the thesis, of between 1,000 and 1,500 words for an M.Litt., and between 1,500 and 2,500 for a D.Phil., prepared by the candidate. This is in addition to the requirement to submit an abstract of not more than 300 words in length required by the Education Committee's regulations. One copy of each abstract prepared at the time of the examination should be bound into each of the examiners' copies of the thesis. Copies of both abstracts shall be bound into the copy of the thesis which shall be deposited in the Bodleian Library. In addition one loose copy of the 300 word abstract, printed on a single page, must be submitted together with the Library copy.

B. MATHEMATICAL, PHYSICAL AND LIFE SCIENCES DIVISION

1. PERMISSION TO WORK IN A WELL-FOUND LABORATORY OUTSIDE THE UNIVERSITY

Applicants who are admitted to undertake research under the supervision of the Mathematical, Physical and Life Sciences Divisional Board may, exceptionally, be permitted by the divisional board to undertake their research in a well-found laboratory outside the University. Such candidates shall be dispensed from the residence requirements, but shall be required to attend the University for such instruction as the division and department concerned shall require. Before admitting a candidate on this basis, the department concerned shall be required to satisfy itself and the divisional board that appropriate arrangements are in place for approving all aspects of the student's academic work, including the following:

(i) the availability of the equipment and facilities necessary for the project in the agency concerned;

(ii) the existence of a wider collaboration between the department and the agency in which the student is based;

(iii) the subject of their doctoral studies;

(iv) satisfactory induction procedures;

(v) satisfactory health and safety arrangements;

(vi) satisfactory supervision arrangements, to include specification of a minimum number of contact hours between student and supervisor, which shall include not less than two face-to-face meetings between student and supervisor, for a total of at least 8 hours, each term;

(vii) satisfactory arrangements for monitoring the student's progress within the department;

(viii) provision for the student to attend the University for such instruction as the division and department shall require.

Dispensation from these rules shall be sought from the Head of the Mathematical, Physical and Life Sciences Division through the departmental Director of Graduate Studies.

2. TRANSFER OF STATUS AND CONFIRMATION OF STATUS

1. *Transfer of Status*

All research students will be admitted to the status of Probationer Research Student in the first instance. The status of Probationer Research Student may be held for a maximum of four terms (other than students registered on a Doctoral Training Centre Programme). Probationer Research Students should normally apply to transfer status to M.Sc by Research or D.Phil. status before the end of the fourth full-term from admission, subject to the further guidance below. Cases to defer applications for the transfer of status must be made by the candidate with the supervisor's support to the departmental Director of Graduate Studies by the end of the fourth full-term after admission. Approval will only be granted in exceptional circumstances, in accordance with the Regulations of the Education Committee, set out in §4.

In the Biological Sciences (the Departments of Plant Sciences and Zoology), candidates should apply to transfer from the status of Probationer Research Student by the end of the fourth full-term after admission as a research student.

In the Mathematical Sciences (the Department of Computer Science, and the Departments of Mathematics, Statistics, and Computer Science), students in Category A (those who have had no previous experience of research work, and normally all candidates in the Computing Laboratory) should apply to transfer from the status of Probationer Research Student between the second and fourth full-term after admission as a research student. Students with no previous experience of research work are advised to apply in the third full-term after admission. Students in Category B (those who have had previous experience of research work who may have completed a taught master's course) should apply to transfer immediately after admission to Probationer Research Student status. (This category is only available to candidates in the Computing Laboratory in exceptional circumstances with the approval of the Director of Graduate Studies.)

In the Physical Sciences (the Departments of Chemistry, Earth Sciences, Engineering Science, Materials and Physics), candidates should apply to transfer from the status of Probationer Research Student in the third or fourth full-term after admission as a research student.

In the *Biological Sciences*, *Mathematical Sciences*, and *Physical Sciences*, a first application for transfer of status must take place within the six term limit of PRS status, as set out in the Regulations of the Education Committee, §4. Any application outside those limits (other than in Regulations of the Education Committee, §4, cl.6), must be approved by or on behalf of Education Committee.

Doctoral Training Centre Programmes The regulations applying to research students following Doctoral Training Centre Programmes are set out in section 7.

Advice on the timing of transfer of status in each department will be provided by the departmental Director of Graduate Studies.

Applications to transfer status should be considered by a minimum of two assessors on behalf of the Board of the Mathematical, Physical and Life Sciences Division, one of whom may be the student's academic advisor, but neither of whom should normally be the student's supervisor or a member of his/her supervisory team. Each department has its own assessment procedures, which should include as a minimum the following four components:

(i) completion of the appropriate graduate studies application forms to be submitted to the Divisional Graduate Studies Office, 9 Parks Road;

(ii) submission of written work by the student. For example: a progress report; a literature review; any required course work; a plan for the development of the student's research; any published papers. Each department will set out its own requirements in this area;

(iii) an interview between the student and his/her assessors. The process of assessment must always include an interview with the candidate if the assessors cannot recommend transfer to D.Phil. status;

(iv) the student should have made a brief presentation or talk whilst a Probationer Research Student. This need not be part of the transfer interview.

A report will be written to provide feedback to the student, their supervisor, and college. The report will include an assessment of the viability and suitability of the proposed research, and of its completion on a reasonable timescale.

A candidate whose first application for transfer to D.Phil. status is not approved, shall be permitted to make one further application, and shall be granted an extension of time for one term if this is necessary for the purposes of making the application.

A candidate who is transferred to M.Sc by Research status, rather than to D.Phil. status, may have one further opportunity to apply to transfer to D.Phil. status, subject to (a) that a sufficient period of time has elapsed from the original transfer attempt to allow for the possibility of significant development; and (b) the candidate's supervisor supports a further application.

These procedures are also set out in the Division's Graduate Studies Handbook.

2. *Confirmation of Status*

Confirmation of status for D.Phil. students must take place no later than nine terms after admission to graduate status. Students are advised to apply for their first attempt at confirmation of D.Phil. status by the end of the eighth full-term after admission as a graduate research student.

Doctoral Training Centre Programmes The regulations applying to research students following Doctoral Training Centre Programmes are set out in section 7.

Students are encouraged very strongly to apply for confirmation of status at least six–twelve months before they expect to submit their thesis for examination to make this process a constructive part of the development of the student's research. The application for confirmation of status must be made and approved before requesting the formal appointment of examiners.

The requirements for confirmation of status may vary for each department within the following framework:

(i) completion of the appropriate graduate studies application forms to be submitted to the Divisional Graduate Studies Office, 9 Parks Road. The candidate and their supervisor are required to provide a clear indication of progress to date, and the timetable for submission of the thesis;

(ii) all applications must be reviewed by one or more assessors, one of whom may be the departmental Director of Graduate Studies. If there is only one assessor this should not be the candidate's supervisor;

(iii) the candidate should produce a brief written report about their research achievements to date. The specific requirements will be set out by the department, for example a publication(s) or draft chapter(s) from the candidate's thesis, a plan and the timetable for submission of the thesis;

(iv) the assessor(s) may request to interview the candidate, and the candidate may request to have an interview with the assessor(s). The process of assessment must always include an interview with the candidate if the assessor(s) are unable to recommend confirmation of D.Phil. status.

The assessor(s) will write a brief report to provide feedback to the candidate, the supervisor, and college. The report will include an assessment of progress and submission of the thesis within the planned timescale.

A candidate whose first application for confirmation of status is not approved, shall be permitted to make one further application, normally within one term of the original application, and shall be granted an extension of time for one term if this is necessary for the purposes of making the application.

If a candidate's application for confirmation of status is unsuccessful, the board may approve a transfer from D.Phil. to M.Sc. by Research status.

Cases to defer applications for the confirmation of status must be made by the candidate with the supervisor's support to the departmental Director of Graduate Studies by the end of the ninth full-term after admission. Approval will only be granted in exceptional circumstances. Students may apply to defer confirmation of status for a maximum of three terms. The Director of Graduate Studies in each department may decide how many terms, up to the maximum, a candidate may be allowed to defer.

These procedures are also set out in the Division's Graduate Studies Handbook.

3. APPOINTMENT OF EXAMINERS

In applying for appointment of examiners, candidates should note that a supervisor is disqualified from appointment, and that the divisional board will not normally appoint as examiner individuals previously closely associated with the candidate or his or her work, representatives of any organisation sponsoring the candidate's research, representatives of any organisation at which a candidate dispensed from residence under the provisions of cl.1 above, is based, or former colleagues of the candidate. In particular, an examiner, whether internal or external, who has played a significant part in advising the candidate is inappropriate and particularly so where the collaboration has led to the publishing of joint papers by the candidate and the examiner. It is accepted that examiners will usually be acquainted with the supervisor, and sometimes the candidate, and that this in itself is not a bar to acting as an examiner. Dispensation from this rule should be sought from the Head of Division through the departmental Director of Graduate Studies.

4. BIOLOGICAL SCIENCES (PLANT SCIENCES AND ZOOLOGY)

All research students will be admitted to the status of Probationer Research Student in the first instance. Individuals may hold this status for a maximum of four terms. The provisions for extension to this time limit are set out in the Regulations of the Education Committee, §4. Candidates should discuss with their supervisors whether to apply for transfer to M.Sc. status or to D.Phil. status, and the most appropriate time at which to apply. It is possible to transfer to M.Sc. status initially and thereafter to D.Phil. status if this is appropriate.

1. *Admission of students to the status of Student for the M.Sc. by Research*

Applicants should submit the material specified in Sect. VII. A. §3, cl. 1; the board does not normally require any further test under §3, cl. 2. Candidates may obtain full details from the Director of Graduate Studies.

2. *Admission of students to the status of Student for the Doctor of Philosophy*

The form of written work to be submitted by candidates for admission as Students for the Doctor of Philosophy, and the manner of its examination, as required by

Sect. VIII, §3, cl. 2, shall be determined by the board acting through the candidate's department or sub-department. Details may be obtained from the Director of Graduate Studies.

3. *Confirmation for Status of Student for the Doctor of Philosophy*

The status of Students for the Doctor of Philosophy will be confirmed by the board under the provisions of Sect. VIII, §4, cl. 2, when it has received a certificate from the candidate's head of department that he or she is continuing satisfactorily to conduct research. Details may be obtained from the Director of Graduate Studies.

4. *Theses*

D.Phil. theses should normally be not more than 50,000 words in length (approximately 170 sides of A4 paper), exclusive of bibliography, appendices, diagrams, and tables. In exceptional circumstances the permission of the board can be sought to exceed this limit, but in no case may a thesis be longer than 75,000 words.

A set of scientific papers prepared as for publication, but not necessarily yet published, that concern a common subject may constitute an acceptable thesis, provided that with the addition of an Introduction, General Discussion, and General Conclusions they constitute a coherent body of work. Such papers should either be incorporated as typescript pages or as offprints bound in to the body of the thesis. Papers written in collaboration should not be included unless the greater part of the work is directly attributed to the candidate himself or herself, and the supervisor so certifies. Joint papers may however be included as appendices in a thesis.

Candidates with some published work may also include that as part of a traditional thesis, normally as an appendix.

Approval to submit a thesis using this format must be sought in advance from the appropriate Director of Graduate Studies.

5. MATHEMATICAL SCIENCES

1. *Admission to the status of Probationer Research Student*

Applicants (other than those from overseas) will be notified individually if they are required to attend for interview before a decision is taken on an application for admission.

2. *Admission to the status of Student for the Degree of Master of Science by Research*

A Probationer Research Student may apply for transfer to M.Sc. status at any time within four terms of admission to the status of Probationer Research Student. Assessment for transfer shall be by oral examination. Two persons appointed by the board shall conduct the examination.

3. *Admission to the status of Student for the Degree of Doctor of Philosophy*

(i) Any person seeking transfer to the status of D.Phil. student must apply to the board, which will approve such application only if two (or, in exceptional cases, three) assessors appointed by the board shall have certified

(a) that they have considered the written work submitted by the applicant and are satisfied that it demonstrates a capability of producing research work of the requisite standard and presenting the findings clearly; and

(b) that together they have interviewed the candidate and satisfied themselves that the planned programme of research is one that may be profitably undertaken at Oxford and that the candidate has a good knowledge and understanding of the work that is likely to be needed to embark on the programme.

(ii) Before making application to the board for transfer to the status of D.Phil. student, the applicant shall, in consultation with his or her supervisor, prepare a body of written work which shall be submitted as evidence of suitability for transfer.

(iii) Applications shall be in one of two categories:

Category A (open to students who have had no previous experience of research work, and normally all candidates in the Department of Computer Science.)

In this category the written work submitted shall consist of a short dissertation on a topic selected in consultation with the supervisor, the preferred length being of between twenty-five and fifty typed pages (or fifteen to thirty printed pages of TEX, depending on font used).

Students in Category A should apply to transfer from the status of Probationer Research Student to the status of Student for the degree of Doctor of Philosophy between the second and fourth term after admission as a research student. Students with no previous experience of research work are advised to apply in the third term after admission. Cases to defer application for the transfer of status must be made by the candidate's supervisor to the departmental Director of Graduate Studies by the end of the fourth full-term after admission. Approval will only be granted in exceptional cases. The provisions governing deferral are set out in the Regulations of the Education Committee, §4. A form of application for the assessment together with a form of application for transfer should be sent to the Graduate Office, MPLS Division, 9 Parks Road. The applicant should include with the application a brief description of the proposed subject of research for the D.Phil. degree and a brief statement (courses attended, texts and publications studied etc.) setting out the steps taken to ensure that he or she has the knowledge and understanding likely to be necessary to embark on the planned research work. The applicant should also name a date (not later than four weeks before the start of the Full Term following the date of application (applications made in vacation to be counted as if they had been made in the following term)) by which time he or she undertakes to make available two (or in exceptional cases three) copies of the written work supporting the application.

A student whose first application for transfer to D.Phil. status under Category A is not approved, shall be permitted to make one further application, and shall be granted an extension of time for one term if this is necessary for the purposes of making the application. A candidate failing to secure a Category B transfer to D.Phil. status will be allowed to apply for transfer under Category A.

Category B (open to applicants who have had previous experience of research work; it is expected that this will include many students who have successfully completed a taught master's course.This category is only available to candidates in the Department of Computer Science in exceptional circumstances with the approval of the Director of Graduate Studies.)

In this category the written work submitted with the application may consist of either

(a) a thesis or dissertation produced in connection with another course of research or study; or

(b) work that has been accepted for publication in a learned journal or journals; or

(c) other work which is in the opinion of the supervisor of comparable standing.

Students under Category B will make applications immediately after admission to Probationer Research Student status. A form of application for assessment together with a form of application for transfer together with two copies of the written work, should be sent to the Graduate Office, MPLS Division, 9 Parks Road. In exceptional cases a third copy may be required. The applicant should include with the application a brief description of the proposed subject of research for the D.Phil. degree and a brief statement (courses attended, texts and publications studied, etc.) setting out the steps taken to ensure that he or she has the knowledge and understanding likely to be necessary to embark on the planned research work.

(iv) In both types of application, on receipt of a form of application for assessment the board will appoint two (or in exceptional cases, three) members of the faculty to advise the board on the suitability of the applicant for transfer. Having considered the work submitted they shall arrange to interview the applicant to assess his/her suitability. They shall subsequently report to the board as to whether or not they are satisfied that the conditions described in clause 3(i) above have been met.

(v) On receipt of the report from the board's advisers, and after due consideration of any supervisor's reports that are available the board shall determine

(*a*) that the application be approved; or

(*b*) that the application be rejected, but that the student be allowed to apply for transfer to the status of Student for the Degree of M.Sc. by Research; or

(*c*) that the candidate make one further application (under Category A).

4. *Transfer from status of Student for the Degree of Master of Science by Research to status of Student for the Degree of Doctor of Philosophy*

(i) Any person seeking transfer to the status of a D.Phil. student must apply to the board, which will approve such application only if two (or, in exceptional cases, three) persons appointed by the board shall have certified:

(*a*) that they have considered written work submitted by the applicant and are satisfied that it demonstrates a capability of producing research work of the requisite standard and presenting the findings clearly; and

(*b*) that together they have interviewed the candidate and satisfied themselves that the planned programme of research is one that may be profitably undertaken at Oxford and that he or she has a good knowledge and understanding of the work that is likely to be needed to embark on the programme.

(ii) Before making application to the board for transfer to the status of D.Phil. student, the applicant shall in consultation with his/her supervisor prepare a body of written work which shall be submitted as evidence of suitability for transfer.

(iii) Application for transfer from M.Sc. status to D.Phil. student status shall consist of a short dissertation on a topic selected in consultation with the supervisor, the preferred length being of between twenty-five and fifty typed pages (or fifteen to thirty printed pages of TEX, depending on fount used), or a part-written thesis.

Application may be made at any time up to the ninth term after admission. A form of application for assessment together with a form of application for transfer should be sent to the Graduate Office, MPLS Division, 9 Parks Road. The applicant should include with the application a brief description of the proposed subject of research for the D.Phil. degree and a brief statement (courses attended, texts and publications studied etc.) setting out the steps taken to ensure that he or she has the mathematical knowledge and understanding likely to be necessary to embark on the planned research work. The applicant should also name a date (not later than four weeks before the start of the Full Term following the date of application (applications made in vacation to be counted as if they had been made in the following term)) by which time he or she undertakes to make available two (or in exceptional cases three) copies of the written work in support of the application.

A student whose first application for transfer from M.Sc. by Research status to D.Phil. status is not approved, shall be permitted to make one further application, and shall be granted an extension of time for one term if this is necessary for the purposes of making the application.

(iv) On receipt of a form of application for assessment the board will appoint two (or in exceptional cases, three) members of the faculty, neither of whom shall normally be the applicant's supervisor, to advise the board on the suitability of the applicant for transfer. Having considered the work submitted they shall arrange to interview the applicant to assess suitability. They shall subsequently report to the board as to whether or not they are satisfied that the conditions described in clause (i) above have been met.

(v) On receipt of the report from the board's assessors, and after due consideration of any supervisor's reports that are available the board shall determine that the application be approved; or that the application be rejected.

5. *Confirmation of D.Phil. status*

Confirmation of D.Phil. Student status, which will normally take place by the end of the eighth term after that in which the candidate was admitted as a Probationer Research Student, will take the form of an oral examination with two assessors appointed by the board, based on the candidate's own written report of progress.

The assessors shall recommend to the board either that D.Phil. status be confirmed or that one further application may be made, normally within one term of the original application. An extension of time for one term shall be granted if this is necessary for the purposes of making the application. If D.Phil. status is not confirmed, the second application shall normally be made by the end of the tenth term after that in which the candidate was admitted as a Probationer Research Student. Two assessors appointed by the board shall require evidence of progress such as written work and shall indicate to the student precisely what is required. A second oral examination may be held.

If, after considering a candidate's second application for confirmation of status, the board concludes that the student's progress does not warrant this, it may approve his or her transfer to the status of Student for the Degree of Master of Science by Research.

6. *Thesis*

Where some part of the thesis is not solely the work of the candidate or has been carried out in collaboration with one or more persons, the candidate shall submit a clear statement of the extent of his or her own contribution.

In *Computer Science*, the text of a thesis submitted for the Degree of D.Phil shall not exceed 250 pages of A4, single-spaced in normal size type, but there is no limit in references, diagrams, tables of empirical data or other forms of computer output, etc. Most theses are between 150 and 200 pages, though what is normal depends on the topic. Theses on certain topics in theoretical computer science tend to be shorter; those that rely on the collection and interpretation of empirical data presented as evidence may be closer to the upper limit.

In *Mathematics* and in *Statistics*, the text of theses submitted for the Degree of D.Phil. shall not exceed 200 pages, A4 size, double-spaced in normal-size type, but there is no limit on references, numerical tables, diagrams, computer output, etc. The normal length of a thesis, however, is nearer 100 pages (exclusive of the material defined above).

7. *D.Phil. in Software Engineering*

For students registered on the programme as Probationary Research Students or *D.Phil.* Students on or before *1 October 2008*

The regulations for this degree are set out at Section 8, below.

6. PHYSICAL SCIENCES

1. *Master of Science by Research*

Applicants for admission as students for the Degree of Master of Science by Research shall in addition to the requirements of Sect. VII. A, §3, cl. 1, be required to undertake such other tests as the department concerned, acting through the candidate's head of department or sub-department shall determine. The Notes of Guidance provided by the department or sub-department will give details of these requirements.

2. *Doctor of Philosophy*

The form of written work to be submitted by candidates for admission as Students for the Degree of Doctor of Philosophy, and the manner of its examination, as required by Sect. VIII, §3, cl. 2, shall be determined by the department concerned, acting through the candidate's head of department or sub-department. The notes of guidance provided by the department or sub-department will give details of these requirements. All candidates will be examined orally.

3. *Confirmation of status of students for the Degree of Doctor of Philosophy*

The status of Students for the Degree of Doctor of Philosophy will be confirmed by the board under the provisions of Sect. VIII, §4, cl. 1, when it has received a certificate from the candidate's head of department or sub-department that he or she is continuing satisfactorily to conduct research. The candidate and the supervisor will be required to provide a clear indication of the proposed time-table for submission of the thesis.

4. *Theses*

(*a*) **Longer abstracts: Earth Sciences, Chemistry, and Engineering**

Candidates for the Degrees of M.Sc. and D.Phil. in Earth Sciences must submit with their theses, in addition to the abstracts of them required of all candidates of up to 300 words, three copies of a longer abstract of not more than 1,500 words for the M.Sc. and 2,500 for the D.Phil., one copy of which shall be bound into the copy of the thesis which, if the application for leave to supplicate for the degree is successful, will be deposited in the Bodleian Library.

Candidates for the Degrees of M.Sc. and D.Phil. in *Chemistry* or *Engineering* may if they wish submit with their theses, in addition to the abstract of them required of all candidates, a longer abstract of not more than 1,500 words for the M.Sc. and 2,500 for the D.Phil.. Should such an abstract be submitted, a copy of it must be bound into the copy of the thesis which, if the application for leave to supplicate for the degree is successful, will be deposited in the Bodleian Library. The fuller abstract may be bound into the other two copies of the thesis if candidates so desire.

(*b*) **Word limits**

Theses submitted by candidates in *Materials* shall not exceed 25,000 words for the M.Sc. and 40,000 words for the D.Phil., A4 size, double-spaced, but there is no limit on references, diagrams, tables, photographs, computer programmes, etc.

Theses submitted by candidates for the Degree of D.Phil. in *Physics* (except *Theoretical Physics*) must not exceed 250 pages, A4 size, double spaced in normal-size type (elite), the total to *include* all references, diagrams, tables, etc.

The text of theses submitted for the degree of D.Phil. in *Theoretical Physics* must not exceed 150 pages as defined above.

Theses submitted by candidates for the Degree of M.Sc. in Physics must not exceed 150 pages as defined above.

Theses submitted by candidates in *Engineering Science* must not exceed 250 pages for the Degree of D.Phil. or 200 pages for the Degree of M.Sc. They should be double spaced on A4 paper, in normal size type (Times New Roman, 12 point), the total to *include* all references, diagrams, tables, appendices, etc.

The text of theses submitted for the Degree of D.Phil. in *Earth Sciences* must not exceed 250 pages as defined above, but there is no limit on diagrams, tables, etc.

In special circumstances the Graduate Studies Committee of the appropriate faculty may, on application made *before* the thesis is submitted, grant leave to exceed the limit by a stated amount. Applications to exceed these limits must explain why the candidate believes the nature of the thesis is such that an exception should be made, and must be supported by the supervisor.

7. DEGREE OF DOCTOR OF PHILOSOPHY IN THE: CENTRE FOR DOCTORAL TRAINING IN HEALTHCARE INNOVATION; DOCTORAL TRAINING CENTRE AT THE LIFE SCIENCES INTERFACE; DOCTORAL TRAINING CENTRE IN SYSTEMS BIOLOGY; INDUSTRIAL DOCTORATE CENTRE IN SYSTEMS APPROACHES TO BIOMEDICAL SCIENCES; FUSION DOCTORAL TRAINING NETWORK; DOCTORAL TRAINING CENTRE IN CYBER SECURITY.

1. *General regulations*

These regulations shall apply to all research students registered on the above named doctoral training programmes, irrespective of the division or department they are based within for their research project. In these regulations the above named doctoral training programmes are described as Doctoral Training Centre Programmes.

The provisions of the following regulations shall apply, except as specifically provided below: Regulations for Admission as a Probationer Research Student; Regulations for the Degree of Master of Science by Research, Regulations for the Degree of Doctor of Philosophy (§1-7); General Regulations of the Education Committee governing the examination of students for the degrees of M.Sc. by Research, M.Litt. and D.Phil., and concerning the maintenance of the register of graduate students; and the Special Regulations of Divisional and Faculty Boards concerning the status of Probationer Research Student and the degrees of M.Litt., M.Sc. by Research, and D.Phil. Mathematical, Physical and Life Sciences Division; and Medical Sciences Division, depending on the department and division in which the student carries out their research.

For the purposes of these regulations 'Board' shall mean the Mathematical, Physical and Life Sciences Divisional Board, or the Medical Sciences Divisional Board, depending on the department and division in which the student carries out their research.

2. *Register of Probationer Research Students*

The board may grant a student suspension from the Register of those admitted to the status of Probationer Research Student or deprive a student of his or her status; and in such cases it shall at all times follow procedures determined by the Education Committee by regulation. The board may also reinstate a student to the Register, provided that the total number of terms a student has spent as a Probationer

Research Student has not exceeded seven terms in the case of a student on the Doctoral Training Centre Programme.

3. *Probationer Research Student Status*

The regulations governing Probationer Research Student Status set out in the Regulations of the Education Committee, §4, apply to those holding the status of Probationer Research Students in the Doctoral Training Centres.

The maximum number of terms that a student on a four-year Doctoral Training Centre Programme may hold the status of Probationer Research Student under §4 cl.9 and §4 cl.10 (i)(a) is six terms, including the term in which the student was admitted. A Probationer Research Student on a Doctoral Training Centre Programme shall normally apply for admission to D.Phil. status after a minimum of five terms and no longer than six terms.

The Education Committee regulations applying to a Probationer Research Student on a Doctoral Training Centre Programme that govern applications for transfer from Probationer Research Student Status are set out under §4 cl.6; and extensions to the maximum number of terms specified above are set out under §4 cl.7.

A Probationer Research Student on a Doctoral Training Centre Programme shall cease to hold such status in accordance with the Education Committee regulations under §4.10 (i)–(iii).

4. *Confirmation of Status as a Student for the Degree of Doctor of Philosophy*

A candidate on a Doctoral Training Centre Programme who has been admitted to the status of Student for the Degree of Doctor of Philosophy must apply to the board for confirmation of his or her status as a D.Phil. Student by the end of the ninth full-term after admission as a research student, and not normally earlier than the eighth term after that in which he or she was initially admitted to the status of a Probationer Research Student or to the status of a student for another higher degree of the University. A Student for the Degree of Doctor of Philosophy shall cease to hold such status unless it has been confirmed within nine terms of his or her admission to that status, in accordance with §4 cl.5.

5. *Other requirements for students for the Degree of Philosophy following a Doctoral Training Centre D.Phil. programme*

A full-time Student for the Degree of Doctor of Philosophy following a Doctoral Training Centre Programme may hold that status for twelve terms. If such a student has been prevented by exceptional circumstances from completing his or her thesis, the board shall have power to grant and extension of time for a period or periods, not exceeding nine terms in all, to be determined by the board. Applications for such extension of time shall be made through the Registrar not later than the term in which the student is due to apply for permission to supplicate.

A Student for the Degree of Doctor of Philosophy following a Doctoral Training Centre Programme shall cease to hold that status if:

(i) he or she shall have been refused permission to supplicate for the Degree of Doctor of Philosophy; or

(ii) the board concerned shall in accordance with the Regulations for the Degree of Doctor of Philosophy, Part A., §2, cl. 3, and with the provisions set down by regulation by the Education Committee and after consultation with the student's college and supervisor, have deprived the student of that status;

(iii) he or she shall have been transferred under the relevant provision to another status;

(iv) he or she shall have failed to complete his or her thesis within twelve terms or within such further extension of time as may have been granted by the board concerned.

8. DEGREE OF DOCTOR OF PHILOSOPHY IN THE OXFORD INTERDISCIPLINARY BIOSCIENCE DOCTORAL TRAINING PARTNERSHIP

1. *General regulations*

The Oxford Interdisciplinary Bioscience Doctoral Training Partnership shall be   5
under the joint supervision of the Boards of the Mathematical, Physical, and Life
Sciences Division, and the Medical Sciences Division, which shall appoint a
Management Board to run the programme. In these regulations, the above named
doctoral training programme is described as the Doctoral Training Partnership
Programme.   10

2. These regulations shall apply to all research students registered on the Oxford
Interdisciplinary Bioscience Doctoral Training Partnership Programme, irrespective
of the division or department they are based within for their research project.

The provisions of the following regulations shall apply, except as specifically
provided below: Regulations for Admission as a Probationer Research Student;   15
Regulations for the Degree of Master of Science by Research, Regulations for the
Degree of Doctor of Philosophy (§1–7); General Regulations of the Education
Committee governing the examination of students for the degrees of M.Sc. by
Research, M.Litt. and D.Phil., and concerning the maintenance of the register of
graduate students; and the Special Regulations of Divisional and Faculty Boards   20
concerning the status of Probationer Research Student and the degrees of M.Litt.,
M.Sc. by Research, and D.Phil. Mathematical, Physical and Life Sciences Division;
and Medical Sciences Division, depending on the department and division in which
the student carries out their research. For the purposes of these regulations 'Board'
shall mean the Mathematical, Physical and Life Sciences Divisional Board, or the   25
Medical Sciences Divisional Board, depending on the department and division in
which the student carries out their research.

3. *Register of Probationer Research Students* The board may grant a student
suspension from the Register of those admitted to the status of Probationer
Research Student or deprive a student of his or her status; and in such cases it shall   30
at all times follow procedures determined by the Education Committee by regulation.
The board may also reinstate a student to the Register, provided that the total
number of terms a student has spent as a Probationer Research Student has not
exceeded seven terms in the case of a student on the Doctoral Training Partnership
Programme.   35

4. *Probationer Research Student Status* The regulations governing Probationer
Research Student Status set out in the Regulations of the Education Committee, §4
apply to those holding the status of Probationer Research Students in the Doctoral
Training Partnership Programme. The particular clauses in those regulations that
apply to students in Doctoral Training Centres shall apply equally to students in the   40
Doctoral Training Partnership Programme.

The maximum number of terms that a student on the four-year Doctoral Training
Partnership Programme may hold the status of Probationer Research Student under
§4 cl.9 and §4 cl.10 (i)(a) is six terms, including the term in which the student was
admitted. A Probationer Research Student on the Doctoral Training Partnership   45
Programme shall normally apply for admission to D.Phil. status after a minimum of
five terms and no longer than six terms.

The Education Committee regulations applying to a Probationer Research Student
on the Doctoral Training Partnership Programme that govern applications for
transfer from Probationer Research Student Status are set out under §4 cl.6; and   50
extensions to the maximum number of terms specified above are set out under §4 cl.7.

A Probationer Research Student on the Doctoral Training Partnership Programme shall cease to hold such status in accordance with the Education Committee regulations under §4.10 (i)–(iii).

5. *Confirmation of Status as a Student for the Degree of Doctor of Philosophy* A candidate on a Doctoral Training Partnership Programme who has been admitted to the status of Student for the Degree of Doctor of Philosophy must apply to the board for confirmation of his or her status as a D.Phil. Student by the end of the ninth full-term after admission as a research student, and not normally earlier than the eighth term after that in which he or she was initially admitted to the status of a Probationer Research Student or to the status of a student for another higher degree of the University. A Student for the Degree of Doctor of Philosophy shall cease to hold such status unless it has been confirmed within nine terms of his or her admission to that status, in accordance with §4 cl.5.

6. *Other requirements for students for the Degree of Doctor of Philosophy following the Doctoral Training Partnership Programme.* A full-time Student for the Degree of Doctor of Philosophy following the Doctoral Training Partnership Programme may hold that status for twelve terms. If such a student has been prevented by exceptional circumstances from completing his or her thesis, the board shall have power to grant and extension of time for a period or periods, not exceeding nine terms in all, to be determined by the board. Applications for such extension of time shall be made through the Registrar not later than the term in which the student is due to apply for permission to supplicate. A Student for the Degree of Doctor of Philosophy following the Doctoral Training Partnership Programme shall cease to hold that status if:

(i) he or she shall have been refused permission to supplicate for the Degree of Doctor of Philosophy; or

(ii) the board concerned shall in accordance with the Regulations for the Degree of Doctor of Philosophy, Part A., §2, cl. 3, and with the provisions set down by regulation by the Education Committee and after consultation with the student's college and supervisor, have deprived the student of that status;

(iii) he or she shall have been transferred under the relevant provision to another status;

(iv) he or she shall have failed to complete his or her thesis within twelve terms or within such further extension of time as may have been granted by the board concerned.

9. D.Phil IN SOFTWARE ENGINEERING

For students registered on the programme as Probationary Research Students or D.Phil. Students on or before 1 October 2008

1. *Admission*

Students to whom these regulations apply will have been admitted as Probationary Research Students or D.Phil. Students under the regulations of the Continuing Education Board as they were at the time of their admission. Students were admitted to study on a part-time basis only.

2. *Attendance requirements*

Students are required to attend for a minimum of thirty days of university-based work each year, to be arranged with the agreement of their supervisor, for the period that their names remain on the Register of Graduate Studies unless individually dispensed by the Mathematical, Physical and Life Sciences Divisional Board.

3. *Admission/transfer to D.Phil. status*

(*a*) Applicants must demonstrate that they are capable of producing research work of the requisite standard and presenting the findings clearly; and that their planned programme of research is one that may be profitably undertaken at Oxford; and that they have a good knowledge and understanding of the work that is likely to be needed to embark on the programme.   5

(*b*) Students who have successfully completed the relevant Oxford Masters degree deemed an acceptable prerequisite by the board, shall normally apply for admission to D.Phil. status up to the twelfth term after their initial admission as a graduate student.   10

(*c*) Students who hold the status of Probationary Research Student, shall normally apply for admission to D.Phil. status after a minimum of six terms and no longer than twelve terms.

(*d*) Admission to D.Phil. status may be made conditional on such requirements as the board may impose.   15

(*e*) Applicants should specify the date by which they undertake to make available two (or in exceptional cases, three) copies of the written work in support of the application. Applicants should do so not later than four weeks before the start of the full term in which they wish to be assessed. Application for transfer should be sent to the Director of Graduate Studies, the Computing   20
Laboratory, Wolfson Building, Parks Road, Oxford OX1 3QD.

(*f*) Applications for transfer to D.Phil. status shall be accompanied by:

(1) a short dissertation on a topic selected in consultation with the supervisor, or a part-written thesis, the preferred length being of between 25 and 50 typed pages.   25

(2) The applicant should include with the application a brief description of the proposed subject of research for the D.Phil. degree and a brief statement setting out the steps taken to ensure that he or she has the knowledge and understanding likely to be necessary to embark on the planned research work.

(3) two copies of a confidential report from the supervisor, which should be   30
sent by the supervisor direct to the Director of Graduate Studies, the Computing Laboratory.

The Director of Graduate Studies shall send one copy of the written work and the confidential report to each of the assessors appointed by the board.

(*g*) Candidates should also note that while as precise a definition of the subject   35
should be given as is possible at this stage of their work, they are not bound to follow the statement precisely, but may reformulate their plan in the light of further study. If reformulation goes so far as to require alteration of the title of the thesis as approved, however, they should seek permission of the relevant board to alter it.   40

(*h*) Candidates shall be assessed by two assessors appointed by the board, neither of whom will normally be the student's supervisor. The assessors shall certify that they have considered the written work submitted by the applicant and interviewed the applicant. The assessors should also provide a written report of the application to the board for approval of their recommendation. In cases   45
where the assessors decide that the application is not of the required standard to transfer to D.Phil. status their written report should outline the areas in which the application is judged to fall short of the required standard.

(*i*) A student who is unsuccessful may be given one further opportunity to apply for transfer (within the limit of twelve terms).   50

4. *Confirmation of D.Phil. status*

(*a*) Assessors are appointed by the board to assess whether a candidate's work on their thesis is developing satisfactorily and that they may be considered ready to be examined within three further terms. D.Phil. status must be confirmed before a candidate may submit their thesis for examination for the degree of D.Phil..

(*b*) Application for confirmation of D.Phil. status, with statements of support from the candidate's society and supervisor, shall normally be presented to the Director of Graduate Studies, the Computing Laboratory, not earlier than four weeks before the end of the twelfth term, and at the latest by four weeks before the end of the eighteenth term, after admission to the status of Probationer Research Student or to status of student for another higher degree of the University.

(*c*) Application for confirmation of D.Phil. status shall normally be accompanied by:

(1) the candidate's own written report of progress, stating how much of the thesis is complete and how much remains to be done (with an estimate of the completion date);

(2) a statement of the title of the thesis and a specimen chapter;

(3) a confidential report from the supervisor which should be sent directly to the Director of Graduate Studies, the Computing Laboratory.

The Director of Graduate Studies should send the written work and the confidential report to the interviewer appointed by the board.

(*d*) Candidates shall be assessed by two assessors appointed by the board, neither of whom will normally be the student's supervisor. The assessment shall include an oral examination. The assessors shall also provide a written report of the application to the board for approval of their recommendation. In cases where the assessors decide that the application is not of the required standard to warrant confirmation of D.Phil. status, their written report should outline the areas in which the application is judged to fall short of the required standard.

(*e*) A student who is unsuccessful may be given one further opportunity to apply for confirmation (within the statutory limit).

5. *Theses*

Theses shall not normally exceed 200 pages, A4 size, in normal sized type.

Any thesis exceeding these limits is liable to be rejected on that ground. It is recognised that in special circumstances it will be necessary for leave to be granted to exceed this limit by a stated amount. In particular it is recognised that the inclusion of essential edited source material, whether as an appendix or as a main part of the thesis, presents special problems in regard to length; and the board will be prepared to consider applications for edited material to be excluded from the word limit otherwise placed on the thesis. Leave to exceed these limits for other reasons will be given only in the most special cases and on the recommendation of the supervisor. Any application for permission to exceed the limit should be submitted with a detailed explanation and statement of the amount of excess length requested, and with a covering letter from the supervisor. Applications should be made as soon as possible and may not be later than the last day of the fifth week of the term before that in which applications made for appointment of examiners.

C. MEDICAL SCIENCES DIVISION

1. ADMISSION OF RESEARCH STUDENTS

All research students will be admitted to the status of Probationer Research Student in the first instance.

2. PROBATIONER STATUS

Students may hold the status of Probationer Research Students for a maximum of four terms. Candidates should discuss with their supervisors whether to apply for transfer to M.Sc. status or D.Phil. status, and the most appropriate time at which to apply. In exceptional circumstances the Board may grant up to two terms' extension to this deadline.

Students on the programmes listed below may hold Probationer Research Student status for a maximum of six terms:

D.Phil. in Cardiovascular Science (BHF)

D.Phil. in Chromosome and Developmental Biology

D.Phil. in Genomic Medicine and Statistics

D.Phil. in Infection, Immunology and Translational Medicine

D.Phil. in Ion Channels and Disease

D.Phil. in Structural Biology

In exceptional circumstances the Board may grant up to one term's extension to this deadline.

3. ADMISSION OF STUDENTS TO THE STATUS OF STUDENT FOR THE DEGREE OF MASTER OF SCIENCE BY RESEARCH

Candidates should submit the statement from the supervisor and the statement from the candidate's society as specified by the regulations governing the degree of Master of Science by Research. In addition, candidates should submit an outline of their project of no more than 500 words and a timetable for completion. Candidates will be required to give a presentation on their work. Further guidance on the form of the written submission and the form of the presentation should be sought from the departmental Director of Graduate Studies.

4. ADMISSION OF STUDENTS TO THE STATUS OF STUDENT FOR THE DEGREE OF DOCTOR OF PHILOSOPHY

Candidates should submit the statement from the supervisor and the statement from the candidate's society as specified by the regulations governing the degree of Doctor of Philosophy. In addition, candidates should submit a report of no more than 3,000 words which should include an abstract, introduction, results, discussion and future plans including a proposed timetable for completion. Students may add appendices as necessary of up to a further 2,000 words including methods, figure legends, and references. Further guidance on the form of report should be sought from the departmental Director of Graduate Studies.

5. PERMISSION TO WORK IN A WELL-FOUND LABORATORY OUTSIDE OF OXFORD

Applicants who are admitted to undertake research under the supervision of the Medical Sciences Divisional Board may, exceptionally, be permitted by the Divisional Board to undertake their research in a well-found laboratory outside of Oxford. Such candidates shall be dispensed from the residence requirements, but shall be required to attend Oxford for such instruction as the Division and department concerned shall require. Before admitting a candidate on this basis, the department concerned shall be required to satisfy itself and the Divisional Board that appropriate arrangements are in place for approving all aspects of the student's academic work, including the following:

    (i) the availability of the equipment and facilities necessary for the project in the agency concerned;

    (ii) the existence of a wider collaboration between the department and the agency in which the student is based;

    (iii) the subject of their doctoral studies;

    (iv) satisfactory induction procedures;

    (v) satisfactory health and safety arrangements;

    (vi) satisfactory supervision arrangements, to include specification of a minimum number of contact hours between student and supervisor, which shall include not less than two face-to-face meetings between student and supervisor, for a total of at least 8 hours, each term;

    (vii) satisfactory arrangements for monitoring the student's progress within the department;

    (viii) provision for the student to attend Oxford for such instruction as the division and department shall require.

6. CONFIRMATION OF STATUS OF STUDENTS FOR THE DEGREE OF DOCTOR OF PHILOSOPHY

Candidates shall normally apply for confirmation of status in the eighth term from their admission as a research student, and no later than the ninth term from their admission as a research student. The Board strongly advises candidates to apply for confirmation of status a minimum of one term before they intend to submit their thesis.

Candidates should submit the statement from the supervisor and the statement from the candidate's society as specified by the regulations governing the degree of Doctor of Philosophy. Candidates must include a statement detailing the skills training that they have undertaken. This paperwork should be accompanied by a full contents list for the thesis, and include the milestones of any remaining work to be undertaken, and dates for the submission of draft chapters to the supervisor(s) for comment.

Candidates shall be required to deliver a formal, oral presentation of their work. The presentation will be attended by two assessors who are deemed to have the appropriate expertise to comment on the content of the project. The assessors will be appointed by the candidate's department; at least one assessor will have had no direct supervisory involvement with the student.

The assessors will report to the Board on the candidate's suitability for confirmation of D.Phil. status. This report will be based on the information provided in the statement from the supervisor and the statement from the candidate's society as specified by the regulations governing the degree of Doctor of Philosophy, and in the supplementary statement from the candidate in conjunction with their presentation. In cases where confirmation of status is not recommended the assessors will attach a short written report detailing where the work submitted falls below the standard required.

7. THESES

For students admitted prior to 1 October 2009.

A set of scientific papers that concern a common subject may exceptionally constitute an acceptable thesis, but only if with the addition of an introduction, general discussion, and general conclusion they constitute a continuous theme. Joint papers may not be included unless the supervisor certifies the extent of the candidate's own contribution. Joint papers may be included as appendices in a thesis. Approval to submit a thesis using this format should be sought from the divisional board (via the Chair, Medical Sciences Graduate Studies Committee, c/o Medical Sciences Office, Level 3 John Radcliffe Hospital, Oxford OX3 9DU) as soon as possible after admission and not later than the date at which the appointment of examiners is requested.

Candidates with some published work may also include that as part of a traditional thesis, normally as an appendix.

The length and scope of theses in each subject area in the Division is set out in the Notes for the Guidance of Graduate Students issued by the Medical Sciences Board.

8. BIOCHEMISTRY: JOINT PROGRAMME WITH THE SCRIPPS RESEARCH INSTITUTE

1. General

(*a*) The University may, in collaboration with The Scripps Research Institute, La Jolla, California (TSRI), through the Department of Biochemistry, admit a candidate to the full-time status of Probationer Research Student, and, on successful transfer of status, of Student for the Degree of Doctor of Philosophy (or, exceptionally, Master of Science) jointly with TSRI and permit such a student to supplicate for the degree of Doctor of Philosophy (or, exceptionally, Master of Science by Research) jointly awarded with TSRI.

(*b*) The Board shall, in consultation with TSRI, elect for the supervision of the programme a Joint Programme Committee, which shall have the power to arrange research supervision, lectures, and other instruction, and shall be responsible to both institutions. The programme directors in each institution will be responsible to the Oxford-Scripps Joint Programme Committee ('the Joint Programme Committee'), membership of which will consist of faculty members from both institutions.

(*c*) All students accepted on this programme will be admitted simultaneously as students of both institutions, and will be subject to the regulations and guidelines of both institutions, **except** as provided in the following regulations. Students admitted to the programme will be matriculated as students of the University of Oxford at the beginning of the programme, which is of five years' duration, irrespective of whether they begin their studies at Oxford or at TSRI; and, for the purpose of University of Oxford regulations, numbers of terms shall be reckoned from the term in which the student is admitted to the joint programme, irrespective of whether they begin their studies at Oxford or at TSRI.

(*d*) The joint programme shall be subject to the following detailed regulations for the conduct of the programme and the admission of students, and the granting of leave to supplicate shall be subject to those regulations and any other relevant provisions agreed by the University and TSRI.

(*e*) For the purposes of these regulations 'Board' shall mean the Medical Sciences Divisional Board of the University of Oxford or any body or person authorised to act on its behalf in these matters.

(*f*) For the purposes of these regulations, 'term' shall mean a term as prescribed in the University of Oxford's Regulations on the Number and Length of Terms, and when the required time in these regulations is reckoned in years, a year shall be deemed to be the equivalent of three terms. (For example, if five years are required, fifteen terms shall be understood.)

(*g*) In the event of a conflict between the regulations and guidelines of the two institutions, the procedure for resolution described in the Inter-Institutional Agreement between the two institutions will apply.

2. Admission

(*a*) All students will be admitted to the status of Probationer Research Student (Joint Oxford/TSRI) in the first instance. The provisions of the University of Oxford Regulations for Admission as a Probationer Research Student, §§1, 2, relating to the Status of Probationer Research Student and to the Admission of Candidates as Probationer   5
Research Students, apply **except** that the Board will discharge its duties under these regulations following consultation with TSRI, through the Joint Programme Committee.

(*b*) Although students may hold this status for a maximum of six terms, candidates should normally apply to transfer from Probationer Research Student (Joint Oxford/TSRI) status in the third term after admission as a research student.   10

3. Induction

All students admitted to the programme will undertake an induction session at TSRI, and thereafter will start the full programme of study at Oxford or TSRI in accordance with the regulations set out above and below. Students starting at Oxford will be required to attend the induction course in the Department of Biochemistry.   15

4. Residence and other requirements

(*a*) With the exception of the references to part-time students, the provisions of the University of Oxford Regulations for Admission as a Probationer Research Student, §4, relating to the Residence and other Requirements of Probationer Research Students, apply to Probationer Research Students (Joint Oxford/TSRI).   20

(*b*) With the exception of the references to part-time students, the provisions of the University of Oxford Regulations for the Degree of Doctor of Philosophy, §6, relating to Residence and other Requirements for Students for the Degree of Doctor of Philosophy, apply to Doctor of Philosophy (Joint Oxford/TSRI) students **except** that he or she shall be deprived of that status if he or she shall have failed to complete   25
his or her thesis within fifteen terms or within such further extension of time as may have been granted by the Board (see 7(*f*) below).

(*c*) In line with the regulations referred to in (*a*) and (*b*) above which make provision that 'time spent outside Oxford during term as part of an academic programme approved by Council shall count towards residence for the purpose of   30
this clause', study at TSRI shall qualify as residence under these regulations; the normal patterns of study, after completion of the induction session under 3. above, shall be as follows:

  (i) *For students commencing the programme at Oxford*: Students will study in Oxford for up to the first three years of the programme, during which period   35
  they will be subject to the regulations and disciplinary procedures of the University of Oxford, and for the remaining years at TSRI.

  (ii) *For students commencing the programme at TSRI*: Students will study at TSRI for up to the first three years of the programme, and for the remaining years in Oxford, during which period they will be subject to the regulations and   40
  disciplinary procedures of the University of Oxford.

5. Fees

The following provisions of Appendix I, Regulations on Financial Matters, apply:

§1 *Fees payable at matriculation*

§2 *Fees payable by candidates on registration, entry for an examination, application for*   45
leave to supplicate, or resubmission of a thesis for certain degrees

§5 *In respect of certificates and personal data*

§6 *Composition fees payable by members of the University*, except that students who begin their study at TSRI shall pay no composition fee in respect of the first two years of their programme.   50

Students who begin their study at Oxford will therefore be liable for composition fees at the HomeEU or Overseas rate as appropriate in respect of their first nine terms of residence under the terms of section 3, thereafter being exempt under the terms of section 4, of §6; and students who begin their study at TSRI will be liable for composition fees at the HomeEU or Overseas rate as appropriate in respect of their final nine terms of residence (noting in both cases that residence, under the terms of 4(*c*) above, includes study at TSRI).

6. Supervision

The Department of Biochemistry and TSRI, in consultation through the Joint Programme Committee, will each appoint academic supervisors for each student, who will be required to make termly reports on students' progress while the student remains in the joint degree programme, i.e. until the thesis has been accepted for the award of the Doctor of Philosophy (Joint Oxford/TSRI).

(i) For Probationer Research Students (Joint Oxford/TSRI), the provisions of the University of Oxford Regulations for Admission as a Probationer Research Student, §3, relating to Supervision of Probationer Research Students, apply.

(ii) For Doctor of Philosophy (Joint Oxford/TSRI) Students, the provisions of the University of Oxford Regulations for the Degree of Doctor of Philosophy, §5, relating to Supervision of Students for the Degree of Doctor of Philosophy, apply.

(iii) For all students, the provisions of the Memorandum of Guidance for Supervisors and Research Students will apply (see 11 below).

7. Student progress

(*a*) *Completion of coursework at TSRI*

(i) All students will be required to undertake a sequence of taught coursework in connection with the proposed field of research at TSRI and to pass the associated examinations in accordance with the TSRI requirements unless exempted from this requirement under (ii) following.

(ii) Candidates may, in advance of registration for the joint degree programme, apply to the Joint Programme Committee for exemption from all or part of this requirement in recognition of study and examinations previously undertaken.

(iii) A student who fails any element of the coursework will be required to resit the examination, or to pass an equivalent element, before proceeding to the next stage of the programme.

(*b*) *Admission of students to the status of Student for the Degree of Doctor of Philosophy (Joint Oxford/TSRI)*

(i) Students who begin their programme of study at TSRI will apply for transfer of status according to the stated requirements, i.e. by entering the TSRI qualifying examination for PhD candidacy, having completed and passed the taught coursework elements as provided under (*a*)(i) and (*a*)(iii) above.

(ii) For students who begin their programme of study at the University of Oxford, the provisions of the University of Oxford Regulations for the Degree of Doctor of Philosophy, §3, Admission of Candidates to the Status of Student for the Degree of Doctor of Philosophy, shall apply, and **in addition**, unless exempted under the provisions of (*a*)(ii) above, such students will be required to undertake the sequence of taught coursework at TSRI, and to pass the coursework examinations, as provided under (*a*)(i) and (*a*)(iii) above, when they have moved to TSRI.

(iii) Application for transfer of status should normally take place during the third term after admission to the programme. However, if a student undertakes work in two or more different laboratories within the particular institution during the first year, application for transfer of status may be delayed until after the third term, but *must* be made before the end of the sixth term. A candidate whose first application for transfer to Doctor of Philosophy (Joint Oxford/TSRI) status is not approved shall be permitted to make one further application, following the procedures laid down in the University of Oxford Regulations for the Degree of Doctor of Philosophy, §3, cll.1 to 4, and shall be granted an extension of time for one term if this is necessary for the purposes of making the application.

(iv) The recommendations open to the assessors of the application for the *first time* shall be:

Transfer to Doctor of Philosophy (Joint Oxford/TSRI) status; or

Transfer to Master of Science by Research (Joint Oxford/TSRI) status; or

Rejection of application to transfer to either Doctor of Philosophy (Joint Oxford/TSRI) status or Master of Science by Research (Joint Oxford/TSRI) status, with the opportunity for submission of a second application, if the candidate chooses.

(v) The recommendations open to the assessors of the application for the *second time* shall be:

Transfer to Doctor of Philosophy (Joint Oxford/TSRI) status; or

Transfer to Master of Science by Research (Joint Oxford/TSRI) status; or

Rejection of application to transfer to either Doctor of Philosophy (Joint Oxford/TSRI) status or Master of Science by Research (Joint Oxford/TSRI) status, with consequent removal from the Register of Graduate Students.

(vi) It is possible to transfer to M.Sc. (Joint Oxford/TSRI) status initially and thereafter apply to transfer to Doctor of Philosophy (Joint Oxford/TSRI) status if this is appropriate.

(*c*) *Admission of students to the status of Student for the Degree of Master of Science by Research (Joint Oxford/TSRI): Guidelines for transfer to M.Sc. status*

If, exceptionally, it is agreed that the student should apply for transfer to the status of student for the degree of Master of Science by Research (Joint Oxford/TSRI), the procedures set out in the programme guidelines will be followed.

The decision to work towards the Degree of M.Sc. by Research (Joint Oxford/TSRI) should be reached in discussion with the supervisor(s) concerned and agreed by the Director of Graduate Studies at Oxford and the Dean of Graduate Studies at TSRI.

(*d*) *Confirmation of Status of Student for the Degree of Doctor of Philosophy (Joint Oxford/TSRI)*

With the exception of the references to part-time students, the provisions of the University of Oxford Regulations for the Degree of Doctor of Philosophy, §4, Confirmation of Status as a Student for the Degree of Doctor of Philosophy, will apply to Doctor of Philosophy (Joint Oxford/TSRI) students. The status of a Student for the Degree of Doctor of Philosophy (Joint Oxford/TSRI) will be confirmed under the provisions above, on the basis of supporting statements from the supervisors from both institutions, when it has been confirmed by the Director of Graduate Studies in consultation with the Dean of Graduates at TSRI that the student is continuing satisfactorily to conduct research. Confirmation of Doctor of

Philosophy (Joint Oxford/TSRI) status exists to give faculties and departments an opportunity to monitor the direction and progress of a student's work in the period between transfer of status and submission of thesis. It intends both to assess the progress of the research work and to support the work of a student and his or her supervisor(s) by ensuring that the Director of Graduate Studies and the Dean of Graduates at TSRI are aware of the state of the research in progress, and the likely timetable for submission. Application for confirmation of Doctor of Philosophy (Joint Oxford/TSRI) status should be made normally after the ninth term, and *must* be made before the fifteenth term; the detailed arrangements for application at Oxford and at TSRI are as set out in the programme guidelines.

A candidate whose first application for confirmation of his or her status is not approved shall be permitted to make one further application following the procedures laid down in this section, normally within one term of the original application, and shall be granted an extension of time for one term if this is necessary for the purposes of making the application. If, after considering a candidate's second application for confirmation of status, the Board concludes that the student's progress does not warrant this, the Board may approve his or her transfer to the status of Student for the Degree of Master of Science by Research (Joint Oxford/TSRI).

(*e*) *Termination of status*

(i) *Probationer Research Student (Joint Oxford/TSRI)*

    The provisions of the University of Oxford Regulations for Admission as a Probationer Research Student, §4, cl.6, apply. Decisions made under these provisions will be the subject of consultation between the two institutions through the Joint Programme Committee.

(ii) *Student for the Degree of Doctor of Philosophy (Joint Oxford/TSRI)*

    The provisions of the University of Oxford Regulations for the Degree of Doctor of Philosophy, §6, cl.8, apply **except** that he or she shall be deprived of that status if he or she shall have failed to complete his or her thesis within fifteen terms or within such further extension of time as may have been granted by the Board (see (*f*) below). Decisions made under these provisions will be the subject of consultation between the two institutions, through the Joint Programme Committee.

(*f*) *Extension of time*

Student for the Degree of Doctor of Philosophy (Joint Oxford/TSRI)

If a full-time Student for the Degree of Doctor of Philosophy (Joint Oxford/TSRI) has held that status for fifteen terms, but has been prevented by exceptional circumstances from completing his or her thesis, the Board shall have power to grant an extension of time for a period or periods, not exceeding nine terms in all, to be determined by the Board. Applications for such extension of time shall be made through the relevant Graduate Studies Assistant at the University of Oxford not later than the term in which the student is due to apply for permission to supplicate; applications made under these provisions will be the subject of consultation between the two institutions through the Joint Programme Committee.

8. Suspension of Graduate Students from the Register

The provisions of the General Regulations of the Education Committee Governing the Examination of Students for the Degrees of M.Sc. by Research, M.Litt., and D.Phil. and Concerning the Maintenance of the Register, cl. 4, apply; action proposed under these provisions will be the subject of consultation between the two institutions through the Joint Programme Committee.

9. Removal of Graduate Students from the Register

The provisions of the General Regulations of the Education Committee Governing the Examination of Students for the Degrees of M.Sc. by Research, M.Litt., and D.Phil. and Concerning the Maintenance of the Register, cl. 5, apply; action proposed under these provisions will be the subject of consultation between the two institutions through the Joint Programme Committee.

10. Reinstatement of Graduate Students to the Register

The provisions of the General Regulations of the Education Committee Governing the Examination of Students for the Degrees of M.Sc. by Research, M.Litt., and D.Phil. and Concerning the Maintenance of the Register, cl. 6, apply; action proposed under these provisions will be the subject of consultation between the two institutions through the Joint Programme Committee.

11. Memorandum of Guidance for Supervisors and Research Students

The provisions of the General Regulations of the Education Committee Governing the Examination of Students for the Degrees of M.Sc. by Research, M.Litt., and D.Phil. and Concerning the Maintenance of the Register, cl. 7, apply.

12. Complaints and appeals

(*a*) While at Oxford students may seek advice on matters of concern from a number of individuals who have responsibility for different aspects of the well-being of graduate students; these include supervisors, Director of Graduate Studies, college tutors, the student's college and departmental advisors, head of department, and college head. If resolution of a complaint or appeal is not possible by means of procedures in place within the Department of Biochemistry, then a student may refer the matter to the Proctors for formal consideration, under the Statutes and Regulations of the University of Oxford relating to the powers of the Proctors.

(*b*) While at TSRI, students may seek advice on matters of concern from numerous individuals and a committee who have responsibility for aspects of the well-being of graduate students. These individuals include the thesis research advisor, the student-chosen Advisory and Qualifying Examination Committee (consisting of at least two members of the TSRI faculty, one Oxford representative, and the student's advisor at TSRI) that meets annually or when requested by the student or a faculty member, and the Dean and the Associate Deans. In the absence of a resolution of a conflict, the student is permitted to present his or her case to the President of TSRI who will make every reasonable effort to resolve the conflict.

13. Appointment of examiners

(*a*) A Student for the Degree of Doctor of Philosophy (Joint Oxford/TSR) who has fulfilled the applicable requirements set out in the preceding clauses of this section and whose status has not expired, may apply to the Board for the appointment of examiners and for leave to supplicate for the Degree of Doctor of Philosophy (Joint Oxford/TSRI).

(*b*) Such applications should be made to the Board through the relevant Graduate Studies Assistant at the University of Oxford. They shall include:

(i) a certificate from the student's college that the application has the approval of that college;

(ii) a certificate from the supervisors that the student has pursued his or her course of study in Oxford and at TSRI in accordance with the preceding clauses of this section;

(iii) a statement by the candidate of what part, if any, of the thesis has already been accepted, or is currently being submitted, for any degree or diploma or certificate or other qualification in the University of Oxford, TSRI, or elsewhere;

(iv) a statement by the candidate that the thesis is his or her own work, except where otherwise indicated.

(*c*) The supervisors shall consult with the candidate concerning possible examiners, and forward to the Board the names of suggested examiners together with details of any special considerations which the candidate wishes to make known about any potential examiners.

(*d*) The candidate shall also submit, to the University of Oxford, for examination, at such time and in such format as provided by the General Regulations of the Education Committee governing the examination of students for the degrees of M.Sc. by Research and Doctor of Philosophy, and by the Special Regulations of the Board as set out in this section:

(i) two printed or typewritten copies of a thesis;

(ii) two printed or typewritten copies of an abstract of the thesis, which shall not normally exceed 300 words.

Submission of additional copies of the thesis, and abstract as appropriate, to the Thesis Committee at TSRI shall be according to the TSRI guidelines.

(*e*) On receipt of an application the Board shall appoint two examiners, in consultation with The Scripps Research Institute, neither of whom shall be the candidate's supervisor. The appointment of examiners by the Board shall be in accordance with the provisions of the Education Committee's Notes of Guidance for Research Degrees, i.e. that it is an absolute requirement for examinations for the Degree of Doctor of Philosophy that one examiner should be external to the University of Oxford, and that this is the preferred convention for the Degree of M.Sc. by Research. In addition, both the examiners appointed by the Board for the Degree of Doctor of Philosophy (Joint Oxford/TSRI) and for the Degree of Master of Science by Research (Joint Oxford/TSRI) should be external to TSRI. For examinations which are undertaken at TSRI (see 15(*a*) below), the examiners shall act together with such members of the candidate's Thesis Committee as shall be determined by TSRI, and for examinations which are undertaken at Oxford, up to two members of the candidate's Thesis Committee, as determined by TSRI, shall take part in the examination; the student's TSRI thesis advisor may attend the examination on a non-participatory basis.

The duties of the examiners (jointly with the members of the Thesis Committee) shall be:

(i) on behalf of the University of Oxford and TSRI, to consider the thesis and the abstract of it submitted by the student, provided that they shall exclude from consideration in making their report any part of the thesis which has already been accepted, or is being concurrently submitted for any degree or other qualification in this University or TSRI or elsewhere, and shall have the power to require the candidate to produce for their inspection the complete thesis so accepted or concurrently submitted;

(ii) to examine the student orally in the subject of his or her thesis;

(iii) to satisfy themselves by examination (oral, written, or both) whether the student possesses a good general knowledge of the particular field of learning within which the subject of the thesis falls;

(iv) to report to the Board through the relevant Graduate Studies Assistant at the University of Oxford on the scope, character, and quality of the work submitted;

(v) to return to the student the copies of the thesis and the abstracts thereof.

14. Theses

The provisions of the General Regulations of the Education Committee Governing the Examination of Students for the Degrees of M.Sc. by Research, M.Litt., and D.Phil. and Concerning the Maintenance of the Register, cll. 1, and 2, apply.

Theses for the Degree of Doctor of Philosophy (Joint Oxford/TSRI) should not normally be more than 50,000 words in length (amounting to approximately 170 sides of A4 paper), exclusive of bibliography, appendices, diagrams, and tables. In exceptional circumstances the permission of the Board can be sought to exceed this limit, but in no case may a thesis be longer than 75,000 words.

15. Conduct of Oral Examinations

(*a*) The oral examination may be held in either institution, as agreed by the student, the supervisors, and the Thesis Committee in consultation and as endorsed by the Joint Programme Committee, in a suitable institutional or college building. It shall, except in special circumstances, begin not earlier than 9 a.m. nor later than 5 p.m., and may be held in term or vacation. The examiners shall be responsible for informing the candidate of the final arrangements made and shall give reasonable time for the candidate to make himself or herself available. It shall be the duty of candidates to ensure that any letter addressed to them at their college or any other address which they have given is forwarded to them if necessary. The examiners shall allow reasonable time for receiving an acknowledgement from the candidate of their summons.

(*b*) Candidates may apply to the Board for the oral examination to be held not later than a certain date, provided that this date shall not be earlier than one calendar month after the date on which the thesis has been received at Oxford by the Examination Schools, or after the date on which the examiners have agreed to act, whichever is the later. If the Board is satisfied that there are special circumstances justifying this application, it will ask the examiners to make arrangements to enable the oral examination to be held within the period specified. In such cases the examiners, when invited to act, will be informed that the candidate has asked that the oral examination be held not later than a certain date, and acceptance of the invitation to examine will be on the understanding that they would seek to meet this request. If it is not practicable to meet the student's request, then the Board shall decide how to proceed.

(*c*) Notice of the examination shall be given in the University of Oxford in one of the following ways:

(i) It may be published in the *University Gazette* not later than the day before it is due to take place;

(ii) Not later than two days before the examination the examiners may inform the relevant Graduate Studies Assistant in writing; and post a notice in the Examination Schools; and if the examination is to be held in Oxford in a place other than the Examination Schools, post a notice also at the place of examination.

(*d*) The notice shall state the name of the candidate, the subject of the thesis, the place, day, and hour of the examination, and the names of the examiners. If an examination is held without the giving of notice required by this regulation it shall be invalid, unless the Proctors, on receipt of a written application from the examiners, shall determine otherwise. The student or his or her college, other society, or approved institution, may within fourteen days of the date of the Proctors' decision in respect of the granting of consent, appeal in writing to the Education Committee (who may nominate another member of the committee, other than one of the Proctors, to adjudicate the appeal).

(*e*) An examination held in Oxford may be attended by any member of the University in academic dress. Up to two members of the candidate's Thesis Committee, as determined by TSRI, may take part in the examination, and the student's TSRI thesis advisor may attend on a non-participatory basis, but otherwise no person who is not a member of the University may attend it except with the consent of the examiners. The Proctors, after consultation with the Board, may decide (either at their own discretion or at the request of the candidate or the supervisor(s) or the department) to forbid the attendance of any person or all persons (other than the examiners, including the agreed members of the candidate's Thesis Committee, and the candidate) or to impose any condition on attendance if and to the extent that such action is in their view necessary to protect the interests of the University or the candidate or both, and the examiners shall be informed accordingly and shall include this information in the notice of examination. The student or his or her college may within fourteen days of the date of the Proctors' decision appeal in writing to the Chair of the Education Committee (who may nominate another member of the committee, other than one of the Proctors, to adjudicate the appeal).

(*f*) Candidates are strongly recommended to take a copy of their thesis to the examination.

(*g*) If, owing to illness or other urgent and unforeseen cause, an examiner is unable to attend the examination, it shall be postponed to a later date; however, if, after appropriate consultation between the Department of Biochemistry and TSRI through the Joint Programme Committee, the Proctors are satisfied that postponement would be a serious hardship to the candidate, they may authorise another member of the Board to attend the examination as a substitute but such substitute shall not be required to sign the report containing the recommendation as described in 16 below. The Proctors shall determine what payment, if any, the substitute examiner shall receive.

(*h*) Oral examinations held at The Scripps Research Institute shall be subject to such detailed regulations of that institute as are relevant.

16. Recommendation of the examiners

Having completed the examination of a candidate *for the first time*, the examiners appointed by the Board and by TSRI may make any one of the recommendations (*a*), (*b*) or (*d*) below *only*. Having completed the examination of a candidate *who has revised and resubmitted his or her thesis*, the examiners may make any one of the recommendations (*a*) to (*f*). The recommendations are:

(*a*) That the Board should grant the candidate leave to supplicate for the Degree of Doctor of Philosophy (Joint Oxford/TSRI). In making this recommendation, the examiners must include in their report statements that:

- the student possesses a good general knowledge of the particular field of learning within which the subject of the thesis falls;

- the student has made a significant and substantial contribution in the particular field of learning within which the subject of the thesis falls;

- the thesis is presented in a lucid and scholarly manner;

- in their opinion the thesis merits the Degree of Doctor of Philosophy (Joint Oxford/TSRI);

- The student has presented a satisfactory abstract of the thesis.

Examiners shall bear in mind that their judgement of the substantial significance of the work should take into account what may reasonably be expected of a capable and diligent student after completing the five-year joint programme. If the examiners are satisfied that the candidate's thesis is of sufficient merit to qualify for the degree but

consider, nevertheless, that before the thesis is deposited the candidate should make minor corrections (which are not sufficiently substantial to justify reference back for re-examination), they must require the candidate to correct the thesis to their satisfaction before they submit their report. If the candidate has not completed these corrections within three calendar months of the date of receipt of the list of minor   5
corrections from the examiners, his or her name shall be removed by the relevant Graduate Studies Assistant at the University of Oxford on behalf of the Registrar from the Register of Students for the Degree of Doctor of Philosophy (Joint Oxford/ TSRI); however, the Board may, on good cause shown by the candidate, grant an extension of time of three further calendar months in which the candidate may fulfil   10
this requirement before the removal of his or her name from the Register. No subsequent extension shall be granted, but it shall be open to a candidate who has failed to fulfil this requirement within those three or six months in total, as the case may be, to apply to the Board for reinstatement as a Student for the Degree of Doctor of Philosophy (Joint Oxford/TSRI), with the support of his or her society and   15
supervisor(s), upon submission to the relevant Graduate Studies Assistant of a copy of his or her thesis incorporating the required corrections, and upon payment of such reinstatement fee as is prescribed by Council at that time. Permission to supplicate shall not be granted until this fee has been paid.

(*b*) That the Board should offer the candidate a choice between (i) reference of the   20
thesis back to him or her in order that he or she may revise it for re-examination for the Degree of Doctor of Philosophy (Joint Oxford/TSRI), and (ii) leave to supplicate for the Degree of Master of Science (Joint Oxford/TSRI), as appropriate, on the basis that the thesis has not reached the standard required for the Degree of Doctor of Philosophy (Joint Oxford/TSRI) but has nevertheless reached that required for the   25
Degree of Master of Science (Joint Oxford/TSRI). If the Board adopts this recommendation, and the student chooses to revise the thesis for re-examination for the Degree of Doctor of Philosophy (Joint Oxford/TSRI), the student shall retain the status and obligations of a Student for the Degree of Doctor of Philosophy (Joint Oxford/TSRI) and shall be permitted to apply again for the appointment of exam-   30
iners in accordance with the provisions of the University of Oxford Regulations for the Degree of Doctor of Philosophy, §7, relating to Examination of Students for the Degree of Doctor of Philosophy. If such permission shall have been given by the Board during a vacation, it shall be deemed to have been given in the term preceding that vacation.   35

(*c*) That the Board should refer the student's thesis back in order that he or she may present it for re-examination for the Degree of Master of Science (Joint Oxford/ TSRI) only. If the Board adopts the recommendation the student shall be transferred forthwith to the status of Student for the Degree of Master of Science (Joint Oxford/ TSRI), and shall be permitted to apply for permission to supplicate for the Degree of   40
Master of Science (Joint Oxford/TSRI) in accordance with the provisions of the University of Oxford Regulations for the Degree of Master of Science by Research, §6, relating to Examination of Students for the Degree of Master of Science by Research. If such permission shall have been given by the Board during a vacation, it shall be deemed to have been given in the term preceding that vacation. The word   45
limit for a thesis submitted under this provision shall be that specified for the Doctor of Philosophy (Joint Oxford/TSRI) under 14 above.

(*d*) That the Board should refer the student's thesis back in order that he or she may present it for re-examination either under (*b*) above for the Degree of Doctor of Philosophy (Joint Oxford/TSRI) or, if the student chooses, under (*c*) above for the   50
Degree of Master of Science (Joint Oxford/TSRI) only. The Board shall adopt such a recommendation only if it is fully satisfied that the thesis as it stands is not of the standard required for the Degree of Doctor of Philosophy (Joint Oxford/TSRI), nor

for the Degree of Master of Science (Joint Oxford/TSRI), but that the candidate could reach the standard required for the Degree of Doctor of Philosophy (Joint Oxford/TSRI). If such permission shall have been given by the Board during a vacation, it shall have been deemed to have been given in the term preceding that vacation.

(*e*) That the thesis has not reached the standard required for the Degree of Doctor of Philosophy (Joint Oxford/TSRI) but has nevertheless reached that required for Master of Science (Joint Oxford/TSRI), and that the candidate may be granted leave to supplicate for that degree on the basis of the thesis as it stands.

(*f*) That the student's application for leave to supplicate should be refused.

If the examiners recommend reference back of the student's application under (*b*), (*c*) or (*d*) above, they shall annex to their report to the Board a statement for transmission to the candidate setting out the respects in which the thesis falls below the standard for the degree in question, and what changes are necessary for it to reach that standard. In exceptional circumstances, examiners of a thesis submitted *for the first time*, and notwithstanding a recommendation under (*b*) or (*d*) above, may certify that they are unable to indicate how the thesis might be changed, within the time allowed, in order to reach the standard required for the degree of Doctor of Philosophy (Joint Oxford/TSRI).

On receipt of the examiners' report, the Board shall reach a decision on whether to accept the examiners' recommendation; no candidate shall be given leave to supplicate for the degree of Doctor of Philosophy (Joint Oxford/TSRI) unless the examiners have made the statements required in clause (*a*) above. A candidate who has been granted leave to supplicate by the Board shall be required to submit to the Examination Schools a copy of his or her thesis, incorporating any amendments or corrections required by the examiners and approved by the Board, with a view to deposit in the Bodleian or other appropriate library of the University of Oxford. Permission to supplicate shall in all cases be conditional upon fulfilment of this requirement.

In an exceptional case in which the Board is unable to accept the examiners' recommendation, or in which the examiners cannot reach an agreed recommendation, the Board shall have power to appoint one or two new examiners as it deems necessary (subject to consultation with the Joint Programme Committee), to conduct such further examination of the candidate as the Board may require. The Board shall make a report on any such case to the Education Committee.

The Board may exempt a candidate who is being re-examined under the provisions of clauses (*b*)–(*e*) above from the oral examination, provided that the examiners are able to certify that they are satisfied without examining the candidate orally that they can recommend to the Board in the terms required by clause (*a*) above that he or she be given leave to supplicate for the Degree of Doctor of Philosophy (Joint Oxford/TSRI).

It shall be the duty of the relevant Graduate Studies Assistant, on behalf of the Registrar, to notify the candidate of the Board's decision as soon as may be. The relevant Graduate Studies Assistant shall also be responsible for publishing at the end of each academic year the names of those candidates to whom permission to supplicate has been granted during that year, together with a statement of the subject of the thesis written by each.

When, on the conclusion of the investigation of a complaint made by a candidate, the Proctors recommend that a candidate be re-examined, the Board shall have power to hold a new examination.

9. D.PHIL IN THE MEDICAL SCIENCES DOCTORAL TRAINING CENTRE

1. General regulations

These regulations shall apply to all students registered for

1. D.Phil. in Biomedical and Clinical Sciences
2. D.Phil in Cardiovascular Science (BHF)
3. D.Phil. in Chromosome and Developmental Biology
4. D.Phil. in Genomic Medicine and Statistics
5. D.Phil. in Infection, Immunology and Translational Medicine
6. D.Phil. in Ion Channels and Disease
7. D.Phil. in Structural Biology

within the Medical Sciences Doctoral Training Centre, irrespective of the division or department they are based within for their research project.

Programme 1 above is a three-year programme. Programmes 2–7 above are four-year programmes.

The provisions of the following regulations shall apply, except as specifically provided below: Regulations for Admission as a Probationer Research Student; Regulations for the Degree of Master of Science by Research, Regulations for the Degree of Doctor of Philosophy (§1–7); General Regulations of the Education Committee governing the examination of students for the degrees of M.Sc. by Research, M.Litt. and D.Phil., and Concerning the Maintenance of the Register of Graduate Students; and the Special Regulations of Divisional and Faculty Boards concerning the status of Probationer Research Student and the degrees of M.Litt., M.Sc. by Research, and D.Phil.

For the purposes of these regulations 'Board' shall mean the Medical Sciences Divisional Board.

2. Register of Probationer Research Students

The Board may grant a student suspension from the Register of those admitted to the status of Probationer Research Student or deprive a student of his or her status; and in such cases it shall at all times follow procedures determined by the Education Committee by regulation. The Board may also reinstate a student to the Register, provided that the total number of terms a student has spent as a Probationer Research Student has not exceeded six terms in the case of a student on a four-year Medical Sciences Doctoral Training Centre programme.

3. Probationer Research Student Status

A student on a four-year Medical Sciences Doctoral Training Centre programme may hold the status of Probationer Research Student for a maximum of six terms, including the term in which the student was admitted. In exceptional circumstances the Board may grant up to one term's extension to this deadline.

4. Confirmation of Status as a Student for the Degree of Doctor of Philosophy

A student on a four-year Medical Sciences Doctoral Training Centre programme who has been admitted to the status of Student for the Degree of Doctor of Philosophy must apply to the Board for confirmation of his or her status as a D.Phil Student not later than the tenth term and normally during the ninth term after admission to the programme. In all other respects the procedure for confirmation of status of such students will follow the procedures for confirmation of status of students within the Medical Sciences Division.

5. Other requirements for students for the Degree of Doctor of Philosophy following a Medical Sciences Doctoral Training Centre four-year D.Phil Programme

A full-time Student for the Degree of Doctor of Philosophy following a four-year Medical Sciences Doctoral Training Centre programme may hold the status of a registered research student for a maximum of twelve terms. If such a student has been prevented by exceptional circumstances from completing his or her thesis by that time, the Board shall have power to grant an extension of time for a period or periods, not exceeding six terms in all, to be determined by the Board. Applications for such extension of time shall be made through the Registrar not later than the term in which the student is due to apply for permission to supplicate.

A full-time Student for the Degree of Doctor of Philosophy following a four-year Medical Sciences Doctoral Training Centre Programme shall cease to hold that status if: (i) he or she shall have been refused permission to supplicate for the Degree of Doctor of Philosophy; or (ii) the Board concerned shall in accordance with the Regulations for the Degree of Doctor of Philosophy, Part A., §2, cl. 3, and with the provisions set down by regulation by the Education Committee and after consultation with the student's college supervisor, have deprived the student of that status; (iii) he or she shall have been transferred under the relevant provisions to another status; (iv) he or she shall have failed to complete his or her thesis within twelve terms or within such further extension of time as may have been granted by the Board concerned.

D. SOCIAL SCIENCES DIVISION

I. ANTHROPOLOGY

1. *Transfer from M.Phil. status to D.Phil. status*

A student who has obtained an M.Phil. may only be admitted direct to D.Phil. status on condition that the research topic is a development of the research contained in the M.Phil. thesis or if the student can otherwise demonstrate his or her competence to undertake the proposed research, and that appropriate supervision can be provided.

2. *Transfer from Probationer Research Student status to M.Litt. or D.Phil. status*

For transfer of status, the student should submit two copies in typescript of a substantial piece of written work relevant to the proposed thesis. The work should not exceed 20,000 words excluding bibliography and any appendixes, but including notes, and should consist of, or incorporate, a detailed research proposal. The student will be required to show that the research already undertaken shows promise of the ability to produce a satisfactory M.Litt. or D.Phil. thesis, as the case may be, on the intended topic. Students should submit their work to the Departmental Office, Institute of Social and Cultural Anthropology, not later than the end of Trinity *full term* after the Michaelmas Term in which they were admitted. An extension of one term (i.e. to the end of the Michaelmas full term in the year after the student was admitted) may be granted in exceptional circumstances. In the case of students admitted in other terms, submission should take place by the end of the third term (i.e. full term) after admission, with the possibility of an extension for a further one term (i.e. to the end of full term) in exceptional circumstances. (NB: alternative provisions apply to probationer research students with coursework, as described in paragraph 3, below). The student's submission will be assessed by two assessors appointed by the Teaching Committee of the School of Anthropology and Museum Ethnography, to which they will submit a written report. In exceptional cases one assessor, but in the case of joint supervision not both, may be the applicant's supervisor. A student whose first application is unsuccessful may be given one further opportunity to apply for transfer of status, for which an extension of one term is automatically granted.

All probationer research students must give presentations on their proposed research projects to the class designated for that purpose or an agreed equivalent to qualify for transfer of status. They will also be expected to attend relevant courses on training and methods, as agreed with, and directed by, their supervisor(s).

3. *Probationer research students with coursework*

Probationer research students entering the Institute of Social and Cultural Anthropology should normally have a prior, full taught-course degree in social or cultural anthropology at either the graduate or undergraduate levels before being admitted to this status. Exceptionally, however, students who have earned a distinction in either (1) a degree in a closely related subject that includes some social or cultural anthropology, or (2) a mixed degree in social or cultural anthropology and another closely related subject may be admitted directly to the status of probationer research student in anthropology. In addition to the standard requirements for probationer research students in anthropology (and except as varied below), students entering the above Institute via this route should satisfy the following conditions:

(1) they enter the Institute as research students in the Michaelmas term of their first academic year and not in any other term;

(2) the topic of their proposed research lies in the general thematic or geographical area covered by their prior degree;

(3) they undertake a full course of eight tutorials in general anthropology, with essays, in the first Michaelmas term of their admission as probationer research students. Three of the essays produced for these tutorials are to be submitted for assessment as described below;

(4) they follow a course in an option (area or topic) offered to master's students in the above Institute in the first Hilary and, where provided for, Trinity terms after their admission as research students. The option must be relevant to their proposed research if one is available (area or topic), except that they may not repeat an option in which they have been examined as part of a prior degree in the University of Oxford. If the student cannot take such an option for either of these reasons, a free choice may be allowed with the agreement of the Director of Graduate Studies for Anthropology or his or her delegate. The student shall write one essay of tutorial standard on the option for assessment as described below;

(5) the proposed supervisor has given his or her approval of this course of action in writing to the Director of Graduate Studies for anthropology or, in case the latter is the proposed supervisor, to the Director of the Institute of Social and Cultural Anthropology.

Note: the work specified in (3) and (4) above shall constitute Part I of the assessment for transfer from probationer research student to full D.Phil student, and the text for transfer that the student will be required to prepare on the basis of his or her proposed research (in the same manner as for ordinary probationer research students in anthropology) shall constitute Part II of the said assessment.

Students following these arrangements must pass an assessment of the work they have carried out under (3) and (4) above (Part I), which shall normally involve scrutiny of three tutorial essays and the option essay. This assessment shall be carried out at the same time as the standard assessment of the text on the proposed research (Part II). An extra assessor or assessors, one of whom in special cases may be the student's supervisor, may but need not be appointed to scrutinise the work carried out for Part I. The extra assessor(s), if any, need not be present at the assessment interview with the student, but should advise the assessors conducting the interview in writing beforehand of the standard of work achieved by the student in Part I.

Both parts of the assessment, i.e. Parts I and II as specified above, must be passed by the student, though not necessarily on the same occasion. If the student fails in either Part I or Part II, or both, he or she will be required to resubmit materials for, and pass, the relevant part(s) within one term of the original submission. Both elements in Part I, as described under (3) and (4) above, must be passed by the student.

The deadline for a student following this path to submit materials for assessment for upgrade to full status as a doctoral student shall normally be the fourth term after admission as a research student (i.e. the Michaelmas Term of the second year in the status of probationer research student). Such students are expected to start work on their text for upgrade during the Hilary term after their admission as probationer research students at the latest.

4. *Confirmation of Status as a student for the Degree of Doctor of Philosophy*

The provisions of the Regulations for the Degree of Doctor of Philosophy (§4) shall apply, except as specifically provided below.

Application for confirmation of D.Phil. status shall normally be made not earlier than the sixth term and not later than the ninth term from admission as a research student in the case of a student admitted first to the status of Probationer Research Student, and normally not earlier than the third term and not later than the sixth term from readmission in the case of a student admitted directly to D.Phil. status from an M.Phil. degree within the School of Anthropology and Museum Ethnography.

For students admitted directly to D.Phil. status from an M.Phil. degree within the School of Anthropology and Museum Ethnography before 1 October 2012:

(i) Application for confirmation of D.Phil. status shall normally be made not earlier than the sixth term and not later than the ninth term from readmission.

For students admitted directly to D.Phil. status from an M.Phil. degree within the School of Anthropology and Museum Ethnography before 1 October 2011:

(i) Application for confirmation of D.Phil. status shall normally be made not earlier than the fourth term and not later than the tenth term from readmission.

The Teaching Committee of the School of Anthropology and Museum Ethnography may in addition, and for good reason, permit a candidate to defer for a maximum of three terms his or her application for confirmation of status.

A student for the Degree of Doctor of Philosophy shall cease to hold such status unless it has been confirmed within nine terms of his or her admission if first admitted as a Probationer Research Student, or within six terms from readmission directly to D.Phil. status from an M.Phil. degree within the School of Anthropology and Museum Ethnography (or within a maximum of twelve terms or nine terms respectively where deferral has been approved in accordance with the paragraph above).

The student will be required to give evidence confirming that the research already carried out gives promise of the ability to produce a satisfactory D.Phil. thesis on the intended topic. For this purpose the applicant must submit: (a) a detailed outline of the whole of the proposed thesis, including an indication of the topics, theories, arguments etc. to be covered in individual chapters (as applicable); and (b) at least one and not more than two sample chapters. In the latter case, the student is advised to submit one chapter that is basically ethnographic in type (if applicable), the other concerning the more general comparative and/or theoretical issues with which the thesis deals, though this advice may be varied in consultation with the supervisor(s). The outline should not exceed 4,000 words, and the submitted chapters should not exceed 20,000 words in total. If these materials do exceed these limits, the assessors are under no obligation to read beyond them, though they are permitted to require the student to submit extra materials to help them in reaching a recommendation. The materials should be submitted, in two copies, to the Departmental Office, Institute of Social and Cultural Anthropology.

On receiving the application the Graduate Studies Committee of the School of Anthropology and Museum Ethnography shall appoint two assessors. In exceptional cases, one assessor may be the applicant's supervisor. The assessors shall read the script and interview the candidate before submitting to the Graduate Studies Committee of the School of Anthropology and Museum Ethnology a reasoned written report supporting their recommendation. A student whose first application is unsuccessful may be given one further opportunity to apply, following the procedures laid down, normally within one term of the original application, and may apply for an extension of time for one term if necessary for the purpose of making the application.

All D.Phil. students must give presentations on their research projects to the class designated for that purpose or an agreed equivalent to qualify for confirmation of status.

5. *Submission of theses*

D.Phil. theses submitted by the students in Anthropology must not exceed 100,000 words, including notes (but excluding bibliography, glossary, and appendices containing ethnographic material and archaeological evidence), unless for exceptional reasons and on the recommendation of the candidate's supervisor the Teaching Committee of the School of Anthropology and Museum Ethnography otherwise determines.

2. ARCHAEOLOGY

1. *General regulations*

These regulations shall apply to all students registered for the D.Phil. in Archaeology, the D.Phil. in Archaeological Science, and the D.Phil. in Classical Archaeology.

2. *Transfer from Probationer Research Student status to D.Phil. status*

This transfer shall normally take place not later than the fourth term after admission as a research student. The student will be required to show that the research already accomplished shows promise of the ability to produce a satisfactory D.Phil. thesis on the intended topic. For this purpose, the candidate must make an oral presentation of their work, and submit to the Archaeology Graduate Studies Committee two copies in typescript of a substantial piece of written work (of between 10,000 and 15,000 words) relevant to the proposed thesis, together with a research proposal. These should normally be submitted to the Graduate Studies Assistant at the School of Archaeology, by the Monday of the fifth week in the term in which the application is made. On receiving the application the Archaeology Graduate Studies Committee shall appoint two assessors, of whom neither shall normally be the student's supervisor. The assessors shall read the scripts and interview the candidate before submitting to the committee a reasoned written report supporting their recommendation. A student whose first application is unsuccessful may be given one further opportunity to apply for transfer, following the procedures laid down, and may apply for an extension of time for one term if necessary for the purpose of making the application.

3. *Confirmation of D.Phil. status*

The status of student for the Degree of Doctor of Philosophy shall be confirmed by the committee under the provisions of Sect. viii, § 4, cl. 1. Candidates should normally apply for confirmation of status by week five of their seventh term after admission as a research student. Candidates must make an oral presentation of their work, and submit a research outline, of approximately 1,000 words, a table of contents indicating how much work has been done on each section of the thesis to date, and a draft chapter or chapters of the thesis of no more than 10,000 words. The committee will appoint two assessors who will consider the applications and will normally interview candidates. A student whose first application is unsuccessful may be given one further opportunity to apply, following the procedures laid down, normally within one term of the original application, and may apply for an extension of time for one term if this is necessary for the purpose of making the application.

4. *Length of D.Phil. theses*

Theses submitted for the Degrees of D.Phil. in Archaeology, Archaeological Science and Classical Archaeology should not normally exceed 80,000 words, excluding bibliography and descriptive catalogue or similar factual matter.

3. **DEPARTMENT OF EDUCATION**

1. *Admission*

All students (whether studying on a full or part-time basis) are normally admitted as Probationer Research Students. A student admitted to study on a full-time basis is not permitted to change the basis of his or her study from full-time to part-time at any stage of his or her registration as a graduate student.

In assessing applications from candidates seeking to undertake a research degree through part-time study, the Graduate Studies Committee shall have regard to evidence that:

(i) the candidate has a minimum of three years' experience as a professional educator and is currently employed in an established post within an educational institution;

(ii) the candidate can meet the attendance requirements relating to part-time study and lives locally to the University;

(iii) the candidate has the written support of their present employer for their proposed course of study and its obligations;

(iv) the candidate's proposed topic of research is related to their present or intended professional work.

Attendance requirements (for part-time students)

Part-time research students are required to attend for a minimum of thirty days of university-based work each year, to be arranged with the agreement of their supervisor, for the period that their names remain on the Register of Graduate Students unless individually dispensed by the Department's Departmental Board.

2. Candidates with Probationer Research Student status, unless or until they have entered upon another status, or have been otherwise dispensed from some or all of the following requirements by the Graduate Studies Committee, are required to undertake the work set out below during the first year.

A first year student shall:

i. satisfactorily complete a course of lectures, seminars and classes, as determined in the Handbook for DPhil students and supervisors and supplemented by his or her supervisor;

ii. satisfactorily complete the First Year portfolio of work completed during the first year of PRS status.

3. *Transfer from Probationer Research Student status to D.Phil status*

This transfer shall normally take place not later than the fourth term after admission as either an M.Sc. in Educational Research Methodology student or Probationer Research Student. The student will be required to show that the research already accomplished shows promise of the ability to produce a satisfactory D.Phil thesis on the intended topic. For this purpose the student must submit to the Graduate Studies Committee of the Department of Education two copies in typescript of a substantial piece of written work as follows:

The submission should be about 10,000 words in length and must include:

   (i) a working title for the research

  (ii) an outline description/draft abstract of the research (one side of A4 paper)

 (iii) an introductory section which provides a rationale, conceptual framework and background for the research, drawing on relevant literature and theoretical perspectives

 (iv) a section which includes key research questions, the overall methodological approach and specific strategies and methods, ethical issues, and a brief preliminary description of planned data analysis, demonstrating evidence of a well thought out and well-argued research design; this may include a pilot study.

The following are also required, thought they are not included in the 10,000 word limit

  (v) CUREC form(s) as required and clear evidence of how commitment to responsible (ethical) conduct of research will be realised

 (vi) Risk assessment form including evidence that the student has considered carefully issues of safety in fieldwork

(vii) A clear timetable for the research which demonstrates that the project is feasible and practicable and can be completed within the timeframe

(viii) A list of references

 (ix) Evidence of presentation of work at a seminar (e.g. PPRS, Work in Progress, Research Group Seminar, etc.)

  (x) A supporting commentary which introduces the thesis and guides the readers specifically to aspects of the work which provide evidence of meeting the criteria listed (500-1000 words).

The Graduate Studies Committee of the Department of Education shall appoint two assessors who will interview the student and make a recommendation to the committee in an agreed written report. Candidates seeking to transfer to D.Phil Status will be expected during the interview to show evidence of research training through successful completion of the requirements of the Department's educational research methods course, unless specifically exempted from all or part of it. A candidate whose first application for transfer to D.Phil status is unsuccessful shall be permitted to make one further application to apply for transfer within one term. Those students who fail at the second attempt may be approved for transfer to M.Litt. status, or transfer to M.Sc. by Research status.

4. *Confirmation of Status*

Confirmation of Status shall normally take place not later than the seventh term after admission as either an M.Sc. in Educational Research Methodology student or a Probationer Research Student. It is intended to be a comprehensive monitoring of progress towards the final thesis.

Students' application for Confirmation of Status will be examined by two assessors appointed by the Graduate Studies Committee for this purpose. For this purpose the student must submit to the Graduate Studies Committee of the Department of

Education two copies in typescript of a substantial piece of written work of about 30,000 words as follows:

- (i) an abstract of the thesis (one side of A4 paper)
- (ii) an outline structure of the thesis, including chapter headings, a brief statement of the contents of each chapter (about 300-500 words for each chapter), which show how the chapters link together and develop the thesis
- (iii) the equivalent of two well-developed but draft chapters from the thesis in progress (one of the chapters should be a chapter presenting findings)
- (iv) a list of references (of work cited in the text submitted) **and** a bibliography of literature relevant to the study as a whole
- (v) a clear outline timetable detailing the work which has already been carried out, and the activities planned for the remaining stages, including a detailed timetable of the future work leading to submission

Candidates whose first application for confirmation of status is not approved shall be permitted to make one further application within one term.

5. *Thesis*

Theses submitted for the degree of D.Phil. should build on and develop the material submitted for Transfer of Status and Confirmation of Status.

A thesis for the Degree of M.Sc. by Research which exceeds 30,000 words, or a thesis for the Degree of M.Litt. which exceeds 50,000 words, or a thesis for the Degree of D.Phil. which exceeds 100,000 words, in each case including footnotes/endnotes but excluding appendices and references or bibliography, is liable to be rejected by the board unless the candidate has, with the support of his or her supervisor, secured the leave of the Department's Departmental Board to exceed this limit.

4. ECONOMICS, SOCIAL POLICY AND INTERVENTION, SOCIOLOGY, AND INTERNATIONAL DEVELOPMENT

1. *Transfer to M.Litt. (or M.Sc. by Research) or D.Phil. status*

Students in these subject areas will normally be expected to transfer out of Probationer Research status in their third or fourth term after admission. Applications should be submitted to the departmental Graduate Studies Committee and will comprise the following:

- (*a*) a transfer of status form, obtainable from the relevant Graduate Studies Assistant, signed by the candidate's supervisor and an appropriate college officer. The candidate should indicate clearly on the form the status to which he or she wishes to transfer; and
- (*b*) a provisional thesis title and a short outline statement of the proposed research topic, which should include sources and methods to be used; and
- (*c*) a piece of written work relevant to the thesis of between 5,000 and 7,000 words.

The Graduate Studies Committee will appoint two assessors, one of whom will normally be a member of the committee, except in cases where neither of the two most appropriate assessors is a member of the committee, who will read the work, examine the candidate orally, and submit a written report to the committee.

The committee will then decide whether transfer to the status applied for will be approved. In the case of applications to transfer to D.Phil. status where the committee is not satisfied that the candidate should be allowed to make the transfer it may approve admission to M.Litt. status, (or exceptionally to M.Sc. by Research Status) or approve an extension of time in order to allow the candidate to resubmit at a later date (but before the end of the sixth term after admission to Probationer Research status). The committee may request additional written work or other evidence, or appoint an additional assessor, whenever it is considered necessary.

Individual Graduate Studies Committees may require additional tests or forms of assessment to be completed. Candidates are advised to consult the Notes of Guidance for Graduate Students issued by each Graduate Studies Committee.

Any candidate who is admitted to M.Litt. status (or M.Sc. by Research Status) may subsequently apply for transfer to D.Phil. status before the end of the sixth term after admission to Probationer Research status. The committee will expect to see evidence of substantial developments in the progress of the research since the transfer to M.Litt status (or M.Sc. by Research Status) before this further transfer is approved.

Additional regulations for the Department of Economics

Probationer Research Students in Economics are required to take a qualifying examination, unless exempted from all or part of the examination by the appropriate Graduate Studies Committee, on the grounds of an appropriate previous graduate degree or substantial professional experience since graduation. The examination consists of the equivalent of five second year papers in the M.Phil. examination, where one first year M.Phil. paper is the equivalent of two second year papers, taken at the times set for that examination in Trinity Term. A student who does not achieve the required mark on a paper is automatically granted a two term extension to Probationer Research Student status and is allowed to resit that paper once in the following Trinity Term examination, unless a special dispensation is obtained from the Graduate Studies Committee.

Probationer Research Students are required to achieve a mark of 64 on each of the papers they sit in order to pass the Qualifying Examination. In exceptional circumstances the Graduate Studies Committee may exempt a student from having to pass the examination is he/she receives marks of 50 or above on each paper. All requests for exemption will require the strong support of the supervisor.

Additional regulations for International Development

Probationer Research Students in International Development who have been admitted to this status but who have not received appropriate postgraduate training in a relevant aspect of development studies or of research techniques for the social sciences may, with the formal approval of the Director of Graduate Studies, the Course Director of the course concerned, and the Graduate Studies Committee for the Department of International Development, be required to attend and pass successfully any course listed for the M.Phil. in Development Studies or appropriate course from another postgraduate degree at Oxford University.

This condition shall be conveyed to the student when the offer of a place is made and in such cases transfer to D.Phil. status shall not normally be permitted until this condition has been fulfilled.

2. *Confirmation of D.Phil. status*

Students who have been admitted to D.Phil. status must, not later than the ninth term or normally earlier than the sixth term after that in which he or she was initially admitted to the status of a Probationer Research Student or to the status of a student for another higher degree of the University, apply for confirmation of that status. Students would normally be expected to apply for confirmation of D.Phil. status before the end of their ninth term after admission to Probationer Research status.

Requirements for confirmation of status are:

(*a*) completion of the appropriate form, obtainable from the relevant Graduate Studies Assistant, signed by the supervisor and an appropriate college officer.

(*b*) a comprehensive outline of the treatment of the thesis topic including details of progress made and an indication of the anticipated timetable for submission.

(*c*) two draft chapters intended to form part of the final thesis.

The application must be submitted to the relevant Graduate Studies Committee, who will appoint assessors as appropriate. A written report on the application will be made to the committee before confirmation of D.Phil. status is approved.

If the committee does not consider that the candidate's progress warrants confirmation of status it may either (*a*) recommend resubmission of the application at a later date within the normal timetable (not later than six terms after admission to D.Phil. status) or (*b*) approve an extension of D.Phil. status in order to allow time for resubmission of the application or (*c*) approve transfer to M.Litt. status, or (*d*) reject the application.

Individual departments may require candidates to complete other tests or assessments before confirmation is approved. Candidates are advised to consult the Notes of Guidance for Graduate Students issued by each Graduate Studies Committee.

Additional regulations for International Development

Probationer Research Student entrants must confirm status by the end of the ninth term after arrival in Oxford, and entrants from the M.Phil in Development Studies must do so by the end of their eleventh term after arrival in Oxford. The comprehensive outline should be up to 3,000 words. The main submission should be between 15,000 and 20,000 words of the main thesis, which can be one chapter or parts of two or more chapters. It should be core material based on the writing up of fieldwork or other research.

Additional regulations for the sub-faculty of Economics

Those applying for confirmation of D.Phil. status in Economics shall present the preliminary results of their research at a departmental seminar or workshop as part of the confirmation process, under arrangements to be approved by the Director of Graduate Studies.

D.Phil students coming from the M.Phil in Economics must confirm status by the end of their eleventh term as a graduate student in Economics at the University of Oxford, inclusive of the time spent on the M.Phil.

3. *Theses*

M.Sc. by Research

Where, exceptionally, transfer has been allowed to M.Sc. by Research status, candidates are required to submit either a thesis or two written papers not exceeding in total 25,000 words in length.

Theses for the Degree of M.Litt. which exceed 50,000 words, theses or written papers for the M.Sc. by Research which exceed in total 25,000 words, and those for the Degree of D.Phil. which exceed 100,000 words, excluding the bibliography, are liable to be rejected unless candidates have, with the support of their supervisors, secured the leave of the appropriate Academic Studies Committee to exceed this limit. These figures are strictly *maxima*. It is not the board's intention that they should be construed as norms, and candidates are advised that many successful theses have been significantly shorter.

Additional regulations for the Department of Social Policy and Intervention

Social Policy D.Phil Pathway:

A D.Phil. thesis may be accepted for examination if it consists of a minimum of four academic papers of publishable quality, framed by an introduction and a conclusion. Only one of the four academic papers may be a co-authored piece of work, with the candidate having contributed at least 70 percent of the work [to be confirmed by the co-author(s)]. Such a body of work shall be deemed acceptable provided it represents a coherent and focused body of research, addressing one overarching research question. Current overall word limits and conditions are detailed in the D.Phil. Notes for Guidance. Candidates wishing to proceed in this manner must be approved at the time of confirmation of D.Phil. status.

Social Intervention D.Phil Pathway:

A D.Phil. thesis may be accepted for examination if it consists of a minimum of three academic papers of publishable quality. Such a body of work shall be deemed acceptable provided it represents a coherent and focused body of research. It should include an Introduction, a Survey of Literature, and a Conclusion. Current word limits and conditions are detailed in the D.Phil. Notes for Guidance. A D.Phil. Thesis submitted under this rubric may include joint publications. Where joint publications are included, all co-authors must certify in writing to the Director of Graduate Studies that the majority of that work represents the work of the candidate. Candidates wishing to proceed in this manner must obtain permission from their supervisor, from the Director of Graduate Studies, and must be approved at the time of confirmation for D.Phil. status. Evidence must be submitted at the time permission is sought that at least one of the three academic papers has been submitted to an identified journal, if not yet accepted or published. If, after a petition is accepted, a candidate wishes to revert to a standard D.Phil. thesis format, the candidate must lodge a petition with his or her supervisor to be approved by the Director of Graduate Studies, showing good cause for the change.

5. GEOGRAPHY

1. *Transfer from Probationer Research Student status to M.Litt, M.Sc, or D.Phil status*

The transfer of status normally takes place not later than the third term after admission as a research student. Students are required to demonstrate that the research already accomplished shows promise of the ability to produce a satisfactory M.Litt, M.Sc, or D.Phil thesis on the intended topic. Students are required to submit to the director of Graduate Studies a report title and abstract (of no more than 300 words/one side of A4) by Friday of eighth week Michaelmas Term. Each student will also give a Transfer of Status Presentation of fifteen minutes (plus ten minutes of questions) during noughth week of Hilary Term. Students should submit two copies (and one electronic copy) of a research proposal of no more than 7,500 words, including an outline of research plans, a preliminary review of the literature, methodology progress to date, bibliography and a timetable for completion to the Director of Graduate studies by Friday of eighth week Hilary Term. On receiving the application, the Director of Graduate studies will, on behalf of the Graduate studies Committee, appoint two assessors (normally two members of the academic staff) neither of whom will normally be the student's supervisor. The interviewers will read the script before submitting to the board their reports and a joint summary statement supporting their recommendation. Students will be required to attend a Transfer of Status Assessment Meeting with their supervisor(s) and transfer of status assessors to discuss their report. These meetings will be held during 1st week of Trinity Term. A student whose first application is unsuccessful may be given one further opportunity to apply for transfer, following the procedures laid down, and may apply for an extension of time for one term if this is necessary for the purpose of making the application.

2. *Confirmation of D.Phil status*

Application for Confirmation of D.Phil status should normally be made not earlier than the sixth term from admission as a research student and not later than the ninth term. The department expects that, in most cases, the conformation will be made immediately after return from field-work and no later than eighth week Trinity Term of the student's third year. No candidate may submit a thesis for the doctoral degree without having first obtained confirmed doctoral status. Any student who does not confirm by the end of their ninth term, will be required to apply for a deferral of confirmation of status and may be allowed up to three terms for this purpose. Any student who fails to confirm status within twelve terms of registering as a PRS will have their student status lapsed. Students who have taken an M.Phil first and were admitted directly to D.Phil status, should confirm status within three terms of starting the D.Phil Any student who fails to confirm within twelve terms of starting the M.Phil will have their status lapsed. The purpose of the submission for confirmed status is to ensure that the candidate is working to a doctoral standard.

The confirmation report should show evidence that the research already accomplished gives promise of the ability to produce a satisfactory D.Phil thesis on the intended topic. For this purpose the candidate must submit to the Director of Graduate Studies two copies (together with an electronic version) of a report describing in approximately 3,000 words the aims and methods of the projected thesis. The student will also be required to include with the written work an outline of the proposed thesis, including the topics to be covered in individual chapters, and a timetable for completion. In addition, two substantive chapters of no more than 10,000 words each must also be submitted. Candidates wishing to undertake the D.Phil via scientific papers should substitute the chapters of the thesis with two papers.

On receiving the application the Director of Graduate studies will appoint two assessors (normally two academic members of staff) neither of whom will normally be the student's supervisor. The assessors will read the script before submitting to the board their written reports and a joint summary statement supporting their recommendation. Students will be required to meet with their assessors and supervisor at an assessment interview to discuss their report. A student whose first application is unsuccessful may be given one further opportunity to apply for confirmation, following the procedures laid down, normally within one term if necessary for the purpose of making the application. Students will be notified of the outcome and they should receive advice from their supervisor(s) on their confirmation assessment.

3. *Submission of theses*

Candidates for the Degrees of M.Sc, M.Litt, and D.Phil are required to submit at least two sets of all maps, diagrams, and other illustrations, one of which should be a reproduction of the original set. The copy of the thesis deposited in the Bodleian should be one of those with a complete set of maps and illustrations.

Applications for leave to present only one set of maps, diagrams and other illustrations may be granted in exceptional circumstances, but such concessions will be granted only very sparingly.

M.Sc theses should be approximately 40,000 words, inclusive of appendices but exclusive of tables, figures, and references.

M.Litt theses should not exceed 50,000 words, exclusive of the bibliography, unless for exceptional reasons and on the recommendation of the candidate's supervisor the board otherwise determines.

D.Phil theses submitted by students in Geography must not exceed 100,000 words, exclusive of the bibliography but including notes, glossary, appendices, etc., unless for exceptional reasons and on the recommendation of the candidate's supervisor the board otherwise determines.

A D.Phil thesis may be accepted for examination if comprised of a minimum of four scientific papers submitted for publication if not yet accepted or published. Such a body of work will be deemed acceptable provided it represents a coherent and focused body or research. It should include an Introduction, a Survey of Literature, and a Conclusion. Current word limits and conditions remain in place.

A D.Phil thesis submitted under this rubric may include joint publications. In that case, all co-authors must certify in writing to the Director of Graduate Studies of the School that the majority of the work represents that of the candidate.

Candidates wishing to proceed in this manner must obtain permission from his/her supervisor, the School, and the Divisional Board and must be approved at the time of confirmation for D.Phil status. Evidence must be submitted at the time permission is sought that the scientific papers have been submitted to identified journals.

If, after a petition is accepted, a candidate wishes to revert to a standard D.Phil thesis format, the candidate must lodge a petition with his/her supervisor, the School, the Divisional Board showing good cause for the change.

6. BOARD OF THE FACULTY OF LAW[1]

1. *The First Research Year*

    (i) All those admitted to a research degree in the Faculty of Law must in the first year follow a course of instruction in Legal Research Method approved by the Law Board (or, for students registered for the D.Phil in Criminology, a course of instruction in Criminal Research Methods), and must satisfy the examiners that they have completed to the required standard such tests or exercises as may be prescribed by the Law Board as part of such a course of instruction. Where the Law Board judges that it has sufficient evidence of a candidate's proficiency in research methods, it may in exceptional circumstances dispense a candidate from this requirement.

    (ii) Candidates admitted in the first instance as Probationer Research Students may, with the consent of the Faculty Board, transfer to the status of a student for the M.St. in Legal Research.

2. *Transfer to the D.Phil. or M.Litt.*

    (i) Candidates wishing to transfer to the status of student for the degree of D.Phil. or M.Litt. must, subject to sub-paragraphs (ii) and (iii) below, undertake both parts of the Qualifying Test (paragraph 3 below).

    (ii) It is not possible to transfer to M.Litt. status, having successfully completed the M.Phil. or M.St. in Legal Research, unless the candidate proposes to write an entirely new thesis. A candidate transferring to D.Phil. status is entitled to incorporate the thesis presented for the M.Phil. or M.St. in Legal Research within the D.Phil. thesis.

    (iii) Candidates who at the time of the transfer will have successfully completed the M.Phil. in Law or the M.Phil. in Criminology and Criminal Justice or the M.St. in Legal Research shall submit for Part B of the Qualifying Test their successful M.Phil. or M.St. thesis. In such a case the word limits for Part B in sub-paragraph (ii) of paragraph 3 below do not apply.

    (iv) Students who have previously been registered for the M.St. in Legal Research or for the M.Phil. in Law or M.Phil. in Criminology and Criminal Justice, and have been granted leave to supplicate for either of these degrees, but have been referred on their application to transfer to D.Phil. status, may conditionally hold the status of Probationer Research Student, provided that the Faculty Board is satisfied that the student fulfils the conditions set out in the appropriate regulation. Probationer Research Student status in this instance may not be held for more than six terms beyond the date at which they first held the

---

[1] For candidates admitted before Michaelmas Term 2007, see *Examination Regulations*, 2004, p. 952, l. 8-p. 953, l. 47.

status of a student for the M.St. in Legal Research or for the M.Phil. in Law or
M.Phil. in Criminology and Criminal Justice.

3. *The Qualifying Test*

(i) Part A of the Qualifying Test requires that the candidate shall submit to the
The Faculty of Law Graduate Studies Office (or, for students registered for
the D.Phil. in Criminology, to the Graduate Studies Administrator within the
Centre for Criminology) two typescript or printed copies of a statement of the
subject of the proposed thesis and details of the manner in which the candidate proposes to treat it. This statement shall not exceed 2,000 words.

(ii) Subject to sub-paragraph (iii) of paragraph 2 above, Part B of the Qualifying
Test requires that the candidate shall submit to the Faculty of Law
Graduate Studies Office (or, for students registered for the D.Phil. in
Criminology, to the Graduate Studies Administrator within the Centre for
Criminology) two typescript or printed copies of a substantial piece of
written work which may or may not be intended to form part of the proposed
thesis but must be relevant to its subject. For transfer to the D.Phil., this
Part B submission must not exceed 10,000 words, for the M.Litt., 6,000
words. In each case the candidate must state the number of words used. The
required format for this submission is the common format prescribed for all
law theses which is printed in the Faculty of Law's Graduate Students'
Handbook.

(iii) Supervisors of candidates offering Part B are required to discuss with the
candidate the names of possible assessors, and to provide the Board (or, for
students registered for the D.Phil in Criminology, the Director of Graduate
Studies (Research)) with the names of three suitable persons who have indicated their willingness to act as assessors if called upon to do so. This
notification may be made before the submission of the material, but must be
made, at the latest, on the day the material is submitted. (For students
registered for the D.Phil in Criminology, two assessors will be appointed by
the Director of Graduate Studies (Research) in consultation with the supervisor).

(iv) Subject to sub-paragraph (v) below, candidates admitted as Probationer
Research Students to the doctoral or M.Litt. programmes, must submit all
materials for the Qualifying Test by the end of the fourth week of Full Term in
the third term after the candidate's admission.

(v) Subject to the general time-limit in sub-paragraph (vi) below, the Graduate
Studies Committee, having consulted with the supervisor, may, for good
cause, allow the Qualifying Test to be deferred.

Applications for deferral must be made through the Faculty of Law Graduate
Studies Office (or, for students registered for the D.Phil. in Criminology, to the
Graduate Studies Administrator within the Centre for Criminology) in time to
allow the Graduate Studies Committee to consider the matter in the second week
of the candidate's third term.

(vi) In no case may the materials for the Qualifying Test be submitted or resubmitted after the end of the fourth term from the admission of the student to the
doctoral or M.Litt. programmes. A student will in any case cease to hold PRS
status if he or she does not gain admission to another status within four terms
of admission as a full-time student.

4. *Assessing the Qualifying Test*

(i) The Director of Graduate Studies shall appoint two assessors and shall report
their appointments to the Board.

(ii) The assessors shall interview the candidate.

(iii) The assessors shall report in writing as to (*a*) the suitability of the candidate's subject for the kind of thesis in question and (*b*) the competence of the candidate to handle it at the required level; and, in accordance with their report, the assessors shall make a recommendation.

(iv) On the original submission for the Qualifying Test, the assessors may recommend (*a*) that the candidate be granted the transfer which has been applied for, or (*b*) that the candidate be permitted to resubmit Part A or, in the case in which the candidate is a Probationary Research Student, Part B or both Part A and Part B; in the case in which the candidate offers a successful M.Phil. or M.St. thesis for Part B within sub-paragraph (iii) of paragraph 2 above, there can be no reference back except in relation to Part A. Hence in a case in which, despite having earned the degree for which it was submitted, the thesis fails to satisfy the assessors of Part B of the Qualifying Test, the permission to transfer must be refused.

(v) Unless, for good cause shown, the Director of Graduate Studies, after consultation with the supervisor, agrees to an extension of time, the assessors must lodge their report and recommendation with the Faculty of Law Graduate Studies Office (or, for students registered for the D.Phil. in Criminology, to the Graduate Studies Administrator, the Centre for Criminology) within one calendar month of the date on which the materials are sent out to them.

(vi) The Faculty of Law Graduate Studies Office (or, for students registered for the D.Phil. in Criminology, to the Graduate Studies Administrator, the Centre for Criminology) shall pass the report and recommendation to the Director of Graduate Studies (or, for students registered for the D.Phil in Criminology, the Director of Graduate Studies (Research)), who has the authority of the Board to inform the candidate without further delay of the nature of the recommendation and to inform the supervisor of the contents of the report.

(vii) Where the assessors have recommended resubmission, the candidate should normally resubmit at any time before the end of the subsequent term following the original submission. On resubmission the assessors may recommend (a) that the candidate be granted the transfer requested or (b) that the candidate be refused permission to transfer. In the case of a Probationary Research Student the effect of the latter recommendation is to entitle the candidate to apply for transfer to the M.St. in Legal Research under the appropriate regulation, with effect retrospective to the original registration as a Probationary Research Student. Such applications will be considered by the Graduate Studies Committee.

(viii) The Director of Graduate Studies shall place the report of the assessors before the meeting of the Graduate Studies Committee next following its receipt by the The Faculty of Law Graduate Studies Office (or, for students registered for the D.Phil. in Criminology, to the Graduate Studies Administrator at the Centre for Criminology).

5. *Confirmation of D.Phil status*

(i) Applications for confirmation of status shall normally be made not earlier than the sixth term, and confirmation of status must normally be completed no later than three terms after the Qualifying Test.

(ii) Application for confirmation of D.Phil status shall be accompanied by (*a*) a statement giving the title of the thesis, and summarising each component chapter in approximately 100 words per chapter, (*b*) an overview of the intended thesis, of approximately 1,000 words, stating how much of the thesis is complete and how much remains to be done (with an estimate of the probable date of completion), and (*c*) a piece of written work, which shall normally be of 20,000–30,000 words in length and intended to form part of the thesis.

(iii) The candidate's supervisor shall provide a report on the candidate's application upon the form provided for this purpose or in a separate communication sent directly to the Graduate Studies Administrator. The report shall comment upon the accuracy of the account and feasibility of the timetable, and upon the candidate's progress, together with an estimate of the probable date of completion.

(iv) The documents described above under (ii) and (iii) shall be considered by two assessors, appointed by the Graduate Studies Committee, one of whom shall, wherever practicable, be one of those who acted at the time of the candidate's transfer to D.Phil status. The assessors shall interview the candidate and submit a joint written report to the Graduate Studies Committee, normally within one month of receiving the application. The report shall include a recommendation as to whether the application should be approved. The faculty may grant the application or refer it back for resubmission. Only one resubmission for confirmation may be submitted, and no such resubmission will normally be permitted after the end of the candidate's ninth term.

6. All theses and dissertations in law must conform to the statement which appears in the Law Faculty's Graduate Students' Handbook under the title 'Format of Theses in the Faculty of Law'.

7. DEPARTMENT OF POLITICS AND INTERNATIONAL RELATIONS

(*See also the general notice at the commencement of these regulations. The current edition of the relevant 'Notes of Guidance for Graduate Students and Supervisors' contains an elaborated version of these regulations.*)

Candidates with Probationer Research Student status, unless or until they have entered upon another status, or have been otherwise dispensed from some or all of the following requirements by the relevant Graduate Studies Committee, are required to undertake the work set out below during the first year.

1. A first-year student shall:

(i) satisfactorily complete a course of lectures, seminars, and classes, as determined in the relevant 'Notes of Guidance for Graduate Students and Supervisors' and supplemented by his or her supervisor;

(ii) satisfactorily complete a course of research methods training, as determined in the relevant 'Notes of Guidance for Graduate Students and Supervisors' and supplemented by his or her supervisor and/or by the relevant Director of Research Training.

2. Applications for transfer from Probationer Research Student status to D.Phil. or M.Litt. status must be submitted in accordance with the requirements in the relevant 'Notes of Guidance'. Applicants in their fourth and final term of Probationer Status must submit their completed application not later than 5 p.m. on the Friday of fifth week of that term. In addition to satisfying the above requirements (i) and (ii), the transfer of status application must include two copies of an outline of the proposed research topic and two copies of the written work-all as specified in the relevant 'Notes of Guidance for Graduate Students and Supervisors'. The relevant Graduate Studies Committee will appoint two assessors, one of whom will normally be a member of the committee, except in cases where neither of the two most appropriate assessors is a member of that committee. The committee will

then decide whether to approve the transfer. In the case of applications to transfer to D.Phil. status where the committee does not so approve, it may authorise an extension of time in order to allow the candidate to resubmit at a later date (but before the end of the sixth term after admission to Probationer Research Student status), or alternatively approve a transfer to M.Litt. status.

3. Candidates whose applications for transfer of status are not successful may, with the approval of the relevant Graduate Studies Committee, submit revised proposals within their first six terms of Probationer Research Student status.

4. Though not in itself sufficient qualification for students wishing to advance to M. Litt. or D.Phil. status, the successful completion of the M.Sc. in Politics Research or the M.Sc. in Political Theory Research may serve in place of 1. (i) and (ii) above, and material submitted as part of the requirements for the M.Sc. may also be used in the transfer application. Probationer Research Students who have already completed the M.Sc. in Politics Research or the M.Sc. in Political Theory Research should normally apply for transfer of status by the end of the Trinity Full Term of their first year of study as a Probationer Research Student.

8. SAÏD BUSINESS SCHOOL

1. *Admissions*

Applicants shall be required to satisfy to the University Admitting Body (UAB) of the Saïd Business School that they have:

(*a*) a 2:1 (or equivalent) undergraduate degree (this is the minimum qualification level that will be considered);

(*b*) a GRE or GMAT score: as a guide, a score in excess of 630 (GRE quantative and verbal sections average) or 610 (GMATn total score);

(*c*) a Test of English as a Foreign Language (TOEFL) or International English Language Test Scheme (IELTS) in excess of 630 (if TOEFL paper) or 109 (if TOEFL internet) or 7.5 for IELTS if English is not their native language or if they have not studied their full degree in an English-speaking country;

(*d*) their University academic transcripts;

(*e*) three references (a minimum of two must be academic);

(*f*) one piece of written work for assessment of approximately 2,000 words. This should be an essay or section of longer work on a topic appropriate to the degree for which they are applying. They must include a signed declaration that the piece is their own work without the assistance of others;

(*g*) a research proposal to help the UAB identify a potential supervisor;

(*h*) the above and any additional criteria which the UAB may from time to time determine.

2. *Probationer Research Students*

All students are normally admitted as Probationer Research Students (PRS).

Unless granted a dispensation by the D.Phil. Committee of the Saïd Business School, during their first year, Probationer Research Students shall:

(*a*) attend such lectures, seminars and classes as his or her supervisor and/or the committee shall determine;

(*b*) satisfactorily complete such courses and coursework as the supervisor and/or the committee shall determine, dependant upon which course the student has already taken prior to commencing the D.Phil.;

(*c*) applications to D.Phil. Committee for exemption from the above will be considered.

3. *Transfer of status*

Students who have taken the M.Sc. in Management Research or MFE prior to commencing their D.Phil. study as a PRS are normally expected to transfer status in their third term. All students must transfer status by the end of their fourth term.

Applications for transfer of status must be submitted to the D.Phil. Committee and should be comprised of the following: 5

(*a*) a transfer of status form (GSO.2), signed by the student's supervisor and an appropriate college officer. The candidate should indicate clearly on the form the status to which he or she wishes to transfer;

(*b*) a good pass in all of the courses and coursework as stated in 2.(b) above, approved by the student's supervisor; 10

(*c*) a satisfactory research proposal or research outline;

(*d*) where appropriate, one draft chapter of the thesis.

Further details of these requirements are set out in the D.Phil Notes for Guidance.

Two assessors nominated by the student and his/her supervisor and appointed by the D.Phil. Committee will examine the student by viva voce and submit a written transfer report to the D.Phil. Committee with recommendations as to whether or not the student should be allowed to transfer to D.Phil status. 15

The D.Phil. Committee will consider the application and the recommendations of the assessors and in light of this will decide whether to approve the transfer of status, or approve admission to M.Litt status (in the case that the Committee is not satisfied that the candidate should be allowed to transfer), or approve an extension of time in order to allow the candidate to carry out further research and make revisions to his/her proposal and to resubmit at a later date (but before the PRS status period expires). The committee may request additional written work (such as a revised research proposal) or other evidence, and/or appoint an additional assessor, and/or state that the student should be re-examined. 20 25

4. *Confirmation of D. Phil status*

Students will normally be expected to apply for their Confirmation of Status by the end of their sixth term after admission. They must apply for their Confirmation of Status by the end of their ninth term. 30

Applications for confirmation of status as a Student for the Degree of Doctor of Philosophy shall comprise the following:

(*a*) a confirmation of status application form (GSO14) signed by the candidate's supervisor and an appropriate officer of the candidate's college; 35

(*b*) a comprehensive outline of the treatment of the thesis topic including details of progress made and an indication, where possible, of the anticipated timetable for submission;

(*c*) two draft chapters totalling no more than 25,000 words which include material particularly central to the thesis. 40

Further details of these requirements are set out in the D.Phil. Notes for Guidance.

The application must be submitted to the D.Phil. Committee and will be considered by two assessors nominated by the student and supervisor and appointed by D.Phil. Committee. These may be the same assessors as were chosen for the transfer of status, but assessors selected at this stage may not be chosen for the final viva voce. The assessors will read the work, interview the candidate (examine viva voce) and make a recommendation to the committee in a written report. 45

If the committee does not consider that the candidate's progress warrants confirmation of status it may either recommend resubmission of the application at a later date within the normal timetable, or approve an extension of D.Phil. status in order to allow time for resubmission of the application, or recommend transfer to M.Litt. status, or reject the application.

5. *Three paper route*

A D.Phil. thesis may be accepted for examination if comprised of a minimum of three academic papers of publishable quality. Such a body of work shall be deemed acceptable provided it represents a coherent and focused body of research. It should include an Introduction, a Survey of Literature, and a Conclusion. Current word limits and conditions are detailed in the D.Phil. Notes for Guidance.

A D.Phil. Thesis submitted under this rubric may include joint publications, providing that, aside from the candidate, none of the named co-authors is a student. Where a joint publication with another student is included, this must be in addition to the minimum of three academic papers required to be included in the D.Phil thesis. Where joint publications are included, all co-authors must certify in writing to the Director of Graduate Studies of the School that the majority of that work represents the work of the candidate.

Candidates wishing to proceed in this manner must obtain permission from his/her supervisor, the Director of Graduate Studies, and the D.Phil. Committee and must be approved at the time of confirmation for D.Phil. status. Evidence must be submitted at the time permission is sought that at least one of the three academic papers has been submitted to an identified journal, if not yet accepted or published.

If, after a petition is accepted, a candidate wishes to revert to a standard D.Phil. thesis format the candidate must lodge a petition with his/her supervisor, the School and D.Phil. Committee showing good cause for the change.

6. *Thesis*

Theses for the Degree of M.Litt. which exceed 50,000 words and those for the Degree of D.Phil. which exceed 100,000, excluding the bibliography, are liable to be rejected unless candidates have, with the support of their supervisors, secured the prior dispensation of the board of Graduate Studies to exceed this limit.

9. OXFORD INTERNET INSTITUTE

1. *Admissions*

Applicants shall be required to satisfy the Graduate Studies Committee of the Oxford Internet Institute that they have:

(*a*) a Master's degree or other advanced degree, normally in one of the social sciences, and normally passed with a mark of at least 67 per cent or an equivalent level of distinction;

(*b*) achieved at least a 2.1 (or its equivalent) at first degree level;

(*c*) for students whose first language is not English, have met the higher level of the University's English language requirements; and that they are;

(*d*) well-fitted to undertake research at doctoral level.

2. *Probationer Research Students*

All students are normally admitted as Probationer Research Students.

Unless granted a dispensation by the Graduate Studies Committee of the Oxford Internet Institute, Probationer Research Students during their first year shall:

(*a*) attend such lectures, seminars, and classes as his or her supervisor and/or the committee shall determine;

(*b*) attend and satisfactorily complete such courses or classes from the Institute's Research Methods Training Programme as directed by the committee;

(*c*) attend and satisfactorily complete the Institute's Social Dynamics of the Internet course.

3. *Transfer to D.Phil. status*

Students will normally be expected to transfer to D.Phil. status in their third or fourth term as a Probationer Research Student at the Oxford Internet Institute. Applications should be submitted to the Graduate Studies Committee of the Oxford Internet Institute and will comprise the following:

    (*a*) a transfer of status form, signed by the candidate's supervisor and an appropriate officer of the candidate's college;

    (*b*) confirmation from the candidate's supervisor that such courses as the candidate has been required to undertake have been satisfactorily completed;

    (*c*) an outline of their research (one side of A4 paper);

    (*d*) a detailed research proposal of no more than 6,000 words. This should:

        (i) draw upon relevant literature to discuss the background to the research, theoretical perspectives, and possible outcomes to the research;

        (ii) state key research questions;

        (iii) discuss the overall methodological approach, and specific strategies, to be employed in answering these research questions, paying particular attention to practical and ethical issues relevant to the research.

    (*e*) a preliminary timetable for the research;

    (*f*) a list of references;

    (*g*) OII Training Needs Assessment Form.

The application will be considered by a specially constituted panel of two assessors appointed by the Graduate Studies Committee of the Oxford Internet Institute. The panel will read the work, interview the candidate and make a recommendation to the committee in a reasoned written report.

Candidates will be expected during the interview to show evidence of their understanding of general theory and research methods in the social sciences applicable to their proposed study and specific research methods appropriate to the study of social aspects of the Internet and related ICTs.

The committee will make a decision on the application in the light of the assessors' report and may request additional written work or other evidence, or appoint an additional assessor, whenever it considers necessary.

4. *Confirmation of status*

Applications for confirmation of status as a Student for the Degree of Doctor of Philosophy submitted to the Graduate Studies Committee of the Oxford Internet Institute shall comprise the following:

    (*a*) a confirmation of status application form signed by the candidate's supervisor and an appropriate officer of the candidate's college;

    (*b*) an abstract of the thesis (one side of A4 paper);

    (*c*) an outline structure of the thesis, consisting of chapter headings, and a brief statement of the intended content;

    (*d*) an outline timetable detailing what work has already been carried out and what activities are planned for the remaining stages;

    (*e*) two completed draft chapters intended to form part of the final thesis.

The application will be considered by a specially constituted panel of two assessors appointed by the Graduate Studies Committee of the Oxford Internet Institute. The panel will read the work, interview the candidate and make a recommendation to the committee in a written report.

    (*f*) OII Training Needs Assessment Form.

5. *Thesis*

The thesis must not exceed 100,000 words, the limit to include abstract, all notes and appendices but not the bibliography. Any thesis exceeding this limit is liable to be rejected on that ground unless prior dispensation has been granted by the Graduate Studies Committee on the advice of the candidate's supervisor.

E. CONTINUING EDUCATION BOARD

1. For the purposes of this section the word 'board' shall include any body that has been authorised by the Continuing Education Board with power to act on its behalf to admit students to read for the Degree of Doctor of Philosophy; and to assess students with PRS or D.Phil. status.

2. *Admission*

(*a*) Students are admitted to study on part-time basis only.

(*b*) Students are admitted *either*

   (i) as Probationer Research Students, *or*

   (ii) as a D.Phil. student. Students may, at the discretion of the Continuing Education Board, be admitted to D.Phil. status under the provisions of Sect. 15, para. 2, cl. 1(i). Students who have successfully completed the M.Sc. in Advanced Cognitive Therapy, the M.Sc. in Applied Landscape Archaeology, the M.Sc. in English Local History, the M.Sc. in Evidence-Based Health Care, the M.St in Mindfulness-Based Cognitive Therapy, the M.Sc. in Professional Archaeology, or any other relevant Oxford Masters degree deemed an acceptable prerequisite by the board, may be admitted under these provisions.

(*c*) In assessing applications from candidates seeking to undertake a research degree through part-time study, the board shall have regard to evidence that:

   (i) the candidates can meet the attendance requirements relating to part-time study;

   (ii) the candidates are well-fitted to undertake research at doctoral level;

   (iii) the candidate's personal and professional circumstances are such that it is both practicable for them to fulfil the requirements of the course, and necessary for them to study on a part-time basis;

   (iv) if appropriate, the candidates have the written support of their present employer for their proposed course of study and its obligations;

   (v) the proposed field of research can be appropriately supervised under the auspices of the Continuing Education Board.

3. *Attendance requirements*

Students are required to attend for a minimum of thirty days of university-based work each year, to be arranged with the agreement of their supervisor, for the period that their names remain on the Register of Graduate Studies unless individually dispensed by the Continuing Education Board.

4. *Probationer Research Student*

A research student in Archaeology or Architectural History or Cognitive-Behavioural Therapy or English Local History or Evidence-Based Health Care admitted to Probationer Research Student status shall normally be required to:

   (i) attend such lectures, seminars, and classes as his or her supervisor shall determine, and provide evidence of his or her attendance; and

   (ii) present one seminar paper which shall be assessed by one or two assessors. Such assessors should not normally include the candidate's supervisor; and

(iii) submit an essay of between 3,000 and 5,000 words, being either a section of the candidate's proposed thesis or an essay on a relevant topic, and a brief statement limited to 500 words, of the subject of the thesis and the manner in which the candidate proposes to treat it.

5. *Admission/transfer to D.Phil. status*

(*a*) Applicants must demonstrate that they are capable of producing research work of the requisite standard and presenting the findings clearly; and that their planned programme of research is one that may be profitably undertaken at Oxford; and that they have a good knowledge and understanding of the work that is likely to be needed to embark on the programme.

(*b*) Students who have successfully completed the M.Sc in Advanced Cognitive Therapy, M.Sc. in Applied Landscape Archaeology, the M.St. or M.Sc. in English Local History, the M.Sc. in Evidence-Based Health Care, the M.St in Mindfulness-Based Cognitive Therapy, the M.St. or M.Sc. in Professional Archaeology, or any other relevant Oxford Masters degree deemed an acceptable prerequisite by the board, shall normally apply for admission to D.Phil. status up to the twelfth term after their initial admission as a graduate student.

(*c*) Students who hold the status of Probationary Research Student, shall normally apply for admission to D.Phil. status after a minimum of six terms and no longer than eight terms.

(*d*) A student may be permitted to hold the status of Probationary Research Student for up to a further four terms subject to the provisions of Chapter 12, Section 4 cl.7.

(*e*) Admission to D.Phil. status may be made conditional on such requirements as the board may impose.

(*f*) Applicants should specify the date by which they undertake to make available two (or in exceptional cases, three) copies of the written work in support of the application. Applicants should do so not later than four weeks before the start of the full term in which they wish to be assessed. Application for transfer should be sent to the Registry, Department for Continuing Education, 1 Wellington Square.

(*g*) Applications for transfer to D.Phil. status shall be accompanied by:

(i) **for research students in Archaeology, Architectural History, Cognitive-Behavioural Therapy, English Local History and Evidence-Based Health Care**

(1) two copies of a brief statement, limited to 500 words, of the subject of the thesis and the manner in which the candidate proposes to treat it;

(2) two copies of a piece of written work, normally 3,000 to 5,000 words long, being *either* (*a*) a section of the proposed thesis, *or* (*b*) an essay on a relevant topic, *or* (*c*) an augmented version of the statement under (1) above;

(3) two copies of a confidential report from the supervisor, which should be sent by the supervisor direct to the Registry of the Department for Continuing Education.

The Registry shall send one copy of the written work and the confidential report each to the assessors appointed by the board.

Candidates should note that if they adopt alternative 2(*c*) above they must also submit the 500 word statement required by general regulation.

(*h*) Candidates should also note that while as precise a definition of the subject should be given as is possible at this stage of their work, they are not bound to follow the statement precisely, but may reformulate their plan in the light of further study. If reformulation goes so far as to require alteration of the title of the thesis as approved, however, they should seek permission of the relevant board to alter it.

(*i*) Candidates shall be assessed by two assessors appointed by the board, neither of whom will normally be the student's supervisor. The assessors shall certify that they have considered the written work submitted by the applicant and interviewed the applicant. The assessors should also provide a written report of the application to the board for approval of their recommendation. In cases where the assessors decide that the application is not of the required standard to transfer to D.Phil. status their written report should outline the areas in which the application is judged to fall short of the required standard.

(*j*) A candidate who is unsuccessful may be given one further opportunity to apply for transfer (within the limit of eight terms). A candidate whose second application for transfer is unsuccessful shall cease to hold the status of a Probationary Research Student.

6. *Confirmation of D.Phil status*

(*a*) Assessors are appointed by the board to assess whether a candidate's work on their thesis is developing satisfactorily and that they may be considered ready to be examined within three further terms. D.Phil. status must be confirmed before a candidate may submit their thesis for examination for the degree of D.Phil.

(*b*) Application for confirmation of D.Phil. status, with statements of support from the candidate's society and supervisor, shall normally be presented to the Registry of the Department for Continuing Education not earlier than four weeks before the end of the twelfth term, and at the latest by four weeks before the end of the eighteenth term, after admission to the status of Probationer Research Student or to status of student for another higher degree of the University.

(*c*) Application for confirmation of D.Phil. status shall normally be accompanied by:

(i) for research students in Archaeology, Architectural History, Cognitive-Behavioural Therapy, English Local History and Evidence-Based Health Care

(1) a statement of the title of the thesis and of the manner in which the candidate proposes to treat it. This should include a proposed chapter structure;

(2) a specimen chapter or part of a chapter not longer than 10,000 words in the case of Archaeology, and Cognitive-Behavioural Therapy and Evidence-Based Health Care or 6,000 words in the case of Architectural History and English Local History;

(3) a confidential report from the supervisor which should be sent directly to the Registry of the Department for Continuing Education.

The Registry should send the written work and the confidential report to the interviewer appointed by the board.

(*d*) Candidates shall be assessed by two assessors appointed by the board, neither of whom will normally be the student's supervisor. The assessment shall include an oral examination. The assessors shall also provide a written report of the application to the board for approval of their recommendation. In cases where the assessors decide that the application is not of the required standard to warrant confirmation of D.Phil. status, their written report should outline the areas in which the application is judged to fall short of the required standard.

(*e*) A student who is unsuccessful may be given one further opportunity to apply for confirmation (within the statutory limit).

7. *Theses*

Theses submitted for the degree of D.Phil. in *Archaeology* should not normally exceed 80,000 words, *excluding* bibliography and descriptive catalogue or similar factual matter.

Theses submitted for the degree of D.Phil in Cognitive-Behavioural Therapy shall not exceed 80,000 words. This shall *include* all notes, appendices, any source material being edited, and all other parts of the thesis whatsoever *excluding only* the bibliography.

Theses submitted for the degree of D.Phil. in *Architectural History* and in, *English Local History* and *Evidence-Based Health Care* shall not exceed 100,000 words. This shall *include* all notes, appendices, any source material being edited, and all other parts of the thesis whatsoever *excluding only* the bibliography.

Any thesis exceeding these limits is liable to be rejected on that ground. It is recognised that in special circumstances it will be necessary for leave to be granted to exceed this limit by a stated amount. In particular it is recognised that the inclusion of essential edited source material, whether as an appendix or as a main part of the thesis, presents special problems in regard to length; and the board will be prepared to consider applications for edited material to be excluded from the word limit otherwise placed on the thesis. Leave to exceed these limits for other reasons will be given only in the most special cases and on the recommendation of the supervisor. Any application for permission to exceed the limit should be submitted with a detailed explanation and statement of the amount of excess length requested, and with a covering letter from the supervisor. Applications should be made as soon as possible and may not be later than the last day of the fifth week of the term before that in which applications made for appointment of examiners.

Theses submitted for the degree of D.Phil. in *Archaeology, Architectural History, Cognitive-Behavioural Therapy, English Local History and Evidence-Based Health Care* must be accompanied with two printed or typewritten copies of an abstract of the thesis, which shall not normally exceed 2,500 words for the D.Phil., prepared by the student. One copy of the abstract shall be bound into the copy of the thesis which shall be deposited in the Bodleian Library. (This is in addition to the requirement to submit an abstract of not more than 300 words in length required by the Education Committee's Regulations.)

8. Candidates admitted exceptionally under Council Regulations 15 of 2002 shall normally be subject to the provisions of (2)–(7) above. Theses submitted for the degree of D.Phil. by students admitted under this provision shall not normally exceed 100,000 words inclusive of all notes, appendices, any source material being edited, and all other parts of the thesis whatsoever excluding only the bibliography. The Continuing Education Board may, in individual cases, determine that alternative provisions shall apply, and in such cases shall notify the candidate on admission.

NOTES

19

REGULATIONS FOR THE DEGREE OF DOCTOR OF ENGINEERING

A

GENERAL REGULATIONS

1. Any member of the University who has been admitted to the status of student for the degree of Doctor of Engineering by the Mathematical, Physical and Life Sciences Board and who has satisfied the conditions prescribed by these regulations may supplicate for the degree of Doctor of Engineering.

2. Candidates shall follow a programme of study consisting of (*a*) coursework and (*b*) research, in engineering or applied science, in the context of industrial or other professional practice. Each candidate must pass a specified number of coursework modules during the programme of study, as detailed in the special regulations for the degree of Doctor of Engineering. Each candidate shall submit for examination a thesis, or portfolio of a coherent set of linked research projects.

3. A student for the degree of Doctor of Engineering shall normally pursue his or her course of study at Oxford for 12 terms.

4. A student for the degree of Doctor of Engineering may be permitted by the Mathematical, Physical and Life Sciences Divisional Board to undertake their research in a well-found research environment outside the University. Such students shall be dispensed from the residence requirements, but shall be required to attend for such instruction as the Division and department concerned shall require, as specified in the Special Regulations and Course Handbook. Before admitting a candidate on this basis, the conditions set out in the Special Regulations of the Mathematical, Physical and Life Sciences Division shall be met.

5. Candidates shall be admitted initially with the status of Probationer Research Student.

6. A member of the University who has held the status of Probationer Research Student and has completed the qualifying test for entry to Doctor of Engineering status prescribed in the

Special Regulations below may be admitted to the status of student for the degree of Doctor of Engineering.

7. A candidate should normally apply for confirmation of his or her status as a student for the degree of Doctor of Engineering no later than the tenth term after that in which he or she was initially admitted to the status of Probationer Research Student. All students for the degree of Doctor of Engineering must have their status confirmed before applying for the appointment of examiners. Candidates applying for confirmation of status must have fulfilled the requirements as specified in the special regulations for the degree of Doctor of Engineering.

8. Examiners of the thesis submitted for the degree of Doctor of Engineering shall bear in mind that their judgement of the substantial significance of the work should take into account what may reasonably be expected of a capable and diligent student after four years of full-time study.

9. If a candidate is not permitted to continue with Doctor of Engineering status, he or she may be permitted to transfer instead to the status of student for the degree of M.Sc. by Research.

10. Except as specifically provided above, and as provided in Special Regulations for the degree of Doctor of Engineering below, the provisions of the following regulations shall apply: Regulations for Admission as a Probationer Research Student; General Regulations for the Degree of Doctor of Philosophy (§1–7); General Regulations of the Education Committee governing the examination of students for the degrees of M.Sc. by Research, M.Litt. and D.Phil. and concerning the maintenance of the register; Special Regulations of Divisional and Faculty Boards concerning the status of probationer research student and the degrees of M.Litt. M.Sc. by Research, and D.Phil.: Mathematical and Physical Sciences Division; provided that, in all cases, 'Doctor of Engineering' shall be substituted for 'Doctor of Philosophy'.

B

(ii) Special Regulations for the degree of Doctor of Engineering in Engineered Metals for High Performance Applications in Aerospace and Related Technologies (ENGMET)

1. Candidates shall follow a programme of study in Engineering, Materials Science and related disciplines, consisting of (*a*) coursework and (*b*) research, and shall have an industrial or other external sponsor.

2. The University of Oxford shall appoint an academic supervisor for each student. The sponsor shall appoint both an external supervisor and a professional mentor for each student. The student shall meet with their academic supervisor

normally at least four times per term, at least one of these meetings taking place in Oxford.

3. In order successfully to fulfil the coursework requirements, candidates are required to pass a specified number of coursework modules in each academic year, as detailed in the Course Handbook. The list of permitted courses is detailed in the   5
Course Handbook, and will be updated annually. If a candidate fails any coursework module they are permitted to resit the module according to the details as stipulated in the Course Handbook.

4. Although students may hold the status of Probationer Research Student for a maximum of 6 terms, students shall normally apply to transfer from Probationer   10
Research Student to the status of student for the degree of Doctor of Engineering by the fourth term after admission as a research student. In order successfully to transfer status candidates must fulfil the specific conditions as detailed in the Course Handbook. The academic supervisor and external supervisor shall each provide a report on the student's progress. A candidate whose first application for transfer to   15
Doctor of Engineering status is not approved shall be permitted to make one further application, following the procedures laid down above, and shall be granted an extension of time for one term (beyond the six term maximum) if this is necessary for the purposes of making the application.

5. Candidates shall normally apply for confirmation of status as a student for the   20
degree of Doctor of Engineering not later than the tenth term, and normally by the ninth term, after that in which they were initially admitted as a research student. Candidates will be required to fulfil the specific conditions, as detailed in the course Handbook, before applying for confirmation of status. A candidate whose first application for confirmation of Doctor of Engineering status is not approved shall   25
be permitted to make one further application, following the procedures laid down above, normally within one term of the original application, and shall be granted an extension of time for one term (beyond the normal maximum of ten terms) if this is necessary for the purposes of making the application.

6. If, after considering a candidate's second application for transfer of status, or a   30
candidate's second application for confirmation of status, the responsible body considers that the student's progress does not warrant this, the responsible body may approve his or her transfer to the status of student for the Degree of Master of Science by Research.

7. In order to supplicate for the degree of Doctor of Engineering, candidates will   35
be required to pass a specified number of coursework modules, as detailed in the Course Handbook. They will also submit for examination a thesis, or portfolio of a coherent set of linked research projects.

8. The coursework modules shall be provided under arrangements approved by the Mathematical, Physical and Life Sciences Division and the Education   40
Committee, as set out in the Course Handbook. Coursework modules offered by another institution shall be provided under the arrangements approved by the Mathematical, Physical and Life Sciences Division and the Education Committee and set out in a collaboration agreement with that institution. Variation of arrangements for the provision of modules will require the approval of the Mathematical,   45
Physical and Life Sciences Division and the Education Committee.

NOTES

20

REGULATIONS FOR THE DEGREES OF DOCTOR OF LETTERS AND DOCTOR OF SCIENCE

1. Any person belonging to one of the following classes may become a candidate for the Degree of Doctor of Letters or of Doctor of Science under the conditions set forth in this Section:*

(*a*) Masters of Arts or Masters of Biochemistry or Chemistry or Earth Sciences or Engineering or Mathematics or Physics (including Masters of Arts or Masters of Engineering of the University of Cambridge, and Masters of Arts of the University of Dublin, who have been incorporated in this University) who have entered upon the thirtieth term from their matriculation (at this University or, if earlier, at Cambridge or Dublin as the case may be);

(*b*) Undergraduates or Bachelors of Arts of the University of Cambridge or Dublin who have been incorporated and have incepted in the Faculty of Arts in this University and have entered upon the thirtieth term from their matriculation at Cambridge or Dublin;

(*c*) Persons on whom the Degree of Master of Arts has been conferred by decree or special resolution, other than a degree *honoris causa,* and who have entered upon the ninth term from their admission to that degree;

(*d*) Doctors of Philosophy, Masters of Science or of Letters, and Bachelors of Letters or of Science who have entered upon the twenty-first term from their matriculation.

2. Any such person may apply for permission to supplicate for the Degree of Doctor of Letters or of Doctor of Science, submitting, with the application, evidence of his fitness. This evidence must

---

* If papers or books published in the calendar year preceding that in which application is made are submitted, the applicant should specify the exact date of publication.

consist of published papers or books, and one year at least must elapse between the publication of any such paper or book and its submission as evidence in support of an application.* The candidate, in his application, shall state whether any part of the work submitted has previously been accepted for a degree.   5

3. *The application shall be made through the Registrar to the board to which the subject of the papers or books in question belongs, and at least two copies of each of such papers or books shall, where possible, be sent with it. The application must further be accompanied by the fee prescribed in the appropriate regulation   10 (see Appendix I) and by a certificate, signed by some officer of, or some person deputed by, the college to which the candidate belongs, showing that his application has the approval of the college. A candidate who submits papers or books which have been produced in collaboration shall state in respect of each item the extent of his   15 own contribution.

Applications for permission to supplicate for the Degree of Doctor of Letters shall be made to one of the following bodies only:

Board of the Faculty of:

Classics;   20

English Language and Literature;

Law;

Linguistics, Philology and Phonetics;

Management.

Medieval and Modern Languages and Literature;   25

History;

Music;

Oriental Studies;

Philosophy;

Theology.   30

Divisional Board:

Social Sciences.

Applications for permission to supplicate for the Degree of Doctor of Science shall be made to one of the following boards only: 35

---

* All applications must be on the agenda of the meeting of the board at which they are to be considered. They should therefore reach the Registrar not less than eight days before the board's meeting.

Divisional Board:

Social Sciences;

Mathematical, Physical and Life Sciences

Medical Sciences.

Committee for:

Archaeology.

4. The board shall appoint judges to consider the evidence submitted by any candidate, and to report thereon to the board. In making their report the judges shall state whether the evidence submitted constitutes an original contribution to the advancement of knowledge of such substance and distinction as to give the candidate an authoritative status in some branch or branches of learning.

5. If the board approves the evidence as of sufficient merit for the degree, it shall give leave to the candidate to supplicate for the degree, and shall notify its decision in the *University Gazette*. One copy of each of the papers and books submitted as evidence shall remain in the possession of the University for deposit in Bodley's Library, provided that no book or paper of which the Library already possesses a copy shall be so deposited except with the consent of the candidate and of the Librarian, unless the copy submitted by the candidate shall be of a different issue or shall contain alterations or additions.

6. The boards shall have power to make, and to vary from time to time, such regulations for carrying out the provisions of this Section as they may deem expedient, provided that all such regulations and any variations in them shall be submitted to the Education Committee for approval.

NOTES

2 1

REGULATIONS FOR DEGREES IN CIVIL LAW AND FOR THE DEGREES OF MAGISTER JURIS AND MASTER OF PHILOSOPHY IN LAW

GENERAL REGULATIONS

§1. Admission of Candidates for the Degrees of Bachelor of Civil Law, Magister Juris, and Master of Philosophy in Law

1. Any person may be admitted by the Board of the Faculty of Law as a candidate for the Degrees of Bachelor of Civil Law, Magister Juris, or Master of Philosophy in Law provided that the following conditions have been satisfied:

(*a*) A candidate must either (i) have passed all the examinations required for the Degree of Bachelor of Arts and have obtained honours in the Second Public Examination, or have obtained honours in a degree examination of another university, such university having been approved by Council for the purpose of the status of Senior Student, or (ii) in the opinion of the Board of the Faculty of Law, be otherwise adequately qualified to undertake the course.

(*b*) A candidate must satisfy relevant provisions prescribed in the regulations made by the board, and any conditions the board may impose.

2. Any student for these degrees who is not a graduate of the University may wear the same gown as that worn by Students for the Degree of Doctor of Philosophy.

§2. Degrees of Bachelor of Civil Law and Magister Juris

Any person who has been admitted under the provisions of §1 above may supplicate for the Degree of Bachelor of Civil Law or the Degree of Magister Juris provided:

(i) that he or she has satisfied the examiners in the examinations prescribed in this section; and

(ii) that he or she has kept three terms of statutory residence as a matriculated member of the University after admission as a Student for the Degree of Bachelor of Civil Law or Magister Juris, whichever is the earlier.

§3. Degree of Master of Philosophy in Law

Any person who has been admitted under the provisions of §1 above may supplicate for the Degree of Master of Philosophy in Law provided:

(i) that he or she has satisfied the examiners in the examinations prescribed in this section; and

(ii) that he or she has kept six terms of statutory residence as a matriculated member of the University after admission as a Student for the Degree of Bachelor of Civil Law or Magister Juris.

§4. Examinations for the Degrees of Bachelor of Civil Law, Magister Juris, and Master of Philosophy in Law

1. The examinations for the Degrees of Bachelor of Civil Law, Magister Juris, and Master of Philosophy in Law shall comprise such subjects as the Board of the Faculty of Law shall from time to time by regulation determine.

2. The examinations shall be under the supervision of the board.

§5. Supervision of Students

Every candidate who elects to offer a thesis or dissertation shall seek approval from the Board of the Faculty of Law as prescribed in the regulations made by the board. Subject to such approval, supervision shall be provided as prescribed in the appropriate regulation, provided that references to the Degree of Master of Studies shall be deemed to refer to the Degrees of Bachelor of Civil Law, Magister Juris, or Master of Philosophy in Law as the case may be.

§6. Admission of Bachelors of Civil Law and Holders of the Degree of Magister Juris or the Degree of Master of Philosophy in Law to the Degree of Doctor of Civil Law

1. Any person who has been admitted to the Degree of Bachelor of Civil Law or to the Degree of Magister Juris or Master of Philosophy in Law, and who has completed fifteen terms from the date of such admission, may apply to the Board of the Faculty of Law for leave to supplicate for the Degree of Doctor of Civil Law. The application shall be made through the Registrar, and shall be accompanied by

(1) evidence that the candidate's application has the approval of his or her college;

(2) the fee prescribed in the appropriate regulation (see Appendix I);

(3) evidence of the candidate's fitness for the degree. This evidence must consist of three copies of a published book or of published books or papers, treating in a scientific manner of one or more legal subjects and consisting of an original contribution to the advancement of knowledge of such substance and distinction as to give the candidate authoritative status in some branch or branches of legal learning. A candidate who submits papers or books which have been produced in collaboration shall state in respect of each item the extent of the candidate's own contribution.

2. On receipt of the application the Board of the Faculty of Law, having determined that the evidence submitted is of the appropriate kind, shall appoint not fewer than two judges, who shall report to the board on the sufficiency of the evidence.

3. If the board, after consideration of the reports of the judges, shall approve the evidence as sufficient for the degree, it shall give leave to the candidate to supplicate for the degree, and shall notify its decision in the *University Gazette*. One copy of the evidence shall remain in the possession of the University for deposit in Bodley's Library, provided that no book or paper of which the Library already possesses a copy shall be so deposited except with the consent of the candidate and of the Librarian, unless the copy submitted by the candidate shall be of a different issue or shall contain alterations or additions.

§7. Admission to the Degrees of Bachelor of Civil Law and Doctor of Civil Law by Accumulation

1. Any person belonging to one of the following classes may apply to the Board of the Faculty of Law for permission to supplicate for the Degrees of Bachelor of Civil Law and Doctor of Civil Law at the same time under the conditions set forth in this subsection:

(*a*) Masters of Arts, except those on whom the degree has been conferred by decree or special resolution, who have entered upon the sixty-sixth term from their matriculation at this University, or, if they have been incorporated in this University, the sixty-sixth term from their matriculation at the University of Cambridge or of Dublin;

(*b*) persons on whom the Degree of Master of Arts has been conferred by decree or special resolution, other than a degree *honoris causa*, and who have entered upon the forty-fifth term from their admission to that degree;

(*c*) Doctors of Philosophy, or Masters of Letters or of Science or of Studies, who have entered upon the sixty-sixth term from their matriculation at this University.

2. The application of any such person shall be made to the board, and dealt with by the board, in the manner prescribed in §6 above.

3. If the board approves the evidence as sufficient for the Degree of Doctor of Civil Law, it shall give leave to the candidate to supplicate for the Degrees of Bachelor of Civil Law and Doctor of Civil Law at the same time, although the candidate shall not have passed the examination for the former degree.

SPECIAL REGULATIONS
Degrees of Bachelor of Civil Law and Magister Juris

1. *Admission criteria*

BCL The Law Board will normally admit to the BCL only candidates whose previous legal training is primarily in the common law.

M.Jur. The Law Board will normally admit to the M.Jur. only candidates whose previous legal training is not primarily in the common law.

2. *Residence*

Candidates for the BCL and M.Jur. must keep three terms statutory residence.

3. *Courses and subjects*

The subjects of the examination are listed in Schedule A below. The details of the courses are set out in the Law Faculty Student Handbook.

Candidates for the BCL and M.Jur. must offer four papers. A dissertation counts as one paper.

Not all subjects will necessarily be taught or examined in any one year. Depending on the availability of teaching resources, the Law Faculty may limit the number of candidates that may offer a subject. Details of those subjects which are available will be published in the Law Faculty Student Handbook for the year of the examination, subject to any amendment posted in the Law Faculty Office by Monday of week minus 1 of the Michaelmas Term before the examination is held.

In addition to the subjects in Schedule A, candidates may offer any other subject that may be approved from time to time by regulation published in the *Gazette* by the end of the Monday of week minus 1 of the Michaelmas Term before the examination is held.

No candidate for the BCL or M.Jur. may:

(*a*) offer a subject with the same title and/or the same syllabus as one which he or she has previously offered in the Final Honour School of Jurisprudence or Diploma in Legal Studies;

(*b*) offer two subjects having the same syllabus.

BCL Subject to compliance with the regulations above, candidates for the BCL may offer:

(*a*) any subject in List I which is offered in the year in question;

(*b*) a dissertation under the provisions in Schedule B below.

M.Jur. Subject to compliance with the regulations above, candidates for the M.Jur. 5 may offer:

(*a*) any subject in List I which is offered in the year in question;

(*b*) any subject in List II which is offered in the year in question;

(*c*) a dissertation under the provisions in Schedule B below.

4. *Examinations* 10

Candidates offering Jurisprudence and Political Theory will be examined under the provisions of Schedule C.

The examiners may award a distinction for excellence in the examination.

Candidates who fail or withdraw from the examination may with the permission of the faculty board and subject to such conditions as it imposes offer themselves for 15 re-examination. Candidates offering themselves for re-examination must retake all of the papers, except that:

(*a*) if all of the written papers are passed and the dissertation failed then only the dissertation need be resubmitted;

(*b*) if the dissertation is passed and one or more of the written papers failed then 20 only the written papers need be re-taken;

provided that nothing in this clause shall prejudice the powers of the Education Committee and Proctors to permit partial resits in exceptional circumstances.

If a candidate, having failed or withdrawn from an examination, successfully applies to sit the examination at a later date, and one or more of the subjects studied 25 by that candidate are not available when the candidate comes to be examined, papers shall nevertheless be set for that candidate in those subjects. These papers may not be taken by other candidates.

5. *Statutes and Other Source Material*

Details of the statutes and other source material which will be available to candi- 30 dates in the examination room for certain papers will be given in a notice circulated to candidates by the examiners.

6. *Notice of options*

The date for notification of the options to be offered by candidates is the fourth week of the Michaelmas Full Term preceding the examination with the exception of 35 the dissertation option [see Schedule B].

7. *Change of option choice*

Save in exceptional circumstances, no student may change their choice of option later than Friday of the first week of Hilary Term.

8. *Examiners* 40

The examiners appointed to examine subjects in List II shall be those appointed to examine the same subjects in the Honour School of Jurisprudence and shall examine those papers in the examination for the Honour School of Jurisprudence.

Degree of M.Phil. in Law

1. *Admissions* 45

Candidates may signify their intention to take the M.Phil. in Law when they apply for the BCL or M.Jur. or M.Sc Law and Finance or after they have been admitted. In either case a formal application must then be made in the Hilary Term preceding the Michaelmas Term in which they wish to study for the M.Phil. The appropriate form, obtainable from the The Faculty of Law Graduate Studies Office, must be returned to the Law Faculty's Student Administration Officer on the same date as that office specifies for the receipt of applications for the M.St. in Legal Research. Admission of those whose thesis topics are approved by the Law Faculty's Graduate Studies Committee and for whom that Committee certifies the availability of supervision will always be conditional on a specified level of performance in the BCL or M.Jur. or M.Sc Law and Finance.

2. *Residence*

Candidates for the M.Phil. in Law must keep 6 terms statutory residence, which may include periods spent in residence while studying for the BCL or M.Jur. or M.Sc Law and Finance.

3. *Courses and examination*

Candidates for the M.Phil. in Law shall satisfactorily complete Part 1 and Part 2. Part 1 and Part 2 shall be taken in that order and shall normally be taken in successive years. A candidate wishing to take Part 2 but not to proceed directly from Part 1 to Part 2 in successive years must seek permission from the Graduate Studies Committee for Law. Part 1 shall consist of the BCL or M.Jur. or M.Sc Law and Finance as the case may be.

In Part 2, candidates for the M.Phil. in Law shall follow a course of instruction in Legal Research Method, satisfy the examiners that they have completed to the required standard such tests or exercises in Legal Research Method as may be prescribed as part of such a course of instruction, and be examined by thesis which must not exceed 30,000 words and should not normally be less than 25,000 words, and by oral examination, under the provisions of cll. 1 to 9 of the regulations for the M.St. in Legal Research, provided that:

(*a*) references to the Degree of Master of Studies shall be deemed to refer to Part 2 of the M.Phil. in Law;

(*b*) in cl. 5, the date of application for examination shall be during the Trinity Term after the candidate began Part 2 of the M.Phil. in Law. A candidate who wishes to apply for examination at a later date must seek the approval of the Graduate Studies Committee for Law by the end of Week Four of the same Trinity Full Term. Only in exceptional circumstances will the Committee extend the M.Phil. deadline. Unless the deadline has been extended, a thesis submitted after the required date will normally be eligible only to be examined for an M.St.

The thesis may cover the same area of Law as a dissertation offered in the BCL or M.Jur. or M.Sc Law and Finance, but the text of the dissertation must not be incorporated into the thesis.

SCHEDULE A

List I

Advanced Property and Trusts;
Commercial Remedies;
Comparative and European Corporate Law;
Comparative and Global Environmental Law;
Comparative Equality Law;
Comparative Human Rights;
Comparative Public Law;
Competition Law;
Conflict of Laws;
Constitutional Principles of the EU;
Constitutional Theory;
Corporate and Business Taxation;

Corporate Finance Law;
Corporate Insolvency Law;
Criminal Justice and Human Rights;
Dissertation;
European Business Regulation (the law of the EU's internal market); 5
European Intellectual Property Law;
European Private Law: Contract;
European Union as Actor in International Law;
Evidence;
International and European Employment Law; 10
International Commercial Arbitration;
International Dispute Settlement;
International Economic Law;
International Law and Armed Conflict;
International Law of the Sea; 15
Jurisprudence and Political Theory;
Law and Society in Medieval England;
Law in Society;
Medical Law and Ethics;
Personal Taxation; 20
Philosophical Foundations of the Common Law;
Principles of Civil Procedure;
Principles of Financial Regulation;
Punishment, Security and the State;
Regulation; 25
Restitution of Unjust Enrichment;
Roman Law (Delict);
The Roman and Civilian Law of Contracts;
Transnational Commercial Law.

List II 30
Commercial Law;
Company Law;
Comparative Law: Contract;
Contract;
European Union Law (may not be taken in conjunction with Constitutional 35
    Principles of the EU from list I);
European Human Rights Law;
Family;
Land;
Public International Law; 40
Tort;
Trusts (may not be taken in conjunction with Advanced Property and Trusts
    from list I);
Copyright, Patent and Allied Rights (may not be taken in conjunction with European
    Intellectual Property Law from List I, or with Copyright, Trade Marks and Allied 45
    Rights);
Copyright, Trade Marks and Allied Rights (may not be taken in conjunction with
    European Intellectual Property Law from List I, or with Copyright, Patent and
    Allied Rights).

SCHEDULE B

Dissertations

Candidates for the BCL and M.Jur. may offer a dissertation, which must be written in English and must not exceed 12,500 words and should not normally be less than 10,000 words (including notes, but excluding tables of cases or other legal sources) on a subject to be proposed by the candidate in consultation with the supervisor, and approved by the Graduate Studies Committee in Law. The dissertation shall be wholly or substantially the result of work undertaken whilst registered for the degree of Bachelor of Civil Law or Magister Juris. In deciding whether to give approval, the committee shall take into account the suitability of the subject matter and availability of appropriate supervision. Candidates should submit the proposed title of the dissertation and a synopsis of its scope in not more than 500 words not later than Monday of Week Minus One of Michaelmas Full Term to the board's Director of Graduate Studies (Taught Courses) who shall, when the topic and supervisor have been confirmed by or on behalf of the board's Committee for Graduate Studies, communicate that information to the Chair of the Examiners for the BCL and M.Jur.

Supervisors or others are permitted to give bibliographical help and to discuss drafts. Every candidate offering a dissertation is entitled to six sessions of supervision, each of approximately one hour, not counting meetings to settle the shape of the dissertation before it was approved.

The examiners must judge the extent to which the dissertation affords evidence of significant analytical ability on the part of the candidate. The required format for this dissertation is the common format prescribed for all law theses, which is printed in the Faculty of Law's Graduate Student's Handbook.

Submission

No later than noon on Friday of the fifth week of Trinity Full Term two copies of your dissertation must be delivered to the Examination Schools, High Street, Oxford OX1 4BG. The package must be clearly marked 'Dissertation for BCL/M.Jur.'. In order to ensure anonymity, the dissertation must bear your examination number. Neither your name nor the name of your college must appear. You must include with the thesis (i) a signed statement that, except where otherwise indicated, the thesis is entirely your own work, and (ii) a second statement indicating which part or parts of the dissertation have formed or will form part of a submission in accordance with the requirements of another course at this or another university. To ensure anonymity these statements must be placed in a sealed envelope. The examiners shall exclude from consideration any part of your dissertation which is not your own work or which has been or will be submitted to satisfy the requirements of another course, and the examiners shall have power to require you to produce for their inspection the work so submitted or to be submitted.

SCHEDULE C

Candidates offering Jurisprudence and Political Theory will be examined in that subject by the submission of three essays. Essay questions will be published by the Board of Examiners on the morning of the Friday of the eighth week of the Hilary Term preceding the examination. Candidates will be contacted with details of how to collect or access the questions. The examiners shall offer a choice of six topics from which candidates shall be required to select three. The total length of the three essays submitted shall be not less than 5,000 words, nor more than 8,000. The essays shall be wholly or substantially the result of work undertaken whilst registered for the degree of Batchelor of Civil Law or Magister Juris. Two copies of each essay submitted must be delivered to the Chair of the BCL/M.Jur. Examiners, Examination Schools, High

Street, Oxford OX1 4BG, by noon on the Friday preceding the beginning of the Trinity Full Term in which the examination is to be taken. The essays must bear the candidate's examination number, but not his or her name or the name of his or her college. Every candidate shall sign a Declaration of Authorship to the effect that the essays are his or her own work. Candidates shall further state the total number of words used in their essays. This Declaration of Authorship shall be presented together with the essays. To ensure anonymity the Declaration of Authorship must be placed in a sealed envelope.

5

NOTES

22

REGULATIONS FOR DEGREES IN MEDICINE AND SURGERY

§1. Qualifications of Candidates for the Degree of Bachelor of Medicine

1. A student who has been admitted to the Degree of Bachelor of Arts with Honours may supplicate for the Degree of Bachelor of Medicine, provided that they shall have passed the examinations hereinafter prescribed.

2. A candidate who has been admitted to the Second Examination for the Degree of Bachelor of Medicine by the Medical Sciences Board under the provisions of §6, cl. 1 of this section may supplicate for the Degree of Bachelor of Medicine without having been admitted to the Degree of Bachelor of Arts with Honours, provided that they shall have passed the Second Examination and shall have kept statutable residence for six terms.

3. A candidate for the Preliminary Examination in Medicine or for the Degree of Bachelor of Medicine who has been admitted under the provisions of §6, cl. 1 of this section and who is not a graduate of the University may wear the same gown as that worn by Students for the Degree of Doctor of Philosophy.

§2. Degree of Bachelor of Surgery

Any person admitted to the Degree of Bachelor of Medicine shall *ipso facto* be admitted also to the Degree of Bachelor of Surgery.

§3. Subjects and Method of the First Examination for the Degree of Bachelor of Medicine

A

1. The First Examination for the Degree of Bachelor of Medicine shall be under the supervision of the Medical Sciences Board. The Board shall have power to require candidates for admission to any

part of the First Examination to produce certificates of attendance at courses of practical instruction, and such other certificates as the Board may from time to time determine, and to define the form of such certificates. It shall be the duty of the Registrar to see that these conditions are observed.

2. The subjects of the First Examination shall be:

Part I

1. Organisation of the Body
2. Physiology and Pharmacology
3. Biochemistry and Medical Genetics
4. Population Health 1: Medical Sociology

Part II

5. Applied Physiology and Pharmacology
6. The Nervous System
7. Principles of Pathology
8. Psychology for Medicine

3. The syllabus of each subject shall be as prescribed from time to time by the Medical Sciences Board by regulation.

4. Subjects 1, 2, 3, 5, 6, and 7 shall each be examined in two Parts, A and B. In each of these subjects, a candidate must offer both Parts A and B at one examination, provided that a candidate who has failed at his or her first attempt to satisfy the examiners in one Part only of a subject may offer that Part alone at a subsequent examination. In each of these subjects, a candidate must pass both Parts, or have accumulated passes in both Parts, in order to pass in that subject. When a candidate who at the first attempt passed only one Part of a subject subsequently passes the remaining Part of that subject, the examiners shall publish his or her name as having passed in that subject.

5. A candidate must offer all four subjects in Part I at one examination, provided that a candidate who has failed at his or her first attempt in any subject or subjects may offer subject 4 or any Part or Parts of subjects 1, 2, or 3 at a subsequent examination (in accordance with clause 4 above), and provided that the Medical Sciences Board may dispense candidates who have already passed a First Public Examination in any subject from the requirement to offer all four subjects at one examination. In Part I, the examiners may publish the name of a candidate as having passed one, two, three, or four subjects, and the examiners may in addition publish the name of a candidate as having passed one Part only of any of

the subjects 1, 2, or 3. In Part II, a candidate must offer all four subjects at one examination, provided that a candidate who has failed at his or her first attempt in any subject or subjects may offer subject 8 or any Part or Parts of subjects 5, 6, or 7 at a subsequent examination (in accordance with clause 4 above). In Part II, the examiners may publish the name of a candidate as having passed one, two, three, or four subjects, and the examiners may in addition publish the name of a candidate as having passed one Part only of any of the subjects 5, 6, or 7.

6. A candidate shall be deemed to have passed the First Examination if he or she has satisfied the examiners in all the subjects of Parts I and II as specified in clause 2 above.

7. A candidate who has passed Part I of the First Examination shall be deemed to have passed the First Public Examination.

8. No candidate shall be admitted to the examination for Part II of the First Examination without first having passed all the subjects of Part I, save in exceptional circumstances at the discretion of the Medical Sciences Board following application from the candidate's society. No candidate may offer any subject or Part of a subject in Parts I and II of the First Examination on more than two occasions, save in exceptional circumstances at the discretion of the Medical Sciences Board following application from the candidate's society.

9. The examiners may award a Distinction to candidates of special merit in either Part I or Part II of the examination, provided that all examinations for all four subjects specified for that Part in clause 2 above have been offered in their entirety and passed at one examination at the first scheduled opportunity which shall be the candidate's first attempt, except in exceptional circumstances at the discretion of the Board of Examiners following application from the candidate's society.

10. The examiners may award a Pass with Merit to candidates of special merit in any of the individual subjects 1, 2, 3, 5, 6, or 7, provided that all four subjects of Part I or of Part II of the examination have been offered in their entirety at one examination. The award of Pass with Merit shall be based on performance in Part B of a subject and shall be confined to candidates who have passed Part A of that subject at the same sitting which shall be the first scheduled opportunity and the candidate's first attempt, except in exceptional circumstances at the discretion of the Board of Examiners following application from the candidate's society.

11. No candidate shall be admitted to the First Examination unless he or she has been through the standard selection procedures

for the standard medical course (including sitting the Biomedical Admissions Test—BMAT), has met the published entry requirements for admission to the standard medical course, and his or her name has been entered on the University Register of Medical Students.

B

A Core Syllabus and a Composite Syllabus (Core plus Extension) for each of Parts I and II will be published annually at the start of Michaelmas Term by the Medical Sciences Board. The syllabuses will make appropriate reference to related issues of clinical significance. In each subject, candidates will be expected to have a general understanding of the components specified in the syllabus, including methods of study and quantitative analysis of experimental results.

In subjects 1, 2, 3, 5, 6, and 7 two papers will be set, Paper A and Paper B. Paper A shall be no longer than 1 hour and 25 minutes in duration, and shall be a computer-based assessment of breadth of knowledge and understanding of the Core Syllabus. Paper B shall be set to examine deeper knowledge and understanding of a choice of topics included in or closely relating to the Composite Syllabus. For Subjects 1, 2, and 3, Paper B shall be two hours in duration, and for Subjects 5, 6, and 7, Paper B shall be three hours in duration.

Part I

1. *Organisation of the Body*
2. *Physiology and Pharmacology*
3. *Biochemistry and Medical Genetics*
4. *Population Health 1: Medical Sociology*

One one-and-a-half-hour paper will be set on the syllabus specified in the Core Syllabus for Part I.

Part II

5. *Applied Physiology and Pharmacology*
6. *The Nervous System*
7. *Principles of Pathology*
8. *Psychology for Medicine*

One two-hour paper will be set on the syllabus specified in the Core Syllabus for Part II.

General Regulations of the First Examination

Candidates shall submit notebooks, initialled as satisfactory by the demonstrators, or other certified evidence of satisfactory practical work in the courses associated with each subject of the First Examination, with the exception of Medical Sociology and Psychology for Medicine. The practical course for Subject 2 includes the course in elementary statistics defined in the Composite Syllabus for Part I. Each notebook shall be accompanied by a certificate signed by the candidate indicating that the notebook submitted is the candidate's own work. The notebooks or evidence shall be available to the examiners at a time prescribed by the examiners prior to the written examination and shall be taken into consideration by them. Candidates whose notebooks or other evidence are unsatisfactory may be required by the examiners to submit to further examination. Failure to submit an initialled notebook or certified evidence shall result in the candidate being failed in the relevant subject of the examination, unless the candidate has an adequate attendance record at the relevant practical classes and provided the examiners are satisfied, after taking account of the candidate's examination script and any further examination as they shall deem necessary, that the candidate has a satisfactory knowledge and understanding of the practical course.

The Director of Pre-Clinical Studies or his or her deputy is required to make 5
available to the examiners evidence (in the form of a list of names, signed by the Director or his or her deputy) to certify that each candidate has a satisfactory attendance record for each practical course defined in the preceding paragraph.

Evidence of satisfactory practical work and of attendance at a practical course is normally admissible by the examiners for a period extending no longer than to the 10
end of the academic year following the year in which the course was pursued.

The Director of Pre-Clinical Studies or his or her deputy is required to make available to the examiners evidence (in the form of a list of names, signed by the Director or his or her deputy) to certify that each candidate has participated satisfactorily in the *Patient and Doctor Course*. 15

Candidates may be required to undergo oral examination.

§4. Qualifying Examination in the Principles of Clinical Anatomy

A

There shall be a Qualifying Examination in the Principles of 20
Clinical Anatomy for medical students who have passed the First Examination for the Degree of Bachelor of Medicine and who are seeking admission to a course in clinical medicine in Oxford or elsewhere. The examination shall be governed by the following provisions. 25

(*a*) The examination shall be under the supervision of the Medical Sciences Board.

(*b*) No candidate shall be admitted to this Qualifying Examination unless his or her name has been entered on the Register of University Medical Students and he or she has pre- 30
viously passed the First Examination for the Degree of Bachelor of Medicine.

(*c*) The syllabus and obligations required of candidates, and the method of examination, shall be as prescribed from time to time by regulations of the Medical Sciences Board. 35

B

The syllabus shall be published annually in Trinity Term by the Medical Sciences Board. Candidates shall submit notebooks, initialled as satisfactory by the demonstrators, or other certified evidence of satisfactory practical work associated with the course. The examination will consist of in-course assessment of a form approved by 40
the Medical Sciences Board. Any candidate whose performance in any part of this assessment is judged to be unsatisfactory may be reassessed during the course or at some duly advertised time during the Long Vacation by such means as may be deemed appropriate by the examiners. In determining whether a candidate has passed the examination, the examiners will take account of the candidate's overall 45

record of assessment without necessarily requiring a satisfactory performance in every constituent part.

The Director of Pre-Clinical Studies or his or her deputy is required to make available to the examiners evidence (in the form of a list of names, signed by the Director or his or her deputy) to certify that each candidate has a satisfactory attendance record at the course in the Principles of Clinical Anatomy. Any candidate whose record of attendance is deemed unsatisfactory by the examiners shall be liable to undergo additional examination by such means as may be deemed appropriate by the examiners, or he or she may be failed at the discretion of the examiners.

Candidates may be required to undergo oral examination.

§5. Subjects and Method of the Examination for the Preliminary Examination in Medicine

A

1. A candidate may be admitted to the Preliminary Examination in Medicine provided that his or her name is on the Register of Clinical Students and he or she has been admitted to the Degree of Bachelor of Arts with Honours or has obtained a degree of another university deemed adequate for the purpose by the Medical Sciences Board, and that he or she has satisfied such additional qualifications as the Medical Sciences Board may from time to time prescribe in its regulations.

2. The Preliminary Examination in Medicine shall consist of two parts. Part I may be offered not earlier than three terms, and Part II not earlier than six terms, from the date of entry onto the Register of Clinical Students.

3. The examination shall comprise such subjects and papers as the Medical Sciences Board shall from time to time by regulation determine.

4. The examiners may award a Distinction to candidates of special merit in either Part I or Part II of the examination, provided that all the subjects in that Part have been offered and passed at one examination.

5. The examination shall be under the supervision of the Medical Sciences Board.

B

The examination will be in two parts. A core syllabus and an extension syllabus for each of Parts I and II will be published annually at the start of the Michaelmas Term prior to the examination by the Medical Sciences Board.

Part I

The examination will assess candidates' core knowledge and understanding of core material, and clinical skills and critical-appraisal skills. Candidates must pass all seven components listed below in order to pass the examination. Candidates who fail any component(s) of the examination at the first attempt need re-sit only the component(s) that they have failed, provided that all components are passed within a single academic year; except that, where a candidate has been granted leave by the Board to sit a component or components for a third time (under the provisions of the General Regulations for Part I of the Preliminary Examination in Medicine), the Board may also, at its discretion, waive the requirement for the candidate to pass all components within a single academic year. 5

1. *Core Material*

Candidates will be required to demonstrate their knowledge and understanding of the principles of basic medical science as defined in the core syllabus for Part I. Two papers will be set. Paper One (one hour) will consist of questions requiring short answers, and may require candidates to select answers from a list of options. Paper 10 Two (two hours) will be in the format of problem-based questions. Each question will be marked pass or fail, and a cumulative pass/fail mark will be given for a candidate's overall performance in the two papers. The marks from these papers will not contribute to the award of a Distinction.

2. *Paper 3: Ethics (one hour)* 15

Candidates will be required to write one essay in response to a choice of question topics.

3. *Paper 4: Systems of the Body (one and a half hours)*

Candidates will be required to write one essay from a choice of questions, which will relate to extension topics notified to candidates at the start of the academic year. 20 Candidates will be given credit for demonstrating their breadth of reading beyond the core syllabus, for their ability to synthesise evidence from different sources and produce a coherent argument, and for discussion of experimental evidence from primary literature. During the examination, candidates will have access to such databases of medical literature as may be prescribed from time to time by 25 the Medical Sciences Board and notified to candidates at the beginning of the academic year.

4. *Paper 5: Critical Appraisal (two hours)*

This paper will assess candidates' ability to critically appraise primary research material. The primary research paper, or extracts from a number of papers, may 30 report laboratory-based or clinical research. The literature will contain experimental, public health or clinical data for interpretation but may also include descriptions of experimental methods. Candidates may be required to offer criticism of the experimental method, or of the interpretation of the results, or to draw their own inferences from the published data. Candidates must attempt all questions. 35

5. *Clinical Skills*

Candidates will be required to demonstrate, in a practical examination, their ability to take a clinical history and to perform a clinical examination of the systems of the body specified in the core curriculum and, to apply such practical skills as may be defined in the core syllabus published by the Medical Sciences Board. The examina- 40 tion will include an assessment of candidates' communication skills with patients, orally and/or in writing, and of their professional behaviour.

6. *Submitted Essay: Systems of the Body*

(i) *Form and subject of the essay*

Candidates will be required to submit an essay on a topic approved by the 45 examiners. The submitted essay shall be of not more than 3,000 words, excluding any tables, figures, diagrams or references. It must be in a format prescribed by the Graduate-entry Education Committee and published in the *Notes of Guidance for the Preliminary Examination in Medicine*.

A list of suggested essay titles, and the topics to which they relate, approved by the Chair of Examiners in consultation with the module organisers, shall be published no later than the end of Week 5 of the Michaelmas Term in the academic year of the examination. Candidates may also propose their own titles. The essay may relate to any of the topics set out in the *Notes of Guidance for the Preliminary Examination in Medicine* except that candidates may not submit an essay that closely relates to work that they have previously submitted for any university examination. A candidate wishing to offer an essay with a title not on the approved list must apply for approval of their proposed title by no later than the end of Week 0 of Hilary Term in the academic year of the examination. Application shall be made via the Course Administrator in the Medical School Office and shall include the proposed title, a brief outline of the subject matter, and the topic or topics to which it relates. Decision on the application shall be made by the Chair of Examiners in consultation with the module organisers and shall be communicated to the candidate as soon as possible and in any case not later than Week 2 of Hilary Term in the academic year of the examination.

(ii) *Registration*

No later than the end of Week 0 of Hilary Term in the academic year of the examination, every candidate must register the title of their essay via the Course Administrator in the Medical School Office.

(iii) *Authorship*

The essay must be the candidate's own work. Candidates' tutors, or their deputies nominated to act as advisors, may discuss with candidates the proposed field of study, the sources available, and the method of treatment, but on no account may they read or comment on any written draft. Every candidate shall sign a certificate to the effect that this rule has been observed and that the essay is their own work. The certificate, sealed in a separate envelope, should be addressed to the Chair of Examiners for the Preliminary Examination in Medicine Part I and submitted alongside the essay.

(iv) *Submission*

The essay (two paper copies and an electronic copy) must be submitted to the Chair of Examiners for the Preliminary Examination in Medicine Part I, c/o the Examination Schools, High Street, Oxford, not later than noon on the Friday of Week 0 of Trinity Term.

7. *Longitudinal Case Study combined with Behavioural Sciences Commentary*

Candidates will be required to complete a Longitudinal Case Study during their clinical course, details of which will be published each year in the clinical course handbook. This coursework must be submitted to the candidate's GP Tutor by Friday of Week 9 of Hilary Term. The clinical course organiser will then forward each case study to the Chair of Examiners by the end of Week 0 of Trinity Term, together with a certificate, signed by the relevant clinical supervisor, of satisfactory performance by the candidate in the Longitudinal Case Study. Candidates will separately submit an essay covering an aspect of Behavioural Sciences, which will relate to the longitudinal case study. This essay will contribute to the award of a Distinction.

(i) *Form and subject of the essay*

Candidates will be required to submit a Behavioural Sciences commentary, relating to the patient described in the Longitudinal Case Study, in the form of an essay of not more than 3,000 words, excluding any tables, figures, diagrams or references. It must be in a format prescribed by the Graduate-entry Education Committee and published in the *Notes of Guidance for the Preliminary Examination in Medicine.*

The essay must refer to aspects of Behavioural Sciences from a list published at the beginning of the academic year by the Graduate-entry Education Committee and included in the *Notes of Guidance for the Preliminary Examination in Medicine.* The   5
number of such topics to be covered in the essay will be determined from time to time by the Graduate-entry Education Committee and will be published with the list and included in the *Notes of Guidance.*

(ii) *Authorship*

The essay must be the candidate's own work. Candidates' tutors, or their deputies   10
nominated to act as advisors, may discuss with candidates the proposed field of study as it relates to the patient, the sources available, and the method of treatment, but on no account may they read or comment on any written draft. Every candidate shall sign a certificate to the effect that this rule has been observed and that the essay is their own work; and the candidate's tutor or advisor shall countersign the certificate   15
confirming that, to the best of their knowledge and belief, this is so. The certificate, sealed in a separate envelope, should be addressed to the Chair of Examiners for the Preliminary Examination in Medicine Part I and submitted alongside the essay.

(iii) *Submission*

The essay (two paper copies and an electronic copy) must be submitted to the   20
Chair of Examiners for the Preliminary Examination in Medicine Part I, c/o the Examination Schools, High Street, Oxford, not later than noon on the Friday of Week o of Trinity Term.

General regulations for Part I of the Preliminary Examination in Medicine

The examination will be set at the end of the extended Trinity Term and at the end   25
of the Long Vacation.

Examiners may award Distinctions for outstanding performance in Papers 3, 4 and 5, together with the Submitted Essay and Behavioural Sciences element of the Longitudinal Case Study, by candidates sitting the examination for the first time.

Candidates may be required, at the discretion of the examiners, to undergo an oral   30
examination which may include a further clinical examination.

No candidate may enter for the examination on more than two occasions, save in exceptional circumstances at the discretion of the Medical Sciences Board following application from the candidate's society.

Part II   35

The examination will consist of seven components. Candidates must pass all seven components listed below in order to pass the examination. Candidates who fail any component(s) of the examination at the first attempt need re-sit only the component(s) that they have failed, provided that all components are passed within a single academic year; except that, where a candidate has been granted leave by the   40
Board to sit a component or components for a third time (under the provisions of the General Regulations for Part II of the Preliminary Examination in Medicine), the Board may also, at its discretion, waive the requirement for the candidate to pass all components within a single academic year.

1. *Paper1: Medicine (two hours)*   45

This paper will test core knowledge and understanding through problem-based questions. This material may include basic and applied science, differential diagnosis of common diseases and simple first-line clinical investigations. The paper will be marked pass/fail only. The marks from this paper will not contribute to the overall mark in the examination, nor to the award of a Distinction.

2. *Paper 2: Clinical Science (two hours)*

This paper will relate to extension topics notified to candidates at the start of the academic year and will require candidates to answer two questions. Candidates will be given credit for demonstrating their breadth of reading beyond the core syllabus, for their ability to synthesise evidence from different sources and produce a coherent argument, and for discussion of primary literature.

3. *Paper 3: Data Interpretation (two hours)*

This paper will assess candidates' ability to critically appraise primary research material. The primary research paper, or papers (normally not more than two), will report clinical research. The literature will contain experimental, epidemiological, or clinical data for interpretation, including public health data. Candidates may be required to offer criticism of the experimental method, or of the interpretation of the published data (including epidemiological data), or to draw their own inferences from the published data. Candidates must attempt all questions.

4. *Extended Essay on a Public Health topic*

(i) *Form and subject of the essay*

Candidates will be required to submit an essay on a topic related to Public Health aspects of the diagnosis or management of a clinical case they have seen during their clinical attachments in the second year of the course. The submitted essay shall be of not more than 3,000 words, excluding any tables, figures, diagrams or references. It must be in a format prescribed by the Graduate-entry Education Committee and published in the *Notes of Guidance for the Preliminary Examination in Medicine*.

The essay must refer to aspects of Public Health from a list published at the beginning of the academic year by the Graduate-entry Education Committee and included in the *Notes of Guidance for the Preliminary Examination in Medicine*. The number of such topics to be covered in the essay will be determined from time to time by the Graduate-entry Education Committee and will be published with the list and included in the *Notes of Guidance*.

(ii) *Validity*

Candidates must submit with their essay a certificate from the Clinical Tutor in Medicine or in Surgery, or from a consultant in charge of the patient, confirming that the student has seen the patient described in the essay.

As a prologue to the essay, candidates should include a summary of the clinical case to which the essay refers. The summary should not usually exceed 250 words, but will not be included in the overall word count for the essay.

(iii) *Authorship*

The essay must be the candidate's own work. Candidates' tutors, or their deputies nominated to act as advisors, may discuss with candidates the proposed field of study, the sources available, and the method of treatment, but on no account may they read or comment on any written draft. Every candidate shall sign a certificate to the effect that this rule has been observed and that the essay is their own work. The certificate, sealed in a separate envelope, should be addressed to the Chair of Examiners for the Preliminary Examination in Medicine Part II and submitted alongside the essay.

(iv) *Submission*

The essay (two paper copies and an electronic copy) must be submitted to the Chair of Examiners for the Preliminary Examination in Medicine Part II, c/o the

Examination Schools, High Street, Oxford, not later than noon on the Friday of Week 1 of Trinity Term.

5. *Extended Synoptic Essay on a Science topic*

(i) *Form and subject of the essay*

Candidates will be required to submit an essay on a topic approved by the examiners, illustrating a technique or scientific application across several fields of clinical or basic science. The submitted essay shall be of not more than 3,000 words, excluding any tables, figures, diagrams or references. It must be in a format prescribed by the Graduate-entry Education Committee and published in the *Notes of Guidance for the Preliminary Examination in Medicine.*

A list of suggested essay titles, and the topics to which they relate, approved by the Chair of Examiners in consultation with the Chair of the Graduate-entry Education Committee, shall be published no later than the end of Week 5 of the Michaelmas Term in the academic year of the examination. Candidates may also propose their own titles. Candidates may not submit an essay that closely relates to work that they have previously submitted for any university examination. A candidate wishing to offer an essay with a title not on the approved list must apply for approval of their proposed title by no later than the end of Week 0 of Hilary Term in the academic year of the examination. Application shall be made via the Course Administrator in the Medical School Office and shall include the proposed title, a brief outline of the subject matter, and the topic or topics to which it relates. Decision on the application shall be made by the Chair of Examiners in consultation with the Chair of the Graduate-entry Education Committee and shall be communicated to the candidate as soon as possible and in any case not later than Week 2 of Hilary Term in the academic year of the examination.

(ii) *Registration*

No later than the end of Week 0 of Hilary Term in the academic year of the examination, every candidate must register the title of their essay via the Course Administrator in the Medical School Office.

(iii) *Authorship*

The essay must be the candidate's own work. Candidates' tutors, or their deputies nominated to act as advisors, may discuss with candidates the proposed field of study, the sources available, and the method of treatment, but on no account may they read or comment on any written draft. Every candidate shall sign a certificate to the effect that this rule has been observed and that the essay is their own work. The certificate, sealed in a separate envelope, should be addressed to the Chair of Examiners for the Preliminary Examination in Medicine Part II and submitted alongside the essay.

(iv) *Submission*

The essay (two paper copies and an electronic copy) must be submitted to the Chair of Examiners for the Preliminary Examination in Medicine Part II, c/o the Examination Schools, High Street, Oxford, not later than noon on the Friday of Week 1 of Trinity Term.

6. *A clinical long case, followed by a viva*

Candidates will be assessed on their clinical history and examination skills, including their communication skills and professional behaviour, and knowledge of differential diagnosis and first-line investigations.

7. *An Objective Structured Clinical Examination or similar problem-based clinical assessment*

Candidates will be assessed on their ability to perform a clinical examination of the systems of the body specified in the core curriculum, and on their practical skills, and on their ability to interpret and use clinical data.

8. In addition to the above examination, candidates will be required to have satisfactorily completed the following courses of instruction during Year 2:

(*a*) Practical skills and procedures (defined in the core curriculum) to be assessed in-course. A completed checklist of these skills and procedures, signed by the appropriate Clinical Tutor or other representative nominated by the Course Director, is required as a qualification for entry to the examination. These skills may be re-sampled during the end-of-year clinical assessment.

(*b*) The Laboratory Medicine Course (as prescribed for the Second Examination for the Degree of BM, Year 1)

(*c*) Medicine (as prescribed for the Second Examination for the Degree of BM, Year 1)

(*d*) Surgery (as prescribed for the Second Examination for the Degree of BM, Year 1)

General regulations for Part II of the Preliminary Examination in Medicine

The examination will be set towards the end of Trinity Term and at a time to be specified by the examiners during the Long Vacation.

Examiners may award Distinctions for outstanding performance in Papers 2 and 3, and the two extended essays, by candidates sitting the examination for the first time.

Candidates may be required, at the discretion of the examiners, to undergo an oral examination which may include a further clinical examination.

No candidate may enter for the examination on more than two occasions, save in exceptional circumstances at the discretion of the Medical Sciences Board following application from the candidate's society.

§6. Subjects and Method of the Second Examination for the Degree of Bachelor of Medicine

A

*1. A candidate may be admitted to the Second Examination if his or her name has been entered on the University Register of Clinical Students and he or she has satisfied one of the following conditions:

(*a*) he or she has passed in all the subjects of the First Examination and the Qualifying Examination in the Principles of Clinical Anatomy and has either been admitted to the Degree of Bachelor of Arts with Honours or obtained a bachelor's degree at another university; or

(*b*) he or she has passed in all the subjects of the Preliminary Examination in Medicine; or

---

* Applications for admission to the Second BM Examination under the provisions of this clause should be addressed to the Medical School Office, Level 2, John Radcliffe Hospital, Headley Way, Oxford OX3 9DU.

(*c*) he or she has both

   (i) successfully completed at a university in the United Kingdom a GMC-approved course of study in medical sciences that has included the subjects of the First Examination and the Principles of Clinical Anatomy, and is deemed by the Medical Sciences Board to qualify the candidate for admission; and

   (ii) obtained a bachelor's degree in science or arts at a university, such degree having been approved by the Board.

2. The Second Examination for the Degree of Bachelor of Medicine shall be under the supervision of the Medical Sciences Board. The Board shall have power to require candidates for admission to any part of the Second Examination to produce certificates of attendance at courses of practical instruction, and such other certificates as the Board may from time to time determine, and to define the form of such certificates. It shall be the duty of the Registrar to see that these conditions are observed.

3. The subject of the Second Examination shall be clinical medicine in all its aspects.

(*a*) The Second Examination shall cover three years, the subjects for each year being prescribed by regulation of the Medical Sciences Board.

(*b*) Each of Years 1 and 2 shall involve a form of assessment prescribed by regulation of the Board which shall be notified to candidates. No candidate shall commence Year 2 or 3 until he or she has satisfactorily completed Year 1 or 2 respectively (except that a candidate shall be permitted to commence Year 2 if he or she has passed in all the subjects in the Preliminary Examination in Medicine), unless the Director of Clinical Studies, at his or her discretion and in exceptional circumstances, decides that the candidate may proceed to the next year of study on condition that he or she should undertake remedial work and if necessary be reassessed at a later date.

(*c*) Year 3 shall involve written and clinical examinations and may involve oral examinations. No candidate shall be examined on the Year 3 Vocational Skills Course until he or she has passed the assessments for Years 1 and 2 and the Year 3 General Clinical Studies Course.

4. A candidate who has passed in all the subjects of the Preliminary Examination in Medicine shall be exempted from the Year 1 assessments of the Second Examination and shall be permitted to proceed directly to commence Year 2.

5. The examiners may award a Distinction for outstanding performance over the three years. Criteria for Distinctions will be determined by the Medical Sciences Board.

6. The examiners may award merits in each of the examined subjects in Years 1, 2 and 3.

7. Breach of the Code of Conduct for Medical Students, as approved and from time to time amended by Council's General Purposes Committee on the recommendation of the Medical Sciences Board, may be deemed to be a ground for removal of a student's name from the University Register of Clinical Students according to procedures which shall always be subject to approval by Council's General Purposes Committee on the recommendation of the Medical Sciences Board.

8. The provisions of the appropriate regulations, concerning the times of holding examinations and the entry of names, and the special regulation concerning dress shall not, unless otherwise prescribed by regulation of the board, apply to Years 1 and 2, except in the case of a formal examination set by the examiners of these stages, as prescribed by regulation of the Board.

B

1. *Syllabus and Examination*
The Second Examination shall be divided as detailed below.

YEAR 1

In Year 1, students are required to satisfy the examiners in:

 (*a*) The Laboratory Medicine Course (concerning the application to human disease of the principles of Laboratory Medicine, including Histopathology, Microbiology and Infection, Clinical Biochemistry, Immunology and Haematology);
 (*b*) Medicine;
 (*c*) Surgery.

Each candidate will be assessed according to the methods approved by the Medical Sciences Board and notified to candidates before the commencement of each course of instruction.

Candidates must satisfy the relevant head of department or his or her deputy, or the Director of Clinical Studies or his or her deputy, that they have attended a course of instruction, and attained the necessary skills, knowledge and understanding in:

 (*a*) The Patient Doctor 2 Course (being an introduction to clinical methods, history taking and physical examination);
 (*b*) Anaesthetics;
 (*c*) Clinical Pharmacology;
 (*d*) Communication Skills;
 (*e*) Medical Ethics and Law;
 (*f*) Primary Health Care;
 (*g*) Radiology;
 (*h*) Special Study approved on behalf of the Medical Sciences Board.

No candidate shall commence Year 2 until he or she has satisfactorily completed Year 1, unless the Director of Clinical Studies at his or her discretion should, in exceptional circumstances, decide that the candidate may proceed to Year 2 on condition that he or she should undertake remedial work and if necessary be reassessed at a later date.   5

YEAR 2

In Year 2, students are required to satisfy the examiners in:

(*a*) Neurology and Neurosurgery;
(*b*) Obstetrics and Gynaecology (including Genito-Urinary Medicine);
(*c*) Orthopaedics, Rheumatology, Trauma and Emergency Medicine;   10
(*d*) Paediatrics;
(*e*) Palliative Care, Primary Health Care, and Population Health 2: Public Health;
(*f*) Psychiatry.

Each candidate will be assessed according to the methods approved by the Medical Sciences Board and notified to candidates before the commencement of each course   15
of instruction.

Candidates must satisfy the relevant head of department or his or her deputy, that they have attended a course of instruction in, and attained the necessary skills, knowledge and understanding in:

(*a*) Clinical Geratology;   20
(*b*) Dermatology;
(*c*) Ophthalmology;
(*d*) Otolaryngology.

No candidate shall commence Year 3 until he or she has satisfactorily completed Year 2, unless the Director of Clinical Studies at his or her discretion should, in   25
exceptional circumstances, decide that the candidate may proceed to Year 3 on condition that he or she should undertake remedial work and if necessary be reassessed at a later date.

YEAR 3

In Year 3, students are required to satisfy examiners in General Clinical Studies   30
and Vocational Skills. Each candidate will be assessed according to the methods approved by the Medical Sciences Board and notified to candidates before the commencement of each course of instruction. Students who fail an assessment will have to forfeit part or all of the elective for a period of intensive clinical training.

1. General Clinical Studies   35

Students are required to satisfy the examiners in:

(*a*) Medicine and Surgery encompassing Communication Skills, Radiology, and
      Clinical Pharmacology; and
(*b*) Specialties studied but not previously formally examined (namely Clinical
      Geratology, Dermatology, Ophthalmology, and Otolaryngology).   40

Candidates must satisfy the Director of Clinical Studies that they have attended a course of instruction in Special Study and Clinical Options approved by the Medical Sciences Board.

2. Vocational Skills

Students are required to satisfy the Director of Clinical Studies or his or her deputy   45
that they have provided work to a satisfactory standard in:

(*a*) Special Study and Clinical Options as approved by the Medical Sciences
      Board;
(*b*) A Course to prepare students for work as a Foundation 1 doctor;

(*c*) An Elective (students who fail an assessment may be required to complete remedial clinical work. These students will forfeit part, or all, of the elective and instead will be required to produce a satisfactory report at the end of an additional clinical attachment);

(*d*) A student assistantship with a clinical team; and

(*e*) An assessment in procedural skills.

2. *Assessment*

YEARS 1, 2, AND 3

Proposals for the assessment of candidates in Years 1, 2, and 3 of the examination shall be drawn up by each specialty group, or in the case of Year 3 by the Board's Clinical Education Committee and submitted for approval to the Medical Sciences Board, at such times as the Board shall determine. The form or forms of assessment are chosen from among the following:

(*a*) clinical examination including long and short cases;

(*b*) competency check sheets, logbooks, or portfolios;

(*c*) examination and comment (written or viva voce) on specimens;

(*d*) objective structured clinical examinations;

(*e*) poster presentations;

(*f*) case presentations;

(*g*) written tests, which may consist in whole or in part of, for example, multiple choice questions, short answer questions, extended matching questions or essays;

(*h*) case histories and commentaries;

(*i*) prepared essays;

(*j*) viva voce examinations; and

(*k*) other tests individually approved by the Board.

In clinical subjects, all assessments shall include a test of clinical competence. In addition, reports on candidates' attendance and general aptitude shown during the course of instruction shall be made by those responsible for the course and taken into consideration in association with the performance of candidates in the assessment.

A candidate shall be warned (in writing with a copy to the Director of Clinical Studies) by those responsible for the course in question before the assessment takes place, if his or her attendance and general aptitude are such as seems likely to jeopardise his or her chances of passing the assessment.

The first assessment of candidates shall be carried out during or at the conclusion of each component of the course by the staff, as appointed by the head of the relevant department, or, in the case of Year 3, by the examiners and/or assessors. Candidates in Years 1 and 3 shall be permitted a maximum of three attempts to pass an assessment. In Year 2 the Examination Board may require candidates to be assessed in a specified module or modules on one further occasion. Candidates in Year 2 shall be permitted a maximum of two attempts in order to pass Year 2.

It shall be the responsibility of the staff concerned, under the supervision of the Medical Sciences Board, to give the candidates and the relevant examiners and/or assessors, reasonable notice of the dates on which the assessments will take place, to decide on the outcome of each assessment, and to keep departmental records of each assessment. A candidate should not normally be assessed exclusively by staff members who have been responsible for his or her instruction.

YEAR 1

A candidate in Year 1 who fails to reach a satisfactory standard in any part of the assessment at the first attempt may offer himself or herself for reassessment on one further occasion and will only be required to be reassessed in the part or parts of the assessment they have failed. If a candidate fails to reach a satisfactory standard at the second attempt in any part of the assessment, the head of department concerned, or his or her deputy, shall require the candidate to be reassessed in the part or parts of the assessment previously failed after completing the necessary coursework; this assessment shall be carried out and adjudged by the staff appointed by the relevant head of department and in the presence of an external examiner. In the event that a candidate's performance is judged to be unsatisfactory at this third attempt then his or her name shall be removed from the Register of Clinical Students subject to appeal to the Medical Sciences Board.

YEAR 2

A candidate in Year 2 who fails to reach a satisfactory standard in any individual course module assessment at the first attempt and is required by the Examination Board to be reassessed, will only be required to be reassessed in the part or parts of the assessment they have failed. A candidate must reach the threshold pass mark for Year 2 (from the sum of cumulative marks awarded from each course module assessment) and satisfy the Examination Board in a minimum of five out of the six modules, or the candidate will be deemed to have failed the second year of the course. A candidate who has been deemed to have failed will be allowed only one further attempt to pass Year 2 and will be required to repeat the second year of the course in its entirety. In the event that a candidate's performance is judged to be unsatisfactory at this second attempt then his or her name shall be removed from the University Register of Clinical Students subject to appeal to the Medical Sciences Board.

YEAR 3

A candidate in Year 3 who fails to reach a satisfactory standard at the first attempt in any part of the assessment in medicine and surgery will be deemed, normally, to have failed the complete assessment and may offer himself or herself for reassessment on one further occasion. This reassessment will be undertaken in the presence of an external examiner. A candidate in this position will usually be required to be reassessed in all parts of the assessment, unless the examiners specifically direct that there be reassessment only in the part or parts in which the candidate has failed to reach a satisfactory standard. If a candidate fails to reach a satisfactory standard at the second attempt in any part of the assessment, then the candidate shall be deemed to have failed the complete assessment. The examiners shall require the candidate to be reassessed after completing the necessary coursework; this assessment shall be carried out and adjudged by the examiners, which shall include an external examiner. In the event that a candidate's performance is judged to be unsatisfactory at this third attempt then his or her name shall be removed from the University Register of Clinical Students subject to appeal to the Medical Sciences Board.

3. *The Duties of the Examiners*

YEAR 1

In the first assessment of candidates in Year 1 each relevant pair of examiners shall be required to attend, and if they so wish participate, on at least one occasion each year.

In the reassessment of any candidate who has been deemed to have failed the whole assessment in Year 1, the external examiner shall be present and may participate if he or she wishes.

Year 3 examiners may assist with the assessment in Year 1.

YEAR 2

In the first assessment of candidates in the individual course module assessments of Year 2 each relevant pair of examiners/specialty advisors shall be required to attend, and if they so wish participate, on at least one occasion in each year.

YEAR 3

Assessment of General Clinical Studies

The examination shall be arranged and conducted by the Year 3 Examination Board under the direction of the Chair of Examiners and the Principal Examiners in Medicine and Surgery. When fewer than ten candidates present themselves the examination shall be arranged and conducted by the Chair of Examiners and the Principal Examiners in Medicine and Surgery. In considering whether a candidate has passed the assessment, the examiners may fail a candidate who does not satisfy them in one part of the assessment, even if he or she has satisfied them in other parts at that stage.

Assessment of Vocational Skills

Candidates shall be required to submit to the examiners such evidence as they require of the successful completion of their work. In considering whether candidates shall have passed the assessment, the examiners may fail a candidate who has provided either none or insufficient evidence of satisfactory completion of one part of the course, even if he or she has satisfied them in other parts of the course.

§7. Degree of Master of Surgery

A

1. Any person may supplicate for the Degree of Master of Surgery provided that:

(*a*) *either*

>> (i) he or she has been admitted to the Degree of Bachelor of Surgery and has entered upon the thirtieth term from his or her matriculation, or in the case of a person who has incorporated as a Bachelor of Surgery, the thirtieth term from the date of matriculation at the University of Cambridge, or in the case of a person who has been admitted to the Second Examination for the Degree of Bachelor of Medicine under the provisions of the appropriate regulation, the twenty-first term from his or her matriculation;

> *or*

>> (ii) he or she holds the Degree of Master of Arts of the University (other than a degree by decree or special resolution or a degree *honoris causa*), has previously been entered in the Register of University Medical Students and has passed the First Examination for the Degree of Bachelor of Medicine of this University, holds a medical degree of another British university qualifying him or her to practise medicine, and has entered upon the thirtieth term from his or her matriculation;

(*b*) he or she has passed the FRCS or equivalent examination, and passed the examination hereinafter prescribed.

2. The examination shall consist of a thesis, and may include a viva voce examination to test the candidate's general competence in his or her own field.

3. No candidate shall be admitted to the examination earlier than the sixteenth term from the date of passing the Second Examination for the Degree of Bachelor of Medicine or an equivalent final medical examination from a university approved by Council.*

4. A candidate shall submit as evidence of his or her fitness to supplicate for the degree a thesis upon a subject previously approved by the Medical Sciences Board, or with the previous approval of that board a book or papers which have already been published under his or her own name. A candidate may submit joint publications provided that a substantial portion of the work submitted has been written solely by him or her. He or she shall make his application to the Medical Sciences Board through the Registrar, and shall at the same time submit:

(*a*) evidence that the subject of his or her thesis or published work has been approved by the Medical Sciences Board;

(*b*) four printed or typewritten copies of an abstract, of around 400 to 450 words and not exceeding 600 words, summarising the scope of the thesis or other evidence, the techniques used, and the principal findings;

(*c*) a certificate from the proper officer of his or her society that his or her application has the approval of that society;

(*d*) the fee prescribed in the appropriate regulation (see Appendix I);

(*e*) such number of copies of his or her evidence in such form as the board may by regulation direct.

The thesis or other evidence shall be accompanied by a certificate signed by the candidate indicating that it is the candidate's own work except where otherwise indicated. If the thesis or published work has not been submitted for examination before the sixteenth term after approval has been given under this clause, the candidate is required to seek reapproval of his or her submission.

5. On receipt of any such application, the Registrar shall submit it to the Medical Sciences Board. The board shall thereupon appoint two examiners whose duties shall be:

---

* i.e. a university approved for the purpose of senior status or a university especially approved for the purpose of this clause.

(1) to consider the evidence sent in by the candidate under the provisions of the preceding clause; provided that they shall exclude from consideration in making their report any part of the evidence that *either*

    (*a*) has already been accepted, or is being concurrently submitted for any degree in this or any other University, and shall have the power to require the candidate to produce for their inspection the complete thesis so accepted or concurrently submitted; *or*

    (*b*) does not represent the candidate's own work;

(2) if they think fit to examine the candidate orally;

(3) to report to the board through the Registrar;

(4) to return to the Registrar, with their report, the copy or copies of the evidence submitted by the candidate.

6. On receipt of the report of the examiners, it shall be the duty of the board to decide whether to permit the candidate to supplicate for the Degree of Master of Surgery, but permission shall in no case be given unless the examiners have reported that the work as embodied in his or her evidence and tested by his or her examination has resulted in an original contribution to knowledge deserving publication (whether or not already published) based on clinical and/or experimental observations, and that it is in their opinion of sufficient merit to entitle the candidate to supplicate for the Degree of Master of Surgery.

7. If the board approves the evidence as of sufficient merit for the degree, the board shall notify its decision in the *University Gazette* and one copy of the thesis or of each of the papers and books submitted as evidence shall remain in the possession of the University for deposit in Bodley's Library.

B

M.Ch.

1. Dissertations, theses, or published work for the M.Ch. must be submitted *in English* unless for exceptional reasons the Medical Sciences Board otherwise determines at the time of approving the subject of a dissertation or thesis, or granting leave to submit published work, as the case may be.

2. Candidates are required to send three copies of any dissertation, thesis, book, or papers submitted. Dissertations or theses must be either printed or typewritten and should not normally exceed 50,000 words (excluding appendices and case reports). Only in exceptional circumstances and with the approval of the Medical Sciences Board is it permitted to exceed this limit.

3. Candidates are required to submit at the same time as their application four printed or typewritten copies of an abstract, of around 400 to 450 words and not exceeding 600 words, summarising the scope of the dissertation, thesis, or published work, the techniques used, and the principal findings. One copy of the abstract will be used for the appointment of judges or examiners. One copy must be bound into the copy of the dissertation or thesis which, if the applicant is successful, will be deposited in the Bodleian Library. The abstract may also be bound into the other two copies of the dissertation, thesis, or published work if the candidate so desires. Each copy of the abstract shall be headed with the title of the dissertation, thesis, or published work, the name and college of the candidate, the degree for which it is submitted, and the term of submission.

4. Unless the board has excused the candidate from this requirement, the dissertation or thesis must be typed on one side of the paper only with a margin of 3 to 3.5 cms on the left-hand edge of each paper. The dissertation, thesis, or published work must have a stabbed binding with covers of stout manila or stiff cardboard and a canvas back, or must be stitched and bound in a stiff case. (It should be noted that the dissertation, thesis, or published work must be bound and that a loose-leaf binder of the screw-in type is not acceptable.)

Candidates are advised to pack each copy of the dissertation, thesis, or published work into a separate parcel, ready in all respects, except the address, to be posted to the judges or examiners when appointed. Each parcel should bear the candidate's name and college and the words 'M.Ch. THESIS' as appropriate in BLOCK CAPITALS in the bottom left-hand corner. The separate copies thus packed should be sent to the Examination Schools, High Street, Oxford OX1 4BG, in one covering parcel.

5. Oral Examination for the M.Ch.

(1) The examination may be attended by any member of the University in academic dress. No person who is not a member of the University may attend it except with the consent of both judges or examiners.

(2) The place, day, and hour of the examination shall be fixed by the judges or examiners, who shall be responsible for informing the candidate thereof by post prepaid, and it shall be the duty of the candidate to ensure that any letter addressed to him is forwarded to him if away. The judges or examiners shall allow reasonable time for receiving an acknowledgement from the candidate of their summons. The day shall be fixed by the judges or examiners to suit their own convenience, but they are asked, in order that the candidate may know what arrangements he may safely make, to give the candidate early information of the date fixed, even though it may be some considerable time ahead.

(3) Notice of the examination shall be given by the judges or examiners to the Registrar.

(4) If, owing to illness or other urgent and unforeseen cause, a judge or examiner is unable to attend the examination, it shall be postponed to a later date, provided that, if the Vice-Chancellor is satisfied that postponement will be a serious hardship to the candidate, he may authorise another person to attend the examination as a substitute. Such substitute shall not be required to sign the report, but he shall receive such remuneration as the Vice-Chancellor and Proctors shall determine.

§8. Status of Student for the Degree of Doctor of Medicine*

1. Any person may supplicate for the Degree of Doctor of Medicine if *either*:

(1) he or she has been admitted to the Degree of Bachelor of Medicine and has entered upon the thirty-sixth term from his or her matriculation, or, in the case of a person who has been admitted to the Oxford Graduate Entry Medical Course, the thirtieth term from the date of his or her matriculation, or, in the case of a person who has incorporated as a Bachelor of Medicine, the thirty-sixth term from the date of his or her matriculation at the University of Cambridge, or, in the case of a person who has been admitted to the Second Examination for the Degree of Bachelor of Medicine under the provisions of §6, cl. 1 of this section, the twenty-seventh term from his or her matriculation; *or*

(2) he or she holds the Degree of Master of Arts of the University (other than a degree by decree or resolution or an honorary degree), has previously been entered in the Register of University Medical Students and has passed the First Examination for the Degree of Bachelor of Medicine of this University, holds a degree qualifying him or her to be placed on the Medical Register, and has entered upon the thirty-sixth term from his or her matriculation.

2. It shall be the duty of the Registrar to keep a Register of those admitted to the status of Student for the Degree of Doctor of Medicine.

3. On application for admission to the status of Student for the Degree of Doctor of Medicine, the applicant shall state whether he or she will wish to submit as his or her dissertation a series of papers or books, as permitted under §12, cl. 3 of this section.

---

* Students whose proposed outlines for submission (or resubmission) of a dissertation have been approved before 1 April 2002 will be examined under the provisions governing the Degree of Doctor of Medicine as they stood before that date (*Examination Decrees*, 2001, pp. 899–902). Students who were first examined before 1 April 2002 but who will be seeking permission to resubmit after that date will also be re-examined under the old provisions. Judges who examine a student who is required to submit under the old provisions may however, should the thesis not meet the requirements for the award of the degree on initial submission, offer the candidate the option of revising his or her thesis for re-examination (on payment of the appropriate fee) in accordance with clause 10 (2) of subsection 12 below under the legislation as it stood on 1 April 2002.

§9. Registration for the Degree of Doctor of Medicine

1. Except in the case of submission of published work as a dissertation for the degree, no student shall submit a dissertation until at least the beginning of the sixth term after the Medical Sciences Board has granted his or her admission.

2. A student must carry out the bulk of the research for the dissertation during the period in which he or she is registered.

3. If the dissertation, including published work submitted as a dissertation, has not been submitted for examination before the fifteenth term after admission has been granted, a student shall be required to seek readmission.

§10. Advisers of Students for the Degree of Doctor of Medicine

1. (1) Except in the case of students submitting published work as a dissertation for the degree, every student on admission as a Student for the Degree of Doctor of Medicine shall be allocated to an Adviser in Oxford appointed by the Medical Sciences Board in the student's area of research.

   (2) In the case of students working outside Oxford, each student shall be required to seek additional advice from a senior member of the academic or clinical staff at the institution at which the research is to be pursued; and the student shall notify the Medical Sciences Board of the name of that person and provide a written statement signed by that person confirming that he or she is willing to undertake the role of an additional Adviser.

2. (1) It shall be the duty of the Adviser to offer support and assistance to the student in the manner prescribed in the *Memorandum of Guidance for Advisers and Students for the Degree of Doctor of Medicine* as published from time to time by the Medical Sciences Board.

   (2) The Adviser shall submit reports on the progress of the student's work at the beginning of each Michaelmas and Trinity Term, and the reports of Advisers outside Oxford shall, in the case of the relevant students, also be received by the Adviser in Oxford.

   (3) It shall be the responsibility of the Adviser at the host institution (whether that is Oxford or elsewhere) to inform the Medical Sciences Board if he or she is of the opinion that the student is unlikely to reach the standard required for the Degree of Doctor of Medicine.

3. (1) Except when approval has been given for submission of published work as a dissertation for the degree, it shall be the duty of every Student for the Degree of Doctor of Medicine to seek the advice of the Adviser (or, in the case of students working outside Oxford, both Advisers) at an early stage of the proposed research and to seek comments on his or her dissertation before its submission.

(2) During the course of the research the student shall maintain contact with the Adviser or Advisers in the manner prescribed in the *Memorandum of Guidance for Advisers and Students for the Degree of Doctor of Medicine*.

§11. Confirmation of status as a Student for the Degree of Doctor of Medicine

1. (1) Except in the case of submission of published work as a dissertation, a student registered for the Degree of Doctor of Medicine must, not later than the sixth term and not earlier than the third term after that in which he or she was admitted to the status of Student for the Degree of Doctor of Medicine, apply to the Medical Sciences Board for confirmation of that status.

(2) Except in the case of students submitting published work as a dissertation, all Students for the Degree of Doctor of Medicine shall have their status confirmed before they may make an application for the appointment of examiners.

2. Students applying for confirmation of status shall submit their application to the Medical Sciences Board through the Registrar; and each application shall be accompanied by:

(1) a report on the work undertaken since registration;

(2) a statement from the Adviser at the place where the work is being undertaken commenting on whether the student's progress provides firm evidence that the work when completed is likely to reach the standard required for the Degree of Doctor of Medicine.

3. (1) If, after considering a student's application for confirmation of status, the Medical Sciences Board concludes that the student's progress does not warrant confirmation, the board may permit the submission of a further application not later than the third term after the original application.

(2) If the second application is unsuccessful, the student's name shall be removed from the Register of Students for the Degree of Doctor of Medicine.

4. Except in the case of submission of published work as a dissertation for the degree, a Student for the Degree of Doctor of Medicine shall cease to hold that status unless it has been confirmed within nine terms of his or her admission to that status.

§12. Examination of Students for the Degree of Doctor of Medicine

1. A Student for the Degree of Doctor of Medicine who has, where applicable, fulfilled the requirements set out in §§9 and 11 of this section, and whose status has not expired, may apply to the Medical Sciences Board for the appointment of examiners and for leave to supplicate for the Degree of Doctor of Medicine.

2. Students admitted to the Degree of Doctor of Medicine prior to April 2002 will be given the option of examination under the regulations introduced in April 2002.

3. (1) A Student for the Degree of Doctor of Medicine may

either

(*a*) submit a dissertation upon a subject which, together with the proposed manner of treating it, has previously been approved by the Medical Sciences Board;

or

(*b*) in exceptional circumstances, submit as his or her dissertation a series of papers or books published at least twelve months before the proposed date of submission, if the previous approval of the Medical Sciences Board has been given after considering the seniority of the student (who shall be required to have held a career-grade post for a period of at least fifteen years prior to submission), and the opinions of any referees who may be consulted.

(2) Submission of published works as a dissertation shall be permitted only when there is evidence of outstanding quality in the scientific papers or other works intended for submission; it shall also be a requirement that the published works be accompanied by a general introduction and a general conclusion and that they form a continuous theme.

4. Applications for the appointment of examiners and for leave to supplicate shall be made to the Medical Sciences

Board through the Medical Sciences Graduate School Office* and shall include:

(1) a statement by the candidate that the thesis is his or her own work, except where otherwise indicated;

(2) a statement by the candidate of what part, if any, of the thesis has already been accepted, or is concurrently being submitted, for any degree or diploma or certificate or other qualification in this University or elsewhere;

(3) a statement, where applicable, from the Adviser at the place where the research was undertaken certifying that the candidate has sought his or her advice as appropriate;

(4) a statement from the candidate's college in support of the application;

(5) two printed or typewritten copies of an abstract of the thesis, which shall not normally exceed 300 words in length.

5. Where the Medical Sciences Board has given approval for submission of published work as a dissertation, two printed or typewritten copies of the thesis may be submitted by the student immediately after approval, in a format which is in accordance with the instructions obtainable from the Medical Sciences Board through the Medical Sciences Graduate School Office.

6. In all other cases, students shall submit an application in accordance with clause 4 above up to four months in advance of submitting two printed or typewritten copies of the thesis in a format which is in accordance with the instructions obtainable from the Medical Sciences Board through the Medical Sciences Graduate School Office.

7. If a student has not submitted his or her thesis for examination within twelve months from submission of the application under the provisions of clause 4 above, then the application shall lapse.

8. (1) On receipt of an application the Medical Sciences Board shall appoint two examiners, neither of whom shall be the student's Adviser, and one of whom shall be external to the University.

---

* Medical Sciences Graduate School Office, Level 3, John Radcliffe Hospital, Headley Way, Oxford, OX3 9DU.

(2) The duties of the examiners shall be:

(*a*) to consider the thesis and the abstract of it submitted by the candidate, except that they shall exclude from consideration in making their report any part of the thesis that either has already been accepted, or is concurrently being submitted, for any degree or diploma or certificate or other qualification in this University or elsewhere, or does not represent the candidate's own work;

(*b*) to examine the candidate orally in the subject of his or her thesis, unless, in exceptional circumstances in the case of submission of published work as a dissertation, the board agrees, on the recommendation of the examiners, to dispense with this requirement;

(*c*) to report to the Medical Sciences Board through the Registrar on the scope, character, and quality of the work submitted, in the manner prescribed in clause 10 below;

(*d*) to return to the candidate the copies of the thesis and abstract.

9. (1) The Medical Sciences Board shall have power to make regulations concerning the notice to be given of the oral examination, and of the time and place at which it may be held.

(2) The examination may be attended by any member of the University in academic dress, while non-members may attend only with the consent of the examiners.

(3) The Vice-Chancellor and Proctors after consultation with the board may decide (either at their own discretion or at the request of the student or the supervisor or department) to forbid the attendance of any person or all persons (other than the examiners and the candidate) or to impose any condition on attendance if and to the extent that such action is in their view necessary to protect the interests of the University or the candidate or both, and the examiners shall be informed accordingly and shall include this information in the notice of examination.

10. Having completed the examination, the examiners may make one of the following recommendations in their report to the Medical

Sciences Board, or they may alternatively proceed in accordance with the provisions of clause 11 below:

(1) that the board grant the student leave to supplicate for the Degree of Doctor of Medicine, if making this recommendation, the examiners shall include in their report statements that:

   (*a*) the student possesses a comprehensive knowledge of the particular field of learning in which the thesis falls;

   (*b*) the thesis embodies original observations on either clinical or experimental material;

   (*c*) the work done by the student and embodied in the thesis has resulted in an original and substantial contribution to medical science;

   (*d*) the thesis is presented in a lucid and scholarly manner;

   (*e*) the student has presented a satisfactory abstract of the thesis;

   (*f*) in their opinion the thesis merits the award of the Degree of Doctor of Medicine;

(2) that the board offer the student the option of reference of the thesis back to him or her in order that he or she may revise it for re-examination for the Degree of Doctor of Medicine on not more than one occasion, on the basis that the thesis has not reached the standard required for the Degree of Doctor of Medicine; if making this recommendation, the examiners shall annex to their report to the board a statement, for transmission to the student, setting out the respects in which the thesis falls below the standard required for the degree and what changes are necessary for it to reach that required standard, and setting a deadline (subject to the agreement of the board) for resubmission;

(3) that, in the case of a student whose thesis has already been referred back on one occasion, the student's application for leave to supplicate be refused; if making this recommendation, the examiners shall annex to their report a statement, for transmission to the student, setting out the respects in which the thesis falls below the standard required for the degree.

11. (1) If the examiners are satisfied that the student's thesis is of sufficient merit to qualify for the degree but consider,

nevertheless, that before the thesis is deposited the student should make minor corrections (which are not sufficiently substantial to justify reference back for re-examination), they shall require the student to correct the thesis to their satisfaction before they submit their report.

(2) If the student has not completed these corrections within three calendar months of the date of the oral examination, his or her name shall be removed by the Registrar from the Register of Students for the Degree of Doctor of Medicine, except that the board may, on good cause shown by the student, grant an extension of time of three further calendar months in which the student may fulfil this requirement before the removal of his or her name from the Register.

(3) No subsequent extension shall be granted, but it shall be open to a student who has failed to fulfil this requirement within those three or six months in total, as the case may be, to apply to the board for reinstatement as a Student for the Degree of Doctor of Medicine, with the support of his or her college and Adviser(s), upon submission to the Registrar of a copy of his or her thesis incorporating the required corrections, and upon payment of such reinstatement fee as may from time to time be prescribed by Council by decree; leave to supplicate shall not be granted until this fee has been paid.

12. The Medical Sciences Board may exempt a candidate who is being re-examined under the provision of clause 10(2) above from a further oral examination, if the examiners are able to certify that they are satisfied without examining the candidate orally that they can recommend to the board in the terms required by clause 10(1) above that he or she be given leave to supplicate for the Degree of Doctor of Medicine.

13. In an exceptional case in which the Medical Sciences Board is unable to accept the examiners' recommendation, or in which the examiners cannot reach an agreed recommendation, the board shall have power to appoint one or two new examiners, as it deems necessary, to conduct such further examination of the candidate as the board may require.

14. (1) A student who has been granted leave to supplicate by the board shall be required to submit to the Registrar a copy of his or her thesis, incorporating any amendments

or corrections required by the examiners and approved by the board, with a view to deposit in the Bodleian or other appropriate university library.

(2) Leave to supplicate shall in all cases be conditional upon fulfilment of this requirement.

15. (1) It shall be the duty of the Registrar to notify the student of the board's decision as soon as may be.

(2) The Registrar shall also be responsible for publishing at the end of each academic year (except in so far as it may be necessary not to publish any name in order to comply with the provisions of the Data Protection Act 1998) the names of those students to whom permission to supplicate has been granted during that year, together with a statement of the subject of the thesis written by each.

16. When, on the conclusion of an investigation of a complaint made by a student, the Proctors recommend that a student be re-examined, the board shall have power to hold a new examination.

DM

1. *Admission*

Students qualified under the appropriate regulation may apply for admission as a Student for the Degree of Doctor of Medicine to the Medical Sciences Board through the Registrar. Such application shall be accompanied by:

(i) a completed application form (obtainable from the Medical Sciences Graduate School Office);

(ii) a statement of not more than 1,500 words outlining the proposed scope of the research to be undertaken and provisional thesis title;

and, in the case of students wishing to submit published work, the following additional information:

(iii) a list of the works to be submitted, details of their publication, and a statement on whether any part of the work to be submitted has previously been accepted for a degree. A student who submits work that has been produced in collaboration shall state in respect of each item the extent of his or her own contribution. This statement must be certified by each of the senior and primary authors (where he or she is not the student) in the case of each piece of collaborative work submitted.

A set of published works may constitute an acceptable dissertation but only if with the addition of a general introduction and general conclusion they form a continuous theme.

2. *Confirmation of Status*

Students who have been admitted to DM status, and intend to submit a dissertation for a thesis, must, not later than six terms and not earlier than three terms after admission to DM status, apply for confirmation of that status.

The requirements for confirmation of status are:

(i) completion by the student of the appropriate form (obtainable from the Medical Sciences Graduate School Office);

(ii) submission by the student of a report of no more than 2,500 words on the work undertaken since registration, including a comprehensive outline of the research topic, details of progress made, and the anticipated timetable for submission of the thesis;

(iii) completion of the appropriate form (obtainable from the Medical Sciences Graduate School Office) by the Adviser at the place where the work is being undertaken.

The application shall be directed to the Graduate Studies Committee of the Medical Sciences Board, which shall appoint two assessors competent in the student's area of research (who may include the Adviser in Oxford in the case of students working outside Oxford). The assessors shall submit to the board's Graduate Studies Committee a report (using a form obtainable from the Medical Sciences Graduate School Office) after considering the student's report and, if necessary, interviewing the student. Before a decision is reached on whether or not confirmation of status should be approved the Graduate Studies Committee shall take into account the comments made on the application by the Adviser at the place of work and that Adviser's biannual reports.

If the Graduate Studies Committee does not consider that the student's progress warrants confirmation of status it may either: (*a*) permit the resubmission of the application on one further occasion not later than the third term after the original application; or (*b*) reject the application.

A copy of the assessors' report, amended as necessary by the Graduate Studies Committee, will normally be made available to the student.

3. *Theses*

The requirements for the submission of a thesis are as follows:

(i) The completion by the student of the appropriate form (obtainable from the Medical Sciences Graduate School Office). The form may be submitted immediately in the case of students submitting published work as a dissertation and up to four months in advance of submitting the thesis in the case of other students.

(ii) The submission of two printed or typewritten copies of the thesis and two printed or typewritten copies of an abstract, formatted and supplied according to the instructions obtainable from the Medical Sciences Board through the Medical Sciences Graduate School Office.

4. *Oral Examination*

(i) The place, day, and hour of examination shall be fixed by the examiners, who shall be responsible for informing the student by post, and it shall be the duty of the student to ensure that any letter addressed to him or her is forwarded to him or her if away. The examiners shall allow reasonable time for receiving an acknowledgement from the student of their summons. The day shall be fixed by the examiners to suit their own convenience but they are asked, in order that the student may know what arrangements he or she may safely make, to give the student early information of the date fixed, even though it may be some considerable time ahead.

(ii) Notice of the examination shall be given by the examiners to the Research Degrees Team at the Examination Schools, High Street, Oxford, OX1 4BG.

(iii) If, owing to illness or other urgent or unforeseen cause, an examiner is unable to attend the examination, it shall be postponed to a later date, except that, if the Proctors are satisfied that postponement will be a serious hardship to the student, the Proctors may authorise another person to attend the examination as a substitute. The substitute shall not be required to sign the report, but he or she shall receive such remuneration as the Vice-Chancellor and Proctors shall determine.

NOTES

23

REGULATIONS FOR DEGREES
IN DIVINITY

GENERAL REGULATIONS

With effect from 1 October 2005 study for the Degree of Bachelor of Divinity will only be permissible for students already registered for the degree. No new applications will be accepted.

§1. Qualifications of Candidates for the Degree of Bachelor of Divinity

1. Any Master of Arts who has incepted in this University or has been incorporated in this University, or any person upon whom the Degree of Master of Arts has been conferred by decree or special resolution may supplicate for the Degree of Bachelor of Divinity, provided that

(1) he shall have either obtained a First or Second Class in the Honour School of Theology or Philosophy and Theology or passed or have been exempted from the Qualifying Examination hereinafter prescribed; and

(2) he shall have obtained from the Board of the Faculty of Theology a certificate that he has presented published work and/or a thesis of a high standard of merit such as entitles him to supplicate for the degree.

2. The Board of the Faculty of Theology shall have power to exempt a candidate for the Degree of Bachelor of Divinity from the requirement that he pass the Qualifying Examination.

§2. Qualifying Examination

1. The Qualifying Examination shall be in Christian Theology as specified in the regulations below.

2. The examination shall be under the supervision of the Board of the Faculty of Theology.

3. No candidate shall be admitted to examination unless either he is a Master of Arts, or has passed all the examinations required

for the Degree of Bachelor of Arts not less than five terms before that in which the examination is held.

4. Candidates holding the Diploma in Theology who satisfied the examiners for the diploma in the same papers as are specified for the Qualifying Examination may, with the approval of the board, be deemed to have passed the Qualifying Examination. Candidates holding the Diploma in Theology who satisfied the examiners for the diploma in three or two of the papers specified for the Qualifying Examination may, with the approval of the board, be deemed to have satisfied the examiners for the Qualifying Examination in those papers, in which case they shall be required, in order to pass the examination, to satisfy the examiners at one examination, in only one other paper or two other papers respectively.

5. Every candidate shall be examined in writing and, unless individually excused by the examiners, viva voce.

§3. Work Submitted and Certificate

1. Every candidate who proposes to present a thesis must notify the Board of the Faculty of Theology, indicating the area of Christian Theology in which he intends to write the thesis. The board shall then assign an Adviser, who shall interview the candidate and advise him on a precise topic. The candidate shall then submit a title and statement of area and method for the board's approval, which must be obtained before the candidate can proceed, and which will not normally be given unless the board is satisfied that the candidate has the linguistic competence appropriate to the subject proposed. The candidate shall be instructed to consult the Adviser further at a point prior to submission of the thesis.

2. A candidate who submits papers or books which have been produced in collaboration shall state in respect of each item the extent of his own contribution.

3. Every candidate must send to the Registrar:

(1) three copies of the published work or typewritten thesis,[*][†] unless the board, on application from the candidate, shall for special reasons order otherwise;

---

[*] Published work submitted should not exceed 100,000 words (excluding only the bibliography); a thesis should not exceed 75,000 words (excluding only the bibliography, which in the case of a thesis is compulsory). Unless the board has excused the candidate from this requirement, the thesis must be typed on one side of the paper only, with a margin of 3 to 3.5 cm on the left-hand edge of each page. The thesis must have a stabbed binding with covers of stout manila or stiff cardboard and a canvas back, or must be stitched and bound in a stiff case. (It should be noted that the thesis must be bound and that a loose-leaf binder of the screw-in type is not acceptable.)

(2) a statement of what part, if any, of his work submitted has already been accepted, or is being concurrently submitted, for any degree in this or any other University;

(3) the fee prescribed in the appropriate regulation (see Appendix I);

(4) evidence that his application has the approval of his society.

4. The work submitted shall be examined by at least two examiners appointed by the board. The examiners shall also publicly examine the candidate in the subject of his submission and in matters relevant thereto.

The examiners shall report[‡] to the board through the Registrar, and it shall be the duty of the board to decide whether leave to supplicate for the degree shall be granted to the candidate, but such leave shall in no case be granted unless the examiners shall have reported that the work submitted by the candidate and as tested by his public examination is of a high standard of merit such as entitles him to supplicate for the degree, provided further that they shall have excluded from consideration in making their report any part of the work which has already been accepted, or is being concurrently submitted, for any degree in this or any other University, and shall have the power to require the candidate to produce for their inspection the whole of the work so accepted or concurrently submitted.

5. A candidate who has failed to obtain leave to supplicate may apply to the board through the Registrar for leave to submit his work again in a revised form. If the board approves the application the candidate shall be permitted to submit his work to the board again after a period, not being less than four months, to be deter-

---

Candidates are advised to pack each copy of the thesis intended for the examiners into a separate parcel, ready in all respects, except the address, to be posted to the examiners when appointed. Each parcel should bear the candidate's name and college and the words 'BD THESIS' in BLOCK CAPITALS in the bottom left-hand corner, and a slip giving the address to which the examiners should write should be enclosed with each copy of the thesis. Candidates are responsible for ensuring that their examiners have no difficulty in communicating with them. The separate copies thus packed, together with the library copy, should be sent to the Registrar in one covering parcel.

† The following instruction is issued to candidates by the Board of the Faculty of Theology and Religion. References should be precise; and, where these are to such works as writings of fathers and schoolmen, the title of the treatise and, when these exist, the number of the book, chapter, and section should be given, not only the volume or page or column of particular editions.

‡ If the examiners are satisfied that the candidate's thesis, as it stands, is of sufficient merit to qualify him for the degree but consider, nevertheless, that before the thesis is deposited the candidate should make minor corrections (which are not sufficiently substantial to justify reference back for re-examination), they may require the candidate to correct the thesis to their satisfaction before they submit their report.

mined by the board, and the provisions of clauses 3 and 4 of this Section shall apply to him.

6. A candidate to whom leave to supplicate has been granted by the board may supplicate for the Degree of Bachelor of Divinity, provided that he has delivered to the Registrar a copy of his thesis for deposit in the Bodleian Library.

§4. Degree of Doctor of Divinity

1. Any person belonging to one of the following classes may become a candidate for the Degree of Doctor of Divinity under the conditions set forth in this section:

(*a*) Masters of Arts who have incepted in this University and have entered upon the thirtieth term from their matriculation;

(*b*) Masters of Arts of the University of Cambridge or Dublin who have been incorporated in this University and have entered upon the thirtieth term from their matriculation at Cambridge or Dublin;

(*c*) Undergraduates or Bachelors of Arts of the University of Cambridge or Dublin who have been incorporated and have incepted in the Faculty of Arts in this University and have entered upon the thirtieth term from their matriculation at Cambridge or Dublin;

(*d*) Persons on whom the Degree of Master of Arts has been conferred by decree or special resolution, other than a degree *honoris causa*, and who have entered upon the ninth term from their admission to that degree;

(*e*) Doctors of Philosophy, Masters of Letters or of Science, and Bachelors of Letters or of Science who have entered upon the twenty-first term from their matriculation.

2. A candidate for the Degree of Doctor of Divinity shall apply to the board through the Registrar and shall submit with his or her application work dealing with some subject or subjects in the area of Theology or the Study of Religions. At least three printed copies of all the work submitted shall be provided by the candidate. This evidence must consist of published papers or books and one year at least must elapse between the publication of any such paper or book and its submission as evidence in support of an application.* The evidence may include published work previously submitted successfully by the candidate for the Degree of Bachelor of Divinity.

---

* If papers or books published in the calendar year preceding that in which application is made are submitted, the applicant should specify the exact date of publication.

A candidate who submits work which has been produced in collaboration shall state in respect of each item the extent of his own contribution.

3. The application shall also be accompanied by the fee prescribed in the appropriate regulation (see Appendix I) and by a certificate signed by some officer of, or some person deputed by, the society to which the candidate belongs, and showing that his or her application has the approval of such society.

4. The work submitted by the candidate shall be examined by at least two judges appointed by the board. They shall report to the board through the Registrar, and it shall be the duty of the board to consider their report, and to decide whether the evidence submitted constitutes an original contribution to the advancement of theological knowledge of such substance and distinction as to give the candidate an authoritative status in this branch of learning.

5. If the board, after consideration of the reports of the judges, shall approve the evidence as sufficient for the degree, it shall give leave to the candidate to supplicate for the degree, and shall notify its decision in the *University Gazette*. One copy of each of the papers and books submitted as evidence shall remain in the possession of the University for deposit in Bodley's Library, provided that no book or paper of which the library already possesses a copy shall be so deposited except with the consent of the candidate and of the librarian, unless the copy submitted by the candidate shall be of a different issue or shall contain alterations or additions.

SPECIAL REGULATIONS FOR THE
DEGREE OF BACHELOR OF DIVINITY

With effect from 1 October 2005 study for the Degree of Bachelor of Divinity will only be permissible for students already registered for the degree. No new applications will be accepted.

I. *Qualifying Examination*

1. The examination shall be held once a year at the end of Trinity Term.

2. Candidates will be required to take the following subjects in the examination for the Postgraduate Diploma in Theology

(1) The Four Gospels.

(2) The New Testament Epistles with special reference to St Paul.

(For papers (1) and (2) the prescribed portions of the texts must be offered in Greek.)

(3) *Either* (i) Old Testament: The Pentateuch and the Historical Books

or (ii) Old Testament: Prophets, Psalms, and Wisdom.

(4) The Christian Doctrines of God, of Human Nature and Salvation.

3. The names must be sent to the Registrar, on a form to be obtained previously from the University Offices, Wellington Square. An examination fee as prescribed in the appropriate regulation (see Appendix I) in respect of each candidate must be forwarded at the same time. (Late entries may be made under the provisions of the appropriate regulation.)

4. In order to pass the examination a candidate must satisfy the examiners in all four papers.

A candidate who, at any one examination, has satisfied the examiners in three out of four papers may offer the remaining paper at a later examination.

II. *Oral Examination*

The place, day, and hour of the examination shall be fixed by the examiners, who shall be responsible for informing the candidate thereof by post prepaid, and it shall be the duty of the candidate to ensure that any letter addressed to him at his college, as well as at any other address which he may have given, is forwarded to him if away. The examiners shall allow reasonable time for receiving an acknowledgement from the candidate of their summons.

24

EXAMINATIONS FOR DIPLOMAS AND CERTIFICATES

DIPLOMA IN APPLIED STATISTICS

GENERAL REGULATIONS

1. The Divisional Board of Mathematical, Physical and Life Sciences shall have power to grant Diplomas in Applied Statistics to candidates who have satisfied the conditions prescribed in this section.

2. The examination for the Diploma in Applied Statistics shall be under the supervision of the Divisional Board of Mathematical, Physical and Life Sciences.

3. The Divisional Board of Mathematical, Physical and Life Sciences shall have power to arrange lectures and courses of instruction for the Diploma in Applied Statistics.

4. Subject to the provisions of this section, any member of the University may be admitted to the course and to the examination who has obtained the leave of the Divisional Board of Mathematical, Physical and Life Sciences, provided that

(*a*) he or she has passed all the examinations required for the Degree of Bachelor of Arts and has obtained First or good Second Class Honours in the Second Public Examination, or has obtained such honours in a degree examination of another university, such university having been approved by Council for the purposes of Senior Status, or

(*b*) he or she is, in the opinion of the board, otherwise adequately qualified to undertake the course.

5. Applications for leave under the preceding clauses shall be sent to the Registrar through the head or tutor of the society to which the applicant belongs or desires to belong. The board shall have power to determine the character and length of a course of study to be followed by the applicant before he may be admitted to the examination.

6. On admitting an applicant as a candidate for the diploma, the board shall appoint a supervisor who shall direct and superintend the work of the candidate. The supervisor shall send a report on the progress of the candidate to the board at the end of each term (except the term in which the student enters for the examination) and at any other time when the board so requests or he believes it expedient. In particular he shall inform the board at once if he is of the opinion that a student is unlikely to reach the standard required for the diploma. The Registrar shall send a copy of each report by the supervisor to the student's society.

7. After admission as a Diploma Student, a candidate must have kept statutory residence and pursued a course of study at Oxford for at least three terms before taking the examination, provided that a candidate for the Degree of Master of Science (Applied Statistics) may, with the approval of the Divisional Board of Mathematical, Physical and Life Sciences, transfer to the status of a Student for the Diploma in Applied Statistics not later than the last day of Hilary Term in the year in which the written examination is to be taken, in which case the date of his admission as a Student for the Degree of Master of Science shall be reckoned as the date of his admission as a diploma student; time spent outside Oxford during term as part of an academic programme approved by Council shall count towards residence for the purpose of this clause.

8. A Student reading for the diploma who is not a graduate of the University may wear the same gown as that worn by Students for the Degree of Doctor of Philosophy.

9. The examiners may award a distinction to a candidate for the diploma.

Special Regulations

1. The Divisional Board of Mathematical, Physical and Life Sciences shall elect for the supervision of the course a standing committee which shall have power to arrange lectures and other instruction.

2. Candidates shall follow for at least three terms a course of instruction in Statistics, and will, when entering their name for the examination, be required to produce from their society a certificate that they are doing so.

3. The examination will consist of a written examination consisting of two papers on the syllabus described in the schedule.

4. In the written examination the examiners will permit the use of bilingual dictionaries.

5. Each candidate will be expected to have displayed evidence of the ability to apply statistical methods to real data.

The examiners will take into account the results of an assessment of ability to apply statistical methods to real data organised by the standing committee. The committee will be responsible for notifying the candidates of the arrangements for the assessment, and for forwarding the assessed material to the Chair of the Examiners before the end of the Trinity Term in the year in which the assessment is made. The supervisory committee may specify that one of the practical assessments will be carried out as group projects, the details of which will be given in the Course Handbook.

Schedule

5

Paper 1: Principles of statistical analysis
  Statistical distribution theory; statistical inference; statistical methods.

Paper 2: Further statistical methodology
  Topics in statistical methodology chosen from a list approved by the standing committee and published in the Course Handbook by the beginning of Michaelmas   10
Term of the academic year in which the written examination is to be taken.

DIPLOMA IN LEGAL STUDIES

GENERAL REGULATIONS

1. The Board of the Faculty of Law shall have power to grant Diplomas in Legal Studies to members of the University who have kept residence and pursued a course of study at Oxford for not less than three terms; time spent outside Oxford during term as part of an academic programme approved by Council shall count towards residence for the purpose of this clause.

2. The examination for the Diploma in Legal Studies shall be under the supervision of the Board of the Faculty of Law.

3. The examiners for the diploma shall be such of the Public Examiners in the Honour School of Jurisprudence as shall be required.

4. A Diploma Student must keep statutory residence and pursue a course of study at Oxford for three terms, and may not take the examination for the Diploma earlier or later than in the second term after that with effect from which he or she was admitted as a Diploma student.

5. The examiners may award a distinction to a candidate for the Diploma in Legal Studies.

SPECIAL REGULATIONS

1. The Diploma will normally only be granted to candidates who on admission had no significant previous education in the common law.

2. The examination for the diploma shall be in each Trinity Term.

3. The examination shall consist of any three standard subjects selected by the candidate from such standard subjects specified for the Honour School of Jurisprudence as notified as available in the Diploma in Legal Studies. Notice of these subjects will be given in the edition of the Law Faculty Handbook for Undergraduate Students for the relevant year, which will be published and made available on the Faculty website by Monday of noughth week of Michaelmas Term that year.

4. Candidates in examinations will not be required to answer more than three questions.

5. Candidates may be required to attend a viva voce examination.

6. The Law Board will approve and offer a Legal Research Skills Programme, as outlined in the Special Regulations for the Honour School of Jurisprudence. Candidates for the Diploma are required to undertake unit one of the course and an additional print resources class (details of which will be notified to the students) and to complete the associated assessments to the satisfaction of the Programme Coordinator appointed by the Law Board.

POSTGRADUATE DIPLOMA IN THEOLOGY

1. It shall be lawful for the Board of the Faculty of Theology and Religion to grant Postgraduate Diplomas in Theology to candidates who have satisfied the conditions prescribed in this Section.

2. The examination shall be under the supervision of the Board of the Faculty of Theology.

3. Subject to the provisions of this Section, any member of the University who has obtained the leave of the Board of the Faculty of Theology and Religion and has kept statutory residence for at least three terms may be admitted to the examination for the Postgraduate Diploma in Theology provided that:

   (*a*) he or she has passed all the examinations required for the Degree of Bachelor of Arts and has obtained First or upper Second Class Honours in the Second Public Examination, or has attained such honours in a degree examination of another university, such university having been approved by Council for the purposes of Senior Status; *or*

   (*b*) he or she is, in the opinion of the board, otherwise adequately qualified to undertake the course.

Time spent outside Oxford during term as part of an academic programme approved by Council shall count towards residence for the purpose of this clause.

4. Applications for leave under cl. 3 shall be sent to the Registrar, through the Head or tutor of the society to which the applicant belongs or desires to belong. The board shall have power to determine the character and length of a course of study in Theology to be followed by the applicant before he or she may be admitted to the examination.

5. The examiners may award a distinction in any subject in the examination.

6. A student reading for the diploma who is not a graduate of the University shall wear the same gown as that worn by Students for the Degree of Doctor of Philosophy.

SPECIAL REGULATIONS

All candidates will be required to offer not less than *three* papers (and not more than *five*), of which at least one must normally be either (1) or (2) and another must be either (3), (4) or (5).

(1) *The Four Gospels*. Candidates will be expected to answer questions on the literature and the religion of the gospels, with portions of the text in *either* Greek *or* English.
The prescribed portions of the Greek text* are:
Matthew 3-17 with synoptic parallels (text of Huck-Lietzmann, *Synopsis of the first Three Gospels*).
The prescribed portions of the English text† are:
Matthew 5-7; Mark; John.

(2) *The New Testament Epistles with special reference to St Paul*. Candidates will be expected to answer questions on the theology of these epistles, with portions of the text in *either* Greek *or* English.
The prescribed portions of the Greek text* are:
Romans 1-8.
The prescribed portions of the English text† are:
Romans; 1 Corinthians (edition of text as for paper 1).

(3) *Old Testament: The Pentateuch and Historical Books*. Candidates must demonstrate in essay questions knowledge of the broad range of the syllabus and also of the issues of method involved. They must also show a detailed knowledge of the texts in *either* Hebrew *or* English.
The prescribed portions of the Hebrew text‡ are: Genesis 1-4.
The prescribed portions of the English text† are: *either* Genesis 1-11 *or* Exodus 1-15; and *either* 2 Samuel 1-12 *or* 2 Kings 18-25.

(4) *Old Testament: Prophets, Psalms, and Wisdom*. Candidates must demonstrate in essay questions knowledge of the broad range of the syllabus and also of the issues of method involved. They must also show a detailed knowledge of texts in *either* Hebrew *or* English.
The prescribed portions of the Hebrew texts‡ are: Isaiah 1, 6, and 7.
The prescribed portions of the English text† are: *either* Isaiah 1-12 *or* Zechariah 1-14; and *either* Psalms 73-89 *or* Proverbs 1-12.

(5) *God, Christ, and Salvation*. As specified for paper (5) in the Honour School of Theology.

(6) *Christian Life and Thought in Europe and the English-Speaking World, 1789-1921*. As specified for paper (9)A in the Honour School of Theology.

(7) *Christian Moral Reasoning*. As specified for paper (12) in the Honour School of Theology.

(8) *World Religions*. Candidates will be expected to make a study of one of the following religions:
(*a*) Islam;
(*b*) Buddhism;
(*c*) Hinduism.
The syllabuses will be as prescribed for papers (16), (18), and (20) in the Honour School of Theology.

---

* The Greek text used will be the text of the United Bible Societies, 4th edn.
† The English text used will be the New Revised Standard Version.
‡ The Hebrew text used will be the *Biblia Hebraica Stuttgartensia* (Stuttgart, 1977).

(9) *Philosophy of Religion.* The subject will include an examination of claims about the existence of God, and God's relation to the world: their meaning, the possibility of their truth, and the kind of justification which can or needs to be provided for them, and the philosophical problems raised by the existence of different religions. One or two questions may also be set on central claims peculiar to Christianity, such as the doctrines of the Trinity, Incarnation, and Atonement. 5

(10) *The Development of Doctrine in the Early Church to AD 451* as specified for paper (4) in the Honour School of Theology.

Every candidate is required to follow for at least three terms a course of instruction in Theology, and he or she will, when he or she enters his or her name for the examination, be required to produce from his or her society a certificate that he or she is following a course of instruction in Theology for at least three terms. 10

*From candidates who wish to be admitted to the examination under cl. 3 (*b*) of the Decree, the Board of the Faculty of Theology will require evidence that they have followed, or have arranged to follow, for three terms a course of instruction in Theology in Oxford to the satisfaction of the board. Application for the board's approval of the course of instruction should be sent to the Registrar, through the Head or a tutor of the candidate's society or prospective society, at the same time as the application for permission to be admitted to the examination. 15

Before admission to the examination every candidate must have kept at least three terms by residence as a matriculated member of the University. Terms kept prior to admission as a student for the diploma may be reckoned for this purpose. 20

The Nomination of Examiners shall be made as early as may be in Michaelmas Term.

Except as may be determined by the board from time to time the examination for the diploma will take place in Trinity Term. 25

---

* Candidates are advised to obtain the approval of the board for their course of instruction not later than the Michaelmas Term preceding the examination.

POSTGRADUATE CERTIFICATE IN EDUCATION

GENERAL REGULATIONS

1. The Departmental Board of the Department of Education shall have power to grant Postgraduate Certificates in Education to candidates who have satisfied the relevant conditions prescribed in this section.

2. The examination for the Postgraduate Certificate in Education shall be under the supervision of the Departmental Board which shall have the power to make regulations concerning the examination and arrange lectures and courses of instruction for the Certificate.

3. (*a*) All applicants for the Postgraduate Certificate in Education must have obtained on entry to the course a grade C or above in GCSE English Language and in GCSE Mathematics, or their equivalent.

   (*b*) Applicants must be graduates. Candidates for admission should normally have at least a good upper second class degree in a subject appropriate for the curriculum area to which they are applying.

4. After admission as a certificate student, a candidate must have kept statutory residence and pursued a course of study in Oxford for at least three terms before taking the examination.

5. A student reading for the Postgraduate Certificate in Education, who is not a graduate of the University, may wear the same gown as that worn by Students for the degree of Doctor of Philosophy.

SPECIAL REGULATIONS

1. *Course*

   (*a*) The course will consist of lectures, tutorials, seminars and classes in the theory and practice of education, together with a serial placement and two extended periods of practical experience in schools or other educational settings.

   (*b*) The subjects of the course of study are as follows:

   Curriculum studies related to the professional knowledge, understanding and skills required for teaching a specific subject across the 11-18 age range: the place of the subject in the school curriculum; the establishment and maintenance of a purposeful learning environment; lesson planning, teaching, and evaluation; formative and summative assessment; the promotion of young people's health and well-being;

professional team work and collaboration In each of the seven subjects offered (English, Geography, History, Mathematics, Modern Foreign Languages, Religious Education and Science) an integrated programme requires students to set theoretical and research-based understandings alongside classroom observation and teaching experience, subjecting both the educational theory and the practice to rigorous critical evaluation. 5

A Professional Development Programme presented through an integrated programme taught within the University and across the partnership schools, concerned with issues of policy and professional practice which transcend individual subjects. This programme is structured around a number of core themes which include: the changing nature of education and the role of schools; the developing school curriculum (secondary phase) and assessment; adolescence; learners and learning; inclusion and issues of social justice; teacher professionalism and collaborative working. It also includes training in research methods appropriate to the conduct of small scale practitioner research studies. 10 15

School Experience. The course includes 120 days' experience in a school or other educational setting nominated for this purpose by the Department of Education.

2. *Examination*
Every candidate will be required to satisfy the examiners in the following:

(*a*) an assignment of 4,000 to 5,000 words (including footnotes/endnotes but excluding appendices, references or bibliography) on an issue of professional practice which transcends individual subjects. 20

Two typewritten/word-processed copies of the assignment must be delivered to the PGCE Examiners, c/o the PGCE Course Administrator, Department of Education, 15 Norham Gardens, Oxford OX2 6PY at such dates and times as the examiners shall determine. Both copies of the assignment should be anonymous except for the candidate number. 25

(*b*) two curriculum assignments of 4,000-5,000 words each (including footnotes/endnotes but excluding appendices, references or bibliography), related to the theory and practice of teaching and learning within the candidate's own subject discipline. 30

Two typewritten/word-processed copies of each assignment must be delivered to the PGCE Examiners, c/o the PGCE Course Administrator, Department of Education, 15 Norham Gardens, Oxford OX2 6PY at such dates and times as the examiners shall determine. Both copies of each assignment should be anonymous except for the candidate number. 35

(*c*) an assessment of the candidate's professional attributes, knowledge, understanding and skills in relation to the Teachers' Standards as determined by the Department for Education. This assessment is carried out by persons representing both the University and its partnership schools who are appointed for this purpose by the Departmental Board of the Department of Education. 40

Details of submission deadlines for the assignments set out under (*a*) and (*b*) above and of the deadlines for the assessment of candidate's professional attributes, knowledge, understanding and skills as set out in (*c*) above shall be published annually in the PGCE course handbook distributed to candidates at the start of the course. 45

The determination of any candidate's fitness to teach during the course of the Postgraduate Certificate of Education programme must be carried out in accordance with the Regulations for procedures concerning fitness to teach during the PGCE programme published annually in the PGCE course handbook and made available to students on the first day of the PGCE term. 50

Candidates may also be called for viva voce examination.

If it is the opinion of the examiners that any or all of the candidate's written assignments are not of the standard required for the award of the Postgraduate Certificate in Education, but that all assignments are nevertheless of sufficient merit to meet the standards required for the Professional Graduate Certificate in Education, then the board may recommend that the candidate should be awarded the Professional Graduate Certificate in Education, provided that the candidate's professional attributes, knowledge, skills and understanding are also assessed as having met the Teachers' Standards.

Candidates who fail the examination may apply to the Departmental Board to be re-examined on not more than one occasion which should normally be within one year of their initial failure.

Those candidates who have failed the examination, but whose assignments meet the standards required for the Professional Graduate Certificate in Education, may apply for re-examination for the Postgraduate Certificate in Education within one academic year. In such cases the Departmental Board may recommend candidates to the Department for Education for the Award of Qualified Teacher Status even before their assignments have been resubmitted provided that they have satisfied the examiners in 2(c) above.

Candidates who fail to satisfy the examiners in 2(c) above shall not be granted permission to re-enter for the examination.

PROFESSIONAL GRADUATE CERTIFICATE IN EDUCATION

GENERAL REGULATIONS

1. The Departmental Board of the Department of Education shall have power to grant Professional Graduate Certificates in Education to candidates who have satisfied the relevant conditions prescribed in this section.

2. The examination for the Professional Graduate Certificate in Education shall be under the supervision of the Departmental Board which shall have the power to make regulations concerning the examination and arrange lectures and courses of instruction for the Certificate.

3. (*a*) All candidates for the Professional Graduate Certificate in Education must have obtained on entry to the course a grade C or above in GCSE English Language and in GCSE Mathematics, or their equivalent.

   (*b*) All candidates must be graduates. They should normally have at least a good upper second class degree in a subject appropriate for the curriculum area to which they are applying.

4. After admission as a certificate student, a candidate must have kept statutory residence and pursued a course of study in Oxford for at least three terms before taking the examination.

5. A student reading for the Professional Graduate Certificate in Education, who is not a graduate of the University, may wear the same gown as that worn by Students for the degree of Doctor of Philosophy.

SPECIAL REGULATIONS

1. *Course*

(*a*) The course will consist of lectures, tutorials, seminars and classes in the theory and practice of education, together with a serial placement and two extended periods of practical experience in schools or other educational settings.

(*b*) The subjects of the course of study are as follows:

Curriculum studies related to the professional knowledge, understanding and skills required for teaching a specific subject across the 11-18 age range: the place of the subject in the school curriculum; the establishment and maintenance of a purposeful learning environment; lesson planning, teaching, and evaluation; formative and summative assessment; the promotion of young people's health and well-being;

professional team work and collaboration In each of the seven subjects offered (English, Geography, History, Mathematics, Modern Foreign Languages, Religious Education and Science) an integrated programme requires students to set theoretical and research-based understandings alongside classroom observation and teaching experience, subjecting both the educational theory and the practice to rigorous critical evaluation.

A Professional Development Programme presented through an integrated programme taught within the University and across the partnership schools, concerned with issues of policy and professional practice which transcend individual subjects. This programme is structured around a number of core themes which include: the changing nature of education and the role of schools; the developing school curriculum (secondary phase) and assessment; adolescence; learners and learning; inclusion and issues of social justice; teacher professionalism and collaborative working. It also includes training in research methods appropriate to the conduct of small scale practitioner research studies.

School Experience The course includes 120 days' experience in a school or other educational setting nominated for this purpose by the Department of Education.

2. *Examination*

Every candidate will be required to satisfy the examiners in the following:

(*a*) an assignment of 4,000 to 5,000 words (including footnotes/endnotes but excluding appendices, references or bibliography) on an issue of professional practice which transcends individual subjects.

Two typewritten/word-processed copies of the assignment must be delivered to the PGCE Examiners, c/o the PGCE Course Administrator, Department of Education, 15 Norham Gardens, Oxford OX2 6PY at such dates and times as the examiners shall determine. Both copies of the assignment should be anonymous except for the candidate number.

(*b*) two curriculum assignments of 4,000-5,000 words each (including footnotes/endnotes but excluding appendices, references or bibliography), related to the theory and practice of teaching and learning within the candidate's own subject discipline.

Two typewritten/word-processed copies of each assignment must be delivered to the PGCE Examiners, c/o the PGCE Course Administrator, Department of Education, 15 Norham Gardens, Oxford OX2 6PY at such dates and times as the examiners shall determine. Both copies of each assignment should be anonymous except for the candidate number

(*c*) an assessment of the candidate's professional attributes, knowledge, understanding and skills in relation to the Teachers' Standards as determined by the Department for Education. This assessment is carried out by persons representing both the University and its partnership schools who are appointed for this purpose by the Departmental Board of the Department of Education.

Details of submission deadlines for the assignments set out under (*a*) and (*b*) above and of the deadlines for the assessment of candidate's professional attributes, knowledge, understanding and skills as set out in (*c*) above shall be published annually in the PGCE course handbook distributed to candidates at the start of the course.

The determination of any candidate's fitness to teach during the course of the Professional Certificate of Education programme must be carried out in accordance with the Regulations for procedures concerning fitness to teach during the PGCE programme published annually in the PGCE course handbook.

Candidates may also be called for viva voce examination.

Candidates who fail the examination may apply to the Departmental Board to be re-examined on not more than one occasion which should normally be within one year of their initial failure.

Candidates who fail to satisfy the examiners in 2(c) above shall not be granted permission to re-enter for the examination. 5

CERTIFICATE AND DIPLOMA IN THEOLOGICAL AND PASTORAL STUDIES

GENERAL REGULATIONS

1. The Board of the Faculty of Theology and Religion shall have the power to grant the following awards to candidates who have satisfied the conditions prescribed in this section and any further conditions which the board may prescribe by regulation:

Certificate in Theological and Pastoral Studies

Diploma in Theological and Pastoral Studies

2. The examinations for these qualifications shall be under the supervision of the Board of the Faculty of Theology and Religion.

3. Candidates who have been admitted under such conditions as the Board of the Faculty of Theology and Religion shall prescribe, to courses at Blackfriars, Campion Hall, Harris Manchester College, Mansfield College, Regent's Park College, Ripon College, Cuddesdon, St Benet's Hall, St Stephen's House, and Wycliffe Hall may be admitted by the board to the examinations for the above mentioned qualifications, provided that they have paid to the Curators of the University Chest, through their colleges or other institutions, the fees prescribed in the appropriate regulation (see Appendix 1).

4. The supervision of the arrangements for the above mentioned qualifications shall be the responsibility of the Supervisory Committee for the Degree of Bachelor of Theology. The committee shall have such powers and duties in respect of the above mentioned qualifications as may from time to time be prescribed by the Board of the Faculty of Theology and Religion.

5. Part-time students for the above mentioned qualifications shall in each case be required to pursue their course of study for twice the number of terms required of an equivalent full-time student.

6. On successful completion of the Certificate in Theological and Pastoral Studies, candidates may offer the remaining papers necessary to complete the Diploma in Theological and Pastoral Studies.

Special Regulations

Admission Requirements

Candidates will normally be expected to have five GCSE passes at grades A-C, one of which must be in English Language, and two passes at Advanced Level (A2); they will normally be expected to meet University residence requirements. Exemptions   5 from these requirements for mature student candidates or those otherwise qualified may be made at the discretion of the BTh Supervisory Committee. Candidates must demonstrate aptitude and vocation for ministry or other church work. Students who can demonstrate completed and accredited previous academic achievement equivalent to the Certificate in Theological and Pastoral Studies may, at the discretion of the   10 Supervisory Committee for the Bachelor of Theology, be admitted directly to study for the Diploma in Theological and Pastoral Studies.

Course Requirements

Candidates for the Certificate in Theological and Pastoral Studies will take at least *four papers* at Level 4* from the syllabus as outlined for the Bachelor of Theology,   15 including at least one of A1 and A2.

Candidates who have satisfied the examiners in four papers including A1 or A2 may supplicate for the Certificate or may take at least *four further papers* at Level 5* from the syllabus as outlined for the Bachelor of Theology, including at least one of C1 and C4.   20

Candidates for the Certificate or Diploma in Theological and Pastoral Studies may not transfer to the CTh or BTh courses, or to any other University of Oxford degree programme.

Examinations

Examination will take place by continuous assessment within colleges, supervised   25 and moderated by the BTh Supervisory Committee and a Faculty Board moderator on behalf of the Faculty Board. Two summative pieces of work will be assessed for each paper. These will take the form of two essays or, alternatively, one essay plus one project. Essays at Level 4 should not exceed 2,500 words, and essays at Level 5 should not exceed 3,000 words. Guidelines for the project will be published in the   30 course handbook issued by the Faculty of Theology and Religion. In addition to submitting these two moderated pieces of work for each paper, candidates must complete a form, countersigned by a college officer, stating that they have attended the relevant course of instruction and passed the required formative, internally assessed work for that paper.   35

The Examiners may award the Certificate and the Diploma at the following grades: Distinction, Merit and Pass.

---

* As defined in the Framework for Higher Education Qualifications (2008).

POSTGRADUATE DIPLOMA IN INTEGRATED IMMUNOLOGY

GENERAL REGULATIONS

1. The Medical Sciences Board shall have the power to grant Postgraduate Diplomas in Integrated Immunology to members of the University who have kept residence and pursued a course of study at Oxford for not less than two terms.

2. The examination shall be under the supervision of the Medical Sciences Board.

SPECIAL REGULATIONS

1. A candidate may be admitted to the Postgraduate Diploma in Integrated Immunology provided that he or she has the status of Probationary Research Student.

2. The Divisional Board of Medical Sciences shall appoint for the supervision of the course an Organising Committee, which shall have the power to arrange the teaching, assessments and other instruction.

3. The Organising Committee shall appoint an academic mentor for each candidate.

4. Each candidate shall:
   (*a*) follow a course of study in Integrated Immunology for two terms and for a substantial part of the intervening vacation, as determined by the course timetable;
   (*b*) attend all organised sessions including lectures, tutorials, class-directed learning, problem-based learning and continuing professional development sessions which are compulsory (a record of attendance is kept).

5. Candidates shall be examined in all of the following ways:
   (i) At the end of Michaelmas Term (normally in Week 10), each candidate must pass a computer-based examination on the topics in the Schedule for Term 1. Candidates who fail the examination once will be permitted to take it again on one further occasion, in order to proceed with the course.
   (ii) At the end of Hilary Term (normally in Week 10), each candidate must pass a computer-based examination on the topics in the Schedule for Term 2. Candidates who fail the examination once will be permitted to take it again on one further occasion, in order to proceed with the course.
   (iii) Each candidate will be required to submit to the examiners two copies of a printed essay of between 3,000-4,000 words by noon, Monday of Week 8 of Michaelmas Term. The subject of the essay must have been approved by the Examining Board. Each candidate shall make a public presentation on their essay to the examiners and will be examined viva voce as required, at the end of Michaelmas Term at a time to be notified by the examiners. Candidates will have the opportunity to revise and re-submit their essay by noon, Friday of the week preceding Week 0 of Hilary Term, in the event that they are deemed not to have passed this element of the examination.

(iv) Each candidate will be required to submit to the examiners two copies each of four clinical commentaries (printed) of 1,000-1,500 words each by noon, Monday of Week 8 of Hilary Term. The subjects of the clinical commentaries must have been approved by the Examining Board. Each candidate will be required to make a public presentation of one or more of their commentaries and will be examined viva voce, at the end of Hilary Term at a time to be notified by the examiners. Candidates will have the opportunity to revise and re-submit their clinical commentaries by noon, Friday of the week preceding Week 0 of Trinity Term, in the event that they are deemed not to have passed this element of the examination.

6. The examiners may examine any candidate viva voce on any part of the examination.

7. Candidates must pass each element of the examination to pass overall.

8. Candidates must pass each element of the examination in each term before being permitted to progress to the next term.

9. Candidates will be allowed one opportunity to retake or resubmit each of the required elements should they fail to reach the necessary standard. Students failing to pass any element on the second attempt will normally be judged to have failed to reach the necessary standard for the award.

10. The examiners may award a distinction for excellence in the whole examination.

11. The required written submissions must be sent to the Chair of Examiners, Postgraduate Diploma in Integrated Immunology, c/o Examination Schools, High Street, Oxford.

Schedule

The syllabus for study will be:

Term 1: Fundamental aspects of immunology
  The dynamic anatomy of immunity
  Innate immunity
  Antigen presentation and recognition
  Adaptive Immunity
  Phylogenetically ancient systems

Term 2: Clinical aspects of immunology
  Infection and immunity
  Failure of immunity
  Aberrant and unwanted immunity
  The immunology of cancer
  Manipulation of Immunity

POSTGRADUATE DIPLOMA IN MUSCULOSKELETAL SCIENCES

GENERAL REGULATIONS

1. The Medical Sciences Board shall have the power to grant Postgraduate Diplomas in Musculoskeletal Sciences to candidates who have satisfied the conditions prescribed in this Section.

2. The Examination shall be under the supervision of the Medical Sciences Board.

SPECIAL REGULATIONS

1. The Medical Sciences Board shall elect for the supervision of the course an Organising Committee, which shall have the power to arrange teaching, assessments and other instruction.

2. The Organising Committee shall appoint for each candidate an academic supervisor.

3. Candidates will hold a first degree in medicine, or exceptionally a biomedical science degree.

4. Candidates shall follow a course of study in Musculoskeletal Sciences on a part-time basis for at least six terms, and including vacations, as determined by the course timetable. The course commences every two years in January and runs until December of the following year.

5. Candidates shall be examined in all of the following ways:

(i) Year 1 (January to December)

    (*a*) Each candidate shall submit a literature review of no more than 4,000 words on a topic selected by the candidate and approved by the Organising Committee. The review must be submitted during the Long Vacation on a date to be specified in the course handbook.

    (*b*) Each candidate must pass an examination in Michaelmas Term. The examination will comprise two elements: the first of these will consist of a one-hour computer-based assessment comprising multiple-choice questions; the second of these will constitute a two-hour written paper. The dates of the examination will be specified in the course handbook.

(ii) Year 2 (January to December)

    (*a*) Each candidate must submit, for assessment of their progress, an outline research proposal. The outline must be submitted in Hilary Term on a date to be specified in the course handbook.

    (*b*) Each candidate will be assessed on their presentation skills by means of a public oral presentation on his or her research topic. The presentation must take place in Trinity Term on a date to be specified in the course handbook.

    (*c*) **[Until 1 October 2014:** Each candidate must pass a written examination in Michaelmas Term on a date to be specified in the course handbook. Part of the written examination will comprise computer-based multiple choice questions.] **[From 1 October 2014:** Each candidate must pass an examination in Michaelmas Term. The examination will comprise two elements: the first of these will consist of a one-hour computer-based assessment comprising multiple-choice questions; the second of these will constitute a two-hour written paper. The dates of the examination will be specified in the course handbook.]

5

6. Candidates may be examined viva voce on their research proposal. The viva voce examination will normally be conducted at the end of the course.

7. Candidates must pass each examination or written assignment in order to pass overall.

10

8. Candidates will be allowed one opportunity to retake or resubmit each of the required elements, normally within six months of the original failure, should they fail to reach the necessary standard. Candidates failing to pass any element at the second attempt will normally be judged to have failed to reach the necessary standard for the award and will not be permitted to continue.

15

9. The required written submissions must be sent to the Chair of Examiners, MSc in Musculoskeletal Sciences, c/o Examination Schools, High Street, Oxford. Submissions must be accompanied by a declaration of authorship and originality.

10. The examiners may award a distinction for excellence in part of or in the whole examination.

20

Schedule

The syllabus for study will include the following components:

Core Subjects

Candidates are required to complete all of the following modules:
1. Principles of Musculoskeletal Diseases

25

2. Research, Statistics and Epidemiology
3. Scientific Aspects of Common Musculoskeletal Diseases

Specialist Subjects

Candidates are required to complete one of the following modules:
1. Advanced Rheumatology

30

2. Advanced Orthopaedics

NOTES

25

EXAMINATIONS FOR DIPLOMAS AND CERTIFICATES OPEN TO NON-MEMBERS OF THE UNIVERSITY

GENERAL REGULATIONS

1. A Register shall be kept by the Registrar of the University of all students who are studying with a view to obtaining a diploma or certificate granted under the provisions of this Decree and who are not members of the University. The Register shall be entitled the Register of Diploma Students.

2. For the purpose of this Register, each of the bodies empowered to grant diplomas or certificates shall make to the Registrar each term, not later than the end of the second week of Full Term, a return of the names and addresses of all students who have been admitted by such body in that term and who are studying with a view to a diploma or certificate and who are not members of the University.

3. No student shall have his or her name entered, replaced, or retained on the Register unless *either* (1) he or she is more than twenty-five years of age and has satisfied the Vice-Chancellor and Proctors that he or she is of good character, *or* (2) he or she is a graduate of a university approved by Council under the appropriate regulation, *or* (3) he or she has been admitted as a student for a Diploma or Certificate by the Continuing Education Board, *or* (4) he or she is a member of a society or institution in Oxford established for the purpose of higher study and approved for the purpose of this decree by Council,* *or* (5) he or she is a member of the Public Service, naval, military, or civil, engaged on a course of higher study or research.

4. Before the name of any person is entered or replaced on the Register, he or she shall pay to the Registrar of the University, through the body returning his or her name in pursuance of clause 2 above, a fee as prescribed in the appropriate regulation (see

---

* The following bodies have been approved under this clause: Ruskin College, Green-Templeton College, Ripon College Cuddesdon, St Stephen's House, Wycliffe Hall, and the Oxford Centre for Hebrew and Jewish Studies.

Appendix I). The Registrar shall pay all fees so received to the University Chest. This clause shall not apply to students admitted as candidates for the Special Diploma in Educational Studies, for Postgraduate Diplomas or Postgraduate Certificates awarded by the Continuing Education Board, for the Diploma in Jewish Studies or for the Diploma in Management Studies.

5. The name of any diploma student may be removed, either temporarily or permanently, from the Register either by the Proctors or by the body by which his or her name was returned. No name which has been removed shall be replaced on the Register except with the consent of the authority which removed it. Nothwithstanding the earlier provisions of this clause, the student may within fourteen days of the date of the Proctors' decision appeal in writing to the Chair of the Education Committee (who may nominate another member of the committee, other than one of the Proctors, to adjudicate the appeal). If the Proctors' decision is not upheld, the Education Committee may replace the student's name on the Register.

6. No one whose name is not on the Register, except a member of the University, shall be entitled to attend any lecture or course of instruction given under arrangements made by a body which grants any such diploma or certificate as aforesaid.

7. No one except a member of the University shall be permitted to be a candidate in the examination, or any part of the examination, for any such diploma or certificate unless his or her name (1) is on the Register in the term in which such examination or part of an examination is held, or, if the examination is held in vacation, in the term immediately preceding such examination, (2) has been on the Register during at least one previous term or such longer period as may be prescribed by the body under whose authority the examination is held, provided that such body may dispense from this second requirement any candidate who before registration has attended only lectures or courses of instruction given in vacation under arrangements made by such body, or who is a member of the Public Service, naval, military, or civil, engaged on a course of higher study or research.

8. The bodies empowered to grant diplomas or certificates shall cause lists of candidates in the examinations or any parts of examinations for any such diplomas or certificates to be distributed in the usual manner at least three days before the day fixed for the beginning of any such examination.

REGULATIONS FOR THE POSTGRADUATE DIPLOMAS IN EDUCATION, IN LEARNING AND TEACHING IN HIGHER EDUCATION, AND IN TEACHING ENGLISH LANGUAGE IN UNIVERSITY SETTINGS

GENERAL REGULATIONS

1. The Departmental Board of the Department of Education shall have power to grant Postgraduate Diplomas in Education and Postgraduate Diplomas in Learning and Teaching in Higher Education and Postgraduate Diplomas in Teaching English in University Settings to candidates who have satisfied the conditions prescribed in this section and any further conditions which the committee may prescribe by regulation.

2. The examinations for the diplomas shall be under the supervision of the Departmental Board which shall have power subject to the approval of the Education Committee to make regulations governing the examinations.

3. Candidates, whether members of the University or not, may be admitted as students for the diplomas under such conditions as the committee shall prescribe, provided that

(i) before admission to a course of study approved by the committee, candidates have satisfied the committee that they have received a good general education, that they have had appropriate educational experience acceptable to the committee, and are well qualified to enter the proposed course of study;

(ii) any person so admitted who is not a member of the University, shall be required to pay to the Curators of the University Chest through the committee the composition fee payable under the provisions of the appropriate regulation, notwithstanding that he or she is not a member of the University.

4. The Departmental Board shall make a return to the Registrar by the end of the sixth week of Michaelmas Term, showing the

names of all persons admitted in that term as students for the diplomas, and the Registrar shall add the names of non-members of the University to the Register of Diploma Students.

5. Any person who has been accepted as a candidate for the diplomas and who has satisfactorily pursued a course, whose character and length have been approved by the committee, may be admitted to the examinations.

6. A candidate must apply to the committee for admission to the examinations at such time as the committee shall, by regulation, prescribe. His or her application must be accompanied by:

(*a*) a certificate from the Secretary of the Committee that he or she is satisfactorily pursuing a course of study approved by the committee;

(*b*) such other information as the committee may, by regulation, require.

SPECIAL REGULATIONS FOR THE POSTGRADUATE DIPLOMA IN EDUCATION

1. Candidates for the Postgraduate Diploma in Education shall be qualified teachers in the United Kingdom, or recognised by the Graduate Studies Committee as being of equivalent status overseas. They shall normally have had not less than three years' educational experience acceptable to the committee. The committee may in exceptional cases admit to the examination candidates with other qualifications.

2. Each candidate for the Postgraduate Diploma in Education will follow a course of study approved by the Graduate Studies Committee. Each candidate shall be required to follow *one* of the following options:

(*a*) A full-time course involving a programme of study of three terms in duration which will consist of: an introduction to research methods; an individual programme of study leading to the submission of the dissertation; and a common programme of studies embracing topics from amongst the following areas of study upon which he will be required to submit essays; the development of the educational system of England and Wales; the nature and control of the curriculum; the organisation, administration, and management of schools; contemporary work in sociology and psychology in relation to the practice of pedagogy in schools; assessment in education; teacher education; comparative education.

(*b*) A course involving a programme of study of three terms in duration in which each candidate will spend at least 40 per cent of the days of these terms in university-based study, and the remainder of these terms working in his or her own school or local education authority and engaged in a research and development project. Each programme of study will consist of an introduction to research methods, a research and development project concerned with a significant aspect of educational practice, which will lead to the submission of the dissertation, and a programme of studies which shall be equivalent in weight to the common programme of studies indicated in 3(*a*) above, which shall incorporate part of that common programme and which shall be related to the research and development project being undertaken by the candidate. The whole programme for each candidate shall be approved by the Graduate Studies Committee, which shall satisfy itself that the programme is suitable in its standards and scope for the Postgraduate Diploma in Education and is practically viable for the candidate for whom it is proposed. Application for approval of programmes is to be received not later than six weeks before the beginning of the term in which the course starts. The Committee, having considered a proposed programme, will inform the candidate of its decision not later than two weeks before the beginning of that term.

(*c*) A course extending over a minimum period of two years and a maximum period not normally exceeding three years from the beginning of the term in which the candidate is admitted for the Postgraduate Diploma course, with no requirements for full-day attendance, but otherwise involving the same requirements as those prescribed in 3(*b*) above.

3. Each student for the Postgraduate Diploma in Education will be assigned to a supervisor, who will be responsible for directing the student's course of study, including the dissertation. The title of the dissertation is to be submitted to the examiners for approval. The examiners shall notify candidates of the date by which the title must be submitted for approval.

4. All candidates for admission as students for the Postgraduate Diploma in Education and must apply to the department not later than two weeks before the start of the term in which the Postgraduate Diploma Courses start.

5. Every candidate for admission to the examination must apply to the Graduate Studies Committee for entry to the examination by the first day of Hilary Full Term in the academic year in which he wishes to take the examination. Candidates for the Postgraduate Diploma in Education must, at the same time, state the subject on which he or she proposes to submit the dissertation.

6. Candidates for the Postgraduate Diploma in Education must offer a dissertation of between 15,000 and 20,000 words. Two typewritten copies of the dissertation must be delivered to the Postgraduate Diploma Examiners, Department of Education, 15 Norham Gardens, Oxford, OX2 6PY, not later than noon on 30 September after the completion of the course of studies. Candidates wishing to submit dissertations later than 30 September must obtain the approval of the Departmental Board by the last day of the preceding Trinity Term, but no dissertation may be submitted later than noon on 30 September in the year following, unless the Departmental Board approves a later date for submission. One bound copy of the dissertation of each candidate who passes the examination shall be retained by the department for deposit in the departmental Library.

7. Candidates for the Postgraduate Diploma in Education may also be required to attend an oral examination.

8. The examiners for the Postgraduate Diploma in Education shall also consider, as part of the examination, reports on the candidate's work submitted by his or her supervisor. Reports shall be submitted at the end of each Full Term except that, in the term in which the candidate takes the examination, a report shall be submitted by the end of the seventh week of Full Term.

9. Candidates for the Postgraduate Diploma in Education who fail the examination may be re-examined on not more than one occasion which normally shall be within one year of their initial failure.

Special Regulations for the Postgraduate Diploma in Learning and Teaching in Higher Education

1. Candidates for the Postgraduate Diploma in Learning and Teaching in Higher Education ('the Diploma') shall be engaged as teachers in higher education.

2. All candidates for admission as students for the Diploma must apply to the Course Director at the Oxford Learning Institute not later than March 31st in the calendar year in which they wish to start the course. The Course Director shall forward his or her recommendations for decision to the Graduate Studies Committee of the Department of Education.

3. All candidates for the Diploma shall follow a course of study approved by the Graduate Studies Committee of the Department of Education.

4. Every candidate for admission to the examination must apply to the Graduate Studies Committee of the Department of Education by submitting an examination entry form to the Course Director at the Oxford Learning Institute no later than the first day of Hilary Full Term preceding the Michaelmas Term in which he or she wishes to be examined. No candidate shall be examined later than in the seventh term following the start of his or her course of study except with the approval of the Graduate Studies Committee of the Department of Education following written application via the Oxford Learning Institute.

5. Candidates for the Diploma must submit a portfolio of written work of between 12,000 and 15,000 words in total. Two typewritten copies of the portfolio and a certificate from the Oxford Learning Institute confirming that the candidate has participated in no fewer than six of the full-day seminars in the Diploma programme must be delivered to the Postgraduate Diploma Examiners, Department of Education, 15 Norham Gardens, Oxford OX2 6PY, not later than noon on the Monday of the first week of the Michaelmas Full Term in which the candidate is to be examined. In exceptional circumstances, following written application in advance via the Oxford Learning Institute, the Graduate Studies Committee of the Department of Education may allow late submission by specifying a revised deadline not later than noon on the Friday of the first week of that Michaelmas Term. One bound copy of the dissertation of each candidate who passes the examination shall be retained for deposit in the Oxford Learning Institute.

6. Candidates for the Diploma in Learning and Teaching in Higher Education may be awarded a distinction.

7. Notwithstanding the provisions in clause 4 above regulating the time allowed for completion of the course, candidates for the Diploma who fail the examination may be re-examined on not more than one occasion which shall be in the Michaelmas Term following their initial failure.

Special Regulations for the Postgraduate Diploma in Learning and Teaching (Part-Time)

1. The Postgraduate Diploma in Learning and Teaching is open only to candidates who are admitted to follow the required programme of study with the intention of proceeding to the M.Sc. in Learning and Teaching. The required programme of study will comprise Part I and Part II of the M.Sc. in Learning and Teaching (or Part II for those candidates who are exempt from Part I), as specified in the examination regulations pertaining to the programme for the degree of Master of Science in Learning and Teaching.

2. As candidates registered for the Diploma, students will follow a course of study that will allow them to progress, on successful completion of Part II, to the MSc in Learning and Teaching. Students who, having successfully completed Part II, choose not to continue with their programme of study will be awarded the Diploma. Those who progress to, and successfully complete Part III of the M.Sc. programme, will be awarded the degree of Master of Science which will subsume the award of the Diploma.

SPECIAL REGULATIONS FOR THE POSTGRADUATE DIPLOMA IN TEACHING ENGLISH LANGUAGE IN UNIVERSITY SETTINGS

1. Candidates for the Postgraduate Diploma in Teaching English Language in University Settings (the Diploma) shall normally have successfully obtained an honours degree. They shall be engaged as teachers of English as a second or foreign language at the time of application, and shall expect to continue this engagement during the Diploma course.

2. All candidates for admission as students for the Diploma must apply to the Course Director at the Department of Education. The Course Director shall forward his or her recommendations for decision to the Graduate Studies Committee of the Department of Education.

3. All candidates for the Diploma shall follow a course of study approved by the Graduate Studies Committee of the Department of Education.

4. Every candidate will be required to complete all eight summatively assessed online modules of the course by carrying out tasks and participating in discussions as directed by the Course Director. Every candidate will also be required to complete both formatively assessed residential modules, or, in exceptional cases and as determined by the Course Director, to give evidence of equivalent learning for one of these two modules.

5. Every candidate will be required to satisfy the examiners in the following:
   (i) Satisfactory participation in the appropriate web-based tasks and discussions for each module
   (ii) Satisfactory performance in the take-home examinations. Every candidate must complete all eight take-home examinations, each examination consisting of an essay which will be given a numerical mark and a reflective portfolio which will be marked on a pass/fail basis.

The overall mark for the Diploma shall be the mean of the seven best marks of the eight essays completed in the take-home examinations. Interim marks will be released to candidates during Hilary Term and Trinity Term of each year after a meeting of the Examination Board for the Diploma.

6. In each of the two years of this part-time course, an electronic copy of each of two module take-home examinations must be sent to the Chair of Examiners, PG Diploma in Teaching English Language in University Settings, Department of Education, no later than noon on the Monday of Week 1 of Hilary Full Term, and an electronic copy of each of two module take-home examinations must be sent in the same fashion no later than noon on the Monday of Week 1 of Trinity Full Term. Each take-home examination must be accompanied by a declaration indicating that it is the candidate's own work.

7. No candidate shall be examined later than in the seventh term following the start of his or her course of study except with the approval of the Graduate Studies Committee of the Department of Education.

8. Candidates for the Diploma who fail the examination may be re-examined on not more than one occasion which shall be in the year following their initial failure. Notwithstanding the provisions in clause 7 above regulating the time allowed for completion of the course, in the case of failure of a student to reach an average passing mark over the seven highest-marked module essays, a resit of all module take-home examinations must be submitted electronically by noon on Monday of Week 1 of Trinity term of the year following the student's final year of taught modules.

9. The examiners may award a distinction for excellence on the whole examination.

Schedule

Summatively assessed modules by distance learning:
   Module 1 Individual and group differences in language learning
   Module 2 Listening to and reading English in university settings
   Module 3 Understanding and teaching the grammar of English
   Module 4 Speaking and writing in university settings
   Module 5 Learning and teaching of vocabulary
   Module 6 Evaluating and designing English language teaching materials for uni-
        versity settings
   Module 7 New technologies and language learning and teaching
   Module 8 Assessing language learning

Formatively assessed residential modules:
   Module 0 Induction
   Module 9 Research methods

POSTGRADUATE CERTIFICATES IN THE SOFTWARE ENGINEERING PROGRAMME (OLD REGULATIONS)

For students registered on the M.Sc., PG Dip, and PG Cert in Software Engineering; the M.Sc., PG Dip, and PG Cert in Software and Systems Security; or the PG Cert in Object Technology before 1 April 2010.

GENERAL REGULATIONS

1. The Mathematical, Physical and Life Sciences Board shall have power to grant Postgraduate Certificates to candidates who have satisfied the conditions prescribed in this section and any further conditions which the board may prescribe by regulation.

2. The examination for each Postgraduate Certificate shall be under the supervision of the Mathematical, Physical and Life Sciences Board which shall have power, subject to the approval of the Education Committee, to make regulations governing the examination.

3. Candidates, whether members of the University or not, may be admitted as students for a Postgraduate Certificate under such conditions as the board shall prescribe, provided that before admission to a course of study approved by the board, candidates shall have satisfied the board that they have had appropriate educational and professional experience acceptable to the board, and are well-equipped to enter the proposed course of study.

4. Any person who has been accepted as a candidate for a Postgraduate Certificate, and who has satisfactorily pursued a course, the character and length of which have been approved by the board, may be admitted to the examination.

SPECIAL REGULATIONS

Object Technology (old regulations)
For students registered on the M.S.c., PG Dip, and PG Cert in Software Engineering; the M.Sc., PG Dip, and PG Cert in Software and Systems Security; or the PG Cert in Object Technology before 1 April 2010.

1. The Mathematical, Physical and Life Sciences Board, in consultation with the Faculty of Computer Science, shall elect for the supervision of the course a standing committee which shall have the power to arrange lectures and other instruction.

2. The course will consist of lectures, tutorials, seminars, and classes in the theory and practice of Object Technology. The course may be taken over a period of not less than one year, and not more than two years.

3. *For candidates enrolled on the M.Sc., PG Dip, and PG Cert in Software Engineering; the M.Sc., PG Dip, and PG Cert in Software and Systems Security; or the PG Cert in Object Technology from October 2008 to March 2010, and available to those who enrolled on those programmes prior to October 2008 and who have not already been awarded the relevant qualification.*

Every candidate will be required to satisfy the examiners in the following:

(*a*) attendance at a minimum of four modules, at least three of which chosen from the Schedule for the Postgraduate Certificate in Object Technology (below), with the remainder chosen from Schedules A or B of the M.Sc. in Software Engineering (old regulations), together comprising a programme of study approved by the Programme Director;

(*b*) submission of at least four written assignments, corresponding to those modules attended.

The assignments under (*b*) shall be forwarded to the examiners for consideration by such dates as the examiners shall determine and shall notify candidates and tutors.

4. Candidates will be expected to attend a viva voce examination at the end of the course of studies unless dispensed by the examiners.

5. The examiners may award a distinction for excellence in the whole examination.

6. The standing committee for the M.Sc. in Software Engineering shall have the discretion to permit any candidate to be exempted from submitting up to one of the total of four written assignments required under 3(b) above, provided the Standing Committee is satisfied that such a candidate has undertaken sufficient study, of an appropriate standard, normally at another institution of higher education.

7. Candidates who fail to satisfy the examiners in the assignments under 3(b) may be permitted to resubmit work in respect of part or parts of the examination which they have failed for examination on not more than one occasion which shall normally be within one year of the original failure. No written assignment shall be submitted to the examiners on more than one occasion.

Schedule

(i) Design patterns
(ii) Distributed objects
(iii) Object orientation
(iv) Object-oriented design
(v) Object-oriented programming
(vi) One other module from the schedule of courses for the M.Sc. in Software Engineering (old regulations).

The Standing Committee for the M.Sc. in Software Engineering shall have the power to add other courses or delete courses from this list. In June and December each year a list of modules shall be published in the *University Gazette*. Each such list, which will have been approved by the Standing Committee and which will be a selection from the full set above, will contain those modules which will be available during the following nine months.

Software and Systems Security (old regulations)

For students registered on the M.Sc., PG Dip, and PG Cert in Software Engineering; the M.Sc., PG Dip, and PG Cert in Software and Systems Security; or the PG Cert. in

Object Technology from October 2008 to March 2010, and available to those who enrolled on the M.Sc., PG Dip, and PG Cert in Software Engineering; the M.Sc., PG Dip, and PG Cert. in Software and Systems Security; or the PG Cert in Object Technology prior to October 2008 and who have not already been awarded the relevant qualification.

   1. The Mathematical, Physical and Life Sciences Board, in consultation with the Faculty of Computer Science, shall elect for the supervision of the course a Standing Committee which shall have the power to arrange lectures and other instruction.

   2. The course will consist of lectures, tutorials, seminars, and classes in the theory and practice of Software and Systems Security. The course may be taken over a period of not less than one year, and not more than two years.

   3. Every candidate will be required to satisfy the examiners in the following:

      (*a*) attendance at a minimum of four modules, at least three of which shall be chosen from Schedule A for the M.Sc. in Software and Systems Security (old regulations), with the fourth chosen from Schedules A or B of that M.Sc., together comprising a programme of study approved by the Programme Director;

      (*b*) submission of at least four written assignments, corresponding to those modules attended.

The assignments under (*b*) shall be forwarded to the examiners for consideration by such dates as the examiners shall determine and shall notify candidates and tutors.

   4. Candidates may, at the discretion of the examiners, be required to attend a viva voce examination.

   5. The examiners may award a distinction for excellence in the whole examination.

   6. The standing committee for the M.Sc. in Software and Systems Security shall have the discretion to permit any candidate to be exempted from attending at, and submitting the written assignment for, up to one of the total of four modules required under 3 above, provided that the standing committee is satisfied that such a candidate has undertaken equivalent study, of an appropriate standard, normally at another institution of higher education.

   7. Candidates who fail to satisfy the examiners in the assignments under 3(*b*) may be permitted to resubmit work in respect of part or parts of the examination which they have failed for examination on not more than one occasion which shall normally be within one year of the initial failure. No written assignment shall be submitted to the examiners on more than one occasion.

Software Engineering (old regulations)

For students registered on the M.Sc., PG Dip, and PG Cert in Software Engineering; the M.Sc., PG Dip, and PG Cert in Software and Systems Security; or the PG Cert in Object Technology before 1 April 2010.

   1. *Course*

The Divisional Board of Mathematical, Physical and Life Sciences, in consultation with the Faculty of Computer Science, shall elect for the supervision of the course a Standing Committee which shall have the power to arrange lectures and other instruction.

   2. The course will consist of lectures, tutorials, seminars, and classes in the theory and practice of Software Engineering. The course may be taken over a period of not less than one year, and not more than two years.

   3. *For students registered on the M.Sc., PG Dip, and PG Cert in Software Engineering; the M.Sc., PG Dip, and PG Cert in Software and Systems Security; or the PG Cert in Object Technology from October 2008 to March 2010, and available to those who enrolled on the M.Sc., PG Dip, and PG Cert in Software Engineering; the*

M.Sc., PG Dip, and PG Cert in Software and Systems Security; or the PG Cert in Object Technology prior to October 2008 and who have not already been awarded the relevant qualification.

Every candidate will be required to satisfy the examiners in the following:

(*a*) attendance at a minimum of four modules, chosen from Schedules A or B of the M.Sc. in Software Engineering (old regulations) together comprising a programme of study approved by the Programme Director;

(*b*) submission of at least four written assignments, corresponding to those modules attended. These shall be forwarded to the examiners for consideration by such dates as the examiners shall determine and shall notify to candidates and tutors;

(*c*) a viva voce examination, unless individually dispensed by the examiners.

The assignments under (*b*) shall be forwarded to the examiners for consideration by such dates as the examiners shall determine and shall notify candidates and tutors.

4. The examiners may award a distinction for excellence in the whole examination.

5. The Standing Committee for the M.Sc. in Software Engineering shall have the discretion to permit any candidate to be exempted from submitting one of the total of four assignments required, provided that the Standing Committee is satisfied that such a candidate has undertaken equivalent study, of an appropriate standard, normally at another institution of higher education.

6. Candidates who fail to satisfy the examiners may re-enter the examination on not more than one occasion which shall normally be within one year of the initial failure. No written assignment shall be submitted to the examiners on more than one occasion.

POSTGRADUATE CERTIFICATES (CONTINUING EDUCATION)

1. The Continuing Education Board shall have power to grant Postgraduate Certificates to candidates who have satisfied the conditions prescribed in this section and any further conditions which the board may prescribe by regulation.

2. The examination for each Postgraduate Certificate shall, in consultation with representatives of collaborating departments or faculties, be under the supervision of the Continuing Education Board which shall have power, subject to the approval of the Education Committee, to make regulations governing the examination.

3. Candidates, whether members of the University or not, may be admitted as students for a Postgraduate Certificate under such conditions as the board shall prescribe, provided that before admission to a course of study approved by the board, candidates shall have satisfied the board that they have had appropriate educational and professional experience acceptable to the board, and are well-equipped to enter the proposed course of study.

4. Any person who has been accepted as a candidate for a Postgraduate Certificate, and who has satisfactorily pursued a course, the character and length of which have been approved by the board, may be admitted to the examination.

SPECIAL REGULATIONS

Archaeology

1. (*a*) The course will consist of lectures, classes, seminars and tutorials in Archaeology. The course, which is available on a part-time basis only, is normally be taken over a period of one year and over a maximum of two years.

(*b*) The subjects of the course of study will include topics relevant to archaeological research methods, landscape archaeology, material culture, and analytical techniques.

2. Every candidate will be required to satisfy the examiners in the following:

(*a*) attendance at the taught courses;

(*b*) three assignments of between 2,000 and 2,500 words based on the taught courses;

(*c*) a practical logbook of up to 5,000 words;

(*d*) a dissertation of up to 10,000 words (including bibliography, appendices, footnotes, figure captions and descriptive catalogues but excluding external reference data under the heading of 'supplementary information') on a topic agreed by the Board of Examiners.

The assignments under 2(*b*), the logbook under 2(*c*) and the dissertation under 2(*d*) shall be submitted electronically to the examiners c/o the Registry, Department for Continuing Education, Wellington Square, Oxford OX1 2JA for consideration by such date as the examiners shall determine and shall notify candidates. The logbook under 2(*c*) and dissertation under 2(*d*) must also be submitted in hard copy.

3. Candidates may be required to attend a viva voce examination at the end of the course of studies.

4. The examiners may award a distinction to candidates for the Postgraduate Certificate.

5. Candidates who fail to satisfy the examiners in the assignments under 2(*b*), or the logbook under 2(*c*) or the dissertation under 2(*d*), may be permitted to resubmit work in respect of the part or parts of the examination which they have failed for examination on not more than one occasion which shall normally be within one year of the initial failure.

Architectural History

1. *Course*

(*a*) The course will consist of lectures and classes on architectural history and on site evaluation and survey. The course may be taken on a part-time basis over a period which shall normally be of one year's duration and shall not exceed two years.

(*b*) The course will consist of three taught units, two of which will be on architectural history and one of which will be on site evaluation and survey, which will be offered in three ten-week terms.

2. Every candidate will be required to satisfy the examiners in the following:

(*a*) attendance at the classroom-based courses;

(*b*) submission of the following portfolio of written work:

  (i) three essays or projects linked to unit one each of which shall not exceed 1,500 words in length;

  (ii) two essays linked to unit two, each of which shall not exceed 2,000 words in length;

  (iii) a workbook linked to unit three;

  (iv) a dissertation which shall not exceed 8,000 words in length on a topic agreed by the Board of Studies.

The assignments under (i)-(iii) and the dissertation under (iv) will be forwarded to the examiners c/o the Registry, Department for Continuing Education, Wellington Square, Oxford OX1 2JA by such dates as the examiners shall determine and shall notify to candidates.

3. Candidates may be required to attend a *viva voce* examination at the end of the course of studies at the discretion of the examiners.

4. The examiners may award a distinction to candidates for the certificate.

5. Candidates who fail to satisfy the examiners in the assignments under 2(i)-(iii), or the dissertation under 2(iv), or both, may be permitted to resubmit work in respect of part or parts of the examination which they have failed for examination on not more than one occasion which shall normally be within one year of the initial failure.

Cognitive Behavioural Therapy for Psychological Trauma

1. The course will consist of lectures, tutorials, seminars, and classes on the principle and practice of cognitive behavioural therapy for psychological trauma, together with clinical practice in cognitive behavioural therapy for psychological trauma. The course will be taken on a part-time basis over a period of not less than three terms and not more than nine terms.

2. Every candidate will be required to satisfy the examiners in the following:

(*a*) attendance at the appropriate classroom-based courses including small group case supervisions;

(*b*) one essay of no more than 4,000 words, to assess critical appreciation of theory, research and practice on topics provided by course tutors and approved by the examiners;

(*c*) one written case report of 4,000 to 6,000 words;

(*d*) one video or audio (-tape or digital equivalent) recording of a therapy session;

(*e*) close clinical supervision of two 'training clients' as evidenced by a log book of supervised clinical practice.

The essay under (*b*), the case report under (*c*) and the audio/video recording under (*d*) shall be forwarded to the examiners for consideration by such date as the examiners shall determine and shall notify the candidates and tutors.

The audio/video- recording will be accompanied by a written reflective analysis on topics provided by course tutors, and students will also be required to keep a log book to provide evidence of their supervised CBT practice with two 'training' clients by the end of block 4.

3. The examiners may award a distinction to candidates for the Postgraduate Certificate.

4. Candidates who fail to satisfy the examiners in the essay under 2(*b*), the case report under 2(*c*) and the audio/video- recording under 2(*d*) may be permitted to resubmit work in respect of the part or parts of the examination that they have failed for examination on not more than one occasion, which shall normally be within three months of the original failure.

Cognitive Behavioural Therapy (Introductory Level)

1. The course will consist of lectures, tutorials, seminars, and classes on the principle and practice of cognitive behavioural therapy, together with clinical practice in cognitive behavioural therapy. The course will be taken on a part-time basis over a period of not less than three terms and not more than nine terms.

2. Every candidate will be required to satisfy the examiners in the following:

(*a*) attendance at the appropriate classroom-based courses including small group case supervisions;

(*b*) two essays, each of no more than 4,000 words, to assess critical appreciation of theory, research and practice on topics provided by course tutors and approved by the examiners;

(*c*) one written case report of 2,000 to 4,000 words;

(*d*) one audio/visual tape (or digital equivalent) recording of a therapy session;

(*e*) close clinical supervision of three 'training clients' as evidenced by a log book of supervised clinical practice.

The essays under (*b*), the case report under (*c*) and the one audio/videotape (or digital equivalent) recording under (*d*) shall be forwarded to the examiners for consideration by such date as the examiners shall determine and shall notify the candidates and tutors.

The audio/videotape (or equivalent recording) will be accompanied by a written reflective analysis on topics provided by course tutors, and students will also be expected to keep a log book to provide evidence of their supervised CBT practice with three 'training' clients in module 3.

3. The examiners may award a distinction to candidates for the Postgraduate Certificate.

4. Candidates who fail to satisfy the examiners in meeting their attendance requirements under 2(*a*), the essays under 2(*b*), the case report under 2(*c*) and the audio/videotape (or digital equivalent) recording under 2(*d*) may be permitted to resubmit work in respect of the part or parts of the examination that they have failed for examination on not more than one occasion, which shall normally be within three months of the original failure.

Contemporary European Institutions and Policy

1. *Course*

(*a*) The course shall consist of lectures, seminars, and tutorials on the subjects shown in 1(*b*) below. The course, which is available on a part-time basis, will normally be of one year's duration and shall not exceed two years.

(*b*) The course will consist of four taught units, as set out below:

  (i) Post-war European History and Politics

  (ii) European Economic Integration

  (iii) Strategic Foreign Direct Investment

  (iv) What is Europe? Conflicts and Controversies in the twentieth and twenty-first Centuries

2. Every candidate will be required to satisfy the examiners in the following:

(*a*) attendance at the classroom-based courses;

(*b*) four written essays, based on the taught courses, each of no more than 2,500 words in length;

(*c*) a dissertation of 9,000–10,000 words in length (excluding footnotes and appendices) on a topic agreed by the Board of Studies;

(*d*) written progress reports on each module from the module tutors.

The assignments under (*b*) and the dissertation under (*c*) will be forwarded to the examiners c/o the Registry, Department for Continuing Education, Wellington Square, Oxford OX1 2JA by such dates as the examiners shall determine and shall notify to candidates except that the dissertation shall be submitted by the end of the last week of September of the Long Vacation.

3. Candidates may be required to attend a viva voce examination at the end of the course of studies.

4. The examiners may award a distinction to candidates for the Certificate.

5. Candidates who fail to satisfy the examiners in the assignments under 2(*b*), the dissertation under 2(*c*), or both, may be permitted to resubmit work in respect of part or parts of the examination which they have failed for examination on not more than one occasion which shall normally be within one year of the initial failure.

Diplomatic Studies

1. Students for the Certificate may hold that status for no more than six terms.

2. Each student will follow a course of study comprising four core courses. The four core courses are:

International Politics;

Economics;

International Law;

Diplomatic Practice.

3. *Examinations.* All candidates will be required to satisfy the examiners in four separate three-hour written examinations covering each of the core areas listed in the preceding paragraph demonstrating that they have mastered the substance of the subjects listed and (where appropriate), that they are able to apply them in their continuing professional careers in the international field.

4. The examiners may award a distinction to candidates for the Certificate.

5. A candidate whose overall average mark falls below 50 shall be eligible to resit the failed elements during the following academic year.

6. Candidates who fail to satisfy the examiners in the written examinations in all four of the core elements of the Certificate course, will not be eligible to qualify for the Certificate.

Ecological Survey Techniques

1. Every candidate must follow for at least one year a part-time course of instruction in the theory and practice of Ecological Survey Techniques, normally over a period of no more than three years.

2. Every candidate will be required to satisfy the examiners in the following:

(*a*) attendance at the one-week module in Schedule A;

(*b*) engagement with and contribution to both online modules in Schedule B;

(*c*) engagement with and contribution to two online modules chosen from those listed in Schedule C;

(*d*) participation in and completion of a Field Project module;

(*e*) participation to the satisfaction of the Programme Director in all other parts of the course;

(*f*) one written assignment of not more than 2,500 words based on the module in Schedule A. This is formative only and the marks do not contribute to the final award;

(*g*) four written assignments of not more than 2,000 words, one from each of the modules from 2(*b*) and one from each of the modules chosen from 2(*c*) above. Depending on the modules chosen, up to two of the written assignments on the modules from 2(*c*) may be replaced by presentations in a media specified by the examiners;

(*h*) One field project of not more than 5,000 words and an associated on-line learning journal of not more than 1,000 words.

The assessed work under Clauses 2 (*f*), (*g*) and (*h*) will be submitted to examiners, in normal circumstances through an electronic submission system, for consideration by such date as the examiners shall determine and of which they shall notify candidates.

3. Candidates may be required to attend a viva voce examination at the end of the course at the discretion of the examiners.

4. The examiners may award a Distinction to candidates for the Certificate.

5. The Course Committee shall have the discretion to deem satisfactory completion of up to two modules listed in Schedule B and C below prior to registration for the award as having met the attendance and examination requirements for that module or modules under 2 above. Such discretion will normally only be exercised if the time elapsed between commencement of the module concerned and registration for the award is not more than two years.

6. Candidates who fail to satisfy the examiners in any part of the assessment listed under 2(*g*) or 2(*h*) may be permitted to resubmit work in respect of the part or parts of the examination which they have failed on not more than one occasion which shall normally be within one year of the original failure.

Core Module Schedule A

Introduction to ecological survey techniques

Core Modules Schedule B

Data analysis
Field techniques for surveying vegetation

Optional Modules Schedule C

Field techniques for surveying mammals and reptiles
Field techniques for surveying birds
Field techniques for surveying invertebrates
Field techniques for surveying fish and amphibians

Evidence-Based Health Care

1. The Divisional Board of Medical Sciences, jointly with the Continuing Education Board, shall elect for the supervision of the course a Standing Committee, which shall have the power to arrange lectures and other instruction.

2. Candidates must follow for at least three and at most nine terms a part-time course of instruction in the theory and practice of Evidence-Based Health Care, which shall normally take place over a period of no more than four years. The postgraduate certificate is only available to students admitted for the degree of M.Sc in Evidence-Based Health Care.

3. Every candidate will be required to satisfy the examiners in the following:

(*a*) attendance at both of the modules listed in Schedule A (below);

(*b*) attendance at one of the modules listed in Schedule B (below);

(*c*) three written assignments, usually of no more than 5,000 words, one on each of the modules from 3(*a*) and 3(*b*) above.

The assessed work set out in clause 3(*c*) shall be forwarded to the examiners c/o Registry, Department for Continuing Education, 1 Wellington Square, Oxford OX1 2JA, for consideration by such date as the examiners shall determine and of which they shall notify candidates.

4. Candidates may be required to attend a viva voce examination at the end of the course of studies at the discretion of the examiners.

5. The examiners may award a distinction to candidates for the Postgraduate Certificate.

6. Candidates who fail to satisfy the examiners in any of the three assignments under 3(*c*) may be permitted, normally within one year of the original failure, to resubmit work in respect of the part or parts they have failed on not more than one occasion for each assignment without being required to repeat attendance at the relevant module or modules under 3(*a*) and/or 3(*b*).

7. The Standing Committee shall have the discretion to permit any candidate to be exempted, in exceptional circumstances, from attendance at one module under 3(*a*) or 3(*b*) and from submitting the associated assignment required under 3(*c*) above, provided that the Standing Committee is satisfied that such a candidate has undertaken equivalent study, or has appropriate work experience to an equivalent standard.

Schedule A

M1: Practice of EBHC

M2: Introduction to Study Design and Research Methods

Schedule B

M3: Knowledge into Action

M4: Clinical Epidemiology

M5: Evidence-Based Diagnosis and Screening

M6: Systematic Reviews

M7: Randomised Control Trials

M8: Essential Medical Statistics

M9: Patient-Based Evidence

M10: Ethics in Health Care

M11: Qualitative Research Methods

M12: Evidence-Based Dentistry

M13: Introduction to Statistics in Health Care Research

Any other module as defined by the Programme Director and approved by the Standing Committee.

Health Research

1. The Medical Sciences Board, jointly with the Continuing Education Board, shall elect for the supervision of the course a Standing Committee, which shall have the power to arrange lectures and other instruction.

2. Candidates must follow for at least three and at most nine terms, a part-time course of instruction in the theory and practice of Health Research, which shall normally take place over a period of no more than three years.

3. Every candidate will be required to satisfy the examiners in the following:

(*a*) attendance at three of the modules listed in the Schedule (below);

(*b*) three written assignments, usually of no more than 5000 words, one on each of the modules from 3(*a*) above.

The assignments set out in clause 3(*b*) shall be forwarded, usually electronically via a specified online submission system, to the examiners c/o Registry, Department for Continuing Education, 1 Wellington Square, Oxford OX1 2JA, for consideration by such date as the examiners shall determine and of which they shall notify candidates.

4. Candidates may be required to attend a viva voce examination at the end of the course of studies at the discretion of the examiners.

5. The examiners may award a distinction to candidates for the Postgraduate Certificate.

6. Candidates who fail to satisfy the examiners in any of the three assignments under 3(*b*) may be permitted, normally within one year of the original failure, to resubmit work in respect of the part or parts they have failed on not more than one occasion for each assignment without being required to repeat attendance at the relevant module or modules under 3(*a*).

7. The standing committee shall have the discretion to permit any candidate to be exempted, in exceptional circumstances, from attendance at any module under 3(*a*) and from submitting the associated assignment required under 3(*b*) above, provided that the standing committee is satisfied that such a candidate has undertaken equivalent study, or has appropriate work experience to an equivalent standard.

Schedule

M1: Practice of EBHC
M2: Introduction to Study Design and Research Methods
M3: Bioethics and Good Clinical Practice

Any other module as defined by the Programme Director and approved by the   5
Standing Committee replacing one of the three above.

Historical Studies

1. Each candidate shall follow for at least three terms and a maximum of six terms
a part- time course of instruction in historical studies.

2. The course will consist of seminars, classes, tutorials, and on-line distance   10
learning.

3. The course will consist of five units listed in the schedule below.

4. Every candidate will be required to satisfy the examiners in the following:

   (*a*) a minimum of 75 per cent attendance at the classroom-based sessions and
   active participation in all parts of the course to the satisfaction of the course   15
   director;

   (*b*) four assignments that shall not exceed 2,500 words based on units one to four
   in the schedule below;

   (*c*) two primary source evaluations of not more than 1,500 words each;

   (*d*) a dissertation of not less than 8,000 words and not exceeding 10,000 words.   20

The assignments under 4(*b*)-(*c*) shall be submitted electronically and the dissertation under 4(*d*) shall be submitted in hard copy and on disc (or equivalent) to the
examiners c/o Registry, Department for Continuing Education, Wellington Square,
Oxford OX1 2JA for consideration by such date as the examiners shall determine and
shall notify candidates.   25

5. Candidates may be required to attend a viva voce examination at the end of the
course of studies at the discretion of the examiners.

6. The examiners may award a distinction to candidates for the Certificate.

7. A candidate who fails to satisfy the examiners in the assignments under 4(*b*)-(*c*)
or in the dissertation under 4(*d*) above may normally be permitted to resubmit work   30
in respect of the part or parts of the examination which they have failed on not more
than one occasion which shall normally be within one year of the original failure.

Schedule

Unit One: Princes, States and Revolutions
Unit Two: European Court Patronage   35
Unit Three: Religious Reformations and Movements
Unit Four: Memory and Conflict
Unit Five: Special Subjects

Nanotechnology

1. The Continuing Education Board shall elect for the supervision of the course   40
a Steering Committee that shall have the power to arrange lectures and other
instruction.

2. Every candidate must follow for at least three terms a part-time course of
instruction in the theory and practice of Nanotechnology normally over a period of
one year and no more than three years.   45

3. Every candidate will be required to satisfy the examiners in the following:

(*a*) participation, to the satisfaction of the Course Director, in all parts of the three modules in the Schedule;

(*b*) a portfolio of assignments (written reports, problem sheets and presentations) for each of the modules in the Schedule, totalling not more than 2500 words in length for Module 1, and not more than 6000 words for each of Modules 2 and 3.

The assessed work set out in clause 3(*b*) shall be forwarded to the examiners c/o Registry, Department of Continuing Education, 1 Wellington Square, Oxford OX1 2JA, for consideration by such date as the examiners shall determine and of which they shall notify candidates.

4. Candidates may be required to attend a *viva voce* examination at the end of the course of studies at the discretion of the examiners.

5. The examiners may award a distinction to candidates for the certificate.

6. Candidates who fail to satisfy the examiners in any part of the examination may be permitted to resubmit work in respect of the part or parts of the examination which they have failed for examination on not more than one occasion which shall normally be within one year of the original failure.

7. The Steering Committee shall have the discretion to permit any candidate to be exempted from one of the three modules in the Schedule, provided that the steering committee is satisfied that such a candidate has undertaken equivalent study, or has appropriate work experience to an equivalent standard.

Schedule

1. The Wider Context of Nanotechnology

2. The Fundamental Science of Nanotechnology

3. Fundamental Characterisation for Nanotechnology.

Psychodynamic Counselling

1. *Course*

(*a*) The course will consist of lectures, tutorials, seminars, classes, and workshops on psychodynamic theory, philosophy, and techniques. Self exploration will be undertaken in small experiential groups. The course will be taken on a part-time basis over a period which shall be of one year's duration.

(*b*) The course will consist of three study terms, each of ten weeks, covering respectively: (i) The Psychodynamic Approach-Definition: (ii) Process and Skills in Early Sessions: (iii) Practicalities, Technique, and Ethical Implications.

2. Every candidate will be required to satisfy the examiners in the following:

(*a*) attendance at weekly classes, a weekend school, individual tutorials, and review and revision days;

(*b*) two written assignments, each of no more than 3,000 words and each on one key psychodynamic concept;

(*c*) one written assignment, of no more than 4,000 words, to provide a critique of interpersonal processes and techniques in action;

(*d*) an extract from the student's Reflective Journal, of no more than 5,000 words;

(*e*) annual reports from a candidate's course tutor.

The assignments under (*b*)-(*d*) will be forwarded to the examiners c/o Registry, Department for Continuing Education, Wellington Square, Oxford OX1 2JA, for consideration by the examiners by such date as the examiners shall determine and shall notify candidates before the start of the academic year in which the assignment is due.

3. Candidates may be required to attend a viva voce examination at the end of the course of studies.

4. Candidates who fail to satisfy the examiners in 2(*b*)-(*d*) above may be permitted to resubmit work in the part or parts of the examination which they have failed for examination on not more than one occasion which shall normally be within one year of the original failure. Approval for deferral must be obtained from the relevant board of studies.

5. The examiners may award a distinction to candidates for the certificate.

Surgical Science and Practice (*old regulations for students registered on the MSc Surgical Science and Practice before 1 October 2012*)

1. The Divisional Board of Medical Sciences, jointly with the Continuing Education Board, shall elect for the supervision of the course a Standing Committee, which shall have the power to arrange lectures and other instruction.

2. Candidates must follow for at least three terms, a part-time course of instruction in the theory and practice of Surgical Science and Practice, which shall normally take place over a period of no more than four years. The Postgraduate Certificate is only available to students admitted for the degree of MSc in Surgical Science and Practice.

3. Every candidate will be required to satisfy the examiners in the following:

(*a*) Active participation, to the satisfaction of the Course Director, in any three of the modules selected from either Schedule A or Schedule B below.

(*b*) Written assignments related to each of the modules selected from Schedule A, each of not more than 4,000 words in length.

(*c*) Assignments consisting of multiple choice questions or structured short questions, online project working and practical tests related to each of the modules selected from Schedule B.

The assignments set out in clause 3(*c*) and 3(*c*) shall be forwarded, usually through a specified electronic submission system, to the examiners c/o Registry, Department for Continuing Education, 1 Wellington Square, Oxford OX1 2JA, for consideration by such date as the examiners shall determine and of which they shall notify candidates.

4. Candidates may be required to attend a viva voce examination at the end of the course of studies at the discretion of the examiners.

5. The examiners may award a distinction to candidates for the Postgraduate Certificate.

6. Candidates who fail to satisfy the examiners in any of the assignments under 3(*b*) and 3(*c*) may be permitted, normally within one year of the original failure, to resubmit work in respect of the part or parts they have failed on not more than one occasion for each assignment without being required to repeat attendance at the relevant module or modules under 3(*a*).

7. The Standing Committee shall have the discretion to permit any candidate to be exempted, in exceptional circumstances, from attendance at any module under 3(*a*) and from submitting the associated assignment required under 3(*b*) and 3(*c*) above, provided that the Standing Committee is satisfied that such a candidate has undertaken equivalent study, or has appropriate work experience to an equivalent standard.

Schedule A

The practice of evidence-based health care
Quality improvement science and systems analysis
Introduction to surgical management and leadership
Becoming a medical educator 5
Any other module as defined by the Course Director and approved by the Standing
Committee

Schedule B

Human factors, teamwork and communication
Surgical technology and robotics. 10

Surgical Science and Practice (exit award only) (*new regulations for students
registering on the award from 1 October 2012 and available to existing students*)

1. The Medical Sciences Board, jointly with the Continuing Education Board,
shall elect for the supervision of the course a Standing Committee, which shall have
the power to arrange lectures and other instruction. 15

2. The Postgraduate Certificate is only available to students admitted for the
degree of M.Sc. in Surgical Science and Practice. The course is available on a part
time basis only and shall consist of instruction in the theory and practice of Surgical
Science and Practice.

3. The policy of the Continuing Education Board on variable intensity part time 20
study shall apply to this award.

4. The minimum period of registration on the Postgraduate Certificate shall be
three terms and the maximum period of registration shall be twelve terms.

5. Every candidate will be required to satisfy the examiners in the following:

(*a*) Participation, to the satisfaction of the Course Director, in any three of the 25
modules selected from either Schedule A or Schedule B below.

(*b*) Written assignments related to each of the modules selected from Schedule A,
each of not more than 4,000 words in length.

(*c*) Assignments consisting of multiple choice questions or structured short questions, online project working and practical tests related to each of the modules 30
selected from Schedule B.

The assignments set out in clause 5(*b*) and (*c*) shall be forwarded, usually through a
specified electronic submission system, to the examiners c/o Registry, Department for
Continuing Education, 1 Wellington Square, Oxford OX1 2JA, for consideration by
such date as the examiners shall determine shall notify candidates. 35

6. Candidates may be required to attend a viva voce examination at the end of the
course of studies at the discretion of the examiners.

7. The examiners may award a distinction to candidates for the Postgraduate
Certificate.

8. Candidates who fail to satisfy the examiners in any of the assignments under 40
5(*b*) or (*c*) above may be permitted to resubmit work in respect of the part or parts
they have failed on not more than one occasion for each assignment without being
required to repeat attendance at the relevant module or modules. The resubmission
shall normally be within one year of the original failure.

9. Provided the Standing Committee is satisfied that a student on the award has 45
undertaken equivalent study, of an appropriate standard, normally at another institution of higher education, or has appropriate work experience to an equivalent
standard, the committee may permit the candidate to be exempted from attendance

and the submission of a written assignment in respect of up to three modules. In exercising this discretion the Standing Committee shall take into consideration the length of time that has elapsed since the study or work experience was undertaken.

10. The Standing Committee may deem satisfactory completion of a module (including the associated assessment) prior to registration for the award as having met the attendance and examination requirements in respect of that module. Such discretion will normally only be exercised if the time elapsed between commencement of the accredited module concerned and registration for the award is not more than two years. The maximum number of modules taken prior to registration for the award that may count in this way shall be three.

Schedule A

The practice of evidence-based health care
Quality improvement science and systems analysis
Introduction to surgical management and leadership
Becoming a medical educator
Any other module as defined by the Course Director and approved by the Standing Committee.

Schedule B

Human factors, teamwork and communication
Surgical technology and robotics.

POSTGRADUATE DIPLOMAS IN THE SOFTWARE ENGINEERING PROGRAMME (OLD REGULATIONS)

GENERAL REGULATIONS

For students registered on the M.Sc., PG Dip, and PG Cert in Software Engineering; the M.Sc., PG Dip, and PG Cert in Software and Systems Security; or the PG Cert in Object Technology before 1 April 2010.

1. The Mathematical, Physical, and Life Sciences Board shall have power to grant Postgraduate Diplomas to candidates who have satisfied the conditions prescribed in this section and any further conditions which the board may prescribe by regulation.

2. The examination for each Postgraduate Diploma shall be under the supervision of the Mathematical, Physical and Life Sciences Board which shall have power, subject to the approval of the Education Committee, to make regulations governing the examination.

3. Candidates, whether members of the University or not, may be admitted as students for a Postgraduate Diploma under such conditions as the board shall prescribe, provided that before admission to a course of study approved by the board, candidates shall have satisfied the board that they have had appropriate educational experience acceptable to the board, and are well-equipped to enter the proposed course of study.

4. Any person who has been accepted as a candidate for a Postgraduate Diploma, and who has satisfactorily pursued a course, the character and length of which have been approved by the board, may be admitted to the examination.

SPECIAL REGULATIONS

Software and Systems Security (old regulations)

For students registered on the M.Sc., PG Dip, and PG Cert in Software Engineering; the M.Sc., PG Dip, and PG Cert in Software and Systems Security; or the PG Cert in Object Technology from October 2008 to March 2010, and available to those who enrolled on the M.Sc., PG Dip, and PG Cert in Software Engineering; the M.Sc., PG Dip, and PG Cert in Software and Systems Security; or the PG Cert in Object

Technology prior to October 2008 and who have not already been awarded the relevant qualification.

1. The Mathematical, Physical and Life Sciences Board, in consultation with the Faculty of Computer Science, shall elect for the supervision of the course a Standing Committee which shall have the power to arrange lectures and other instruction.

2. The course will consist of lectures, tutorials, seminars, and classes in the theory and practice of Software and Systems Security. The course may be taken over a period of not less than one year, and not more than three years.

3. Every candidate will be required to satisfy the examiners in the following:

(a) attendance at eight modules chosen from those in Schedules A and B for the M.Sc. in Software and Systems Security (old regulations), of which at least six should come from Schedule A for that M.Sc., comprising a programme of study approved by the Standing Committee;

(b) submission of eight written assignments based on the modules chosen in 3(a) above. These shall be forwarded to the examiners for consideration by such dates as the examiners shall determine and shall notify to candidates and tutors;

(c) a viva voce examination, unless individually dispensed by the examiners.

4. The examiners may award a distinction for excellence in the whole examination.

5. The Standing Committee for the M.Sc. in Software and Systems Security shall have the discretion to permit any candidate for the postgraduate diploma to be exempted from submitting up to two of the total of eight assignments required under 3(b) above, provided that the Standing Committee is satisfied that such a candidate has undertaken equivalent study, of an appropriate standard, normally at another institution of higher education.

6. The Standing Committee shall have the discretion to permit any assignments submitted as part of the course for the Postgraduate Certificate in Software Engineering, or the Postgraduate Certificate in Software and Systems Security, or the Postgraduate Certificate in Object Technology, to be submitted for the examination for the Diploma, so long as the choice of assignments complies with the requirements of cll. 3(a) and (b) above. The corresponding period of study undertaken for the Postgraduate Certificate shall be counted towards the maximum period of study for the Diploma.

7. If any candidate who is successful in the examination for the Postgraduate Diploma in Software and Systems Security has previously successfully completed the Postgraduate Certificate in Software Engineering, or the Postgraduate Certificate in Sofware and Systems Security, or the Postgraduate Certificate in Object Technology, and for that examination has incorporated the assignments submitted for the Postgraduate Certificate into the Postgraduate Diploma, then the Postgraduate Diploma will subsume his or her Certificate.

8. Candidates who fail to satisfy the examiners may re-enter the examination on not more than one occasion which shall normally be within one year of the initial failure. No written assignment shall be submitted to the examiners on more than one occasion.

Software Engineering (old regulations)

For students registered on the M.Sc., PG Dip, and PG Cert in Software Engineering; the M.Sc., PG Dip, and PG Cert in Software and Systems Security; or the PG Cert in Object Technology from October 2008 to March 2010, and available to those who enrolled on the M.Sc., PG Dip, and PG Cert in Software Engineering; the M.Sc., PG Dip, and PG Cert in Software and Systems Security; or the PG Cert in Object

Technology prior to October 2008 and who have not already been awarded the relevant qualification.

1. The Mathematical, Physical and Life Sciences Board, in consultation with the Faculty of Computer Science, shall elect for the supervision of the course a Standing Committee which shall have the power to arrange lectures and other instruction.　　　5

2. The course will consist of lectures, tutorials, seminars, and classes in the theory and practice of Software Engineering. The course may be taken over a period of not less than one year, and not more than three years.

3. Every candidate will be required to satisfy the examiners in the following:

(*a*) attendance at eight modules chosen from those in Schedules A and B for the　　10 M.Sc. in Software Engineering (old regulations), comprising a programme of study approved by the Standing Committee;

(*b*) submission of eight written assignments based on the modules chosen in 3(*a*) above. These shall be forwarded to the examiners for consideration by such dates as the examiners shall determine and shall notify to candidates and　　15 tutors;

(*c*) viva voce examination, unless individually dispensed by the examiners.

4. The examiners may award a distinction for excellence in the whole examination.

5. The Standing Committee for the M.Sc. in Software Engineering shall have the discretion to permit any candidate for the postgraduate diploma to be exempted from　　20 submitting up to two of the total of eight assignments required under 3(*b*) above, provided that the Standing Committee is satisfied that such a candidate has undertaken equivalent study, of an appropriate standard, normally at another institution of higher education.

6. The Standing Committee shall have the discretion to permit any assignments　　25 submitted as part of the course for the Postgraduate Certificate in Software Engineering, or the Postgraduate Certificate in Software and Systems Security, or the Postgraduate Certificate in Object Technology, to be submitted for the examination for the Diploma. The corresponding period of study undertaken for the Postgraduate Certificate shall be counted towards the maximum period of study for　　30 the Diploma.

7. If any candidate who is successful in the examination for the Postgraduate Diploma in Software Engineering has previously successfully completed the Postgraduate Certificate in Software Engineering, or the Postgraduate Certificate in Software and Systems Security or the Postgraduate Certificate in Object Technology,　　35 and for that examination has incorporated the assignments submitted for the Postgraduate Certificate into the Postgraduate Diploma, then the Postgraduate Diploma will subsume his or her Certificate.

8. Candidates who fail to satisfy the examiners may re-enter the examination on not more than one occasion which shall normally be within one year of the initial　　40 failure. No written assignment shall be submitted to the examiners on more than one occasion.

POSTGRADUATE DIPLOMAS
(CONTINUING EDUCATION)

General Regulations

1. The Continuing Education Board shall have power to grant Postgraduate Diplomas to candidates who have satisfied the conditions prescribed in this section and any further conditions which the board may prescribe by regulation.

2. The examination for each Postgraduate Diploma shall be under the supervision of the Continuing Education Board which shall have power, subject to the approval of the Education Committee, to make regulations governing the examination.

3. Candidates, whether members of the University or not, may be admitted as students for a Postgraduate Diploma under such conditions as the board shall prescribe, provided that before admission to a course of study approved by the board, candidates shall have satisfied the board that they have had appropriate educational experience acceptable to the board, and are well-equipped to enter the proposed course of study.

4. Any person who has been accepted as a candidate for a Postgraduate Diploma, and who has satisfactorily pursued a course, the character and length of which have been approved by the board, may be admitted to the examination.

Special Regulations

Advanced Cognitive Therapy Studies (*old regulations for students registered on the PG Diploma ACTS before 1 October 2012*)

1. The course will consist of lectures, tutorials, seminars, and classes on the principle and practice of advanced cognitive therapy studies, together with clinical practice and practice in supervision of cognitive therapy trainees. The course will be taken on a part-time basis over a period of not fewer than three terms.

2. Every candidate will be required to satisfy the examiners in the following:

(*a*) attendance at the appropriate classroom-based courses including small group supervision of supervision practice;

(*b*) attendance at two independent advanced level clinical therapy training workshops;

(*c*) skill in treating simple and complex cases with cognitive therapy;

(*d*) skill in supervising cognitive therapy trainees, as demonstrated in a video-recording of a supervision session delivered by the candidate, together with written reflection and critical review, and supervisee feedback;

(*e*) one written research proposal (1,500 words);

(*f*) one extended written case study of a complex case (no more than 6,000 words);

(*g*) two written assignments, each of no more than 4,000 words, one covering the design, delivery and evaluation of a training event, and one describing and evaluating the development of a service initiative;

(*h*) a presentation of a brief interactive cognitive therapy training event.

The presentations under (*d*) and (*h*), the assessed work under (*e*), (*f*) and (*g*), shall be forwarded to the examiners for consideration by such dates as the examiners shall determine and shall notify the candidates and tutors.

3. Candidates may be expected to attend a viva voce examination at the end of the course of studies at the discretion of the examiners.

4. The examiners may award a distinction to candidates for the Postgraduate Diploma.

5. Candidates who fail to satisfy the examiners in the presentations under 2(*d*) and (*h*), or the assessed work under (*e*), (*f*) and (*g*), may be permitted to resubmit work in respect of the part or parts of the examination which they have failed for examination on not more than one occasion which shall normally be within one year of the original failure.

Advanced Cognitive Therapy Studies (*new regulations for students registering on the award from 1 October 2012 and available to existing students*)

1. The course will consist of lectures, tutorials, seminars, and classes on the principles and practice of advanced cognitive therapy studies, together with clinical supervision and practice in the supervision and training of cognitive therapists. The course will be taken on a part-time basis.

2. The policy of the Continuing Education Board on variable intensity part-time postgraduate study applies to this award.

3. The minimum period of registration for the award of the Postgraduate Diploma shall be three terms and the maximum period shall be nine terms.

4. Candidates may be permitted by the Continuing Education Board in certain circumstances to intermit for a maximum of six terms. Any such period shall not count to the maximum or minimum permitted period of registration and no fee liability will be incurred during such periods.

5. Where a candidate undertakes a module for credit under Cl. 10 below the date of registration for the award shall retrospectively be deemed to be first day of the term in which the module was taken.

6. Every candidate will be required to satisfy the examiners in the following:

(*a*) attendance at the modules listed below;

(*b*) attendance at two independent advanced level clinical therapy training workshops;

(*c*) one video of a supervision session together with a reflective commentary and a written critique of no more than 2,000 words in respect of Module 1;

(*d*) one written report of no more than 4,000 words covering the design, delivery and evaluation of a CBT training event in respect of Module 2;

(*e*) one recorded clinical session of a 'complex case' together with a written case study of no more than 4,000 words of that patient in respect of Module 3;

(*f*) one written research proposal of no more than 1,500 words in respect of Module 4;

(*g*) one written assignment of no more than 4,000 words describing and evaluating the development of a service initiative in respect of Module 5.

The assessed work under (*c*), (*d*), (*e*), (*f*) and (*g*), shall be forwarded to the examiners for consideration by such dates as the examiners shall determine and shall notify the candidates and tutors.

7. Candidates may be required to attend a viva voce examination at the end of the course of studies at the discretion of the examiners.

8. The examiners may award a distinction to candidates for the Postgraduate Diploma.

9. Candidates who fail to satisfy the examiners in any of the assignments under 6 (*c*) to (*g*) above may be permitted to resubmit work in respect of the part or parts they have failed on not more than one occasion for each assignment without being required to repeat attendance at the relevant module or modules. The resubmission shall normally be within one year of the original failure.

10. Provided the Programme Committee is satisfied that a student on the award has undertaken equivalent study, of an appropriate standard, normally at another institution of higher education, or has appropriate work experience to an equivalent standard, the Committee shall have the discretion to permit the candidate to be exempted from attendance and the submission of a written assignment in respect of up to two modules. In exercising this discretion the Programme Committee shall have consideration to the length of time that has elapsed since the study or work experience was undertaken.

11. The Programme Committee shall have the discretion to deem satisfactory completion of a module including the associated assessment prior to registration for the award as having met the attendance and examination requirements in respect of that module. Such discretion will normally only be exercised if the time elapsed between commencement of the accredited module concerned and registration for the award is not more than two years. The maximum number of modules taken prior to registration for the award that can contribute to the achievement of the award of the Postgraduate Diploma shall be two.

Modules

Module 1. Supervision theory, principles and practice
Module 2. Training skills, in the context of adult learning theory
Module 3. Updates in clinical theory, research and practice in Anxiety Disorders and Depressive Disorders
Module 4. Research methodology and skills for the practicing clinician
Module 5. Organisational development, particularly as it relates to establishing, maintaining and developing cognitive therapy service

Cognitive Behavioural Therapy

1. The course will consist of lectures, tutorials, seminars, and classes on the principle and practice of cognitive behavioural therapy, together with clinical practice in cognitive behavioural therapy. The course will be taken on a part-time basis over a period of not less than three terms and no more than nine terms.

2. Every candidate will be required to satisfy the examiners in the following:

(*a*) attendance at the appropriate classroom-based courses including small group case supervisions;

(*b*) supervised treatment of at least five patients by cognitive behavioural therapy;

(*c*) six audio- or videotape presentations of behavioural therapy sessions;

(*d*) three written case presentations, each of no more than 4,000 words;

(*e*) a dissertation of no more than 10,000 words on a topic approved by the examiners.

The six audio- or videotape presentations under (*c*), the three case presentations under (*d*), and the dissertation under (*e*) shall be forwarded to the examiners for consideration by such date as the examiners shall determine and shall notify candidates and tutors.

3. Candidates may be required to attend a viva voce examination at the end of the course of study at the discretion of the examiners.

4. The examiners may award a distinction to candidates for the Diploma.

5. Candidates who fail to satisfy the examiners in the audio- or videotape presentations under 2(*c*), the three case presentations under 2(*d*), or the dissertation under 2(*e*) may be permitted to resubmit work in respect of the part or parts of the examination which they have failed for examination on not more than one occasion which shall normally be within one year of the original failure.

5

Diplomatic Studies

1. Students for the Diploma may hold that status for no more than six terms.

2. Candidates are only eligible to be admitted to the Diploma in Diplomatic Studies if they have achieved a satisfactory standard in the first term of study for the Certificate in Diplomatic Studies. Admission to the Diploma will take place at the end of the first term in the year of study, on the basis of a transfer proposal and the first term's assessed written work, as approved by the Admissions Committee for the programme.

10

3. Each student will follow a course of study comprising four core courses. The four core courses are:

International Politics. Key concepts in international relations leading to central issues in world politics, with particular emphasis on change in the international system and the evolving role of diplomacy in consequence.

15

Economics. Basics of international trade theory and macroeconomics, focusing on such applied and political economy topics as trade liberalisation, globalisation, and international resource transfers.

20

International Law. Principles of international law and the processes of legal reasoning, and their application to current world problems ranging from the nature of international law to the use of force and conflict settlement.

Diplomatic Practice. Overview of different regions of the world, major international organisations, and current world problems as they affect diplomats. Review of practical aspects of diplomacy and their application to discussion of practical action by means of which governments can address these problems.

25

In addition, candidates will be required to submit a dissertation of between 10,000 and 12,000 words.

4. *Examinations.* Candidates will be required to take papers in International Politics, International Law, Economics, and Diplomatic Practice.

30

5. *Syllabus*

 I. Four core modules: International Politics, Economics, International Law, and Diplomatic Practice.

 II. Each candidate will be required to present a dissertation of not more than 12,000 words, on a subject approved by the examiners, to the examiners c/o the Registry, Department for Continuing Education, 1 Wellington Square, Oxford OX1 2JA, by 12 noon on Friday of sixth week of Trinity Term in the year in which he or she completes the course. All material submitted for the dissertation shall be accompanied by a certificate signed by the candidate indicating that it is the candidate's own work.

35

40

6. The examiners may award a distinction to candidates for the Diploma. To be awarded a distinction, a candidate must obtain **either** an average of 70 overall in the five programme elements; **or** a mark of 70 or above in three of the five programme elements, of which one shall normally be the dissertation.

7. A candidate for the Diploma who fails to meet the standard required for award of the Diploma, but who has met the examination standards and requirements stipulated in the regulations governing the Certificate in Diplomatic Studies, may be offered the option of resitting the examination for the Diploma, or (having satisfied the examination standards and requirements of that qualification) of being awarded the Certificate.

45

8. A candidate whose overall average mark falls below 50 shall be eligible to resit the failed elements on one occasion during the following academic year. Compensation in one paper is allowed.

50

9. Candidates who fail to satisfy the examiners in the written examinations in all four of the core elements of the Certificate course, or who fail to submit a dissertation of the necessary standard will be eligible to resit on one occasion.

Evidence-Based Health Care

1. The Divisional Board of Medical Sciences, jointly with the Continuing Education Board, shall elect for the supervision of the course a Standing Committee, which shall have the power to arrange lectures and other instruction.

2. Candidates must follow for at least three and at most nine terms a part-time course of instruction in the theory and practice of Evidence-Based Health Care, which shall normally take place over a period of no more than four years. The postgraduate diploma is only available to students admitted for the degree of M.Sc. in Evidence-Based Health Care.

3. Every candidate will be required to satisfy the examiners in the following:

(*a*) attendance at both of the modules listed in Schedule A (below);

(*b*) attendance at four of the modules listed in Schedule B (below);

(*c*) six written assignments, usually of no more than 5,000 words, one on each of the modules from 3(*a*) and 3(*b*) above.

The assessed work set out in clause 3(*c*) shall be forwarded to the examiners c/o Registry, Department for Continuing Education, 1 Wellington Square, Oxford OX1 2JA, for consideration by such date as the examiners shall determine and of which they shall notify candidates.

4. Candidates may be required to attend a viva voce examination at the end of the course of studies at the discretion of the examiners.

5. The examiners may award a distinction to candidates for the Postgraduate Diploma.

6. Candidates who fail to satisfy the examiners in any of the six assignments under 3(*c*) may be permitted, normally within one year of the original failure, to resubmit work in respect of the part or parts they have failed on not more than one occasion for each assignment without being required to repeat attendance at the relevant module or modules under 3(*a*) and/or 3(*b*).

7. The Standing Committee shall have the discretion to permit any candidate to be exempted, in exceptional circumstances, from attendance at a module under 3(*a*) or 3(*b*) and from submitting an assignment required under 3(*c*) above, provided that the Standing Committee is satisfied that such a candidate has undertaken equivalent study, or has appropriate work experience to an equivalent standard.

Schedule A

M1: Practice of EBHC
M2: Introduction to Study Design and Research Methods

Schedule B

M3: Knowledge into Action
M4: Clinical Epidemiology
M5: Evidence-Based Diagnosis and Screening
M6: Systematic Reviews
M7: Randomised Control Trials
M8: Essential Medical Statistics
M9: Patient-Based Evidence
M10: Ethics in Health Care
M11: Qualitative Research Methods

M12: Evidence-Based Dentistry

M13: Introduction to Statistics in Health Care Research

Any other module as defined by the Programme Director and approved by the Standing Committee.

Experimental Therapeutics (exit award only) (*old regulations for students registered on the MSc Experimental Therapeutics before 1 October 2012*)

1. The Medical Sciences Board, in consultation with the Continuing Education Board, shall elect for the supervision of the course a Standing Committee that shall have the power to arrange lectures and other instruction.

2. Every candidate must follow for at least six terms a part-time course of instruction in the theory and practice of Experimental Therapeutics, which shall normally take place over a period of two years and no more than four years.

3. Every candidate will be required to satisfy the examiners in the following:

(*a*) active participation, to the satisfaction of the Programme Director, in each of the modules listed below.

(*b*) six written assignments of not more than 5,000 words in length, one from each of the six modules specified.

The assessed work set out in cl. 3(*b*) shall be forwarded to the examiners c/o Registry, Department for Continuing Education, 1 Wellington Square, Oxford OX1 2JA, for consideration by such date as the examiners shall determine and of which they shall notify candidates. The assessed work will, in normal circumstances, be submitted through an electronic submission system.

4. The examiners may award a distinction to candidates for the Postgraduate Diploma.

5. Candidates who fail to satisfy the examiners in any part of the examination may be permitted to resubmit work in respect of the part or parts of the examination that they have failed, for examination on not more than one occasion which shall normally be within one year of the original failure.

6. The Standing Committee shall have the discretion to permit any candidate to be exempted from submitting an assignment of the total of six written assignments required under 3(*b*) above, provided that the Standing Committee is satisfied that such a candidate has undertaken equivalent study, or has appropriate work experience to an equivalent standard.

Schedule

(1) Structure of clinical trials and experimental therapeutics

(2) Pharmacokinetics and Drug Therapy

(3) Pharmacodynamics, Biomarkers and Personalised Therapy

(4) Adverse drug reactions, drug interactions, and pharmacovigilance

(5) How to do research on therapeutic interventions: protocol preparation

(6) Biological Therapeutics

(7) Any other module as defined by the Programme Director and approved by the Standing Committee

Experimental Therapeutics (exit award only) (*new regulations for students registering on the award from 1 October 2012 and available to existing students*)

1. The Medical Sciences Board, in consultation with the Continuing Education Board, shall elect for the supervision of the course a Standing Committee that shall have the power to arrange lectures and other instruction.

2. The Postgraduate Diploma is only available to students admitted for the degree of M.Sc. in Experimental Therapeutics. The course is available on a part time basis only and shall consist of instruction in the theory and practice of Experimental Therapeutics.

3. The policy of the Continuing Education Board on variable intensity part-time postgraduate study shall apply to this award.

4. The minimum period of registration on the PG Diploma shall be three terms and the maximum period of registration shall be twelve terms.

5. Candidates may be permitted in certain circumstances to suspend status, for a maximum of six terms. Any such period shall not count to the maximum or minimum permitted period of registration and no fee liability will be incurred during such periods.

6. Every candidate will be required to satisfy the examiners in the following:

(*a*) participation, to the satisfaction of the course director, in each of the modules listed below;

(*b*) six written assignments of not more than 4,000 words in length, one from each of the six modules specified.

The assessed work set out in clause 6(*b*) shall be forwarded to the examiners c/o Registry, Department for Continuing Education, 1 Wellington Square, Oxford OX1 2JA, for consideration by such date as the examiners shall determine and shall notify candidates. The assessed work will, in normal circumstances, be submitted through an electronic submission system.

7. Candidates may be required to attend a viva voce examination at the end of the course of studies at the discretion of the examiners.

8. The examiners may award a distinction to candidates for the PG Diploma.

9. Candidates who fail to satisfy the examiners in any of the assignments under 6b above may be permitted to resubmit work in respect of the part or parts they have failed on not more than one occasion for each assignment without being required to repeat attendance at the relevant module or modules. The resubmission shall normally be within one year of the original failure.

10. Provided the Standing Committee is satisfied that a student on the award has undertaken equivalent study, of an appropriate standard, normally at another institution of higher education, or has appropriate work experience to an equivalent standard, the committee may permit the candidate to be exempted from attendance and the submission of a written assignment in respect of up to three modules. In exercising this discretion the Standing Committee shall take into consideration the length of time that has elapsed since the study or work experience was undertaken.

11. The Standing Committee may deem satisfactory completion of a module (including the associated assessment) undertaken prior to registration for the award as having met the attendance and examination requirements in respect of that module. Such discretion will normally only be exercised if the time elapsed between commencement of the accredited module concerned and registration for the award is not more than two years. The maximum number of modules taken prior to registration for the award that may be counted in this way shall be three.

Module Schedule

(1) Structure of clinical trials and experimental therapeutics*

(2) Drug development, pharmacokinetics and imaging*

(3) Pharmacodynamics, biomarkers and personalised therapy*

(4) Adverse drug reactions, drug interactions, and pharmacovigilance*

(5) How to do research on therapeutic interventions: protocol preparation*

(6) Biological therapeutics*

---

* Also available to students on the PG Certificate and Diploma in Health Research

(7) Any other module as defined by the programme director and approved by the Standing Committee.

Health Research

1. The Medical Sciences Board, jointly with the Continuing Education Board, shall elect for the supervision of the course a Standing Committee, which shall have the power to arrange lectures and other instruction.

2. Candidates will normally be expected to have satisfactorily completed the Postgraduate Certificate in Health Research. Applications for dispensation from this requirement will be considered, in exceptional circumstances only, by the Standing Committee. To be dispensed from this requirement, candidates must demonstrate that they have undertaken equivalent study, or have appropriate work experience to an equivalent standard.

3. Candidates must follow for at least three and at most six terms, a part-time course of instruction in the theory and practice of Health Research. For candidates who have successfully completed the Postgraduate Certificate in Health Research, the number of terms in excess of three taken to complete the study of the Postgraduate Certificate will count towards the maximum number of terms permitted to complete the study of the Postgraduate Diploma. The period of study for the Postgraduate Diploma shall normally be no more than two years, so long as, for candidates who completed the Postgraduate Certificate in Health Research, the total period of study on the Postgraduate Certificate and Diploma in Health Research shall be no longer than three years from the commencement of the Postgraduate Certificate.

4. Every candidate will be required to satisfy the examiners in the following:

(*a*) attendance at three of the modules listed in the Schedule (below);

(*b*) three written assignments, usually of no more than 5000 words, one on each of the modules from 4(*a*) above.

The assignments set out in clause 4(*b*) shall be forwarded, usually electronically via a specified online submission system, to the examiners c/o Registry, Department for Continuing Education, 1 Wellington Square, Oxford OX1 2JA, for consideration by such date as the examiners shall determine and of which they shall notify candidates.

5. Candidates may be required to attend a viva voce examination at the end of the course of studies at the discretion of the examiners.

6. The examiners may award a distinction to candidates for the Postgraduate Diploma.

7. Candidates who fail to satisfy the examiners in any of the three assignments under 4(*b*) may be permitted, normally within one year of the original failure, to resubmit work in respect of the part or parts they have failed on not more than one occasion for each assignment without being required to repeat attendance at the relevant module or modules under 4(*a*).

8. The standing committee shall have the discretion to permit any candidate to be exempted, in exceptional circumstances, from attendance at any module under 4(*a*) and from submitting the associated assignment required under 4(*b*) above, provided that the standing committee is satisfied that such a candidate has undertaken equivalent study, or have appropriate work experience to an equivalent standard.

Schedule

M4: Evidence in Practice (Clinical Epidemiology and Decision Making)
M5: Systematic Reviews
M6: Randomized Control Trials
M7: Qualitative Research Methods
M8: Introduction to Statistics in Health Care Research

M9: The power of bioinformatics in modern research
M10: Evidence-Based Diagnosis
M11: Knowledge into Action

Any other module as defined by the Programme Director and approved by the Standing Committee.

History of Design (exit award only)
  1. Candidates must follow a course of instruction in History of Design. The course will be taken on a part-time basis over a period of not fewer than two years and not more than three years within a maximum period of five years. The postgraduate diploma is only available to students admitted for the degree of MSt in the History of Design.

  2. The examination will consist of the following parts:

A Core Papers

Every candidate must submit a written assignment for each of the three core course papers taught in Year 1:

    I. Techniques and Materials (Object Case Study: 2,500 words)

    II. Historical Methods (Methodology and Critical Sources Review: 3,000 words)

    III. Research Project (Extended Essay: 5,000 words)

B Advanced Papers

Every candidate must follow two Advanced Papers courses form the options listed in the Schedule below, and submit one written assignment of no more than 5,000 words in length for each paper. Candidates will select two Advanced Papers in Year 2 of the MSt from a list of available options.

  3. Each candidate must attend a viva voce examination when required to do so by the examiners.

  4. The examiners may award a distinction for excellence in the Postgraduate Diploma.

  5. A candidate who fails the assessment for a core module or advanced paper, may be permitted to resubmit the written work, on one further occasion only, not later than one year after the initial attempt.

Schedule

Advanced Papers are available in the following areas:
- Decoration in Modern France
- The Arts and Crafts Tradition in Modern Britain
- Design in the Machine Age
- Design, Body, Environment
- Visual Cultures of the World Wars
- Academic Writing and Contemporary Practice*
- Medieval Period or Early Modern Option
- Papers from the existing MSc English Local History:

---

* This Advanced Paper will be assessed by means of two written assignments: a Documentation Project and a Critical Sources Review; each 1,500 words in length.

A.7 The social history of English architecture, 1870–1940

A.8 The English suburb, 1800–1939

A.4 English architecture 1500–1640

Not all advanced papers will be available in any one year and the definitive list of advanced papers available in any one year will be circulated to candidates and their supervisors during the second week of Michaelmas Term. 5

Recanati-Kaplan Centre Postgraduate Diploma in International Wildlife Conservation Practice

1. The Mathematical, Physical and Life Sciences Board, jointly with the Continuing Education Board, shall elect for the supervision of the course a Standing Committee 10 that shall have the power to arrange lectures and other instruction.

2. The diploma shall be entitled the Recanati-Kaplan Centre Postgraduate Diploma in International Wildlife Conservation Practice.

3. Candidates must follow for a period of eight months a course of instruction in International Wildlife Conservation Practice. 15

4. Every candidate will be required to satisfy the examiners in the following:

   (*a*) the submission of five written assignments of not more than 2,000 words each, one on each of the modules listed in the Schedule below; and

   (*b*) the attendance on two projects (at least one of which may take the form of a placement) approved by the Standing Committee, and the submission of two 20 reports of not more than 7,000 words each, one on each of the projects.

The assignments under (*a*) and the reports under (*b*) shall be forwarded to the examiners c/o the Registry, Department for Continuing Education, 1 Wellington Square, Oxford OX1 2JA, for consideration by such date as the examiners shall determine and of which they shall notify candidates. 25

5. Candidates may be required to attend a viva voce examination at the end of the course of studies at the discretion of the examiners.

6. The examiners may award a distinction to candidates for the Postgraduate Diploma.

7. Candidates who fail to satisfy the examiners in any part of the examination may be permitted to resubmit work in respect of the part or parts of the examination 30 which they have failed for examination on not more than one occasion which shall normally be within one year of the original failure.

Schedule of Modules

   (*a*) Wildlife Ecology and Behaviour

   (*b*) Species and Biodiversity Monitoring 35

   (*c*) Population Management

   (*d*) Habitat Assessment

   (*e*) Human Populations/Actions and Conservation

Any other module as defined by the Programme Director and approved by the Standing Committee. 40

Mathematical Finance (*old regulations*)

For students registered on the PG.Dip. in Mathematical Finance in or before January 2011

1. The Mathematical, Physical and Life Sciences Board, jointly with the Continuing Education Board, shall elect for the supervision of the course a Standing Committee 45 which shall have the power to arrange lectures and other instruction.

2. Every candidate must follow for at least five and at most eight terms a part-time course of instruction in the theory and practice of Mathematical Finance.

3. The subjects of the course will consist of all four modules listed in Section A of the Schedule for the M.Sc. in Mathematical Finance and one module chosen from Section B of the Schedule.

4. Every candidate must normally:

(*a*) attend four modules from Section A of the Schedule and one from Section B. Candidates may, in exceptional circumstances, and with the permission of the Standing Committee, be exempt from attendance at part of module 1;

(*b*) submit four assignments, one on each of the modules in Section A of the Schedule. These assignments will be assessed formatively and will not contribute towards the final award;

5. Every candidate will be required to satisfy the examiners in the following:

(*a*) two written examinations, covering material relevant to modules 1 to 4 in Section A of the Schedule;

(*b*) one assignment chosen from the advanced modules in Section B of the Schedule. The assignment should be of no more than ten sides of A4 in length (excluding tables, appendices, footnotes and bibliography);

(*c*) a project report of no more than twenty-five sides of A4 in length (excluding tables, appendices, footnotes and bibliography), on a topic approved by the Standing Committee.

(*d*) With the permission of the Standing Committee, a candidate for the Postgraduate Diploma may attend one or two additional advanced modules from Section B of the Schedule and may submit the associated assignment(s), to be counted towards the requirements for the M.Sc. in Mathematical Finance if the candidate is later accepted onto the M.Sc., subject to the provisions of the regulations for the M.Sc.

The assignments under clauses (*b*) and (*d*) and the project report under (*c*) above shall be submitted electronically, in accordance with details given in the handbook for the Postgraduate Diploma, by such date as the examiners shall determine and shall notify candidates. In exceptional cases where a candidate is unable to submit work electronically, he or she must apply to the Standing Committee for permission to submit the work in paper form to the Examiners c/o Registry, Department for Continuing Education, 1 Wellington Square, Oxford OX1 2JA. Such applications must reach the Registry two weeks before the deadline for submitting the work.

6. Candidates may be required to attend a viva voce examination at the end of the course of studies at the discretion of the examiners.

7. The examiners may award a distinction to candidates for the Diploma.

8. Candidates who fail to satisfy the examiners in the written examinations under 5 (*a*), the assignment under 5(*b*), or the project report under 5(*c*) may be permitted to resubmit work in respect of the part or parts of the examination which they have failed. In the case of the written examinations, this shall normally be on the occasion of the written examinations next following; in the case of assignments or the project report, the work shall normally be resubmitted within one year of the decision of the examiners.

Paediatric Infectious Diseases

1. The course will consist of lectures, written assignments and online interactive case studies in the field of paediatric infectious disease. The course may be taken on a part-time basis over a period which shall normally be of two years' duration but shall not exceed three years' duration.

2. Every candidate must normally:

(*a*) Attend a residential course held annually in Oxford entitled 'Infection and Immunity in Children'.

(*b*) Attend a second residential course held annually in Oxford entitled 'Infection and Immunity in Children' (with a different course syllabus each year).

(*c*) Attend the residential PENTA-ESPID (Tr@inforPedHIV) training course in paediatric HIV medicine.

(*d*) Complete Online PENTA-ESPID (Tr@inforPedHIV) module in paediatric HIV medicine.

(*e*) Actively participate in seven ESPID Online Case Rounds.

(*f*) Actively participate in one four week PENTA-ESPID (Tr@inforPedHIV) Online Case Discussion in paediatric HIV medicine.

(*g*) Actively participate in six online multiple choice sessions.

3. Every candidate shall be required to satisfy the examiners in the following:

(*a*) Active participation, to the satisfaction of the Course Director, in all parts of the course.

(*b*) A written assignment consisting of either:

i. An audit of clinical practice in paediatric infectious disease of no more than 4000 words.

Or

ii. A case study and literature review of no more than 4000 words.

And

iii. A short oral presentation.

(*c*) A written assignment consisting of either:

i. A dissertation in an area of special interest of no more than 8000 words.

Or

ii. A project report describing a research study in the field of paediatric infectious diseases undertaken by the candidate of no more than 8000 words written in the style of a scientific paper with abstract, introduction/background, methods, results and conclusion.

(*d*) An examination consisting of multiple choice questions in paediatric infectious diseases covering the topics outlined in the schedule for training in paediatric infectious disease summarised below.

The assignments under 3(*b*) and 3(*c*) shall be forwarded to the examiners c/o Registry, Department of Continuing Education, 1 Wellington Square, Oxford OX1 2JA, for consideration by such date as the examiners shall determine and of which they shall notify candidates. The assessed work will, in normal circumstances, be submitted through an electronic submission system.

4. Candidates may be required to attend a viva voce examination at the end of the course of studies at the discretion of the examiners.

5. The examiners may award a distinction to candidates for the Postgraduate Diploma.

6. A candidate who fails to satisfy the examiners in the assignments under 3(*b*) and 3(*c*) or the examination under 3(*d*) above may normally be permitted to resubmit work in respect of the part or parts of the examination which they have failed on not more than one occasion which shall normally be within one year of the original failure.

Professional Archaeology

1. Every candidate must follow for three terms (full-time) or six terms (part-time) a course of instruction in Professional Archaeology.

2. The course will consist of lectures, seminars, individual tutorials and, in the case of full-time students, three approved ten week placements, or in the case of part-time students, approved work-place projects undertaken.

3. The examination will consist of the following parts:

    (*a*) a portfolio which shall include:

        (i) a written report of 5,000 words maximum of the work undertaken at the first placement;

        (ii) a written report of 5,000 words maximum of the work undertaken at the second placement;

        (iii) a written report of 5,000 words maximum of the work undertaken at the third placement;

    (In the case of part-time students, a written report of 15,000 words maximum on work-place projects undertaken with an approved relevant organisation). The portfolio material for each placement must represent ten weeks of professionally competent work;

        (iv) three written assignments of 2,000–2,500 words each, one during each of the placements on an agreed topic;

        (v) five written reports of 1,000 words maximum each, one on each of the following courses: four optional short courses and a survey week.

The portfolio shall be forwarded to the examiners, c/o Registry, Department for Continuing Education, 1 Wellington Square, Oxford OX1 2JA for consideration by such a date as the examiners shall determine and shall notify the candidates and tutors at the start of each academic year.

    (*b*) a viva voce examination.

    4. The examiners may award a distinction for excellence in the whole examination.

    5. A candidate who fails to satisfy the examiners in 3(*a*) may be permitted to resubmit work in respect of the part or parts of the examination which they have failed for examination on one further occasion, not later than one year after the initial attempt.

Psychodynamic Practice

    1. *Course*

    (*a*) The course will consist of lectures, tutorials, seminars, classes, and supervised practice on the theory and practice of Psychodynamic Practice. Candidates will be required to undertake personal therapy. The course will be taken on a part-time basis over a period which shall be of two years' duration.

    (*b*) The course places equal emphasis on theory, practice, and the candidate's personal and professional development. In the first year candidates will study the Historical and Theoretical Perspective, the Psychiatric Perspective, the Contemporary Perspective, and the Developmental Perspective, and be introduced to core clinical models. The organisational perspective will be taught to complement candidates' clinical placements. Candidates will study long term counselling and psychotherapy. The second year will include the study of time limited counselling and psychotherapy and the application of the core theoretical model to varied contexts and clinical populations.

    2. Every candidate will be required to satisfy the examiners in the following:

    (*a*) attendance at weekly classes, sensitivity group sessions, individual tutorials, a weekend school, and review sessions and revision days;

    (*b*) five written assignments as follows:

        (i) an initial case study of no more than 3,000 words.

        (ii) a second case study, of no more than 3,000 words.

        (iii) an extract from a candidate's placement log of no more than 3,000 words.

        (iv) an extract from the candidate's Reflective Journal, of no more than 3,000 words.

        (v) an essay, of no more than 3,000 words, based on theoretical material covered in the course.

(c) a dissertation of no more than 10,000 words (including appendices and foot-notes but excluding bibliography). The subject of the dissertation must be submitted for approval by the external examiner following consultation with the course director by noon of Friday of fourth week of Hilary Full Term in the second year of the course.

(d) participation in a minimum of 17 placement supervisions to include at least 100 hours of client/patient contact;

(e) participation in a minimum of 80 hours of personal therapy and submission of a statement of hours completed from the candidate's personal therapist;

(f) submission of annual reports from the candidate's course tutor and clinical seminar leader;

(g) confirmation from the sensitivity group conductor that there are no ethical reasons why the candidate should be discouraged from commencing profes-sional work.

The assignments under (b) and three typewritten or printed copies of the disserta-tion under (c) will be forwarded to the examiners c/o Registry, Department for Continuing Education, Wellington Square, Oxford OX1 2JA for consideration by such date as the examiners shall determine and shall notify candidates before the start of the academic year in which the assignment is due.

3. Candidates may be required to attend a viva voce examination at the end of the course of studies.

4. Candidates who fail to satisfy the examiners in any of the assignments in 2(b) or the dissertation may be permitted to resubmit work in the part or parts of the examination which they have failed for examination on not more than one occasion which shall normally be within one year of the original failure. Approval for deferral must be obtained from the relevant board of studies. Candidates who fail to obtain a satisfactory report of their placement at the end of the first year will be given additional support. Candidates who fail to obtain a satisfactory report at the end of the second year may be permitted by the examiners to continue in the placement until the required standard is reached, for a period of no more than one year after the end of the second year.

5. The examiners may award a distinction to candidates for the diploma.

Surgical Science and Practice (exit award only) (*old regulations for students registered on the MSc Surgical Science and Practice before 1 October 2012*)

1. The Divisional Board of Medical Sciences, jointly with the Continuing Education Board, shall elect for the supervision of the course a Standing Committee, which shall have the power to arrange lectures and other instruction.

2. Candidates must follow for at least three terms and at most nine terms, a part-time course of instruction in the theory and practice of Surgical Science and Practice, which shall normally take place over a period of no more than four years. The Postgraduate Diploma is only available to students admitted for the degree of MSc in Surgical Science and Practice.

3. Every candidate will be required to satisfy the examiners in the following:

(a) Attendance at the modules in Schedule A and Schedule B below and other teaching sessions as required.

(b) Active participation in all parts of the course to the satisfaction of the Course Director.

(c) Four written assignments related to the modules in Schedule A, each of not more than 4,000 words in length.

(d) Two assignments consisting of multiple choice questions or structured short questions, online project working and practical tests related to the modules in Schedule B.

The assignments set out in clauses 3(*c*) and 3(*d*) shall be forwarded, usually through a specified electronic submission system, to the examiners c/o Registry, Department for Continuing Education, 1 Wellington Square, Oxford OX1 2JA, for consideration by such date as the examiners shall determine and of which they shall notify candidates.

4. Candidates may be required to attend a viva voce examination at the end of the course of studies at the discretion of the examiners.

5. The examiners may award a distinction to candidates for the Postgraduate Diploma.

6. Candidates who fail to satisfy the examiners in any of the assignments under 3(*c*) and 3(*d*) may be permitted, normally within one year of the original failure, to resubmit work in respect of the part or parts they have failed on not more than one occasion for each assignment without being required to repeat attendance at the relevant module or modules under 3(*a*).

7. The Standing Committee shall have the discretion to permit any candidate to be exempted, in exceptional circumstances, from attendance at any module under 3(*a*) and from submitting the associated assignment required under 3(*c*) and 3(*d*) above, provided that the Standing Committee is satisfied that such a candidate has undertaken equivalent study, or has appropriate work experience to an equivalent standard.

Schedule A

The practice of evidence-based health care
Quality improvement science and systems analysis
Introduction to surgical management and leadership
Becoming a medical educator
Any other module as defined by the Course Director and approved by the Standing Committee.

Schedule B

Human factors, teamwork and communication
Surgical technology and robotics.

Surgical Science and Practice (exit award only) (*new regulations for students registering on the award from 1 October 2012 and available to existing students*)

1. The Medical Sciences Board, jointly with the Continuing Education Board, shall elect for the supervision of the course a Standing Committee, which shall have the power to arrange lectures and other instruction.

2. The Postgraduate Diploma is only available to students admitted for the degree of M.Sc. in Surgical Science and Practice. The course is available on a part time basis only and shall consist of instruction in the theory and practice of Surgical Science and Practice.

3. The policy of the Continuing Education Board on variable intensity part time study shall apply to this award.

4. The minimum period of registration on the Postgraduate Diploma shall be three terms and the maximum period of registration shall be twelve terms.

5. Every candidate will be required to satisfy the examiners in the following:

(*a*) Attendance at the modules in Schedule A and Schedule B below and other teaching sessions as required.

(*b*) Active participation in all parts of the course to the satisfaction of the Course Director.

(*c*) Four written assignments related to the modules in Schedule A, each of not more than 4,000 words in length.

(*d*) Two assignments consisting of multiple choice questions or structured short questions, online project working and practical tests related to the modules in Schedule B.

The assignments set out in clauses 5(*c*) and (*d*) shall be forwarded, usually through a specified electronic submission system, to the examiners c/o Registry, Department for Continuing Education, 1 Wellington Square, Oxford OX1 2JA, for consideration by such date as the examiners shall determine and shall notify candidates.

6. Candidates may be required to attend a viva voce examination at the end of the course of studies at the discretion of the examiners.

7. The examiners may award a distinction to candidates for the Postgraduate Diploma.

8. Candidates who fail to satisfy the examiners in any of the assignments under 5 (c) or (d) above may be permitted to resubmit work in respect of the part or parts they have failed on not more than one occasion for each assignment without being required to repeat attendance at the relevant module or modules. The resubmission shall normally be within one year of the original failure.

9. Provided the Standing Committee is satisfied that a student on the award has undertaken equivalent study, of an appropriate standard, normally at another institution of higher education, or has appropriate work experience to an equivalent standard, the committee may permit the candidate to be exempted from attendance and the submission of a written assignment in respect of up to three modules. In exercising this discretion the Standing Committee shall take into consideration the length of time that has elapsed since the study or work experience was undertaken.

10. The Standing Committee may deem satisfactory completion of a module (including the associated assessment) prior to registration for the award as having met the attendance and examination requirements in respect of that module. Such discretion will normally only be exercised if the time elapsed between commencement of the accredited module concerned and registration for the award is not more than two years. The maximum number of modules taken prior to registration for the award that may count in this way shall be three.

Schedule A

The practice of evidence-based health care
Quality improvement science and systems analysis
Introduction to surgical management and leadership
Becoming a medical educator
Any other module as defined by the Course Director and approved by the Standing Committee.

Schedule B

Human factors, teamwork and communication
Surgical technology and robotics.

Sustainable Urban Development (exit award only)

1. The Continuing Education Board shall elect for the supervision of the course a course committee that shall have the power to arrange lectures and other instruction.

2. Every candidate must follow for at least six terms a part-time course of instruction in the theory and practice of Sustainable Urban Development, which shall normally take place over a period of two years and no more than four years. The Postgraduate Diploma is only available to students admitted for the degree of MSc in Sustainable Urban Development.

3. Every candidate will be required to satisfy the examiners in the following:

(*a*) Attendance at classes, tutorials, group seminars and other teaching sessions;

(*b*) seven written assignments, each being on one of the units listed in the Schedule below, and each of not more than 3000 words in length;

The assessed work set out in clause 3(*b*) shall be forwarded in normal circumstances through an electronic submission system to the examiners c/o Registry, Department for Continuing Education, 1 Wellington Square, Oxford OX1 2JA, for consideration by such date as the examiners shall determine and of which they shall notify candidates.

4. Candidates may be required to attend a viva voce examination at the end of the course of studies at the discretion of the examiners.

5. The examiners may award a distinction to candidates for the Postgraduate Diploma.

6. Candidates who fail to satisfy the examiners in any part of the examination may be permitted to resubmit work in respect of the part or parts of the examination that they have failed for examination on not more than one occasion which shall normally be within one year of the original failure.

7. The course committee shall have the discretion to permit any candidate to be exempted, in exceptional circumstances, from submitting an assignment, provided that the committee is satisfied that such a candidate has undertaken equivalent study, or have appropriate work experience to an equivalent standard.

Schedule

Concepts of the City and Environmental Change
Climate Change and the Built Environment
Placemaking
Financing Sustainability
Transportation and Sustainability
Urbanism and the Design Process
The Flexible City? Urban Theory, Practice and Project Management
Urbanisation and the Global South
Any other subject approved by the course committee.
Not all units will be available in any one year.

UNDERGRADUATE CERTIFICATES (CONTINUING EDUCATION)

GENERAL REGULATIONS

1. The Continuing Education Board shall have the power to grant Certificates to candidates who have satisfied the conditions prescribed in this section and any further conditions which the board may prescribe by regulation.

2. The examination for each Certificate (Continuing Education) shall be under the supervision of the Continuing Education Board, which shall have power, subject to the approval of the Education Committee, to make regulations governing the examination.

3. Candidates, whether members of the University or not, may be admitted as students for an Undergraduate Certificate (Continuing Education) under such conditions as the board shall prescribe, provided that before admission to a course of study approved by the board, candidates shall have satisfied the board that they have appropriate educational experience acceptable to the board, and are well-equipped to enter the proposed course of study.

4. Any person who has been accepted as a candidate for an Undergraduate Certificate (Continuing Education), and who has satisfactorily pursued a course, the character and length of which have been approved by the board, may be admitted to the examination.

SPECIAL REGULATIONS

Archaeology

1. *Course*

(a) The course will consist of lectures, tutorials, seminars and classes on the subject of Archaeology. The course, which is available on a part-time basis only, may be taken over a period of a minimum of two, and no more than three years.

(b) The subjects of the course will be taught in two one-year modules. One module shall be offered each year. Candidates must complete the introductory module *Discovering Archaeology: its purpose and practice* (Module A) before proceeding to Module B. To qualify for the award of the Certificate, candidates must satisfy the examiners in modules A and B.

2. Every candidate will be required to satisfy the examiners in the following:

(a) Attendance at a minimum of 75 per cent of class-based sessions;

(b) Attendance at one week of fieldwork (and associated written work) and study visits to the satisfaction of the Course Director;

(*c*) Attendance at a minimum of two one-hour tutorials in the second year of the course;

(*d*) Three practical assignments, of which two shall be between 1,000 and 1,500 words in length, and one shall be between 2,000 and 2,500 words, based on the practical work undertaken in Module A;

(*e*) Three written assignments of normally between 1,400 and 1,600 words in length, based on the subjects taught in Module A;

(*f*) Three practical assignments, each of which shall be between 1,000 and 1,500 words in length, based on the practical work undertaken in Module B;

(*g*) Three written assignments of normally between 1,800 and 2,000 words in length, based on the subjects taught in Module B;

(*h*) One written assignment totalling no more than 1,000 words in length, and a field notebook, covering work done in the fieldwork week;

(*i*) One two-hour written examination, covering the subjects taught in Module A;

(*j*) One extended project of between 4,500 and 5,500 words in length consisting of a subject of the candidate's choice relating to the course material in Module B and agreed with the Course Director.

The written work under clauses 2(*b*), (*d*)-(*j*) will be forwarded to the examiners for consideration by such dates as the examiners shall determine and shall notify candidates.

3. Candidates may be required to attend a viva voce examination at the end of the course.

4. The examiners may award a distinction to candidates for the Certificate.

5. Candidates who fail to satisfy the examiners in the assessed work specified in clauses (*b*), (*d*) to (*j*) may be permitted to resubmit work in respect of the part or parts of the examination which they have failed on not more than one occasion which shall normally be within one year of the initial failure.

Archaeology: Themes and Methods (*for students admitted from October 2011*)

1. The course shall consist of lectures, tutorials, seminars and classes on the subject of Archaeology. The course, which is available on a part-time basis only, may be taken over a period of a minimum of one, and no more than two, years.

2. Every candidate will be required to satisfy the examiners in the following:

(*a*) attendance at class-based sessions;

(*b*) attendance at study visits;

(*c*) attendance at two seminars;

(*d*) participation in on-line study forums;

(*e*) three written assignments each of no more than 1,500 words in length based on methods in Archaeology. The first of these is formative only and marks do not contribute to the final award;

(*f*) two written assignments each of no more than 2,000 words in length based on the periods covered;

(*g*) a Practical Logbook of up to 5,000 words in length offering a choice of tasks to include reports of fieldwork, visits and contributions to Discussion Forum.

The written work under clauses 2(*e*)-(*g*) will be forwarded to the examiners for consideration by such dates as the examiners shall determine and shall notify candidates.

3. The examiners may award a distinction to candidates for the Certificate.

4. Candidates who fail to satisfy the examiners in the assessed work specified in clauses 2(*e*)-(*g*) may be permitted to resubmit work in respect of part or parts of the examination which they have failed on not more that one occasion which shall normally be within one year of the initial failure.

Higher Education

1. The Certificate shall consist of accredited classes and other courses of study provided by the Department for Continuing Education. The Certificate is available on a part-time basis and may be taken over a period of not fewer than two years and no more than four years.

2. The main subjects for the Certificate shall be Archaeology, Art History, Architectural History, Creative Writing, History, Italian, Literature, Philosophy, and Spanish, together with such other subjects as may be approved by the Continuing Education Board. Candidates must select one of these as their main subject. A list of classes and other courses available in any one year that can be taken for the Certificate, including those identified as qualifying courses, will be published annually by the Department.

3. Every candidate will be required to satisfy the examiners in the following:

(*a*) accumulation of 120 Credit Accumulation and Transfer Scheme (CATS) points from classes and courses provided by the Department for Continuing Education. These 120 points must include the following:

  (i) 5 points from either three study skills day schools or the online study skills course;

  (ii) 10 points from a course approved as a qualifying course in the candidate's main subject;

  (iii) no fewer than 50, and no more than 70, additional points, in the candidate's main subject;

  (iv) no fewer than 30 points, and no more than 50 points, from eligible classes or courses in other subjects;

  (v) a reflective learning journal of not more than 2,000 words submitted in two parts (5 CATS points).

(*b*) Two assignments, each of no more than 2,500 words or equivalent, based on topics relating to two separate classes or courses in the candidate's main subject area.

(*c*) One assignment of not more than 3,500 words or equivalent based on a topic relating to a class or course in the candidate's main subject area other than those referred to in 3(*b*) above.

(*d*) Attendance at a minimum of 70 per cent of each class or course.

4. Timing

(*a*) The study skills day schools or online study skills course referred to in 3(*a*)(i) above must normally be undertaken during the first term of registration;

(*b*) The first part of the reflective journal referred to in 3(a)(v) above shall normally be submitted after completion of the first 60 CATS points of study and the second part after completion of at least 100 CATS points.

(*c*) The assignment referred to in 3(*c*) above shall normally be submitted during the last year of registration for the Certificate.

5. Credit may not be counted as part of the Certificate of Higher Education if it contains a significant proportion of material (normally 30 per cent or more)

duplicated from a class or course already counted towards any certificate, diploma or other award of the University.

6. The Director of the Certificate shall have the discretion to permit any candidate to count towards the Certificate up to 30 CATS points from any class or course offered by the Department for Continuing Education so long as these shall have been obtained no more than four years before formal registration on the Certificate.

7. Candidates may count up to 105 CATS points towards the Certificate of Higher Education from courses studied online.

8. A candidate may be required to attend a viva voce examination.

9. The examiners may award a distinction to candidates for the Certificate.

10. Candidates who fail any accredited class or course they intent to count towards the Certificate under 3(*a*) above, or who fail to satisfy the examiners in the reflective journal under 3(*a*)(v) may be permitted to resubmit work in respect of that class or course, or resubmit the reflective journal on not more than one occasion.This shall normally be within one month of the initial failure. Candidates who fail to satisfy the examiners in the assignments under 3(*b*) or 3(*c*) above may be permitted to resubmit the assignment or assignments on not more than one occasion. This shall normally be within three months of the initial failure. All resubmissions of work must be within one year of the initial failure.

History of Art

1. *Course*

(*a*) The course shall consist of lectures, tutorials, seminars, and classes on the subjects of the History of Art. The course, which is available on a part-time basis only, may be taken over a period of a minimum of two, and no more than three years.

(*b*) The subjects of the course will be taught in two one-year modules. One module shall be offered each year. Students must complete Module 1 before proceeding to Module 2.

2. Every candidate will be required to satisfy the examiners in the following:

(*a*) Attendance at the theoretical courses; students must attend a minimum of 75 per cent of the equivalent of sixty two-hour sessions;

(*b*) Attendance at six study visits;

(*c*) Four written assignments of not more than 1,500 words and four of not more than 2,000 words based on the subjects taught;

(*d*) Two long essays one of 3,000 words and one of 5,000 words on a subject approved by the Course Director;

(*e*) Six class tests.

The written work under (*c*) and (*d*), and the class tests under (*e*), will be forwarded to the examiners for consideration by such dates as the examiners shall determine and shall notify candidates.

3. Candidates may be required to attend a viva voce examination at the end of the course.

4. The examiners may award a distinction to candidates for the Certificate.

5. Candidates who fail to satisfy the examiners in the written work under (*c*) and (*d*), or the class tests under (*e*), may be permitted to resubmit work in respect of part or parts of the examination which they have failed on not more that one occasion which shall normally be within one year of the initial failure.

History of Art (*for students admitted from October 2011*)

1. The course shall consist of lectures, tutorials, seminars and classes on the subject of the History of Art. The course, which is available on a part-time basis only, may be taken over a period of a minimum of one, and no more than two, years.

2. Every candidate will be required to satisfy the examiners in the following:

(*a*) attendance at the theoretical courses, including study visits; students must attend a minimum of 75 per cent of the equivalent of thirty two-hour sessions;

(*b*) one written assignment of nor more than 1,000 words. This assignment is formative only and marks do not contribute to the final award;

(*c*) five written assignments of not more than 1,500 words based on the subjects taught;

(*d*) one extended essay of not more than 3,000 words on a subject approved by the course director.

The written work under (*c*) and (*d*) will be forwarded to the examiners for consideration by such dates as the examiners shall determine and shall notify candidates.

3. Candidates may be expected to attend a viva voce examination at the end of the course.

4. The examiners may award a distinction to candidates for the Certificate.

5. Candidates who fail to satisfy the examiners in the written work under (*b*) and (*c*) may be permitted to resubmit work in respect of part or parts of the examination which they have failed on not more that one occasion which shall normally be within one year of the initial failure.

Theology and Religious Studies

1. The course shall consist of lectures, tutorials, seminars and classes on the subject of Theology and Religious Studies. The course, which is available on a part-time basis only, may be taken over a period of a minimum of one, and no more than two, years.

2. Every candidate will be required to satisfy the examiners in the following:

(*a*) Attendance at the theoretical courses, including study visits; students must attend a minimum of 75% of the equivalent of 30 two-hour sessions;

(*b*) One written assignment of not more than 1,000 words. This assignment is formative only and marks do not contribute to the final award.

(*c*) Five written assignments of not more than 1,500 words based on the subjects taught.

(*d*) One case study of not more than 3,000 words on a subject approved by the course director. The written work under (*c*) and (*d*) will be forwarded to the examiners for consideration by such dates as the examiners shall determine and shall notify candidates.

3. Candidates may be expected to attend a viva voce examination at the end of the course.

4. The examiners may award a distinction to candidates for the Certificate.

5. Candidates who fail to satisfy the examiners in the written work under 2(*c*) and (*d*) may be permitted to resubmit work in respect of part or parts of the examination which they have failed on not more that one occasion which shall normally be within one year of the initial failure.

UNDERGRADUATE DIPLOMAS (CONTINUING EDUCATION)

GENERAL REGULATIONS

1. The Continuing Education Board shall have the power to grant Diplomas to candidates who have satisfied the conditions prescribed in this section and any further conditions which the board may prescribe by regulation.

2. The examination for each Diploma (Continuing Education) shall be under the supervision of the Continuing Education Board, which shall have power, subject to the approval of the Education Committee, to make regulations governing the examination.

3. Candidates, whether members of the University or not, may be admitted as students for an Undergraduate Diploma (Continuing Education) under such conditions as the board shall prescribe, provided that before admission to a course of study approved by the board, candidates shall have satisfied the board that they have appropriate educational experience acceptable to the Board and are well-equipped to enter the proposed course of study.

4. Any person who has been accepted as a candidate for an Undergraduate Diploma (Continuing Education), and who has satisfactorily pursued a course, the character and length of which have been approved by the committee, may be admitted to the examination.

SPECIAL REGULATIONS

Biblical and Theological Studies (Regents Park College)

1. *Course*

The course shall consist of lectures, tutorials, seminars, and classes on the subject of Biblical and Theological Studies. The course, which is available on a part-time basis only, may be taken over a period of a minimum of two, and no more than five years. Candidates shall take twelve subjects chosen from the Schedule below.

2. Every candidate will be required to satisfy the examiners in the following:

(*a*) Attendance at the theoretical courses; students must attend a minimum of 75 per cent of the equivalent of 60 two-hour sessions;

(*b*) Ten coursework assignments, each of which shall not exceed 2,000–2,500 words or equivalent in length, based on the theoretical courses;

(*c*) A dissertation of no more than 5,000 words, on a topic of theological interest to the candidate, normally in the field of pastoral theology, the title of which shall be approved by the Course Director.

The assignments under (*b*) and the dissertation under (*c*) will be forwarded to the examiners for consideration by such dates as the examiners shall determine and shall notify candidates.

3. Candidates may be required to attend a viva voce examination at the end of the course.   5

4. The examiners may award a distinction to candidates for the Diploma.

5. Candidates who fail to satisfy the examiners in the assignments under 2(*b*) and dissertation under 2(*c*) may be permitted to resubmit work in respect of the part or parts of the examination which they have failed on not more than one occasion which shall normally be within one year of the initial failure.   10

Schedule

Candidates must complete two of the three subject groups shown below. Only one subject group is available each year. *The definitive list of subjects for any one year will be circulated to candidates before the start of Michaelmas Term of that year.*

Subject Group A   15
  1 Pastoral theology
  2 The Atonement
  3 The Reformation
  4 'Romans'
  5 Covenant in the Old Testament   20
  6 Ethics

Subject Group B
  1 The Sacraments
  2 The Church and the Kingdom
  3 The Early Church   25
  4 The Psalms
  5 Social Context of Theology
  6 The Corinthian Letters

Subject Group C
  1 Old Testament Prophets   30
  2 Mission
  3 Luke and Acts
  4 Philosophy
  5 Modern Church History
  6 God and Revelation   35

Biblical and Theological Studies (Wycliffe Hall)

1. *Course*

(*a*) The course shall consist of lectures, tutorials, seminars and classes on the subjects of Biblical and Theological Studies. The course, which is available on a part-time basis only, may be taken over a minimum period of two years,   40 and a maximum period of five years.

(*b*) Candidates shall take twelve subjects, all nine from Group A and three from Group B. The definitive list of subjects from Group B for any one year will be circulated to candidates before the start of Michaelmas Term of that year.

Group A

1. Old Testament I
2. Old Testament II
3. New Testament I
4. New Testament II   5
5. Christian Doctrine I
6. Christian Doctrine II
7. Church History and Historical Theology I
8. Church History and Historical Theology II
9. Theological Reflection (part-taught, leading to dissertation)   1(

Group B

10. Christian Ethics
11. The Study of Christian Mission
12. Pastoral Theology
13. Christian Worship and Prayer   1
14. The Study of Christian Apologetics
15. The Study of Christian Evangelism
16. The Study of an Influential Christian Thinker
17. Christianity, Communication and Culture
18. Christian Homiletics   2(

Wycliffe Hall reserves the right to not offer a subject in Group B if it is significantly under-subscribed.

2. Every candidate will be required to satisfy the examiners in the following:

(*a*) Attendance at the subject teaching; students must attend a minimum of 75 per cent of the equivalent of 60 two-hour sessions;   2

(*b*) Attendance at six out of eight Study Days;

(*c*) Ten coursework assignments, each of which shall not exceed 2,500 words or equivalent in length or equivalent work for non-essay assigment, based on the subject teaching;

(*d*) A dissertation of no more than 5,000 words, on a topic of theological interest   3(
to the candidate, normally in the field of pastoral theology, the title of which shall be approved by the Course Director.

Assignments under (*c*) and the dissertation under (*d*) will be forwarded to the examiners for consideration by such dates as the examiners shall determine and shall notify candidates.   3

3. Candidates may be required to attend a viva voce examination at the end of the course.

4. The examiners may award a distinction to candidates for the Diploma.

5. Candidates who fail to satisfy the examiners in the assignments under 2(*c*) or dissertation under 2(*d*) may be permitted to resubmit work in respect of the part or   4(
parts of the examination which they have failed on not more than one occasion which shall normally be within one year of the initial failure.

British Archaeology

1. *Course*

(*a*) The course shall consist of lectures, tutorials, seminars and classes on the   4.
subject of British Archaeology. The course, which is available on a part-time

basis only, may be taken over a period of a minimum of two, and no more than five years.

(*b*) The subjects of the course will be taught in three one-year modules. One module is offered each year. Modules currently available are:

Module 1: Early Prehistoric Britain;

Module 2: Later Prehistoric and Roman Britain;

Module 3: Anglo-Saxon, Viking and Medieval Britain.

2. Every candidate will be required to satisfy the examiners in the following:

(*a*) Attendance at the theoretical courses; candidates must attend a minimum of 75 per cent of the equivalent of sixty two-hour sessions;

(*b*) Attendance in each module at either two practical weekends (four days) *or* approved archaeological training (minimum six days or equivalent);

(*c*) At least four one-hour tutorials; five if the extended project is undertaken;

(*d*) Ten coursework assignments, each of which shall not exceed 2,500 words in length, based on the theoretical courses;

(*e*) In the first module, one practical logbook, which shall not exceed 8,000 words;

(*f*) In the second module, one practical logbook which shall not exceed 8,000 words or an extended project which shall not exceed 8,000 words on a topic approved by the Course Director.

Assignments under 2(*d*), 2(*e*), and 2(*f*) will be forwarded to the examiners for consideration by such dates as the examiners shall determine and shall notify candidates.

3. Candidates may be required to attend a viva voce examination at the end of the course.

4. The examiners may award a distinction to candidates for the Diploma.

5. Candidates who fail to satisfy the examiners in the assignments under 2(*d*)-(*e*), may be permitted to resubmit work in respect of the part or parts of the examination which they have failed on not more than one occasion which shall normally be within one year of the initial failure.

Computing

1. *Course*

(*a*) The course will comprise twelve units drawn from the Schedule below, and will be taught in two one-year modules, each comprising six units.

(*b*) The course, which is available on a part-time basis only, may be taken over a period of a minimum of two, and no more than five years. The course may be taken either in a distance learning mode or a face-to-face mode.

2. Every candidate will be required to satisfy the examiners in the following:

(*a*) Active participation in all parts of the course to the satisfaction of the Course Director;

(*b*) Active participation in group discussions under the guidance, and to the satisfaction, of the Student's tutor;

(*c*) Attendance at two one-week summer schools in Oxford (normally in July/August) *or* six weekend schools;

(*d*) Ten coursework assignments, each of which shall not exceed 2,000–2,500 words or equivalent in length, based on the theoretical courses;

(*e*) Two summer school assignments *or* two weekend school assignments each of which shall not exceed 2,000–2,500 words or equivalent in length;

(*f*) Two written three-hour examination papers, each covering the subjects taught in one module.

Assignments under (*d*) and (*e*) will be forwarded to the examiners for consideration by such dates as the examiners shall determine and shall notify candidates.

3. Candidates will be required to achieve an overall pass for the assignments under 2(*d*) and (*e*) above and the examination papers under 2(*f*) above.

4. Candidates may be required to attend a viva voce examination at the end of the course.

5. The examiners may award a distinction to candidates for the Diploma.

6. Candidates who fail to satisfy the examiners in the assignments under 2(*d*)-(*e*) and 3, may be permitted to resubmit work in respect of the part or parts of the examination which they have failed, for examination on not more than one occasion which shall normally be within one year of the initial failure.

Schedule of units

1 The Basics of Hardware and Software

2 Networks of Data Structures

3 File Structures and Databases

4 Computer Architecture

5 Human Computer Interaction

6 New Frontiers

7 Concepts of Programming

8 Further Programming

9 Multimedia Applications

10 World Wide Web 1

11 World Wide Web 2

12 An Introduction to Systems Analysis and Development Software

13 Any other unit as defined by the Director of Studies and approved by the Board of Studies

The Board of Studies shall have the power to add other units or delete units from this list. In June and December each year a list of units will be published. Each such list, which will have been approved by the Board of Studies and which will be selected from the above schedule, will contain those units which will be available during the following academic year.

Creative Writing

1. *Course*

(*a*) The course shall consist of lectures, tutorials, seminars and classes on the subject of Creative Writing. The course, which is available on a part-time basis only, may be taken over a period of a minimum of two, and no more than five years.

(*b*) The course will cover the study and practice of the craft of writing. A range of literary genres and sub-genres will be considered, and directed approaches to the analytical reading of work by other writers will be undertaken.

2. Every candidate will be required to satisfy the examiners in the following:

(*a*) Attendance at the theoretical courses; students must attend a minimum of 75 per cent of the class based sessions;

(*b*) Attendance at twelve forty-five minute individual tutorials, six day schools and one one-week summer school;

(*c*) Nine written assignments, each of no more than 2,000 words in length of prose, or 15 pages of drama , or 100 lines of poetry;

(*d*) Two end-of-year portfolios of written work, each of not more than 6,000 words of prose, or 30 pages of drama or 300 lines of poetry.

Assignments under (*c*) and (*d*) will be forwarded to the examiners for consideration by such dates as the examiners shall determine and shall notify candidates.

3. Candidates may be required to attend a viva voce examination at the end of the course.

4. The examiners may award a distinction to candidates for the Diploma.

5. Candidates who fail to satisfy the examiners in the assignments under 2(*c*)–(*d*) may be permitted to resubmit work in respect of the part or parts of the examination which they have failed on not more than one occasion which shall normally be within one year of the initial failure.

English Local History

(*Note: For candidates enrolled on the programme prior to 1 October 2011 one module will be assessed by a three hour written examination paper, covering the subjects taught in that module, rather than by portfolio*)

Regulations

1. The course shall consist of lectures, seminars and classes on the subject of English Local History. The course, which is available on a part-time basis only, may be taken over a period of a minimum of two, and no more than five, years. The subjects of the course will be taught in two one year modules, offered in alternate years:

Module 1: English Local History to *c.*1530

Module 2: English Local History from *c.*1530

2. Every candidate will be required to satisfy the examiners in the following:

(*a*) attendance at classes; students must attend a minimum of 75 per cent of seventy two-hour teaching sessions;

(*b*) attendance at two residential weekends;

(*c*) eight coursework assignments, each of which shall not exceed 2,500 words in length;

(*d*) two extended essays, each of which shall not exceed 5,000 words in length, based on material taught during the course;

(*e*) two portfolios which shall not exceed 5,000 words in length commenting on selected primary sources.

Assignments under (*c*), (*d*) and (*e*) will be forwarded to the examiners for consideration by such dates as the examiners shall determine and shall notify candidates.

3. Candidates may be required to attend a viva voce examination at the end of the course.

4. The examiners may award a distinction to candidates for the Diploma.

5. Candidates who fail to satisfy the examiners in the assignments under 2(*c*), (*d*) or (*e*), may be permitted to resubmit work in respect of the part or parts of the examination which they have failed on not more than one occasion which shall normally be within one year of the initial failure.

Environmental Conservation

1. *Course*

(a) The course shall consist of lectures, tutorials, seminars and classes on the subject of Environmental Conservation. The course, which is available on a part-time basis only, may be taken over a period of a minimum of two, and no more than five years.

(b) The subjects of the course will be taught in two one-year modules, offered in alternate years:

Module 1: Conservation and the Environment;

Module 2: Getting Involved with Environmental Conservation.

2. Every candidate will be required to satisfy the examiners in the following:

(a) Attendance at the theoretical courses; for each module, students must attend a minimum of 75 per cent of ten day school sessions (held on Saturdays);

(b) Attendance at three linked weekend schools per module (or one one-week summer school per module);

(c) Six coursework assignments, each of which shall not exceed 2,000–2,500 words in length, based on the theoretical courses;

(d) Two long assignments, each of which shall not exceed 5,000 words in length, based on practical work;

(e) Two field notebook assignments, each of which shall not exceed 3,500 words in length;

(f) Two written three-hour examination papers, each covering the subjects taught in one module.

Assignments under (c), (d) and (e) will be forwarded to the examiners for consideration by such dates as the examiners shall determine and shall notify candidates.

3. Candidates may be required to attend a viva voce examination at the end of the course.

4. The examiners may award a distinction to candidates for the Diploma.

5. Candidates who fail to satisfy the examiners in the assignments under 2(c)–(e), or the examination under 2(f), or both, may be permitted to resubmit work in respect of the part or parts of the examination which they have failed on not more than one occasion which shall normally be within one year of the initial failure.

History of Art

1. *Course*

(a) The course shall consist of lectures, tutorials, seminars and classes on the subject of the History of Art. The course, which is available on a part-time basis only, may be taken over a period of a minimum of two, and no more than five years.

(b) The subjects of the course will be taught in four one-year modules of which candidates must offer two. Two modules will be available each year. Modules currently available are:

Module 1: The Late Middle Ages and the Early Renaissance

Module 2: The High Renaissance and Baroque

Module 3: Revolution to Modernity: 1848–1914

Module 4: Modern Art and Contemporary Visual Culture

2. Every candidate will be required to satisfy the examiners in the following for each of the two modules to be offered:

(a) Attendance at the theoretical courses; students must attend a minimum of 75 per cent of the equivalent of 30 two-hour sessions;

(*b*) Attendance at five Saturday Study Days;

(*c*) i) Two essays, each of which shall not exceed 3,000 words in length;

ii) A research project consisting of no more than 8,000 words in length each, based on a subject of the candidate's choice relating to the course material and agreed with the Course Director;

iii) A written three-hour examination paper.

The essays under (*c*)i) and the project under (*c*)ii) will be forwarded to the examiners for consideration by such dates as the examiners shall determine and shall notify candidates.

3. Candidates may be required to attend a viva voce examination at the end of the course.

4. The examiners may award a distinction to candidates for the Diploma.

5. Candidates must achieve a pass mark (40 per cent) in each element of assessment in each module: the two essays under 2(*c*)i) taken together; the research project under 2(*c*)ii) and the examination under 2(*c*)iii). Candidates who fail to satisfy the examiners in any element may be permitted to resubmit work in respect of that element on not more than one occasion which shall normally be within one year of the initial failure.

Theological Education and Ministry

1. Candidates for admission to the Diploma must have completed the Undergraduate Certificate in Theological Education and Ministry offered by St. Albans and Oxford Ministry Course and the Department for Continuing Education or an equivalent course of study approved by the Board of Studies.

2. The Diploma shall consist of lectures, tutorials, seminars and classes on the subject of Theological Education and Ministry. The course, which is available on a part-time basis only, may be taken over a period of a minimum of two, and no more than four years.

3. Every candidate will be required to satisfy the examiners in the following:

(*a*) Attendance at the theoretical courses; students must attend a minimum of 75 per cent of 60 two-hour sessions;

(*b*) Attendance at twelve Study Weekends and two one-week Summer Residence;

(*c*) A minimum of 160 hours of church placement work;

(*d*) Two block placements, each of at least 35 hours of supervised practical work;

(*e*) Three coursework assignments, each of which shall not exceed 2,000 words in length, based on the theoretical courses;

(*f*) Twelve coursework assignments, each of which shall not exceed 3,000 words in length, based on the theoretical courses;

(*g*) Submission of satisfactory reports from placement supervisors covering the block placements and from academic and personal tutors covering the student's progress on the remainder of the course.

Assignments under (*e*) and (*f*) will be forwarded to the examiners for consideration by such dates as the examiners shall determine and shall notify candidates.

4. Candidates may be required to attend a viva voce examination at the end of the course.

5. The examiners may award a distinction to candidates for the Diploma.

6. Candidates who fail to satisfy the examiners in the assignments under 2(*e*)-(*f*) may be permitted to resubmit work in respect of the part or parts of the examination which they have failed on not more than one occasion which shall normally be within one year of the initial failure.

UNDERGRADUATE ADVANCED DIPLOMAS (CONTINUING EDUCATION)

General Regulations

1. The Continuing Education Board shall have power to grant Advanced Diplomas (two-year part-time), Advanced Diplomas (one-year full-time), and Advanced Diplomas (one-year part-time) to candidates who have satisfied the conditions prescribed in this section and any further conditions which the Board may prescribe by regulation.

2. The examination for each Advanced Diploma (Continuing Education) shall be under the supervision of the Continuing Education Board, which shall have power, subject to the approval of the Education Committee, to make regulations governing the examination.

3. Candidates, whether members of the University or not, may be admitted as students for an Advanced Diploma (Continuing Education) under such conditions as the Board shall prescribe, provided that before admission to a course of study approved by the Board, candidates shall have satisfied the board that they have appropriate educational experience acceptable to the committee and are well-equipped to enter the proposed course of study.

4. Any person who has been accepted as a candidate for an Advanced Diploma (Continuing Education), and who has satisfactorily pursued a course, the character and length of which have been approved by the Board, may be admitted to the examination.

Special Regulations

(i) ADVANCED DIPLOMAS (TWO YEAR PART-TIME)
Undergraduate Advanced Diploma in Archaeological Practice
1. *Course*
   (*a*) The course will consist of lectures, classes, seminars and tutorials in Archaeological Practice. The course, which is available on a part-time basis only, will normally be taken over a period of two, and no more than five, years.
   (*b*) The subjects of the course of study will include topics relevant to landscape archaeology, material culture, environmental and scientific archaeology.
2. Every candidate will be required to satisfy the examiners in the following:
   (*a*) Attendance at the taught courses and at one week's prescribed practical fieldwork;

(*b*) Six assignments of between 2,000 and 2,500 words based on the taught courses;

(*c*) One long assignment of up to 5,000 words (including appendices);

(*d*) A practical logbook of up to 5,000 words per module which is assessed separately at the end of each module but also extends to both years as a continuing project;

(*e*) A dissertation of up to 10,000 words (including appendices) on a topic agreed by the Board of Studies.

Assignments under 2(*b*)–2(*c*), the logbook under 2(*d*), and the dissertation under 2(*e*) will be forwarded to the examiners for consideration by such dates as the examiners shall determine and shall notify candidates.

3. Candidates may be required to attend a viva voce examination at the end of the course of studies.

4. The examiners may award a distinction to candidates for the Advanced Diploma.

5. Candidates who fail to satisfy the examiners in the assignments under 2(*b*)–2(*c*), or the logbook under 2(*d*), or the dissertation under 2(*e*), may be permitted to resubmit work in respect of the part or parts of the examination which they have failed for examination on not more than one occasion which shall normally be within one year of the initial failure.

Advanced Diploma in Environmental Conservation

1. *Course*

(*a*) The course will consist of lectures, classes, seminars, and tutorials in Environmental Conservation. The course, which is available on a part-time basis only, will normally be taken over a period of two, and no more than five, years.

(*b*) The subjects of the course of study will be taught in two one-year modules, entitled:

1 Environmental Change and Issues

2 Conservation Management

One module will be offered each year.

2. Every candidate will be required to satisfy the examiners in the following:

(*a*) Attendance at the taught courses and at practical fieldwork sessions;

(*b*) Eight assignments of between 2,000 and 2,500 words in length, based on the taught courses;

(*c*) Two field notebooks based on the practical fieldwork, each of which shall not exceed 5,000 words in length;

(*d*) One long assignment of up to 5,000 words (excluding appendices and bibliography);

(*e*) A dissertation of up to 10,000 words (excluding appendices and bibliography) on a topic agreed by the Board of Studies.

Assignments under 2(*b*)–2(*d*) and the dissertation under (*e*) will be forwarded to the examiners for consideration by such dates as the examiners shall determine and shall notify candidates.

3. Candidates may be required to attend a viva voce examination at the end of the course of studies.

4. The examiners may award a distinction to candidates for the Advanced Diploma.

5. Candidates who fail to satisfy the examiners in the assignments under 2(*b*)-2(*d*), or the dissertation under 2(*e*), or both, may be permitted to re-submit work in respect of the part or parts of the examination which they have failed for examination on not more than one occasion which shall normally be within one year of the initial failure.

Advanced Diploma in the History of Art

1. *Course*

(*a*) The course will consist of lectures, classes, seminars, and tutorials in the History of Art. The course, which is available on a part-time basis only, will normally be taken over a period of two, and no more than five, years.

(*b*) The subjects of the course will be taught in two one-year modules, entitled:

  1 Art and Architecture from 1900 to 1945

  2 Art and Architecture since 1945

One module will be offered each year. Students must complete Module 1 before proceeding to Module 2.

2. Every candidate will be required to satisfy the examiners in the following:

(*a*) Attendance at the taught courses and at study visits;

(*b*) Ten assignments, each of 2,000 words in length, based on the taught courses;

(*c*) One long assignment of up to 5,000 words (including appendices);

(*d*) A dissertation of up to 10,000 words (including appendices) on a topic agreed by the Board of Studies.

Assignments under 2(*b*)–2(*c*) and the dissertation under 2(*d*) will be forwarded to the examiners for consideration by such dates as the examiners shall determine and shall notify candidates.

3. Candidates may be required to attend a viva voce examination at the end of the course of studies.

4. The examiners may award a distinction to candidates for the Advanced Diploma.

5. Candidates who fail to satisfy the examiners in the assignments under 2(*b*)-2(*c*), or the dissertation under 2(*d*), or both, may be permitted to re-submit work in respect of the part or parts of the examination which they have failed for examination on not more than one occasion which shall normally be within one year of the initial failure.

(ii) ADVANCED DIPLOMAS (ONE YEAR FULL-TIME)

Advanced Diploma in British and European Studies

1. *Course*

(*a*) The course will consist of lectures, tutorials, and classes in the culture of Britain and Europe, with accompanying study in English language. Every candidate must take the course under the supervision of the Continuing Education Board for at least one year. Such study shall be pursued at Oxford.

(*b*) The course will consist of four core subjects as follows:

  (i) Pre-sessional course

  (ii) English language

  (iii) British and European Studies

  (iv) Extended essay option.

2. Candidates will normally be expected to pass an examination at the end of the pre-sessional course before being permitted to proceed to the remainder of the course.

3. In addition, every candidate will be required to satisfy the examiners in the following:

    (*a*) A written portfolio of exercises based on the contents of the English language 5
course, which will be of no more than 10,000 words in total;

    (*b*) Six assignments based on the theoretical courses in British and European Studies, each of a maximum of 2,000 words;

    (*c*) An extended essay normally of between 4,000 and 5,000 words in length (the limit to include notes) on a topic related to one of the core subjects of study. 10

Assignments under 3(*a*)–3(*c*) will be forwarded to the examiners for consideration by such dates as the examiners shall determine and shall notify candidates.

4. Candidates may also be called for viva voce examination.

5. The examiners may award a distinction to candidates for the Advanced Diploma. 15

6. Candidates who fail to satisfy the examiners in any part of the examination may be permitted to re-submit work in respect of the part or parts of the examination which they have failed for examination on not more than one occasion which shall normally be within one year of the initial failure.

Advanced Diploma in Globalisation Studies 20

    1. (*a*) The course will consist of lectures, tutorials, and classes in Globalisation Studies with accompanying study in English language. Every candidate must take the course under the supervision of the Continuing Education Board for at least one year. Such study shall be pursued at Oxford.

    (*b*) The course will consist of four core subjects as follows: 25

    (i) Pre-sessional course

    (ii) English language

    (iii) Globalisation studies

    (iv) Extended essay

2. Every candidate will be required to satisfy the examiners in the following: 30

    (*a*) Attendance at the taught courses;

    (*b*) A pre-sessional examination at the end of the presessional course. The candidate must normally pass this before being permitted to proceed to the remainder of the course.

    (*c*) A written portfolio of exercises based on the contents of the English language 35
course, which will be of no more than 10,000 words in total;

    (*d*) Six assignments based on the theoretical courses in Globalisation Studies, each of a maximum of 2,000 words;

    (*e*) An extended essay normally of between 4,000 and 5,000 words in length (the limit to include notes) on a topic related to one of the core subjects of study. 40

Assignments under 2(*c*)–2(*e*) will be forwarded to the examiners for consideration by such dates as the examiners shall determine and shall notify candidates.

3. Candidates may also be called for *viva voce* examination.

4. The examiners may award a distinction to candidates for the Advanced Diploma. 45

5. Candidates who fail to satisfy the examiners in 2(*c*)-2(*e*) above of the examination may be permitted to resubmit work in respect of the part or parts of the examination which they have failed for examination on not more than one occasion which shall normally be within one year of the initial failure.

(iii) ADVANCED DIPLOMAS (ONE YEAR PART-TIME)

Biblical and Theological Studies (offered at Regent's Park College)

1. *Course*

(*a*) The course will consist of lectures, tutorials, seminars, and classes, on the subject of Biblical and Theological Studies. Candidates will be required also to undertake supervised pastoral practice and preaching. Candidates will be expected to have completed the Undergraduate Diploma in Biblical and Theological Studies offered by the College (formerly the Undergraduate Certificate in Biblical and Theological Studies) or an equivalent course of study approved by the Board of Studies.

(*b*) The course may be taken on a part-time basis only over a period of at least one year and no more than two years. Candidates shall follow six subjects from the Schedule below.

2. Every candidate will be required to satisfy the examiners in the following:

(*a*) Attendance at the theoretical courses; students must attend a minimum of 75 per cent of the equivalent of 30 two-hour sessions;

(*b*) Three coursework assignments, each of which shall not exceed 3,000 words or equivalent in length, based on the theoretical courses;

(*c*) A dissertation of no more than 10,000 words, on a topic of theological interest to the candidate, the title of which shall be approved by the Course Director;

(*d*) Completion of a placement of a minimum of eighty hours of supervised pastoral practice and preaching.

(*e*) A satisfactory report of the period of supervised pastoral practice and preaching from a candidate's supervisor appointed for this purpose by the Course Director.

Assignments under (*b*) and (*c*) will be forwarded to the examiners for consideration by such dates as the examiners shall determine and shall notify candidates.

3. Candidates may be expected to attend a viva voce examination at the end of the course.

4. The examiners may award a distinction to candidates for the Advanced Diploma.

5. Candidates who fail to satisfy the examiners in the assignments under 2(*b*)-(*c*) may be permitted to resubmit work in respect of part or parts of the examination which they have failed on not more than one occasion which shall normally be within one year of the initial failure.

Schedule

Candidates must complete one group of the three subject groups shown below. Only one subject group is available each year. The definitive list of subjects for one year will be circulated to candidates not later than Friday of the third week of Michaelmas Term of that year. Candidates may not offer for the Advanced Diploma any subject group undertaken as part of the Undergraduate Diploma in Biblical and Theological Studies.

Subject Group A
1. Pastoral theology
2. The Atonement
3. The Reformation
4. 'Romans'
5. Covenant in the Old Testament
6. Ethics

Subject Group B
1. The Sacraments
2. The Church and the Kingdom
3. The Early Church
4. The Psalms
5. Social Context of Theology
6. The Corinthian Letters

Subject Group C
1. Old Testament Prophets
2. Mission
3. Luke and Acts
4. Philosophy
5. Modern Church History
6. God and Revelation

Data and Systems Analysis

1. *Course*

(*a*) The course will comprise four taught units (selected from the list below) and a group project.

(*b*) The course is available on a part-time basis and will normally be taken over a period of one year, and may not be taken over a period of more than two years. The course may either be taken in a distance learning mode or a face-to-face mode.

2. Every candidate will be required to satisfy the examiners in the following:

(*a*) active participation in all parts of the course to the satisfaction of the Course Director;

(*b*) active participation in group discussions under the guidance, and to the satisfaction, of the student's tutor;

(*c*) four assignments of 4,000 words each (or equivalent), based on the units 1–4 below;

(*d*) a group project report of 4,000 words (or equivalent).

Assignments under 2(*c*) and 2(*d*) above will be forwarded to the examiners for consideration by such dates as the examiners shall determine and shall notify candidates.

3. Candidates will be required to achieve an overall pass for the four assignments under 2(*c*) above and the report under 2(*d*) above. All assignments under 2(*c*) and the project report under 2(*d*) carry equal weight.

4. Candidates may be required to attend a viva voce examination at the end of the course.

5. The examiners may award a Distinction to candidates for the Advanced Diploma.

6. Candidates who fail to satisfy the examiners in the requirements under 2(c)–2(d) and 3 may be permitted to resubmit work in respect of the part or parts of the examination which they have failed for examination on not more than one occasion which shall normally be within one year of the examiners' decision to permit the candidate the opportunity to resubmit the work.

Schedule

Unit 1: The System Development Life-cycle and Management
Unit 2: Systems Analysis and Design—Data Driven and Procedural Techniques
Unit 3: Systems Analysis and Design—Data Organisation
Unit 4: Systems Analysis and Design—Objects and Architectures
Unit 5: Group Project

Any other unit (or units), defined by the Course Director and approved by the Board of Studies, may be substituted in place of one of Units 2, 3, or 4 above.

Local History

1. *Course*

The course will comprise two modules:

Module 1 Concepts and Methods for Local History

Module 2 Databases for Historians

The course, which is available on a part-time, distance learning basis only, will normally be taken over a period of one year, and may not be taken over a period of more than two years.

2. Every student will be required to satisfy the examiners in the following:

(a) participation in all parts of the course to the satisfaction of the Course Director;

(b) participation in electronic group discussions under the guidance, and to the satisfaction, of the student's academic tutor;

(c) one assignment of not more than 2,000 words, one assignment of not more than 2,500 words, one assignment of not more than 2,000 words plus supporting tables, and one assignment of not more than 3,000 words, based on the work covered in the Concepts and Methods module (Module 1);

(d) one assignment of not more than 2,500 words, based on the work covered in the Databases module (Module 2);

(e) one assignment of not more than 5,000 words, which will be a Local History project involving the use of a database of historical data.

Assignments under 2(c)–(e) above will be forwarded to the examiners for consideration by such dates as the examiners shall determine and shall notify students.

3. Students will be required to pass all assignments in both modules to be awarded the Advanced Diploma. Students who fail to satisfy the examiners in the assignments under 2(c)–(e) may be permitted to resubmit work which they have failed for examination on not more than one occasion which shall normally be within in one year of the date on which the assignment was first due to be submitted.

4. Students may be required to attend a viva voce examination at the end of the course of studies.

5. The examiners may award a Distinction to candidates for the Advanced Diploma.

POSTGRADUATE DIPLOMA
IN LEGAL PRACTICE

GENERAL REGULATIONS

1. The University of Oxford, jointly with Oxford Brookes University, shall have power to grant Postgraduate Diplomas in Legal Practice to candidates recommended by the Legal Practice Course (LPC) Examination Committee, constituted as prescribed in clause 4 below.

2. The course will be open to all persons who under the Law Society's regulations are qualified to enter the Legal Practice Course. Candidates may be admitted under such conditions as the Oxford Institute of Legal Practice (OILP), a joint venture between the University of Oxford and Oxford Brookes University, shall prescribe. Candidates will not, by virtue of their admission to the course, become members of the University.

3. Any person who has been accepted as a candidate for the Postgraduate Diploma in Legal Practice and who has satisfactorily pursued a course the character and length of which have been approved by the Board of Studies of OILP may be admitted to the examination.

4. The LPC Examination Committee shall comprise:

(*a*) the Director of OILP (convenor);

(*b*) the Course Manager of the LPC;

(*c*) all full-time academic staff of OILP;

(*d*) all other staff responsible for units of the LPC;

(*e*) at least three external examiners approved by the Law Society on the recommendation of the Legal Practice Course Committee;

(*f*) one person nominated by the University of Oxford;

(*g*) one person nominated by Oxford Brookes University;

(*h*) the Chief Training Officer of the Law Society or that officer's nominee.

The Chair of the Examination Committee shall be the Director of OILP or the Director's nominee.

5. The Examination Committee shall:

(*a*) consider each candidate's performance in the examinations, assessed coursework, and skills assessments and make recommendations to the University of Oxford and Oxford Brookes University for the award of the Postgraduate Diploma in Legal Practice, and the two institutions shall have no power to alter such recommendations;

(*b*) consider whether, under the assessment regulations, the performance of any candidate justifies a recommendation for the award of the Postgraduate Diploma with Commendation or Distinction.

6. In the case of a referred or deferred examination or referred or deferred skills assessment, a recommendation for the award of the Postgraduate Diploma in Legal Practice may be made by the Chair of the Examination Committee after approval of the recommendation by the external examiners. A decision either to fail a candidate or to permit a candidate, who has failed a referred or deferred examination or referred or deferred skills assessment, to repeat the entire diet of assessments may be made by the Chair of the Examination Committee after approval of the recommendation by the external examiners.

7. No recommendations under clause 5 (*a*) or (*b*) above may be made by the Examination Committee unless a majority of the external examiners approves the recommendation.

Special Regulations

1. Candidates will be examined in the following compulsory subjects: Litigation and Advocacy; Conveyancing and Wills; Business Law and Practice; Probate and Administration.

2. Candidates will be examined in two options from the following: Commercial Law; Corporate Finance; Commercial Property; Family Law; Housing Law; Planning and Environmental Law.

3. Examination under cll. 1 and 2 will be by written examination (accounting for 75 per cent of the mark) and coursework (accounting for 25 per cent of the mark).

4. The pass mark in the compulsory subjects and the options shall be 50 per cent. A minimum mark of 50 per cent should normally be obtained in both the examination element and each element of the coursework assessment. However a mark of not less than 45 per cent in one element may be compensated by the mark obtained in the other element, provided the overall mark scored in this subject is 50 per cent or more.

5. The coursework element of each compulsory subject shall consist of two pieces of coursework. The coursework element of each option shall consist of one piece of coursework.

6. Candidates will be assessed on their competence in the following pervasives: Introduction to Revenue Law; Professional Conduct; European Community Law; Financial Services Act.

7. Assessment of the pervasives shall be by means of two assessed exercises in each pervasive. Assessment of the pervasives shall be on a competent/non-competent basis.

8. Candidates will be assessed on their competence in the following skills: Writing and Drafting; Negotiation and Advocacy; Interviewing and Advising; Legal Research.

9. Each skill shall be assessed by means of two practical exercises in that skill. The assessment of each exercise shall be on a competent/non competent basis. If the exercise is oral in form, then the assessment shall be undertaken by two members of staff. The oral exercise will be videotaped, and the tape made available to the external examiners.

10. The Legal Practice Course Committee may, exceptionally, exempt a candidate from taking some or all of the skills assessments or may vary the candidate's assessment programme. Medical evidence of a disability which might prevent or distort a skills assessment must be presented to the Legal Practice Course Committee. The agreement of the external examiners must be obtained for an exemption or variation from any skills assessment.

11. In order to be awarded the Postgraduate Diploma in Legal Practice a candidate will normally be required to pass each of the four compulsory subjects, and to pass two of the optional subjects and be judged competent in each skill and in each pervasive subject.

12. A candidate who has satisfied the conditions in cl. 11 above and has achieved an average of 60 per cent or greater over the compulsory subjects and options and a mark of at least 60 per cent in four subjects or more may be recommended for the award of Postgraduate Diploma in Legal Practice with Commendation.

13. A candidate who has satisfied the conditions in cl. 11 above and has achieved an average of 70 per cent or greater over the compulsory subjects and options and a mark of at least 70 per cent in four subjects or more may be recommended for the award of Postgraduate Diploma in Legal Practice with Distinction.

14. A candidate who fails to be judged competent in one skills assessment exercise shall be given one further opportunity to pass another similar exercise in the same skill.

15. The Examination Committee may, exceptionally, on medical grounds condone a finding that a candidate is not competent in one legal skill provided that the candidate is competent in all other skills assessments.

16. A candidate who fails to submit coursework by the required date for submission or who fails to attend or submit any skills assessment other than for reason of illness or some other cause considered reasonable by the Legal Practice Course Committee shall be deemed to have failed that component of the assessment.

17. The Legal Practice Course Committee shall have power to refer a candidate who fails to achieve a mark of 45 per cent or more in one coursework assessment only. The Legal Practice Course Committee shall require resubmission of a similar coursework on such terms as it shall determine. Under such circumstances, the Postgraduate Diploma cannot be awarded the Commendation or Distinction.

18. The Examination Committee may allow a candidate's overall performance to compensate for failure in one compulsory subject or one option, provided that the failure is within the range of 45–49 per cent of the total marks available for that subject and provided that the candidate has achieved a minimum of 55 per cent of the total marks available in at least one other subject.

19. A candidate who fails at the first attempt to satisfy the Examination Committee in one subject or one skill may be allowed to repeat the assessment

component on one further occasion. The referral will normally be in the September following but must be within two years of the meeting of the Examination Committee at which the decision was made.

20. The Examination Committee has discretion to determine the form, conditions, and time of the referral. If a component is assessed by more than one form of assessment and one form has been passed, then the form that has been passed will not be retaken. The maximum mark attainable for a referred subject is 50 per cent. Under such circumstances, the Postgraduate Diploma cannot be awarded with Commendation or Distinction.

21. A candidate who fails at the first attempt to satisfy the Examination Committee in more than one subject or skill may be permitted to repeat the entire diet of assessments (including skills assessments) on one further occasion within two years. Under such circumstances, the Postgraduate Diploma cannot be awarded with Commendation or Distinction.

POSTGRADUATE DIPLOMA IN MANAGEMENT STUDIES

GENERAL REGULATIONS

1. The Executive Committee of the Saïd Business School shall have power to grant Postgraduate Diplomas in Management Studies to candidates who have satisfied the conditions prescribed in this section and any further conditions which the Committee may prescribe by regulation.

2. The examination for the Postgraduate Diploma shall be under the supervision of the Executive Committee of the Saïd Business School which shall have power, subject to the approval of the Social Sciences Divisional Board, to make regulations governing the examination.

3. Candidates, whether members of the University or not, may be admitted as students for the Postgraduate Diploma under such conditions as the committee shall prescribe, provided that before admission to a course of study approved by the Committee, candidates shall have satisfied the committee that they have had appropriate educational experience acceptable to the committee, have relevant industrial or commercial experience and are well-equipped to enter the proposed course of study.

4. Any person who has been accepted as a candidate for the Postgraduate Diploma, and who has satisfactorily pursued the course prescribed by the Committee, may be admitted to the examination.

SPECIAL REGULATIONS

1. Students of the diploma may hold that status for no more than nine terms.

2. The Standing Committee shall appoint an academic supervisor to supervise the work of the candidate. The supervisor shall send a report of the work of the candidate to the board at the end of each period of study. The supervisor will inform the board if it is thought that the student is unlikely to reach the standard required by the diploma.

3. Each student will follow a course of study comprising four core courses and a business project. The four core courses are:

Managing the organisation: Functional and cross-functional management, finance and accounts, information management, operations management, and human resources.

Managing strategically: Corporate strategy, securing competitive advantage, strategic approaches to leadership, investment, product development, and human resources.

Managing change: Managing personnel and organisational change, reward strategies for change, leading change and change through teamwork, change in manufacturing and services.

A fourth core course from a range of options to be notified to candidates at the start of the course.

Each candidate must submit a business project to be undertaken as part of a group assignment on a subject to be approved by their supervisor. Candidates must submit, no later than Friday of the sixth week of the Michaelmas Term in the year after their Part I examination, a report of no more than 6,000 words to their supervisor.

4. The examination will be in three parts:

(*a*) Part I

The examination shall be held after the first two core courses. It shall consist of one written paper covering elements of the first two core courses.

(*b*) Part II

No candidate shall enter the Part II examination unless he or she has already passed Part I. The Part II examination shall consist of one written paper covering elements of the third and fourth core courses.

(*c*) Each candidate will be required to propose, research, and submit a dissertation not exceeding 10,000 words on a topic agreed by the examiners. The dissertation must be submitted to the Chair of Examiners, c/o the Postgraduate Secretary, Saïd Business School, by Friday of the first week of July in the year in which it is intended to finish the course.

5. The examiners shall also consider, as part of the examination, a report on the candidate's business project submitted by his or her supervisor.

6. The examiners, of whom two shall be appointed, shall have a duty to examine the student in accordance with any regulations prescribed by regulation and to submit a written report to the Graduate Studies Committee of the Saïd Business School which shall decide whether the diploma should be awarded.

7. Candidates may also be required to attend a viva voce examination.

8. The examiners may award a distinction to candidates for the diploma.

9. Candidates who fail an examination may be re-examined on not more than one occasion which normally shall be within one year of their initial failure.

POSTGRADUATE DIPLOMA IN INTELLECTUAL PROPERTY LAW AND PRACTICE

GENERAL REGULATIONS

1. The Board of the Law Faculty shall have the power to grant Postgraduate Diplomas in Intellectual Property Law and Practice to candidates who have satisfied the conditions prescribed in this section and any further conditions which the Board may prescribe by regulation.

2. The examination for the Postgraduate Diploma shall be under the supervision of the Board of the Law Faculty which shall have power, subject to the approval of the Divisional Board, to make regulations governing the examination.

3. Persons may be admitted to read for the Postgraduate Diploma under such conditions as the Board shall prescribe, provided that before admission candidates shall have satisfied the Board that they have appropriate educational experience acceptable to the Board, and are well equipped to enter the proposed course of study.

4. Any person who has been accepted as a candidate for the Postgraduate Diploma, and who has satisfactorily pursued the course prescribed by the Board, may be entered for the examination.

SPECIAL REGULATIONS

1. Each candidate will follow a course of study comprising a two-week residential programme in Intellectual Property Law and Practice and five Legal Practice workshops in the area of Intellectual Property.

2. The examination will be in two parts:

(*a*) *Part I*

Each candidate will be required to complete and submit five written coursework assignments of at least 3,000 words each in response to questions set by the examiners. Those coursework assignments must be submitted to the Chair of Examiners for the Diploma in Intellectual Property Law and Practice, Examination Schools, High Street, Oxford, OX1 4BG, on the date stipulated in the year in which the written examination is taken. The submission date will be published in the course handbook before the first Monday on the first term in which students commence the course.

(*b*) *Part II*

The Part II examination shall consist of two written papers covering elements of the courses covered in the residential programme.

3. The examiners may award a distinction to candidates for the Diploma.

4. Candidates who fail an examination may be re-examined on not more than one occasion which shall normally be within one year of their initial failure.

POSTGRADUATE CERTIFICATE IN MANAGEMENT STUDIES

GENERAL REGULATIONS

1. The Academic Policy Committee of the Saïd Business School shall have the power to grant Postgraduate Certificates in Management Studies to candidates who have satisfied the conditions prescribed in this section and any further conditions which the Committee may prescribe by regulation.

2. The examination for the Postgraduate Certificate in Management Studies shall be under the supervision of the Academic Policy Committee of the Saïd Business School which shall have the power, subject to the approval of the Social Sciences Divisional Board, to make regulations governing the examination.

3. Candidates may be admitted as students for the Postgraduate Certificate of Management Studies under such conditions as the committee shall prescribe, providing that before admission, candidates shall have satisfied the committee that they have appropriate educational experience acceptable to the committee, have relevant professional experience, and are well equipped to enter the proposed course of study.

4. Any person who has been accepted as a candidate for the postgraduate certificate, and who has satisfactorily pursued the course prescribed by the committee, may be admitted to the examination.

5. Every person who has been accepted as a candidate for the postgraduate certificate shall be laced by the committee under the supervision of a member of the University or other competent person selected by the committee. It shall be the duty of the supervisor to direct and superintend the work of the candidate and to submit a report to the examiners on the candidate's work.

SPECIAL REGULATIONS

1. Candidates of the postgraduate certificate may hold that status for no more than three terms.

2. Candidates are only eligible to be admitted to the Postgraduate Certificate of Management Studies if they have first satisfactorily completed a programme of study approved for this purpose by the Executive Committee of the Saïd Business School.

3. Every candidate for the postgraduate certificate shall pursue a course of study approved by the Academic Policy Committee of the Saïd Business School.

4. Every candidate will be required to satisfy the examiners in the following:

(*a*) An extended project of no more than 20,000 words on a subject falling within any field of Management Studies to be agreed by the Programme Director. Three typewritten/word-processed copies of the project must be submitted to the Chair of Examiners c/o Examinations Office, Said Business School, Park End Street, Oxford, not later than 12 noon on the first Friday of September. The project must be accompanied by a statement by the candidate indicating that it is the candidate's own work;

(*b*) A report by the supervisor on the candidate's work;

(*c*) A viva voce examination.

5. Candidates who fail to satisfy the examiners may re-submit their project on not more than one occasion which shall normally be within six months of the initial failure.

6. (*a*) If for good cause a student is temporarily unable to carry out his or her coursework, the Executive Committee may grant him or her temporary suspension of status for a minimum of one term and a maximum of three terms. Applications for suspension of status should be made to the Diploma and Accredited Programmes Committee c/o the relevant Graduate Studies Assistant and should be accompanied by a statement of support from the student's supervisor.

(*b*) The Academic Policy Committee may for sufficient reason, and after consultation with the student's supervisor, temporarily suspend him or her from the Register on its own initiative.

POSTGRADUATE DIPLOMA IN FINANCIAL STRATEGY (PART-TIME)

GENERAL REGULATIONS

1. The Executive Committee of the Saïd Business School shall have the power to grant Postgraduate Diplomas in Financial Strategy to candidates who have satisfied the conditions prescribed in this section and any further conditions which the Committee may prescribe by regulation.

2. The examination for the Postgraduate Diploma shall be under the supervision of the Executive Committee of the Saïd Business School which shall have power, subject to the approval of the Social Sciences Divisional Board, to make regulations governing the examination.

3. Candidates may be admitted as students for the Postgraduate Diploma under such conditions as the Committee shall prescribe, provided that before admission candidates shall have satisfied the Committee that they have appropriate educational experience acceptable to the Committee, have relevant professional experience, and are well equipped to enter the proposed course of study.

4. Any person who has been accepted as a candidate for the Postgraduate Diploma, and who has satisfactorily pursued the course prescribed by the Committee, may be admitted to the examination.

SPECIAL REGULATIONS

1. Candidates must follow a course of instruction in Financial Strategy for at least twelve months and not more than fourteen months. Candidates must complete:

(*a*) Four core courses, and satisfy the examiners in the assessment associated with each course. The four core courses are:

Strategy;

Finance I;

Finance II;

Corporate Valuation.

Details can be found in the course handbook.

(*b*) Courses may be assessed by one or more of the following: written examinations, individual assignments, and group assignments, subject to the constraint that at least 50 per cent of marks in any course must be assigned to individual work.

(*c*) A project report not exceeding 10,000 words on a topic agreed by the examiners. Three typewritten/wordprocessed copies of the project report must be submitted to the Chair of Examiners for the Postgraduate Diploma in Financial Strategy, c/o Saïd Business School, Park End Street, Oxford, not later than 12 noon *on the date stipulated in the year in which the written examination is taken. The submission date will be published by the Course Director before the first Monday of the first term in which students commence the course.* All material submitted for the project report shall be accompanied by a statement signed by the candidate indicating that it is the candidate's own work.

2. Candidates may be examined viva voce on any assessment, the project report, or both.

3. The examiners may award a distinction for excellence in the whole examination.

4. Candidates who fail an assessment may be re-examined on not more than one occasion which normally shall be within one year of their initial failure.

POSTGRADUATE DIPLOMA
IN STRATEGY AND INNOVATION
(PART-TIME)

*For candidates admitted after 1 October 2009; candidates
admitted before this date will be examined according to the
regulations in the* Examination Regulations *2008*

GENERAL REGULATIONS

1. The Executive Committee of the Saïd Business School shall
have the power to grant Postgraduate Diplomas in Strategy and
Innovation to candidates who have satisfied the conditions prescribed in this section and any further conditions which the
Committee may prescribe by regulation.

2. The examination for the Postgraduate Diploma shall be under
the supervision of the Executive Committee of the Saïd Business
School which shall have power, subject to the approval of the Social
Sciences Divisional Board, to make regulations governing the
examination.

3. Candidates may be admitted as students for the Postgraduate
Diploma under such conditions as the Committee shall prescribe,
provided that before admission candidates shall have satisfied the
Committee that they have appropriate educational experience
acceptable to the Committee, have relevant professional experience,
and are well equipped to enter the proposed course of study.

4. Any person who has been accepted as a candidate for
the Postgraduate Diploma, and who has satisfactorily pursued the
course prescribed by the Committee, may be admitted to the
examination.

SPECIAL REGULATIONS

1. Candidates must follow a course of instruction in Strategy and Innovation
either for at least twelve months and not more than fourteen months, or for at
least twenty-four months and not more than twenty-six months. Candidates must
complete:

(*a*) four courses, and satisfy the examiners in the assessment associated with each
course. The four courses are:
Strategy
Innovation Strategy
Globalisation and Strategy
Strategy in Action

(*b*) Courses may be assessed by one or more of the following: written examinations, individual assignments, and group assignments, subject to the constraint that at least 50 per cent of marks in any course must be assigned to individual work.

(*c*) a project report not exceeding 10,000 words on a topic agreed by the examiners. Three typewritten/word processed copies of the project report must be submitted to the Chair of Examiners for the Postgraduate Diploma in Strategy and Innovation, c/o Saïd Business School, Park End Street, Oxford, not later than 12 noon on the date stipulated in the year in which the written examination is taken. The submission date will be published by the Course Director before the first Monday of the first term in which students commence the course. All material submitted for the project report shall be accompanied by a statement signed by the candidate indicating that it is the candidate's own work.

2. Candidates may be examined viva voce on one or more of the written examinations, assignments, and the project report.

3. The examiners may award a distinction for excellence in the whole examination.

4. Candidates who fail an examination may be re-examined on not more than one occasion which shall normally be within one year of their initial failure.

POSTGRADUATE DIPLOMA
IN ORGANISATIONAL LEADERSHIP
(PART-TIME)

GENERAL REGULATIONS

1. The Executive Committee of the Saïd Business School shall have the power to grant Postgraduate Diplomas in Organisational Leadership to candidates who have satisfied the conditions prescribed in this section and any further conditions which the Committee may prescribe by regulation.

2. The examination for the Postgraduate Diploma shall be under the supervision of the Executive Committee of the Saïd Business School which shall have power, subject to the approval of the Divisional Board, to make regulations governing the examination.

3. Candidates may be admitted as students for the Postgraduate Diploma under such conditions as the Committee shall prescribe, provided that before admission candidates shall have satisfied the Committee that they have appropriate educational experience acceptable to the Committee, have relevant professional experience, and are well equipped to enter the proposed course of study.

4. Any person who has been accepted as a candidate for the Postgraduate Diploma, and who has satisfactorily pursued the course prescribed by the Committee, may be admitted to the examination.

SPECIAL REGULATIONS

1. Candidates must follow a course of instruction in Organisational Leadership for at least twelve months and not more than fourteen months. Candidates must complete:
   (*a*) Four courses, and satisfy the examiners in the assessment associated with each course. The four courses are:
   Understanding Management Success;
   The Strategic Mindset;
   Meeting the Organisational Challenge;
   The Strategic Leader.
   Details can be found in the course handbook.
   (*b*) Courses may be assessed by one or more of the following: written examinations, individual assignments, and group assignments, subject to the constraint that at least 50 per cent of marks in any course must be assigned to individual work.

(*c*) A project report not exceeding 10,000 words on a topic agreed by the examiners. Three typewritten/wordprocessed copies of the project report must be submitted to the Chair of Examiners for the Postgraduate Diploma in Organisational Leadership, c/o Saïd Business School, Park End Street, Oxford, not later than 12 noon *on the date stipulated in the year in which the written examination is taken. The submission date will be published by the Course Director before the first Monday of the first term in which students commence the course.* All material submitted for the project report shall be accompanied by a statement signed by the candidate indicating that it is the candidate's own work.

2. Candidates may be examined viva voce on any assessment, the project report, or both.

3. The examiners may award a distinction for excellence in the whole examination.

4. Candidates who fail an assessment may be re-examined on not more than one occasion which normally shall be within one year of their initial failure.

POSTGRADUATE DIPLOMA IN GLOBAL BUSINESS (PART-TIME)

GENERAL REGULATIONS

1. The Executive Committee of the Saïd Business School shall have the power to grant Postgraduate Diplomas in Global Business to candidates who have satisfied the conditions prescribed in this section and any further conditions which the committee may prescribe by regulation.

2. The examination for the Postgraduate Diploma shall be under the supervision of the Executive Committee of the Saïd Business School which shall have power, subject to the approval of the Divisional Board, to make regulations governing the examination.

3. Candidates may be admitted as students for the Postgraduate Diploma under such conditions as the committee shall prescribe, provided that before admission candidates shall have satisfied the committee that they have appropriate educational experience acceptable to the committee, have relevant professional experience, and are well equipped to enter the proposed course of study.

4. Any person who has been accepted as a candidate for the Postgraduate Diploma, and who has satisfactorily pursued the course prescribed by the committee, may be admitted to the examination.

SPECIAL REGULATIONS

1. Candidates must follow for at least twelve months and not more than fourteen months a course of instruction in Global Business. Candidates must complete:
    (*a*) Four courses, and satisfy the examiners in the assessment associated with each course. The four courses are:
    Global Strategy
    Risk and Reputation
    Corporate Diplomacy in a Global Context
    The Challenges of Business in Emerging Markets
    Details can be found in the course handbook.
    (*b*) Courses may be assessed by one or more of the following: written examinations, individual assignments, and group assignments, subject to the constraint that at least 50 per cent of marks in any course must be assigned to individual work.
    (*c*) A project report not exceeding 10,000 words on a topic agreed by the examiners. Three typewritten/word-processed copies of the project report must be submitted to the Chair of Examiners for the Postgraduate Diploma in Global Business, c/o Saïd Business School, Park End Street, Oxford, not later than 12 noon *on the date stipulated in the year in which the written examination is taken.*

The submission date will be published by the Course Director before the first Monday of the first term in which students commence the course. All material submitted for the project report shall be accompanied by a statement signed by the candidate indicating that it is the candidate's own work.

2. Candidates may be examined viva voce on any assessment, the project report, or both.

3. The examiners may award a distinction for excellence in the whole examination.

4. Candidates who fail an assessment may be re-examined on not more than one occasion which normally shall be within one year of their initial failure.

CERTIFICATE IN THEOLOGY
CERTIFICATE FOR THEOLOGY
GRADUATES

GENERAL REGULATIONS

1. The Board of the Faculty of Theology and Religion shall have power to grant the following certificates to candidates who have satisfied the conditions prescribed in this section and any further conditions which the board may prescribe by regulation:

Certificate in Theology;

Certificate for Theology Graduates.

2. The examinations for the above mentioned certificates shall be under the supervision of the Board of the Faculty of Theology and Religion.

3. Candidates, both members of the University and others, who have been admitted, under such conditions as the Board of the Faculty of Theology and Religion shall prescribe, to courses at Campion Hall, Mansfield College, Regent's Park College, St. Benet's Hall, Blackfriars, Ripon College Cuddesdon, St. Stephen's House, Wycliffe Hall, and Harris Manchester College may be admitted by the board to the examinations for the above mentioned certificates, provided that they have paid to the Curators of the University Chest, through their colleges or other institutions, the fee or fees prescribed in the appropriate regulation (see Appendix I).

4. The supervision of the arrangements for the above mentioned certificates shall be the responsibility of the Supervisory Committee for the Degree of Bachelor of Theology and the Theology Certificates. The committee shall have such powers and duties in respect of the above mentioned certificates as may from time to time be prescribed by the Board of the Faculty of Theology and Religion.

5. Part-time students for the above mentioned certificates shall in each case be required to pursue their course of study for twice the number of terms required of an equivalent full-time student.

6. On successful completion of part I or of the entire course, candidates for the Certificate in Theology may, with the approval of the Supervisory Committee, offer the remaining papers necessary to meet the requirements for the award of the Bachelor of Theology.

SPECIAL REGULATIONS

A. THE CERTIFICATE IN THEOLOGY

A. 1. *Admission requirements*

Candidates will normally be expected to have five GCSE passes, one of which must be in English Language and two of which must be at Advanced Level. Exemptions from this requirement for mature student candidates or those otherwise qualified may be made at the discretion of the Supervisory Committee.

A. 2. *Course requirements*

The length of the course is two years. A minimum of eight papers must be taken from the syllabus as outlined for the Bachelor of Theology. In Part 1 candidates must take all four papers. In Part 2 they must take one paper each from sections B, C, and D. The Supervisory Committee may dispense a candidate from individual compulsory papers on the basis of previous academic work, but not from the total number of papers required.

B. THE CERTIFICATE FOR THEOLOGY GRADUATES

B. 1. *Admission requirements*

Candidates for the Certificate for Theology Graduates must have obtained an Honours or Joint Honours Degree in Theology. Candidates for the one-year course must have obtained at least second class honours. Candidates for the one-year course who have not taken the Honour School of Theology in Oxford must apply to the Supervisory Committee.

B. 2. *Course requirements*

One-year candidates must take at least four papers. Two-year candidates must take at least eight papers. There are no compulsory papers. All papers will be examined at the same level. Each paper will be examined by an essay of 7,000 words, except that:

(*a*) candidates may integrate two papers in a single essay of 12,000 words (which will still count as two papers);

(*b*) one-year candidates may substitute a written examination in one paper, and two-year candidates in up to three papers, except for paper D.1;

(*c*) candidates may take papers additional to the minimum requirement by written examination, except for paper D.1.

C. REGULATIONS OF GENERAL APPLICATION

C. 1. *Registration and fees*

Not later than the end of the second week of Michaelmas Term, colleges shall forward the names of non-members of the University who wish to be registered as candidates for either of the two certificates, together with the registration fee prescribed (see Appendix I) in accordance with the appropriate regulation. No registration fee is payable for matriculated members of the University, but colleges shall, by the stated time, notify the Registrar of all such students commencing certificate courses.

C. 2. *Examination*

Further provisions governing the examination for the Certificates in Theology are given in the regulations for the Bachelor of Theology.

FOUNDATION CERTIFICATES

GENERAL REGULATIONS

1. The Continuing Education Board shall have power to grant Foundation Certificates to candidates who have satisfied the conditions prescribed in this section and any further conditions which the Committee may prescribe by regulation.

2. The examination for each certificate shall be under the supervision of the Continuing Education Board which shall have the power subject to the approval of the Education Committee, to make regulations governing the examination.

3. The Director of the Department for Continuing Education shall keep a register of attendance of students for the Certificate. No student shall be granted leave to take the examination unless the register shows satisfactory attendance by him or her.

4. Candidates, whether members of the University or not, may be admitted as students for the Certificate under such conditions as the Continuing Education Board shall prescribe provided that, before admission to the course, candidates have satisfied the Committee that they are well qualified to enter the proposed course of study.

5. Examination for the certificate shall be by written examination, by coursework essays, and (if the examiners think fit) by oral examination, under such conditions as the Continuing Education Board may by regulation prescribe.

SPECIAL REGULATIONS

English Literature *(for candidates admitted from October 2011)*

1. The course which is available on a part-time basis only, may be taken over a period of two, and no more than four years.

2. The examination will consist of:

    I. Six papers, of which there will be two on each of the topics set out below. Each paper will be of two hours, with an additional fifteen minutes allowed as reading time in respect of each of the two papers in (*c*) below. One of the two papers on each of these topics shall be taken during the third term of study:

        (*a*) Early Modern Literature;

        (*b*) Victorian and Modern Literature;

        (*c*) Criticism: History, Theory, and Practice.

II. Eleven coursework essays, of not more than 2,000 words in length. Essays must be the candidate's own work and every candidate must submit a statement to that effect. The coursework essays will be forwarded to the examiners for consideration by such dates as the examiners shall determine and shall notify candidates.

III. Candidates may, at the discretion of the examiners, be required to attend a *viva voce* examination at the end of the course of study.

3. The examiners may award a distinction to candidates for the Certificate.

4. Candidates who fail to satisfy the examiners in the assessed work specified in clause 2 may be permitted to resubmit work in respect of the part or parts of the examination which they have failed on not more than one occasion which shall normally be within one year of the initial failure.

History

1. The course which is available on a part-time basis only, may be taken over a period of two, and no more than four years.

2. The examination will consist of:

  (i) Four papers as set out below, each of three hours' duration.

   (*a*) Two papers on British History, 1485–1603 and 1900–1979.

   (*b*) One paper on European History, 1815–1914.

   (*c*) One optional paper (source-based) to be chosen from a list to be published annually before the end of the last week of Trinity Term.

  (ii) Nine coursework essays, each of up to 2,000 words in length.

  (iii) One extended essay of up to 4,000 words on a candidate's optional subject.

  (iv) Candidates may be required to attend a viva voce examination at the end of the course of studies at the discretion of the examiners.

The coursework essays in 2 (ii) and the extended essay in 2 (iii) will be forwarded to the examiners for consideration by such dates as the examiners shall determine and shall notify the candidates. Essays must be the candidate's own work and every candidate must submit a statement to that effect.

3. The examiners may award a distinction to candidates for the Certificate.

4. Candidates who fail to satisfy the examiners in the assessed work specified in clause 2 may be permitted to resubmit work in respect of the part or parts of the examination which they have failed on not more than one occasion which shall normally be within one year of the initial failure.

DEGREE OF DOCTOR OF CLINICAL PSYCHOLOGY

GENERAL REGULATIONS

1. The Medical Sciences Board shall have power to admit as Students for the Degree of Doctor of Clinical Psychology candidates nominated by the Directorate of the Oxford Doctoral Course in Clinical Psychology.

2. The Directorate of the Oxford Doctoral Course shall make a return to the Registrar by the end of the first week of Michaelmas Full Term, showing the names of all persons nominated in that term as Students for the Degree of Doctor of Clinical Psychology, and the Registrar shall keep a register of such students.

3. The Medical Sciences Board shall have power, on the advice of the Directorate of the Oxford Doctoral Course, to remove temporarily or permanently the name of a student from the register. This power shall include cases where students have been found under the procedures of the course and the Oxford Health NHS Foundation Trust guilty of gross misconduct or in breach of the British Psychological Society's Code of Ethics and Conduct.

4. Students shall be admitted to the doctoral programme for a probationary period. The external examiner shall conduct a formal mid-course review during the second half of the second year of the course (i.e. between eighteen and twenty-four months after the commencement of the course). Candidates shall be required to complete successfully all elements of the work required before they are permitted to progress onto the second part of the course.

5. Subject to the provisions of clauses 3 and 4 above, students for the Degree of Doctor of Clinical Psychology may hold that status for a maximum of five years.

6. An appeal against a decision of the Board of Examiners for the Doctorate in Clinical Psychology may be made only through the University's procedures and those laid down in the course handbook. No procedures arising from a candidate's status as employee or former employee of the Oxford Health NHS Foundation Trust may affect a decision of the examiners.

7. The Proctors shall be responsible for overseeing the proper conduct of the examinations for the Degree in Clinical Psychology.

The Proctors shall have power to investigate any complaint or appeal concerning the conduct of the examination and to impose upon any candidate for the examination any penalty equivalent to that which they would be empowered to impose upon a member of the University in similar circumstances.

8. Should any Students for the Degree of Doctor of Clinical Psychology have access to University services and facilities, they will be required to observe the appropriate statutes, decrees, regulations, and/or rules governing the use of such services and facilities. The Proctors shall have power to investigate any alleged breaches of those statutes, decrees, regulations, and/or rules and to deal with the matter and impose any penalty equivalent to that which they would have been empowered to impose upon a member of the University in similar circumstances.

Special Regulations

1. Candidates shall follow a course of training in Clinical Psychology for a period of at least three years. The training shall consist of Clinical, Academic, and Research elements, and candidates will be required to demonstrate their competence in all three elements. The precise periods of training, and the amount of time to be spent on each element, will be notified to candidates by the Course Director prior to the commencement of the course.

2. Candidates shall be examined in all of the following ways:

(*a*) Clinical Activity

Each candidate shall develop competence in five or six supervised clinical areas normally including the following:

(i) Adult; (ii) Child; (iii) Disabilities; (iv) Older People; (v) Specialist (to be chosen by the candidate in consultation with the course tutors, subject to the availability of appropriate supervision. Final year candidates will normally either develop competence in one (twelve month) or two (six month) elective areas).

Candidates shall submit to the Board of Examiners a report on five of the above clinical areas. Normally, at least one report will concern clinical work which is other than individually based. Each report shall consist of not more than 6,000 words including tables and diagrams but excluding references and appendices. Candidates shall also submit to the Clinical Tutor a notebook (Log Book) for each clinical area. The candidate's supervisor in each clinical area shall complete, in consultation with the Clinical Tutor, an Evaluation of Clinical Competence (ECC). The Reports and ECC Forms shall be assessed as part of the examination. The notebooks shall be available to the examiners.

(*b*) Academic Activity

Candidates shall be required to follow a programme of study, as prescribed by the Director of the Course, normally in each of the following areas:

(i) Adult mental health; (ii) Children; (iii) Disabilities; (iv) Older People; (v) Specialist teaching.

Candidates are required to submit an extended essay in three of these areas. The essay shall not exceed 5,000 words including tables and diagrams but excluding references, and shall be on a subject approved in advance by the Course Directorate. One essay will take the form of a Critical Review.

(*c*) Research Activity

Candidates shall offer the following:

    (i) One service-related project of approximately 4,500 words in length including tables and diagrams but excluding references and appendices. The project shall normally be carried out within a clinical context within the first two years of training and shall be of direct relevance to the clinical work.

    (ii) A research dissertation of between 15,000 and 25,000 words, including tables, diagrams, references and appendices. The Research Dissertation shall consist of a research report of a significant and substantial investigation with human participants and shall be of clinical relevance. The subject of the Research Dissertation must be approved in advance by the Course Directorate. All candidates will be examined on the Dissertation viva voce.

3. Candidates shall be required to satisfy examiners in each of the assessment units described in clause 2 above.

4. Guidelines on the preparation and submission of all written work will be updated annually as required and will be included in the Course Handbook.

5. Deadlines for the submission of all assessed work (i.e. essay titles, essays, service-related projects, integrated clinical reports, critical reviews, dissertation proposals and dissertations) will be published annually by the Directorate in the 'Annual Course Syllabus Book' at the start of the academic year. They will also be lodged with the Proctors, and posted in the Course Office.

6. All material submitted for examination must be sent to the Chair of Examiners of the Doctorate in Clinical Psychology, c/o the Course Manager, Isis Education Centre, Warneford Hospital, Headington, Oxford. It shall be accompanied by a certificate signed by the candidate indicating that it is the candidate's own work, except where otherwise specified. In the case of the integrated clinical report, service-related project, and dissertation, this must be supported by a signed statement from the candidate's supervisor indicating that the material submitted is the candidate's own work. These certificates must be submitted separately in a sealed envelope addressed to the Chair of Examiners for the Doctorate in Clinical Psychology.

NOTES

26

RECOGNIZED STUDENTS

1. There shall be a Register of Recognized Students who are not members of the University.

2. The Board of a faculty or divisional board may place the name of any applicant on the Register of Recognized Students:

Provided that the applicant:

(*a*) is not a member of the University,

(*b*) possesses the qualifications required from candidates for admission to the status of Senior Student except that persons not so qualified may in exceptional cases be admitted,

(*c*) is placed under an academic adviser appointed by the board. It shall be the duty of the academic adviser to advise on the work of the student but not to give systematic instruction. He or she shall submit a report on the progress of the student to the Board at the end of each term.

3. Application for admission as a Recognized Student shall be made to the Registrar for submission to the appropriate faculty board and shall be accompanied by

(*a*) evidence of the degrees previously obtained by the applicant,

(*b*) a statement of the proposed subject of study,

(*c*) a certificate from a professor or head of a department of the University of Oxford supporting the application.

4. If an applicant for admission as a Recognized Student shall propose a subject of study which is outside the scope of the board of any faculty or divisional board but which may in the opinion of the Education Committee be profitably studied at Oxford, that committee may, on the recommendation of a delegacy or committee constituted under the provisions of the appropriate regulation, deal with his or her case as if it were the board of a faculty.

5. For each term for which his or her name is on the Register, every Recognized Student shall pay to the Curators of the University Chest, within fourteen days from the beginning of Full Term (or from the date of the decision to place his or her name on the Register, in the case of a decision taken during Full Term and

applying to that term), a fee at the annual rate specified in the appropriate regulation.

6. A Recognized Student shall cease to hold that status

(a) if he or she shall have failed to pay the fees required under clause 5,

(b) if his or her name shall have been removed from the Register by the faculty or divisional board concerned.

7. Every Recognized Student shall be entitled

(i) to use the University Libraries subject to the provision of the statutes governing particular Libraries,

(ii) to attend lectures advertised in the lists of boards of faculties and other bodies:

Provided that attendance

(a) at lectures described as seminars or classes or informal instruction shall be subject to the permission of the holder,

(b) at lectures given in any college building shall be subject to the right of the college concerned to refuse admission.

(iii) to work in any University department or institution subject to the agreement of the head of that department or institution.

8. No Recognized Student shall have his or her name on the Register of Recognized Students for more than three terms.

9. A faculty or divisional board shall have power to remove from the Register the name of any Recognized Student which it has placed on the Register.

27

VISITING STUDENTS

1. There shall be a Register of Visiting Students who are members of a college or other society but who are not members of the University. Council may determine from time to time conditions for admission to the Register and the maximum numbers of the members of each college or other society who may be admitted as Visiting Students in any one year.

2. Application for admission as a Visiting Student shall be made to the Registrar through the candidate's society within fourteen days after the society has admitted the candidate. The application shall provide such particulars as Council shall from time to time specify, and shall include an undertaking by the candidate, in terms approved from time to time by Council, (i) as to conduct and (ii) as to payment when due of the fees payable to the University while holding the status of Visiting Student.

3. For each term in which his or her name is on the Register, every Visiting Student shall pay:

    (*a*) to his or her college or other society for transmission to the Curators of the University Chest, within fourteen days from the beginning of Full Term (or, in the term of admission, within fourteen days from the day on which his or her name was entered on the Register), a fee at the annual rate specified in the appropriate regulation .

4. A Visiting Student shall cease to hold that status (i) after three terms, or (ii) forthwith if:

    (*a*) he or she shall have failed to pay the fees required under cl. 3;

    (*b*) he or she ceases to be a member of a college or other society;

    (*c*) he or she is matriculated, or his or her name is placed on the Register of Diploma Students or the Register of Recognized Students; or

    (*d*) in accordance with the prescribed procedure, he or she is found to have committed a breach of his or her undertaking as to conduct and it is held that his or her status is to cease as a consequence.

5. Every Visiting Student shall be entitled:

(*a*) to use the university libraries subject to the provisions of the statutes or decrees governing particular libraries, and to the general regulations and rules of the libraries concerned.

(*b*) to attend lectures advertised in the lists of boards of faculties and other bodies, provided that:

(i) attendance at lectures described as seminars or classes or informal instruction shall be subject to the permission of the holder, and

(ii) attendance at lectures given in any college building shall be subject to the right of the college concerned to refuse admission.

6. A Visiting Student may be permitted to work, and receive teaching or supervision, in any university laboratory, subject to prior arrangement agreed between his or her society and the head of department, and subject to such conditions as may be determined, by the head of department in accordance with arrangements approved from time to time by Council.

7. No Visiting Student shall be eligible to be a candidate for any examination, or scholarship, prize, or other award of the University.

APPENDIX I

REGULATIONS ON FINANCIAL MATTERS

Section I. Fees and Dues payable to the University

§1. *Fees payable by candidates on registration, entry for an examination, application* 5
for leave to supplicate, or resubmission of a thesis for certain degrees

   (*a*) On admission to the Status of Student for the Degree of DM and
      for each subsequent year that the name of the student remains on the
      register of students for the degree   £336

   (*b*) On entering for certain university examinations: 10
      Certificates in Theology   £62
      Certificate and Diploma in Theological and Pastoral Studies   £62
      Degree of B.Mus   £284
      Degree of M.Ch.,   £119

   (*c*) On re-entering the university examination for[1]:   15
      Degrees of B.Phil., M.Phil., M.Th., M.Sc. (by Coursework), M.St.,
      MBA, MFA, MPP and any diploma or certificate (other than those
      listed under §5 cl. 3(a)(xi) (a)-(i)):   £150

   (*d*) On applying for leave to supplicate:
      for the degree of M.Ch.,   £449   20
      for the degree of DM   £473
      for the degrees of DD, DCL, D.Litt, D.Sc., and D.Mus.   £710

   (*e*) On resubmission of a thesis for the degree of M.Litt., M.Sc.
      (by Research), D.Phil., or EngD, or on reinstatement on the
      Register of Students for the degree of M.Litt., M.Sc. (by Research),   25
      D.Phil., or EngD   £215

   (*f*) On resubmission for the degree of DM   £473

§2. *Fee payable by candidates on registration for courses validated by the University*
For the Degree of Doctor of Clinical Psychology   £1,568

§3. *Fees payable in respect of degrees*   30
   1. Every person shall pay £10 on supplicating for admission to the degree of MA,
provided that:

---

[1] The fee is payable only if required by §5, cl. 3, below.

(i) no fee shall be payable by any person on whom a degree has been conferred by special resolution or who incorporates in virtue of having obtained an educational position in the University;

(ii) no fee shall be payable by a Master of Surgery on supplicating for admission to the Degree of Master of Arts.

2. The following fees shall be paid by every person:

(*a*) accumulating the Degrees of Bachelor and Doctor of Civil Law   £44

§4. *In respect of certificates, transcripts and personal data*

1. Every person shall pay the fee prescribed below in each case for certificates issued, on request, to Degree Conferrals Office, Examination Schools, Oxford OX1 4BG:

(*a*) for the first certificate attesting admission to any degree, which shall include a statement of the class obtained: no charge

(*b*) for each replacement certificate attesting admission to any degree (the request must be accompanied by a written statement declaring the original lost, stolen or damaged):   £30

2. Every person shall pay the fee prescribed below in each case for transcripts issued, online or by request to University of Oxford, c/o Examination Schools, High Street, Oxford OX1 4BG:

(*a*) for the first transcript provided upon successful completion: no charge

(*b*) for each transcript provided during the course and any subsequent transcripts upon completion: £5

3. Every person making a request to be supplied with personal data under Section 7 of the Data Protection Act 1998 shall pay the fee determined from time to time by Council.[2]

§5. *Composition fees payable by members of the University*

1. Every member of the University shall pay a composition fee as specified in cl. 14 below for each academic year in which he or she is working in Oxford:

(i) For the Degree of BA or the Degree of M.Biochem. or the Degree of M.Chem. or the Degree of M.Math.Comp.Sci. or the Degree of M.Earth Sc. or the Degree of M.Eng. or the Degree of M.Math. or the Degree of M.Comp.Sci. or the Degree of M.Comp.Phil. or the Degree of M.Phys. or the Degree of M.Phys.Phil. or the Degree of M.Math.Phil. (Those working for an honour school requiring the study of one or more languages for an academic year outside Oxford or for Law with Law Studies in Europe, or for an honour school requiring a period of study shorter than a year outside Oxford, or for Part II in Chemistry or Metallurgy and Science of Materials or Molecular and Cellular Biochemistry, or for Part II in the Honour Schools of Engineering Science or Engineering, Economics, and Management or Materials, Economics, and Management, shall be deemed for all the purposes of this clause to be working in Oxford for the degree of BA or the Degree of M.Biochem. or the Degree of M.Chem. or the Degree of M.Eng., whether or not their work is being undertaken in Oxford);

---

[2] Such requests should be addressed to the Data Protection Officer, University Offices, Wellington Square, Oxford OX1 2JD, from whom details of the current fee can be obtained. The fee is subject to a maximum prescribed from time to time by the Home Secretary under the Act.

   (ii) for the Degree of BFA;

   (iii) for the Degree of BCL or Magister Juris;

   (iv) for a second Final Honour School;

   (v) for the First Examination for the Degree of BM;

   (vi) for the Diploma in Theology;

   (vii) for the Diploma in Legal Studies;

  (viii) for the Certificate in Diplomatic Studies;

   (ix) for the Postgraduate Diploma in Diplomatic Studies;

   (x) for the Postgraduate Diploma in Education; or

   (xi) for the Postgraduate Certificate in Education (those working for the certificate shall be deemed for all the purposes of this clause to be working in Oxford, whether or not their work is being undertaken in Oxford).

The fee shall be paid as follows:

(*a*) in the case of those whose fees are paid under the terms of the Education (Student Support) Regulations (or under corresponding arrangements approved by the Scottish Executive, Northern Ireland Assembly, Welsh Assembly or the States Assembly of Jersey, States Assembly of Guernsey or Isle of Man Government) the fees shall be paid in accordance with the arrangements laid down in those regulations;

(*b*) in all other cases, the fee shall be collected in accordance with the provisions of cl. 13 below;

On application by their society, and subject to the approval of Council's Education Committee, some part of the fee for an academic year may subsequently be returned to those who do not work in Oxford for the whole of that year.[3]

2. Every member of the University shall pay a composition fee at the appropriate annual rate specified in cl. 14 below for each term from and including the term in which he or she begins to work for the Second Examination for the Degree of Bachelor of Medicine up to and including the term in which he or she completes all the stages of the examination, or ceases to work for the examination.

3. (*a*) Subject to the provisions of cll. 4 and 5 below, every member of the University shall pay a composition fee at the appropriate annual rate specified in cl. 14 below for each term in which he or she is registered as a Probationer Research Student or is working for one of the qualifications listed below, from and including the term in which he or she is first so registered or begins working for such qualification, up to and including the term in which he or she takes the examination[4] or (in the case of a degree or diploma by thesis only) submits his or her thesis:[5]

   (i) the Degree of B.Phil.;

   (ii) the Degree of M.Sc.;

   (iii) the Degree of M.St.;

   (iv) the Degree of MBA;

   (v) the Degree of MPP;

---

[3] The general rule agreed by Council is that, for each complete term not spent working in Oxford, one third of the annual fee shall be returned.

[4] Where the examination comprises a written examination *followed* by the submission of a dissertation, the relevant term is that in which the written examination is taken, save that the relevant term for a student for the Degree of M.Th. is that in which his or her dissertation is submitted (subject to the provisions of cl. 5 of this sub-section).

[5] A thesis submitted other than during Full Term shall be deemed for this purpose to have been submitted during the preceding term.

(vi) the Degree of M.Litt.;

(vii) the Degree of M.Phil.;

(viii) the Degree of M.Th.;

(ix) the Degree of M.F.A.;

(x) the Degree of D.Phil.;

(xi) any diploma or certificate other than:

    (*a*) the Diploma in Theology;

    (*b*) the Diploma in Legal Studies;

    (*c*) the Postgraduate Diploma in Education;

    (*d*) the Postgraduate Certificate in Education;

    (*e*) the Certificate in Management Studies;

    (*f*) the Certificate in Theology;

    (*g*) the Certificate in Diplomatic Studies;

    (*h*) the Postgraduate Diploma in Diplomatic Studies; or

    (*i*) certificates issued by the Board of Studies in Education under the provisions of the appropriate regulation.

Candidates who continue to work for one of the qualifications listed above after failing an examination shall pay a composition fee for each term in which they receive tuition or supervision; but if they receive no further tuition or supervision, they shall pay no further composition fees but shall pay the fee prescribed in §1 above when they re-enter. Candidates whose thesis submitted for the degree of M.Litt., M.Sc., or D.Phil., has been referred back shall pay no further composition fees, but shall pay the fee prescribed in §1 above when they apply for re-examination; and candidates whose dissertation for the degree of M.Sc. in Education did not satisfy the examiners shall pay the fee prescribed in §1 above before a revised or new dissertation for Part II of the examination is examined. For the purposes of this clause 'term' shall include any period of forty-two days' residence reckoned as a term of residence under the Regulations for Residence in the University provided that not more than three composition fees shall be payable in the same academical year.

(*b*) the fee shall be collected in accordance with cl.13 below.

4. The number of composition fees payable under cl. 3 above by those working for the degree of D.Phil. shall not exceed nine provided that:

(*a*) **[for candidates admitted to graduate study before 1 September 2006]** candidates for the D.Phil. may count towards this figure up to six composition fees paid while working for any one of the degrees of M.St., M.Sc. by Coursework, M.Phil., M.Th., M.F.A., M.Juris., B.Phil., or BCL; **[for candidates admitted from 1 September 2006 onwards]** candidates for the D.Phil. may count towards this figure up to three composition fees paid while working for the degree of M.Phil., M.St. in Legal Research, or B.Phil.;

(*b*) candidates for the D.Phil. who have held the status of Probationer Research Student, or of Student for the Degree of M.Sc. by Research or M.Litt. or for the Diploma in Law, before transferring[6] to work for the degree of D.Phil. shall be deemed for the purpose of this sub-section to have been working for the D.Phil. from the term in which they began working for the course from which they have transferred, and may count towards their D.Phil. fee liability

---

[6] A candidate is not deemed to be '*transferring* to work for the Degree of D.Phil.', when he or she is admitted as a D.Phil. student after satisfying the examiners for the Degree of M.Sc. by Research or M.Litt., or for the Diploma in Law.

any fees paid while holding their previous status, subject to the payment on transfer of any consequent additional fees for which they are liable;

(c) the number of composition fees payable by candidates for the Doctor of Engineering shall not exceed twelve;

(d) the number of composition fees payable by candidates for the D.Phil. in the Doctoral Training Centre at the Life Sciences Interface, the D.Phil in the Doctoral Training Centre in Systems Biology, the D.Phil in the Centre for Doctoral Training in Healthcare Innovation, and the D.Phil in the Industrial Doctorate Centre in Systems Approaches to Biomedical Sciences shall not exceed twelve;

(e) the number of composition fees payable by candidates for a D.Phil in the Medical Sciences Doctoral Training Centre who have been admitted to a four-year doctoral programme shall not exceed twelve;

(f) the number of composition fees payable by candidates for a D.Phil in Biomedical Sciences under the NIH-Oxford programme shall not exceed six.

5. The number of composition fees payable under cl. 3 above by those working for any qualification other than the degree of D.Phil. shall not exceed six in respect of each qualification, save that those receiving tuition or supervision after failing an examination shall continue to pay composition fees for each term in which they receive tuition or supervision, and those who are part-time Students for the Degree of Master of Science in Applied Social Studies or Education shall pay not more than twelve composition fees, those who are students for the Degree of Master of Science in Bioinformatics or Evidence-Based Health Care or Experimental Therapeutics or Software and System Security or Software Engineering shall pay not more and not fewer than six composition fees (at the half rate) irrespective of the period for which they are registered for that degree, and those who are Students for the Degree of Master of Theology shall not pay more than six fees (at the half rate) while working for Part II of that degree. Students studying for the Degree of Master of Studies in International Human Rights Law shall pay not more than six composition fees save for those students receiving tuition or supervision after failing an examination or those students requiring an extension of time shall continue to pay composition fees for each term in which they receive tuition or supervision.

6. Every member of the University who, not holding an academic appointment in the University or the colleges, has been matriculated in order to study in the University otherwise than for a degree, diploma, or certificate of the University shall pay a composition fee at the appropriate annual rate specified in cl. 14 below for each term in which he or she is studying in the University.

7. Every member of the University shall pay such other fees applicable to him or her as may be prescribed by any statute or regulation.

8. Fee requirements relating to full-time students holding the status of Probationer Research Student or that of a Student for the Degrees of D.Phil., B.Th., M.Litt., or M.Sc. by Research shall also apply to part-time students holding the same status, save that part-time students shall be required to pay half the applicable full-time fee over twice the applicable length of time for full-time students.

9. Notwithstanding the provisions of cl. 14 below, the University shall remit three-fifths of the prescribed composition fees payable by any overseas student who establishes, by information certified to the Secretary of the Chest by an officer of the student's college or society, that at least half of the cost of the student's maintenance (as distinct from university or college fees) in the relevant year has been provided by resident Junior Members of the University (otherwise than from funds of common rooms contributed directly or indirectly by local education authorities or

other grant-paying authorities in payment of membership fees); provided that the number of students whose fees are remitted under this clause shall not in any one year exceed thirty-five and that any arrangements required for determining the allocation between colleges or other societies of the benefits available under this clause shall be subject to approval from time to time by Council's Education Committee.

10. Council's Education Committee shall have power to approve exchange arrangements with other universities under which no fees are payable on either side. Any of the fees prescribed in cl. 14 below, which would otherwise have been payable by any person working in Oxford under those exchange arrangements shall be remitted.

11. (*a*) Where admission as a graduate student is reckoned from a term earlier than that in which the application for admission was approved, on the grounds that:

(i) a term or terms had been spent at another university on a course of study directly relevant to the work subsequently undertaken for the degree of M.Litt., M.Sc., or D.Phil., and.

(ii) the earlier study had not led to the award of a qualification of any university, and was under the supervision of a person who has subsequently taken up an appointment at Oxford.

Subject to the approval of Council's Education Committee any fees payable under cl. 3 above in respect of such term or terms may be remitted either wholly or in part. For the purposes of determining the appropriate fee level, the student will usually be deemed to have commenced the programme of study in the term to which their admission has been antedated.

(*b*) Subject to the approval of Council's Education Committee where a clinical student has already spent at least three terms working full-time for the Degree of M.Sc. by research and has paid at least three composition fees in respect thereof, any further fees payable in respect of the M.Sc. course for terms in which he or she is also working as a clinical student at a university clinical school outside Oxford may be remitted.

12. (*a*) Not later than the fourteenth day after the last day of every Full Term the Head or Bursar of every society, or the Head of the student's department for programmes where fees are usually paid directly to the department, shall send to the Secretary of the Chest a schedule signed by himself or herself containing the names of all members of the society who were liable to pay the composition fees referred to in cll. 1-3 and cl. 6 above, in respect of that term.

(*b*) The Head or Bursar of every society shall pay to the Secretary of the Chest such University composition fees as were due for that term in accordance with the mechanisms agreed between the colleges and the University from time to time. Where University composition fees are collected by a department these shall be paid to the Secretary of the Chest in accordance with the mechanisms that are agreed from time to time.

13. (*a*) The annual university composition fee shall be paid on or before the seventh day of Michaelmas Full Term (or of the term in which the student commences his or her course, as the case may be) unless the Bursar of the student's college or the Head of the student's department for programmes where fees are usually paid directly to the department, certifies in writing that:

(i) the college has approved the student's application to pay by instalments, the first such instalment having been paid; and/or

(ii) the student has applied for, and is *prima facie* eligible for, a contribution to his or her fee from his or her local authority (or other fee-paying body), and the college is of the opinion that no contribution will be required from the student;

(iii) the student's programme did not commence on the first day of the relevant term, and payment is due on the seventh day after the actual commencement of the student's programme.

(*b*) In the event that any fee or continuation charge payable by the student, or the relevant instalment towards such a fee, remains unpaid after the due date of payment it shall be the duty of the Bursar of the student's college, or the Registrar for programmes where fees or charges are usually paid directly to the University, or the Head of the student's department for programmes where fees or charges are usually paid directly to the department, to notify the student concerned that, in the event that the fees or charges due have not been paid in full within four weeks from the date of such notification, the student shall be liable for suspension from access to the premises and facilities of the University (including the Examination Schools and other places of examination) from the end of such four-week period until such time as outstanding fees have been paid. The Bursar/or Head shall also inform the Registrar that he or she has so notified the student concerned; and if the fees or charges due have not been paid in full within the specified four-week period, the Bursar/or Head shall inform the Registrar of the position, whereupon, subject to the other provisions of this clause, the University shall have the right forthwith to suspend the student concerned from access to the premises and facilities of the University.

(*c*) On application by their society, or by the Head of the student's department for programmes where fees are usually paid directly to the department, and subject to the approval of Council's Education Committee, some part of the fee for an academical year may subsequently be returned to those who do not work in Oxford as a result of suspension or withdrawal, for the whole of that year.[3] In addition if a student withdraws or suspends their status on or before Monday of Week 4 of any term the fees payable in respect of that term will be reimbursed to the student.[7]

(*d*) Applications for the remission or waiver of university fees, for the resolution of issues relating to the non-payment of university fees, and for all other questions of doubt or difficulty relating to the liability of individual students for university fees, including those covered under (*a*) to (*c*) above, and for questions of doubt or difficulty relating to the charging of deposits for course fees, or for tuition charge waivers or bursaries as covered in §6, or for liability for the continuation charge as covered in §7 shall be determined by the Fees Panel. The Panel, shall be chaired by the Assessor and consist of two members nominated by Conference of Colleges, two members nominated by Council's Education Committee, and the Assessor-elect. Applications for dispensation from residence requirements, other than those specified above, shall be determined by the Proctors, on condition that if the Fees Panel or the Proctors, as the case may be, are unable to agree on how to deal with any individual application they shall refer the application to Council's Education Committee for decision.

(*e*) There shall be no appeal against a decision of the Fees Panel. A student may, however, make a further application under the procedures outlined above for relief from suspension or such terms as may have been imposed by a Fees Panel if the Bursar of his or her college supports an application on the basis that the student's financial circumstances have changed for reasons beyond his or her control.

---

[3] The general rule agreed by Council is that, for each complete term not spent working in Oxford, one third of the annual fee shall be returned.

[7] Certain programmes which have been granted permission to charge non-refundable deposits and programmes within the Department for Continuing Education and the Saïd Business School may have different refund policies.

14. (i) For 2013–14 composition fees payable under cl. 1 above shall be of the following amounts, and those payable under cll. 2 and 6 shall be at the following annual rates:[8]

(a) for members of the University (other than part-time students) entitled, in accordance with the Special Appendix to this subsection, to be charged fees at the appropriate 'home' rate and who commenced the programme of study on or after 1 September 2012 the fee shall be £9,000 except that for those working for an honour school requiring the study of one or more languages for an academic year outside Oxford, or for Law with Law Studies in Europe, and where the period of full-time study in Oxford is not more than ten weeks in total in the year, the fee, during that year, shall be £4,500;

(b) for members of the University (other than part-time students) entitled, in accordance with the Special Appendix to this subsection, to be charged fees at the appropriate 'home' rate and who commenced the programme of study on or after 1 September 2006 and before 1 September 2012 the fee shall be £3,465, except that for those working for an honour school requiring the study of one or more languages for an academic year outside Oxford, or for Law with Law Studies in Europe, and where the period of full-time study in Oxford is not more than ten weeks in total in the year, the fee, during that year, shall be £1,725, and except that those who commenced the programme of study on or after 1 September 2009 and where that programme of study leads to a qualification that is of an equivalent or lower level to one the student has already been awarded shall pay fees at the appropriate Island rate as described in (m) below unless the programme of study has been designated a strategically important and vulnerable subject or is otherwise exempt from having a higher fee charged, as determined by Council's Planning and Resource Allocation Committee from time to time;

(c) for members of the University (other than part-time students) entitled, in accordance with the Special Appendix to this subsection, to be charged fees at the appropriate 'home' rate and who commenced the programme of study before 1 September 2006 the fee shall be £1,380, except that for those working for an honour school requiring the study of one or more languages for an academic year outside Oxford, or for Law with Law Studies in Europe, and where the period of full-time study in Oxford is not more than ten weeks in total in the year, the fee, during that year, shall be £690;

(d) for members of the University working for the degree of B.Th. or for the Certificate in Theology, and who commenced the programme of study on or after 1 September 2006 but before 1 September 2008, the 'home' fee rate shall be £1,725;

(e) for members of the University working for the degree of B.Th. or for the Certificate in Theology, and who commenced the programme of study on or after 1 September 2008 but before 1 September 2009, the 'home' fee rate shall be £2,315;

(f) for members of the University working for the degree of B.Th. or for the Certificate in Theology, and who commenced the programme of study on or after 1 September 2009 but before 1 September 2012, the 'home' fee rate shall be £3,465;

(g) for members of the University working for the degree of B.Th. or for the Certificate in Theology, and who commenced the programme of study on or after 1 September 2012, the 'home' fee rate shall be £9,000;

---

[8] The fee payable each term will be one-third of the specified figure.

(*h*) for members of the University working for the Certificate or Diploma in Theological and Pastoral Studies or for the Certificate in Theology who commenced the programme of study on or after 1 September 2010 but before 1 September 2012, the 'home' rate shall be £3,465 and the 'overseas' rate shall be £13,860;

(*i*) for members of the University working for the Certificate or Diploma in Theological and Pastoral Studies who commenced the programme of study on or after 1 September 2012, the 'home' rate shall be £7,350 and the 'overseas' rate shall be £13,860;

(*j*) for members of the University entitled, in accordance with the Special Appendix to this subsection, to be charged fees at the appropriate 'home' rate and liable to pay a composition fee under cl. 6 above, the rate specified in (*a*) above;

(*k*) for Visiting Students, fees shall be payable at 50% of the 'overseas' under-graduate fee rate specified for the relevant subject area in the Schedule below; in cases where the subject is not offered at undergraduate level, fees shall be payable at 50% of the 'overseas' graduate research fee rate as specified for the relevant subject area in the Table of Fees or Schedule below; in cases where a Visiting Student is studying across subject areas in different categories of the Schedule, the applicable fee rate shall be that which applies to the larger portion of their studies;

(*l*) for Recognised Students, fees shall be payable at 50% of the 'overseas' graduate research fee rate specified for the relevant subject area in the Table of Fees or Schedule below; in cases where a Recognised Student is studying across subject areas in different categories of the Table of Fees or Schedule, the applicable fee rate shall be that which applies to the larger portion of their studies;

(*m*) for members of the University resident in the Isle of Man or the Channel Islands, who commenced the programme of study before 1 September 2012, fees in one of four bands, details of which may be obtained from the University Offices (Planning and Resource Allocation Section), or from College offices, unless (*p*) applies;

(*n*) for members of the University resident in the Isle of Man or the Channel Islands, who commenced the programme of study on or after 1 September 2012, the fee shall be £9,000 except that for those working for the Second Examination for the degree of BM (i.e. clinical medical students) the fee shall be £22,820, unless (*p*) applies;

(*o*) for all other members of the University, the appropriate amount or rate as specified in the schedule below, unless (*p*) applies;

(*p*) for members of the University who commenced the programme of study on or after 1 September 2011 and who are working for an honour school requiring the study of one or more languages for an academic year outside Oxford, or for Law with Law Studies in Europe, and where the period of full-time study in Oxford is not more than ten weeks in total in the year, the fee, during that year, shall be half of the fee that would be payable if they were studying in Oxford for the full year.

(ii) For 2013–14, composition fees payable under cl. 3 above (other than those admitted by the Continuing Education Board or by any other Board to undertake a programme with a modular fee and assessment structure) shall be at the following annual rates:[9]

---

[9] A student shall be deemed to have *commenced a programme of study* on commencing study towards any new qualification aim.

(*a*) For members of the University entitled, in accordance with the Special Appendix to this subsection, to be charged fees at the appropriate 'home' rate, £3,900, or half that rate if part-time students for Degrees, Diplomas or Certificates not specified in items (b) to (hx) below; except that those who commenced the programme of study on or after 1 September 2009 and before 1 September 2011 and where that programme of study leads to a qualification that is of an equivalent or lower level to one the student has already been awarded shall pay fees at the appropriate rate as determined by Council's Planning and Resource Allocation Committee on the basis of the relevant Island rate as described in (i) (*m*) above or at the rate specified in the table below whichever is the higher unless the programme of study has been designated a strategically important and vulnerable subject, is a research programme of study or is otherwise exempt from having a higher fee charged, as determined by Council's Planning and Resource Allocation Committee from time to time.

Table : Fees[10]

Sub-section	Programme title	'home' rate[11]	'overseas' rate[12]
(a)	see 14(ii)(*a*) above		
(b)	MSc African Studies	£7,665	£15,910
(c)	MSt Ancient Philosophy	£7,665	£15,910
(d)	DPhil Anthropology (entry on or after 1 September 2012)	£10,815	£17,010
(e)	DPhil Anthropology (entry on or after 1 September 2011 and before 1 September 2012)	£7,665	£17,010
(f)	MSc Applied Linguistics & Second Language Acquisition (entry on or after 1 September 2013)	£7,665	£14,755
(g)	MSc Applied Linguistics & Second Language Acquisition (entry on or after 1 September 2012 and before 1 September 2013)	£6,510	£13,860
(h)	MSc Applied Statistics (entry on or after 1 September 2013)	£6,510	£17,010
(i)	MTh Applied Theology (entry on or after 1 September 2012)	£5,935	£15,910
(j)	MTh Applied Theology (entry on or after 1 September 2011 and before 1 September 2012)	£5,355	£15,910
(k)	PGDip Applied Theology (entry on or after 1 September 2012)	£5,935	£15,910
(l)	DPhil Archaeological Science (entry on or after 1 September 2012)	£6,510	£15,910

[10] Rates are given in this table for 2013 entry only for one-year courses, for 2012 and 2013 entry only for two-year courses and for 2011, 2012 and 2013 entry only for research programmes. Rates for students who started prior to these dates may be obtained from the University Offices (Planning and Resource Allocation Section).

[11] i.e. the rate to be charged to members of the University entitled, in accordance with the Special Appendix to this subsection, to be charged fees at the appropriate 'home' rate.

[12] i.e. the rate to be charged to members of the University who are not entitled, in accordance with the Special Appendix to this subsection, to be charged fees at the appropriate 'home' rate.

(m)	DPhil Archaeological Science (entry on or after 1 September 2011 and before 1 September 2012)	£5,355	£15,910	
(n)	MSc Archaeological Science	£7,665	£15,910	
(o)	MSt Archaeological Science	£6,510	£14,755	
(p)	DPhil Archaeology (entry on or after 1 September 2012) (for part-time rate see cl. 14 (iv))	£6,510	£14,755	5
(q)	DPhil Archaeology (entry on or after 1 September 2011 and before 1 September 2012) (for part-time rate see cl. 14 (iv))	£5,355	£14,755	
(r)	MPhil Archaeology (entry on or after 1 September 2012)	£6,510	£14,755	10
(s)	MSt Archaeology	£6,510	£14,755	
(t)	DPhil Astrophysics (entry before 1 September 2012)	£3,900	£16,275	
(u)	MSc(Res) Astrophysics (entry before 1 September 2012)	£3,900	£16,275	15
(v)	DPhil Atmospheric, Oceanic & Planetary Physics (entry before 1 September 2012)	£3,900	£16,275	
(w)	MSc(Res) Atmospheric, Oceanic & Planetary Physics (entry before 1 September 2012)	£3,900	£16,275	20
(x)	DPhil Atomic & Laser Physics (entry before 1 September 2012)	£3,900	£16,275	
(y)	MSc(Res) Atomic & Laser Physics (entry before 1 September 2012)	£3,900	£16,275	
(z)	BCL Bachelor of Civil Law	£14,755	£19,480	25
(aa)	MSt Bible Interpretation	£5,935	£15,910	
(ab)	MSc Biodiversity, Conservation & Management	£10,815	£15,190	
(ac)	MSc Biomechanical Engineering (entry on or after 1 September 2013)	£6,510	£19,480	
(ad)	MBA Business Administration[13]	£41,000	£41,000	30
(ae)	EMBA Business Administration[14]	£57,000	£57,000	
(af)	MPhil Celtic Studies (entry on or after 1 September 2011)	£5,935	£15,910	
(ag)	MSt Celtic Studies	£5,935	£15,910	
(ah)	DPhil Chemical Biology (entry before 1 September 2012)	£3,900	£16,275	35
(ai)	MSc(Res) Chemical Biology (entry before 1 September 2012)	£3,900	£16,275	
(aj)	MSt Chinese Studies	£5,935	£15,910	
(ak)	DPhil Classical Archaeology	£6,510	£14,755	40

[13] Notwithstanding any general provisions to the contrary, 15% of this fee shall be payable by the student as a non-refundable deposit at the time of his or her acceptance of the offer by the University of admission to the course.

[14] Part-time fee applies to whole programme and is payable over two years; including college fees. Notwithstanding any general provisions to the contrary, 15% of this fee shall be payable by the student as a non-refundable deposit at the time of his or her acceptance of the offer by the University of admission to the course.

(al)	MPhil Classical Archaeology (entry on or after 1 September 2012)	£6,510	£14,755
(am)	MSt Classical Archaeology	£6,510	£14,755
(an)	MSt Classical Armenian Studies	£5,935	£15,910
(ao)	MSt Classical Hebrew Studies	£5,935	£15,910
(ap)	MPhil Classical Indian Religion (entry on or after 1 September 2011)	£5,935	£15,910
(aq)	MSc Clinical Embryology	£29,400	£29,400
(ar)	MSc Cognitive Evolutionary Anthropology	£10,815	£17,010
(as)	MPhil Comparative Social Policy (entry on or after 1 September 2013)	£10,815	£17,010
(at)	MPhil Comparative Social Policy (entry on or after 1 September 2011 and before 1 September 2013)	£7,665	£15,910
(au)	MSc Comparative Social Policy (entry on or after 1 September 2013)	£10,815	£17,010
(av)	DPhil Computer Science (entry on or after 1 September 2012 and before 1 September 2013)	£3,900	£14,230
(aw)	MSc(Res) Computer Science (entry on or after 1 September 2012 and before 1 September 2013)	£3,900	£14,230
(ax)	MSc Computer Science (entry on or after 1 September 2013)	£6,510	£17,010
(ay)	DPhil Condensed Matter Physics (entry before 1 September 2012)	£3,900	£16,275
(az)	MSc(Res) Condensed Matter Physics (entry before 1 September 2012)	£3,900	£16,275
(ba)	MSc Contemporary India	£10,815	£15,910
(bb)	MSc Criminology & Criminal Justice (all programmes)	£5,935	£13,860
(bc)	MPhil Cuneiform Studies (entry on or after 1 September 2011)	£5,935	£15,910
(bd)	DPhil Development Studies (entry on or after 1 September 2010)	£7,665	£15,910
(be)	MPhil Development Studies (entry on or after 1 September 2010)	£14,755	£19,480
(bf)	DPhil Earth Sciences (entry before 1 September 2012)	£3,900	£16,275
(bg)	MSc(Res) Earth Sciences (entry before 1 September 2012)	£3,900	£16,275
(bh)	MPhil Eastern Christian Studies: Oriental Studies (entry on or after 1 September 2011)	£5,935	£15,910
(bi)	MPhil Eastern Christian Studies: Theology (entry on or after 1 September 2012)	£5,935	£15,910
(bj)	MPhil Economic & Social History (entry on or after 1 September 2011)	£5,935	£15,910
(bk)	MSc Economic & Social History	£5,935	£15,910
(bl)	MPhil Economics (entry on or after 1 September 2012)	£10,815	£13,860

(bm)	MSc Economics for Development	£14,755	£19,480
(bn)	DPhil Education (entry on or after 1 September 2010)	£6,510	£13,860
(bo)	MSc and MSc(Res) Education (all programmes)	£7,665	£14,755
(bp)	MPhil Egyptology (entry on or after 1 September 2011)	£5,935	£15,910
(bq)	MSc Endovascular Neurosurgery	£14,755	£28,105
(br)	EngD Engineered Metals (entry before 1 September 2012)	£3,900	£16,275
(bs)	DPhil Engineering Science (entry before 1 September 2012)	£3,900	£16,275
(bt)	MSc(Res) Engineering Science (entry before 1 September 2012)	£3,900	£16,275
(bu)	MSt English & American Studies	£5,935	£15,910
(bv)	MSt English (all programmes)	£5,935	£15,910
(bw)	MSt English Language	£5,935	£15,910
(bx)	MPhil English Studies (Medieval) (entry on or after 1 September 2011)	£5,935	£15,910
(by)	DPhil Environmental Change (entry on or after 1 September 2010)	£10,815	£15,910
(bz)	MSc Environmental Change & Management	£10,815	£15,910
(ca)	MPhil Evidence–Based Social Intervention (entry on or after 1 September 2013)	£10,815	£17,010
(cb)	MPhil Evidence–Based Social Intervention (entry on or after 1 September 2011 and before 1 September 2013)	£7,665	£15,910
(cc)	MSc Evidence–Based Social Intervention	£10,815	£17,010
(cd)	MSt Film Aesthetics	£5,935	£15,910
(ce)	MSc Financial Economics	£31,500	£31,500
(cf)	PGDip Financial Strategy (PT, January 2014 entry)[15]	£19,200	£19,200
(cg)	MFA Fine Art	£7,665	£17,010
(ch)	MPhil General Linguistics & Comparative Philology (entry on or after 1 September 2011)	£5,935	£15,910
(ci)	MSt General Linguistics & Comparative Philology	£5,935	£15,910
(cj)	DPhil Geography & the Environment (entry on or after 1 September 2010)	£10,815	£15,910
(ck)	MPhil Geography & the Environment	£10,815	£15,910
(cl)	MSc(Res) Geography & the Environment (entry on or after 1 September 2010)	£10,815	£15,910
(cm)	MSt Global & Imperial History	£5,935	£15,910
(cn)	PGDip Global Business (PT, January 2014 entry)[15]	£19,200	£19,200
(co)	MSc Global Governance & Diplomacy	£14,755	£19,480
(cp)	MSc Global Health Science	£11,920	£28,105

[15] Fee applies to whole programme and is not an annual rate.

(cq)	MPhil Greek &/or Latin Languages & Literature (entry on or after 1 September 2011)	£5,935	£15,910
(cr)	MSt Greek &/or Latin Languages & Literature	£5,935	£15,910
(cs)	MPhil Greek &/or Roman History (entry on or after 1 September 2011)	£5,935	£15,910
(ct)	MSt Greek &/or Roman History	£5,935	£15,910
(cu)	DPhil Healthcare Innovation Centre for Doctoral Training (entry before 1 September 2012)	£3,900	£16,275
(cv)	MSt History of Art & Visual Culture	£5,935	£15,910
(cw)	MPhil History of Science, Medicine & Technology (entry on or after 1 September 2011)	£5,935	£15,910
(cx)	MSc History of Science, Medicine & Technology	£5,935	£15,910
(cy)	DPhil Information, Communication and the Social Sciences (entry on or after 1 September 2011)	£6,510	£15,910
(cz)	DPhil Inorganic Chemistry (entry before 1 September 2012)	£3,900	£16,275
(da)	MSc(Res) Inorganic Chemistry (entry before 1 September 2012)	£3,900	£16,275
(db)	PGDip Intellectual Property Law & Practice (PT) (entry on or after 1 September 2013)	£6,510	£6,510
(dc)	DPhil International Development (entry on or after 1 September 2011)	£7,665	£15,910
(dd)	DPhil International Relations (entry on or after 1 September 2011)	£7,665	£17,010
(de)	MPhil International Relations (entry on or after 1 September 2012)	£10,815	£17,010
(df)	MPhil Islamic Art & Archaeology (entry on or after 1 September 2011)	£5,935	£15,910
(dg)	MSt Islamic Art & Archaeology (all programmes)	£5,935	£15,910
(dh)	MPhil Islamic Studies & History (entry on or after 1 September 2011)	£5,935	£15,910
(di)	MSt Japanese Studies	£5,935	£15,910
(dj)	MSt Jewish Studies	£7,665	£17,010
(dk)	MPhil Jewish Studies in the Graeco–Roman Period (entry on or after 1 September 2011)	£5,935	£15,910
(dl)	MSt Jewish Studies in the Graeco–Roman Period	£5,935	£15,910
(dm)	MPhil Judaism & Christianity in the Graeco–Roman World (entry on or after 1 September 2012)	£5,935	£15,910
(dn)	MSt Korean Studies	£5,935	£15,910
(do)	MPhil Late Antique & Byzantine Studies (entry on or after 1 September 2011)	£5,935	£15,910
(dp)	MSt Late Antique & Byzantine Studies	£5,935	£15,910
(dq)	MPhil Latin American Studies (entry on or after 1 September 2012)	£6,510	£15,910
(dr)	MSc Latin American Studies	£6,510	£15,910

(ds)	MSc Law & Finance[13] (entry on or after 1 September 2013)	£23,900	£23,900
(dt)	MSc Learning & Teaching (PT)[16]	£1,950	£4,500
(du)	DPhil Life Sciences Interface Doctoral Training Centre (entry before 1 September 2012)	£3,900	£16,275
(dv)	MJur Magister Juris	£14,755	£19,480
(dw)	MSc Major Programme Management (PT) (entry on or after 1 September 2013)[14]	£29,875	£29,875
(dx)	Cert Management Studies (PT) (entry on or after 1 September 2012)	£9,740	£9,740
(dy)	DPhil Management Studies (entry on or after 1 September 2012)	£13,860	£13,860
(dz)	MPhil Material Anthropology & Museum Ethnography (entry on or after 1 September 2011)	£7,665	£17,010
(ea)	DPhil Materials (entry before 1 September 2012)	£3,900	£16,275
(eb)	MSc(Res) Materials (entry before 1 September 2012)	£3,900	£16,275
(ec)	EngD Materials Science (entry before 1 September 2012)	£3,900	£16,275
(ed)	MSc Mathematical & Computational Finance[17] (entry on or after 1 September 2013)	£23,900	£23,900
(ee)	MSc Mathematical Modelling and Scientific Computing (entry on or after 1 September 2013)	£5,355	£14,755
(ef)	DPhil Mathematics (entry before 1 September 2013)	£3,900	£14,230
(eg)	MSc(Res) Mathematics (entry before 1 September 2013)	£3,900	£14,230
(eh)	MSc Mathematics & the Foundations of Computer Science (entry on or after 1 September 2013)	£5,355	£14,755
(ei)	MPhil Medical Anthropology (entry on or after 1 September 2012)	£10,815	£17,010
(ej)	MSc Medical Anthropology	£10,815	£17,010
(ek)	MPhil Medieval Arabic Thought (entry on or after 1 September 2011)	£5,935	£15,910
(el)	MSt Medieval History	£5,935	£15,510
(em)	MSt Medieval Studies	£5,935	£15,910

---

[13] Notwithstanding any general provisions to the contrary, 15% of this fee shall be payable by the student as a non-refundable deposit at the time of his or her acceptance of the offer by the University of admission to the course.

[16] Part-time fee being one half of equivalent full-time fee.

[14] Part-time fee applies to whole programme and is payable over two years; including college fees. Notwithstanding any general provisions to the contrary, 15% of this fee shall be payable by the student as a non-refundable deposit at the time of his or her acceptance of the offer by the University of admission to the course.

[17] Notwithstanding any general provisions to the contrary, 10% of this fee shall be payable by the student as a non-refundable deposit at the time of his or her acceptance of the offer by the University of admission to the course.

(en)	MSc Migration Studies	£14,755	£19,480
(eo)	MPhil Modern British and European History (entry on or after 1 September 2011)	£5,935	£15,910
(ep)	MSt Modern British & European History	£5,935	£15,910
(eq)	MPhil Modern Chinese Art (entry on or after 1 September 2010)	£7,665	£15,910
(er)	MPhil Modern Chinese Studies (entry on or after 1 September 2011)	£10,815	£17,010
(es)	MSc Contemporary Chinese Studies	£10,815	£17,010
(et)	MPhil Modern Japanese Studies (entry on or after 1 September 2011)	£5,355	£13,860
(eu)	MSc Modern Japanese Studies	£5,355	£13,860
(ev)	MPhil Modern Jewish Studies (entry on or after 1 September 2011)	£5,935	£15,910
(ew)	MSt Modern Jewish Studies	£5,935	£15,910
(ex)	MPhil Modern Languages (entry on or after 1 September 2011)	£5,935	£15,910
(ey)	MSt Modern Languages	£5,935	£15,910
(ez)	MPhil Modern Middle Eastern Studies (entry on or after 1 September 2011)	£5,935	£15,910
(fa)	MPhil Modern South Asian Studies (entry on or after 1 September 2011)	£5,935	£15,910
(fb)	MSt Modern South Asian Studies (entry on or after 1 September 2012)	£5,935	£15,910
(fc)	MSc Musculoskeletal Sciences (PT, January 2014 entry)	£2,680	£14,050
(fd)	MPhil Music (all programmes) (entry on or after 1 September 2011)	£5,935	£17,010
(fe)	MSt Music (all programmes)	£5,935	£17,010
(ff)	MSc Nature, Society & Environmental Policy	£10,815	£15,910
(fg)	DPhil Numerical Analysis (entry before 1 September 2013)	£3,900	£14,230
(fh)	MSc(Res) Numerical Analysis (entry before 1 September 2013)	£3,900	£14,230
(fi)	DPhil Organic Chemistry (entry before 1 September 2012)	£3,900	£16,275
(fj)	MSc(Res) Organic Chemistry (entry before 1 September 2012)	£3,900	£16,275
(fk)	PGDip Organisational Leadership (PT, January 2014 entry)[15]	£19,200	£19,200
(fl)	MSt Oriental Studies	£5,935	£15,910
(fm)	MPhil Ottoman Turkish Studies (entry on or after 1 September 2011)	£5,935	£15,910
(fn)	DPhil Particle Physics (entry before 1 September 2012)	£3,900	£16,275

---

[15] Fee applies to whole programme and is not an annual rate.

(fo)	MSc(Res) Particle Physics (entry before 1 September 2012)	£3,900	£16,275
(fp)	MSc Pharmacology	£5,935	£15,910
(fq)	MPhil Philosophical Theology (entry on or after 1 September 2012)	£5,935	£15,910
(fr)	MSt Philosophical Theology (entry on or after 1 September 2012)	£5,935	£15,910
(fs)	BPhil Philosophy (entry on or after 1 September 2011)	£7,665	£15,910
(ft)	MSt Philosophy	£7,665	£15,910
(fu)	MSt Philosophy of Physics	£7,665	£15,910
(fv)	DPhil Physical & Theoretical Chemistry (entry before 1 September 2012)	£3,900	£16,275
(fw)	MSc(Res) Physical & Theoretical Chemistry (entry before 1 September 2012)	£3,900	£16,275
(fx)	DPhil Plant Sciences (entry before 1 September 2012)	£3,900	£16,275
(fy)	MSc(Res) Plant Sciences (entry before 1 September 2012)	£3,900	£16,275
(fz)	MSc Political Theory Research	£10,815	£17,010
(ga)	DPhil Politics (entry on or after 1 September 2011)	£7,665	£17,010
(gb)	MSc Politics Research	£10,815	£17,010
(gc)	MPhil Politics (all programmes) (entry on or after 1 September 2012)	£10,815	£17,010
(gd)	MPP Public Policy	£31,500	£31,500
(ge)	MSc Public Policy in Latin America	£6,510	£15,910
(gf)	MSc Refugee & Forced Migration Studies	£14,755	£19,480
(gg)	MPhil Russian & East European Studies (entry on or after 1 September 2012)	£6,510	£15,910
(gh)	MSc Russian & East European Studies	£6,510	£15,910
(gi)	MSt Science & Religion	£5,935	£15,910
(gj)	MPhil Slavonic Studies (entry on or after 1 September 2011)	£5,935	£15,910
(gk)	MSt Slavonic Studies	£5,935	£15,910
(gl)	DPhil Social & Cultural Anthropology (entry on or after 1 September 2011 and before 1 September 2012)	£7,665	£17,010
(gm)	DPhil Social & Cultural Anthropology (entry on or after 1 September 2010 and before 1 September 2011)	£6,510	£15,910
(gn)	DPhil Social & Cultural Anthropology (entry on or after 1 September 2009 and before 1 September 2010)	£5,355	£13,860
(go)	MPhil Social Anthropology (entry on or after 1 September 2012)	£10,815	£17,010
(gp)	MSc Social Anthropology (all programmes)	£10,815	£17,010
(gq)	MSt Social Anthropology	£10,815	£17,010

(gr)	DPhil Social Intervention (entry on or after 1 September 2011)	£7,665	£15,910	
(gs)	DPhil Social Policy (entry on or after 1 September 2011)	£7,665	£15,910	
(gt)	MSc Social Science of the Internet	£10,815	£15,910	5
(gu)	DPhil Sociology (entry on or after 1 September 2013)	£5,355	£13,860	
(gv)	MPhil Sociology	£6,510	£13,860	
(gw)	MSc Sociology	£7,665	£15,910	
(gx)	DPhil Statistics (entry before 1 September 2013)	£3,900	£14,230	1
(gy)	MSc(Res) Statistics (entry before 1 September 2013)	£3,900	£14,230	
(gz)	PGDip Strategy & Innovation (PT, January 2014 entry)[15]	£19,200	£19,200	
(ha)	MSt Study of Religion	£5,935	£15,910	
(hb)	MSt Syriac Studies	£5,935	£15,910	1
(hc)	DPhil Systems Approaches to Biomedical Sciences Industrial Doctorate Centre (entry before 1 September 2012)	£3,900	£16,275	
(hd)	DPhil Systems Biology Doctoral Training Centre (entry before 1 September 2012)	£3,900	£16,275	2
(he)	MSc and PGDip Teaching English Language in University Settings (TELUS) (PT)	£5,960	£5,960	
(hf)	MPhil Theology (entry on or after 1 September 2012)	£5,935	£15,910	
(hg)	MSt Theology	£5,935	£15,910	
(hh)	PGDip Theology (entry on or after 1 September 2011)	£5,355	£15,910	2
(hi)	Certificate for Theology Graduates (entry on or after 1 September 2012)	£5,935	£15,910	
(hj)	MSc Theoretical Chemistry (entry on or after 1 September 2013)	£5,355	£15,910	3
(hk)	DPhil Theoretical Physics (entry before 1 September 2012)	£3,900	£16,275	
(hl)	MSc(Res) Theoretical Physics (entry before 1 September 2012)	£3,900	£16,275	
(hm)	MPhil Tibetan & Himalayan Studies (entry on or after 1 September 2011)	£5,935	£15,910	3
(hn)	MPhil Traditional East Asia (Classical, Medieval, & Early-Modern) (entry on or after 1 September 2011)	£5,935	£15,910	
(ho)	MSt US History	£5,935	£15,910	
(hp)	MPhil Visual, Material, & Museum Anthropology (entry on or after 1 September 2012)	£10,815	£17,010	4
(hq)	MSc Visual, Material, & Museum Anthropology	£10,815	£17,010	
(hr)	MSc Water Science, Policy & Management	£10,815	£15,910	
(hs)	MSt Women's Studies	£5,935	£15,910	
(ht)	MSt World Literatures in English	£5,935	£15,910	4

[15] Fee applies to whole programme and is not an annual rate.

(hu)	MSt Yiddish Studies	£5,935	£15,910
(hv)	DPhil Zoology (entry before 1 September 2012)	£3,900	£16,275
(hw)	MSc(Res) Zoology (entry before 1 September 2012)	£3,900	£16,275
(hx)	For all other members of the University, the appropriate rate specified in the Schedule below, or half that rate if part-time students as aforesaid.		

(iii) For 2013–14, composition fees payable under cl. 3 above for members of the University who are admitted as students by the Continuing Education Board to a part-time programme that has a modular fee structure or by any other Board to a programme with a modular fee and assessment structure shall pay an annual programme fee at either the 'home'[11] or 'overseas'[12] rate and a module fee for each module undertaken as given in (*a*) to (*f*):

Sub-section	Programme Title	'home' rate[11] programme fee	'overseas' rate[12] programme fee	module fee
(a)	MSc Evidence-Based Healthcare	£1,260	£5,200	£1,575
(b)	MSc Experimental Therapeutics	£1,260	£5,200	£1,575
(c)	MSc Software & Systems Security	£1,840	£2,970	£1,690
(d)	MSc Software Engineering	£1,840	£2,970	£1,690
(e)	MSc Surgical Science & Practice	£1,260	£5,960	£1,575
(f)	MSc Sustainable Urban Development	£1,420	£6,825	£1,525

(iv) For 2013–14, composition fees payable under cll. 1 or 3 above for members of the University who are admitted as students by the Continuing Education Board to a programme that has an annual fee structure shall be at the following annual rates[18] except that those who commenced the programme of study on or after 1 September 2009 and before 1 September 2011 and where that programme of study leads to a qualification that is of an equivalent or lower level to one the student has already been awarded shall pay fees at the appropriate rate as determined by Council's Planning and Resource Allocation Committee. Unless stated to the contrary, the fees in the table below are for part-time study:

---

[11] i.e. the rate to be charged to members of the University entitled, in accordance with the Special Appendix to this subsection, to be charged fees at the appropriate 'home' rate.

[12] i.e. the rate to be charged to members of the University who are not entitled, in accordance with the Special Appendix to this subsection, to be charged fees at the appropriate 'home' rate.

[18] Rates are given in this table for 2013 entry only for one year courses and for 2012 and 2013 entry only for two year courses unless otherwise stated. Rates for students who started prior to these dates details may be obtained from the Department for Continuing Education.

Sub-section	Programme Title	'home'[11] rate	'overseas'[12] rate
(a)	MSc Advanced Cognitive Therapy Studies (entry after 1 September 2011)	£5,200	£7,955
(b)	MSc Applied Landscape Archaeology (entry after 1 September 2011)	£2,075	£6,930
(c)	DPhil Archaeology	£2,075	£6,930
(d)	MSt Creative Writing	£4,225	£7,375
(e)	MSt Diplomatic Studies (entry after 1 September 2012)	£8,505	£8,505
(f)	PGCert/PGDip Diplomatic Studies (Foreign Service Programme) (FT)	£15,910	£15,910
(g)	MSc English Local History (entry after 1 September 2012)	£2,680	£6,930
(h)	MSt History of Design (entry on or after 1 September 2013)	£2,970	£6,930
(i)	MSt History of Design (entry on or after 1 September 2012 and before 1 September 2013)	£2,680	£6,930
(j)	MSt International Human Rights Law	£9,295	£9,740
(k)	MSt Literature & Arts (entry on or after 1 September 2013)	£4,225	£7,375
(l)	MSt Literature & Arts (entry on or after 1 September 2012 and before 1 September 2013)	£3,835	£7,375
(m)	MSc Mathematical Finance (entry after 1 September 2012)[19]	£26,400	£29,900
(n)	MSt Mindfulness-Based Cognitive Therapy	£8,505	£10,975
(o)	MSt Psychodynamic Practice (entry after 1 September 2012)	£2,680	£6,930

(v) For non-matriculated students studying subjects listed under cl. 14 (iii) or (iv) above fees are as published by the Department for Continuing Education except that for subjects listed under (iii) (*c*) or (*d*) above fees are as published by the Department of Computer Science.

---

[11] i.e. the rate to be charged to members of the University entitled, in accordance with the Special Appendix to this subsection, to be charged fees at the appropriate 'home' rate.

[12] i.e. the rate to be charged to members of the University who are not entitled, in accordance with the Special Appendix to this subsection, to be charged fees at the appropriate 'home' rate.

[19] Whole course fee.

Schedule

Category A. Composition fees of £11,920 (or at that annual rate) shall be paid by:

(i) those liable to pay a composition fee under the provisions of §5 cl. 1 above, **who commenced the programme of study before 1 September 2005**[9], and who are studying for an Undergraduate Degree in:

Ancient and Modern History;

Archaeology and Anthropology;

Classical Archaeology and Ancient History;

Classics and English;

Classics and Modern Languages;

Classics and Oriental Studies;

Economics and Management;

English Language and Literature;

English and Modern Languages;

European and Middle Eastern Languages;

Geography;

History;

History and Economics;

History and English;

History and Modern Languages;

History and Politics;

History of Art;

Human Sciences;

Jurisprudence;

Mathematics;

Mathematics and Statistics;

Modern Languages;

Oriental Studies;

Philosophy and Modern Languages;

Philosophy, Politics and Economics;

Theology (BA);

(ii) those liable to pay a composition fee under the provision of §5 cl. 1 above, **who commenced the programme of study before 1 September 2006**[9], and who are studying for an Undergraduate Degree in:

Mathematics and Philosophy;

Physics and Philosophy.

(iii) those liable to pay a composition fee under the provisions of §5 cl.1 above, **who commenced their programme of study before 1 September 2008**[9], and who are studying for an Undergraduate Degree in:

Literae Humaniores;

Philosophy and Theology;

---

[9] A student shall be deemed to have *commenced a programme of study* on commencing study towards any new qualification aim.

(iv) those liable to pay a composition fee under the provisions of §5 cl. 1 above **who commenced the programme of study before 1 September 2010**[9], who are studying for an Undergraduate Degree in:

Theology (B.Th.);

(v) those liable to pay a composition fee under the provisions of §5 cl. 3 above, **who commenced the programme of study before 1 September 2005**[9], and who are admitted as students by:

(*a*) the Humanities Board;

(*b*) the Social Sciences Board;

(*c*) the Continuing Education Board;

(vi) those liable to pay a composition fee under the provisions of §5 cl.3 above, **who commenced their programme of study before 1 September 2008**[9], and who are working within the Faculty of Philosophy;

(vii) those liable to pay a composition fee under the provisions of §5 cl. 3 above, **who commenced their programme of study before 1 September 2010**[9], who are admitted as students by:

(*a*) the Humanities Board to work towards the M.Th. or Postgraduate Diploma in Applied Theology;

(*b*) the Social Sciences Board, to work within any of the following Faculties or Departments: Department of Economics, Department of Education, Department of Politics and International Relations, Oxford Internet Institute, Faculty of Law, Saïd Business School, Department of Social Policy and Intervention, Department of Sociology, Department of International Development and who are in their second or subsequent year of study towards a graduate research degree.

Category B. Composition fees of £13,860 (or at that annual rate) shall be paid by:

(i) those liable to pay a composition fee under the provisions of §5 cl. 1 above, **who commenced the programme of study on or after 1 September 2005**[9], and who are studying for an Undergraduate Degree in:

Ancient and Modern History;

Archaeology and Anthropology;

Classical Archaeology and Ancient History;

Classics and English;

Classics and Modern Languages;

Classics and Oriental Studies;

English Language and Literature;

English and Modern Languages;

European and Middle Eastern Languages;

Geography;

History;

History and Economics;

History and English;

History and Modern Languages;

History and Politics;

History of Art;

Jurisprudence;

---

[9] A student shall be deemed to have *commenced a programme of study* on commencing study towards any new qualification aim.

Modern Languages;
Oriental Studies;
Philosophy and Modern Languages;
Philosophy, Politics and Economics;
Theology (BA);
Theology and Oriental Studies.

(ii) those liable to pay a composition fee under the provisions of §5 cl. 1 above, **who commenced their programme of study on or after 1 September 2005 and before 1 September 2013**[9], and who are studying for an Undergraduate Degree in:

Mathematics;

Mathematics and Statistics;

(iii) those liable to pay a composition fee under the provisions of §5 cl. 1 above, **who commenced their programme of study on or after 1 September 2005 and before 1 September 2009**[9], and who are studying for an Undergraduate Degree in:

Economics and Management;

(iv) those liable to pay a composition fee under the provisions of §5 cl. 1 above, **who commenced their programme of study on or after 1 September 2005 and before 1 September 2010**[9], and who are studying for an Undergraduate Degree in:

Human Sciences;

(v) those liable to pay a composition fee under the provision of §5 cl. 1 above, **who commenced the programme of study on or after 1 September 2006 and before 1 September 2013**[9], and who are studying for an Undergraduate Degree in:

Mathematics and Philosophy;

Physics and Philosophy.

(vi) those liable to pay a composition fee under the provisions of §5 cl.1 above, **who commenced their programme of study on or after 1 September 2008**[9], and who are studying for an Undergraduate Degree in:

Literae Humaniores;

Philosophy and Theology;

(vii) those liable to pay a composition fee under the provisions of §5 cl. 1 above, **who commenced their programme of study on or after 1 September 2010**[9], and who are studying for an Undergraduate Degree in:

Theology (B.Th.)

(viii) those liable to pay a composition fee under the provision of §5 cl. 1 above, **who commenced the programme of study on or after 1 September 2005**[9], and who are studying for the:

Diploma in Theology;

Diploma in Legal Studies;

Postgraduate Certificate in Education;

(ix) those liable to pay a composition fee under the provisions of §5 cl. 3 above, **who commenced the programme of study on or after 1 September 2005**[9], and who are admitted as students by:

(*a*) the Humanities Board to work within any Faculty or Department (other than the Faculty of Philosophy (except that those admitted to work in Philosophy in

---

[9] A student shall be deemed to have *commenced a programme of study* on commencing study towards any new qualification aim.

or after 1 September 2008 pay fees as specified under cl. (x) below), the Faculty of Music or the Ruskin School of Art, or for the M.Th. or Postgraduate Diploma in Applied Theology);

(*b*) the Continuing Education Board;

(x) those liable to pay a composition fee under the provisions of §5 cl.3 above, **who commenced their programme of study on or after 1 September 2008**[9], and who are admitted as students to work in the Faculty of Philosophy;

(xi) those liable to pay a composition fee under the provisions of §5 cl. 3 above, **who commenced their programme of study on or after 1 September 2005 and before 1 September 2009**[9], by the Social Sciences Board:

(*a*) to work within the School of Geography and the Environment;

(*b*) to work within the Department of Politics and International Relations and who are in their first year of study towards a graduate research degree;

(xii) those liable to pay a composition fee under the provisions of §5 cl. 3 above, **who commenced their programme of study on or after 1 September 2005 and before 1 September 2010**[9], by the Social Sciences Board:

(*a*) to work within the Schools of Anthropology or Archaeology;

(*b*) to work within any of the following Faculties or Departments: Department of Economics, Department of Education, Oxford Internet Institute, Faculty of Law, Saïd Business School, Department of Social Policy and Intervention, Department of Sociology, Department of International Development and who are in their first year of study towards a graduate research degree;

(xiii) those liable to pay a composition fee under the provisions of §5 cl. 3 above, **who commenced their programme of study on or after 1 September 2010**[9], by:

(*a*) the Humanities Board to work towards the M.Th. or Postgraduate Diploma in Applied Theology;

(*b*) the Social Sciences Board, to work within any of the following Faculties or Departments: School of Archaeology, Department of Economics, Department of Education, Faculty of Law, Saïd Business School, Department of Sociology;

(xiv) those liable to pay a composition fee under the provisions of §5 cl. 3 above, **who commenced their programme of study on or after 1 September 2010 and before 1 September 2011**[9], by the Social Sciences Board, to work within the Oxford Internet Institute or the Department of Social Policy and Intervention;

(xv) those liable to pay a composition fee under the provisions of §5 cl. 6 above, and who are studying a subject listed in (i) or (vi) above, or which falls within the scope of any board of any division as specified in (ix), (x) and (xiii) above.

Category C. Composition fees of £14,755 (or at that annual rate) shall be paid by:

(i) those liable to pay a composition fee under the provisions of §5 cl. 1 above, **who commenced their programme of study on or after 1 September 2013**[9], and who are studying for an Undergraduate Degree in:

Mathematics;

Mathematics and Statistics;

Mathematics and Philosophy;

Physics and Philosophy.

---

[9] A student shall be deemed to have *commenced a programme of study* on commencing study towards any new qualification aim.

(ii) those liable to pay a composition fee under the provisions of §5 cl. 3 above, **who commenced the programme of study on or after 1 September 2013**[9], and who are admitted as students by the Mathematical, Physical and Life Sciences Board to work within the Mathematical Institute, or who are working for the Diploma in Education;

(iii) those liable to pay a composition fee under the provisions of §5 cl. 6 above, and who are studying a subject listed in (i) above, or which falls within the scope of any board of any division as specified in (ii) above.

Category D. Composition fees of £15,910 (or at that annual rate) shall be paid by:
(i) those liable to pay a composition fee under the provisions of §5 cl. 1 above, who are studying for an Undergraduate Degree in:

Biomedical Sciences;

Cell and Systems Biology;

Experimental Psychology;

Fine Art;

Molecular and Cellular Biochemistry;

Music;

Neuroscience;

[Until 1 October 2014: Physiological Sciences;]

Psychology and Philosophy;

Psychology, Philosophy, and Linguistics

[Until 1 October 2014: Psychology, Philosophy and Physiology.]

(ii) those liable to pay a composition fee under the provisions of §5 cl. 1 above, **who commenced their programme of study on or after 1 September 2009**[9], and who are studying for an Undergraduate Degree in:

Economics and Management;

(iii) those liable to pay a composition fee under the provisions of §5 cl. 1 above, **who commenced their programme of study on or after 1 September 2010**[9], and who are studying for an Undergraduate Degree in:

Human Sciences;

(iv) those liable to pay a composition fee under the provisions of §5 cl. 1 above, **who commenced their programme of study before 1 September 2012**[9], and who are studying for an Undergraduate Degree in:

Biological Sciences;

Chemistry;

Computer Science;

Computer Science and Philosophy;

Earth Sciences;

Geology;

Engineering Science;

Engineering, Economics and Management;

Materials, Economics and Management;

Materials Science;

---

[9] A student shall be deemed to have *commenced a programme of study* on commencing study towards any new qualification aim.

Mathematics and Computer Science;

Physics.

(v) those liable to pay a composition fee under the provisions of §5 cl. 1 above, who are studying for the:

Bachelor of Medicine (First Examination, Parts I and II);

Preliminary Examination in Medicine (Part I);

(vi) those liable to pay a composition fee under the provisions of §5 cl. 3 above, who are admitted as students by:

(*a*) the Mathematical, Physical and Life Sciences Board to work towards the M.Sc/ Postgraduate Diploma in Applied Statistics or the M.Sc in Theoretical Chemistry;

(*b*) the Medical Sciences Board to work towards the M.Sc in Psychological Research or the M.Sc in Neuroscience or the M.Sc in Pharmacology.

(vii) those liable to pay a composition fee under the provisions of §5 cl. 3 above, **who commenced their programme of study before 1 September 2012**[9], who are admitted as research students by:

(*a*) the Mathematical, Physical and Life Sciences Board to work within the Departments of Chemistry, Earth Sciences, Engineering Science, Materials, Physics, Plant Sciences, Zoology, the Life Sciences Interface Doctoral Training Centre, the Systems Biology Doctoral Training Centre, the Healthcare Innovation Doctoral Training Centre, the Biomedical Science Industrial Doctorate Centre;

(*b*) the Medical Sciences Board to work within the Departments of Biochemistry and Experimental Psychology, and the Medical Sciences Doctoral Training Centre;

(viii) those liable to pay a composition fee under the provisions of §5 cl. 3 above, **who commenced their programme of study before 1 September 2012**[9], who are admitted as students by the Mathematical, Physical and Life Sciences Board to work towards the M.Sc. in Biomedical Engineering or the M.Sc. in Computing Science;

(ix) those liable to pay a composition fee under the provisions of §5 cl. 3 above, **who commenced the programme of study on or after 1 September 2005**[9], and who are admitted as students by the Humanities Board to work within the Faculty of Music or the Ruskin School of Art (except that those admitted **on or after 1 September 2011**[9] for a taught graduate degree pay a composition fee as given under Category E below);

(x) those liable to pay a composition fee under the provisions of §5 cl. 3 above, **who commenced the programme of study before 1 September 2005**[9], and who are admitted as students by the Medical Sciences Board to work within the Departments of Pathology, Pharmacology or Physiology, Anatomy and Genetics;

(xi) those liable to pay a composition fee under the provisions of §5 cl. 3 above, **who commenced their programme of study on or after 1 September 2009**[9], by the Social Sciences Board, to work within the School of Geography and the Environment;

(xii) those liable to pay a composition fee under the provisions of §5 cl. 3 above, **who commenced their programme of study on or after 1 September 2009 but before 1 September 2011**[9], by the Social Sciences Board, to work within the Department of Politics and International Relations;

---

[9] A student shall be deemed to have *commenced a programme of study* on commencing study towards any new qualification aim.

(xiii) those liable to pay a composition fee under the provisions of §5 cl. 3 above, **who commenced their programme of study on or after 1 September 2010**[9], by the Social Sciences Board, to work within the Department of International Development;

(xiv) those liable to pay a composition fee under the provisions of §5 cl. 3 above, **who commenced their programme of study on or after 1 September 2010 but before 1 September 2011**[9], by the Social Sciences Board, to work within the School of Anthropology;

(xv) those liable to pay a composition fee under the provisions of §5 cl. 3 above, **who commenced their programme of study on or after 1 September 2011**[9], by the Social Sciences Board, to work within the Oxford Internet Institute or the Department of Social Policy and Intervention;

(xvi) those liable to pay a composition fee under the provisions of §5 cl. 6 above, and who are studying a subject listed in (i) to (iii) or (v) above, or which falls within the scope of any board of any division as specified in (ix), (xi), (xiii) or (xv) above.

Category E. Composition fees of £17,010 (or at that annual rate) shall be paid by:

(i) those liable to pay a composition fee under the provisions of §5 cl. 3 above, **who commenced the programme of study on or after 1 September 2011**[9], and who are admitted as students by:

(*a*) the Humanities Board to work within the Faculty of Music or the Ruskin School of Art for a taught graduate degree;

(*b*) by the Social Sciences Board, to work within the Department of Politics and International Relations or the School of Anthropology;

(ii) those liable to pay a composition fee under the provisions of §5 cl. 3 above, **who commenced their programme of study on or after 1 September 2012**[9] who are admitted as research students by:

(*a*) the Mathematical, Physical and Life Sciences Board to work within the Departments of Chemistry, Earth Sciences, Engineering Science, Materials, Physics, Plant Sciences, Zoology, the Life Sciences Interface Doctoral Training Centre, the Systems Biology Doctoral Training Centre, the Healthcare Innovation Doctoral Training Centre, the Biomedical Science Industrial Doctorate Centre;

(*b*) the Medical Sciences Board to work within the Departments of Biochemistry and Experimental Psychology, and the Medical Sciences Doctoral Training Centre;

(iii) those liable to pay a composition fee under the provisions of §5 cl. 3 above, **who commenced their programme of study on or after 1 September 2013**[9] who are admitted as students by:

(a) the Mathematical, Physical and Life Sciences Board to work within the Department of Computer Science or the Department of Statistics;

(b) the Medical Sciences Board.

(iv) those liable to pay a composition fee under the provisions of §5 cl. 3 above, **who commenced their programme of study on or after 1 September 2012 but before 1 September 2013**[9] who are admitted as students by the Mathematical, Physical and Life Sciences Board to work towards the M.Sc. in Biomedical Engineering or the M.Sc. in Computer Science;

---

[9] A student shall be deemed to have *commenced a programme of study* on commencing study towards any new qualification aim.

(v) those liable to pay a composition fee under the provisions of §5 cl. 6 above, which falls within the scope of any board of any division as specified in (i)(*b*), (ii) or (iii) above.

Category F. Composition fees of £19,480 (or at that annual rate) shall be paid by:
(i) those liable to pay a composition fee under the provisions of §5 cl. 1 above, **who commenced their programme of study on or after 1 September 2012 and before 1 September 2013**[9], who are studying for an Undergraduate Degree in:

Biological Sciences;
Chemistry;
Computer Science;
Computer Science and Philosophy;
Earth Sciences;
Geology;
Engineering Science;
Engineering, Economics and Management;
Materials, Economics and Management;
Materials Science;
Mathematics and Computer Science;
Physics.

Category G. Composition fees of £20,405 (or at that annual rate) shall be paid by:
(i) those liable to pay a composition fee under the provisions of §5 cl. 1 above, **who commenced their programme of study on or after 1 September 2013**[9], who are studying for an Undergraduate Degree in:

Biological Sciences;
Chemistry;
Computer Science;
Computer Science and Philosophy;
Earth Sciences;
Geology;
Engineering Science;
Engineering, Economics and Management;
Materials, Economics and Management;
Materials Science;
Mathematics and Computer Science;
Physics.

(ii) those liable to pay a composition fee under the provisions of §5 cl. 6 above, and who are studying a subject listed in (i) above.

Category H. Composition fees of £28,100 (or at that annual rate) shall be paid by:
(i) those liable to pay a composition fee under the provisions of §5 cl. 2 above, who are studying for the:

Bachelor of Medicine (Second Examination)

---

[9] A student shall be deemed to have *commenced a programme of study* on commencing study towards any new qualification aim.

Preliminary Examination in Medicine (Part II)

(ii) those liable to pay a composition fee under the provisions of §5 cl. 3 above, **who commenced their programme of study before 1 September 2013**[9], and who are admitted by the Medical Sciences Board to work within departments in the Faculty of Clinical Medicine.

(iii) those liable to pay a composition fee under the provisions of §5 cl. 3 above, **who commenced the programme of study on or after 1 September 2005 and before 1 September 2013**[9], and who are admitted as students by the Medical Sciences Board to work within the Departments of Pathology, Pharmacology or Physiology, Anatomy and Genetics;

(iv) those liable to pay a composition fee under the provisions of §5 cl. 6 above, and who are studying a subject listed in (i) above.

Special Appendix

Definition of persons entitled to be charged University composition fees at the appropriate 'home' rate

The University currently applies the following definition of persons entitled to be charged University composition fees at the appropriate 'home' (and EU) rate.

1. A person who on the relevant date

(*a*) is settled in the United Kingdom within the meaning of the Immigration Act 1971, and

(*b*) meets the residence conditions referred to in paragraph 8.

2. A person who on the first day of an academic year of the course

(*a*) is a refugee; and

(*b*) is or was ordinarily resident in the United Kingdom and Islands on the relevant date and has not ceased to be so ordinarily resident since he or she was recognised as a refugee, or

(*c*) is the spouse, civil partner or child of such a refugee and who were such at the time of the principal's asylum application to the Home Office, and who were ordinarily resident in the United Kingdom and Islands on the relevant date and have not ceased to be so resident since recognition as a refugee.

(*d*) for the purposes of this paragraph 'child' has the meaning given in paragraph 9(*a*).

3. A person who on the first day of an academic year of the course

(*a*) has been granted Humanitarian Protection as a result of an application for asylum, and

(*b*) has been granted leave to enter or remain accordingly, and

(*c*) is or was ordinarily resident in the United Kingdom and Islands on the relevant date and has not ceased to be so ordinarily resident since being granted Humanitarian Protection; or

(*d*) who is the spouse, civil partner or child of such a person and who were such at the time of the principal's asylum application to the Home Office and who were ordinarily resident in the United Kingdom and Islands on the relevant date and have not ceased to be so resident since being granted Humanitarian Protection.

(*e*) for the purposes of paragraph 3 'child' has the meaning given in paragraph 9(*a*).

---

[9] A student shall be deemed to have *commenced a programme of study* on commencing study towards any new qualification aim.

4. A person who on the relevant date

(*a*) is a national of a member state of the European Community, or

(*b*) who is the family member of such a national, and

(*c*) who meets the residence conditions referred to in paragraph 8.

(*d*) For the purposes of paragraph 4, 'family member' has the definition given in paragraph 9*(b)*.

5. A person who on the relevant date

(*a*) is

    (i) an EEA[20] migrant worker or an EEA[20] self-employed person; or

    (ii) a Swiss employed person or a Swiss self-employed person; or

    (iii) a family member of a person mentioned in paragraph (i) or (ii); or

    (iv) an EEA[20] frontier worker or an EEA[20] frontier self-employed worker; or

    (v) a Swiss frontier employed person or a Swiss frontier self-employed person; or

    (vi) a family member of a person mentioned in paragraph (iv) or (v); and

(*b*) is ordinarily resident in the United Kingdom and Islands on the first day of the first academic year of the course; and

(*c*) meets the residence conditions referred to in paragraph 8.

(*d*) Paragraph 6(*b*) does not apply where the person falls within paragraph 6(*a*)(iv), (v) or (vi).

(*e*) For the purposes of paragraph 6 'family member' has the definition given in paragraph 9(*c*).

6. A person who on the relevant date

(*a*) is the child of a Swiss national that is entitled to support in the United Kingdom by virtue of article 3(6) of Annex 1 to the Switzerland Agreement; and

(*b*) is or was ordinarily resident in the United Kingdom and Islands on the first day of the first academic year of the course; and

(*c*) meets the residence conditions referred to in paragraph 8.

7. A person who on the relevant date

(*a*) is the child of a Turkish worker in the UK; and

(*b*) is or was ordinarily resident in the United Kingdom with the Turkish worker on the first day of the first academic year of the course; and

(*c*) meets the residence conditions referred to in paragraph 8.

8. The residence conditions referred to above are that:

(*a*) the person has been ordinarily resident throughout the three-year period preceding the relevant date, in the case of a person mentioned in paragraph 1, in the United Kingdom and Islands, or, in the case of a person mentioned in paragraphs 4 to 6, in the EEA[20], Switzerland or EU overseas territories, or, in the case of a person mentioned in paragraph 7, in the EEA[20], Switzerland, EU overseas territories or Turkey; and

(*b*) in the case of a person mentioned in paragraph 1, 4 or 6 his or her residence in the United Kingdom and Islands, or in the EEA[20], Switzerland, EU overseas territories or Turkey, as the case may be, has not during any part of the period

---

[20] The European Economic Area (EEA) is made up of the countries in the EU plus Iceland, Liechtenstein and Norway.

referred to in paragraph 8(*a*) been wholly or mainly for the purpose of receiving full-time education.

(*c*) A person shall be treated as ordinarily resident in the United Kingdom or the EEA[20], Switzerland, EU overseas territories, or Turkey as the case may be if he or she would have been so resident at the relevant time but for the fact that a spouse or civil partner, parent, guardian, or any other person having parental responsibility for him or her, is or was temporarily employed outside the area in question. For these purposes, temporary employment includes:

(i) in the case of members of the regular navy, military or air forces of the Crown, any period which they serve outside the United Kingdom as members of such forces; and

(ii) in the case of members of the regular armed forces of a Member State of the EEA[20] or Switzerland, any period which they serve outside of the territory comprising the EEA[20] and Switzerland as members of such forces.

9. (*a*) For the purposes of paragraphs 2 and 3, 'child' refers to a person who was under 18 at the time of the principal's asylum application to the Home Office and includes a person adopted in pursuance of adoption proceedings and a stepchild.

(*b*) For the purposes of paragraph 4, 'family member' includes the spouse or civil partner of such a national, and the direct descendants of his or her spouse or civil partner who are under 21 or who are dependents of his or her spouse or civil partner.

(*c*) For the purposes of paragraph 5, 'family member' includes

(i) in relation to EEA[20] nationals, the spouse or civil partner of such a national, the direct descendants of his or her spouse or civil partner, and dependants in the ascending line of the EEA[20] national or their spouse or civil partner;

(ii) in relation to Swiss nationals, the spouse or civil partner or his child or the child of his spouse or civil partner.

10. A reference in this Appendix to the relevant date in paragraphs 1 to 3 or 8, or to the first day of the first academic year of the course is a reference to 1 September, 1 January, 1 April, 1 July closest to the beginning of the first term of the first year of the person's course. A reference in this Appendix to the relevant date in paragraphs 4 to 7 is a reference to 1 September, 1 January, 1 April, 1 July closest to the beginning of the first term of an academic year of the person's course.

11. A person who was admitted to his or her course in pursuance of arrangements with an institution outside the United Kingdom for the exchange of students on a fully reciprocal basis.

12. A person who commenced a programme of undergraduate study before 1 September 2011 who is spending a year abroad on an approved course required by the honour school for which he or she is working.

13. Any student who does not meet the criteria outlined above is charged University composition fees at the appropriate 'overseas' rate. In determining whether students are liable for University composition fees at 'home' or 'overseas' rates, the University applies the above criteria. It should however be noted that these are liable to be changed from time to time to conform to national legislation.

---

[20] The European Economic Area (EEA) is made up of the countries in the EU plus Iceland, Liechtenstein and Norway.

§6. *Regulations for Oxford Bursaries and Tuition Fee Reductions*

1. The arrangements described in this section apply to members of the University, entitled, in accordance with the Special Appendix to §5, to be charged fees at the appropriate 'home' (and EU) rate, who are working in Oxford:

   (i) For the Degree of BA or the Degree of MBiochem or the Degree of MChem or the Degree of MMathCompSci or the Degree of MEarth Sc or the Degree of MEng or the Degree of MMath or the Degree of MCompSci or the Degree of MCompPhil or the Degree of MPhys or the Degree of MPhysPhil or the Degree of MMathPhil, or the degree of BTh (full time mode only);

   (ii) For the degree of BFA;

   (iii) For the First Examination for the Degree of BM;

   (iv) For the Preliminary Examination in Medicine;

   (v) For the Second Examination for the degree of BM;

   (vi) For the full time Certificate or Diploma in Theological and Pastoral Studies;

   (vii) For the Postgraduate Certificate in Education.

2. All students described in cl 1 above, who are entitled to receive support from a funding agency as described in cl 6 below, will be eligible to be assessed for an Oxford bursary, subject to cl 4. Bursary levels will be at the rates determined from time to time by Council's Education Committee and Planning and Resource Allocation Committee. Bursary amounts are set out on the University website. Members of the University described in cl 1. (i), (ii) and (iii) who are in their first year of study will be eligible to be assessed for an additional start-up bursary. Special regulations for members of the University described in cl 1. (iv), (v), (vi) and (vii) are set out in cll 12 to 15.

3. All students described in cl 1, who are entitled to receive support from a funding agency as described in cl 6 below, who commenced their programme of study on or after 1 September 2012, and who would otherwise be liable for the full University composition fee as described in §5, will be eligible to be assessed for a reduction in their fee, subject to cl 4. The level of the fee reduction will be at the rates determined from time to time by Council's Education Committee and Planning and Resource Allocation Committee. The levels of fee reductions are set out on the University website. Special regulations for members of the University described in cl 1 (iv), (v), (vi) and (vii) are set out in cll 12 to 15. Students will not be entitled to a cash equivalent of a fee reduction.

4. If a student who is eligible to be charged the university composition fee at the 'home' rate is not entitled to means-tested maintenance support from his or her funding agency, he or she will not be eligible to be assessed for a bursary or tuition fee reduction in that academic year. Students who are entitled to be assessed by the Student Finance European Team, and who are entitled, in accordance with the Special Appendix to §5, to be charged fees at the appropriate 'home' (and EU) rate, are eligible to be assessed for a bursary or tuition fee reduction, subject to the conditions referred to in paragraph 10.

5. Students who are repeating a year of their studies at Oxford will be eligible to be assessed for a bursary and/or tuition fee reduction subject to cl 4. Students repeating their first year or transferring to year one of a new course described in cl 1 will not be eligible for any start-up bursary, and will receive a fee reduction at the level received by eligible students after their first year.

6. Requirements for the assessment of student's household income are as follows:

   (i) A member of the University as described in cl 1 can only be considered for a bursary or tuition fee reduction if he or she is first financially assessed by his or her funding agency and if consent has been given for the University to access this information. Financial assessments will only be accepted from Student Finance England, Student Finance Northern Ireland, Student Finance Wales, the Student Awards Agency for Scotland, the Student Finance Services European Team, the Student Loans Company (SLC) or the National Health Service (NHS). The University will only base a student's bursary and/or tuition fee reduction upon income information provided to it via the SLC;

(ii) Special regulations for financial assessments apply to members of the University who are working in Oxford for the Preliminary Examination in Medicine and Second Examination for the degree of BM. These are set out in cll 12 and 13;

(iii) Home students are obliged to accept any maintenance grant they become eligible for as a result of financial assessment by their funding agency in order to be eligible to be assessed for a bursary and/or a tuition fee reduction. They are not required by the University to take out a maintenance loan or tuition fee loan from their funding agency to be eligible to be assessed for a bursary or for a tuition fee reduction respectively.

7. The annual deadlines for the assessment of bursaries and tuition fee reductions shall be as follows:

(i) To be assessed for an Oxford bursary and/or tuition fee reduction students must comply with the application deadlines set by their funding agency. Students who fail to comply with requests to provide information to their agency will not be assessed by the University after the deadlines listed in cl 7 (ii) and (iii);

(ii) To be assessed, or reassessed, for an Oxford bursary students must ensure that they have provided all information to their funding agency in time to ensure their assessment is complete and available to the University from the SLC by 30 May of the academic year in which they wish to be considered for a bursary;

(iii) To be assessed, or reassessed, for a tuition fee reduction students must ensure that they have provided all information to their funding agency in time to ensure their assessment is complete and available to the University from the SLC by 20 December of the academic year in which they wish to be considered for a tuition fee reduction;

(iv) Any student who wishes to be considered for a bursary and/or tuition fee reduction, or a change in their bursary and/or tuition fee reduction after the dates listed in cl 7 (ii) and (iii) must submit their case for a re-assessment to the Student Financial Support section (Examination Schools, Oxford OX1 4BG) by 30 May of that academic year. The request must detail when the student applied for funding, what difficulties he or she had in being assessed correctly, and what action he or she took to rectify this. It must also contain the final financial notification for that year, if available, and any evidence of the difficulties which he or she has experienced. If the final financial notification received by the student from the funding agency for that academic year is still not available to the University by 30 May of that academic year, the student will have until 20 December of the following academic year to submit the final financial notification for a re-assessment to be completed by the University.

8. The arrangements for adjustments to bursaries during an academic year are as follows:

(i) Each of the regulations in this section will be subject to the dates and regulations listed in cl 7;

(ii) Students who have received an overpayment of their bursary following a revised household income assessment will not be asked to repay any funds, unless the bursary was obtained due to incorrect information being knowingly submitted to the student's funding agency by the student or his or her sponsor;

(iii) If a student's revised household income assessment results in an increased bursary entitlement, subsequent bursary payments will be adjusted upwards to reflect the student's increased entitlement for the whole year. The increased bursary payments will be calculated as if the student had been eligible for that level from the start of the academic year;

(iv) If a student fails to provide information requested by their funding agency, as a result of which the financial assessment is withdrawn, the University will suspend bursary payments until the student's assessment has been completed by the funding agency, at which point their bursary entitlement will be re-assessed;

(v) The amount paid per term will be one third of the total annual bursary to which they are eligible. Students will be expected to repay their bursary for any term where they have suspended or withdrawn before the Monday of Week 2.

9. The arrangements for adjustments to fee liability and tuition fee reductions during an academic year are as follows:

(i) Each of the regulations in this section will be subject to the dates and regulations listed in cl 7;

(ii) Students whose revised household income assessment has increased will not be liable for an increased tuition fee, unless the initial tuition fee reduction was obtained due to incorrect information being knowingly submitted to the student's funding agency by the student or his or her sponsor;

(iii) If a student's revised household income assessment has reduced, resulting in an entitlement to a larger tuition fee reduction, he or she will receive an additional tuition fee reduction. The level of the fee reduction will calculated as if the student had been eligible for that level from the start of the academic year.

10. Household income will be assessed in the first year of study only for students who are entitled to be financially assessed by the Student Finance European team, and who are entitled, in accordance with the Special Appendix to §5, to be charged fees at the appropriate 'home' (and EU) rate. These students will not be automatically re-assessed each year. Students who wish to have their household income reassessed must submit a request to the Student Financial Support section, Examination Schools, Oxford OX1 4BG.

11. The arrangements for changes to bursary and tuition fee reduction entitlement between years are as follows:

(i) Students entitled, in accordance with the Special Appendix to §5, to be charged fees at the appropriate 'home' rate, and who are entitled to be financially assessed by Student Finance England, Student Finance Northern Ireland, Student Finance Wales, the Student Awards Agency for Scotland, the Student Loans Company or the National Health Service, are required by these funding agencies to apply for financial support each year if they wish to access means-tested support. The assessment of their household income by their funding agency may change from year to year, and consequently their entitlement to a bursary and/or tuition fee reduction is subject to change each year. Special regulations are set out in cll 12 and 13 for financial assessments for members of the University working for the Preliminary Examination in Medicine (Part II) and Bachelor of Medicine (Second Examination);

(ii) Students will only be eligible to be assessed for a bursary and/or tuition fee reduction for the period in which they are entitled, in accordance with the Special Appendix to §5, to be charged fees at the appropriate 'home' (and EU) rate.

12. Special regulations apply for members of the University who are working in Oxford for the Preliminary Examination in Medicine (Part II) and Bachelor of Medicine (Second Examination) where these students were admitted on the accelerated four-year course. These are as follows:

(i) The household income of students in years two to four of their course will be estimated on the basis of the financial assessment of their household income in year one of their course;

(ii) Students will be eligible to be assessed for a tuition fee reduction in the first year of their course. The level of the fee reduction will correspond to the reduction available to students described in cl 1 (i), (ii) and (iii) after their first year of studies;

(iii) Students will be eligible to be assessed for a bursary for all years of the course. They will not be eligible for any start-up bursary available to students in cl 1 (i), (ii) and (iii) in their first year of study.

13. Special regulations apply for members of the University who are working in Oxford for the Bachelor of Medicine (Second Examination) in years four to six of the six-year medicine course:

(i) The household income of students in years five and six of the six-year medicine course will be estimated on the basis of the financial assessment of their household income in year four of their course;

(ii) Students in year four of the course will be eligible to be assessed for a tuition fee reduction. The level of the fee reduction will correspond to the reduction available to those eligible students described in cl 1 (i), (ii) and (iii) after their first year of studies;

(iii) Students will be eligible to be assessed for a bursary for all years of the course. They will not be eligible for any start-up bursary available to students in cl 1 (i), (ii) and (iii) in their first year of study.

14. Special regulations apply for members of the University who are working in Oxford for the Certificate or Diploma in Theological and Pastoral Studies.

(i) Students will be eligible to be assessed for the tuition fee reductions advertised on the Faculty of Theology website, and determined from time to time by Council's Education Committee and Planning and Resource Allocation Committee;

(ii) Students will be eligible to be assessed for a bursary for all years of the course. They will not be eligible for any start-up bursary available to students in cl 1 (i), (ii) and (iii) in their first year of study.

15. Members of the University working in Oxford for the Postgraduate Certificate in Education will be eligible to be assessed for a tuition fee reduction determined from time to time by Council's Education Committee and Planning and Resource Allocation Committee. The level of the fee reduction will correspond to the reduction available to those eligible students described in cl 1 (i), (ii) and (iii) after their first year of studies. They will only be eligible to be assessed for an Oxford bursary if they do not receive a Training and Development Agency (TDA) bursary. They will not be eligible for any start-up bursary available to students in cl 1 (i), (ii) and (iii) in their first year of study.

16. Students who have completed the part time Foundation Certificate in History or English Language and Literature at Oxford with the Department for Continuing Education and who progress directly to the second year of the BA in History or the BA in English Language and Literature are eligible to be assessed for any start-up bursary and/or enhanced tuition fee reduction that is normally available to students described in cl 1 (i), (ii) and (iii) in their first year.

17. If a student believes that his or her bursary or fee reduction has not been processed according to these regulations and/or the bursary and fee reduction rates approved by Council's Education Committee and Planning and Resource Allocation Committee, he or she should contact the Student Financial Support section, Examination Schools, Oxford OX1 4BG. Any question of doubt or difficulty relating to the eligibility of individual students for tuition fee reductions and/or Oxford bursaries shall be determined by the Fees Panel, as described in § 5, cl 13 (*d*) and (*e*).

§7. *Continuation charge*

A candidate admitted to graduate research study (that is, a student for the DPhil, EngD, MLitt, MSc(Res), or any other programme of study designated as a research programme) who commenced their current programme of study in or after September 2011 and who has reached the end of the period of fee liability, as defined at §5, cl. 4, and who thereafter remains registered as a graduate research student, shall pay a continuation charge for each subsequent term up to and including the term in which the thesis is submitted. Candidates whose thesis has been referred back shall pay no further composition fee or continuation charge, but shall pay the fee prescribed in §1 above when they apply for re-examination.

A student who is paying composition fees in respect of any given term shall not be liable for a continuation charge in the same term.

The continuation charge will first become payable in 2013–14, and the level of the charge in that year will be £400 per term.

Divisions may remit the continuation charge (subject to approval by PRAC) for graduate research students on a specified course or courses of study, provided that the remission applies to all students on that course in a specified term or terms of study.

§8. *Fees payable by certain students*

1. If a person who is not a member of the University is admitted to work, and receive instruction or supervision, in any university department by the head of the department, he or she shall pay to the Secretary of the Chest such fee or fees as shall be prescribed by the head of the department in accordance with arrangements approved from time to time by Council's Education and Planning and Resource Allocation Committees.

2. The head of each department shall have discretion to fix a fee or fees for any member of the University who is working in his or her department, unless that member is liable to pay a composition fee under the provisions of §5 of this Section or would be liable but for the provisions of cll. 4 or 5 thereof.

3. The head of each department shall maintain, and on request send to the Secretary of the Chest not later than the end of the third week of Full Term, or in the case of students working in the vacation only, as soon as may be, a list of the names of the students attending lectures or working in his or her department other than those liable to pay a fee covering that term under §5, cll. 1 and 3 of this section.

4. No fee shall be payable under the provisions of this subsection by any person who is paying a fee under the provisions of §9 of this Section, or whose name is on the

Register of Recognized Students or the Register of Visiting Students, or by any salaried employee who is receiving instruction or supervision in the department in which he or she is working.

5. For the purposes of this subsection the word 'Term' shall include the vacation following.

§9. *Fees payable by certain Clinical Students*

1. Every person attached to the clinical school under regular instruction for a qualifying medical examination of another university or of a recognised professional institution shall, unless liable to pay a composition fee under the provisions of §5 of this section, pay to the Regius Professor of Medicine a fee of £10 on admission and a composition fee every three months at the annual rate specified in cl. 14 of the said §5 which would be applicable to him or her if liable for fees under cl. 2 thereof.

2. The Regius Professor of Medicine shall have discretion to fix fees for persons attached to the clinical school who are not under regular instruction but who would otherwise be liable to pay a fee or fees under cl. 1 above.

3. Within fourteen days of the last day of every Full Term the Regius Professor of Medicine shall

(i) send to the Secretary of the Chest a schedule specifying (*a*) the names of all the persons who were liable to pay any of the fees referred to in cll. 1 and 2 above since the preparation of the previous schedule, and (*b*) the particular fees payable by such persons, and

(ii) account to the curators for the fees so specified between those at the 'home' and 'overseas' rates, for the remainder of the course then being undertaken.

OTHER FEES PAYABLE

1. *Late entry for examinations*

(*a*) where a candidate proposes to offer a book or subject or part of the examination which has already been offered by a candidate who entered by the due date and no change in the conduct of the examination is involved   £40.00

(*b*) where the provisions of (*a*) are not satisfied but the chair of examiners is willing to consent   £40.00

2. *Late alteration of options*

(*a*) where a candidate proposes to offer a book or subject or part of the examination which has already been offered by a candidate who entered by the due date and no change in the conduct of the examination is involved   £40.00

(*b*) where the provisions of (*a*) are not satisfied but the chair of examiners is willing to consent   £40.00

NOTES

APPENDIX II

REGULATIONS FOR CANDIDATES SUPPLICATING FOR DEGREES

DEGREE DAYS 2013–15

A new system for degree ceremonies is being introduced from July 2013. Please consult the University website (http://www.ox.ac.uk/students/graduation/ceremonies/dates/) for further information.

Ceremonies will normally be held in the Sheldonian Theatre for the purpose of granting graces and conferring degrees on the days shown below.

MICHAELMAS TERM 2013

Friday, 4 October (11.00 a.m. only) St Peter's College and New College only
Friday, 8 November (11.00 a.m. and 2.30 p.m.)
Saturday, 9 November (11.00 a.m. and 2.30 p.m.)
Saturday, 16 November (11.00 a.m. only)

HILARY TERM 2014

Saturday, 8 March (11.00 a.m. and 2.30 p.m.)

TRINITY TERM AND LONG VACATION 2014

Saturday, 10 May (11.00 a.m.) Keble College and Christ Church only
Saturday, 10 May (2.30 p.m.)
Saturday, 12 July (11.00 am and 2.30 pm)
Monday, 21 July (11.00 am and 2.30 pm)
Tuesday, 22 July (11.00 am and 2.30 pm)
Wednesday, 23 July (11.00 am only)
Friday, 25 July (11.00 am and 2.30 pm)
Saturday, 26 July (11.00 am and 2.30 pm)
Monday, 28 July (2.30 pm only)
Friday, 1 August (11.00 am and 2.30 pm)
Saturday, 2 August (11.00 am and 2.30 pm)
Monday, 15 September (11.00 am only)
Friday, 19 September (11.00 am and 2.30 pm)
Saturday, 20 September (11.00 am and 2.30 pm)

MICHAELMAS TERM 2014

Friday, 3 October (11.00 am only) St Peter's College and New College only
Friday, 7 November (11.00 am and 2.30 pm)
Saturday, 8 November (11.00 am and 2.30 pm)
Saturday, 15 November (11.00 am only)

HILARY TERM 2015

Saturday, 7 March (11.00 am and 2.30 pm)
Saturday, 9 May (11.00 am) Keble College and Christ Church only
Saturday, 9 May (2.30 pm)

If you are unable to graduate on a Saturday or Friday afternoon for reasons of religion or belief, please contact your college office to discuss the possibility of graduating on a Friday morning.

Names of candidates must be entered, through the authorities of a college or hall, with Degree Conferrals, Examination Schools, High Street, Oxford OX1 4BG, not later than 12 noon on the Friday, fifteen days before the ceremony. The doors of the Sheldonian Theatre will normally open to visitors half an hour before the commencement of the ceremony. Tickets will be required by visitors.

Candidates are presented for degrees by the appropriate officers. Where presentation is by a professor, the professor should be notified in advance through the candidate's society.

INDEX